THE ROUGH GUIDE TO

The Greek Islands

This ninth edition updated by

Nick Edwards, John Fisher, Rebecca Hall and
John Malathronas

ROUGH
GUIDES

roughguides.com

Contents

Introduction to
The Greek Islands

It would take a lifetime of island-hopping to fully appreciate the 227 inhabited Greek islands scattered across the Aegean and Ionian seas. With sapphire water lapping at rocky coastlines sprinkled with secret coves and sandy beaches, they are the stuff of dreamy travel posters, the very definition of the eulogized Greek summer of sun, sea and sand. Easy as it is to wax lyrical in general terms, however, the islands are by no means a homogeneous holiday cluster – no Bahamas or Seychelles here. Each one has its distinctive personality, architecture and flora as well as its own loyal tourist base.

The sea, surprisingly **unpolluted** and beautifully clear, is undoubtedly the major selling point: as well as offering gorgeous swimming, there are **watersports** galore, from snorkelling and kayaking to banana boating and windsurfing – indeed, the Greek islands are home to some of the best windsurfing spots in the world. Yacht charter, whether bare-boat or skippered, is big business, particularly out of Rhodes, Kálymnos, Kos, Lefkáda, Páros and Pireás. When the sea is less welcoming during the spring and winter months and the crowds have abated a little, there's plenty of land-based activity including **walking** through lush, wild flower-strewn meadows, **hiking** and **rock climbing** to enjoy.

But the islands are far from simply good-looking outdoor playgrounds: like the rest of Greece, they exude a colossal sense of **history**, sheltering vestiges of occupying foreign forces. Romans, Arabs, Byzantines, Genoese, Venetians, French, British, Italians and Ottomans have all controlled different islands since the time of Alexander the Great, and countless monuments have been left behind by these waves of power: frescoed Byzantine churches, fortified Venetian towns, conventional castles built by the Genoese and Knights of St John, Ottoman mosques and the Art Deco edifices of the interwar Dodecanese Italian administration make up this historical patchwork. Couple these with the lovely cities and temples of ancient Greece itself and the fascinating jumble is complete.

ABOVE FROM LEFT COLOURFUL HOUSES, FISKÁRDHO, KEFALONIÁ; PRIEST STROLLING IN KÁLYMNOS; CHEZ LUCIEN, ATHENS **OPPOSITE** WINDMILL, ÍOS

The biggest surprise – for the first-time visitor at least – is the ecologically sensitive absorption of **mass tourism**, from the untainted beaches to the traditional, still inhabited, inland capitals. Of course, there are overblown resorts, tavernas aplenty, sophisticated bars and clubs, even the obligatory Irish pub. But, with a few loutish exceptions, the sense of history, accompanied by stringent planning regulations, has ensured that life on the islands more or less appears as it has for centuries. This is becoming even more pronounced in the second decade of the tumultuous, debt-ridden twenty-first century as more and more Greeks eschew their urban jails and change to a lower gear by starting new lives where their ancestors began their long cultural journey so many centuries ago.

Where to go

After an almost mandatory stop in **Athens** – the big, sprawling capital of Greece – perhaps the best approach for first-time visitors is to sample islands from the Argo-Saronic archipelago. Crete, the Dodecanese, the Cyclades and the northeast Aegean are all reasonably well connected with each other in high season, though the Sporades and Ionian groups offer limited possibilities for island-hopping, and to get there usually involves a long mainland traipse.

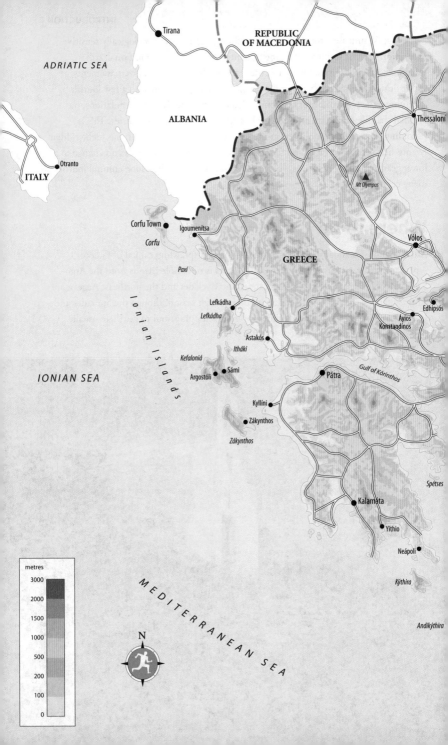

FACT FILE

• There are around 6000 **Greek islands**, of which 227 are inhabited. Around one million people live on the islands, nearly half of these in towns with over five thousand inhabitants.

• Greek structures such as doors, windowsills, furniture, and church domes are often painted a bright royal **blue**, especially in the Cyclades, following an ancient belief that this shade of blue keeps evil away.

• No point in Greece is more than 137km from water. Greece has about 14,400km of **coastline**, the tenth longest in the world.

• **Tourism** is the country's main foreign-currency earner, hitting nineteen million overseas visitors in 2014; export of agricultural products – especially olive oil, olives, citrus, wine and raisins – is another top industry.

• With over 370 brands and 190 distilleries scattered about the islands, anise-flavoured **ouzo** is Greece's most famous and popular beverage. Come the evening, the Greeks sip it with a little ice and water while tucking into mezédhes. *Stin uyeia sou!* (Cheers!)

If time and money are short, head for well-preserved, atmospheric Ýdhra in the Argo-Saronic Gulf, a short ferry ride from **Pireás** (the main port of Athens); alternatively, **Kéa**, one hour from the port of Lávrio close to Athens airport, has a Neoclassical charm and few foreign tourists. Of the Sporades, **Skýros** and **Skópelos** remain the most traditional and attractive, with forests, pale-sand beaches and well-preserved capitals. Among the Cyclades, cataclysmically volcanic **Santoríni** (Thíra) and **Mýkonos** with its perfectly preserved harbour-town rank as must-see spectacles, but mountainous **Náxos** and gently rolling **Sífnos** have a life independent of cruise-ship tourism and are better for longer stays. Cliff-bound **Amorgós** and **Folégandhros**, rocky **Sýros** with its Italianate main town, artistic **Tínos**, secluded **Sérifos** and lonely **Anáfi** with its balmy, south-facing beaches are less obvious but equally satisfying choices. **Crete** can fill an entire Rough Guide itself, but the highlights have to be Knossós and the nearby Iráklio Archeological Museum, the other Minoan palaces at Festós and Ayía Triádha, and the west in general – Réthymno and Haniá, whose hinterland extends to the relatively unspoilt southwest coast, reachable via the remarkable Samariá Gorge.

Rhodes, with its Unesco Heritage Old Town, is the capital of the Dodecanese, but scenic **Sými** and austere **Pátmos**, the island of St John's Revelation, have beaches just as lovely. **Kárpathos**, marooned between Rhodes and Crete, has arguably the best coastline in the Dodecanese, while **Léros** and **Níssyros** will appeal to the adventurous. From Pátmos or Léros, it's easy to continue north via **Sámos** – one of Greece's most attractive islands – or **Híos**, with its striking medieval architecture, to balmy, olive-cloaked **Lésvos**, perhaps the most traditional of all islands in its way of life.

The Ionian islands are primarily package-holiday territory but, especially if you're exiting Greece towards Italy, be sure to stop at **Corfu**, which along with neighbouring **Paxí** islet escaped damage from the 1953 earthquake which devastated the southern Ionians. Little **Itháki**, most easily reached from the mainland, is relatively untouristy, given its lack of beaches, though big brother **Kefaloniá** is well and truly in the spotlight owing to spectacular scenery – and (over)exposure in Louis de Bernière's *Captain Corelli's Mandolin*.

BEST ISLAND FOR ...

Watersports Kárpathos (see p.291). The *meltémi* winds are the best and strongest here, which makes for great windsurfing conditions.

Food and drink Lésvos (see p.387). As this island is the main producer of both olive oil and ouzo, you can expect top-quality ingredients served up in the tavernas and bars.

Parties Mýkonos (see p.141). From energetic superclubs to chilled, sophisticated beach bars, the nightlife here is seriously hot – be prepared to party hard and pay for it.

Classical sights Crete (see p.211, p.215 & p.233). Knossós, Festós, Zákros … to mention just a few. Take your pick from a number of Cretan classics.

Seclusion Alónissos (see p.436). If you're keen for some peace and quiet, this traditional little island has it in spades.

Luxury Ýdhra (see p.96). With mule the only way of getting around, this cute and charming island hasn't escaped the attention of the rich and famous, so expect pricey boutique hotels and chic restaurants to indulge your sophisticated side.

Views Santoríni (see p.188). There are few views in the whole world that compare with the dizzying panoramas of this island's marine caldera, subject of a thousand blog posts and a million snaps.

ABOVE VLYHÓS, ÝDHRA **OPPOSITE** WILD FLOWERS ABOVE THE GULF OF MIRABELLO, CRETE

When to go

Most islands and their inhabitants are far more agreeable outside the **busiest period** of early July to late August. The first Monday in August traditionally marks the arrival of the largest number of holiday-makers in Greece in one day; in 2014 this amounted to 760 flights bringing 148,000 passengers. In order to cope with such an influx, bus and ferry schedules change almost weekly, hours are extended, prices skyrocket and, occasionally, service standards slip.

The peak period also coincides with the arrival of the infamous **meltémi**, a cool, fair-weather wind which appears during daytime but disappears at night; those picturesque windmills on Mýkonos weren't built for show. The *meltémi* originates in high-pressure systems over the far north Aegean, gathering momentum as it travels southwards and ending up in gusts by the time it reaches Crete. It is responsible for the occasional cancellation of a catamaran service, although large ferries are unaffected. North-facing Cretan coasts, the Cyclades and western Dodecanese bear the full brunt; the wind is less pronounced in the north or northeast Aegean, where continental landmasses provide some shelter for the islands just offshore.

As for climate (see box, p.48), you won't miss out on **warm weather** if you come between late May and the end of June, or in September, though at these times you'll find little activity on the northernmost islands of Thássos, Límnos and Samothráki and in the Western Cyclades. During October you'll probably hit a week's stormy spell, but for

GODS AND MONSTERS

A high proportion of the ancient sites still seen on the Greek islands today were built as **shrines and temples to the gods**. They include spectacular sites such as **Delos** (see p.147) or the **Temple of Aphaea** in Égina (see p.87), but also many other sanctuaries, great and small, throughout the islands – everywhere, in fact, because the gods themselves were everywhere.

There were many lesser and local gods like the Nymphs and Pan, but the great gods known to all were the **twelve** who lived on **Mount Olympus**, including **Zeus** and his wife and sister, **Hera**. They had human form, and were born and had sexual relations among themselves and humankind, but they never ate human food, nor did they age or die.

As well as fearsome gods, tales of **monsters** and demons proliferate from the Greek islands, of which the half-bull, half-man **Minotaur** (see p.211) is probably the best known. Dwelling within the Cretan labyrinth at Knossós, in the grounds of his father's palace, he was fed a diet of youths and maidens until Theseus turned up and destroyed him. The Minotaur's notoriety is equalled by the **Cyclops**, one-eyed giants who were said to live on the island of Sérifos (see p.116) and supplied Zeus with regular thunderbolts. The three horrifyingly ugly **Gorgon** sisters with snakes for hair and a gaze that could turn a mortal to stone, Euryale, Stheno and (the ill-fated) Medusa, were feared to such a degree that their figures were carved onto buildings throughout the Greek islands; check out the pediment on the Temple of Artemis in the Archeological Museum in Corfu (see p.467). Add to this motley crew the giant, winged **Sirens**, who lived on the rocks in the sea and reputedly lured sailors to their watery deaths, and one thing is for sure – the Greeks certainly had imagination.

much of that month the "little summer of Áyios Dhimítrios", the Greek equivalent of Indian summer, prevails. While restaurants and nightlife can be limited in spring and autumn, the light is softer, and going out at midday becomes a pleasure rather than an ordeal. The most reliable venues for late autumn or early winter breaks are Rhodes and balmy southeastern Crete, where it's possible to swim in relative comfort as late as November.

December to March are the **coldest** and least reliably sunny months, particularly on the Ionian islands, typically the rainiest area from November onwards. The high peaks of northerly or lofty islands wear a brief mantle of snow around the turn of the year, with Crete's mountainous spine staying partly covered well into April. Between January and April the glorious lowland **wild flowers** start to bloom, beginning in the southeast Aegean. April weather is more reliable, the air is crystal-clear and the landscape green. May is more or less settled, though the sea is still cold.

Another factor that affects the timing of a Greek island visit is the level of tourism and the related amenities provided. If you can only visit during midsummer, it is wise to reserve a package well in advance, plan an itinerary off the beaten track and buy all your ferry tickets beforehand. Between November and Easter, you'll have to contend with pared-back ferry and plane schedules plus skeletal facilities when you arrive. However, you should be able to find adequate services to the more populated islands, and at least one hotel and taverna open in the port or main town of all but the tiniest isles.

ABOVE GORGON, MOSAIC IN RHODES TOWN

Author picks

Our authors hopped from island to island, testing out the best beaches, sampling the tastiest tzatziki, taking to the water on boats, kayaks or windsurfers and exploring countless ancient ruins. Here are their highlights:

Marine sanctuary Take a boat trip to the Alónissos Marine Park (see p.442) for stunningly clear water, even by Greek standards. If you're lucky, you might catch sight of dolphins or an elusive monk seal.

Must-do museum The Archeological Museum in Iráklio, newly reopened after years of refurbishment, is a real eye-opener; a fresh look at Europe's earliest civilization (see p.206).

Biggest time bubble To experience what Greek holidays were like thirty years ago, before the Age of Resorts, book a ferry to the tiny island of Áno Koufoníssi (see p.174).

Skópelos cheese pie Never have calories tasted so good than in this helical filo pie, fried in olive oil rather than baked in the oven (see p.431).

A climb to remember The twenty-minute strenuous vertical climb to Hotzoviótissas monastery in eastern Amorgós (see p.177) can just about convince anyone that its precarious structure was indeed built by angels.

Alternative islands Pockets of alternative culture exist, such as the lesbian and spiritual influence at Skála Eressoú, on Lésvos (see p.400), and the hippy colony around Nas, on Ikaría (see p.372).

Moonwalking on Níssyros Not literally, but it certainly feels like it once you step foot on the plains of the extra-terrestrial landscape of the Stéfanos volcano crater floor (see p.312). Completely otherworldly.

> Our author recommendations don't end here. We've flagged up our favourite places – a perfectly sited hotel, an atmospheric café, a special restaurant – throughout the guide, highlighted with the ★ symbol.

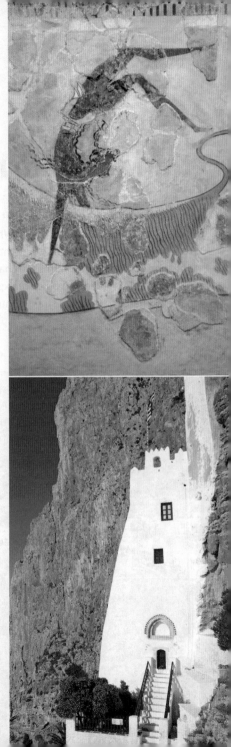

FROM TOP FRESCO, IRÁKLIO ARCHEOLOGICAL MUSEUM, CRETE; MONASTERY OF HOTZOVIÓTISSAS, AMORGÓS

21

things not to miss

It's not possible to see everything that the Greek Islands have to offer in one trip – and we don't suggest you try. What follows, in no particular order, is a selective taste of the region's highlights, including beautiful beaches, outstanding Classical monuments, charming seaside towns and unforgettable wildlife and outdoor experiences. All the highlights have a page reference to take you straight into the guide, where you can find out more. Coloured numbers refer to chapters in the Guide section.

1

5 KLÉFTIKO, MÍLOS
Two hours by boat from Adhámas, this otherwise unreachable cove is as close to being marooned on a deserted beach as you will get.

6 THE CLIFFS OF KÁLYMNOS
The island's limestone cliffs and dry weather attract climbers from all over the world.

7 DELOS
Pay your respects to the most sacred site of the Eastern Mediterranean and the biggest port of the Cyclades in the ancient world.

8 SÝMI
Take a leap into the past and stroll among the grand mansions of Sými's picturesque harbour, built with wealth from the sponge trade.

9 AUGUST 15
The feast of the Assumption of the Virgin provides a spectacular explosion of Orthodox devotion in the Cyclades, especially on Tínos.

10 CHURCH OF EKATONDAPYLIANÍ, PÁROS
Built by St Helen in the fourth century AD over an old pagan temple, this may well be the most continuous place of worship in Europe.

5

6

7

11 HANIÁ HARBOUR
Page 246
Crete's most charming city, Haniá displays the haunting vestiges of its Venetian and Ottoman past with pride.

12 SAMARIÁ GORGE
Page 253
The 16km descent of this leafy gorge enclosed by high rock faces is an unforgettable hike.

13 ISLAND WINES
Pages 38, 193 & 214
Have a go at wine tasting in the vineyards of Santoríni, Crete or Sámos, and sample the delights of local grape varieties.

14 KOURÉMENOS BEACH
Page 232
Kourémenos, on Crete's unspoilt east coast, is one of the finest windsurfing beaches in all of Greece.

15 ÓLYMBOS VILLAGE, KÁRPATHOS
Page 295
Ólymbos village, built spectacularly on a saddle between two mountain peaks, has goosepump-inducing views of Northern Kárpathos.

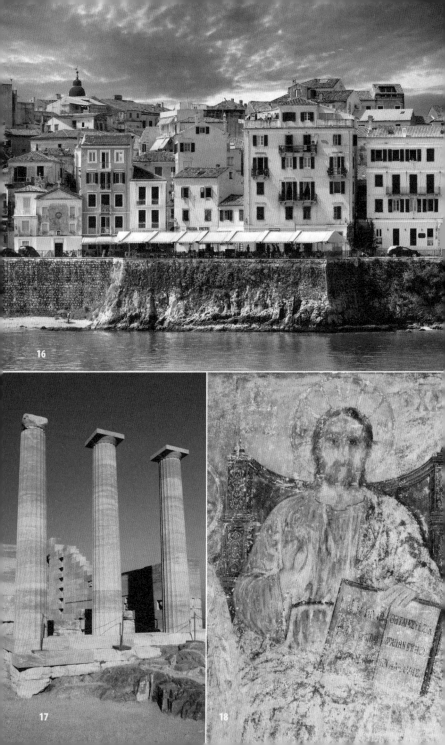

19

16 CORFU HISTORIC CENTRE
Page 463

With its elegant Venetian architecture and fine museums, Corfu's capital is the beating heart of the Ionian islands.

17 THE OTHER ACROPOLIS
Page 278

From the Hellenistic Acropolis of Líndhos, high above the modern village, look north along the length of Rhodes island for one of the most stunning views of the Dodecanese.

18 PÁTMOS, MONASTERY OF ST JOHN
Page 341

Built around the cave where St John wrote the Book of Revelation, this monastery is a warren of fresco-strewn courtyards, arcades and roof terraces.

19 MARINE PARK, ALÓNISSOS
Page 442

The sea around the island is a haven for the endangered Mediterranean monk seal.

20 MELISSÁNI CAVE, KEFALONIÁ
Page 499

Visit the underwater Melissáni Cave to admire the rock formations and play of light on the cave walls.

21 SHIPWRECK BAY, ZÁKYNTHOS
Page 514

Lie back and enjoy the unforgettable scenery of one of Greece's poster beaches.

20

21

Itineraries

Although there are as many itineraries as there are islands, the ultimate Greek summer experience is island-hopping, and in particular around the Cyclades. If you want to combine some history with blissful beach living, then head for the Dodecanese, while if you haven't got your sea legs and prefer driving to sailing, base yourself in Crete. The other islands, especially the Ionians, are best explored individually.

HOPPING AROUND THE CYCLADES

Ferry routes connect all of these islands; in the summer months be sure to book tickets in advance and check the most recent timetables. You'll need at least 2–3 weeks to cover this itinerary depending on ferry frequency.

❶ **Ándhros** Green and fertile, with some terrific walking trails and a fantastic selection of beaches, this is a great introduction to the Cyclades. **See p.132**

❷ **Mýkonos** The party island for as many sensuous, fun-filled days as your body can take and your wallet can stand. **See p.141**

❸ **Páros** A little bit of everything – beautiful beaches, pretty fishing harbours, graceful monasteries and an energetic nightlife defined by its "happy hours". **See p.154**

❹ **Náxos** The activity centre of the Cyclades, this is the place to go trekking, diving or kitesurfing. **See p.164**

❺ **Santoríni** Don't forget your camera – the crater that makes up this island is particularly photogenic at sunset. **See p.188**

❻ **Mílos** Join a boat ride around the island and swim in some of its kaleidoscopic coves. **See p.124**

❼ **Sérifos** Glorious beaches and with a breathtaking inland capital, Sérifos is a perfect chill-out zone. **See p.116**

DISCOVERING THE DODECANESE

The starting point for this itinerary, Rhodes, is served by several flights daily, while all the other islands are connected by regular ferries. The whole itinerary should take a minimum of 2–3 weeks depending on how often ferries are running.

❶ **Rhodes** With its lovely medieval Old Town and numerous sandy beaches, this is rightfully one of the most visited of the Greek islands. **See p.266**

❷ **Sými** Italian architecture, cobbled streets in the Horió and the everyday comings and goings of Greek life makes Sými a very attractive island getaway. **See p.297**

❸ **Tílos** Quiet, volcanic and part-protected with a national park, this is one of the most relaxing of the Dodecanese chain. **See p.303**

❹ **Níssyros** Home to a dormant volcano, there are some rather unearthly moonscape panoramas to enjoy here. **See p.307**

❺ **Kálymnos** The sponge capital of the Mediterranean has reinvented itself as a rock-climbing, hiking and scuba-diving destination. **See p.327**

❻ **Pátmos** Despite the awe-inspiring cave where St John the Divine wrote the Book of

ABOVE FROM LEFT CLIMBING, KÁLYMNOS; TREKKING, NÁXOS

Revelation, beaches are still the island's principal attraction. **See p.338**

THE GREAT ISLAND

Ancient Minoan palaces, beautiful port towns, high mountains and plentiful beaches all make Crete more than just the biggest of the Greek islands. To explore properly, hire a car and give yourself a couple of weeks.

❶ **Haniá** The island's sophisticated second city is the gateway to the mountains of the west, as well as a beautiful place to relax and people-watch. **See p.286**

❷ **Loutró** Accessible only on foot or by boat, Loutró is the perfect escape after you've hiked the Samariá Gorge. **See p.256**

❸ **Réthymno** A university city with an enchanting old town and a big, sandy beach right in the centre. **See p.236**

❹ **Iráklio** Crete's capital boasts a world-class archeological museum and is the easiest base for exploring the ruins at Knossós. **See p.203**

❺ **Áyios Nikólaos** Home to the finest of the luxury hotels, plus great food and nightlife. See p.222

❻ **Káto Zákros** A tiny, isolated seaside hamlet, with a lovely pebble beach and one of the four great Minoan palaces. **See p.232**

SARONIC SAILING

Ideal for exploring by yacht or on a flotilla holiday, the Saronic Gulf also lends itself to a short trip from Athens, with frequent, fast hydrofoils and catamarans. Allow a week.

❶ **Égina** An easy first day's sail, or less than two hours by ferry, Égina has a lively harbour and, inland, the beautiful Temple of Aphaea, one of the most visually compelling in Greece. **See p.83**

❷ **Póros** The narrow channel between Póros Town and the mainland is the highlight of many a sailing trip; great moorings, plenty of beaches and some lively bars. **See p.92**

❸ **Ýdhra** The most dramatic of the Argo-Saronic islands, its town like an amphitheatre around a horseshoe harbour. Sailors can expect crowds and short tempers, but it's worth it. **See p.96**

❹ **Spétses** A family holiday island with developed infrastructure, good beaches and excellent, upmarket tavernas; yachties in the know anchor off *Loula*, a taverna at the island's eastern tip. **See p.101**

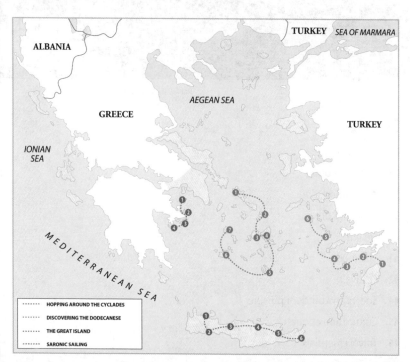

TOUR BOATS, SPINÁLONGA, CRETE

Basics

Getting there

By far the easiest way to get to the Greek islands is to fly. An increasing number of islands have international airports that see charters and occasional scheduled flights from Britain, Ireland and the rest of northern Europe. Other islands can be reached on domestic flights, connecting with international scheduled arrivals in Athens and Thessaloníki. Even if your starting point is North America, Australia, New Zealand or South Africa, the most cost-effective way to Greece may well be to get to London, Amsterdam, Frankfurt or another Northern European hub, and pick up an onward flight from there.

Airfares are highest in July, August and during Easter week. But May, June and September are also popular, and since far fewer flights operate through the winter, bargains are rare at any time.

When **buying flights** it always pays to shop around and bear in mind that many websites don't include charter or budget airlines in their results. Be aware too that a **package deal**, with accommodation included, can sometimes be as cheap as, or even cheaper than, a flight alone: there's no rule that says you have to use your accommodation every night, or even at all.

Once in Greece, you'll find a vast **ferry** network which connects even the smallest of islands (see p.29). Details of the main ports are covered in the "Athens and the ports" chapter (see p.54).

Overland alternatives from the UK or Northern Europe involve at least three days of nonstop travel. If you want to take your time over the journey, **driving** or travelling **by train** can be enjoyable, although invariably more expensive than flying. We've included only brief details of these routes here.

Flights from the UK and Ireland

The vast majority of flights to the islands are with budget or charter airlines. The latter mostly offer flight-only seats in much the same way as budget operators, albeit with clunkier booking systems and often less convenient flight times; most of them fly only in the summer months, from May to September. **Regular scheduled flights** include: British Airways (Ⓦbritishairways.com) from Heathrow to Mýkonos and Santoríni (Thíra); easyJet (Ⓦeasyjet.com) from Gatwick to Corfu, Haniá (Chania, Crete), Irákio (Heraklion, Crete), Kefaloniá, Kos, Mýkonos, Rhodes, Santoríni and Zákynthos, from Luton to Corfu, Irákio and Mýkonos, from Bristol to Corfu and Irákio, from Manchester to Corfu, Irákio, Mýkonos and Santoríni, from Edinburgh to Irákio, from Glasgow to Kos, and from Liverpool to Rhodes; Jet2 (Ⓦjet2.com) from Manchester, East Midlands, Leeds Bradford, Newcastle and Glasgow to Irákio, Corfu, Ródhos and Zákynthos, from Leeds, East Midlands and Manchester also to Kos, and from Leeds and Manchester to Kefaloniá; Ryanair (Ⓦryanair.com) from Stansted to Corfu, Haniá, Kefaloniá and Rhodes, from Bristol and East Midlands to Haniá, from Bournemouth to Rhodes, Glasgow to Corfu, and Liverpool to Kos; and Norwegian (Ⓦnorwegian.com) from Gatwick to Corfu and Santoríni. In addition, **charter operators** go from a variety of UK regional airports to all of the above plus Skiáthos, Sámos, Lésvos and Límnos, as well as mainland airports at Kavála (for Thássos), Vólos (for the Sporades) and Préveza (for Lefkádha). The main operators with whom you can book direct are Monarch (Ⓦmonarch.co.uk), Thomas Cook (Ⓦflythomascook.com) and Thomson (Ⓦthomson.co.uk); others may be available indirectly, through travel agencies or third-party websites.

Don't expect any of the above to be cheap: unless you book far in advance, there are few bargain **fares** to Greece or its islands. Seats are available on the budget airlines for less than £50 each way, but you'll have to move very fast indeed (or travel way out of season) to find fares this low. Realistically you can expect to pay £75–200 each way at most times of the year.

A BETTER KIND OF TRAVEL

At Rough Guides we are passionately committed to travel. We believe it helps us understand the world we live in and the people we share it with – and of course tourism is vital to many developing economies. But the scale of modern tourism has also damaged some places irreparably, and climate change is accelerated by most forms of transport, especially flying. All Rough Guides' flights are carbon-offset, and every year we donate money to a variety of environmental charities.

Indirect flights

If you can't get a direct flight, or the island you're heading for has no airport, you'll have to make at least one stop along the way and continue by **domestic flight** (see p.30) or by **ferry**. Most obviously this means via Athens, but there are also plenty of connecting flights to the islands from Thessaloníki, while ferry connections may be better from nearby islands: if you're travelling to Pátmos, for example, look at flights to Kos or Rhodes; for Skópelos consider Skiáthos or Vólos (on the mainland). Details of how to get to and through Athens and the other mainland ports can be found in Chapter 1 (see p.54), where there's also a map showing island airports and the major ferry routes (see pp.62–63).

Scheduled flights include Aegean (W aegeanair .com) from Heathrow, Birmingham and Manchester to Athens; British Airways from Heathrow to Athens and Gatwick to Thessaloníki; easyJet from Gatwick, Manchester or Edinburgh to Athens and Gatwick to Thessaloníki; and Ryanair from Stansted to Athens. From Dublin to Athens, Aer Lingus (W aerlingus .com) have three direct flights a week from April to September, with fares starting at around €115 each way, though you can easily pay twice that. Almost all airlines, including charter operators, allow you to book one-way tickets at no extra cost, so you can fly into Athens with one and leave from an island with another.

Flights from the US and Canada

Delta (W delta.com) operate **direct nonstop flights** from New York JFK to Athens, daily for most of the year, while US Airways (W usair.com) flies daily from Philadelphia to Athens between May and October. Code-sharing airlines can quote through fares with one of the above, or a European partner, from **virtually every major US city**, connecting either at New York or a European hub such as London or Frankfurt. From Athens, there are reasonably priced add-on flights to the islands (see p.30).

Fares vary greatly, so it's worth putting in a little time on the internet, or using a good travel agent; book as far ahead as possible to get the best price. Round-trip prices range from US$900 out of season to $1400 in high summer; from the west coast, expect to pay ten to twenty percent more. Remember too that you may be better off getting a domestic flight to New York or Philadelphia and heading directly to Athens from there, or flying to London (beware of changing airports) or another European city and travelling on from there.

Flights from Australia and New Zealand

There are **no direct flights** from Australia or New Zealand to Greece; you'll have to change planes in Southeast Asia or Europe. Tickets purchased direct from the airlines tend to be expensive; travel agents or Australia-based websites generally offer much better deals on fares and have the latest information on limited specials and stopovers. For a simple return fare, you may also have to buy an add-on internal flight to get you to the international departure point.

Fares **from Australia** start from around Aus$1200, rising to around Aus$2600 depending on season, routing, validity, number of stopovers, etc. The shortest flights and best fares are generally with airlines like Singapore (W singaporeair.com), Etihad (W etihadairways.com) and Emirates (W emirates .com) who can fly you directly to Athens from their Asian or Gulf hubs, though you'll also find offers on Swiss (W swiss.com), KLM (W klm.com) and other European carriers. **From New Zealand**, prices are slightly higher: from around NZ$1800, rising to over NZ$3000 in high season.

Flights from South Africa

There are currently no direct flights from **South Africa** to Athens. Alternative routes include EgyptAir (W egyptair.com) via Cairo, Emirates (W emirates.com) or Etihad (W etihadairways.com) via the Gulf, or just about any of the major European airlines through their domestic hub. Prices start at around R7000 for a good low-season deal, to double that in high season or if the cheaper seats have gone.

FLIGHT AGENTS

Charter Flight Centre UK ☎ 020 8714 0010, W charterflights .co.uk. Booking for a huge range of charter flights from the UK and Ireland.

Flight Centre W flightcentre.com. Low-cost airfares worldwide from their local websites, plus rail passes and more.

North South Travel UK ☎ 01245 608 291, W northsouthtravel .co.uk. Friendly, competitive flight agency, offering discounted fares worldwide. Profits are used to support projects in the developing world, especially the promotion of sustainable tourism.

Skyscanner W skyscanner.net. Comprehensive flight search site that includes charter and budget airlines.

STA Travel UK ☎ 0333 321 0099, US ☎ 1 800 781 4040, Australia ☎ 134 782, New Zealand ☎ 0800 474 400, South Africa ☎ 0861 781 781; W statravel.com. Worldwide specialists in independent travel; also student IDs, travel insurance, car rental, rail passes, and more. Good discounts for students and under-26s.

Trailfinders UK ☎ 020 7368 1200, Ireland ☎ 01 677 78880; Ⓦ trailfinders.com. One of the best-informed and most efficient agents for independent travellers.

Travel CUTS Canada ☎ 1800 667 2887, Ⓦ travelcuts.com. Popular, long-established student-travel organization, with good worldwide offers; not only for students.

Trains

As a result of the economic crisis, **Greek rail routes** have been greatly reduced, and for a while all international services were suspended. Travelling to Greece by train is possible, however (though not to the islands), and the most practical route **from Britain** doesn't actually involve any Greek trains; you cross France and Italy by rail before embarking on the **ferry from Bari** or Brindisi to Pátra (Patras), with connecting buses to Athens (see box, below). Many of the ferries from Italy call at Corfu on the way, and there are connections to other Ionian islands. If you're determined to go **all the way to Greece by train**, there are a number of alternate routes across Europe to either Belgrade or Sofia, each of which has connections to Thessaloníki, from where you can get an onward train to Athens, or ferries from local ports to islands in the northeast Aegean. The quickest route (though still slower and more expensive than using the ferry from Italy) is via Paris, Munich and Zagreb to Belgrade.

Either way, the journey to Athens from the UK takes **two-and-a-half days** at least and will almost always work out more expensive than flying. It also takes a fair bit of planning, since there's no through train and **tickets** have to be bought from several separate operators. However, you do have the chance to stop over on the way, while with an **InterRail** (for European residents only; Ⓦ interrail .eu) or **Eurail** (for all others; Ⓦ eurail.com) pass, you can take in Greece as part of a wider rail trip around Europe. Booking well in advance (essential in summer) and going for the cheapest seats on each leg, you can theoretically buy individual tickets for around £170 each way, to and from London, not including the incidental expenses along the way. Using rail passes will cost you more, but give far more flexibility. For full details, check out the Man in Seat 61 website (Ⓦ seat61.com).

Car and ferry

Driving to Greece can be a pleasant proposition if you have plenty of time to dawdle along the way, though fuel, toll and ferry costs ensure it's not a cheap option. It's only worth considering if you want to explore en route, or are going to stay for an extended period. The most popular **route** from the UK is down through France and Italy to catch one of the Adriatic ferries (see box, below); this is much the best way to get to the Ionian Islands, and to Athens for ferries to most other islands. The far longer alternative through Germany, Austria, Slovenia, Croatia, Serbia and the FYROM only makes sense if you are heading for the northeast Aegean islands or want to explore northern Greece on the way.

Tour operators

Every mainstream **tour operator** includes Greece in its portfolio. You'll find far more interesting alternatives, however, through the small **specialist agencies**. As well as traditional village-based accommodation and less-known islands,

---

ITALY–GREECE FERRIES

Sailing from **Italy to Greece**, you've a choice of four ports; ferries run year-round, but services are reduced December to April. The shortest routes and most frequent ferries link Bari and Brindisi with Corfu, Igoumenítsa (the port of the western Greek mainland) and Pátra (at the northwest tip of the Peloponnese). Ferries also sail from Venice, Ravenna and Ancona to Pátra via Igoumenítsa/Corfu. These longer routes are more expensive, but the extra cost closely matches what you'll pay in Italian motorway tolls and fuel to get further south. On most ferries, you can stop over in Corfu for no extra charge. For direct access to Athens and the Aegean islands head for Pátra, from where you can cut across country to Pireás.

The following companies operate ferries: schedule and booking details for all of them are also available at Ⓦ openseas.gr and Ⓦ viamare.com.

ANEK Ⓦ anek.gr. Ancona and Venice to Corfu, Igoumenítsa and Pátra.

Grimaldi Lines Ⓦ grimaldi-lines.com. Brindisi and Ravenna to Igoumenítsa and Pátra.

Minoan Lines Ⓦ minoan.gr. Ancona to Igoumenítsa and Pátra.

Superfast Ferries Ⓦ superfast.com. Ancona and Bari to Corfu, Igoumenítsa and Pátra.

Ventouris Ferries Ⓦ ventourisferries.it. Bari to Corfu, Igoumenítsa, Kefaloniá and Zákynthos.

many also offer **walking** or **nature holidays** and other special interests such as **yoga**, **art** and above all **sailing**, with options ranging from shore-based clubs with dinghy tuition, through organized yacht flotillas to bareboat or skippered charters.

PACKAGE OPERATORS

Grecian Tours Australia ☏ 03 9663 3711, Ⓦ greciantours.com.au. A variety of accommodation and sightseeing tours, plus flights.

Greek Sun Holidays UK ☏ 01732 740317, Ⓦ greeksun.co.uk. Good-value package holidays mainly in smaller islands of the Dodecanese, northeast Aegean and Cyclades; also tailor-made island-hopping itineraries.

Hidden Greece UK ☏ 020 8758 4707, Ⓦ hidden-greece.co.uk. Specialist agent putting together tailor-made packages to smaller destinations at reasonable prices.

Homeric Tours US ☏ 800 223 5570, Ⓦ homerictours.com. Hotel packages, individual tours, escorted group tours and fly-drive deals. Good source of inexpensive flights.

Olympic Holidays UK ☏ 020 8492 6868, Ⓦ olympicholidays.com. Huge package-holiday company serving a wide variety of islands; all standards from cheap and cheerful to five-star, and often a good source of last-minute bargains and cheap flights.

Sun Island Tours Australia ☏ 1300 665 673, Ⓦ sunislandtours .com.au. Greece specialist offering an assortment of island-hopping, fly-drives, cruises and guided land-tour options, as well as tailor-made.

Sunvil Holidays UK ☏ 020 8758 4758, Ⓦ sunvil.co.uk. High-quality outfit with a wide range of holidays to many islands.

True Greece US ☏ 1 800 817 7098, Ⓦ truegreece.com. Luxury hotels and villas, plus cruises, customized trips, weddings and more.

VILLA AND APARTMENT AGENTS

Cachet Travel UK ☏ 020 8847 8700, Ⓦ cachet-travel.co.uk. Attractive range of villas and apartments in the more unspoilt south and west of Crete, plus Híos, Sámos, Ikaría and Foúrni.

CV Villas UK ☏ 020 7563 7999, Ⓦ cvvillas.com. High-quality villas, principally in the Ionian islands and Crete.

Greek islands Club UK ☏ 020 8232 9780, Ⓦ gicthevillacollection .com. Specialist in upmarket villas with private pools, especially in the Ionian islands and Sporades.

Ionian Island Holidays UK ☏ 020 8459 0777, Ⓦ ionianislandholidays.com. Villas and small hotels, not just in the Ionians but also in the Sporades and mainland.

Pure Crete UK ☏ 01444 880 404, Ⓦ purecrete.com. Lovely, converted cottages and farmhouses in western Crete, plus walking, wildlife and other special-interest trips.

Simpson Travel UK ☏ 020 8392 5742, Ⓦ simpsontravel.com. Classy villas, upmarket hotels and village hideaways in selected areas of Crete, the Ionians, Skópelos, Sámos and more.

Travel à la Carte UK ☏ 01635 33800, Ⓦ travelalacarte.co.uk. Villas and apartments on Corfu, Paxí, Kefaloniá, Sými and more, plus Paxí painting, photography, yoga and creative writing courses.

SMALL GROUP TOURS, YOGA AND ART HOLIDAYS

Hellenic Adventures US ☏ 1 800 851 6349 Ⓦ hellenicadventures.com. Small-group escorted tours led by enthusiastic expert guides, as well as itineraries for independent travellers, cruises and other travel services.

Free Spirit Travel UK ☏ 01273 564230, Ⓦ freespirituk.com. Yoga and meditation in western Crete.

Painting Alonissos UK ☏ 01905 25460, Ⓦ paintingalonissos .com. Painting holidays and art courses on the island of Alónissos.

Skyros Holidays UK ☏ 01983 865566, Ⓦ skyros.com. Holistic yoga, dance, art, music, "personal growth" and more on the island of Skýros, as well as well-regarded writers' workshops.

Yoga Plus UK ☏ 01582 724214, Ⓦ yogaplus.co.uk. Ashtanga yoga courses in a remote part of southern Crete.

WALKING AND CYCLING

ATG Oxford UK ☏ 01865 315678, Ⓦ atg-oxford.co.uk. Somewhat pricey but high-standard guided walks on Crete and elsewhere.

Classic Adventures US ☏ 800 777 8090, Ⓦ classicadventures .com. Spring or autumn rural cycling tours crossing the north Peloponnese to Zákynthos and on Crete.

Exodus UK ☏ 0845 869 9179, Ⓦ exodus.co.uk. Week-long treks exploring southern Évvia.

Explore Worldwide US ☏ 1 800 715 1746, Can ☏ 1 888 216 3401, UK ☏ 0843 634 6057, Aus ☏ 1300 439 756; Ⓦ exploreworldwide.com. A variety of tours, many combining hiking with sailing between the islands.

Freewheeling Adventures Canada & US ☏ 800 672 0775, Ⓦ freewheeling.ca. Eight-day cycling tours of Crete.

Hooked on Cycling UK ☏ 01506 635 399, Ⓦ hookedoncycling .co.uk. Guided and self-guided cycle tours, including island-hopping on a private boat.

Inntravel UK ☏ 01653 617001, Ⓦ inntravel.co.uk. Walking holidays on Crete and some smaller islands.

Jonathan's Tours ☏ 0033 5610 46447, Ⓦ jonathanstours.com. Family-run walking holidays on Crete and smaller islands.

Ramblers Holidays UK ☏ 01707 331133, Ⓦ ramblersholidays .co.uk. A huge variety of walking trips including spring hiking in Crete, Dodecanese island-hopping and combined island and mainland treks.

Walking Plus UK ☏ 020 8835 8303, Ⓦ walkingplus.co.uk. Enthusiastic Gilly and Robin Cameron Cooper offer guided and self-guided off-season walks in the Cyclades.

WILDLIFE HOLIDAYS

Naturetrek UK ☏ 01962 733051, Ⓦ naturetrek.co.uk. Fairly pricey but expertly led one- or two-week natural history tours; offerings include springtime birds and flora on Lésvos, and wildlife of Crete.

The Travelling Naturalist UK ☏ 01305 267994, Ⓦ www .naturalist.co.uk. Wildlife holiday company that runs excellent bird-watching and wild-flower-spotting trips to Crete, Lesvós and Kós.

SAILING AND WATERSPORTS

Northwest Passage US ☎ 1 800 RECREATE, ⓦ nwpassage.com.
Excellent sea-kayaking tours in Crete and other islands; also yoga, climbing, hiking and art in Crete and Santoríni.

Nautilus Yachting UK ☎ 01732 867445, ⓦ nautilusyachting .com. Bareboat yacht charter, flotillas and sailing courses from a wide variety of marinas.

Neilson UK ☎ 0333 014 3351, ⓦ neilson.co.uk. Half a dozen excellent beach activity clubs, plus flotillas and bareboat charter.

Seafarer UK ☎ 020 8324 3117, ⓦ seafarercruises.com. Small-boat island cruises, including tall-ship and mega-yacht vessels.

Sportif UK ☎ 01273 844919, ⓦ sportif.travel. Wind- and kitesurfing packages and instruction on Crete, Kos, Rhodes, Sámos, Lésvos, Límnos and Kárpathos.

Sunsail UK ☎ 0844 463 6817, ⓦ sunsail.com. Mainland beach club, plus flotillas and bareboat mainly in the Ionians and Sporades.

Swim Trek US ☎ 1 877 455 SWIM, UK ☎ 01273 739 713, ⓦ swimtrek.com. Week-long open-water swimming tours of small islands in the Cyclades and Sporades, in which you swim between the islands.

Valef Yachts US ☎ 1 800 223 3845, ⓦ valefyachts.com. Small-boat cruises around the islands and luxury crewed yacht or motorboat charter.

Getting around

Inter-island travel mostly means taking ferries, catamarans or occasionally hydrofoils, which will eventually get you to any of the sixty-plus inhabited isles. Internal flights are relatively expensive, but can save literally days of travel: Athens–Rhodes is just 2 hours return, versus 28 hours by boat. The standard public transport on the Greek islands is the bus, although services vary from rudimentary to quite comprehensive. The best way to supplement buses is to rent a scooter, motorbike or car – in any substantial town or resort you will find at least one rental outlet.

By sea

There are several varieties of sea-going vessels: **ordinary ferries**, which never exceed 17 knots; the new generation of "**high-speed**" boats (*tahyplóö*) and catamarans, which usually carry cars, and are capable of attaining 27 knots; **roll-on-roll-off** short-haul barges, nicknamed *pandófles* ('slippers'); **hydrofoils**, similarly quick but which carry only passengers; and local **kaïkia**, small boats which do short hops and excursions in season.

Ferry connections are indicated both on the route **map** (see pp.62–63) and in the "Arrival and Departure" sections throughout the book. Schedules are notoriously erratic, however, and must be verified seasonally; details given are for departures between late June and early September. When sailing in season from **Pireás** to the Cyclades or Dodecanese, you should have a choice of at least two, sometimes three, daily departures. **Out-of-season** departure frequencies drop sharply, with less populated islands connected only two or three times weekly.

Reliable departure information is available from the local **port police** (*limenarhío*) at all island and mainland harbours of any size; around Athens there are offices at Pireás (☎ 210 455 0000), Rafína (☎ 22940 28888) and Lávrio (☎ 22920 25249). Busier port police have automated phone-answering services with an English option for schedule information. Many companies produce annual **schedule** booklets, which may not be adhered to as the season wears on – check their **websites** (if any) for current information, or refer to ⓦ gtp.gr or, even better, ⓦ openseas.gr.

Ferries

Except for some subsidized peripheral routes where older rust-buckets are still used, the Greek **ferry fleet** is fairly contemporary. **Routes and speed** can vary enormously, however; a journey from Pireás to Santoríni, for instance, can take anything from five to ten hours.

Tickets are best bought a day before departure, unless you need to reserve a cabin berth or space for a car. During holiday periods – Christmas/New Year, the week before and after Easter, late July to early September – and around the dates of elections, ferries need to be booked at least ten days in advance. Ticketing for most major routes is computerized and you cannot **buy** your ticket on board, although booths on the quay sell last-minute tickets. Many companies allow you to reserve places and pay online but tickets must still be picked up at the port at least fifteen minutes before departure.

The cheapest **fare class**, which you'll automatically be sold unless you specify otherwise, is *ikonomikí thési*, which gives you the run of most boats except for the upper-class restaurant and bar. Most newer boats seem expressly designed to frustrate summertime travellers attempting to sleep on deck. For long overnight journeys, it's worth considering the few extra euros for a **cabin bunk**;

second-class cabins are typically quadruple, while **first-class** double cabins with en-suite bathrooms can cost as much as a flight.

Motorbikes and cars get issued separate tickets, which can cost as much as five times the passenger fare, depending on size and journey duration – the shortest crossings are most expensive in comparison to a passenger ticket. For example, Keramotí–Thássos is €3 per person/€16 per car, while Sámos–Ikaría costs €10/€35 and Sámos–Pireás is €39/€88. It's really only worth taking a car to the larger islands like Crete, Rhodes, Híos, Lésvos, Sámos, Corfu or Kefaloniá, and only if staying a week or more. Otherwise, it is cheaper to leave your car on the mainland and rent another on arrival.

Hydrofoils, catamarans and high-speed boats

Hydrofoils – commonly known as *dhelfínia* or "Flying Dolphins" – are at least twice as expensive as ordinary ferries. Their network neatly fills gaps in ferry scheduling, but the service has been drastically reduced in recent years. The other drawback is that they are the first vessels to get cancelled in bad weather and even in moderate seas are not for the seasick-prone. Many don't operate – or are heavily reduced in frequency – from October to June. Hydrofoils aren't allowed to carry scooters or bicycles.

Catamarans and high-speed boats (tahýplia) are ruthlessly air-conditioned, usually without deck seating and with Greek TV blaring at you from multiple screens – paying extra for *dhiakikriméni thési* (upper class) merely gets you a better view. Car fares are normal, though passenger **tickets** are at least double a comparable ferry journey, ie similar to hydrofoil rates. Similarly, many don't run between October and April.

Small boats

In season, small boats known as **kaïkia** and **small ferries** sail between adjacent islands and to a few of the more obscure satellite islets. These are extremely useful and often very pleasant, but seldom cheaper than mainline services. The more consistent *kaïki* links are noted in the text, though the only firm information is to be had on the quayside. Swarms of **taxi-boats** are a feature of many islands; these shuttle clients on set routes to remote beaches or ports which can only be reached arduously, if at all, overland. Costs on these can be pretty stiff, usually per person but occasionally per boat.

By plane

Scheduled Greek **domestic flights** are run by the merged partnership of Olympic Air (☎801 801 0101, ⊛olympicair.com) and Aegean Airlines (☎801 112 0000, ⊛aegeanair.com), as well as minor operators Sky Express (☎2810 223 800, ⊛skyexpress.gr) and Astra Airlines (☎2310 489 390, ⊛ astra-airlines.gr), plus several new routes operated by Ryanair (⊛ryanair.com). Together they cover a broad network of island and mainland destinations, though most routes, especially on Aegean/Olympic, are to and from Athens or Thessaloníki. All these airlines are geared to web and call-centre **e-ticket sales**, as there are few walk-in town offices. Tickets bought through travel agencies attract a minimum €10 commission charge.

Fares to/between the islands cost at least double the cost of a deck-class ferry journey, but on inter-island routes poorly served by boat (Rhodes–Sámos, for example), consider this time well bought, and indeed some subsidized peripheral routes cost less than a hydrofoil/catamaran journey. The cheapest web fares on Aegean/Olympic are non-changeable and non-refundable, so it may be worth paying a little extra for a flexi-fare.

Island flights are often full in peak season; if they're an essential part of your plans, make **reservations** at least a month in advance. Waiting lists exist and are worth signing on to, as there are almost always cancellations. Small prop planes, which won't fly in strong winds or (in some cases) after dark, are used on many routes to less popular destinations. A 15kg baggage **weight limit** can be strictly enforced; if, however, you are connecting with an international flight or purchased your ticket outside Greece, you're allowed the standard 20–23kg limit.

By bus

Bus services on **major routes** in Greece are efficient and frequent, departing promptly at scheduled departure times. On the islands there are usually buses to connect the port and main town (if different) for ferry arrivals or departures. The national network is run by a syndicate of private operators based on each island, known as the **KTEL** (*Kratikó Tamío Ellinikón Leoforíon;* ☎14505 premium call charge and no national online timetable).

In island capitals or large cities in Crete, the **ticketing** is often computerized, sometimes with assigned seating, but otherwise it's first-come, first-served, with some standing allowed, and tickets dispensed on the spot by a conductor (*ispráktoras*). Prices are fixed according to distance and there are no cheap advance booking fares; Iráklio–Haniá costs €13.80, for example, but no other island except Évvia and Lésvos will have fares much in excess of €5.

By car, motorcycle and taxi

The Greek islands are blessed with dramatic coastal and mountain scenery, which is undoubtedly a joy to drive through. You should, however, bear in mind that Greece has one of the highest fatal **accident rates** in Europe. Local driving habits can be atrocious; overtaking on bends, barging out from side roads and failing to signal manoeuvres are common practices. **Drunk driving** is also a major issue, especially on Sunday afternoons, public holidays or late at night.

Road conditions can be very poor, from bad surfaces and inadequate signposting to unmarked railway crossings. The larger islands have some fast dual carriageways but, unlike the mainland, no toll motorways. **Fuel**, whether regular unleaded (*amólyvdhi*), super or diesel, is currently over €1.65 per litre across the country, often €1.80-plus in remoter areas. Be aware that many petrol stations close after 8pm and on Sundays.

Parking in the biggest island towns is inevitably a nightmare owing to oversubscription. **Pay-and-display** systems, plus residents-only schemes, are common, and it's often unclear where to obtain tickets.

Rules of the road

As in all of continental Europe, you **drive on the right** in Greece. Uphill drivers demand their **right of way**, as do the first to approach a one-lane bridge; **flashed headlights** usually mean the opposite of what they do in the UK or North America, here signifying that the other driver insists on coming through or overtaking. However, this gesture rapidly repeated from someone approaching means they're warning you of a police control-point ahead. One extraordinary fact is that there is no national law about who has the right of way at **roundabouts** – more often than not it is the vehicle entering the roundabout, but proceed with care.

Seat-belt use (and helmet wearing on scooters and motorcycles) is compulsory and children under the age of 10 are not allowed to sit in the front seats of cars; infractions of these rules are punishable by fines. It's illegal to drive away from any kind of **accident** – or to move the vehicles before the police appear – and where serious injury has resulted to the other party you can be held at a police station for up to 24 hours.

Car rental

Car rental in Greece starts at around €250 a week in peak season for the smallest vehicle from a one-off outlet or local chain, including unlimited mileage, tax and insurance. At other times, at smaller local outfits, you can get terms of €25–30 per day, all inclusive, with even better **rates** for three days or more – or prebooked on the internet. Rates for open **jeeps** vary from €60 to €90 per day.

Rental prices in Greece almost never include **collision damage waiver** (CDW) and personal insurance. The CDW typically has a deductible charge of €400–700, which may be levied for even the tiniest scratch or missing mudguard. To avoid this, it is strongly recommended that you pay the €5–7 extra per day for full coverage. Frequent EU-based travellers should consider **annual**

SIX MEMORABLE JOURNEYS

Kefaloniá's West Coast The road route north from Argostóli offers vistas of the Lixoúri Peninsula, Mýrtos beach and picturesque Ássos. See p.500.

The approach to Samothráki The ferry from Alexandhroúpoli allows Samothráki's profile, dominated by majestic Mount Fengari, to loom into focus. See p.410.

Mount Psilorítis, Crete Drive via Týlissos and Anóyia for sweeping views of the green valleys around Mount Psilorítis. See p.221.

Náxos to Amorgós Take the ferry from fertile Náxos via the delightful minor Cyclades to the imposing coast of Amorgós. See p.172.

Mastic villages, Híos Glimpse the alluring Mastic coast and marvel at the unique architecture of the villages on a drive through southern Híos. See p.380.

The Zákynthos circuit The anticlockwise boat tour of the island takes you to the famous Blue caves and Shipwreck Bay. See p.507.

excess insurance through Insurance 4 Car Hire
(Ⓦinsurance4carhire.com).

Almost all agencies will require a blank **credit
card** slip as a deposit (destroyed when you return
the vehicle safely); minimum **age requirements**
vary from 21 to 23. **Driving licences** issued by any
European Economic Area state are honoured, but
an **International Driving Permit** is required by all
other drivers (despite claims by unscrupulous
agencies). You can be arrested and charged if
caught by the traffic police without an IDP if you
require one.

Avance, Antena, Payless, Kosmos, National/Alamo,
Reliable, Tomaso and Eurodollar are dependable
Greek, or smaller international, chains with
branches on many islands; all are cheaper than
Hertz, Sixt or Avis. Specific local recommendations
are given in the guide.

Bringing your own car

If you intend to **drive your own car to and within
Greece**, remember that insurance contracted in
any EU state is valid in any other, but in many cases
this is only third-party cover. Competition in the
industry is intense, however, so many UK insurers
will throw in full, pan-European cover for free or for
a nominal sum, for up to sixty days. Those with
proof of AA/RAC/AAA membership are given free
road assistance from ELPA, the Greek equivalent,
which runs **breakdown services** on several of the
larger islands; in an emergency ring ❶10400.

EU citizens bringing their own cars are free to
circulate in the country for six months, or
until their home-based road tax or insurance
expires, whichever happens first; keeping a car in
Greece for longer entails more paperwork. **Non-EU
nationals** will get a car entered in their passport;
the carnet normally allows you to keep a vehicle in
Greece for up to six months, exempt from road tax.

Scooter and motorcycle rental

Small **motor scooters** with automatic transmission,
known in Greek as *mihanákia* or *papákia* (little
ducks), are good transport for all but the steepest
terrain. They're available for rent on most islands for
€12–18 per day. Prices can be bargained down out
of peak season, or for a longer rental period. Only
models of 80cc and above are powerful enough for
two riders in mountainous areas, which includes
most islands.

True **motorbikes** (*mihanés*) with manual trans-
missions and safer tyres are less common. With the
proper licence, bikes of 125cc and up are available
in many resorts for around €20 per day. **Quads** are

also increasingly offered – without doubt the most
stupid-looking and impractical conveyance yet
devised, and very unstable on turns – make sure
helmets are supplied.

Reputable establishments demand a full **motorcycle driving licence** (Class B) for any engine over
80cc and sometimes even for 50cc models, which is
the official legal requirement. You will sometimes
have to leave your passport as a deposit. Failure to
carry the correct licence on your person also
attracts a stiff fine, though some agencies still
demand this rather than a passport as security.

Many rental outfits will offer you (an often
ill-fitting) **crash helmet** (*krános*), and some will
make you sign a waiver of liability if you refuse it.
Helmet-wearing is required by law, with a €185 fine
levied for failure to do so; on some smaller islands
the rule is laxly enforced, on others random police
roadblocks do a brisk commerce in citations, to
foreigners and locals alike.

Before riding off, always check the **brakes** and
electrics; dealers often keep the front brakes far too
loose, with the commendable intention of
preventing you going over the handlebars. Make
sure also that there's a kick-start as backup to the
battery, since ignition switches commonly fail. If
you **break down** on a scooter or motorcycle you're
often responsible for returning the machine,
although the better outlets offer a free retrieval
service.

Taxis

Greek **taxis** are among the cheapest in the
Mediterranean – so long as you get an honest
driver who switches the meter on and doesn't use
high-tech devices to doctor the reading. Use of the
meter is mandatory within city or town limits,
where Tariff 1 applies, while in rural areas or
between midnight and 5am Tariff 2 is in effect. On
certain islands, set rates apply on specific fixed
routes – these might only depart when full.
Otherwise, throughout Greece the meter starts at
€1.20, though the minimum **fare** is €3.40; baggage
in the boot is charged at €0.40 per piece. Additionally, there are surcharges of €2.60 for leaving or
entering an airport, and €1.07 for leaving a harbour
area. If you summon a taxi by phone on spec,
there's a €1.92 charge; the meter starts running
from the moment the driver begins heading
towards you. All categories of supplemental
charges must be set out on a card affixed to the
dashboard. For a week or so before and after
Orthodox Easter, and Christmas, a *filodhórima*
(gratuity) of about ten percent is levied.

By bike

Cycling in the Greek islands is not such hard going as you might imagine (except in summer), especially on one of the mountain bikes that are now the rule at rental outfits; they rarely cost more than €8 a day. You do, however, need steady nerves, as roads are generally narrow with no verges or bike lanes and Greek drivers are notoriously inconsiderate to cyclists.

If you have your own bike, consider taking it along on the **plane** (it's free if within your 20–23kg international air allowance, but arrange it in writing with the airline beforehand to avoid huge charges at check-in). Once in Greece you can take a bike for free on most ferries and in the luggage bays of buses. Any small spare parts you might need are best brought along, since specialist shops are rare.

Accommodation

There are vast numbers of tourist beds throughout the Greek islands, and most of the year you can rely on simply turning up and finding something. At Easter and in July and August, however, you can run into problems if you haven't booked in advance. The economic crisis and subsequent loss of domestic tourism has tended to depress prices, and what you pay may depend on how far you are willing to bargain.

Many of the big hotels and self-catering complexes are pre-booked by **package-holiday** companies for the whole season. Although they may have vacancies if you just turn up, non-package visitors are far more likely to find themselves staying in smaller, simpler places which usually describe themselves simply as **"rooms"**, or as apartments or studios. Standards here can vary from spartan (though invariably clean) to luxurious, but the vast majority are purpose-built blocks where every room is en suite, and where the minimal furnishings are well adapted to the local climate – at least in summer.

Seasons

There are typically three **seasons** which affect prices: October to April (low), May, June and September (mid) and July and August (high) – though **Easter** and the first two weeks of August may be in a higher category still. Urban hotels with a predominantly business clientele tend to charge the same rates all year. Elsewhere, places that have significant domestic tourism, such as the Argo-Saronic islands, frequently charge significantly more at weekends.

Many of the smaller places offering rooms **close from October to April**. In winter, then, you may have to stay in hotels in the main towns or ports. On smaller islands, there may be just one hotel and a single taverna that stays open year-round. Be warned also that resort or harbour hotels which do operate through the winter are likely to have a certain number of prostitutes as long-term guests; licensed prostitution is legal in Greece, and the management may consider this the most painless way to keep the bills paid.

ACCOMMODATION PRICES

The price we quote is for the establishment's **cheapest double room in mid season** – there may well be other rooms that cost more, and occasionally the cheapest price will mean a shared bathroom. Depending on where you are, the price may rocket in the first two weeks of August, sometimes by as much as double: for much of the year, however, you can expect to pay a bit less. In rooms establishments and the cheaper hotels, the price of a basic double room starts at around €20–25 a night out of season, though the same room may be €50 or more in August. For a bit more luxury and in more touristy areas, you'll probably be paying €40–50 in mid-season, €70–90 if you add a pool and other facilities; 5-star hotels charge €200 and above.

Prices are for the room only, except where otherwise indicated; fancier places often include breakfast in the price – we indicate this in the listing, but check when booking.

By law, **prices must be displayed** on the back of the door of your room, or over the reception desk. You should never pay more than this, and in practice it is rare to pay as much as the sign says. If you feel you're being overcharged, threaten to make a report to the tourist office or police, who will generally take your side in such cases.

Hotels

The tourist police set official **star categories** for hotels, from five-star down; all except the top category have to keep within set price limits. You may still see the old letter system (L, luxury, is five-star, then A to E). Ratings correspond to the facilities available (lifts, dining room, pool etc), a box-ticking exercise which doesn't always reflect the actual quality of the hotel; there are plenty of 2-star hotels which are in practice smarter and more comfortable than 3-star outfits. A new "boutique" category allows some hotels to escape the straitjacket on the grounds of location or historical significance.

Hotels with 2-star and below have only to provide the most rudimentary of continental **breakfasts** – sometimes optional for an extra charge – while 3-star and above will usually offer buffets with cheese, cold meats, eggs and cereals.

Single rooms are rare, and generally poor value – you'll often have to pay the full double-room price or haggle for a small discount; on the other hand, larger groups and families can almost always find triple and quadruple rooms, and more upmarket hotels may have **family suites** (two rooms sharing one bathroom), all of which can be very good value.

Private rooms and apartments

Many places categorized as apartments or rooms are every bit as comfortable as hotels, and in the lower price ranges are usually more congenial and better value. At their most basic, **rooms** (*dhomátia* – but usually spotted by a "Rooms for Rent" or Zimmer Frei sign) might be literally a room in someone's house, a bare space with a bed and a hook on the back of the door, and washing facilities outside, but the sparse facilities are offset by the disarming hospitality you'll be offered as part of the family. However, these days almost all are purpose-built, with comfortable en-suites and balconies – at the fancier end of the scale you'll find studio and apartment complexes with marble floors, pools, bars and children's playgrounds. Many have a variety of rooms at different prices, so ask to see the room first. Places described as studios usually have a small kitchenette, while apartments generally have at least one bedroom and separate kitchen/living room.

Areas to **look for rooms**, along with recommendations of the best places, are included in the guide. The rooms may also find you, as owners descend on ferry or bus arrivals to fill any space they have, sometimes with photos of their premises. This can be great, but you can also be in for a nasty surprise – usually because the rooms are much further than you had been led to believe, or bear no relation to the pictures. In some places the practice has been outlawed. In the more developed island resorts, where package holiday-makers predominate, room owners may insist on a minimum stay of a few days, or even a week (specified in our reviews if that is the case).

Rooms proprietors sometimes ask to keep your **passport**: ostensibly "for the tourist police", but in reality to prevent you leaving with an unpaid bill. They'll almost always return the documents should you ask for them.

If you are **stranded**, or arrive very late in a remote village, you may well find someone with an unlicensed room prepared to earn extra money by putting you up. This should not be counted on, but things work out more often than not.

Villas and longer-term rentals

Although one of the great dreams of Greek travel is finding an idyllic coastal villa and renting it for virtually nothing for a whole month, there's no chance at all of your dream coming true in modern Greece. All the best **villas** are contracted out to

---

HOT WATER AND AIR CONDITIONING

When checking out a room, always ask about the status of **air conditioning** and **wi-fi**. Almost all modern rooms and apartments have air conditioning (indicated by a/c in our listings), but it's sometimes an optional extra, in which case you'll be charged an additional €5 or so a night for it. Hot water should always be available, though there may not be enough: rooftop solar heaters are popular and effective, but shared solar-powered tanks tend to run out in the post-beach shower crunch around 6–7pm, with no more available until the next day. A water heater, either as a backup or primary source, is more reliable. **Wi-fi** is spreading very rapidly, and these days even the most basic places tend to have it. There's very rarely a charge, but wi-fi may not extend to the rooms (or if it does, not to every room) and it's often pretty slow.

SEVEN SPECIAL PLACES TO STAY

Mýlos tou Markétou, Mílos A sixteenth-century windmill converted into a stylish apartment. See p.128

Heaven, Páros Individually decorated rooms, crisp white sheets and views to die for at this heavenly B&B. See p.161

Polikandia, Folégandhros A well-priced, well-designed boutique hotel on one of Greece's less discovered islands. See p.185

Míliá Eco Village, Crete Abandoned mountain hamlet restored as lovely, candlelit accommodation. See p.257

Spirit of the Knights, Rhodes Exquisite B&B with a lovely courtyard tucked away in Rhodes Old Town. See p.274

Maison des Couleurs, Léros Fabulous Italian manor house cleverly refurbished with bold colours and original features and furnishings. See p.336

Karimalis Winery, Ikaría A winery and organic farm running wine and cooking courses on little-visited Ikaría. See p.371

agents and let through **foreign operators**. Even if you do find one empty for a week or two, renting it locally usually costs far more than it would have done to arrange from home. There, specialist operators (see p.28) represent some superb places, from simple to luxurious, and costs can be very reasonable, especially if shared between a few people. Several of the companies listed will arrange stays on two islands over two weeks.

That said, if you do arrive and decide you want to drop roots for a while, you can still strike lucky if you don't mind avoiding the obvious coastal tourist spots, and are happy with relatively modest accommodation. Pick an untouristed village, get yourself known and ask about; you might still pick up a wonderful deal. **Out of season** your chances are much better – even in touristy areas, between October and March (sometimes as late as April and May) you can bargain a very good rate, especially for stays of a month or more. **Travel agents** are a good source of information on what's available locally, and many rooms places have an apartment on the side or know someone with one to rent.

Hostels and backpackers

Over the years most traditional youth **hostels** in the islands have closed down; competition from inexpensive rooms meant that they were simply not cost-effective. However, those that survive are generally very good, and there's a new generation of youth-oriented **backpackers** on the more popular islands, big on social life and a party atmosphere. Few of them are members of any official organization – though an IYHF card or student ID may save you a few euros – and virtually none will have a curfew or any restrictive regulations. Prices for a dorm bed vary from as little as €10 in a simple, traditional hostel to as much as €30 in high season in the fancier backpackers.

If you're planning to spend a few nights in hostels, **IYHF membership** is probably a worthwhile investment. By no means all Greek hostels offer discounts, but there are other membership benefits – the card may be accepted as student ID, for example. You may be able to buy membership at official hostels; otherwise visit ⓦhihostels .com from where you can apply via your local youth hostel association. To book hostels online try ⓦhostelworld.com.

Camping

Partly thanks to the economic crisis, Greek **camping** has undergone something of a revival in recent years. **Officially recognized campsites** range from ramshackle compounds to highly organized and rather soulless complexes, often dominated by camper vans. Most places cost in the region of €5–7 a night per person, plus €4–6 per tent and the same again for a car, or €7–10 per camper van; at the fanciest sites rates for two people plus a tent can almost equal the price of a basic room. You will need at least a light sleeping bag, since even summer nights can get cool and damp. The website of the official Greek camping organization (ⓦwww .greececamping.gr) lists all authorized campsites, with booking for many of them.

Camping **outside an official campsite** (with or without a tent) is against the law – enforced in most tourist areas and on beaches. If you do camp rough, exercise sensitivity and discretion. Police will crack down on people camping (and especially littering) if a large community of campers develops.

Off the beaten track nobody is very bothered, though it is always best to ask permission in the local taverna or café, and to be aware of rising crime, even in remote areas. If you want to camp near a beach, the best strategy is to find a sympathetic taverna, which in exchange for regular patronage will probably be willing to guard small valuables and let you use their facilities.

Food and drink

Although many visitors get by on moussaká or kalamári almost every night, there is a huge range to Greek cuisine, not least its wonderful mezédhes, seafood and juicy, fat olives. Despite depressed wages, most Greeks still eat out with friends or family at least once a week. The atmosphere is always relaxed and informal, with pretensions rare. Drinking is traditionally meant to accompany food, though a range of bars and clubs exists.

Breakfast

Greeks don't generally eat **breakfast**, more often opting for a mid-morning snack (see below). This is reflected in the abysmal quality of most hotel "continental" offerings, where waxy orange squash, stewed coffee, processed cheese and meats, plus pre-packaged butter, honey and jam (confusingly called *marmeládha*), are the rule at all but the top establishments. There might be some fresh fruit, decent yoghurt and pure honey, if you are lucky. The only egg-and-bacon kinds of places are in resorts where foreigners congregate, or where there are returned North American- or Australian-Greeks. Such outlets can often be good value (€4–7 for the works, including coffee), especially if there's competition.

Picnics and snacks

Picnic ingredients are easily available at supermarkets, bakeries and greengrocers; sampling produce like cheese or olives is acceptable. Standard white **bread** is often of minimal nutritional value and inedible within a day of purchase, although rarer brown varieties such as *olikís* (wholemeal), *sikalísio* (rye bread) or *oktásporo* (multigrain) fare better. Olives are ubiquitous; the Kalamáta and Ámfissa varieties usually surpass most local picks in quality.

Honey is the ideal topping for the famous local **yoghurt**, which is widely available in bulk. Sheepmilk yoghurt (*próvio*) is richer and sweeter than the more common cow's-milk kind. **Feta cheese** is found everywhere, often with a dozen varieties to choose from, made from goat's, sheep's or cow's milk in varying proportions. Harder *graviéra* is the second most popular cheese.

Greece imports very little produce from abroad, aside from bananas, the odd pineapple and a few mangoes. **Fruit** is relatively expensive and available mainly by season. Reliable picnic fruits include cherries (June–July); *krystália*, small, heavenly green pears (Sept–Nov); *vaniliés*, orange- or red-fleshed plums (July–Oct); and kiwi (Oct–May). Less portable, but succulent, are figs, whose main season is August and September. Salad **vegetables** are more reasonably priced; besides the famous, enormous tomatoes (June–Sept), there's a bewildering variety of cool-season greens, including rocket, dill, enormous spring onions and lettuces.

Restaurants

Greek cuisine and **restaurants** are usually straightforward and still largely affordable – typically €12–20 per person for a substantial meal with house wine. Even when preparation is basic, raw materials are usually wholesome and fresh. The best strategy is to **go where Greeks go**, often less obvious backstreet places that might not look much from outside but deliver the real deal. The

---

FAST FOOD GREEK STYLE

Traditional hot **snacks** are still easy to come by, although they are being elbowed aside by Western fast food at both international and nationwide Greek chains such as *Goody's* (burgers, pasta and salad bar), *Everest*, *Grigoris* and *Theios Vanias* (baked pastries and baguette sandwiches), and various pizzerias. Still, thousands of kebab shops (*souvladzídhika*) churn out *souvlákia*, either as small shish on wooden sticks or as *yíros* – doner kebab with garnish in pítta bread. Other snacks include cheese pies (*tyrópites*), spinach pies (*spanokópites*) and, less commonly, minced meat pies (*kreatópites*); these are found either at the baker's or some of the aforementioned chains.

TAVERNA TIPS

Since the idea of **courses** is foreign to Greek cuisine, starters, main dishes and salads often arrive together unless you request otherwise. The best strategy is to order a selection of mezédhes and salads to share, in local fashion. Waiters encourage you to take *horiátiki saláta* – the so-called Greek **salad**, including feta cheese – because it is the most expensive. If you only want tomato and cucumber, ask for *angourodomáta*. Cabbage-carrot (*láhano-karóto*) and lettuce (*maroúli*) are the typical cool-season salads.

Bread is generally counted as part of the "cover" charge (€0.50–1 per person), so you have to pay for it even if you don't eat any. Though menu prices are supposedly inclusive of all taxes and service, an extra **tip** of around five percent or simple rounding up of the bill is in order.

---

two most common types of restaurant are the **estiatório** and the **taverna**. Distinctions are slight, though the former is more commonly found in the larger island towns and emphasize the more complicated, oven-baked casserole dishes termed *mayireftá* (literally, "cooked").

As one might expect, the identikit tavernas at resorts dominated by foreigners tend to make less effort, bashing out speedily grilled meat with pre-cut chips and rice containing the odd pea. You should beware of **overcharging** and bill-padding at such establishments too. In some island capitals and chic resorts, growing numbers of pretentious restaurants boast fancy decor and Greek nouvelle (or fusion) cuisine with speciality wine lists, while producing little of substance.

Greeks generally eat very late in the evening, rarely venturing out until after 9pm and often arriving at midnight or later. Consequently, most restaurants operate flexible hours, varying according to the level of custom, and thus the **opening times** given throughout the listings should be viewed as approximate at best.

Estiatória

With their long hours and tiny profit margins, **estiatória** (sometimes known as *inomayiría*, "wine-and-cook-houses") are, alas, a vanishing breed. An *estiatório* will generally feature a variety of *mayireftá* such as *moussaká*, *pastítsio* (macaroni pie), meat or game stews, stuffed tomatoes or peppers, the oily vegetable casseroles called *ladherá*, plus oven-baked meat and fish. Usually you point at the steam trays to choose these dishes. Batches are cooked in the morning and then left to stand, which is why the food is often **lukewarm**; most such dishes are in fact enhanced by being allowed to steep in their own juice.

Tavernas and psistariés

Tavernas range from the glitzy and fashionable to rough-and-ready beachside ones with seating under a reed canopy. Really primitive ones have a very limited (often unwritten) menu, but the more elaborate will offer some of the main *mayireftá* dishes mentioned above, as well as standard taverna fare: **mezédhes** (hors d'oeuvres) or **orektiká** (appetizers) and **tís óras** (meat and fish, fried or grilled to order). **Psistariés** (grill houses) serve spit-roasted lamb, pork, goat, chicken or *kokorétsi* (grilled offal roulade), and often *yíros* by the portion. They will usually have a limited selection of mezédhes and salads (*salátes*), but no *mayireftá*. In rural areas, roadside *psistariés* are often called *exohiká kéndra*.

The most common mezédhes are tzatzíki (yoghurt, garlic and cucumber dip), *melitzanosaláta* (aubergine/eggplant dip), fried courgette/zucchini or aubergine/eggplant slices, *yígandes* (white haricot beans in hot tomato sauce), *tyropitákia* or *spanakopitákia* (small cheese or spinach pies), *revythókeftedhes* (chickpea patties similar to falafel), octopus salad and *mavromátika* (black-eyed peas).

Among **meats**, *souvláki* and chops are reliable choices; pork is usually better and cheaper than veal, especially as *pantséta* (spare ribs). The best *souvláki*, not always available, is lamb; more commonly encountered are rib chops (*païdhákia*); lamb roasted in tin foil (*exohikó*) is another favourite. *Keftédhes* (breadcrumbed meatballs), *biftékia* (pure-meat patties) and the spicy, coarse-grain sausages called *loukánika* are cheap and good. Chicken is widely available but typically battery-farmed. Other dishes worth trying are stewed goat (*yídha vrastí*) or baked goat (*katsíki stó foúrno*) – goat in general is typically free-range and organic.

Fish and seafood

Seafood can be one of the highlights of a trip to the Greek islands, though there are some tips to bear in mind when ordering fish at a taverna or *psaro-*

VEGETARIANS

Vegetarians will find scarcely any dedicated **meat-free restaurants** at all in Greece. That is not to say that they cannot enjoy excellent food, however. The best solution in tavernas or ouzerís is to assemble a meal from vegetarian mezédhes and salads and, in *estiatória* especially, keep an eye open for the delicious *ladherá*, vegetables baked in various sauces.

tavérna (specialist seafood restaurant). The standard procedure is to go to the glass cooler and pick your specimen, then have it weighed (uncleaned) in your presence. Overcharging, especially where a printed menu is absent, is not uncommon; have weight and price confirmed clearly.

Taverna owners often comply only minimally with the requirement to indicate when seafood is **frozen** – look for the abbreviation "kat", "k" or just an asterisk on the Greek-language side of the menu. If the price, almost invariably quoted by the kilo, seems too good to be true, it's almost certainly farmed. The choicest varieties, such as red mullet, *tsipoúra* (gilt-head bream), sea bass or *fangrí* (common bream), will be expensive if wild – €45–70 per kilo. Less esteemed species tend to cost €20–35 per kilo but are usually quoted at €6–9 per portion.

Fish caught in the summer months tend to be smaller and drier, and so are served with *ladholé-mono* (oil and lemon) sauce. An inexpensive May–June treat is fresh, grilled or fried *bakaliáros* (hake), the classic UK fish-and-chip shop species. *Gávros* (anchovy), *atherína* (sand smelts) and *sardhélles* (sardines) are late-summer fixtures, at their best in the northeast Aegean. *Koliós* (mackerel) is excellent either grilled or baked in sauce. Especially in autumn you may find *psarósoupa* (fish soup) or *kakaviá* (bouillabaisse).

Cheaper **seafood** (*thalassiná*) such as fried baby squid (usually frozen); *thrápsalo* (large, grillable deep-water squid) and octopus are summer staples; often mussels, cockles and small prawns will also be offered at reasonable sums (€20–30 per kilo).

Wine

All tavernas will offer you a choice of bottled **wines**, and most have their own house variety: kept in barrels, sold in bulk (*varelísio* or *hýma*) by the quarter-, half- or full litre, and served in glass flagons

or brightly coloured tin "monkey-cups". Per-litre prices depend on locale and quality, ranging from €4–5 (Skýros) to €10–12 (Santoríni, Rhodes). Non-resinated wine is almost always more than decent; some people add a dash of soda water or lemonade. Barrelled **retsina** – pine-resinated wine, often an acquired taste – is far less common than it used to be, though you will find bottled brands everywhere: Yeoryiadhi from Thessaloníki, Liokri from Ahaïa and Malamatina from central Greece are all quaffable.

Among **bottled wines** available throughout the islands, Cambas Attikos, Zítsa and Rhodian CAIR products are good, inexpensive whites, while Boutari Naoussa and Kourtakis Apelia are decent, mid-range reds. For a better but still moderately priced red, choose either Boutari or Tsantali Merlot, or Averof Katoï from Epirus.

Travelling around **wine-producing islands** such as Límnos, Lésvos, Santoríni, Kefaloniá, Náxos, Ikaría, Rhodes and Crete you will also have the chance to sample local bottlings. Curiously, island **red wines** are almost uniformly mediocre, so you are better off ordering mainland varieties from Carras on Halki-dhikí, and various spots in the Peloponnese and Thessaly. Particularly notable local vintages are mentioned throughout the guide. The best available current guide to the emerging Greek domaines and vintners is Konstantinos Lazarakis' *The Wines of Greece*.

Finally, CAIR on Rhodes makes "**champagne**" ("naturally sparkling wine fermented en bouteille", says the label), in both brut and demi-sec versions. It's not Moët & Chandon quality by any means, but at about €6 per bottle, nobody's complaining.

Cafés and bars

A venerable institution, under attack from the onslaught of mass global culture, is the **kafenío**, still found in every Greek town but dying out in many resorts. In greater abundance, you'll

TOURING WINERIES IN GREECE

An increasing amount of Greek **wineries** are opening their doors to visitors for **tastings and tours**, which are usually free or for a nominal charge. There are a number of wineries dotted around the islands – check out ⓦnewwineries ofgreece.com for more info.

THE STRONG STUFF

Ouzo and the similar **tsípouro** (some north Aegean islands and increasingly elsewhere) and **tsikoudhiá** (Crete) are simple spirits of up to 48 percent alcohol, distilled from the grape-mash residue of winemaking. The former is always flavoured with anise, the latter two mostly unadulterated but may have a touch of anise, cinnamon, pear essence or fennel. There are nearly thirty brands of ouzo or *tsípouro*, with the best reckoned to be from Lésvos and Sámos. Note that ouzo has the peculiar ability to bring back its effect when you drink water the morning after, so make sure you don't plan to do anything important (not least driving) the next day.

encounter **patisseries** (*zaharoplastía*), swish modern **cafeterias and trendy bars**.

Kafenía, cafeterias and coffee

The **kafenío** (plural *kafenía*) is the traditional Greek coffee house. Although its main business is "Greek" (Middle Eastern) **coffee** – prepared unsweetened (*skétos* or *pikrós*), medium (*métrios*) or sweet (*glykós*) – it also serves instant coffee, ouzo, brandy, beer, sage-based tea known as *tsáï vounoú*, soft drinks and juices. Some *kafenía* close at siesta time, but many remain open from early in the morning until late at night. The chief summer socializing time for a preprandial ouzo is 6–8pm, immediately after the afternoon nap.

Cafeterias are the province of fancier varieties of coffee and **kafés frappé**, iced instant coffee with sugar and (optionally) condensed milk – uniquely Greek despite its French name. Like Greek coffee, it is always accompanied by a glass of water. *Freddoccino* is a newer, cappuccino-based alternative to the traditional cold frappé. "Nes"(café) is the generic term for all instant **coffee**, regardless of brand. Thankfully, almost all cafeterias now offer a range of foreign-style coffees – filter, dubbed *fíltros* or *gallikós* (French); cappuccino; and espresso – at overseas prices. Alcohol is also served and many establishments morph into lively bars late at night.

Sweets and desserts

The **zaharoplastío**, a cross between café and patisserie, serves coffee, a limited range of alcohol, yoghurt with honey and sticky cakes. The better establishments offer an amazing variety of pastries, cream-and-chocolate confections, honey-soaked Greco–Turkish sweets like *baklavás*, *kataïfi* (honey-drenched "shredded wheat"), *loukoumádhes* (deep-fried batter puffs dusted with cinnamon and dipped in syrup), *galakto-boúreko* (custard pie) and so on. For more dairy-based products, seek out a **galaktopolío**, where you'll often find *ryzógalo* (rice pudding), *kréma*

(custard) and locally made *yiaoúrti* (yoghurt). Both *zaharoplastía* and *galaktopolía* are more family-oriented places than a *kafenío*. **Traditional specialities** include "spoon sweets" or *glyká koutalioú* (syrupy preserves of quince, grape, fig, citrus fruit or cherry).

Ice cream, sold principally at the parlours which have swept across Greece (Dhodhoni is the posh home-grown competition to Haägen-Dazs), can be very good and almost indistinguishable from Italian prototypes. A scoop (*baláki*) costs €1.20–1.50; you'll often be asked if you want it in a cup (*kypelláki*) or a cone (*konáki*), and whether you want toppings like *santiyí* (whipped cream) or nuts.

Ouzería, mezedhopolía and spirits

Ouzería (often called **tsipourádhika** in Vólos, Thessaloníki and increasingly elsewhere), found mainly in select neighbourhoods of larger island towns, specialize in ouzo and *mezédhes*. In some places you also find **mezedhopolía**, a bigger, more elaborate kind of ouzerí. These places are well worth trying for the marvellous variety of mezédhes they serve. In effect, several plates of mezédhes plus drinks will substitute for a more involved meal at a taverna, though it works out more expensive if you have a healthy appetite. Faced with an often bewilderingly varied menu, you might opt for a *pikilía* (assortment) available in several sizes, the most expensive one usually emphasizing seafood.

Ouzo is served by the glass, to which you can add water from the accompanying glass or ice to taste. The next measure up is a *karafáki* – a 200ml vial, the favourite means of delivery for *tsípouro*. Once, every ouzo was automatically accompanied by a small plate of **mezédhes** on the house: cheese, cucumber, tomato, a few olives, sometimes octopus or a couple of small fish. Nowadays "ouzomezés" is a separate, pricier option. Often, however, this is "off-menu" but if you order a *karafáki* you will automatically be served a selection of snacks.

Bars, beer and mineral water

Bars (*barákia*) are ubiquitous throughout the islands, ranging from clones of Spanish bodegas to musical beachside bars more active by day than at night. At their most sophisticated, however, they are well-executed theme venues in ex-industrial premises or Neoclassical houses, with both Greek and international soundtracks. Most Greek bars have a half-life of about a year; the best way to find current hot spots, especially if they're more club than bar, is to look out for posters advertising bar-hosted events in the neighbourhood.

Shots and **cocktails** are invariably expensive at €5–8, except during well-advertised happy hours; beer in a bar will cost €4–6 in most establishments. **Beers** are mostly foreign lagers made locally under licence at just a handful of breweries on the central mainland. **Local brands** include the palatable Fix from Athens, milder Mythos and Veryina from Komotiní. There is, however, a growing number of quality **microbreweries**: the original is Craft in Athens, who produce lager in three grades (blonde, "smoked" and black), as well as a red ale, and now distribute quite widely. Other highly rated but strictly local microbreweries have sprung up on Crete (Réthymno), Corfu, Híos and Santoríni. Genuinely **imported** German beers, such as Bitburger, Fisher and Warsteiner (plus a few British and Irish ones), are found in Athens and at busier resorts.

The ubiquitous Loutraki **mineral water** is not esteemed by the Greeks themselves, who prefer various brands from Crete and Epirus. In many tavernas there has been a backlash against plastic bottles, and you can now get mineral water in glass bottles. Souroti, Epsa and Sariza are the principal labels of naturally **sparkling** (*aerioúho* in Greek) water, in small bottles; Tuborg club soda is also widespread. Note that despite variable quality in taste **tap water** is essentially safe all over Greece, though persuading restaurants to provide it can be difficult on many islands.

Health

There are no required inoculations for Greece, though it's wise to ensure you are up to date on tetanus and polio. The main health risks faced by visitors involve overexposure to the sun, overindulgence in food and drink, or bites and stings from insects and sea creatures.

British and other EU nationals are entitled to free medical care in Greece upon presentation of a European Health Insurance Card (see box, below). The US, Canada, Australia and New Zealand have no formal healthcare agreements with Greece (other than allowing for free emergency trauma treatment), so insurance is highly recommended.

Doctors and hospitals

For serious medical attention you'll find English-speaking **doctors** (mainly private) in all the bigger towns and resorts: if your hotel can't help, the tourist police or your consulate should be able to come up with some names. There are **hospitals** on all the bigger islands, and some kind of medical centre on virtually every one. For an ambulance, phone ❶ 166.

Pharmacies, drugs and contraception

For minor complaints it's enough to go to the local **pharmacy** (*farmakío*). Greek pharmacists are highly trained and dispense a number of medicines which elsewhere could only be prescribed by a doctor. In the larger towns and resorts there'll usually be one who speaks good English. Pharmacies are usually closed evenings and Saturday mornings, but all should have a schedule on their door showing the night and weekend duty pharmacists in town.

THE EUROPEAN HEALTH INSURANCE CARD

If you have an **EHIC** (🌐 ehic.org.uk, 🌐 ehic.ie) you are entitled to free consultation and treatment from doctors and dentists. At hospitals you should simply have to show your EHIC; for free treatment from a regular doctor or dentist, you should call the IKA (the Social Insurance Institute, who administer the scheme) on their national appointments hotline, ❶ 184. For prescriptions from pharmacies you pay a small fixed charge plus 25 percent of the cost of the medicine; if you are charged in full, get a receipt and keep the original prescription to claim it back. You can also claim back for private treatment; take the original receipts and your EHIC to the IKA within one month, and they will reimburse you up to the limit allowed for similar treatment by the IKA.

If you regularly use any form of **prescription drug**, you should bring along a copy of the prescription, together with the generic name of the drug; this will help you replace it, and avoids problems with customs officials. In this regard, you should be aware that **codeine** is banned in Greece. If you import any you might find yourself in serious trouble, so check labels carefully; it's a major ingredient of Panadeine, Veganin, Solpadeine, Codis and Nurofen Plus, to name just a few.

Contraceptive pills are sold over the counter at larger pharmacies, though not necessarily the brands you may be used to; a good pharmacist should come up with a close match. **Condoms** are inexpensive and ubiquitous – just ask for *profylaktiká* (less formally, *plastiká* or *kapótes*) at any pharmacy, sundries store or corner *períptero* (kiosk). Sanitary towels and **tampons** are widely sold in supermarkets.

Common health problems

The main health problems experienced by visitors – including many blamed on the food – have to do with **overexposure to the sun**. To avoid these, cover up, wear a hat, and drink plenty of fluids to avoid any danger of **sunstroke**; remember that even hazy sun can burn. **Tap water** meets strict EU standards for safety, but high mineral content and less than perfect desalination on many islands can leave a brackish taste not suited to everyone. For that reason many people prefer to stick to bottled water (see opposite). Hayfever sufferers should be prepared for a pollen season earlier than in northern Europe, peaking in April and May.

Hazards of the sea

To avoid hazards in or by the sea, goggles or a dive mask for swimming and footwear for walking over wet or rough rocks are useful. You may have the bad luck to meet an armada of **jellyfish** (*tsoúkhtres*), especially in late summer; they come in various colours and sizes ranging from purple "pizzas" to invisible, minute creatures. Various over-the-counter remedies are sold in resort pharmacies to combat the sting, and baking soda or diluted ammonia also help to lessen the effects. Less vicious but far more common are spiny sea urchins, which infest rocky shorelines year-round. If you step on or graze against one, an effective way to remove the spines is with a needle (you can crudely sterilize it with heat from a cigarette lighter) and olive oil. If you don't remove the spines, they'll fester.

Bites and stings

Most of Greece's insects and reptiles are pretty benign, but there are a few that can give a painful bite. Much the most common are **mosquitoes**: you can buy repellent devices and sprays at any minimarket. On beaches, sandflies can also give a nasty (and potentially infection-carrying) sting. Adders (*ohiés*) and scorpions (*scorpií*) are found throughout Greece. Both creatures are shy, but take care when climbing over drystone walls where snakes like to sun themselves, and – particularly when camping – don't put hands or feet in places, like shoes, where you haven't looked first.

Finally, watch out for the pine processionary **caterpillar**, which takes its name from the long, nose-to-tail convoys it. In addition to munching its way through a fair amount of Greece's surviving pine forests, it sports highly irritating hairs, with a venom worse than a scorpion's. If you touch one, or even a tree trunk they've been on recently, you'll know all about it for a week, and the welts may require antihistamine to heal.

If you snap a **wild-fig shoot** while walking, avoid contact with the highly irritant **sap**. The immediate antidote to the active alkaloid is a mild acid – lemon juice or vinegar; left unneutralized, fig "milk" raises welts which take a month to heal.

The media

Greeks are great devourers of newsprint – although few would propose the Greek mass media as a paradigm of objective journalism. Papers are almost uniformly sensational, while state-run TV and radio are often biased in favour of whichever party happens to be in government. Foreign news is widely available, though, in the form of locally printed newspaper editions and TV news channels.

Newspapers and magazines

British newspapers are widely available in resorts and the larger towns at a cost of €2–4 for dailies, or €4–6 for Sunday editions. Many, including the *Times*, *Mail* and *Mirror*, have slimmed-down editions printed in Greece which are available the same day; others are likely to be a day old. In bigger newsagents you'll also be able to find *USA Today*, *Time* and *Newsweek* as well as the *International New York Times*, which has the bonus of including an abridged English edition of the same day's *Kathimerini*, a respected Greek daily, thus allowing you to keep up with Greek news too. From time to time you'll also find various English-language magazines aimed at visitors to Greece, though none seems to survive for long.

Radio

Greece's airwaves are cluttered with **local and regional stations**, many of which have plenty of music, often traditional. In popular areas many of them have regular news bulletins and tourist information in English. The mountainous nature of much of the country, though, means that any sort of **radio reception** is tricky: if you're driving around you'll find that you constantly have to retune. The two state-run networks are ER1 (a mix of news, talk and pop music) and ER2 (pop music).

The BBC World Service no longer broadcasts to Europe on short wave, though Voice of America can be picked up in places. Both of these and dozens of others are of course available as internet broadcasts, however, or via satellite TV channels.

Television

Greece's state-funded **TV stations**, ET1, NET and ET3, nowadays lag behind private channels – Mega, Star, Alpha, Alter and Skai – in the ratings, though not necessarily in quality of offerings. Most foreign films and serials are broadcast in their original language, with Greek subtitles; there's almost always a choice of English-language movies from about 9pm onwards, although the closer you get to the end of the movie, the more adverts you'll encounter. Although hotels and rooms places frequently have TVs in the room, reception is often dire: even where they advertise satellite, the only English-language channels this usually includes are CNN and BBC World.

Festivals

Most of the big Greek popular festivals have a religious basis, so they're observed in accordance with the Orthodox calendar: this means that Easter, for example, can fall as much as three weeks to either side of the Western festival.

On top of the main religious festivals, there are scores of local festivities, or **paniyíria**, celebrating the patron saint of the village church. Some of the more important are listed below; the *paramoní*, or **eve of the festival**, is often as significant as the day itself, and many of the events are actually celebrated on the night before. If you show up on the morning of the date given you may find that you have missed most of the music, dancing and drinking. With some 330-odd possible saints' days, though, you're unlikely to travel round for long without stumbling on something. Local tourist offices should be able to fill you in on events in their area.

Easter

Easter is by far the most important festival of the Greek year. It is an excellent time to be in Greece, both for the beautiful and moving religious ceremonies and for the days of feasting and celebration which follow. If you make for a smallish village, you may well find yourself an honorary member for the period of the festival. This is a busy time for Greek tourists as well as international ones, however, so check dates (see opposite) and book ahead.

The first great ceremony takes place on **Good Friday** evening, as the Descent from the Cross is lamented in church. At dusk, the *Epitáfios*, Christ's funeral bier, lavishly decorated by the women of the parish, leaves the sanctuary and is paraded solemnly through the streets. Late **Saturday** evening sees the climax in a majestic Mass to celebrate Christ's triumphant return. At the stroke of midnight, all the lights in each crowded church are extinguished and the congregation plunged into darkness until the priest lights the candles of the nearest worshippers, intoning "*Dévte, lévete Fós*" ("Come, take the Light"). The burning candles are carried home through the streets; they are said to bring good fortune to the house if they arrive still burning.

The lighting of the flames is the signal for celebrations to start and the Lent fast to be broken. The traditional greeting, as fireworks and dynamite explode all around you in the street, is *Khristós Anésti* ("Christ is risen"), to which the response is *Alithós Anésti* ("Truly He is risen"). On **Easter Sunday** there's feasting on roast lamb.

The Greek equivalent of **Easter eggs** is hard-boiled eggs (painted red on Holy Thursday), which are baked into twisted, sweet bread-loaves (*tsourékia*) or distributed on Easter Sunday. People rap their eggs against their friends' eggs, and the owner of the last uncracked egg is considered lucky.

Name days

In Greece, everyone gets to celebrate their birthday twice. More important, in fact, than your actual birthday, is the **"Name Day"** of the saint who bears the same name. If your name isn't covered, no problem – your party is on All Saints' Day, eight weeks after Easter. If you learn that it's an acquaintance's name day, you wish them *Khrónia Pollá* (literally, "many years").

The big name-day celebrations (Iannis/Ianna on Jan 7 or Yeoryios on April 23 for example) can involve thousands of people. Any church or chapel bearing the saint's name will mark the event – some smaller chapels will open just for this one day of the year – while if an entire village is named after the saint, you can almost guarantee a festival. To check out when your name day falls, see ⓦ sfakia-crete.com.

Festival calendar

JANUARY

January 1: New Year's Day (Protokhroniá) In Greece this is the feast day of Áyios Vassílios (St Basil). The traditional New Year greeting is "Kalí Khroniá".

January 6: Epiphany (Theofánia/Tón Fóton) Marks the baptism of Jesus as well as the end of the twelve days of Christmas. Baptismal fonts, lakes, rivers and seas are blessed, especially harbours (such as Pireás), where the priest traditionally casts a crucifix into the water, and local youths compete for the privilege of recovering it.

FEBRUARY/MARCH

Carnival (Apokriátika) Festivities span three weeks, climaxing during the seventh weekend before Easter. The Ionian islands, especially Kefaloniá, are also good for Carnival, as is Ayiássos on Lésvos, while the outrageous Goat Dance (see p.444) takes place on Skýros in the Sporades.

Clean Monday (Katharí Dheftéra) The day after Carnival ends and the first day of Lent, 48 days before Easter, marks the start of fasting and is traditionally spent picnicking and flying kites.

March 25: Independence Day and the feast of the Annunciation (Evangelismós) Both a religious and a national holiday, with, on the one hand, military parades and dancing to celebrate the beginning of the revolt against Ottoman rule in 1821, and, on the other, church services to honour the news given to Mary that she was to become the Mother of Christ. There are major festivities on Tínos, Ýdhra and any locality with a monastery or church named Evangelístria or Evangelismós.

APRIL/MAY

Easter (Páskha: April 12, 2015; May 1, 2016; April 16, 2017; April 8, 2018) The most important festival of the Greek year (see opposite). The island of Ýdhra, with its alleged 360 churches and monasteries, is the prime Easter resort; other famous Easter celebrations are held at Corfu,

Pyrgí on Híos, Ólymbos on Kárpathos and St John's monastery on Pátmos, where on Holy Thursday the abbot washes the feet of twelve monks in the village square, in imitation of Christ doing the same for his disciples. Good Friday and Easter Monday are also public holidays.

April 23: The feast of St George (Áyios Yeóryios) St George, the patron saint of shepherds, is honoured with big rural celebrations and much feasting and dancing at associated shrines and towns. At the mountain town of Asigonía in Crete, this is a major event. If it falls during Lent, festivities are postponed until the Monday after Easter.

MAY/JUNE

May 1: May Day (Protomayiá) The great urban holiday when townspeople traditionally make for the countryside to picnic and fly kites, returning with bunches of wild flowers. Wreaths are hung on their doorways or balconies until they are burnt in bonfires on St John's Eve (June 23). There are also large demonstrations by the Left for Labour Day.

May 21: Feast of St Constantine and St Helen (Áyios Konstandínos & Ayía Eléni) Constantine, as emperor, championed Christianity in the Byzantine Empire; St Helen was his mother. It's a widely celebrated name day for two of the more popular Christian names in Greece.

May 20–27: Battle of Crete The anniversary of one of the major World War II battles is celebrated in the Haniá province of Crete with veterans' ceremonies, sporting events and folk dancing.

Whit Monday (Áyio Pnévma) Fifty days after Easter, sees services to commemorate the descent of the Holy Spirit to the assembled disciples. Many young Greeks take advantage of the long weekend, marking the start of summer, to head for the islands.

June 29 & 30: SS Peter and Paul (Áyios Pétros and Áyios Pávlos) The joint feast of two of the more widely celebrated name days is on June 29. Celebrations often run together with those for the Holy Apostles (Áyii Apóstoli), the following day.

JULY

July 17: Feast of St Margaret (Ayía Marína) A big event in rural areas, as she's an important protector of crops. Ayiá Marina village on Kássos will be en fête, as will countless other similarly named towns and villages.

July 20: Feast of the Prophet Elijah (Profítis Ilías) Widely celebrated at the countless hilltop shrines of Profítis Ilías.

July 26: St Paraskevi (Ayía Paraskeví) Celebrated in parishes or villages bearing that name.

AUGUST

August 6: Transfiguration of the Saviour (Metamórfosis toú Sotíros) Another excuse for celebrations, particularly at Khristós Ráhon village on Ikaría, and at Plátanos on Léros. On Hálki the date is marked by messy food fights with flour, eggs and squid ink.

August 15: Assumption of the Blessed Virgin Mary (Apokímisis tís Panayías) This is the day when people traditionally return to their home village, and the heart of the holiday season, so in many places there will be no accommodation available on any terms. Even some Greeks will resort to sleeping in the streets at the great

---

CULTURAL FESTIVALS

Festivals of music, dance and theatre take place in summer throughout the islands, many at atmospheric outdoor venues. Some are unashamedly aimed at drawing tourists, others more seriously artistic. Some of the more durable include:

Domus Festival, Náxos July–early Sept ⓦ naxosfestival.com

Ippokrateia Festival, Kos July

Iráklio Festival, Crete July–Aug

Lefkádha Arts and Folklore festivals last week of Aug

Philippi Festival, Thássos July–Aug ⓦ philippifestival.gr

Réthymno Cretan Diet Festival July ⓦ www
.rethymnowinefestival.gr, ⓦ www.cretandietfestival.gr

Thíra Music Festival Sept ⓦ santorinimusicfestival.com

---

pilgrimage to Tínos; also major festivities at Páros, at Ayiássos on Lésvos, and at Ólymbos on Kárpathos.

August 29: Beheading of John the Baptist (Apokefálisis toú Prodhrómou) Popular pilgrimages and celebrations at Vrykoúnda on Kárpathos. On Crete a massive name-day pilgrimage treks to the church of Áyios Ioánnis on the Rodhópou peninsula.

SEPTEMBER

September 8: Birth of the Virgin Mary (Yénnisis tís Panayías) Sees special services in churches dedicated to the event, and a double cause for rejoicing on Spétses where they also celebrate the anniversary of the battle of the straits of Spétses. Elsewhere, there's a pilgrimage of childless women to the monastery at Tsambíka, Rhodes.

September 14: Exaltation of the Cross (Ípsosis toú Stavroú) A last major summer festival, keenly observed on Hálki.

September 24: Feast of St John the Divine (Áyios Ioánnis Theológos) Observed on Níssyros and Pátmos, where at the saint's monastery there are solemn, beautiful liturgies the night before and early in the morning.

OCTOBER

October 26: Feast of St Demetrios (Áyios Dhimítrios) Another popular name day; in rural areas the new wine is traditionally broached on this day, a good excuse for general inebriation.

October 28: Óhi Day A national holiday with parades, folk dancing and speeches to commemorate prime minister Metaxas' one-word reply to Mussolini's 1940 ultimatum: "Óhi!" ("No!").

NOVEMBER

November 7–9: Arkádhi The anniversary of the 1866 explosion at Arkádhi monastery in Crete is marked by an enormous gathering at the island's most revered shrine.

November 8: Feast of the Archangels Michael and Gabriel (Mihaïl and Gavríil, or tón Taxiárhon) Marked by rites at the numerous churches named after them, particularly at the rural monastery of Taxiárhis on Sými, and the big monastery of Mandamádhos, Lésvos.

DECEMBER

December 6: Feast of St Nicholas (Áyios Nikólaos) The patron saint of seafarers, who has many chapels dedicated to him.

December 25 & 26: Christmas (Khristoúyenna) If less all-encompassing than Greek Easter, Christmas is still an important

religious feast, and one that increasingly comes with all the usual commercial trappings.

December 31: New Year's Eve (Paramoní Protohroniá) As on the other twelve days of Christmas, a few children still go door-to-door singing traditional carols, receiving money in return. Adults tend to sit around playing cards, often for money. A special baked loaf, the *vassilópitta*, in which a coin is concealed to bring its finder good luck throughout the year, is cut at midnight.

Sports and outdoor pursuits

The Greek seashore offers endless scope for watersports, from waterskiing and parasailing to yachting and windsurfing. On land, the greatest attraction lies in hiking; often the smaller, less developed islands are better for this than the larger ones crisscrossed by roads. As for spectator sports, the twin Greek obsessions are football (soccer) and basketball, with volleyball a close third. You'll see youths playing impromptu games everywhere, but as of the 2014–15 season only Crete, Corfu and Lesvos boasted top-flight teams on the islands.

Watersports

Windsurfing and kitesurfing are very popular around Greece: the islands' bays and coves are ideal for beginners, with a few spectacularly windy spots

---

FIVE OF THE BEST WINDSURFING SPOTS

Sánta María, Páros (see p.160).

Kourémenos, eastern Crete (see p.232).

Prassoníssi, Rhodes (see p.281).

Kokkári, Sámos (see p.360).

Vassilikí, Lefkádha (see p.488).

for experts (see opposite). Board rental rates are reasonable and instruction is generally also available. **Waterski** boats spend most of their time towing people around on bananas or other inflatables, though usually you can waterski or wakeboard as well, while **parasailing** (*parapént*) is also on offer at all the big resorts. **Jet skis** can be rented in many resorts, too, for a fifteen-minute burst of fuel-guzzling thrills.

A combination of steady winds, appealing seascapes and numerous natural harbours has long made the islands a tremendous place for **sailing**. All sorts of bareboat and flotilla yacht trips are on offer (see p.29), while dinghies, small cats and motorboats can be rented at many resorts. For yachting, spring and autumn are the most pleasant seasons; *meltémi* winds can make for nauseous sailing in July and August when you'll also find far higher prices and crowded moorings. The Cyclades suffer particularly badly from the *meltémi*, and are also relatively short on facilities: better choices are to explore the Sporades from Skiáthos; to set out from Athens for the Argo-Saronic islands; or to sail around Corfu and the Ionians, though here winds can be very light.

Because of the potential for pilfering submerged antiquities, **scuba diving** is still restricted, though relaxation of the controls has led to a proliferation of dive centres across the Dodecanese, Ionians, Cyclades and Crete. There's not a huge amount of aquatic life surviving around Greece's over-fished shores, but you do get wonderfully clear water, while the rocky coast offers plenty of caves and hidden nooks to explore.

Walking and cycling

If you have the time and stamina, **walking** is probably the single best way to see the quieter islands. The bigger islands offer greater choice, especially the well-organized Corfu Trail (see p.479), mountainous Évvia and above all Crete, with its famous gorge descents. This guide includes some of the more accessible hikes, from gentle strolls to long-distance mountain paths; there are also plenty of companies offering walking holidays (see p.28). In addition, you may want to acquire a countrywide or regional **hiking guidebook**, available in the more popular spots, though detailed **maps** (p.50) may be better bought in advance.

Cycling is less popular with Greeks, but in an increasing number of resorts you can hire **bikes**, and many of the rental places lead organized rides, which vary from easy explorations of the countryside to serious rides up proper mountains. Again, there are specialist companies offering cycling breaks in Greece (see p.28). Summer heat can be fierce, but spring and autumn offer great riding and walking conditions.

Culture and etiquette

In many ways, Greece is a thoroughly integrated European country, and behaviour and social mores differ little from what you may be used to at home. Dig a little deeper, however, or travel to more remote, less touristed areas, and you'll find that traditional Greek ways survive to a gratifying degree. It's easy to accidentally give offence – but equally easy to avoid doing so by following a few simple tips, and to upgrade your status from that of tourist to xénos, a word that means both stranger and guest.

In general, Greeks are exceptionally friendly and curious, to an extent that can seem intrusive, certainly to a reserved Brit. Don't be surprised at being asked personal questions, even on short acquaintance, or having your **personal space** invaded. On the other hand, you're also likely to be invited to people's houses, often to meet a large extended family. Should you get such an invitation, you are not expected to be punctual – thirty minutes late is normal – and you should bring a small **gift**, usually flowers, or cakes from the local cake shop. If you're invited out to dinner, you can offer to **pay**, but it's very unlikely you'll be allowed to do so, and too much insistence could be construed as rude.

SHHHH! SIESTA TIME

The hours **between 3 and 5pm**, the midday **siesta** (*mikró ýpno*), are sacrosanct – it's not acceptable to visit people, make phone calls to strangers or cause any sort of loud noise (especially with motorcycles) at this time. Quiet is also legally mandated **between midnight and 8am** in residential areas.

Dress codes and cultural hints

Though **dress codes** on the beach are entirely informal, they're much less so away from the sea; most Greeks will dress up to go out, and not doing so is considered slovenly at the least. There are quite a number of **nudist** beaches in remote spots, with plenty of locals enjoying them, but on family beaches, or those close to town or near a church (of which there are many along the Greek coast), even toplessness is often frowned on. Most monasteries and to a lesser extent churches impose a fairly strict **dress code** for visitors: no shorts, with women expected to cover their arms and wear skirts (though most Greek women visitors will be in trousers); the necessary wraps are sometimes provided on the spot.

Two pieces of **body language** that can cause unintentional offence are hand gestures; don't hold your hand up, palm out, to anybody, and don't make an OK sign by forming a circle with your thumb and forefinger – both are extremely rude. Nodding and shaking your head for yes and no are also unlikely to be understood; Greeks use a slight forward inclination of the head for yes, a more vigorous backward nod for no.

Bargaining and tipping

Most shops have fixed prices, so **bargaining** isn't a regular feature of tourist life. It is worth negotiating over rooms – especially off season – or for vehicle rental, especially for longer periods, but it's best not to be aggressive about it; ask if they have a cheaper room, for example, rather than demanding a lower price. **Tipping** is not essential anywhere, though taxi drivers generally expect it from tourists and most service staff are very poorly paid. Restaurant bills incorporate a service charge; if you want to tip, rounding up the bill is usually sufficient.

Smoking also deserves a mention. Greeks are the heaviest smokers in Europe, and although legally you're not allowed to smoke indoors in restaurants, bars or public offices, in practice the law is almost universally disregarded. Effective no-smoking areas are very rare indeed.

Women and lone travellers

Thousands of **women** travel independently around the islands without being harassed or feeling intimidated. With the westernization of relationships between unmarried Greek men and women, almost all of the traditional Mediterranean macho impetus for trying one's luck with foreign girls has faded. Foreign women are more at risk of **sexual assault** at certain notorious resorts (including Kávos in Corfu, Laganás in Zákynthos and Faliráki in Rhodes) by northern European men than by ill-intentioned locals. It is sensible not to bar-crawl alone or to accept late-night rides from strangers (**hitching** at any time is not advisable for lone female travellers). In more remote areas intensely traditional villagers may wonder why women travelling alone are unaccompanied, and may not welcome their presence in exclusively male *kafenía*. Travelling with a man, you're more likely to be treated as a *xénos*.

Lone men need to be wary of being invited into bars in the largest island ports; these bars are invariably staffed with hostesses (who may also be prostitutes) persuading you to treat them to drinks. At the end of the night you'll be landed with an outrageous bill, some of which goes towards the hostess's commission; physical threats are brought to bear on reluctant payers.

Travel essentials

Costs

The **cost of living** in Greece has increased astronomically since it joined the EU, particularly after the adoption of the euro and further increases in the VAT rate in 2011. Prices in shops and cafés now match or exceed those of many other EU member countries (including the UK). However, outside the chintzier resorts, travel remains affordable, with the aggregate cost of restaurant meals, short-term accommodation (see p.33) and public transport falling somewhere in between that of cheaper Spain or France and pricier Italy.

Prices depend on where and when you go. Island capitals, as well as the trendier tourist resorts and small islands (such as Sými, Ýdhra, Mýkonos, Paxí and Pátmos), are more expensive and costs everywhere increase sharply during July–August and during other holiday periods such as Easter.

On most islands a daily per-person **budget** of €50/£40/US$64 will get you basic accommodation and meals, plus a short ferry or bus ride, as one of a couple. Camping would cut costs marginally. On €100/£80/US$128 a day you could be living quite well, plus sharing the cost of renting a large motorbike or small car. Note that accommodation costs (see p.33) vary greatly over the seasons.

A basic taverna **meal** with bulk wine or a beer costs around €12–20 per person. Add a better bottle of wine, pricier fish or fancier decor and it could be up to €20–30 a head; you'll rarely pay more than that. Even in the most developed of resorts, with inflated "international" menus, there is often a basic but decent taverna where the locals eat.

Crime and personal safety

Greece is one of Europe's safest countries, with a **low crime rate** and a deserved reputation for honesty. Most of the time if you leave a bag or wallet at a café, you'll probably find it scrupulously looked after, pending your return. Although muggings and other violent crimes are still very rare outside Athens, petty theft has been on the rise with the economic crisis. With this in mind, it's best to lock rooms and cars securely, and to keep your valuables hidden. **Civil unrest**, in the form of strikes and demonstrations, is also on the increase, but while this might inconvenience you, you'd be very unlucky to get caught up in any trouble as a visitor.

Though the chances are you'll never meet a member of the national **police force**, the Elliniki Astynomia, Greek cops expect respect, and many have little regard for foreigners. If you do need to go to the police, always try to do so through the **Tourist Police** (☎ 171), who should speak English and are used to dealing with visitors. You are officially required to carry suitable ID on you at all times, either a passport or a driving licence, though in reality nobody would expect you to have such valuable documents with you at the beach, for example.

The most common causes of a brush with the law are beach nudity, camping outside authorized sites, **public inebriation** or lewd behaviour. In 2009 a large British stag group dressed as nuns was arrested in Mália and held for several days,

having managed to combine extreme drunkenness with a lack of respect for the church. Also avoid taking **photos in forbidden areas** such as airports (see p.52).

Drug offences are treated as major crimes – the maximum penalty for "causing the use of drugs by someone under 18", for example, is life imprisonment and an astronomical fine. Foreigners caught in possession of even small amounts of marijuana get long jail sentences if there's evidence that they've been supplying the drug to others.

Electricity

Voltage is 220 volts AC. Standard European two-pin plugs are used; **adaptors** should be purchased beforehand in the UK, as they can be difficult to find locally; standard 5-, 6- or 7.5-amp models permit operation of a hair dryer or travel iron. Unless they're dual voltage, North American appliances will require both a step-down transformer and a plug adaptor (the latter easy to find in Greece).

Entrance fees

All the major **ancient sites**, like most **museums**, charge **entrance fees** ranging from €2 to €12, with an average fee of around €3. Entrance to all state-run sites and museums is **free** on Sundays and public holidays from November to March.

Entry requirements

UK and all other EU nationals need only a valid **passport, which remains unstamped,** to enter Greece. US, Australian, New Zealand, Canadian and most non-EU Europeans receive mandatory entry and exit stamps in their passports and can stay, as tourists, for ninety days (cumulative) in any six-month period. Such nationals arriving by flight or boat from another EU state not party to the

---

DISCOUNTS

Full-time students are eligible for the **International Student ID Card** (ISIC; ⓦ isiccard.com), which entitles the bearer to cut-price transport and discounts at museums, theatres and other attractions, though often not accepted as valid proof of age. If you're not a student but aged under 26, you can qualify for the **International Youth Travel Card**, which provides similar benefits to the ISIC. Teachers qualify for the **International Teacher Identity Card** (ITIC), offering insurance benefits but limited travel discounts.

Seniors are entitled to a discount on bus passes in the major cities; Olympic Airways also offer discounts on full fares for domestic flights. Proof of age is necessary.

AVERAGE MONTHLY TEMPERATURES AND RAINFALL

	Jan	Feb	Mar	Apr	May	Jun	Jul	Aug	Sep	Oct	Nov	Dec
ATHENS												
Maximum °C/°F	13/55	14/57	16/61	20/68	25/77	30/86	33/91	33/91	29/84	24/75	19/66	15/59
Minimum °C/°F	6/43	7/45	8/46	11/52	16/61	20/68	23/73	23/73	19/66	15/59	12/54	8/46
Rainfall mm	62	37	37	23	23	14	6	7	7	51	56	71
CYCLADES (NÁXOS)												
Maximum °C/°F	15/59	15/59	16/62	20/68	23/73	26/79	27/81	28/82	26/79	24/75	20/68	17/63
Minimum °C/°F	10/50	10/50	11/52	13/55	16/62	20/68	22/72	22/72	20/68	18/64	15/59	12/54
Rainfall mm	91	73	69	19	12	11	2	1	11	45	48	93
CRETE (IRÁKLIO)												
Maximum °C/°F	16/62	16/62	17/63	20/68	23/73	27/81	29/84	29/84	27/81	24/75	21/70	18/64
Minimum °C/°F	9/48	9/48	10/50	12/54	15/59	19/66	22/72	22/72	19/66	17/63	14/57	11/52
Rainfall mm	95	46	43	26	13	3	1	1	11	64	71	79
DODECANESE (RHODES)												
Maximum °C/°F	15/59	16/62	17/63	21/70	25/77	30/86	32/90	33/91	29/84	25/77	21/70	17/63
Minimum °C/°F	7/45	8/46	9/48	12/54	15/59	19/66	21/70	22/72	19/66	15/59	12/54	9/48
Rainfall mm	201	101	92	23	21	1	1	0	15	75	114	205
IONIANS (CORFU)												
Maximum °C/°F	14/57	15/59	16/62	19/66	23/73	28/82	31/88	32/91	28/82	23/73	19/66	16/61
Minimum °C/°F	6/43	6/43	8/46	10/50	13/55	17/63	19/66	19/66	17/63	14/57	11/52	8/46
Rainfall mm	196	132	100	70	41	14	4	20	95	184	237	259

Schengen Agreement may not be stamped in routinely at minor Greek ports, so make sure this is done in order to avoid unpleasantness on exit. Your passport must be valid for three months after your arrival date.

Unless of Greek descent, visitors from **non-EU** countries are currently not, in practice, being given extensions to tourist visas. You must leave not just Greece but the entire Schengen Group and stay out until the maximum 90-days-in-180 rule, as set forth above, is satisfied. If you **overstay** your time and then leave under your own power – ie are not deported – you'll be hit with a huge fine upon departure, and possibly be banned from re-entering for a lengthy period of time; no excuses will be entertained except (just maybe) a doctor's certificate stating you were immobilized in hospital. It cannot be overemphasized just how exigent Greek immigration officials have become on this issue.

Greek embassies abroad

Australia 9 Turrana St, Yarralumla, Canberra, ACT 2600 ☎ 02 6273 3011, ⓦ mfa.gr/sydney.
Canada 80 Maclaren St, Ottawa, ON K2P 0K6 ☎ 613 238 6271, ⓦ mfa.gr/ottawa.
Ireland 1 Upper Pembroke St, Dublin 2 ☎ 01 676 7254, ⓦ mfa.gr/dublin.

New Zealand Petherick Tower, 38–42 Waring Taylor St, Wellington 6142 ☎ 04 473 7775, ⓦ mfa.gr/wellington.
South Africa 1267 Pretorius St, Hatfield 0001 ☎ 012 434 7351, ⓦ mfa.gr/pretoria.
UK 1A Holland Park, London W11 3TP ☎ 020 7221 6467, ⓦ mfa.gr/london.
USA 2217 Massachusetts Ave NW, Washington, DC 20008 ☎ 202 939 1300, ⓦ mfa.gr/washington.

Gay and lesbian travellers

Greece is deeply ambivalent about **homosexuality**: ghettoized as "to be expected" in the arts, theatre and music scenes but apt to be closeted elsewhere. "Out" gay Greeks are rare, and "out" local lesbians rarer still; foreign same-sex couples will be regarded on most islands with some bemusement but accorded the standard courtesy as foreigners – as long as they refrain from public displays of affection, taboo in rural areas. There is a sizeable **gay community** in Athens, plus a fairly obvious scene at resorts like Ýdhra, Rhodes and Mýkonos. Skála Eressoú on Lésvos, the birthplace of Sappho, is (appropriately) an international mecca for lesbians. Even in Athens, however, most gay nightlife is underground (often literally so in the siting of clubs), with no visible signage for nondescript premises.

Insurance

Despite the EU healthcare privileges that apply in Greece (see p.40), you should consider taking out an **insurance policy** before travelling, to cover against theft, loss, illness or injury. Before paying for a whole new policy, however, it's worth checking whether you are already covered: some home insurance policies may cover your possessions when overseas, and many private medical schemes (such as BUPA or WPA in the UK) offer coverage extensions for abroad. **Students** will often find that their student health coverage extends during the vacations.

Make any claim as soon as possible. If you have medical treatment, keep all receipts for medicines and treatment. If you have anything stolen or lost, you must obtain an **official statement** from the police or the airline which lost your bags – with numerous claims being fraudulent, most insurers won't even consider one unless you have a police report.

Internet

With the proliferation of portable wi-fi devices, **internet cafés** have all but disappeared except in the larger island capitals. Nearly all accommodations, most cafés (but not old-style *kafenía*) and an increasing number of tavernas offer free wi-fi access to patrons. An increasing number of municipalities are introducing free wi-fi hotspots; a full list is available in Greek only at Ⓦ free-wifi.gr.

Laundry

Laundries or *Plindíria*, as they're known in Greek, are available in the main resort towns; sometimes an attended service wash is available for little or no extra charge over the basic cost of €8–10 per wash and dry. Self-catering villas will usually be furnished with a drying line and a selection of plastic wash-tubs or a bucket. Most larger hotels have laundry services, but charges are quite steep.

Living in Greece

EU (and EEA) nationals are allowed to stay indefinitely in any EU state, but to ensure avoidance of any problems – eg, in setting up a bank account – you should, after the third month of stay, get a **certificate of registration** (*vevéosi engrafís*). Residence/work permits for **non-EU/non-EEA nationals** can only be obtained on application to a Greek embassy or consulate outside of Greece; you have a much better chance of securing one if you are married to a Greek, are of Greek background by birth or have permanent-resident status in another EU state.

As for **work**, non-EU nationals of Greek descent and EU/EEA native speakers of English (ie Brits and Irish) have a much better chance than anyone else. **Teaching English at a private language school** (*frontistírio*) is not as well paid as it used to be and is almost impossible to get into these days without a bona fide TEFL certificate.

Many people find **tourism-related work**, especially on the islands most dominated by foreign visitors, April and May being the best time to look around. This is often as a rep for a package company, although they recruit the majority of staff from the home country; all you need is EU nationality and the appropriate language, though knowledge of Greek is a big plus. Jobs in bars or restaurants are a lot easier for women to come by than men. Another option if you have the requisite skills is to work for a **windsurfing** school or **scuba-diving** operation.

Mail

Post offices are open Monday to Friday from 7.30am to 2pm, though certain main branches are also open evenings and Saturday mornings.

Airmail letters take 3–7 days to reach the rest of Europe, 5–12 days to North America, a little longer for Australia and New Zealand. Postal rates for postcards are €0.80, and for letters up to 20g €0.90 to all overseas destinations. For a modest fee (about €3) you can shave a day or two off delivery time to any destination by using the **express service** (*katepígonda*). **Registered** (*systíméno*) delivery is also available for a similar amount but is slow unless coupled with express service. Stamps (*grammatósima*) are widely available at newsagents and other tourist shops, often for a small surcharge.

Parcels should (and often can) only be handled in the island capitals. For non-EU/EEA destinations, always present your box open for inspection, and come prepared with tape and scissors.

Ordinary **post boxes** are bright yellow, express boxes dark red, but it's best to use those adjacent to an actual post office, since days may pass between collections at boxes elsewhere.

Maps

The most reliable **general touring maps** of Greece are those published by Athens-based Anavasi (Ⓦanavasi.gr), Road Editions (Ⓦroad.gr) and newcomer Orama (Ⓦnakas-maps.gr). Anavasi and Road Editions products are widely available in Greece at selected bookshops, as well as at petrol stations and general tourist shops throughout the islands. In Britain they are found at Stanfords (☎020 7836 1321, Ⓦstanfords.co.uk) and the Hellenic Book Service (☎020 7267 9499, Ⓦhellenicbookservice. com); in the US, they're sold through Omni Resources (☎910 227 8300, Ⓦomnimap.com).

Hiking/topographical maps are gradually improving in quality and availability. Anavasi publishes a series covering the White Mountains and Psiloritis on Crete and Mt Dhýrfis on Évvia.

Money

Greece's currency is the **euro** (€). Up-to-date **exchange rates** can be found on Ⓦxe.com. Euro notes exist in denominations of 5, 10, 20, 50, 100, 200 and 500 euros, and coins in denominations of 1, 2, 5, 10, 20 and 50 cents and 1 and 2 euros. Avoid getting stuck with **counterfeit euro notes** (€100 and €200 ones abound). The best tests are done by the naked eye: genuine notes all have a hologram strip or (if over €50) patch at one end, there's a watermark at the other, plus a security thread embedded in the middle. If you end up with a fake note, you'll have no recourse to a refund. Note that

shopkeepers do not bother much with shortfalls of 10 cents or less, whether in their favour (especially) or yours.

Banks and exchange

Greek **banks** normally open Monday to Thursday 8.30am–2.30pm and Friday 8.30am–2pm. Always take your passport with you as proof of identity and expect long queues. Large hotels and some travel agencies also provide an exchange service, though with hefty commissions. On small islands with no full-service bank, "authorized" bank agents will charge an additional fee for posting a travellers' cheque to a proper branch.

A number of authorized brokers for **exchanging foreign cash** have emerged in Athens and other major tourist centres. When changing small amounts, choose those bureaux that charge a flat percentage commission (usually 1 percent) rather than a high minimum. There is a small number of 24-hour **automatic foreign-note-changing machines**, but a high minimum commission tends to be deducted. There is no need to **purchase euros** beforehand unless you're arriving at some ungodly hour to one of the remoter frontier posts. **Travellers' cheques** (best in euros rather than dollars), can be cashed at most banks, though rarely elsewhere. Cashing the cheques will incur a minimum charge of €1.20–2.40 depending on the bank; for larger amounts, a set percentage will apply.

ATMs and credit cards

Debit cards have become the most common means of accessing funds while travelling, by withdrawing money from the vast network of Greek

---

PUBLIC HOLIDAYS

January 1 New Year's Day.
January 6 Epiphany.
February/March Clean Monday (*Katharí Dheftéra*), 7 weeks before Easter.
March 25 Independence Day.
April/May Good Friday and Easter Monday (see p.43).
May 1 May Day.
May/June Whit Monday, 7 weeks after Easter.
August 15 Assumption of the Virgin Mary.
October 28 Óhi Day (see p.44).
December 25/26: Christmas Day/ Boxing Day.

PHONE CODES AND NUMBERS

All Greek phone numbers require dialling of all ten digits, including the area code. Land lines begin with 2; mobiles begin with 6. All land-line exchanges are digital, and you should have few problems reaching any number from either overseas or within Greece. Mobile phone users are well looked after, with a signal even in the Athens metro.

PHONING GREECE FROM ABROAD

Dial ☏0030 + the full number

PHONING ABROAD FROM GREECE

Dial the country code (below) + area code (minus any initial 0) + number

Australia	☏0061	UK	☏0044
New Zealand	☏0064	Ireland	☏00353
Canada	☏001	USA	☏001
South Africa	☏0027		

GREEK PHONE PREFIXES

Local call rate	☏0801	Toll-free/Freefone	☏0800

USEFUL GREEK TELEPHONE NUMBERS

Ambulance	☏166	Police/Emergency	☏100
Fire brigade, urban	☏199	Speaking clock	☏141
Forest fire reporting	☏191	Tourist police	☏171 (Athens);
Operator	☏132 (Domestic)		☏210 171 (elsewhere)
Operator	☏139 (International)		

ATMs. Larger airports have at least one ATM in the arrivals hall and any town or island with a population larger than a few thousand (or substantial tourist traffic) also has them. Most accept Visa, MasterCard, Visa Electron, Plus and Cirrus cards; American Express holders are restricted to the ATMs of Alpha and National Bank. There is usually a charge of 2.25 percent on the sterling/dollar transaction value, plus a commission fee of a similar amount. Using **credit cards** at an ATM costs roughly the same; however, inflated interest accrues from the moment of use.

Major credit cards are not usually accepted by cheaper tavernas or hotels but they can be essential for renting cars. Major travel agents may also accept them, though a **three-percent surcharge** is often levied on the purchase of ferry tickets.

Opening hours and public holidays

It's difficult to generalize about Greek **opening hours**, which are notoriously erratic. Most shops open 8.30/9am and close for a long break at 2/2.30pm. Most places, except banks, reopen around 5.30/6pm for three hours or so, at least on Tuesday, Thursday and Friday. Tourist areas tend to adopt a more northern European timetable, with supermarkets and travel agencies, as well as the most important archeological sites and museums, more likely to stay open throughout the day. If you find yourself needing to tackle Greek bureaucracy, you can't count on getting anything essential done except from Monday to Friday, between 9.30am and 1pm.

As far as possible, times are quoted in the text for tourist sites but these change with exasperating frequency, especially since the economic crisis. Both winter and summer hours are quoted throughout the guide, but to avoid disappointment, either phone ahead or time your visit during the core hours of 9am–2pm. **Monasteries** are generally open from approximately 9am to 1pm and 5 to 8pm (3.30–6.30pm in winter) for limited visits. Again, the opening times given for **restaurants**, **cafés** and **bars** can also be very flexible.

Phones

Three **mobile phone networks** operate in Greece: Vodafone-Panafon, Cosmote and Q-Telecom/WIND. **Coverage** is good, though there are a few "dead" zones on the most mountainous islands or really remote islets. Contract-free plans are heavily promoted in Greece, so if you're here for more than a week or so, buying a **pay-as-you-go** SIM card (for €15–20) from any of the mobile phone outlets will pay for itself very quickly. Top-up cards – starting from €8–10 – are available at all *períptera* (kiosks). Since July 2014, roaming charges within the EU have been capped at €0.19 per minute (or €0.05 to receive calls). North American users will only be able to use tri-band phones in Greece.

Land lines and public phones are run by OTE who provide phonecards (*tilekártes*), available in denominations starting at €4, from kiosks and newsagents. If you plan on making lots of international calls, you'll want a **calling card**, all of which involve calling a free access number from either certain phone boxes or a fixed line (not a mobile) and then entering a twelve-digit code. OTE has its own scheme, but competitors generally prove cheaper. Avoid making calls direct **from hotel rooms**, as a large surcharge will be applied, though you will not be charged to access a free calling-card number.

Photography

You can feel free to snap away pretty much anywhere in Greece, although some churches display "No photography" signs, and museums and archeological sites may require permits at least for professional photographers. The main exception is around **airports** or **military installations** (usually clearly indicated with a "No pictures" sign). The ordeal of twelve British plane-spotters who processed slowly through Greek jails and courts in 2001–2 on espionage charges should be ample deterrent.

Time

Standard Greek time is two hours ahead of GMT, but the clocks move forward one hour onto **summer time** along with the rest of Europe between the last Sunday in March and the last Sunday in October. For North America, the difference is usually seven hours for Eastern Standard Time, ten hours for Pacific Standard Time.

Toilets

Public toilets are usually in parks or squares, often subterranean; otherwise try a bus station. Except in tourist areas, public toilets tend to be filthy – it's best to use those in restaurants and bars. Remember that throughout Greece, you drop paper in the adjacent **wastebins**, not the toilet bowl.

Tourist information

The **National Tourist Organization of Greece** (Ellinikós Organismós Tourismoú, or EOT; Visit Greece abroad, Ⓦ visitgreece.gr) maintains offices in most European capitals, plus major cities in North America and Australia. It publishes an array of free, glossy, regional pamphlets, invariably several years out of date, fine for getting a picture of where you want to go, though low on useful facts.

In Greece, you will find official **EOT offices** in many but by no means all of the larger islands where, in addition to the usual leaflets, you can find weekly **schedules** for the inter-island **ferries** – rarely entirely accurate, but useful as a guideline. EOT staff may be able to advise on local **buses** as well as current opening hours for local sites and museums and occasionally can assist with accommodation.

Where there is no EOT office, you can get information from municipally run tourist offices – these can be more highly motivated and helpful than EOT branches. In the absence of any of these, you can visit the **Tourist Police**, essentially a division (often just a single room) of the local police. They can sometimes provide you with lists of rooms to let, which they regulate, but they're really the place to go if you have a **serious complaint** about a taxi, or an accommodation or eating establishment.

Greek national tourist offices abroad

Australia & New Zealand 37–49 Pitt St, Sydney, NSW 2000 ☎ 02 9241 1663, Ⓔ hto@tpg.com.au.

UK & Ireland 4 Great Portland St, London W1W 8QJ ☎ 020 7495 9300, Ⓔ info@gnto.co.uk.

USA 305 E 47th St, New York, NY 10017 ☎ 212 421 5777, Ⓔ info@ greektourism.com.

Travellers with disabilities

In general **disabled** people are not especially well catered for in Greece though, as relevant EU-wide legislation is implemented, the situation is gradually improving. In cities, wheelchair ramps and beeps for the sight-impaired are rare at pedestrian crossings, and outside Athens few buses are of the "kneeling" type. Only Athens airport, its metro and airline staff in general (who are used to handling wheelchairs) are disabled-friendly. Ancient monuments, one of the country's main attractions, are usually inaccessible or hazardous for anyone with mobility impairments.

Some advance planning will make a stress-free holiday in Greece more likely. The Greek National Tourist Office is helpful; they also publish a useful questionnaire that you might send to hotels or self-catering accommodation. Before purchasing **travel insurance**, ensure that pre-existing medical conditions are not excluded. A **medical certificate** of your fitness to travel is also extremely useful; some airlines or insurance companies may insist on it.

Travelling with children

Children are worshipped and indulged in Greece, and present few problems when travelling. They are not segregated from adults at meal times, and early on in life are inducted into the typical late-night routine – kids at tavernas are expected to eat (and up to their capabilities, talk) like adults. Outside of certain all-inclusive resorts with children's programmes, however, there are very few amusements specifically for them – certainly nothing like Disney World Paris. Water parks, tourist sites and other places of interest that are particularly child-friendly are noted throughout the guide.

Luxury hotels are more likely to offer some kind of **babysitting** or **crèche service**. All the same basic baby products that you can find at home are available on the islands, though some may be more expensive, so it can pay to load up on nappies, powders and creams before leaving home.

Most domestic ferry-boat companies and airlines offer child **discounts**, ranging from fifty to one hundred percent depending on their age; hotels and rooms won't charge extra for infants, and levy a modest supplement for "third" beds which the child occupies by him/herself.

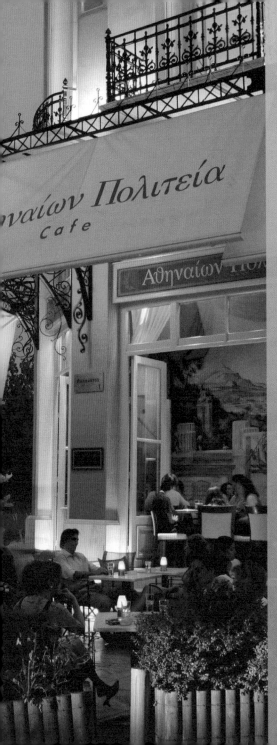

Athens and the mainland ports

CAFÉ LIFE, THISSÍO, ATHENS

Athens and the mainland ports

Although a growing number of islands have their own airports served by direct international flights, the majority still have to be reached by ferry. In this chapter you'll find survival guides to all the significant ports on the Greek mainland; how to get there, where to find the ferries, and suggestions for places to stay and eat if you need to do so.

Most commonly, you'll find yourself travelling to or from the islands via **Athens**, and here you may well want to break your journey to take in the exceptional array of ancient sites and museums, while sampling some of the country's best food and nightlife. A couple of nights' stopover will allow you to take in the Acropolis and the other major sites and museums, and get a feel for a few of the city's neighbourhoods. Even in a single day, a morning arrival would give you time for a look at the Acropolis and Pláka before heading down to the port of **Pireás** (Piraeus) to catch an overnight ferry.

Note that **ferry timetables** are seasonal and complicated, with the same ferry taking different routes on different days and journey times that vary wildly, so take the schedules listed in this chapter (accurate at the time of research) as a rough guide.

Athens and Pireás

ATHENS is home to more than a third of Greece's population and, while history looms large, the twenty-first-century capital is also a vibrant, hectic place, buzzing with life into the early hours of its warm summer nights. While on first acquaintance it may not be a beautiful city, new roads, rail and Metro, along with extensive pedestrianization in the centre, have transformed Athens' aesthetics over recent years. The clamorous port at **Pireás** is quickly and easily reached from the centre or airport.

The vestiges of the ancient Classical Greek city, most famously represented by the **Parthenon** and other remains that top the **Acropolis**, are an inevitable focus, along with the magnificent **National Archeological Museum**. Even on a brief stopover, though, you should also take the time to explore some of the city's **neighbourhoods**. **Eating out** is great, with establishments ranging from traditional tavernas to gourmet restaurants. In summer, much of the action takes place outdoors, from dining on the street or clubbing on the beach, to **open-air cinema**, **concerts** and **classical drama**. There's a diverse **shopping** scene, too, ranging from colourful bazaars and lively street markets to chic suburban malls. And with good-value, extensive public transportation allied to inexpensive taxis, you'll have no difficulty getting around.

Acropolis

The rock of the **Acropolis** dominates almost every view of Athens. Easily defensible and with plentiful water, its initial attractions are obvious. Even now, with no function apart from tourism, it is the undeniable heart of the city, around which everything else clusters, glimpsed at almost every turn. Surrounded by pedestrianized streets, it can be appreciated from almost every angle.

ESSENTIALS   **ACROPOLIS**

Getting there The summit of the Acropolis can be entered only from the west, where there's a big coach park at the bottom of the hill: bus #230 from Sýndagma will take you almost to the entrance. On foot, the obvious approach is from Metro Akrópoli. Crowds at the Acropolis can be horrendous – to avoid the worst come very early in the day, or late.

CAPTION

Highlights

❶ Acropolis, Athens Rising above the city, the great rock of the Acropolis topped by the Parthenon symbolizes not just Athens, but the birth of European civilization. **See opposite**

❷ National Archeological Museum, Athens Quite simply the world's finest collection of ancient Greek art and sculpture. **See p.64**

❸ Pireás The port of Athens is constantly alive with the movement of ferries and cruise liners – if this is not enough, the small boat harbours boast some of the city's best fish restaurants. **See p.64**

❹ Gázi, Athens The heart of Athens' nightlife, packed with bars, cafés and restaurants that are buzzing till late at night. **See p.68**

❺ Áno Póli, Thessaloníki In the city's Upper Town, restored Ottoman architecture vies for space with Roman and Byzantine remains, and it's also home to a burgeoning nightlife scene. **See p.75**

❻ Archeological Museum, Thessaloníki Home to the Gold of Macedon exhibition, displaying finds from the royal tombs at Vergina. **See p.75**

HIGHLIGHTS ARE MARKED ON THE MAP ON P.58 &63

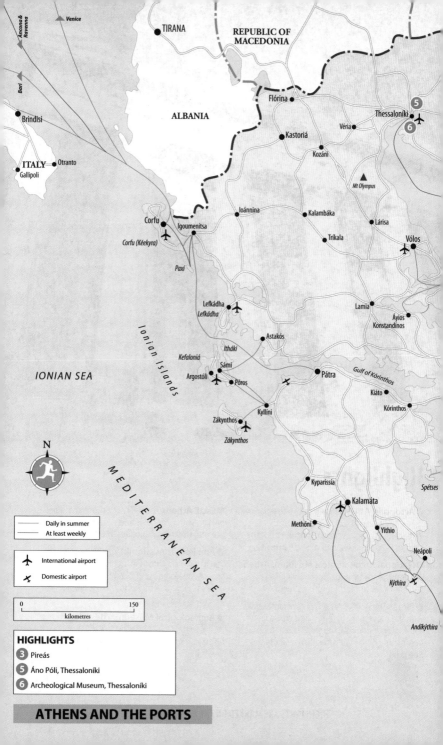

ATHENS AND THE PORTS

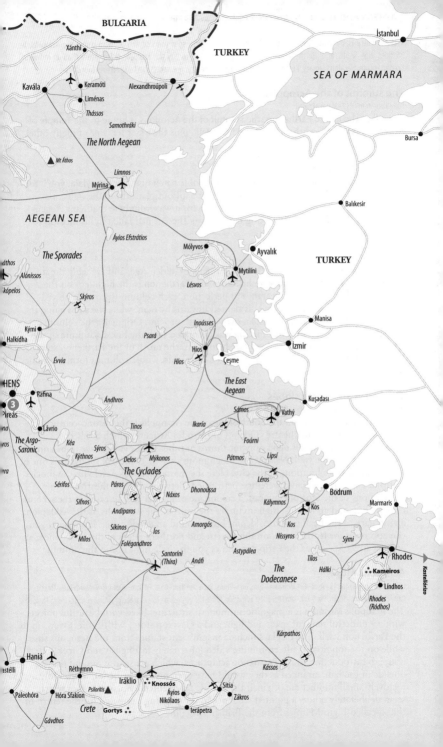

1

Tickets Entry is by a multiple ticket (€12) which also includes the South and North Slopes, Ancient Agora, Roman Forum, Hadrian's Library, Kerameikos and Temple of Zeus, so if you visit any of them before the Acropolis, be sure to buy this multiple ticket rather than an individual entry; the tickets can be used over four days.

The summit of the Acropolis

Daily 8am–8pm • €12 • Metro Akrópoli

As well as the iconic **Parthenon**, the **summit of the Acropolis** is home to the **Temple of Athena Nike**, the Erechtheion and the Propylaia, plus the lesser remains of many other ancient structures.

Temple of Athena Nike

Entering the Acropolis via the monumental double gatehouse, the **Propylaia**, you'll see the elegant, tiny **Temple of Athena Nike** on a precipitous platform to the right, overlooking Pireás and the Saronic Gulf. In myth, it was from here that King Aegeus threw himself to his death, thinking that his son Theseus had failed in his mission to slay the Minotaur on Crete.

Parthenon

The first and greatest project of Pericles' Athenian Golden Age, and arguably the finest achievement of Classical Greek architecture, the **Parthenon** is the highlight on the Acropolis. To achieve the appearance of perfection, each column (its profile bowed slightly to avoid seeming concave) is slanted inwards by 6cm, while the steps along the sides of the temple incline just 12cm over a length of 70m. Originally the columns were brightly painted and the building was decorated with the finest sculpture of the Classical age, also lavishly coloured (see below). To the north of the Parthenon stands the **Erechtheion** and its striking Porch of the Caryatids, whose columns form the tunics of six tall maidens.

The South and North slopes

Daily 8am–8pm • €2 (or joint Acropolis ticket) • Metro Akrópoli

The dominant structure on the **South Slope** of the Acropolis is the second-century Roman **Herodes Atticus Theatre** (Odeion of Herodes Atticus), which has been extensively restored but is open only for shows; at other times, you'll have to be content with spying over the wall. Nearby, the much more ancient **Theatre of Dionysos** is one of the most evocative locations in the city. Here the masterpieces of Aeschylus, Sophocles, Euripides and Aristophanes were first performed. Between the two theatres lie the foundations of the **Stoa of Eumenes**, a colonnade of market stalls erected in the second century BC, and above this, high up under the walls of the Acropolis, is the **Asklepion**, a sanctuary to the healing god Asklepios built around a sacred spring. From here, you can approach the **North Slope**, on the eastern and northern edges of the rock, where an ancient street known as the **Peripatos** allows you to circle right round the summit.

Acropolis Museum

Dhionysíou Areopayítou 15 • April–Oct Mon 8am–4pm, Tues–Thurs, Sat & Sun 8am–8pm, Fri 8am–10pm; Nov–March Tues–Thurs 9am–5pm, Fri 9am–10pm, Sat & Sun 9am–8pm; last admission 30min before closing • €5 • ⓦ theacropolismuseum.gr • Metro Akrópoli

The **Acropolis Museum** is a magnificent modern structure, filled with beautiful objects, with a wonderful sense of space and light and a glass top storey with a direct view up to the Parthenon itself. The displays include magnificent statues from the Acropolis sites, while on the top floor, a fifteen-minute video (alternately in English and Greek) offers a superb introduction to the **Parthenon sculptures**, which are set out around the outside of the hall, arranged as they would have been on the Parthenon itself. Only a relatively small number are original; the rest are represented by plaster copies which seem deliberately crude, a pointed reference to the ongoing campaign for the return of the so-called Elgin Marbles from the British Museum.

1

The Ancient Agora

Daily 8am–8pm (museum opens at 11am Mon) • €4 (or joint Acropolis ticket) • Metro Monastiráki

The **Agora** or market was the heart of ancient Athenian city life; the chief meeting place of the city, where orators held forth, business was discussed and gossip exchanged. Today, it's an extensive and confusing jumble of ruins, dating from the sixth century BC to the fifth century AD. The best overview is from the exceptionally well-preserved **Hephaisteion**, or Temple of Hephaistos, where there's a terrace overlooking the rest of the site and an explanatory map. For some background, head for the **Stoa of Attalos**, where a small **museum** occupies the lower level of the building.

Pláka

The largely pedestrianized area of **Pláka**, with its narrow lanes and stepped alleys climbing towards the Acropolis, is arguably the most attractive part of Athens, and certainly the most popular with visitors. Although surrounded by traffic-choked avenues, Pláka itself provides a welcome escape from concrete and exhaust fumes. With scores of **cafés and restaurants** to fill the time between museums and sites, and streets lined with touristy **shops**, it's an enjoyable place to wander. Of the sights, don't miss the **Folk Art Museum** (Kydhathinéon 17; Tues–Sun 8am–3pm; €2; ⑩melt.gr), with five floors devoted to displays of weaving, pottery, regional costumes and embroidery along with other traditional Greek arts and crafts, or the **Roman Forum** (daily 8am–8pm; €2, or joint Acropolis ticket), built during the reign of Julius Caesar and his successor Augustus as an extension of the Greek Agora.

Monastiráki and Psyrrí

Monastiráki, to the north of Pláka, is substantially less touristy than its neighbour. The area has been a marketplace since Ottoman times, and still preserves, in places, a bazaar atmosphere; from Platía Monastirakíou, you'll see signs in both directions that proclaim you're entering the famous **Athens Flea Market**. Psyrrí, northwest, is a once run-down but rapidly gentrifying area with plenty of nightlife as well as some quirky shops. This is also a great place to **eat and drink**: between them, Monastiráki and Psyrrí probably have more eating places per square metre than anywhere else in Athens.

Sýndagma

All roads lead to **Sýndagma** – you'll almost inevitably find yourself here sooner or later for the Metro and bus connections. With the Greek Parliament building (the Voulí) on its uphill side, **Platía Syndágmatos** – Constitution Square – is the political and geographic heart of Athens; the principal venue for mass demonstrations and political rallies. In front of the **Voulí**, goose-stepping **evzónes** in tasselled caps, kilt and woolly leggings change their guard at regular intervals before the **Tomb of the Unknown Soldier** (not open to the public), while behind it spread the shady **National Gardens** (entrances on Amalías, Vasilíssis Sofías and Iródhou Attikoú; sunrise–sunset; free) – a luxuriant tangle of trees whose shade and duck ponds provide palpable relief from the heat of summer.

Platía Omonías and the bazaar

While Pláka and Sýndagma are resolutely geared to tourists and the Athenian well-heeled, **Platía Omonías** (Omónia Square) and its surroundings represent a much more gritty city, revolving around everyday commerce and trade. The **bazaar area** around Odhós Athinás is home to a bustling series of markets and small shops spilling into the streets and offering some of urban Athens' most compelling sights and sounds,

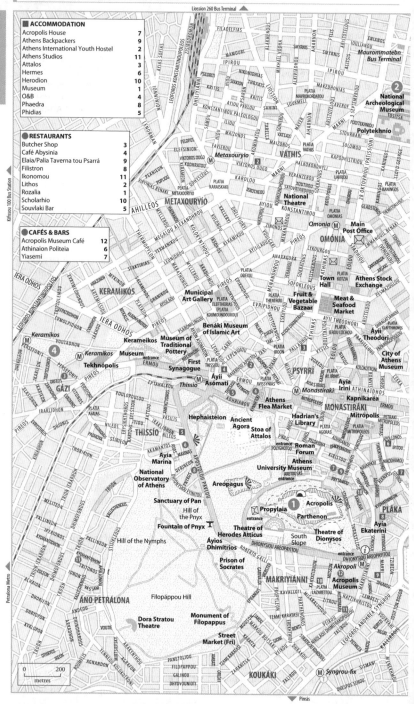

Liossion 260 Bus Terminal

ACCOMMODATION

Acropolis House	7
Athens Backpackers	9
Athens International Youth Hostel	2
Athens Studios	11
Attalos	3
Hermes	6
Herodion	10
Museum	1
O&B	4
Phaedra	8
Phidias	5

RESTAURANTS

Butcher Shop	3
Café Abysinia	4
Elaia/Palia Taverna tou Psarrá	9
Filistron	8
Ikonomou	11
Lithos	2
Rozalia	1
Scholarhio	10
Souvlaki Bar	5

CAFÉS & BARS

Acropolis Museum Café	12
Athinaion Politeia	6
Yiasemi	7

Pireás

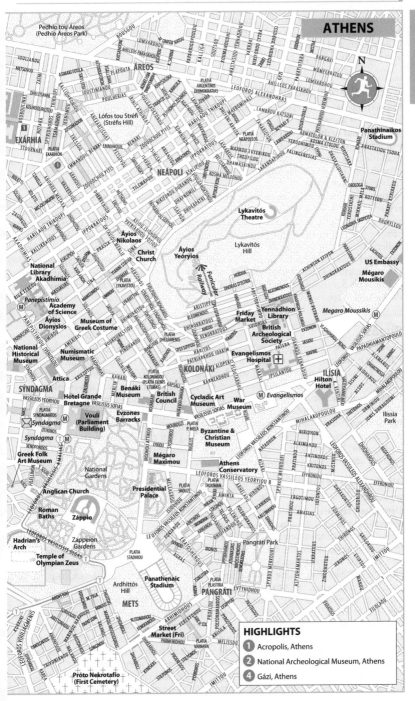

ATHENS

HIGHLIGHTS

1 Acropolis, Athens

2 National Archeological Museum, Athens

4 Gázi, Athens

1

as well as an ethnic mix that is a rare reminder of Greece's traditional role as a meeting place of East and West. It's also a neighbourhood being increasingly recolonized by the drug addicts and prostitutes who were cleared out in time for the Olympics – a process accelerated by the economic crisis.

National Archeological Museum

Patissíon 44 • Daily 8am–8pm • €7 • ⓦ www.namuseum.gr • Metro Viktorías or Omónia; also dozens of buses, including trolleys #2 and #5 – look for those labelled *Mousseio*

The **National Archeological Museum** is an unrivalled treasure-trove of ancient Greek art. You could easily spend an entire morning or afternoon here, but it's equally possible to scoot round the highlights in an hour or two. Arriving early in the morning or late in the afternoon should mean you won't be competing with the tour groups for space.

Highlights include the **Mycenaean halls** – where the gold **Mask of Agamemnon**, arguably the museum's most famous piece, is almost the first thing you see – and a vast collection of Classical **sculpture**, following a broadly chronological arrangement around the main halls of the museum. Don't ignore, either, the less well-known collections hidden away at the rear of the museum and upstairs. These include the **Stathatos collection**, with some truly exquisite jewellery; a wonderful **Egyptian** room; the **bronze collection**; hundreds of **vases**; and a display on the excavations of Akrotíri on Santoríni (see p.195), including some of the famous **Minoan frescoes** discovered there.

Pireás

Metro Pireás • Buses #40 from Sýndagma, #49 from Omónia, #X96 from the airport; you can also get here by ferry (see opposite)

PIREÁS (Piraeus) has been the port of Athens since Classical times, when the so-called Long Walls, scattered remnants of which can still be seen, were built to connect it to the city. Today, it's a substantial metropolis in its own right. The port and its **island ferries** are the reason most people come here; if you're spending any time, though, the real attractions of the place are around the small-boat harbours of **Zéa Marina** and **Mikrolímano** on the opposite side of the small peninsula. Here, the upscale residential areas are alive with attractive waterfront cafés, bars and restaurants offering some of the best seafood in town, and there's an excellent archeological museum and a small beach – all are accessible by local trolley bus #20 from the Metro station.

ARRIVAL AND DEPARTURE

BY PLANE

Elefthérios Venizélos (Athens International) Airport Located at Spáta, 33km southeast of the city, Athens' modern and efficient airport (☎ 210 353 0000, ⓦ www.aia.gr) has facilities including free wi-fi (max 1hr), ATMs and banks with money-changing facilities on all levels, the usual array of travel agencies and car rental places. Aegean (ⓦ aegeanair.com), Astra (ⓦ astra-airlines. gr), Olympic (ⓦ olympicairlines.com), Ryanair (ⓦ ryanair .com) and Sky Express (ⓦ www.skyexpress.gr) operate daily domestic flights in summer.

Domestic destinations Alexandroúpoli; Astypálea; Haniá (Chania; Crete); Híos; Ikaría; Iráklio (Heraklion; Crete); Ioánnina; Kálimnos; Kárpathos; Kastoriá; Kavála; Kefaloniá; Kérkyra (Corfu); Kos; Kozáni; Kýthira; Léros; Límnos; Mílos; Mýkonos; Mytilíni (Lésvos); Náxos; Páros; Rhodes; Santoríni (Thíra); Sitía (Crete); Sámos; Skiáthos; Skýros; Sýros; Thessaloníki; Zákynthos.

FROM THE AIRPORT INTO TOWN

By Metro and rail The Metro and suburban trains share a station at the airport, and departures for both are displayed in the terminals. Metro Line 3 takes you straight into the heart of the city in 45min (every 30min, 6.30am–11.30pm; single €8, return €14, discounts for multiple tickets) where you can change to the other lines at either Monastiráki or Sýndagma. The suburban train (same fares) offers direct trains to the northern suburbs and Corinth, but for Laríssis station in the centre and Pireás you have to change at SKA, or to Metro Line 1 at Neratzíotissa.

By bus Buses can be slower than the Metro (1hr–1hr 30min), especially at rush hour, but they're also cheaper,

1

more frequent (3–4 per hr during the day, every 30min through the night), run all night and offer direct links to other parts of the city: the #X95 runs to Sýndagma square; #X96 to the port at Pireás via Glyfádha and the beach suburbs; #X93 to the bus stations. Tickets cost €5 from a booth beside the stops or on board – be sure to validate your ticket once on the bus. There are also regional bus services to local destinations including the ports of Rafína (hourly, 6am–9pm; €5, buy ticket on the bus) and Lávrio (20 daily, 6.30am–10pm; €6). Electronic boards in the airport show all bus departures.

By taxi Taxis can take anything from 35min to 1hr 35min (at rush hour) to reach the centre; there's a fixed fare to the centre of €35, or €50 at night, and no extras should be added. The fare to Ráfina should be similar, Pireás or Lávrio €10–15 more.

BY FERRY FROM PIREÁS

Hundreds of ferries leave Pireás daily, so it's perhaps not surprising that a comprehensive list is hard to find: even the tourist office simply look up individual queries online (at ⓦ openseas.gr). There are also smaller ferry terminals

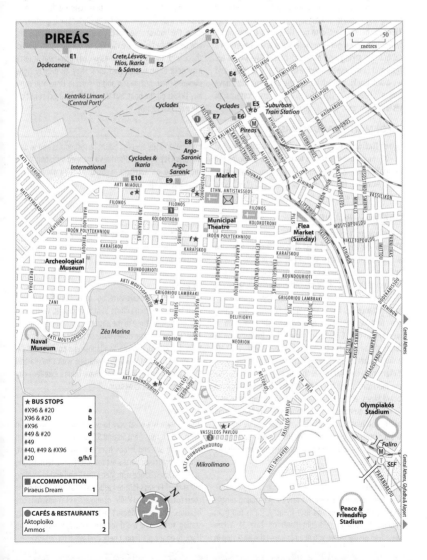

PIREÁS

0   50
metres

E1 Dodecanere
Crete, Lésvos, Hios, Ikaria & Sámos E2
a ★
E3
E4

Kentrikó Limani (Central Port)
Cyclades
Cyclades E5 ★ b
E7 E6
Suburban Train Station
Pireás Ⓜ

E8 ★ c
Argo-Saronic

International
Cyclades & Ikaria
Argo-Saronic
E10 E9
Market
e ★
d ★
ETHN. ANTISTASSEOS

FILONOS FILONOS FILONOS
KOLOKOTRONI **Municipal Theatre** KOLOKOTRONI **Flea Market (Sunday)**
IROÓN POLYTEKHNIOU IROÓN POLYTEKHNIOU
KARAÏSKOU f ★ KARAÏSKOU KARAÏSKOU

Archeological Museum
KOUNDOURIOTI KOUNDOURIOTI
AKTI MOUSOPOULOU GRIGORIOU LAMBRAKI GRIGORIOU LAMBRAKI
ZANI ★ g
DELIYIORYI
NEORION NEORION

Naval Museum
Zéa Marina
SIRANGIOU
AKTI KOÚNDOURIÓTI ★ h

★ i
VASSILEOS PAVLOU
AKTI KOUMOUNDHOUROU
Mikrolímano

Olympiakós Stadium

Faliro Ⓜ
SEF

Peace & Friendship Stadium

Central Athens
Central Athens, Glyfádha & Airport

★ BUS STOPS	
#X96 & #20	a
X96 & #20	b
#X96	c
#49 & #20	d
#49	e
#40, #49 & #X96	f
#20	g/h/i

■ ACCOMMODATION	
Piraeus Dream	1

● CAFÉS & RESTAURANTS	
Aktoploiko	1
Ammos	2

1

at Rafína (see p.74) and Lávrio (see p.72).

Getting there The easiest way to travel between the port and central Athens is on Metro line 1; the journey takes about 20min from Omónia. Alternatively, there are buses: #40 (about every 10min from 5am–midnight; hourly 1–5am) runs to and from Sýndagma, while #49 from Omónia (roughly every 15min from 5am–midnight; hourly 1–5am) will drop you slightly closer to the ferries. Both are very slow, however – allow an hour to be safe. From the airport, you can take express bus #X96 (around 1hr 20min). Taxis cost about €10 at day tariff from the centre of Athens. It can be hard to get a taxi amid the throng disgorging from a ferry.

Tickets There's no need to buy tickets for conventional ferries before you get here, unless you want a berth in a cabin or are taking a car on board; during Greek holidays (Aug and Easter especially) these can be hard to get and it's worth booking in advance – the big companies have online booking. Hydrofoil and fast catamaran reservations are also a good idea at busy times,

especially Fri night/Sat morning out of Athens, and Sun evening coming back. In general, though, the best plan is simply to get to Pireás early and check with some of the dozens of shipping agents around the Metro station and along the quayside Platía Karaïskáki (there are plenty of agents in central Athens, too). Most of these act only for particular lines, so for a full picture you will need to ask at three or four outlets.

Departure points Boats for different destinations leave from a variety of points around the main harbour: it can be helpful to know the gate number, though these are primarily for drivers. Free, airport-style buses run from gate E5, near the Metro, as far as E1, for the big ferries to Crete, the Dodecanese and the northwest. The main gates and departure points are marked on our map, but always check with the ticket agent as on any given day a ferry may dock in an unexpected spot. They all display signs showing their destination and departure time; you can't buy tickets on the boat, but there's usually a ticket hut on the quayside nearby.

INFORMATION AND TOURS

Greek National Tourist Office Dhionysíou Areopayítou 18–20, just by the entrance to the South Slope of the Acropolis (Mon–Fri 9am–8pm, Sat & Sun 10am–4pm; Metro Akrópoli). This is a useful first stop and they have a good free map as well as information sheets on current

museum and site opening hours, bus schedules and so on.

Athens City Tourism Provides a manned infopoint at the airport and an excellent website, ⓦ thisisathens.org – check out the interactive maps.

GETTING AROUND

BY PUBLIC TRANSPORT

Tickets The easiest and least stressful way to travel on public transport is with a pass. A one-day *imerísio* costs €4 and can be used on buses, trolleybuses, trams, Metro and the suburban railway in central Athens (everything except the airport route beyond Doukissis Plakentias and some long-distance bus lines). You validate it once, on starting your first journey, and it is good for 24hr from then. A weekly pass costs €14. A single ticket, valid for 90min on all forms of transport (and transfers between them), is €1.40; a single ticket for one journey by bus or tram only is €1.20. Tickets must be validated at the start of your journey – in the machines at the top of the stairs in Metro stations, on board buses, and on the platform or on board for trams. Tickets and passes can be bought from any Metro ticket office, machines at tram stations, blue-and-yellow bus ticket booths (near most major stops) and many newsstands. You can buy several at once and then validate them as necessary.

BY METRO

The Metro is much the easiest way to get around central Athens; it's fast, quiet and user-friendly. Trains run from roughly 5.30am to midnight (later on Line 1). When travelling on the Metro you need to know the final stop in

the direction you're heading, as that is how the platforms are identified; there are plenty of maps in the stations. Further information at ⓦ stasy.gr.

BY BUS

The bus network is extensive, but crowded and confusing; most buses run from around 5am to midnight, with just a few – including those to the airport – continuing all night. Easiest to use are the trolleybuses: #1 connects the Laríssis train station with Omónia, Sýndagma and Koukáki; #2, #4, #5, #9, #11 and #15 all link Sýndagma with Omónia and the National Archeological Museum. There's excellent city bus information at ⓦ oasa.gr.

BY TRAM

Athens' tram is a great way to get to coastal suburbs and the beach. It runs from around 5.30am to 1am, or 2.30am on Fri and Sat and heads from Sýndagma to the coast, where it branches: northwest towards Pireás, terminating at SEF, an interchange with Metro line 1 and within walking distance of Pireás's leisure harbours; southwest along the coast to Glyfádha and Voúla, giving access to numerous city beaches. The tram doesn't automatically stop at every station, so push the bell if you're on board, or wave it down if you're on the platform. Check ⓦ stasy.gr for details.

BY TAXI

Athenian taxis can seem astonishingly cheap – trips around the city centre will rarely run above €5, and Pireás is €9–12 from the centre; the exact amount is determined by traffic and amount of luggage. One legitimate way that taxi drivers increase their income is to pick up other passengers along the way. There is no fare-sharing: each passenger (or group of passengers) pays the full fare for their journey. So if you're picked up by an already-occupied taxi, you'll pay from that point on, plus the €1.16 initial tariff. When hailing an occupied taxi, call out your destination, so the driver can decide whether you suit him or not.

ACCOMMODATION

HOTELS

★**Acropolis House** Kódhrou 6, Pláka ☎ 210 322 2344, ⓦ acropolishouse.gr; Metro Sýndagma; map pp.62–63. A rambling, slightly dilapidated 150-year-old mansion, much loved by its regulars, most of whom are students and academics who often leave behind books for other guests to read. Furnishings are individual, and some rooms have (sole use) bathrooms across the hall; there's a/c and free wi-fi throughout. There's a variety of prices, and discounts for longer stays. Breakfast included. €60

Athens Studios Veïkóu 3a, Makriyiánni ☎ 210 923 5811, ⓦ athensstudios.gr; Metro Akrópoli; map pp.62–63. Furnished apartments for up to six people, with kitchen, sitting room, TV, free wi-fi, a/c and linen provided. They are managed by the people who run *Athens Backpackers* (see below), and include use of the hostel's bar and facilities. Great value for groups. €90

★**Attalos** Athinás 29, Monastiráki ☎ 210 321 2801, ⓦ attaloshotel.com; Metro Monastiráki; map pp.62–63. Modern from the outside but traditional within, the *Attalos* has bright, comfortable rooms (some triples available), well insulated from the noisy street, all with a/c, TV and free wi-fi (plus free computer terminals in the lobby). Some balcony rooms on the upper floors have great views, but rooms facing the internal courtyard at the back are generally larger and quieter. There's also a roof-terrace bar in the evenings. Buffet breakfast available at extra cost. €70

★**Hermes** Apóllonos 19, Pláka ☎ 210 323 5514, ⓦ hermeshotel.gr; Metro Sýndagma; map pp.62–63. Friendly and welcoming three-star with marble bathrooms, polished wood floors and designer touches in every room, plus TV, a/c, fridge and wi-fi (small charge). Some rooms are rather small; others have big balconies. Interconnecting rooms also available. Breakfast included. €120

Herodion Robérto Gálli 4, Makriyiánni ☎ 210 923 6832, ⓦ www.herodion.gr; Metro Akrópoli; map pp.62–63. This lovely four-star hotel – albeit not quite as luxurious as the exterior and lobby might lead you to believe – enjoys an enviable position right behind the Acropolis. The roof terrace looks almost straight down to the south slope of the Acropolis. €150

Museum Bouboulínas 16, Exárhia ☎ 210 380 5611, ⓦ museum-hotel.gr; Metro Viktorías/Omónia; map pp.62–63. Very pleasant, international-style hotel (part of the Best Western chain), right behind the National Archeological Museum and the Polytekhnío. Rooms in the new wing, which has triples, quads and small suites, are more luxurious but slightly more expensive. €55

★**O&B** Leokoríou 7, Psyrrí ☎ 210 331 2950, ⓦ oandbhotel.com; Metro Thissío; map pp.62–63. Understated designer hotel with exceptional service and just 22 rooms including a couple of large suites with private terrace and Acropolis views. All rooms have free wi-fi and satellite TV, classy bathrooms and toiletries, plus DVD and CD players with a library of titles to borrow. Friendly and comfortable as well as elegant, plus a great location on the fringes of Psyrrí. €155

Phaedra Herefóndos 16, at Adhrianoú, Pláka ☎ 210 323 8461, ⓦ hotelphaedra.com; Metro Akrópoli; map pp.62–63. Small, simple rooms with bare tiled floors, TV and a/c, not all en suite (but you get a private bathroom). Polite, welcoming management looks after the place well and it's quiet at night, thanks to a location at the junction of two pedestrian alleys. One of the best deals in Pláka. €55

Phidias Apostólou Pávlou 39, Thissío ☎ 210 345 9511, ⓦ phidias.gr; Metro Thissío; map pp.62–63. With an enviable position overlooking the Acropolis, at the heart of a newly fashionable area crammed with designer cafés, the *Phidias* has cosy if rather dated rooms, with TV and a/c. Service with a scowl, and overdue for a makeover, but it's decent value; almost all rooms have balconies and fabulous views. Breakfast included. €70

HOSTELS

★**Athens Backpackers** Mákri 12, Makriyiánni ☎ 210 922 4044, ⓦ backpackers.gr; Metro Akrópoli; map pp.62–63. Very central Athenian-Australian-run hostel with few frills, but clean rooms, communal kitchen, internet access, bar, fabulous rooftop view and great atmosphere. Dorm €22

Athens International Youth Hostel Víktoros Ougó 16 ☎ 210 523 2540, ⓦ athens-international.com; Metro Metaxouryío; map pp.62–63. A huge affair, with 140 beds over seven floors in two-, four- and six-bed dorms, all a/c and en suite, some women-only. Cheap and always busy, it is much the most traditionally "youth-hostelly" of Athens' hostels. Dorm €9, double €31

PIREÁS

Piraeus Dream Fílonos 79–81 & Notára 78–80, Pireás ☎ 210 411 0555, ⓦ piraeusdream.gr; Metro

Pireás; map p.65. It's easy to get from the centre to Pireás, but if you do have a very early departure or late ferry arrival, this friendly hotel is a solid option. It has

quiet, recently refurbished rooms (with spectacular lighting), a/c and TV. Buffet breakfast included. **€65**

EATING AND DRINKING

Athens has arguably the best and most varied **restaurants** and **tavernas** in the country, though most tourists, sticking to the obvious central choices, never discover that. While **Pláka**'s hills and narrow lanes can provide a pleasant, romantic evening setting, they also tend to be marred by high prices and tourist hype: areas like **Psyrrí** and **Thissío** (or Gázi and Exárhia a little further afield) are where the locals go for a meal out. The pleasure harbours of **Pireás**, meanwhile, are a favourite Sunday lunchtime destination.

RESTAURANTS, TAVERNAS AND OUZERÍS

Butcher Shop Persefónis 19, Gázi ☎210 341 3440; map pp.62–63. As the name and the decor – a modernist take on a traditional butchers – suggest, this is not one for the vegetarians (though if seafood is more your thing, note that the next-door fish restaurant, *Sardelles*, is under the same management and can serve to the same tables). There's all sorts of high-quality meat, from lamb chops (€15.40) to game birds (€12), plus a huge variety of burgers (€10–12.50), exotic sausages (€7.50–9) and the fanciest *yíros* in town (with shank and pancetta of free-range pork, €11.50). Great chips, too. Daily noon–2am.

★**Café Abysinia** Kynétou 7, Platía Avysinnías ☎210 321 7047, ⍟avissinia.gr; map pp.62–63. With two floors and a delicious, modern take on traditional Greek cooking (wild-boar meatballs, €15, for example, or mussel pilaf for €10.50), *Café Abysinia* is always busy, with a local alternative crowd. Though more expensive than many, it's still decent value, and there's live music most weekday evenings and weekend lunchtimes. Tues–Sat 11am–1am, Sun till 7pm.

Elaia/Palia Taverna tou Psarrá Erekhthéos 16, at Erotókritou ☎210 324 9512321 8733; map pp.62–63. Though they appear to be separate restaurants, these two actually share a menu and kitchen; given that, the best place to sit is on the roof terrace at *Elaia*, which offers wonderful views; there are also plenty of tables below, both inside and on a tree-shaded and bougainvillea-draped pedestrian crossroads. You're best making a meal of the mezédhes (€6–9) which include humble standards as well as seafood and fish concoctions. There's live music Thurs–Sat evenings and Sun lunchtime. Mon–Sat 1pm–1am, Sun from noon.

Filistron Apóstolou Pávlou 23, Thissío ☎210 342 2897, ⍟filistron.com; map pp.62–63. Somewhat touristy, but worth it for the roof terrace with its great Acropolis view, this restaurant has a short menu of tasty, well-presented mezédhes from all over Greece (small plates €5–8.50, large €8–13.50), which means some interesting and unusual dishes. It's good value given the location. Mon–Thurs & Sun noon–midnight, Fri & Sat till 1am.

★**Ikonomou** Tróon 41, at Kydhantidhón, Áno Petrálona ☎210 346 7555; map pp.62–63. Wonderful,

traditional taverna where home-cooked food is served to packed pavement tables in summer. No menu, just a dozen or so inexpensive daily specials: check out what others are eating as the waiters may not know the names of some of the dishes in English. Mon–Sat dinner only.

Lithos Aisópou 17, Psyrrí ☎210 324 7797, ⍟lithospsiri.gr; map pp.62–63. Lively restaurant with plenty of locals who appreciate the slightly modern take on Greek classics and the live music every night (and weekend lunchtimes). Excellent cheese or fennel pies to start (around €5), followed perhaps by lamb with honey and thyme (€15), octopus, or seafood risotto (around €10). Daily lunch & dinner.

Rozalia Valtetsíou 58, Exárhia ☎210 330 2133, ⍟rozalia.gr; map pp.62–63. Ever-popular mid-range taverna, with excellent chicken and highly palatable barrelled wine. You order mezédhes (mostly €3.50–7) from the tray, as the waiters thread their way through the throng; there's also a regular menu of grilled fish and meat (€10.50–13). Garden seating in summer. Daily noon–midnight.

★**Scholarhio** Tripódhon 14, Pláka ☎210 324 7605, ⍟scholarhio.gr; map pp.62–63. Attractive, split-level ouzerí with a perennially popular summer terrace, sheltered from the street. It has a great selection of mezédhes (all €3–6) brought out on trays so that you can point to the ones that you fancy. Especially good are the flaming sausages, *bouréki* (thin pastry filled with ham and cheese) and grilled aubergine. The house red wine is also palatable and cheap. All-inclusive deals at €14 a head. Daily 11am–2am.

Souvlaki Bar Thissíou 15, Monastiráki ☎210 515 0550, ⍟facebook.com/souvlakibar.gr; map pp.62–63. Modern take on a classic *souvladzídhika* (kebab shop), close to Thissío Metro. Great *yíros* (€2.50) and *souvláki* (including veggie versions; portion €6.50–8.50) in designer surroundings, plus excellent burgers (€6.50–9) and more. Daily lunch & dinner till late.

CAFÉS AND BARS

★**Acropolis Museum Restaurant** Acropolis Museum, Dhionysíou Areopayítou, Makriyiánni ☎210 900 0915, ⍟theacropolismuseum.gr;

map pp.62–63. Despite the name, this is really a café, where they serve light meals such as octopus with pasta (€12.50) and baked red beans with sausage & fennel (€8), as well as salads, cakes and drinks. There's a large, cool, smoke-free internal area and a shaded terrace looking up towards the Parthenon. Quality is superb and the prices reasonable. Don't make the mistake of going to the ground-floor café; grab a free pass to the second floor for the same menu in far nicer surroundings. April–Oct Mon 8am–4pm, Tues–Fri till midnight, Sat & Sun till 8pm; Nov–March Tues–Thurs 9am–5pm, Fri till midnight, Sat & Sun till 8pm.

Athinaion Politeia Akamántos 1, at Apóstolou Pávlou, Thissío ☎210 341 3795, ⬤athinaionpoliteia.gr; map pp.62–63. Housed in an old mansion, in an enviable position with great views from the terrace towards the Acropolis, this is (not surprisingly) a popular meeting place and a decent spot to relax over a frappé. Rather pricey light meals (mains €8.50–14) are also served. Daily 9am–3am.

★**Yiasemi** Mnisikléous ☎2130 417 937, ⬤yiasemi.gr; map pp.62–63. A café-bistro on a steep, stepped street, Yiasemi is a victim of its own success – it's almost always packed with locals. If there are no tables on the street, check inside, where it's warm in winter for soup and hot chocolate, and stairs lead up to a less-known outdoor terrace. There are hot drinks and fresh juices, big breakfast for €8 and inexpensive lunchtime specials (many

vegetarian, such as cheese pie with black-eye pea salad) for €5. Daily 10am–2am.

PIREÁS
If you're looking for food to take on board a ferry, or breakfast, you'll find numerous places around the market area and near the Metro station, as well as all along the waterfront. There are plenty of bakeries and souvláki joints here, including a handy branch of Everest on the corner of Aktí Kalimassióti by the Metro. Otherwise there's little good food in the port area, but some superb fish tavernas over at Mikrolímano.

Aktoploiko Aktí Tsélegi 4; map p.65. Less manic than most places around the port, with tables outside on a pedestrianized part of the waterfront just off Platía Karaïskáki, this café serves breakfast and light meals – souvláki, salads, pasta – throughout the day. Daily morning till late.

★**Ammos** Aktí Koumoundhoúrou 44, Mikrolímano ☎210 422 4633; map p.65. In contrast to the high-luxe places around it, Ammos goes for an island feel, with hand-painted tables and beach scenes. Still mainly fish (drunkard's mussels €7.80, grilled prawns or fisherman's pasta €15), but also a wide variety of meze (€5–9) and slightly lower prices and a younger crowd than its neighbours. Reservations recommended at weekends. Daily lunch & dinner.

Alexandhroúpoli

The modern city of **ALEXANDHROÚPOLI**, almost on the Turkish border in the northwest corner of Greece, has daily ferries to Samothráki. It's not the most exciting of places, but there's a lively seafront promenade and, if you have a few hours to spare, the excellent **Ethnological Museum** (14 Maïoú 63; March–Sept Tues & Wed 9am–3pm, Thurs & Fri 9am–3pm & 6–9pm, Sat & Sun 10am–3pm; Oct–Feb Tues–Sat 9am–3pm, Sun 10am–3pm; €3; ☎25510 36663, ⬤emthrace.org), about 500m north of the ferry terminal, is one of the best in Greece.

ARRIVAL AND DEPARTURE

ALEXANDHROÚPOLI

By plane The airport is 4km west of town. Frequent local buses stop by en route to town.
Destinations Athens (2–3 daily; 1hr); Sitía, Crete (3 weekly; 1hr 45min).
By train The train station is next to the port.
Destination Thessaloníki (2 daily; 6hr–6hr 40min); Komotiní (55min–1hr); Xánthi (1hr 25min–1hr 35min).
By bus The KTEL station is at Venizélou 36 (☎25510

26479), four blocks inland from the port.
Destinations Dhadhiá (2 daily; 1hr); Dhidhymótiho (every 30min–1hr; 1hr 30min); Komotiní (hourly; 1hr); Thessaloníki (6 daily; 4hr).
By ferry Alexandhroúpoli is the only access port for ferries to Samothráki (1–3 daily, 2hr 30min; ☎25510 38503, ⬤saos.gr).

ACCOMMODATION AND EATING

Erika K. Dhimitríou 110, just east of the port entrance ☎25510 34115, ⬤hotel-erika.gr. Smart seafront hotel, recently upgraded, with comfortable rooms and a hearty breakfast (extra). **€60**

O Glaros K. Dhimitríou 126, opposite port entrance ☎25510 32899. The one surviving seafront café-cum-ouzerí is a great spot to wait for a ferry with a glass of ouzo and a few cheap mezédhes, mostly under €5. Daily 10am–midnight.

1

Astakós

ASTAKÓS ("Lobster") is a small port on the western mainland with frequent ferries to Kefaloniá and Itháki. Despite the name, there's no lobster served at any of the mediocre tavernas lining the quay; around the marketplace many Neoclassical buildings from the 1870s hint at a more prosperous past.

ARRIVAL AND DEPARTURE   ASTAKÓS

By bus The KTEL is at the end of the quay; buses from Athens should coincide with the ferry.

By ferry Ferry timetables change from month to month throughout summer. See ⓦ ionionpelagos.com or call ☎ 26460 38020 for the latest departure times.

Destinations Sámi, Kefaloniá (at least 2 daily; 2hr 30min); Pisaetós, Itháki (1–2 daily, less in winter; 2hr 30min); Vathý, Itháki (1–2 daily, less in winter; 1hr 30min) both have a reduced service year-round.

ACCOMMODATION

Stratos By the quay ☎ 26460 41911. The only hotel in the centre of town, dingy and overpriced *Stratos* overlooks the tiny, gravelly beach; in peak season it might be worth asking around to see if cheaper rooms are available elsewhere. €50

Áyios Konstandínos

ÁYIOS KONSTANDÍNOS is the closest port to Athens for the Sporades islands, with daily departures to Skiáthos, Skópelos and Alónissos. There's little to hang about for and, with frequent buses along the coastal Athens–Lamía motorway, no real need to do so.

ARRIVAL AND DEPARTURE   ÁYIOS KONSTANDÍNOS

By bus The bus station is located about 200m south of the ferry landing. As well as the regular buses to and from Athens' Liossíon terminal, there are also dedicated buses from central Athens in high season, timed to coincide with ferries, run by Alkyon Travel (☎ 210 383 2545, ⓦ alkyontravel .gr) for Hellenic Seaways and Jeta Tours (☎ 210 323 0582, ⓦ jeta-tours.gr) for Aegean Flying Dolphins.

Destinations Athens (hourly; 2hr 30min); Pátra (1 daily; 3hr 30min).

By ferry In summer, Hellenic Seaways fast catamarans and ferries (☎ 21041 99000, ⓦ hsw.gr) and Aegean Flying Dolphins hydrofoils (ⓦ aegeanflyingdolphins.gr)

run to Alónissos, Skópelos and Skiáthos. Prebooking is recommended: local agents are Alkyon (☎ 22350 32444, ⓦ alkyontravel.com) and Stavrianos (☎ 22350 32609). Edipsos Ferries (☎ 22260 23330, ⓦ ferriesedipsos.gr) also runs a frequent service from Arkítsa, 16km east of Áyios Konstandínos, to Edhipsós on Évvia, while in peak season only there are also departures direct from Áyios Konstandínos to Áyios Yeóryios on Évvia.

Destinations Alónissos (summer 3 daily; 2hr 25min–5hr 5min); Évvia (June–Aug at least every 2hr; 25–45min); Skiáthos (summer 3 daily; 1hr 20min–2hr 40min); Skópelos (summer 3 daily; 2hr 5min–4hr 15min).

Igoumenítsa

IGOUMENÍTSA is Greece's third passenger port after Pireás and Pátra, with frequent ferries to **Corfu** and **Italy**. It's also the country's leading cargo port, so away from the waterfront it's far from attractive; levelled during World War II, it was rebuilt in bland utilitarian style. You should be able to get a ferry out immediately; every day in season there are sailings to Italy in the morning, and throughout the evening. If you end up stuck for the day, you're better off taking an excursion out of Igoumenítsa than hanging around.

ARRIVAL AND DEPARTURE   IGOUMENÍTSA

By bus The KTEL is about 700m north of the ferry terminal on Leoforos 49 Martiron.

Destinations Athens (6 daily, 8hr); Ioánnina (10–14 daily; 2hr); Párga (2 daily Mon–Fri; 1hr).

By ferry Almost all international ferries depart from the New Port Egnatía at the far south end of town, although a few do still use the old port; drivers must check in at least 2hr before departure. Local ferries operate from the domestic ferry quay just north of the new terminal; tickets for these services are purchased at waterside booths.

Domestic destinations Corfu Town (every 10–45min; 1hr 15min–2hr); Lefkími, southern Corfu (4–6 daily; 40min); Paxi (1–2 daily in summer; 1hr).

International destinations Ancona (2–3 daily; 14hr 30min–15hr 30min); Bari (1–2 daily; 9hr–10hr 30min); Brindisi (1–4 daily; 6hr 30min–9hr); Ravenna (5 weekly; 26hr); Venice (1 daily on Mon, Tues, Fri & Sat; 22–25hr).

ACCOMMODATION AND EATING

Akti Roudou 13, at Agion Apostolon ☎ 26650 23763. This simple taverna is much more authentic than the usual choices along the strip. The menu has all the Greek standards, plus fresh catch of the day, for around €10–12 a head. Daily lunch & dinner.

Stavrodhromi Soulíou 16 ☎ 26650 22343, ⓦ stavrodromihotel.gr. The best budget hotel in town, on the street leading diagonally uphill and northeast from the square. Simple, air-conditioned rooms with small kitchenettes, plus a ground-floor bar-restaurant that sometimes hosts live music. **€30**

Kalamáta

KALAMÁTA, famous for its olives, is by far the largest city in the southern Peloponnese; quite a metropolitan shock after the small-town life of the rest of the region. There's a weekly, summer-only ferry to Kýthira and western Crete. With time to kill it's worth visiting the **Kástro** (Mon–Fri 8.30am–3pm; free), a small Byzantine fortress twenty minutes' walk north of the centre. On Wednesdays and Saturdays, one of the region's most colourful produce **markets** (roughly 8am–3pm) is held just below here, and there are also a couple of small **museums**, as well as the simple pleasures of eating at tavernas among the Neoclassical houses on the waterfront.

ARRIVAL AND DEPARTURE — KALAMÁTA

By air The airport (☎ 27210 69442) is 8km west of town on the highway; regular buses run along this road, but it's far easier to get a taxi into town.

By bus The bus station (☎ 27210 28581; ⓦ ktelmessinias .gr) is nearly 1km north of the centre along Nédhondos; again, it's easiest to get a taxi down to the port.

Destinations Athens (4 direct daily; 2hr 45min); Kórinthos (7 daily; 3hr 15min–4hr); Messíni (1–2 hourly; 30min); Pátra (2 daily; 3hr–3hr 30min).

By ferry June–Sept, 1 weekly to Kýthira (5hr 10min) and Kastélli, Crete (9hr 20min) with Lane Lines (☎ 27210 20704).

ACCOMMODATION AND EATING

Elektra Hotel & Spa Psaron 152, at Bouboulinas ☎ 27210 99100, ⓦ elektrahotelspa.gr. Convenient for the ferries, this swish hotel offers a dozen different spa treatments and has the largest and most comfortable beds you are likely to sink into in Greece. Gym, rooftop pool, sauna and Turkish bath all add up to a great stay. Breakfast included. **€100**

Kannás Poseidonos 12 ☎ 27210 91596, ⓦ kannas.gr.

Facing the water, with seating on a pretty terrace, this restaurant has good fish and pasta dishes. Try their shrimp risotto for €12. Daily noon–midnight.

Routsis Navarínou 127 ☎ 27210 80830. Old-fashioned beachside taverna offering fresh local olives, home-made feta, steamed greens, catch of the day or fish soup (mains around €6). Daily 11am–1am.

Kavála

KAVÁLA is one of the main departure points for Thássos (see p.414), as well as Límnos (see p.404) and other northeast Aegean islands. Although its attempt to style itself the "Azure City", on account of its position at the head of a wide bay, is going a little overboard, it does have an interesting **historic centre**, focused on the harbour area and the few remaining tobacco warehouses. A picturesque **citadel**

1

(daily 8am–9pm, winter till 4pm; €2) looks down from a rocky promontory to the east, and an elegant Ottoman **aqueduct** leaps over modern buildings into the old quarter on the bluff.

ARRIVAL AND DEPARTURE   KAVÁLA

By plane Megas Alexandhros airport is about 25km east of Kavála; there are charter flights from the UK and domestic connections with Athens (1–2 daily; 1hr 5min). There is no convenient bus to town, and taxis cost at least €40.

By bus The main bus station is on the corner of Mitropolítou Khryssostómou and Filikís Eterías, an easy walk from the port.

Destinations Alexandhroúpoli (5 daily; 3hr); Athens (2 daily; 9hr); Thessaloníki (hourly; 2hr).

By ferry Details for the services below are available from

the port authority (☎2510 223 716) and tickets from agencies such as Zolotas (☎2510 835 671), around the harbourfront towards the terminal/customs house. Note that Keramotí, 46km southeast of Kavála, offers a more frequent, shorter and marginally cheaper ferry crossing to Thássos (6–12 daily; 40min).

Destinations Híos (2 weekly; 12hr); Ikaría (1 weekly; 17hr); Lésvos (2 weekly; 10hr); Límnos (2 weekly; 5hr); Sámos (2 weekly; 15hr); Thássos (Skála Prínou; 6 daily; 1hr 15min).

ACCOMMODATION AND EATING

Esperia Erythroú Stavroú 42 ☎2510 229 621, ⓦesperiakavala.gr. A decent hotel offering comfortable a/c rooms – ask for the quieter side or back ones. Breakfast, served on a terrace, is included. **€50**

Imaret Poulídhou 6 ☎2510 620 151, ⓦimaret.gr. This unique and expertly refurbished Ottoman medrese offers rooms and suites that have been faultlessly fashioned, while keeping the original building intact. Services include

a traditional hammam with massage, a restaurant serving Ottoman dishes and a womb-like indoor pool. **€300**

O Kanadhos Poulídhou 27 ☎2510 835 172. Grilled meat and fish for around €7–9 are the forte at this friendly place run by returnees from Toronto – hence the name and the English-speaking management. They also do very cheap bulk wine. Daily 11am–1am.

Kyllíni

The small port of **KYLLÍNI**, south of Pátra, is the main departure point for the Ionian island of Zákynthos and also has boats to Póros and Sámi on Kefaloniá. It's not a particularly attractive place, and there should be no need to stay, if you time things right.

ARRIVAL AND DEPARTURE   KYLLÍNI

By bus KTEL buses from Athens and Pátra continue on to the ferry to Zákynthos (ⓦktel-zakynthos.gr).

Destinations Athens (2–4 daily; 4hr); Pátra (2–4 daily; 1hr).

By ferry Ferries from Kyllíni are run by Ionian Ferries (ⓦionianferries.gr) and Kefalonian Lines (ⓦkefalonianlines

.com). The timings below are summer frequencies; a heavily reduced service operates year-round.

Destinations Póros, Kefaloniá (5–7 daily; 1hr 30min); Sámi, Kefaloniá (at least 1 daily; 2hr–2hr 30min); Zákynthos (8–10 daily; 1hr).

Lávrio

LÁVRIO lies close to the southern tip of Attica, some 60km from the centre of Athens; easily accessed from there or direct from the airport. Its ferries mainly serve **Kéa** and **Kýthnos**, but there are also services to the northeast Aegean and to many of the Cycladic islands via Sýros. Lávrio is a major yachting centre, and there are plenty of cafés and restaurants around the harbour, plus the **Archeological Museum** (Tues–Sun 8am–3pm; €2), which is excellent, but given the frequent connections there's absolutely no need to stay here.

ARRIVAL AND DEPARTURE

By bus KTEL buses run between Lávrio and Athens airport (20 daily; 30min), as well as the Mavrommatéon terminal in Athens (hourly; 1hr 40min).

By ferry Operators are Goutos Lines (☏ 22920 26777), Karystia (☏ 22920 60370) and NEL (🖥 www.nel.gr).

Destinations Peak season departures include: Ándhros (1 weekly; 9hr 15min); Áyios Efstrátios (4 weekly; 8hr 30min–11hr 50min); Folégandhros (1 weekly; 14hr 10min); Kavála

(4 weekly; 17hr–19hr 30min); Kéa (3–5 daily; 1hr); Kímolos (1 weekly; 16hr); Kýthnos (1–3 daily; 1hr 40min–2hr 45min); Íos (1 weekly; 12hr 25min); Límnos (4 weekly; 10hr 30min–13hr 40min); Mílos (1 weekly; 17hr 15min); Mýkonos (1 weekly; 7hr 10min); Náxos (1 weekly; 10hr 10min); Páros (1 weekly; 8hr 40min); Síkinos (1 weekly; 13hr 15min); Sýros (2–4 weekly; 5hr 45min); Tínos (1 weekly; 6hr 50min).

Neápoli

A small port at the southern foot of the Peloponnese, **NEÁPOLI** (full name Neápoli Voión) is a mix of old buildings and modern Greek concrete behind a grey-sand beach with views of Kýthira and Elafónissos islands. For such an out-of-the-way place, it is surprisingly developed, catering mostly to Greek holiday-makers.

ARRIVAL AND DEPARTURE

By bus The KTEL bus station is on the main road down towards the sea, at Leofóros Dhimokratías 7 (☏ 27340 23222).

Destinations Athens (3–4 daily; 6hr); Spárti (3–4 daily, 2hr).

By ferry The ferries leave from the jetty at the junction of

Voion and Ayias Triadhas streets (☏ 276340 22228). Ferry tickets are available from the office of the Vatika Bay Shipping Agency (☏ 27340 24004 or ☏ 27340 29004, 🖥 vatikabay.gr), just west of the pier.

Destination Kýthira (1–2 daily; 1hr 15min).

ACCOMMODATION

Aïvalí Akti Voion 164 ☏ 27340 22287, 🖥 aivali-neapoli .gr. This clean, unpretentious hotel is right on the seafront, near the ferry for Kýthira. Rooms have a/c and balconies, all of which face the water, plus there's wi-fi at reception. Breakfast included. **€45**

Vergina ☏ 27340 23443, 🖥 verginahotel.com. This hotel is quietly situated, a block away from the harbour. It's modestly modern, with internet access, a/c, parking and basic rooms with balconies. Breakfast included. **€30**

Pátra

PÁTRA (Patras) is the largest city in the Peloponnese and, after Pireás, the major port of Greece; it's the chief terminal for **ferries from Italy** as well as having connections to most of the **Ionian islands**. The city is also a hub of the mainland transport network, with connections throughout the Peloponnese and, via the ferry at Río, across the straits to Delphi or western Greece. Unless you arrive late in the day from Italy, you shouldn't need to spend more than a few hours in the city – though it's not a bad place to spend time, with a large student population and a newly pedestrianized centre.

ARRIVAL AND DEPARTURE

By bus The main bus station (☏ 2610 623 886, 🖥 ktelachaias.gr) is next to the Pátra Infocenter at Agora Argyri. Buses for Mesolóngi, Agrínio and Náfpaktos leave from the old Deck 5 (☏ 2610 421 205), about 15min walk north.

Destinations Athens (2 hourly, 3hr); Itéa, for Delphi (Mon–Sat 2 daily; 3–4hr); Itháki via Kefaloniá (1 daily; 6hr); Kalamáta (2 daily; 4hr); Kefaloniá via Kyllíni (3 daily; 4hr);

Mesolóngi (8–10 daily; 1hr); Náfpaktos (1–7 daily; 1hr); Thessaloníki (2–3 daily; 7hr); Vólos (4 weekly; 6hr).

By train The train station, on Óthonos & Amalías, serves only the commuter line Pátras–Rio. The new line to Athens is planned for completion by 2016; in the meantime, there are frequent replacement buses to Kiáto, where you can pick up the Athens suburban train.

By ferry All ferries now leave from Néo Limáni (New Port)

at the south of the city. A taxi to the centre costs €5, and bus #18 will also take you through the centre to the KTEL station (hourly 10.30am–5.30pm; €1.10). Italy-bound ferries (see box, p.27) leave from early afternoon to midnight. You must check in at the agent's embarkation booth at least 2hr before departure (ⓦpatrasport.gr).

International destinations Ancona (2–3 daily; 19hr 30min/20hr 30min); Bari (1–2 daily; 14hr 30min/16hr); Brindisi (1 daily; 14hr 30min); Venice (1 daily; 31hr).
Domestic destinations Corfu (1–2 daily; 6hr 15min/6hr 45min); Igoumenítsa (3–5 daily; 4hr 45min–7hr).

ACCOMMODATION AND EATING

Don't expect too much of Pátra's hotels; most cater for a very passing trade and don't try too hard. The pedestrianized seaward end of Ayíou Nikoláou is a very lively area at night, with busy cafés spread across the street.

Astir Ayíou Andhréou 16 ☎2610 277 502, ⓦhotel astirpatras.gr. Pleasantly modernist styling in the public spaces, handsome large rooms, great harbour views plus a rooftop terrace restaurant with a pool make this the best choice in town. Greek PMs stay in the VIP suite when visiting. Extras include wi-fi, covered parking and a sauna. Breakfast included. €80

Atlanta Zaïmi 10 ☎2610 220 019, ⓔatlanta@pat .forthnet.gr. Plain but central hotel, just across from the bus station, with small but comfortable rooms. Free wi-fi. Breakfast €5. €40

Due Piani Ayíou Nikolaou 47 ☎2610 279 222. You can come here three times in the same day and find a very different crowd and atmosphere – it's a café in the mornings, swish restaurant during the day and a live-music and DJ venue in the evenings. Try the medium *pikilía* (a meze platter) for €12 if you dare. Daily 8am–2am.

Olympic Star Ayíou Nikoláou 46 ☎2610 622 939, ⓦolympicstar.gr. Stylish hotel with large rooms, each with its own balcony, LCD TV, wi-fi, jet showers and a desktop computer in every room. If you can afford it, ask for the suite. Breakfast included. €58

Rafína

The port of **RAFÍNA**, about 30km from central Athens, has fast ferries and catamarans to the **Cyclades**, as well as to Marmári on nearby **Évvia**. Many Athenians have summer homes overlooking the attractive, rocky coast, but the beaches are tricky to reach even with a car, so for visitors the chief attraction, ferries aside, is gastronomic. Overlooking the harbour is a line of excellent **seafood restaurants**, many with roof terraces and a ringside view of the comings and goings at the harbour. The pedestrianized square above the harbour is also a lively place, ringed with cafés and rather cheaper eating options.

ARRIVAL AND DEPARTURE

RAFÍNA

By bus The bus terminal is right on the seafront at the outer edge of the harbour, facing the sea; get your ticket on the bus.
Destinations Athens airport (12 daily; 40min); Athens Mavrommatéon (every 30min; 1hr).

By ferry There are ticket agents for the multitude of operators all round the port.
Destinations Peak season departures include: Amorgós (6 weekly; 4hr 30min); Ándhros (1–3 daily; 2hr); Íos (1 daily; 7hr 20min); Irakliá (3 weekly; 4hr 30min); Koufoníssi (6 weekly; 4hr); Marmári, Évvia (at least 5 daily; 1hr); Mýkonos (1–7 daily; 2hr 5min–4hr 40min); Náxos (1–4 daily; 3hr 5min–5hr 50min); Páros (1–3 daily; 2hr 50min–4hr 50min); Skhinoússa (4 weekly; 4hr 10min); Santoríni (6 weekly; 3hr 15min–5hr 40min); Tínos (1–5 daily; 1hr 40min–3hr 50min).

ACCOMMODATION AND EATING

Hotel Avra Arafinidhón Alón 3 ☎22940 22780, ⓦhotelavra.gr. Occupying a prime position high above the harbour, this business-style designer hotel has luxury rooms and suites, many with sea views. €70

Ouzeri Limeni Platía Plastíra 17 ☎22940 24750. The best choice on the lively square above the harbour, with excellent meze and Greek standards, for less than you'll pay down at the harbour. Tues–Sun lunch & dinner.

Ta Kavoúria tou Asimáki Rafína harbour ☎22940 24551. The pick of Rafína's seafood restaurants is the first you'll come to as you descend towards the harbour from the square; though it looks fancier than its neighbours, with linen tablecloths and proper wine glasses, it's no more expensive. Head for the roof terrace, which has a great view of the harbour activity. Daily noon–midnight.

Thessaloníki

Greece's second city and capital of the north, **THESSALONÍKI** – or Salonica, as it is sometimes known to English-speakers – has a distinctly Balkan feel but also an unusually wide ethnic mix and a prosperous air, stimulated by a major university and a famously avant-garde live music and entertainment scene. Local food is some of the best in Greece: there are some very sophisticated restaurants, but also wholesome traditional fare on offer in a great number of old-fashioned Turkish-influenced ouzería and tavernas.

Though in no way a tourist resort, the city has plenty to offer: **churches**, **Ottoman buildings** and excellent **museums** above all. Of these, the undoubted champion is the **Archeological Museum** (Platía H.A.N.TH.; May–Oct daily 8am–8pm, Nov–April Tues–Sun 8am–3pm; €6; ☎ 2310 830 538, ⓦ amth.gr), which displays many of the finds from the royal tombs of Philip II of Macedon (father of Alexander the Great). Monumental highlights of Thessaloníki include the **White Tower (Lefkós Pýrgos**; east end of Leofóros Níkis; Tues–Sun 8.30am–3pm; €3; ☎ 2310 267 832, ⓦ lpth.gr), the city's graceful symbol; Roman remains including the **Arch of Galerius** and nearby **Rotónda**, now the church of **Áyios Yeóryios** (Platía Ayíou Yeoryíou; Tues–Sun 8.30am–3pm; free; ☎ 2310 968 860); the many Ottoman survivals in the heart of the **Upper Town (Áno Póli)**; and Byzantine churches, above all **Ayía Sofía** (between Egnatía and Platía Navarínou; daily 7am–1pm & 5–6.30pm; free; ☎ 2310 270 253) and **Áyios Dhimítrios** (Ayíou Dhimitríou; Mon 12.30–7pm, Tues–Sat 8am–8pm, Sun 10.30am–8pm; free; ☎ 2310 968 843).

ARRIVAL AND DEPARTURE

THESSALONÍKI

By plane Thessaloníki "Makedonia" airport (☎ 2310 985 000, ⓦ thessalonikiairport.com) is located 15km south of the city centre. City bus #78 shuttles back and forth from the airport to the KTEL bus terminal via the town centre once or twice hourly all day, and #78N goes once an hour through the night. A taxi ride into town comes to nearly €20, including extras (see p.32).

Domestic destinations Athens (14–16 daily; 50min); Corfu (4 weekly; 1hr); Haniá (Chania), Crete (1–2 daily; 1hr 30min); Híos (4 weekly; 1hr); Iráklio (Heraklion), Crete (1–2 daily; 1hr 15min); Lésvos (5 weekly; 55min); Límnos (6 weekly; 45min); Rhodes (1–2 daily; 1hr 15min); Sámos (4 weekly; 1hr 5min); Santoríni (2 weekly; 1hr 5min).

By train The train station is on the west side of town, with convenient bus links and a taxi rank. If you want to buy tickets or make reservations in advance, you'll find that the OSE office at Aristotélous 18 (Mon–Fri 8am–3.30pm) is far more central and helpful than the station ticket-windows.

Destinations Alexandhroúpoli (2 daily; 6hr–6hr 45min); Athens (8 daily; 4hr 40min–6hr); Édhessa (8 daily; 1hr 20min–1hr 30min); Flórina (3 daily; 2hr 30min); Lárissa (19 daily; 1hr 20min–1hr 35min); Litóhoro (11 daily; 1hr); Véria (8 daily; 45min–1hr); Xánthi (2 daily; 4hr 40min–5hr 15min).

By bus Most KTEL buses use the main terminal ("Makedonia"), 3km west of the city centre at Yiannitsón 194 (☎ 2310 500 111, ⓦ ktel-thes.gr); local buses #1, #31 & #78 go to the train station and Egnatía.

Destinations Alexandhroúpoli (7–8 daily; 4hr); Athens (10 daily; 7hr); Édhessa (hourly; 1hr 45min); Igoumenítsa (2 daily; 4hr); Ioánnina (5–6 daily; 4hr); Kalambáka (4 daily; 4hr 30min); Kastoriá (6 daily; 2hr 30min); Kavála (hourly; 2hr–2hr 30min); Litóhoro (11–12 daily; 1hr 15min); Pélla (hourly; 1hr); Véria (every 15–30min; 1hr); Vólos (8 daily; 3hr); Xanthi (9–10 daily; 2hr 30min).

By ferry All ferries leave from the port located at the western end of the seafront. The most convenient agent is Ferry Traveller, located inside the domestic passenger terminal (☎ 2310 500 800, ⓦ ferrytraveller.gr). Currently, only one reliable route operates to: Límnos, Lésvos, Híos and Sámos (1 weekly).

ACCOMMODATION

Augustos Ptoleméou 1 ☎ 2310 522 550, ⓦ augustos .gr. Charming and recently renovated 1920s hotel with arty decor, on a quiet corner near Egnatía, with all en-suite high-ceilinged rooms and a spacious breakfast-lounge-cum-bar. **€45**

The Bristol Hotel Oplopíou 2 ☎ 2310 506 500, ⓦ bristol.gr. Thessaloníki's original boutique hotel, with twenty period-furnished rooms and suites in an impeccably restored 1870 building. There's a good Italian/Argentinian restaurant, and a lavish buffet breakfast is included. Best

1

deals are online. **€110**
Le Palace Tsimiskí 12 ☎ 2310 257 400, ⊚ lepalace.gr.
This Art Deco hotel offers spacious, stylishly decorated
rooms with modern baths and double-glazing. Lovely

common areas comprise a mezzanine lounge, a ground-
floor café and a restaurant, in which you can eat the
outstanding buffet breakfast that's included in the rates.
Good online deals. **€60**

EATING

Iy Gonia tou Merakli Avyerinoú, alley off Platía
Áthonos ☎ 2310 287 726. Inexpensive seafood, better
than average portions, a quality free dessert and highly
palatable barrelled wine make this the best of several
ouzerís in these atmospheric surrounding lanes. Mezé
specials, plus drink deals for €4 or less. Daily
noon–2am.
Myrovolos Smyrni In arcade in the Modhiáno off
Komninón 32 ☎ 2310 274 170. Friendly, crowded ouzerí,
also known as *Tou Thanassi*. Typical dishes (all €3–7)
include cheese-stuffed squid, Smyrna-style meatballs,
stuffed potatoes and grilled baby fish. Reservations
recommended. Daily noon–2am, closed Sun eve.

Ta Bakaliarakia tou Aristou Katoúni 3, Ladhádhika
☎ 2310 542 906. Heapings of cod and chips, served on
greaseproof paper for around €6–7, make this joint in a
pedestrianized portside alley quite memorable. There's a
second branch one block away at Fasianoú 2. Daily
9am–7pm.
Zythos Platía Katoúni 5, Ladhádhika ☎ 2310 540 284,
⊚ zithos.gr. Imaginative Greek mezédhes are on offer
here, plus a range of sausages and pasta dishes for
around €10, along with an excellent selection of wines
and beers, both draught and bottled. Reservations
recommended at weekends. Daily: food noon–9.30pm,
drinks 10am–2am.

Vólos

VÓLOS is the major port of Thessaly, in central Greece, with frequent ferries
and hydrofoils to the **Sporades**. The industrial outskirts and mostly lacklustre
centre evoke nothing of a mythological past as the spot from which Jason and
the Argonauts embarked on their quest for the Golden Fleece. University of
Thessaly students do make it a lively city, however, so it's not a bad place to spend
a few hours or even a night while waiting for a boat. The most attractive place to
linger is along the eastern **waterfront esplanade**, between landscaped **Platía
Yeoryíou** and the **Archeological Museum** (Athanasáki 1; summer 8am–5pm, winter
8am–3pm; €3).

ARRIVAL AND DEPARTURE   VÓLOS

By air The airport (serving international charter and
budget airlines, but no domestic flights) is 26km southwest
of the city. Buses generally meet flights and transfer
passengers to Vólos.
By train The train station is just off Platía Ríga Feréou, a
short walk to the waterfront and ferries.
Destinations Athens (10 daily via Lárissa; 4hr 30min–5hr);
Lárissa (12 daily; 50min).
By bus The KTEL city bus terminal is on Sekéri, just off
Grigoríou Lambráki, a 10min walk southwest of the
main square, Platía Ríga Feréou. There is a taxi rank
outside.
Destinations Athens (10 daily; 3hr 30min); Thessaloníki
(8–9 daily; 3hr)
By ferry In the summertime, Vólos has frequent car ferries

to the Sporades (plus faster, passenger-only hydrofoils and
catamarans). Hellenic Seaways (☎ 21041 99000,
⊚ hellenicseaways.gr), ANES Ferries (☎ 22460 71444;
⊚ anes.gr) and Aegean Flying Dolphins (☎ 21042 21766;
⊚ aegeanflyingdolphins.gr) run most of the routes, and
publish up-to-date timetables online.
Destinations Alónissos (6 weekly car ferries in summer,
5hr; plus 1–2 daily passenger catamarans/hydrofoils, 2hr
25min–3hr 20min); Mantoudi, Évvia (3 weekly; 5hr
30min); Skiáthos (1–3 daily car ferries in summer; 2hr
50min; 1–3 daily passenger catamarans/hydrofoils 1hr
35min); Skópelos, both ports (1–2 daily car ferries
depending on season; 2hr 5min–3hr 35min; 1–2 daily
passenger catamarans/hydrofoil in summer, 2hr–2hr
30min).

ACCOMMODATION AND EATING

Aegli Argonafton 24 ☎ 24210 24471 ⊚ aegli.gr. Right
by the port and close to the best restaurants and nightlife,
Aegli has clean, simple rooms with high ceilings (though

some lack daylight), plus a modern breakfast room with
stone-clad walls. **€50**
Haliambalias (aka Zafiris) Kondarátou 8, at Skýrou.

Founded in 1947 and the place to go for affordable *mayireftá*; the menu never varies much from vegetarian *tourloú*, baked *pérka* (perch) fish and a few stews. Expect to pay €10–15 per person. Mon–Sat.
Xenia Domotel Plastíra 1 ☎ 24210 92700, ⓦ domotelxeniavolouhotel.gr. This crisply modern seafront luxury resort has a pool, spa, fitness centre, plush rooms in blue-green and white, plus free in-room wi-fi and free use of a laptop, as well as a range of other amenities and a copious buffet breakfast. **€102**

Yíthio

YÍTHIO (Gythion), Sparta's ancient port, is the eastern gateway to the dramatic Máni peninsula, and one of the south's most attractive seaside towns in its own right. Its low-key harbour, with **ferries to Pireás and Kýthira**, gives onto a graceful nineteenth-century waterside of tiled-roof houses. There are beaches within walking distance, and rooms are relatively easy to find. The islet of **Marathoníssi**, ancient Kranae, in the bay, is where Paris of Troy, having abducted Helen from Menelaus's palace at Sparta, dropped anchor, and where the lovers spent their first night.

ARRIVAL AND DEPARTURE
YÍTHIO

By bus The bus station is close to the centre of town; with your back to it, the main waterfront street, Vassiléos Pávlou, lies ahead of you.
Destinations Athens (6 daily; 5hr); Areópoli (4 daily; 30min); Ítylo (2 daily; 1hr); Spárti (6 daily; 1 hr).

By ferry The local agent is Rozakis, on the waterfront (☎ 27330 22207).
Destinations Andikýthira (1 weekly; 4hr 45min); Kastélli, Crete (1 weekly; 6hr 55min); Kýthira (1 weekly; 2hr 30min).

ACCOMMODATION AND EATING

Gythion Vassiléos Pávlou 33 ☎ 27330 23452, ⓦ gythionhotel.gr. A fine old (1864) hotel with period decorated rooms, all with 5m-high ceilings and views of the waterfront. Guests can use the Gythion Bay campsite's beach and private beach facilities. Free wi-fi, and breakfast included. **€40**

Saga Tzanetáki ☎ 27330 23220. Above-average fish taverna overlooking the Marathoníssi islet, and run by a friendly, knowledgeable French-Greek family who specialize in seafood. Choose your fish from the ice bucket knowing it arrived the same day, and be sure to try the fish soup as a starter (€6). Daily noon–midnight.

The Argo-Saronic islands

TEMPLE OF APHAEA

The Argo-Saronic islands

The rocky, partly volcanic Argo-Saronic Islands, most of them barely an olive's throw from the mainland, differ to a surprising extent not just from the land they face but also from one another. The northernmost island of the Argo-Saronic group, Salamína, is effectively a suburb of Pireás, with its narrow strait, barely a kilometre across, crossed by a constant stream of ferries. There's little to attract you on the other side, however, and the island is covered only briefly in this Guide. Égina, important in antiquity and more or less continually inhabited since then, is infinitely preferable: the most fertile of the group, it is famous for its pistachio nuts and home to one of the finest ancient temples in Greece. Tiny Angístri is often treated as little more than an adjunct of Égina (Aegina), but it's a lovely place in its own right, ideal for a few days' complete relaxation. The three southerly islands – green Póros, tiny, car-free Ýdhra (Hydra) and upmarket Spétses – are comparatively infertile and rely on water piped or transported in rusting freighters from the mainland.

Given their proximity to Athens and their beauty, the Argo-Saronics are hugely popular destinations – **Égina** almost becomes a city suburb at weekends. **Póros**, **Ýdhra** and **Spétses** are similar in the summer, though their visitors include a higher proportion of foreign tourists. More than any other group, these islands are best out of season and midweek, when visitor numbers (and prices) fall dramatically and the ports return to a quieter, more provincial pace. You'll also notice a significant difference between Ýdhra and Spétses, the furthest of the islands, and those closer to Athens: because of the distance, and because they're accessible only by **hydrofoil** and **catamaran** rather than the cheaper conventional **ferries**, they're markedly more expensive and exclusive, with significant expat populations. The islands were not extensively settled until medieval times, when refugees from the mainland established themselves here and adopted seagoing commerce (and piracy) as livelihoods. Today, foreigners and Athenians have replaced locals in the depopulated harbour towns; hydrofoils, water-taxis and yachts are faint echoes of the massed warships, schooners and *kaïkia* (traditional wooden boats) once at anchor.

GETTING THERE   THE ARGO-SARONIC

BY FERRY, HYDROFOIL AND CATAMARAN
Virtually all services from Pireás to the Argo-Saronic islands leave from between gates E8 and E9, where there are ticket booths. For all of these islands, hydrofoil or catamaran services are faster and more frequent than ferries, though they cost around twice as much. Fri evening and Sat morning sailings, as well as the returns on Sun night, can be very busy; for these, or if you hope to bring a vehicle for the weekend on a regular ferry, reserve your trip well in advance.

Tickets and agencies Contact details for Pireás are as follows (local island agencies are given in the individual island accounts): Aegean Flying Dolphins (to Égina and Angístri) ☎ 210 422 1766, ⌨ aegeanflyingdolphins.gr; Alexandros (fast ferry to Souvála and Ayía Marína, Égina) ☎ 210 482 1002, ⌨ www.alexcruises.gr; Ayios Nektarios Eginas (ferry to Égina) ☎ 210 422 5625, ⌨ anes.gr; Hellenic Seaways (hydrofoils and Flying Cat to all points) ☎ 210 419 9000, ⌨ hsw.gr; Saronic Ferries (all other ferries to Égina, Angístri and Póros, including Hellenic Seaways ones) ☎ 210 411 7341, ⌨ saronicferries.gr.

The Battle of Salamis p.83   Hiking on Ýdhra p.100
Excursions to the Peloponnese p.93 Spétses on foot p.105
Ýdhra's festivals p.99

SPÉTSES ISLAND

Highlights

❶ Temple of Aphaea, Égina The best-preserved ancient temple on any Greek island, in an evocative setting on a wooded hill with magnificent views towards the mainland and Athens. **See p.87**

❷ Angístri Island Little known to outsiders, this dot of land is less than an hour from Athens by hydrofoil yet preserves the feel of an unspoilt hideaway. **See p.89**

❸ Sailing into Póros Whether navigating your own yacht or arriving by hydrofoil, the busy, narrow channel between Póros and the mainland is quite an experience; an

ever-changing spectacle of small, and not-so-small, craft. **See p.92**

❹ Ýdhra Town Ýdhra's perfect, horseshoe-shaped harbour, surrounded by grand eighteenth-century mansions and genuinely traffic-free streets, is one of the most evocative in all of Greece. **See p.98**

❺ Zoyeriá Beach, Spétses Some of the most alluring beaches in the Argo-Saronics can be found along Spétses' pine-speckled coastline; at hard-to-reach Zoyeriá is a wonderful, isolated taverna, most of whose customers arrive by boat. **See p.102**

HIGHLIGHTS ARE MARKED ON THE MAP ON P.82

Salamína

SALAMÍNA is the quickest possible island-hop from Pireás, and indeed much of its population commutes to the city to work. The island itself, however, is highly developed, has few tourist facilities, and is close enough to the Athenian dockyards to make swimming unappealing. The island's port is at **Paloúkia**, facing the mainland, just a short hop across a narrow, built-up isthmus to **Salamína Town** on the west coast. Five kilometres or so beyond Salamína Town, **Eándio** has the island's cleanest and most attractive beaches. A similar distance from Salamína Town to the north is the **monastery of Faneroméni** (daily 8.30am–12.30pm & 4pm–sunset), a working nunnery with impressive frescoes, beautifully sited amid pine woods overlooking the mainland.

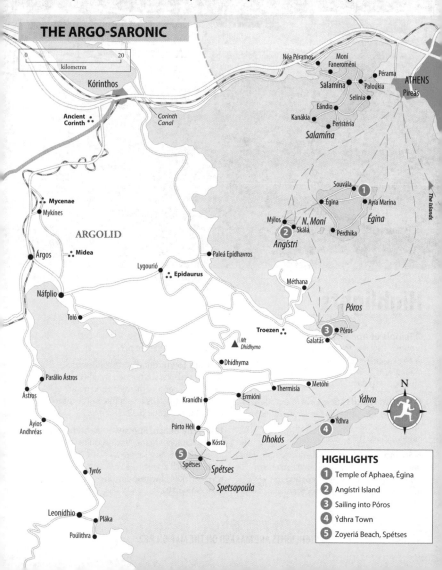

HIGHLIGHTS

1. Temple of Aphaea, Égina
2. Angístri Island
3. Sailing into Póros
4. Ýdhra Town
5. Zoyeriá Beach, Spétses

THE BATTLE OF SALAMIS

Perhaps the main reason to head to Salamína is for the **boat trip** itself, through an extraordinary industrial seascape of docks and shipworks. The waters you cross were the site of one of the most significant **sea battles** of ancient times; some would say of all time, given that this was a decisive blow in preventing a Persian invasion, thus allowing the development of Classical Athens and with it modern Western culture.

In 480 BC, the Greeks were in full retreat from the vast **Persian army** under Xerxes following the defeat of the Spartans at Thermopylae. Many Greek cities, including Athens, had been sacked and burned by the invaders – indeed, smoke from the ruins on the Acropolis probably formed a backdrop to the **Battle of Salamis**. The Greeks had roughly 370 triremes supplied by around twenty cities, the bulk from Athens, Corinth and Aegina; the Persian fleet was twice the size, with heavier ships that were even more diverse, with many from subject nations whose loyalty was questionable.

Through false information and strategic retreats, the Greeks managed first to tire many of the Persian crews – who rowed all night to cut off a nonexistent escape attempt – and then to lure them into the narrow strait off Salamína. Crowded in and unable to manoeuvre, and with the wind in the wrong direction, the Persians found themselves at the mercy of the more nimble Greek triremes, and the battle eventually became a rout. Some two hundred Persian ships were sunk, against forty-odd on the Greek side, and few of their heavily armoured crews or marines survived.

ARRIVAL AND DEPARTURE   SALAMÍNA

By boat There are small passenger boats every 30min from Pireás throughout the day (Gate E8; 45min), and a constant stream of small boats and roll-on, roll-off car ferries, day and night, from Pérama, on the mainland directly opposite (5min). Pérama is easily reached by bus: #843 from Pireás, G18 or B18 from Omónia in central Athens. There are also ferries every 20min or so between Faneroméni and Néa Péramos (aka Megára) on the mainland.

GETTING AROUND

By bus Salamína has a pretty impressive bus system, with departures from the ferry dock in Paloúkia to Salamína Town every 15min. Buses also run hourly to numerous other destinations on the island, including Eándio and Faneroméni.

Égina

A substantial and attractive island with a proud history, less than an hour from Pireás, **ÉGINA (Aegina)** is not surprisingly a popular weekend escape from Athens. Despite the holiday homes, though, it retains a laidback, island atmosphere, especially if you visit midweek or out of season. Famous for its **pistachio orchards** – the nuts are hawked from stalls all around the harbour – the island can also boast substantial ancient remains, the finest of which is the beautiful fifth-century BC **Temple of Aphaea**, which commands superb views towards Athens from high above the northeast coast.

ARRIVAL AND DEPARTURE   ÉGINA

BY FERRY AND HYDROFOIL

In Égina Town, ferries dock on the outer wall of the harbour and hydrofoils inside it, very close to each other and pretty much at the heart of things. The *Angístri Express* (see p.89) can be found among the pleasure and fishing boats a short distance to the south. The schedule summaries below are for summer weekday services; sailings are more frequent and significantly busier at weekends (Fri–Sun) and less regular from mid-Sept to June. Ayía Marína and Souvála are linked to Pireás two or three times daily in high season.

Tickets and agencies Immediately in front of the docks in Égina Town is a row of cabins displaying timetables and selling tickets for Aegean Flying Dolphins (to Pireás and Angístri ☎ 22970 25800, ⓦ aegeanflyingdolphins.gr), Ayios Nektarios Eginas (ferry to Pireás ☎ 22970 25625, ⓦ anes .gr), Hellenic Seaways (hydrofoils and Flying Cat to Pireás and Angístri ☎ 22970 26430, ⓦ hsw.gr) and Saronic Ferries (ferries to Pireás, Angístri, Méthana and Póros ☎ 22970 24200, ⓦ saronicferries.gr). They're open through the day, and the relevant ones will also open 30min or more before early-morning or late-night departures. Alexandros Ferries

2

Angístri

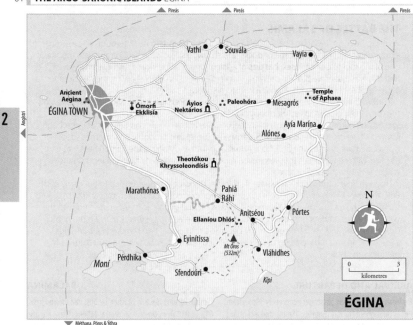

ÉGINA

Méthana, Póros & Ýdhra

(to Pireás from Ayía Marína ☎ 22970 52210 and Souvála ☎ 22970 32234, ⊛ www.alexcruises.gr) has quayside booths open an hour or so before departure. For the *Angístri Express* (☎ 6947 118 863), buy tickets on the boat.
Destinations Angístri (6 hydrofoils and 1 or 2 ferries daily, plus *Angístri Express* 2–3 daily except Sun; 15min); Pireás (from Égina Town 12 hydrofoils and 11 ferries daily, 40min–1hr 30min; from Ayía Marína 1–2 ferries daily, 1hr 15min; from Souvála 1–3 daily, 40min); Póros (via Méthana 1 ferry daily; 1hr 15min).

INFORMATION

Information There's no tourist office, but ⊛ aeginagreece .com and ⊛ discoveraegina.gr are useful resources.
Services There are numerous banks around Égina Town harbour, many with ATMs. The post office is at the rear of Platía Ethneyersías, where the buses stop.

GETTING AROUND

By bus The bus station is on Platía Ethneyersías, immediately north of the dock; buy your tickets at the little booth, in summer located on the waterfront, the rest of the year in the square by the bus stop. Three to five buses a day head to Souvála and to Ayía Marína, four to six along the coast to Pérdhika; on arrival, they turn round and head straight back. All buses towards Ayía Marína stop at Áyios Nektários and most at the Temple of Aphaea; on the return journey, they all stop at both.
By car and motorcycle Several places on and behind Égina Town's main waterfront rent scooters, cars, motorbikes and mountain bikes – Égina is large and hilly enough to make a motor worthwhile for anything other than a pedal to the local beaches: Trust (☎ 22970 27010), in a narrow alley off the harbour behind Alpha Bank, has the best prices, though some of their mopeds are fairly battered. There are also hire places in Ayía Marína.
By taxi The taxi rank (☎ 22970 32010) is at the base of the ferry jetty, opposite the ticket cabins; taxis meet ferry arrivals in Ayía Marína and Souvála too.

Brief history

Inhabited from the earliest times, ancient **Aegina** was a significant regional power as far back as the Bronze Age. It traded to the limits of the known world, maintained a sophisticated silver coinage system (the first in Greece) and fostered prominent athletes and craftsmen. The Aeginian fleet played a major role in the Battle of Salamis (see p.83). After this, however, the islanders made the political mistake of siding with the

Spartans, which gave Athens a pretext to act on long-standing jealousy; her fleets defeated those of the islanders in two separate sea battles and, after the second, the population was **expelled** and replaced by more tractable colonists.

Subsequent history was less distinguished, with a familiar pattern of occupation – by Romans, Franks, Venetians, Catalans and Ottomans – before the War of Independence brought a brief period of glory as seat of government for the fledgling Greek nation, from 1826 to 1828. For many decades afterwards, Égina was a penal island, and you can still see the enormous **jail** undergoing restoration on the edge of town; the building was originally an **orphanage** for victims of the independence struggle, founded by first president Kapodhístrias in 1828.

2

Égina Town

ÉGINA TOWN, the island's capital, makes an attractive base, with some grand old buildings around a large, busy harbour. The Neoclassical architecture is matched by a sophisticated ethos: by island standards this is a large town, with plenty of shopping and no shortage of tempting places to eat and drink. Life revolves around the **waterfront**, where ferries come and go, yachts moor, fishermen tend their nets and *kaïkia* (traditional wooden boats) tie up to sell produce from the mainland.

Markellos Tower

Thomaïdhou, inland from the harbour • No admission except during the occasional special exhibition

The restored Pýrgos Markéllou, or **Markellos Tower**, is an extraordinary miniature castle that was the seat of the first Greek government after independence. Despite appearances, it was built only around 1800 by members of the Friendly Society (see p.537) and the local politician Spýros Márkellos. You can't usually go inside, but walking here, through the cramped inland streets, is enjoyable in itself.

Folklore Museum

Spýrou Ródhi 16 • Fri 4.30–7.30pm, Sat 11am–1pm & 4.30–7.30pm, Sun 11am–1pm • Free • ☎ 22970 26401

Égina's **Folklore Museum** is a lovely example of its type, housed in a nineteenth-century mansion. Its upper rooms are packed with fine old furniture, traditional costumes, and many of the trappings of island life a century ago, along with a small local historical archive. Downstairs are rooms devoted to fishing, with model boats and fishing gear, and to agriculture, with a collection of the basics of village life.

Ancient Aegina

Beyond the town beach, 600m north of the harbour • Daily 8am–3pm, museum closed Mon • €3 • ☎ 22970 22248

The site of **Ancient Aegina** lies north of the centre on a promontory known as **Kolóna**, after the lone column that stands there. The extensive remains, centring on a Temple of Apollo at the highest point, are well signed, and some reconstruction makes it easier to make out the various layers of settlement from different eras. Near the entrance, a small but worthwhile **archeological museum** houses finds from the site, along with information on the island's ancient history. Highlights of the display include a room of Minoan-influenced Middle Bronze Age pottery, rescued from a nearby building site.

The beaches

On the north edge of town, between the port and Kolóna, there's a tiny but popular **beach** with remarkably shallow water. This was the site of the ancient city's harbour, of which various underwater remains are clearly visible. You can swim south of town, too, but there are more enticing spots further north – immediately beyond Kolóna there's an attractive bay with a small, sandy beach, while other small coves lie off the road which heads further out of town in that direction. Only a couple have any facilities, with loungers and beach bars.

ACCOMMODATION

Aeginitiko Archontiko Cnr Thomaïdhou and Ayíou Nikólaou ☎ 22970 24968, ⊛ aeginitikoarchontiko.gr. Brick-red Neoclassical mansion opposite the Markellos Tower, lovingly restored with period furnishings and a conscious attempt to preserve traditional island culture. About as far from a bland business hotel as you can get – there's lots of lace, old pictures on the walls, creaking, springy beds and a wonderful breakfast (included) with home-made preserves, cakes and pastries. The suite has painted ceilings; other rooms can be pretty basic, though all have a/c, TV and fridge. €65

Elektra Leonándrou Ladhá 25 ☎ 22970 26715, ⊛ aegina-electra.gr. Friendly, quiet establishment, on the first street directly inland from the ferry quay, whose compact but comfortable rooms come with small balconies and free wi-fi. €40

★**Fistikies** Logiotatídhou 1 ☎ 22970 23783, ⊛ fistikies.gr. Lovely modern apartments around a small pool, slightly inland on the southern edge of town, near the

football stadium. The well-equipped apartments typically have a small bedroom, large living room and kitchen, all classily furnished and with cable TV. €90

Hotel Brown Waterfront ☎ 22970 22271, ⊛ hotel brown.gr. Housed in a former sponge factory dating from 1886 and facing the southern part of the harbour, the *Hotel Brown* has a fabulous position and an excellent modern café-restaurant. The rooms, though, are a little dated: those at the front have great views of the harbour activity, but the garden bungalows are quieter; a galleried family suite sleeps four. Breakfast included. Open June–Oct. €65

Plaza Kazantzáki 4 ☎ 22970 25600. One of a series of small waterfront hotels close to the town beach, the place offers refurbished rooms with quality bathrooms and elegant dark-wood decor, plus double-glazing, a/c and TV. There are great sea views from the marginally more expensive rooms at the front and little balconies from which to appreciate them. €55

EATING AND DRINKING

There are plenty of good places to eat and drink in Égina, particularly at the south end of pedestrianized **Panayióti Irióti**, behind the fish market, and at the far ends of the waterfront – fussy Athenian patronage keeps the standards fairly high. The cafés near the ferry jetty and in the centre of the waterfront tend to be less good value. In the **backstreets**, you'll find an extraordinary number of bakeries and cake shops.

★**Agora** Panayióti Irióti ☎ 22970 27308. Also known as *Yeladhakis*, this is the best of the rival seafood ouzerís behind the fish market (though the others are very good too). Not the most attractive location, but it serves wonderful, inexpensive, authentic Greek food (around €8 per fish plate): accordingly, it's usually mobbed, and you may have to wait for a table. Summer seating is in the cobbled lane, and in winter it's up in the loft. Daily Mon–Thurs dinner, Fri–Sun lunch and dinner.

Avli Panayióti Irióti 17 ☎ 22970 26438. This large place in an alley behind the harbour is popular with expats and open all day serving coffee, breakfast (€4–8.50), lunch and dinner (mains €6–10; spaghetti and pizza as well as Greek dishes and pricier steaks), while in the early hours it transforms into a bar with Latin/jazz sounds. Daily 10am–late.

Babis Waterfront ☎ 22970 23594. The last building at the southern end of the waterfront, *Babis* is a design-conscious modern taverna that also has tables right on the seafront over the road, where it's candlelit at night. The menu is modern Greek, with plenty of well-cooked standards as well as innovative dishes like chicken roll with local pistachios and ricotta. There's a BBQ every Fri

night for €14. Daily 10am–late.

Elia Koumoundhoúrou 4 ☎ 22975 00205. A modern taverna in an alley that emerges close to the Markellos Tower, with a menu of inventive meze such as octopus with peppers and ouzo (€6.50) or red mullet croquettes with garlic sauce (€7.50) as well as salads, pasta and more traditional Greek dishes. Live music many evenings. Thurs–Sun lunch from 1pm, dinner from 8pm.

Flisvos Kazantzáki 8 ☎ 22970 26459. An excellent spot for grilled fresh fish and traditional dishes at fair prices (*moussaká* or *souvláki* €7.50, swordfish steak €12), towards the end of a line of similar establishments behind the town beach. Good-value lunchtime specials. Daily lunch and dinner.

Melenio Mitropóleos 4 ☎ 22970 26133. Close to the Markellos Tower, this is an exceptional modern *zaharo-plastío* with fine ice cream and beautiful displays of cakes and sweets. Daily 8.30am–11.30pm.

Skotadis Harbourfront ☎ 22970 24014. Popular with locals, this is the best of a cluster of taverna-ouzerís just south of the market. It has a small menu, predominantly fish and meze at €6–7 a dish, but what it does it does well. Daily 10am–1am.

NIGHTLIFE

Ellinikon Seaside Aktí Hatzí 10 ☎ 6936 111 213, ⊛ ellinikon.net. A big, enjoyable, somewhat touristy club on the seafront at the southern fringe of town, with

mainstream and Greek dance music. It has a sister club in town, *Ellinikon Vintage* (Kapodístria Ioánni 7). Weekends in summer 10.30pm–late.

Heaven Dhimokratías 48 ☎ 22970 28872. All-day café-bar, on the harbourfront just beyond *Skotadis* restaurant (see opposite), that gets more raucous the later it gets; there's dancing, DJs and occasional live music in the evenings. A couple of similar places are nearby. Daily 10am–late.

Inn on the Beach Aktí Hatzí ☎ 22970 25116, ⓦ innonthebeach.gr. Just beyond the southern edge of town, *Inn on the Beach* is an elegant café, lounge and cocktail bar by day, with DJs as the night wears on. Daily 10am–3am.

ENTERTAINMENT

Open-air cinemas There are three summer open-air cinemas – Anesis on Eákou close to the Pýrgos Markéllou, Olympia on Faneroménis opposite the football ground, and

Akroyiali out beyond this on the Pérdhika road; indoor Titina, opposite the Pýrgos Markéllou, is open year-round.

Across the island

Two main routes lead east towards Ayía Marína and the Temple of Aphaea: you can head directly **inland** from Égina Town across the centre of the island or follow the **north coast** road via Souvála. Along this north coast there are plenty of scruffy beaches and clusters of second-home developments, between which is a surprisingly industrial landscape, with boatyards and working ports. Souvála itself is something of an Athenian resort, with a couple of direct daily ferries to Pireás but little other reason to stop.

Áyios Nektários

Halfway between Égina Town and Ayía Marína, passed by 3–5 buses daily between the two • Daily, hours dependent on church routine and coach tours, but should be at least 9am–1pm & 4–6pm • Free • ☎ 22970 53800

On the route inland you'll pass the modern convent of **Áyios Nektários**, a site of Orthodox pilgrimage whose vast church is said to be the largest in Greece. The convent was founded by **Saint Nektarios**, who died in 1920 and was canonized in 1961. His tomb lies in the chapel of the original monastery, Ayía Triádha. Miracles surrounded Nektarios from the moment of his death, when nurses put some of his clothing on an adjacent bed, occupied by a man who was paralysed; the patient promptly leapt up, praising God.

Paleohóra

Unrestricted • Free

On the hillside opposite Áyios Nektários is the ghost town of **PALEOHÓRA**, the island capital through the Middle Ages. Established in early Christian times as a refuge against piracy, it thrived under the Venetians (1451–1540) but was destroyed by Barbarossa in 1537. The Turks took over and rebuilt the town, but it was again destroyed, this time by the Venetians, in 1654, and finally **abandoned** altogether in the early nineteenth century. The place now consists of some **thirty stone chapels** dotted across a rocky outcrop, an extraordinary sight from a distance. Little remains of the town itself – when the islanders left, they simply dismantled their houses and moved the masonry to newly founded Égina Town. At the entrance, a helpful map shows the churches and the paths that lead up the hill between them; many are semi-derelict or locked, but plenty are open too, and several preserve remains of frescoes. Despite their apparent abandonment, many chapels have candles burning inside, and prayers left alongside the icons.

If you climb right to the top, you're rewarded with wonderful **views** in all directions – you can also appreciate the defensive qualities of the site, from which both coasts can be watched, yet which is almost invisible from the sea.

Temple of Aphaea

12km east of Égina Town • Tues–Sun 9.30am–5.30pm; museum 10.30am–1.30pm • €4 • ☎ 22970 32398

The Doric **Temple of Aphaea** stands on a pine-covered hill, with stunning views all around: Athens, Cape Soúnio, the Peloponnese and Ýdhra are all easily made out. Built

2

between 500 and 480 BC, it slightly predates the Parthenon, and is one of the most complete and visually complex ancient buildings in Greece, its superimposed arrays of columns and lintels evocative of an Escher drawing. Aphaea was a Cretan nymph who, fleeing from the lust of King Minos, fell into the sea, was caught by some fishermen and brought to ancient Aegina; her cult, virtually unknown anywhere else, was established on the island as early as 1300 BC. Two hundred years ago, the temple's pediments were intact and essentially in perfect condition. However, like the Elgin marbles, they were "purchased" from the Turks – this time by Ludwig I of Bavaria – and they currently reside in Munich's Glyptothek museum. The small temple **museum** offers a great deal of information about the history and architecture of the building. A well-signed path leads from the temple to Ayía Marína; an easy walk down, slightly tougher coming up.

Ayía Marína and around

The island's major beach resort, **AYÍA MARÍNA**, lies steeply below the Temple of Aphaea on the east coast. There's a good, clean, sandy **beach** that shelves very gently, plus there are rentable pedaloes and plenty of places to eat, many of them catering to day-trippers – direct boats arrive from Pireás daily. The place has clearly seen better days, as the number of empty premises and the ugly, half-built hotel overshadowing the beach attest, but package tourism seems to be on the up, and it can be lively and enjoyable in a bucket-and-spade sort of way, with plenty of hotels and rooms, and a main street lined with shops, bars and pubs; the occasional summer beach party sees an overnight invasion of young Athenians.

Pórtes

PÓRTES, 8km south of Ayía Marína, is a hamlet with a distinctly end-of-the-road feel, a partly sandy beach with decent snorkelling and a couple of good tavernas. From here, the road climbs steeply inland, beneath the island's highest peak and heads back towards Égina Town via the villages of **Anitséou** and **Pahiá Ráhi**. The latter, with fine views eastwards, has been almost entirely rebuilt in traditional style by foreign and Athenian owners.

ACCOMMODATION AND EATING   AYÍA MARÍNA AND AROUND

AYÍA MARÍNA

Argo Spa Hotel ☎ 22970 32266, ⓦ argohotel.com. In a great position directly above the bay as you come into town, the *Argo* has a pool and small "spa" (sauna and hot tub) and often offers good, all-in deals. Refurbished, modern rooms mostly have sea views. **€60**

Barracuda Beach Bar ☎ 22970 32095, ⓦ barracuda bar.gr. With a precarious wooden terrace hanging over the beach, the *Barracuda* also offers service on the beach itself. Milkshakes, coffee and sandwiches by day; cocktails and a DJ at night. July & Aug daily 10am–3am, plus some weekends in May, June and Sept.

Hotel Liberty 2 ☎ 22970 32105, ⓦ hotelliberty2.gr. An ochre-coloured building overlooking the end of the beach; simple and old-fashioned, with marble floors, but

all rooms have sea views as well as a/c and TV. **€40**

Neromilos ☎ 22970 32198. Just above the tiny fishing harbour, *Neromilos* (the "Watermill") is a big, popular place with a terrace above the water where they serve no-nonsense Greek food (starters €3–5, mains €5–9). June–Oct daily lunch and dinner.

PÓRTES

Akroyiali ☎ 22970 31335. A fine *psarotavérna* (seafood restaurant) with a terrace above the sea, close to the beach. Good-quality fish and mezédhes attract visitors from around the island at weekends. Nearby *Thanasis* offers a slightly more meaty menu. May–Sept lunch and dinner daily; winter weekends only.

The west coast

The road south of Égina Town, along the **west coast** of the island, is flat and easy. Sprawling **Marathónas**, 5km from Égina, has the biggest if not the prettiest of the west coast's sandy beaches, which offers fine views and loungers, along with a scattering of rooms, tavernas and cafés. The next settlement, **Eyinítissa**, has a popular, sheltered cove backed by eucalypts and a beach bar.

Pérdhika

PÉRDHIKA, scenically set on a little bay packed with yachts at the end of the coastal road, is the most picturesque village on Égina. The pedestrianized **waterfront** esplanade at the southern edge of the village, overlooking Moní islet and the Peloponnese, is the heart of tourist life. From the harbour, you can take a boat to **Moní** (10min; €5 return), most of which is fenced off as a nature conservation area but is worth the trip for a swim in wonderfully clear water. Pérdhika Bay itself is shallow and yacht-tainted, though you can swim from the rocky shore further round.

On the headland opposite the harbour, along with crumbling wartime bunkers, is a **Camera Obscura** built by two Austrian artists. In the darkened interior, twelve narrow slits project an inverted 360-degree image of the landscape outside. If you have your own transport, a couple more **cove beaches** are accessible beyond Pérdhika, where new holiday homes are reached by steep concrete tracks.

2

ACCOMMODATION AND EATING — THE WEST COAST

MARATHÓNAS

Ostria ⊕ 22970 26738. This place has an idyllic setting, with tables set out under the trees at the southern end of the beach and the water lapping almost to your feet. The food is great too, especially the calamari and the cheese pies, and they also have apartments. Daily lunch and dinner.

PÉRDHIKA

Andonis ⊕ 22970 61443. One of a long line of tavernas along the waterfront, this is the best of the bunch for fish, with a big outdoor charcoal grill. There's plenty of Athenian and yachtie patronage here, so prices are a little higher than you might expect – fish is priced by the kilo. Daily lunch and dinner.

Antzi Studios ⊕ 22970 61446, ⊛ antzistudios.gr.

Large studio and apartment complex with a good-sized pool. The modern apartment units with separate kitchens, some for four people, are greatly preferable to the older studios. **€50**, new apartments **€90**

Hermes ⊕ 22970 61200. Bars and cafés are concentrated towards the end of the esplanade, where they can afford to turn the music up louder: *Hermes* is usually the busiest late-night spot, but there are plenty of other choices nearby. Daily 10am–late.

Hotel Hippocampus ⊕ 22970 61363, ⊛ hippocampus-hotel-greece.com. Friendly, simple two-star hotel built around a leafy garden courtyard, complete with private chapel. All rooms have balcony, a/c and TV, and there's a small roof terrace. **€50**

Angístri

ANGÍSTRI, fifteen minutes by fast boat from Égina, is a tiny island, obscure enough to be overlooked by most island-hoppers, though the visitors it does have are a diverse mix: Athenian weekenders, retirees who bought and restored property here years ago, plus a few British and Scandinavian package holiday-makers. There's a small, not terribly attractive strip of development on the north coast facing Égina, but the rest of the island is pine-covered, timeless and beautiful – albeit with very few beaches. It's also strangely contradictory: holiday weekends can see hordes of young Greeks camping out on otherwise empty beaches, while in Skála a few small, classy hotels are juxtaposed with cafés serving English breakfasts to the package-trippers.

ARRIVAL AND DEPARTURE — ANGÍSTRI

BY FERRY

There are ferries and hydrofoils to and from Pireás via Égina; ferries dock at Skála, hydrofoils at Mýlos. The *Angístri Express* (⊕ 6947 118 863) calls at both on its route to and from Égina.

Agencies Hellenic Seaways (ferry and hydrofoils; ⊕ 22970

91171, ⊛ hsw.gr or ⊛ saronicferries.gr) and Aegean Flying Dolphins (hydrofoils; ⊕ 22970 91221, ⊛ aegeanflying dolphins.gr).

Destinations Égina (*Angístri Express* 2–3 daily; 15min); Pireás via Égina (ferries 1 or 2 daily; 25min/1hr 30min; hydrofoils 12 daily in summer, 6 out of season; 10min/1hr).

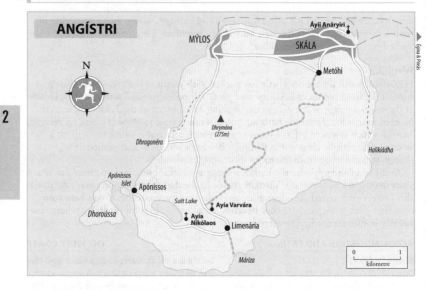

ANGÍSTRI

MÝLOS

SKÁLA

Ayii Anáryiri

Metóhi

Égina & Pireás

Dhragonéra

▲ Dhrymóna (275m)

Halikiádha

Apónissos Islet

Apónissos

Salt Lake

Ayía Varvára

Dhoroússa

Ayía Nikólaos

Limenária

Máriza

N

0 — 1 kilometre

2

GETTING AROUND

By bus In summer, the island bus connects Skála and Mýlos with Dhragonéra, Limenária and Apónissos several times a day; the day's timetable (timed to match ferry and hydrofoil arrivals) is chalked up at its starting point, outside the church in Skála.

By scooter and bike Scooters and mountain bikes are available for rent from several outlets in Skála and Mýlos; Kostas Motorent in Skála (☎ 22970 91021) is particularly

helpful. It is less than 10km to the furthest point of the island, so in cooler weather you can comfortably cross Angístri by pedal power – albeit with a couple of steep climbs.

On foot The island is small enough to cross on foot, via Metóhi along a winding dirt track through the pines.

By water-taxi Water-taxis (☎ 6977 618 040; about €30/ boat from Skála to Dhragonéra, for example) serve the beaches and Égina.

Skála and around

SKÁLA is Angístri's main tourist centre, its sandy beach backed by a straggle of modern development. Thanks to the weekending Athenian youth, there are lively bars and cafés here, and an unexpectedly busy nightlife; in summer, there's even an open-air cinema. The beach, and most of the new development, lies to the right (west) from the jetty, beyond the big church, but there are some far more attractive places to stay, which look out over a rocky coastline, left of the dock.

From the paved road's end in this direction, beyond the *Alkyoni Hotel* (see opposite), a path leads along the clifftop to secluded **Halikiádha**. This pebble beach, backed by crumbling cliffs, is predominantly nudist; at busy weekends there may be crowds of young Greeks camping nearby, but the rest of the time it's almost deserted. The scary scramble down is rewarded by the island's best swimming in crystalline water. On the main town beach, you can rent sun-loungers, pedaloes and kayaks.

METÓHI, the hillside hamlet just above Skála, was once the island's main village, but now consists chiefly of holiday homes. If you can face the steep climb, you'll get the chance to take in some wonderful views out towards Égina.

ACCOMMODATION

SKÁLA AND AROUND

Aktaion Hotel Immediately right from the jetty ☎ 22970 91222, ⓦ hotelaktaion.gr. The best option in the main part of town, this hotel has a small swimming

pool, and most rooms have big balconies with sea views. All rooms also have TV, fridge and kitchenette. They also rent out larger apartments. **€45**

★**Alkyoni Hotel** Left of the jetty ☎ 22970 91377, ⓦ alkyoni-agistri.gr. The large, stone-floored rooms on the seafront side of this hotel, southeast of the jetty, have balconies directly above the water with stunning views. Best of all are the duplex rooms on the upper floor, big enough for a family, with a raised sleeping area and kitchenette below. There's also a friendly coffee/breakfast bar. €35

★**Rosy's Little Village** Left of the jetty ☎ 22970 91610, ⓦ rosyslittlevillage.com. Delightful spot on the rocks southeast of the jetty, with a variety of rooms, most with sea views. *Rosy's* has direct access to its own rocky swimming spot, free kayaks and bikes for guests, and a small sailing boat and motorboat for hire, plus a good restaurant. €62

EATING, DRINKING AND NIGHTLIFE

2

Moskhos Opposite the church, beneath Saronis Hotel ☎ 22970 91394. Blue-and-white checked tablecloths lend a relaxed feel to this long-established taverna, which offers a more interesting and authentic menu than many of the restaurants here. Stuffed mushrooms, *hórta* (greens) and *saganáki* (fried cheese) feature, as well as fresh fish, prawns and octopus. Daily lunch and dinner.

Quattro Beach road ☎ 22970 91447. Beachside café-bar that trumps its neighbours by offering not just free wi-fi, but a laptop brought to your table. Open all day for breakfast, coffee and cocktails, plus good, chilled out sounds at night. Daily 10am–late.

Taboo Main road on the western edge of town ☎ 6909 585 559, ⓦ tabooclub.gr. The one real club on the island, which can be packed, sweaty and thumping or deserted, depending on the visiting crowds – watch out for posters advertising special events like beach parties and funk and soul nights. Summer Fri–Sun from 11pm, plus special events year-round.

Taverna Parnassos Metóhi ☎ 22970 91339. The roof terrace here, close to the village's highest point, has perhaps the best views on the whole island, and there's excellent, home-cooked traditional food to appreciate while you enjoy them. Daily lunch and dinner.

Mýlos (Megalohóri)

The least attractive aspect of Angístri is the windblown road along the coast between Skála and **MÝLOS**. Mýlos itself has an attractive, traditional village centre with a church and platía, but there's only a tiny beach, so relatively few people stay here. Access to the rest of the island is easy, however, and there are plenty of rooms and tavernas.

ACCOMMODATION AND EATING   MÝLOS

Fotis On the main street, village centre ☎ 22970 91325. This centrally located year-round taverna used to double as the local butcher, so the meat here is particularly good. It's worth checking out the day's specials in the kitchen – they're often absolutely delicious. Daily lunch and dinner.

Kouros Harbourside ☎ 22970 91357. This café is in a lovely position looking out over the goings-on at the harbour. They serve breakfasts, ice cream and waffles and

full meals, plus there's free wi-fi and even live music some evenings. Daily 10am–10pm.

Meltemi Studios Above the harbour ☎ 22970 91057, ⓦ meltemistudios.gr. Purpose-built studios in a prime position, with views back along the coast towards Skála as well as over the harbour. Rooms are clean and cheerful, and there's a tiny deep pool that operates as a pool bar in high season. €45

Rest of the island

There's basically just one road on Angístri, and it runs from Skála and Mýlos round the west coast to the bottom of the island. Midway around, **Dhragonéra** is a beautiful but rocky pine-fringed beach with a dramatic panorama across to the mainland and a seasonal *kantína*; other small coves are accessible across the rocks. Despite the warning signs, many people camp in the woods around these beaches. **LIMENÁRIA**, a small farming community at the edge of a fertile plateau in the southern corner of the island, is largely unaffected by tourism. The closest swimming is a few hundred metres east down a cement drive, then steps, at **Máriza**, where a diminutive concrete lido gives access to deep, ice-clear water. The little anchorage of **Apónissos** lies 2km west, past a shallow salt marsh; there's lovely swimming here in a tiny, warm lagoon, idyllic when uncrowded, or off the rocks in deeper, cooler water.

EATING AND DRINKING

REST OF THE ISLAND

Aponisos Taverna Apónissos. This simple ouzerí has a matchless beachside setting, where wooden chairs are set on a terrace above the water. Simple meze dishes are the order of the day. June–Sept lunch and dinner daily.

O Tasos Limenária ☎ 22970 91362. Hugely popular with visiting mainlanders – and hence packed at weekend lunchtimes – *O Tasos* produces traditional cooking using local produce. Pricier than you'd expect for the location. Daily lunch and dinner.

Póros

Separated from the mainland by a 350m strait, **PÓROS** ("the ford") barely qualifies as an island at all. Popular with Brits and Scandinavians – more than any other Argo-Saronic island, Póros attracts package-holiday operators – it is also busy with weekending Athenians, who can get here by road (via Galatás) or on cheap ferries from Pireás, and with yachties taking advantage of the extensive mooring. There are in fact two islands, **Sferiá** (Póros Town) and the far larger **Kalávria**, separated from each other by a miniature canal spanned by a bridge. The town is a busy place, with constant traffic of shipping and people: if your stay is longer than a couple of nights, you may want to base yourself on Kalávria for a little more peace, and come into town for the food, nightlife and shopping.

ARRIVAL AND DEPARTURE

PÓROS

BY FERRY

In addition to regular ferry and hydrofoil connections with Pireás and the other Argo-Saronics, Póros has frequent, almost round-the-clock passenger boats shuttling across from the mainland port of Galatás to Póros Town (5min; €1), plus a car ferry every 30min. Small passenger boats tie up among the yachts and other small vessels on the southerly side facing Galatás, hydrofoils next to them near the northwestern end of the waterfront, and ferries further round at the northern end of town.

Destinations Pireás via Méthana and Égina (1–2 ferries daily, 2hr 15min; 4–6 hydrofoils and Flying Cats, 1hr); Spétses (4–6 hydrofoils and Flying Cats, 1hr 30min); Ýdhra (4–6 hydrofoils and Flying Cats, 35min).

Tickets and agents Hydrofoils and catamarans that serve the island are operated by Hellenic Seaways (ⓦ hsw.gr), whose local agent is Marinos Tours (☎ 22980 23423); ferries by Saronic Ferries (ⓦ saronicferries.gr), represented by Askeli Travel (☎ 22980 24566, ⓦ poros -accommodation.gr). These and many other travel and accommodation agencies are on the waterfront between the hydrofoil and ferry docks.

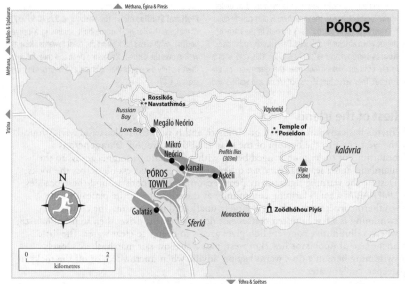

EXCURSIONS TO THE PELOPONNESE

You can easily get to mainland Peloponnese from Póros – boats shuttle constantly between Póros Town and **Galatás**, from where there are numerous potential excursions. Local travel agents run a variety of **tours**, or you'll see hire cars on offer in Galatás from around €25 a day.

TROEZEN

Ancient Troezen is an unenclosed site near the modern village of Trizína, barely 10km from Galatás. Legendary birthplace of Theseus, the scattered site is most easily understood if you purchase a map in the village – this also recounts the stories of Theseus' life. A short walk up a gorge from the site takes you to the spectacular natural rock arch of the Dhiavoloyéfyro, the Devil's Bridge.

EPIDAURUS / EPÍDHAVROS

Most famous for its fourth-century BC theatre, one of the finest ancient monuments in Greece, **Epidaurus** is also an extensive sanctuary to Asklepios, god of healing. The theatre is used for productions of Classical Greek drama on Friday and Saturday nights from June to August, as part of the annual Athens & Epidaurus Festival (☻greekfestival.gr; organized excursions from many island travel agents).

NÁFPLIO

A long day-trip, but arguably the most rewarding destination in the Peloponnese, **Náfplio** is a gorgeous nineteenth-century town in a stunning coastal setting protected by forbidding fortresses. The town has plenty of excellent restaurants and cafés.

INFORMATION

Tourist information Check ☻poros.com.gr for information on the island and for accommodation listings.

Services A couple of banks (with ATMs) and the post office are on Platía Iroön in the centre of Póros Town.

GETTING AROUND

By bus Buses (€1.50) depart to Kalávria, west to Russian Bay or east to the monastery, hourly on the hour from the road across from Platía Iroön (less frequent out of season).

By taxi The taxi rank (☎22980 23003) is close to Platía Iroön; a taxi to most beaches is less than €6; €10 will take you right across the island to Vayioniá.

By car or bike Travel agents in town can rent you a car, or a quad bike or scooter, though for the latter much the best

service and prices are from Fotis (☎22980 25873); their office is over the bridge, on the road towards Askéli, but if you call they can deliver a bike to you.

Island tours In high season, thrice-weekly boat trips around the island depart from the central waterfront, while a *trenaki* offers a variety of tours from the car park by the ferry dock, including a regular evening haul all the way up to the Temple of Poseidon.

Póros Town

PÓROS TOWN rises steeply across the western half of tiny volcanic Sferiá, a landmark clocktower at its summit. There's a two-room **Archeological Museum** on the waterfront (Korizi square; Tues–Sun 8.30am–3pm; €2; ☎22980 23276) whose local finds will fill a spare half an hour, but otherwise there are few sights here. This is a place to eat, drink, shop and watch the world go by. Away from the waterfront, you'll quickly get lost in the labyrinth of steep, narrow streets, but nowhere is far away and most of the restaurants are reasonably well signed. For a fine view over the rooftops and the strait, climb up to the **clocktower** (signed "Roloï") – the tower itself is structurally suspect and fenced off, but you can still enjoy the outlook.

ACCOMMODATION   PÓROS TOWN

Rooms in **Póros Town** itself can be in very short supply at weekends and during holiday periods, when prices are inevitably high (they can be dramatically lower out of season); some noise is always likely too. Over on **Kalávria** (see p.94) there's considerably more choice, with plenty of apartments and small hotels in the touristy enclaves of Askéli – close to good beaches – or less attractive Mikró Neório. Travel agencies all along the waterfront act as representatives for many of these.

2

★**Hotel Dionysos** Waterfront, opposite the ferry dock ☎22980 23511, ⓦhoteldionysos.eu. Set in an imposing mansion, this hotel has large, newly refurbished rooms, most of which have bare stone walls, and some have four-poster beds and wonderful old baths. Great value. **€45**

Manessi Waterfront, under the clocktower ☎22980 22273, ⓦmanessi.gr. Classy place in the centre of town, with lots of dark wood and designer touches. The larger rooms have impressive power showers, while those at the front have fabulous views; new windows mean they're well soundproofed, too. **€45**

Poros Town Waterfront ☎22980 23900, ⓦporostours .gr. A comfortable hotel set above a waterfront travel agency; a couple of rooms have balconies out front. If full, they can book you in at a variety of other places around town. **€40**

Villa Tryfon Near main square, on clocktower side of the hill ☎22980 25854, ⓦporos.com.gr/tryfon-villa. Facilities here are somewhat basic, but the cheerful blue-and-white studio rooms do all have kitchenettes, a/c and stunning views – and you'll get an exceptionally friendly welcome. **€40**

EATING, DRINKING AND NIGHTLIFE

The central waterfront is mostly given over to competing **cafés**, all of which are open from breakfast till late, as well as bars and souvenir shops: the better tavernas lie towards the southeastern end of the waterfront or up in the steep streets of the hilltop town. The southeastern end of the waterfront is also the place for good-value cafés – on Platía Dhimarhíou, for example, or next to the archeological museum. The better **bars and clubs** are in this direction too, becoming livelier as you head out along the coast road, though nightlife is highly seasonal. The open-air Cine Diana, functioning in the summer only, is on the northern waterfront towards the ferry dock.

★**Karavolos** Behind the northern waterfront, above and directly behind Cine Diana ☎22980 26158. Rightly popular with locals and expats, friendly *Karavolos* serves excellent traditional cuisine such as *kolokythokeftédhes* (courgette and cheese fritters) or pork roasted with garlic; the name means snail, and you'll also find these on the menu. Daily, evenings only.

Malibu Southeastern waterfront ☎22980 22491. One of the first of the bars you come to at this end of the harbourfront, and the most reliably open year-round. Popular with expats, yachties and tourists alike, and a good place to start your evening – though many never leave. Daily 9pm–late.

Naftis Southeastern waterfront ☎22980 23096. Excellent *psarotavérna* (seafood restaurant) with an attractive waterside terrace overlooking the yachts, south of the centre. As the evening wears on, the owners have been known to put on an impromptu Greek dancing display. Daily, evenings only.

Oasis Central waterfront ☎22980 22955. Despite being right in the centre and one of the most heavily touted spots on the waterfront, *Oasis* is actually pretty good. Plenty of locals eat here, and the simple, charcoal-grilled meats, squid and octopus are excellent. The service is very friendly, too. Daily lunch and dinner.

Platanos On the main square of the upper town ☎22980 25409. *Platanos* serves earthy, rural food on a vine-covered terrace, washed down with powerful retsina. The owners also have a butcher's shop, so charcoal-grilled meat is the speciality – *kondosoúvli* (hunks of pork roasted on a spit) or pricier steaks. Daily, evenings only.

★**Yiahni Sokaki** In the alley behind the fish market ☎22980 22522. Unsigned, old-fashioned *mayireftá* establishment. Take a look at the kitchen to see what's been prepared that day – meatballs, *moussaká* or more original dishes like chicken roasted with potatoes and cherry tomatoes, all for €6–7. When it's all gone, they close. Daily, lunchtime only.

Kalávria

KALÁVRIA, Póros's "mainland", is covered in pine forest and barely inhabited, though there are a couple of fertile plateaus on the northern side with olive terraces, vineyards and magnificent panoramic views.

Western Kalávria

Kanáli and **Míkro Neório**, immediately across the canal from Póros Town, are overdeveloped, though they do have some good seafront restaurants looking back toward town. The first place worth a stop in its own right, though, is **MEGÁLO NEÓRIO**, arguably the island's most pleasant resort: small-scale, with a sandy beach, an excellent waterski centre with courses to professional level (☎22980 42540, ⓦwww.passage.gr), and some fine beachside tavernas. **Love Bay**, immediately west, has a lovely sandy beach, but is tiny and always packed; there's a friendly seasonal *kantína*, and kayaks and snorkel gear can be hired here.

The **Rossikós Navstathmós** on Russian Bay, a crumbling early nineteenth-century Russian naval base, marks the end of the route for the westward bus. There's a very busy, mostly shadeless beach here.

Askéli

Askéli, with its strip of hotels and villas, is the first place you reach as you head east on Kalávria. There are plenty of cafés and places to eat, many of which overlook the narrow, crowded beach. A good watersports centre (✆697 801 6500) hires out kayaks and small sailing boats, and they also have a powerboat for ringo rides and the like.

Monastiríou

The eighteenth-century **monastery of Zoödhóhou Piyís** (daily sunrise–1pm & 5pm–sunset), next to the island's only spring, is the terminus of Póros's eastward bus. Steps from the bus stop lead down to the pleasant sandy beach of **Monastiríou**, overlooked by pine-covered slopes. Surprisingly, this is usually one of the less crowded beaches, though hardly empty, as the taverna and *kantína* here will testify.

Temple of Poseidon

Daily 8am–5pm • Free • ⊛ kalaureia.org

The remains of the **Temple of Poseidon** overlook the island's northern and western coasts, with great views towards Égina. The temple lay at the heart of **ancient Kalaureia**, whose heyday was in the fourth century BC, and it's an extensive site. Despite plenty of signage and an ongoing Swedish excavation, there's not a great deal to see above ground level – many of the stones were carted off to be used as building materials in the seventeenth and eighteenth centuries (much of which ended up on Ýdhra), and some of the more interesting sections are roped off while they are excavated. It was here that Demosthenes, fleeing from the Macedonians after encouraging the Athenians to resist their rule, took poison rather than surrender.

Vayioniá

Vayioniá, just about the only accessible beach on the island's north shore, was the port of ancient Kalaureia. The bay is beautiful when viewed from above; close up the pebbly beach is narrow and can be windy, but it's still a very pleasant spot, with a seasonal beach bar/café, and loungers to rent.

ACCOMMODATION AND EATING   **KALÁVRIA**

MEGÁLO NEÓRIO

★**Pavlou** ✆22980 22734, ⊛ pavlouhotel.gr. Family-run hotel with pool and tennis court, right on one of the island's best beaches (where they also have a great restaurant). Rooms are simple, with no frills, but spacious, with big balconies, half of which have great sea views. Breakfast included. **€60**

MIKRÓ NEÓRIO

Aspros Gatos Labraki 49, Waterfront ✆22980 25650. Friendly taverna serving good seafood dishes, such as rice pilaf with mussels and pine nuts, on a waterfront terrace with views back over Póros Town. Only about 20min walk from town, or you can take the free water-taxi service for groups of five or more. Daily lunch and dinner.

MONASTIRÍOU

Sirene ✆22980 22741, ⊛ sireneblueresort.gr. Large, modern hotel with pool and tennis courts, spectacularly sited on a steep slope above the sea, with a small private beach below. The stunning location ensures fabulous views from the balconies, though the refurbished rooms are small. Good off-peak deals. **€140**

VAYIONIÁ

Paradisos ✆22980 23419. Well signed on the main road just east of the turning down to Vayioniá, this rural taverna serves plenty of local produce, including rabbit *stifádho* and spit-roasted pork, plus charcoal-grilled squid or lamb, washed down with local retsina and home-made bread. Live Greek music on Sun. Daily noon–midnight.

2

Ýdhra

The island of **ÝDHRA (Hydra)** is one of the most atmospheric destinations in Greece. With its harbour and main town preserved as a **national monument**, it feels like a Greek island should, entirely **traffic-free** (even bicycles are banned) with a bustling harbour and narrow stone streets climbing steeply above it. Away from the main settlement the rest of the island is roadless, rugged and barely inhabited. The charm hasn't gone unnoticed – Ýdhra became fashionable as early as the 1950s, and in the 1960s characters ranging from Greek painter Nikos Hatzikyriakos-Ghikas to Canadian songster Leonard Cohen bought and restored grand old houses here. There's still a sizeable expat community, which contributes to a relatively sophisticated atmosphere and noticeably **high prices**. But even the seasonal and weekend crowds, and a very limited number of beaches, can't seriously detract from the appeal. When the town is overrun, it's easy enough to leave it all behind on foot or by excursion boat. The **interior** is mountainous and little-visited, so with a little walking you can find a dramatically different kind of island – one of rural cottages, terraces of grain to feed the donkeys, hilltop monasteries and pine forest.

ARRIVAL AND DEPARTURE   ÝDHRA

BY FERRY
Hellenic Seaways hydrofoils and Flying Cats connect Ýdhra to Pireás via Póros. In the other direction they continue to Spétses, some via Ermióni or on to Pórto Héli on the mainland. Small passenger boats also cross to Metóhi on the nearby mainland.

Tickets and agencies The local agent for Hellenic Seaways tickets (ⓦhsw.gr) is Hydreoniki Travel (☎22980

54007, ⓦhydreoniki.gr), located in an alley at the eastern end of the harbour. Metóhi boats are operated by Hydra Lines (☎6947 325 263, ⓦhydralines.gr).

Destinations Ermióni (3 daily; 20min); Metóhi (5 daily in season; 15min); Pireás (5 daily, more in midsummer; 1hr 20min); Póros (5 daily, more in midsummer; 35min); Pórto Héli (3 daily; 1hr); Spétses (5 daily, more in midsummer; 45min).

INFORMATION

Tourist information The local municipality's website, ⓦhydra.gr, is an excellent resource.
Internet There's free wi-fi at many cafés.

Services Several banks with ATMs can be found round the waterfront, while the post office is on the market square just inland.

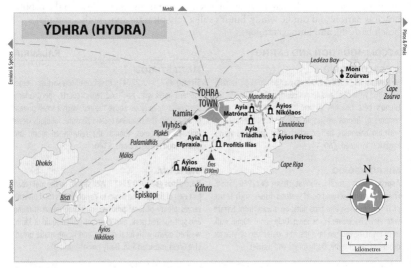

ÝDHRA (HYDRA)

GETTING AROUND

On foot There's only one paved road on Ýdhra, and it leads east from the harbour to Mandhráki just a couple of kilometres away, so to explore the island you either walk or take a boat (see below). The largely shadeless trails mean that in midsummer walking can be a mercilessly hot experience. There are excellent, part-cobbled tracks which lead west of town to the beaches at Kamíni (about 20min), Vlyhós (30min) and Plákes (40min). Steeper, rougher paths lead into the interior and towards the south coast (see box, p.100).

By boat Small boats shuttle constantly in season from the harbour to the beaches, at prices ranging from about €3 per person one way to Mandhráki or Vlyhós, to €12 return to Bísti. You can also hire private water-taxis – good value for groups, at around €15 per boat to Vlyhós or €55 to Bísti.

By mule If you are carrying luggage or might struggle on the sometimes steep cobbles in Ýdhra Town, you can hire a mule at the harbour; fixed prices for various destinations are posted. The fancier hotels may provide a mule if they know when you are arriving – or more likely a porter with a handcart for your luggage.

Ýdhra Town

ÝDHRA TOWN, with tiers of grey-stone mansions and humbler white-walled, red-tiled houses rising from a perfect horseshoe harbour, makes a beautiful spectacle. Around the **harbour**, trippers flock to cafés and chic boutiques, but it's also worth spending time wandering the backstreets and narrow alleys.

The magnificent houses you'll encounter everywhere were mostly built during the eighteenth century on the accumulated wealth of a remarkable merchant fleet, which traded as far afield as America and – during the Napoleonic Wars – broke the British blockade to sell grain to France. In the 1820s, the town's population was nearly twenty thousand – an incredible figure when you reflect that today it is under three thousand – and Ýdhra's merchants provided many of the ships for the Greek forces during the War of Independence, and consequently many of the commanders. At each side of the harbour, cannons facing out to sea and statues of the heroes of independence remind you of the island's place in history.

The Koundouriótis mansions

The mansions of the wealthy eighteenth-century merchant families are still the great monuments of the town; some labelled at the entrance with "*Oikía*" ("Residence of …") followed by the family name. Among the finest are the **Koundouriótis mansions**, built by two brothers: Lázaros (see below) and **Yíoryios**. The latter was a leading politician of the fledgling Greek nation and grandfather of Pávlos, president of Republican Greece in the 1920s – consequently, the house, periodically open for art exhibitions, is usually known as the **Pávlos Koundouriótis Mansion**.

Lázaros Koundouriótis Museum

High above the western side of town • April–Oct daily 10am–2pm & 5.30–8.30pm • €4 • ☎ 22980 52421

The hot climb up stepped alleyways to the **Lázaros Koundouriótis Museum** is rewarded with great views down over the town and port. The ochre-coloured landmark building, whose eponymous original owner played a prominent role in the struggle for Greek independence, boasts a lovingly restored interior that looks ready to move into. The red-tiled floors, panelled wooden ceilings and period furnishings outshine the contents of the museum, which includes paintings, folk costume and independence paraphernalia.

Historical Archives Museum

Eastern waterfront • Daily 9am–4pm, July & Aug also 7.30–9.30pm • €5 • ☎ 22980 52355

The **Historical Archives Museum** occupies one of Ýdhra's great houses, looking out across the harbour. It's a small, crowded and enjoyable display mostly of naval memorabilia – ships' prows and sidearms from the independence struggle and later conflicts – as well as clothing and period engravings. The **Melina Mercouri Centre**, next door, often has interesting temporary art exhibitions (look out for posters around town).

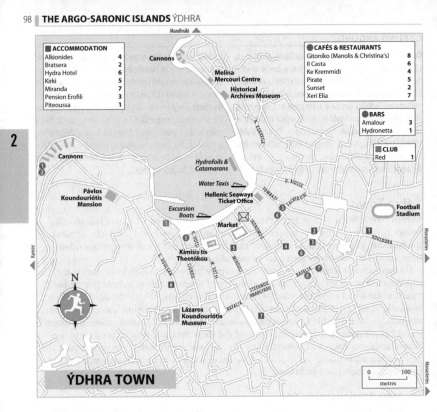

ACCOMMODATION
Alkionides	4
Bratsera	2
Hydra Hotel	6
Kirki	5
Miranda	7
Pension Erofili	3
Piteoussa	1

CAFÉS & RESTAURANTS
Gitoniko (Manolis & Christina's)	8
Il Casta	6
Ke Kremmidi	4
Pirate	5
Sunset	2
Xeri Elia	7

BARS
Amalour	3
Hydronetta	1

CLUB
Red	1

ÝDHRA TOWN

0 — 100
metres

Kímisis tís Theotókou

Harbour • Museum Tues–Sun 10am–2.30pm, Aug also 7–9pm • €2 • ☎ 22980 54071

The most obvious and important of Ýdhra's many churches is **Kímisis tís Theotókou** by the port, with its distinctive clocktower. The cloistered courtyard houses the small but rich collection of the **ecclesiastical museum** – silver-bound books, icons, vestments, bejewelled crosses and the like.

ACCOMMODATION   ÝDHRA TOWN

Most accommodation in Ýdhra Town is high quality, though prices tend to be equally elevated. Midweek or out of season you should be able to negotiate significant reductions on the official rates. The nature of the old buildings and the closely packed streets mean that some noise is inevitable, especially near the waterfront. Addresses and street signs are almost nonexistent, so ask for directions when you book, or refer to our map.

★**Alkionides** ☎ 22980 54055, ⓦ alkionidespension .com. Lovely pension, quietly tucked away yet central, with an attractive courtyard and helpful management; the rooms are extremely comfortable and well equipped, and there's a wonderful studio apartment with its own roof terrace. **€70**, studio **€85**

Bratsera ☎ 22980 53971, ⓦ bratserahotel.com. This classy four-star hotel occupies a stylishly renovated former sponge factory; the extensive common areas (including bar, restaurant and courtyard pool) serve as a museum of the industry, displaying photos and artefacts. Lovely rooms

have flagstone floors and beamed ceilings, though only superior and above have balconies. **€160**

★**Hydra Hotel** ☎ 22980 53420, ⓦ hydra-hotel.gr. Set in a mansion high above the harbour, this stunning boutique hotel offers glorious views from many of its rooms. Each room is different, from simple doubles up to a split-level family apartment. **€150**

Kirki ☎ 22980 53181, ⓦ hydrakirki.gr. *Kirki*'s unprepossessing entry leads to a delightful old house, with a small courtyard garden and simple, island-style rooms; all have a/c and balconies, though the attractive large terraces at the back do get some early-morning noise from the market. €55

Miranda ☎ 22980 52230, ⊕ mirandahotel.gr. A bougainvillea-draped 1810 mansion converted into a popular hotel, with highly individual rooms; best are nos. 2 and 3, both with painted, coffered ceilings and large sea-view terraces. Large breakfasts in the shaded courtyard are another big plus and there's a basement bar for winter. €120

Pension Erofili ☎ 22980 54049, ⊕ pensionerofili.gr. The simple but spacious rooms at this quiet, friendly and relatively inexpensive pension are set around a court-yard; all have a/c, fridge and television. A small apartment upstairs has its own kitchen. €45

★**Piteoussa** ☎ 22980 52810, ⊕ piteoussa.com. Named after the three giant pines at the front, this friendly small inn is exceptional value, its units equipped with iPod speakers, CD and DVD players and Korres toiletries in the marble-floored bathrooms. Downstairs rooms are larger, but all have balconies and designer touches. €55

EATING AND DRINKING

Brace yourself for some of the steepest food and drink prices in the Greek islands outside of Mýkonos and Rhodes. The permanently busy quayside cafés and bars offer an incomparable people-watching experience, but there are few worthwhile restaurants on the harbour. If you want something to take down to the beach with you, try the excellent bakery, with *tyrópittes* (cheese pies) and cakes, that's tucked into the western corner of the harbour by the *Pirate* bar.

★**Gitoniko (Manolis & Christina's)** ☎ 22980 53615. Hidden away inland, near Áyios Konstandínos church, this traditional taverna serves excellent, well-priced *mayireftá* at lunch, such as stuffed marrow (€7) – which runs out early – plus grills (including succulent fish) in the evening; there's an extensive roof-terrace in summer. Daily lunch and dinner.

Il Casta ☎ 22980 52967. Neapolitan restaurant serving up tasty Italian specialities, including excellent home-made pasta, elegantly presented in a lovely courtyard that's candle-lit at night; a little pricier than most. Daily lunch and dinner.

Ke Kremmidi ☎ 22980 53099, ⊕ kekremmidi.gr. A *souvláki* joint with style, where they serve inexpensive *yíros* (meat-filled) pita as well as more inventive and interesting stuff including good cheese and meat pies and a variety of Turkish-style dishes. Daily 10am–2am.

Pirate ☎ 22980 52711. Café by day and an increasingly lively bar as the evening wears on, *Pirate* attracts a young crowd and plays Western music. Among the lowest prices on the waterfront for coffee, breakfast and sandwiches. Daily 10am–2am.

Sunset ☎ 22980 52067, ⊕ sunsethydra.com. Behind the cannons on the western edge of town, *Sunset* offers an incomparable setting for an end-of-holiday treat or romantic tryst; the modern Greek and Italian cuisine is on the pricey side (pasta dishes €12–22, steak €28), but the views justify the cost. Daily lunch and dinner.

Xeri Elia ☎ 22980 52886. Busy, large taverna with a lovely setting in a vine-shaded inland platía. All the standards are served, along with good seafood, and there's often live music in the evenings. Daily lunch and dinner.

NIGHTLIFE

Nightlife in Ýdhra Town is tame on the whole, though a number of bars do play music into the early hours; there's also an open-air cinema in summer, on Ikonómou, inland from the market.

Amalour ☎ 6977 461 357. Laidback cocktail bar with an eclectic playlist – plenty of Latin and jazz – and 30-to-40-something crowd. Almost always the busiest place in town in the early evening; sometimes hosts special events or theme nights. Daily 7pm–2am.

Hydronetta ☎ 22980 54160. The classic sunset-watching bar, with steps down the rocks into the water, where the music carries on into the small hours. Limited seating gives it an exclusive, chill-out vibe. The place is also open during the day for swimming, coffee and an early start on the booze. Daily 9am–2am.

Red ☎ 6974 421 398. The closest thing you'll find to a dance club in town, *Red* is a late-night joint right on the waterfront, where they play Sixties and Seventies rock plus a few dance tunes and the odd Greek number. Fri–Sun 10pm–3am, plus some weekdays in summer.

ÝDHRA'S FESTIVALS

Over the weekend closest to June 21, Ýdhra Town celebrates the **Miaoulia**, in honour of Admiral Andreas Miaoulis whose fire boats, packed with explosives, were set adrift downwind of the Turkish fleet during the War of Independence. The highlight of the celebrations is the burning of a boat at sea as a tribute to the sailors who risked their lives in this dangerous enterprise.

Orthodox Easter is also a colourful and moving experience, especially on the evening of Good Friday when the fishermen's parish of Áyios Ioánnis at Kamíni carries its *Epitáfios*, or symbolic bier of Christ, into the shallows to bless the boats and ensure calm seas.

2

HIKING ON ÝDHRA

Many of the **paths** that track across the island's interior have recently been signed, at least at their starting points, and a **map** of them is displayed on the harbour waterfront (you can also download maps and a guide from ⓦ hydra.gr). Don't be misled into assuming that these walks are easy, however; once off the main coastal track, the terrain is rocky and unforgiving, there's little shade, and the trails are in places very hard to follow. These are the main routes:

WESTERN BEACHES

Very easy walking as far as **Palamidhás** (see below) where the track runs out and a path heads uphill towards the hamlet of **Episkopí**. The route avoids the village and eventually there's a fork: left to **Áyios Nikólaos** or straight on along the main path to **Bísti**. From either of the beaches you should be able to get a boat back. It's at least four hours to Bísti.

PROFÍTIS ILÍAS AND MOUNT ÉROS

The monastery of **Profítis Ilías** and nearby convent of **Ayía Efpraxía** are about an hour-and-a-half's climb above Ýdhra Town. What must be the longest stairway in Greece (or alternatively a zigzag path) constitutes the final approach to Profítis Ilías (closed noon–4pm, but water and *loukoúm* (Turkish delight) are hospitably left at the gate). If you want to go further, take the rather tougher, harder-to-follow trail which continues south before splitting: left will take you to the 590m summit of **Mount Éros**, the Argo-Saronic islands' highest point (another 30min); right to the chapel of **Áyios Mámas**, on whose feast day of September 2 there's a pilgrimage of people and animals to be blessed, and eventually on to **Episkopí** (another 2hr), from where you can head on to Bistí or circle back round via Palamidhás.

ÁYIOS NIKÓLAOS

The path from Ýdhra Town towards deserted **Áyios Nikólaos** monastery offers spectacular views back down over the harbour before reaching, at the top, a broad, easy dirt track heading straight across a high plateau towards the monastery. Just beyond Áyios Nikólaos is a small settlement, from where you can in theory head down to **Limnióniza**, a scenic cove on the south coast an hour and a quarter from Ýdhra Town. However, it's a steep scramble on a path which is hard to find and there are no boats back unless you arrange to be picked up by water-taxi. A far easier alternative is to follow the broad track down from Áyios Nikólaos to **Mandhráki**, where you can have a swim before taking the boat back to town.

CAPE ZOÚRVA

This is Ýdhra's eastern tip and is about four hours' walk from town, on a path that heads east from Áyios Nikólaos. There are several small chapels along the way, along with the substantial **Moní Zoúrvas** (three hours). Water-taxis can drop off and pick up at the bay below the monastery, and perhaps the best way to do this trip is to take an early-morning water-taxi to **Ledéza Bay**, hike to the cape, and then back to town: with the return from the cape to the monastery, this will take over five hours.

Beaches

There's no big sandy beach on Ýdhra, just a series of small, mainly shingly, coves. **Mandhráki** is the closest to town, dominated by the *Miramare Hotel* (see opposite) which occupies the imposing former shipyard of independence war hero Admiral Miaoulis. In season there's windsurfing, waterskiing, pedaloes to hire and floating trampolines.

Walk west from Ýdhra Town and you'll find several spots where you can clamber down to swim from the rocks in crystal-clear water, but the first tiny pebble beach lies just beyond the picturesque village of **Kamíni**. Next up is a popular swimming cove at **Kastéllo** and then **Vlyhós**, a small hamlet with a rebuilt nineteenth-century bridge and a shingle beach with loungers and umbrellas; there's pleasant swimming in the lee of an offshore islet here. **Plákes**, a long, pebbly stretch with loungers, *palapa* shelters and a small resort hotel, is followed by the rather scruffy cove of **Palamidhás**, with the island's only surviving shipyard. This marks the end of the easy path; **Mólos**, just beyond, is not accessible on foot. At the western tip of the island, a very tough walk or easy journey by boat, are two coves sheltering perhaps the island's best beaches: **Bísti** has a smallish, white-pebbled beach surrounded by pine trees that offer shade; **Áyios Nikólaos** is larger and sandier, but with less shade and fewer boats. Both have seasonal snack-bars as well as loungers and kayaks to rent.

ACCOMMODATION, EATING AND DRINKING   BEACHES

MANDHRÁKI

Mandraki 1800 ☎ 22980 52112. Above a tiny cove as you enter Mandhráki, this café/ouzerí has loungers and umbrellas, free for customers, and serves good fresh fish as well as meze and drinks. April–Oct daily, all day.

Miramare Hotel ☎ 22980 52300, ⓦ miramare.gr. All-in-one restaurant, beach-bar and hotel right on the beach. The rather crude beachside bungalows are not great value, but you can eat or simply have a coffee on a beautiful waterside terrace, and they have their own boat transfer to town. Easter & June–Oct daily, all day.

KAMÍNI

Antonia ☎ 22980 52481. Just one delightfully old-fashioned room and one apartment for up to five people are available here, both with balconies that hang right over the sea; with no frills at all (though there is a/c) and virtually no English spoken, this feels like the Greece of thirty years ago. €60

Pension Petroleka ☎ 6942 523 338, ⓦ ostria-hydra .gr. Immediately behind *Antonia* (see above), there are just a couple of well-equipped apartments here, simply furnished but with wi-fi and a/c. The larger and more expensive one has two rooms with separate bathroom and kitchen and huge balcony. €70

Taverna Kodylenia ☎ 22980 53520, ⓦ www.hydra -kodylenia.gr. With a beautiful terrace overlooking the little harbour, *Kodylenia* is famous for its seafood and wonderful sunset views. Crowds of weekend trippers mean slightly higher-than-average prices: *moussaká* for €9, seafood spaghetti €15, pork with mushroom and wine sauce €12. March–Oct daily lunch and dinner.

VLYHÓS

Antigonis ☎ 22980 53228, ⓔ antigone@freemail.gr. Just above the jetty where the boats drop you, *Antigonis* has good-value apartments overlooking the water; the small ones have a bedroom and living room/kitchenette, the larger have two bedrooms and separate kitchen. There's also a decent restaurant and snack-bar. June–Oct. €65

PLÁKES

Four Seasons ☎ 22980 53698, ⓦ fourseasonshydra.gr. An incongruously luxurious small suite hotel for this isolated spot, complete with a decent waterfront restaurant and organized beach. Accommodation is in beautiful, spacious suites and studio apartments (sleeping up to four people), with modern facilities including wi-fi and satellite TV. There are evening boat trips to the restaurant (April–Oct) from town. €190

Spétses

A popular, upmarket escape for Athenians, **SPÉTSES** had brief fame and a vogue as a package destination, largely thanks to John Fowles, who lived here in the early 1950s and used the place, thinly disguised, as the setting for his cult novel *The Magus*. But the island never developed the mass infrastructure – or the convenient beaches – to match. Today, the town is much the biggest in the Saronic Islands, with **apartments and villas** spreading for several kilometres along the northeast coast, while the rest of the island remains almost entirely uninhabited, with **pine forest** inland and numerous excellent **small beaches** around the coast.

ARRIVAL AND DEPARTURE   SPÉTSES

BY FERRY

At least five daily Hellenic Seaways hydrofoils and Flying Cats connect Spétses with Pireás (2hr 20min) via Ýdhra (45min) and Póros (1hr 25min). Around three a day call at mainland Ermióni en route, and in the other direction continue to Pórto Héli. A car ferry and seasonal passenger boats also run several times daily to Kósta on

the nearby mainland (though you can't bring a car to the island). All of them dock pretty much in the heart of town at the cannon-studded main harbour known as the Dápia.

Tickets and agencies The local agent for Hellenic Seaways is Bardakos (☎ 22980 73141, ⓦ hsw.gr), on the east side of the Dápia.

INFORMATION

Tourist information Mimoza Travel (☎ 22980 75170) and Alasia Travel (☎ 22980 74098, ⓦ alasiatravel.gr),

both on the waterfront immediately east of the Dápia, can help with accommodation and local information. A useful

2

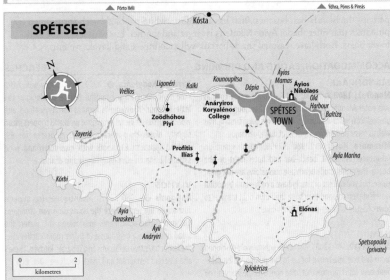

website is ⓦ spetsesdirect.com.

Internet Many of the harbour cafés have free wi-fi, but *Café 1800* (daily all day, till late), on the waterfront towards Kounoupítsa, is the only central internet café.

Services There are banks with ATMs all around the Dápia.

GETTING AROUND

By bus There are two bus services to the beaches in high season: west to Kounoupítsa, Ligonéri and Vréllos from the waterfront by the *Hotel Poseidonion* (roughly hourly during the day); east and then around the island to Áyii Anáryiri and Ayía Paraskévi from behind the town beach (4–5 daily).

By boat Seasonal *kaïkia* (traditional wooden boats) offer shuttles to the beaches (€10 return to Áyii Anáryiri, for example) or round-the-island trips, and there are plentiful water-taxis (€18–80 per boatload depending on destination; ☎ 22980 72072).

By bike Bike Center (daily 10am–3.30pm & 5.30–10pm;

☎ 22980 72209), about halfway along the shopping street behind the seafront hotels, has good mountain bikes for €6 a day, plus maps and suggested routes; there are a few stiff slopes, but you could easily circle the island in a couple of hours.

By scooter and motorbike Several rental places can be found behind the town beach. Try Bratopoulos (☎ 6932 333 014), often the cheapest if you bargain (from €15/day), or Nautilus (☎ 22980 77068); Stanathiotis (☎ 22980 75364) on Bótasi, the main street inland, generally has the newest machines (all three high season daily around 9am–10pm; low season depends on demand).

Spétses Town

SPÉTSES TOWN shares with Ýdhra a history of late eighteenth-century mercantile adventure and prosperity, and a leading role in the War of Independence, which made its foremost citizens the aristocrats of the new Greek state. Plenty of fine old homes and public buildings survive, but here there's been little restriction on new building, which spreads along the shore in both directions. And although most cars are banned in town, you won't notice it, as they're replaced by thousands of **mopeds and scooters** that pay little attention to whether a street is pedestrianized or not. In short, it's much less pretty than Ýdhra Town, but also a great deal more lively and earthy, and full of pricey shops, bars and restaurants.

For most visitors, shopping, eating and drinking are the principal attractions of Spétses, but it's a very enjoyable place to wander, with majestic old houses and gardens scattered through the narrow streets. The harbour, the **Dápia**, marks pretty much the centre of town, with the main square tucked in behind. To the east lies the **town beach** of Áyios

Mámas, with the older part of town behind it. Beyond, via a lovely walk around the point, lies the **Old Harbour**, upmarket focus of the island's nightlife, where private yachts moor up. West of the Dápia is **Kounoupítsa** – much of the simpler accommodation is here, and there are small beaches and waterfront tavernas. It's a big place; to walk from Kounoupítsa to the far end of the Old Harbour will take at least forty minutes.

Bouboulína's Mansion

100m behind the Dapia · Guided tours (30min) up to a dozen times daily; times are posted outside, on boards around town and online · €6 · ☎ 22980 72416, ⓦ bouboulinamuseum-spetses.gr

Local heroine **Laskarína Bouboulína** was a wealthy widow who commanded her own small fleet in the War of Independence, reputedly seduced her lovers at gunpoint and was shot in 1825 by the father of a girl her son had eloped with. Her former home – the so-called **Bouboulína's Mansion** – signposted not far behind the Dápia, is now a private museum. On the entertaining tour, you'll hear the story of how she spent much of her fortune on ships and men for the independence struggle, while highlights among the arms, furniture, pictures and correspondence are a gorgeous wooden ceiling in the main room and a model of Bouboulína's flagship, the *Agamemnon*.

Spétses Museum

On the hill above the town beach · Tues–Sun 8.30am–2.45pm · €3 · ☎ 22980 72994

Spétses' enjoyable local **museum** is housed in one of the town's grandest mansions, the Hatziyánnis Méxis family home, perched high up in the eastern half of town. Apart from the house itself, highlights include magnificent polychrome wooden ships' prows from the revolutionary fleet, as well as its flag, plus (out of sight in a plain wooden ossuary) the bones of Laskarína Bouboulína (see above).

ACCOMMODATION   SPÉTSES TOWN

Accommodation, especially at the cheaper end of the range, tends to be widely scattered. On busy weekends and in Aug it can be in short supply, so it may be easier to arrange it through an agency (see p.101). At quiet times, big discounts can be negotiated.

Athina Apartments Just behind the town beach ☎ 22980 74089, ⓦ athina-spetses.com. Comfortable, well-equipped self-catering apartments in a quiet spot near the beach, run by a friendly and helpful Anglo-Greek couple. **€60**

Kastro Hotel Towards Kounoupítsa, behind Nissia hotel ☎ 22980 75152, ⓦ kastrohotel-spetses.gr. An attractive complex of comfy studios and duplex apartments, arranged around a small pool and bar, that come with kitchen, a/c, TV and balcony. **€85**

Klimis 200m east of the Dápia ☎ 22980 73725, ⓦ klimishotel.gr. Right on the front, *Klimis* may be a little run-down, but is convenient, open all year and excellent value given its position, with wonderful views from the balconied rooms at the front and some kind of sea view from almost every room. Downstairs there's a superb, old-fashioned *zaharoplastío* (confectionary shop) with excellent ice cream, where breakfast (included) is served. **€60**

Poseidonion Immediately west of the Dápia ☎ 22980 74553, ⓦ poseidonion.com. Vast, imposing, *fin-de-siècle* edifice which reopened in 2009 after years of meticulous refurbishment. Grand, high-ceilinged rooms in the main building, many with freestanding claw-foot baths. There are bungalows at the back, behind the pool, and an amazing cupola suite in the tower. Prices to match, unfortunately. **€240**

Roumani Dápia ☎ 22980 72244, ⓦ hotelroumani.gr. Prime location right on the Dápia, which means rooms at the front have stunning views – though they can also be noisy and are overdue for a refurb, hence the reasonable prices. **€65**

★**Villa Christina** 200m inland from the Dápia, just off Bótasi ☎ 22980 72218, ⓦ villachristinahotel.com. Friendly, well-maintained restored inn occupying a rambling old building with two courtyards, set in a peaceful location. A/c rooms and studios (with kitchens) for up to four people are available. Breakfast in the courtyard usually included. **€45**

Villa Orizontes 500m directly uphill from the back of Platía Oroloyíou ☎ 22980 72509, ⓦ villaorizontes.gr. Simple hotel in a quiet spot, high up – look for the large veranda and blue shutters – with a variety of different-sized rooms and apartments with fridge, a/c and TV; more than half have knockout views across town and out to sea. **€40**

Zoe's Club 200m east of the Dápia ☎ 22980 74447, ⓦ zoesclub.gr. Lovely, designer-decorated studios, apartments and houses on a quiet inland corner, set around a large pool. All have flat-screen satellite TV, DVD players and espresso machines in the fully equipped kitchens, and almost all have a great sea view. Expect it to be fully booked for Aug and summer weekends and almost empty the rest of the time, though there are few bargains even then. **€150**

2

EATING AND DRINKING

Spétses is almost as pricey as Ýdhra, especially in the cafés around the Dápia and romantic spots on the old harbour, and on summer weekends you may need to book.

★**Akroyialia** Waterfront towards Kounoupítsa ☎ 22980 74749, ⓦ akrogialia-restaurant.gr. Excellent seafood taverna which enjoys a wonderful setting, with candlelit tables on the beach and the water lapping almost to your feet as you eat. Prices reflect its popularity: pork chops in honey and lemon sauce €9.80, mussel risotto €13.80 and prawn spaghetti €19. Daily lunch and dinner.

Exedra Old Harbour ☎ 22980 73497. A smarter, older crowd tends to come here to enjoy standard dishes like *moussaká*, *angináres ala políta* (artichokes with dill sauce, both €7.50) and fresh fish, served in an unbeatable waterside setting. Despite the upmarket image, prices are just a little higher than at neighbouring establishments. Daily noon–4pm & 7pm–midnight.

Kafeneion Dápia ☎ 22980 72202. Pebble mosaics underfoot and sepia photos indicate that this was the island's first watering hole. A prime people-watching spot, open all day for coffee and snacks, progressing later to a full range of *mezédhes*; or just have a drink while waiting for a hydrofoil. Daily 10am–1am.

Lazaros Bótasi ☎ 22980 72600. A stiff climb 500m uphill leads to this most traditional of tavernas, its cavernous interior decked out with an old jukebox, dangling gourds and wine barrels. It serves a limited but savoury menu of grills, goat in lemon sauce, superior *taramás* and decent barrelled wine. Evening only, late March–early Oct.

Patralis Kounoupítsa ☎ 22980 75380, ⓦ patralis.gr. Old-fashioned, bourgeois *psarotavérna* (fish restaurant), very popular with Greek visitors, which can mean slow service and a wait for a table. The fish is excellent, though, and there are plenty of less expensive meaty alternatives (such as roast lamb for €7) plus good barrelled wine if you don't like the prices on the extensive wine list. Better value for decent fish and sea views than places on the Old Harbour. Daily lunch and dinner.

To Liotrivi Old Harbour ☎ 22980 72269. The "old olive oil press" offers an upmarket, Greek-Mediterranean menu – pirate risotto, grilled prawns, *Spetsiot* fish – to a Latin and jazz soundtrack, with occasional live music. Some tables enjoy a stunning position on a jetty that extends right out into the harbour. Daily lunch and dinner.

To Nero tis Agapis Kounoupítsa ☎ 22980 74009, ⓦ nerotisagapis.gr. Virtually adjacent to *Patralis* (see above) and with a similar seafood-based menu (excellent seafood spaghetti), "The Water of Love" could hardly be a greater contrast in style and decor – self-consciously modern, island-style, with decent music and enthusiastic young staff. Mains such as tagliatelle with fresh fish and shellfish sauce, or cuttlefish with mustard and lemon sauce go for €16–18. Daily lunch and dinner.

NIGHTLIFE AND ENTERTAINMENT

Late-night nightlife is mostly centred on **Baltíza**, the furthest of the inlets at the old harbour; here there are several seasonal clubs, though even in Aug they only really come to life at the weekend. Closer to town, **Áyios Mámas** beach also has a couple of lively music bars. Two **cinemas** operate in summer, close to the main square – Titania (with a roof for shelter, but open sides; ☎ 22980 72434) and open-air, rooftop Marina (☎ 22980 72110).

Balkoni East of the Dápia ☎ 22980 72594. The elegant alternative to nearby *Socrates* (see below); sip your wine or cocktails on a candlelit balcony overlooking the waterfront. They are also open for coffee during the day. Daily 10am–2am.

Bar Spetsa Áyios Mámas ⓦ barspetsa.org. Chilled-out bar playing decent retro rock, mainly Sixties and Seventies. Strong, keenly priced drinks and a great atmosphere most nights. Nightly 8pm–3am.

La Luz Old harbour ☎ 22980 74244. Classy music bar spread over two upstairs floors in a beautifully restored mansion with plenty of exposed brickwork. Open from 4pm for coffee and drinks, but the main action is late at night – live music or DJs most weekends from 11.30pm. Daily 4pm–late.

Mama's Beach Café Áyios Mámas beach ☎ 22980 75250. Lively café and lunch spot by day, with sandwiches, milkshakes and waffles, while at night the upstairs music bar (playing summer party stuff) takes over. Daily 10.30am–2am.

Socrates East of the Dápia ☎ 22980 77007. English-pub-style bar on the waterfront (main entry from the shopping street behind) serving draught beer, including Guinness, and showing big-screen sports. A popular hangout for local expats, especially on football nights. Daily 7pm–2am.

Beaches

A single paved road circles Spétses, mostly high above a rocky coast but with access to beaches at various points. In season you can get to most of them by bus or excursion boat, and none is too far to cycle, or even walk (see box opposite).

Kaïki and Vréllos

Kaïki, or College Beach, is just twenty minutes' walk west of town, with a frequent bus service and extensive facilities including loungers, bars and a waterski outfit that also rents jet skis. **Vréllos**, a small, pebbly cove in a pretty, wooded bay, is the end of the line for buses heading west out of Spétses. Thanks to paved access and a beach cocktail bar pumping out loud Greek rock, it's almost always packed at weekends.

Zoyeriá

At the western extremity of the island, **Zoyeriá** is reached down a track that soon degenerates into a path (which doesn't stop locals riding their scooters) past a series of rocky coves. If you follow this, you'll eventually climb over a small headland to arrive at a sandy beach with a large and popular summer-only taverna, *Loula*. Many of the patrons here arrive the easy way, by boat.

Ayía Paraskeví

The bay of **Ayía Paraskeví**, on the southwest coast, shelters a part-sand beach that is almost always quieter than its near neighbour, Áyii Anáryiri (see below). The end of the eastern bus route, it has a seasonal café-bar, but no other development at all.

Áyii Anáryiri

Áyii Anáryiri is the largest and most popular beach on Spétses: a long, sheltered, partly sandy bay, with a taverna, offshore swimming pontoon and a watersports centre offering kayaks, pedaloes, windsurfers and catamarans to rent, as well as a waterski boat. At the end of the beach concrete steps lead round to the **Bekiris Cave**, a low-ceilinged, shallow cavern; you can clamber in through a narrow entrance at the back and then swim out, though best to have something on your feet for the sharp rocks.

Xylokériza

Almost at the southern tip of the island a long, steep concrete track leads down to a cove of pale-coloured pebbles at **Xylokériza**. There's no sand at all here, but it's a beautiful spot, surrounded by pines and phoenix palms, and rarely crowded. There's a café and volleyball court.

Ayía Marína

Ayía Marína, or Paradise Beach, is a busy, almost suburban, pebble beach, within walking distance of the eastern edge of Spétses Town. Packed with loungers, it also has a popular bar-restaurant and a watersports operation offering kayaks and waterski and ringo rides. There are views offshore towards the tempting but off-limits islet of **Spetsopoúla**, the private property of the heirs of shipping magnate Stavros Niarchos.

SPÉTSES ON FOOT

If you want to explore **Spétses on foot**, you can strike directly across the island to many of the beaches. The easiest route is to follow **Bótasi** out of town, past the *Lazaros* taverna; as you leave town a sign (the only one you'll see) points you up a **paved road**. The paving soon runs out, but a good broad track heads up towards the heights. At the top there are no signs at all: one track leads directly down the other side, to rejoin the road halfway between Áyii Anáryiri and Xylokériza (the other end of this track is optimistically signposted "Profítis Ilías 5", but in practice is virtually impassable, on two wheels or four). The better option is to turn right along the spine of the island, from where you'll have increasingly impressive views across towards the mainland over both coasts. Before long there's an obvious (unsigned) path heading down towards Áyii Anáryiri. Continue beyond this, and there's a less obvious path to Ayía Paraskeví, while the main trail curls back around towards the north, eventually descending to the coast road near Vréllos.

The Cyclades

SANTORÍNI AT SUNSET

The Cyclades

Named from the circle they form around the sacred island of Delos, the Cyclades (Kykládhes) offer Greece's best island-hopping. Each island has a strong, distinct character based on traditions, customs, topography and its historical development. Most are compact enough for a few days' exploration to show you a major part of their scenery and personality in a way that is impossible in Crete, Rhodes or most of the Ionian islands.

The islands do have some features in common. The majority are arid and rocky, and share the "Cycladic" style of brilliant-white cuboid architecture, a feature of which is the central **kástro** of the old island capitals. The typical kástro has just one or two entrances, and a continuous outer ring of houses with all their doors and windows on the inner side, so forming a single protective perimeter wall.

The impact of mass tourism has been felt more severely in the Cyclades than anywhere else in Greece; yet whatever the level of development, there are only three islands where it completely dominates their character in season: **Íos**, the original hippie island and still a paradise for hard-drinking backpackers; the volcanic cluster of **Santoríni**, a dramatic natural backdrop for luxury cruise liners; and **Mýkonos**, by far the most popular of the group, with its teeming old town, selection of gay, nudist and gay-nudist beaches, and sophisticated restaurants, clubs and hotels. After these, **Páros**, **Náxos** and **Mílos** are the most popular, their beaches and main towns packed at the height of the season. The once-tranquil **Lesser Cyclades** southeast of Náxos have become fashionable destinations in recent years, as have nearby **Amorgós**, and **Folégandhros** to the west. To avoid the hordes altogether the most promising islands are **Kýthnos** or **Sérifos** and for an even more remote experience **Síkinos**, **Kímolos** or **Anáfi**. For a completely different picture of the Cyclades, try the island of **Tínos** with its imposing pilgrimage church, or **Sýros** with its elegant Italianate townscape. Due to their proximity to Attica, **Ándhros** and **Kéa** are predictably popular weekend havens for Athenian families, while **Sífnos** remains a chic destination for tourists of all nationalities. The UNESCO site of **Delos** is certainly worth making time for, visited easily on a day-trip from Mýkonos. Note that the Cyclades is the group worst affected by the *meltémi*, which scatters sand and tablecloths with ease between mid-July and mid-August. Delayed or cancelled ferries are common, so if you're heading back to Athens to catch a flight, leave yourself a day's leeway.

ARRIVAL AND DEPARTURE
THE CYCLADES

BY PLANE
There are airports on Páros, Mýkonos, Santoríni, Sýros, Mílos and Náxos. In season, or during storms when ferries are idle, you have little chance of getting a seat on any flight at less than three days' notice, and tickets are predictably expensive. Expect off-season (Nov–April) frequencies to drop by at least eighty percent.

BY FERRY
Most of the Cyclades are served by main-line ferries from Pireás. Boats for Kéa, and seasonally elsewhere, depart from Lávrio. There are regular services from Rafína to Ándhros, Tínos and Mýkonos, with seasonal sailings elsewhere. Between May and Sept there are also a few weekly sailings to the most popular islands from Crete and

FOLÉGANDHROS

Highlights

❶ **Beaches of Mílos** Spectacular shorelines characterized by multicoloured rocks and volcanically heated sand. **See p.124**

❷ **Mýkonos Town** Labyrinthine lanes crammed with restaurants, boutiques and nightlife. **See p.142**

❸ **Delos** The Cyclades' sacred centre and holiest ancient site, birthplace of Apollo and Artemis. See p.147

❹ **Ermoúpolis, Sýros** The elegant capital of the Cyclades, an Italianate architectural jewel and once Greece's busiest port. **See p.150**

❺ **Church of Ekatondapylianí, Parikiá** An

imposing and ornate Paleochristian church on Páros, incorporating a number of impressive architectural styles. **See p.156**

❻ **Mount Zas, Náxos** The only must-do trek in the Cyclades: climb the archipelago's highest mountain. **See p.171**

❼ **Hóra, Folégandhros** The "town of five squares", free of traffic and sitting atop a spectacular cliff, arguably the most beautiful island capital. **See p.185**

❽ **Caldera of Santoríni** The geological wonder of a crater left by a colossal volcanic explosion, offering unforgettable sunset views. **See p.190**

HIGHLIGHTS ARE MARKED ON THE MAP ON P.110

the eastern Aegean. The best website for Greek ferry routes is ⓦ gtp.gr.

Agents and tickets In high season (particularly Easter, Aug and during elections), popular routes may be booked up, so it's important to check availability upon arrival in Greece and book your outward and inbound pre-flight ferry tickets well ahead (particularly those returning to Pireás from the most popular islands). That said, agents may have little advance information on ferry schedules, and purchasing a ticket too far in advance can lead to problems with delayed or cancelled boats.

Timetables The frequency of Pireás, Lávrio and Rafína sailings given in the chapter is from June to Aug, and the timings are for both direct and indirect services. For other

islands the listings are intended to give an idea of services from late June to early Sept, when most visitors tour the islands. During other months, expect schedules to be at or below the minimum level listed, with some ferries cancelled entirely because of the weather.

Catamaran and small-boat services These operate during the summer season from Pireás and Rafína, replacing winter ferries on some routes. Catamaran travel is expensive, but when time is an issue these high-speed craft are a welcome addition to the conventional fleet. The slower *Express Skopelitis* sails daily in season between Náxos and Amorgós, overnighting at the latter and connecting Irakliá, Skhinoússa, Áno Koufoníssi and Dhonoússa – for current info call Prekas agency on Amorgos ☎ 22850 71256.

Brief history

The Cyclades are the most quintessentially Greek of all the islands and their long history reflects that. The mining of **obsidian**, the black, sharp-edged volcanic glass used

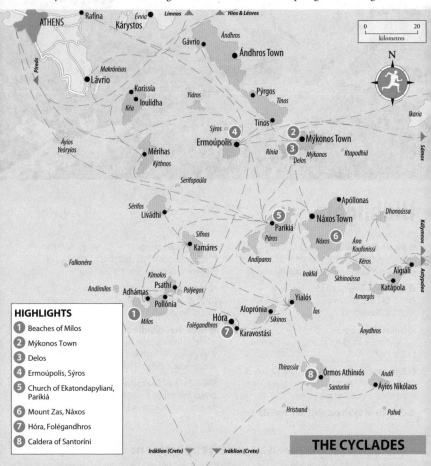

HIGHLIGHTS

1. Beaches of Mílos
2. Mýkonos Town
3. Delos
4. Ermoúpolis, Sýros
5. Church of Ekatondapylianí, Parikiá
6. Mount Zas, Náxos
7. Hóra, Folégandhros
8. Caldera of Santoríni

THE CYCLADES

for making implements, originated on Mílos; shards dating to 11,000 BC have been found deep in the Peloponnese, demonstrating early seaborne Paleolithic trade. The Bronze Age started here around 2800 BC and with it came the **Cycladic civilization**, notable for its sought-after geometric, minimalist figurines made of marble from **Páros** or **Náxos. Mining** for copper, silver and gold, combined with the islands' strategic position, turned them into trading centres.

By 2000 BC the Cretan Minoans had become influential in the area, particularly on **Santoríni**. Such influence, however, came to an end with a catastrophic volcanic eruption around 1600 BC. The Ionian Greeks arrived around 1000 BC and within two hundred years the first cities had appeared. **Delos** became a great religious centre in antiquity.

During and after the Persian wars, **Athens** gradually stripped away the wealth and influence of the **Delian Confederacy**. The Cyclades only regained prosperity during the Hellenistic period, as demonstrated by the construction of numerous large, impressive watchtowers, most notably on Náxos. The subsequent Roman occupation converted Delos back into a successful commercial centre, until a series of raids from the east eventually destroyed it. Under **Byzantine** rule, with little control or support from distant Constantinople, the islands were vulnerable to **pirates**, and settlements moved from the coast to inland, defensive **kástros**, where you find them today.

With the fall of Constantinople to the Crusaders in 1204, the Cyclades came under **Venetian** control and were divided up by adventurers under **Marco Sanudo** who set up the Náxos-based Duchy of the Aegean. Catholicism prospered, some vestiges of which are still found today on Sýros and Tínos. Most of the islands were taken by the **Ottomans** from the 1530s onwards, though Tínos held out until 1715. As they rightly considered the West a bigger threat, the Turks encouraged the Orthodox Church to fight a resurgence against the former Catholic majority.

After the revolution against the Ottoman Empire in 1821, the Cyclades became part of the Greek state in 1832 and **Sýros**, in particular, prospered, as the new state's largest port and a major industrial base. However, the development of **Pireás** and the 1893 opening of the **Corinth Canal** led to a sharp industrial and commercial decline. This was only reversed in the 1960s when the discovery of the pleasures of **Mýkonos** kick-started the tourism boom that continues unabated today.

Kéa

KÉA (Tziá), the nearest of the Cyclades to the mainland, is extremely popular with Athenian families in August and at weekends year-round; their impact has spread beyond the small resorts, and much of the coastline is peppered with holiday homes built with the locally quarried green-brown stone. Because so many visitors self-cater, there is a preponderance of villa accommodation and not as many tavernas as you might expect. However, outside August or weekends, the island, with its rocky, forbidding perimeter and inland oak and almond groves, is an enticing destination for those who enjoy a rural ramble: ten separate walking paths have been earmarked and are well signposted.

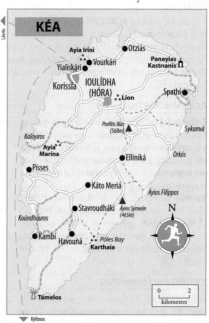

ANCIENT KARTHAIA

The only remains of any real significance from Kéa's past are fragments of temples of Apollo and Athena at **ancient Karthaia**, tucked away on the southeastern edge of the island above Póles Bay, with an excellent deserted twin beach. It is a good ninety-minute round-trip walk from the hamlet of Stavroudháki (on the paved road linking Ioulídha and Havouná), and the inland paved road is worth following along the island's summit from Ioulídha, as it affords fine views over the thousands of magnificent oaks, Kéa's most distinctive feature.

ARRIVAL AND GETTING AROUND

KÉA

By ferry There are regular ferries to Kéa from Lávrio on the mainland; only a few agents in Athens sell tickets for this service, so you'll probably need to get them in Lávrio. Once there, ferries dock at Korissía, on the northwest coast. You can buy ferry tickets from Kea Travel in Korissía (☎ 22880 21920, ⓦ keatravel.gr).

Destinations Ándhros (1 weekly; 8hr); Folégandhros (1 weekly; 12hr 30min); Íos (1 weekly; 11hr); Kýthnos (3 weekly; 1hr 15min); Lávrio (3–5 daily; 1hr); Mílos (1 weekly; 16hr); Mýkonos (1 weekly; 5hr 50min); Náxos (1 weekly; 9hr 40min); Páros (1 weekly; 7hr 20min); Síkinos (1 weekly; 12hr); Sýros

(3 weekly; 4hr); Tínos (1 weekly; 4hr 50min).

By bus Most visitors bring their cars along from Athens, so there are not many extensive bus services. You may need one of the six taxis available that meet boat arrivals. From mid-June to Sept there's a regular bus on a short route (every 30–45min) but with only a few stops.

By car or motorbike There is only one, expensive, rental outlet, so it's best to rent a car or motorbike in Athens – or at Athens International Airport, which is very close to Lávrio – and take it to Kéa, like Athenians do. The island has three petrol stations, all on the road to the port.

INFORMATION AND TOURS

Tourist office At the seafront in Korissía (daily 8am–2pm & 5pm to last boat arrival; ☎ 22880 21500).

Services There are two banks and one ATM in Korissía. Ioulídha has one bank and one ATM. The island's only post

office is opposite the archeological museum (see opposite) in Ioulídha.

Tours Kea Tours (☎ 22880 22004, ⓦ keatours.gr) in Korissía offers walks and excursions around the island.

Korissía

The small port of **KORISSÍA** is unlike any other in the Cyclades; with its red-tiled roofs and Neoclassical houses, it could be Pláka-by-the-Sea. It is very convenient as a base; from there you can easily get by bus to Otziás (6km), Ioulídha (6km) or Písses (16km). Although the port beach, **Áyios Yeóryios**, is adequate, there is better swimming at **Yialiskári**, a small, eucalyptus-fringed cove after the eastern promontory on the road to Vourkári.

ACCOMMODATION

KORISSÍA

Brillante Zoi ☎ 22880 22685/86, ⓦ brillante-hotel.gr. A comfortable hotel on the middle of the port beach, with a beautifully overgrown garden, idiosyncratic furnishings, spacious rooms and a sumptuous breakfast. The chatty, welcoming owner will feel more like an old acquaintance than your landlady. **€70**

Karthea ☎ 22880 21204, ⓦ hotelkarthea.gr. Dated 1970s hotel, but very centrally located at the beginning of the port beach. Followers of modern history will be interested to learn that this is where Greek junta leaders were held under house arrest in 1974. Breakfast included. **€60**

★**Keos Katoikies** ☎ 22880 21661, ⓦ keos.gr. Cool, contemporary minimalist studios, each one with its own large balcony in a dramatic setting overlooking Korissía bay. Make sure you watch the sunset from the adjoining café. The room price includes an excellent English buffet breakfast. Free wi-fi at reception. Easter–Oct. **€100**

Porto Kea ☎ 22880 22870, ⓦ portokea-suites.com. Luxurious hotel behind the main road and by the church of Áyios Yeóryios, with a large swimming pool and complimentary internet access. It has its own trendy bar, *Ammos*, on the beach in front offering free chairs for hotel clients. Breakfast included. Easter–Oct. **€410**

EATING AND DRINKING

En Plo ☎ 6948 605 176. Opposite the ferry disembarkation point, this snack-bar serves delicious desserts. Try the

chocolate soufflé with a cappuccino for €5 while watching the world go by and the ferries dock. It's a lively spot in the early evening. April–Oct daily 8am–1am; Nov–March Fri & Sat 8am–1am.

★**Fillipas** ☎ 22880 21690. Built in local Kéa stone and sitting on the hill above Keos Katoikies, this is the best grill restaurant on the island. Although often booked for functions, they will always find you a table and serve you promptly. Try the giant steaks or its signature beefburger filled with local cheese (€8). April–Oct daily 6pm–1am;

Nov–March Fri & Sat 6pm–1am.

Magazés ☎ 22880 21104, ⊛ kearestaurant.gr. The best in the cluster of the port restaurants, this traditional taverna with a small but tasty range of Greek dishes also offers fresh fish, often caught by the speargun of the owner. If you crave meat instead, try the baked pork with potatoes for €9. April–Oct daily 9am–midnight.

Ioulídha

Kéa's capital, **IOULÍDHA** (Hóra), with its winding flagstoned paths, is beautifully situated in an amphitheatric fold in the hills. It is by no means a typical Cycladic town, but is architecturally the most interesting settlement on the island. Accordingly it has numerous bars and bistros, much patronized in August and at weekends, but during other times the town is quiet, its atmospheric, labyrinthine lanes excluding vehicles.

The lower reaches of the town stretch across a spur to the **kástro**, a tumbledown Venetian fortress incorporating stones from an ancient temple of Apollo. Ioulídha's **Archeological Museum** (summer Tues–Sat 8.30am–3.30pm; winter Thurs–Sun 8am–3pm; €3; ☎ 22880 22079) displays extensive finds from the four ancient city-states of Kéa, its highlight being thirteen female Minoan-style statues. Fifteen-minutes' walk northeast of Ioulídha on the path toward Otziás, you pass the **Lion of Kéa**, a sixth-century BC sculpture carved out of an outcrop of rock, 6m long and 3m high.

ACCOMMODATION AND EATING   **IOULÍDHA**

En Lefko ☎ 22880 22155. On the street between Hóra's two squares, this coffee shop has one of the most romantic gardens, suspended over the cliffs and overlooking the port and beyond. Dimly lit, this is the perfect place to snuggle up with a cappuccino (€4). April–Oct daily 8am–2am.

Hotel Serie ☎ 22880 22355. Only 100m from the Ioulídha bus stop and employing a tasteful colour combination of blue and orange throughout – from the stone

building itself to the furnishings – this is maybe the best-situated boutique hotel on the island with views both of Ioulídha and the valley below. Easter–Oct. **€70**

★**Rolandos** Main square ☎ 22880 22224. The chef, Rolandos, comes from Corfu and serves a traditional Greek menu with an Ionian flavour. His *moussaká* (€8) – using courgettes instead of potatoes – is as famed as his house wine. Easter–Oct daily 10am–2am.

The north coast

Kéa's **north coast** attracts the most visitors. **VOURKÁRI**, strung out around the next bay, a couple of kilometres northeast of Korissía, is a fishing village, arguably more attractive than Korissía, serving as a hangout for the yachting set. Another 4km further, **OTZIÁS** has the biggest and best beach on the northern shore though it's more exposed to prevailing *meltémi* winds.

The eighteenth-century monastery of **Panayías Kastrianís** (June–Sept sunrise–sunset) is 7km east along a surfaced road from Otziás. From here you can take the pleasant walk on dirt tracks and occasional paths to Ioulídha in another two hours. Further on, **Spathí**, 3km south of the monastery on a dirt road, is by far the island's finest beach.

ACCOMMODATION AND EATING   **THE NORTH COAST**

Anemousa Otziás ☎ 22880 21335, ⊛ anemousa.gr. A modern cluster of villas alternating the brown-gold Kéa stone with whitewashed walls. The colour scheme extends to the tasteful furnishings inside the spacious studios which can accommodate up to four adults. April–Oct. **€90**

Aristos Vourkári ☎ 22880 21475. Don't be fooled by the look of this sleepy fish and seafood taverna at the entrance

to the village; it is renowned for its crayfish spaghetti (€20–30), drawing customers from all over the island. April–Oct daily noon–midnight; Nov–March Fri & Sat noon–midnight.

Strofi tou Mimi Vourkári ☎ 22880 21480. The locals are almost equally divided on whether this place, on the corner of the road towards Otziás, or *Aristos* (see above) is the best fish taverna on the island. You'll have to make up your own mind by dining in both. *Strofí tou Mimi* is only slightly cheaper. April–Oct daily 7pm–midnight.

Tis Annas Otziás ☏ 22887 21137. Located at the end of the beach, this is a small but popular taverna with a traditional island interior. Anna is long gone but the family cooks on: specialities include pork stew with haloumi cheese and a variation of coq au vin with pasta (€8). Decent house wine, too. Daily noon–midnight.

The south

The road southwest of Ioulídha twists around a scenic agricultural valley and emerges at a large sandy beach at **Písses**. Beyond here, the asphalt peters out at the end of the 5km road south to **Koúndhouros beach**, which consists of two sheltered coves popular with yachters. A further 2km south, at **Kambí**, there's a nice little beach and a good taverna of the same name.

Kýthnos

One of the lesser known and most low-key of the larger Cyclades, **KÝTHNOS** is an antidote to the overdevelopment you may encounter elsewhere, so much so that credit cards are still not accepted in many places. Few foreigners visit, and the island – known also as Thermiá, after its renowned hot springs – is even quieter than Kéa, particularly to the south where drives or long hikes from **Dhryopídha** to its coastal coves are the primary diversion. This is truly a place to sprawl on sunbed-free beaches without having to jostle for space.

ARRIVAL AND GETTING AROUND

KÝTHNOS

By ferry Boats dock at the west coast in Mérihas. There's a frequent service from/to Lávrio and Pireás, but ferries to nearby Kéa, Sérifos or other islands are sparse.

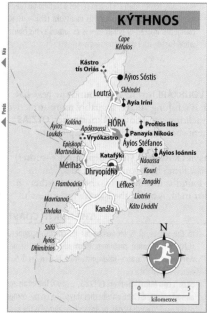

Destinations Folégandhros (1–2 weekly; 8hr 30min); Íos (1 weekly; 9hr 20min); Kéa (2–4 weekly; 1hr 10min); Kímolos (1–2 weekly; 13hr); Lávrio (1–3 daily; 1hr 40min– 2hr 45min); Mílos (2–4 weekly; 4hr); Náxos (1 weekly; 7hr); Mýkonos (1 weekly; 4hr); Páros (1 weekly; 5hr 30min); Pireás (4–5 weekly; 3hr); Sérifos (3–5 weekly; 1hr 30min); Sífnos (2–4 weekly; 2hr 15min); Síkinos (1 weekly; 7hr 30min); Sýros (2 weekly; 2hr 40min); Tínos (1 weekly; 3hr 50min).

By bus Buses run from Mérihas port around six times daily from early June to Sept, serving Hóra (15min), Loutrá (30min), Dhryopídha (30min) and Kanála (45min).

By boat There's a *kaïki* from Mérihas (4 daily; ☏ 22810 32104) to the northern beaches of Apókrousi and Kolóna.

By car or motorbike Halivelakis rental agency (☏ 22810 32506, ⓦ halivelakis.gr) operate a stand at the port during ship arrivals even late at night.

INFORMATION AND ACTIVITIES

Tourist office A helpful information office is open by the jetty during ferry arrivals, even on Sundays or late at night.

Services There's one bank and two ATMs in Mérihas: one up the steps near the disembarkation point, and a second on the harbour road. Hotels and restaurants do not as a rule accept credit cards. Hóra has the only post office (Mon–Fri 9.30am–2pm).

Diving Aqua Team (☎ 22810 31333, ⓦ aquakythnos .com), is located opposite the spa in Loutrá. They offer PADI, ANDI and IAHD diving courses; they also provide special offer package deals of varying prices, some of which include accommodation.

Mérihas and around

MÉRIHAS is an attractive ferry and fishing port – but not really the place to base your stay. The closest beach of any repute is the fine sandy cove of **Martinakia**, a ten-minute stroll north of the port, while **Episkopí**, a 500m stretch of clean grey sand, is thirty minutes' walk further north. About an hour's walk northwest of Episkopí are the better and more popular beaches of **Apókroussi** and **Kolóna**, the latter a very picturesque sand spit joining Kýthnos to the islet of **Áyios Loukás**.

ACCOMMODATION AND EATING | MÉRIHAS AND AROUND

Martinos Studios ☎ 22810 32469, ⓦ martinos -kythnos.gr. Studios only 30m from the sea and over-looking the harbour, with local furnishings, stone floors, fridge, a/c, TV, kitchenette and phone. Reception is closed in the afternoon. Room size varies and some can be spacious while others are on the small side. No breakfast. May–Sept. **€40**

★ **To Kandouni** ☎ 22810 32220. For those who fancy meat in a sea of fish tavernas: here is an excellent grill – situated near the port police – with many different starters and salads as well as specialities such as *sfoungáto* (local cheese croquettes) for €6. April–Oct daily noon–1am.

Villa Elena Martinakia ☎ 22810 32275, ⓦ villa-elena .gr. Two-storey self-catering maisonettes situated on a slope with superb sea views over the Aegean and a stone's throw from the best beach near Mérihas. Fully equipped kitchenette, TV, parking and port transfers available. April–Sept. **€70**

Hóra

HÓRA lies 7.5km northeast of Mérihas, in the middle of the island. Though the town looks unpromising at first sight, wander into the narrow streets beyond the initial square and you'll find a wonderful network of alleyways, weaving their way past shops, churches and through tiny squares with colourful cafés. The early nineteenth-century church of **Áyios Ioánnis Theológos** is worth a visit for its elaborate wooden iconostasis. However, its most valuable possession is a miraculous seventeenth-century icon of the three matriarchs (Elisabeth, Anne and Virgin Mary), said to have been found floating in the sea by local fishermen.

ACCOMMODATION AND EATING | HÓRA

Apocalypse ☎ 22810 31272. Relatively cheap (beer €3) café-bar, opposite the main church of – appropriately enough – St John, playing anything from trance to Greek popular tunes. Daily 7am–midnight.

Filoxenia ☎ 22810 31644, ⓦ filoxenia-kythnos.gr. Welcoming *pension* next to the main square, with clean, basic rooms arranged around a flowery courtyard. It's a convenient base if you want to travel by bus around the island, but still sample whatever nightlife there is after-wards. **€50**

Messaria ☎ 22810 31672/73. Large restaurant by the village entrance that offers the Hóra speciality of local coq au vin for €9. Unlike other establishments in Hóra that close during the day as the clients are out on the beaches, this one's open for lunch, as well as dinner. Daily noon–midnight.

Loutrá and around

The resort of **LOUTRÁ**, 4.5km north of Hóra, is named after its mineral thermal baths. Its nineteenth-century **spa** was designed by Ernst Ziller, the architect of many of Greece's finest Neoclassical public buildings; it's rather grotty inside, but you can enjoy the hot springs for free on the right-hand side of Loutrá's small beach, where they run into the sea. A nicer spot for a dip, though, is the bay of **Ayía Iríni**, 1km east.

Just north of Loutrá, at **Maroula**, Mesolithic graves dating to about the eighth millennium BC suggest Kýthnos may have been one of the earliest inhabited Cycladic islands; other sites indicate copper mining and smelting. About a ninety-minute walk from Loutrá, on Cape Kéfalos, lie the picturesque ruins of the medieval capital **Kástro tís Oriás**, once home to around five thousand people, but now abandoned.

ACCOMMODATION   LOUTRÁ AND AROUND

Meltemi ☎ 22810 31271, ⓦ meltemihotel-kythnos.gr. On the road out of Loutrá this hotel offers dependable value, with its beautifully tiled walls, a landscaped garden and different colour schemes in each room. Breakfast €6; half board €20; free wi-fi; pick-ups from Mérihas €10. April–Oct. **€85**

★**Porto Klaras** ☎ 22810 31276, ⓦ porto-klaras.gr. A hotel worth making the trip to Loutrá just to stay in; its rooms are huge, with decorated carved recesses and large, sculpted beds, while its balconies – some of which come with sofas – have great port views. Free wi-fi, safebox, and, for those who dislike a/c, there are ceiling fans as well. April–Oct. **€60**

EATING

Araxovoli ☎ 22810 31082, ⓦ araxovoli.gr. A fish taverna conveniently situated in the middle of the quay that also offers tasty cooked meals (dish of the day €10). If you want to eat calamari, octopus, crayfish or lobster on the island, this is the place to make a beeline for. Daily 8am–1am.

Sofrano ☎ 22810 31436. A waterfront restaurant for the yachting jet-set, this is the most romantic establishment on the island, complete with candlelit tables, flower-filled vases, pink tablecloths and bundles of atmosphere. Thankfully, the food (mains €12) matches the decor. March–Nov daily 9am–midnight.

Dhryopídha and the south

From Hóra you can drive south to **DHRYOPÍDHA**; more visually appealing than Hóra by virtue of spanning a well-watered valley, its red-tiled roofs are reminiscent of Spain or Tuscany. It was once the island's capital, built around one of Greece's largest **caves**, the Katafýki, that served as a hiding place from corsairs. South of Dhryopídha, **KANÁLA** is a relaxed alternative to Loutrá, with its **Panayía Kanála** church set in a tiny but pleasant pine woodland and home to a miracle-working icon by the seventeenth-century Cretan master, Skordhilis.

ACCOMMODATION AND EATING   DHRYOPÍDHA AND THE SOUTH

Akroyali Áyios Dhimítrios ☎ 22810 32208. Modern villa complex at the end of Áyios Dhimítrios beach decorated in lime-washed white and comprising large suites with sea views and separate, fully equipped kitchens. Restaurant in the premises. May–Sept. **€40**

Bouritis Kanála ☎ 22810 32350. Large self-catering apartments and studios on the beach, all with balcony, sea views, a/c, TV and kitchen, sharing a delightfully tended garden with a BBQ. There is also a well-stocked supermarket in the premises. **€40**

Sérifos

SÉRIFOS has long languished outside the mainstream of history and modern tourism. Little has happened here since Perseus returned with Medusa's head in time to save his mother, Danaë, from being ravished by the local king Polydectes – turning him, his court and the green island into stone. Many would-be visitors are deterred by the apparently barren, hilly interior, which, with the stark, rocky coastline, makes Sérifos appear uninhabited until the ferry turns into postcard-picturesque Livádhi Bay. This element of surprise continues as you slowly discover a number of lovely **beaches** around the island. Sadly, there are still scars from a 2013 forest fire that reached the port; thankfully, the businesses and locals survived intact. Still, because of a tourism downturn after this event, this may well be the best-value Greek island at the moment, with prices stable or inching downwards.

Sérifos is also great for serious **walkers**, who can head for several small villages in the under-explored interior, plus some isolated coves. Many people still keep livestock and produce their own cognac-red wines, which are an acquired taste.

SÉRIFOS

Platýs Yialós
Sykamiá
Taxiarhón
Mónastery
Galaní
Kallítsos
Kéndarhos
Pýrgos
Panayía
Áyios Ioánnis
Avéssalos
Reservoir
Psilí Ámmos
HÓRA
Áyios Sóstis
Megálo Horió
Kástro tís Griás
Liá
Megálo Livádhi
Koutalás
Livádhi
Gánema
Livadhákia
Voús
Kaló Ambéli
Kardví
Rámos

N
0   2
kilometres

Páros
Kýthnos
Sífnos & Mílos

3

ARRIVAL AND GETTING AROUND
SÉRIFOS

By ferry There's a fast catamaran service to Pireás taking only 2hr, and there are good connections in the summer to many other islands. The port is at the Livádhi promontory. Destinations Folégandhros (0–1 weekly; 2hr 30min); Íos (0–1 weekly; 4hr 30min); Kéa (1 weekly; 6hr 30min); Kímolos (1–2 weekly; 3hr 30min); Kýthnos (4 weekly; 1hr 25min); Lávrio (1 weekly; 8hr); Mílos (2–4 daily; 1hr 45min); Mýkonos (1 weekly; 3hr 45min); Páros (1 weekly; 2hr 10min); Pireás (6–8 weekly; 2–4hr); Santoríni (1 weekly; 6hr); Sífnos (2–4 daily; 35min); Síkinos (0–1 weekly; 3hr 40min); Sýros (1–2 weekly; 3hr 20min–5hr 45min).

By bus The bus stop and timetable are at the base of the

yacht and fishing-boat jetty. There's a circular bus route serving Panayía–Galaní–Kéndarhos–Áyios Ioánnis–Psilí Ámmos (2–7 daily; circular route 1hr), Hóra (every 30min in summer; 15min; the last weekend bus from Hóra is after midnight) and Panayía–Galaní–Kéndarhos–Áyios Ioánnis–Psilí Ámmos–Méga Livádhi–Koutalás (2 daily; 30min). The bus stop has a list of the taxis on the island and their phone numbers (Port–Hóra €7).

By car or motorbike For car and motorbike rental try Blue Bird (☎ 22810 51511, ⓦ rentacar-bluebird.gr), next to the petrol station in Livádhi, or Kartsonaki Bros (☎ 22810 51534, ⓦ kartsonakis.gr) on the hill towards Livadhákia.

INFORMATION AND ACTIVITIES

Tourist information Krinas Travel (daily 9am–9pm; ☎ 22810 51500) opposite the disembarkation point has become by default the starting point for help to visitors on the island.

Services There are two ATMs along the seafront in Livádhi. The island's post office is in the lowest quarter of Hóra.

Diving, snorkelling and boat trips Avlómonas beach (see below) is the headquarters of Sérifos Scuba Divers (☎ 6932 570 552, ⓦ serifosscubadivers.gr), who operate scuba-diving and snorkelling trips plus day-long boat excursions during July and August.

Livádhi and around

Most visitors stay in the port, **LIVÁDHI**, which is set in a wide greenery-fringed bay and handy for most of the island's beaches. The usually calm bay is a magnet for yachts, here to take on fresh water which, despite its barren appearance, Sérifos has in abundance. Livádhi and the neighbouring cove of Livadhákia are certainly the easiest places for finding rooms, along with any amenities you might need, which are scarce elsewhere.

The beaches

The very attractive curve of **Avlómonas**, the long Livádhi town beach, has the advantage of overlooking the inland capital, so that when you're swimming in the sea you have a great inland view. Heading away from the dock, climb over the southerly headland to reach **Livadhákia**, a golden-sand beach, shaded by tamarisk trees. A further ten-minutes' stroll across the southern headland brings you to the smaller **Karávi** beach, with its blue-green clear waters but no shade or facilities.

North of Livádhi Bay and accessible by bus in summer – or a 45-minute walk (3km) along a (mostly) surfaced road – is **Psilí Ámmos**, a long, sheltered, award-winning white-sand beach, backed by a large reservoir, and considered the island's best. It's possible to continue on the road, then by path for ten minutes to the larger, but more exposed, **Áyios Ioánnis** beach. Additionally, two more sandy coves, **Liá** (naturist) and **Áyios Sóstis**, hide at the far eastern flank of the island opposite the islet Voús; they are popular with the locals, and accessible via a dirt track off the road to Psilí Ámmos.

ACCOMMODATION
LIVÁDHI AND AROUND

Areti Headland overlooking Livádhi ☎ 22810 51479, ⓦ serifosisland.gr/areti/. Attractively positioned hotel, with a lovely communal terrace fronting a tiny beach and the entrance to the bay. They also have studios and apartments further out for around €50. Breakfast included. April–Oct. **€50**

★**Coralli Camping** Livadhákia Beach ☎ 22810 51500, ⓦ coralli.gr. Superbly located and managed camping with a communal pool, restaurant, bar, minimarket and free wi-fi. This has been named by the Greek *Vima* newspaper as the best campsite in Greece. They also run the more modern four-person *Coralli Studios* (€100), closer to town. April–Oct. **€16**

Maïstrali Beginning of Livádhi beach ☎ 22810 51220, ⓦ hotelmaistrali.com. Seventies-built and furnished hotel but, being the tallest building in town, it has balconies (many frequented by nesting birds) with the best views. It's at the start of the beach, so is situated conveniently for everything: nightlife, beach and restaurants. Breakfast and transfers included. April–Oct. **€55**

Naïas Between Livádhi and Livadhákia ☎ 22810 51749, ⓦ naiasserifos.com. A slightly dated, but comfortable, good-value hotel on the headland between Livádhi and Livadhákia, with a sociable owner; come here to make friends, not just pass through. All rooms with balconies, some with sea views. Twenty percent deposit for reservations required. Breakfast included. **€55**

Vasso Road to Livadhákia ☎ 22810 51346. Very basic but spacious and spotless rooms – some with kitchens – looking inwards into a common courtyard. If airiness and roominess are your thing, look no further – these are simply exceptional value. **€40**

EATING AND DRINKING

Kalis Waterfront ☎ 6942 467 987. One of the most popular ouzerí, where you may have to queue to get a table; you may be tempted to stuff yourself with just its excellent mezédhes, but hang on and try the delicious crayfish spaghetti for €14. Daily 1am–1am.

Metalleio Livádhi ☎ 22810 51755. Hidden behind the coastal road, this is one of the few restaurants in the Cyclades where you may have to book. Great service and food without having to break the bank; imaginative mains from €12 and desserts that can't be finished. After midnight it becomes a club with occasional live bands. Easter–Oct daily 6pm–1am.

NIGHTLIFE

Nightlife is lively and mostly clustered in or near the Livádhi seafront mini-mall.

Shark Livádhi ☎ 6932 411 657. Set in a conspicuous roof garden above the seafront mini-mall, this is an institution on the island and plays mostly Top 10 hits. It has a good selection of bottled beers for €5 and some strong cocktails from €7. May–Sept daily 9pm–5am.

Yacht club Livádhi Beach ☎ 22810 51888. Hard to imagine that this was the first and only taverna in Livádhi back in 1938. It seems that every person under 30 on the island will come here to be seen at some point during the night, every night. Easter–Oct daily 8am–4am.

Hóra

Quiet and atmospheric, **HÓRA** – only 2km from Livádhi – is one of the most unspoilt villages of the Cyclades. The best sights are in the **upper town**: follow signs to the kástro to reach the top via steep and occasionally overgrown stairways. The central square, Ayíou Athanasíou, just northwest of the summit, has an attractive church and a small but colourful Neoclassical town hall. From the main bus stop, starting from the

Vátrahos Bar (see below), a circular signposted loop ("route A") takes you to the church of Áyios Konstandínos where on a clear day you can see as far as Sífnos.

EATING AND DRINKING HÓRA

Aloni ☎ 22810 52603. A restaurant 100m below the bus stop with superb westerly views over Livádhi, that offers tasty Mediterranean specialities (including rabbit in lemon sauce for €8). More locals than tourists frequent it at weekends because of its live Greek music evenings. Definitely book ahead. Daily 6pm–1am.

Stou Stratou ☎ 22810 52566, ⓦ stoustratou.com. An atmospheric café on the main square with a poetry-strewn

menu which offers a nice alternative to eating on the busy seafront down below. Its chocolate cake (€5) is renowned all over the island. April–Sept daily 9am–2am.

Vatrahos Bar ☎ 22810 52687. Just up from the final bus stop, this is a cosy bar/pub for people who just want to drink cold beer, sit at the bar and listen to the bass bouncing off the walls and down their solar plexus. April–Oct daily 9am–3am.

The north and west

If you venture north from Psilí Ámmos (see opposite) your best bet for a swim is the sheltered cove of **Platýs Yialós** at the extreme northeastern tip of the island, reached easily by a partly paved road. Immediately after the Platýs Yialós turn is the fortified fifteenth-century monastery of **Taxiarhón**, once home to sixty monks but currently inhabited by only one. Treasures of the monastic **katholicón** include an ivory-inlaid bishop's throne, silver lamps from Egypt (to where many Serifiots emigrated during the nineteenth century) and the finely carved **iconostasis**. Call before you arrive (☎ 22810 51027) to arrange a visit; donations are expected.

If you drive north from Hóra, you reach a junction in the road; follow the signs west for Megálo Horió and on to **Megálo Livádhi**, a remote but lovely beach resort 10km west of Hóra. Iron and copper ores were once exported from here, via a loading bridge that still hangs over the water.

An alternative turning just below Megálo Horió leads 3.5km to the small mining and fishing port of **Koutalás**, that suffered the most from the forest fires of 2013. The winding track above the village leads east back to Livádhi, but there are no places to buy refreshments on the two-hour journey back. A side track en route leads down to the very pretty but shadeless **Kaló Ambéli** beach.

Sífnos

SÍFNOS is prettier, tidier and more cultivated than its northern neighbours. In keeping with the island's somewhat high-class clientele, camping rough is forbidden, and nude sunbathing is not tolerated. The island's modest size makes it eminently explorable, and there's a vast network of paths that are mostly easy to follow. The areas to head for are the port, **Kamáres**, the island's capital **Apollonía**, as well as the east and south coasts. There is nothing in the north worth a peek, except maybe the small fishing village of **Herrónisos**, but even that is too far and offers too little for the first-time visitor. Sífnos has a strong tradition of **pottery** (going back as early as the third century BC) and has long been esteemed for its distinctive cuisine, with sophisticated casseroles baked in the clay-fired *gástres* (pots), from where the word gastronomy derives. The island is perhaps best appreciated today, however, for its many beautifully situated **churches** and **monasteries**, and for the beautiful scenery around **Vathý** in the far southwest (see p.124).

ARRIVAL AND GETTING AROUND SÍFNOS

By ferry Sífnos is better connected with the mainland and with the rest of the Cyclades than its northern neighbours. Ferries dock at the port in Kamáres on the east coast.

Destinations Folégandhros (2–6 weekly; 1hr 30min–4hr); Íos (1–3 weekly; 3hr); Kéa (1 weekly; 7hr 40min); Kímolos (2–3 weekly; 1hr 30min–2hr); Kýthnos (1–3 weekly;

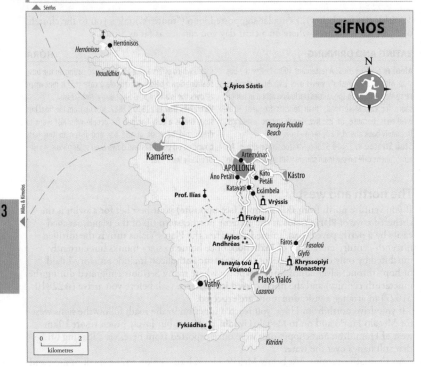

2hr 15min); Mílos (2–5 daily; 1hr–1hr 20min); Mýkonos (1 weekly; 5hr); Páros (2 weekly; 3hr 20min); Pireás (3–5 daily; 2hr–5hr 30min); Santoríni (2 weekly; 5hr 30min); Sérifos (2–3 daily; 25min–1hr); Síkinos (2–3 weekly; 2–5hr); Sýros (1–2 weekly; 3hr–5hr 30min).

By bus The bus service is excellent, and most of the roads are good. Buses leave regularly from Kamáres to Apollonía/Artemónas (every 30min; 20min); for all other destinations you have to change at Apollonía. Buses leave for Kamáres

(8–10 daily) from Apollonía's central square, Platía Iróon. There is a second station by the *Anthoussa* hotel (see opposite) for Platys Gialós (6–8 daily; 30min), Fáros (5–6 daily; 20min), Kástro (5–6 daily; 20min), Vathý (3–4 daily; 50min) and Herrónisos (3 daily; 1hr).

By car or motorbike For rental try *Stavros Hotel* (see opposite) and No1 (☏ 22840 33791/93, ⊛ protomotocar.gr), right by the disembarkation point in Kamáres.

INFORMATION

Tourist office There's an information centre opposite the ferry disembarkation point (Mon–Fri 8am–3pm).

Services There are three banks and four ATMs in Apollonía; the post office is beside the central square. *Stavros Hotel* (see opposite) in Kamáres operates an internet and fax hub available to nonresidents at €4/hr.

Travel agents Katsoularis Travel on Stenó in Apollonía (☏ 22840 31004) can help you find accommodation, tours and ferry tickets. Aegean Thesaurus (☏ 22840 33151/33527), on Kamáres main street, can arrange accommodation across the island.

Kamáres

KAMÁRES, the island's port, with its gorgeous, clean, sheltered beach stretching to the headland of **Ayía Marína** opposite the port, is tucked away in a long, steep-sided valley that cuts into the cliffs of the island's western side. A compact resort, though with concrete blocks of accommodations edging up to the base of the hill-slopes, Kamáres' seafront road is crammed with bars, travel agencies, ice-cream shops and restaurants.

ACCOMMODATION

Boulis ☎ 22840 32122, ⓦhotelboulis.gr. If you want to wake up and head straight for a swim, this hotel – arranged around a hedged and vine-covered courtyard in the middle of Kamáres beach – is the place for you. Optional breakfast (€8) in the adjoining, atmospheric café. Easter–Oct. **€65**

Dina's rooms Ayía Marína ☎ 22840 32364. On the furthest side of the beach, these spotless rooms have the best views in Kamáres and are best suited to those who prefer quieter, more secluded accommodation. "Rooms" here is a misnomer – there are hotels that offer much less. May–Sept. **€50**

Makis Camping ☎ 22840 32366 or ☎ 6945 946 339, ⓦmakiscamping.gr. A campsite on Kamáres beach with excellent facilities such as a café-bar, free wi-fi, minimarket and a laundry open to nonguests. The obliging, friendly owner is a mine of information about the island. There are also on-site double studios. May–Sept. Camping **€16**, studios **€30**

★ **Stavros** ☎ 22840 33383, ⓦ sifnostravel.com. A first-class, extremely helpful and reasonably priced hotel on the harbourfront with spacious rooms, free wi-fi and internet facilities. With a wide range of services, it can serve as a one-point information and booking centre for trips and the like. **€60**

EATING AND DRINKING

Follie Ayía Marína ☎ 22840 31183, ⓦcafefolie.gr. Is it a bar? Is it a beach club? Is it a nightspot? A bit of everything, really; Athenian-owned and operated, it is full for breakfast, is rather muted in the afternoon, but packs them in again for evening drinks and dinner (€8). Don't let all this multi-functioning confuse you, though; the food in the restaurant is very good. Easter–Sept daily 8am–3am.

Ísalos Ayía Marina ☎ 22840 33716. Café-bar and restaurant with a shaded terrace offering more classy cuisine than anywhere else on the island. Its Greek and International menu is highly imaginative, matching the assiduously sophisticated decor. Try its marinated fish selection for €10. Easter–Sept daily 8am–midnight.

The Old Captain Bar Kamáres ☎ 22840 31990. A beach bar offering deckchairs during the day, this place really comes alive after sunset when a DJ plays eclectic rock music catering for the young people who haven't made it to Apollonía. Cocktails €8. Easter–Oct daily 11am–3am.

★ **Simos** ☎ 22840 32353. Family-run, popular taverna on the Kamáres main street with a reputation second to none among the islanders, offering meat and vegetables from the owners' farm. Their casseroles (€8) are as traditional as they are tasty and an absolute must. Daily noon–midnight.

Apollonía and around

A steep bus ride from Kamáres takes you 5.5km up to **APOLLONÍA**, the centre of an amalgam of five hilltop villages that have merged over the years into one continuous community: immediately north is **Áno Petáli**, which then runs into **Artemónas**, about fifteen minutes away on foot. With white buildings, stepped paths, belfries and flower-draped balconies, it is very scenic, though not self-consciously so.

Sights in Apollonía include numerous churches, while on the central square, the **folk museum** (April–Oct daily 9.30am–2pm & 6–10pm; €1) with its collection of textiles, lace, costumes and weaponry, is worth a visit. Behind and parallel to the square runs the pedestrian street, **To Stenó**, lined with restaurants, bars and fancy shops. The main pedestrian street north from the square leads via Áno Petáli to Artemónas, past the eighteenth-century church of **Panayía Ouranofóra**, which incorporates fragments of a seventh-century BC temple of Apollo and a relief of St George over the door.

Taking the road south to **Katavatí** you'll pass, after a few minutes, the beautiful empty monastery of Firáyia; fifteen minutes further along there's a turning to a vast Mycenaean **archeological site** (Tues–Sun 8.30am–3pm; €2). Next to it stands the church of **Áyios Andhréas**, from where there are tremendous views over the neighbouring islands.

ACCOMMODATION

Anthoussa Hotel Apollonía ☎ 22840 31431, ⓦhotel anthousa-sifnos.gr. A good and solid enough hotel with comfortable rooms, balconies with views and tasteful light-blue decor, plus a terrific patisserie below: try its home-made cakes, chocolates and ice cream for breakfast, if you dare. Free wi-fi. Breakfast €7.50. Easter–Nov. **€50**

Mrs Dina Áno Petáli ☎ 22840 31125. A string of well-furnished rooms and studios in a peaceful position with panoramic views, next to the four-star *Petali Village* (see p.122) in the cathedral area but at a fraction of the price. The landlady is almost never there and will leave you to chill out in peace. May–Oct. **€45**

★**Petali Village** Áno Petáli ☎22840 33024, ⓦhotel petali.gr. A luxurious hotel in a quiet position, easy to fall in love with, offering parking, jacuzzi, pool and free wi-fi.

Its nautical decoration and verandas overlooking the east of the island offer relaxation worth the price tag. Breakfast included. **€125**

EATING AND DRINKING

Mamma Mia Apollonía ☎22840 33086. On the Áno Petáli steps, this is the surprising meeting point of the island's youth, but don't let that put you off. If you find yourself tired of *moussaká* and *pastítsio* and, of course, fish, then have a large wood-fired pizza here for €10; that's what the Sifniots themselves do. A branch also operates on Platys Yialós. June–Sept daily 7pm–2am.

Okyalos Apollonía ☎22840 32060, ⓦen.okyalos-sifnos .gr/. This restaurant on the main street is established as the

in-place to dine, though with loud music while you eat it's worth making a reservation for the roof garden – if you can. Try their *Mastelo* roast lamb for €15. Daily 7pm–late.

Tou Apostoli to Koutoúki Stenó ☎22840 33186. One of the better eating establishments but rather pricey, offering island and other Greek specialities. This is the best place to try the Sifniot casseroles; choose either from its selection of veal- or pork-baked dishes (€13). April–Sept daily 7am–11am.

NIGHTLIFE

Argo Stenó ☎22840 31114, ⓦargobar.gr. Long-standing island club playing everything from classical music to modern rock. While weekdays are mostly the realm of young tourists with their drunken antics, the live music shows on Fridays and Saturdays attract all ages and are

considerably better behaved. April–Oct daily 11pm–late.

Xodos Stenó ☎6972 558 857. Out of Apollonía on the way to Platys Yialós, this is a dance club with local and international DJs catering to a mostly young clientele. June–Sept Fri & Sat midnight–6am.

The east coast

Most of Sífnos' coastal settlements are along the less precipitous **east coast**, within a modest distance of Apollonía and its surrounding cultivated plateau. **Kástro** may be more appealing than the resorts of **Fáros** and **Platýs Yialós**, which can get very overcrowded in July and August.

Kástro

KÁSTRO, the ancient capital of the island, retains much of its medieval character. It's essentially a sinuous main street along the ridge of a hilltop, the houses on either side, all of the same height, forming the outer defence wall. Their roofs slope inwards in order to collect rainwater inside in case of siege. There are some fine sixteenth- and seventeenth-century churches with ornamental floors; Venetian coats of arms, ancient wall fragments and cunningly recycled Classical columns are still on some of the older dwellings, while the occasional ancient sarcophagus lies incongruously on the pavement. In addition, there are the remains of the ancient acropolis, as well as a small **Archeological Museum** (Tues–Sun 9am–3pm; €2) operating in a former Catholic church in the higher part of the village.

You can walk along Kástro's northeastern peripheral path overlooking the picture-postcard church of the **Eptá Mártyres** (Seven Martyrs), which juts out into the sea. There's nothing approximating a **beach** near Kástro, as defence and not easy access was the aim of the inhabitants. For a swim you can use the Eptá Mártyres rocks, or possibly the rocky cove of **Serália**, just south of Kástro, or the small shore at **Panayía Pouláti**, 1.3km to the northwest; both have facilities.

The fantastic views over the valley below might inspire you to tackle two well-signposted **walks** to Fáros (1hr 30min) and to Vrýsis monastery (50min) that start from the *Konáki* snack-bar (see opposite). If you're driving, best park along the ridge and walk up as the car park at the end is small with little room to manoeuvre.

ACCOMMODATION AND EATING   KÁSTRO

Aris & Maria ☎22840 31161, ⓦarismaria-traditional .com. Rooms and studios in six century-old houses all over

Kástro, fully renovated, but retaining all of the traditional Cycladic features such as wooden ceilings and stone floors.

THE MONASTERY OF KHRYSSOPIYÍ

From the beach at Glyfó (see below), a hillside path leads in fifteen minutes to the longer beach of **Apokoftó**, where there are a couple of good grill tavernas. Flanking Apokoftó to the south, marooned on a sea-washed promontory, is the seventeenth-century **Khryssopiyí Monastery**, which features on every poster of the island. According to legend, the cleft in the rock (under the entrance bridge) appeared when two village girls, fleeing to the spit to escape the attentions of menacing pirates, prayed to the Virgin to defend their virtue. To celebrate the story, a large festival takes place forty days after Easter and involves the spectacular arrival of a holy icon on a large high-speed ferry, and its – often dramatic – transfer to a small boat to be brought ashore.

As no cars are allowed inside Kástro, you will need to carry your luggage for about 100m uphill to the reception following the signs to "Ancient Wall". **€55**

★ **Konaki** ☏ 22840 33165. Complete with a striking pink decor, this café-cum-snack-bar at the entrance to Kástro has good, strong cappuccino and home-made local pastries (€5). Shaded and with comfortable seats, it's the perfect place to laze about and gaze across to Apollonía beyond the valley below. April–Oct daily 9am–10pm.

To Astro ☏ 22840 31476. The oldest taverna in the village, feeding people since 1969. Enjoy your food slowly and unhurriedly to match the service, but you can speed it up by choosing from the day's *gastra* dishes (€12) that should already have been prepared. May–Sept daily noon–midnight.

Fáros

To the south of Kástro, the small fishing village of **FÁROS** is a possible fall-back base, though the beaches are relatively small. The main beach is partly shaded and crowded in season while **Fasoloú**, a 400m walk to the southeast past the headland, is better and shaded by many tamarisk trees. Head off west through the older part of the village to find the picturesque **Glyfó** beach, arguably the best of the three.

ACCOMMODATION AND EATING   FÁROS

Gorgona ☏ 22840 71460/1. A lively hippy and alternative commune on the main street that also offers rooms. Don't be put off by the tattooed arms on display, or the rock music blasting out of the speaker; this is the hangout of mellow souls who welcome strangers. May–Sept daily noon–late. **€40**

Sifnéïko Arhontikó Fáros ☏ 22840 71422/71454, Ⓦ sifneiko-arxontiko.gr. Don't be taken in by its Greek name ("Sífnos Manor"); this modern hotel is not housed in an old mansion, but was built in 1992 in typical Cycladic style. Rather hard to find because it's not signposted, but worth tracking down, as it offers the most comfortable option in Fáros – convenient both for the buses and the beach. April–Sept. **€50**

Thalatta Glyfó ☏ 22840 71485. Built on a slope and inaccessible to vehicles, this villa complex is as close to pure solitude as you can hope for – although you do have access to a minimarket, bars and several tavernas within 200m. Four-night minimum stay. May–Sept. **€65**

Yórgos-Dimítris Fasoloú Beach ☏ 22840 71493. An excellent and well-priced taverna offering only produce from its own farm and good house wine. The shady location under the tamarisk trees and the nearby parking facilities make it the best beach eating option in this part of the island (mains start from €5). Easter–Sept daily noon–midnight.

Platýs Yialós

PLATÝS YIALÓS is 12km from Apollonía, near the southern tip of the island, and has a long stretch of beach that takes four bus stops to cross in its entirety. Buffeted by occasional strong winds, a continuous row of buildings – many of them pottery workshops – lines the entire stretch of beach, which can be slightly off-putting. A five-minute walk from the last bus stop over the southwestern headland brings you to **Lazárou Beach**, a tiny pebble bay entirely occupied by the eponymous beach bar and restaurant behind the water's edge.

Alexandros ☏ 22840 71300, ⓦ hotelalexandros.gr. Getting off at the first bus stop at Platýs Yialós, you encounter this unmistakeably luxurious – as the large swimming pool indicates – but surprisingly affordable hotel where the focus is on room size rather than elaborate reception areas. Large, home-made buffet breakfast included. Mid-May to Sept. **€83**

★**Ariadne** ☏ 22840 71277. An excellent restaurant in a shady courtyard under the beach salt cedar trees near bus stop

#3. It is featured regularly in every Greek gourmet publication, specializing in octopus macaroni, lobster spaghetti and seafood risotto (€11). March–Oct daily noon–midnight.

Cyclades Beach ☏ 22840 71276, ⓦ cycladesbeach.gr. Reputable hotel by the third beach bus stop that's been operating since 1979 and offers the best-priced rooms on the island. Its restaurant, open to nonresidents, has a good buffet breakfast (€5) and, later, traditional Greek food. Daily noon–10pm. **€45**

Vathý

A fishing village on the shore of an almost circular, almost enclosed bay, **VATHÝ** is the most attractive base on the island, with little to do but relax on the beach or in a waterfront taverna. Even the surfaced road and the opening of the luxury *Elies* resort (see below) seems not to have destroyed the character of this previously remote spot, a character accentuated by the poster-pretty all-white monastery of **Taxiárhis** on the promontory bisecting the beach.

Elies Resort ☏ 22840 34000, ⓦ eliesresorts.com. This gated top-class resort on the slopes outside Vathý – where every employee is attired in white clothes, giving it a semblance of the village in the *Prisoner* TV series – offers luxurious surroundings and claims to have the largest pool in the Cyclades. Drop in to play spot-the-VIP, as it is frequented by celebrities, politicians and industrialists. May–Oct. **€210**

Studios Nikos ☏ 22840 33244, ⓦ sifnosrooms.com. A villa compound right on the beach, with attractive, comfortable studios sharing a front grass garden with uninterrupted views to the sea. With large balconies and verandas, separate kitchens and a lot of room inside for three or four people, they are great value for a family self-catering stay. April–Nov. **€52**

EATING

To Tsikali ☏ 22840 71177. One of the better-known family tavernas on Sífnos, it has the best spot on the seafront beyond the monastery and can occasionally surprise the most discerning of palates with its home-made cheese, mezédhes, chunky chips, goat *gástres* and lemony rabbit dishes (€7). Easter–Oct daily noon–midnight.

Tou Koutsouno ☏ 22840 71156. Signposted just before the hairpin that descends to the village, this is a restaurant that claims with good reason to have the best views over Vathý. It has some imaginative croquettes based on courgettes, tomatoes and chick peas (€6) which are all worth sampling before moving to its grills. Take it easy and don't hurry the two old dears who own it. Daily noon–midnight.

Mílos

Volcanic **MÍLOS** is a geologically diverse island with weird rock formations, hot springs and odd outcrops off the coast. Minoan settlers were attracted by obsidian; this and other products of its volcanic soil made it one of the most important of the Cyclades in the ancient world. Today, the quarrying of many rare minerals has left huge scars on the landscape but has given the island a relative prosperity which today translates into several gourmet restaurants with better wine lists than many of its neighbours. With some 75-odd **beaches** and sensational views, Mílos hasn't had to tart itself up to court tourism – indeed, the wealthy mining companies that employ a quarter of the population are happy to see tourism stay at low levels. It helps that the western half of Mílos, as well as the other islands around it, including **Kímolos**, is a nature reserve protecting three endemic species: the extremely rare **Mediterranean seal**, the **Mílos viper**, and the one you are most likely to encounter, the long, crocodile-shaped **Mílos wall lizard**. Note that the importance of the **archeological finds**, museums and sites here is surpassed only by Delos and Santoríni.

ARRIVAL AND GETTING AROUND

By plane The island's tiny airport (☏ 22870 22831), 5km southeast of the port, is served by Olympic with flights from/to Athens (2–4 daily; 45min).

By ferry Mílos is the best-connected island of the Western Cyclades. Ferries dock at the main port of Adhámas. In addition, a small car ferry to the neighbouring island of Kímolos leaves regularly from Pollónia on Mílos' north-western tip – a quicker and cheaper option than the larger ferries.

Destinations Áno Koufoníssi (0–1 weekly; 4hr); Amorgós Katápola (0–1 weekly; 3hr 30min); Anáfi (0–1 weekly; 5hr); Iráklio (Heraklion), Crete (1 weekly; 10hr 20min); Crete Sitía (1 weekly; 14hr); Folégandhros (1–3 daily; 2hr); Íos (3–5 weekly; 3hr 30min); Kéa (1 weekly; 10hr); Kárpathos and Kássos (1 weekly; 16hr–23hr); Kímolos, Adhámas (2–3 daily; 1hr); Kímolos, Pollónia (5–7 daily; 20min); Kýthnos (5 weekly; 3hr); Lávrio (1 weekly; 11hr); Mýkonos (3–6 weekly; 6hr–9hr); Náxos (3 weekly; 4–6hr);

MÍLOS

Páros (3–4 weekly; 6hr 30min–8hr); Pireás (3–5 daily; 2hr 20min–6hr); Rhodes and Hálki (1–2 weekly; 25hr–26hr); Santoríni (1–2 daily; 2hr–5hr); Sérifos (1–3 daily; 1hr 30min); Sífnos (1–3 daily; 2hr); Síkinos (1–2 weekly; 3hr 50min); Sýros (2–3 weekly; 5hr–12hr).

By bus Services start from the main square of Adhámas by *Hotel Portiani* and are sometimes inconveniently timed in the shoulder season: Pláka/Tripití (every 30min; 20min), Pollónia (4–10 daily; 30min), Paleohóri via Zefyría (3–7 daily; 40min), Hivadholímni (8–10 daily; 15min), Sarakíniko (2–4 daily; 30min).

By taxi Taxis seem to be used on Mílos more than on other islands. The taxi rank is near the Adhámas bus stop (☏ 22870 22219). The fare to Pollónia is around €12.

By car or motorbike Rental is available on the Adhámas waterfront near the jetty from many places including Sea, Sun, Sophia (☏ 22870 22120/21994) and Milos Cars (☏ 22870 23484/23397, ⊛ miloscars.gr)

3

INFORMATION

Tourist office Situated opposite the ferry dock (daily 9am–5pm & 7–11pm; ☏ 22870 22445, ⊛ milos.gr), with

a daily updated list of available rooms around the island, as well as maps and detailed bus and ferry timetables.

Services The post office is by the main square in Adhámas and there are several several banks and ATMs behind it.

Pláka has a post office near the archeological museum.

Adhámas

The lively main port of **ADHÁMAS** was a small hamlet until it was populated by refugees from a failed rebellion in Crete in the 1840s. Because it is so recent, you may find it architecturally disappointing compared to some of the Cycladic ports, despite the marble-paved esplanade around its natural headland. There's an ill-defined centre just inland of the esplanade, at the junction of the Pláka road and the Mílos Bay coastal road, where restaurants, cafés and shops abound.

Ecclesiastical Museum

Behind the quayside • April–Oct Mon–Sat 9.15am–1.15pm & 6.15–10.15pm • Free • ☎ 22870 23956

Housed in the ninth-century church of Ayía Triádha, the unmissable **Ecclesiastical Museum** has a superb collection of liturgical paraphernalia and rare icons that arrived in Adhámas when the inland capital, Zefyría, was abandoned. This is the place to admire the work of the Cretans Emmanouel Skordhílis and his son, Antonis, two of the prime icon-makers in eighteenth-century Greece.

Mining Museum of Mílos

On the seafront, 500m east of the centre of town • April daily 9.30am–2pm; May & Oct daily 9.30am–2pm & 5.30–8.30pm; June–Sept daily 9am–2pm & 5–10pm; Nov–March Sat 9am–2pm • €4 • ☎ 22870 22481, ⓦ milosminingmuseum.com

The well-organized **Mining Museum of Mílos** gives an interesting insight into how mining has shaped the island, with an extensive collection of mining equipment, mineral samples and geological maps of Mílos, plus informative displays on the extraction, processing and uses of minerals. The museum is well worth a visit at the start of your stay in order to make more sense of the island's appearance and economy. Don't miss the two moving short films where old miners describe their working conditions (English subtitles).

ACCOMMODATION   **ADHÁMAS**

★**Aeolis** ☎ 22870 23985, ⓦ aeolis-hotel.com. Great-value hotel with palatial rooms and designer furniture but a bit difficult to find: behind the main square, in the street by the dry rivulet. Built with modern specifications, it provides baby cots on request and has two rooms specially adapted for disabled travellers. Two-night minimum stay in the summer. Breakfast €6. **€58**

Meltemi ☎ 22860 22284/21955, ⓦ hotelmeltemi.gr. Basic, centrally positioned hotel behind the main square, clean, a bit noisy (ask for a room at the back) but with all

amenities, this is the cheapest option in town. Suffers from occasional water pump pressure, so your showers may be quite lengthy. **€60**

Ostria ☎ 22870 28127, ⓦ ostria-hotel.gr. A beautiful and comfortable hotel in a quiet position to the east of town (near the mining museum) with excellent breakfast (included). The ivy-covered common areas and its candlelit roof garden are as relaxing as the rooms themselves. May–Sept. **€120**

Portiani ☎ 22870 22940, ⓦ hotelportiani.gr. The most

MÍLOS BOAT TOURS

One of the absolute must-dos on Mílos is a **boat tour**, either down the bizarre western coastline, making several stops at otherwise inaccessible swimming spots like the magnificent **Kléftiko**, or to **Kímolos** and **Polýaigos** to spot the rare Mediterranean seal. Weather permitting, the boats normally leave at 10am from the **Adhámas quayside** and return at 6–7pm.

Chrysovalandou ☎ 6944 587 574, ⓦ sailcatgreece .com. Offers two excursions per day from Adhámas.

Excellent Yachting ☎ 22870 41292. Provides alternative "snorkel safaris" from Pollónia or Adhámas aimed at

younger travellers for €50 including lunch and free drinks.

★**Panormos** ☎ 22870 23533 or ☎ 6945 778 809, ⓔ skipper20@in.gr. Excursions to sheltered coves whatever the weather and the wind direction.

central hotel (in the main square), partly renovated, with excellent buffet breakfast, free wi-fi and a spectacular sea-view terrace. The reception can organize everything for you, from car rental to daily excursions. It can be a bit noisy, though, if you're an early sleeper. **€65**

EATING AND DRINKING

★ **Flisvos** ☎ 22870 22275. An award-winning waterfront restaurant in the same family for three generations. Wide menu offering everything from fried calamari to grilled meats (€8) and a variety of savoury filo pastries accompanied by a good wine list of Santoríni vintages. April–Oct daily noon–midnight.

Kinigos ☎ 22870 22349. Another popular waterfront place to eat, with a varied menu and excellent people-watching potential. Its specialities are the various meatball dishes (€7) made with a secret house recipe, as well as its famed *moussaká* (€6.50). Come early to find a table. April–Oct daily noon–midnight.

Pláka and around

PLÁKA, the capital of the island, is the largest of a cluster of traditional villages that huddle beneath a small crag on the road northwest of Adhámas. Steps beginning near the *Fóras* taverna lead up to the **kástro**, its upper slopes clad in stone and cement to channel precious rainwater into cisterns. The **Folk Museum** (Tues–Sat 10am–2pm & 6–9pm, Sun 10am–2pm; €3; ☎ 22870 21292) has a well-presented array of artefacts related to the history of arts, crafts and daily life on Mílos. The small church of the **Dormition** nearby offers one of the best views in the Aegean, particularly at sunset.

On a long ridge 1km south of Pláka, the narrow, attractive village of **Trypití** ("perforated"), which takes its name from the cliff-side catacombs nearby, is less busy with traffic than Pláka. At the very bottom of the cliff edge and accessed via a road from the southern end of Trypití or steps down from the catacombs, **Klíma** is the most photogenic of the island's fishing hamlets, with its picturesque boathouses tucked underneath the colourful village dwellings.

Archeological Museum

Behind the lower car park • Tues–Sun 8.30am–3pm – it doesn't always look open, even when it is • €3 • ☎ 22870 28026

This Neoclassical jewel of a building, built by Ernst Ziller (see p.115) in the 1840s, contains numerous Neolithic obsidian implements, plus finds from ancient Phylakope (see p.129); highlights include a votive lamp in the form of a bull and a Minoan-looking terracotta idol, the **Lady of Phylakope**. You'll also recognize the plaster-cast copy of the **Venus de Milo**, the original of which was found on the island in 1820. It's not clear whether it was discovered with the arms already separated from the torso, or if they were broken off in a skirmish between French sailors and locals.

Catacombs

1km south of Pláka and 400m from Trypití • Summer Tues–Sat 9.30am–6.30pm, Sun 8.30am–3pm; winter Tues–Sun 8am–3pm • €3 • Groups of ten allowed at a time

From Pláka's archeological museum, signs point you towards the early **Christian catacombs**, a fifteen-minute walk south of town; once there, steps lead down from the road to the inconspicuous entrance. Some five thousand bodies lie buried in three tomb-lined corridors with side galleries, stretching 200m into the soft volcanic rock, making these the largest catacombs in Greece. Bear in mind that only the first 50m are illuminated and accessible by boardwalk and the guided tour lasts only about fifteen minutes.

Ancient Melos

1km south of Pláka, near the catacombs

Just above the catacombs are the ruins of **Ancient Melos** whose focal point is a well-preserved Roman **amphitheatre**. En route to the theatre from the surfaced road is the signposted spot where the *Venus de Milo* was found in what may have been the compound's gymnasium.

3

ACCOMMODATION

PLÁKA AND AROUND

★**Mylos tou Marketou** Tripití ☎ 22870 22147, ⓦ mylosgreece.com. A sixteenth-century windmill on the furthest, eastern side of the village that has been fully adapted to a four-bed apartment (€170). The adjoining auxiliary buildings have been converted to more conventional studios, all with a fantastic view of Mílos Bay. May–Oct. **€70**

Spiti tis Makhis ☎ 22870 41353/22129. A hotel with refurbished rooms employing cherry-wood furniture and bright orange colours that make a difference from the Cycladic blue, it occupies the house where the *Venus de Milo* was hidden following its discovery. Conveniently situated for the bus, but set back from the main road, it also has plenty of parking space. June–Oct. **€75**

EATING AND DRINKING

Arhontoula ☎ 22870 21384, ⓔ arhontoula3@yahoo .gr. One of the oldest and more reputable family restaurants in Pláka occupying the same spot in the main street for over a hundred years, offering Greek and international cuisine – even Indian curry dishes – plus a carefully selected wine list. Mains start from €7. April–Nov daily noon–midnight.

Foras ☎ 22870 23954. An old-style *mezedhopolío* (like they don't make them any more) on the main road into Pláka. Greek coffee, a variety of ouzo bottles, many small-plate mezédhes (€6) and an elderly clientele that has been coming here to enjoy the food for decades. Daily noon–midnight.

The south

The main road to **southern Mílos** splits at Kánava junction, near the large power station. The sea there contains underwater hot vents resulting in fizzy hotspots that locals use for jacuzzi-like baths. The eastern fork leads to **Zefyría**, which was briefly the capital until an eighteenth-century earthquake (and subsequent plague) drove out the population. There's little to see in the old town but a magnificent seventeenth-century church with beautifully painted walls and ceilings. The original iconostasis was transferred to the church of the Dormition in Adhámas, while the icons are displayed in the Ecclesiastical museum.

South of Zefyría, it's a further 8km down a winding, surfaced road to the coarse sand of **Paleohóri**, one of the island's best beaches, warmed by underground volcanism. A little rock tunnel leads west to a second beach, which is backed by extraordinarily coloured cliffs and where steam vents heat the shallow water. **Ayía Kyriakí**, further to the west of Paleohóri, is a pebble beach under imposing sulphurous and red oxide cliffs.

ACCOMMODATION AND EATING

THE SOUTH

Artemis Paleohóri ☎ 22870 31222. A restaurant and apartment complex, difficult to categorize because its fish taverna (with an excellent wine list) is as good and as well known as its comfortable lodgings. May–Oct daily 9am–6pm. Apartments for 2–3 people **€100**

★**Sirocco** Paleohóri ☎ 22870 31201, ⓦ restaurant

sirocco.gr. An institution on the island, using the hot volcanic sand – that reaches a constant temperature of 100°C only 30cm below the surface – to bake casseroles of lamb, veal, pork and fish (€12) in clay pots overnight. May–Oct daily noon–10pm.

Hivadholímni and the west

The westerly road from the Kánava junction leads past the airport entrance to **Hivadholímni**, the best beach on Mílos Bay itself. Behind the beach is a salty lagoon where in May and September you can observe migrating birdlife. Just before Hivadholímni, you can fork south to **Provatás**, a short beach closed off by multicoloured cliffs to the east. It's easy to get to so it hasn't escaped development.

Forking to the east before Provatás, the road leads to the trendy and very popular beach of **Firipláka**. Further east, on a dirt road, is sandy **Tsigrádho**, excellent for swimming and usually uncrowded. Going west from the Kanava junction the surfaced road ends at **Ayía Marína**, although a dirt road continues into **Hálakas** and the small fishing village of **Embourió**, where there's a perfectly acceptable beach.

For the most part, the southwestern peninsula of Hálakas, centred on the wilderness of Mount Profítis Ilías (748m), is an uninhabited nature reserve with unsurfaced dirt tracks, two of which lead to the fine, unspoilt beaches of **Triádhes** and **Ammoudharáki Kléftiko** in the southwest corner. It's only reachable by boat, but repays the effort to get there with its stunning rock formations and semi-submerged tunnels.

ACCOMMODATION HIVADHOLÍMNI

Milos Camping ☎ 22870 31410/1, ⓦ miloscamping .gr. Large campsite overlooking Mílos Bay and above Hivadholímni beach; its minibus meets ferries, and in summer there are frequent buses to and from Adhámas. There's a decent restaurant next door with a swimming pool. Check for special deals online. Mid-May to Sept. **€14**

The north coast

From either Adhámas or the Pláka area, good roads run roughly parallel to the **north coast** which, despite being windswept and sparsely inhabited, is not devoid of geological interest. **Sarakíniko**, in particular, is an astonishing sculpted inlet, with a sandy seabed and gleaming white rocks popular with sunbathing local youth. Nearby **Mýtakas** is another good beach, accessible via a 500m dirt road, with dramatic views west along the rocky coastline.

Eastwards you reach another of Mílos' coastal wonders, **Papáfranga**, a short ravine into which the sea flows under a rock arch – the tiny beach at its inland end is accessed by rock-carved steps. To the right of the Papáfranga car park, the remains of three superimposed Neolithic settlements crown a small knoll at **Phylakope** (Tues–Sun 8.30am–3pm; free). **Pollónia**, the end of the road 12km northeast of Adhámas, is a small harbour within a semicircular bay with a long, curved, tamarisk-lined beach. This is where you take the small ferry to Kímolos (see below) opposite.

ACTIVITIES THE NORTH COAST

Diving and watersports Pollónia is immensely popular with windsurfers and divers; the Apollon Diving Center (☎ 22870 41451) offers PADI courses, snorkelling trips and equipment rental.

ACCOMMODATION

Andreas Pollónia ☎ 22870 41262, ⓦ andreas-rooms. gr. Villa complex at the western edge of Pollónia with triple studios, stunning views and easy access to the quiet neighbouring bay, plus its own boat, *Perseas*, bookable for trips and fishing expeditions to nearby islands. Help yourself to vegetables from the garden. **€50**

Kapetan Tasos Pollónia ☎ 22870 41287, ⓦ kapetan tasos.gr. One of the more luxurious options in the quay area that has been fully renovated; the "superior" suites are as big as a two-bedroom flat. Organizes transfers, and has free wi-fi, mini-gym and optional breakfast until 2pm. April–Oct. **€120**

EATING AND DRINKING

★ **Armenaki** Pollónia ☎ 22870 41061, ⓦ armenaki.gr. Claiming never to use anything frozen and nothing but olive oil, this is one of the best restaurants on Mílos, packed day and night, so it's wise to make a reservation. Its fish casseroles (€12) and seafood pasta go down well with its diligently chosen white wines. April–Oct daily noon–late.

Yialos Pollónia ☎ 22870 41208, ⓦ gialos-pollonia.gr. Small but stylish restaurant with a well-thought-out menu and a wide range of seafood and fish dishes. Try the prawn tartare or sea bream carpaccio (€15), and follow that with an imaginative dessert such as caramelized strawberries. April–Oct daily noon–midnight.

Kímolos

Of the three islands off the coast of Mílos, only rugged, scenic **KÍMOLOS** is inhabited. Volcanic like Mílos, it profits from its geology and used to export chalk (*kimolía* in Greek) until the supply was exhausted. Bentonite is still extracted locally, and the fine dust of this clay is a familiar sight on the northeastern corner of the island. Apart from the inhabited southeast, the rest of the island is a nature reserve, which explains lack of surfaced roads.

3

Even in August Kímolos isn't swamped by visitors. Just as well, since, although there are around 450-odd beds on the whole island, there is little in the way of other amenities. There's only one bus, no car or motorbike rental (rent your vehicle from Mílos) and few restaurants. Those visitors who venture here come for the tranquillity and for trekking in pristine nature.

ARRIVAL AND DEPARTURE   KÍMOLOS

By ferry Whether you arrive from Adhámas or from Pollónia on Mílos (see p.129), you'll dock at the tiny port of Psáthi on the southeast coast. Ferry tickets for onward journeys – unless bought in advance up in Hóra (see below) – are only sold an hour or so before the arrival of the boat. Larger ferries call briefly on their way to and from Adhámas, but the best option for Milos is the ferry *Panagia Faneromeni* (☎22870 51184, ⊛kimolos-link.gr) that serves Pollónia (see p.129).

Destinations Folégandhros (3 weekly; 45min–1hr); Íos (2–3 weekly; 4hr 30min); Kéa (1 weekly; 9hr); Kýthnos (1 weekly; 3hr 30min–7hr); Mílos, Adhámas (2–3 daily; 1hr); Mílos, Pollónia (7–8 daily; 20min); Mýkonos (1 weekly; 9hr 30min); Páros (3–4 weekly; 4hr 30min); Pireás (1–2 daily; 3hr 30min); Náxos (1 weekly; 5hr 45min); Santoríni (2 weekly; 4hr 30min); Sérifos (2 weekly; 2hr); Sífnos (1–3 daily; 1hr); Síkinos (2 weekly; 1hr 30min); Syros (12 weekly; 4–11hr).

Travel agents There are two shipping agencies, both highly reputable: Kimolos Travel (☎22870 51219) and Maganiotis (☎22870 51000, ⊜smagan@otenet.gr).

GETTING AROUND AND INFORMATION

By bus There is one regular bus in high season to the capital, Hóra (8–10 daily; 10min) from the port as well as connecting with the ferries (☎6973 700 033). Alternatively, Hóra can be reached on foot in about 30min from the port. Other destinations around the island are on paths that are 2–3hr on foot from Hóra.

By taxi There's only one taxi on the island (☎22870 51552 or ☎6945 464 093).

Services There is one bank and one ATM in Hóra; the island's post office is in the west of the village.

Hóra

Dazzlingly white **HÓRA** (known locally as Horió) is perched on the ridge above Psáthi behind a few old windmills overlooking the bay. The magnificent, two-gated, sixteenth-century **kástro** was built against marauding pirates. The perimeter houses are still intact and inhabited, though its heart is a jumble of ruins except for the small church of **Christós** (1592) and the chapel of the island's own saint **Ayía Methodhía**, beatified in 1991. Just outside the kástro to the north stands the conspicuously unwhitewashed, late seventeenth-century church of **Khryssóstomos**, the most beautiful on the island. Near the church is the **Archeological Museum** (July–Sept Tues–Sun 8.30am–3pm; free), displaying pottery from the Geometric to the Roman period. In a restored house near the eastern gateway is the privately run **Folk and Maritime Museum** (July–Sept daily 9am–1.30pm; €1).

ACCOMMODATION   HÓRA

★**Meltemi** ☎22870 51360/86, ⊛kimolos-meltemi .gr. A superlative option in the west of the village, with modern, recently renovated rooms, airy balconies, terrific views and an excellent restaurant below. The owner is the captain of the *Panagia Faneromeni* and can arrange for your pick-up at Psáthi. €50

Villa Maria ☎22870 51392. Central hotel, right by the entrance to Hóra, with rooms and studios that are up there with the most comfortable in the Cyclades; however, check carefully (and then reconfirm) whether it is block-booked, something that happens often. €50

EATING

★**Panorama** ☎22870 51351. Near the northeastern gate of the kástro, this is the best place to eat on the island. It offers well-cooked dishes (mains €6) with fresh ingredients, a tasteful marine decor and a pretty veranda. Most importantly in an island as sleepy as this, the place is almost constantly open. Daily 9am–midnight.

To Kyma Psáthi ☎22870 51001. An excellent taverna midway along the beach, specializing in fresh seafood (€8) and vegetarian dishes that come directly from their own farm. This is the place to try fried rather than the normally grilled octopus. April–Oct daily noon–late.

Rest of the island

The hamlet of **Alykí** on the south coast is about thirty minutes' walk on the paved road that forks left from Psáthi; it's named after the saltpan that sprawls behind a pebbly beach. Here you can indulge in some serious bird-watching or try to spot the rare, endemic Mílos wall lizard. If you stroll west one cove, you arrive at **Bonátsa**, which has better sand and shallower water. Passing another cove you come to the even more attractive beach of **Kalamítsi**, with decent shade.

There are three signposted beaches next to each other starting from the dirt track at the end of the asphalted road off **Fykiádha**, a 45-minute walk west of Alykí. The first one, dotted with caves and ancient tombs, is **Dhékas**. It's divided by a low bluff from the long coarse-sand beach of **Elliniká**, itself separated by a rocky promontory from **Mavrospiliá**, the best spot to watch the sunset. There are no facilities on any beach.

Some 7km northeast from Hóra is **Prása**, arguably the best easily accessible beach on the island, with crystal-clear water, fine sand and radioactive thermal springs. The route takes in impressive views across the straits to the island of **Políaigos**, and there are several peaceful coves where it's possible to swim in solitude. In the northwest, on Kímolos's 361m summit, are the scant ruins of a Venetian fortress known as **Paleókastro** which can be reached after a reasonable trek (2hr 30min) from the dirt road off Prása. The road forks by the peak to Sklavos, with one branch leading to **Skiadhi**, an odd rock formation like a mushroom which has been adopted as the island landmark.

ACCOMMODATION AND EATING   REST OF THE ISLAND

Bonatsa Studios Bonátsa ☎ 6945 779 594, ⓦ bonatsa .gr. Right behind a string of salt cedars, this apartment complex offers studios of exceptional quality in bright red and yellow colours. A good restaurant belonging to the owner operates next door (7pm–midnight). June– Sept. **€40**

Kimolia Yi Prássa ☎ 22870 51192, ⓦ kimoliagi.gr. Set at 200m from the beach, this is the only, but still pretty good, accommodation option here, eye-catchingly

decorated, with much ornamental bric-a-brac on show. Children under the age of four pay nothing. Breakfast included. April–Sept. **€50**

Sardis Alykí ☎ 22870 51458, ⓦ kimolosrooms.com. Comfortable hotel with enormous rooms 50m from the sea. Recommended for birdwatchers especially outside the peak season as the saltpan (Alykí) that gives the beach its name attracts many waders. Good restaurant on-site. June–Sept. **€60**

Ándhros

ÁNDHROS, the second largest and northernmost of the Cyclades, is also one of the most verdant, its fertile, well-watered valleys and hillsides sprouting scores of holiday villas. Still home to a very hospitable people, an attractive capital, numerous good beaches, plus some idiosyncratic reminders of the Venetian period – such as the *peristereónes* (dovecote towers) and the *frákhtes* (dry-stone walls) – Ándhros has a special charm. Driving is also a joy, with precipitous coastal roads offering panoramic views over the Aegean.

The only cloud in your enjoyment of the island may be the current shutdown of all state museums on Ándhros; check if they have opened before you visit.

ARRIVAL AND GETTING AROUND   ÁNDHROS

By ferry Ándhros has limited connections to the rest of the islands. All ferries and catamarans arrive at the main port, Gávrio, on the east coast.
Destinations Mýkonos (2–4 daily; 2hr 30min); Rafína (up to 3 daily; 2hr); Sýros (1 weekly; 2hr 45min); Tínos (2–6 daily; 1hr 40min).

By bus Buses run from the port's waterfront where the schedules are posted: Batsí (6–8 daily; 20min); Hóra (4–6 daily; 50min); Kórthi (2–3 daily; 1hr). Buses to Hóra and Korthi connect with boat arrivals.

By car or motorbike Gávrio is the easiest place on the island for car rental, with several competing

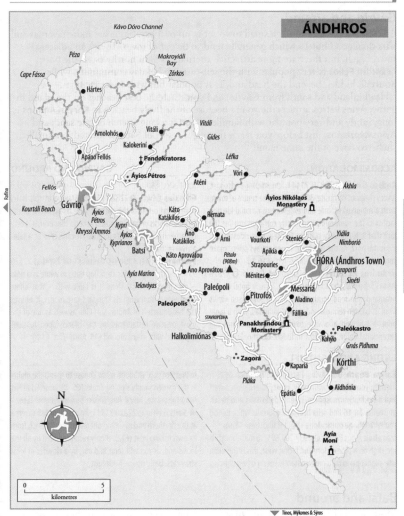

ÁNDHROS

Kávo Dóro Channel

Péza
Makroyiáli
Bay
Cape Fássa
Zórkos
Hártes
Amolohós
Vitáli
Vitáli
Kalokeríni
Gídes
Apáno Fellós
† Pandokratoras
Léfka
Áyios Pétros
Aténi
Vóri
Ákhla
Fellós
Áyios Nikólaos
Monastery
Kourtáli Beach
Gávrio
Áyios
Pétros
Káto
Katákilos
Rémata
Kypri
Khryssi Ammos
Áyios
Kyprianos
Batsí
Áno
Katákilos
Árni
Vourkotí
Steniés
Yiália
Nimborió
Apíkia
HÓRA (Ándhros Town)
Káto Aprovátou
Pétalo
(908m)
Strapouriés
Paraporti
Ayía Marína
Áno Aprovátou
Ménites
Sinéti
Telavóyas
Paleópoli
Messariá
Pitrofós
Aladino
Paleópolis
STAVROPÉDHA
Fállika
Paleókastro
Panakhrándou
Monastery
Kohylo
Gnás Pídhuma
Halkolimiónas
Kórthi
Zagorá
Kapariá
Pláka
Epátia
Aïdhónia

N

0   5
kilometres

Rafína

Tínos, Mýkonos & Sýros

3

---

establishments. Try the reliable and friendly Euro Car (☎ 22820 72440, ✆ rentacareuro.com) right in front of the disembarkation point. As the island is very large and tricky to explore, and the bus services limited, you are advised to book your transport before arriving.

Travel agents Batis (☎ 22820 71489), Kyklades Travel (☎ 22820 72363/71750) and Porto Andros (☎ 22820 71222, ✉ portoand@otenet.gr), all operate near the centre of the port.

INFORMATION

Tourist offices A tiny converted dovecote by the disembarkation point in Gávrio houses an unmanned information booth. There's also an unmanned but signposted info kiosk by the jewellers' in Batsí (the island's main resort).

Services There are two banks and three ATMs on the waterfront in Gávrio, and the post office is at the southern

end. *Carlíto's* café-bar (daily 9am–3am; ☎ 6977 729 268), also at the waterfront, offers free wi-fi as well as internet facilities (€2.50/hr). Batsí has an ATM behind the *Dodóni* café-bar. There are several banks and two ATMs in Hóra, and the post office is on the main street. There is one ATM in Ormos Korthíou, on Yeoryíou Psálti, parallel to the esplanade.

Gávrio and around

GÁVRIO is a pleasant enough small town set in an oval bay, but it has more tavernas and bars than good hotels, which generally tend to be out of town. There's an adjacent town beach, but there are more attractive alternatives 5km northwest of the port: beautiful **Fellós** is very popular with the self-catering holiday community, while **Kourtáli**, hidden beyond the headland, is as popular but with fewer facilities.

Head inland and south from Gávrio, and you reach the best beaches on the island in a row: **Áyios Pétros** attracts the young because of the lively beach bar; **Khryssí Ámmos** is long, sandy and very popular with families; **Kyprí** is a long stretch of fine sand; and **Áyios Kyprianos**, just before you reach the major resort of **Batsí**, is located in a small sheltered cove of the same name.

ACCOMMODATION   GÁVRIO AND AROUND

Andros Gávrio ☎ 22820 71444, ⓦ campingandros.gr. A very pleasant campsite, 300m behind the centre of town, with a minimarket, café and excellent communal kitchen facilities. The swimming pool partly compensates for the fact that it is not very close to the sea. Free rides to and from the port. As the reception is not always open, make sure they're waiting for you. May–Oct. **€16.50**

★Andros Holidays 400m south of Gávrio ☎ 22820 71443, ⓦ androsholidayhotel.com. Luxury hotel on the headland side road south of town with lovely sea views from its garden terraces and arched verandas. With a large pool, a bar, and a private cove in front, its rooms are exceptional value. Breakfast included. Good online deals.

April–Oct. **€80**

Galaxias Gávrio ☎ 22820 71228. Staying at this hotel right at the centre of the port feels like living in one of the faceless blocks of flats in Central Athens. However, it is very cheap and, because of its location, it can serve as a late-arrival fallback. **€35**

Perrakis Between Khryssí Ámmos and Kyprí ☎ 22820 71456, ⓦ hotelperrakis.com. Top hotel in white and gold – matching the local stone it is built with – that offers great views from even its standard-rate rooms. It houses the headquarters of Andros Surf Club as well as one of the most creative restaurants on the island (open to non-residents) with mains around €15. April–Oct. **€100**

EATING AND NIGHTLIFE

Kaliva Beach Bar Áyios Pétros ☎ 6977 352 662. A friendly, youthful bar with lively, chatty international staff and a studenty atmosphere. It rents deckchairs and beach umbrellas for €6 and sells beer and cocktails while lulling you with lounge music. June–Sept daily 10am–8pm.

Marabou Áyios Pétros ☎ 6937 101 695, ⓦ marabouclub .gr. High on a promontory and facing west, this is the main late-night option for a predominantly young crowd dancing

to Western pop, although many choose to spend the nights in the garden simply sipping drinks (€6–8). June Fri & Sat midnight–late, July & Aug Thurs–Sun midnight–late.

★Sails Gávrio ☎ 22820 71333. An excellent fish taverna at the northern end of Gávrio offering the daily catch from its own fishing boat (€12). Highly recommended by all the locals and, as you will soon find out, by a clowder of local stray cats. Daily noon–midnight.

Batsí and around

Most visitors head 8km south to **BATSÍ**, the island's main resort with its hotels, rooms and bars set around a fine natural harbour. The beautiful though often crowded beach curves twice around the bay, and the sea is cold, calm and clean. South of town, a coastal road leads to the small, picturesque sandy cove of **Ayía Marína** and, further on, the gorgeous beach of **Telavóyas**.

There's a good archeological site of the ancient city of **Paleópolis**, 8km south from Batsí, which flourished from the sixth century BC to the end of the eighth century AD, covering a large area just southwest of the modern village. It is reached via a shady, pleasant signposted path from the village to the eponymous beach.

ACCOMMODATION   BATSÍ AND AROUND

★Chryssí Akti Batsí ☎ 22820 41236, ⓦ hotel -chryssiakti.gr. Right on the main beach, this hotel, which depends mainly on package tours, is solid, central, efficient and comfortable. Good swimming pool, and even better

interior café-bar with a first-class range of patisseries. Free parking next to the hotel. Breakfast included. April–Oct. **€60**

Villa Rena Batsí ☎ 22820 41024, ⓦ villarena.gr. Reached both by car from the ring road (limited parking) and via a five-minute climb from the beach, this hotel has a super collection of tastefully decorated apartments around a sloping shady garden and a surprisingly deep swimming pool. March–Oct. **€50**

EATING AND DRINKING

Balkoni tou Aigaiou Áno Aprovátou ☎ 22820 41020. Accessed via a narrow, winding hill road to the village of Áno Aprovátou, 3km from the highway south of Batsí, the "Balcony of the Aegean", set high above the coast, has superior, well-priced rural food; try its home-made Ándhros sausage (€9). The panoramic views are legendary. Easter–Oct daily noon–4pm & 6–11pm; Nov–Easter Fri & Sat noon–4pm & 6–11pm, Sun noon–3pm.

Café Scala Batsí ☎ 22820 41656. The largest and most popular hangout in the village with a DJ playing easy-listening music after sunset. Good selection of beers from €5. Don't forget to check out the hilarious Adam and Eve theme in the toilets. Easter–Oct daily 9am–5am; Nov–Easter Fri & Sat 9am–5am.

★**Stamatis** Batsí ☎ 22820 41283. An old-style family taverna – the locals' choice – with a balcony for balmy nights and a large indoor area for when the *meltémi* hits. Try the Batsí speciality, chicken roll with local cheese for €9. Daily noon–1am.

Hóra and around

Stretched along a rocky spur that divides a huge bay 32km from Gávrio, the capital **HÓRA** (also known as **Ándhros Town**) is the most attractive town on the island. Paved in marble and schist from the still-active local quarries, the buildings near the bus station are grand nineteenth-century edifices, and the squares with their ornate wall fountains and gateways are equally elegant. The old port, **Plakoúra**, on the west side of the headland, has a yacht supply station and a former ferry landing from where occasional boats run to the isolated but superbly idyllic **Ákhla** beach in summer. More locally, there are beaches on both sides of the town headland: **Nimborió** to the north and the less developed **Parapórti** to the southeast, though both are exposed to the *meltémi* winds in summer – the reason Gávrio (see opposite), on the other side of the island, became the main port instead.

From the Theófilou Kaïri square, right at the end of Hóra's main street, Embiríkou (aka "Agorá"), you pass through an archway and down through the residential area of Paleá Póli past the town theatre to **Ríva Square**, with its Soviet-donated statue of an unknown sailor scanning the sea.

Archeological Museum

On the main street near Kaïri Square, Hóra • Winter Fri–Sun 9am–4pm; summer Tues–Sat 9am–4pm • €3 • ☎ 22820 23664/29134

The **Archeological Museum** has well laid-out and clearly labelled displays, mostly from Paleópolis (see opposite). There are funerary stelae, a *kouros* and a torso of Artemis, but its prize item is the fourth-century *Hermes of Ándhros*, reclaimed from a prominent position in the Athens archeological museum. This is a remarkably preserved Roman copy of the Hermes of Praxiteles, attributed to one of antiquity's greatest sculptors.

Goulandhrís Museum of Contemporary Art

Kaïri square, Hóra • April–June & Oct Wed–Mon 10am–2pm; July–Sept Mon 11am–3pm, Wed–Sun 11am–3pm & 6–9pm; Nov–March Sat–Mon 10am–2pm • Summer €5, winter €3 • ⓦ moca-andros.gr

Behind the Archeological Museum (see above) there is the surprisingly good **Goulandhrís Museum of Contemporary Art**. A four-storey mansion, it has a permanent collection with works by prominent Greek sculptors as well as international artists such as Hundertwasser, Warhol, Rodin and Giacometti, plus regular temporary exhibitions.

North of Hóra

The tidy village of **Apikía**, 6km north of Hóra, is the source of the Sáriza mineral water brand. An uphill turn at the southwestern end of the village leads, via a signed fifteen-minute path, to the **Rematiá Pytháras**, a pretty wooded stream with small

3

> ## PANAYÍA PANAKHRÁNDOU
>
> Two hours' pleasant walk from Hóra via the village of Fállika, or via a signposted turn-off on the road to Kórthi, you arrive at the finest monastery on the island, **Panayía Panakhrándou** (closed 1–4.30pm). Founded around 961 and with an icon said to be by St Luke, it's still defended by massive walls but is occupied these days by just one monk. From the entrance door, a long passageway leads in past gushing springs to the atmospheric *katholicón* dedicated to the Dormition of the Virgin with its impressive and colourful iconostasis. Its lower decoration with **Ottoman Iznik tiles** is unique in the Aegean and it represents a gift to the monastery by Patriarch Dionysius III in the 1660s.

waterfalls. The road continues to **Vourkotí** and, after a turn-off to Ákhla (a dirt track continuing for 8km), it then becomes a broad, mostly unused highway, via Árni, to the west coast. There are some wonderful views of the northeast from along this road, particularly where it crosses the **Kouvára ridge** at an altitude of 700m.

ACCOMMODATION AND EATING   HÓRA AND AROUND

Alcioni Nimborió beach ☏ 22820 23652/23805, ⓦ alcioni.gr. These pink-and-cyan studios right by Nimborió beach have been expanded to fill all available space, cutting down on common areas, such as reception; consequently they are on the large side, with local wooden furniture, though some tend to be a bit noisy from the traffic in front. April–Oct. **€70**

Andria Studios Hóra ☏ 22820 22905, ⓦ andriastudios .com. Just one block away from the main road, behind Nimborió beach, you can hear a pin drop in these huge, well-furnished studios with their own kitchenette – the best priced in Hóra. Easter–Oct. **€50**

Madouris Nimborió ☏ 22820 24620. Simple and unassuming, you'll wonder why its tables are all taken while the surrounding tavernas are empty. Then you'll taste the fresh fried calamari, with portions that feed two adults (€9)

and you'll understand. April–Sept daily noon–midnight.

Onar Residence Ákhla beach ☏ 6932 563 707, ⓦ onar -andros.gr. Extremely difficult to reach and a pain to get to – 40km from Gávrio including 8km on a dirt road – but worth it. This is an ecolodge in the middle of one of the best beaches of Ándhros, with self-catering bungalows composed of stone, wood and reeds, but supplied with all modern facilities; as close to feeling stranded on a desert island as you could dream of. May–Nov. **€170**

Paradise Hotel Entrance to Hóra ☏ 22820 22187/8/9, ⓦ paradiseandros.gr. If you have your own transport, this hotel, though far from the beach and the town centre, makes an appealing holiday sanctuary, with modern art paintings in the common areas, a striking swimming pool, a tennis court, free wi-fi, regal furnishings and even a small folklore museum next door. Easter–Sept. **€85**

The south

If you're exploring **the south** from Hóra, take the road that runs through the dramatic **Dipotámata** valley; at the seaward end, the fine, sheltered cove of **Sinéti** is worth a detour, though the access road is somewhat steep.

Paleókastro

Two kilometres south of Sinéti, the entry road to Kohýlo village forks: the left goes 2km (partly surfaced) to **Paleókastro** (aka Kástro Fanerroménis), a ruined Venetian castle perched on a rocky crest at 586m, with amazing views overlooking Kórthi Bay. Legend has it that an old woman, who betrayed the stronghold to the Turks, jumped from the top in remorse, and she remains as a column of rock in the sea off Griás Pídhima beach (see below) where she landed.

Kórthi

A short distance south of Paleókastro is the resort of **Kórthi** (or Órmos Korthíou or simply Órmos), a small town, with a new seafront esplanade that's waking up to its tourist potential and is popular with windsurfers; this is where the Greek Olympic team practises. Set on a large bay, isolated from the rest of the island by the high ridge and relatively unspoilt, it is pleasant enough to merit a stay. Lovely **Griás Pídhima** beach is accessible via a signed road and dirt track from near the northern end of the esplanade, while **Kandoúni** beach covers the southern half of the main bay.

EATING AND DRINKING
THE SOUTH

★ **Lithodhomi** Kórthi ☎ 22820 61093/61130. One of those surprise finds that make your heart beat faster with excitement: a restaurant in the middle of the Kórthi esplanade with great rustic stone decor, an inventive menu offering many vegetarian options (€10), good service, fresh ingredients and a great wine list. A must if you've come all this way. Daily noon–1am.

Tínos

TÍNOS still feels like one of the most Greek of the larger islands in the Cyclades. A few foreigners have discovered its beaches and unspoilt villages, but most visitors are Greek, here to see the church of **Panayía Evangelístria**, a grandiose shrine erected on the spot where a miraculous icon with healing powers was found in 1822. A local nun, now canonized as Ayía Pelayía, was directed in a vision to unearth the relic just as the War of Independence was getting under way, a timely coincidence that served to underscore the links between the Orthodox Church and Greek nationalism. Today, there are two major annual pilgrimages, on March 25 and August 15, when Tínos is inundated by the faithful, and at 11am, the icon bearing the Virgin's image is carried in state down to the harbour.

The Ottoman tenure here, and on adjoining Sýros, was the most fleeting in the Aegean. **Exóbourgo**, the craggy mount dominating southern Tínos and surrounded by most of the island's sixty-odd villages, is studded with the ruins of a Venetian citadel that defied the Turks until 1715, long after the rest of Greece had fallen; an enduring legacy of the long Venetian rule is a **Catholic minority**, which accounts for almost half the population. Hills are dotted with distinctive and ornate **dovecotes**, even more in

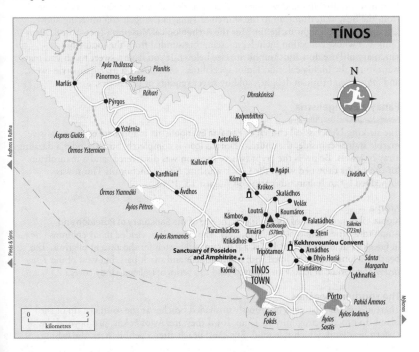

evidence here than on Ándhros. Aside from all this, the inland village architecture is striking, and there's a flourishing folk-art tradition that finds expression in the abundant local marble.

ARRIVAL AND DEPARTURE   TÍNOS

By ferry All ferries dock at Tínos Town at any one of three different marinas: one for yachts, one for catamarans and one for normal ferries, all next to each other.
Destinations Amorgos Katápola (1–3 weekly; 2hr 15min); Ándhros (2–6 daily; 1hr 30min); Áno Koufoníssi (0–3 weekly; 2hr 30min); Irakliá (0–3 weekly; 2hr 50min); Mýkonos (3–7 daily; 30min); Náxos (1–2 daily; 1hr 30min); Páros (1–2 daily; 1hr); Pireás (1 daily; 5hr); Rafina (up to 5 daily; 1hr 40min–3hr 50min); Santoríni (5 weekly; 3hr); Skhinoússa (0–3 weekly; 2hr 20min); Sýros (5–6 weekly; 30min–1hr).

GETTING AROUND AND INFORMATION

By bus Buses leave from a small parking area on the inner quay and serve: Áyios Fokás (8–9 daily; 15min); Falatádos/Stení (6 daily; 20min); Kalloní via Xinára (3 daily; 20min); Kiónia (2 hourly; 10min); Pánormos via Pýrgos (4 daily; 45min); Kalloní (3 daily; 45min); Pórto (1 hourly; 20min). Info in Greek is available at ⊛ kteltinou.gr.
By car or motorbike Not only a much more reliable means of exploring the island than bus, especially in the shoulder season, but also the only way to reach some of the beaches of the island. Vidalis at 2 Ierarhon St (☎ 22830 23400, ⊛ vidalis-rentacar.gr) is a reputable rental agency

– they have four smaller rental outlets around town.
Day-trip to Delos In season (July–Sept) there are day-trips by boat to Delos (Tues–Sun; €50 round trip); this makes it possible to see Delos without the expense of staying overnight on Mýkonos. The time on Delos itself (about 2hr 30min) compares favourably with tours from Mýkonos.
Services There is no shortage of banks or ATMs in Tínos Town.
Travel agents Windmills Travel (☎ 22830 23398, ⊛ windmillstravel.com) on the front towards the new jetty can help with information as well as tour bookings to Delos and hotel bookings both here and on Mýkonos.

Tínos Town and around

TÍNOS TOWN is large and commercial, possessing a unique mixture of religion and commerce: trafficking in devotional articles certainly dominates the streets leading from the busy waterfront up to the church of Panayía Evangelístria towering above. On the way, you might make time for the **Archeological Museum** (Tues–Sun 8.30am–3pm; €2) whose collection includes a fascinating sundial from the local Roman sanctuary of Poseidon and Amphitrite (see below). If you have a sweet tooth you may want to try the highly calorific Tiniot specialities: *amygdalotó*, a marzipan-style sweet, and *loukoúmia* (Turkish delight), sold by street vendors or patisseries.

Panayía Evangelístria
Leofóros Megalóharis • Daily 8am–8pm

The striking Neoclassical church of **Panayía Evangelístria** is approached via a massive marble staircase; inside, the church's famous **icon** is completely buried under a dazzling array of jewels. Below is the crypt (where the icon was discovered) and a mausoleum for the sailors drowned when the Greek warship, *Elli*, at anchor off Tínos, was torpedoed by an Italian submarine on August 15, 1940.

Kiónia
Kiónia, 3km northwest of the capital, is the site of the **Sanctuary of Poseidon and Amphitrite** (Tues–Sun 8.30am–3pm; free). The excavations yielded many columns (*kiónia* in Greek), but also a temple, baths, a fountain and hostels for the ancient pilgrims. The **beach** is a long thin strip, lined with rooms to rent and snack-bars, but west of the *Tinos Beach Hotel* you can follow an unpaved road to a series of isolated sandy coves.

The southern beaches
There are several first-class but mostly unshaded beaches at the southern tip of the island. In order of proximity to Tínos Town they are: **Áyios Fokás**, just beyond the eastern headland, which is a good, fine-sand beach after a pebbly start, the fishing

village beach of Áyios Sóstis, shallow **Áyios Ioánnis** (served by six daily buses), and beyond that the idyllic **Pahiá Ámmos**, with a view of Mýkonos.

ACCOMMODATION   TÍNOS TOWN AND AROUND

Avra Konstandínou 4–6, Tinos Town ☎ 22830 22242. Charming Neoclassical building on the waterfront with fully renovated spacious rooms and modern bathrooms, some with balconies, and an attractive plant-filled communal atrium area. Port transfers, breakfast and free wi-fi included. May–Oct. **€50**

Cavos Áyios Sóstis ☎ 22830 24224, ⓦ cavos-tinos.com. Well situated for the beach and adorned with flowers and palm trees, these large apartments and suites can sleep up to four people and are ideal for families; everything from a baby cot to laundry services can be provided. April–Nov. **€90**

Favie Suzanne Antoníou Sohou 22, Tinos Town ☎ 22830 22693, ⓦ faviesuzanne.gr. An attractive hotel about 200m from the waterfront, fully renovated with facilities for disabled guests, marble balconies and a large swimming pool plus free jacuzzi and wi-fi. Breakfast included. March–Oct. **€70**

★**Tinion Hotel** Alavánou 1, Tinos Town ☎ 22830

22261, ⓦ tinionhotel.gr. A 1920s Neoclassical hotel just back from the waterfront, full of faded grandeur and resonating with history; a Greek prime minister once resigned in the dining room in a fit of pique. Spacious rooms, some with balconies. Port transfers, free wi-fi and breakfast included. March–Nov. **€70**

Tinos Beach Kiónia ☎ 22830 22626, ⓦ tinosbeach.gr. Typical 1970s modernist hotel that dominates the beach, offering comfortable rooms with verandas. Good swimming pool, large breakfast, fair pricing, a range of facilities and regular shuttle into town makes this rather anonymous resort a more attractive option than expected. April–Oct. **€82**

Tinos Camping Louisas Sohou 5, Tinos Town ☎ 22830 22344/23548 ⓦ tinoscamping.gr. One of the nicer and more laidback campsites in the Cyclades, shady and roomy and very close to the centre of town, but reception only open 8am–4pm. En-suite studios are also on offer. May–Oct. Camping **€12**, studios **€35**

EATING

Symposion Evangelistrias 13, Tínos Town ☎ 22830 24368, ⓦ symposion.gr. Sophisticated restaurant at the top of a converted Neoclassical house offering an imaginative menu (€14) that makes no concessions to normal meagre pilgrim fare as is usual around town. It's worth trying its huge English brunch for €17 at least once during your stay. April–Oct daily 9am–4pm & 7.30pm–midnight.

★**To Koutouki tis Elenis** G. Gafou 5, Tínos Town ☎ 22830 24857, ⓦ koutouki-elenis.gr. A gem of a restaurant in an 1812 building with a creative chef who mixes international and traditional cooking with superb results. Try its baked cheeses for a starter, the pork with feta (€9) for a main and finish with its irresistible walnut pie. Daily noon–midnight.

THE DOVECOTE TRAIL

From the port of Tínos drive up Evangelistrías, turn right and follow the signs to **Tripótamos** where you can visit the only still-functioning clay pot workshop on the island. Nearby **Ktikádhos** is a fine village with two superb churches and a very good taverna. Heading northwest from the main road junction beyond Ktikádhos, you can see several beautifully restored **dovecote houses** on the turn-off to **Tarambádho** – it's worth stopping there and following an hour-long signed path through the village, to get as close to these dovecotes as possible, as they are the most photogenic you are likely to encounter.

Driving further north from the Tarambádho turn-off, you can break your trip at **Ystérnia** by turning off to **Órmos Ysterníon**, a pretty, compact beach, and even prettier Skhináki beach at the far end.

There are a number of eating options en route; here are the best:

Drosia Ktikádhos ☎ 22830 41215. A good, vine-shaded, sea-view taverna with mains around €8. One of the few that if booked in advance still offers baked pigeons (*pitsounia*), the age-old traditional Tínos staple food and the *raison d'être* of the dovecotes. April–Oct daily noon–midnight.

★**To Thalassaki** Órmos Ysterníon ☎ 22830 31366,

✉ tothalassaki@gmail.com. Award-winning fish taverna right on the beach providing an exceptional range and quality of food for something so out of the way. Most dishes (€13) are marinated in an infusion of herbs before cooking. Just the sunset views and its extensive ouzo selection are worth making a detour for. March–Oct daily noon–midnight.

The north

A good beginning to a foray into **northern Tínos** is to drive the so-called **Dovecote Trail** (see box, p.139). The ornate dovecotes are mostly found in the villages off the main road between **Tínos Town** and **Ystérnia**.

Pýrgos

Five daily buses along the Dovecote Trail finish up at **PÝRGOS**, a few kilometres beyond Ystérnia and in the middle of the island's marble-quarrying district, as can be surmised by the magnificently crafted marble bus stop. The artisans of this beautiful village are renowned throughout Greece for their skill in producing marble ornamentation; ornate fanlights and bas-relief plaques fashioned here adorn houses throughout Tínos. Pýrgos is also home to a School of Fine Arts, and the **Museum Of Marble Crafts** (March–Oct Wed–Mon 10am–6pm; Nov–Feb Wed–Mon 10am–5pm; €3; ☎ 22830 31290) contains numerous representative works from some of the island's finest pupils. Nearby is the **Yiannoúlis Halepás Museum** (March–Oct daily 11am–2.30pm & 5.30pm–9pm; €3), devoted exclusively to the work of the artist who spent many years here and is generally lauded as the most important Neoclassical Greek sculptor. The small cemetery up and left from the main square offers a free showcase of the villagers' talent over the ages.

Pánormos

Pýrgos' marble products were once exported from **Pánormos** harbour, 4km northeast, with its small, shaded **Stafída** beach. The village itself gives access to a number of good beaches reachable on foot: **Róhari** is to the southeast, facing north, and with deep clear waters and massive waves, while **Ayía Thálassa** and **Kaválargos** are much more sheltered on the northwest side of the bay.

EATING AND DRINKING | THE NORTH

Marina Pánormos ☎ 22830 31314, ✉ marina-taverna @hotmail.com. A seaside ouzerí with a great ouzo and mezédhes selection; spoilt for choice, you may want to order a starters platter (€7) but, unless there are two of you, wait until you've finished before you venture into a main; the portions are quite large. May–Sept daily 10am–midnight.

Myronia Pýrgos ☎ 22830 31229, ✉ iliasofi@otenet.gr. The best of the tavernas and patisseries on the attractive main village square, with seats around the 150-year-old

plane tree. It still serves baked pigeon with pasta (€8) if you pre-order; but there are some excellent veal burgers if you want something more conventional. Easter–Oct daily noon–midnight.

Tis Irinis Pýrgos ☎ 22830 31165. A friendly, popular taverna opposite the stunning marble bus stop that offers good, traditional family favourites such as *pastítsio* (€6) and a quick turnaround service for those pressed for time to visit the museums opposite. Easter–Oct daily noon–midnight.

Around Exóbourgo

The ring of villages around the mountain of **EXÓBOURGO** is a worthwhile visit. The fortified pinnacle itself (570m), with the ruins of three Venetian churches and a fountain, is reached by steep steps from **Xinára** (near the island's major road junction), the old seat of the island's Roman Catholic bishop. Most villages in north-central Tínos have mixed populations, but Xinára and its immediate neighbours are purely Catholic; the inland villages also tend to have a more sheltered position, with better farmland nearby – the Venetians' way of rewarding converts and their descendants.

At **Loutrá**, an almost deserted village north of Xinára (population 17), there's an Ursuline convent, and a small **Folk Art Museum** (daily 9.30am–2.30pm; free) in the seventeenth-century Jesuit monastery. From Krókos, 1km northwest of Loutrá, you can turn to tiny **Voláx**, the most spectacular village on the island: a windswept oasis surrounded by hundreds of giant granite boulders, as far from a typical Greek landscape as you can get in the Cyclades. Alternatively you can continue to **Kómi**, 5km beyond Krókos, where you can take a detour for **Kolymbíthra**, a magnificent double beach: one part wild, huge and windswept and the other balmy and sheltered.

From either Skaládho or Voláx you go on to **Koúmaros**, towards the agricultural villages of **Falatádhos** and **Stení**, which appear as white speckles against the fertile Livádhia valley. Falatádhos has a number of whitewashed churches, including Áyios Ioánnis, notable for its marble decoration. From Stení, which has fewer amenities but plenty of postcard-perfect whitewashed buildings to admire, you can catch the bus back to Tínos Town.

EATING

AROUND EXÓBOURGO

To Katoï Falatádhos ☎ 22830 41000. A good restaurant that draws customers from all around the island, based in a low-ceilinged old warehouse that reminds you of Central European bierkellers; it specializes in grills (€12) and meat on the spit. June–Sept daily 7pm–midnight.

Mýkonos

MÝKONOS has become the most popular, the most high-profile and the most expensive of the Cyclades. Boosted by direct air links with Europe, it sees several million tourists a year pass through, producing some spectacular August overcrowding on the island's 85 square kilometres. But if you don't mind the tourist hordes, or you come in the shoulder season, its striking capital is still one of the most photogenic Cycladic towns, with whitewashed houses concealing a dozen little churches, shrines and chapels.

The sophisticated nightlife is hectic, amply stimulated by Mýkonos's former reputation as *the* gay resort of the Mediterranean, although today gay tourists are well in the minority. While everywhere on the island is at least gay-friendly, gay tourists prefer to congregate in Mýkonos Town itself or the beaches of Super Paradise and Eliá. The locals take it all in their stride, ever conscious of the important revenue generated by their laissez-faire attitude. When they first opened up to the hippy tourists who began appearing on Mýkonos in the 1960s, they assumed their eccentric visitors were sharing cigarettes due to lack of funds. Since then, a lot of the innocence has

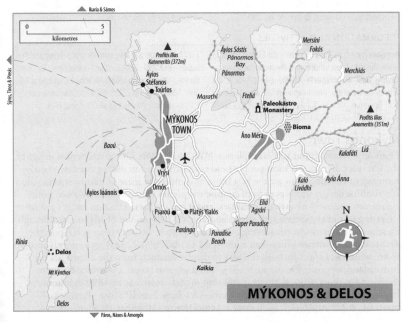

MÝKONOS & DELOS

evaporated, and you shouldn't come for scenery, solitude or tradition, but Mýkonos offers lovely and lively beaches and a party lifestyle second to none.

ARRIVAL AND DEPARTURE
MÝKONOS

By plane The airport is 20min outside Mýkonos Town in the centre of the island.

Destinations Athens (2–7 daily with Aegean and Olympic; 35min); London (2 weekly each with EasyJet/BA; 4hr); Thessaloníki (5 weekly with Aegean; 1hr); Santoríni (daily; 30min).

By ferry Most arrive by ferry at the old port at the north end of Mýkonos Town. Cruise ships and any overflow anchor at the new port, which is 1km further north. Check your ticket before leaving to see if you have an old or a new port stamp. Boats for Delos leave from the waterfront in town.

Destinations Áno Koufoníssi (0–5 weekly; 9hr); Amorgós Aegiáli (0–2 weekly; 2hr 20min); Amorgós Katápola (2–6

weekly; 2hr); Ándhros (1–2 daily; 2hr 30min); Dhonoússa (0–2 weekly; 5hr 30min); Folégandhros (1 daily; 4hr); Irakliá (0–4 weekly; 10hr 15min); Iráklio (Heraklion), Crete (1 daily; 4h 30min); Ikaría (5–6 weekly; 2hr); Íos (1–3 daily; 1hr 15min); Kímolos (1–4 weekly; 11hr 30min); Mílos (1–5 weekly; 5hr 10min–12hr); Náxos (2–3 daily; 45min–1hr); Páros (2–4 daily; 35min–1hr 30min); Pireás (3–4 daily; 4hr–5hr 30min); Rafína (up to 7 daily; 2hr 5min–4hr 40min); Sámos (6–7 weekly; 3hr 40min); Santoríni (2–4 daily; 2hr 15min–3hr 30min); Skhinoússa (0–5 weekly; 10hr); Sérifos (1 weekly; 3hr 30min); Sífnos (1 weekly; 3hr 30min); Síkinos (1–3 weekly; 6hr 45min); Sýros (2–5 daily; 45min–1hr 15min); Tínos (3–7 daily; 30min).

GETTING AROUND

By bus The north bus station for Toúrlos, Áyios Stéfanos, Kalafáti, Eliá and Áno Méra is located by the old port; the south bus station for all western and the popular southern beaches is just outside the pedestrianized area at the other end of town. If you choose to use public transport to the beaches from Paránga to Paradise, you certainly won't be alone – on any sunny day in season the beaches and transport range from busy to overcrowded. Buses to Paradise run every hour through the night in high season. Chartered buses to Super Paradise leave from near the Old Port disembarkation every 30min in season (11am–11pm). All timetables are online at ⓦ mykonosbus.com.

By car or motorbike Rental agencies are concentrated around the two bus stops. The only free parking area near the town is by the north bus station. Parking spaces at most beaches are inadequate and signposting surprisingly poor.

By taxi Taxis run from Mantó square on the main seafront and from the south bus station; the rates are fixed but if there's more than one passenger and it's late at night, you may be asked each to pay the full fare. Try Mykonos Radio Taxi (☎ 22890 22400).

By boat *Kaïkia* head from town and Orkós to all of the southern beaches. A regular boat service (Seabass) runs between the old and new ports (€2).

INFORMATION AND ACTIVITIES

Services There is no shortage of banks or ATMs in Mýkonos Town. The island post office is near the south bus station.

Diving and watersports Kalafáti (see p.146) is the activity centre of the island between late May and early Oct. Operators include Kalafati Dive Center (☎ 22890

71677, ⓦ mykonos-diving.com) for scuba diving, and Pezi-Huber (☎ 22890 72345, ⓦ pezi-huber.com) for wind-surfing. Alternatively, behind Paradise beach (see p.146), Dive Adventures (☎ 22890 24808, ⓦ diveadventures.gr) offer introductory scuba and a full range of PADI.

Mýkonos Town

Don't let the crowds put you off exploring **MÝKONOS TOWN**, the quintessential image of the Cyclades. In summer most people head out to the beaches during the day, so early morning or late afternoon are the best times to wander the maze of narrow streets. The labyrinthine design was supposed to confuse the pirates who plagued Mýkonos in the eighteenth and early nineteenth centuries, and it has the same effect on today's visitors.

Getting lost in the convoluted streets and alleys is half the fun of Mýkonos, although there are a few places worth seeking out. Coming from the ferry quay you'll pass the **Archeological Museum** (Tues–Sun 9am–4pm; €2; ☎ 22890 22325) on your way into town, which was specially built in 1905 to display artefacts from the cemeteries on Rínia island, opposite Delos (see p.147). The town also boasts a **Maritime Museum** displaying various nautical artefacts and ship models as well as an 1890 lighthouse lantern re-erected in the back garden (April–Oct Tues–Sun 10.30am–1pm & 6.30–9pm; €4; ☎ 22890 22700). Next door is **Lena's House** (Mon–Sat 10.30am–2pm &

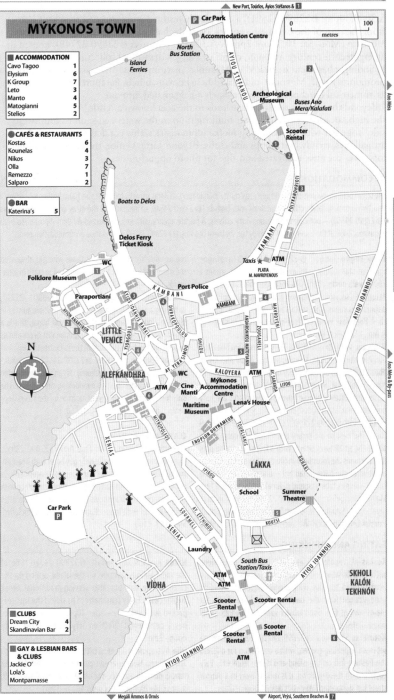

MÝKONOS TOWN

■ ACCOMMODATION
Cavo Tagoo	1
Elysium	6
K Group	7
Leto	3
Manto	4
Matogianni	5
Stelios	2

● CAFÉS & RESTAURANTS
Kostas	6
Kounelas	4
Nikos	3
Olla	7
Remezzo	1
Salparo	2

● BAR
Katerina's	5

■ CLUBS
Dream City	4
Skandinavian Bar	2

■ GAY & LESBIAN BARS & CLUBS
Jackie O'	1
Lola's	5
Montparnasse	3

5.30–8.30pm; ☎22890 22591), a completely restored and furnished merchant home from the turn of the twentieth century. Near the base of the Delos jetty, the **Folklore Museum** (Mon–Sat 10.30am–2pm & 5.30–8.30pm; free; ☎22890 22748), housed in an eighteenth-century mansion, crams in a larger-than-usual collection of bric-a-brac, including a basement dedicated to Mýkonos' maritime past. The museum shares the promontory with Mýkonos' oldest and best-known church, **Paraportianí**, a fascinating asymmetrical hotchpotch of four chapels amalgamated into one.

Beyond the church, the shoreline leads to the area known as **Little Venice** because of the high, arcaded Venetian houses built right up to the water's edge on its southwest side. Together with the adjoining **Alefkándhra** district, this is a dense area packed with art galleries, trendy bars, shops and clubs. Beyond Little Venice, the famous **windmills** look over the area, renovated and ripe for photo opportunities.

ACCOMMODATION   MÝKONOS TOWN

The scrum of room-owners by the old port jetty can be intimidating, so if you arrive by ferry press on 100m further, where you'll find two accommodation offices; one deals with **hotels** (☎22890 24540, ⓦmha.gr) and the other with **rented rooms** (☎22890 24860) – both are open during ferry arrivals. A private agency with longer hours (daily 9am–9pm) deals with accommodation at the lower end of town by the southern bus stop (☎22890 23160; ⓦmykonos-accommodation.com).

Cavo Tagoo Tangoú ☎22890 20100, ⓦcavotagoo .gr. Five-star luxury hotel overlooking the sea, about a 700m walk north of the Old Port disembarkation point. Attentive service, spacious rooms, roof pool with panoramic views and restaurant with specialist sushi chef. Breakfast included; four-night minimum stay July & Aug. May–Oct. **€450**

K Group Vrýsi ☎22890 23415, ⓦmyconiancollection .gr. A cluster of hotels, *Kalypso*, *Kochyli*, *Korali* and *Kyma*, about 1km south of town. Many of the comfortable rooms have wonderful views and there's also a pool and restaurant. Often available when smaller places are fully booked. Breakfast included. Easter–Oct. **€160**

★**Leto** Old Port ☎22890 22207/22918, ⓦletohotel .com. The best of the luxury town hotels, slightly raised above the small town beach, with a large swimming pool that becomes the focus both in the daytime and, fully lit, at night when the hotel restaurant – one of the best on the island – lays its tables around it. Breakfast included. **€120**

Manto Evangelistrías 1 ☎22890 22330, ✉mantohotel1 @yahoo.gr. Situated in a small side street, the hotel's exterior belies its Tardis-like interior expanse. Good, simple

rooms with a/c and fridge for those who are always on the move and just want a comfortable bed to crash in afterwards. March–Nov. **€75**

Matogianni Matogianni Str ☎22890 22217, ⓦmatogianni.gr. Living proof that it's possible to stay in Mýkonos Town without mortgaging your home, this is a comfortable hotel with classically minimalist decor and as peaceful as can be in the buzz of the backstreets. **€60**

Stelios Above the old port ☎22890 24641. This white-washed Mykoniot-style building is an excellent-value pension in a prime location overlooking the old port. The only hitch may be hauling your luggage up the steep steps behind the OTE office. April–Oct. **€60**

GAY AND LESBIAN

Elysium By the School of Fine Arts ☎22890 23952, ⓦelysiumhotel.com. Exclusively gay hotel with beautiful views, boasting a poolside bar open to nonresidents, a popular setting for an early-evening party complete with go-go dancers and drag shows. Occasional all-night parties in conjunction with international DJs. Breakfast included. May–Oct. **€160**

EATING AND DRINKING

Kostas Mitropoléos 5 ☎22890 23326. Buried deep within Alefkándhra, this restaurant serves everything from seafood to grills with a good wine list including wine straight from the barrel (€6/half litre). Prices for mains start at €14. Good lobster spaghetti for €25. Daily noon–2am.

Kounelas Svorónou ☎22890 28220. Seafood taverna set in an appealing garden, with a reputation for offering the freshest fish on the island and dishes from €15. Very popular with the gay crowd, it is tucked away in a narrow street but signposted. May–Oct daily 6.30pm–2am.

Nikos Ayías Monís square ☎22890 24320. One of the most famous tavernas on the island, strong on the catch of the day but also serving traditional Greek cuisine (€15). Every centimetre of its side of the square is packed with customers after 10pm, which sometimes has a detrimental effect on seryice. April–Oct daily noon–2am.

Olla Mitropoléos 11 ☎22890 77177, ⓦolla-mykonos .gr. Inspired Mediterranean cuisine in cheerful designer surroundings in a cul-de-sac off Mitrópoleos. Salads €10, mains €14–20. April–Oct daily 10am–1am.

Remezzo Old Port ☎ 22890 25700, ⓦ remezzomykonos
.com. Stylish, expensive restaurant, offering nouvelle
cuisine dishes from €20 and alternative sunset views to
those at Little Venice. April–Oct daily 8pm–late.
★**Salparo** Kaminaki Waterfront ☎ 22890 78950.

The old *Baboulas* changed its name but only that: it still
offers the best coal-grilled seafood mezédhes on Mýkonos,
all personally supervised by Petroúla, the owner and chef.
Try the mussels cooked in seawater (€13) and marvel.
April–Nov daily noon–midnight.

NIGHTLIFE

Dream City Lákka ☎ 22890 24100. Offshoot of the
successful Athens club of the same name, this is a club that
plays feelgood dance music with the best sound system
this side of Ibiza. Entrance varies by night and includes first
drink. Mid-April to May & Sept Fri & Sat midnight–8am;
June–Aug daily midnight–8am.
Katerina's Little Venice ☎ 22890 23084. Owned by the
first female captain in the Greek navy, Katerina, this low-
key bar-restaurant with sea and sunset views from the
balcony, is one of the most laidback places for a drink
(cocktails €10). April–Oct daily noon–late.
Skandinavian Bar Áyios Ioánnis Barkiá ☎ 22890
22669, ⓦ skandinavianbar.com. For some serious
drinking, head for the *Skandinavian*, which has been
thumping out dance music, beer (€6) and cocktails (€8)
until the early hours since 1978. VIP table service can be
booked. May–Sept daily 8pm–late.

GAY AND LESBIAN

Jackie O' Near Paraportianí ☎ 22890 77168, ⓦ jackieo
mykonos.com. The busiest gay club in town, it attracts a
crowd of all sexual persuasions who like to dance to relentless
funky house mixed with the occasional disco hit. On two
floors, although trying to reach the top bar through the crowd
is sometimes impossible. Easter–Oct daily 10pm–6am.
Lola's Pittaraki St ☎ 22890 78391. Chic bar owned by
long-standing Mýkonos residents Dimitris and Gilles, with
gay icons on the wall, camp decor and torch songs on the
radio. Try the kick of their espresso martini (€12) and never
touch a vodka Red Bull again. April–Oct 8pm–3am.
Montparnasse Ayíon Anargýron 24, Little Venice
☎ 22890 23719, ⓦ thepianobar.com. With great
cocktails (€8) and a balcony over the sea, this gay piano bar
is a very good place to warm up for the night ahead. Sunset
views followed by cabaret and live music. May–Oct daily
7pm–3am.

Around Mýkonos Town

The closest **beaches** around Mýkonos Town are those to the north, at **Toúrlos**
(only 2km away but not up to the usual standard) and **Áyios Stéfanos** (3km away,
much better), both developed resorts and connected by a very regular bus service
to Mýkonos Town. There are tavernas and rooms (as well as package hotels) at
Áyios Stéfanos. You'll need your own transport, a bus or *kaïki*, to get to most
of them.

The undistinguished but popular beaches southwest of the town are tucked into
pretty bays. The nearest, 1km away, is **Megáli Ámmos**, a good but often windy beach
backed by flat rocks and pricey rooms, but nearby Kórfos Bay is unpleasant, thanks to
the town dump and machine noise. Buses serve **Ornós**, a package resort on a low-lying
area between the rest of the island and the Áyios Ioánnis peninsula. The south side has
a reasonable beach, plus *kaïkia* to other beaches, a handful of tavernas, and numerous
accommodation options.

Two kilometres west is **Áyios Ioánnis**, the island's westernmost bay and small,
namesake church, overlooking Delos – the tiny public beach achieved a moment of
fame as a location for the film *Shirley Valentine*. Accessed by a 500m dirt track
northwest from Áyios Ioánnis is the small but popular beach at **Kápari**, with good views
of Delos and the sunset.

ACCOMMODATION

AROUND MÝKONOS TOWN

Dionysos Ornós ☎ 22890 23313, ⓦ dionysoshotel.gr.
Easily the most comfortable hotel in the area with a
pool and adjoining bar, free wi-fi, satellite TV, children's
area and a fitness room, as well as parking space – a
mission impossible in Ornós. Breakfast included. May–
Oct. **€150**

Manoulas Beach Áyios Ioánnis ☎ 22890 22900,
ⓦ hotelmanoulas.gr. A surprisingly affordable high-class
hotel, blindingly set in white against the background of
the deep blue of the Aegean. The panoramic view from its
restaurant (mains from €12) across to Delos is breathtaking.
Breakfast included. May–Oct. **€120**

The south coast

The western half of the **south coast** is the busiest part of the island. *Kaïkia* and buses head from town to all of its beaches. Drivers will find that car-parking spaces at most beaches are inadequate and signposting surprisingly poor.

Platýs Yialós and Psaroú

You might begin with **Platýs Yialós**, 4km south of town: one of the longest-established resorts on the island, where the sand is monopolized by end-to-end hotels. **Psaroú**, just a steep hairpin road away to the west, is much prettier – 150m of white sand backed by foliage and reeds.

Paránga and Paradise beach

Just over the headland to the east of Platýs Yialós lies **Paránga**, actually two beaches separated by a smaller headland, the first of which is quieter than its neighbour. Next is the golden crescent of **Paradise beach**. Here, as on many of Mýkonos' most popular beaches, it can be difficult to find an opening big enough to fit a towel in high season, and any space clear of people is likely to be taken up by straw umbrellas, rentable (usually along with two accompanying loungers) for about €16 per day.

Super Paradise beach and Agrári

The next bay east contains **Super Paradise beach**, accessible by *kaïki*, or by a surfaced but extremely steep access road. It is one of the most fun spots on the island, with its main beach bar staging a party every evening at 6pm. The western part is dominated by the *Jackie O'* gay complex (daily 9am–9pm; ☎22890 77298) which has a separate signposted entrance for cars. The more secluded **Agrári** beach is 300m to the east.

Eliá and Kaló Livádhi

One of the more scenically attractive beaches on Mýkonos is **Eliá**, the last port of call east for the *kaïkia*, also reachable via an inland road. A broad, sandy stretch, with plenty of parking and a mountainous backdrop at the eastern end, it's the longest beach on the island, though divided by a rocky area, and almost exclusively gay later in the season. East from the Eliá road is **Kaló Livádhi** (seasonal bus service), long and sandy, and fronting an agricultural valley scattered with little farmhouses.

ACCOMMODATION — THE SOUTH COAST

★**Mykonos Camping** Paránga ☎22890 25915/6, ⓦmycamp.gr. This campsite and hostel on the Paránga beach has one of the most pleasant settings on the island. It offers a wood-fired pizzeria, a pool with an adjoining cocktail bar, restaurant and minimarket, as well as relative peace and quiet from the relentless Mykoniot buzz. May–Oct. Camping €12.50, dorm €10/person

Paradise Beach Resort Paradise ☎22890 22852, ⓦparadise-greece.com. An industrial-size (and feel) campsite operating since 1969, also offering a huge accommodation choice including cabins and bungalows. Totally self-sufficient with a restaurant, various bars, a clothes shop and its own club with resident DJs. April–Oct. Camping €30, cabins €30, bungalows €90

NIGHTLIFE

★**Cavo Paradiso** Paradise ☎22890 27205, ⓦcavo paradiso.gr. The after-hours club in the Cyclades, regularly voted as one of the top ten in the world, where die-hard party animals of all persuasions come together, united by world-famous DJs. The €20 entrance charge includes first drink, but check for discounts/guest list online. Mid-June to mid-Sept (daily in July & Aug) 11.30pm–8am.

The east and north

The main road **east** via the unexciting village of **Áno Méra** leads to **Ayía Ánna**, on a double-headed headland with a shingle beach and taverna, just before the larger, more attractive **Kalafáti**, the island's cleanest beach. **Liá**, roughly 4.6km east by road from Áno Méra, is smaller than Kalafáti, but as pleasant and with as clear water.

The **north coast** suffers persistent battering from the *meltémi* and for the most part is bare, brown and exposed. The deep inlet of **Pánormos Bay** is the exception to this, with the lovely, relatively sheltered beaches of **Pánormos** and **Áyios Sóstis**; although not served by buses, they are becoming increasingly popular, but still remain among the least crowded on the island. At the southern, inner end of the bay, **Fteliá** is a good windsurfers' beach and legendary burial site of Ajax, one of *The Íliad*'s mythical heroes. If you are driving there, stop by at the only – but excellent – vineyard on the island, **Bíoma** (☎22890 71883), for some wine tasting.

ACCOMMODATION AND EATING
THE EAST AND NORTH

★**Aphrodite Beach** Kalafáti ☎22890 71367, ⓦaphrodite-mykonos.gr. A four-star hotel 18km from Mýkonos Town, and completely self-sufficient should you want to sample Mýkonos without the crowds. There is also a selection of hostel-style accommodation with four bunk beds per room, so it draws a very hip young crowd. April–Nov. Dorms €45, doubles €110

Liasti Liá ☎22890 72150, ⓦliasti.com. The furthest restaurant east, but don't let that deter you if you have your own transport. Once there, you will be surprised as to how busy it is, but once you sample the Italian menu (€12) you'll understand. April–Sept daily 10am–9pm.

Thalassa Kalafáti beach ☎22890 72081. Happening beach bar during the day and one of the best places to eat on Mýkonos for dinner. Its pork in cheese and mushroom sauce (€17) is one of the top gastronomic experiences on the island. All this and free wi-fi, too. May–Sept daily noon–midnight.

Delos

The remains of **ANCIENT DELOS (Dhílos)**, the Cyclades' sole UNESCO Heritage Site, manage to convey the past grandeur of this small, sacred isle a few kilometres west of Mýkonos. The ancient town lies on the west coast on flat, sometimes marshy ground that rises in the south to **Mount Kýnthos**.

The site

Tues–Sun 9am–3pm • €5 • ☎22890 22259

As you disembark from the boat, the Sacred Harbour is on your left, the Commercial Harbour on your right and straight ahead lies the **Agora of the Competaliasts**. The

---

OLD DELOS DAYS

Delos's ancient fame arose because **Leto** gave birth to the divine twins **Artemis** and **Apollo** here, although the island's fine, sheltered harbour and central position in the Aegean did nothing to hamper development from around 2500 BC. When the Ionians colonized the island about 1000 BC it was already a cult centre, and by the seventh century BC it had also become a major commercial and religious port. Unfortunately Delos attracted the attention of Athens, which sought dominion over this prestigious island; the wealth of the **Delian Confederacy**, founded after the Persian Wars to protect the Aegean cities, was harnessed to Athenian ends, and for a while Athens controlled the Sanctuary of Apollo. Athenian attempts to "purify" the island began with a decree (426 BC) that no one could die or give birth on Delos – the sick and the pregnant were shipped to the neighbouring island of **Rínia** – and culminated in the simple expedient of banishing the native population.

Delos recovered in Roman times and reached its peak of prosperity in the third and second centuries BC, after being declared a free port by its Roman overlords; by the start of the first century BC, its population was around 25,000. In the end, though, its undefended wealth brought ruin: first **Mithridates** of Pontus (88 BC), then the pirate **Athenodorus** (69 BC) plundered the treasures, and the island never recovered.

Competaliasts were Roman merchants who worshipped the Lares Competales, the guardian spirits of crossroads; offerings to Hermes would once have been placed in the middle of the agora (market square), their positions now marked by one round and one square base.

Sacred Way and Sanctuary of Apollo

The **Sacred Way** leads north from the far left corner of the Agora of the Competaliasts and was formerly lined with statues and the grandiose monuments of rival kings; walk up it to reach the three marble steps of the **Propýlaia** leading into the **Sanctuary of Apollo**.

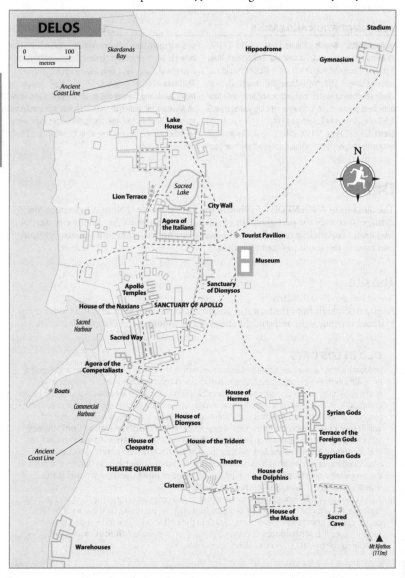

On your left is the Stoá of the Naxians, while against the north wall of the House of the Naxians, to the right, is the spot where a huge statue of Apollo (c.600 BC) stood in ancient times; parts of it can be seen behind the **Temple of Artemis** to the left. In 417 BC the Athenian general Nikias led a procession of priests across a bridge of boats from Rínia to dedicate a bronze palm tree whose circular granite base you can still see. Three **Temples to Apollo** stand in a row to the right along the Sacred Way: the massive Delian Temple, the Athenian, and the Porinos, the earliest, dating from the sixth century BC. To the east stands the **Sanctuary of Dionysus** with its colossal marble phallus.

Lions' Quarter

Northwest of the Sanctuary of Dionysus, behind the small **Letóön** temple, is the huge **Agora of the Italians**, while on the left are replicas of the famous **lions**, their lean bodies masterfully executed by Naxians in the seventh century BC to ward off intruders who would have been unfamiliar with the fearful creatures. Of the original lions, three have disappeared and one – looted by Venetians in the seventeenth century– adorns the Arsenale in Venice. The remaining originals are in the site **museum** whose nine rooms include a marble statue of Apollo, mosaic fragments and an extensive collection of phallic artefacts. Opposite the lions, tamarisk trees ring the site of the **Sacred Lake**, where Leto gave birth, clinging to a palm tree. On the other side of the lake is the City Wall, built – in 69 BC – too late to protect the treasures.

Theatre Quarter

Bear right from the Agora of the Competaliasts and you enter the residential area, known as the **Theatre Quarter**. The remnants of impressive private mansions are now named after their colourful main **mosaic** – Dionysus, Trident, Masks and Dolphins. The **theatre** itself seated no fewer than 5500 spectators; just below it and structurally almost as spectacular is a huge underground cistern with arched roof supports. Behind the theatre, a path leads towards the **Sanctuaries of the Foreign Gods**, serving the immigrant population. It then rises steeply up Mount Kýnthos for a **Sanctuary of Zeus and Athena** with spectacular views out to the surrounding islands. Near its base, a small side path leads to the **Sacred Cave**, a rock cleft covered with a remarkable roof of giant stone slabs – a Hellenistic shrine to Hercules.

ARRIVAL AND DEPARTURE   **DELOS**

By boat In season, two excursion boats to Delos leave from the west end of Mýkonos harbour Tues–Sun at 9am, 11am, 1pm and 5pm, returning from the site at 12.15pm, 1.30pm, 3pm & 7.30pm (€18 return from a kiosk at the front). Guided day-trips are also possible from Mýkonos as well as Tínos (see p.137). Note that it is illegal to remove anything from Delos as well as anchor, swim or dive at or near the island. Allow 4hr if you want to walk the whole site and see the museum.

Sýros

SÝROS is a living, working island with only a fleeting history of tourism, rendering it the most Greek of the Cyclades. There's a thriving, permanent community, the beaches are busy but not overflowing and the villages don't sprawl widely with new developments. As well as being home to a number of excellent restaurants, the island is known for its numerous shops selling *loukoúmia* (Turkish delight), *mandoláta* (nougat) and *halvadhópita* (soft nougat between disc-shaped wafers). In addition Sýros still honours its contribution to the development of **rembétika** music: Markos Vamvakaris, one of its prime proponents, hailed from Áno Sýros where a square has been named after him.

The island's sights – including the best beaches – are concentrated in the south and west; the north is unpopulated and barren, offering little interest. Most people tend to stay in **Ermoúpolis**, the island's and the Cyclades' capital, which offers better connections to a variety of beaches, none further than 15km away.

ARRIVAL AND GETTING AROUND

By plane The island is served by Athens (via Olympic, 6 weekly; 45min). There's no bus service from the airport, so you'll need to arrange a pick-up or take a taxi.

By ferry All ferries dock at Ermoúpolis, on the east coast. Destinations Amorgós (3–4 weekly; 5–6hr); Anáfi (3 weekly; 10hr); Ándhros (2–3 weekly; 2hr 30min); Astypálea (1 weekly; 6hr 30min); Folégandhros (5 weekly; 5hr 30min); Ikaría (6–7 weekly; 3hr); Íos (3–5 weekly; 4hr); Koufoníssi/Lesser Cyclades (3 weekly; 3hr–7hr 30min); Lávrio via Kéa/Kýthnos (2–4 weekly; 4hr); Mílos/Kímolos (3–5 weekly; 5–7hr); Mýkonos (2–5 daily; 1hr); Náxos (2–5 weekly; 2hr); Páros (2–5 weekly; 1hr 10min–1hr 30min); Pátmos (1 weekly; 3hr 30min); Pireás (2–3 daily; 3–4hr); Sámos (6 weekly; 4hr 30min); Santoríni (3–5 weekly; 5–7hr); Sérifos (3 weekly; 2–5hr); Sífnos (3 weekly; 2hr 30min–6hr); Síkinos (3–5 weekly; 5hr); Tínos (2–6 daily; 30–50min).

By bus The buses inside the city are free, but there are moves to start charging soon. There are two hourly route loops running in opposite directions: Ermoúpoli to Galissás (20min), Fínikas (25min), Posidonía (30min), Mega Yialos, Vari, Azólimnos then back to Ermoúpoli; and vice versa, from Ermoúpoli to Azólimnos (15min), Vari (20min), Mega Yialos (25min), Posidonía (30min), Fínikas and Galissas. There is also a seasonal route from Ermoúpoli to Kini (20min).

By taxi Sýros drivers tend not to use the taximeter, so insist. If you're unsuccessful, be aware that a fare inside the city should cost around €3 and from the port to Áno Sýros €5 (☎ 22810 86222).

SÝROS

By car or motorbike There are many car and motorbike rental agencies on the Ermoúpolis waterfront, including Gaviotis, Akti Papagou 20 (☎ 22810 86610). Note that the police are pretty stringent here about giving drivers alcohol tests or fines for speeding.

INFORMATION AND TOURS

Tourist office TeamWork at Aktí Papágou 18 on the waterfront in Ermoúpolis (☎ 22810 83400, ⊕ teamwork .gr) is a useful source of information and is able to help with your accommodation, excursion and ticket needs. In the summer there's an accommodation kiosk on the waterfront open during ferry arrivals.

Services There are several banks and about a dozen ATMs in Ermoúpolis, mostly around the waterfront. The post office is on Protopapadháki St. Laundry facilities are

available at Krinos, Protopapadháki 34 (☎ 22810 88554). In Spot, on the seafront at Papágou, has internet but requires that you become a member, the cheapest option being €5 for 3hr. It's open 24hr daily.

Tours Starting from Platía Miaoúli in Ermoúpolis, a small tourist train runs a 40min tour of the town's main sights (€4), while horse-drawn carriages (☎ 22810 81517) start from the centre of the waterfront in season, doing city tours of various durations (€10–50).

Ermoúpolis

Possessing an elegant collection of grand townhouses that rise majestically from the bustling, café-lined waterfront, **ERMOÚPOLIS** – once Greece's chief port – is one of the most striking towns in the Cyclades, and is certainly worth at least a night's stay.

Medieval Sýros was largely Catholic, but the influx of refugees from Psará and Híos during the nineteenth century created two distinct communities. Today, the Orthodox community accounts for two-thirds of the population; Lower Ermoúpolis is mostly Orthodox while the Catholics live in the Upper Town and in the majority of the villages. They do, however, commonly celebrate each other's festivals (including Easter on the Orthodox dates only), lending a vibrant mix of cultures that gives the island its colour.

Platía Miaoúli and around

The long, central square, **Platía Miaoúli**, is named after an admiral of the War of Independence whose statue stands there, and in the evenings the population parades in front of its arcades. The bougainvillea-covered pedestrian street of Roïdi and side streets east of Miaoúli square are peppered with most of the better eating options.

Up the stepped street (Benáki) to the left of the town hall is the small **Archeological Museum** (Tues–Sun 8.30am–3pm; free; ☎22810 88487) with three rooms of finds from Sýros, Páros and Amorgós. To the left of the clocktower more steps climb up to **Vrondádho**, the hill that hosts the Orthodox quarter. The wonderful church of the

Anástasis stands atop the hill, with its domed roof and panoramic views over Tínos and Mýkonos.

Below Miaoúli square, and down a side street you can find the elaborate **Casino** and the **Church of the Dormition** (April–Aug 7.30am–noon & 5.30–6.30pm; Sept–March 7.30am–12.30pm & 4.30–5.30pm; free), which contains the town's top art treasure: a painting of the Assumption by **El Greco**, executed while he was around 20 years old.

North to Vapória

Up from the right of Miaoúli square is the **Apollon Theatre**, built like an Italian provincial opera house, which occasionally hosts performances (during morning rehearsals you can enter and watch for free or visit its small museum for €1.50). Further on up is the handsome Neoclassical Orthodox church of **Áyios Nikólaos**, which was built in 1848–70 and has an impressive marble iconostasis (7am–2pm & 5–8pm). Beyond it lies the **Vapória** district, where the island's wealthiest shipowners, merchants and bankers built their mansions.

Áno Sýros

On the taller hill to the left from Miaoúli square is the intricate medieval quarter of **Áno Sýros**, with a clutch of Catholic churches below the cathedral of St George. Just below it lies the **Capuchin monastery of St Jean**, founded in 1535 to do duty as a poorhouse. Once up here it's worth visiting the local art and rembétika exhibitions, as well as personal items of the man himself at the **Markos Vamvakaris museum** (June–Sept daily 11am–2pm & 7–10pm; €1.50).

ACCOMMODATION   **ERMOÚPOLIS**

Hermes Kanári Square ☏ 22810 83011/88011, ⓦ hermes-syros.com. Modernist Sixties hotel in a prime location, home to a very popular seafront restaurant (mains €10). Ask specifically for a room with sea views. Breakfast included. **€65**

Omiros Omírou 43 ☏ 22810 84910, ⓦ hotel-omiros.gr. One of the most romantic options in town, on a quiet road above the Orthodox cathedral, in the direction of Áno Sýros. Classically styled rooms set in an elegant nineteenth-century mansion once owned by Tiniot sculptor Yeóryios Vitalis. Breakfast €5. **€60**

Palladion Proïou 60 ☏ 22810 86400, ⓦ palladion-hotel.com. Not far from the casino, yet quiet, clean, recently renovated and with rooms overlooking a garden; overall excellent value. **€60**

Paradise Omírou 3 ☏ 22810 83204, ⓦ paradiserooms.gr. Basic en-suite rooms in a quiet part of town. All rooms have access to a pleasant shaded courtyard, while rooms on the top floor have good views. Breakfast €7. **€40**

Sea Colours Apartments Athinás 10 ☏ 22810 81181. Traditionally decorated apartments for up to six people, with sea views, just above the swimming platforms of Áyios Nikólaos, a 5min walk from Platía Miaoúli. April–Nov. **€40**

★**Sýrou Mélathron** Babayiótou 5 ☏ 22810 85963, ⓦ syroumelathron.gr. Regal hotel, recently renovated, set in a restored 1856 mansion in the quieter Áyios Nikólaos area of town. Has suites as well as spacious rooms, some with sea views (about €10 extra). Breakfast included. **€80**

EATING

Amvix Aktí Papágou 26 ☏ 22810 83989. Owned by Roberto, an Italian chef from Padua, since 1995, this trattoria offers a taste of real Italy. Best pizzas on the island for €12. Daily noon–midnight.

Archontariki tis Maritsas Roïdi 8 ☏ 22810 86771. Very popular rustic taverna that serves island specialities, including its signature dish of casserole of mushrooms and spicy local sausage with peppers (€8). Daily noon–midnight.

Lilis Piazza, Áno Syros ☏ 22810 88087. An institution in the old town, with an unmatched view by the Kamares entrance, this is the taverna where Vamvakaris (see above)

played. It's been going since 1953, offering Greek specialities from Asia Minor (€9). Daily noon–midnight.

★**Stin Ithaki tou Aï** Klonos, corner with Ayíou Stefánou 1 ☏ 22810 82060, ⓦ ithakitouai.gr. Welcoming taverna serving traditional *ladherá* dishes (various vegetables cooked in oil), as well as a good, cheap *souvláki* (€10). Daily noon–midnight.

Yiannena Kanári Square ☏ 22810 82994. Popular, friendly spot, seemingly unchanged since the 1950s, serving great seafood and other Greek standards (€7). A smaller branch is on Venizelou 2. Daily 11am–1am.

NIGHTLIFE

Casino Aigeou Proïou 74 ☏22810 84400, ⓦcasino syros.gr. Large casino that draws in well-dressed punters (no T-shirts, shorts or flip-flops) from as far as Russia. Minimum bid roulette €2.50; Black Jack €5; slot machines open 24hr. Over-21s only. Daily 8pm–3.50am.

Piramatiko Platía Miaoúli ☏22810 83734. Busy, sophisticated bar, playing a varied and eclectic mix from

indie rock to house music. Starts off as a café and ends up as a club. Cheap beers start at €3. Daily 9am–3am.

Theia Methi Chiou 43 ☏6908 520 165. If you want to hear contemporary rembétika, then take an early seat at this *mezedhopolío* on the western side of Platía Miaoúli, which often has live music after 9.30pm; order your mains (€8) and enjoy the show. Daily 7pm–late.

The beaches

Syros offers a decent choice of **beaches**, which rarely become overwhelmingly crowded, even in high season. The best are located on the south and west coasts, within easy reach of Ermoúpolis – and many are served by the circular bus route around the island (see p.150).

Galissás and Armeós

The first stop on the bus round-trip from Ermoúpolis is well-developed **Galissás**, the largest beach on the island. If you feel the urge to escape the crowds, walk ten minutes around the *Dolphin Bay Hotel* to reach the nudist beach of **Armeós**. You can also drive southwest to the end of the dirt road over the ridge of Charassónas and walk down (30min) to the **sea cave** of Áyios Stéfanos (signposted), which has a remarkable chapel built inside it.

Fínikas and Posidhonía

A rural forty-minute walk, or a ten-minute bus ride south from Galissás, brings you to the more mainstream resort of **Fínikas**, with its long and narrow beach protected from the road by a row of tamarisk trees. Fínikas is separated by a small headland from its neighbour **Posidhonía** (or Delagrazia after the local church).

Agathopés, Komitó and Mégas Yialós

From Fínikas, it's worth walking ten minutes further south, past the naval yacht club and its patrol boat, to **Agathopés**. This is the best sandy beach on the island, facing a little islet, Skhinónisi, just offshore. **Komitó**, at the end of the road leading south 500m from Agathopés, is a small, quiet sandy bay below a private olive grove.

From Posidhonía the road swings southeast to **Mégas Yialós**, a diffuse, elongated resort. There are two beaches, Mégas Yialós and Ambélia; the long, eponymous beach is lined with shady trees and there are pedal boats for hire.

Akhládhi, Vári and Azólimnos

The cove of **Akhládhi** is sheltered and family-friendly, while **Vári**, just beyond, is more – though not much more – of a town, with its own small fishing fleet. As it is the most sheltered of the island's bays – something to remember when the *meltémi* is up – it attracts mostly families and little children; the younger crowd are attracted by the beach bars of Agathopés and Komito above. The final resort on the circular tour is **Azólimnos**, accessed by a narrow road from Vári, or a wider one from the northern end.

Kíni

A bus also goes to **Kíni**, in the west of the island, 7km from Ermoúpolis. This is an ideal resort for families with small children as it has a sheltered, sandy beach and shallow waters. There are umbrellas, sunbeds and tamarisk trees for shade, with several beachside tavernas operating in season.

3

ACCOMMODATION

Akrothalasia Azólimnos ☎ 22810 61653, ⊛ akrothalasia .com. Astonishingly good value hotel, offering self-catering studios next to the beach with a pool and children's pool, parking space, wi-fi, and a cafeteria on the premises. May–Sept. **€35**

Brazzera Fínikas ☎ 22810 79173, ⊛ brazzera.gr. Modern, well-situated hotel close to the beach, whose green furnishings tastefully match the green of the salt

THE BEACHES

cedars in front. Large rooms with tiled floors adorned with flowers make this one of the most pleasant stays outside Ermoúpolis. Breakfast included. April–Oct. **€65**

Dolphin Bay Galissás ☎ 22810 42924, ⊛ dolphin-bay .gr. Luxurious hotel, amphitheatrically built with impressive views over the bay from its large swimming pool and bar. The complex includes an excellent restaurant (mains €15). Free wi-fi everywhere, breakfast included. May–Sept. **€50**

EATING

Niriídhes Akhládhi ☎ 6978 830 332. This fish taverna, the beach offshoot of the *Archontariki tis Maritsas* (see p.152) in Ermoúpolis, specializes in imaginative seafood dishes such as shrimp omelette, yet still has a place for time-honoured platters like grilled octopus (€9). May–Oct 10am–midnight.

To Iliovasilema Galissás ☎ 22810 43325. A small

seaside taverna with an inventive menu, it punches well above its weight in the reputation stakes. The owner has his own boat and nothing from the catch goes to waste: small fish are used for the bouillabaisse, shellfish are added to the pasta sauce, while the larger items are grilled with lemon and herbs. Daily April–Oct noon–midnight; Nov–March 7pm–midnight.

Páros

With a gentle and undramatic landscape arranged around the central peak of Profítis Ilías, **PÁROS** has a little of everything one expects from a Greek island: old villages, monasteries, fishing harbours, nice beaches and varied nightlife. However, **Parikiá**, the capital, can be touristy and expensive, and it is very difficult finding rooms and beach space here in August, during which the other settlements, the port of **Náoussa** and the satellite island of Andíparos (see p.162), handle most of the overflow. Drinking and carousing is many people's idea of a holiday on Páros, so it's not surprising that both Parikiá and Náoussa have a wealth of pubs, bars and discos, offering staggered happy hours. Happily, culture is also available, in the form of the astonishing paleo-Christian **church of Ekatondapyliani**.

ARRIVAL AND GETTING AROUND

By plane The island is served by regular flights from Athens (via Olympic; 2–4 daily; 35min). The airport is 12km south of Parikiá. There are buses waiting for the flights during the summer months.

By ferry Parikiá is a major hub for inter-island ferry services and serves almost all islands in the Cyclades. There are two ferries from Páros to Andíparos: the first is a passenger ferry from Parikiá and the second is a car ferry from Poúnda, 7km south of Parikiá (see opposite). The latter leaves every 30–45min during the summer months; 7.15am–1.30am. For more information on ferries, call ☎ 22840 21240.

Destinations Amorgós (2–3 daily; 3hr); Áno Koufoníssi (1–2 daily; 3hr); Anáfi (1 weekly; 9hr 30min); Andíparos (hourly in season; 40min); Astypálea (1–4 weekly; 5hr); Dhonoússa (1–2 weekly; 3hr 15min); Iraklliá (1–3 weekly; 3hr); Iráklio (Heraklion), Crete (1 daily; 3hr 45min); Folégandhros (3–5 weekly; 3hr 15min); Íos (1–3 daily; 2hr); Kálymnos (1 weekly; 8hr); Kímolos (2 weekly; 4hr 30min); Kós (1 weekly; 9hr); Lávrio via Kéa/Kýthnos (1 weekly; 8hr); Mílos (4–6 weekly; 5hr 45min); Mýkonos

PÁROS

(2–4 daily; 30–45min); Náxos (3–6 daily; 35min–1hr); Nísyros (1 weekly; 11hr); Pireás (3–5 daily; 3–4hr); Rhodes (1 weekly; 15hr); Santoríni (2–3 daily; 2–3hr); Skhinoússa (1–3 weekly; 2hr 20min); Sérifos (1–2 weekly; 2hr 15min); Sífnos (1–2 weekly; 3hr 10min); Síkinos (2–3 weekly; 4hr); Sýros (1–3 weekly; 1hr 35min–3hr)); Tílos (1 weekly; 12hr 30min); Tínos (1–2 daily; 50min–1hr 10min).

Travel agents Polos Tours (☎ 22840 22092/3, ⊛ polos tours.gr) in Parikiá is one of the better travel agencies, issuing air tickets for Olympic, and acting as agents for virtually all the boats.

By bus The bus station is 100m or so west of the ferry dock. Note that there are two places called Poúnda on Páros, one being the west-coast port, the other a beach on the east coast (see p.161). Destinations include Náoussa (hourly through the night in high season; 20min), Poúnda for Andíparos (1–2 hourly; 20min) and Dhryós (3–5 daily; 1hr).

By car or motorbike Rental outfits in Parikiá include European (☎ 22840 21771, ⊛ paroscars.gr) and Avant

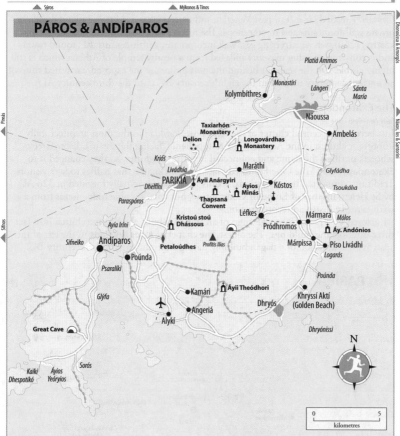

PÁROS & ANDÍPAROS

Travel (☎ 22840 22302, ⓦ avant.gr) on the western and eastern waterfronts respectively. Note that traffic rules are strictly enforced, and that various streets are one way. Parking is only allowed in designated areas and parts of the Parikiá seafront are closed to traffic during summer evenings.

INFORMATION

Tourist information There is no official tourist office on the island; bus timetables are posted by the bus station in Parikiá and there's a kiosk by the windmill with general accommodation information on the island. Your best bet is to go to a travel agent (see opposite). There is also *Parola*, a bilingual (Greek-English) annual listings magazine also available online at ⓦ issuu.com/parolaparos.

Services There is no shortage of banks or ATMs in Parikiá. The island's only post office is west of the windmill, past the ancient cemetery. Cybercookies (☎ 22840 21610, ⓦ cyber cookies.gr; €3/hr) off the main square is the best internet café. Luggage can be left at various travel agents (look for signs) along Parikiá's waterfront.

Parikiá and around

Bustling **PARIKIÁ** sets the tone architecturally for the rest of Páros, its ranks of typically Cycladic white houses punctuated by the occasional Venetian-style building and church domes. The town's sights apart, the real attraction of Parikiá is simply to wander the town itself, especially along the meandering **old market street** (Agorá) and adjoining

Grávari. Arcaded lanes lead past Venetian-influenced villas, traditional island dwellings, ornate wall-fountains and trendy shops. The market street culminates in a formidable **kástro** (1260), whose surviving east wall incorporates a fifth-century BC round tower and is constructed using masonry pillaged from a nearby temple of Athena which is still highly visible. On the seafront behind the port police are the exposed, excavated ruins of an **ancient cemetery** used from the eighth century BC until the third century AD.

The Ekatondapylianí

Daily 7am–9pm • Free

Just beyond the central clutter of the ferry port, Parikiá has the most architecturally important church in the Aegean – the **Katopoliani** ("facing the town"). Later Greek scholars purified the name and connected it with past glories, so they changed it to **Ekatondapylianí** ("The One Hundred Gated"), a nickname that baffles today's visitors. Tradition, supported by excavations, claims that it was originally founded in 326 AD by St Helen, mother of Emperor Constantine, but what's visible today stems from a sixth-century Justinian reconstruction.

Enclosed by a great front wall, sign of an Imperial-built church, the church is in fact three interlocking buildings. The oldest, the chapel of **Áyios Nikólaos** to the left of the apse, is an adaptation of a pagan building dating from the early fourth century BC.

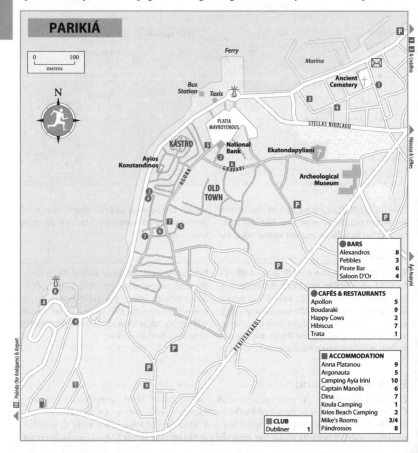

PARIKIÁ

0 — 100 metres

N

Ferry

Marina

Bus Station

Taxis

Ancient Cemetery

PLATIA MAVROYENOUS

STELLAS NIKOLAOU

KÁSTRO

National Bank

Ekatondapylianí

Áyios Konstandinos

AGORA

GRÁVARI

OLD TOWN

Archeological Museum

PERIFEREAKOS

● BARS	
Alexandros	8
Pebbles	3
Pirate Bar	6
Saloon D'Or	4

● CAFÉS & RESTAURANTS	
Apollon	5
Boudaraki	9
Happy Cows	2
Hibiscus	7
Trata	1

■ ACCOMMODATION	
Anna Platanou	9
Argonauta	5
Camping Ayía Iríni	10
Captain Manolis	6
Dina	7
Koula Camping	1
Krios Beach Camping	2
Mike's Rooms	3/4
Pándrossos	8

■ CLUB	
Dubliner	1

Poúnda (for Andíparos) & Airport

Livádhia

Náoussa & Léftes

Ayí Anáryiri

On the right, there is another building attached, housing a Paleochristian **baptistry**, where the initiate used to dip in a cross-shaped pool.

Byzantine museum

Daily 7am–9pm · €2 · ☎ 22840 21243

Inside the church courtyard there is a small **Byzantine museum** displaying a collection of icons. Look through the iconostasis (which still retains its ancient marble frame) to observe two unique features: at the back, a set of amphitheatric steps, the **synthronon**, where the priests used to chant, and, at the front, the **ciborium**, a marble canopy over the altar.

Archeological Museum

Behind Ekatondapyliani · Tues–Sun 8am–3pm · €2 · ☎ 22840 21231

Parikiá's **Archeological Museum** has a good collection and is definitely worth a visit. Its prize exhibits are a large Gorgon, a fifth-century winged Nike by **Skopas** and – hidden at the back of the main room – a piece of the **Parian Chronicle**, a social and cultural history of Greece up to 264 BC engraved in marble.

Áyii Anáryiri monastery

2.5km east of central Parikiá

If you're staying in Parikiá, you'll want to get out at some stage. The shortest **excursion** is along the road starting from the northern end of the ring road up to the **Áyii Anáryiri** monastery. Perched on the bluff above town, this makes a great picnic spot, with cypress groves, a gushing fountain and some splendid views.

Beaches near Parikiá

Less than 1km north of the harbour lies the twin crescent of **Livádhia** beach, with shallow waters and shaded by salt cedars; further on lies **Kriós** beach, much better, served by *kaïki* from just to the right of the ferry terminal (€4). The beaches south along the asphalt road are even better: the first unsurfaced side track leads to the small, sheltered **Dhelfíni**; fifteen minutes further on is **Paraspóros** near the remains of an ancient temple to Asklepios, the god of healing. Continuing for 45 minutes (or a short hop by bus) brings you to arguably the best of the bunch, **Ayía Iríni**, a palm-fringed beach with fine sand, a taverna and a beautiful **campsite** (see p.158).

Petaloúdhes

Not far from the turning to Ayía Iríni, 7km from Parikiá, is the "**Valley of the Butterflies**"(Petaloúdhes), a walled-in private oasis where millions of Jersey tiger moths perch on the foliage in summer (June–Sept 9am–8pm; €2; ☎ 22840 91211/91554). The trip can be combined with a visit to the eighteenth-century nunnery of **Áyios Arsenios**, at the crest of a ridge 1km to the north. Only women are allowed in the sanctuary, although men can wait in the courtyard. Petaloúdhes can also be reached from Parikiá by bus during the summer months.

ACCOMMODATION	PARIKIÁ AND AROUND

Anna Platanou 600m southwest of the port, Parikiá ☎ 22840 21751, ⓦ annaplatanou.gr. This smart, family-run and family-friendly hotel has clean, refurbished rooms in a peaceful location overlooking a garden. The owners also have much larger studios and apartments at the junction of the Alykí–Poúnda roads for €50. Port transfers available. April–Oct. €75

Argonauta Parikiá ☎ 22840 21440, ⓦ argonauta.gr. Stylish hotel in the white-and-blue Cycladic fashion with smart rooms arranged around a beautiful stone courtyard

next to the National Bank. There's a good restaurant underneath. April–Oct. €85

★**Captain Manolis** Manto Mavrogenous Square, Parikiá ☎ 22840 21244, ⓦ paroswelcome.com. Central – behind the National Bank – but unbelievably quiet; all rooms have ivy-covered balconies facing the garden, as well as a/c and fridge. Breakfast €4. Free wi-fi. May–Oct. €58

Dina Agorá, Parikiá ☎ 22840 21325, ⓦ hoteldina.com. Small family pension, right in the middle of the night action in the Agorá opposite the Ayía Triádha church. There is occasional noise from the *Pirate's Bar* opposite, so either come home when they close at 3am or ask for a room at the back. May–Oct. **€50**

Mike's Rooms Opposite the ferry dock, Parikiá ☏ 22840 22856, ⊚ roomsmike.com. Clean, comfortable studios with hospitable staff, and a recommendations diary as long as the *Encyclopedia Britannica*. Mike, the owner, is a tirelessly enthusiastic source of information and assistance. **€35**

Pandrossos Parikiá ☏ 22840 22903, ⊚ pandrossos hotel.com. Perched magnificently on a high hill overlooking the port and beyond, this four-star hotel has a good restaurant, a deep swimming pool and colourful rooms with balconies offering exceptional sunset views. Breakfast included. March–Oct. **€80**

CAMPING

★ **Camping Ayia Irini** Ayía Iríni ☏ 22840 91496, ⊚ campingai.gr. One of the most atmospheric campsites

in the Cyclades: you're right on the beach, but it feels like you're camping in someone's overgrown garden. It has its own cheap taverna, although the olive, citrus and summer-ripening fruit trees can provide you with free sustenance. Bus transfers organized. June to mid-Sept. **€16**

Koula Camping Parikiá, 900m east of the bus station ☏ 22840 22081, ⊚ campingkoula.gr. For those who need to be very close to the town, this campsite is a reasonable choice for a night or two, with 24hr reception, a wide range of cabins or bungalows, and even a covered area for just sleeping bags. The owners also operate a cheap but good restaurant next door. April–Oct. **€17**

★ **Krios Beach Camping** Krios ☏ 22840 21705, ⊚ krios -camping.gr. Excellent facilities, including a pool and wi-fi, in a shady, flat site, 2km east from Parikiá, supplemented by a cool beach bar next door. Occasional Greek parties, which include plate smashing, see crowds specially bussed in from Parikiá; they finish early enough so that you can enjoy your sleep. Free pick-ups from port. June–Sept. **€16.50**

EATING

Apollon Off Agorá, Parikiá ☏ 22840 21875, ⊚ apollon garden.gr. Housed in a converted 1920s olive press with a large garden near the market, this is one of the island's classiest restaurants. Despite high prices, its popularity never wanes. Try the pork with prunes (€15) – highly recommended. April–Oct daily 7pm–late.

★ **Boudaraki** Waterfront, Parikiá ☏ 22840 22297. The locals rate this ouzerí at the southern beachfront by the bridge as the best one on Páros. Expect good service even when packed, an excellent selection of *mezédhes* and mains (€12), as well as home-made *baklavá* to finish the meal off. May to mid-Oct daily noon–1am.

Happy Cows Off Gravari, Parikiá ☏ 22840 24691. Remarkably eclectic vegetarian restaurant in a side street behind the National Bank under new management that

makes some concessions to carnivores including chicken and fish. Not cheap (mains around €17), yet imaginative, with unexpected local ingredients that make you want to play "name that vegetable". April–Oct daily 7pm–2am.

Hibiscus Waterfront, Parikiá ☏ 22840 21849. One of the oldest restaurants on the island, in a great, central spot on the waterfront south of the windmill, overlooking the sea; it offers the usual Greek dishes, but is famous mainly for its selection of generous-sized, wood-oven-baked pizzas for €10. April–Oct daily 6pm–2am.

Trata Parikiá ☏ 22840 24651. Behind the ancient cemetery off the road heading out of town, this popular, family-run taverna specializes in serving large plates of tasty seafood and grilled meats (€12) in a vine-covered patio. April–Oct daily noon–midnight.

NIGHTLIFE

Alexandros Parikiá ☏ 6930 671 269, ⊚ alexandros -cafe.gr. The best possible location for a sophisticated evening drink in a fabulously romantic spot around a real windmill. Set apart from the town, on an elevated promontory at the southern end of the promenade, it has wonderful sunset views which you can enjoy while listening to classical music. Cocktails €9. June–Sept daily 6.30pm–3am.

Dubliner Parikiá ☏ 22840 21113, ⊚ dubliner.gr. Large, brash and youthful dance complex set back from the main drag just off the seafront bridge. It comprises five loud bars – opening gradually as the summer hots up – a main club and an outdoors chill-out area. Entrance with first drink €5. June–Sept daily 11pm–6am.

★ **Pebbles** Parikiá. Upstairs bar at the seafront, east of the windmill and up the steps from the kiosk, playing jazz

and lounge music, with good sunset views and excellent cocktails (€7). It attracts a mixed-age crowd, who pack the place to watch the sunset around 8pm and then return after midnight. Daily noon–3am.

Pirate Bar Parikiá. Popular, established jazz and blues bar near the town hall, opposite *Dina*. It's rather small, so it's convenient for smokers as most of its clientele tend to stand outside. Cocktails €8. April–Oct daily 10am–2pm & 6.30pm–3am.

Saloon D'Or Parikiá ☏ 22840 22176. Rowdy but fun spot on the seafront south of the windmill, with cheap drinks and reggae music. It offers hookahs in various flavours, as well as comfortable oriental divans and settees to sink in and enjoy them. Cocktails €7. May–Sept daily 8.30pm–3.30am.

The southwest

There's little to stop for southwest of Parikiá until **Poúnda**, 6km away, the watersports centre of the island. A further 6km south, past the airport, you reach **Alykí**, a pretty resort on a picturesque bay with two beach sections: one pebbly and bare and the other sandy and shaded.

Skorpios Cycladic Folk Museum

Entrance to Alykí • Daily May–Sept 9.30am–2pm • Free • ☏ 22840 91129

The deeply idiosyncratic **Skorpios Cycladic Folk Museum** houses a collection of model boats and miniatures of various typical buildings from the Cyclades. You can find here painstakingly reconstructed examples, from the dovecotes of Tínos to Náxos cereal grinding mills, and from the Lion Avenue of Delos to the windmills of Mýkonos. It's all a bit kitsch, but fascinating nevertheless.

ACTIVITIES	THE SOUTHWEST

Diving and watersports Paros Watersports in Poúnda (☏ 22840 92229, ⊚ paros-watersports.gr) offers courses and rents equipment for all levels of kitesurfing, wakeboarding and scuba diving leading to a PADI certification course.

ACCOMMODATION AND EATING

Galatis Alykí ☏ 22840 91355, ⊚ galatishotel.gr. This is the best hotel outside Parikiá and Náoussa, several notches up from merely comfortable, offering a pool, a restaurant and (mostly) sea-view rooms. Free wi-fi. Breakfast included. Cheap car rental possible. April–Nov. **€45**

Náoussa and around

Many consider **NÁOUSSA** a more fashionable alternative to Parikiá. Although a major resort town, with modern concrete hotels and attendant trappings, it has developed around a charming little port whose layout has not been adversely affected. The local festivals are still celebrated with enthusiasm, especially the re-enactment on August 23 of a naval victory over the pirates, followed by a fireworks display.

Although the nightlife is on a par with that of Parikiá, most people are here for the local beaches. **Áyii Anáryiri** is just off the path that goes east of Náoussa's harbour, while **Pipéri** is a couple of minutes' walk west. To the northwest, 4km on the road around the bay brings you to **Kolymbíthres**, with its wind- and sea-sculpted rock formations. A few minutes beyond, **Monastíri beach**, below the abandoned Pródhromos monastery, is similarly attractive for diving and snorkelling. A regular summer *kaïki* service connects them for €6 return.

Go northeast of town and the sands are better still: after the glorious sandbank of **Xínari** you reach the barren **Viglákia** headland, also reached by *kaïki*. It is dotted with good surfing beaches such as **Platiá Ámmos**, which lies on the northeastern tip of the island, and **Lángeri** which is backed by dunes; a walk ten minutes south of the main beach brings you to the mostly gay section. The best surfing beach, though, is at **Sánta María**, an expanse of sand 6km by road from Náoussa.

Ambelás, 3km southeast of Náoussa, has a safe, sheltered beach, as you might guess from the number of fishing boats moored here. It is also the start of a long, rough coastal 6km track that leads south, passing several undeveloped shady coves on the way such as **Glyfádha** and the almost deserted **Tsoukália**, until you reach the impressive spread of **Mólos beach**, never particularly crowded. From here you can pick up again the asphalted road straight back to Náoussa or through the **inland villages** back to Parikiá.

ACCOMMODATION	NÁOUSSA AND AROUND

Astir of Paros Kolymbíthres ☏ 22840 51976, ⊚ astirofparos.gr. Superb and lavish five-star resort on the road to Kolymbíthres with marble baths, huge balconies and excellent service. Its sixteen-acre site includes two restaurants, large pool, tennis court, three-hole golf course, heliport and even two small chapels for weddings. April–Oct. **€225**

Christiana Ambelás ☎ 22840 51573, ⊛ christiana hotel.gr. A good-value hotel, 3km from Náoussa, with great fresh fish and local wine in the in-house restaurant and extremely friendly proprietors; they have both rooms and fully equipped apartments, all with balconies facing the beach. Breakfast included. May–Sept. **€45**

Heaven Náoussa ☎ 22840 51549, ⊛ heaven-naoussa .com. As it is difficult to find (walk up the steps above the bus station car park), this feels like a true discovery: an elegant, cool and spotlessly clean boutique hotel belonging to a Scandinavian Greek and his family. Wi-fi, breakfast and parking available. May–Sept. **€60**

Sea House Náoussa ☎ 22840 52198. This was one of the first places in Náoussa to let rooms and has one of the best locations above Pipéri beach with beautiful views from all of its balconies. Recommended for those who prize location over extravagance. April–Oct. **€50**

Stella Náoussa ☎ 22840 21367, ⊛ hotelstella.gr. Out of season, you should be able to haggle for reduced prices at this basic but well-located hotel with rooms arranged around its own garden, several blocks inland from the old harbour. **€55**

Surfing Beach Village Sánta María ☎ 22840 52492/3, ⊛ surfbeach.gr. A well-organized campsite where surfers rub shoulders with families. From late June to July it runs a summer camp for 7–14-year-olds. Also offers beach huts and bungalows with a/c and private WC (€50). Courtesy minibus to and from Parikiá. May–Sept. Camping **€10**, beach huts **€20**

3

EATING AND DRINKING

Meltemi Náoussa ☎ 22840 51263. On the quiet side of the bridge, this excellent grill restaurant offers Cretan specialities (€12) with a smile. The owner is friendly and chatty and you'll undoubtedly be offered a free shot of *tsikoudhiá* "for digestion". Easter–Oct daily 6pm–late.

Ouzeri ton Naftikon Náoussa ☎ 22840 51662. Probably the best *mezedhopolío* in the harbour area. Offers fresh fish and a rather standard Greek menu (mains €8),

but has a reputation second to none. Come before 9pm or else you won't find a seat. April–Oct daily 6.30pm–late.

Yemeni Náoussa ☎ 22840 51445, ⊛ yemeni.gr. Popular family restaurant in the winding streets of central Náoussa, offering well-cooked, traditional Greek dishes for around €8–10. Everything comes from the family farm – from the pork and chicken to the oil you will pour on your salad. Easter–Oct daily 6pm–late.

NIGHTLIFE

Barbarossa Náoussa ☎ 22840 51391. Chic bar bathed in candlelight at the far end of the harbour (not to be confused with the expensive restaurant at the opposite end). Frequented mostly by twenty-something Greeks, this may be the place to try your language skills. Cocktails €10. April–Oct daily 6pm–4am.

Shark Náoussa ☎ 6937 306 037. On a first-floor balcony overlooking the harbour, this is a bar for alternative rockers

and where ale rather than cocktails is the drink of choice. A good selection of bottled beers on offer (€5). May–Sept daily 9pm–3am.

Vareladhiko Potami district, Naoussa. Classic club playing pop hits and frequented mainly by under-30s. The script is predictable: beer will flow, patrons will dance on the tables and holiday romances will blossom. It's still great fun, though. July to mid-Sept (days vary) 11pm–6am.

The southeast coast

The coast southeast of the inland junction at **Marpíssa** – itself a maze of winding alleys and ageing archways overhung by floral balconies – is comparatively off the tourist radar, yet it is easily reachable by regular buses during the summer and boasts some magnificent beaches.

The first resort you reach, **Píso Livádhi**, was once a quiet fishing village, but it is now dominated by open-air car parks and relatively indifferent tavernas. However, between here and **Dhryós** to the south there are no fewer than four excellent beaches. **Logarás** just over the promontory from Píso Livádhi has a superb stretch of sand, while the next beach, **Poúnda** (not to be confused with the port of the same name on the west coast), is home to a beach club with parties that go on well into the night. The final two are the twin windsurfing beaches of **New** and **Old Khrissí Akti** (Golden Beach), which have been established as the main resorts of the southeast.

Dhryós, the end of the bus routes, is the only settlement of any size in this part of Páros. Although the village is mostly modern and characterless, it has an attractive, quiet beach.

3

THE INLAND VILLAGES

Most people bypass Páros interior, but on a cooler day try walking the **medieval flagstoned path** that once linked both sides of the island. Start from the main square of the village of **Mármara** and go west. First up is **Pródhromos**, an old fortified farming settlement with defensive walls girding its nearby monastery. **Léfkes** itself, 5km from Pródhromos, is perhaps the most unspoilt settlement on Páros. The town flourished from the seventeenth century on, its population swollen by refugees fleeing from coastal piracy; indeed it was the island's capital during most of the Ottoman period. Léfkes' marbled alleyways and amphitheatrical setting are unparalleled – and undisturbed by motor vehicles, which are forbidden in the middle of town. Another 5km towards Parikiá and you hit **Maráthi**, from where Parian marble was supplied to much of Europe. Considered second only to Carrara marble, the last slabs were mined here by the French in 1844 for **Napoleon's tomb** in Les Invalides. Just east of the village, marked paths lead to two huge entrances of ancient marble mines which can be visited with an organized tour only. From Maráthi, it's easy enough to pick up the bus on to Parikiá.

ACCOMMODATION AND EATING   THE SOUTHEAST COAST

Fisilanis Logarás ☎ 22840 41734, ⊛ fysilanis.com.gr. In operation since 1964, this is an outstanding-value family hotel and taverna (mains €6) worth experiencing if only for a few days. Well-stocked rooms with sea views, friendly service and unbeatable prices. Breakfast included. April–Oct. **€52**

Golden Beach Khrissí Aktí ☎ 22840 41366, ⊛ golden beach.gr. The dominant hotel on the "Old" Golden Beach with windsurfing facilities available next door, an adjoining restaurant open for breakfast through to dinner and a beach bar open until 2am (beer €3). Free wi-fi and breakfast included. April–Oct. **€77**

Andíparos

ANDÍPAROS is no longer a secret destination: the waterfront is lined with new hotels and apartments, and in high season it can be full, though in recent years families have displaced the former young, international crowd. However, the island has retained its friendly backwoods atmosphere and has a lot going for it, including good sandy beaches and a remarkable cave. Furthermore, rooms and hotels here are much less expensive than on Páros.

ARRIVAL AND GETTING AROUND   ANDÍPAROS

By ferry There are two ferries going to two different places on Páros: the passenger-only ferry goes to Parikiá (see p.155) and the car ferry goes to Poúnda, 7km below Parikiá (see p.161).
By bus The bus stop is by the ferry disembarkation point;

from here you can get to the Great Cave (30min) and Áyios Yeóryios (50min).
By car or motorbike Antiparos Europcar (☎ 22840 61346, ⊛ antiparos-cars.com) is a good rental outlet near the ferry dock.

INFORMATION AND ACTIVITIES

Services There's a bank at the waterfront, as well as a small post office.
Travel agents Oliaros Tours (☎ 22840 61231, ⊛ antiparostravel.gr) on the main shopping street can help with accommodation, boat and plane tickets, excursions

and car rental. They also operate a currency exchange and a postal courier service.
Diving Blue Island Divers (☎ 22840 61767, ⊛ blueisland -divers.gr) on the waterfront offer two-day PADI diving courses (€200). They also rent underwater scooters.

Andíparos Town

Most of the population live in the large low-lying **ANDÍPAROS TOWN**, across the narrow straits from Páros, the new development on the outskirts concealing an attractive traditional settlement. A long, flagstoned pedestrian street forms its backbone, leading from the jetty to the Cycladic houses around the outer wall of the **kástro**. It was built by Leonardo Loredano in the 1440s as a fortified settlement safe from pirate raids – his family coat of arms can still be seen on a house in the courtyard. The only way in is through a pointed archway from the main square, where several cafés are shaded by a giant eucalyptus. Inside, more whitewashed houses surround two churches and a cistern built into the surviving base of the central tower. The town has also developed into a prime **diving** centre.

ACCOMMODATION   ANDÍPAROS TOWN

Camping Antiparos ☎ 22840 61221, ⓦ camping -antiparos.gr. This fully equipped campsite is a 10min walk northeast of town along a track, next to its own nudist beach; the water here is shallow enough for campers to wade across to the neighbouring islet of Dhipló. May–Sept. **€16**

Kouros Village ☎ 22840 61084/5, ⓦ kouros-village.gr. If any proof were needed that Andíparos is value for money you need only visit this extensive resort. Large, clean pool, a restaurant with a panoramic view (mains €6),

an open-air dancefloor and apartment-sized rooms. Breakfast included. May–Oct. **€70**

Mantalena ☎ 22840 61206, ⓦ hotelmantalena.gr. In 1960 a Greek film, *Mantalena*, was shot on Andíparos by director George Roussos. Three years later his brother built this hotel north of the jetty, which is still run by his family. This is one of the more fashionable places on Andíparos and offers large rooms and balconies with wi-fi and satellite TV – plus some apartments in the old town. Breakfast included. May–Oct. **€50**

EATING AND DRINKING

Anargyros ☎ 22840 61204. The taverna with the most central location in the port, where you can rest assured that the daily special (around €8) will be also be consumed by the owner's family later. Also offers basic, clean rooms at the back for €50. June–Sept daily 10am–midnight.

Yannis Place ☎ 22840 61469. A restaurant that mutates into a late-night bar. This is a laidback place for the young and the very young, and will make you feel nostalgic for your salad days, if you are but over 30. June–Sept daily 8pm–midnight.

The beaches

Andíparos' **beaches** begin right outside town: **Psaralíki**, just to the south with golden sand and tamarisks for shade, is much better than **Sifnéïko** on the opposite side of the island. Villa development is starting to follow the surfaced road down the east coast, but has yet to get out of hand. **Glýfa**, 4km down, is another good beach, while, in the southeast of the island, **Sorós** is by far the most bewitching beach on the island. On the southwest coast there are some fine sand dunes at **Áyios Yeóryios**, the end of the surfaced road. From there, one *kaïki* makes an 11am daily trip to the uninhabited, but archeologically rich, island of **Dhespotikó**, opposite.

ACCOMMODATION AND EATING   THE BEACHES

Delfini Áyios Yeóryios ☎ 22840 24506, ⓦ dolphin antiparos.gr. Modern studios sleeping up to four people, with large verandas. There's a café-bar for breakfast and

lunch as well as a grill for dinner. Although off the beaten track, this is a lively establishment, offering a range of excursions and activities. May–Sept. **€100**

The Great Cave

Áyios Ioánnis Hill · Summer daily 10am–3.30pm · €5 · Buses from Andíparos Town (30min)

The **Great Cave** in the centre of the island is the chief attraction for day-trippers. In these eerie chambers the Marquis de Nointel, Louis XIV's ambassador to Constantinople, celebrated Christmas Mass in 1673 while a retinue of five hundred, including painters, pirates, Jesuits and Turks, looked on; at the exact moment of midnight explosives were detonated to emphasize the enormity of the event. Although electric lights and cement steps have diminished its mystery and grandeur, the cave remains impressive. Check out the historical graffiti carved over the centuries.

Náxos

NÁXOS is the largest and most fertile of all the Cyclades islands and with its green and mountainous highland scenery it appears immediately dissimilar to its neighbours. The difference is accentuated by the **unique architecture** of many of the interior villages: the Venetian Duchy of the Aegean, headquartered here from 1204 to 1537, left towers and fortified mansions scattered throughout the island, while medieval Cretan refugees bestowed a singular character upon Náxos' eastern settlements.

Today Náxos could easily support itself without visitors by relying on its production of potatoes, olives, grapes and lemons, but it has thrown in its lot with mass tourism, so that parts of the island are now almost as busy as Páros (see p.154) in season. The island has plenty to see if you know where to look: the highest mountains in the Cyclades, intriguing central valleys, a spectacular north coast and long, marvellously sandy beaches in the southwest. It is also renowned for its wines, cheese and *kítron*, a sweet liqueur distilled from the leaves of this citrus tree and available in green, yellow or clear varieties depending on strength and sugar level.

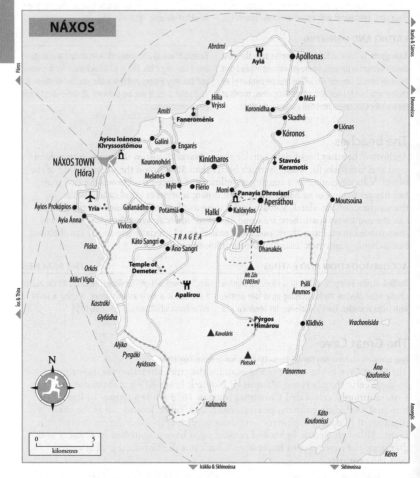

ARRIVAL AND GETTING AROUND

By plane Náxos is served by regular flights from Athens (via Olympic, 1–3 daily; 45min). From the airport it's a 10min bus ride to Náxos Town (€12).

By ferry Ferries dock in the northern harbour quay of Náxos Town.

Destinations Amorgós Aegiáli (3–4 weekly; 3hr); Amorgós Katápola (1–2 daily; 4hr); Anáfi (1 weekly; 8hr); Áno Koufoníssi (1–2 daily; 2hr 30min); Astypálea (1–3 weekly; 3hr 45min); Dhonoússa (3–5 weekly; 1hr 10min); Folégandhros (1–2 daily; 3hr 40min); Íos (1 daily; 1hr–1hr 30min); Iráklio (Heraklion), Crete (4–5 weekly; 3hr); Irakliá (1–2 daily; 1hr 30min); Kálymnos (1 weekly; 6hr 30min); Lávrio via Kéa-Kýthnos (1 weekly; 7hr); Mílos (2–4 weekly; 4–7hr); Mýkonos (2–5 daily; 1hr 10min–3hr); Nísyros (1 weekly; 9hr 30min); Páros (2–3 daily; 25–45min); Pireás (3–5 daily; 4hr–6hr 30min); Rafína (up to 4 daily; 3hr 5min–5hr 50min); Rhodes (1 weekly; 14hr); Santoríni (3–6 daily; 2–6hr); Skhinoússa (1–2 daily; 2–6hr); Sérifos (1 weekly; 3hr 30min); Sífnos (1–3 weekly; 4hr 30min); Síkinos (1–3 weekly; 2hr 40min); Sýros (2–3 weekly; 3hr); Tílos (1 weekly; 11hr); Tínos (4–8 weekly; 1hr 20min).

By bus The bus station (☎22850 22291, ⓦnaxos destinations.com/naxos-ktel-destinations.html) is opposite the main dock. Printed timetables are available and change almost monthly.

Destinations Aperáthou (4–5 daily; 1hr); Apóllonas (2–3 daily; 1hr; 2hr via scenic coastal route); Áyios Prokópios/Ayía Ánna/Pláka (10 daily; July & Aug every 30min; 15min); Filóti/Hálki (7–8 daily; 45min); Kastráki-Pyrgáki (1–2 daily; 45min); Pláka (10 daily; July & Aug every 30min; 30min).

By car or motorbike Auto Tour Rent-a-Car by the bus station in Náxos Town (☎22850 25480, ⓦnaxos rentacar.com) rents cars and offers a wealth of information. In town, parking immediately next to accommodation is not always possible. The best one-day drive is Halkí–Filóti–Aperáthou–Apóllonas returning via the northern coastal route.

By taxi The central taxi call number is ☎22850 22444.

INFORMATION AND ACTIVITIES

Services The post office is north of the Town Hall square in Náxos Town.

Travel agents Excursions around Náxos and to other islands are conveniently booked at Zas Travel (☎22850 23330) on the seafront near the jetty. Further down the promenade Naxos Tours (☎22850 23043, ⓦnaxostours .net) can also help with all kinds of arrangements.

Proto Tourism (☎22850 24949, ⓦproto-tourism.com) opposite the bus station has left luggage facilities (lockers €6/day or bags €1.5/piece) and can help with private room accommodation.

Windsurfing Flisvos Sportsclub (☎22850 22935, ⓦflisvos-sportclub.com) is based at Áyios Yeóryios beach, offering windsurfing courses and other activities.

Náxos Town

As your ferry approaches **NÁXOS TOWN**, you can't help sensing that this is a really special place, if only because of the looming, fortified **kástro**. Indeed, this is where Marco Sanudo – the thirteenth-century Venetian who founded the town and established the Duchy of the Aegean – and his descendants ruled over the Cyclades. A superficial glance at the waterfront may be enough to convince you that most of the town's life occurs by the crowded port esplanade, but don't be deceived. There is a lot more life in Náxos Town in the vast network of backstreets and low-arched narrow alleys that lead up through the old town, **Boúrgo**, to the **kástro** itself. And don't miss out on the second centre of activity to the south, around the main square, **Platía Evripéous**, where there are more tavernas, shops and cafés.

Portára

A long causeway, built to protect the harbour to the north, connects Náxos Town with the islet of Palátia – the place where, according to legend, Theseus was duped by

---

> **NÁXOS MUSIC FESTIVAL**
>
> One of the highlights of Naxiot evenings is the **Domus Festival** of classical, jazz, choral, Byzantine and traditional music held at the Venetian Museum (see p.166) in either the garden or the basement, depending on the season and weather (ⓦnaxosfestival.com/naxos-domus -festival). Tickets should be booked in advance at the museum (☎22850 22387) and include a glass of local wine or *kítron*.

Dionysos into abandoning Ariadne on his way home from Crete. The famous stone **Portára** that has greeted visitors for 2500 years is the portal of a temple of Apollo, built on the orders of the tyrant Lygdamis around 530 BC, but never completed.

The kástro

Tours in English offered by the Venetian Museum at 11am Tues–Sun in season (€15, includes entrance to all kástro museums)

The **kástro** is normally entered through the **north gate** (also known as the Traní Pórta or "Majestic Gate"), a splendid example of a medieval fort entrance. A few of the Venetians' Catholic descendants still live in the old mansions that encircle the site, many with ancient coats of arms above the doorways. In the centre of the kástro are the plain stone remains of a **rectangular tower**, said to have been the residence of Marco Sanudo. Opposite the tower stands the restored **Catholic cathedral**, still displaying a thirteenth-century crest inside. Behind the tower you can find the seventeenth-century **Ursuline convent**. Nearby is what was to become one of Ottoman Greece's first schools, the **French Commercial School**, now a cultural centre; opened by Jesuits in 1627 for Catholic and Orthodox students alike, its pupils included, briefly, writer Nikos Kazantzakis (see p.206).

The Venetian Museum

Kástro • Daily: mid–May to June & Sept–Oct 10am–3pm & 6.30–9.pm; July & Aug 10am–10pm (but opening times can vary year by year; phone to check) • €5 • ☎ 22850 22387

A mansion next to the Traní Pórta, the **Venetian Museum** (Domus Della-Rocca-Barozzi), is open to the public and offers the best views from the kástro, with concerts (see box, p.165); the guided tour includes a tasting from the family's wine cellar.

The Archeological Museum

Kástro • Tues–Sun 8.30am–3pm • €3 • ☎ 22850 22725

The French Commercial School building now houses an excellent **Archeological Museum**, which includes an important collection of Early Cycladic figurines (note how most of the throats were cut in some kind of ritual), Archaic and Classical sculpture, pottery dating from Neolithic to Roman times, as well as obsidian knives and spectacular gold rosettes. Sadly, labelling is mostly in Greek. On the terrace, a Hellenistic-period mosaic floor shows a Nereid (sea nymph) astride a bull surrounded by deer and peacocks.

Mitropóleos Museum

Kástro • Tues–Sun 8.30am–3pm • Free

In front of the Orthodox cathedral, the **Mitropóleos Museum** has walkways over a recently excavated tumulus cemetery from the Mycenaean era – thirteenth to eleventh century BC – with funerary remnants including a *hermax*, a pile of the stones that were traditionally thrown behind on leaving a cemetery. In the general area, items dating from the early Cycladic period (3200 BC) right through to late Roman (300 AD) have been found.

Town beaches

Grótta, just to the northeast of the town, is the easiest **beach** to reach. It's not ideal for swimming but snorkellers can see the remains of submerged Mycenaean buildings. The other town beach, **Áyios Yeóryios**, is an improvement: a long sandy bay fringed by the town's southern accommodation area, within ten minutes' walking distance from Platía Evripéous.

ACCOMMODATION   **NÁXOS TOWN**

Apollon Fontana ☎ 22850 22468, ⊛ apollonhotel -naxos.gr. Comfortable, modern doubles, all with balconies, in a quiet spot near the Mitropóleos Museum and convenient for the port, the nightlife and Grótta beach. Breakfast included. **€60**

Despina's Rooms Boúrgo ☎ 22850 22356. Hidden (but

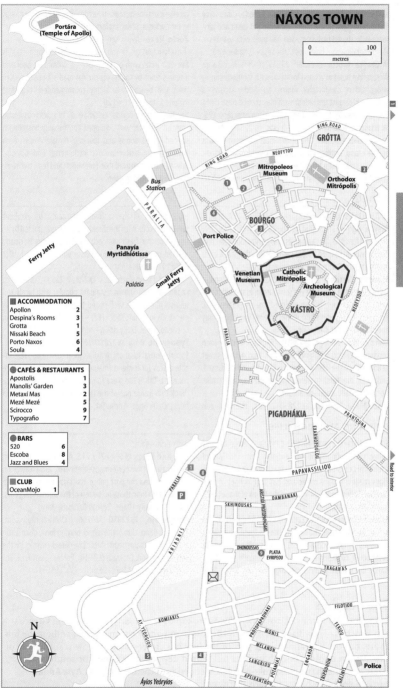

NÁXOS TOWN

Portára (Temple of Apollo)

0   100
metres

GRÓTTA

RING ROAD

NEOFYTOU

RING ROAD

Bus Station

Mitropoleos Museum

Orthodox Mitrópolis

PARALIA

Port Police

BOÚRGO

APOLLONOS

Panayía Myrtidhiótissa

Palátia

Small Ferry Jetty

Ferry Jetty

Venetian Museum

Catholic Mitrópolis

Archeological Museum

KÁSTRO

NEOFITOU

PARALIA

PIGADHÁKIA

PRANTOUNA

EKARHOPOULOU

PAPAVASSILIOU

PARALIA

P

SKHINOUSSAS

DAMBANAKI

ARISTIDI PROTOPAPADAKI

DHONOUSSAS

PLATIA EVRIPEOU

TRAGANAS

FILOTIOU

PROTOPAPADHAKI

AY. YEORYIOU

KOMIAKIS

MONIS

FENIOU

ENGARON

MELANON

SANGRIOU

TRIPODHON

GALINIS

POTAMIS

APEIRANTHOU

Police

Áyios Yeóryios

N

Road to interior

6 & Airport

ACCOMMODATION

Apollon	2
Despina's Rooms	3
Grotta	1
Nissaki Beach	5
Porto Naxos	6
Soula	4

CAFÉS & RESTAURANTS

Apostolis	1
Manolis' Garden	3
Metaxí Mas	2
Mezé Mezé	5
Scirocco	9
Typografio	7

BARS

520	6
Escoba	8
Jazz and Blues	4

CLUB

| OceanMojo | 1 |

3

well signposted) beneath the castle; you'll need to climb some distance to reach it. The rooms are small but clean and airy, some with shared bathroom, and balconies with sea views. The owner organizes boat trips to the Lesser Cyclades. €35

★**Grotta** Grótta ☎ 22850 22215, ⓦ hotelgrotta.gr. Welcoming hotel in a good location, with fabulous sunset views. Offers comfortable rooms, an indoor jacuzzi, a fantastic breakfast (included) with pies cooked fresh daily, free pick-ups plus free wi-fi and cable internet access. €75

★**Nissaki Beach** Áyios Yeóryios ☎ 22850 25710, ⓦ nissaki-beach.com. One of the most luxurious options on the island, oozing minimalist but comfortable Cycladic elegance. If the palm trees around the pool area don't tempt you, then the boundless views to the Aegean surely will. Its excellent seaside restaurant has one of the best wine menus in the Cyclades. Breakfast included. April–Oct. €170

Porto Naxos Áyios Yeóryios ☎ 22850 25710, ⓦ porto -hotels-naxos.gr. If you have your own transport, this five-star hotel with parking space, a swimming pool and a tennis court by the Náxos circular road – but only 200m from the beach – is highly recommended. Breakfast included. April–Oct. €120

Soula Áyios Yeóryios ☎ 22850 23196, ⓦ soulahotel .com. A modern, well-equipped and friendly hostel with six-bed mixed dorms and four-bed female dorms, each with its own bathroom/WC, kitchenette, and balcony. Private rooms also available. Free sheets and ferry transfers. Breakfast €6. €15/person

EATING

★**Apostolis** Old Market, Hóra ☎ 22850 26777. Always busy, a sign of its regard in the town, with invariably excellent family dishes and grills (€8) plus a good selection of local wines. Beware its side salads (€5) – they are a meal in themselves. Daily noon–midnight.

Manolis' Garden Boúrgo ☎ 22850 25168. Popular taverna, located in a large yet cosy garden in the old town, with a small but well-considered menu (mains €8). Although not vegetarian it has many vegetable-only options. May–Oct daily 6pm–1am.

Metaxi Mas Boúrgo ☎ 22850 26425. Friendly ouzerí serving excellent, well-priced food (€7) on a little street heading up to the kástro. Service is friendly and unhurried, and even the fussiest demands are met with a smile. April–Oct daily noon–midnight.

Meze-Meze Seafront ☎ 22850 26401. The best and most popular of the seafront restaurants. Its excellent service can cope with the throngs of tourists attracted by its reputation for fresh seafood; anything frozen is clearly marked on the menu. Good house wine, too. April–Oct daily 11am–midnight.

Scirocco Platía Evripéous ☎ 22850 25931, ⓦ scirocco -naxos.gr. Well-known restaurant popular with locals and tourists alike for its well-priced traditional dishes such as meatballs in tomato sauce (€7) – hence the occasional long queue to get in. Daily noon–midnight.

Typografio Hóra ☎ 22850 22375, ⓦ typografio.com. Superb central location, delicious local cuisine and reasonable prices for a menu (mains €9) as imaginative as the wine list. This is the place to go for a romantic tête-à-tête (book in advance one of the tables with the best views in front). Daily 6pm–midnight.

DRINKING AND NIGHTLIFE

520 Old Market ☎ 6944 680 629. On a huge balcony above the harbourfront but entered from Old Market street, this café-bar attracts all ages throughout the day. Plays mellow lounge music and has a quirky set of own cocktails based on the 24 letters of the Greek alphabet (€8). Daily 10am–late.

Escoba Waterfront ☎ 22850 23567. The best option in the cluster of bars and clubs in the southern waterfront, it serves large cocktails (€8) and is bigger than its neighbours, so there's less of a crush. Normally plays Latin music, but it has a popular rock night on Tues. June–Sept daily 6pm–4am.

Jazz and Blues ☎ 6944 701 215. A petite jazz bar, with the occasional live performance thrown in, tucked away on a street behind the port police. Its classy drinks are much cheaper (€5) than those in the rest of the surrounding bars. April–Oct daily 10am–2pm & 8.30pm–3am.

OceanMojo ☎ 22850 26766, ⓦ oceanmojo.com. The main dance club of the island, playing funk, disco/Latin and groove mainstream hits. Live Greek music in the shoulder season. Cocktails (€8–10). Easter–Sept Fri & Sat (daily in season) 11pm–6am.

The beaches

Lying just 4km from Náxos Town, **Áyios Prokópios** is regularly voted among Greece's top **beaches**. The village itself lies in the southern part of the main road and on the bus route, but the best and quieter part of the beach is closer to Náxos Town, at the base of the distinct double cone of Stelídha hill. Rapid development along the southwestern stretch means that Áyios Prokópios has blended into the next village, **Ayía Ánna**, further along the busy southern highway.

Beyond the Ayía Ánna headland is 5km-long **Pláka beach**, a vegetation-fringed expanse of white sand accessed by a flat, unsurfaced road from the north where purely for convenience this part of the beach is called **Marágas**. Some parts of Pláka are naturist where shielded from the road by dunes, and at the southern end is **Orkós**, the playground of the young and intrepid with plenty of wind- and kitesurfers in high season.

You'll find more windsurfers along the coastal stretch south from Pláka through remote **Glyfádha** down to **Alykó** and nearby **Pyrgáki**, where the coastal road ends and the asphalted highway to Náxos begins. On the juniper-covered promontory by Alykó there is another nudist beach, known locally as **Hawaii** for the vibrant blue colour of its waters, while 4km beyond by unsurfaced road is the **Ayiassós** beach – this is where Marco Sanudo landed in 1207 to conquer the island from the Byzantines and promptly burned his ships so that there could be no way back.

ACCOMMODATION THE BEACHES

Finikas Pyrgáki ☎ 22850 75230, ⓦ finikashotel.gr. At the end of the coastal dirt road and away from it all, this is a fully self-sufficient hotel, offering everything from a restaurant and free wi-fi to a sauna and a gym. It also organizes watersports activities. Breakfast included. May–Sept. **€150**

Naxos Imperial Resort and Spa Stelídha ☎ 22850 26620, ⓦ naxosimperial.com. The best deluxe hotel of many on the Stelídha peninsula, it is also close to the best section of Áyios Prokópios beach. There's volleyball, gym, spa, restaurant, bar and a pool. Breakfast included. May–Sept. **€100**

Orkos Beach Mikrí Vígla ☎ 22850 75194, ⓦ orkosbeach.eu. Next to the Flisvos Kite Center, with a cool pool and even cooler customers. Its garden alone is perfect to laze in. Internet, wi-fi, parking and breakfast included. May–Oct. **€70**

Stella Ayía Anna ☎ 22850 42526, ⓦ stella-apartments

-naxos.gr. Clean and close to the sea but not far from the village itself, these studios with kitchenette and bougainvillea-bursting balconies are possibly the best option south of Náxos Town. Wi-fi in the reception only. April–Oct. **€55**

CAMPING

Maragas Ayía Anna ☎ 22850 42552, ⓦ maragascamping.gr. A suitably laidback shaded campsite with a taverna, beach bar and watersports facilities. There's a regular bus service to Náxos Town. April–Oct. Camping **€32**, cabins **€40**

Plaka Pláka ☎ 22850 42700, ⓦ plakacamping.gr. Near the beginning of the Cyclades' longest beach, this is the newest campsite on Náxos with a pool, restaurant and café. It's flanked by its imaginatively named *Plaka I* and *Plaka II* sister hotels (€45–60). Bus service to Náxos Town every 20min in season. April–Oct. **€16**

EATING AND DRINKING

Gorgóna Ayía Anna ☎ 22850 41007. Cool, large, shaded, family-run beach bar that becomes a fish restaurant with reasonable prices (€10) in the evening and continues functioning as a late-night bar until the morning. Known locally for its delicious home-made *rizógalo*, a spiced rice pudding. Daily 8am–3am.

Molos Áyios Prokópios ☎ 22850 26980. Fish taverna offering only fresh fish caught on the day and assorted seafood – which tends to be fried, however, rather than grilled. Occupying the best spot on the beach, it is unsurprisingly popular. Two deckchairs plus one umbrella €10. May–Oct daily 9am–1am.

Central Náxos

After its beaches, **Central Náxos** is the island's second unique selling point, with its lush green valleys, mountains, painfully picturesque villages, historic churches, old forts and Classical sites. Because of the sheer size of the island these are best enjoyed via two day-long drives: one short and one much longer. The short drive is Náxos–Galanádho–Sangrí–Halkí–Moní–Kinídharos–Flério--Náxos, while the longer drive is Náxos–Galanádho–Sangrí–Halkí–Filóti–Aperáthou–Apóllonas–Náxos via the northern coastal road.

Galanádho and Sangrí

From Náxos Town, head for the market village of **Galanádho** to reach the twin villages of **SANGRÍ**, on a vast plateau at the head of a long valley. On the way have a look at the domed eighth-century church of **Áyios Mámas**, neglected since the Ottoman conquest. Káto Sangrí has the ruins of a Venetian castle, while Áno Sangrí is an attractive little place, all cobbled streets and fragrant courtyards. From there, it's also only about ninety minutes' walk to the Byzantine castle of **Apalírou**, at 474m, which held out for two months against the besieging Marco Sanudo. Its fortifications are relatively intact and the views magnificent. Thirty minutes' stroll away on a path leading south out of the village, or 3km by surfaced lane, are the partially rebuilt remains of a **Classical temple of Demeter** (Tues–Sun 8.30am–3pm; free) from 530 BC, over which was constructed an early Christian basilica.

The Tragéa and Halkí

From Sangrí, the road twists northeast into the **Tragéa** region, scattered with olive trees and occupying a vast highland valley. The area is the only part of the Cyclades to have a regular winter snowfall, and the only part with traditional songs about snow. It's a good jumping-off point for all sorts of exploratory rambling. **HALKÍ**, 16km from Náxos Town, is a fine introduction of what is to come; set high up, it's a quiet town with some lovely churches, including the **Panayía Protóthronis** church (daily 10am–1pm; free), with its eleventh- to thirteenth-century frescoes. Just behind is the restored seventeenth-century Venetian **Grazia-Barozzi Tower**, and nearby is the distillery (1896) and shop of **Vallindras Naxos Citron**, whose charming proprietors explain the process of producing *kítron* followed by a little tasting session.

Moní

Driving from Halkí to Moní you pass the sixth-century church of **Panayía Dhrosianí** (daily 11am–5pm; donation expected), historically the most important church on the island with some of the oldest frescoes in Greece. **MONÍ** itself, at an altitude of 550m, enjoys an outstanding view of the Tragéa and Mount Zas, and has numerous woodcarving workshops.

Kinídharos and Flério

From Moní you can loop back to Náxos Town, and the first village you encounter on the way is **KINÍDHAROS**, with its marble quarries and daily folk evenings; it has a reputation of staging one of the best carnivals in the Cyclades. Five kilometres beyond is the village of **FLÉRIO**. Nearby is the most interesting of the ancient marble quarries of the seventh- to sixth-century BC on Náxos, home to two famous **koúroi**, left recumbent and unfinished; even so, they're finely detailed figures, over 5m in length. The Koúros Flerioú (Koúros Melánon), from around 570 BC, is a short walk along the stream valley; the Koúros Farangioú (Koúros Potamiás) is a steeper walk up the hillside. Both are well signposted.

CLIMBING MOUNT ZAS

If you're arriving by bus and intend to climb **Mount Zas** you should start from the steps opposite the taverna *Baboulas* on Filóti's main square. This is a round-trip walk of three to four hours on partly marked trails to the summit, a climb that rewards you with an astounding panorama of virtually the whole of Náxos and its Cycladic neighbours. The initial path out of the village climbs up to rejoin the road to Apóllonas. The final approach trail begins beside the small **Ayía Marína chapel**. You can return to Filóti via the trail to the150m-deep **Zas Cave**, which is also accessed by a separate route through **Ariés**, ten minutes' drive from Filóti.

If you have your own transport, you can drive all the way to the trailhead at Ayía Marína and continue on from there.

Filóti and Aperáthou

At the far side of the gorgeous Tragéa valley, **FILÓTI**, the largest village in the region, lies on the northwestern slopes of **Mount Zas**, which at 1001m is the highest point in the Cyclades. **APERÁTHOU** (officially Apíranthos), 8km beyond Filóti, is hilly, winding and highly picturesque; it shows the most Cretan influence of all interior villages and gave Greece one of its prime ministers, **Petros Protopapadakis** (it's unfortunate that he was executed for high treason in 1922). Its location high in the mountains means it is noticeably cooler and greener than the coast. There are two Venetian **fortified mansions**, Bardáni and Zevgóli, and, amazingly, four small private **museums**: Natural History, Geological, Fine Arts and a Folklore Museum (all daily: April, May, Sept & Oct 10.30am–2.30pm; June & July 10.30am–7.30pm; Aug 10.30am–9pm; €2 combined entry for all; ☎ 22850 61622) as well as a state Archeological Museum (Tues–Sun 8.30am–3pm; free; ☎ 22850 61725). There's some good **shopping** in Aperáthou, as well: **Epilekton** in the main street is an excellent delicatessen with a selection of local cheeses, hot peppers and sun-dried aubergines.

Pýrgos Himárrou and Kalandós

A turning at the southern end of Filóti is signposted to the **Pýrgos Himárrou** (12.5km), a remote 20m-high Hellenistic watchtower – one of the tourist landmarks of the island – and onward (another 12km) to the deserted but excellent in all respects **Kalandós** beach on the south coast. Bring your own water and food supplies if you're planning to stop here.

EATING   CENTRAL NÁXOS

Lefteris Aperáthou ☎ 22850 61333. A restaurant with an unmatched reputation on Náxos and, as a bonus, not as full as others closer to the main road, which are always busy. At the end of your meal (mains €13) try the homemade *glyká koutalioú*, stewed syrupy fruit which are so sweet that a few teaspoonfuls constitute a serving. April–Oct daily 10am–1am.

Panorama Moní ☎ 22850 31070. Small family restaurant with exceptional views. Whatever the dish of the day is (€6), order it; it will most likely involve some kind of meat, as this part of Náxos is famous for its tender beef and veal. Daily 11am–11pm.

Platanos Aperáthou ☎ 22850 61192. Rare mountain decor, good balcony views and food standards to rival *Leftéris* (see above). This is one of those old-fashioned Greek restaurants where you can go in the kitchen to check what's available (mains €9) and whether you like the look of it. April–Oct daily 9am–11pm.

Northern Náxos

The route to **Northern Náxos** through the mountains from Aperáthou to Apóllonas is very scenic, and the road surface is in reasonable condition all the way. Jagged ranges and hairpin bends confront you after **Kóronos**, past **Skadhó**, to the remote emery-miners' village of **Koronídha** – the highest village on the island. **Apóllonas** is a small resort with two good beaches: a tiny and crowded stretch of sand backed by a line of cafés and restaurants, and a longer and quieter stretch of shingle, where *Kouros Hotel* lies. The major attraction in Apóllonas is a 12m-long **koúros**, approached by a path from the main road just above the village. Lying *in situ* at a former marble quarry, this is the largest of Náxos' abandoned stone figures, but less detailed than those at Flério. The return to Náxos Town is via the northern coastal road, which is spectacular, set high above the sea. Stop for a break at the village of **Engarés** to visit a 200-year-old **olive press**, now a museum (mid-April to Sept daily 9am–7pm; free; ☎ 22850 62021, ⓦ olivemuseum.com).

ACCOMMODATION   NORTHERN NÁXOS

Kouros Apóllonas ☎ 22850 67000, ⓦ hotelkouros .blogspot.com. Relaxing, dreamy hotel standing alone in the middle of the shingle beach with spacious, quiet rooms and a well-stocked beach bar. Despite it being out of the way, it attracts a surprisingly young clientele. May–Sept. **€60**

Lesser Cyclades

Four of the six small islands in the patch of the Aegean between Náxos and Amorgós have slid from obscurity into fashion in recent years. Inhabited since prehistoric times, the group is known commonly as the **Lesser Cyclades** and includes **Ikliá, Skhinoússa, Áno Koufoníssi** and **Dhonoússa**. The islands' popularity has hastened the development of better facilities and higher prices, but, with only limited ferry services, they've managed to avoid mass tourism so far. This is likely to change, however, as Áno Koufoníssi has been added to the large ferry and catamaran routes between mid-June and early September.

ARRIVAL AND INFORMATION   LESSER CYCLADES

By ferry Blue Star ferries call at Náxos linking up with the smaller *Express Skopelitis*, which serves the Lesser Cyclades daily throughout the year. Speedboats and ferries from Pireás operate in the high season, and most now stop at Áno Koufoníssi.

Day-trips from Náxos A boat trip from Náxos takes in Irakliá and Skhinoússa or Áno Koufoníssi.

Island transport Apart from a seasonal bus on Áno

Koufoníssi, there are no buses or taxis on the islands; hotels will organize your transport to and from the port. There is also no car or scooter rental.

Health Note that there are no pharmacies on any island, but some drugs are dispensed from the rural GP practices. In case of emergency there are speedboats on call 24/7, so make sure you have good travel insurance.

Irakliá

IRAKLIÁ, the westernmost of the Lesser Cyclades, and with the least spoilt scenery, has just over 150 permanent residents. As the first stop on the ferry service from Náxos, the island is hardly undiscovered by tourists, but with fewer amenities than some of its neighbours, it retains the feel of a more secluded retreat.

The port of **Áyios Yeóryios** is a small but sprawling settlement behind a sandy tamarisk-backed beach that gets quite crowded in August. **Livádhi**, a big, shallow beach, is 2km southeast of the port and its crystal-clear waters are the main tourist

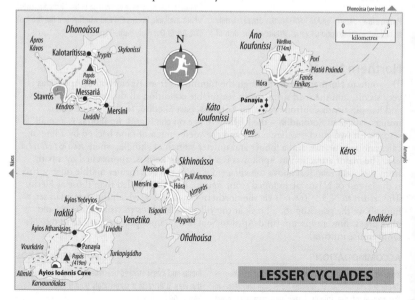

LESSER CYCLADES

attraction of the island. The asphalted road continues 3km on to the tiny capital **Panayía (Hóra)**. In season, a local boat sails from the port to make a tour of the island, stopping at the small sandy beach at **Alimiá** and the nearby pebble beach of **Karvounólakos**, which is surrounded by coloured rock formations.

On August 28, the feast of St John the Baptist, a 4pm service is held inside the large cave where his miraculous icon is said to have been found.

ARRIVAL AND INFORMATION
IRAKLIÁ

By ferry Ferries dock at Áyios Yeóryios.
Destinations Áno Koufoníssi (1–2 daily; 2hr); Amorgós (Aegiáli and Katápola; 3–4 weekly; 3hr 30min); Dhonoússa (3 weekly; 2hr 10min); Mýkonos (2 weekly; 5hr); Náxos (3–4 weekly; 1hr); Páros (2 weekly; 1hr 25min); Pireás (0–1 weekly; 7hr); Skhinoússa (1–2 daily;

15min); Sýros (1 weekly; 4hr 45min); Tínos (3–4 weekly; 2hr 35min).
Services There's an ATM at Áyios Yeóryios. A sub-post office is a short distance above the *Perigiali* taverna.
Travel agents Aegeon (☏ 22850 71539) can take care of all your travel and ticket needs.

ACCOMMODATION AND EATING

Anna's Place ☏ 22850 74234, ✉ annas.place.rooms @gmail.com. Family lodgings on the slope at the back of the village with great views. All rooms have a/c, private bathrooms and wi-fi. **€50**
Iliovasilema ☏ 22850 71569, ⊛ sunset-iraklia.gr. Four very large apartments on top of a small hill 500m from the port and with magnificent sunset views, a/c, TV, fridge and

a common kitchen. May–Sept. **€35**
Maïstrali ☏ 22850 71807, ⊛ maistraliclub.com. The best place to eat on the island, with a menu of seafood, especially crustaceans, as well as standards like *moussaká* (€6). The veranda has a good view of the port below and there is free wi-fi for clients. June–Sept daily 6pm–midnight.

Skhinoússa

A little to the northeast of Irakliá, the island of **SKHINOÚSSA** is just beginning to awaken to its tourist potential. Its indented outline, sweeping valleys and partly submerged headlands – such as the sinuous, snake-like islet Ofidhoúsa (Fidoú) – provide some of the most dramatic views in the group.

An asphalted road leads up from the port of **Mersíni** to the capital, **Hóra** (also called **Panayía**). From Hóra you can reach no fewer than sixteen beaches dotted around the island, accessible by a network of dirt tracks. **Tsigoúri**, the most developed, is a ten-minute steep walk downhill from Hóra. The locals' preferred choice of beaches are **Alygariá** to the south, **Psilí Ámmos** to the northeast, and **Almyrós**, half an hour southeast. All have beach bars during high season.

ARRIVAL AND INFORMATION
SKHINOÚSSA

By ferry Boats dock at the small port of Mersíni.
Destinations Amorgós (Aegiáli and Katápola; 3–4 weekly; 1hr 30min–2hr); Áno Koufoníssi (1–2 daily; 30min); Dhonoússa (1–2 daily; 3hr 40min); Irakliá (1–2 daily; 15min); Náxos (3–4 weekly; 1hr 30min–6hr); Páros (2–3 weekly; 1hr 10min–7hr 40min); Pireás (1–2 weekly;

7hr 45min); Sýros (1 weekly; 5hr).
Travel agents Grispos Tours (☏ 22850 29329) can help you with tickets and information.
Services There's an ATM at Hóra, as well as several mini-markets, bars and tourist shops plus a sub-post office.

ACCOMMODATION AND EATING

Grispos Villas Tsigoúri ☏ 22850 71930, ⊛ grisposvillas .com. Perched above Tsigoúri beach at the northwest end, this complex offers everything – from rooms with conti-nental breakfast to large studios with cooking facilities; they also sell ferry tickets in season. Breakfast included; there's also a half-board option (€14). **€45**

Iliovasilema ☏ 22850 71948/71161, ⊛ iliovasilema hotel.gr. Well-priced friendly hotel, comfortable rather than luxurious, whose veranda bar enjoys spectacular views of the harbour. They operate a free shuttle to and from every beach for their customers. No credit cards accepted. June–Sept. **€60**

3

3

Áno Koufoníssi

ÁNO KOUFONÍSSI (usually referred to simply as Koufoníssi) is the flattest, most developed and most densely inhabited island of the group. With some of the least-spoilt beaches in the Cyclades, the island is attracting increasing numbers of Greek and foreign holiday-makers. As it's small enough to walk round in a day, it feels overcrowded in July and August.

Hóra, on a low hill behind the ferry harbour, has been engulfed by new room and hotel development, but the town, with great views across the water to mountainous Keros island, still retains its affable, small-island atmosphere. All the good **beaches** are in the east and southeast of the island, improving as you go east along a road that skirts the gradually developing coastline along the edge of low cliffs. **Fínikas** (or **Harokópou**), a fifteen-minute walk from town, is the first of four wide coves with gently shelving golden sand. The next beach, **Fanós**, is the youngsters' favourite, because of the beach bar that dominates the stretch of sand in season. Next is **Platiá Poúnda** (or **Italídha**), which is a small, pretty and clothing-optional beach. From here, the path rounds a rocky headland to **Porí**, a much longer and wilder beach, backed by dunes and set in a deep bay. It can be reached more easily from the town by following the asphalt road heading inland through the scrub-covered hills.

You can also travel by pleasure boat for a swim to the beaches of **Káto Koufoníssi**, but not to **Kéros** which is out of bounds; the whole island and its waters are an archeological area (much like Delos), which is still being excavated.

ARRIVAL AND INFORMATION
ÁNO KOUFONÍSSI

By ferry Boats dock at the jetty below Hóra.

Destinations Amorgós (Aegiáli and Katápola; 1–2 daily; 1–2hr); Dhonoússa (3 weekly; 2hr 20min); Irakliá (1–3 daily; 45min); Mýkonos (2–3 weekly; 1hr 20min); Náxos (1–3 daily; 30min–2hr 20min); Páros (4–5 weekly; 5hr); Pireás (1–2 daily; 5hr); Santoríni (2–4 weekly; 1hr 30min–3hr); Skhinoússa (1–2 daily; 30min); Sýros (1 weekly; 6hr); Tinos (2–4 weekly; 2hr).

By bus In July & Aug, an hourly bus (10am–9pm) makes the trip from Hóra to Porí, stopping at Fínikas.

Travel agents Koufonissia Tours (☎ 22850 74091, ⓦ koufonissiatours.gr; open during ferry arrivals) deals with accommodation, while Prásinos Tours (☎ 22850 71438; 7am–10pm) deals with ferry tickets. The latter can also charter a boat for island excursions or, for travel emergencies, to the town of Volakas on Naxos, opposite (€40–50).

Services There's a sub-post office with an ATM behind the *Myrtó* hotel.

ACCOMMODATION

Aeolos ☎ 22850 74206, ⓦ aeoloshotel.com. Modern, exceptionally well-designed hotel with a great pool overlooked by bougainvillea-draped balconies and large rooms in bright colour schemes. Free wi-fi and big breakfast buffet included. June–Sept. €100

Koufonissia Hotel & Resort ☎ 22850 74067, ⓦ hotel koufonisia.gr. On the road leading to Porí, this is a great-value spa resort with rooms built around its landscaped gardens and pool. Try its range of massages that include

a chocolate therapy treatment. Breakfast included. Mid-May to Sept. €100

★ **Myrto** ☎ 22850 74400, ⓦ myrto-hotel.com. Inaugurated in 2014, this is the new kid on the block, and it's a winner: 50m to the beach, balconies with smashing views of Keros opposite, high ceilings, marble baths and smiling service. Wi-fi at reception, cable LAN in the rooms and breakfast included. June–Sept. €75

EATING

Capetan Nicolas ☎ 22850 71690. After many decades, this is still the best place to eat seafood on the island. At the west end of the village, it offers a fine array of fresh grilled seafood from the owner's fishing boat. Try the shrimp risotto for €11.50 and home-made *taramosaláta* (€4) that bears no resemblance to supermarket varieties. May–Oct daily 12.30pm–late.

Gastronautis ☎ 22850 71468. Chef Petros acquired a cosmopolitan view of Mediterranean food in Berlin and brought gourmet food at reasonable prices to the island. Try his slowly cooked veal, chicken or lamb stews (€10) complemented by his eclectic choice of wines. Mid-April to mid-Oct daily 9am–noon & 2pm–1am.

Dhonoússa

DHONOÚSSA is a little out on a limb compared with the other Lesser Cyclades, and ferries call less frequently. Island life centres on the pleasant port settlement of **Stavrós**, spread out behind the harbour and its first-rate beach. Most sunbathers head for **Kéndros**, a long and sheltered stretch of shadeless sand twenty minutes over the ridge to the east; a World War II German wreck can be easily spotted by snorkellers. The village of **Mersíni** is an hour's walk from Stavrós, while a nearby path leads down to **Livádhi**, an idyllic nudist beach with tamarisks for shade. In high season a beach-boat runs from the port to all beaches.

ARRIVAL AND DEPARTURE	DHONOÚSSA

By ferry Ferries dock at Stavrós.
Destinations Amorgós (Aegiáli and Katápola; 3–4 weekly; 1hr); Áno Koufoníssi (2–3 weekly; 3hr 20min); Astypálea (1 weekly; 2hr 20min); Irakliá (3–4 weekly; 4hr 20min);

Náxos (1–2 daily; 1hr 10min–5hr); Páros (1–3 weekly; 2hr 30min–7hr); Pireás (1–3 weekly; 7hr); Skhinoússa (3–4 weekly; 1hr 40min–4hr 30min); Sýros (1 weekly; 8hr).

ACCOMMODATION AND EATING

Chryssa ☏ 22850 51575, ⓦ donoussarooms.gr. Set back from Stavrós, this pension has basic but large rooms and balconies overlooking the port. Every room has its own kitchenette and cooking implements but not all have a/c. May–Oct. **€60**

Corona Borealis Café-bar that slowly becomes the soul of the party in Stavrós playing alternative indie rock until the early hours. Young clientele, because, well, there are not many other places to go. June–Sept daily 10am–3am.

Amorgós

AMORGÓS, with its dramatic mountain scenery and laidback atmosphere, is attracting visitors in increasing numbers. The island can get extremely crowded in midsummer, the numbers swollen by film buffs paying their respects to the film location of Luc Besson's *The Big Blue*, although few venture out to **Líveros** at the island's western end to see the wreck of the *Olympia* which figures prominently in the film. In general it's a low-key, escapist clientele, happy to have found a relatively large, interesting, uncommercialized and hospitable island with excellent walking possibilities. Families tend to herd around **Katápola**, while younger tourists

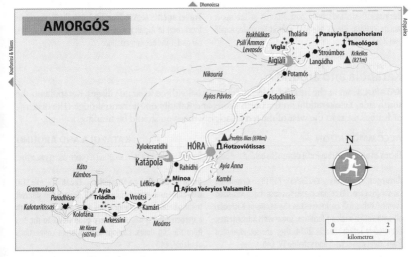

prefer **Aigiáli**. However, if you rent a car, **Hóra**, the island capital, is the best base from which to explore the island.

Almost every hotel will offer you a glass of *rakómelo* as a welcome drink. It's a kind of fermented grappa with honey, herbs and spices, drunk in shots as an aperitif.

ARRIVAL AND DEPARTURE
AMORGÓS

Most ferries and catamarans call either at **Katápola** in the southwest or **Aigiáli** in the north, while some dock at both. Be aware that it is those destinations, rather than "Amorgós", that are named on **ferry schedules**. There are more onward connections from Katápola than Aigiáli. Prekas (☎ 22850 71256) in Katápola, just along from the ferry dock, is the one-stop **boat-ticket agency** (as well as an ouzerí).

KATÁPOLA

By ferry The ferries stop at the town jetty; some continue on to Aigiáli (15min).

Destinations Anáfi (1 weekly; 2hr); Áno Koufoníssi (1–2 daily; 25min); Dhonoússa (3–4 weekly; 2hr); Irakliá (1–2 daily; 1hr 50min); Íos (1 weekly; 5hr 20min); Kos (July & Aug 1 weekly; 5hr); Léros (July & Aug 1 weekly; 3hr 20min); Mýkonos (0–1 daily; 1hr 50min); Náxos (1–2 daily; 1hr); Páros (1–2 daily; 2hr 30min); Pátmos (1 weekly; 2hr); Pireás (1–2 daily; 4–9hr); Rhodes (July & Aug 1 weekly; 8hr); Santoríni (6 weekly; 1hr); Skhinoússa (1–2 daily;

2hr –4hr 15min); Sýros (1 weekly; 7hr), Tínos (2–3 weekly; 2hr 40min).

AIGIÁLI

By ferry The ferries stop at the town jetty; some continue on to Katápola (15min).

Destinations Áno Koufoníssi (3 weekly; 2hr 30min); Astypálea (1 weekly; 1hr 30min); Dhonoússa (3–4 weekly; 50min); Irakliá (3 weekly; 3hr 30min); Náxos (1–2 daily; 5hr); Páros (4–5 weekly; 3hr 15min); Pireás (4 weekly; 6hr); Skhinoússa (5 weekly; 2hr 20min).

GETTING AROUND

By bus A bus shuttles between Katápola and Hóra (3 daily; 15min) and continues to Ayía Ánna and Hotzoviótissas monastery. There is a bus from Katápola to Aigiáli (2 daily; 1hr) and another (2–7 times weekly at 9.45am) out to the "Káto Meriá", made up of the hamlets of Kamári-Vroútsi, Arkessíni and Kolofána. From Aigiáli there's a bus service up to Langádha and Tholária, the two villages east of and 200m above Aigiáli bay, with 3 departures daily up and down (a timetable is posted by the harbour bus stop).

By boat From Katápola there's a *kaïki* service to the nearby beaches at Maltézi and Plákes (€3 return) and a daily excursion *kaïki* to the islet of Gramvoússa off the western end of Amorgós (€8 return).

By car or motorbike There are several car/bike-rental outfits; the one that has been around the longest is Thomas (☎ 22850 71777, ⊕ thomas-rental.gr) with branches in Katápola, Hóra and Aigiáli.

INFORMATION

Services The island's main post office is in the upper square in Hóra. There's one ATM each at Katápola, Aigiáli and Hóra.

Travel agents Aegialis Tours (☎ 22850 73393, ⊕ aegialis tours.com) in Aigiáli can help you with tickets, transfers, car rental and accommodation.

Katápola and around

KATÁPOLA, set at the head of a deep inlet, is actually three separate villages: **Katápola** on the south side, **Xylokeratídhi** on the north shore, and **Rahídhi** on the central ridge. The beach of Káto Krotíri to the west of the ferry dock is where you should be heading, though.

ACCOMMODATION
KATÁPOLA AND AROUND

There's an on-off free municipal **campsite** behind the beach in front of Rahídhi; enquire whether it's open when you arrive.

Amorgos Katápola ☎ 22850 71013, ⊕ pension -amorgos.com. No common areas as such, but good-sized rooms (with small bathrooms) in the centre of Katápola, all with coffee-making facilities, some with kitchenettes. Completely refurbished in 2014, they are soundproofed from street noise. Wi-fi and satellite TV. **€40**

Anna Studios Katápola ☎ 22850 71218, ⊕ studioanna-amorgos.com. Well signed and difficult to miss because of its height, this hospitable *pension* with a garden setting has some very good views to the sea from the top floors. Laptops with internet connections available. **€40**

Eleni Kato Krotiri ☎ 22850 71628, ⓦ roomseleni.gr. Great location for basic but good-value rooms complex above the Káto Krotíri beach. All rooms have kitchenette, wi-fi and from some you can see the three Roman tombs adjacent to the property. No breakfast but free washing facilities. Easter–Nov. **€40**

EATING

Mourayio Katápola ☎ 22850 71011. The most popular taverna in town, cooking a wide range of seafood since 1980, including a good fish soup, lobster spaghetti (around €25–35) and marinated octopus (€9), all worth the wait while you enjoy the waterfront views. April–Oct daily noon–midnight; Nov–March daily 5pm–midnight.

Vitzentzos Xylokeratídhi ☎ 22850 71518. Serves traditional Amorgós dishes that include island slow-roasted goat with potatoes and a range of vegetable dishes cooked in oil and tomato sauce (€6). Easter to early Oct daily noon–midnight.

Hóra and around

HÓRA is one of the better-preserved settlements in the Cyclades, with a scattering of tourist shops, cafés, tavernas and rooms. Dominated by an upright volcanic rock plug, wrapped with a chapel or two, the thirteenth-century **Venetian fortifications** look down on nearly thirty other **churches**, some domed, and a line of decapitated windmills beyond.

Monastery of Hotzoviótissas

Above Ayía Anna beach. Daily 9am–1pm & 5–7pm • Donation expected

The spectacular **Monastery of Hotzoviótissas**, gleaming white at the base of a towering, vertical cliff, can be reached on foot via a steep, cobbled path starting from a car park 150m below. Modest dress is required: no shorts for men while women must be fully covered. Only three monks occupy the fifty rooms now, but they are quite welcoming considering the crowds who file through. The main church is dominated by the miraculous **icon** around which the monastery was founded, along with other treasures. Tradition, supported by evidence, has it that in the ninth century AD, a precious icon of the Virgin was brought here by beleaguered monks from the monastery of **Khotziba** in Palestine, who settled here to escape Arab raids. Sitting and admiring the view from the terrace, while being treated to a shot of *rakómelo* and a sweet by the monks, is one of the highlights of visiting Amorgós.

Monastery of Áyios Yeóryios Valsamítis

5km south of Hóra on the way to Mouros Beach • Daily 9am–1pm & 5–7pm • Donation expected • ☎ 22857 70199

After a hiatus of 250 years during which the monastery was simply a church, a nun now lives again in the **Monastery of Áyios Yeóryios Valsamítis**. The *katholikón* is built in the old hydromanteion (water oracle) of Apollo where the priests predicted the future by divining the waters of a sacred fountain. This custom of "consulting the waters" continued until the 1950s on Amorgós, until the Orthodox Church cemented the fountain. You can still see the fountain enclosure, and also the (stagnant) waters of the now defunct spring.

Beaches

The nearest **beach** to Hóra, at **Ayía Ánna**, is small but more than adequate. If you skip the first tiny coves, the path will take you to the nudist bay of **Kambí**; bring food and water for the day. An alternative is **Moúros**, 5km west, with clean, crystal-clear waters and a seasonal taverna.

The best beach, however, is at the end of the road west, about 20km from Hóra, at spectacular **Kalotarítissas Bay**, its tiny fishing jetty and small sand and pebble beach partly enclosed and sheltered by a rocky headland. A beach hut selling snacks and drinks operates in season, and in July and August there are **boat trips** (€4) from here to the uninhabited but picturesque islet of **Gramvoússa**, opposite; boats leave at 11am, returning at 7pm. About 1.8km before Kalotarítissas, the **wreck of the Olympia** is visible down to the right, in **Líveros Bay**.

ACCOMMODATION — HÓRA AND AROUND

★Emprostiada Hóra ⓣ22850 71814, ⓦemprostiada.gr. A guesthouse built and decorated in the style of a Cycladian manor, in the middle of a spacious landscaped garden. Great furnishings that include several traditional hole-in-the-wall double beds. Free wi-fi and coffee facilities in all rooms. €50

Panorama Hóra ⓣ22850 74016/71606, ⓦpanorama-amorgos.gr. Rooms and studios in two different sites in Hóra, large and comfortable with fitted kitchens; some have balconies with western views towards the kástro. Wi-fi and parking available. €40

EATING AND DRINKING

Liotrivi Hóra ⓣ22850 71700. With a roof terrace facing the kástro, this taverna, down the steps from the bus stop, is where you should try the local casseroles such as veal with aubergines (€8) or goat stew. Its home-made wine straight from the barrel is also excellent (€3/half litre). Mid-May to mid-Oct daily 12.30pm–1am.

Yasemi Hóra ⓣ22850 74017, ⓔjazzminamorgos@yahoo.com. Bars rise and disappear like shooting stars but Yasemí has been quietly going since 2004, and is still popular both for its breakfasts and for its late-night cocktails (€8.50). Daily 9am–4am.

3

Aigiáli and around

The road from Hóra to **AIGIÁLI** (Eyiáli), 15km away, is one of the most impressive in the Cyclades, overlooking several beautiful small coves. The town itself is smaller and more picturesque than Katápola, and so tends to be more popular. The main Aigiáli **beach** is more than satisfactory, getting better and better as you stroll further north. A trail here leads over various headlands to three bays: sandy **Levrósos** (a 20min walk), the most popular, which has a taverna; **Psilí Ámmos** (30min walk), which is mixed sand and gravel; and **Hókhlakas** (20min), where naturism is tolerated; there are no facilities in the last two so bring along what you need. The best of all beaches north is **Áyios Pávlos**, 5km from Aigiáli, while boats also leave in season for the beaches of the island of **Nikouriá** opposite.

ACCOMMODATION — AIGIÁLI AND AROUND

★Aegialis Aigiáli ⓣ22850 73393, ⓦamorgos-aegialis.com. High on the hillside on the far side of the bay, this is the largest hotel on the island, and has superb views, a large pool, spa with thalassotherapy treatments using saltwater and natural island products, sauna, jacuzzi, gym and a good restaurant (mains €15). It offers Greek cooking courses in season. €130

Aegiali Camping Aigiáli ⓣ22850 73500, ⓦaegialicamping.gr. Usually busier than the one in Katápola but not necessarily better, this is a tree-covered, cheerful campsite 100m from the middle of the beach. Free wi-fi at reception and in the campsite's restaurant. May–Oct. €11

Karkisia Aigiáli ⓣ22850 73180, ⓦkarkisia-hotel.gr. Well-priced option that's very comfortable and easy on the eye, near the Aigiáli beach over which the top floor balconies have views. Every double room has a sofabed that can be used to sleep a third person at no extra cost. All rooms have kitchenette and cooking facilities. Breakfast €5. Mid-May to mid-Oct. €40

★Lakki Village Aigiáli ⓣ22850 73253/73505, ⓦlakkivillage.com. Literally a village with well-equipped studios and rooms in labyrinthine pebbled alleys. Don't just stop by the pool; this huge site extends all the way from the Tholária road to the beach. Good restaurant where a €15 half-board option is offered. Breakfast included. April–Oct. €90

EATING AND DRINKING

Embassa Aigiáli ⓣ22850 73277. The coolest café-bar to lounge about and chill at while watching the sunset, favourite of backpackers and the itinerant European youth. Very strong cocktails for €8. Easter to mid-Oct daily 9am–late.

Limani Aigiáli ⓣ22850 73269, ⓦlimani.amorgos.net. Also known as *Kyra-Katinas* after the taverna's former matriarch who sadly is no more: her two sons carry on the taverna tradition. One of them has married a Thai lady who offers authentic Thai home cooking on Fri. Otherwise, it's the usual Greek staples (mains €8). Easter to mid-Oct daily 9am–1am.

Íos

Though not terribly different –
geographically or architecturally – from
its immediate neighbours, no other
Greek island attracts the same vast
crowds of young people as **ÍOS**.
Although it has worked hard to shake
off its late-twentieth-century reputation
for alcoholic excesses and to move the
island's tourism up a class, with some
success, Íos is still extremely popular
with the young backpacker set, who
take over the island in July and August.

The only real villages – **Yialós** (for
families), **Hóra** and **Mylopótas** (for the
18–25s) – are clustered in a western
corner of the island, and development
elsewhere is restricted by poor roads.
As a result there are still some very
quiet beaches with just a few rooms to
rent. Most visitors stay along the arc
delineated by the port – at Yialós, where you'll arrive, in Hóra above it, or by the beach
at Mylopótas. Despite its past popularity, sleeping on the beach on Íos is strictly
banned these days and so is nudism.

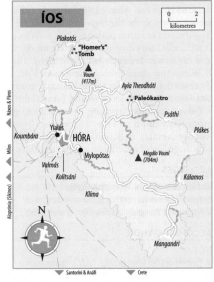

3

ARRIVAL AND GETTING AROUND ÍOS

By ferry Ferries dock in Yialós, an easy 20min trek from the capital, Hóra, or a short hop by bus.

Destinations Áno Koufoníssi (0–2 weekly; 1hr 40min); Amorgós Katápola (1 weekly; 3hr); Anáfi (1–2 weekly; 6hr); Folégandhros (1 weekly; 1hr 40min); Iráklio (2–4 weekly; 2hr 30min); Kímolos (1–2 weekly; 2hr 45min); Lávrio via Kéa/Kýthnos (1 weekly; 10–11hr); Mílos (1–4 weekly; 4hr); Mýkonos (1–2 daily; 1hr 40min–2hr); Náxos (1–3 daily; 50min–3hr); Páros (1–3 daily; 1hr 35min–3hr); Pireás (1–2 daily; 3hr–4hr 30min); Rafina (1 daily; 7hr 30min); Santoríni (2–3 daily; 40min); Sérifos (1 weekly; 5hr–6hr 30min); Sífnos (1–3 weekly; 3hr 30min–5hr 30min); Síkinos (2–4 weekly; 20min); Sýros (1–3 weekly; 5hr 15min); Tínos (0–3 weekly; 3hr 20min).

By bus Buses constantly shuttle between Yialós, Hóra and Mylopótas (every 20–30min 8am–midnight). There are occasional public and private buses running to the beaches at Manganári and Ayía Theodhóti; they sell return tickets only and are quite pricey (€6).

By boat From Yialós, daily boats depart at around 10am for the beaches on the south coast, returning in the late afternoon (€12 return).

By car or motorbike Hiring a car is not as necessary as on other islands; the main strip, Yialós to Mylopótas, is walkable and a very nice stroll. To rent your own transport in Hóra try Vangelis Bike Rental (☎ 22860 91919) or Jacob's Car & Bike Rental (☎ 22860 91700, ⌨ jacobs-los.gr) in Yialós.

Travel agents Aktaion Travel (☎ 22860 91343) has a branch (closed 2–5pm) in the main church square in Yialós.

INFORMATION AND TOURS

Tourist office The unofficial tourist information office is Aktaion, right in the middle of the port (daily 9am–2pm & 5–9pm), which also has a branch in Hóra.

Services There's an ATM near the quay. The post office is in the new town of Hóra, a block behind the town hall.

Boat tours For a quick escape from the packed beaches at the height of the season, try one of the daily excursions around quieter nearby beaches on the wooden Leigh Browne sailing vessel moored in the harbour (€25), available on demand.

Hóra and around

HÓRA (also called Íos Town) is a twenty-minute walk up behind Yialós port, and is one
of the more accessible picturesque towns in the Cyclades, filled with meandering

arcaded lanes and whitewashed chapels. Still, it gets pretty raunchy when the younger crowd moves in for the high season, and the laddish logos and inscriptions available on T-shirts and at tattoo parlours clash with its superior aspirations. The main road divides it naturally into two parts: the **old town** climbing the hillside to the left as you arrive, and the **newer development** to the right. The **Archeological Museum** (Tues–Sun 8.30am–3pm; free) in the yellow town hall, is part of an attempt to attract a more diverse range of visitors to the island. It contains some interesting finds from ancient **Skárkos**, a few kilometres inland from Yialós.

Yialós – with its surprisingly peaceful and uncrowded beach – isn't as attractive as Hóra above but it provides a refreshing, breezy escape from the hot, noisy capital. Twenty minutes' walk on the other side of Hóra there's the popular **Mylopótas**, the site of a magnificent beach, lots of water activity outlets but surprisingly little nightlife.

ACTIVITIES   HÓRA AND AROUND

Watersports Meltemi Watersports (☏6932 153 912, ⊛meltemiwatersports.com) is a British-owned outlet on Mylopótas and Manganári beaches, offering waterskiing, windsurfing and wakeboarding lessons. They also hire out canoes, pedaloes, snorkelling equipment and sailing boats (April–Oct).

ACCOMMODATION

HÓRA

★ **Francesco's** Old Town ☏22860 91223, ⊛francescos .net. An excellent hostel made up mostly of super-clean doubles and relatively few dorm beds. With free pick-ups and wi-fi, a bar, pool and jacuzzi plus spectacular views over the port, it offers the best value for money on the island. May–Sept. Dorms €17, doubles €40

Lofos New Quarter ☏22860 91481. Right up from the archeological site, this family-owned, shaded complex, with simple but well-furnished rooms, is very convenient for access both to the bus stop and Hóra's nightlife opposite. Best of all, for something so close to the action, it's quiet. May–Oct. €30

Lofos Village New Quarter ☏22860 92481, ⊛lofos village.com. A luxurious set of modern villas further up the hill with panoramic views over Hóra from its swimming pool. Currency exchange, free port transfers, jacuzzi and parking are some of the many facilities on offer. Check for online deals. May–Oct. €130

YIALÓS

Galini Rooms ☏22860 91115, ⊛galini-ios.com. A good, quiet choice in a rural setting just over 200m down the lane by the centre of the beach; relaxing in the well-tended large garden is as big a delight as lying on the beach. April–Oct. €60

★ **Golden Sun** ☏22860 91110, ⊛iosgoldensun.com. Family-owned hotel about 300m up the road to Hóra, with meticulously clean, brightly painted rooms offering nice views over the bay and large, well thought-out common areas around a swimming pool. Mid-May to Sept. €40

Yialos Beach ☏22860 91421, ⊛yialosbeach.gr. Stylish hotel, just behind the hospital, offering smart doubles and studios with their own private gardens, built around a large pool with a children's pool nearby. Two-night minimum stay in high season. May–Oct. €55

MYLOPÓTAS

Dionysos ☏22860 91215, ⊛dionysos-ios.gr. Both attractive and luxurious, with buildings arranged around a swimming pool, this complex comes up trumps on location and services offered including free wi-fi, children's pool, a fitness studio and tennis courts. Online deals offer huge discounts. May–Oct. €120

Far Out Beach Club ☏22860 91468, ⊛faroutclub.com. Large campsite with well-organized facilities, including a pool, laundry, internet, bungalows and a good-value cafeteria. However, it can get very noisy and crowded in Aug. May–Sept. Camping €9, dorms €18, bungalows €50

Íos Palace ☏22860 92000, ⊛iospalacehotel.com. Luxury hotel that has appropriated part of the beach with its own deckchairs (free to residents). Despite its opulent looks, this is a place for all budgets offering a range of differently priced rooms from basic and undersized, to massive suites with their own balcony pool. May–Oct. €130

Purple Pig/Stars Camping ☏22860 91302, ⊛purplepigstars.gr. A friendly, laidback hostel complex by the road up to Hóra, with a range of facilities, including its own club, minimarket, pool and poolside bar. It offers film shows, twice-weekly live music and watersports rental. Dorms €12, bungalow with private bathroom €35

EATING

HÓRA

Lord Byron Old Town ☏22860 92125. A *mezedhopolío* off

the main square that tries hard to re-create a traditional atmosphere, with old rembétika music, a good Greek menu

(mains €12) and a well-chosen Santoríni wine list. Extremely popular, so make a booking or come early. Daily 6pm–1am.
The Nest Old Town ☎22860 91778. Signposted from everywhere in Hóra, this is where the locals go to eat and you'll soon find out why: from the moment you sit down the service and sociability are exceptional. Try the *yiuvétsi* (veal baked in pasta), a snip at €7. April–Oct daily noon–1am.

YIALÓS

Octopus Tree ☎6972 754 365. A warm, intimate space a bit out of the way by the fishing boats on the Yialós waterfront, which serves fresh seafood caught by the owner. With mains starting at €12 it's not exactly cheap but

you pay for the freshness. Daily 9am–3pm & 7pm–1am.

MYLOPÓTAS

Drakos ☎22860 91281. Right at the water's edge, this is the best fish taverna on Mylopótas offering mostly fried seafood dishes (€10). If you want to challenge your tastebuds, try its cod in garlic sauce, which is thankfully based mostly on mashed potato. May–Sept daily noon–2am.
Marios ☎22860 91130. Perched alone on a curve on the road to Hóra at the top of the steps to the beach, this chalet-like restaurant has spectacular views, excellent service and enormous pizzas for €10. Easter–Oct noon–3.30pm & 6pm–midnight.

DRINKING AND NIGHTLIFE

Every evening during the summer, Hóra is the centre of the island's **nightlife**, its streets throbbing with music from ranks of competing discos and clubs – mostly free, or with a nominal entrance charge, and inexpensive drinks. Most of the smaller **bars** and **pubs** are tucked into the narrow streets of the old village on the hill, offering something for everyone, and you'll have no trouble finding them.

Fun Pub Hóra, Old Town ⓦfunpubios.com. An early starter and late finisher, this is a lively, Irish-themed and Irish-owned pub in the narrow backstreets of Hóra. From karaoke, quiz nights and internet to free films and a pool table, you can come here seven nights a week and still be entertained. April–Oct daily 6pm–3am.
Íos Club Entrance to Hóra ⓦiosclub.gr. Established in 1969, this snack-bar at the top of the stairs leading to Yialós starts off the evening with classical music while the clients

sit back and enjoy the sweeping sunset views over Yialós. May–Sept daily 6pm–late.
Skorpion 200m on the road to Mylopótas. Cavernous club with an excellent sound and lighting system; its frenetic atmosphere is up there with the best on Mýkonos. This is where everyone ends up when the clubs in Hóra close, so large queues start forming around 3am. Entrance €10 with first drink free. June–Sept daily midnight–8am.

The beaches

The best **beach** on the Yialós side is **Koumbára**, a twenty-minute stroll from Yialós over the headland, where the scenery is rockier and more remote. There is also a smaller beach further on with a cove backed by extraordinary green cliffs and a rocky islet to explore. Its western-facing setting and string of palm trees makes it ideal to watch the sunset, and attracts many amateur photographers.

On the south coast, there's a superb beach at **Manganári** easily reached by boat or bus (see p.179). Another decent beach is at **Kálamos**: get off the Manganári bus at the turning for Kálamos, which leaves you with a 4km walk, or else take a *kaïki* from Yialós. There's more to see, and a better atmosphere, at **Ayía Theodhóti** up on the east coast. You can get there on a paved road across the island – the daily excursion bus costs €6 return. A couple of kilometres south of Ayía Theodhóti is **Paleókastro**, a ruined Venetian castle which encompasses the remains of a marble-finished town and a Byzantine church.

HOMER'S TOMB

Homer's tomb can be reached by car or motorbike (signposted from the road to Ayía Theodhóti, 4.5km from Hóra). An ancient town has long since slipped down the side of the cliff, but the rocky ruins of the entrance to a tomb remain, as well as some graves. There is certainly an ancient tradition, from Pausanias and Pliny, that Homer was buried on the island; furthermore, Hellenistic coins from Íos bear his name and his head. However, it was Dutch archeologist Pasch van Krienen who first discovered these tombs in 1771 and immediately claimed one of them as Homer's – in reality, though, it probably dates only to the Byzantine era.

In the unlikely event that the beach at Ayía Theodhóti is too crowded, try the one at **Psáthi**, 14km to the southeast, although you may need your own transport to get there.

EATING   THE BEACHES

KUMBÁRA

Polidoros ☎ 22860 92072. This grill taverna is one of the better places to eat on Íos, offering coal-grilled meats and local specialities such as pork with celery casserole (€12) and stuffed courgette flowers. June to mid-Sept daily noon–10pm.

AYÍA THEODHÓTI

Koukos ☎ 22860 92420. A very good family restaurant, rated highly by the locals, because it offers produce such as honey, milk products, eggs and chickens from its own farm next door (mains €8). Accompanied by bread baked in a wood-fired oven, organic food never tasted so good. May–Sept daily noon–8pm.

Síkinos

SÍKINOS has so small a population – around 240 – that the mule ride or walk from the port up to the capital was only replaced by a bus in the late 1980s. At roughly the same time the new jetty was completed; until then Síkinos was the last major Greek island where ferry passengers were still taken ashore in launches. With no dramatic characteristics and no nightlife to speak of, few foreigners make the short trip over here from neighbouring Folégandhros or Íos. The end result, however, is the most unspoilt countryside in the Cyclades where the clichéd image of a priest riding a donkey can suddenly materialize from over a hill.

ARRIVAL AND DEPARTURE   SÍKINOS

By ferry Ferries dock at the far end of the port of Aloprónia, on the east coast. There are fewer connection options than in many of the neighbouring islands. If you cannot find any ferries to your choice destination, check if you can change at Íos.

Destinations Anáfi (1–2 weekly; 5hr 30min); Folégandhros (2–5 weekly; 40min); Íos (4–5 weekly; 30min); Kímolos (1–3 weekly; 2hr 15min); Lávrio via Kéa/Kýthnos (1 weekly; 12hr); Mílos (3 weekly; 3hr 45min); Mýkonos (2 weekly; 6hr 20min); Náxos (3–5 weekly; 2hr 45min); Páros (3–4 weekly; 4hr); Pireás (2–4 weekly; 6–10hr); Santoríni (4–5 weekly; 2–3hr); Sérifos (0–2 weekly; 4–6hr); Sífnos (2–5 weekly; 2hr 50min–5hr); Sýros (2–3 weekly; 6hr).

SÍKINOS & FOLÉGANDHROS

Santoríni, Crete & Dodecanese ▼

GETTING AROUND AND INFORMATION

By bus There's a single island bus, which in the high season shuttles regularly between the harbour and Hóra (4–8 daily; 7.15am–11.45pm). Note that the bus is replaced by a normal four-seater car out of season.

By car or motorbike The island's only rental office is at the Eko petrol station 50m back from Aloprónia; it mostly rents scooters.

Services There's a bank with an ATM in Kástro, while the post office is at the entrance to Kástro.

Aloprónia

Such tourist facilities that exist are concentrated in the little harbour of **ALOPRÓNIA**, with its crystal-clear water, sandy beach, breakwaters and jetty. Many of the few dozen houses around the bay are summer holiday homes owned by expat Sikiniots now resident in Athens or beyond.

ACCOMMODATION AND EATING   ALOPRÓNIA

Lucas ☎22860 51075, �🌐sikinoslucas.gr. Family studios at the water's edge on the opposite side of the dock, as well as rooms and studios among a cluster of buildings at the back of the village, 700m from the harbour along the road to Hóra. The family also operate a taverna which in May and June is your only eating option in the port (mains €10). April–Oct. **€40**

Maïstrali 22860 51087, 🌐maistrali-sikinos.gr. Modern hotel behind the lighthouse, unimaginatively built like a square, urban two-storey house, but offering large, well-furnished rooms with the best views over the port. April–Oct. **€50**

★ **Porto Sikinos** ☎22860 51220, 🌐portosikinos.gr. The place to stay in Aloprónia, a pricey option but on the swish side, offering free wi-fi, fridge, TV, a/c, island furnishings and everything else you might require for a restful stay. May–Sept. **€65**

Hóra

HÓRA consists of the double village of **Kástro** and **Horió**. As you slowly drive or walk up from Aloprónia, the scenery turns out to be less desolate than initial views from the ferry suggest, while the village itself, draped across a ridge overlooking the sea, is a delightfully unspoilt settlement. Most of the facilities are in the larger, northeastern Kástro, whereas Horió is purely residential. The fortress-monastery of **Zoödhóhou Piyís** ("Life-giving Fountain") crowns the cliff-edged hill above, and is accessed by a stepped path out of the top of Kástro. The architectural highlight of the village is the **kástro** itself, a quadrangle of eighteenth-century mansions arrayed defensively around the blue-domed church of **Panayía Pantánassa**, which opens for evensong at around 6pm. Although tourists don't tend to stay here, eating options cater for the locals and are surprisingly varied and better than in Aloprónia.

EATING AND DRINKING   HÓRA

★ **Anemelo** ☎22860 51216. A friendly café-bar with the only shade in town; it has only a few tables outside, but you can share a table with strangers. Good cup of coffee and a snack menu that goes from omelettes (€5) to homemade syrupy desserts. May–Oct daily 10am–midnight.

To Steki tou Garbi ☎22860 51215. Unpretentious and cheap with a first-class selection of traditional Greek island cooking (€6–12), along with its own barrel wine, which has been made in the same traditional way for generations. March–Nov daily noon–midnight.

Around the island

Ninety minutes' walk northeast from Hóra lies **Paleókastro**, the patchy remains of an ancient fortress. In the opposite direction, another ninety-minute walk takes you by an old path or higher road through a steeply terraced landscape to **Episkopí**, where elements of an ancient temple-tomb have been incorporated into a seventh-century church – the structure is known formally as the Heröön, though it is now thought to have been a Roman mausoleum rather than a temple of Hera. Note the weathered wooden door, and the cistern under long stone slabs in the courtyard.

The beaches of **Dhialiskári** and **Áyios Yeóryios** are reachable by road – though only the latter is asphalted – while **Málta** is only reachable by *kaïki* from Aloprónia. A more feasible journey by foot is to the pebble beach at **Áyios Pandeleïmonas**: just under an hour's trail walk southwest of Aloprónia, it's the most sheltered on the island, and is also served by a small boat in season.

Folégandhros

The sheer cliffs of **FOLÉGANDHROS** rise 300m from the sea in places, and until the early 1980s they were as effective a deterrent to tourists as they had historically been to pirates. Folégandhros was used now and then as an island of political exile from Roman times right up until 1969, and life in the high, barren interior was only eased in 1974 by the arrival of electricity and the subsequent construction of a road running from the harbour to Hóra and beyond. Development has been given further impetus by the recent increase in tourism and the ensuing commercialization. The island is becoming so trendy that Greek journalists speak of a new Mýkonos in the making, a fact that is reflected in its swish jewellery and clothes shops. Yet away from showcase Hóra and the beaches, the countryside remains mostly pristine. Donkeys are also still very much in evidence, since the terrain on much of the island is too steep for vehicles.

ARRIVAL AND GETTING AROUND

FOLÉGANDHROS

By ferry The recent popularity of Folégandhros has resulted in a slew of new ferry routes to almost every other port in the Cyclades. Ferries dock at Karavostási on the southeast coast.

Destinations Amorgós Katápola (1 weekly; 4hr); Anáfi (0–2 weekly; 1hr 30min); Áno Koufoníssi (0–1 weekly; 4hr 30min); Íos (4–8 weekly; 1hr 15min); Kéa/Lávrio (1 weekly; 10–11hr); Kýthnos (2 weekly; 6–10hr); Mílos (0–2 daily; 1hr–2hr 30min); Mýkonos (5–6 weekly; 3hr 30min); Náxos (2–3 weekly; 3hr 30min); Páros (1–3 weekly; 2hr 45min–5hr 20min); Pireás (1–2 daily; 3hr 30min–4hr); Santoríni (3–6 weekly; 45min–3hr); Sérifos (0–2 weekly; 4hr 30min); Sífnos (1–3 weekly; 1hr 45min);

Síkinos (3–6 weekly; 45min); Sýros (3–4 weekly; 7hr–9hr); Tínos (0–1 weekly; 6hr 30min).

By bus There are hourly buses daily in summer from Karavostási to Hóra, from where further buses run to Áno Meriá (6 daily; 30min) or Angáli beach (4 daily; 30min). Off season the bus to Angáli leaves you 1km away on the road to Áno Meriá.

By car or motorbike It may be worthwhile renting a car for a day – try Spyros' Motorbike Rental in Karavostási (☎22860 41448), which is cheaper than its counterparts in Hóra – but generally the buses will, as a rule, take you where you want to go.

INFORMATION

Services There's an ATM at Dhoúnavi square and the island's post office is at Poúnda square.

Travel agents Diaplous (☎22860 41158, ⓦdiaplous travel.gr) and Folegandros Travel (☎22860 41273/41198,

ⓦfolegandros-travel.gr) – both closed 2–5pm – are between Doúnavi and Poúnda squares; Folegandros Travel also has an office at the port.

Karavostási and around

KARAVOSTÁSI, the port, serves really as a last-resort base. There are several hotels and plenty of rooms but compared to the beauty of Hóra, just above, hardly any atmosphere. The closest **beach**, other than the narrow main shingle strip, is the smallish, sand-and-pebble **Várdhia**, signposted just north over the tiny headland. Some fifteen minutes' walk south lies **Livádhi**, a family beach with tamarisk trees. Just before Livádhi are the much smaller but more romantic beaches of **Vitséntzou** and **Poundáki**, reached by steep paths.

Touted as the island's most scenic beach, **Kátergo** is a 300m stretch of pea-gravel with two offshore islets, on the southeastern tip of the island. Most visitors come on a boat excursion from Karavostási or Angáli, but you can also get there on foot (20min) from the hamlet of Livádhi, itself a fifteen-minute dirt-road walk inland from Livádhi beach. Be warned, though, that it's a rather arduous and stony trek, with a final 80m descent on loose-surfaced paths; there is no shade on the walk or the beach. The narrow sea passage between the beach's southern cliffs and the right-hand islet, **Makrí**, has very strong currents and swimming through is not recommended.

ACCOMMODATION AND EATING KARAVOSTÁSI AND AROUND

Kalymnios Karavostási ☎ 22860 41146. Fish taverna said to have the freshest seafood on the island. Whether crab claws, fried calamari (€10) or lobster spaghetti, you order and pay by the kilo. Also open for breakfast. April–Oct daily 7am–1am.

Livadhi Camping Livádhi ☎ 22860 41204, ⓦfolegandros.org. A friendly and more than adequate campsite with a café-restaurant and minimarket, plus

a rental office for cars and motorbikes. They also rent apartments for two people (€50). June–Sept. **€17**

Vardia Bay Várdhia ☎ 22860 41277, ⓦvardiabay.com. Grand hotel with luxurious rooms and studios in a great location above the jetty, right on the beach of the same name. Everything is on the large side: from the rooms and the verandas with their stupendous sea views to the breakfast buffet. **€100**

Hóra

The island's real character and appeal are rooted in the spectacular **HÓRA**, perched on a cliff-edge plateau, a steep 3km from the port. Locals and foreigners mingle at the cafés and tavernas under the trees of the five adjacent squares, passing the time undisturbed by traffic, which is banned from the village centre. Towards the northern cliff-edge and entered through two arcades, the defensive core of the medieval **kástro** neighbourhood is marked by ranks of two-storey residential houses, with almost identical stairways and slightly recessed doors.

Kímisis tis Theotókou

From the cliff-edge Poúnda square, where the bus stops, a path zigzags up – with views along the northern coastline – to the wedding-cake church of **Kímisis tis Theotókou**, whose unusual design includes two little fake chapels mounted astride the roof. The church, formerly part of a nunnery, is on the gentlest slope of a pyramidal hill with 360m cliffs dropping to the sea on the northwest side and is a favourite spot for watching some of the Aegean's most spectacular sunsets.

The Khryssospiliá

Beyond and below Kímisis tis Theotókou hides the **Khryssospiliá**, a large **cave** with stalactites and ancient inscriptions, centre of a strange ancient youth cult, but closed to the public for archeological excavations. However, a minor, lower grotto can still be visited by excursion boat from the port.

ACCOMMODATION HÓRA

Aegeo ☎ 22860 41468, ⓦaegeohotel.com. A reasonably priced hotel option, just before Poúnda square, which includes free wi-fi and breakfast, but gets booked quickly. The same family manages a more basic (but immaculately clean) option at *Evgenía* rooms (☎ 22860 41006) next door. April–Sept. **€80**

Anemomilos Apartments ☎ 22860 41309, ⓦanemomilosapartments.com. Wonderfully appointed at the cliff's edge with dramatic vistas, these are super-luxurious apartments from which watching the sunset becomes an artistic experience. "Blue" coded rooms have

better views and are more expensive than "green" ones. April–Sept. **€180**

Chora Resort & Spa ☎ 22860 41590–4, ⓦchoraresort .com. Grand luxury resort at the northern end of town, spanning a couple of acres, that offers a large pool, fitness centre, designer rooms, mini-golf and even its own church for weddings and baptisms. Larger rooms have their own jacuzzi. Breakfast included. April–Sept. **€145**

★**Polikandia** ☎ 22860 41322, ⓦpolikandia -folegandros.gr. Centred around a large swimming pool, this is a superbly designed boutique hotel before Poúnda

3

square, paying great attention to detail: free wi-fi, communal jacuzzi and individual massage showers that

have to be seen to be believed. Breakfast €8. April–Sept. **€70**

EATING AND DRINKING

★ **Eva's Garden** ☎ 22860 41110. If proof be needed that Folégandhros is sophisticated, this elegant restaurant-bar provides it with an unusually inventive menu (mains €8) in a very romantic atmosphere. Easter–Oct daily 6am–1am.
Kritikos ☎ 22860 41219. A Cretan grill in the fourth square with the best *dakos* (feta, crispy roll and tomato salad) in the Cyclades and some good Cretan wines.

Excellent barbecued and grilled steaks from €8. April–Oct daily noon–1am.
Pounta ☎ 22860 41063, ⓦ pounta.gr. On Poúnda square, this is the best restaurant for breakfast and for the local *matsáta* (hand-drawn tagliatelle with veal, chicken or goat) for €10. Easter–Oct daily 8am–3pm & 6pm–midnight.

NIGHTLIFE

The town's burgeoning **nightlife** – a few dance bars along with a number of music pubs and ouzerís – is to the south, away from most accommodation.

Astarti ☎ 22860 41091. A very popular bar in the third square with an alternative feel, elegant furnishings, carefully chosen wooden decor and large cocktails (€12). The clubbers come here and then continue to *Patitiri*, a few doors down, that stays open after everything else has closed. May–Sept daily 6pm–3am.

★ **BaRaki** On the same road as *Astarti*, this is a cosy, friendly bar with a good selection of cocktails for €9. Occasional music with a DJ whose booth takes up almost half the space inside, but who cares when you'd rather be outside anyway? June–Sept daily 10pm–3am.

Áno Meriá and around

West of Hóra, a paved road threads its way along the spine of the island towards sprawling **ÁNO MERIÁ** – in fact a multitude of tiny hamlets. In the middle of the settlement stands the large parish church of Áyios Yeóryios (1905), with an unusual white, carved iconostasis. Ask the bus driver to drop you off at the long footpaths down to the beaches on the western half of the island. Muleteers await the buses here and will, for €5, transport tourists down dirt roads to the beaches at **Ambéli**, **Ligariá** and **Áyios Yeóryios**; the first two are small and can get crowded, the last is a much better beach but faces north and is only comfortable when the wind blows from the south. **Livadháki beach** is accessed by signed path from just beyond Taxiárhis.

The best swimming in this part of the island is at the attractive and popular sheltered south-coast beach of **Angáli**, where there are several tavernas. (Off-season the bus leaves you 1km away on the road to Áno Meriá.) Naturists should take the paths which lead twenty minutes east to **Firá** or west to **Áyios Nikólaos** beaches respectively. The latter is particularly fine, with many tamarisks, coarse sand and views back over the island. A lone taverna operates at Áyios Nikólaos, while Firá has no facilities.

ACCOMMODATION AND EATING

ÁNO MERIÁ AND AROUND

Blue Sand Angáli ☎ 22860 41042, ⓦ bluesand.gr. A three-star boutique option in this well-connected beach with white, minimalist undulating staircases and rooms with verandas offering mesmerizing sea views. Free wi-fi, port transfers, breakfast included. May–Sept. **€130**
Profítis Ilías Bakery At Profítis Ilías, a well-concealed, yet signposted, bakery is along a short lane to the left of

the road. It offers the local cheese-and-onion pie called *kalasoúna* for €2. Mon–Sat 8am–3pm.
Synantisi ☎ 22860 41208. A taverna at the last but one bus stop in Áno Meriá with a bit of everything: fresh fish, home-grown vegetables and hotpots of local meat such as rabbit, goat or chicken (€9). This is a good place to try the local *kalasoúna* pies as well as *matsata*. June–Sept 11am–midnight.

Santoríni

As the ferry manoeuvres into the great caldera of **SANTORÍNI (Thíra)**, the land seems to rise up and clamp around it. Gaunt, sheer cliffs loom hundreds of metres above the deep blue sea, nothing grows or grazes to soften the awesome view, and the only colours are the reddish-brown, black and grey pumice layers on the cliff face of Santoríni, the largest island in this mini-archipelago. The landscape tells of a history so dramatic and turbulent that legend hangs as fact upon it.

These apocalyptic events, though, scarcely concern modern tourists, who come here to take in the spectacular views, stretch out on the island's dark-sand beaches and absorb the peculiar, infernal geographic features. The tourism industry has changed traditional island life, creating a rather expensive playground. There is one time-honoured local industry, however, that has benefited from all the outside attention: **wine**. Santoríni is one of Greece's most important producers, and the fresh, dry white

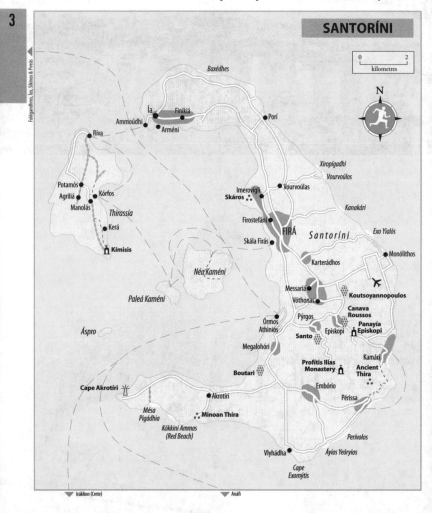

wines it is known for (most from the *assýrtiko* grape for which the region is known) are the perfect accompaniment to the seafood served in the many restaurants and tavernas that hug the island's cliffs.

Brief history

From as early as 3000 BC, Ancient Thíra developed as a sophisticated outpost of Minoan civilization, until some time between 1650–1600 BC when catastrophe struck: the volcano-island erupted some 60 cubic kilometres of magma over a period of months. The island's heart sank below the sea, leaving a caldera 10km in diameter. Earthquakes and tsunami reverberated across the Aegean (one full metre of ash was discovered on Rhodes), Thíra was destroyed, and the great Minoan civilization on Crete was dealt a severe blow by the ensuing ash fallout and tsunami. The island's history has become linked with the legend of Atlantis, all because of Plato. Although he dated the cataclysm to approximately 9500 BC, he was perhaps inspired by folk memories.

ARRIVAL AND DEPARTURE

SANTORÍNI

By plane The airport is on the east side of the island, near Monólithos. Buses are not frequent, so make sure you've arranged a pick-up.

Destinations Athens (Aegean, 3–4 daily; 45min); Iráklio (Heraklion), Crete (Aegean, 1 daily; 30min); London (Easyjet, 3hr 55min); Rhodes (2 weekly; 50min); Thessaloníki (Aegean, 2–4 daily; 1hr 5min).

By ferry All ferries dock at the port of Órmos Athiniós on the west coast, 10km south of the island's main town, Firá. The old ports of Skála Firás (just below Firá) and Ammoúdi (near Ía, in the north of the island) are used only by local excursion boats and cruise ships. Note that the old, traditional route of 580 steps from Skála Firás up to Firá is a difficult 45min walk; you can also go by mule (€5) or cable car (April–Oct daily 6.30am–11pm; Nov–March daily 7.30–10.30am & 2.30–4.30pm; €5, luggage €2.50; ☎ 22860 22977).

Destinations Amorgós Katápola (5–6 weekly; 1hr 5min); Anáfi (3 weekly; 2hr 35min); Áno Koufoníssi (0–1 daily; 2hr 40min); Astypálea (1 weekly; 3hr); Chálki (2 weekly, 11hr); Crete Sitía (1 weekly; 10hr); Iráklio (Heraklion), Crete (5–6 weekly; 1hr 30min–6hr); Folégandhros (1–2 daily; 1hr 30min–3hr); Íos (1–3 daily; 30min–1hr); Kárpathos/ Kássos (1–2 weekly; 6–13hr); Kímolos (1–2 weekly; 2hr 30min); Kos (3–4 weekly; 6hr); Lávrio via Kéa/Kýthnos (1 weekly; 12hr); Mílos (1–3 daily; 2hr 40min); Mýkonos (July & Aug 1–3 daily; 2hr–2hr 30min); Náxos (2–4 daily; 1hr 40min); Páros (2–4 daily; 2hr 30min–3hr 30min); Pireás (3–5 daily; 4hr 30min–8hr); Rhodes/Hálki (6–7 weekly; 8–14hr); Sífnos (2–4 weekly; 5hr 30min–7hr); Síkinos (6–8 weekly; 2hr); Sýros (4 weekly; 3hr 15min– 8hr 45min); Thirassía (4–6 daily from Órmos and 2–3 daily from Ammoúdhi; 15min); Tínos (5–7 weekly; 3hr).

GETTING AROUND AND INFORMATION

By bus Buses leave Firá, the island's capital, from just south of Theotokopoúlou square to Períssa, Perívolos, Kamári, Monólithos (via the airport), Akrotíri, Órmos Athiniós and Vliháda. For the timetable consult ⬤ ktel -santorini.gr.

By taxi The island's taxi base (☎ 22860 22555) is near the Firá bus station, within steps of the main square. There are fewer than forty in the whole island, so make sure you have your onward transport arranged well in advance.

By car or motorbike If you want to see the whole island in a couple of days, a rented motorbike or car will be essential. There are many rental places all over the island and your hotel or any travel agent can arrange it for you. Nomikos Travel (☎ 22860 24940, ⬤ nomikostravel.gr) opposite the OTE building in Firá is a good, reliable agency.

Day-trips and tours There are many travel agents clustered around Firá's main square: Santo Star (☎ 22860

23082, ⬤ santostar.gr) and Kamari Tours (☎ 22860 31390, ⬤ kamaritours.gr) organize excursions and trips to ancient Thíra, as well as day tours to Nea and Paleá Kaméni and Thirassía. Prices for the latter range from €15 for simple transport to about €40–50 for a more intimate guided tour on a traditional *kaïki*. The glass-bottom *Calypso* (☎ 22860 22958, ⬤ dakoutrostravel.gr) makes an excursion to the islands of the archipelago daily at 1pm in season (€20) and hovers over the volcanic reefs to allow passengers a peek into the depths of Santoríni's flooded crater. In Kamári (see p.193) Ancient Thira Tours (☎ 22860 32474) also operate guided tours of the ruins of Ancient Thíra (€8; 2hr stopping time at site).

Services There are many cafés clustered on Firá's main square; others offer free wi-fi to their customers all over the island. The post office (Mon–Fri 7.30am–2.30pm) is opposite and up from the museum of Prehistoric Thira.

Firá and around

Half-rebuilt after a devastating earthquake in 1956, **FIRÁ** (also known as Hóra) clings precariously to the edge of the enormous **caldera**. The rising and setting of the sun are especially beautiful when seen here against the Cycladic buildings lining the clifftop, and are even enough to make battling through the high-season crowds worthwhile. Although Firá's restaurants are primarily aimed at the tourist market, the food can be very good; views of the crater add considerably to the price. Similarly, accommodation isn't cheap and rooms facing the caldera tend to be particularly expensive.

Using a spectacular two-hour footpath along the lip of the caldera you reach the village of **Firostefáni** and further to the north, **Imerovígli**, both of which have equally stunning views and prices. The only alternative location, where you don't have to pay as much for the view, is **Karterádhos**, a small village about twenty minutes' walk southeast of Firá.

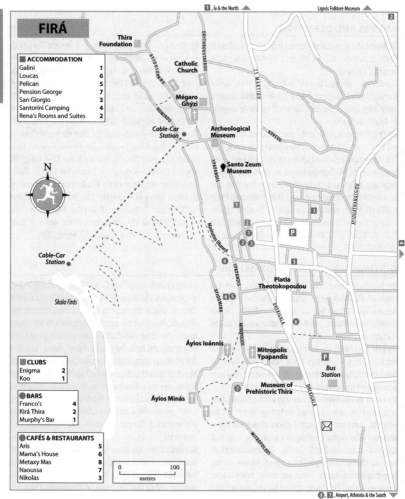

FIRÁ

ACCOMMODATION
Galini	1
Loucas	6
Pelican	5
Pension George	7
San Giorgio	3
Santorini Camping	4
Rena's Rooms and Suites	2

CLUBS
Enigma	2
Koo	1

BARS
Franco's	4
Kirá Thira	2
Murphy's Bar	1

CAFÉS & RESTAURANTS
Aris	5
Mama's House	6
Metaxy Mas	8
Naoussa	7
Nikolas	3

Museum of Prehistoric Thira
Between the cathedral and bus station • Wed–Mon 8am–3pm • €3 • ☎ 22860 23217

Fira's **Museum of Prehistoric Thira** has informative displays of fossils, Cycladic art and astonishing finds from submerged Akrotíri (see p.195) that include plaster casts of prehistoric furniture such as tables, lamps and a portable oven.

The Archeological Museum
Near the cable car to the north of town • Tues–Sun 8am–3pm • €3 • ☎ 22860 22217

The **Archeological Museum** is well presented, and has a collection from the later Homeric Classical and Hellenistic eras, much of which came from the excavations of Ancient Thira. The highlight is a mourning woman from the seventh century BC whose coloration has been remarkably preserved.

Mégaro Ghýzi
Just north of the Archeological Museum • May–Oct Mon–Sat 10am–4pm • €3 ☎ 22860 23077, ⊛ megarogyzi.gr

The handsome **Mégaro Ghýzi**, housed in an old mansion owned by the Catholic diocese of Santoríni, has been restored as a cultural centre, and has a good collection of old prints and maps as well as photographs of the town before and after the 1956 earthquake.

3

Santo Zeum
May–Oct daily 10am–6pm • €5 • ⊛ santozeum.com

Santo Zeum is the latest stunner in the Santoríni cultural milieu. Operating only since July 2011, this is a one-trick museum – but what a trick it is: it contains photographic reproductions (using a technique specially invented by Kodak) of the Akrotíri murals, which can be reasonably assumed to mark the beginning of the art of painting per se.

Lignós Folklore Museum
Kondohóri • Daily 10am–2pm & 6–8pm • €3 • ☎ 22860 22792

Located in the north of Firá, the extensive **Lignós Folklore Museum** features a completely furnished local "cave home" with period winery, chapel, garden and workshops, as well as a gallery and historical archive.

ACCOMMODATION   FIRÁ AND AROUND

Galini Firostefáni ☎ 22860 22095, ⊛ hotelgalini.gr. Possibly the cheapest hotel with a caldera view, situated in a relatively quiet spot a 10min walk from Firá. Great café terrace, too. March–Nov. **€100**

Loucas Firá ☎ 22860 22480, ⊛ www.loucashotel -santorini.com. Traditional caldera-side hotel below the Cathedral of Ypapandís, with rooms in caves carved into the cliff-side with 180-degree views of the precipice below and a beautiful pool and jacuzzi. Breakfast included. April–Oct. **€150**

Pelican Firá ☎ 22860 23113/4, ⊛ pelicanhotel.gr. Large hotel off the central square with spacious rooms but no views; it's owned by a travel agency a few blocks away, so they can organize your stay completely. Free wi-fi, satellite TV, 24hr reception, parking possible nearby. Breakfast included. **€75**

Pension George Karterádhos ☎ 22860 22351, ⊛ pensiongeorge.com. Comfortable rooms and studios, pool and a good welcome, just a 15min walk from Firá. Unlike other hotels, this one also has a well-attended garden where you can relax among the palm trees.

Breakfast €6. Free transfers upon arrival. **€60**

San Giorgio Firá ☎ 22860 23516, ⊛ sangiorgiovilla.gr. Tucked away to the left of the parking area next to the main square, you can find this hospitable, clean hotel with simple rooms, all with balconies; excellent value for budget travellers. It offers a ten percent discount for Rough Guide readers booking directly with the hotel. April–Nov. **€55**

Rena's Rooms and Suites Firá ☎ 22860 28130, ⊛ renasuites.com. Comfortable, friendly hotel, a 10min walk towards the Folklore Museum, whose rooms are furnished individually in bright, non-standard Cycladic colours, some overlooking a large pool. Minibus transfers available for a charge. April–Oct. **€120**

CAMPING

Santorini Camping Firá, 300m east of the centre ☎ 22860 22944, ⊛ santorinicamping.gr. A shady campsite with a pool, restaurant, games room, 24hr reception, own security and free internet access. Double rooms also available. Breakfast €5. March–Nov. Camping **€20**, doubles **€35**

EATING

Aris Firá ☎22860 22480. Dependably good Greek and international food plus an excellent wine list in a relaxed, unhurried atmosphere, with a sensational view – and prices to match (€20); not always busy, as the steep steps down below *Hotel Loucas* act as a deterrent to some customers. April–Oct daily noon–midnight.

Mama's House Firá. Right below the main square, this is a cheap, backpacker-friendly spot with hearty continental and English breakfasts, filling pasta dishes (€8), a shaggy dog and the overwhelming chatty presence of Mama herself, a distinguished old lady straight out of the photo album of Greek stereotypes. March–Nov daily 8am–midnight.

Metaxy Mas Exo Gonia ☎22860 31323, ⓦsantorini -metaximas.gr. On terraces overlooking the eastern side of the island and a 15min drive from Firá, this restaurant offers several Cretan dishes with an international twist and an alternative view than the caldera. Feb–June & Sept–Dec daily 2.30pm–midnight; July & Aug daily 12.30pm–midnight.

★**Naoussa** Firá ☎22860 24869/21277, ⓦnaoussa -restaurant.gr. Good traditional Greek cuisine and the cheapest place to eat and watch the sunset at Firá. Dishes as close to home-made as you'll get anywhere in town; start with the celebrated *moussaká* for €10.50. Daily noon–midnight.

Nikolas Erythroú Stavroú, Firá ☎22860 24550. An old and defiantly traditional taverna, insisting on using nothing frozen or not in season; the locals know this and prefer it, so it can be very hard to get a table. Mains around €10. Daily noon–midnight.

DRINKING AND NIGHTLIFE

Most of the first-rate **nightlife** is northwest of the central square, on Erythroú Stavroú, often not starting long before midnight and busiest between 1am and 4am.

Enigma Central square, Firá. Long-established dance club with three large barrel-roofed arches and outdoor area with a palm-tree bar. Its VIP room has seen some of the most famous world celebrities and still attracts the island's *beau monde*. June–Sept daily midnight–late.

Franco's Firá ☎22860 24428, ⓦfrancos.gr. Exclusive, expensive cocktail bar in a fabulous location by the steps to the old port offering opera, champagne and sunbeds. Try the Maria Callas cocktail (€9) and watch the sunset while listening to the Diva herself singing *Norma*. Easter–Oct daily 5pm–late.

Kira Thíra Central square, Firá. Going back more than three decades, this small, laidback venue with live DJs and music has fanatic followers who pack the place to the rafters year after year for its famous sangria, despite its less-than-ideal acoustics. May–Oct daily 8pm–late.

Koo Central square, Firá ☎22860 22025, ⓦkooclub.gr. In direct competition with *Enigma* (see above), it offers less frenetic chill-out and trance music, with candles and cocktails, three bars, and a reservation service if you want to book a table in the VIP room. June–Sept Wed, Thurs, Fri & Sat midnight–late; July & Aug daily midnight–late.

Murphy's Bar Central square, Firá ☎22860 22248. Reasonably priced Irish pub with all the obligatory hilarity. Established in 1999 it hasn't looked back since; in 2014 it took over another floor and expanded to twice its size. The wall of drinks behind the bar reaches to the ceiling and this is a rather tall venue. March–Oct daily noon–3am.

Ía

ÍA (Oía), the most photographed town on the island, was once a major commercial centre in the Aegean, but it has declined in the wake of economic depression, wars, earthquakes and depleted fish stocks. Partly destroyed in the 1956 earthquake, the town has been sympathetically reconstructed, its white and cyan houses clinging to the cliff face. Apart from the **caldera** and the town itself, there are a couple of things to see, including the **Naval Museum** (Mon & Wed–Sun 10am–2pm & 5–8pm; €3; ☎22860 71156) and the very modest remains of a Venetian castle. It is a quieter, though still touristy, alternative to Firá except during sunset, for which people are coached in from all over the island, creating traffic chaos and driving up prices. Public buses are extremely full around this time (after 6pm, although in the summer the sunset occurs around 8.30pm).

Below the town, two sets of 220-odd steps lead to two small harbours: one to **Arméni** for the fishermen, and the other to **Ammoúdi**, where the excursion boats dock.

ACCOMMODATION

Much of the town's accommodation is in restored **cave houses**, with caldera views adding at least €100/day to a room.

★**Andronis Suites** ☎22860 72041, ⓦandronis -suites.com. With its central location, superlative views, spa, apartments carved deep into the cliffs, and balconies that can induce vertigo, this may well be the most prestigious spot in the Cyclades and the price reflects it. Some apartments sleep up to five, mind you. Breakfast included. April–Oct. €610

Oia Youth Hostel ☎22860 71465, ⓦsantorinihostel.gr.

Well signposted from the bus terminal, this excellent hostel has a terrace and a shady courtyard, laundry, free wi-fi, life-size chess board, a good café-bar and clean dormitories (mixed and single-sex). May to mid-Oct. €17

Pension Delfini ☎22860 71600, ⓦdelfinihotel.gr. By far the best middle-price option, this small boutique hotel offers rooms with jacuzzis and private balconies with caldera views. Breakfast included. Doubles €150, four-person suite €370

EATING AND DRINKING

At the older, western end of town, **restaurant** prices can be as steep as the cliffs. In general the further east you go along the central ridge the better the price.

1800 ☎22860 71485, ⓦoia-1800.com. Regarded as one of the best restaurants on the island, and serving highly refined, French-inspired cuisine, the interiors here have a fin-de-siècle feel and the roof garden offers unique unhindered views over the caldera. Its wines are excellent and, like the food (mains around €30), accordingly expensive. May–Oct daily 6.30pm–midnight.

★**King Neptune** ☎22860 71294. With a rooftop bar to rival the best for views and dishes for €15 that don't break the bank, this is the best-value combination of good food, view and atmosphere in Ía. Come early for dinner before the sunset buses invade, get a front-row table and chill. April–Nov daily noon–late.

The east coast

Santoríni's **beaches**, on the island's **east coast**, are long black stretches of volcanic sand that get blisteringly hot in the afternoon sun. They're no secret, and in the summer the crowds can be a bit overpowering. Among the resorts lie the substantial and beautifully sited remains of **ancient Thíra**.

In the southeast, the family resort of **Kamári** is popular with package-tour operators, and hence more touristy. Nonetheless it's quieter and cleaner than most, with a well-maintained seafront promenade.

THE WINERIES

Some of Santoríni's most important **wineries** are scattered around Pýrgos and the south, and offer excellent-value **tours**. Whichever tour you go on, none is complete without a taste of Santoríni's prized dessert wine, **vinsánto**, which is among the finest wines produced in Greece and used by the Orthodox Church in Holy Communion. Tour prices at the smaller wineries usually include tastings, while samples are available from the larger wineries for a nominal fee.

Boutari Megalohóri ☎22860 81011, ⓦboutari.gr. This is the Santoríni branch of one of the largest wineries of Greece with an exceptional Estate Argyros Vinsanto. Easter–Oct daily 10am–6pm.

Canava Roussos Episkopí ☎22860 31349, ⓦcanavaroussos.gr. Making wines since 1836, this is one of the most traditional Greek family wineries producing a famed white called Nyktéri. May–Oct daily 11am–8pm.

Koutsoyannopoulos Kamári ☎22860 31322, ⓦwine-museum-koutsoyannopoulos.gr. The best-known winery; it has a 300m-long cellar that's home to a wine museum offering a more intimate glimpse of the winemaking process. Dec–March Mon–Sat 9.30am–2pm; April, May & Nov daily 10am–5pm; June–Oct 10am–7pm.

Santo Pýrgos ☎22860 28058, ⓦsantowines.gr. Offers the most comprehensive tours, complete with multimedia presentations. Book online. April–Nov daily 10am–sunset.

3

Things are considerably scruffier at **Aríssa**, around the cape. Because of its beach and abundance of cheap rooms, it's crowded with backpackers. The beach itself extends several kilometres to the west, through Perívolos to Áyios Yeóryios, sheltered by the occasional tamarisk tree and with beach bars dotted along at intervals. An interesting attraction in Períssa is the **Museum of Minerals and Fossils** (summer daily 10am–2pm; winter Sun only 10am–2pm; free), with exhibits that include rare palm-tree fossils from pre-eruption Santoríni.

Ancient Thira

Between Kamári and Períssa • Tues–Sun 8.30am–2.30pm • €1.50 • Excursion minibuses depart from Kamári (see p.193); alternatively, walk the looping cobbled road – Archaias Thiras – starting from Ancient Thira Tours in Kamári

Kamári and Períssa are separated by the Mésa Vounó headland, on which stood **ancient Thira**, the post-eruption settlement, dating from 915 BC through to the Venetian period. Starting from Períssa, a stony shadeless path to the site passes a chapel dating back to the fourth century AD before skirting round to the **temple of Artemidoros** with bas-relief carvings of a dolphin, eagle and lion representing Poseidon, Zeus and Apollo. Next, the trail follows the sacred way of the ancient city through the remains of the **agora** and past the **theatre**. The path meets the paved road to Kamári at a saddle between Mésa Vounó and Profítis Ilías, the only remaining visible components of the pre-eruption landscape.

ACTIVITIES   THE EAST COAST

Diving Kamári is the base of Navy's Diving Centre (☎ 22860 31006, ⓦ navys.gr), which offers PADI courses for beginners and volcanic reef diving for certified divers.

ACCOMMODATION

Anny Studios Períssa ☎ 22860 82669, ⓦ annystudios .com. One of the most pleasant hostels you're likely to find on the Greek islands. Offers a range of modern, well-fitted rooms with balconies from studios with kitchenettes to dorms, set around a central pool and bar in a quiet cul-de-sac close to the beach. Free wi-fi, laptops also available. Breakfast €4. Doubles €38, dorms €15

★**Chez Sophie** Kamári ☎ 22860 32912, ⓦ chezsophie .gr. A stunningly designed boutique hotel with large rooms set around a swimming pool towards the southern end of the beach. Superb service that includes free wi-fi, parking, free air and ferry transfers, plus a delicious home-made buffet breakfast. May–Oct. €90

Perissa Beach Períssa ☎ 22860 81343, ⓦ perissa -camping.com. Right behind the coastal road, this camp-site has plenty of space and shade. It's also next to a route of noisy late-night bars, but if you choose to stay here you're more likely to be carousing than resting. Has special overflow space for sleeping bags only. €17

Rose Bay Hotel Kamári ☎ 22860 33650, ⓦ rosebay.gr. A less pricey option than other luxurious hotels in the north part of town, with a pleasant pool setting, set back from the beach. Breakfast included. April–Oct. €140

EATING AND DRINKING

Períssa's young crowds aren't so choosy when it comes to food, so the **restaurants** at Kamári catering to over-35s are much better. The best of the **bars** at Kamári are towards the southern end of the beach, offering staggered happy hours 8pm–midnight, and there's a good open-air licensed **cinema** at the north end of the town.

Kritikos North of Kamári ☎ 22460 44277. A taverna much frequented by locals, this is one of the better grill places to eat on the island (mains €15). It's a long way out of Kamári on the road up to Messariá, and too far to walk, but the bus stops outside. April–Nov daily noon–midnight.

★**Meli & Thymari** Kamári ☎ 22860 31835, ⓦ melithymari-santorini.com. Old restaurant with new management and a female chef who has taken Kamári by storm. Tasty variations on traditional dishes such as beef fillet in vinsanto sauce (€14) and chicken in a clay pot with cheese and vegetables (€10). Easter–Oct daily noon–midnight.

West to Pýrgos

As you drive west of Kamári towards Pýrgos you can't miss the sight of **Panayía Episkopí**, the most important Byzantine monument on the island. Built in the eleventh

THE ARCHIPELAGO

The best and most popular **day-trip** from Firá is to the three islands of the **inner archipelago**. Most people stick to the still volcanically active Paleá and Néa Kaméni, although, if you have time, it is worth staying overnight in Thirassía for a glimpse of what Santoríni used to feel like before the cruise ships arrived.

PALEÁ AND NÉA KAMÉNI

Local ferries from either Skála Firás or Ía (Ammoúdhi), venture to the charred volcanic islets of **Paleá Kaméni** (active 46–1458 AD) and **Néa Kaméni** (active 1707–1950). At Paleá Kaméni you can swim from the boat to warm mineral-laden springs, while Néa Kaméni (€2 entrance fee), with its own mud-clouded hot springs, features a demanding hike to a smouldering, volcanically active crater.

THIRASSÍA

The boat excursions also continue to the relatively unspoilt islet of **Thirassía** (ⓦthirasia.gr), which was once part of Santoríni until sliced off by an eruption in the third century BC. It's an excellent destination, except during the tour-boat rush of lunch hour. At other times, the island is one of the quietest in the Cyclades, with views as dramatic as any on Santoríni. The downside is that there's no proper beach and the tavernas in Kórfos close early after the last ferry has gone. There's an ATM at the Citizen's Service office (KEP) and credit cards are normally not accepted on the island.

Tour boats head for the village of **Kórfos**, a stretch of shingle backed by fishermen's houses and high cliffs, while ferries dock at **Ríva**. There should be no problem taking a car or rental bike over, but fill up with petrol first. From Kórfos a steep, stepped path climbs up to **Manolás**, nearly 200m above, where donkeys are still used for transport. Manolás straggles along the edge of the caldera, an attractive small village that gives an idea of what Santoríni was like before tourism arrived there.

ACCOMMODATION

Zacharo Rooms Manolás ☎22860 29102. All rooms have a/c, private bathroom and TV with amazing views over Manolás, Kórfos and Santoríni itself. No credit cards accepted. Easter–Oct. **€45**

---

century, it was the setting of centuries of conflict between Orthodox Greeks and Catholics, but is most notable today for its carved iconostasis of light blue marble with a white grain.

Further west is **PÝRGOS**, one of the oldest settlements on the island, a jumble of weather-beaten houses and alleys that form several concentric circles around the village kástro. It climbs to another Venetian fortress crowned by the seventeenth-century church of the **Presentation of the Virgin**. You can clamber around the battlements for sweeping views over the entire island and its Aegean neighbours.

EATING

PÝRGOS

Kallisti ☎22860 34108. If you can't get a table at *Selene* (see below), worry not. This cosy, covered taverna on the main square has excellent cheap food and a tradition of good service; its lamb casserole (€6) literally melts in the mouth. April–Oct daily noon–midnight.

★**Selene** ☎22860 22249, ⓦselene.gr. Santoríni's most famous restaurant, awarded Greece's top gastronomic accolade in 2011 and 2014, has moved to Pýrgos from Firá, but still serves delicious, inventive food. Choose from dishes such as rabbit quintet or cod in sea urchin risotto (all around €30) or the taster menu from €60/person. Booking essential. April–Oct daily noon–11pm.

Akrotíri and the south coast

Evidence of the Minoan colony that once thrived here has been uncovered at the ancient site of **AKROTÍRI** (summer 8am–8pm; winter 8am–3pm; €5; ☎22860 81366) at the southwestern tip of the island; the site was inhabited from the Late Neolithic period through to the seventeenth century BC. Allow at least an hour to visit the site.

Kókkini Ámmos (Red Beach) is about 500m from the site and is quite spectacular, with high reddish-brown cliffs above sand of the same colour. It's a better beach than the one below the site, but gets crowded in season. More secluded black-sand beaches lie under the surreal, pockmarked pumice stone that dominates the lunar coast around **Cape Exomýtis** at the island's southern extremity. Both **Vlyhádha** to the west and **Áyios Yeóryios** to the east of the cape are accessed by decent roads branching off from the main one to Embório, though no buses run here and there are no amenities to speak of. An hour's walk west of ancient Akrotíri, a lighthouse marks the tip of **Cape Akrotíri**, which offers better views of the caldera than even Ía itself.

ACCOMMODATION AND EATING   AKROTÍRI AND THE SOUTH COAST

Caldera View Resort Megalohóri ☎ 22860 82010, ⓦ calderaview-santorini.com. Situated 6km from Firá and 2km from the Red Beach, this modern bungalow complex, opened in May 2011, has arguably better sunset and caldera views than other more expensive locations on the island. You'll need your own wheels to move around,

though. June–Sept. **€75**

Delfinia Akrotíri ☎ 22860 81151. Wonderfully situated at the water's edge, just below the bus stop, this is a grill taverna that offers fresh seafood and the catch of the day. Try the lightly fried calamari (€15), which is perfectly cooked. Daily noon–10pm.

Anáfi

A ninety-minute boat ride to the east of Santoríni, **ANÁFI** is the last stop for ferries and is something of a travellers' dead end. It was so for the Argonauts who prayed to Apollo for some land at which to rest; he let the island emerge from the sea for their repose. If rest is what you crave, you'll have it here in abundance. Not that this is likely to bother most of the visitors, who come here for weeks in midsummer to enjoy exactly that: its seclusion. Although idyllic geographically, Anáfi is a harsh place, its mixed granite and limestone core overlaid by volcanic rock spewed out by Santoríni's eruptions. Apart from the few olive trees and vines grown in the valleys, the only plants that seem to thrive are prickly pears. The quiet, unassuming capital, **Hóra**, provides a daring dash of white in a treeless, shrub-strewn hillock, its narrow, winding streets offering protection from the occasionally squally *gharbís* wind that comes unencumbered from the southwest.

The beaches

The glory of Anáfi is a string of south-facing beaches starting under the cliffs at **Áyios Nikólaos**. These – along with two nearby monasteries – are accessible by bus, although walking is still an option. The nearest beach is **Klisídhi**, east of the harbour,

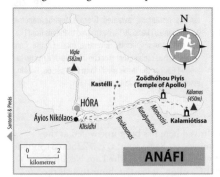

which has 200m of gently shelving sand. The next big beach is **Roúkounas** with some 500m of broad sand rising to tamarisk-stabilized dunes where free camping is allowed. Beyond Roúkounas, it's another half-hour on foot to the first of the exquisite half-dozen coves of **Katalymátsa**, the ancient port. On the craggy hill of **Kastélli**, an hour's scramble above the beach, is the site of **ancient Anáfi**; a further forty-five minutes takes you to **Monastíri**, where the bus stops.

The monasteries

Monastíri in Anáfi means the **monastery of Zoödhóhou Piyís**. The bus stops only a few hundred metres before the building. A ruined temple of Apollo, supposedly built by the grateful Argonauts, is incorporated into the monastery, while the courtyard, with a welcome cistern, is the venue for the island's major festivals, celebrated eleven days after Easter and September 7–8. Go left immediately before the monastery to join the spectacular onward path to **Kalamiótissa**, another monastery perched atop the abrupt limestone pinnacle at the extreme southeast of the island. It takes another hour to reach, but is eminently worthwhile for the stunning scenery and views over the entire south coast – there is no accessible water up here, so bring enough with you.

ARRIVAL AND DEPARTURE
ANÁFI

By ferry All ferries dock at the small port of Áyios Nikólaos, on the south coast. Buses always wait for ferries to take arriving passengers to Hóra (5min).

Destinations Iráklio (Heraklion), Crete (1 weekly; 4hr); Crete, Sitía (1 weekly; 8hr); Folégandhros (2 weekly; 4hr 30min); Íos (2 weekly; 6hr); Kárpathos/Kássos/Hálki (2 weekly; 5–10hr); Lávrio via Kéa/Kýthnos (1 weekly; 14–17hr); Mílos (1 weekly; 6hr 40min); Mýkonos (3 weekly; 5hr 15min); Náxos (2–3 weekly; 8hr 15min); Páros (2–3 weekly; 9hr 30min); Pireás (2 weekly; 9–11hr); Rhodes (2 weekly; 19hr); Santoríni (2–4 weekly; 50min–1hr 30min); Síkinos (0–2 weekly; 5hr 30min); Sýros (2 weekly; 13hr); Tínos (1–2 weekly; 4hr 50min).

Travel agents Anafi Travel (☎22860 61408/61220, ✉roussoanafi@yahoo.gr) sells boat tickets.

GETTING AROUND AND INFORMATION

By bus There are buses from Hóra to Áyios Nikólaos (7–8 daily; 15min) and Monastíri (3–4 daily), via the beaches.
By car or motorbike You can rent both cars and motorbikes at Moto Manos (☎22860 61430).

Services There's an ATM at Áyios Nikólaos and the island's sub-post office in Hóra. There's no pharmacy on the island (some drugs are dispensed from the GP's practice).

ACCOMMODATION

Apollon Village Klisídhi ☎22860 28739, ⊛apollon village.gr. Some 800m from the port, this complex has twelve elegant maisonettes on the hillside overlooking Klisídhi beach, each named after Muses or Olympian gods and every one designed accordingly. Breakfast included. May–Sept. **€90**

Ta Plagia Hóra ☎22860 61308, ⊛taplagia.gr. Rooms (with ceiling fans) and studios with kitchenette (and a/c) for up to four people with their own balconies and unhindered pelagic views. Internet and good home-made breakfasts (€5) charged separately. April–Oct. Doubles **€60**, studios **€70**

EATING

Alexandhra Hóra ☎22860 61212. A good, solid restaurant, as laidback as the island itself, offering both grilled fresh fish and seafood by the kilo as well as casseroles and prepared dishes (€6). Daily 9am–11pm.

Liotrivi Hóra ☎22860 61209. A good family taverna where you're invited to come to the kitchen and choose among the prepared dishes (€9) or pick up the fresh ingredients for your own individual fish soup, which is then cooked on the spot. May–Sept daily noon–midnight.

★**Roukounas** Roukounas beach ☎22860 61206. Popular family taverna 150m from Roukounas beach. Try its local pasta (€8) or signature baked aubergine dish, all served with its own freshly baked bread. May–Oct 10am–midnight.

Crete

FALÁSARNA BEACH, WESTERN CRETE

Crete

Crete (Kríti) is a great deal more than just another Greek island. In many places, especially in the cities or along the developed north coast, it doesn't feel like an island at all, but rather a substantial land in its own right. Which of course it is – a mountainous, wealthy and at times surprisingly cosmopolitan one with a tremendous and unique history. At the same time, it has everything you could want of a Greek island and more: great beaches, remote hinterlands and hospitable people.

With a thriving agricultural economy (and some unexpectedly good vineyards), Crete is one of the few Greek islands that could probably support itself without visitors. Nevertheless, tourism is an important part of the economy, particularly along the **north coast**, where many resorts cater to rowdy young revellers lured by thumping bars and cheap booze. The quieter, less commercialized resorts and villages lie at either end of the island – west, towards **Haniá** and the smaller, less well-connected places along the south and west coasts, or east around Sitía. The **high mountains** of the interior are still barely touched by tourism.

Of the cities, sprawling **Iráklio** (Heraklion) can give a poor first impression, but it's a place that grows on you. The wonderful archeological museum here is an essential visit, Minoan **Knossós** is a short bus ride away, and there are more Minoan sites at **Festós** and **Ayía Triádha** to the south, with Roman **Górtys** to provide contrast. Further east, the upmarket resort of **Áyios Nikólaos** provides sophisticated restaurants and hotels, while laidback **Sitía** is a perfect base for exploring the eastern coastline. In the west, **Réthymno** boasts a pretty old town and an excellent beach, though **Haniá** (Chania) in the extreme west arguably beats it in terms of style and atmosphere. South of here is the **Samariá Gorge**, one of the best hikes in Greece.

In terms of **climate**, Crete has the longest summers in Greece, and you can get a decent tan here right into October and swim at least from May until early November. The one seasonal blight is the *meltémi*, a northerly wind, which regularly blows harder and more continuously here than anywhere else – the locals may welcome its cooling effects, but it's another reason (along with crowds and heat) to avoid an August visit if you can.

Brief history

Crete's strategic position between east and west has ensured a history far richer than many a full-grown nation. The island is distinguished above all as the home of Europe's earliest civilization, the **Minoans** (see p.522), whose remarkably advanced society lay at the centre of a far-reaching maritime trading empire as early as 2000 BC. Control of the island subsequently passed from **Greeks** to **Romans** to **Saracens**, through the **Byzantine empire** to Venice, and finally to Turkey for more than two centuries. During **World War II**, Crete was occupied by the Germans and attained the dubious distinction of being the first place to be successfully invaded by paratroops.

Highlights

❶ Archeological Museum, **Iráklio** The finest collection of Minoan artefacts in the world, gloriously displayed. **See p.206**

❷ Knossós Even with the crowds, the Minoan palace of Knossós is the standout archeological site on the island. **See p.211**

❸ Lasíthi Plateau This fertile high mountain plateau is a taste of traditional Crete, with a cave that's the mythological birthplace of Zeus. **See p.219**

❹ Palékastro Great beaches and simple accommodation in the far east, plus access to gorge walks and ancient sites. **See p.232**

❺ Amári Valley Wonderfully scenic mountain drives, white-walled villages and olive groves, plus some lovely hiking country. **See p.241**

❻ Haniá old town Atmospheric city centre where vibrant modern life coexists with the beautiful architectural legacies of Venetian and Turkish history. **See p.246**

❼ Samariá Gorge A magnificent gorge, offering a chance to see brilliant wild flowers, golden eagles and perhaps a Cretan ibex. **See p.253**

❽ Sfakiá coast Having made it through the Samariá Gorge, you'll find some of Crete's least-visited coastline. **See p.255**

HIGHLIGHTS ARE MARKED ON THE MAP ON PP.202–203

ARRIVAL AND DEPARTURE CRETE

By plane Crete has two international airports, Iráklio (Heraklion) and Haniá (Chania), both served by direct flights from the UK and Europe between April and Oct; Sitía also sees the occasional summer international charter. From Athens and Thessaloníki there are daily flights year-round to Iráklio and Haniá with Aegean (w aegeanair.com) and Ryanair (w ryanair.com), while Astra (w astra-airlines. gr) offer daily connections between Athens and Sitía, Sky Express (w www.skyexpress.gr) fly from Iráklio and Sitía to a number of islands and mainland cities, and Olympic (w olympicair.com) connects Sitía with Kássos, Kárpathos and Rhodes.

By ferry There are daily year-round ferry connections from Pireás to both Iráklio and Haniá, and there are also ferries linking Kastélli in the west with Kýthira and the Peloponnese, and Sitía in the east with the islands of the Dodecanese. Fast cats run from Iráklio and Réthymno to Santoríni and other Cycladic islands.

GETTING AROUND

By bus There are excellent bus connections across most of Crete. Fast buses run constantly along the north-coast highway, linking the major towns, while less frequent connections from the main hubs of Iráklio, Áyios Nikólaos, Réthymno and Haniá head inland and to the south coast. Timetables are available on w bus-service-crete.com, or official sites w ktelherlas.gr for the east, w e-ktel.com for the west.

By car or motorbike The main routes across the island and to the south are generally well surfaced and fairly well signposted. Beware of heading off on unsurfaced roads though, particularly on mountain tracks, which often just peter out before coming to a dead end. In Iráklio 25-Avgoústou is lined with companies offering car and motorbike rental, but you'll often find better deals on the backstreets nearby. Try Blue Sea, Kosmá Zótou 7, just off the bottom of 25-Avgoústou (☎ 2810 241 097, w bluesearentals.com); Alianthos, at the airport and in Amoudhára (☎ 2810 390 482, w alianthos-group.com); or Ritz in the *Hotel Rea*, Kalimeráki 1 (☎ 2810 223 638, w hotelrea.gr). All offer free delivery to hotels and airport.

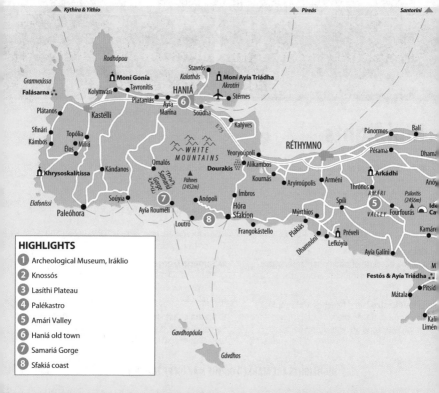

HIGHLIGHTS

1 Archeological Museum, Iráklio
2 Knossós
3 Lasíthi Plateau
4 Palékastro
5 Amári Valley
6 Haniá old town
7 Samariá Gorge
8 Sfakiá coast

Central Crete

Crete's heartland, centred on the island capital, **Iráklio**, is busier with tourists than anywhere else on the island. They come for two simple reasons: the string of big resorts to the east of the city, just an hour or so from the airport, and the great Minoan sites, almost all of which are concentrated in the centre of the island. The **resorts**, especially those closest to the capital, are dominated by package tours and are not the island's most attractive, but they're well-connected and in easy reach of the capital, with its magnificent **Archeological Museum**, and of the sites of **Knossós** and **Mália**. West of Iráklio mountains drop straight into the sea virtually all the way to Réthymno, with just two significant coastal settlements, at **Ayía Pelayía** and **Balí**. **Inland** lies agricultural country, some of the richest on the island, including a cluster of Crete's better vineyards and a series of wealthy villages; the **Lasíthi Plateau** makes a particularly striking contrast to the coastal development just a few kilometres away. To the south lie more ancient sites at **Górtys**, **Festós** and **Ayía Triádha**, all of which could potentially be visited in a full day, with a lunchtime or evening swim on the south coast at **Mátala** or **Léndas**.

Iráklio

IRÁKLIO (Heraklion) is a big, boisterous city – the fifth largest in Greece. Strident and modern, it's a maelstrom of crowded thoroughfares, building work and dust, and, in high summer, its great sites are packed. Penetrate behind this facade, however, and you can discover a vibrant working city with a myriad of attractive features that do much to

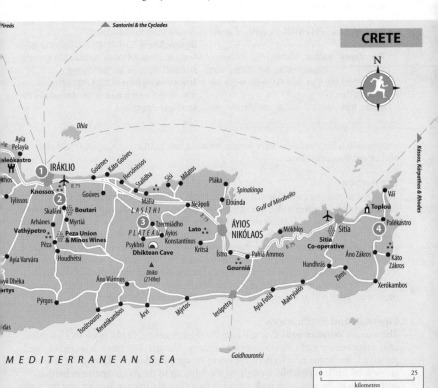

4

ADVENTURE SPORTS

Crete is a great place for **adventure holidays**, and there are numerous companies across the island offering everything from mountain biking and canyoning to trekking and horseriding. Here's a selection of what's on offer. Watersports and diving operators are also listed throughout the chapter.

CLIMBING/ADRENALINE SPORTS

Liquid Bungy ☎ 6937 615 191, ⓦ bungy.gr. White-knuckle bungee jumping (Europe's second highest) at the Arádhena Gorge, Haniá.

Trekking Plan ☎ 6932 417 040, ⓦ cycling.gr. Rock climbing, mountaineering, canyoning, rapelling, kayaking and mountain biking in Haniá province.

HORSERIDING

Horse Riding Center ☎ 28320 31851, ⓦ cretehorse riding.com. Horse and donkey rides and instruction outside Plakiás.

Melanouri ☎ 28920 45040, ⓦ melanouri.com. Horseriding and instruction, from an hour-long jaunt to a week's riding holiday, at a stable near Mátala.

Odysseia ☎ 28970 51080, ⓦ horseriding.gr. One- to six-day guided and unguided horse treks from their base at Avdhoú near the Lasíthi Plateau.

Zoraïda's Horseriding ☎ 28250 61745, ⓦ zoraidas -horseriding.com. Horseriding holidays and treks from their stables in Yeoryioúpoli, Haniá.

WALKING AND CYCLING

Cretan Adventures ☎ 28103 32772, ⓦ cretan adventures.gr. Hiking, cycling and a huge variety of other adventure and family activities throughout Crete.

Crete-Cycling.Com ☎ 6986 927 706, ⓦ crete-cycling .com. Hard-core cycling with high-quality equipment from bases in Ayía Galíni and Mókhlos; spring and autumn training camps.

The Happy Walker Tombázi 56, Réthymno ☎ 28310 52920, ⓦ happywalker.com. Walking tours ranging from day-hikes near Réthymno to ten-day mountain hikes.

Hellas Bike ☎ 28210 60858, ⓦ hellasbike.net.

One- to seven-day bike tours at anything from family to committed mountain-biker level, from Ayía Marína in Haniá province.

Korifi Tours ☎ 28930 41440, ⓦ korifi.de. Hiking tours from a tiny village in southwest Crete; also climbing and enduro motorbiking.

Olympic Bike ☎ 28310 72383, ⓦ olympicbike.com. Gentle bike tours and serious mountain biking, mostly in central Crete from a base in Réthymno.

Strata Walking Tours ☎ 28220 24336, ⓦ stratatours .com. Guided trekking holidays and day-walks in the Kastélli area of the far west.

---

temper initial impressions: hefty fortifications, a fine market, atmospheric old alleys and interesting museums.

The harbour

The obvious starting point for any exploration of Iráklio is the **harbour**, now home only to small craft but still guarded over by an impressive sixteenth-century **Venetian fortress**, generally known by its Turkish name of **Koúles**. Though it withstood a 22-year Ottoman siege, time has caught up with its underwater foundations and the building is closed to visitors pending restoration; nonetheless the causeway leading to and around the fort is a favourite place for a stroll and for locals to fish. On the landward side of the harbour, the vaulted **Arsenáli** are marooned in a sea of traffic scooting along the harbour road. Now undergoing a long process of renovation, in their heyday these shipyards were at the water's edge and as many as fifty galleys at a time could be built or repaired here.

City walls and fortifications

The massive **Venetian walls** that still encircle the city centre, in places up to 15m thick, offer more evidence of Iráklio's turbulent history. Though their fabric is incredibly well preserved, and many new sections are being excavated and restored along the seafront, access is tricky. It is possible, though, to scramble up to the Áyios Andhréas Bastion, over the sea in the west, and walk round as far as the Martinengo Bastion and the **tomb**

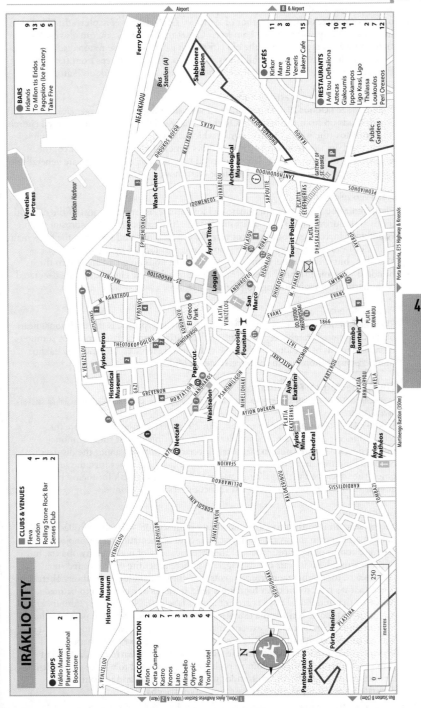

IRÁKLIO CITY

● **SHOPS**
Iráklio Market	2
Planet International Bookstore	1

■ **CLUBS & VENUES**
Fleva	4
London	1
Rolling Stone Rock Bar	3
Senses Club	2

■ **ACCOMMODATION**
Atrion	2
Creta Camping	8
Kastro	7
Kronos	1
Lato	3
Mirabello	5
Olympic	9
Rea	6
Youth Hostel	4

● **BARS**
Iridanós	9
To Mílon tis Eridos	13
Pagopiíon (Ice Factory)	6
Take Five	5

● **CAFÉS**
Kirkor	11
Mare	3
Utopia	8
Veneris	15
Bakery Cafe	

● **RESTAURANTS**
I Avli tou Defkaliona	4
Aztecas	10
Giakoumis	14
Ippokampos	1
Ligo Krasí, Ligo Thálassa	2
Loukoulos	7
Peri Orexeos	12

Airport

& Airport

Ferry Dock

4

of Nikos Kazantzakis, Cretan author of *Zorba the Greek*, whose epitaph reads: "I believe in nothing, I hope for nothing, I am free." Closer to the centre, you can also explore the **Gateway of St George** – one of the old city's main gateways whose restored subterranean vaults now house temporary exhibitions. It's approached down steps from the middle of Platía Eleftherías, and you emerge at the bottom beside the car park on Ikárou Avenue.

25-Avgoústou Street and around
Pedestrianized **Odhós 25-Avgoústou**, lined with shipping and travel agencies, banks and stores, heads up from the harbour. On the left as you climb is the much-revered church of **Áyios Títos** (the island's patron saint), which commands a lovely little plaza, while just beyond are the **Venetian City Hall** with its famous **loggia**, and **San Marco**, the cathedral in the Venetian era, later converted to a mosque. The last two are generally open to house some kind of exhibition or craft show.

Platía Venizélou
Platía Venizélou (aka Fountain Square or Lion Square) is crowded most of the day with locals and tourists sitting outside its many cafés. Its focal point is the **Morosini Fountain**, which dates from the final years of Venetian rule and was once the city's main source of fresh water. Originally the whole thing was topped by a giant statue of Poseidon, but even without him it's impressive: the lions on guard are two to three hundred years older than the rest of the structure, while the eight basins are decorated with marine themes including dolphins and Tritons.

Platía Eleftherías
Platía Eleftherías, with seats shaded by palms and eucalyptuses, is the traditional heart of the city, though rarely very peaceful; traffic swirls around it constantly, on summer evenings crowds of strolling locals come to fill its café terraces, and most of Iráklio's more expensive shops are in the streets leading off here.

The Archeological Museum
Xanthoudhídhou 2 • April–Oct daily 8am–8pm; Nov–March Mon 11am–5pm, Tues–Sun 8am–3pm • €6, joint ticket with Knossós €10 • ☏ 2810 279 000

Iráklio's **Archeological Museum** reopened in 2014 after a seven-year closure for refurbishment. At first sight it's not clear where the time or vast sums of money involved went – there's nothing remotely spectacular or flashy about the displays. Spend a little time here, however, and you realize just how clever it is; the superb objects are displayed with sparkling clarity and allowed to speak for themselves. For anyone who remembers the fusty old collection, it's a revelation.

Ground floor
You go straight into the museum's most important section – the finest collection of **Minoan artefacts** in the world – arrayed in a series of thematic and chronologically arranged rooms on the ground floor. The sheer quantity of high-quality objects, most of them around 4000 years old, is staggering: there are entire walls covered in arrowheads, for example, or bronze ingots, or Minoan double-axe symbols. There's so much that it's hard to pick out **highlights** (and if there's one criticism to be made, it would be that individual objects are not always labelled). Nonetheless, exhibits to look out for in particular include the extensive collection of **Kamares ware** pottery, whose polychrome decoration seems extraordinarily modern; gold jewellery including the famous **bee pendant** from the Palace of Mália; a beautiful **axe head** shaped like a leopard; a clay **model house**, complete with balcony; the **Town Mosaic**, a series of painted plaques depicting buildings, probably once attached to a piece of wooden furniture; the enigmatic and still-undeciphered **Festos disc**; and the intricately decorated black stone **Harvesters Vase** from Ayía Triádha.

First floor

Upstairs is the **fresco gallery**, where the most famous frescoes from Knossós are displayed. Only tiny fragments of the originals survived, but they have been almost miraculously reconstituted to give an impression of the entire fresco; the displays also show alternative interpretations of some of them. Beyond are galleries featuring the **Classical, Hellenistic and Roman eras**, perhaps most interesting in showing the continuity of art and ideas. Giant *píthoi* (clay storage jars), for example, are identical in shape and function to those made almost two thousand years earlier, but with very different decoration.

Odhós 1866: the market

Daily 8am–8pm (individual stalls vary; some close on Sun, while many take a siesta around 2–5pm)

Odhós 1866 is packed throughout the day with the stalls and customers of Iráklio's **market**. This is one of the few living reminders of an older city, with an atmosphere reminiscent of an eastern bazaar. There are luscious fruit and vegetables, as well as butchers' and fishmongers' stalls and others selling a bewildering variety of herbs and spices, cheese and yoghurt, leather and plastic goods, CDs, tacky souvenirs, an amazing array of cheap kitchen utensils, pocket knives and more.

Historical Museum

Sófokli Venizélou 27 • April–Oct Mon–Sat 9am–5pm; Nov–March Mon–Sat 9am–3.30pm • €5 • ☎ 2810 283 219, ⓦ historical-museum.gr

The **Historical Museum** offers a comprehensive overview of Cretan history. There are sculptures and architectural pieces from the Byzantine, Venetian and Turkish periods as well as documents and photos recalling the German invasion of Crete, plus exhibits on island folklore. Local memorabilia include the reconstructed studies of the writer Nikos Kazantzakis and of Cretan statesman (and Greek prime minister) Emanuel Tsouderos. There's enough variety and interactivity to satisfy just about anyone, plus the only **El Greco** paintings on the island of his birth, the small *View of Mount Sinai and the Monastery of St Catherine* (painted around 1570) and the even smaller *Baptism of Christ* (1567).

Natural History Museum

Sófokli Venizélou • Daily 9am–9pm • €8 • ☎ 2810 282 740, ⓦ www.nhmc.uoc.gr

Spectacularly housed in a converted seafront power plant, the **Natural History Museum** examines the ecosystems of the eastern Mediterranean along with Crete's geological evolution, the arrival of man, and the environment as it would have appeared to the Minoans. There's also an **earthquake simulator**, a planetarium and, for kids, the interactive **Discovery Centre**, with plenty of dinosaurs.

The beaches

If cultural pursuits become overwhelming, it's easy to escape the city for a few hours to lie on the **beach**. The simplest course is to head east, beyond the airport, to the municipal beach at **Amnísos** or marginally quieter **Tobróuk**. Beaches to the west, around **Amoudhára**, are less prone to aircraft noise but also more commercialized and more exposed; getting to the sand can be tricky too, with few access roads penetrating the line of hotels. You'll find food, drink and other facilities at all of them; bus details are given in "Getting Around" (see p.208)

ARRIVAL AND DEPARTURE **IRÁKLIO**

BY PLANE

Iráklio Airport The airport (Heraklion; ☎ 2810 397 800) is right on the coast, 4km east of the city. Plans for a new airport, originally due to open in 2014, seem indefinitely on hold; meantime the old one barely copes at peak times. Bus

#1 leaves for Platía Eleftherías from outside the terminal (every 10min 6am–11.45pm; €1.10); buy your ticket at the booth before boarding. There are also plenty of taxis, with prices to major destinations posted – it's €10–12 to the centre of town; agree on the fare before taking the cab.

Airlines Aegean (airport office ☎2810 344 321, ⓦaegeanair.com) operates scheduled flights to Athens, Thessaloníki and Rhodes; Sky Express (airport office ☎2810 223 500, ⓦskyexpress.gr) and Minoan Air, Vosporóu 1 (☎2810 333 183, ⓦminoanair.com) operate small planes to Athens and the islands.

Domestic destinations Athens (7 daily; 50min); Ikaría (1 weekly; 50min); Kós (5 weekly; 50min); Kýthira (2 weekly; 50min); Mytilíni (Lésvos, 6 weekly; 1hr 15min); Rhodes (at least 1 daily; 1hr); Santoríni (3 weekly; 30min); Thessaloníki (1 daily; 1hr 15min).

BY FERRY

From the port cut straight up the stepped alleys behind the bus station (from where city buses depart to all areas) towards Platía Eleftherías (about a 15min walk) or follow the main road west along the coast, past the bus station and the Venetian harbour, then cut up towards the centre along 25-Avgoústou.

Operators and destinations Minoan Lines, 25-Avgoústou 17 (☎2810 229 602, ⓦminoan.gr) and ANEK/Superfast, Dhimokratías 11 (☎2810 223 067, ⓦanek.gr) have nightly ferries to Athens (9/9.30pm; 9hr); ANEK also operate the *Prevelis*, departing Sat am (and Wed in summer) to Sitía, Kássos (6hr), Kárpathos (8hr), Hálki (10hr) and Rhodes (12hr), Sun night to Santoríni (4hr) and Mílos (8hr). Hellenic Seaways (ⓦhsw.gr; April–Sept) and Seajets (ⓦseajets.gr; June–Sept) operate daily fast catamarans to Santoríni (2hr), Íos (2hr 50min) or Náxos (2hr 50min), Páros (4hr) and Mýkonos (4hr 50min).

Agents The local agent for Hellenic Seaways and Seajets is Paleologos Travel, 25-Avgoústou 5 (☎2810 346 185,

ⓦferries.gr), who display current timetables and can sell tickets for all ferries.

BY BUS

Timetables ⓦktelherlas.gr or ⓦbus-service-crete.com.
Bus Station A On the main road between the ferry dock and the Venetian harbour, Bus Station A serves all the main north coast routes – west to Réthymno and Haniá, east to Hersónisos, Mália, Áyios Nikólaos and Sitía – as well as southeast to Ierápetra and points en route. There's a left luggage office here (daily 6am–9pm; €2/bag/day). Note that fewer services run on Sun.

Destinations Ay. Nikólaos (18 daily; 1hr 30min); Haniá (17 daily; 3hr); Hersónisos (every 15min; 45min); Ierápetra (7 daily; 2hr 30min); Mália (every 15min; 1hr); Réthymno (17 daily; 1hr 30min); Sitía (6 daily; 3hr 15min).

Bus Station B Buses for the southwest (Festós, Mátala and Ayía Galíni) and along the inland roads west (Týlissos and Anóyia) operate out of Bus Station B just outside Pórta Haníon, a 15min walk from the centre down Kalokerinoú (or jump on any city bus heading along this street).

Destinations Anóyia (3 daily; 1hr); Ay. Galíni (6 daily; 2hr); Festós (6 daily; 1hr 30min); Mátala (4 daily; 2hr); Míres (11 daily; 1hr 15min).

BY CAR

Arriving in town by car, the best bet is to head for one of the signposted city-centre car parks (€3–6/day depending on location). One of the best is the large museum car park on Doúkos Bófor, 70m downhill from the Archeological Museum, which uses space below the city walls and has plenty of shade.

GETTING AROUND

By bus Only the further-flung sites and beaches really justify taking a bus. For the beaches, head for Platía Eleftherías; westbound bus #6 stops outside the *Capsis Hotel* (every 15min); eastbound #7 departs from the tree-shaded stop opposite (every 20min). Knossós buses start from the city bus stands alongside Bus Station A (every 15min) and pass through Platía Eleftherías; airport buses also pass through the square. Buy tickets before you board,

from machines in Platía Eleftherías and elsewhere, or from many kiosks (€1.10 for city and airport, €1.50 to the beach or Knossós; day pass €5). Bus info can be found at ⓦastiko-irakleiou.gr.
By taxi Major taxi stands are in Platía Eleftherías, Platía Kornarou, opposite the harbour and at the bus stations; or call ☎2810 210 102/168. Prices should be displayed on boards at the taxi stands.

INFORMATION AND TOURS

Tourist office Xanthoudhídhou 1 opposite the Archeological Museum (Mon–Fri 9am–2.30pm; ☎2810 246 298, ⓦheraklion.gr). There's a second office at the airport (May–Sept daily 8am–8pm).
City tours Two rival companies (ⓦher-openbus.gr and ⓦcretecitytour.com) operate hop-on, hop-off bus tours

with stops at all the major sights and museums. The route stays almost entirely outside the walls, so doesn't include the city centre, but they do go out as far as Knossós. In high season they run every 40min or so; a 24hr ticket costs €20, though if you hesitate their ubiquitous touts may offer you a better deal.

ACCOMMODATION

Finding a room can be difficult in high season. **Inexpensive places** are mainly concentrated in the streets above the Venetian harbour to the west of Odhós 25-Avgoústou. More **luxurious hotels** mostly lie closer to Platía Eleftherías and near the eastbound bus station. Noise can be a problem wherever you stay; all of the following have free wi-fi.

★**Atrion** Hronáki 9 ☎2810 246 000, ⓦatrion.gr. This attractive, modern, business-style hotel, with all the comforts that implies – marble bathrooms, minibar, silent a/c – combines luxury with a personal touch and friendly welcome. Top-floor suites have stunning views. Breakfast included. **€85**

Kastro Theotokopoúlou 22 ☎2810 284 185, ⓦkastro -hotel.gr. Very comfy mid-range hotel with a/c rooms, flat-screen TV and modern en-suite bathrooms. Rooms look brand new, though the Olympic theme feels dated. Breakfast included. **€75**

Kronos Agárthou 2, west of 25-Avgoústou ☎2810 282 240, ⓦkronoshotel.gr. This friendly two-star hotel is located on a busy street (so there's some traffic noise) by the central seafront. En-suite rooms with a/c, TV, fridge and balcony, some with wonderful sea views (at extra cost). **€60**

★**Lato** Epimenídhou 15 ☎2810 228 103, ⓦlato.gr. Stylish boutique hotel in a great central location, with luxurious rooms sporting a/c, minibar, TV and fine balcony views over the port (higher floors have better views; some cheaper rooms in a new extension across the road). Excellent rooftop bar and restaurant in summer. Breakfast included. **€89**

Mirabello Theotokopoúlou 20 ☎2810 285 052, ⓦmirabello-hotel.gr. Slightly old-fashioned, family-run hotel featuring balcony rooms, a couple with shared bath, but most en suite with new windows and bathrooms, a/c and TV. Shared bath **€45**, en suite **€55**

Olympic Platía Kornarou ☎2810 288 861, ⓦhotel olympic.com. Modern, business-style hotel in a great location. Rooms, with laminated wooden flooring and blonde wood furnishings, are quiet and well equipped, with a/c, TV, minibar and strongbox, if a little small. Breakfast included. **€64**

★**Rea** Kalimeráki 1 ☎2810 223 638, ⓦhotelrea.gr. A good budget option, this friendly, comfortable and clean *pension* enjoys a quiet but central position. Some rooms with washbasin, others en suite; there can be some internal noise, and wi-fi doesn't reach all rooms. Shared bath **€35**, en suite **€45**

Youth Hostel Výronos 5 ☎2810 286 281, ⓔheraklio youthhostel@yahoo.gr. The youth hostel occupies a wonderful old building with high ceilings and tiled or wood floors and you certainly can't complain about the price, though the dorms – single sex, with eight to ten bunks – and bathrooms are very basic indeed. Simple private rooms too. Dorm **€10**, room **€27**

CAMPING

Creta Camping Káto Goúves, 16km east of Irákli ☎28970 41400, ⓦcretacamping.com. The surroundings are bleak, but this is a big, well-organized site right on the seafront, with facilities including restaurant, minimarket, wi-fi, beach bar and beach loungers, as well as car hire and organized tours. **€18**

EATING

There's no shortage of excellent places to **eat** in Irákli, though prices are generally slightly higher than elsewhere on the island. For good quality and reasonably priced food, you need to get away from the more obvious tourist haunts, above all the main squares of Venizélou and Eleftherías (though the former is a great coffee stop). The **market** has plenty of fresh produce, and you can also find **picnic** food at the minimarkets in tourist areas or at the supermarket on the north side of El Greco Park.

RESTAURANTS

Aztecas Hándhakos 22 ☎2810 220 334. Warm Mexican decor and classic Tex-Mex dishes, beers and jugs of sangria make a change from the usual Greek fare. Around €8 for tacos or enchiladas, combo plate €9. Daily summer 7pm–12.30am; winter 1pm–12.30am.

Giakoumis Fotíou Theodosáki 5 ☎2810 284 039. The little alley connecting the market with Odhós Evans boasts several tavernas catering for market traders and their customers as well as tourists. Established in 1935, *Giakoumis* is very touristy these days, but it claims to be the city's oldest taverna and locals still reckon it serves up some of the best *païdhákia* (lamb chops; €10) on the island – some tribute, given the competition. Also traditional *mayiréfta* (€8–10). Mon–Sat 10am–late.

★**I Avli tou Defkaliona** Kalokairinoú 8 ☎2810 244 215. Very popular taverna-ouzerí with a great little terrace behind the Historical Museum, serving up excellent meat and fish dishes (mains €8–12). In high summer, you may need to book to ensure an outdoor table; if you despair of getting one, note that there are a couple of excellent modern ouzerís on the square opposite. Daily 5pm–1am.

★**Ippokampos** Sófokli Venizélou 3 ☎2810 280 240. The first of a row of places with glassed-in, sea-view terraces immediately west of the harbour, *Ippokampos* serves excellent fish at competitive prices (sardines €6.50, red mullet €12). Highly popular with locals, it's often crowded late into the evening, and you may have to queue or turn up earlier than the Greeks eat. Mon–Sat 1pm–midnight.

Ligo Krasi, Ligo Thálassa Marinéli at Mitsotákis ☎2810 300 501, ⓦligokrasiligothalassa.gr. This ouzerí with a small terrace on a busy corner facing the harbour is very popular with locals and serves up a good selection of seafood mezédhes (meze €2.80–5, sea bass €11, fried fish for two €28). You order by ticking the items you want from a list, and there's often an excellent free dessert. Daily 11.30am–1am.

4

Loukoulos Koraí 5 ☎2810 224 435, ⓦloukoulos -restaurant.gr. With a leafy courtyard terrace and an Italian slant to its international menu, this is one of the more elegant tavernas in Iráklio. Not as pricey as it looks (wood-oven pizza from €6, grilled meats €9–15, fish €10–12), though the wine list can bump prices up. Daily 1pm–midnight.

Peri Orexeos Koraí 10 ☎2810 222 679. This popular taverna with cool modern decor and a roof that opens over an upper floor to create a roof terrace is a good bet for creative Cretan cooking. As well as more straightforward options, dishes include the likes of chopped squid with basil pesto and pitta (€7), mussels with mustard and feta (€8.50) or rolled chicken stuffed with cheese, sundried tomatoes and basil (€10). Daily 1pm–1am.

CAFÉS

Kirkor Platía Venizélou 29 ☎2810 242 705. The cafés on Platía Venizélou that specialize in luscious pastries to accompany a mid-morning coffee are an essential visit. *Kirkor* is *the* place to sample authentic *bougátsa* (creamy cheese pie served warm and sprinkled with sugar and cinnamon); also excellent *loukoumadhes* (dough fritters in honey) and *tyrópita*. Daily 6am–11pm.

Mare Sófokli Venizélou, opposite the Historical Museum ☎2810 241 946. Stylish coffee and drinks bar with a wonderful setting and spectacular glass seafront terrace. Serves a range of snacks and light lunches (burger or risotto €7.50), and good cocktails at night. Daily 8am–2am.

Utopia Hándhakos 51 ☎2810 341 321. Locals flock here for the cakes and biscuits, served on fancy cake stands, and above all for the chocolate fondue and chocolate fountains – not cheap, but irresistibly indulgent. At night they also serve more than sixty different beers from all over the world, along with "beer meze" (sausages, mainly), but even then, most people are here for the chocolate and cake. Daily 9am–2am.

Veneris Bakery Cafe Yiannitsón 12 at Smyrnis ☎2810 280 161. Simple, self-service place with tables in a courtyard alongside an excellent bakery, serving inexpensive coffee, bread and cakes hot from the oven, fresh juices and tasty sandwiches. Mon–Fri 6.30am–9pm, Sat 6.30am–6pm.

DRINKING AND NIGHTLIFE

As a university town, Iráklio has plenty of late-night spots, though young Cretans tend to be more into sitting and chatting over background music than energetic dancing; consequently large areas of **Koraï** and the surrounding pedestrianized streets are packed with alfresco cafés which transform into **bars** as the lights dim and the volume ramps up. The bigger **clubs** are generally away from the central zone; most don't open their doors before 11pm, with the crowds drifting in after 1am and dancing until dawn. For livelier, and earlier, partying head to one of the nearby resorts or look out for posters advertising beach parties in summer.

BARS

Iridanos Andróyeo 8, cnr Perdhíkari. Bar-café spread over two floors offering a bit of everything – cool, old-fashioned decor with exposed brick and swirling fans; big-screen sport; free wi-fi; and a constantly changing crowd. Daily 9am–3am.

Pagopiion (Ice Factory) Platía Áyios Títos ☎2810 346 028. Stunning bar with arty decor inside Iráklio's former ice factory. Much of the old building has been preserved, including a lift for hauling the ice from the basement freezer and a fascistic call to duty in German Gothic script – a remnant of the Nazi occupation. Be sure to visit the toilets, which are in an artistic league of their own. Daily 9am–late.

Take Five Arkoléondos 7, El Greco Park ☎2810 226 564. One of the oldest bars in Iráklio, *Take Five* began as a rock bar in the 1980s and is now a slick pavement café with an indoor bar, playing jazzy music; a favourite late-night hangout for a slightly older crowd. Daily 9am–4am.

To Mílon tis Eridos Platía Koraí ☎2810 241 820. Café-bar that serves everything from twelve types of coffee to cocktails and herbal teas, including *diktamo* (Cretan dittany), a panacea the Cretans have been sipping for thousands of years. Daily 9am–3am.

CLUBS

Fleva Milátou 16 ☎6970 203 232. Downtown club where you can dance to house, techno and Greek pop until the sun rises. Look out for their beach parties. Wed–Sun 11.30pm–8am.

London Makaríou 17 at Venizélou ☎2810 288 011. Dance club that's part of a huge complex including a 24hr sports bar/internet café and *Baloo* live music venue. The playlist features Greek pop and international chart sounds. Tues–Sun 11pm–late.

Rolling Stone Rock Bar Ayiostefanitón 19. Rock club with sweaty, late-night live rock and punk bands, and rock DJs – Wed is Greek Rock night. Great atmosphere. Tues–Sat 10.30pm–4am.

Senses Club Papandréou 277, Amoudhára ☎6944 2697339. A lively, summer-only club with a party atmosphere, 5km west of the city, by Amoudhára beach, playing various types of international music including dance and R&B. Good theme nights and special events. Summer daily 9pm–late.

SHOPPING

In addition to Iráklio's **central market** (see p.209) there's a huge **street market** every Sat in an open area at Itánou and Leonídhou, southeast of the centre, and a smaller, local one every Tues on Irodhótou in the airport suburb of Alikarnassós. Upmarket **shops**, especially those selling jewellery, clothes and fabrics, cluster around Dedhálou, Odhós 1821 and Odhós Evans (east and west of the market respectively) and along Kalokerinoú heading west from here.

Planet International Bookstore Hándhakos 73 ☎ 2810 289 605. This excellent bookshop has the island's biggest stock of English-language titles. Mon, Wed & Sat 8am–2pm, Tues, Thurs & Fri 9am–2pm & 5.30–8pm.

DIRECTORY

Banks There are ATMs all over town, but the main bank branches are on 25-Avgoústou.

Hospital The closest is the Venizélou Hospital, on the Knossós road south out of town (☎ 2810 368 000).

Internet The municipality has free wi-fi at many central locations; two central internet cafés are Papercut, a comic-book store and gaming place at Hándhakos 30 (open 24hr) and Netcafé, Odhós-1878 4 (daily 10am–2am).

Laundry Washsalon, cnr Evgenikoú and Ayiostefanítón (Mon & Wed 9am–6pm, Tues, Thurs & Fri 9am–9pm, Sat 9am–3pm) and Wash Center, Epimenídhou 38, near the *Lato* hotel (Mon–Fri 8.30am–3pm & 5.30–9pm, Sat 8.30am–3pm); both do good service washes.

Pharmacies Plentiful on the main shopping streets – at least one is open 24hr on a rota basis; check the list on the door of any pharmacy. There are also traditional herbalists in the market.

Post office Main office in Platía Dhaskaloyiánni, off Eleftherías (Mon–Fri 8.30am–7pm), with a temporary sub-office in summer in El Greco Park.

Knossós

5km southeast of Iráklio • Daily: May–June 8am–5pm; July–Sept 8am–8pm; Oct–April 8.30am–3pm • €6, or €10 joint ticket with Iráklio Archeological Museum • ☎ 2810 231 940

4

KNOSSÓS is the largest and most important of the **Minoan palaces**, and the most visited. The mythological home of King Minos and the Minotaur (see below), it dates from the second millennium BC, and its labyrinthine interconnected rooms and corridors provide a fitting backdrop to the legend.

The discovery of the palace is among the most extraordinary tales of modern archeology. **Heinrich Schliemann**, the German excavator of Troy, suspected that a major Minoan palace lay under the various tumuli here, but was denied permission to dig by the local Ottoman authorities. His loss was Englishman **Sir Arthur Evans's** gain. Evans excavated and liberally "restored" the palace from 1900 onwards, and though his restorations have been the source of furious controversy among archeologists ever since, his guess as to what the palace might have looked like is arguably as good as anyone's. It makes Crete's other Minoan sites infinitely more meaningful if you have seen Knossós first.

To avoid the hordes, try get to the site early, before the coach tours arrive, or in the late afternoon when they've left.

THE LEGEND OF THE MINOTAUR

Knossós was the court of the legendary **King Minos** whose wife Pasiphae, cursed by Poseidon, bore the **Minotaur**, a creature half-bull, half-man. The **labyrinth** was constructed by Daedalus to contain the monster, and every nine years (some say every year) seven youths and seven maidens were brought from Athens as human sacrifice, to be devoured by the beast. Finally **Theseus**, son of the king of Athens, volunteered as one of the youths, vowing to slay the Minotaur. In Crete, Minos' daughter **Ariadne** promptly fell in love with Theseus and showed him how to escape the labyrinth using a ball of thread. It ended well for nobody: Ariadne left with Theseus, but was abandoned on Naxos; Daedalus, imprisoned in his own maze by a furious king, constructed the wings that bore him away to safety – and his son **Icarus** to his untimely death; and Theseus' father killed himself, believing that his son's mission had failed.

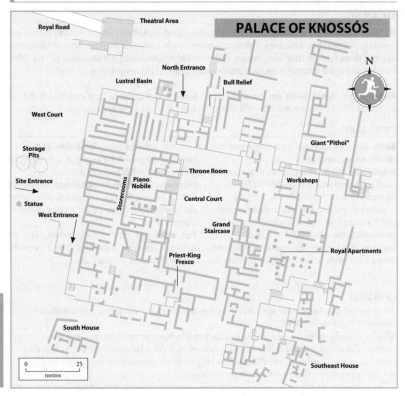

PALACE OF KNOSSÓS

Royal Road · Theatral Area · North Entrance · Lustral Basin · Bull Relief · West Court · Storage Pits · Giant "Pithoi" · Site Entrance · Throne Room · Piano Nobile · Workshops · Storerooms · Statue · Central Court · West Entrance · Grand Staircase · Royal Apartments · Priest-King Fresco · South House · Southeast House

0 — 25 metres

The site

As soon as you enter the **Palace of Knossós** through the West Court, the ancient ceremonial entrance, it is clear how the legends of the labyrinth grew up around it. Even with a map and description, it can be very hard to work out where you are. If you are worried about missing the highlights, you can always tag along with a group for a while, catching the patter and then backtracking to absorb the detail when the crowd has moved on. You won't get the place to yourself, whenever you come, but exploring on your own does give you the opportunity to appreciate individual parts of the palace in the brief lulls between groups, though the **walkways** that channel visitors around the site severely restrict the scope for independent exploration.

For some idea of the size and complexity of the palace in its original state, take a look at the cutaway drawings (wholly imaginary but probably not too far off) on sale outside.

Royal Apartments

The superb **Royal Apartments** around the central staircase are plainly the finest of the rooms at Knossós. The **Grand Stairway** is a masterpiece of design, its large well bringing light into the lower storeys. At the bottom is the **Queen's Suite**, decorated with the celebrated **dolphin fresco** and with running friezes of flowers and abstract spirals. Remember, though, that all this is speculation; the dolphin fresco, for example, was found on the courtyard floor, not in the room itself, and would have been viewed from an upper balcony as a sort of trompe l'oeil, like looking through a glass-bottomed boat. A dark passage leads around to the queen's **bathroom** and a clay tub, the famous "flushing" toilet (a hole in the ground with drains to take the waste away – it was flushed by throwing a bucket of water down).

Above the queen's domain are the **King's Quarters**, where the staircase opens into a grandiose reception chamber known as the **Hall of the Royal Guard**, its walls decorated in repeated shield patterns. Immediately off here is the **Hall of the Double Axes** (or the King's Room); believed to have been the ruler's personal chamber, its name comes from the double-axe symbol carved into every block of masonry.

The Central Court and Throne Room

The paved **Central Court** at the heart of the palace covers the oldest remains found on the site, dating back to the Neolithic era. In Minoan times high walls would have hemmed the courtyard in on every side, and the atmosphere would have been very different from the open, shadeless space which survives. Off the northwestern corner is the entrance to the **Throne Room**. Here, a worn stone throne sits against the wall of a surprisingly small chamber; along the walls around it are ranged stone benches, suggesting a king ruling in council, and behind there's a reconstructed fresco of two griffins.

The rest of the palace

Don't miss the giant *pithoi*, the storage chambers (which you see from behind the Throne Room), or the many other frescoes (all reproductions) including the Priest-King looking down on the south side of the central court, or the relief of a charging bull on its north side. The much-perused **drainage system**, evident in various locations, was a series of interconnecting terracotta pipes running underneath most of the palace. Guides to the site never fail to point these out as evidence of the advanced state of Minoan civilization.

Just outside the North Entrance is the **theatral area**, an open space a little like a stepped amphitheatre, which may have been used for ritual performances or dances. From here the **Royal Road**, claimed as the oldest road in Europe, sets out. Circling back around the outside of the palace, you can get an idea of its scale by looking up at it; on the south side are a couple of small reconstructed Minoan houses which are worth exploring.

4

ARRIVAL AND INFORMATION   **KNOSSÓS**

By bus Local bus #2 (every 15min) starts from the city bus stands alongside Bus Station A, passes through Platía Elefterías, and leaves town along Odhós-1821 and Evans.

By taxi A taxi from the centre of Iráklio will cost around €12.

By car From the centre of Iráklio head out through Evans gate; from anywhere else on the island turn directly off the bypass onto the badly signed Knossós road. There's a free car park immediately before the site entrance; avoid paying exorbitant rates for the private car parks, whose touts will attempt to wave you in.

Website The British School at Athens has a useful website dedicated to Knossós, with detail on its history and excavations in addition to a virtual tour; check out ⓦ bsa .ac.uk/knossos/vrtour.

Inland from Iráklio: wine country

Heading south from Knossós you immediately leave any crowds behind as you enter the rich agricultural countryside dominated by **Mount Yioúhtas** (811m), said by ancient Cretans to be the final resting place of Zeus. Seen from the northwest, the mountain has an unmistakeably human profile. This is one of Crete's major **wine-producing** areas (see box, p.214), with a particular concentration of wineries around the village of **Péza**, and there are also some fascinating minor Minoan sites near **Arhánes**.

Arhánes

ARHÁNES, at the foot of Mount Yioúhtas, is a sizeable, wealthy farming town, as it was in Minoan times. The main square has several tavernas, cafés and bars, while 100m to the north is an excellent **Archeological Museum** (daily except Tues 8.30am–2.30pm;

WINE TASTING IN CRETE

The Péza region is Crete's major wine-producing area, but there are also **vineyards** in eastern Crete, around Sitía, and smaller ones in the west around Haniá. Wine has been being made in this area for four thousand years (see below), probably using grape varieties not far removed from the Kotsifáli and Mandilariá (for red), Plytó and Vilána (white) that are extensively cultivated today. A growing number of **wineries** open their doors to visitors, though most require appointments; the following are some of the bigger operations. There's a well-signposted **wine trail** around Péza – see ⓦ winesofcrete.gr.

Boutari Skaláni, Iráklio ☎ 2810 731 617, ⓦ boutari .gr. Not far south of Knossós lies the spectacular modern Fantaxometocho estate, owned by one of Greece's biggest winemakers. Specializing in organic production methods, they make excellent wines. Mon–Fri 9am–5pm.

Dourakis Alíkambos, Vrýsses, near Haniá ☎ 28250 51761, ⓦ dourakiswinery.gr. On the main road towards Hóra Sfákion, this small, friendly family-owned winery offers tasting and tours (from €6), and there's a small one-room museum of old farming implements. Mon–Sat 11am–5pm.

Minos Wines Péza, Iráklio ☎ 2810 741213, ⓦ minoswines.gr. On the main street in Pezá village, the epicentre of Cretan wine production, Minos is one of the island's biggest producers. There are tours (€2) of the winemaking plant approximately hourly, but at any time you can watch a video about the history of Cretan wine production, look at some traditional equipment, and taste and buy the house brands. The vineyard of their premium brand, Milliarakis, is east of here in the village of Sambá, visited by appointment. May–Oct Mon–Fri 9am–4pm, Sat 10.30am–3pm.

Peza Union Pezá, on the Kastélli road at the eastern edge of town ☎ 2810 741 945, ⓦ pezaunion .gr. The union of agricultural cooperatives of Pezá produces olive oil as well as wine, from the vines and trees of many small producers. Free tours of their exhibition centre are followed by wine tasting and a small meze. May–Oct Mon–Sat 9am–5pm.

Sitia Union On the main road towards Áyios Nikólaos, 1km from Sitía. ☎ 28430 29991. The famous wines of Sitía are produced here. Tours (€2.50) include a tasting in the cellar and an audiovisual presentation. Mon–Fri 8am–2.30pm.

free; ☎ 2810 752 712), which displays a series of exceptional finds from the town and surrounding sites. Check here for details of the nearby sites, and their current opening status. These include the burial ground at **Foúrni** (July & Aug Tues–Sun 8.30am–2.30pm; at other times check at the museum), immediately west of town, and **Anemospiliá** (not normally open, but viewable through fence), 2km northwest of town. The latter has caused huge controversy since its excavation in the 1980s: many traditional views of the Minoans have had to be rethought in the light of the discovery of an apparent human sacrifice. From Arhánes you can also drive (or walk, with a couple of hours to spare) to the summit of Mount Yioúhtas to see the imposing remains of a Minoan **peak sanctuary** and enjoy spectacular panoramic **views**.

Vathýpetro
3km south of Arhánes • Tues–Sun 8.30am–2.30pm • Free

At **Vathýpetro** the remains of a large **Minoan villa** are surrounded by a vineyard with a valid claim to be the oldest in the world – winemaking has apparently been carried on here almost continuously since the second millennium BC. The house was originally a substantial building of several storeys, and inside was discovered a wonderful collection of everyday agricultural items, many of them in the basement workrooms. Most remarkable is an exceptionally well-preserved **winepress**, which can still be seen *in situ*.

GETTING AROUND

By bus Buses from Iráklio (Bus Station A) serve many of the villages in this region.
Destinations Arhánes (Mon–Fri 15 daily, Sat 9 daily, Sun 3 daily; 30min); Péza (Mon–Sat 4 daily, Sun 7.30am only; 35min).

INLAND FROM IRÁKLIO: WINE COUNTRY

By car The old road out via Knossós is much the most pleasant route, but directions can be confused by the presence of the new road, which cuts across the island via Peza and Houdhétsi, often extremely close to the older road.

The Messára and the south coast

The route southwest from Iráklio climbs through the mountains before winding down to **Áyii Dhéka** and the Messará plain. Here on the fertile Messará lie three major archeological sites – Minoan **Festós** and **Ayía Triádha**, and Roman **Górtys** – while beyond them it's an easy drive to the south-coast resort of **Mátala**, or a rather longer, hillier one to quieter **Léndas**.

Áyii Dhéka

ÁYII DHÉKA is for religious Cretans a place of pilgrimage; its name, "The Ten Saints", refers to ten early Christians martyred here under the Romans. The old Byzantine church in the centre of the village preserves the stone block on which they are supposed to have been decapitated, and in a crypt below the modern church on the village's western edge you can see the martyrs' (now empty) tombs. It's an attractive village to wander around, with several places to eat.

Górtys

600m west of Áyii Dhéka • Daily: July–Sept 8am–8pm; Oct–June 8am–3pm • €4 • ☎ 28920 31144

The remnants of the ancient city of **GÓRTYS**, once capital of a Roman province that included not only Crete but also much of North Africa, are scattered across a large area, covering a great deal more than the fenced site beside the road that most people see. The best way to get some idea of the scale is to follow the path through the fields on the south side of the main road from Áyii Dhéka, an easy walk of less than 1km; along the way you'll skirt most of the major remains.

In the **fenced site**, to the north of the road, are the ruins of the still impressive sixth-century **basilica of Áyios Títos**, and beyond this the **Odeion**, which houses the most important discovery on the site, the **Law Code**. Written in an obscure early Doric-Cretan dialect, this is, at 9m by 3m, the largest Greek inscription ever found. The laws set forth reflect a strictly hierarchical society: five witnesses were needed to convict a free man of a crime, only one for a slave; raping a free man or woman carried a fine of a hundred *staters*, a serf only five. A small **museum** holds a number of large and finely worked sculptures found at Górtys, more evidence of the city's importance.

Festós

15km west of Míres • Daily: June–Sept 8am–8pm; Oct–May 8am–3pm • €4, joint ticket with Ayía Triádha €6

In a wonderfully scenic location on a ridge at the eastern end of the Messará plain, the **palace of Festós** enjoys a stunning setting, overlooked by the snowcapped peaks of Psilorítis and with magnificent views east across the plain. While no traces of frescoes were found here, and few other artworks, this doesn't imply that the palace wasn't luxurious: the materials were of the highest quality, there were sophisticated drainage and bathing facilities, and remains suggest a large and airy dining hall on the upper floors overlooking the court.

Excavated by the Italian Federico Halbherr (also responsible for the early work at Górtys) at almost exactly the same time as Evans was working at Knossós, Festós is a huge contrast. Here, to the approval of most traditional archeologists, reconstruction was kept to an absolute minimum – it's all bare foundations, and walls which rise at most 1m above ground level. It's interesting to speculate why the palace was built halfway up a hill rather than on the plain below – certainly not for defence, for this is in no way a good defensive position. Psychological superiority over the peasants or reasons of health are both possible, but it seems quite likely that it was simply the magnificent **view** that finally swayed the decision.

Once you start to explore, the strong similarities between Festós and the other palaces are unavoidable: the same huge rows of storage jars, the great courtyard with its monumental stairway, and the theatral area. Unique to Festós, however, is a third courtyard, in the middle of which are the remains of a **furnace** used for metalworking.

4

Ayía Triádha

4km west of Festós, on the far side of the hill • Daily: May–Sept 9.30am–4.30pm; Oct–April 8.30am–3pm • €4, joint ticket with Festós €6

Some of the finest artworks in the museum at Iráklio came from **Ayía Triádha**, 4km west of Festós. No one is quite sure what this site is, but the most common theory has it as some kind of royal summer villa. It's smaller than the palaces but, if anything, even more lavishly appointed and beautifully situated. In any event, it's an attractive place to visit, far less crowded than Festós, with a wealth of interesting little details. Look out in particular for the row of **stores** in front of what was apparently a marketplace, and the remains of a **paved road** that probably led down to a harbour on the Gulf of Messará. There's a fourteenth-century **chapel** – dedicated to Áyios Yeóryios – at the site, worth visiting in its own right for the remains of ancient frescoes.

Mátala

MÁTALA is known above all for the **caves** cut into the cliffs above its beautiful sands. These are ancient tombs first used by Romans or early Christians, but more recently inhabited by a sizeable hippy community in the 1960s and 1970s (including some famous names such as Bob Dylan and Joni Mitchell). The caves have long since been cleared and cleaned up, and these days they are an archeological site (April–Sept daily 10am–7pm; €3), open by day to visitors but searched by the police – and floodlit – every night.

Outside of high summer the resort still has an agreeably laidback feel, but July and August see the **beach** packed to overflowing, above all in the early afternoon when the tour buses pull in for their swimming stop. The town beach is beautiful, though, and if the crowds get excessive you can climb over the rocks in about twenty minutes to another excellent stretch of sand, known locally as "Red Beach". Stay the night and you can start to experience the real Mátala, and enjoy the waterside bars and restaurants in relative peace.

Léndas

The reputation of **LÉNDAS** as a hippy resort, a fishing village where you can hang out by the beach and camp for free, is somewhat outdated: the hippies grew up and now they come back with their families to stay in comfortable rooms and eat at excellent restaurants. For a quiet break, you could hardly choose better: it's small, low-key (though busy with locals at the weekend) and a little alternative, but it's no longer especially cheap, nor the sort of place where campers are welcomed on the beach. Having said that, scores of people *do* camp on the sand at **Dytikós**, just over the headland to the west, a predominantly nudist beach where the old ethos is still very much alive and where there are some good taverna/bars with rooms.

GETTING AROUND   THE MESSÁRA AND THE SOUTH COAST

By bus Buses from Iráklio's Bus Station B head for Míres (Mon–Sat 11 daily, fewer on Sun; 1hr 15min), the transport hub of the Messará plain. From here they continue variously to Festós (6 daily; 1hr 40min), Mátala (4 daily; 2hr), Ayía Galíni (6 daily; 2hr) and Lendás (Mon–Fri 1 daily; 2hr 20min); the majority of these buses call at Áyii Dhéka and Górtys before Míres.

By car The main road is the fast route via Veneráto and Ayía Varvára, but you can also follow a scenic detour via Voutés, Áyios Míronas and Pírgou, an undulating ride through some lovely out-of-the-way villages.

ACCOMMODATION

MÁTALA

Much of the accommodation in Mátala is on "Hotel Street", left off the main road as you enter town, which is almost entirely lined with purpose-built places, all of them with parking, wi-fi and a/c.

Matala Camping Above the car park, close to the beach ☎ 28920 45720. Campsite with shady tamarisk trees. Fine if you don't mind camping on sand; there's a busy bar, and Aug can bring a rowdy party atmosphere. May–Oct. €12

Matala View Hotel St ☎ 28920 45114, ⟨w⟩ matala -apartments.com. Simple rooms, mostly with small balconies, as well as some larger studios and apartments, on the quiet side of Hotel St. Breakfast available at extra cost. May–Oct. **€40**

Nikos Hotel St ☎ 28920 45375, ⓦ matala-nikos.com. The fanciest of the places on Hotel St, with very well kept rooms around a charming plant-filled courtyard and one "penthouse" with a sea view. Direct access to town from the back. May–Oct. **€45**

Sunshine Matala Hotel St ☎ 28920 45110, ⓦ matala -holidays.com. Friendly, comfortable *pension* offering classily renovated rooms with fridge, and one- and two-room apartments with kitchens, on the quieter side of the street. May–Oct. **€40**

LÉNDAS

Nikis Rooms Centre of the village, behind El Greco ☎ 28920 95246, ⓦ nikisrooms-lentas.gr. Super-friendly place with inexpensive rooms equipped with kettle and fridge, around a lovely flower-filled courtyard; a couple of upper-floor rooms have views (at extra cost), but there's a shared roof terrace for those who don't. April–Oct. **€30**

Villa Tsapakis Dytikós Beach ☎ 28920 95378, ⓦ villa -tsapakis.gr. These bougainvillea-fronted rooms come with a sea view, fridge and TV. They also have studios and apartments, and their taverna, *Odysseas*, is the meeting point for everyone staying or camping at Dytikós. April–Oct. **€35**

EATING AND DRINKING

ÁYIOS IOÁNNIS

Taverna Ayios Ioannis On the main road just south of Festós ☎ 28920 42006. Picturesque roadside taverna serving excellent food at tables set under a shady vine trellis; the house speciality of charcoal-grilled rabbit is recommended, and the lamb is tasty, too. Service tends to be slow at busy times. Daily noon–11pm.

LÉNDAS

★**Taverna El Greco** ☎ 28920 95322. A particularly good restaurant with a large leafy terrace above the beach. The food is mostly traditional Greek – the day's baked dishes are on display in the kitchen – but cooked with exceptional care using the best local ingredients. There's an unusually good wine list, too, and they also have rooms. April–Oct daily 11am–midnight.

MÁTALA

Eleni Behind the central section of the beach ☎ 28920 45711. One of the smaller places with a terrace hanging over the beach, *Eleni* has, like all the others, a plastic menu with pictures of food that you can point at. However they also have a handwritten list of daily specials (fresh grilled sardines or traditional lamb casserole, for example, for

around €8), often just scrawled on a notepad, and these are the ones to go for. May–Oct daily noon–midnight.

Giannis Main street beyond the market ☎ 6983 619 233, ⓦ giannisfamily.com. Usually the busiest place in town (partly because of a reputation for being inexpensive, which is no longer entirely justified), this is an earthy, family-run taverna specializing in grilled meats and fish (mixed fish plate €12). You may have to wait, though they can often find space to set up another table somewhere. April–Oct daily noon–late.

Hakuna Matata Main street at far end of town ☎ 6947 343 688. A bar/café/taverna that's open all day, distinguished by the pirate ship's prow hanging out over the water, and the fact that you have to walk through to reach the far end of town. There's plenty of choice of food, but that's not really the point; the place really comes alive at night, serving cocktails (around €7) and with dancing and frequent live bands. April–Oct daily 11am–early hours.

La Scala Far end of the beach above the harbour ☎ 28920 45489. Atmospheric little fish restaurant with a wonderful terrace overlooking the bay; more elegant than most and only marginally more expensive. Mixed fish for two €30, *kakaviá* (traditional fish soup) €8. May–Oct daily noon–midnight.

East of Iráklio: the package-tour coast

East of Iráklio, the main package-tour resorts are at least 30km away, at **Hersónissos** and **Mália**, although there is a string of rather unattractive developments all the way there. There are one or two worthwhile highlights along the way, though: the impressive **Cretaquarium** at Goúrnes, the **old villages** in the hills behind Hersónissos, a couple of **water parks**, and, beyond the clubbing resort of Mália, a fine **Minoan palace** that will transport you back three and a half millennia.

Cretaquarium

Goúrnes • Daily: June–Sept 9am–9pm; Oct–May 9.30am–7pm • €8, children 5–17 €6; audio-guide €3 • ☎ 2810 337 788, ⓦ cretaquarium.gr

A former NATO air base is home to the **Cretaquarium**, a spectacular marine aquarium boasting thirty tanks (some huge), that house everything from menacing sharks to dazzling jellyfish. A non-profit-making part of the Hellenic Centre for Marine Research, it includes most of the island's fish and crustaceans among the 250 species

---

CRETE'S WATER PARKS

Crete can boast three major **water parks** as well as a number of smaller ones, two of them in the resort strip east of Iráklio.

Acqua Plus 3km inland from Hersónissos ☎ 28970 249507, ⓦ acquaplus.gr. A big water park that comes close to rivalling Water City, but doesn't quite match up in terms of size or number of slides. It's a good day out nonetheless, with an attractive setting in a natural bowl of hills and a fair amount of natural shade. Admission is €24/person (children 5–12 €17) and there are cut-price late-entry deals. May–Oct daily 10am–7pm.

Limnoupolis Varýpetro, 8km southwest of Haniá ☎ 28210 33246, ⓦ limnoupolis.gr. Not quite as fancy as its eastern rivals, but still with plenty of big slides and an attractive setting in the foothills of the White

Mountains; entry is €23/person (children 4–12 €17) and like Acqua Plus it offers cut-price late-entry deals. June–Sept daily 10am–6pm; limited opening May & Oct.

Water City Anópoli, 4km inland from Goúrnes, 15km from Iráklio ☎ 2810 781 317, ⓦ watercity.gr. The largest and probably the most impressive on the island, with many of the rides taking advantage of the natural hillside over which the place is built. There's the usual array of slides, pools, snack-bars and fast-food outlets. Admission is €25/person (children 90–140cm €17). May–Oct daily 10am–6.30pm.

---

and over 2500 specimens on display. Unless you're a marine biologist the audio-guide (easily shared between two or three) is pretty well indispensable and gives loads of fascinating background information on the creatures you're looking at.

Hersónissos

The first of the really big resorts, **HERSÓNISSOS** – or more accurately **Límin Hersonísou**, the Port of Hersónisos – is a sprawling and rather seedy place overrun with bars, touristy tavernas and nightclubs. Beach and clubs excepted, the main attractions are the **Lychnostatis Open-air Museum of Folklore** (Mon–Fri & Sun 9am–2pm; €5; ⓦ lychnostatis.gr), an unexpectedly rewarding museum of traditional Crete with imaginative reconstructions of island life past and present, and, a short distance inland, the three pretty **hill villages** of Koutoulafári, Piskopianó and "old" Hersónissos. A glimpse of more traditional Crete, they offer some attractive rooms and good tavernas; Piskopianó also boasts an impressive **Museum of Rural Life** (June–Oct Mon, Wed & Sat 10am–6pm; €4; ⓦ historical-museum.gr), one of the best of its kind on the island.

Mália

MÁLIA is, perhaps, the most notorious resort in Crete: brash, commercial, with a reputation for wild nightlife. The **beach**, long and sandy as it is, becomes grotesquely crowded at times. That said, it can be a great place to stay if you're prepared to enter into the spirit of things – party all night and sleep all day – with the bonus of a genuine town that existed before the tourists came, and a fabulous **Minoan palace** just down the road.

The Palace of Malia

3km east of Mália, just off the old highway • June–Sept Tues–Sun 8am–5pm; Oct–May Tues–Sun 8.30am–3pm • €4 • ☎ 28970 31957 • Any bus passing along the main highway should stop at the turn-off for the site

Much less imposing than either Knossós or Festós, the **Palace of Malia** in some ways surpasses both. For a start, it's a great deal emptier and you can wander among the remains in relative peace. While no reconstruction has been attempted, the palace was never reoccupied after its second destruction in the fifteenth century BC, so the ground plan is virtually intact.

From this site came the famous **gold pendant** of two bees and the beautiful **leopard-head axe**, both of which are displayed in Iráklio's Archeological Museum. Look out for the strange indented stone in the central court (which probably held ritual offerings), for the remains of ceremonial stairways and for the giant *píthoi*, which stand like sentinels around the palace. To the north and west of the main site, archeological digs are still going on as the large town which surrounded the palace comes slowly to light.

The most enjoyable way to get here is by **bike**: it's a pleasant, flat ride from Mália town, where bicycle rental is widely available. Leaving the archeological zone, you can follow the road down to a lovely stretch of clean and relatively peaceful **beach**.

GETTING AROUND   **EAST OF IRÁKLIO: THE PACKAGE-TOUR COAST**

By bus Buses from Iráklio (Bus Station A) serve the coastal resorts, running at least every 30min until 11pm to Hersónissos and Mália, with stops near all the major hotels. Major attractions like Cretaquarium and Water City also feature on tours from all the resorts.

By car The new E75 Highway runs a short way inland, bypassing all the major attractions and resorts; you'll need to turn off onto the old road to access any of them.

The Lasíthi Plateau

Every day, scores of bus tours toil up to the **LASÍTHI PLATEAU** to view the "thousands of white-cloth-sailed windmills" which irrigate the high plain. In reality there are very few working windmills left, although many roadside tavernas have adopted them as marketing features. The drive alone is worthwhile, however, and the plain is a fine example of rural Crete at work, every inch devoted to the cultivation of potatoes, apples, figs, olives and a host of other crops; stay in one of the **villages** for a night or two – good targets include **Tzermiádho**, **Áyios Konstantínos**, **Áyios Yeóryios** and **Psykhró** (bring some warm clothing, as the nights can get extremely cold) – and you'll see real life return as the tourists leave.

The Dhiktean Cave

1km southwest of Psykhró • Daily: April–Oct 8am–8pm; Nov–March 8.30am–3pm • €4 • From Psykhró a signed side road takes you up to a car park (the €2 parking charges are strictly enforced) from where the cave is a 10min climb on a steep, rocky path, or a longer but easier walk up a paved track; you can also go up by mule (€10 each way)

According to legend, it was in the **Dhiktean Cave** that Zeus was born to Rhea. Zeus' father, Kronos, had been warned that he would be overthrown by a son, and accordingly ate all his offspring. On this occasion, however, Rhea gave Kronos a stone to eat instead and left the baby Zeus concealed within the cave, protected by the Kouretes, who beat their shields outside to disguise his cries. The cave was a cult centre from the Minoan period onwards, and offerings to the Mother Goddess and to Zeus dating through to Classical Greek times have been found here.

Concrete steps and electric lighting have made the cave an easy place to visit, although some of the magic and mystery has inevitably been lost. The steps lead you on a circular tour, passing the bottom of the cave where you are confronted with an artificial **lake**. The one experience that has survived the alterations is the view back from the depths of the cave towards the peephole of light at the entrance. It's not hard to believe the tales that this was the infant Zeus' first sight of the world destined to become his kingdom. To avoid the crowds, try to arrive early (coaches start to arrive around 11.30am) or after 5pm.

ARRIVAL AND GETTING AROUND   **THE LASÍTHI PLATEAU**

By bus There are no public buses to the plateau, though tours run from all parts of the island.

By car The quickest and easiest routes up to the plateau are from the north and northwest, from Mália and Hersónissos (see opposite). The approach from Áyios Nikólaos via Neápoli is far slower – a tortuous 30km climb.

On foot On the plateau you can easily walk through the fields from one village to another – the paths between Áyios Yeóryios and Káto Metóhi via Psykhró even form part of the E4 Pan-European walking route: crossing the whole plain, from Psykhró to Tzermiádho, takes 1hr 30min or less. More ambitiously, you can also hike up to the plateau, most directly from Kritsá in the east, or on the E4 path from Kastélli in the west. A good time to take a walk here is the early evening, when you'll encounter the villagers on their carts, donkeys and pick-ups making their way back home.

ACCOMMODATION AND EATING

TZERMIÁDHO

Kronio Village centre ☎ 28440 22375. Traditional Cretan dishes with a French twist thanks to the proprietor's Gallic wife. It's terrific value – if you're hungry and in no hurry, try the meze selection, with eighteen dishes, wine and dessert for around €15 – and excellent cooking. Watch out for the occasional coach party, though. Daily 11am–10pm.

ÁYIOS KONSTANTÍNOS

★ **Taverna Vilaeti** On the main street ☎ 28440 31983, ⓦ vilaeti.gr. A beautifully restored old stone building, much more elegant than you'd expect in this setting, serving exceptionally good traditional food (most of it local and organic) at standard prices (mains €10–14). Daily 9am–late.

Vilaeti Traditional Guesthouses Info at Taverna Vilaeti ☎ 28440 31983, ⓦ vilaeti.gr. Lovely, fully equipped restored village apartments and stone-built

cottages, all with fireplaces for winter and full kitchens with the basics supplied, sleeping up to seven. Two-night minimum stay. **€70**

ÁYIOS YEÓRYIOS

Hotel Maria Hidden away in the backstreets ☎ 28440 31774. Sweet, old-fashioned place with framed embroidery on the walls and tiny bathrooms. Some of the double beds are exceptionally small too – they also have three- and four-bed rooms. April–Oct. **€35**

PSYKHRÓ

Taverna Halavro Above the Dhiktean Cave car park ☎ 28440 31402. Better than you'd expect, considering the captive audience; fresh juices and snacks for cave visitors as well as meze (€3–5), and lamb (€12) and pork (€10) roast in a wood oven. They also have rooms nearby. Daily: April–Oct roughly 8am–8pm; Nov–March 8am–3.30pm.

West of Iráklio

Heading west from Iráklio the **E75 highway**, cut into the cliffs, is fast and efficient. It's a spectacular drive too, but with very little in the way of habitation; there are just a couple of developed beach resorts, at **Ayía Pelayía** and **Balí**, until the final, flat stretch towards Réthymno. If you're in no hurry, take the **older roads west**; these curl up amid stunning mountain scenery and archetypal rural Crete, with tracks tramped by herds of sheep and goats, isolated chapels or farmsteads beside the road, and occasionally a village beneath the heights of the **Psilorítis** range.

Ayía Pelayía

AYÍA PELAYÍA, some 15km from Iráklio, appears irresistibly inviting from the highway far above, a sprinkling of white cubes set around a deep blue bay. Closer up, you're likely to find the narrow, taverna-lined beach packed to capacity. However, the water is clear and calm, the **swimming** excellent and there's a superb view, at night, of the brightly lit ferries heading out of Iráklio. Despite the development, Ayía Pelayía retains a slightly **exclusive** feel; one of Crete's most luxurious hotel resorts nestles on the promontory beyond the beach.

Balí

BALÍ, about halfway between Iráklio and Réthymno, is a resort set around a series of little coves. The place is much bigger than it first appears, especially as the streets are winding and hilly – it's a couple of kilometres from the main road to the village, more to the best beach. Sadly, although the beaches are spectacular, they're very much overrun, and Balí has become a package resort too popular for its own good. It's lively and friendly, but only really tempting well out of season, when there are bound to be bargains given the number of rooms.

Týlissos

15km southwest of Iráklio; the archeological site is signed to the left off the main street of the modern village • Daily 9am–4pm • €2 • ☎ 2810 831 498

Týlissos is a name famous in the annals of Minoan archeology as one of the first sites to be excavated, and the thriving modern village has a fair claim to four thousand years of continuous human occupation. Its reputation is based more on the discoveries made here (many are in the Iráklio Archeological Museum) than what remains: three large villas that were once part of a thriving community, or possibly a staging post on the route west towards as yet undiscovered centres. Still, it's worth a look for a glimpse of Minoan life away from the big palaces, and for the tranquillity of the pine-shaded remains.

Anóyia

ANÓYIA, a small town perched beneath the highest peaks of the Psilorítis range, is the obvious place from which to approach the **Idean Cave** and, for the committed, the **summit of Psilorítis** itself (see below). The weather, refreshingly cool when the summer heat lower down is becoming oppressive, is one good reason to come, but most people are drawn by the proximity of the mountains or by a reputation for some of the best woven and embroidered **handicrafts** in Crete. This is a slight exaggeration but the exceptionally friendly town still makes a pleasant break from the coast. The town also has a reputation as a centre of **lýra** playing and has a buoyant sheep-farming sector; don't miss the **spit-roast lamb** if you're carnivorously inclined.

Mount Psilorítis and the Idean cave

Above Anóyia, a smooth road ascends 21km to the **Nídha Plateau** at the base of Mount Psilorítis. Here, at the end of the road, is the path up to the celebrated Idean cave (about a 15min walk) and the start of the way to the summit of **Mount Psilorítis** (2456m), Crete's highest mountain. The **Idean cave** (Idhéon Ándhron) is a rival of that on Mount Dhíkti for the title of Zeus' birthplace. It was certainly associated from the earliest times with the cult of Zeus, and at times ranked among the most important centres of pilgrimage in the Greek world: Pythagoras visited; Plato set *The Laws* as a dialogue along the pilgrimage route here; and the finds within indicate offerings brought from all over the eastern Mediterranean. Visiting today, though, is something of a letdown – it's not an impressive cavern, and there's little to see.

GETTING AROUND	WEST OF IRÁKLIO
By bus Buses from Iráklio (Bus Station A) to Réthymno along the main coastal highway run at least hourly, and stop at the exit roads to Ayía Pelayía, Balí and Fódhele; you'll then have a 2–3km walk to each village, though in	Balí the local "happy train" (road train) meets most arrivals. Ayía Pelayía also has two direct buses a day from Iráklio. Three buses a day head for Anóyia (1hr) via Týlissos from Iráklio's Bus Station B.

ACCOMMODATION AND EATING

AYÍA PELAYÍA

Creta Sun Hotel On the road behind the village ☎ 28108 11626, ⓦ cretasunhotel.gr. Pleasant studio complex with a pool, and well-kept a/c rooms with fridge and balcony, most with fine views. Free wi-fi and friendly proprietors. April–Oct. **€41**

Irini Beach road ☎ 28108 11455, ⓦ irini-hotel -apartments.gr. Cheery two-room apartments above *The Home*, a lurid pink ice-cream parlour/café, just a few metres from the beach. Apartments sleep 2–6, with a/c, balcony, TV and kitchen. April–Oct. **€45**
Out of the Blue ☎ 28108 11112, ⓦ capsis.com. This

CLIMBING MOUNT PSILORÍTIS

For experienced and properly equipped hikers, climbing **Mount Psilorítis** is not especially arduous. The **route**, which diverts from the path to the Idean Cave just beyond a small chapel, forms a stretch of the E4 Pan-European footpath and is marked with red arrows and E4 waymarkers. It should be a 6–8hr return journey to the summit, although in spring, thick snow may slow you down. Don't attempt the walk alone as you could face a very long wait should you run into trouble.

If you're prepared to camp on the Nídha plateau (it can be very cold), or rent a room at the *Taverna Nida* (see p.222), you could continue on foot the next day down to the southern slopes of the range. It's a beautiful hike and also relatively easy, five hours or so down a fairly clear path to **Vorízia** or **Kamáres**. There are also routes, and guided hikes, up Psilorítis from the Amári Valley in the west (see p.241)

five-star luxury resort complex sits on a private peninsula, comprising five hotels, seven pools, luxury villas with private pools and three private beaches. It even has its own zoo. April–Oct. **€190**

BALÍ

Bali Blue Bay Hotel On the ridge between Varkotopos cove and Limáni ☎ 28340 20111, ⊛ balibluebay.gr. Comfortable, modern hotel with great views from most rooms and even better ones from the rooftop pool. Buffet breakfast included. Free wi-fi in lobby. April–Oct. **€65**

Mira Mare Above Varkotopos cove ☎ 28340 94256. Handily located above a supermarket, these en-suite balcony rooms with a/c, fridge and sea views are excellent value. May–Oct. **€35**

ANÓYIA

Aetos Main street, upper village ☎ 28340 31262. Excellent local taverna with a wood-fired grill and spacious terrace. Specialities include *souvláki* and goat dishes as well as a mouthwatering *ofto* (wood-fire-roasted lamb). Daily 11am–11pm.

Aristea Ring road, upper village ☎ 28340 31459, ⊛ hotelaristea.gr. Friendly, modernized hotel offering smart a/c en-suite rooms with TV and sensational balcony views, as well as studios and apartments for up to six people. Free wi-fi. **€35**

Hotel Marina Ring road, upper village ☎ 28340 31817, ⊛ marinahotelanogia.gr. Three-star modern hotel with studio rooms with kitchenette and fabulous views from the terrace balconies. Free wi-fi. Enquire at *Rooms Arís* a short way down the hill if no one's around. **€43**

MOUNT PSILORÍTIS

Taverna Nida Nihda plateau ☎ 28340 31141. Serves up hearty mountain dishes featuring lamb, pork and chicken, and has a couple of simple rooms sharing a bathroom. Plenty of local knowledge on offer (though little English), so it's a good base for hikes in the surrounding mountains. June–Sept daily breakfast, lunch and dinner; Oct–May Sat & Sun only. **€25**

4

Eastern Crete

Eastern Crete is dominated by the resort of **Áyios Nikólaos** and the upmarket tourism it attracts. Nearby **Eloúnda** is the home of many of the island's most luxurious hotels, as well as the gateway to the mysterious islet of **Spinalónga**. Inland, **Kritsá**, with its famous frescoed church and textile sellers, and the imposing ruins of **ancient Lato** make for good excursions. Far fewer people venture further: **Sitía**, an attractive, traditional town where tourism has had little visible effect, is the gateway to the far east and some of Crete's finest **beaches**, as well as a dramatic Minoan palace at **Káto Zákros**; while the south coast offers attractive small resorts at **Mírtos** and **Makriyialós**.

Áyios Nikólaos

Set on a hilly peninsula around a supposedly bottomless **lake**, in a lovely setting overlooking the **Gulf of Mirabéllo** ("Beautiful View"), **ÁYIOS NIKÓLAOS** is wonderfully picturesque, with dozens of excellent cafés, restaurants and bars around the lake, the harbour and the nearby coast. Curiously, what it doesn't have is a beach of any significance, so the five-star hotels are all some way out – mostly to the north, around Eloúnda – where they have private access to the coast.

By day, things to do in town are pretty limited – most people stroll the area around **Lake Voulisméni**, nose around in the shops, or walk to one of the municipal **beaches**, all of which have Blue Flag status. There's also a wide choice of **boat trips** around the bay (see opposite). Only an interesting **Folk Museum** (Tues–Sun 10am–2pm; €3; ☎ 28410 25093) near the tourist office is worth seeking out.

ARRIVAL AND DEPARTURE

ÁYIOS NIKÓLAOS

By bus The bus station is north of the centre in the new town. There are local buses to the centre hourly, or it's a steep up-and-down walk. For timetables, see ⊛ ktelherlas.gr or ⊛ bus-service-crete.com.

Destinations Eloúnda (every 30min–1hr; 20min);

Ierápetra (7 daily; 1hr); Iráklio (18 daily; 1hr 30min); Kritsá (9 daily; 20min); Pláka (every 2hr; 30min); Sitía (7 daily; 1hr 45min).

By car If you plan to rent a car, you'll find good deals at Club Cars, 28-Oktovríou 24 (☎ 28410 25868, ⊛ clubcars.net).

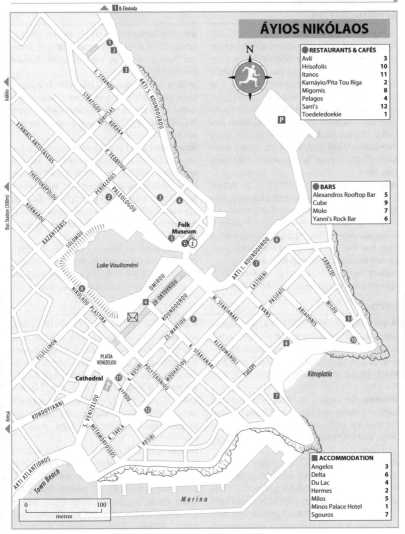

ÁYIOS NIKÓLAOS

● RESTAURANTS & CAFÉS	
Avlí	3
Hrisofolis	10
Itanos	11
Karnáyio/Píta Tou Ríga	2
Migomis	8
Pelagos	4
Sarri's	12
Toedeledoekie	1

● BARS	
Alexandros Rooftop Bar	5
Cube	9
Molo	7
Yanni's Rock Bar	6

■ ACCOMMODATION	
Angelos	3
Delta	6
Du Lac	4
Hermes	2
Milos	5
Minos Palace Hotel	1
Sgouros	7

INFORMATION AND ACTIVITIES

Tourist information The tourist office (April–June & Oct daily 9am–5pm; July–Sept 8am–9.30pm; ☎ 28410 22357, ⓦ aghiosnikolaos.gr/index), by the bridge, is particularly helpful, if often busy. They have lots of maps and brochures, as well as currency exchange at good rates and cheap internet access.

Post office 28-Oktovríou, halfway up, on the right.

Boat trips Daily trips to Spinalónga (€25 with lunch, €15 without), and various fishing, barbecue, beach and sunset tours, often with meals included, leave from around the harbour.

Bike rental and tours Martinbike at the Sunlight Hotel (☎ 28410 26622, ⓦ martinbike.com), on the coast road towards Eloúnda, rent quality mountain and road bikes, and organize tours.

Diving and watersports Pelagos Dive Centre, based at the *Minos Beach Hotel* (☎ 28410 24376, ⓦ divecrete.com), is a quality operation that also rents out motorboats and sailing dinghies by the hour, and can arrange private sailing excursions.

ACCOMMODATION

★**Angelos** Aktí S. Koundoúrou 16 ☎ 28410 23501. Welcoming small hotel on the seafront, offering excellent a/c balconied rooms with TV and fridge plus fine views over the Gulf. No breakfast, but there's a supermarket, owned by the same people, directly underneath; check here for information if there's no one around. **€40**

Delta Tselépi 1 ☎ 28410 28893, ⓦ agiosnikolaos-hotels .gr. Modern, refurbished a/c studios and apartments overlooking Kitroplatía beach, a 5min walk from the centre; those at the front have sea-view balconies. The same owners have good-value two-room family apartments at the nearby *Creta*. **€60**

★**Du Lac** 28 Oktovríou 17 ☎ 28410 22711, ⓦ dulac hotel.gr. Perhaps the most unexpected bargain in Áyios Nikólaos. The rooms and studios are classily renovated in designer style with all facilities including a/c, TV and wi-fi, in an absolutely prime location overlooking the lake. Not all rooms have lake views, however, and night-time noise can be a problem, as you're right in the heart of things. **€50**

Hermes Aktí S. Koundoúrou 21 ☎ 28410 28253, ⓦ hermeshotel.info. Luxurious four-star seafront hotel

with a large rooftop pool and every facility from minibar to satellite TV. Out of season, prices fall by up to 50 percent and there are often big online discounts. Breakfast included. **€115**

★**Milos** Sarolídi 2 ☎ 28410 23783. Sweet little pension east of the Kitroplatía beach, with some of the best rooms in town for the price. Spotless, en-suite a/c balcony rooms (no. 2 is a dream) with TV, fridge and spectacular sea views over the Gulf. April–Oct. **€35**

Minos Palace Hotel On the promontory 1km north of town ☎ 28410 23801, ⓦ minospalace.com. The most appealing of a clutch of luxury hotels just outside town, this is a veritable village in its own right, with views out across the Gulf as well as back towards town – the pricier suites come with private pool. Lovely rooms and every facility including private beach with watersports. Breakfast included. **€160**

Sgouros Nikoláou Pagálou 3 ☎ 28410 28931, ⓦ sgourosgrouphotels.com. Modern hotel overlooking Kitroplatía beach, with a/c balcony rooms with fridge and TV, and plenty of tavernas nearby. Breakfast included. **€55**

EATING

★**Avlí** Odhós P. Georgíou 12 ☎ 28410 82479. Delightful garden ouzeri offering a wide *mezédhes* selection as well as more elaborate dishes such as *kounéli krasato* (rabbit in wine) or lamb slow-cooked in a traditional oven (both €9.80). Booking advisable. May–Oct daily 12.30–3pm & 7–11pm.

Hrisofolis Aktí Pagálou ☎ 28410 22705. Attractive, stylish and creative *mezedhopolío* with reasonably priced fish, meat and veggie *mezédhes* served on a sea-facing terrace close to Kitroplatía beach. Meze from €4.50. Daily 3pm–2am.

Itanos Kýprou 1 ☎ 28410 25340. Popular with locals, this traditional taverna serves reasonably priced Cretan food such as *yemista* (rice-stuffed vegetables, €5) – check what's on offer from the trays in the kitchen – and barrel wine. The surroundings don't match up to the food, sadly, with a choice of tables on the street or in the cavernous, dark interior. Daily 11am–midnight.

★**Karnáyio/Píta Tou Ríga** Paleológou 24 ☎ 28410 25968. What appear to be two separate establishments in fact share a colourful terrace above the lake, where you can order from either menu. *Karnáyio* is a modern incarnation of a traditional ouzeri serving tasty *mezédhes* (€4–5 each, or order the excellent value wine- or ouzo-meze combos), while *Píta tou Ríga* is an upmarket kebab joint – their speciality *píta tou ríga* (€3.80) comes with added bacon and cheese. The place attracts a young, local crowd and there's *lýra* and *laoúto* (lute) music most Fri and Sat evenings. Daily noon–1am.

Migomis Nikoláou Plastíra 24 ☎ 28410 24353. High above the lake, *Migomis* has a matchless view, arguably the best in town, and prices no higher than at any other fancy café; a great place for a coffee or evening drinks. The elegant piano restaurant next door is a little over the top in terms of both price – €21–25 for fish, steaks €25, pasta from €12 – and decor, but worth it if you've booked a terrace-edge table to feast on that panoramic vista. Daily: café 8am–2am, restaurant noon–midnight.

Pelagos Stratígou Kóraka and Kateháki 10 ☎ 28410 25737. Housed in an elegant mansion, this stylish, upmarket fish taverna has an attractive leafy garden terrace that complements the excellent food: grilled prawns €16.50, octopus with honey €10.50, seafood *souvláki* €18. They also have pasta and simple meat dishes. Booking advisable. April–Oct daily noon–3pm & 7pm–1am.

Sarri's Kýprou 15 ☎ 28410 28059. Great little economical neighbourhood café-taverna in a quiet corner, with a shady terrace across the road overlooking an ancient church. Good for breakfast, grills and *souvláki*, with exceptionally good-value daily specials (meze and wine, €8). Daily 9am–midnight.

Toedeledoekie Aktí S. Koundoúrou 19 ☎ 28410 25537. Friendly, low-key café run by a Dutch-Greek couple. There are international papers to read, tasty sandwiches and milkshakes, and at night it morphs into a chilled bar. Daily 10.30am–2am.

CLOCKWISE FROM TOP LEFT IRÁKLIO MUSEUM (P.206); LYRA MAKER, RÉTHYMNO (P.236); PALACE OF KNOSSÓS (P.211) >

DRINKING AND NIGHTLIFE

A string of **bars** along Aktí I. Koundoúrou on the east side of the harbour play cool sounds on their waterside terraces, and many have dancefloors inside that fill as the night wears on. More raucous music venues and **clubs** crowd the bottom of 25-Martíou (known as "Soho Street") as it heads up the hill – though few seem to survive in the same incarnation for long.

Alexandros Rooftop Bar Kondhiláki ☎ 28410 24309. The name says it all; a great eyrie for a relaxed drink overlooking the lake, becoming increasingly rowdy as the cocktails take effect and the music, dating from the Sixties to present day but mostly oldies, gets louder. Happy hour till 10.30pm. Daily 8pm–early hours.

Cube 25-Martíou 9. One of the longest-established of the clubs on 25-Martíou, *Cube* boasts theme nights, local DJs and a broad sweep of music. June–Sept Thurs–Sat midnight–8am.

Molo Akti I. Koundoúrou 6 ☎ 28410 26250. One of a string of harbourside cafés with waterside terraces, *Molo* rarely closes; it's a café and local hangout by day and a cocktail bar in the evening; later on the action moves inside for dancing, club nights and occasional live music. Daily 8am–early hours.

Yanni's Rock Bar Akti I. Koundoúrou 1 ☎ 28410 23581. Long-running classic rock music bar, with a party atmosphere and a soundtrack of Seventies and Eighties music, blues, hard rock and heavy metal. Daily 10pm–4am.

Eloúnda and around

The busy little resort of **ELOÚNDA** has a strangely split personality: surrounded by the most expensive hotels in Crete and boasting plenty of jewellery and fashion stores and pricey seafront restaurants, it also has a much more earthy side, with plenty of inexpensive rooms and cafés that compete to provide the biggest, cheapest English breakfast. There are small beaches all around, though many of the best are monopolized by the big hotels; a good, sandy **municipal beach** stretches out north from the centre, and there are numerous popular swimming spots further out in this direction. Just before the centre of the village, a road (signposted) leads downhill to a natural causeway leading to the ancient "sunken city" of **Olous**. Here you'll find restored windmills, a short length of canal, Venetian saltpans and a well-preserved Roman dolphin **mosaic**, but nothing of the sunken city itself beyond a couple of walls in about 70cm of water.

Pláka

PLÁKA, some 5km north of Eloúnda, lies directly opposite the islet of Spinalónga and was once the mainland supply centre for the leper colony there. Boats still make the short trip across, nowadays carrying tourists, and the formerly decaying hamlet has become quite chichi; it's overlooked by a vast luxury hotel and many of its houses have been done up by foreign owners or villa companies. It's still an attractive, tranquil place, with a couple of excellent tavernas and crystal-clear water – though the beach is made up of large, uncomfortable pebbles.

Spinalónga

April, May & Oct daily 9am–3pm; June–Sept daily 9am–7pm; Nov–March Sat & Sun 9am–3pm • €2 • Boats run every 30min in season from both Eloúnda (€10 return) and Pláka (€8); most give you 1hr on the island, though you can take a later boat if there's room; it's also on many day-trips from Áyios Nikólaos

As a bastion of the Venetian defence, the fortress-rock of **Spinalónga** withstood the power of the Ottoman Empire for 45 years after the mainland had fallen. The most infamous part of the islet's history, however, is more recent; it served as a **leper colony** for five decades until 1957. Even today, despite the crowds of visitors, there's a real sense of the desolation of those years as you walk through the gated tunnel entrance and emerge on a narrow street below the castle, with the roofless shells of houses once inhabited by the unfortunate lepers all around. A short row of buildings here, which were once stores, has been restored and houses a small **museum** with photos and artefacts.

ARRIVAL AND INFORMATION

By bus Frequent buses run between Áyios Nikólaos and Eloúnda (every 30min–1hr; 20min) and some continue to Pláka (every 2hr; 30min).

Information Friendly Olous Travel (☎ 28410 41324,

ⓦ olous-travel.gr), on the main square in Eloúnda, can provide information and assist with finding accommodation, as well as changing money and arranging tours and car rental.

ELOÚNDA AND AROUND

ACTIVITIES

Boat trips From Eloúnda harbour boats leave every 30min from 9am for the trip to Spinalónga (€10 return; ☎ 6974 385 584, ⓦ eloundaboat.gr); longer day-trips taking in local beaches are also available. In Pláka boats depart from the quaysides beside the *Gorgona* and *Spinalonga* tavernas (April–Oct every 30min 9am–6pm; €8 return);

the *Spinalonga*'s boat also offers fishing trips (€80/hr, up to four people) with the catch cooked up at the taverna on your return.

Watersports Everything from windsurfing and ringos to kayaking and motorboat hire is on offer on the beach in Pláka (☎ 6944 932 760, ⓦ spinalonga-windsurf.com).

ACCOMMODATION

ELOÚNDA

Akti Olous On the road to the causeway ☎ 28410 41270, ⓦ eloundaaktiolous.com. An attractive seventy-room seafront hotel where comfortable balcony rooms come with a/c, TV and fridge. There's a bar and pool on the roof, with great views, and a seashore terrace café flanked by a small beach. Breakfast included. May–Oct. €65

Corali Studios Behind the far end of the town beach ☎ 28410 41712, ⓦ coralistudios.com. A sizeable complex, *Corali* (together with neighbouring *Portobello Apartments*, under the same management) has good modern a/c studios and apartments with cooking facilities, all with a sea view, and a pool and bar in the garden area behind. May–Oct. €60

Elounda Peninsula 2km south of Elounda ☎ 28410 68250, ⓦ eloundapeninsula.com. Spectacular hotel draped across its own private peninsula. Accommodation is in duplex suites or larger villas, all with private pools, and there's virtually every facility you could wish for, from an elegant spa to tennis courts, nine-hole golf course, sandy beach and kids' clubs and activities. Part of a complex with

the *Elounda Mare* and *Porto Elounda* hotels, which share the same beaches and facilities, but offer some more standard hotel rooms. May–Oct. €420

Milos Rooms Upper part of town ☎ 28410 41641, ⓦ pediaditis.gr. This small complex of rooms, studios and apartments is set around a pool and bar: all are a/c and larger units have kitchens; they also have simpler seafront places for the same price. Info is available at Info at Pediaditis Bookshop on the main square. May–Oct. Rooms €45, apartments €60

PLÁKA

Athina Villas ☎ 28410 41342, ⓦ spinalonga.com. A modern complex of comfortable a/c studios and apartments with balconies, wi-fi and TV, many with sea views, right in the heart of the village. €45

Blue Palace Immediately south of the village ☎ 28410 65500, ⓦ bluepalace.gr. Spectacularly sited on a slope above the bay, the *Blue Palace* offers sybaritic luxury in its suites and villas, many with private pool. Watersports, spa, gym and tennis courts all on site. €320

EATING AND DRINKING

Eloúnda has a huge choice of **restaurants**, mostly strung out along the waterfront or around the harbour; you'll probably need to book to get into any of those below. There are plenty of all-day **café-bars** interspersed between them, a couple of which have dancefloors inside and stay open to the early hours. Pláka is far quieter, and there's nowhere to eat at all on Spinalónga.

ELOÚNDA

★**Ferryman** Waterfront, south of the harbour ☎ 28410 41230. Glitzy place named for the 1970s BBC TV series *Who Pays the Ferryman?* in which it featured. Justly popular for the candlelit tables right above the water and short menu of interesting variations on traditional Greek recipes, many cooked in the hi-tech wood oven or giant barbecue – pork belly *yíros*-style €13.80, mussels steamed in ouzo €12.40, vegetarian special €8.80. April–Oct daily noon–4pm & 7pm–midnight.

★**Okeanis** Far end of the town beach ☎ 28410 42246. A very attractive terrace overlooking the town beach, with

elegant table settings and old-fashioned service. Expect traditional, home-style Cretan dishes (Mama's aubergines or excellent *moussaká*) with the occasional gourmet twist. Three-course menus for €12–20. Daily 12.30–4pm & 6–11pm.

Old Mill In the Elounda Mare hotel, 2km south of town ☎ 28410 68200. If you want to push the boat out, this is the place to do it; one of the finest restaurants in Crete, dressy and relatively formal, though still in an outdoor garden setting with sea views. Superb modern Greek/ Mediterranean cuisine, at a price – think starters like prawn "cappuccino" (around €20) or mains of rabbit in a honey and

4

walnut sauce (around €40). There's an excellent local wine list too. April–Oct daily noon–4pm & 6pm–midnight.

PLÁKA
Taverna Spinalonga ☎ 28410 41804. With an outdoor terrace facing the sea and Spinalónga, this big taverna at the far end of the village has very helpful owners and some of the lowest prices locally (*moussaká* or grilled octopus €9), especially for fish (priced per kilo), fresh from the day's catch. Daily lunch and dinner.

SHOPPING

Eklektos A. Papandreou 13 ☎ 28410 42086. Great little English bookshop 50m uphill from the square in the direction of Áyios Nikólaos, on the steps down to the water. Mon–Sat 9.30am–9.30pm, Sun 10.30am–9.30pm.

Kritsá

The "traditional" village of **KRITSÁ**, 9km inland of Áyios Nikólaos, is a popular destination for tour buses and day-trippers. Despite some commercialization, it's a trip well worth making for a break from the frenetic pace of the coast. Along the way are a remarkable church, the **Panayía Kerá**, and an ancient site, **Lató**, both worth a visit.

Kritsá is known for its **crafts**, and the main street is lined with tourist stores selling local weaving, ceramics, carved olive wood, leather goods and embroidery. Once you get past the touristy shops and explore the maze of streets winding up the hillside, with their wonderful valley views, you get a real sense of a genuinely Cretan village.

Church of Panayía Kerá

About 1km before Kritsá on the Áyios Nikólaos road • Tues–Sun 9am–4pm • €3

Inside the lovely Byzantine **church of Panayía Kerá** is preserved perhaps the most complete and certainly the most famous set of **Byzantine frescoes** in Crete. The biblical scenes were originally created in the fourteenth and early fifteenth centuries, though all have been retouched and restored to such an extent that they're impossible to date accurately.

Lato

4km north of Kritsá • Tues–Sun 8am–3pm • €2 • ☎ 28410 22462

On the outskirts of Kritsá a surfaced road leads off to the archeological site of **Lato**, where the substantial remains of a **Doric city** are coupled with a grand hilltop setting. The city itself is extensive, but largely neglected, presumably because visitors and archeologists on Crete are more concerned with the Minoan era. Ruins aside, you could come here just for the **views**: west over Áyios Nikólaos and beyond to the bay and Olous (which was Lato's port); inland to the Lasíthi mountains.

ARRIVAL AND DEPARTURE   KRITSÁ

By Bus There's a regular service from Áyios Nikólaos to Kritsá (9 daily; 15min).

ACCOMMODATION

Argyro Main road as you enter Kritsá ☎ 28410 51174, ⓦ argyrorentrooms.gr. Clean, pleasant and economical en-suite rooms (plus a couple with shared bath) with wi-fi, some with TV, many with views across the olive-tree-lined valley. There's a small courtyard café. **€30**

East to Sitía

From Áyios Nikólaos the main road heads south and then east, above the occasional sandy cove, through barren hills sprinkled with new developments and villas. In places the engineering of the new road (an ongoing process still years from completion) is breathtaking. Just past the remarkable Minoan site of **Gourniá** is the turn-off to Ierápetra and the south coast: from here on the road to **Sitía** is one of the most exhilarating in Crete. Carved into cliffs and mountainsides, the road teeters high above the coast much of the way. Of the beaches you see below, only the one at **Mókhlos** is easily accessible, some 5km below the main road.

Gourniá

Signed off the E75, 20km east of Áyios Nikólaos • Tues–Sun 8am–3pm • €3 • ☎ 28410 22462

Gourniá, slumped in the saddle between two low peaks, is the most completely preserved **Minoan town**. Its narrow alleys and stairways intersect a throng of one-roomed houses centred on a main square, and the rather grand house of what may have been a local ruler or governor. Although less impressive than the great palaces, the site is strong on revelations about the lives of the ordinary people – many of the dwellings housed craftsmen, who left behind their tools and materials to be found by the excavators. Its desolation today only serves to heighten the contrast with what must have been a cramped and raucous community 3500 years ago, though bear in mind that the site occupies only part of the original town, which would have stretched all the way to the sea and a small harbour.

Mókhlos

In a sleepy way, **MÓKHLOS** is a surprisingly developed place. Small as it is, almost every house seems to advertise rooms for rent, and there are several good tavernas around the little harbour. The village beach is very small and pebbly, but there's a slightly larger beach (also pebble) to the west. For those who stay there's not a great deal to do – hang out in the harbour taverna-cafés or swim out to the **islet of Mókhlos** just offshore, where there are remains of Minoan houses – but it's very easy to do nothing in this laidback place.

4

GETTING AROUND   EAST TO SITÍA

By bus There are 6 buses daily from Áyios Nikólaos to Sitía, and 7 to Ierápetra; any of them can drop you very close to Gourniá, but only the Sitía buses pass Mókhlos: be warned that you'll be dropped on the main road, a full hour's walk above the village (and a sweaty slog back up).

ACCOMMODATION AND EATING

★Limenaria Overlooking the new harbour, 600m west of Mókhlos ☎ 28420 27837, ⓦ mochlos-crete.gr. A tranquil hideaway with attractive, fully equipped sea-view terrace apartments sleeping up to four; big balconies front and back allow you to appreciate the view. **€55**

★Mesostrati On Mókhlos harbour ☎ 28430 94170.

Traditional Cretan cuisine from family recipes, as well as fresh fish, served on a pretty seaside terrace; also good breakfasts and a weekly Cretan cooking demonstration Wed at 5pm. Delicious daily specials €7–10, mixed meze €11. April–Oct daily 9am–late.

Sitía

After the excesses of Mália or Áyios Nikólaos, arriving in **SITÍA** can seem something of an anticlimax. But don't be fooled: the town's charms are subtle. Allow yourself to adjust to the more leisurely pace of life here and you may, like many other visitors before you, end up staying much longer than intended. An ideal base from which to visit the local attractions, Sitía hasn't entirely escaped the tourist boom; many of the visitors are French or Italian. Things to do include a sandy **town beach**, stretching far into the distance south of town; an excellent **Archeological Museum** (Tues–Sun 9.30am–4pm; €3; ☎ 28430 23917); a Venetian **fortress** (Tues–Sun 9am–4pm; free); and a small **Folklore Museum** (Mon–Sat 10am–2pm; €2). A colourful weekly **market** takes place on Tuesdays between 7am and 2pm along Odhós Itanou near the Archeological Museum.

ARRIVAL AND DEPARTURE   SITÍA

By bus The bus station (☎ 28430 22272) is on the southwest fringe of the centre; head north along Odhós Venizélou to get into town. Info is available at ⓦ ktelherlas .gr or ⓦ bus-service-crete.com.
Destinations Ay. Nikólaos (6 daily; 1hr 45min); Ierápetra (4 daily; 1hr 30min); Iráklio (6 daily; 3hr 15min); Káto

Zákros (Mon, Tues & Fri 2.15pm; 1hr); Makriyialós (4 daily until 2.30pm; 1hr); Palékastro (4 daily until 2.15pm; 30min); Vái (2–3 daily; 30min).

By ferry The ferry dock is 500m northeast of the centre. Just one ferry currently calls at Sitía, the *Prevelis* (☎ 28430 28555, ⓦ anek.gr). It departs Wed & Sat to Kássos (3hr), Kárpathos (5hr), Hálki (8hr) and Rhodes (10hr); and Sun to Iráklio (3hr), Anáfi (8hr), Santoríni (10hr), Mílos (14hr) and Pireás (19hr).

By plane Sitía Airport (☎ 28430 24424) lies immediately north of town. There's no public transport, but it's a taxi ride of just 5min (less than €10). Although it can cater for international flights, so far there's only a very occasional charter. Astra Airlines (☎ 28430 28200, ⓦ astra-airlines.gr) fly daily to Athens; Olympic (☎ 210 355 0500, ⓦ olympicair .com) daily to Rhodes via Kássos and Kárpathos; and Sky Express (☎ 28430 23500, ⓦ skyexpress.gr) 3 weekly to Alexandhroúpoli and Préveza.

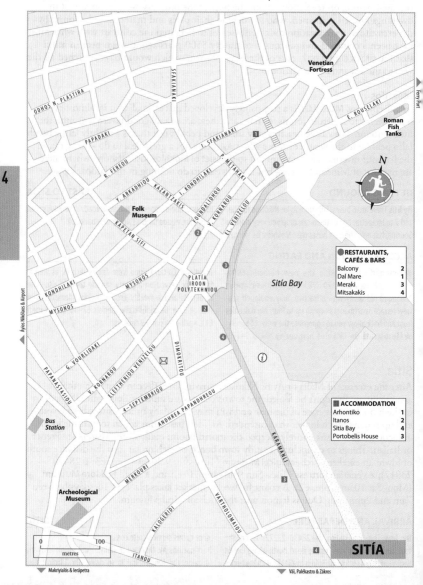

RESTAURANTS, CAFÉS & BARS

Balcony	2
Dal Mare	1
Meraki	3
Mitsakakis	4

ACCOMMODATION

Arhontiko	1
Itanos	2
Sitia Bay	4
Portobelis House	3

SITÍA

INFORMATION

Tourist office The municipal tourist office, on the seafront along the Beach Rd (Mon–Fri 9.30am–2.30pm & 5–9pm, Sat 9.30am–2.30pm; ☎ 28430 28300, ⓦ sitia.gr) can supply accommodation lists, town maps and a free guide to the region that also describes some walking routes.

ACCOMMODATION

★ **Arhontiko** Kondhiláki 16 ☎ 28430 28172. The pick of the budget places, in a lovely, little-modernized traditional house with a shady garden. Only one of the rooms is en suite, but they're spotless and attractive. **€30**

Itanos Platía Iróon Polytehníou ☎ 28430 22900, ⓦ itanoshotel.com. Smart hotel just off the town's main square. A/c balcony rooms mostly have good views, but be sure to check out a few as not all have been refurbished. Free wi-fi in reception area. Breakfast included. **€50**

Portobelis House Karamánli 34 ☎ 28430 22370, ⓦ portobelis-crete.gr. Studios and two-room apartments with kitchens for up to four people, plus some rooms. All are modern and well equipped, and some have sea-view balconies, though most overlook a small garden. Rooms/studios **€45**, apartments **€75**

★ **Sitia Bay** Trítis Septemvríou 8 ☎ 28430 24800, ⓦ sitiabay.com. Purpose-built apartment complex overlooking the town beach, with a large pool. Lovely modern studios and two-room apartments, all with sea-view balconies and fully equipped kitchens, plus a very warm welcome. Substantial discounts out of season. **€100**

EATING AND DRINKING

A line of enticing outdoor **tavernas** crowds the harbourfront, while Sitía's **nightlife**, mostly conducted at an easy pace, centres on the music bars and cafés at the northern end of Venizélou.

Balcony Foundalídhou 19 ☎ 28430 25084, ⓦ www .balcony-restaurant.com. Stylish restaurant on the upper floor of an elegant townhouse, with a menu that combines traditional Cretan dishes with Mexican- and Asian-influenced cuisine, usually to great effect. Four-course menu for two €32. Mon–Sat noon–3pm & 7–11pm.

Dal Mare Venizélou 193 ☎ 28430 20660. Big café-bar with three separate seaside terraces, open most of the day and night. By day there's coffee, snacks – burgers, club sandwiches – and sofas for lounging, and at night there are cocktails and music. Daily 9am–early hours.

★ **Meraki** Venizélou 151 ☎ 28430 23640. The best of a group of fashionable *rakádhika* (like an ouzerí, but serving *raki*) on the seafront. You can order (by ticking items off on a sheet) from a substantial menu combining modern and traditional, but the best deal is to go for a drink with meze (around €7), which will come with about five small dishes of whatever is fresh that day; not quite a meal, but you'll probably want another drink anyway, or you can order a few extras. The wine from Toplóu monastery is also excellent. Daily 9am–late.

Mitsakakis Karamánli 6 ☎ 28430 20200. Wonderful traditional *zaharoplastío* with a terrace facing the harbour, always busy with locals. Try their delicious *loukoumádhes* (dough fritters) with vanilla ice cream (€3.70); they also have sandwiches and crêpes. Daily 8am–midnight.

The far east

Crete's eastern edge is among its most tempting destinations, at least if it's beaches and isolation you're after. You won't find much solitude at **Vái beach**, which features on almost every Cretan travel agent's list of excursions, but it's a beautiful spot, and there are plenty of escapes roundabout. Nearby **Palékastro** is a lovely small town within easy reach of many less well-known beaches, as well as some of Crete's best windsurfing. From here a road winds south to still less-visited country at **Zákros**, site of the fourth great Minoan palace, and little-known **Xerókambos**.

Monastery of Toplóu

On the road to Vái, 15km east of Sitía • Daily: April–Sept 9am–6pm; Oct–March 9am–4pm • €3

The **Monasterty of Toplóu**'s forbidding exterior reflects a history of resistance to invaders, and doesn't prepare you for the gorgeous flower-decked cloister within. The blue-robed monks keep out of the way as far as possible, but in quieter periods their cells and refectory are left discreetly on view. In the church is one of the masterpieces of Cretan art, the **eighteenth-century icon** *Lord Thou Art Great* by Ioannis Kornaros. This marvellously intricate work incorporates 61 tiny scenes, each illustrating a phrase from the Orthodox prayer that begins with this phrase. In the monastery's shop you can buy expensive reproductions of the work as well as olive oil and wine made by the monks (a track opposite the monastery leads to their **winery**, open for visits Mon–Fri 9am–4pm in summer).

Vái

The beach at **Vái** is famous above all for its **palm trees**. The sudden appearance of what is claimed to be Europe's only indigenous wild date-palm grove is indeed an exotic surprise, and dreams of Caribbean beaches are easy to indulge. Rarely for long, however, since throughout summer the beach fills to overflowing as buses pour in and cars unable to squeeze into the car park (€2.50) line the access road for hundreds of metres. On the sand, only the boardwalks guarantee a route through the mass of baking bodies. Pricey sun loungers are available and a watersports centre offers waterskiing, ringos and other high-speed rides. There's a café and expensive taverna, and you'll pay again to have a shower or use the toilet. You may find a bit more solitude by climbing the rocks or swimming to one of the smaller beaches which surround Vái. **Ítanos**, twenty minutes' walk north by an obvious trail, has a couple of tiny beaches and some modest ruins from the Classical era.

Palékastro

A substantial village with easy access to numerous excellent beaches, and with plenty of accommodation both in town and in the surrounding area, **PALÉKASTRO** makes an enjoyable, quiet base. There are several good tavernas and just about every other facility you might need.

Ancient Palékastro

Close to Hióna beach, about a 20min walk from Palékastro village • Tues–Sun 8am–3pm; in practice rarely locked • €3, if there's anyone to collect it

For archeologists the Minoan site of **Palékastro** is a very significant excavation, the largest Minoan town yet discovered and a rich source of information about everyday Minoan life. For an amateur it's less enthralling, but there's plenty to see (though signage could be improved), and continuing excavation means that new finds are still coming to light. Recent explorations on the site's northern side, for example, have revealed a road leading from the town to a nearby harbour (no trace of which has yet been found), while beneath the olive groves to the south and west more of the Minoan town lies waiting to be revealed.

Hióna beach

2km east of Palékastro

Hióna beach, a good stretch of blue-flagged pebble and sand, lies to the south of a flat-topped hill named Kastrí which dominates the coastal landscape. The closest beach to Palékastro, it's less than twenty minutes' walk via the hamlet of **Angathiá**. Though far from crowded, it is probably the most popular beach hereabouts: you can walk to still quieter coves around the bay to the south.

Koureménos beach

2.5km northeast of Palékastro

Koureménos beach, to the north of the Kastrí bluff, is Crete's top **windsurfing** spot. Not surprisingly, it can be windy (a funnel effect creates ideal windsurfing conditions), but it's a fine, long sand-and-pebble beach, with several tavernas and rooms places – even a bar – directly behind. There's also quite a community of camper vans in summer, and a couple of excellent windsurf centres, too.

Káto Zákros

From the first spectacular view as you approach along the clifftop road, **KÁTO ZÁKROS** – "Lower" Zákros – is a delight. There's a pebbly beach, half a dozen waterfront

WALKS AROUND ZÁKROS

The most obvious and best-known of the **walks** around Zákros is the 6km **Gorge of the Dead**, a beautiful ravine that leads from the larger village of Áno ("Upper") Zákros, on the main road, to Káto Zákros, passing the palace en route. It makes up the final stage of the E4 trans-European footpath, so it's pretty well marked. This is just the start of the local hiking possibilities, though: the owners of *Stella's* (see p.234) have waymarked several other 3–4hr walks in the surrounding hills; there's a map at the entrance to the apartments. Best of them is perhaps the **Hokhlakiés Gorge**, halfway between Palékastro and Áno Zákros, a well-signed 3km route to a deserted beach. From the bottom you can either return up the gorge (1hr 10min) or strike out along the coast in either direction; north to Palékastro, south to Káto Zákros, each about 6km further.

tavernas and café-bars, and a few places offering rooms and apartments; along with a tiny harbour with a few fishing boats, this is about all the place amounts to. It's best to bring cash and anything else you might need: there's no shop, or anything else much. But if it's laidback tranquillity you're after, you've come to the right place.

Palace of Zákros

50m behind Káto Zákros beach • Daily: June–Oct 8am–6pm; Nov–May 8am–3pm • €3 • ☎ 28430 26897

Though the **Palace of Zákros** is small, it is full of interest, and can match any of the more important Minoan centres for quality of construction and materials. It's also much easier to understand than many of the other Minoan sites: here, the remains are of one palace only, dating from between 1600 and 1450 BC. Although there is an earlier settlement at a lower level, it is unlikely ever to be excavated – mainly because this end of the island is gradually sinking. Even the exposed parts of the palace are marshy and often waterlogged: there are terrapins living in the green water in the cistern. When it's really wet, you can keep your feet dry and get an excellent view of the overall plan of the palace by climbing the streets of one of Zákros's unique features; the **town** – a place very like Gourniá (see p.229) – that occupied the hill above it.

Xerókambos

Straggling across a little coastal plain in the lee of the Sitían mountains, the tiny hamlet of **XERÓKAMBOS** is not especially attractive, but it's as isolated and peaceful as you could wish for. There's no real centre, just a street along which, between fields of olive groves, are spaced some houses, a few tavernas and a couple of basic minimarkets, with rooms and apartment places scattered along the road and down by the beach. Despite the stirrings of development, this **main beach** is more than long enough to find seclusion if you want it, and there are isolated coves either side where you might never see another soul. The crystal-clear waters here are great for **snorkelling** too.

GETTING AROUND AND INFORMATION · THE FAR EAST

By bus There are services from Sitía to Káto Zákros (Mon, Tues & Fri 2.15pm; 1hr), Palékastro (4 daily until 2.15pm; 30min) and Vái (2–3 daily; 30min). There is no public transport south of Zákros.

Tourist information There's no tourist office, but a number of locally run websites have details of attractions and comprehensive accommodation listings: check out ⓦ eastcrete-holidays.gr, ⓦ eastern.cretefamilyhotels.com and ⓦ palaikastro.com.

ACTIVITIES

Cycling Freak Mountain Bike Centre (☎ 6975 810 240, ⓦ freak-mountainbike.com), at the edge of Palékastro on the Vái road, offers bike rental, guided day-trips and cycle holiday packages.

Windsurfing There are two rival operations at Koureménos, both offering lessons and quality gear rental; Freak (☎ 6979 253 861, ⓦ freak-surf.com) and Gone Surfing (ⓦ gonesurfing.gr).

ACCOMMODATION AND EATING

PALÉKASTRO

Hellas On the main square **☎** 28430 61240, **🖰** palaikastro.com/hotelhellas. Simple a/c rooms come with balcony, TV, wi-fi and fridge; a little impersonal, but could hardly be closer to the action. There's a good traditional taverna on the terrace beneath the hotel, facing the square. Daily 10am–late. **€35**

Hiona Hióna beach **☎** 28430 61228. Stunningly beautiful seafood restaurant on a promontory at the northern end of the beach, a touch more formal than anywhere else in the area and a little pricier, but worth it. Try the *kakaviá* traditional fish stew (€25 for two). Often booked up in season. May–Oct daily noon–midnight.

Kouremenos Beach Apartments Koureménos beach **☎** 28430 56825, **🖰** kouremenosbeach.gr. A couple of small studios for two in the olive groves immediately behind the beach, as well as some larger apartments for up to six people, all with a/c, TV and fridge, the larger ones with separate kitchen. April–Oct. Studios **€40**, apartments **€60**

★ Kouremenos Villas/Panorama Apartments On the hillside beyond Koureménos beach **☎** 28430 61370, **🖰** palaikastro.com/kouremenos_apts. A glorious setting with great views over beach and countryside and an exceptionally friendly welcome, make this place special; very comfortable apartments with modern kitchen, a/c, satellite TV, and a pool. April–Oct. **€61**

Marina Village Off the Hióna Beach road, about 600m from Hióna, 800m from Koureménos **☎** 28430 61284, **🖰** marinavillage.gr. A peaceful haven with well-furnished a/c balcony rooms, surrounded by olive groves and a garden of bougainvillea and banana plants, plus pool and tennis court. They also have a tiny house (for up to four people) right by Hióna beach. Buffet breakfast included. April–Oct. **€58**

KÁTO ZÁKROS

★ Akrogiali End of the beach road **☎** 28431 10710, **🖰** kato-zakros.gr. The last of the places on the waterfront, with a particularly attractive terrace away from the road. Excellent, simple Greek food (mains €6–10) and the friendly owner, Nikos, is a fount of information and acts as an agent for several room options nearby. March–Nov daily 9am–late.

Coral & Athina On the rise immediately beyond Taverna Akrogiali **☎** 28430 26893, **🖰** kato-zakros.gr. Rooms directly above the beach, with great sea views from large communal terraces; clean and simply furnished, with a/c, fridge and TV. Ask at the taverna. March–Nov. **€45**

★ Stella's Traditional Apartments About 500m inland, beyond the palace **☎** 28430 23739, **🖰** zakros.gr. Large, elegantly decorated, stone-built a/c apartments, with hammocks and lovely views in the verdant gardens, and some slightly simpler studios. Exceptionally well equipped, well run and friendly. Studios **€50**, apartments **€70**

Zakros Palace Apartments On the entry road above the village **☎** 28430 29550, **🖰** katozakros-apts.gr. Perched high above the coast with spectacular views; a/c rooms have balconies overlooking both the bay and the gorge, TV, fridge (kitchenette in studios) and wi-fi. **€50**

XERÓKAMBOS

Asteras In the hills above the main road **☎** 28430 26787, **🖰** asterasapartments.gr. Set in their own garden, above the olive groves, these modern a/c studio rooms and two-room apartments all come with kitchenette, fridge and good sea views. May–Oct. **€40**

Liviko View Off the main street **☎** 28430 27000, **🖰** livikoview.gr. Excellent rooms and taverna run by a couple of Greek-Australians. Rooms come with a/c and balcony with sea view, and there are also apartments sleeping up to four; food is served on a lovely terrace, and cooked with organic ingredients grown on the family farm. Vegetarian dishes from €4. Daily 10am–late. **€35**

Ierápetra and the southeast coast

There are three main approaches to Crete's southeastern corner: the long haul across the centre of the island from Iráklio via Áno Viánnos in order to approach from the west; the road south from Sitía that emerges on the coast close to **Markryialós**; or the short cut across the isthmus from Pahiá Ámmos to Ierápetra.

IERÁPETRA itself has various claims to fame – the southernmost town in Europe, the most hours of sunshine, the largest town on the south coast of Crete – but charm is not really one of them. Though there's an excellent **beach**, it's a sprawling place and a major supply centre for the farmers who have grown rich from the plastic greenhouses that scar much of the surrounding coast. In recent years some resources have been devoted to smartening the town up, and on the **seafront**, where a string of restaurants and bars stretches out in either direction, Ierápetra can be genuinely picturesque. However tourism seems very much an afterthought, and things to do by day – apart from lie on the beach – are limited to a decent **Archeological Museum** (Tues–Sun 8.30am–3pm; €2; **☎** 28420 28721) and a visit to the **Venetian fort** (Tues–Sun 8.30am–3pm; free) that guards the harbour.

ISLAND ESCAPE: GAIDHOURONÍSI

The most popular way to escape Ierápetra's often stifling summer temperatures is to take a boat trip to **Gaidhouronísi** (aka Donkey Island or Chrissi Island) some 10km offshore. A real desert island a little over 4km in length, with a cedar forest and a couple of tavernas, Gaidhouronísi has some excellent sandy **beaches** and plenty of room to escape – although you wouldn't want to miss the boat back. There's a waymarked **walking route** around the island, passing the fabulous "**Shell Beach**" covered with millions of multicoloured mollusc shells. Two competing companies, Chrysi Cruises (☎ 28420 20008, ⓦ chrysicruises.com) and Zanadu (☎ 28420 26649), run **daily trips** to Gaidhouronísi, on large boats with on-board bars, from the jetty on the seafront (May–Oct; peak-season departures 10.30am, 11am & 12.30pm, returning 4pm, 5pm & 6pm; 55min). Tickets are sold by agents throughout town, or at the boat; officially they cost €25 but off season, or if you bargain, you may get them for much less.

Makryialós

MAKRYIALÓS, some 27km east of Ierápetra, is strung out along the coastal road and at first sight not at all attractive. Turn off the road, though, and there are plenty of quiet corners, plus one of the best **beaches** at this end of Crete, with fine sand that shelves so gently you almost feel you could walk the two hundred nautical miles to Africa. There's an attractive little harbour too, plenty of other beaches nearby, and some interesting walks into the hills behind.

Mýrtos

MÝRTOS, just off the main road 15km west of Ierápetra, is an unexpected pleasure: a charming, white-walled village with a long shingle beach. Even in August, when the place can get pretty full, the pace of life remains slow. A one-room village **museum** (Mon & Fri 10am–2pm, Wed 5–8pm; free) houses some of the finds from a couple of nearby **Minoan sites**, a villa at Pýrgos and a small settlement at Fournoú Korifí; both are immediately west of Mýrtos, signed off the main road, and generally left unlocked in daylight hours.

ARRIVAL AND DEPARTURE | IERÁPETRA AND THE SOUTHEAST COAST

By bus Ierápetra bus station (☎ 28420 28237) is on Lasthénous, the Áyios Nikólaos road, a 5min walk from the centre.

Destinations Áyios Nikólaos (7 daily; 1hr), Iráklio (7 daily; 2hr 30min), Makriyialós (7 daily; 30min), Mýrtos (5 daily; 30min), Sitía (4 daily until 2.30pm; 1hr 30min).

ACCOMMODATION

IERÁPETRA

Camping Koutsounari 7km east of Ierápetra on the Makryialós road ☎ 28420 61213, ⓦ camping -koutsounari.gr. The only campsite on this stretch of the south coast, with a taverna, store and pool, and although the ground is a bit gritty there's a good beach and plenty of shade. May–Oct. **€18**

Cretan Villa Lakérdha 16 ☎ 28420 28522, ⓦ cretan -villa.com. Close to the bus station; sparkling a/c rooms with TV and fridge overlook the flower-bedecked patio of a beautiful 180-year-old stone house. **€48**

Ersi Platía Eleftherías 19 ☎ 28420 23208. The good-value rooms at this refurbished hotel come with fridge, a/c (€5 extra), TV and balcony – the higher the better for peace and sea views. The owner also has some apartments nearby, with kitchen and lounge, for the same price. **€35**

MAKRYIALÓS

★**Aspros Potamos Traditional Houses** 600m up a signed track at the eastern end of town ☎ 28430 51694, ⓦ asprospotamos.com. This back-to-nature version of *White River Cottages* (see p.236) is slightly further up the valley. Here another group of tiny stone houses cut from the rock has been delightfully converted into studios and apartments, but in this case there's only solar power; rooms have a fridge, single bathroom light and LED reading lamp (plus solar hot water), and in reception there's wi-fi and power for rechargers, otherwise you are reliant on oil lamps and candles for lighting, and a fireplace to warm you in winter (extra charge for firewood). **€50**

Maria Tsankalioti Apartments Seaward side of the main road, halfway through town ☎ 28430 51557, ⓦ makrigialos-crete.com. The friendly proprietor offers bright beachfront studio rooms and apartments – some with sea view and terrace – with kitchenette, a/c, TV and wi-fi. **€40**

★**White House** On the harbour ☎28430 29183, ⓦmakrigialos.com. Three houses and two apartments in beautifully restored harbour buildings, each one architect-designed and unique. Equipment includes everything from wi-fi and washing machine to champagne glasses. Closed Dec. **€105**

White River Cottages 500m up a signed track at the eastern end of town ☎28430 51120, ⓔwriver@otenet.gr. An abandoned hamlet of traditional stone dwellings has been restored as a warren of studios and apartments (for up to four people) around a small pool. Built partly into the rocks, with the original stone floors and whitewashed walls, they come with kitchens, a/c, wi-fi and private terraces. Minimum three-day stay. **€78**

MÝRTOS

Big Blue Apartments West side of village ☎28420 51094, ⓦbig-blue.gr. Lovely rooms with fridge, studios with kitchenette, and larger two-bedroom apartments, all with a/c and sea-view balconies in a stunning position high above the beach. Rooms **€40**, apartments **€80**

Nikos House At the heart of the village ☎28420 51116. Very simple studios or two-room apartments with fans, bath and kitchenette; the upstairs studio, especially, is lovely, and you feel very much part of village life here. **€40**

EATING AND DRINKING

MAKRYIALÓS

Cafe Olympio Overlooking the beach beside the harbour ☎28430 52135. Friendly café-bar that's a good source of information on the local area, and has sunbeds on a sandy strip of beach. Breakfasts, light lunches, cocktails and draft beer. Daily 8am–late.

Faros Overlooking the beach beside the harbour ☎28430 52456. Big taverna in a great position, with everything from pizza and pasta to octopus and calamari; good fish from their own boat too (fish dishes €10–12). Daily noon–late.

★**Kalliotzina** Koutsourás, 3km west of Makriyialós ☎28430 51207. An absolutely classic old-fashioned taverna, serving home-cooked food and excellent fish on a tree-shaded terrace right by the sea. There's no written menu, so check out what's on offer in the kitchen or listen carefully as the day's dishes are reeled off at speed; mains are around €7, or less for the veggie options. There's often music on summer weekends. Daily 11am–late.

★**Piperia** Pefkí, 5km inland from Makriyialós ☎28430 52471. A lovely spot under a spreading pepper tree, with authentic, traditional food and great views over the coast. Mains like okra with lamb or rabbit in wine sauce go for around €8; they have live Greek music some summer evenings (with a set menu); and they sell their own jams, olives and liqueurs. Daily noon–midnight.

MÝRTOS

Katerina's On a pedestrian alley in the heart of the village ☎28420 51451. Self-described as "the only gourmet restaurant in the region", colourful *Katerina's* attempts to be a cut above the rest and mostly succeeds, with dishes like Martini-marinated pork filet mignon as well as old favourites such as *kléftiko*, and plenty of veggie choices – around €20 per head including wine. Chef Yiannis Zervakis also runs half-day cooking workshops and excursions into the mountains to forage for herbs and wild greens. Daily 6–11pm.

Réthymno and around

The province of **Réthymno** has something for everyone. Réthymno Town itself is a relaxed university town overlooked by one of the most imposing Venetian fortresses on the island. It also retains a picturesque old quarter, redolent of traditional urban life, plus a fine beach. Inland, the countryside is dominated by mountains, with Psilorítis in the east and the White Mountains in the west. Between them the **Amari Valley** offers pretty villages and magnificent hiking, while on the south coast, in particular around **Plakiás**, are more excellent beaches.

Réthymno Town

Although it's the third largest town in Crete, **RÉTHYMNO TOWN** never feels like a city, as Haniá and Iráklio do. Instead, it has an easy-going provincial air; it's a place that moves slowly and, for all the myriad bars springing up along the seafront, the **old town** still preserves much of its Venetian and Turkish appearance. There are hundreds of tavernas, bars, cafés and clubs, but the big hotels are all out of town, stretching away along the shore to the east. Dominating everything from the west is the superbly preserved outline of the **fortress**.

The harbour and old town

The Venetian or inner **harbour** is the most attractive part of Réthymno's waterfront, although these days its elegant sixteenth-century lighthouse looks down on a line of bars and tavernas, rather than the sailing ships and barges of bygone eras. Immediately behind spreads the atmospheric **old town**, a warren of ancient buildings with ornate wooden doors and balconies, of fountains and rickety old stores, some still with traditionally dressed craftsmen sitting out front. Look out for the **Venetian loggia**

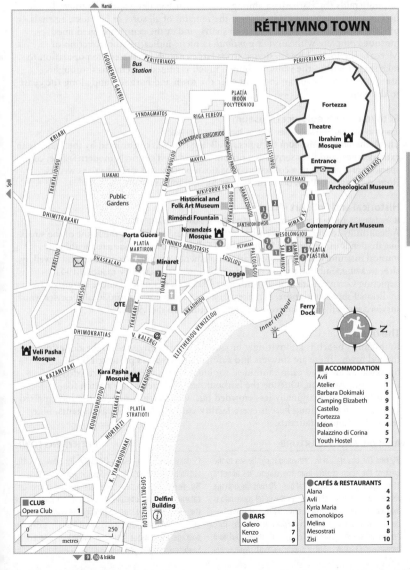

RÉTHYMNO TOWN

ACCOMMODATION
Avli	3
Atelier	1
Barbara Dokimaki	6
Camping Elizabeth	9
Castello	8
Fortezza	2
Ideon	4
Palazzino di Corina	5
Youth Hostel	7

CAFÉS & RESTAURANTS
Alana	4
Avli	2
Kyria Maria	6
Lemonokipos	5
Melina	1
Mesostrati	8
Zisi	10

CLUB
| Opera Club | 1 |

BARS
Galero	3
Kenzo	7
Nuvel	9

which houses a shop selling Classical art reproductions; the **Rimóndi Fountain**, another of the more elegant Venetian survivals; and the **Nerandzés mosque** with its **minaret**, currently serving as a music school. Ethnikís Andístasis, the street leading straight up from the fountain, is the town's **market** area.

The Venetian fortress

Daily: May–Sept 8.30am–8pm; Oct–April 8.30am–6pm • €4 • ☎ 28310 28101

Overlooking the old town from a rise at the western end of the seafront stands the massive **Fortezza** or **Venetian fortress**. Said to be the largest Venetian castle ever built, this was a response, in the last quarter of the sixteenth century, to a series of **pirate raids** (by Barbarossa among others) that had devastated the town. Inside now is a vast open space dotted with the remains of all sorts of barracks, arsenals, officers' houses, earthworks and deep shafts, and at the centre a large domed **mosque** complete with surviving *mihrab* (a niche indicating the direction of Mecca). The fortress was designed to be large enough for the entire population to take shelter within the walls. Although much is ruined, it remains thoroughly atmospheric, and you can look out over the town and harbour, and along the coast to the west.

Réthymno Archeological Museum

Opposite the entrance to the Fortezza • Tues–Sun 8am–3pm • €3 • ☎ 28310 54668

The **Archeological Museum** occupies a building that was constructed by the Turks as an extra defence, and later served as a prison. Nowadays it's entirely modern inside; cool, spacious and airy, with a collection of Minoan pottery and sarcophagi, as well as Roman coins, jewellery, pots and statues, all of it found locally.

Historical and Folk Art Museum

M. Vernárdhou 28, near the Nerandzés mosque • Mon–Sat 9.30am–2.30pm • €4 • ☎ 28310 23398

A beautifully restored seventeenth-century Venetian mansion is the home of the small but tremendously enjoyable **Historical and Folk Art Museum**. Gathered within are musical instruments, old photos, farm implements, traditional costumes and jewellery, lace, weaving, embroidery (including a traditional-style tapestry made in 1941 depicting German parachutists landing at Máleme), a couple of entire reconstructed traditional shops, and more. It makes for a fascinating insight into local lifestyles which survived virtually unchanged from Venetian times to the 1960s.

The beach

Réthymno's **beach** is an invitingly broad swathe of tawny sand, right alongside the old town. There are showers and cafés, and the waters protected by the breakwaters are dead calm (and ideal for kids). Sadly, they're also crowded and often none too clean. Outside the harbour, less sheltered sands stretch for kilometres, only marginally less crowded but with much cleaner water. Interspersed among the hotels along here is every facility you could need – travel agents, bike rental, bars and restaurants.

ARRIVAL AND DEPARTURE   **RÉTHYMNO TOWN**

By bus The bus station in Réthymno is by the sea to the west of the town centre; from the station, it's about a 10min walk to the harbour; local bus #20 runs through the centre and east along the coast to the hotel zone. Info is available at ⓦ e-ktel.com or ⓦ bus-service-crete.com.

Destinations Amári (Mon–Fri 5.30am & 2.30pm; 1hr); Anóyia (Mon–Fri 5.30am & 2pm; 1hr 30min); Arkádhi monastery (3 daily until 2.30pm; 40min); Ayía Galíni (5 daily; 1hr 30min); Haniá (18 daily; 1hr 30min); Iráklio (18 daily; 1hr 30min); Plakiás (5 daily; 50min).

By ferry In summer, there are two or three fast catamarans a week to Santoríni (2hr 30min), leaving in the early morning and returning the same evening. Book through any local travel agent (usually a day-trip package including a tour and meals) or direct with SeaJets (ⓦ seajets.gr)

INFORMATION

Tourist office Based in the Delfini Building, on the seafront (Mon–Fri 7.30am–3pm, Sat 10am–4pm; ☏ 28310 29148, ⊛ rethymno.gr), the tourist office provides maps, timetables and accommodation lists.

ACCOMMODATION

★**Atelier** Himáras 25 ☏ 28310 24440, ⊛ frosso-bora .com. This small place near the fortress is run by a talented potter with a studio in the basement. The attractive en-suite a/c rooms come with kitchenette and satellite TV. Free wi-fi. **€45**

★**Avli** Xanthoudhídhou 22 ☏ 28310 58250, ⊛ avli.gr. Luxury apartments and suites from the people who run arguably the best restaurant around (see below). They're located in a couple of lovingly restored old townhouses, with services including rooftop terrace and hot tub, free wi-fi, and a superb breakfast. **€140**

Barbara Dokimaki Platía Plastíra 7 ☏ 28310 22607, ⊛ barbarastudios.gr. Strange warren of a place, with one entrance on Platía Plastíra, just off the harbourfront, and another on Dambergi. Offers a/c studios and apartments with kitchenette and TV; the more attractive options are on the top floor. Free wi-fi. April–Oct. **€50**

Castello Karaolí 10 ☏ 28310 23570, ⊛ castello -rethymno.gr. A very pleasant small *pension* in a 300-year-old Turkish mansion; a/c en-suite rooms come with fridge and TV and there's a delightful patio garden for taking breakfast (extra). **€50**

Fortezza I. Melissínou 16 ☏ 28310 55551, ⊛ fortezza .gr. Stylish, good-value hotel in a central location with everything you'd expect for the price, including a/c rooms (most with balcony, some with terrace), bar, pool and restaurant. Breakfast included. Free wi-fi. May–Oct. **€77**

Ideon Platía Plastíra 10 ☏ 28310 28667, ⊛ hotelideon .gr. Upmarket hotel in an excellent location just north of the ferry dock – try to get a balcony room with a sea view. Rooms come with a/c, TV and internet and there's a pool. Breakfast included. Free wi-fi. April–Oct. **€78**

Palazzino di Corina Damvérgi 7–9 ☏ 28310 21205, ⊛ corina.gr. Sumptuous luxury suites with a/c, minibar and satellite TV in a stunningly restored Venetian palace; the charming patio squeezes in a small pool. Breakfast included. Free wi-fi. **€112**

★**Youth Hostel** Tombázi 41 ☏ 28310 22848, ⊛ yhrethymno.com. The cheapest beds in town, in six- to eight-bed dorms. Large, clean, very friendly and popular, it has a café, laundry facilities, internet access and a multilingual library. **€10**

CAMPING

Camping Elizabeth About 4km east of town ☏ 28310 28694, ⊛ camping-elizabeth.net. A large, appealing beachside site with all facilities, and regular bus connections to the city. **€15.50**

EATING

The most touristy **restaurants** are arrayed immediately behind the town beach and have menu picture boards outside – many of them overpriced and mediocre – while around the inner harbour there's a cluster of expensive and intimate **fish tavernas**. The most inviting and best-value places to eat tend to be scattered in less obvious parts of the old town.

Alana Salamínos 15 ☏ 28310 27737, ⊛ alana -restaurant.gr. An attractive, tree-filled courtyard provides the setting for an elegant restaurant serving both traditional and updated Cretan dishes. Among the former try *arnáki aginarato* (lamb with artichokes in an egg-lemon sauce, €9.50), the latter includes the likes of sea bass cooked sous-vide with citrus sauce (€18.50). Also good house wine and a range of bottles. Daily noon–2am.

★**Avli** Xanthoudhídhou 22 ☏ 28310 26213, ⊛ avli.gr. Probably Réthymno's finest restaurant; an upmarket place in a Venetian mansion with an exquisite garden patio serving top-notch food. Traditional Cretan dishes are updated with wider Mediterranean touches: for lunch try the *moussaká* (€11.20) or *Avli* salad (€8.50) or, if you're settling in, one of the excellent three-course menus (€29–39). There's also an extensive wine list. Daily 11am–1am.

Kyria Maria Moskhovítou 20 ☏ 28310 29078. Tucked down an alley behind the Rimóndi Fountain, this unassuming little taverna serves tasty *mezédhes* and good-value fish and meat dishes (chicken *souvláki* €7.50, rabbit in lemon sauce €9, set menu for 2 with wine from €23); after the meal, everyone gets a couple of Maria's delicious *tyropitákia* with honey on the house. Daily 8am–midnight.

Lemonokipos Andistásis 100 ☏ 28310 57087, ⊛ lemonokipos.com. Beautiful courtyard restaurant serving modern Greek cuisine under the lemon trees from which it takes its name. Good set menu for €20 (veggie version €11.90); somewhat pricey wine. Daily 10am–12.30am.

Melina Himáras 22 ☏ 28310 21580, ⊛ melina -rethymno.gr. Traditional café/taverna handy for the Fortezza, specializing in meat from the outdoor barbecue (€12–18); give them an hour or so's notice and they'll barbecue an entire joint for you. There are great views over the town from the terrace. Daily 10am–1am.

★**Mesostrati** Yerakári 1 ☏ 28310 29375. An excellent and economical little neighbourhood taverna-ouzerí serving well-prepared country dishes on a shady small terrace. Try their tasty *apákia* (smoked pork) or *loukánika* (sausage), each €6. Live Cretan *lyra* and *laoúto* (lute) performances most Fri and Sat eves, with big-name performers known to drop in for impromptu jam sessions. Mon–Sat 11am–3pm & 6pm–2am, Sun 6pm–2am.

★ **Zisi** Mákhis Krítis 63, Misíria, in the hotel zone 2km east of town ☎ 28310 28814, ⦿ taverna-zisis.gr. *Zisi* is one of the great Réthymno institutions, where local families get together for celebrations, especially on Sun lunchtimes, when booking is advised. The place is large and elegant with real table linen, *mayireftá* (traditional baked dishes) laid out in heated display cabinets and a menu filled with other tempting fish and meat dishes; and it's exceptionally good value (*yemistá* – stuffed vegetables – €4.40; chicken dishes €6). It's accessible by taxi from the centre. Daily 11am–midnight.

DRINKING AND NIGHTLIFE

Galero Platía Petiháki ☎ 28310 54345. Large beers, toasted sandwiches and snacks served on a terrace overlooking the Rimóndi Fountain right at the heart of the action make this one of the most popular places in town for tourists, and deservedly so. Daily 8am–2am.

Kenzo Platía Plastíra 4 ☎ 28310 51488. Music café with lively terrace favoured by the town's students. Similar stylish bars fill the rest of this square. Daily 9am–2am.

Nuvel Inner harbour ☎ 28310 52478. Chic café-bar with a large terrace by the harbourfront. Open all day, the music gets louder as night falls. Daily 9am–late.

Opera Club Salamínos 12 ☎ 6944 333 282. One of the town's bigger dance clubs with an eclectic mix of Greek and western rock and lots of strobe pyrotechnics; forms a bit of a nightlife hub with neighbouring *Ola Ellinika* and *Caramela* clubs. May–Oct daily 11pm–dawn; Nov–April weekends only.

Into the mountains

The main road south from Réthymno offers a fairly easy, flat drive towards Plakiás and the south coast (see opposite). There's far more of interest to be found by heading further east, into the foothills of the **Psilorítis range**. Here the **monastery of Arkádhi** is a popular and easy short trip. Beyond the monastery you can either head east towards Anóyia (p.221), a spectacular mountain drive, or south into the beautiful **Amári Valley**.

Monastery of Arkádhi

25km southeast of Réthymno • Daily: April–Oct 9am–7pm; Nov–March 9am–4pm • €2.50 • ☎ 28310 83135, ⦿ arkadimonastery.gr

The **Monastery of Arkádhi** is, for Cretans, a shrine to the struggle for independence. During the 1866 rebellion against the Turks, the monastery became a rebel strongpoint in which, as the Turks gained the upper hand, hundreds of Cretan independence fighters and their families took refuge. Surrounded and on the point of defeat, the defenders ignited a powder magazine just as the Turks entered the compound. Hundreds were killed, Cretan and Turk alike, and the tragedy did much to promote international sympathy for the cause of Cretan independence. Nowadays, you can peer into the roofless vault where the explosion occurred and wander about the rest of the well-restored grounds. The sixteenth-century **church** survived, and is one of the finest Venetian structures left on Crete.

HIKING THE AMÁRI VALLEY

A good base for touring the **Amári Valley** is Thrónos, a sizeable village at the valley's northern end with an inviting place to stay, *Aravanes* (see opposite). The proprietor here – Lambros Papoutsakis – is a keen walker and conducts guided treks (€20 /hr) around the valley and (for €70, including meals) to the peak of **Mount Psilorítis** (see p.221). His preferred approach is during the full moons of June, July and August, which avoids the extreme summer temperatures. It's not a difficult climb, but you'll need sturdy footwear and a sleeping bag. The summit is reached at around dawn, and the sunrise is always spectacular: on clear days the mountain offers a breathtaking view of the whole island.

Other hikes from Thrónos include a relatively easy path leading north through the foothills in a couple of hours to the monastery of Arkádhi (see above), or a variety of routes south into the valley.

The Amári Valley

The little-travelled route south via the **Amári Valley** is a delight. Although there's not a great deal specifically to see or do (a number of frescoed Byzantine churches are hidden away en route), it's an impressive drive under the flanks of the mountains and a reminder of how, in places, rural Crete continues to exist regardless of visitors. The countryside here is delightfully green even in summer, with rich groves of olive and assorted fruit trees, and if you **stay** you'll find that the nights are cool and quiet. It may seem odd that many of the villages along the way are modern: they were systematically destroyed by the German army in reprisal for the 1944 kidnapping of General Kreipe, and many have poignant roadside monuments commemorating those tragic events.

Spíli

The pleasant country town of **SPÍLI** is tucked beneath the mountains about 30km south of Réthymno. A popular lunch break for drivers and coach tours passing this way, it doesn't look much as you drive through. If you get off the main road, however, narrow alleys of ancient houses wind upwards from an attractive platía with a prodigious 25-spouted **fountain**. It's good hiking country too, and a peacefully rural place to stay once the day-trippers have moved on.

GETTING AROUND

INTO THE MOUNTAINS

By bus From Réthymno there are 3 daily buses (2 at weekends; 40min) to Arkádhi (as well as countless tours); 2 buses on weekdays to the village of Amári (5.30am & 2.30pm; 1hr); and 5 daily to Ayía Galíni that will drop you in Spíli (1hr).

By car Head east out of Réthymno before turning inland for Arkádhi and Amári. Watch out for the road layout

around the monastery: the Amári road passes the monastery on one side, the route east towards Anóyia on the other; they're connected only by the unpaved track through the monastery's car park. Spíli lies on the main road south of Réthymno; you can also reach it on a good new road that cuts across from the western edge of the Amári Valley.

ACCOMMODATION AND EATING

THRÓNOS

Aravanes Thrónos ☎ 28330 22760, 🌐 aravanes-rooms -taverna.gr. The stone-built *Aravanes* has stunning panoramic views across the valley to Mount Psilorítis. The owners rent five en-suite rooms with large balconies and run the attractive taverna below, together with a small shop selling mountain herbs and home-made honey; there's also advice on walking (see opposite) and maps of suggested hikes. €40

SPÍLI

Heracles Just off the main road ☎ 28320 22111, 🌐 heracles-hotel.eu. Friendly *pension* with spotless a/c

balcony rooms with TV and fridge; excellent breakfast (extra), and free wi-fi. The genial proprietor can advise on some superb walks in the surrounding hills, and rents out mountain bikes. He also has exceptionally well-equipped apartments, sleeping up to four, in his grandparents' newly converted house in the old part of town. Doubles €40; apartments €80

Plateia Fountain square ☎ 28320 22555, 🌐 spilicafe platia.gr. Pleasant taverna-café with an elevated terrace above the fountain and an excellent kitchen serving up traditional dishes such as *katsikaki krasatos* (kid in wine; €9.50) and *hortopitakia* (vegetable pies; €5). Daily 8am–midnight.

The south coast

The main road south from Réthymno heads straight out from the centre of town, an initially featureless drive across the middle of the island. About 20km out, two smaller roads cut off to the right for **Plakiás** and **Mýrthios**; the first via the **Kotsifóu gorge**, the second, slightly more direct route, following the course of the even more spectacular **Kourtaliótiko ravine**. The main road continues towards **Ayía Galíni** via Spíli (see above).

Plakiás

PLAKIÁS is the biggest attraction on Réthymno's south coast. A well-established resort, it's still a long way from the big league, with plenty of simple accommodation, few big hotels and a relatively young crowd. Don't come for sophisticated nightlife or for a picturesque white Greek island village: what you'll find is a lively, friendly place that makes a good base for **walks** in the beautiful countryside and is in easy reach of some great **beaches**. Among the best of these are three splashes of yellow sand, divided by rocky promontories, that together go by the name **Dhamnóni**, a thirty- to forty-minute walk away.

Mýrthios

The village of **MÝRTHIOS** hangs high above Plakiás, with wonderful views over the bay. There are few facilities beyond a couple of small shops and a post office, so you really need transport. You can, however, walk down to Plakiás, about twenty minutes steeply downhill, or to several of the nearby beaches – the walk back up is considerably tougher, though.

Préveli Monastery

11km east of Plakiás • April & May daily 9am–6pm; June–Oct Mon–Sat 9am–1.30pm & 3.30–9pm, Sun 8am–7pm; in winter, knock for admission • €3 • In summer 4 buses a day run from Réthymno, and 6 from Plakiás; you can also get here by taking a boat to Palm Beach from Plakiás or Ayía Galíni and climbing up – a strenuous 30min or so • ⓦ www.preveli.org

The celebrated **Moní Préveli**, perched high above the sea, is justifiably proud of its role in centuries of Cretan resistance, and famed above all for the shelter provided to Allied troops, many of them Australian, stranded on the island after the Battle of Crete in World War II. The monks supported and fed many soldiers and helped organize them into groups to be taken off nearby beaches by submarine. Today there's a monument to these events, a small museum, and scintillating sea views.

Palm Beach

Below Préveli Monastery • Constant boat tours from Plakiás and Ayía Galíni, or take the bus to Préveli and climb down; drivers can park in the Prevéli car park or in the valley 2km away, and walk down

A sand-filled cove at the mouth of the Kourtaliótiko gorge, where a stream feeds a little oasis complete with palm grove and cluster of oleanders, **Palm Beach** certainly looks beautiful – but for much of the year it's overwhelmed by visitors. Behind the beach, you can escape up the palm-lined riverbanks on foot or take a pedalo through the icy water. Further upstream, before the gorge becomes too steep to follow, are a couple of deep **pools** to swim in. On the beach, a small **bar-taverna** provides basic food and sells drinks, snacks and a few provisions. It's strange to think, as you bask on the crowded sands, that from here, in 1941, many of the Allied soldiers who sought refuge at Moní Préveli (see above) were evacuated by submarine.

Ayía Galíni

AYÍA GALÍNI is a picturesque place nestling in a fold in the mountains. Once an idyllic, isolated spot, it now swarms with package tourists throughout the season; the beach, a short walk to the east of town, can barely cope. Nonetheless there's something about Ayía Galíni that attracts a loyal following, and there are certainly plenty of excellent restaurants and bars, a lively nightlife scene, well-priced rooms and a friendly atmosphere that survives and even thrives on all the visitors.

GETTING AROUND   THE SOUTH COAST

By bus 5 buses a day connect Réthymno with Mýrthios and Plakiás (50min). In high season, there are also 4 buses a day from Réthymno to Préveli (50min) and 6 between Plakiás and Préveli (20min). Ayía Galíni has connections with both Réthymno (5 daily; 1hr 30min) and Iráklio (bus station B; 6 daily; 2hr).

ACTIVITIES

Boat trips Both Plakiás and Ayía Galíni have a wide choice of daily boat trips from their harbours, not just to Palm Beach but to a variety of other beaches and islets, as well as fishing and occasional dolphin-spotting trips.

FROM TOP SPINALÓNGA ISLAND (P.226); BYZANTINE CHURCH WEST OF IRÁKLIO >

Diving There's good diving around Plakiás; try Dive2gether (☎ 28320 32313, ⓦ dive2gether.com) or Kalypso Rocks Dive Centre (☎ 28310 74687, ⓦ kalypsodivecenter.com).

Horseriding Treks and lessons near Plakiás are offered by the Horse Riding Center (☎ 28320 31851, ⓦ crete horseriding.com; info at Alianthos Travel).

ACCOMMODATION

PLAKIÁS

Anna Plakias Apartments Inland, towards the youth hostel ☎ 6974 078 308, ⓦ anna-plakias.gr. Classy modern apartments and studios with a/c, free wi-fi and kitchenettes, plus a suite with a tiny swimming pool, in a quiet spot shaded by palm trees. **€45**

Gio-ma Western end of the seafront ☎ 28320 31942, ⓦ gioma.gr. In a prime position overlooking the harbour, these fabulously sited, if basic, rooms (with wi-fi, fridge and a/c) sit above the taverna of the same name, right on the water. Over the road are studios and two-room apartments, also with sea views. April–Oct. Rooms **€35**, apartments **€45**

Morpheas Apartments On the seafront, above Plakiás Market ☎ 28320 31583, ⓦ morpheas -apartments-plakias-crete-greece.com. Fine modern rooms, studios and duplex apartments with balconies overlooking the beach (although not all have sea view). Double-glazed against the potentially noisy location, with a/c, TV, fridge and, in the larger apartments, even a washing machine. Rooms **€38**, apartments **€60**

★**Youth Hostel** 500m inland, signed from the seafront ☎ 28320 32118, ⓦ yhplakias.com. The best hostel on Crete – friendly, relaxed and well run, in an attractively rural setting, with a terrace for breakfast and evening drinks and a busy social scene. Hot showers and wi-fi included. Dorms **€10**

MÝRTHIOS

★**Anna Apartments** Mýrthios ☎ 6973 324 775, ⓦ annaview.com. These classy apartments, built with traditional stone and wood, are beautifully furnished and have fantastic views over Plakiás Bay. All come with kitchenette, balcony, a/c, satellite TV and wi-fi. March–Nov. **€50**

AYÍA GALÍNI

Camping No Problem Behind the beach ☎ 28320 91386. Big campsite with a pool, shop and restaurant, with sandy, tree-shaded pitches. April–Oct. **€18**

Hariklia On entry road from Réthymno just before the descent ☎ 28320 91257, ⓦ hotelhariklia.gr. Delightful, spotless *pension* with good harbour views and en-suite a/c rooms with fridge. Guests also have use of kitchen to prepare breakfasts and snacks. Free wi-fi. **€35**

★**Minos** Entry road from Réthymno on left ☎ 28320 91292, ⓦ minos.agiagalini.com. Welcoming hotel with excellent refurbished a/c rooms with fridge, TV and room safe. Many enjoy the best sea views in town (cheaper rooms have partial views). Breakfast available. Free wi-fi. **€30**

Romantika Behind the beach ☎ 28320 91388, ⓦ romantika-kreta.gr. Attractive modern rooms and apartments, all with free wi-fi, satellite TV and a/c, just 30m from the beach. The complex also has a restaurant and crazy golf. Rooms **€45**, apartments **€60**

EATING AND DRINKING

PLAKIÁS

★**Medousa** At the eastern end of the inland street, near the back of the Alianthos Garden hotel ☎ 28320 31521, ⓦ medousa-plakias.com. A welcoming taverna (with good rooms) serving excellent traditional dishes and a special of the day that's usually delicious and unusual (like fried cod with beetroot garlic sauce, €8). Daily noon–3pm & 6.30–10.30pm.

Ostraco On the waterfront, close to the harbour. Long-established music bar set over two storeys and an upstairs terrace, with a rock-based playlist and fun atmosphere. Daily 9am–3am.

Sofia On the seafront near the harbour ☎ 28320 31226. The best of the tavernas right by the sea, with a slightly less touristy menu than some of its neighbours. House specials (€5.50–8) include Cretan *saganáki*, *kotópoulo Sofia* (pot-stewed chicken) and *piri-piri* (spicy oven-baked beef). Daily noon–midnight.

★**Tassomanolis** Facing west along the shore beyond the harbour ☎ 28320 31229. One of three or four good places around this end of the beach. Seafood is king here,

most of it caught by the proprietor from his own boat. Try the oven-baked *dorada* (bream, €22/kg) or their three-fish *souvláki*. Daily noon–midnight.

MÝRTHIOS

Taverna Plateia ☎ 28320 31560. This long-established taverna has arguably the most spectacular terrace view of any taverna on the island. A recent makeover hasn't affected the food: tasty Cretan cuisine with the odd creative twist. Traditional *mayiréfta* are the best bet: the likes of octopus *stifádho* or spicy *soutzoukákia* for around €8–9. It can get busy, especially at Sun lunchtimes, so turn up early if you don't want to wait (they don't accept bookings). Daily noon–11pm.

AYÍA GALÍNI

Onar Taverna Street ☎ 28320 91288. One of the best tavernas on this row, with a great rooftop terrace and views over the harbour, serving wholesome food; try their excellent charcoal-grilled fish and meat or specials such as meatballs with feta cheese (€6). Daily noon–1am.

To Petrino Just off the platía ☎ 28320 91504. Friendly little gem of an ouzerí whose proprietor is an ex-sea captain. Serves breakfast and coffee plus excellent mezédhes later in the day (selection €6.50), and retains some of the flavour of the pre-tourist days. Daily 8am–1pm & 4.30pm–midnight.

Yeoryioúpoli and around

To the west of Réthymno, the main road climbs for a while above a rocky coastline before descending to the sea, where it runs alongside sandy **beaches** for perhaps 14km. About 7km before Yeoryioúpoli, the beach widens and scattered hotel development appears along the coast. If you have your own vehicle, you'll come across plenty of places to stop for a swim, some with hardly anyone else around – but beware of some very strong currents.

On arriving in **YEORYOÚPOLI** (Georgioupolis) you'll find a place with a distinctly split personality: on the one hand it's a pretty **old town** by the river, with ancient eucalyptus trees shading the huge square in the centre; on the other it's a lively **package resort**, with development spreading further every year along the beach to the east of town. As long as you don't expect to find too many vestiges of traditional Crete, it's a very pleasant spot to pass a few days. Yeoryioúpoli's central beach is narrow and busy; walk east a few hundred metres for the quieter and wider sands.

Lake Kournás

Crete's only freshwater lake, **Lake Kournás**, shelters in a bowl of hills 4km inland from Yeoryioúpoli, 4km below the hilltop village of **Kournás**. As lakes go, it's small and shallow, but it nevertheless makes for an interesting excursion; for hikers there's a beautifully scenic route via the hamlet of **Mathés**. Spring, when the mountain views and profusion of wild flowers are stunning, is the best time to visit the lake; in high summer you could be in a completely different place, as the winter waters recede and the lake-shore "beach" is packed with umbrellas and sunloungers.

ARRIVAL AND DEPARTURE   **YEORYIOÚPOLI AND AROUND**

By bus Yeoryioúpoli is easily reached from both Réthymno and Haniá; the main-line buses, which run virtually hourly until midnight along the main highway, stop here.

ACTIVITIES

Boat trips Sofía Cruises (☎ 28250 61100) runs boat trips from the river just below the bridge: in particular "turtle trips" up the river (they're actually terrapins), or a day's outing to the beach at Maráthi, at the mouth of Soúdha Bay.
Cycling Adventure Bikes (☎ 28250 61830, ⓦ adventure bikes.org) organize easy bike tours all around the western end of the island with transport to get you up the steep bits.
Horseriding Horse rides along the beach or treks into the local countryside can be booked through local travel agencies, or direct with Zoraïda's (☎ 28250 61745, ⓦ zoraidas-horseriding.com).

ACCOMMODATION AND EATING

YEORYIOÚPOLI

Anna On the old road west of town across the river ☎ 28250 61556, ⓦ annashouse.gr. Spectacular new rooms and fully equipped apartments around a full-size pool, with all facilities including free wi-fi, café and pool bar. Breakfast available. March–Nov. €80
Babis On the cross street between the square and the beach ☎ 28250 61760. Traditional taverna with good-value, simple Cretan food; try their excellent rabbit *stifádho* (€7.50). Daily 11am–midnight.
Sunlight Seafront, just east of the centre ☎ 28250 61396, ⓦ sunlight-geo.gr. Modern apartment complex that's ugly from the outside, but friendly and comfortable within, with good sea-view balconies and rooms for 2 to 6 people with free wi-fi. It also has an inexpensive beachfront taverna where breakfast (extra) is served. April–Oct. €45
Zorba's Close to the square on the road towards the church ☎ 28250 61381, ⓦ zorbashotel.gr. Larger than average a/c rooms and apartments above a good taverna. The rooms come with kitchenette, the family apartments with a complete kitchen, and there's a tiny courtyard swimming pool. Breakfast included. April–Oct. Rooms €55, apartments €65

KOURNÁS

★**Kali Kardia** Main street, Kournás village ✆ 28250 96278. Popular taverna serving some of the best lamb (€8) and sausages (€6) in the province, together with tasty *souvláki* and super salads – and don't forget to try their noted *galaktoboúreko* dessert, a lemony egg-custard pudding. May–Oct daily 9am–11pm; Nov–April weekends only (same hours).

Korissia North end of the lake ✆ 28250 61653, ⓦ kournas-lake-apartments.gr. Superbly sited taverna-rooms place with a/c lake-view balcony rooms; in Aug (when prices double) it's well away from the worst of the crowds, with its own beach and paddle-boat rentals. The food is also some of the best around the lake, especially spit-roasted meats on the barbecue (from €8). Mosquitoes can be a problem, as anywhere around the lake. **€20**, half board **€40**

Western Crete

Although tourist development is spreading fast, and has already engulfed much of the coast around the city of Haniá, Crete's westernmost quarter is still one of the emptier parts of the island, partly because there are few beaches suited to large resort hotels, and partly because the great archeological sites are a long way from here. In their place are some of the classic elements of the island: scattered coves, unexploited rural villages, and a spectacular vista of mountains.

Haniá (Chania) itself is the most enjoyable of Crete's larger towns, littered with oddments from its Venetian and Turkish past, and bustling with harbourside life. The coast around the city is not particularly exciting; if you want beaches head for the south coast or the far west. Here, **Paleóhora** is the only place which could really be described as a resort, and even this is on a thoroughly human scale; others are emptier still. Elsewhere on the south coast, **Ayía Rouméli** and **Loutró** can be reached only on foot or by boat; **Hóra Sfakíon** sees hordes passing through but few who stay; **Frangokástello**, nearby, has a beautiful castle and the first stirrings of development. Behind these lie the **White Mountains** (Lefká Óri) and the famed walk through the **Samariá Gorge**. In the far west, great beaches at **Falásarna** and **Elafonísi** are mostly visited only as day-trips.

Haniá

HANIÁ, as any of its residents will tell you, is spiritually the capital of Crete, even if the political title was long ago passed back to Iráklio. It is also the island's most attractive city, especially if you can catch it in spring, when the White Mountains' snowcapped peaks seem to hover above the roofs. Although it is for the most part a modern place, you might never know it as a tourist. Surrounding the harbour is a wonderful jumble of **Venetian streets**, a maze-like old town contained by ancient city walls and littered with Ottoman, Byzantine and Minoan ruins.

The harbour

The **harbour** area is at its busiest and most attractive at night, when the lights from bars and restaurants reflect in the water and crowds of visitors and locals turn out to promenade. By day, things are quieter. Straight ahead from Platía Sindriváni (also known as Harbour Square) lies the curious domed shape of the **Mosque of the Janissaries**, built in 1645 (though heavily restored since) and the oldest Ottoman building on the island. It is usually open for some kind of temporary exhibition. Further east, on the inner harbour, the arches of sixteenth-century **Venetian arsenals**, a couple of them beautifully restored, survive alongside remains of the outer walls.

The Naval Museum and Exhibition of Traditional Shipbuilding

Mon–Sat 9am–5pm, April–Oct also Sun 10am–6pm • Naval Museum €3, Exhibition €2, joint ticket €4 • ⓦ mar-mus-crete.gr

A hefty bastion at the western end of the harbour houses Crete's **Naval Museum**, while one of the Arsenali at the opposite, eastern end of the harbour is home to the museum's **Exhibition of Traditional Shipbuilding**. The former displays model ships and other naval

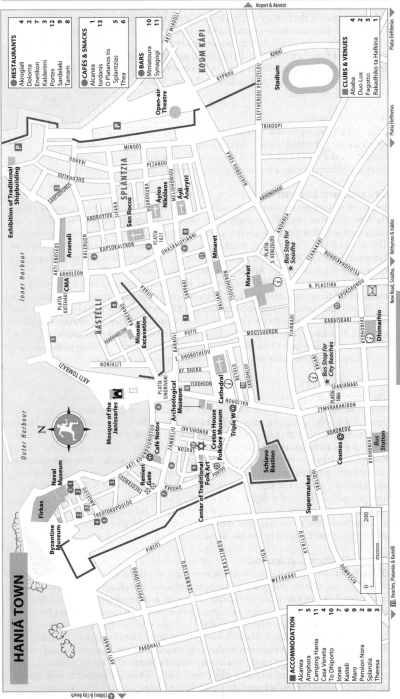

HANIÁ TOWN

RESTAURANTS

Akrogiali	4
Doloma	2
Enetikon	7
Kalderimi	3
Portes	12
Sardelaki	9
Tamam	8

CAFÉS & SNACKS

Alcanea	1
Iordanis	13
O Platanos tis	
Splantziás	5
Thea	6

BARS

Miniatoura	10
Synagogi	11

CLUBS & VENUES

Ababa	4
Duo Lux	2
Fagotto	3
Rakadhiko ta Halkina	1

ACCOMMODATION

Alcanea	1
Amphora	5
Camping Hania	11
Casa Veneta	4
To Dhiporto	10
Ionas	7
Kasteli	6
Maro	9
Pension Nora	2
Splanzia	8
Theresa	3

ephemera tracing the history of Greek navigation, plus a section on the 1941 Battle of Crete which has fascinating artefacts and poignant photos depicting the suffering here under the Nazis. From the **Fírkas**, the fortress behind the museum, the modern Greek flag was first flown on Crete, in 1913. The highlight of the Exhibition is a reconstruction of a fifteenth-century BC **Minoan ship**. This was rowed to Athens for the start of the 2004 Olympics and, with the vast boat shed itself, it easily outshines the rest of the exhibits.

Byzantine Museum

Theotokopóulou 78 • Tues–Sun 9am–4pm • €2, combined ticket with Archeological Museum €3 • ☎ 28210 96046

The **Byzantine Museum**, in the Venetian chapel of San Salvatore, has a tiny but beautifully displayed collection of mosaics, icons, jewellery, coins, sculpture and everyday objects, giving a fascinating insight into an era that's largely overlooked.

City walls and backstreets

From the waterfront west of the Byzantine Museum, Odhós Pireós cuts inland outside the best-preserved stretch of the **city walls**, which are impressive, weighty and threatening. Following them on the inside is rather trickier, but far more enjoyable. This is where you'll stumble on some of the most picturesque little alleyways and finest Venetian houses in Haniá, and also where the pace of renovation and gentrification is most rapid. The arch of the **Renieri Gate** is particularly elegant. There are also interesting art and craft stores here, around Theotokopóulou and in the many alleys that lead off the outer harbour. Haniá's renovated **synagogue** (Mon–Thurs 10am–5pm, Fri 10am–3pm; free; ⓦetz-hayyim-hania.org), fifteenth-century Etz Hayyim, lies down one such alley, a poignant reminder of a Jewish population that was entirely wiped out in 1944. Nearby at Skúfon 20, is the **Centre of Traditional Folk Art & Culture**, which is actually a shop but feels more like a museum and displays the amazing embroideries created by the owner, some of which are worth thousands of euros.

Kastélli and Splántzia

The section of the old town behind the inner harbour is far less touristy, though is rapidly being colonized by boutique hotels, chic restaurants and alternative bars. The little bluff rising behind the mosque is **Kastélli**, site of the earliest habitation in Haniá. Archeologists believe that they may have found the remains of a Minoan palace, the "lost" city of **Kydonia**, in the excavations being carried out – and open to view – along Kanevárou. It's also here that you'll find traces of the oldest **walls**; there were two rings, one defending Kastélli alone, a later set encompassing the whole of the medieval city. The adjoining area to the east, still known by its Turkish name of **Splántzia**, is full of unexpected architectural delights, with carved wooden balconies and houses arching across the street at first-floor level. Many of the streets between here and the inner harbour have been re-cobbled and refurbished, and they're among the most atmospheric and tranquil in the old town.

Odhós Hálidhon and around

Odhós Hálidhon is perhaps the most touristy street in Haniá, and the major junction at the inland end (Platía 1866) marks the centre of town as well as anywhere. If you stand facing north at this junction, everything in front of and below you is basically the old, walled city; behind and to either side lie the newer parts. To the east, **Odhós Yiánnari** leads past the **market** and eventually out to the main road or onto the Akrotíri peninsula, while to the west, **Skalídhi** leads out of town towards Kastélli Kissámou. Ahead of you, Hálidhon descends to the harbour and into the heart of the old town; some 70m from the junction is the animated **Odhós Skridhlóf** ("Leather Street"), where, traditionally, leather-makers plied their trade. While the shops are now geared to tourists, prices for leather sandals, bags and the like remain the best in Crete.

4

Archeological Museum

Odhós Hálidhon 28 • Tues–Sun 8am–3pm • €2, combined ticket with Byzantine Museum €3 • ☎ 28210 90334

Haniá's **Archeological Museum** is housed in the Venetian-built church of San Francesco. The building has been substantially restored and contains a fine display, covering the local area from Minoan through to Roman times. In the courtyard garden a huge fountain and the base of a minaret survive from the period when the Ottomans converted the church into a mosque; around them are scattered various other sculptures and architectural remnants.

Cretan House Folklore Museum

Odhós Hálidhon 46b • Mon–Fri 9am–3pm & 6–9pm, Sat & Sun 9am–3pm • €2 • ☎ 28210 90816

The **Cretan House Folklore Museum** is a cluttered collection of artefacts, tapestries and traditional crafts equipment set out in a replica of a "traditional" house (though few can have been quite so packed). On your way out, take a look at Haniá's elegant **Roman Catholic church** in the same hidden courtyard.

The beaches

Áyii Apóstoli, Khrissi Akti and Kalamáki are accessible on city bus #21 from Platía 1866, while Áyía Marína, Kalathás and Stavrós are served by KTEL buses from the main station

Haniá's beaches lie to the west of the city and on the Akrotíri peninsula to the northeast. The **city beach** (Néa Hóra) is no more than a ten-minute walk west, following the shoreline from the Naval Museum, but for more expansive beaches you're better off heading further west along the coast to the beaches of **Áyii Apóstoli**, **Khrissi Akti** and **Kalamáki**. Further afield there are even better beaches at **Áyía Marína** (see p.253) to the west, or **Kalathás** and **Stavrós** (p.253) out on the Akrotíri peninsula.

4

ARRIVAL AND DEPARTURE   HANIÁ

By plane Haniá Airport (Chania) lies 15km northeast of the city on the Akrotíri peninsula. As well as international scheduled and charter flights, there are domestic services from/to Athens (6 daily; 50min) and Thessaloníki (2 daily; 1hr 15min) with Aegean (🌐 aegeanair.com) and Ryanair (🌐 ryanair.com). Local buses run to the city (roughly hourly 5am–11pm; €2.30), and a taxi will cost about €20. The driving route into Haniá is pretty clear: for all other destinations it's quicker and easier to take the left turn signed to Soúdha at the roundabout some 7km from the airport; this will take you down past the head of Soúdha Bay and out onto the main E75 highway, bypassing Haniá's congestion.

By ferry Arriving by ferry, you'll dock about 10km east of Haniá at the port of Soúdha: take a bus (every 15min; 20min; €1.60) or taxi (around €12) to the city; KTEL buses to Réthymno and Kastélli also meet most ferries. If you're stuck in Soúdha you can find just about everything you need on the square right by the ferries, but it's not an attractive place. Ferry tickets are available from the ANEK office on Venizélou, opposite the market (☎ 28210 27500; 🌐 anek.gr), or any travel agent. There are daily overnight sailings to Pireás (8–9hr), with extra daytime sailings in July and Aug.

By bus The bus station is on Kydhonías, an easy walk from the centre; you'll find info at 🌐 e-ktel.com or 🌐 bus-service-crete-ktel.com.

Destinations Elafonísi (1 daily at 9am; 2hr 15min); Falásarna (3 daily; 1hr 30min); Hóra Sfakíon (2 daily 8.30am & 2pm; 1hr 40min); Iráklio via Réthymno (hourly; 3hr); Kastélli (15 daily; 45min); Omalós (Samariá Gorge; 3 daily 6.15am–8.45am; 1hr 40min); Paleóhora (4 daily; 2hr); Soúyia (3 daily until 2pm; 1hr 45min); Stavrós (7 daily; 25min).

GETTING AROUND AND INFORMATION

By car, motorbike or bicycle For car rental try around the top of Hálidhon, where Tellus, Hálidhon 108 (☎ 28210 91500, 🌐 tellustravel.gr) is one of many. Alianthos is another reliable outlet (☎ 28320 32033, 🌐 alianthos-group.com) with offices at the airport and in Áyía Marína. Summertime, Dhaskaloyiánni 7 and other local branches (☎ 28210 45797, 🌐 strentals.gr), has a huge range, including cars, motorbikes and good bikes.

By taxi The main taxi ranks are on Platía 1866 and at the bottom of Karaiskáki, just off Yiánnari. For radio taxis call ☎ 18300, ☎ 28210 94300/98700.

Tourist office Milonoyiánni 53, at the side of the town hall (Mon–Fri 8.30am–2.30pm; ☎ 28210 41665, 🌐 chania tourism.com). In summer there are information booths on Platía Mitropóleos and in front of the market (July–Sept daily 10am–1.30pm).

TOURS AND ACTIVITIES

Boat trips A number of boats run trips from the harbour (around €15 for 2hr), mainly to the nearby islands of Áyii Theódori and Lazarétta, for swimming and *kri-kri* (ibex) spotting: alternatives include sunset cruises and all-day trips to the Rodhopoú peninsula.

Diving Blue Adventures Diving, Dhaskaloyiánni 69 (☎ 28210 40403, ⓦ blueadventuresdiving.gr), runs daily diving and snorkelling trips.

Waterpark Limnoupolis ⓦ limnoupolis.gr.

ACCOMMODATION

There are thousands of rooms to rent in Haniá, as well as a number of excellent boutique hotels. Even so you may face a long search for a bed at the height of the season. Perhaps the most desirable rooms are those overlooking the **harbour**, which are sometimes available at reasonable rates: this is often because they're noisy at night. Places further back are likely to be more peaceful: **Theotokopóulou** and the alleys off it make a good starting point. In the eastern half of the old town, rooms are far more scattered and in the height of the season your chances are often better over here. Dozens of small rooms places can be found at ⓦ chaniarooms.gr.

HARBOUR AREA

★**Alcanea** Angélou 2 ☎ 28210 75370, ⓦ alcanea .com. Gorgeous eight-room boutique hotel in a historic building beside the Naval Museum. Rooms come with all facilities including free wi-fi, satellite TV and iPod docks, with Nespresso machines and traditional seats in the communal areas. The pricier rooms (at least twice the price of the most basic) have stunning views and balconies. Excellent breakfast included. March–Dec. **€75**

★**Amphora** 2 Párodhos Theotokopóulou 20 ☎ 28210 93224, ⓦ amphora.gr. Hotel in a beautifully renovated fourteenth-century Venetian building, with spiral staircases and four-poster beds. Balcony rooms (such as Room 20) with harbour view are the best value; those without a view are cheaper. Free wi-fi. April–Oct. **€100**

Casa Veneta Theotokopóulou 57 ☎ 28210 90007, ⓦ casa-veneta.gr. Well-equipped, comfortable a/c studios and apartments, some with balcony, behind a Venetian facade. Free wi-fi in reception area and an exceptionally helpful proprietor. April–Oct. **€55**

Maro Párodhos Portoú 5 ☎ 28210 54981. Probably the cheapest rooms in the old town, hidden away in a quiet, unmarked alley off Portoú not far from the Schiavo Bastion. Rooms come with free wi-fi, a/c and fridge; basic, but friendly and clean. **€30**

Pension Nora Theotokopóulou 60 ☎ 28210 72265, ⓦ pension-nora.com. Charming a/c rooms in a refurbished wooden Turkish house. Also appealing studios (same price) in a building nearby. Nice café below. **€40**

Theresa Angélou 8 ☎ 28210 92798, ⓦ pensiontheresa .gr. Beautiful old *pension* in a great position with stunning views from its roof terrace and some rooms; classy decor too, and a kitchen for guests' use. Very popular, so book ahead. Free wi-fi. **€50**

THE OLD TOWN

Ionas Sarpáki, cnr Sórvolou ☎ 28210 55090, ⓦ ionas hotel.com. Small boutique hotel in a lovingly restored Venetian mansion in Splántzia. Very comfortable rooms and beautiful architectural detail. April–Oct. **€85**

★**Kasteli** Kanevárou 39 ☎ 28210 57057, ⓦ pension chania.com. Comfortable, reasonably priced *pension*, very quiet at the back. All rooms come with a/c, fridge and wi-fi. The proprietor is very helpful and also has a few studios, apartments and a couple of beautiful houses to rent nearby. **€50**

★**Splanzia** Dhaskaloyiánni 20 ☎ 28210 45313, ⓦ splanzia.com. Attractive and friendly boutique hotel in an elegantly refurbished Venetian mansion, with stylish rooms, some with four-poster beds draped with mosquito net, and free wi-fi. Breakfast, included, is served in a pretty courtyard. **€95**

To Dhiporto Betólo 41 ☎ 28210 40570, ⓦ todiporto.gr. The "Two Doors" runs between Betólo and pedestrian Skridhlóf: the balcony rooms over the latter, especially, are quiet. Friendly and good value, with a/c, TV, fridge and coffee machine in the rooms. Free wi-fi. **€40**

CAMPING

Camping Hania Behind the beach in Áyii Apóstoli, 5km west of the city ☎ 28210 31138, ⓦ camping -chania.gr. A rather small site, hemmed in by new development, but with a pool and all the usual facilities, just a short walk from some of the better beaches, and a regular local bus to town. May–Oct. **€18**

EATING

The harbour is encircled by a succession of pricey **restaurants**, **tavernas** and **cafés** which are usually better for a drink than a meal. Away from the water, there are plenty of more interesting possibilities.

CAFÉS AND SNACKS

Alcanea Angélou 2 ☎ 28210 75377. Appealing terrace bar with great harbour view beneath the hotel of the same name; it's good for breakfast, coffee and mezédhes and, after sunset, cocktails and Cretan wines. Occasional live acoustic music at night. March–Dec daily 8am–2am.

Iordanis Bougatsa Apokorónou 24 ☎ 28210 88855. Specializes in traditional *bougátsa* (creamy cheese pie served warm and sprinkled with sugar and cinnamon) to eat in or take away. Mon–Sat 6am–2.30pm, Sun 6am–1.30pm.

O Platanos tis Splantzias Platía 1821 ☎ 28210 58930. Retro café-bar-ouzéri on this quiet square that serves interesting Thai food and snacks alongside more traditional mezédhes. April–Oct daily 8am–2am.

Thea Platía Sindriváni ☎ 28210 73377. Café-bar overlooking the harbourside crowds from a first-floor terrace, for peaceful people-watching. Daily 9am–3am.

RESTAURANTS

★**Akrogiali** Aktí Papanikolí 19, Néa Hóra ☎ 28210 73110. Opposite the city beach, with a summer terrace, this excellent, reasonably priced fish and seafood taverna is well worth the 15min walk or short taxi ride. Always packed with locals, so may be worth booking – though there are plenty of alternatives along the same street. Daily lunch and dinner.

Doloma Kapsokalývon 5, behind the Arsenali ☎ 28213 01008. Fine little taverna set back off the street, with a shady terrace, serving well-prepared and economical Cretan dishes with good local wine. Mains such as rice-stuffed tomatoes or *pastítsio* from €4. April–Oct noon–11pm.

Enetikon Zambelíou 57 ☎ 28210 88270, ⓦ enetikon

-crete.gr. A very good taverna whose proprietor is a wine buff and where the house wine comes from the excellent Lyrarakis vineyard in Pezá. The food is also top-notch and anything with lamb is recommended: try the *árni me stamnágathi* (lamb with chicory €8.50). April–Oct daily 11am–midnight.

Kalderimi Theotokopóulou 53 ☎ 28210 76741. A little gem of a place serving traditional Cretan dishes such as lamb *tsigariastó* with fried potatoes (€10.80) or *bouréki* (cheese, potato and courgette pie, €7). Occasional live traditional music too. Mon–Sat noon–1am.

★**Portes** Portoú 48 ☎ 28210 76261. A small group of restaurants nestles under the walls along Portoú. *Portes* is smarter than most, with a particularly adventurous menu, plenty of veggie options and delicious daily specials putting a modern twist on age-old dishes: roast chicken with saffron hazelnuts and honey (€7.50), stuffed courgette flowers (€5.50), spicy meatballs with couscous (€8). Mon–Sat noon–1am, Sun 5pm–1am.

Sardelaki Dhaskaloyiánni 33 ☎ 28210 08880. Exceptional fish and seafood, keenly priced, at this on-trend place at the heart of a newly fashionable area, where young locals hang out at a series of bars, restaurants and ouzerí. Go for the catch of the day, or there's an excellent *Psarósoupa* (fish soup, €5.50) or Okhtapódhi Krasáto (octopus in red wine €8.50). Mon–Sat noon–midnight.

Tamam Zambelíou 49 ☎ 28210 96080. Popular place where the adventurous Greek menu includes much vegetarian food, with added spices giving an eastern flavour. The original restaurant is housed in an old Turkish baths, while opposite is a less atmospheric annexe. The tables squeezed into the alley between the two are very cramped, and you're likely to be jostled by the passing crowds. Mains from €6. Daily noon–12.30am.

DRINKING AND NIGHTLIFE

The harbour area contains dozens of beautifully set but touristy **bars**; locals tend to head to the fringe of the old town. In summer the action moves to the vibrant **club** scene in the resorts west of town.

Ababa Isodhíon 12. Funky bar with childishly colourful decor, open all day, offering snacks, books and board games; chilled sounds and cocktails in the evening through to the early hours. Daily 10am–late.

Duo Lux Sarpidhónos 8 ☎ 28210 52515. Comfy café-bar in a street full of similar places, just off the inner harbour; regular DJs and club nights inside after midnight. Daily 10am–late.

★**Fagotto** Angélou 16 ☎ 28210 71877. Cosy, atmospheric backstreet jazz bar housed in an impressively restored Venetian mansion. Great cocktails, and high-quality live performances in season. Daily 8pm–late.

Miniatoura Daliáni 4 ☎ 6979 526 340. Tiny bar, with cocktails and good music, set in an ancient, arched stone vault,

at the heart of the latest nightlife hotspot. Daily 8pm–4am.

★**Rakadhiko ta Halkina** Aktí Tombázi 29–30 ☎ 28210 41570, ⓦ chalkina.com. Live Cretan music every evening, though the place doesn't really liven up till well after midnight, when the locals start to dance. There's also good meze (mixed plates €5–7) and wine, but it's the traditional music everyone comes for. Hugely popular, but they can usually squeeze you in somewhere. Daily noon–late, music from 9pm.

Synagogi Párodhos Kondhiláki, between Kondhiláki and Skúfon ☎ 28210 95242. Taking its name from the restored synagogue next door, this is a beautiful open-air bar set in a bombed-out Venetian mansion. Good music and cocktails, too. Daily 1pm–3am.

4

SHOPPING

Stores aimed at tourists are mainly found in the old town, especially **jewellery** and **souvenirs** on Hálidhon and all around the harbour, plus **leather** goods on Skridhlóf. Around the junction of Hálidhon and Yiánnari and down towards the market you'll find pharmacies, newspaper stores, photographic shops and banks, and there's a sizeable **supermarket** at the top of Pireós, close to the Schiavo Bastion.

Centre of Traditional Folk Art & Culture Skúfon 20 ☎ 28210 92677. A wonderful place that feels more like a museum than a shop, displaying the astonishing embroideries made by the owner, some of which fetch thousands of euros. April–Nov daily 10.30am–7pm.

Haniá market Odhós Yiánnari, with another entrance on Tsoudherón. Haniá's market, an imposing and rather beautiful cross-shaped structure, has some interesting souvenirs among the stalls of meat, fish and veg. Mon–Sat 8am–2pm.

Mediterraneo Bookstore Aktí Koundouriótou 57, near the Naval Museum, ☎ 28210 86904. Impressively stocked bookshop, with lots of English-language titles. Daily 8am–11pm.

Street market Minöos. There's a fabulous weekly street market inside the eastern city wall, where local farmers sell their produce. Sat mornings.

DIRECTORY

Banks and exchange The main branch of the National Bank of Greece, with ATMs, is opposite the market. There's a cluster of banks with more ATMs around the top of Hálidhon, and lots of out-of-hours exchange places on Hálidhon, in the travel agencies.

Internet Good internet cafés include: Triple W, Odhós I. Baladhinou just off Hálidhon; Café Notos, Aktí Koundouriótou 31 under the *Hotel Lucia*; and Cosmos, on Koronéou near the bus station. Most bars and many restaurants have free wi-fi.

Laundry Service washes at Old Town Laundromat, Karaóli 40 (Mon–Fri 8am–3pm & 6–9pm, Sat 8am–3pm; cheap self-service at easywash, Dhaskaloyiánni 8 (daily 7am–midnight).

Post office The main post office is on Odhós Péridhou just off Kydhonías (Mon–Fri 7.30am–8pm, Sat 9am–1pm).

Around Haniá

Northeast of Haniá, the **Akrotíri peninsula** loops around, protecting the magnificent anchorages of the Bay of Soúdha. On its northeast coast are a number of coves and **beaches**, above all sandy **Kalathás** and spectacular **Stavrós**. Inland you can visit the monasteries of **Ayía Triádha** and **Gouvernétou**.

West of Haniá, the E75 speeds you towards Kastélli with little to see along the way. The **old road**, meanwhile, follows the coastline through a string of small towns and growing resorts. Occasionally it runs right above the water, more often 100m or so inland, but never more than easy walking distance from the sea. There are hotels and apartments the whole way, but the first real resort area starts at **Káto Stalós**, which runs into **Ayía Marína** and then into **Plataniás** without a break, creating the most built-up, touristy strip in the west of the island.

Monastery of Ayía Triádha

Akrotíri peninsula, 2km north of the airport • Daily: summer 8am–sunset; winter 8am–2pm & 4pm–sunset • €2 • ⓦ agiatriada-chania.gr

The majestic three-domed **Ayía Triádha** monastery, established in the seventeenth century and built in Venetian style, is one of the few on Crete to preserve real monastic life to any degree. Its imposing ochre frontage is approached through carefully tended fields of vines and olive groves – all the property of the monastery, which now bottles and markets its own wine and organic olive oil. Inside, you can wander freely around the shady complex, and visit the church and a small museum.

Gouvernétou and Katholikó monasteries

4km north of Ayía Triádha • Easter–Oct Mon, Tues & Thurs 9am–noon & 5–7pm, Sat & Sun 9–11am & 5–8pm; Oct–Easter afternoon hours are 4–7pm • Free • Gouvernétou is enclosed within a compound – leave any transport at the gate and approach on foot; a path beyond Gouvernétou continues 1km to Katholikó

Gouvernétou is one of the oldest monasteries on Crete, dating to around 1537, and it's an isolated, contemplative and strict place; visitors are expected to respect

FESTIVAL ISLAND

The Cretans love a *glendi* (party) and **festivals** are celebrated with plenty of eating, drinking, live music and dancing. Here are some of those which celebrate local harvests (check locally for specific dates):

Chestnut Festival Élos and Prásses, West Crete, end of Oct. The village squares are packed with tables and chairs as the villages celebrate the local chestnut harvest with eating, drinking, dancing, and roast chestnuts, of course.

Sardine Festival Néa Hóra, Haniá. The first Mon in Sept is the date for this annual festival at the small harbour by the town beach, with plentiful free fish and wine, and local musicians and dancers.

Sultana Festival Sitía, in Aug. The region is well known for its sultana production, and the harvest is celebrated with traditional Cretan music and dance in the main square, accompanied by food and wine.

Tsikoudiá (Raki) Festival Haniá, Iráklio, Sitía and Voukoliés, mid-Oct and early Nov. At the end of the grape harvest the must-residue from the wine press is boiled and distilled to make *tsikoudiá*, the local fire water. Hot *tsikoudiá*, with an alcohol content as high as 60 percent, is scooped from the vats and proffered in shot glasses, and so the merriment begins.

this. From the outside, where two towers stand guard, the monastery looks like a fortress; inside there's a refreshingly shaded patio, ancient frescoes in the church and a tiny museum. Beyond Gouvernétou a steep path heads down a craggy ravine towards the sea, passing the ruined **monastery of Katholikó**, the island's most ancient, abandoned long ago following repeated pirate raids. It's an exceptional place, surrounded by caves where there's evidence of still earlier Christian and pre-Christian worship.

Stavrós

Akrotíri peninsula, 15km northeast of Haniá • 7 daily buses from the city (25min)

Stavrós beach is superb if you like the calm, shallow water of an almost completely enclosed lagoon; this one sits right beneath the imposing "Zorbas" mountain (the cataclysmic climax of *Zorba the Greek* was filmed here). It's not very large, so it does get crowded, but rarely overpoweringly so. There's a makeshift café/*kantína* on the beach, and a couple of tavernas across the road.

Ayía Marína

AYÍA MARÍNA, 8km west of Haniá, is a developed resort of some size, known locally for its beach bars and clubs, which attract hordes of young locals and tourists late into the summer nights. The west end of the long sandy beach is quieter and there are good **watersports** facilities here, including jet skiing and paragliding. Just offshore is **Theodorou** island, said to be a sea monster petrified by Zeus before it could swallow Crete. Seen from the west, its "mouth" still gapes open.

The Samariá Gorge

May–Oct 7am–sunset, weather conditions permitting, last entry to hike through 3pm • €5 • ☎ 28210 67179

The 18km hike down the spectacular **SAMARIÁ GORGE**, which claims to be Europe's longest, is one of the most popular day-trips on the island; still better if you make it part of a longer excursion to the south. Although often crowded it's not a walk to be undertaken lightly, particularly in the heat of summer; it's strenuous – you'll know all about it next day – the path is rough, and walking boots or sturdy trainers are vital, as is plenty of water.

The **gorge** begins at the *xylóskalo*, or "wooden staircase", a stepped path plunging steeply down from the southern lip of the Omalós plain. The descent is at first through almost alpine scenery: pine forest, wild flowers and greenery – a verdant shock in the spring, when the stream is at its liveliest. About halfway down you pass the abandoned village of **Samariá**, now home to a wardens' station, with picnic facilities and toilets. Further down, the path levels out and the gorge walls close in until, at the narrowest point (the *sidherespórtes* or "iron gates"), you can practically touch both tortured rock faces at once and, looking up, see them rising sheer for well over 300m.

At an average pace, with regular stops, the walk down takes between five and seven hours (though you can do it quicker). Beware of the kilometre markers; these mark only distances within the **National Park** and it's a further 2km of hot walking before

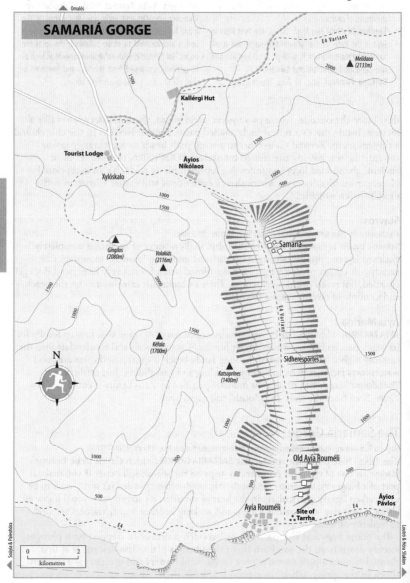

SAMARIÁ GORGE

Omalós

E4 Variant

Melídaou (2133m)

Kallérgi Hut

Tourist Lodge

Áyios Nikólaos

Xylóskalo

Samariá

Gíngilos (2080m)

Volakiás (2116m)

E4 Variant

Kéfala (1700m)

Sidherespórtes

Katsoprínes (1400m)

Old Ayía Rouméli

Ayía Rouméli

Site of Tarrha

Áyios Pávlos

E4

E4

N

0   2
kilometres

Soúyia & Paleochóra

Loutró & Hóra Sfakíon

you finally reach the sea at **Ayía Rouméli** (see p.256). On the way down there is usually plenty of water from springs and streams, but nothing to eat. The park that surrounds the gorge is a refuge of the Cretan wild ibex, the *krí-krí*, but don't expect to see one; there are usually far too many people around.

Omalós

OMALÓS lies in the middle of the mountain plain from which the Samariá Gorge descends. The climate is cooler here all year round and the many paths into the hills surrounding the plateau are a welcome bonus; in spring a profusion of wild flowers and birdlife is to be seen. There are plenty of **tavernas** and some surprisingly fancy **rooms** with all facilities, should you want to stay overnight to get an early start into the gorge. Another significant advantage to staying up here would be if you wanted to undertake some other **climbs** in the White Mountains; the **Kallérgi mountain hut** (☎28210 44647 or ☎6976 585 849, ⓦkallergi.net; €12/person) is about ninety minutes' hike (signed) from Omalós or the top of the gorge.

ARRIVAL AND DEPARTURE	THE SAMARIÁ GORGE

WITH A TOUR
Tours to the Samariá Gorge run from virtually everywhere on the island: they involve a very early bus to the top, walk down by early afternoon, boat from Ayía Rouméli to Hóra Sfakíon and bus from there back home.

BY PUBLIC TRANSPORT
Buses to the gorge You can take regular buses to the top of the gorge from Haniá (3 daily at 6.15am, 7.45am & 8.45am), or marginally less straightforwardly from Soúyia (daily at 7am) or Paleóhora (daily at 6.15am). Early-morning buses from Iráklio and Réthymno connect at Haniá. Be sure

to buy a return ticket if you're coming back the same day.
Ferries from Ayía Rouméli Once at Ayía Rouméli, at the bottom of the gorge, you'll see a kiosk selling boat tickets as you approach the beach; there are ferries (ⓦanendyk .gr) to Loutró/Hóra Sfakíon (May–Oct at least 3 daily; 40min/1hr) and Soúyia/Paleohóra (April–Oct daily 5.30pm; 45min/1hr 20min). Alternatively you can walk to any of these on the coastal path.
Return buses Return bus journeys from Hóra Sfakíon (at 6.30pm) or Soúyia (at 6.15pm) are timed to coincide with the ferries and will wait for them – theoretically, no one gets left behind.

ACCOMMODATION AND EATING

Wardens ensure that no one remains in the gorge overnight, where camping is strictly forbidden. The nearest accommodation is at Omalós, where there are several options: those below offer lifts to the top of the gorge in the morning.

Hotel Exari Omalós village ☎28210 67180, ⓦexari.gr. Impressive new, stone-built hotel with comfortable balcony rooms with TV and a decent restaurant. Free wi-fi in bar. Daily 6am–midnight. **€30**
Hotel Neos Omalos Omalós village ☎28210 67269,

ⓦneos-omalos.gr. Perhaps the pick of the hotels in Omalós, and certainly the busiest taverna, this has pleasant balcony rooms with bath, central heating, satellite TV and free wi-fi. Daily 7am–10pm. **€35**

The Sfakiá Coast

The ancient capital of the Sfakiá region, **Hóra Sfakíon**, lies 70km south of Haniá, reached via a spectacular twisting road over the mountains. It's the main terminus for gorge walkers, with a regular boat service west along the coast to **Ayía Rouméli** and **Loutró**, both accessible only on foot or by boat. **Frangokástello**, with its castle and sandy **beaches**, lies a few kilometres east of Hóra Sfakíon.

Hóra Sfakíon

HÓRA SFAKÍON sees thousands of people passing through daily; those who have walked Samariá Gorge come striding, or staggering, off the boat from Ayía Rouméli to pile onto waiting coaches. Relatively few stay, although there are plenty of great-value **rooms** and some excellent waterfront **tavernas**. Though there are a couple of pebbly coves, what is missing in Hóra Sfakíon is a decent **beach**; to get to one, you could walk

4

WALKS AROUND THE SFAKIÁ COAST

Many people arrive at this part of Crete by walking down the Samariá Gorge, but that's just the start of the local hiking possibilities; there are other **gorges** with far fewer people and infinitely more sense of adventure, plus a **coastal path** linking all the settlements as far as Paleóhora and the island's western tip.

ARÁDHENA AND ÍMBROS

The two most accessible local gorges are Arádhena, west of Loutró, and Ímbros, east of Hóra Sfakíon. The classic **Arádhena** walk is to climb up from Loutró, back and forth across an intimidating-looking cliff face, to Anópoli, and from there by a broad track to the top of the gorge, where there's a spectacular bridge and bungee jump. The descent into the gorge is on an impressive, ancient stone path, but this soon runs out and it's quite a rugged descent to Mármara beach, where you should be able to pick up a boat back to Loutró. It's about 11km to Mármara, or at least 6 hours. **Ímbros Gorge** (April–Oct 8am–sunset; €2) is rather more straightforward. The walk starts from the village of Ímbros on the main Hóra Sfakíon road, easily reached by bus, car or taxi; it's a well-marked and relatively easy 3hr hike down to the village of Komitádhes, above the coast 5km from Hóra Sfakíon. You can either walk this last bit, hitch, or take a local taxi.

THE COASTAL PATH

The **coastal path** is well-marked and well-used, which is not to say it's easy: there's little shelter from a relentless summer sun, and in places it's intimidatingly narrow and uneven. The most travelled and most straightforward section is **between Loutró and Hóra Sfakíon** – about 8km (2hr) – with an inviting swimming spot halfway at Sweetwater beach. West from **Loutró to Ayía Rouméli** is twice as far and significantly tougher, though again there are potential swim stops, and seasonal tavernas, at Mármara beach and the chapel of Áyios Pávlos.

(or for much of the year take an excursion boat) west to **Sweetwater**; there are also numerous opportunities for a dip along the coast road east towards Frangokástello and beyond.

Loutró

Of all the south coast villages, **LOUTRÓ** perhaps best sums up what this coast ought to be all about. It's a soporific place, where there's nothing to do but eat, drink and laze – and where you fast lose any desire to do anything else. The big excitements of the day are the occasional arrivals and departures of the ferries. Loutró itself has beautifully clear water but not much of a beach; if you're prepared to walk, however, there are plenty of lovely **beaches** along the coast in each direction; these can also be reached by hired **canoe**, and some (particularly Sweetwater to the east and Mármara to the west) by regular excursion boats.

Ayía Rouméli

AYÍA ROUMÉLI, the small coastal settlement at the end of Samariá Gorge, is visited daily by hundreds of weary walkers for whom the sea is a welcome shimmering mirage after their long hike. After an iced drink, a plunge in the sea to cool the aching limbs, and lunch at one of the cluster of tavernas, there's nothing much else to stay for, although if you miss the last boat there are plenty of **rooms** to choose from.

Frangokástello

FRANGOKÁSTELLO, 14km east of Hóra Sfakíon, is named after a four-square, crenellated thirteenth-century **castle** (May–Oct daily 10am–8.30pm; €1.50) isolated below a chiselled wall of mountains. Though impressive from a distance, at close quarters the castle turns out to be a bare shell, with little to see inside. There's a lovely, fine-sand **beach** immediately below the castle, and marginally less attractive sands spreading in each direction. Behind them has sprung up a rather straggling resort, with no real centre but plenty of decent places to stay and to eat.

GETTING AROUND

By bus There are buses from Hóra Sfakíon to Haniá (3 daily at 7am, 11am & 6.30pm; 1hr 45min).
By boat There are ticket booths for the local ferries (ⓦanendyk.gr) close to the departure points in all the coastal villages. Boat trips run to local beaches from both

THE SFAKIÁ COAST

Loutró and Hóra Sfakíon, where you can also hire taxi-boats.
Destinations from Hóra Sfakíon Gávdhos (2–3 weekly; 3hr); Loutró/Ayía Rouméli (May–Oct at least 3 daily; 20min/1hr).
Destinations from Ayía Rouméli Soúyia/Paleohóra (April–Oct daily 5.30pm; 45min/1hr 20min).

ACCOMMODATION AND EATING

HÓRA SFAKÍON
Finding food is never a problem in Hóra Sfakíon, and the excellent seafront tavernas have a good array of vegetarian options. There's little to choose between them, though you'll find cheaper cafés and takeaway places on the east side of the bay, towards the ferry jetty.
Stavris ⓣ 28250 91220, ⓦ hotel-stavris-sfakia-crete .com. A variety of en-suite rooms and studios, all with balconies, increasing in price as you add a/c, kitchenette, or sea views, plus smarter apartments on the edge of town. Free wi-fi in bar. **€35**
Xenia ⓣ 28250 91202, ⓦ xeniacrete.com. This former state-owned hotel, now refurbished, has the best location in town with amazing views across the Libyan Sea. All rooms have a/c, fridge, satellite TV and balcony with sea view. **€50**

LOUTRÓ
★**Blue House** ⓣ 28250 91035, ⓦ bluehouse.loutro .gr. One of the original places here, and still one of the

friendliest and best. Good-value a/c, sea-view rooms with fridge, plus superior rooms in a wonderful (more expensive) top-floor extension. Free wi-fi and some of the best food in town at the taverna downstairs. April– Oct. **€40**
★**Nikolas** ⓣ 28250 91352. Virtually the last building in Loutró and probably the quietest you'll find; friendly proprietors rent simple but comfortable a/c rooms at the back and some lovely top-floor a/c balcony rooms with fridge above the water. Free wi-fi. April–Oct. **€38**

AYÍA ROUMÉLI
Calypso Western end of the village ⓣ 28250 91314, ⓦ calypso.agiaroumeli.gr. Simple, airy rooms with a/c, fridge, TV and balcony, most with sea view. The restaurant is one of the quieter spots, serving the usual suspects – oven-baked lamb, stuffed aubergines, *moussaká* (from €5) – on a sea-view terrace. April–Oct daily from breakfast to dinner. **€40**

Kastélli and the far west

Apart from being Crete's most westerly town, and the end of the main coastal highway, **KASTÉLLI** (Kíssamos, or Kastélli Kissámou, as it's variously known) has little obvious appeal. It's a bustling place with a long seafront, a rather rocky strand to the east and a small sandy **beach** to the west. This very ordinariness, however, has real charm: life goes on pretty much regardless of outsiders, and there's every facility you might need. The town was important in antiquity, when the Greco-Roman city-state of **Kísamos** was a major regional power.

To the west of Kastélli lies some of Crete's loneliest and, for many visitors, finest coastline. On the far western tip, **Falásarna** has beautiful beaches and ancient ruins, while **Elafonísi's** "pink" beaches and lagoon lie in the southwest corner; the spectacular

MILIÁ: AN ECOTOURIST VILLAGE
Off the inland route south from Kastélli towards Paleóhora lies **Miliá** (ⓣ 28210 46774, ⓦ milia.gr), an abandoned hamlet of stone houses that has been restored by a cooperative of local people and is now a wonderful eco-retreat. The cottages (€75, breakfast included) have only solar power and candles, while the taverna uses organic local ingredients. Visitors are welcome to get involved in the life of the farm, and there are cookery courses and other **activities** – you can even help make *raki* at the village's still. Otherwise you can walk in the nearby hills – the easier paths are signed – or simply contemplate the natural surroundings; nights up here are truly magical.

4

coastal road connecting them has little development along the way, just a couple of villages high above rocky coves. Other main routes south over the mountains head to the small town of **Paleóhora** and to the laidback seaside village of **Soúyia**.

The Archeological Museum

Platía Tzanakáki • Tues–Sun 8.30am–3pm • €3 • ☎ 28220 83308

Kastélli's superb **Archeological Museum** houses stunning Roman-era **mosaics**; mosaic production was a local speciality, and many more are being excavated around town. Other exhibits include prehistoric and Minoan relics from excavations in the town and from nearby ancient Polyrínia.

Falásarna

The ruins of an ancient city and port are ignored by most visitors to **FALÁSARNA** in favour of some of the best beaches on Crete, wide and sandy with clean water, though far from undiscovered. There's a handful of **tavernas** and an increasing number of **rooms** for rent, and plenty of people **camp** out here too. Although the beach can occasionally be afflicted by washed-up tar and discarded rubbish, this doesn't detract from the overall beauty of the place. Crowds of locals on summer weekends can always be escaped if you're prepared to walk, and the beaches are worth it.

Sfinári and Kámbos

A little-travelled and wildly spectacular road follows Crete's western coastline, with just a couple of spots where there's any development at all. **SFINÁRI** is a sleepy village with a number of rooms to rent on the road down to a quiet pebble beach, that's sandy in patches. At the bottom is a cluster of tavernas which offer free sunloungers to customers.

KÁMBOS is similar, but even less visited. Its stony beach is a good hour's walk down a well-marked gorge path – a branch of the E4 – starting from the village square. Alternatively there's a steep asphalted track, which is driveable.

Moní Khrysoskalítissa

5km north of Elafonísi • Daily 8am–8pm • €2 • ☎ 28220 61261

Moní Khrysoskalítissa (the Monastery of the Virgin of the Golden Step), is a weathered, white-walled nunnery beautifully sited on a rocky promontory with marvellous views along the coastline. There may have been a Minoan shrine on this spot, and the earliest church was built in a cave in the thirteenth century. Look out today for a much-venerated thousand-year-old icon of the Virgin, a small **museum**, and the **golden step** (*hrissí skála*), one of the ninety leading up to the monastery, which appears gold only to those who are pure of spirit.

Elafonísi

The tiny uninhabited islet of **Elafonísi** shelters an almost tropical lagoon, where white sand tinged pink by coral borders aquamarine waters. The water is incredibly warm, calm and shallow and the islet itself is a short wade across the sandbar.

The arrival of crowds to the beach has brought lines of loungers, but little else in the way of infrastructure: there are stalls selling cold drinks and basic food, along with portable toilets and an incongruous phone box. If you're here on a day-trip, the best option is to bring your own picnic.

Paleóhora

The only real resort in the southwest, **PALEÓHORA** retains an enjoyably end-of-the-line feel, helped by extensive sands and the fact that there are no big hotels. Other than head for the beach, eat and drink, there's not a great deal to see or do here, which of course is a major part of its attraction. Built across the base of a narrow peninsula with a harbour and pebble beach on the eastern side, wide sands on the west, Paleóhora is overlooked by the ruins of its Venetian fortress. In the evening the narrow main street closes to traffic so diners can spill out of the restaurants and bars onto tables set out in the road.

Soúyia

A small village slowly on its way to becoming a resort, **SOÚYIA** is not a particularly attractive place on first sight, but it does grow on you. Its best feature is an enormous swathe of bay with a long, grey pebble beach and sparkling clear water. At the far end of this bay most summers there's something of a nudist and camping community – known locally as the Bay of Pigs. Otherwise, sights are few – the local church has a sixth-century Byzantine mosaic as the foundation, although most of it is in Haniá's archeological museum – but there are a couple of fabulous walks: down the beautiful **Ayía Iríni Gorge** or a wonderful hour-long hike over to the nearby ancient site of **Lissós**, with its temples and mosaics.

ARRIVAL AND DEPARTURE

By bus Frequent buses ply the main road between Haniá and Kastélli, with onward connections from there to the far west; Paleóhora and Soúyia have direct connections with Haniá but not Kastélli. For more info, see ⓦe-ktel.com or ⓦbus-service-crete-ktel.com.

Destinations from Kastélli Haniá (15 daily; 45min); Elafonísi (May–Sept 1 daily at 10am, returning 5pm; 1hr 20min); Falásarna (May–Sept 3 daily; 40min).

Destinations from Paleóhora Elafonísi (May–Sept 1 daily 10am, returning 4pm; 1hr 30min); Haniá (4 daily; 1hr 30min); Soúyia (2 daily 1pm & 5.15pm; 1hr).

KASTÉLLI AND THE FAR WEST

Destinations from Soúyia Elafonísi (May–Sept 1 daily 9am, returning 4pm; 1hr 30min); Haniá (3 daily 7.15am–6.15pm; 1hr 45min); Paleóhora (2 daily 9am & 6.15pm; 1hr).

By ferry Kastélli's port is 3km west of town; ferries (ⓦlane.gr) depart four times a week to Andikýthira (2hr) and Kýthira (4hr), continuing once a week each to Yíthio (7hr) and Kalamáta (9hr 30min) in the Peloponnese, once to Pireás (24hr). There's a daily morning ferry (ⓦanendyk .gr) from Paleóhora to Ayía Rouméli (1hr 20min) via Soúyia (30min); on Mon and Wed this continues to Gávdhos (6hr).

INFORMATION AND TOURS

Tourist office The only official tourist office in the region is in Paleóhora, behind Pebble Beach (June–Sept daily except Tues 10am–1pm & 6–9pm; ☎ 28230 41507).

Tours and boat trips Daily boat trips (ⓦgramvousa .com) run from Kastélli port to the beautiful beaches at Gramvoússa and Bálos Bay, at the far northwestern tip of Crete; there are also a variety of boat trips from Paleóhora, including daily runs to Elafonísi and dolphin spotting. Walking with Strata Tours (☎ 28220 24249; ⓦstratatours .com).

ACCOMMODATION AND EATING

KASTÉLLI

Argo Western end of central seafront ☎ 28220 23322, ⓦpapadakisargo.gr. Simply furnished rooms on the central seafront with a/c, TV, fridge and balconies with sea view. April–Oct. €40

Maria Beach On the western beach ☎ 28220 22610, ⓦmariabeach.gr. The best location in town, right on the sandy beach, for a couple of separate buildings housing well-equipped modern a/c rooms, studios and apartments; breakfast included in rates for rooms, not for apartments. Free wi-fi. April–Nov. Rooms €55, apartments €60

Papadakis Western end of the seafront promenade ☎ 28220 22340. There are plenty of good tavernas along Kastélli's waterfront, but Papadakis is one of the most consistent, with decent, reasonably priced seafood (as well as good veggie and meat dishes; mains around €8) and courteous service. You can also bring your own wine. Daily noon–midnight.

FALÁSARNA

Sunset By the car park, at the end of the road ☎ 28220 41204, ⓦsunset.com.gr. With an enviable location, right above the beach, and a good taverna, the long-established *Sunset* has a lot going for it, though some of its rooms (a/c, with balcony) could do with modernization. They also have very basic seafront apartments and, nearby, luxurious two-storey stone villas overlooking the sea. Free wi-fi. April–Oct. Rooms/ apartments €40, villas €180

ELAFONÍSI

Rooms Elafonisi ☎ 28220 61274, ⓦelafonisi-resort .com. Probably the best of Elafonísi's few rooms places, with its own taverna and minimarket, and a/c balcony rooms with fridge and sea view. Also some attractive apartments and villas nearby. April–Oct daily 8am–midnight. €40

PALEÓHORA

Anonymous Homestay In a backstreet off Venizélos ☏ 28230 41509, ⊚ cityofpaleochora.gr. Among the least expensive places in town, and something of a travellers' meeting place. Simple rooms, with use of a communal kitchen, off a charming garden courtyard, plus two two-bedroom apartments. A/c €5 extra. Rooms €25, apartments €50

Camping Grammeno 4km along the coast to the west ☏ 28230 42125, ⊚ grammenocamping.gr. The better of two local campsites (though further from town), this is a friendly place with youthful management and close to an attractive beach. Free wi-fi. €17.50

Caravella Seafront, just south of the ferry jetty ☏ 28230 41131, ⊚ caravella.gr. Paleóhora's best seafood restaurant, with locally caught fish, priced by weight – try the *kathári* (black snapper) – and excellent local *hyma* (barrelled wine). They also serve some meat, plus a daily selection of *mayireftá*. April–Nov daily 9am–11.30pm.

★**Castello Rooms** Overlooking the southern end of Sandy Beach ☏ 28230 41143. Exceptionally friendly place, most of whose simple rooms come with a/c and fridge and have balconies overlooking the beach; a few rooms at the back without view are less expensive (singles available too), and you can still get the views from the terrace taverna. Free wi-fi. €37

★**Oriental Bay** Northern end of Pebble Beach ☏ 28230 41322. With an inviting, tamarisk-shaded terrace fronting the sea, *Oriental Bay* serves some of the best traditional food in town, with daily specials such as roast chicken with lemon and garlic sauce, stuffed courgette flowers or "granny's meatballs" for €5–6. There's occasional live music and also fresh juices and breakfasts. Daily noon–11pm.

The Third Eye Inland from Sandy Beach ☏ 28230 42223, ⊚ thethirdeye-paleochora.com. Excellent vegetarian restaurant run by a Greek-New Zealand couple. Sometimes brusque service, but great food and flavours rarely seen on Crete, from curries to *gado-gado* and bean salads, as well as more conventional Greek dishes; mains around €7. There are regular concerts of *lyra*, Greek and Asian music in summer. Daily 8am–3pm & 5.30–11.30pm.

Villa Marise and Europa Studios North end of Sandy Beach ☏ 28230 83018, ⊚ villamarise.com. Two separate seafront blocks with a variety of well-equipped, a/c rooms, studios and apartments for up to six people, and direct access to the beach. The pool at the *Europa* is open to all guests. Rooms €50, apartments €80

SOÚYIA

★**Captain George** Signed off the main street ☏ 28230 51133, ⊚ sougia.info/hotels/captain_george. Clean and comfortable rooms, studios and apartments, set in gardens a few hundred metres from the beach, with a/c, balcony, TV, fridge and kettle (kitchenette in studios/ apartments). The owner also runs local boat trips. March–Nov. €41

Santa Irene Seafront ☏ 28230 51342, ⊚ santa-irene .gr. Smart, modern studios and apartments in a great waterfront location, all with a/c, TV, kitchenette and balcony (some with sea view). €60

Syia Main street ☏ 28230 51174, ⊚ syiahotel.com. Incongruously chic, boutique-style hotel; the most comfortable studios and apartments in town, if not the most beautiful surroundings. Free wi-fi. Breakfast included. April–Oct. €70

Rembetiko Halfway up the main street ☏ 28230 51510. Home-cooked traditional dishes including plenty of vegetarian options such as rice-stuffed tomatoes and peppers (€5), and meat reared on their own farm, are served on a pleasant garden terrace. Daily 1pm–midnight.

Gávdhos

GÁVDHOS, some 50km of rough sea south of Crete, is the southernmost island in Greece (and Europe if you don't count Spain's Canary Islands). Gávdhos is small (about 10km by 7km) and barren, but it has one major attraction: the enduring **isolation** which its inaccessible position has helped preserve. If all you want is a beach and a taverna that will grill you some fish, this remains the place for you. There's a semi-permanent community of campers and would-be "Robinson Crusoes" on the island year-round, swelling to thousands in August – but just six indigenous families.

Most people choose to base themselves near to one of the three largest beaches; at the most popular of all, **Sarakíniko**, there are several beachfront tavernas and cafés and a few rooms places. **Áyios Ioánnis**, 2km to the northwest, boasts a thriving hippy-type community of nudist campers. The third, quieter choice is pebbly **Kórfos**, south of the port and capital at **Karabé**.

ARRIVAL AND DEPARTURE

By ferry In windy or bad weather the ferry will not operate, so don't plan to leave the day before your flight home. Sometimes people are stranded here for days, even in mid-summer. There are high-season departures from Hóra Sfakíon on Tues, Thurs & Sun at 10.30am, and from Paleóhora via Soúyia and Ayía Rouméli on Mon & Wed at 8.30am; return sailing at 2.30pm same day; check the current timetable at ⓦ anendyk.gr.

GETTING AROUND AND INFORMATION

By bus An ancient bus (€2) meets the ferry and makes the trip to Sarakiníko and Áyios Ioánnis beaches, with a return trip from the beaches about 1hr before the ferry departs. The same bus offers an afternoon tour of the island (€5) in summer.

By mopeds or car Gavdos Travel (☎ 28230 42458), on the road behind the beach at Sarakiníko, rents cars (around €35–40/day plus petrol) and mopeds (around €15–20/day including petrol; cash only).

Services There are well-stocked minimarkets at Sarakiníko and Áyios Ioánnis, but no banks on the island so remember to bring plenty of cash with you.

ACCOMMODATION AND EATING

If you turn up in Aug without a booking you may well find yourself camping on the beach. Travel agents in Paleóhora or Hóra Sfakíon can arrange **rooms**.

Consolas Gavdos Studios Sarakíniko ☎ 28230 42182, ⓦ gavdostudios.gr. A collection of rooms and studios on the hillside above the bay, with kitchen, fridge and terrace. They will pick you up from the ferry if you've prebooked. Satellite TV and internet are available at their taverna. **€45**

Vailakakis (Gerti & Manolis) Sarakíniko ☎ 28230 41103, ⓦ gavdos-crete.com. Simple a/c rooms (with 24hr power) and rather fancier stone-built houses for four to six people. It also has probably the best food on the beach, with excellent, good-value seafood caught daily by Manolis himself. Also a minimarket selling essentials and basics. **€40**

Yiorgos and Maria's Kórfos ☎ 28230 42166. Spotless en-suite a/c rooms with showers in this friendly, family-run taverna-rooms place. They'll collect you from the harbour if you ring ahead. The taverna serves excellent fish and other local dishes on a terrace overlooking the beach. Daily 9am–11pm. **€35**

4

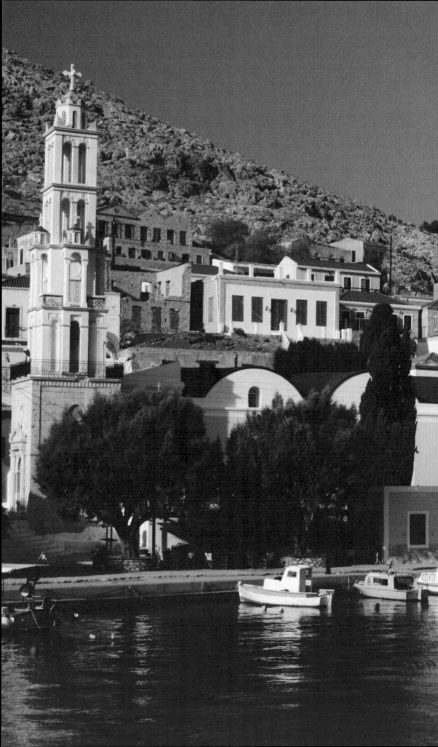

The Dodecanese

HALKI - QUAYSIDE

5

The Dodecanese

Curving tightly against the Turkish coast, almost within hailing distance of Anatolia, the Dodecanese (Dhodhekánisos) are the furthest island group from the Greek mainland. They're hardly a homogeneous bunch. The two largest, Rhodes (Ródhos) and Kos, are fertile giants where traditional agriculture has almost entirely been displaced by a tourist industry focused on beaches and nightlife. Kastellórizo, Sými, Hálki, Kássos and Kálymnos, on the other hand, are essentially dry limestone outcrops that grew rich enough from the sea – especially during the nineteenth century – to build attractive port towns. Níssyros is a real anomaly, created by a still-steaming volcano that cradles lush vegetation, while Kárpathos is more variegated, its forested north grafted onto a rocky limestone south. Tílos, despite its lack of trees, has ample water, Léros shelters soft contours and amenable terrain, and further-flung Pátmos and Astypálea offer architecture and landscapes more reminiscent of the Cyclades.

Major Dodecanese attractions include the beaches on Rhodes and Kos; the wonderful medieval enclave of Rhodes Old Town; the gorgeous ensemble of Neoclassical mansions that surrounds the harbour on Sými; the rugged landscapes of Kálymnos, Kárpathos and Níssyros; the cave and monastery on Pátmos, where St John had his vision of the Apocalypse; and the hilltop village of Hóra on Astypálea. Each island has its own subtler pleasures, however; every visitor seems to find one where the pace of life and friendly ambience strike a particular chord.

Thanks to their position en route to the Middle East, the Dodecanese – too rich and strategic to be ignored, but never powerful enough to rule themselves – have had a turbulent history. The scene of ferocious battles between German and British forces in 1943–44, they only joined the modern Greek state in 1948 after centuries of rule by Crusaders, Ottomans and Italians.

That historical legacy has given the islands a wonderful blend of **architectural styles** and **cultures**; almost all hold Classical remains, a Crusaders' castle, a clutch of vernacular villages and whimsical or grandiose public buildings. For these last, the Italians, who held the Dodecanese from 1912 to 1943, are responsible. Determined to turn them into a showplace for Fascism, they undertook ambitious public works, excavations and reconstruction.

GETTING AROUND   THE DODECANESE

The largest islands in the group are connected by regular ferries and catamarans, as well as flights; only Kastellórizo, Tílos and Astypálea are relatively difficult to reach. Rhodes is the main transport hub, with connections for Crete, the northeastern Aegean and the mainland too. The fastest, most useful connections are provided by twin catamarans, the *Dodekanisos Express* and the *Dodekanisos Pride*, which follow a busy schedule between Rhodes, Pátmos and other islands in the chain; see ⑫ 12ne.gr.

Windsurfing at Prassoníssi p.281	Hiking on Télendhos p.332
Hiking in northern Kárpathos p.296	Italian architecture in the
Hiking on Sými p.302	Dodecanese p.334
Hiking on Níssyros Island p.311	Saint John on Pátmos p.341
Hippocrates p.318	Hóra Festivals p.342
Sponges and sponge diving p.328	Miracle of Lipsí p.345

RHODES OLD TOWN

Highlights

❶ Rhodes Old Town One of Europe's most magnificently preserved medieval towns. See p.269

❷ Lindos Acropolis, Rhodes Occupied for over 3000 years, this hilltop citadel enjoys great views over the town and coast. See p.278

❸ Northern Kárpathos Old walking trails thread through a spectacular mountainous landscape to reach isolated villages. **See p.295**

❹ Sými Graceful Neoclassical mansions soar to all sides of Sými's gorgeous harbour. **See p.297**

❺ Níssyros Volcano Explore the still-bubbling craters of the volcano that created the island. See p.312

❻ Bros Thermá, Kos Relax in shoreline hot springs which flow into the sea, protected by a boulder ring. See p.320

❼ Hóra, Astypálea Wrapped around a beautiful Venetian kástro, the windswept island capital perches proudly above the sea. See p.325

❽ Télendhos islet, Kálymnos Whether admired at sunset from western Kálymnos, or visited via local ferries, beach-fringed little Télendhos should not be missed. See p.332

❾ Hóra, Pátmos With its fortified monastery dedicated to St John of the Apocalypse, this is the Dodecanese's most atmospheric village. See p.342

HIGHLIGHTS ARE MARKED ON THE MAP ON P.266

5

Rhodes

Rhodes (**Ródhos**) is deservedly among the most visited of all Greek islands. Its star attraction is the beautiful **medieval Old Town** that lies at the heart of its capital, Rhodes Town – a legacy of the crusading Knights of St John, who used the island as their main base from 1309 until 1522. Elsewhere, the ravishing hillside village of **Líndhos**, topped by an ancient acropolis, should not be missed. It marks the midpoint of the island's long

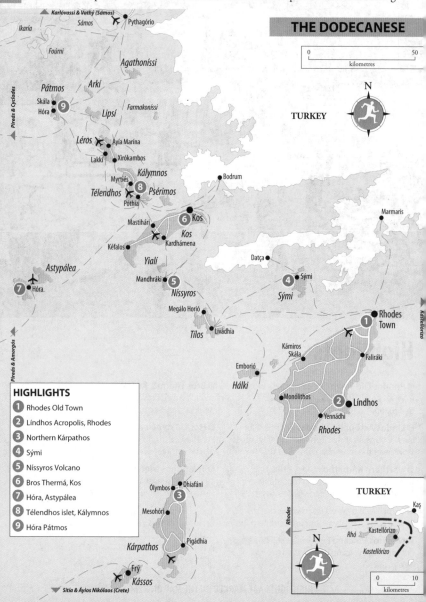

THE DODECANESE

0   50
kilometres

N

TURKEY

Karlóvassi & Vathý (Sámos)

Ikaría
Sámos   Pythagório
Foúrni

Agathoníssi

Pátmos   Arkí
Skála   **9**   Farmakoníssi
Hóra   Lipsí

Léros   Ayía Marína
Lakkí   Xirókambos

Myrtiés   Kálymnos   Bodrum
Télendhos   **8**   Psérimos
Póthia

Mastihári   **6**   Kos
Kos
Kéfalos   Kardhámena
Yialí

Astypálea   Mandhráki   **5**   Datça   **4**   Sými
7   Hóra   Níssyros   Sými

Megálo Horió
Tilos   Livádhia   **1**   Rhodes Town

Kámiros
Skála   Faliráki

Emborió   Monólithos   **2**   Líndhos
Hálki   Yennádhi
Rhodes

HIGHLIGHTS

1. Rhodes Old Town
2. Líndhos Acropolis, Rhodes
3. Northern Kárpathos
4. Sými
5. Níssyros Volcano
6. Bros Thermá, Kos
7. Hóra, Astypálea
8. Télendhos islet, Kálymnos
9. Hóra Pátmos

Ólymbos   Dhiafáni
3
Mesohóri
Pigádhia

Kárpathos

Frý
Kássos

Sitía & Áyios Nikólaos (Crete)

TURKEY
Kaş
Rhó   Kastellórizo
Kastellórizo

N

0   10
kilometres

Pireás & Cyclades

Pireás & Amorgós

Rhodes

Kastellórizo

5

eastern shoreline, adorned with numerous sandy **beaches** that have attracted considerable resort development. At the southern cape, **Prassoníssi** is one of the best windsurfing spots in Europe. If you want to escape the summer crowds, take a road trip into the island's craggy and partly forested interior: worthwhile targets include the castles near **Monólithos** and **Kritiniá**, and frescoed churches at **Thárri**, **Asklipió** and **Áyios Yeóryios Várdhas**.

Brief history

Blessed with an equable climate and strategic position, Rhodes, despite its lack of good harbours, was important from the very earliest times. The finest natural port served the ancient town of **Lindos** which, together with the other Dorian city-states **Kameiros** and **Ialyssos**, united in 408 BC to found a new capital, **Rodos** (Rhodes), at the windswept northern tip of the island. The cities allied themselves with Alexander, the Persians, Athenians or Spartans as conditions suited them, generally escaping retribution for backing the wrong side by a combination of seafaring audacity, sycophancy and burgeoning wealth as a trade centre. Following the failed siege of Macedonian general Demetrios Polyorketes in 305 BC, Rhodes prospered even further, displacing Athens as the major venue for rhetoric and the arts in the east Mediterranean.

Decline set in when the island became involved in the Roman civil wars and was sacked by Cassius; by late imperial times, it was a backwater. The Byzantines ceded Rhodes to the Genoese, who in turn surrendered it to the Knights of St John. After the second great **siege** of Rhodes, in 1522–23, when Ottoman Sultan Süleyman the Magnificent ousted the stubborn knights, the island once again lapsed into relative obscurity, though heavily colonized and garrisoned, until its seizure by the Italians in 1912.

ARRIVAL AND DEPARTURE
RHODES

BY PLANE
Rhodes' airport lies on the island's west coast, 14km south-west of Rhodes Town, alongside Paradhísi village. Buses to and from town stop between the two terminals (turn left out of arrivals; frequent services 6.30am–midnight; €2.30). A taxi ride into town should cost around €22.

Destinations Astypálea (2–3 weekly); Athens (4–5 daily); Iráklio (Heraklion), Crete (1 daily); Kos (2 weekly); Léros (2–3 weekly); Thessaloníki (1 daily); Kárpathos (1–2 daily); Kássos (1 daily); Sitía (1 daily).

BY FERRY
Ferries to Rhodes use three separate harbours in Rhodes Town. Large boats dock at Akándia, catamarans at Kolóna, immediately outside the Old Town, while smaller vessels and excursion craft use the yacht harbour of Mandhráki facing the New Town.

Ticket offices Triton Tours (Plastria 9; ☎ 22410 21690, ⊛ tritondmc.gr), can book all ferry, hydrofoil and day-trip tickets; ANES (88 Australis St; ☎ 22410 37769, ⊛ anes.gr), for catamarans and hydrofoil to Sými; Dodhekanisos

Seaways have a kiosk at their departure point in Kolóna Harbour (☎ 22410 70590, ⊛ 12ne.gr); Tsangaris (☎ 22410 36170) for GA boats; Skevos (111 Amerikis St; ☎ 22410 22461, ⊛ www.bluestarferries.gr), for Blue Star; Zorpidhis (☎ 22410 20625) for LANE; and Stefanakis, Alex Diakou St, for Sea Star.

Destinations Anafi (1–2 weekly; 17hr); Astypálea (1 weekly; 9hr 10min); Crete (1–2 weekly; 12hr 30min); Hálki (3–4 weekly; 1hr 25min–2hr); Kálymnos (1–2 daily; 2hr 40min–8hr 15min); Kárpathos (2–3 weekly; 5hr); Kássos (2–3 weekly; 6hr 30min); Kastellórizo (3 weekly; 2hr 20min–3hr 40min); Kos (2–3 daily; 2hr 10min–6hr 15min); Léros (1–2 daily; 4hr–5hr 15min); Lipsí (6 weekly; 5hr 10min–8hr 20min); Milos (1 weekly; 23hr); Níssyros (4 weekly; 3hr 10min–4hr 45min); Pátmos (1 daily; 4hr 45min–9hr 45min); Pireás (1–2 daily; 12hr 30min–17hr); Santoríni (4–5 weekly; 7–20hr); Sitía (1–2 weekly; 9hr 20min); Sými (3–4 daily; 50min–1hr 40min); Sýros (3 weekly; 9hr); Tílos (4 weekly; 1hr 20min–2hr 15min). The tiny port at Kámiros Skála, 45km southwest of Rhodes Town, is used only by regular boats to Hálki (daily except Sun; 1hr 15min).

INFORMATION AND ACTIVITIES

Tourist offices The municipal tourist office is at Platía Rimínis, just north of the Old Town (June–Sept Mon–Sat 7.30am–9.30pm, Sun 9am–3pm; Oct–May daily 7.30am–3pm). A short walk from here up Papágou, on the corner of Makaríou, the Greek National Tourist Office (Mon–Fri 8.30am–2.45pm) dispenses bus and ferry schedules.

Scuba diving For scuba diving, contact Waterhoppers (⊛ waterhoppers.com) at Mandhráki quay; as well as running beginners' courses in the bay at Kallithéas beach, they offer more challenging deep-wall dives at Ladhikó, just south of Faliraki, and near Líndhos.

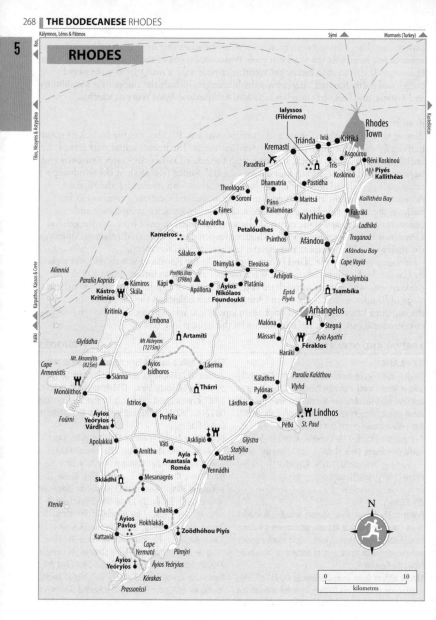

RHODES

GETTING AROUND

By bus Buses from Rhodes Town to the west and east coasts leave from adjacent terminals on Avérof in the New Town, immediately north of the Old Town just outside the Italian-built New Market. The main local operator is KTEL (☎ 22410 27706, ⌨ ktelrodou.gr).

By taxi The main taxi rank is at Platía Rimínis, immediately north of Rhodes Old Town, across from the bus stops. A taxi

to the airport officially costs €22; the fare to Líndhos is €44. Taxi drivers won't normally enter Rhodes Old Town – expect to walk to your hotel from the nearest gate.

By car Major car rental chains have outlets at the airport. In Rhodes Town, try Budget, Plastíra 9 (☎ 22410 21690, ⌨ tritondmc.gr); Etos, Venizélou 33 (☎ 22410 22511, ⌨ etos.gr); or Kosmos, Papaloúka 31 (☎ 22410 74374,

ⓦcosmos-sa.gr). Driving is not permitted in Rhodes Old Town, while parking outside can be hard to find; the best bet is along Filellínou on the south side, between the Ayíou Athanasíou and Koskinoú gates.

By bike and motorcycle Outlets that rent bikes, scooters and motorcycles include Kiriakos (Apodhímon Amerikís 16; ☎ 22410 36047, ⓦmotorclubkiriakos.gr), who will deliver to Rhodes Old Town and shuttle you back once you've finished; Bicycle Centre (Griva 39; ☎ 22410 28315); and Mike's Motor Club (Ioánni Kazoúli 23; ☎ 22410 37420).

DIRECTORY

Hospital/clinic The modern state hospital, just northwest of town, is understaffed and has a deservedly poor reputation; especially if you're insured, head for the well-signed Euromedica clinic in Koskinoú, 6.5km south (24hr; English-speaking staff; ☎ 22410 45000 for their ambulances).

Rhodes Town

By far the largest town on the island, **Rhodes Town** straddles its northernmost headland, in full view of Turkey less than 20km north. The ancient city that occupied this site, laid out during the fifth century BC by Hippodamos of Miletos, was almost twice the size of its modern counterpart, and with over a hundred thousand residents, held more than double its population.

While the fortified enclave now known as the **Old Town** is of more recent construction, created by the Knights Hospitaller in the fourteenth century, it's one of the finest medieval walled cities you could ever hope to see. Yes, it gets hideously overcrowded with day-trippers in high season, but at night it's quite magical, and well worth an extended stay. It makes sense to think of it as an entirely separate destination to the **New Town**, or **Neohóri**, the mélange of unremarkable suburbs and dreary resort that sprawls out from it in three directions.

It was the entrance to **Mandhráki** harbour, incidentally, that was supposedly straddled by the **Colossus**, an ancient statue of Apollo erected to commemorate the 305 BC siege. In front of the New Town, the harbour is today used largely by yachts and excursion boats.

Rhodes Old Town

The Citadel of Rhodes was designated a UNESCO World Heritage Site in 1988 and is one of the best-preserved Old Towns in the world. It is an absolute gem, a superb medieval ensemble that's all but unique in retaining the feel of a genuine lived-in village – it neither grew to become a city nor became overly prettified for visitors. Still entirely enclosed within a double ring of mighty sandstone walls, it stands utterly aloof from the modern world.

Although the newly arrived Knights encircled the local population as well as their own castle within their fourteenth-century walls, they took the precaution of keeping whatever they needed for survival north of the straight-line street of **Sokrátous**, which could be sealed off in times of emergency. Broadly speaking, that distinction remains, with the monumental district, now also scattered with Ottoman mosques and minarets, set somewhat apart.

While it does hold some fascinating sights and museums, however, what makes the Old Town so special is the sheer vibrancy of the place as a whole. Its busiest commercial lanes, packed with restaurants, cafés, and souvenir stores selling anything from T-shirts to fur coats, and *gelati* to jewellery, can be overpoweringly congested in summer – Sokrátous itself is the worst culprit – but it's always possible to escape into the time-forgotten tangle of **cobbled alleyways** that lie further south, and away from the sea. No map can do justice to what a labyrinth it all is, or quite how much is missing; mysterious ruins lie half-buried, overrun with cats or wild flowers, while isolated Cyclopean arches suddenly rear into view, without a trace of the buildings they used to hold up.

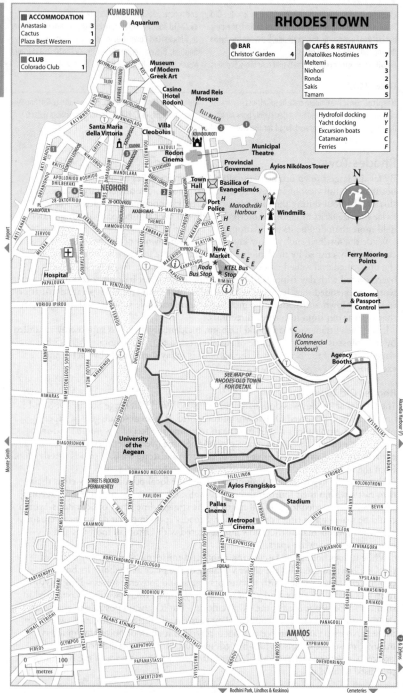

5

Palace of the Grand Masters

Summer daily 8am–7.45pm; winter Tues–Sun 8.30am–3pm • €6, free Sun Nov–March • ☎ 22413 65270

The **Palace of the Grand Masters** dominates the northwestern corner of the Old Town's walls. Destroyed by an ammunition explosion in 1856, it was reconstructed by the Italians as a summer home for Mussolini and King Vittore Emmanuele III, although neither one ever visited Rhodes. While its external appearance, based on medieval engravings and accounts, remains reasonably authentic, free rein was given in its interior to Fascist delusions of grandeur.

The two splendid ground-floor galleries jointly constitute the best **museums** in town. They often close due to staff shortages; check whether they're open before you pay for admission, because otherwise there's precious little to see. One covers ancient Rhodes, documenting everyday life around 250 BC; highlights include a Hellenistic floor mosaic of a comedic mask. The other, across the courtyard, covers the medieval era, stressing the importance of Christian Rhodes as a trade centre. The Knights are represented with a display on their sugar-refining industry and a gravestone of a Grand Master; precious manuscripts and books precede a wing of post-Byzantine icons.

Street of the Knights

The Gothic, heavily restored **Street of the Knights** (Odhós Ippotón) leads east from Platía Kleovoúlou in front of the Palace of the Grand Masters. The various "Inns" along the way lodged the Knights of St John, according to linguistic and ethnic affiliation, until the Ottoman Turks forced them to leave for Malta in 1523. Today the Inns house government offices, foreign consulates or cultural institutions vaguely appropriate to their past. Several stage occasional exhibitions, but the overall effect of the Italian renovation is sterile and stagey.

Archeological Museum

Summer daily 8am–7.45pm; winter Tues–Sun 8.30am–3pm • €6 • ☎ 22413 65256

At the foot of the Street of the Knights, the Knights' Hospital now houses the town's **Archeological Museum**. A very lovely complex in its own right, which takes at least an hour to explore, it consists of several galleries in the medieval hospital itself, plus a delightful raised and walled garden where extensions and outbuildings hold further displays. Rather too many rooms simply hold glass cases filled with small artefacts, displayed with little contextual information, but there's a lot of interesting stuff including votive offerings from Egypt and Cyprus found in the Kamiros acropolis, and an amazing array of ancient painted pottery. The grandest hall upstairs is lined with the tomb slabs of fourteenth- and fifteenth-century Knights, but the light-filled gallery of **Hellenistic statues** nearby is the true highlight. *Aphrodite Adioumene*, the so-called "Marine Venus" beloved of Lawrence Durrell, stands in a rear corner, lent a sinister aspect by her sea-dissolved face that makes a striking contrast to the friendlier *Aphrodite Bathing*.

Turkish Rhodes

Many of the mosques and *mescids* (the Islamic equivalent of a chapel) in which the old town abounds were converted from Byzantine churches after the Christians were expelled in 1522. The most conspicuous of all is the rust-coloured, candy-striped **Süleymaniye Mosque**, rebuilt during the nineteenth century on 300-year-old foundations. Like most local Ottoman monuments, it's not open to visitors, though the purpose-built (1531) **Ibrahim Pasha Mosque** on Plátonos, for example, is still used by the sizeable Turkish-speaking minority.

The Ottomans' most enduring civic contributions are the **Ottoman Library**, opposite the Süleymaniye (Mon–Sat 9.30am–4pm; tip custodian), which has a rich collection of early medieval manuscripts and Korans; the **imaret** (mess-hall) at Sokrátous 179, now an exceptionally pleasant café (*Palio Syssitio*); and the imposing 1558 **Mustafa Hammam** (Turkish bath) on Platía Aríonos (Mon–Fri 10am–5pm, Sat 8am–5pm, last admission

5

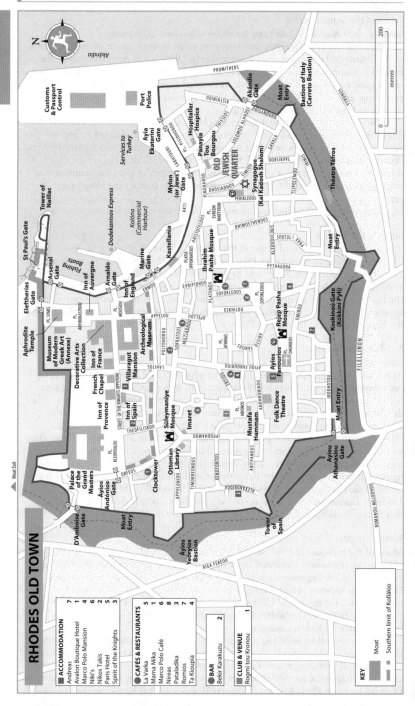

RHODES OLD TOWN

■ ACCOMMODATION	
Andreas	7
Avalon Boutique Hotel	1
Marco Polo Mansion	6
Niki's	2
Nikos Takis	5
Paris Hotel	5
Spirit of the Knights	3

● CAFÉS & RESTAURANTS	
La Varka	5
Mama Mika	1
Marco Polo Café	6
Nireas	8
Pataladika	3
Romios	7
Ta Kioupia	4

● BAR	
Bekir Karakuzu	2

■ CLUB & VENUE	
Rogmi tou Kronou	1

KEY	
Moat	
Southern limit of Kollákio	

N

200

0   metres

4pm; €5). Bring everything you need – soap, shampoo, towel, loofah – to enjoy separate, *au naturel* men's and women's sections.

Jewish Rhodes

Beyond the tiled central fountain in Platía Ippokrátous, Odhós Aristotélous leads to **Platía tón Evréon Martýron** ("Square of the Jewish Martyrs"), named in memory of the 2100 Jews of Rhodes and Kos who were sent to the concentration camps in 1944; a black granite column honours them. Of four **synagogues** that once graced the nearby Jewish quarter, only ornate, arcaded, pebble-floored **Kal Kadosh Shalom** (Mon–Fri & Sun 10am–3pm; donation) on Odhós Simíou, just south, survives. To one side of the synagogue, a well-labelled, three-room **museum** thematically chronicles the Jewish community's life on Rhodes.

New Town (Neohóri)

What's now known as the **New Town** – in Greek, **Neohóri** – dates originally to the Ottoman era, when Orthodox Greeks excluded from the fortified city built their own residential districts outside the walls. Only **Kumburnú**, the area immediately north of the Old Town, at the tip of the headland, bears any relevance to visitors. On its eastern side, Mandhráki yacht harbour serves as the base for excursion boats and some ferry companies, while the streets immediately inland hold the workaday shops, offices and agencies that keep the town as a whole ticking along. The headland itself is surrounded by a continuous **beach** of gritty shingle (loungers, parasols and showers), particularly at **Élli**, the more sheltered east-facing section. Despite being so close to the city, the water offshore is exceptionally clean, which explains the many hotels and restaurants hereabouts. However, judged on its own merits, the New Town makes a poor holiday destination.

Aquarium

Kos St • Daily: April–Oct 9am–8.30pm; Nov–March 9am–4.30pm • €5.50 • ⓦ rhodes-aquarium.hcmr.gr

Perched at the northernmost point of the island, Rhodes' **Aquarium** is as much a museum as a conventional aquarium. It does hold tanks of live fish, not necessarily captioned correctly, but most of its space is taken up with displays on the history and function of the building itself, as well as a monk seal buried as an ancient family's pet, and a stuffed Cuvier's beaked whale.

Museum of Modern Greek Art

Pl. G. Harítou • **Museum** Tues & Thurs–Sat 9am–3pm, Wed 4–10pm; **annexe** Tues–Sat 8am–2pm • €3 (includes annexe) • ⓦ visitrhodes.gr

Near the northernmost tip of the New Town, on what's colloquially known as "100 Palms Square", is Rhodes' **Museum of Modern Greek Art**, which holds the most important collection of twentieth-century Greek painting outside Athens. All the heavy hitters – Hatzikyriakos-Ghikas, surrealist Nikos Engonopoulos, naive artist Theophilos, neo-Byzantinist Fotis Kontoglou – are amply represented. Some of Kontoglou's greatest frescoes, dating from 1951–61, are in the **Evangelismós basilica** at Mandhráki.

What used to be the main, cramped home of the museum, on Platía Sýmis 2 in the Old Town, is now the **annexe**, devoted to maps, prints and special exhibits. Both premises have excellent gift shops.

Hellenistic Rhodes

2km west of the Old Town

A half-hour uphill hike from the Old Town – a hike best undertaken just before sunset, both for the views and the temperature – leads to the unenclosed remains of the **acropolis of Hellenistic Rhodes**, atop Monte Smith. Formerly known as Áyios Stéfanos, this hill was renamed for a British admiral during the Napoleonic Wars. While the ruins cover an extensive area, there's not really all that much to see – a restored theatre

5

and stadium, plus three columns of a temple to **Apollo Pythios**. It's striking to realize, however, that the ancient city stretched from here all the way down to the sea.

The cemeteries

While the vast **municipal cemeteries** at Korakónero, just inland from Zéfyros beach 2km southeast of the centre, might not sound like a hot tourist destination, they can be strangely compelling. This is one of the very few remaining spots in the Balkans where the dead of four faiths lie in proximity, albeit separated by high walls. The easterly **Greek Orthodox section**, the largest, holds the fewest surprises. The small **Catholic section** is not only the last home of various north European expatriates, but also demonstrates that a fair number of Italians elected to accept Greek nationality and stay on after the 1948 unification with Greece. The **Jewish section** (Mon–Fri 8am–1pm) has, understandably, seen little activity since 1944, and is full of memorials in French to those who were deported. Opposite its gate, across the busy road, a small **Allied War graves** plot holds 142 burials. Just south of the Jewish section, the "**Muslim**" **section** (ie Turkish) is the most heavily used and best maintained of the three minority cemeteries.

ACCOMMODATION   **RHODES TOWN**

OLD TOWN

★ **Andreas** Omírou 28D ☎ 22410 34156, ⓦ hotelandreas .com; map p.272. Perennially popular *pension*, imaginatively converted from an old Turkish mansion, with switched-on, international management. The seven rooms vary in size and price; some sleep three, and there's a fabulous "penthouse". All have a/c; five have en-suite bathrooms, while the other two have the key to their own dedicated bathroom down the corridor. Excellent breakfast included. Two-night minimum stay; reservations essential. **€130**

Avalon Boutique Hotel Háritos 9 ☎ 22410 31438, ⓦ avalonrhodes.gr; map p.272. Fourteenth-century manor house, tucked into a quiet courtyard very near the Grand Masters' palace, and stylishly re-modelled to hold six bright, modern and very luxurious suites, each with open-air terrace. The friendly family team serve breakfast (included) in your unit, the courtyard café, or the vaulted bar. **€170**

★ **Marco Polo Mansion** Ayíou Fanouríou 42 ☎ 22410 25562, ⓦ marcopolomansion.gr; map p.272. Superb conversion of an old Turkish mansion, off one of the old town's most charming lanes, with a hammam on site. All rooms are exquisitely furnished with antiques from the nearby eponymous gallery and equipped with handmade mattresses. Large buffet breakfasts (included) are provided in the garden snack-bar, open to all later in the day (see opposite). Reservations and credit-card deposit mandatory. April–Oct. **€110**

Niki's Sofokléous 39 ☎ 22410 25115, ⓦ www .nikishotel.gr; map p.272. Attractive and welcoming little hotel. All rooms are en suite, most have a/c, and those on the upper storey have fine views; there's also a shared roof terrace, and guests have use of a washing machine. Pay a little extra for a private balcony, or a room that sleeps three. Breakfast included. **€55**

Nikos Takis Panetíou 26 ☎ 22410 70773, ⓦ nikostakis hotel.com; map p.272. Set up by two of Greece's most

celebrated fashion designers, whose flamboyant 1960s' work is on show throughout (and sold in the ground-floor boutique), the eight rather extraordinary units in this little hotel range through themes from Moroccan to medieval, with opulent furnishings. Pebble-mosaic courtyard, with fine views over town, for breakfast (included) and drinks. **€160**

Paris Hotel Ayíou Fanouríou 88 ☎ 22410 26356, ⓦ paris-hotel-rhodes.gr; map p.272. On the corner of Omirou, opposite Ag. Fanourios church, this Greek-run establishment offers stylishly decorated doubles, studios and two luxury suites. Courtyard bar open all day for snacks and drinks – a delightful location to digest breakfast (included) and while away the hours. May–Oct. **€75**

★ **Spirit of the Knights** Alexandhridhou 14 ☎ 22410 39765, ⓦ rhodesluxuryhotel.com; map p.272. Gorgeous traditional home in a very quiet back alleyway of the Old Town, in full view of a peaceful stretch of walls. Sensitively converted to create a lovely boutique hotel, with excellent service from an extended English family, it holds six exquisitely furnished and very distinct suites. Local produce breakfast is included and served in a pleasant garden courtyard that also holds a large jacuzzi. Front desk 24hr. **€145**

NEW TOWN

Anastasia 28-Oktovríou 46 ☎ 22410 28007, ⓦ anastasia-hotel.com; map p.270. Italian-era mansion, with high ceilings and tiled floors, that's been converted to a congenial, family-run guesthouse. The simple a/c rooms sleep up to four; there's a bar in the garden, with its resident tortoises. Breakfast extra. **€45**

Cactus Hotel Kó 14 ☎ 22410 26100, ⓦ cactus-hotel.gr; map p.270. The best-value beachfront hotel in the New Town, an updated 1960s high-rise with graceful curving glass-fronted balconies, facing the best stretch of Élli beach near the tip of the headland, and with a pool. **€110**

5

Plaza Best Western Ieroú Lóhou 7 ☎22410 22501, ⓦrhodesplazahotel.com; map p.270. Crisp, modern four-star hotel, convenient for Mandhráki harbour, with a pool, garden and sauna. There's also a restaurant, and they offer buffet English breakfasts. €115

EATING AND DRINKING

While the Old Town holds a quite staggering number of restaurants, prices are rather high, and both value and quality tend to improve away from the main commercial lanes. Most places serve those with children from about 6.30pm, tourists until perhaps 10pm, and locals till midnight or later.

OLD TOWN

La Varka Sofokléous 5; map p.272. Indoor-outdoor ouzerí, with live Greek music and a table-filled terrace right on a busy bar-filled alleyway. The interior makes a cosy retreat in the cooler months. Good salads, *pikilíes* for two at €30, grilled *thrápsalo*, fried or salt-cured seafood titbits, cheapish ouzo and *soúma* by the carafe. Daily 11.30am–1am.

Mama Mika Orféos 23 ☎22410 33427; map p.272. Good, reasonably priced home cooking – a main meat dish of grilled chicken with salad is €12 – served in a friendly atmosphere, across from the clocktower and minaret in the northwest corner of the Old Town. Sit at the plentiful street-level tables, which make for great people-watching. Daily 10am–midnight.

★**Marco Polo Café** Ayíou Fanouríou 42 ☎22410 25562; map p.272. Extremely lovely, deservedly popular hotel restaurant, in a garden courtyard; the lack of a street sign is to keep the crowds down. Traditional adapted recipes, blending subtle flavours, include pilaf with lamb and raisins, turnovers with *pastourmá*, and *psaronéfri* with *manoúri* cheese, fig and red peppercorn sauce. Roughly €30 per head. Excellent wine list and desserts of the day. Reservations essential. April–Oct daily till midnight, dinner only.

Nireas Sofokléous 22 ☎22410 21703; map p.272. This long-standing, family-run fish specialist, on a quiet square just away from the bustle, has earned its sky-high reputation thanks to the hard work and friendly professionalism of its owners, its still-reasonable prices, and its atmospheric indoor/outdoor seating. Individual seafood dishes, like mussels *saganáki*, cost around €10, and unusually they have a range of Italian desserts too. Around €70 for two including dessert and wine. Daily lunch and dinner.

Pataladika Sokrátous 41 ☎22410 24272; map p.272. Despite the address, this large restaurant opens onto a small square just south of the main pedestrian drag. Tables are laid out in flowery gardens that surround the compound, and the rambling interior is charming too, in an old townhouse with assorted dining rooms. Reckon on €70 for dinner for two. A good mixed *mezédhes* plate costs €10.50, while the sliced-up whole stuffed squid is excellent. Daily noon–10pm.

★**Romios** Sofokleous 15 ☎22410 25549; map p.272. Friendly restaurant with courtyard and indoor seating. Traditional local dishes are on offer, as well as international fare. Fresh seafood, grilled meat and home-made pastas plus desserts to die for ensure repeat clientele. Roughly €30 per head. Daily 1pm till late.

Ta Kioupia Menekléous 22 ☎22410 30192; map p.272. Friendly, high-quality restaurant, towards the top of the Old Town. Its contemporary twists on classic Greek cuisine are consistently delicious – you'll remember the smoked aubergine with feta and the blue cheese mousse for a long time. It works out expensive, though, especially as they charge for the various little extra plates they bring to your table (around €40 per head). Daily lunch and dinner, Sun till 6pm.

NEW TOWN

Anatolikes Nostimies Klavdhíou Pépper 109, Zéfyros Beach ☎22410 29516; map p.270. The name means "Anatolian Delicacies": Thracian Pomak/Middle Eastern dips and starters, plus beef-based kebabs. Beach-hut atmosphere, but friendly, popular and reasonably priced (around €15 per head). Post-meal hubble-bubble on request. Daily noon–midnight.

★**Meltemi** Platía Koundourióti 8, Élli beach ☎22410 30480; map p.270. Beachfront ouzerí, with a nicely shaded beach-level patio, offering such delights as *karavidhópsyha* (crayfish nuggets), octopus croquettes, chunky hummus, and superb roast aubergine with beans and onions to a local crowd at roughly €14 a head. Pleasant winter salon inside. Daily lunch and dinner.

Niohori Ioánni Kazoúli 29, Neohóri ☎22410 35116; map p.270. Alias "*Kiki's*" after the jolly proprietress, this homely, inexpensive local is tops for meat grills, sourced from their own butcher/farm; veal liver is €6, a mixed grill €8. There's usually a cooked vegetable dish like okra too. Daily lunch and dinner.

Ronda Platía Koundourióti 6, Neohóri ☎22410 76944; map p.270. Built by the Italians as a waterfront spa complex, and every bit as round as the name implies, this large-domed room now houses a very spacious café. There's nothing remarkable about the food or drink, but it's a lovely place to sit, with views through its huge arched windows of the beach and harbour. Daily 9am–1am.

Sakis Kanadhá 95, at Apostólou Papaïoánnou, Zéfyros ☎22410 21537; map p.270. A friendly old favourite with pleasant patio and indoor seating, equally popular with Rhodians and foreigners. Known for its shellfish (such as

5

limpets and snails), meat (chops, Cypriot *seftaliés*) and the usual starters; a three-course meal costs roughly €15 each. Mon–Sat 5pm–1am, Sun 12.30pm–12.30am.

Tamam Yeoryíou Léondos 1, Neohóri ☎ 22410 73522; map p.270. This small but enormously popular New Town newcomer serves good but expensive traditional cuisine. Steaks cost €25–30 each, and there's a wine list to match. If you're happy to spend a lot, you'll have a real feast; show any reluctance, and the charming service will turn off like a tap. Daily lunch and dinner.

NIGHTLIFE AND ENTERTAINMENT

In the Old Town, an entire alley (Miltiádhou) off Apelloú is home to a score of loud, annually changing music bars and clubs, extending towards Plátonos and Platía Dhamayítou, and frequented mostly by Greeks (in winter too).

Bekir Karakuzu Sokrátous 76, Old Town; map p.272. The last traditional Turkish *kafenío* in the Old Town, with an Oriental-fantasy interior, simply oozes atmosphere. Yoghurt, *loukoúmi*, sage tea and coffees are on the expensive side – consider it admission to an informal museum. Daily 11am–midnight.

Christos' Garden Dhilberáki 59, Neohóri; map p.270. This combination art gallery/bar/café occupies a carefully restored old house and courtyard with pebble-mosaic floors throughout. Daily 10pm till late.

Colorado Club Orfanídhou 57, at Aktí Miaouli, Neohóri ☎ 22410 75120, ⓦ colorado.com.gr; map p.270. Triple venue, just back from the sea on the west side of the New Town, comprised of a "disco-house" dance club, a live music venue and "Heaven", the top-floor chill-out bar. Daily 9pm till late.

Metropol Cnr Venetokléon and Výronos ☎ 22410 28410; map p.270. Southeast of the Old Town, opposite the stadium, this multiplex cinema shows first-run action films year-round.

★**Rogmi tou Kronou** Platía Aríonos 4, Old Town ☎ 22410 25202; map p.272. Rock-oriented bar and music venue, with outside tables, taking up two storeys of a fine old house on one of the Old Town's most attractive squares. Live music or DJs every night till late. Daily noon till late.

The east coast

From the capital as far south as Líndhos, the **east coast** of Rhodes has been built up with a succession of sprawling towns and resorts. Some, such as **Faliráki**, have long since lost any charm they may once have possessed, but there are still some pleasant lower-key alternatives, including **Stegná** and **Haráki**.

Piyés Kallithéas

7km south of Rhodes Town • Daily 9am–late • €2.50 • ⓦ kallitheasprings.gr

A prize example of orientalized Art Deco from 1929, the former spa at **Piyés Kallithéas** was the work of a young Pietro Lombardi who, in his old age, designed Strasbourg's European Parliament building. Accessed via a short side road through pines, has an upmarket bar which serves from inside artificial grottoes at the swimming lido, just below the dome of the **Mikrí Rotónda** in its clump of palms. The main **Megáli Rotónda** higher up is now a small showcase area, with changing modern art exhibits.

Faliráki

The overblown and unappealing resort of **Faliráki**, 10km south of the capital, is a town of two halves. The half-dozen high-rise family hotels in its northerly zone sit uneasily alongside the cheap-and-nasty southern zone, notorious for its drink-fuelled brawls, rapes and even murder. Since the island police forcefully curbed the local club-crawling culture, the place is now a shadow of its former self.

Faliráki's sandy sweep is closed off on the south by the cape of **Ladhikó**. For the best swimming, head for the main cove, south of the promontory. The scenic bay of "**Anthony Quinn**", on its northern flank, is named after the late Mexican American actor, whom Greeks took to their hearts following his roles in *Zorba the Greek* and *The Guns of Navarone*. Quinn bought much of this area and constructed the first road to the beach, but during the 1980s the Greek government swindled him out of his claim; legal battles continue to this day.

5

Afándou Bay

South of Ladhikó, the coastline is adorned, all the way to Líndhos, by striking limestone turrets that punctuate long stretches of beach. The first is the pebble-and-sand expanse of **Afándou Bay**, the least developed large east-coast beach, with just a few showers and clusters of inexpensive sunbeds. Spare a moment, heading down the main access road to mid-beach, for the atmospheric sixteenth-century church of **Panayía Katholikí**, paved with a *votsalotó* floor and decorated with frescoes.

Kolýmbia

Immediately north of the Tsambíka headland, 25km south of Rhodes Town, is **Kolýmbia**, which was laid out by the Italians not long before World War II, as a model farming village. Its original little grid of streets now serves a fast-growing resort that's become a favourite with more upscale package travellers. Reasonable beaches lie to either side of the low hill at road's end; the northern one has more facilities.

Tsambíka

The enormous promontory of **Tsambíka**, 26km south of town, offers unrivalled views along some 50km of coastline. From the main highway, a steep, 1500m cement drive leads to a small car park from where steps mount to the summit. On its September 8 festival childless women climb up – on their hands and knees in the final stretches – to an otherwise unremarkable **monastery** to be cured of their barrenness. Shallow **Tsambíka Bay**, south of the headland (2km access road), has an excellent if packed beach.

Stegná

A kilometre or so south of Tsambíka Bay, a steep road drops for 3.5km down to the sea from the main highway, in huge sweeping curves. It ends at the scruffy but appealing semicircular bay of **Stegná**, where for once no large hotels lurk behind the fine-gravel shore, just some relatively tasteful apartment complexes.

Haráki and around

Haráki is a very likeable little crescent bay, overlooked by the stubby ruins of **Feraklós castle**, the last Knights' citadel to fall to the Turks. There's no road along the shoreline, just a walkway beside a part pebble, part grey-sand **beach** that's backed by a solid row of small two- or three-storey studios, interspersed with the occasional café.

The long straight shoreline south of Haráki is lined with beaches of sand and fine gravel, such as **Paralía Kaláthou**. It ends after 8km, just short of Líndhos, at the little cove of **Vlyhá**, which holds a couple of enormous hotels.

ACCOMMODATION   THE EAST COAST

Atrium Palace Paralía Kaláthou ☎ 22440 31601, ⓦ atrium.gr. Surprisingly unobtrusive despite its 300-plus luxurious rooms, this upscale hotel is one of the few developments on Kaláthou Beach, with expensively land-scaped grounds and curved pools. The remoter villa wings, towards the spa, are best. April–Oct. **€180**

Haraki Village Haráki ☎ 6946 350 401, ⓦ harakivillage .gr. Eight little pastel-coloured studios and apartments, all with balconies or outdoor space, at the north end of the beach below the castle. **€100**

Lindos Blu Vlyhá ☎ 22440 32110, ⓦ lindosblu.gr.

Very opulent, very stylish modern resort hotel, tumbling down the slopes of a pretty bay immediately north of Líndhos, with a spa, infinity pools, and on-site restaurants. All seventy units have sea views, and are intended for adults only; villas/maisonettes have private pools. Minimum stay 4 nights in high season. **€420**

Panorama B&B Stegná ☎ 22440 22516. Laidback B&B, in a peaceful setting a short walk back from Stegná beach, with simple good-value a/c studios and rooms and a breezy shared terrace. **€50**

EATING AND DRINKING

Argo Restaurant Haráki ☎ 6946 351 410. Behind its weathered, custard-yellow exterior, this seafront

restaurant, squeezed among the toothy rocks at the southern end of Haráki beach, is surprisingly smart and

5

offers views of the castle and a good Greek menu, with mussels, chicken or shrimp main dishes (€8–12). Daily noon–10pm.

★ **To Periyiali** Stegná ☎ 22440 23444. The best taverna in Stegná, down by the fish anchorage. Greeks flock here for seafood, hand-cut round chips, home-made *yaprákia* and substantial salads washed down with good bulk wine (€15 or under per head); the travertine-clad loos must be the wackiest, yet most charming, on the island. Daily lunch and dinner.

Líndhos

Set on a stark headland 50km south of Rhodes Town, **LÍNDHOS** is almost too good to be true. A classic Greek village of crazily stacked **whitewashed houses**, poised between a stupendous castle-topped acropolis above and sandy crescent beaches below, it's the island's number-two tourist attraction. Inevitably, it's so tightly packed with day-trippers in summer that you can barely breathe, let alone move along its impossibly narrow lanes. Almost all its shining white homes have long since been bought up by foreigners; most of those along the ancient agora, or serpentine main alleyway, are now run as restaurants, cafés and souvenir stores, while discreetly advertised rental properties lie to either side.

Arrive outside peak season, or if that's not possible at least in the early morning, and strolling through the village is still hugely atmospheric. The belfried, post-Byzantine **Panayía church** (daily 9am–3pm, Mon–Sat also 6.30–8pm) is covered inside with well-preserved eighteenth-century frescoes. The most imposing **medieval captains' residences** are built around *votsalotó* courtyards, their monumental doorways often fringed by intricate stone braids or cables supposedly corresponding in number to the fleet owned.

The acropolis

Early April to late Oct daily 8am–7.45pm; early Nov to late March Tues–Sun 8.30am–2.40pm • €6

Although the dramatic battlements that circle the **acropolis** on the bluff directly above Líndhos belong to a **Knights' castle**, the precinct they enclose is much more ancient. A sanctuary dedicated to local deity Lindia was founded here in the ninth century BC, while the surviving structures were started by local ruler Kleoboulos three hundred years later.

A short climb up steep steps from the centre of the village, or a longer walk (or even donkey ride) up a gentler but more exposed pathway, brings you to the stairway to the castle itself. The relief sculpture of a ship's prow at its foot dates from the second century BC. Once you pass through the sole **gateway**, restrain the impulse to head straight for the summit, and explore the site from the bottom upwards instead. That way the **temple of Athena Lindia** at the top, set on a level platform that commands magnificent coastline views to both north and south, will appear in a stunning climax. Almost all the buildings are recent **reconstructions**, replacing older restoration work now deemed inaccurate, though some ancient stones have been incorporated.

Come early or late in the day if you can, to avoid the crowds and enjoy the best light. And be warned that many of the stairways, parapets and platforms have precipitous, unrailed drop-offs.

Beaches

Líndhos's main **beach**, once the principal ancient harbour, tends to get very overcrowded; quieter options lie one cove beyond at **Pállas beach**. The small, perfectly sheltered **St Paul's harbour**, south of the acropolis and well away from town, has excellent swimming. According to legend, the Apostle landed here in 58 AD on a mission to evangelize the island.

ARRIVAL AND INFORMATION

LÍNDHOS

By car No cars are allowed in the village or to access the acropolis. Arriving drivers instead have to perform an elaborate U-turn at the tiny main square to reach car parks towards the beach, some of which are free.

THE ACROPOLIS, LÍNDHOS >

5

ACCOMMODATION

★**Melenos** ☏ 22440 32222, ⊛ melenoslindos.com. The only hotel in Líndhos itself is an absolute gem, exquisite and highly exclusive, discreetly sited on the second lane above the north beach, by the school. No expense has been spared in laying out the twelve luxurious suites with semi-private, *votsalotó* terraces and tasteful furnishings; there's also a swanky garden-bar and restaurant. Year-round. **€270**

EATING AND DRINKING

The lanes of Líndhos are crammed with run-of-the-mill restaurants, but there are still a few standouts. Almost all have roof terraces with castle views; most diners end up sitting on bare concrete patios in a parallel rooftop world.

Acropolis Roof Garden Trapeza 26 ☏ 22440 32160. The best option along the lanes, with a solid menu of Greek specialities such as rabbit *stifhádo* (€9.50) and a fine array of mezhédes, including tasty *dolmádhes*, all served on a castle-view terrace. Daily lunch and dinner.

★**Mavrikos** Main Square ☏ 22440 31232. Prominent restaurant, on the fig-tree square where all traffic has to turn around. Starters such as *yígandes* in carob syrup (€7.50) or sweet marinated sardines are accomplished, as are superior traditional recipes or fish mains such as skate timbale with sweetened balsamic, or *dolmádhes* and *tyrokafterí*. Typically €23–30 per head. Daily noon–midnight.

Village Café ☏ 22440 31554, ⊛ lindostreasures.com /village. Friendly café and snack-bar, set around a little pebbled courtyard, with a fine array of pastries, juices, sandwiches and light bites. Daily 10am–5pm.

The southeast coast

Until recently, tourist development petered out south of Líndhos, but these days Rhodes' **southeast coast** holds plenty of facilities for travellers seeking to escape the hectic atmosphere of the northern resorts. **Péfki** and **Yennádhi** are the best overnight stops, while **Prassoníssi** at the southern tip is popular with windsurfers. Even if you're not staying down here, it's worth touring in your own vehicle, stopping off perhaps in the villages just inland, like **Asklipió**, with its wonderful church.

Péfki

A couple of kilometres around the headland beyond Líndhos, **PÉFKI** was originally the garden annexe of its illustrious neighbour, but has now burgeoned as a resort in its own right. Its principal **beach**, a gorgeous little cove lined with sand and lapped by sparkling clear waters, inevitably becomes very crowded in summer, but there are other, more secluded little beaches tucked at the base of the low cliffs to the west.

Lárdhos

Although the village of **LÁRDHOS** stands well in from the sea, it has lent its name to dense beachfront development a little further south. Its main beach, 2km south of the centre, is gravelly and heavily impinged upon by hotels; Glýstra cove, 3km south, is a small and more sheltered crescent, at its best in low season.

Asklipió

Nine kilometres south of Lárdhos, close to the unexciting resort of Kiotári, a side road heads 3.5km inland to **ASKLIPIÓ**, a sleepy village enlivened by a crumbling Knights' castle and Byzantine **Kímisis Theotókou church**.

Kímisis Theotókou church

Daily: spring/autumn 9am–5pm; summer 9am–6pm • €1

Asklipió's central **Kímisis Theotókou church** dates from 1060, and has a pebble-floored ground plan, to which two apses were added during the eighteenth century. Thanks to the dry local climate, the **frescoes** inside remain in breathtaking condition. Didactic "cartoon strips" extend completely around the church and up onto the ceiling, featuring Old Testament stories alongside the more usual lives of Christ and the Virgin. Half of the adjacent **Asklipió Museum** (same hours and ticket) is devoted to ecclesiastical treasures; the other, housed in a former olive mill, holds a folklore gallery, full of craft tools and antiquated machinery.

Yennádhi and Lahaniá

The drab outskirts of **YENNÁDHI**, 13km south of Lárdhos and the only sizeable settlement on the southeast coast, mask the attractive older village core inland. Though the present, barrel-vaulted structure of the village cemetery and church, **Ayía Anastasía Roméa**, dates from the fifteenth century, it's built on sixth-century foundations, and covered inside with post-Byzantine **frescoes**. Yennádhi's dark-sand-and-gravel **beach**, clean and offering the usual amenities, extends for kilometres in either direction.

The tiny and picturesque village of **LAHANIÁ**, 10km south of Yennádhi, then 2km inland, was abandoned after a postwar earthquake, though since the 1980s its older houses have been mostly occupied and renovated by foreigners.

Prassoníssi

The main circular island highway doesn't run all the way down its southernmost tip. Branch south at Kattaviá, however, and a paved 8km spur road will bring you to **Prassoníssi**, a two-hour, 90km drive south of Rhodes Town. This gloriously desolate spot has become a major rendezvous for **windsurfers** (see box below).

ACCOMMODATION   THE SOUTHEAST COAST

Effie's Dreams Yennádhi ☎22440 43410, ⓦeffies dreams.com. Six serviceable, good-value a/c studios, overlooking a fountain-fed oasis at the northern end of Yennádhi, plus free wi-fi and a bar. **€55**

Lindian Village Lárdhos ☎22440 35900, ⓦlindian village.gr. Sumptuous beachfront resort, 5km south of Lárdhos, with an attractive complex of individual bungalows (suites have their own plunge pools), plus several gourmet restaurants, a spa/gym and a private beach. **€210**

Pefkos Blue Hotel Péfki ☎22440 48017. Good-value all-studio hotel on the hillside just above Péfki; 35 clean, comfortable apartments sleeping two to four, with kitchens, a/c and panoramic views. **€65**

Prasonisi Light House Prassoníssi ☎22440 91030, ⓦprasonisilighthouse.com. Marginally better of the two accommodation options at the island's southernmost tip, with a range of options, from good-value "eco rooms" to larger rooms with sea-view balconies and fully fledged apartments. Rates include breakfast and dinner. **€84**

EATING AND DRINKING

Kyma Beach Restaurant Péfki ☎22440 48213. High-class restaurant at the midpoint of Péfki beach, with lovely sunset views. They serve delicious Greek specialities with a creative twist; try the octopus carpaccio. A little pricey: starters

and main (without drinks) will set you back about €30 – you pay for the view. Book ahead in summer. Daily noon–10pm.

★**Platanos** Lahaniá Prassoníssi ☎6944 199 991, ⓦlachaniaplatanostaverna.com. On the tiny little main

---

WINDSURFING AT PRASSONÍSSI

Situated at the very southern tip of Rhodes, **Prassoníssi** is regarded as one of the finest **windsurfing** sites in Europe. Strictly speaking, the name refers to "Leek Island", the sturdy little islet just offshore, which is connected to the mainland by a long, low and very narrow sandspit through which a small natural channel frequently opens.

Not only do the waters here belong to different seas – the **Aegean** to the west of the spit, and the **Mediterranean** to the east – but in season they usually offer dramatically contrasting conditions. Thanks to the prevailing **meltémi** wind, and the funnelling effect of the islet, the Aegean side is generally much rougher, with head-high waves. On summer days it therefore becomes the area for expert windsurfers and daredevil kitesurfers. The Mediterranean side, meanwhile, tends to be much calmer, almost lagoon-like, and its shallow sandbars make it especially ideal for beginners.

The **season** at Prassoníssi lasts from May until mid-October. Of the three **windsurfing schools** that operate here, the Polish-run Prasonisi Center (late April–Oct; ☎22440 91044, ⓦprasonisicenter.com) is the keenest and friendliest.

5

platía at the lower, eastern end of Lahaniá village, this welcoming rural taverna has superb mezédhes platters like hummus and *dolmadhákia*. Sit outside at the front, under the eponymous plane tree, or in the dining room, overlooking a deep wooded valley. Around €12 per head. Daily lunch and dinner.

The west coast

While Rhodes' windward **west coast** is damp, fertile and forested, its beaches are exposed and often rocky. None of this has deterred development and, as on the east coast, the first few kilometres of the busy main road have been surrendered entirely to tourism. From Rhodes Town to the airport, the shore is lined with generic hotels, though **Triánda**, **Kremastí** and **Paradhísi** are still nominally villages, with real centres.

Kameiros

Daily: summer 8am–7.45pm; winter 8.30am–2.40pm • €4

The site of ancient **KAMEIROS**, which united with Lindos and Ialyssos to found the city-state of Rhodes, stands above the coast 30km southwest of Rhodes Town. Soon eclipsed by the new capital, Kameiros was only rediscovered in 1859, leaving a well-preserved Doric townscape in a beautiful hillside setting. Visitors can make out the foundations of two small **temples**, the re-erected pillars of a Hellenistic **house**, a Classical **fountain**, and the **stoa** of the upper agora, complete with a water cistern. Kameiros had no fortifications, nor even an acropolis – partly owing to the gentle slope of the site, and also to the likely settlement here by peaceable Minoans.

Kámiros Skála

The tiny anchorage of **KÁMIROS SKÁLA** (aka Skála Kamírou), 45km southwest of Rhodes Town, is noteworthy only as the home port for a regular ferry service to the island of Hálki (see p.286). It does have a handful of restaurants, however, while off-puttingly named **Paralía Krapiás** ("Manure Beach") is 400m southwest.

Kástro Kritinías

From afar, **Kástro Kritinías**, 2km south of Kámiros Skála, is the most impressive of the Knights' rural strongholds; the paved access road is too narrow and steep for tour buses. Close up, it proves to be no more than a shell, albeit a glorious one, with fine views west to Hálki, Alimniá, Tílos and Níssyros.

Monólithos

The tiered, flat-roofed houses of **MONÓLITHOS**, high atop the cliffs 22km south of Kámiros Skála, don't themselves justify the long trip out, but the view over the Aegean is striking. Local diversions include yet another **Knights' castle**, out of sight of town 2km west, which is photogenically perched on its own pinnacle but encloses very little, and the sand-and-gravel beaches at **Foúrni**, five paved but curvy kilometres below the castle.

ACCOMMODATION AND EATING — MONÓLITHOS

Hotel Thomas ☏ 22460 61264, ⓦ thomashotel.gr. At the top of the village, behind its somewhat grim exterior this welcoming hotel has plain, fair-sized rooms with kitchen facilities and panoramic balconies. **€37**

O Palios Monolithos ☏ 22460 61276. Opposite the church, this is the best of several tavernas in the village. Mains are a bit pricey (roughly €25), but it's known for grilled meat and starters like wild mushrooms, *tyrokafterí* and mixed *dolmádhes*, accompanied by good bread and non-CAIR bulk wine. Daily lunch and dinner, Sat & Sun only off season.

Inland Rhodes

Inland Rhodes is hilly and still part-forested (despite the ongoing efforts of arsonists), with soft-contoured, undulating scenery, and villages showing the last vestiges of agrarian life. Most people under retirement age are away working in the tourist industry, returning only at weekends and during winter.

GETTING AROUND   INLAND RHODES

By car You'll need a vehicle to get around inland; no single spot justifies the expense of a taxi or battling with the inconveniently sparse bus schedules.

Ialyssos

10km southwest of Rhodes Town • Summer Mon 8am–7.45pm, Tues–Sun 8.30am–7.45pm; winter Tues–Sun 8.30am–2.40pm • €3

From the scanty acropolis of ancient **Ialyssos**, on flat-topped Filérimos hill, Süleyman the Magnificent directed the 1522 siege of Rhodes. Filérimos means "lover of solitude", after tenth-century Byzantine hermits who dwelt here; **Filérimos monastery** is the most substantial structure. Directly in front of the church sprawl the foundations of third-century temples to Zeus and Athena, built atop a far older Phoenician shrine.

Petaloúdhes

Daily 9am–5pm • Mid-June to Sept €5, Oct to mid-June free

The one "tourist attraction" in the island's interior, **Petaloúdhes** ("Butterfly Valley"), is reached by a 7km side road that bears inland between Paradhísi and Theológos. It's actually a rest stop for **Jersey tiger moths**, which congregate here between mid-June and September, attracted for unknown reasons by the abundant *Liquidambar orientalis* trees growing abundantly in this stream canyon. The moths, which roost in droves on the tree trunks and cannot eat during this final phase of their life cycle, rest to conserve energy, and die of starvation soon after mating. When stationary, the moths are a well-camouflaged black and yellow, but in flight they flash cherry-red overwings.

Eptá Piyés to Profítis Ilías

Eptá Piyés ("Seven Springs"), 4km inland from Kolýmbia junction on the main east-coast highway, is an oasis with a tiny irrigation dam created by the Italians. A trail and a rather claustrophobic Italian aqueduct-tunnel both lead from the vicinity of the springs to the reservoir. Continuing on the same road, you reach **ELEOÚSSA** after another 9km, in the shade of dense forest. Built as the planned agricultural colony of Campochiaro in the mid-1930s, it's now a bizarre **ghost town**, with a central square lined by eerily derelict Italian structures that visitors can wander through at will. From the vast, yellow-trimmed Art Deco fountain-cum-pool just west of the village, stocked with endangered *gizáni* fish, keep straight 3km further to the gorgeous little late Byzantine church of **Áyios Nikólaos Foundouklí** ("St Nicholas of the Hazelnuts").

Émbona

All tracks and roads west across Profítis Ilías converge on the road from Kalavárdha bound for **ÉMBONA**, a large but unremarkable village backed up against the north slope of 1215m **Mount Atávyros**. Émbona lies at the heart of the island's most important **wine-producing districts**.

Thárri monastery

Katholikón Daily, all day • Free

Accessible from Apóllona and Laerma to the north, or via a rough but passable road from Asklipió 11km south, the Byzantine **Thárri monastery** is the oldest religious foundation on Rhodes, re-established as a vital community in 1990 by charismatic abbot Amfilohios. In the striking *katholikón*, successive cleanings have restored damp-smudged **frescoes** dated 1300–1450 to a pale approximation of their original glory.

ACCOMMODATION AND EATING   **INLAND RHODES**

★**Elafos Hotel** Profítis Ilías ☎22410 44808, ⓦelafos hotel.gr. Rather splendid, restored Italian, 1929-vintage chalet-hotel, in a village west of Áyios Nikólaos church, where its 22 high-ceilinged rooms ooze retro charm, and the arcaded ground-floor common areas include a restaurant and a sauna. **€90**

★**Piyi Fasouli** Psínthos ☎22410 50071. Excellent taverna, at the edge of Psínthos village, 6km southeast of Butterfly Valley (see p.283), serving excellent grills and appetizers as well as a few tasty *mayireftá* at tables overlooking the namesake spring. Daily lunch and dinner.

Kastellórizo

Although **KASTELLÓRIZO**'s official name of Meyísti means "Biggest", it's actually among the very smallest Dodecanese islands; it's just the biggest of a local archipelago of islets. It's also extremely remote, located more than 100km east of Rhodes and barely more than a nautical mile off mainland Asia. At night, its lights are outnumbered by those of the Turkish town of Kaş opposite, with which Kastellórizo has excellent relations.

The island's population has dwindled from around ten thousand a century ago to perhaps just three hundred today. An **Ottoman** possession from 1552, it was occupied by the **French** from 1915 until 1921, and then by the **Italians**. When Italy capitulated to the Allies in 1943, 1500 **Commonwealth** commandos occupied Kastellórizo. Most departed that November, after the Germans captured the other Dodecanese, which left the island vulnerable to looters, both Greek and British. By the time a fuel fire in 1944

triggered the explosion of an adjacent arsenal, demolishing half the houses on Kastellórizo, most islanders had already left. Those who remain are supported by remittances from more than thirty thousand emigrants, as well as subsidies from the Greek government to prevent the island reverting to Turkey.

Yet Kastellórizo has a future of sorts, thanks partly to repatriating "Kassies" returning each summer to renovate their crumbling ancestral houses as **second homes**. Visitors tend either to love Kastellórizo and stay a week, or crave escape after a day; detractors dismiss it as a human zoo maintained by the Greek government to placate nationalists, while devotees celebrate an atmospheric, little-commercialized outpost of Hellenism.

ARRIVAL AND DEPARTURE

KASTELLÓRIZO

By air Kastellórizo's airport, 1km above the harbour, is served by regular Olympic/Aegean Air flights from Rhodes (1 daily; 25min). Passengers are accommodated in the island's lone taxi, at €5 per passenger.

By ferry Day-trips to Turkey leave regularly from the port in summer, for around €20.

Designations Astypálea (1 weekly; 16hr); Kalymnós

(2 weekly; 11hr 40min); Kos (2 weekly; 10hr); Níssyros (2 weekly; 8hr 30min); Pireás (2 weekly; 28hr); Rhodes (3 weekly; 2hr 20min–4hr); Sými (2 weekly; 3hr 50min–6hr 25min); Tílos (2 weekly; 7hr).

Travel agents Papoutsis, by the harbour, sells all sea and air tickets (☎ 22410 70630, ⓦ papoutistravel.4ty.gr).

Kastellórizo Town

The island's population is concentrated in **KASTELLÓRIZO TOWN** on the north coast – neatly arrayed around what's said to be the finest natural harbour between Beirut and Fethiye on the Turkish coast – and its "suburb" of Mandhráki, just over the fire-blasted hill and boasting a half-ruined Knights' castle. In summer, it's what Greeks call a *klouví* (bird cage) – the sort of place where, after two strolls up and down the pedestrianized quay, you'll have a nodding acquaintance with your fellow visitors and all the island's characters.

Most of the town's surviving original **mansions** are ranged along the waterfront, sporting tiled roofs, wooden balconies and blue or green shutters on long, narrow windows. Derelict houses in the backstreets are being attended to, and even the hillside is sprouting new constructions in unconventional colours, though the cumulative effect of World War I shelling, a 1926 earthquake, 1943 air raids and the 1944 explosions will never be reversed. The black-and-white posters and postcards depicting the town in its prime, on sale everywhere, are poignant evidence of its later decline.

ACCOMMODATION

KASTELLÓRIZO TOWN

★**Karnayo** ☎ 22460 49266, ⓦ karnayo.gr. An excellent mid-range choice, off the platía at the west end of the south quay, spread over two quiet, sensitively restored buildings, and offering four double a/c en-suite rooms as well as two studios, one of which sleeps four. **€70**

★**Kastellorizo Hotel** ☎ 22460 49044, ⓦ kastellorizo hotel.gr. Right in the thick of things in the middle of west quay, this lovely hotel has friendly management and some of the best amenities on the island. All its fourteen individually styled suites have kitchenettes, four have balconies, and there's a Thalasso-spa-pool as well as waterfront lido. March–Nov. **€130**

Megisti Hotel ☎ 22460 49219, ⓦ megistihotel.gr. Beautiful hotel in an unbeatable location, at the northwest corner of the harbour, with fabulous views and fifteen

spotless, attractively decorated rooms plus four large and very lavish suites. There's great swimming immediately off the spacious patio. **€160**

Pension Mediterraneo ☎ 22460 4900, ⓦ mediterraneo -kastelorizo.com. Simple rooms at the end of the northwest quay, furnished with mosquito nets and wall art. There's an arcaded, waterside basement suite, worth the extra cost for the privilege of being able to roll out the door and into the sea. Breakfast included. **€80**

Poseidon ☎ 22460 49257, ⓦ kastelorizo-poseidon.gr. Newly built houses in traditional style, set back from the platía at the west end of the south quay, and offering a total of twenty-one well-appointed studios spread over five houses, some with balconies. **€70**

5

EATING AND DRINKING

Kastellórizo's harbour quayside is a wonderfully romantic spot to enjoy a leisurely meal, though taverna prices are significantly higher than elsewhere. The island has its own fish, goat meat and wild-fig preserves, and assorted produce is smuggled over from Kaş, but otherwise food and drinking water have to be shipped here from Rhodes. Note that the mains water is contaminated by goat droppings, and tap water on the island is not safe to drink.

Alexandra's ☎ 22460 49019. Along the waterfront, yet a quiet location near the west end of the quay, this taverna offers large, great-value grills and salads with four different dishes of the day (mains around €13). Daily 10am till late.

Radio Café ☎ 22460 49029. Café with great views, close to the ferry jetty, which as well as coffee and breakfast offers internet access and *ouzomezédhes*. Daily 9am–late.

★Ta Platania ☎ 22460 49206. Set well back from the sea, up the hill on the Horáfia platía, this welcoming place

is festooned with film posters, and a good option for daily-changing *mayireftá* and desserts, though the prices are much the same as down by the port. June–Sept only, daily lunch and dinner.

To Mikro Parisi ☎ 22460 49282. Long-established seafood specialist alongside the port, with succulent soups and stews and zestful meat and fish grills. Not the cheapest, but good for a special occasion. Daily lunch and dinner.

The rest of the island

Kastellórizo's austere **hinterland** is predominantly bare rock, flecked with stunted vegetation; incredibly, until 1900 this was carefully tended, producing abundant wine of some quality. A rudimentary paved road system links points between Mandhráki and the airstrip, and a dirt track heads towards Áyios Stéfanos, but there are few specific attractions, and no scooters for rent. Karstic cliffs drop sheer to the sea, offering no anchorage except at the main town, Mandhráki and Návlakas fjord (see below).

The shoreline

Swimming on Kastellórizo is made difficult by the total lack of beaches, and the abundance of sea urchins and razor-sharp limestone reefs. Once clear of the **shoreline**, however, you're rewarded by clear waters with a rich variety of marine life, and amphora shards that testify to the ancient wine trade. Many visitors simply dive in from the lidos on the northwest quay; otherwise the safest entries near town lie beyond the graveyard at Mandhráki and the cement jetty below the power plant at road's end. **Taxi-boats** can take you to otherwise inaccessible coves such as **Plákes**, along the western shoreline of the town bay, where the flat surfaces of a former quarry are equally good for sunbathing on, or swimming off.

Návlakas fjord and Perastá grotto

Halfway along Kastellórizo's southeastern coast, **Návlakas fjord** is a favourite mooring spot for yachts and fishing boats. Uniquely for the island, Návlakas is free of sea urchins. Freshwater seeps keep the temperature brisk, and there's superb snorkelling to 20m depths off the south wall. Another popular stop for boat excursions, a little further south, is **Perastá grotto** (Galázio Spílio), which deserves a visit for its stalactites and strange blue-light effects. The low entrance, negotiable only by inflatable raft, gives little hint of the enormous chamber within, with monk seals occasionally sheltering in an adjacent cave.

Hálki

The little island of **Hálki**, a waterless limestone speck west of Rhodes, continues to count as a fully fledged member of the Dodecanese, even if its population has dwindled from three thousand to barely three hundred in the century since its Italian rulers imposed restrictions on sponge fishing.

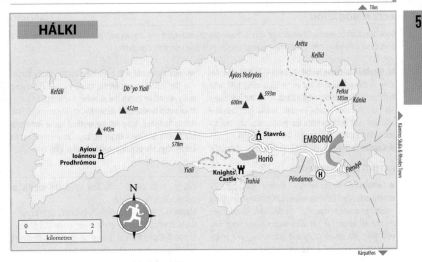

While tourism has brought the island back to life, except at the height of summer Hálki tends to be very quiet indeed. That said, in the middle of the day in high season, when day-trippers from Rhodes vastly outnumber locals in its broad quayside-cum-square, Emborió can feel more like a stage set than a genuine town.

ARRIVAL AND INFORMATION
HÁLKI

By ferry Hálki's port is in Emborió. Zifos Travel sell ferry tickets (☎ 22460 45028, ✆ zifostravel.gr).

Destinations Anáfi (2 weekly; 9hr 50min); Iráklio (Heraklion), Crete (2 weekly; 7hr 20min); Kárpathos (2 weekly; 2hr 40min); Kássos (3 weekly; 5hr); Kos (2 weekly;

2hr 45min); Níssyros (2 weekly; 1hr 40min); Pireás (2 weekly; 20–24hr); Rhodes Kámiros Skála (daily; 1hr 15min); Rhodes Town (4 weekly; 1hr 25min–2hr); Santoríni (2 weekly; 11hr 20min); Sítia, Crete (2 weekly; 4hr 10min); Sými (2 weekly; 2hr 20min); Tílos (2 weekly; 35min).

GETTING AROUND

By bus A sixteen-seat bus shuttles between the waterfront, Póndamos and Ftenáya.

Emborió

With its photogenic ensemble of restored Italianate houses rising from the waterfront, **EMBORIÓ**, facing east towards Rhodes from the head of a large bay, is a sort of miniature version of Sými (see p.297). Hálki's port as well as the only inhabited town, its skyline is pierced by the tallest freestanding **clocktower** in the Dodecanese, as well as – a bit further north – the **belfry** of Áyios Nikólaos, which holds a fine *votsalotó* (pebble-mosaic) courtyard. The **waterfront** has been paved with fieldstones, generally prettified and declared off limits to vehicles in season.

Although there's no **beach** at Emborió, many visitors swim anyway, simply lowering themselves into the water from the quayside or shoreline rocks. If that doesn't suit you, you'll find two beaches within easy walking distance, both equipped with good seaside tavernas. The island's only sandy beach, long narrow **Póndamos**, a fifteen-minute walk west over the hilltop, along the grandly named Tarpon Springs Boulevard, fills with day-trippers in summer. The best alternative, the tiny pebble cove and the gravel sunbed-lido at **Ftenáya**, lies a few minutes south of Emborió, along a well-signposted path that starts behind the *Ai. Nicolas Boutique Hotel* (see p.288); it too can get heavily over-subscribed.

ACCOMMODATION   EMBORIÓ

Book ahead for accommodation in high season. Some places perch right over the sea with access ladders for swimmers. Both ⓦnissiaholidays.com and ⓦzifostravel.gr offer an extensive selection of properties.

Ai. Nicolas Boutique Hotel ☎ 22460 45333, ⓦainicolas .com. Nicely refurbished, but exceedingly overpriced hotel in the old sponge factory on the south side of the bay, barely 5m from the sea. Tasteful en-suite rooms with sea-view balconies and ladders from the terrace into the sea for swimming. Expect erratic service. April–Oct. €130

★**Captain's House** ☎ 22460 45201. Two delightful en-suite a/c rooms, with a sea-view terrace, shady garden and the feel of an old French country hotel. The owner really makes her guests feel at home. April–Oct. €35

Marianthi House ☎ 22460 45028, ⓦzifostravel.gr. Fine, simply furnished stone cottage perched above Pondomos beach, with fabulous views of the bay. Can be rented out for longer stays. Sleeps four, in two bedrooms. €90

EATING AND DRINKING

★**Lefkosia's Paradosiako** Known for her TV appearances, chef Lefkosia believes in making everything – from her cheese to her pasta – from scratch. Baked dishes are the highlights at her waterfont taverna, including wild goat with lemon sauce and potatoes as well as her speciality "Halki pasta", baked with onions and feta. Daily lunch and dinner.

Magefseis ☎ 22460 45028. Simple grill house with a cluster of little tables outside along the harbour, which as well as excellent *gyros* for around €7, serves pretty much the gamut of tourist-favoured Greek cuisine; from mixed grills and salads to vegetarian dishes. Daily noon–late.

Maria ☎ 22460 45300. Well-shaded café, tucked behind the post office, that's dependable for substantial portions of island staples such as lamb stew, or pasta baked with bubbling feta cheese. Daily lunch and dinner.

Theodosia's Zaharoplastio ☎ 22460 45218. Also known as "The Parrot Café" on account of its resident bird, this friendly joint, with a cushioned wooden bench facing the base of the jetty, serves puddings and home-made ice cream to die for as well as good breakfasts. Daily 7am–late.

Horió and beyond

Still crowned by its Knights' castle, the old pirate-safe village of **HORIÓ**, looming 3km west of Emborió, beyond Pondamos, was abandoned in the 1950s. Except during the August 14–15 festival, the church here is locked to protect its frescoes. Across the valley, little **Stavrós monastery** hosts another big bash on September 14. There's little else inland, though Tarpon Springs Boulevard continues all the way across the island to reach the quite charming monastery of **Ayíou Ioánnou Prodhrómou** (festival Aug 28–29; *kantína* otherwise). The terrain en route is bleak, but compensated for by views over half the Dodecanese and Turkey.

Trahiá and Aréta

Hálki's remotest **beaches** can be reached either on boat excursions from Emborió quay – for example, aboard the *Kiristani* (☎69361 16229) – or via demanding hiking trails. **Trahiá**, directly below Horió's castle, and served by a very rough path from Yialí, consists of two coves to either side of an isthmus.

On the north coast, **Aréta fjord** is an impressive, cliff-girt place where seabirds roost and soar. There's some morning and afternoon shade at the small-pebble beach, but only a brackish well for the inquisitive sheep, so bring plenty of water. Experienced hillwalkers can get here on foot in around an hour and a half from the main harbour.

Kássos

The southernmost Dodecanese island, less than 48km northeast of Crete, **KÁSSOS** is very much off the beaten tourist track. Ever since 1824, when an Egyptian fleet punished Kássos for its active participation in the Greek revolution by slaughtering most of the 11,000 Kassiots, the island has remained **barren and depopulated**. Sheer

5

gorges slash through lunar terrain relieved only by fenced smallholdings of midget olive trees; spring grain crops briefly soften usually fallow terraces, and livestock somehow survives on a thin furze of scrub. The remaining population occupies five villages facing Kárpathos, leaving most of the island uninhabited and uncultivated, with crumbling old houses poignantly recalling better days.

ARRIVAL AND INFORMATION   KÁSSOS

By air The island's airport is 1km west of Frý.

Destinations Kárpathos (1–2 daily; 15min); Rhodes, via Karpathos (1–2 daily; 1hr 15min); Sitía, Crete (1–2 daily; 25min).

By ferry The island's port is in Frý, where the main ferry tickets agent is Kasos Maritime & Travel Agency (☎ 22450 41495, ⓦ kassos-island.gr). In season, to no fixed schedule, in addition to the scheduled times listed below, excursion boats also run to Frý from tiny Finíki on Kárpathos' west coast. Try the *M/v Kasos Princess*, which sails roughly three

times a week, or as a day-trip to Kárpathos every Wed in season (8.30am–5pm).

Destinations Anáfi (2 weekly; 4hr 30min–10hr 30min); Hálki (3 weekly; 5hr 20min); Iráklio (Heraklion), Crete (2 weekly; 6hr); Karpathós (7 weekly; 1hr 20min); Mílos (1 weekly; 17hr 15min); Pireás (2 weekly; 15–22hr); Rhodes (3 weekly; 7hr 40min); Santoríni (2 weekly; 7–15hr 30min); Sitía, Crete (2 weekly; 2hr 30min).

Tourist information The official island website is ⓦ kasos.gr.

GETTING AROUND

By bus A Mercedes van connects all the island's villages several times daily in summer, for a flat fare of €0.80.

By car and scooter Oasis in Frý rents out cars and scooters (June–Sept; ☎ 22450 41746).

Frý

The capital of Kássos, **FRÝ** (pronounced "free"), is halfway along the island's north coast, with views towards northwest Kárpathos. It's a low-key little place, with most of its appeal concentrated in the **Boúka** fishing port, protected by two crab-claws of breakwater and overlooked by Áyios Spyrídhon cathedral. Inland, Frý is engagingly unpretentious, even down-at-heel in spots; there are few concessions to tourism, though some attempts have been made to prettify a scruffy little town that's quite desolate out of season.

There's no **beach** in Frý itself: what's generally regarded as the town beach is the sandy cove at **Ammouá**, a half-hour walk along the coastal track west, beyond the airstrip.

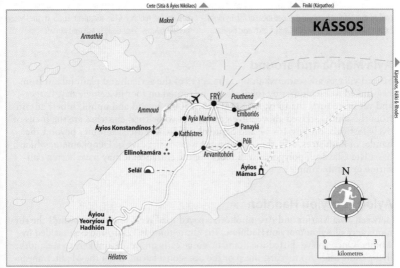

5

The first section you reach is often caked with seaweed and tar, but keep going another five minutes and you'll find cleaner pea-gravel coves. Determined swimmers also use the little patch of sand at **Emboriós**, fifteen minutes' walk east from Frý, where there's also a more private pebble stretch off to the right. Once you've got this far, however, it's worth continuing ten minutes along the shore to the base of the **Pouthená ravine**, which cradles another secluded pebble cove.

In high season, boat excursions head to far better beaches on two islets visible to the northwest, **Armáthia** and **Makrá**. Armáthia has five white-sand beaches to choose from, while Makrá has just one large cove. There are no amenities on either islet, so bring all you need.

ACCOMMODATION   FRÝ

Accommodation is very hard to find. Don't leave it until you arrive; be sure to book ahead.

Angelica's ☎ 22450 41268, ⊛ angelicas.gr. Four bright, roomy kitchenette apartments in a converted mansion 200m above Boúka harbour, with traditional furnishings, and, courtesy of the owner's mother, some rather extraordinary floor-paintings. All have outside space, but only two enjoy sea views. **€50**

Borianoula Apartments ☎ 22450 41495, ⊛ borianoula -apartments.gr. Seven basic but well-equipped en-suite apartments with balconies, on the beach about 600m from the harbour. Friendly service, and they offer airport or port pick-up. **€50**

★ **Evita Village** ☎ 22450 41731, ⊛ evita-village.gr. Small complex of five impeccable and very spacious modern studios, 200m uphill from Emboriós, with comfortable new furnishings and plenty of room to spread out. **€60**

Fantasis Apartments ☎ 22450 41695, ⊛ fantasis -hotel.gr. Six plain en-suite rooms, four with sea-view balconies, in a prominent yellow-trimmed modern structure, 5min climb up from the port towards Panayía. **€40**

EATING AND DRINKING

Iy Orea Bouka Summer-only taverna with a small terrace overlooking the port at Boúka, and a good range of inventive and tasty Kassiot dishes for roughly €10 which you select by visiting the kitchen. June–Sept daily lunch and dinner.

O Mylos ☎ 22450 41825. Frý's finest full-service taverna, overlooking the ferry port, is also the only one that stays open year-round. Excellent food, with a selection of slow-cooked *mayireftá* at lunch, and grilled meat or fish by night. Expect to pay around €12 each. Daily lunch and dinner.

Taverna Emborios ☎ 22450 41586, ⊛ emborios.com. This lively and very welcoming taverna, facing the eponymous cove, is renowned for its fresh-caught seafood, supplemented with hand-picked local herbs and vegetables. Summer daily 11am–2am.

To Koutouki ☎ 22450 41545. This bustling little place, up the steps from the quayside at Boúka, deserves its reputation for sizeable servings of old-fashioned Greek cooking for roughly €15; succulent lamb is the house speciality. June–Sept daily lunch and dinner.

Ayía Marína and around

Several villages are scattered around the edges of the agricultural plain inland from Frý, linked to each other by road; all can be toured on foot in a single day. Larger and yet more rural than Frý, **AYÍA MARÍNA**, 1500m inland and uphill, is best admired from the south, arrayed above olive groves; its two belfried churches are the focus of lively **festivals**, on July 16–17 and September 13–14. Fifteen minutes beyond the hamlet of **Kathístres**, a further 500m southwest, is the cave of **Ellinokamára**, which has a late Classical, polygonal wall blocking the entrance; it may have been a cult shrine or tomb complex.

Ayíou Yeoryíou Hadhión

Between Ayía Marína and Arvanitohóri, a paved road veers southwest towards the rural monastery of **Ayíou Yeoryíou Hadhión**. The entire route is 12km, and best tackled by scooter. Once you've skirted the dramatic gorge early on, you're unlikely to see another living thing aside from goats, sheep or the occasional falcon. Soon the Mediterranean appears; when you reach a fork, take the upper, right-hand turning, following the phone lines. Cistern water is always available in the monastery grounds, which only come to life around the April 23 **festival** (see p.43).

Kárpathos

Despite being the third-largest Dodecanese island, poised halfway between Rhodes and Crete, long, narrow **KÁRPATHOS** has always been a wild and underpopulated backwater. The island's usually cloud-capped mountainous spine, which rises to over 1200m, divides it into two very distinct sections – the low-lying **south**, with its pretty bays and long beaches, and the exceptionally rugged **north**, where deeply traditional villages nest atop towering cliffs. If you prefer to stay in a sizeable town, then **Pigádhia** on the east coast, Kárpathos' capital and largest port, is a good choice, with a wide range of hotels as well as a good beach, though it caters mostly for the Scandinavian and German package-holiday crowd. Several smaller resorts and isolated coves also hold lovely beachfront accommodation.

Touring Kárpathos' magnificent, windswept **coastline** is consistently superb, with its verdant meadows, high peaks, isolated promontories and secluded **beaches**, lapped by crystalline waters. The **interior**, however, isn't always as alluring: the central and northern forests have been scorched by repeated fires, while agriculture plays a minor role. The Karpathians are too well off to bother much with farming; emigration to North America and the resulting remittances have made this one of Greece's wealthiest islands.

Although the Minoans and Mycenaeans established trading posts on what they called Krapathos, the island's four Classical cities figure little in ancient **history**. Kárpathos was held by the Genoese and Venetians after the Byzantine collapse and so has no castle of the Knights of St John, nor any surviving medieval fortresses of note.

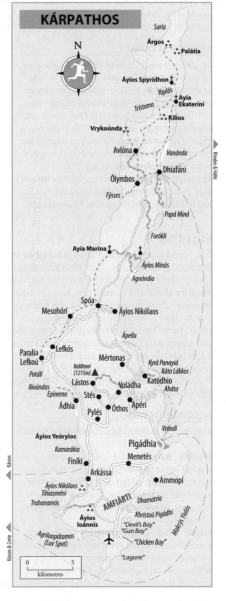

5

ARRIVAL AND DEPARTURE — KÁRPATHOS

By air Kárpathos's airport is on the flatlands at the island's extreme southern tip, 14km south of Pigádhia. There's no bus service, so renting a car at the airport can save you a steep taxi fare (from €18 to Pigádhia).
Destinations Athens (1 daily; 1hr 5min); Rhodes (1–2 daily; 40min); Sitía, Crete, via Kássos (1 daily except Fri; 1hr).
By ferry The island's main port is at Pigádhia. One weekly ferry to each of the destinations below also calls at Dhiafáni on Kárpathos's north coast. The main ferry agent in Pigádhia is Possi Travel (T 22450 22235, E possitvl@hotmail.com), who also sell day-trips to Hálki by ferry (Tues), and Kássos by air and ferry (Sat).
Destinations Anáfi (2 weekly; 6hr 15min–12hr); Hálki (2 weekly; 2hr 40min); Iráklio (Heraklion), Crete (2 weekly; 7hr 20min); Kássos (4 weekly; 1hr 20min); Mílos (2 weekly; 17hr 30min); Pireás (2 weekly; 21hr); Rhodes (4 weekly; 5hr); Santoríni (2 weekly; 12hr); Sítia, Crete (2 weekly; 4hr 10min).

GETTING AROUND

By car The airport's car rental outlet, Houvarda Maria (T 22450 61249), is the agent for Budget (E budgetkarpathos@yahoo.gr) and Drive (E drivekarpathos@yahoo.gr). Several more agencies are based in Pigádhia; especially helpful are Euromoto (T 22450 23238, E euromotokarpathos@yahoo.gr) who can deliver cars to the airport and offer competitive prices. The only petrol stations are immediately north and south of Pigádhia, so it's impossible to tour the whole island in one day by scooter.
By bus Pigádhia's "bus station" is a car park at the western edge of the town centre. Regular buses, run by KTEL (T 22450 22338), go to Pylés, via Apérí, Voládha and Óthos (3–4 daily); Ammopí (5–6 daily). Less frequent services run to Menetés, Arkássa, Finíki and Lefkos, with some continuing to Mesohóri; and to Kyrá Panayía, Ápella and Spóa.
By taxi Set-rate, unmetered taxis congregate two blocks inland from the harbour. Typical fares range from €10 to Ammopí up to €42 to Lefkos.
Boat excursions Boat day-trips run regularly from Pigádhia to isolated east-coast beaches. In addition, *Chrisovalandou III* (T 02410 51292) sails to and from Dhiafáni every day, typically leaving Pigádhia at 8.30am and Dhiafáni around 4.30pm, for a one-way fare of €15.

Pigádhia

The island capital of **PIGÁDHIA** (**Kárpathos Town**) lies on the southeast coast, at the southern end of scenic, 3km-long **Vróndi Bay**. The town itself makes little of its spectacular setting, typically reaching just one or two streets back from its long curving **waterfront**. All the main action is concentrated along its **southernmost section**. From the jetty where ferries and excursion boats dock, at the far end, the quayside curls north, lined initially by seafood restaurants and then an increasing number of cafés and music bars. The only buildings that catch the eye are a group of stately but fading Italian-era port police and county-government buildings, overlooking the port from a low bluff at its northern end. Beyond them, another hotel or two, most large but reasonably tasteful, seem to join the procession along the bay each year, stretching Pigádhia ever further northwards. While there's nothing special to see, Pigádhia does offer most conceivable facilities, albeit with a package-tourism slant.

ACCOMMODATION — PIGÁDHIA

A long line of hotels snakes northwards along Vróndi Bay; you're likely to enjoy Pigádhia more if you stay closer to the harbour.

Amarylis Hotel T 22450 22375, W amarylis.gr. Nice little budget hotel, on the hillside just above the bus terminal and central car park, with sixteen clean, whitewashed and surprisingly large studios and apartments. All have a/c, showers and kitchenettes, half have sea-view balconies. €30
Astron Hotel & Bungalows T 22450 22404, W astronhotel.gr. A good 30min walk from the harbour, this large complex of studios, apartments and rooms, all with balconies, is spread over four properties circling the large pool. Buffet-style breakfast (included) is served on the patio. Efficient management and good rates; mainly filled with Scandinavian tour groups. €35
Atlantis Hotel T 22450 22777, W atlantishotelkarpathos.gr. Welcoming little hotel, with helpful management and pleasant rooms, in a great central location facing the Italian "palace" just up from the port. Pay €5 extra for a sea view. €51
Electra Beach Hotel T 22450 23256, W electrabeachhotel.gr. Imposing modern hotel a 5min walk along the beach from the harbour. Each of its somewhat small but tastefully modernized rooms has its own balcony, with

dazzling views of the bay, and there's also a good pool. Buffet breakfast included. Usually filled with Scandinavian groups in summer, but good bargain low-season rates available. **€100**

EATING AND DRINKING

Mezedhopolio To Ellinikon ☎ 22450 23932. Serving what's unquestionably Pigádhia's finest food, this cosy indoor dining room is set back a block inland from the middle of the harbour. Diners are invited up to the raised kitchen to choose from daily specials like fabulous stuffed aubergine for €5, or a substantial grilled bream for €12; expect free trimmings such as a rich tapenade. Daily lunch and dinner.

★**Orea Karpathos ☎** 22450 22501. The best island restaurant along the harbour front strip near the southern end, running for over 25 years; almost nothing costs more than €10. *Trahanádhes* soup for €4.50, spicy sausages for €7.50, plus there are marinated artichokes, manouri cheese, great spinach pie and palatable local bulk wine. Locals use it as an ouzerí, ordering just mezédhes. April–Oct, dinner only.

Sofia's Place ☎ 22450 23152. Sit and enjoy the life of the port from the blue chairs on the terrace of this pretty, bustling and popular little restaurant in the heart of the action. Very friendly service and good local seafood at slightly above-average prices (around €15 each without wine), plus tasty grilled-meat specials. Daily noon–late.

The south

Immediately south of Pigádhia, reached by a detour off the main road down the other side of a low headland, the purpose-built resort of **AMMOPÍ** (also known as "Amoopi") is not so much a town as a succession of sand-and-gravel, tree- or cliff-fringed coves. There's no commercial centre to it, let alone anything that could be called authentic, but for a beachside holiday, any of the hotels here could make an appealing base. Keep going beyond them all to find some delightful little **turquoise bays**, usually deserted except at the height of summer.

Back on the main road, the further south you go, the flatter and more desolate Kárpathos becomes. The long windswept beach that leads all the way down to the airport has become popular with foreign **windsurfers**, who take advantage of the prevailing northwesterlies, especially during the annual summer European championships. As such, different segments are known these days by their windsurfing nicknames, such as Gun Bay. For non-surfers, the best beach here is **Chicken Bay**, a few metres from the airport runway, though it's a bit too exposed to spend a whole day here.

ACTIVTITIES   THE SOUTH

Windsurfing The most established windsurf school in southern Kárpathos is Pro Center Kárpathos (**☎** 22450 91063 or **☎** 697 788 6289, **ⓦ** chris-schill.com), which makes use of three separate bays and caters to different abilities.

ACCOMMODATION AND EATING

Esperida Ammopí **☎** 22450 81002, **ⓦ** esperida.gr. Large, very welcoming taverna, set well back from the sea halfway down the approach road to Ammopí. Delicious local food, including island cheese, wine and sausage, roast aubergine, and pickled wild vegetables (look out for what they call "capers"). Main dishes around €8, mezes half that. They also offer clean, good-value rooms and apartments (€50). Daily lunch and dinner.

Irini Beach Hotel Gun Bay **☎** 22450 91000, **ⓦ** karpathos

-windsurfing.gr. Upscale hotel complex on the island's prime windsurfing beach, with large comfortable rooms, a good pool, equipment rental and instruction. **€50**

★**Vardes Studios** Ammopí **☎** 22450 81111, **ⓦ** hotel vardes.gr. Ammopí's most peaceful studios, set amid orchards 400m back from the beach. Ten comfortable units, all with shower and balcony; some sleep up to five. House fruit and jam for breakfast (included) plus a bar, but no restaurant. **€45**

The west

Although it's much less developed than the area around Pigádhia, the **western shoreline** of Kárpathos holds several of the island's most attractive **beaches**. Small resorts such as Finíki and Lefkós make great bases for low-key holiday relaxation, amid scintillating scenery.

5

Arkássa

The main road from Pigádhia reaches the west coast at the little town of **ARKÁSSA**. Hardly anything survives of the original village – the rocky coastal frontage now consists of unremarkable studios and tavernas. Head a few hundred metres south, and you'll come to the signposted side road that leads to the whitewashed chapel of **Ayía Sofía**. Remains of a much larger Byzantine basilica here feature several mosaic floors with geometric patterns.

The finest **beach** hereabouts is also located just south of Arkássa. The broad 100m stretch of good-quality sand known as **Áyios Nikólaos** still feels pleasantly rural, even though a newly built hotel has just joined its long-standing taverna.

Finíki

A couple of kilometres north of Arkássa, facing it from the northern end of a long bay, the even smaller resort of **FINÍKI** is still very recognizable as the fishing village it used to be. A brief detour down from the main road, the port is arrayed along the curve of a minuscule beach, and has several welcoming tavernas. In summer, excursion boats head across from here to Kássos.

Lefkós

To reach the attractive resort of **LEFKÓS** – also known as **Paralía Lefkoú** – take a side turning that drops back down from the main road as it climbs through the dense forest around 10km north of Finíki. While considerably more developed than Finíki, it started out as a fishing village. Its best tavernas are concentrated around the **harbour**, which also holds a great sheltered beach, and accommodation is plentiful too. Several more beaches lie nearby, separated by a striking topography of cliffs, islets and sand spits.

Mesohóri

The main road climbs northeast from Lefkos through the pine forest to the dramatically sited village of **MESOHÓRI**. Tumbling seaward along narrow, stepped alleys, Mesohóri comes to a halt at the edge of a bluff that's dotted with three tiny, ancient chapels, separated from the village proper by extensive orchards.

ACCOMMODATION   THE WEST

Arhontiko Studios Finíki ☎ 22450 61473, ⓦ hotel arhontiko.gr. Simple, well-run hotel on the main coast road just above Finíki, where all seven comfortable studios and five larger apartments have sea-view balconies. **€42**

Finiki View Hotel Finíki ☎ 22450 61400, ⓦ finikiview .gr. Pleasant modern hotel, dropping down towards the port from the coast road. Eighteen well-equipped studios and two apartments, set in attractive gardens and sharing use of a pool. Great views at sunset. March–Oct. **€40**

Hotel Krinos Lefkos ☎ 22450 71410, ⓦ hotel-krinos .com. Low-rise complex, just before the road reaches the centre of town, that's especially popular with returning German guests. All its mix of rooms, studios and apartments are en-suite and has either balcony or terrace. March–Oct. **€35**

★Pine Tree Ádhia ☎ 6977 369 948, ⓦ pinetree -karpathos.gr. Simple but very attractive rooms in an utterly gorgeous rural location, with long-range sea views, a short walk up the hillside from the *Pine Tree Restaurant* (see opposite). A little higher up is a lovely stand-alone studio, with traditional sleeping platform, and there's free camping. **€35**

EATING AND DRINKING

Dhramoundana 1 Mesohóri ☎ 22450 71373. The finest eating option in this hillside village, but fiendishly difficult to find; it's near the church of Panayía Vryssianí, low down at the far north end. A couple of outdoor tables enjoy fabulous views, but the food is the main attraction, featuring capers, sausages, home-made *dolmadhes* and marinated "sardines". Daily lunch and dinner.

Dhramoundana 2 Lefkos ☎ 22450 71373. The pick of the three restaurants grouped together at the western end of Lefkos's harbour is slap in the middle. Its friendly owner, whose wife runs the sister restaurant *Dhramoundana 1* (see above), is a Greek-American who lived in Baltimore – hence the fabulous crab cakes. Expect a great meal for around €15. Daily lunch and dinner.

Glaros Áyios Nikólaos, Arkássa ☎ 22450 61015, ⓦ glarosrestaurant-karpathos.com. Stay in one of five tastefully furnished, good-value studios beside one of Kárpathos' nicest beaches. The returned Karpathian-Virginians hosts also run the *Glaros* beach taverna, with open-air dining. **€60**

Marina Finíki ☎ 22450 61100. Finíki's finest waterfront taverna, with a shady patio right by the beach. A quarter chicken is €5, otherwise most meat and fish dishes cost €8, though you'll pay more when there's fresh lobster. Live Greek music on summer evenings. Daily 9am–late.

Pine Tree Restaurant Ádhia ☎ 6977 369 948, ⓦ pinetree-karpathos.gr. Delightful restaurant, set amid orchards and lush gardens in an isolated spot, just up from the sea, 7km north of Finíki. Relax on the flower-decked terrace and sample such delights as home-baked bread, lentil soup and octopus *makaronádha*, washed down by sweet Óthos wine. Daily noon–8pm.

The centre

Central Kárpathos supports a group of villages blessed with commanding hillside settings, ample running water and a cool climate, even in August. Nearly everyone here has "done time" in North America before returning home with their nest eggs; the area is said to have the highest per capita income in Greece.

You're more likely to take a driving tour through the interior than to spend much time in any one place. Villages to look out for include **ÓTHOS**, which is the highest (around 400m) and the chilliest, on the flanks of 1215m Mount Kalilímni, and is noted for its bread, sausages and sweet, tawny-amber wine. **VOLÁDHA**, downhill to the east, cradles a tiny Venetian citadel, while the most attractive, **PYLÉS**, faces west atop a steeply switchbacking road that branches from the main west-coast road 6km north of Finíki.

The north

Despite the now fully asphalted road north from Spóa, the hairpin route remains a frightening prospect for all but the hardiest mountain drivers, and **Northern Kárpathos** still feels very much a world apart. Most visitors, therefore, still arrive by boat at the little port of **Dhiafáni**, and then take a bus up to the traditional hilltop village of **Ólymbos**. All the beaches in northern Kárpathos are pebbly, but don't let that put you off.

Spóa

The gateway to northern Kárpathos, where the road to Ólymbos branches off the main circle-island road, is the village of **SPÓA**, just east of the island's central spine. No road enters the village itself. If you're heading this way along the east coast, you might prefer to take a break at the best beach in these parts, down at **Ápella**, though from the taverna at the road's end you still have to walk a short pathway to reach the scenic 300m gravel strand.

Dhiafáni

The sleepy seafront village of **DHIAFÁNI** only springs to life twice a week, when its rare mainline ferries – one heading towards Rhodes, the other towards Crete – call in. Otherwise, the daily excursion boats from Pigádhia (see p.292) keep a low-key tourist industry – including several tavernas and lodging options – ticking along.

Dhiafáni itself has a reasonable fringe of shingle beach, and there's a quieter alternative at **Vanánda** cove; follow the pleasant signposted path north through the pines for thirty minutes, short cutting the road. Naturist beach **Papá Miná**, with a few trees and cliff shade, lies an hour's walk south via the cairned trail which starts from the road by the ferry dock.

Ólymbos

Founded in Byzantine times as a refuge from pirates, the windswept village of **ÓLYMBOS** straddles a long ridge below slopes studded with ruined windmills. Isolated for centuries, the villagers speak a unique dialect, with traces of its Doric and Phrygian

5

HIKING IN NORTHERN KÁRPATHOS

Northern Kárpathos is renowned for excellent **hiking**. While the most popular walk of all simply follows the jeep track down from Ólymbos to the superb west-coast beach at **Fýsses**, a sharp drop below the village, most local trails head more gently north or east, on waymarked paths.

Ólymbos to Dhiafáni An easy ninety-minute walk leads back down to Dhiafáni, starting just below the two working windmills. The way is well marked, with water twenty minutes along, and eventually drops to a ravine amid extensive forest.

Ólymbos to Vrykoúnda Heading north from Ólymbos, it takes around an hour and a half to reach sparsely inhabited Avlóna, set on a high upland devoted to grain. From there, less than an hour more of descending first moderately, then steeply, along an ancient walled-in path, will bring you to the ruins and beach at Vrykoúnda. Once you've seen the Hellenistic/Roman masonry courses and rock-cut tombs here, and the remote cave-shrine of John the Baptist on the promontory (focus of a major Aug 28–29 festival), there's good swimming in the pebble coves to one side.

Avlóna to Trístomo Starting just above Avlóna, a magnificent cobbled way leads in two and a half hours, via the abandoned agricultural hamlets of Ahordhéa and Kílios, to Trístomo, a Byzantine anchorage in the far northeast of Kárpathos. The views en route, and the path itself, are the thing; Trístomo itself is dreary, with not even a beach.

Trístomo to Vanánda If you've hiked to Trístomo, and would prefer not to retrace your steps to Avlóna, you can hook up, via a shortish link trail east from Trístomo, with a spectacular coastal path back to Vanánda (3hr 30min). Once clear of abandoned agricultural valleys and over a pine-tufted pass, it's often a corniche route through the trees, with distant glimpses of Dhiafáni and no real challenge except at the steep rock-stairs known as Xylóskala.

origins. Their home has long attracted foreign and Greek ethnologists for **traditional dress**, **crafts**, **dialect and music** that have vanished elsewhere in Greece. Here too the traditions are dwindling by the year; only older women, or those who work in the tourist shops, now wear striking, colourful clothing – while flogging trinkets imported from much further afield. Live folk music is still played regularly, especially at festival times (Easter and Aug 15), when visitors have little hope of finding a bed.

Women still play a prominent role in daily life, however: tending gardens, carrying goods on their shoulders or herding goats. Nearly all Ólymbos men historically emigrated to Baltimore or work outside the village, sending money home and returning only on holidays.

ACCOMMODATION AND EATING   THE NORTH

DHIAFÁNI

★**Gorgona** ☎ 22450 51509, ⓦ gorgonakarpathos.it. Located behind the seafront fountain, this Italian-run place is a favourite local rendezvous, featuring light dishes, wonderful desserts, proper coffees and *limoncello* digestif. Daily 9am–late.

★**Hotel Studios Glaros** ☎ 22450 51501. Run by the very welcoming George and Anna Niotis, these sixteen huge units, some of which sleep four and all with sea view, are top of the range in all senses in Dhiafáni, ranged in tiers up the southern slope. **€45**

Maistrali Studios ☎ 22450 51020, ⓦ maistrali karpathos.gr. Centrally located above the *Gorgona* restaurant, these seven a/c and en-suite rooms, plus one apartment, offer a simple yet comfortable place to stay, within short walking distance of Dhiafáni's beach. **€30**

ÓLYMBOS

Hotel Aphrodite ☎ 22450 51307, ⓦ discoverolympos .com. Little hotel, run by the same management as the nearby *Parthenonas* restaurant, with just four spacious double rooms, one of which has a kitchen. All have phenomenal views, to the windmills and the sea. **€35**

Hotel Astro ☎ 22450 51421. Smart en-suite rooms with traditional furnishings and a warm welcome from its owners – the two sisters who run *Café-Restaurant Zefiros* on the other side of the village, where breakfast (included) is taken. **€35**

Pension Olymbos ☎ 22450 51009. This friendly little place, near the village entrance, offers modern units with baths, as well as ones with traditional furnishings such as platform beds. It also has an excellent, inexpensive restaurant, specializing in traditional home cooking and with some unusual shellfish. **€30**

ÁVLONA

Restaurant Avlona ☎ 6946 018 521. This offshoot of the restaurant at *Pension Olymbos* (see opposite) lies on a spur road away from the Dhiafáni–Ólymbos road. The signature dish is *makaroúnes*, home-made pasta with onions and cheese. Four en-suite rooms make it an ideal base for walkers. **Daily lunch and dinner.**

Sými

For sheer breathtaking beauty, the Greek islands can offer nothing to beat arriving at **SÝMI**. While the island as a whole is largely barren, its one significant population centre, **Sými Town**, is gorgeous, a magnificent steep-walled bay lined with Italian-era mansions.

With its shortage of fresh water and relative lack of sandy beaches, Sými has never developed a major tourist industry. Sými Town, however, has a wide range of small hotels, as well as abundant delightful rental properties, while day-trippers from Rhodes – and yachties lured by the enticing harbour – mean it can support some very good restaurants too. In the height – and searing heat – of summer, it can get uncomfortably

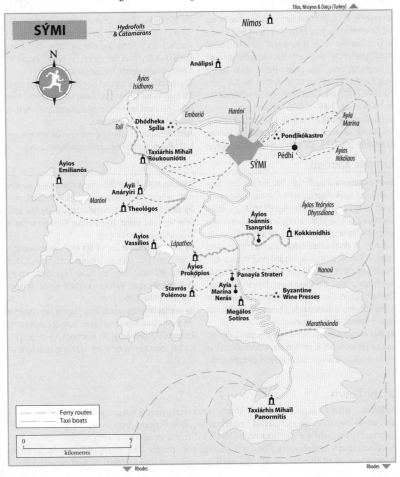

5

crowded, with a large influx of Italian visitors as well as mainland Greeks, but in **spring and autumn** it's wonderful, and even in winter a substantial expat community keeps many businesses open.

Visitors who venture beyond the inhabited areas find an attractive island that has retained some **forest** of junipers, valonea oaks and even a few pines – ideal walking country in the cooler months. Dozens of tiny, privately owned **monasteries** dot the landscape; though generally locked except on their patron saint's day, freshwater cisterns are usually accessible. Near the southern tip of the island, the much larger monastery of **Taxiárhis Miháïl Panormítis** is an important pilgrimage destination.

Little more than a century ago, Sými Town was home to more people than Rhodes Town, thanks to the wealth generated by its twin ancient skills of **shipbuilding** and **sponge diving**. Many of the **mansions** built during that age of prosperity have long since tumbled into decay – a process hastened in September 1944, when an ammunition blast set off by the retreating Germans levelled hundreds of houses up in Horió. While restoration is gradually bringing them back to life, the scattered **ruins** lend the island an appealing sense of time-forgotten mystery.

ARRIVAL AND INFORMATION

SÝMI

By ferry Ferries to and from the islands listed below use the main harbour in Sými Town. Most ferries from Rhodes to Sými Town also call in at Panormítis monastery, at the island's southern tip; only the Proteus sails from Sými Town to Panormítis, three times weekly. Tickets can be bought from Kalodoukas Holidays at the foot of the Kalí Stráta (☎22460 71077, ⊛kalodoukas.gr), and Sými Tours on the harbourfront (☎22460 71307, ⊛symitours.com).
Destinations Astypálea (1 weekly; 9hr); Hálki (2 weekly; 2hr 20min); Kálymnos (9 weekly; 2hr 10min–6hr 20min); Kastellórizo (3 weekly; 3hr 20min–6hr); Kos (7 weekly;

1hr 30min–4hr 50min); Léros (6 weekly; 3hr 20min–5hr 50min); Lipsí (6 weekly; 3hr 45min–7hr); Níssyros (3 weekly; 3–4hr); Pátmos (6 weekly; 5hr 10min–8hr 10min); Pireás (2 weekly; 17–21hr); Rhodes (3–4 daily; 50min–1hr 40min); Tílos (3 weekly; 1hr 30min–3hr 10min).
Tourist office Sými does not have an official tourist office, but Sými Visitor, based above Pahos café by the taxi-boat jetty, sells books and maps of local interest, and runs their own website, ⊛symivisitor.com.
Tours Sými Tours (see above) operates regular trips in season to the Byzantine Wine Press and Panormítis monastery.

GETTING AROUND

Boat excursions Between late May and late Sept, taxi-boats from Yialós harbour run to the east-coast beaches (see opposite), and north to Emborió (see p.301). In Aug, several a day make it possible to beach-hop; in lower season, pick a single day-trip destination. Fares range up to €15 for the round-trip to Marathoúnda. Larger boats offer circle-island cruises in summer, with snorkelling and picnic stops, or day-trips to Turkey, for around €40. You can also take a day-trip to Kastellórizo aboard the Dodekanisos Express catamaran (Mon only; €36; ⊛12ne.gr). On Sat only, the same catamaran makes a day-trip to Datca in Turkey; excursion boats run that route to no fixed schedule in summer.
By bus A year-round bus service operates from a tiny car park on the south side of the harbour. A coach shuttles at regular intervals between Yialós and Pédhi via Horió, while

a minibus makes two or three round-trips daily all the way south to Panormítis monastery (both €1.50 flat fare).
By taxi Sými's six taxis, based alongside the bus stop, serve the entire island. Expect to pay €5 to get between Yialós and Horió with baggage.
By car and scooter There's not much point renting a vehicle on Sými, with its minimal road network, but should you want one, try Glaros (☎22460 71926, ⊛glarosrentacar.gr), Katsaras (☎22460 72203) or Sými Tours (⊛symitours.com).
By tourist train Every hour, from 11am to 4pm, the little red tourist train takes beachgoers from the harbour to **Emborió** (Nimborió) Bay. This 40min ride (€6; children €3) is a fun alternative for those not wishing to walk (☎6941 474 514).

Sými Town

SÝMI, the island's capital and only town, is arrayed around a superb natural harbour in an east-facing inlet on the island's north shore. Inter-island ferries arrive right in the heart of town, while excursion boats jostle for room in summer with mighty Mediterranean cruisers. Immediately behind the straight-line quaysides that enclose the main segment of the port, scattered with sponge stalls and souvenir stores targeted at

5

day-trippers, the lowest row of **Italian-era mansions** clings to the foot of the hillsides. Each is painted in the officially ordained palette of ochres, terracotta, cream or the occasional pastel blue, and topped by a neat triangular pediment and roof of ochre tiles. The hills are steep enough that the houses seem to stand one above the other, to create a gloriously harmonious ensemble.

The lower level of the town, known as **Yialós**, extends northwards to incorporate the smaller curving **Haráni Bay**. Traditionally this was the island's shipbuilding area, and you'll still see large wooden boats hauled out of the water. Yialós also stretches some way inland from the head of the harbour, beyond the main town square, which is used for classical and popular Greek performances during the summer-long **Sými Festival**.

On top of the high hill on the south side of the port, the old village of **Horió** stands aloof from the tourist bustle below. It's hard to say quite where Yialós ends and Horió begins, however; the massive **Kalí Stráta** stair-path, which climbs up from the harbour, is lined with grand mansions, even if some are no more than owl-haunted shells. Another similar stairway, the **Katarráktes**, climbs the west side of the hill, from further back in Yialós, but it's more exposed, and used largely by locals.

Horió

As the 350-plus steps of Kali Stráta deter most day-trippers from attempting to reach **Horió**, the old hilltop village makes a great refuge whenever Yialós is too hot or crowded. It too holds its fair share of Italianate splendours and impressive basilicas. Once you venture away from the main pedestrian lane, it can be quite a tangle to explore – the part you can see from the harbour is just a small portion of the village, which stretches a long way back above Pédhi Bay. At the very pinnacle of things, a **Knights' castle**, largely destroyed by the wartime explosion, occupies the site of Sými's ancient acropolis; you may glimpse a stretch of Classical polygonal wall on one side. The **church of the Assumption**, inside the fortifications, is a modern replacement. One of the bells in the new belfry is the nose cone of a thousand-pound bomb, hung as a memorial.

Folk Museum
Closed indefinitely

A series of arrows leads deep into Horió to the excellent local **Folk Museum**, which, unfortunately, was closed indefinitely at the time of writing. Housed in a fine old mansion, its collection highlights Byzantine and medieval Sými, particularly frescoes in isolated, often locked churches. Displays continue in the eighteenth-century **Hatziagapitos mansion** below, with superb carved wooden chests and allegorical wall paintings.

Beaches

There's no **beach** in Sými Town. Some visitors clamber into the sea from the harbour wall in Haráni Bay, but neither there nor at the tiny, man-made **Sými Paradise** "beach", adjoining a restaurant just around the headland beyond Haráni, is the water clean enough for swimming to be advisable.

Keep walking along the paved coast road from Haráni, however – there's no shade, but the views are nice, and there's seldom any traffic – and in around half an hour you'll come to quiet **Emborió** (Nimborió) Bay. The beach is just a narrow strip of coarse shingle, but it's a great place to while away an afternoon of swimming, snorkelling, and eating at the friendly taverna. In summer, the beach is served by regular taxi-boats, so you're not obliged to walk both ways.

ACCOMMODATION	SÝMI TOWN

Albatros Marketplace, Yialós ☎22460 71707, ⓦ www.albatrosymi.gr. This classy little hotel has four a/c rooms, a pleasant second-floor breakfast salon, and distant sea views. The website is also the booking venue for a number of magnificent apartments in Neoclassical villas. **€53**

5

Aliki Haráni quay, Yialós ☎ 22460 71665, ⓦ hotelaliki .gr. Upscale waterfront hotel, housed in a renovated 1895 mansion, just around the corner from the main harbour. The fifteen tasteful rooms have wood floors and some antique furnishings, plus a/c and large bathrooms. All have at least partial sea views, some have balconies, and three suites. Mid-April to Oct. €140

Fiona Near the top of the Kalí Stráta, Horió ☎ 22460 72088, ⓦ www.fionahotel.com. The large, simply furnished but attractive and airy rooms upstairs at this village hotel enjoy stunning views and have small balconies. There are also three studios next door. Breakfast, on the terrace, included €50

Hotel Chorio Horió ☎ 22460 71800, ⓦ hotelchorio.gr. Opposite *The Windmill* restaurant (see opposite), these seventeen en-suite a/c rooms all have balconies, some with lovely views over the harbour. Expect somewhat erratic service. €75

Iapetos Village Yialós ☎ 22460 72777, ⓦ iapetos -village.gr. Tucked into walled, landscaped grounds just back from the main square at the head of the harbour, this smart complex includes a roofed-over pool. All the rooms, studios and apartments are exceptionally large and have kitchens; some sleep up to six. A good buffet breakfast is included. €135

Kalodoukas Holidays Sými harbour ☎ 22460 71077, ⓦ kalodoukas.gr. Rental agent for a wide array of generally irresistible houses and apartments, all with kitchen facilities and many featuring traditional furnishings plus harbour-view balconies and/or courtyard gardens. 2-person apartment €50, 4-person house €140

Nireus Hotel Yialós ☎ 22460 72400, ⓦ nireus-hotel.gr. Sými's most conspicuous hotel, in prime position near the clocktower at the harbour entrance, with a lovely waterfront bar and decent restaurant. The stunning sea views from the adequate but unexceptional seafront rooms just about justify the high prices; don't even consider the cheaper rear-facing ones. April to mid-Oct. €120

Niriides Apartments Emborió ☎ 22460 71784, ⓦ niriideshotel.com. Ten simply furnished, spacious and quiet rental units, spread over five hillside buildings on the hillside just above the nice little beach at Emborió, 2km north of Yialós. All sleep four and have a/c; friendly management and on-site "lounge-café", with a good taverna immediately below. €115

★ The Old Markets Not far up the Kali Stráta, Yialós ☎ 22460 71440, ⓦ theoldmarkets.com. Boutique B&B hotel, housed in an imposing and very elegant converted mansion, with magnificent harbour views. Each of the four en-suite rooms is luxuriously furnished; the "Sými Suite", which costs double, is quite superb. €195

Opera House Yialós platía ☎ 22460 72034, ⓦ symi operahouse.gr. This unexpectedly large complex, a short walk inland from Yialós' main square, consists of several separate houses, newly built in traditional style. They're divided into apartment suites for two to six people; all have balconies and though few have views to speak of, the rates for the sheer space you get are remarkably low, especially off season. €70

★ Sými Visitor Accommodation ☎ 22460 71785, ⓦ symivisitor.com. Wendy Wilcox and Adriana Shum offer great-value rental stays in restored houses in Yialós and Horió. Ranging from simple studios to family mansions, these are private homes let in their owners' absence, and come with all sorts of idiosyncrasies. Great option for the "real Symi" experience. Two-person €85, 4-person €115

EATING AND DRINKING

RESTAURANTS

George & Maria's Top of Kalí Stráta, Horió. Jolly, much-loved Sými institution, with a pebble-mosaic courtyard. Expect to be invited to inspect the pots in the kitchen before making your choice – perennial dishes (around €10), include feta-stuffed peppers, beans with sausage, lemon chicken, and a full range of grills. Dinner daily, plus random lunchtimes in season.

Muses Yialós Platía ☎ 6958 734 503. With lovely open-air seating beneath trailing vines, *Muses* offers a distinctive, delicious, very contemporary and rather pricey take on Greek cuisine. The cucumber salad is a deconstructed tzatsiki, while the octopus with ouzo foam and orange is fabulously succulent; like most dishes, it's available as a meze (€10) or a main (€20). Daily 7.30–11.30pm.

★ Mythos South quay, Yialós ☎ 22460 71488. This dinner-only, harbour-view roof terrace near the bus stop serves some of the tastiest food on the island. Chef-owner Stavros' specialities include *psaronéfri* with mushrooms and sweet wine sauce, lamb *stifádho* and feta *saganáki* in fig sauce. Best is the phenomenal meze menu, with sharing dishes such as scallops in cheese sauce. Around €29 per head. Late May to late Sept daily 7.30–11pm.

Syllogos Platía Syllógou, Horió. Vast but not impersonal place with indoor/outdoor seating, great for taverna standards like *skordhaliá*, *arní lemonáto*, fried fish and aubergine *imám*, with good *hýma* wine on offer – only skimpy portion sizes deprive it of an "author pick" symbol. Roughly €20 a head. Daily lunch and dinner.

Tholos Haráni quay ☎ 22460 70203. The last restaurant you come to as you walk around Haráni bay, with waterside tables laid out right on the headland. A fabulously romantic spot for a fine meal of grilled fresh fish (around €15 per head); the cheese-topped aubergine is pretty good too. May–Oct daily lunch and dinner.

Trata Platía Trata, Yialós ☎ 22460 71411. This lively, very informal local hangout fills most of the small square

5

at the foot of the Kalí Stráta. The fresh seafood is great, but it's also a place to go off piste and simply see what delights – especially vegetable dishes – may be lurking in the kitchen. Daily 9am–late.

★ **The Windmill** Horió ☎ 6955 973 695. This delightful *mezédhes* restaurant, run by a welcoming Greek-British duo, has open-air tables laid out around the old windmill in the Horió. Expect favourites such as home-made hummus and *briám*, plus a host of vegetarian and meat dishes along with deliciously simple salads and excellent service. *Mezédhes* from €7. Daily 7.30pm till late.

BARS AND CAFÉS

Bar Tsati Haráni quay ☎ 22460 72498. You can't get any closer to the water than this friendly Italian-run little café-bar, a short walk from the clocktower around Haráni bay. A cluster of pastel-coloured tables and chairs in a harbour-front nook, plus cushions on the sea wall itself. Proper Italian espresso and tasty titbits, and a lively late-night scene. Daily 11am–1am or later.

Evoi Evan Yialós platía. With a large terrace sprawling beneath the spreading ficus trees, and a cavernous interior that includes a pool table upstairs, *Evoi Evan* is open from breakfast onwards, serving coffee, smoothies and juices first thing, and a full drinks menu later on. Daily 8am–late.

★ **The Olive Tree** Horió ☎ 22460 72681, ⓦ olivetree symi.eu. Friendly English-run café, across from the *Fiona* hotel (see opposite); a meeting place for energetic local

expats. Free wi-fi, top-quality coffee and home-made cakes, excellently priced juices and smoothies, good sandwiches and healthy breakfasts and dinner Sat in spring and autumn. Fantastic views over the harbour below. Daily 8am–3pm.

Pahos Yialós. Classic *kafenío*, in operation since World War II. Facing the west quay south of Yialós bridge, this is still the spot for an evening ouzo or coffee and people-watching. Pahos himself has retired but can sometimes be found sitting out front as a customer; otherwise it's hardly changed – including the prices, significantly lower than elsewhere. Daily 8am–late.

The Secret Garden Pédhi ☎ 22460 72153. Michalis and Katya operate a lovely establishment, tucked away in a courtyard garden but well signposted on the road to Pédhi. Breakfasts such as Katya's eggy-bread speciality, and delicious *mezédhes* in the evening guarantee a repeat clientele of both expats and locals. Daily 9am till late.

To Steno Yialós ☎ 22460 72767. Traditional locally popular *kafenío* near the *Albatros* hotel (see opposite) offering your everyday Greek frappé, ouzo and beers, but all served with meze home-produced from owner Mercure's farm. Six meze dishes plus ouzo or beer for €20. Daily 8am till late.

Sunrise Café/Anatoli Iliou Horió ☎ 22460 72720. Cosy English/Austrian-run café, on the eastern edge of Horió. Well-priced drinks, breakfasts, good salads and light snacks, plus courtyard with a book swap. Daily mornings, plus afternoons after siesta till late.

The rest of the island

Away from Sými Town, the only other settlements on the island are little **Pédhi**, on the shoreline below Horió, and **Panormítis** down at the southern tip. The main attractions for visitors are isolated pebbly **beaches** that stand at the heads of the deeply indented bays along the eastern coast – accessible by taxi-boat in summer – and the tiny scattered **monasteries** that make great targets for hikers.

Pédhi

The hugely indented bay lying south of Sými Town, on the far side of the ridge that stretches away from Horió, is home to the separate little community of **PÉDHI**. Somewhat further than it may look from Horió – it takes about half an hour to walk down the hillside – it's served by regular buses.

Originally a fishing hamlet with a sideline in boatbuilding, Pédhi has slowly expanded over the past twenty years. Much of the waterfront is now lined with new houses built in the standard Italian-influenced Sými style. Even if there's nothing authentic about it, it's reasonably pretty; locals fear the construction of an ugly new marina may spoil things, but there's been little progress so far. While the waterfront has a hotel and a couple of tavernas, Pédhi doesn't have a beach.

Ayía Marína

A small indentation in the headland that separates Sými Town from Pédhi Bay, known as **Ayía Marína**, has been developed as a miniature beach. With wonderful turquoise water, and a monastery-capped islet within easy swimming distance just offshore, it's an attractive spot, but in summer it tends to fill up (largely with Italians) the moment the

5

HIKING ON SÝMI

Sými has become an extremely popular **hiking** destination. With midsummer temperatures high even by Greek-island standards, spring and autumn are much the best seasons to come. Most trails lead through depopulated and waterless areas, so you need to have good equipment and provisions, and ideally relevant experience. Lance Chilton's *Walks in Sými*, sold locally packaged with his *Walker's Map of Sými*, is a very good investment for all hikers. Neil Gosling of **Sými Dream** (☎6936 421 715, ☯symidream.com) – located three-quarters of the way up the Kali Strata – offers twice weekly small group photography walking tours of the island. From beginner to advanced photographer, or even just for the stroll, the knowledge of the island that Neil imparts makes this a brilliant way to explore the area (Wed & Sun 9.25am–noon; €10; meet at Symi Dream office).

One excellent trail takes three hours (one way) to cross the island from Yialós to its westernmost tip, where the tiny monastery of **Áyios Emilianós** is tethered to the mainland by a slender causeway. Some of the route lies through forest. Along the way there, you'll pass Sými's oldest monastery, **Taxiárhis Mihaïl Roukouniótis** (daily 9–11am & 5–6pm), which contains naive eighteenth-century frescoes. For a shorter walk, you can drop down a dirt track from the monastery to reach small, pebbly **Tolí Bay**, which has a summer-only taverna. An eastward trail over the hilltop from there drops down to **Emborió**, to complete a potential loop back to Yialós.

Another meaty hike crosses the island from Horió in ninety minutes to scenic **Áyios Vassílios** gulf; for the final forty minutes, follow a paint-splodge-marked path from the road's end. Immediately above **Lápathos beach** is a little monastery which has some interesting frescoes and accessible water.

The finest frescoes on the island are at the hilltop, **Kokkimídhis monastery** (dates from 1697, usually open), reached by a steep track off the Panormítis road, where a complete cycle shows the acts of the Archangel and the risen Christ.

It's also possible to hike all the way from Horió to **Nanoú beach** (see below) in around three hours. That leaves you with time for a meal and swim before catching the boat back to Yialós. Alternatively, as the route leads first to the chapel at **Panayía Strateri** on the main road, you could take a scooter that far and only walk the final 45 minutes, through a scenic forested gorge, down to the beach.

day's first taxi-boat arrives. The waterfront is an unbroken row of sunbeds, and the one taverna does a brisk trade.

It's possible to beat the crowds by walking here, either along a paint-splodge-marked path from Pédhi or over the top of the ridge from the east end of Horió, but the best time to hike is in low season, when the taxi-boats aren't running and you may have the place to yourself.

Áyios Nikólaos

An exposed fifteen-minute footpath along the south side of Pédhi Bay – simply push your way through the gate at the end of the quayside, then follow the cairns along the slope – leads to **Áyios Nikólaos**, the only all-sand cove on Sými. Also served by regular taxi-boats in season, this offers sheltered swimming, shady tamarisks, a bar, beach volleyball and a relaxing taverna.

Áyios Yeóryios Dhyssálona

The first significant bay to interrupt Sými's eastern coastline south of Pédhi is **Áyios Yeóryios Dhyssálona**. This spectacular fjord can only be accessed by boat. No path could find a foothold in the smooth limestone that soars at its inland end. There's no taverna, and the whole place falls into shade in the early afternoon.

Nanoú

The largest east-coast bay, **Nanoú**, holds the most popular beach for boat-trippers. A 200m stretch of gravel, sand and small pebbles, with a scenic backdrop of pines, it offers good snorkelling, and has a decent, seafood-strong **taverna**. Nanoú isn't on a paved road, but it is possible to hike down here, from the main trans-island road (see box opposite).

Marathoúnda

The southernmost taxi-boat stop, **Marathoúnda**, is a magnificent bay, fringed by a long beach of coarse pebbles and ideal for tranquil swimming. It's also accessible via a paved road, which branches off the main road just after it switchbacks down from the island's central spine towards the monastery at Panormítis. Just back from the beach, the valley floor is flat enough to support a few fields, as well as goats who regularly stroll along the waterfront in search of titbits.

Taxiárhis Mihaïl Panormítis monastery

Museums daily 8.30am–2pm & 3–4pm • €1.50 combined admission

In summer, at least one daily inter-island ferry, as well as countless excursion boats from Rhodes, calls in at the large **Taxiárhis Mihaïl Panormítis monastery**, located in a gorgeous (albeit beachless), almost entirely closed little bay in the far south of Sými. You can also get here by road, on one of the daily buses that heads down from Yialós. A shop, bakery and simple taverna cater to the needs of day-trippers.

Built in honour of the Archangel Michael (*Taxiárhis* in Greek), patron saint of the island, the monastery was thoroughly pillaged during World War II, so – except for its lofty belfry – don't expect much of the building or its contents. Away from its spruce main **courtyard**, which has an attractive pebble-mosaic floor, most of the complex is gently fading. Lit by an improbable number of oil lamps, the central *katholikón* is also graced by a fine *témblon* and of course the cult icon, though frescoes are unremarkable.

The monastery courtyard contains two small **museums**. One, devoted entirely to artefacts related to the monastery's religious significance, contains a strange mix of precious antiques, exotic junk, and votive offerings including bodybuilding and motocross trophies. A small boat is piled with messages-in-bottles carried here by the Aegean currents – the idea is that if the bottle or toy boat arrives, the sender's prayer is answered. In the opposite corner, a folklore museum holds displays on costumes, weaving, and domestic activities.

ACCOMMODATION AND EATING   **THE REST OF THE ISLAND**

Katsaras Pédhi ☎ 22460 71417. With a shaded terrace right at the water's edge, this large taverna, in the middle of Pédhi Bay, makes a great place for a full meal or a sunset drink. Vegetable and seafood mezes cost around €8, grilled meat more like €12. Daily noon–9pm.

Pédhi Beach Hotel Pédhi ☎ 22460 71981, ⓦ pedi beachhotel.gr. Large, simply furnished a/c rooms in the middle of the bay; there's a patio laid out with sunbeds, though no beach. A small proportion of rooms have

sea-view balconies; rates include dinner at the on-site restaurant, and drop significantly outside Aug. €120

★**Taverna** Marathoúnda. Run by the Kalodoukas family, who also offer rental studios here, and supplied with fresh organic produce from their adjoining fields, this excellent waterfront taverna offers top-quality mezes for around €8, or beautifully prepared fish from around €12.50. Mid-May to mid-Sept daily lunch and dinner.

Tílos

Stranded midway between Kos and Rhodes, the small, usually quiet island of **TÍLOS** is among the least frequented and most unpredictably connected of the Dodecanese. For visitors, however, it's a great place simply to rest on the beach, or hike in the craggy hinterland.

Tílos shares the characteristics of its closest neighbours: limestone **mountains** like those of Hálki, plus volcanic lowlands, pumice beds and red-lava sand as on Níssyros. With ample groundwater and rich volcanic soil, the islanders could afford to turn their backs on the sea, and made Tílos the **breadbasket** of the Dodecanese. Until the 1970s,

5

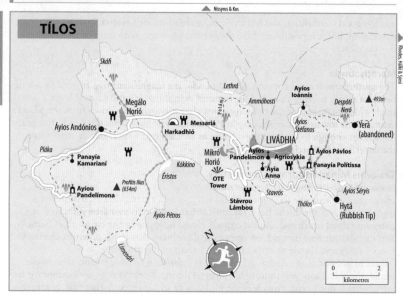

Nissyros & Kos

TÍLOS

travellers were greeted by the sight of shimmering fields of grain bowing in the wind. Nowadays, the hillside terraces languish abandoned, and the population of five hundred dwindles to barely a hundred in winter.

While recent development has turned the port of **Livádhia** ever more towards tourism, Tílos remains low-key. This is still a place where visitors come to get away from it all, often for extended stays. If you're here to **walk**, little may seem striking at first glance, but after a few days you may have stumbled on several small Knights' **castles** studding the crags, or found some of the inconspicuous, often frescoed, often locked **medieval chapels** that cling to the hillsides.

ARRIVAL AND INFORMATION

TÍLOS

By ferry The island's port is at Livádhia; buy ferry tickets from Stefanakis, close to the jetty (☎ 22460 44310, ⓦ tilos-travel.com).

Destinations Astypálea (1 weekly; 7hr 15min); Hálki (2 weekly; 45min); Kálymnos (2 weekly; 5hr 30min); Kastellórizo (2 weekly; 6hr 35min–10hr); Kos (4 weekly; 2–3hr); Níssyros (4 weekly; 50min); Pireás (2 weekly;

14–19hr); Rhodes (7 weekly; 1hr 20min–2hr 15min); Sými (3 weekly; 1hr 30min–3hr 10min).

Maps The best maps on Tílos are published by SKAI, while walking guides Iain and Lyn Fulton (☎ 22460 44128 or ☎ 6946 054 593, ⓦ tilostrails.com) offer itineraries geared towards all levels.

GETTING AROUND

By bus A blue-and-white bus, charging €1.20, links Livádhia and Megálo Horió, to coincide with ferry arrivals. It also makes up to five runs daily between Livádhia and the beaches at Áyios Andónios and Éristos, plus a €4 round

trip to Ayíou Pandelímona monastery on Sun mornings.

By car and scooter Iris Rent a Car (☎ 6972 842 665) and Drive (☎ 22460 44173) in Livádhia.

Livádhia

At its core, the port-cum-resort of **LIVÁDHIA**, at the head of a splendid bay on the island's north shore, is still recognizable as a traditional harbourfront village. A row of little tavernas, hotels and studios stretches away to the east, however, taking advantage of a narrow strip of beach that offers pleasant family swimming. The entire seafront is now lined by a broad pedestrian promenade, which is great for visitors even if it does diminish the "authentic" feel of the place.

GETTING AROUND

By car and moped The bypass road that was supposed to take all vehicles around the back of the village hasn't quite materialized, so even the shortest journey by road can require labyrinthine detours. Once you're settled in you'll almost certainly walk everywhere local anyway.

ACCOMMODATION
LIVÁDHIA

Anna's Studios ☎ 22460 44334, ⓦ tilosrooms.gr. The immaculate nine units in this bright whitewashed building, on the west hillside immediately above the jetty, vary in size, but all have pastel-hued furnishings and kitchenettes, and three have enormous sea-view balconies. **€40**

Blue Sky ☎ 22460 44294. Nine well-appointed apartments, right on the harbour just above the ferry jetty, and available year-round, but call ahead to check out of season. Each is designed for three, with a galleried sleeping area, kitchen, and sea-view balcony. **€40**

Dream Island Hotel ☎ 22460 70707, ⓦ dreamisland .gr. Eleven very spacious one- and two-bedroom apartments, within a few metres of the water roughly two-thirds of the way around the bay. All have at least partial sea views, and are decorated in cool contemporary colours. Rates include breakfast and sunbeds. **€120**

★ **Faros Hotel** ☎ 22460 44068, ⓦ farosroomstilos .com. Family-run, friendly hotel-cum-taverna, out on its own at the far east end of the bay. Peaceful, well-cared-for three-bedded rooms, plus what's effectively its own beach. It's a 25min walk back to the main strip of restaurants, though the food here is perfectly good, plus the service and peacefulness of the place ensure repeat clientele, year after year. Breakfast included. **€55**

Ilidi Rock ☎ 22410 44293, ⓦ tilosholidays.gr. Tílos' largest and newest hotel, dropping in bright-white tiers to the water's edge at the west end of the bay, a 5min walk from the ferry. State-of-the-art studios and apartments; one wing has disabled access. Two little private pocket beaches, plus gym facilities. Mainly caters to Scandinavian tour groups; open all year, though breakfast (not included) in summer only. A/c costs extra. **€60**

Irini Hotel ☎ 22410 44293, ⓦ tilosholidays.gr. Lushly landscaped low-rise hotel, 200m inland from the middle of the beach. The large pool, good breakfasts (included) from the on-site café, wi-fi signal and pleasant gardens make up for somewhat small, mock-antique furnished rooms. **€60**

Tilos Fantasy ☎ 22460 44425, ⓦ tilosfantasy.gr. Substantial modern complex of studios, with mainly Italian clientele, in a quiet hillside location 400m back from the sea. The rooms are perfectly presentable, though the furnishings look out of an IKEA catalogue, and there are two single beds in each room. **€55**

EATING AND DRINKING

CaféBar Georges ☎ 22460 44257. Traditional old bar on the main square, where the outdoor tables are filled nightly with locals watching the world go by. Daily 8am–late.

Iy Omonoia ☎ 22460 44287. Enduringly popular traditional café, also known as *Tou Mihali*, stretching under trees strung with light bulbs beside the square, just up from the sea. A good venue for breakfast or a sundowner; its inexpensive, tasty, generous mezédhes will stand in for a formal meal. Daily 8am–late.

Mediterranean Delights Popular bar, grill and seafood restaurant next to the bakery in the paltia. Chef Anthony is American trained and offers excellent breakfast choices such as omelettes and eggs benedict for €8; you can enjoy your food or drinks on the roof terrace, with a view of the harbour. Daily 8am–late.

Mihalis ☎ 22460 44359. Welcoming taverna, set in attractive gardens a short walk back from the sea, 50m east of the central square. No-nonsense fish for around €10, roast goat for a little less, as well as good vegetable platters and non-CAIR bulk wine. Daily 8am–late.

★ **Oneiro/Dream** Very popular "grill-and-fish house", open to the sea breezes near the centre of the beachfront promenade. Excellent grills and spit-roasts, typically costing €8 for meat and €12 for fish. Be prepared to wait for your food in high season. Daily lunch and dinner.

Taverna Trata ☎ 22460 44364. Relaxed taverna, 100m inland from the beach at the first bend in the road, serving good local food on a nice open-air terrace. Check in the kitchen to see what's cooking, or sample grilled meat or fish for around €10. Daily lunch and dinner.

To Armenon ☎ 22460 44134. Professionally run and salubrious beach-taverna-cum-ouzerí, right by the sea in the middle of the bay, with large portions of octopus salad (€8.50), white beans, meaty mains and fish platters (typically €12.50), plus pasta and pizza, all washed down by Alfa beer on tap. Daily 10am–late.

To Mikro Kafé Pretty little shoreline cottage, nicely restored to create a buzzing, music-oriented bar and café that also offers a reasonable snack menu. The rooftop terrace is a great spot for late-night stargazing. Daily 5pm–late.

5

Beaches near Livádhia

It's easy to spend days on end lazing on the beach at Livádhia itself, but quieter alternatives lie within easy walking distance. An obvious trail heads north to the pebble bay of **Lethrá**, a walk that takes around an hour one way. Two-thirds of the way along, a side path drops to the tiny red-sand beach of **Ammóhosti**, which you're unlikely to have to yourself.

Stavrós

An hour-long hike from Livádhia, to the secluded cove of **Stavrós** on the south coast, starts between the *Tilos Mare Hotel* and the *Castellania Apartments*; once up to the saddle with its paved road, you've a sharp drop to the beach. Ignore the cairns in the ravine bed; the true path is up on the right bank.

Thólos and Áyios Séryis Bay

The trail (1hr) to the similar cove of **Thólos**, just east of Stavrós, begins by the cemetery and the chapel of **Áyios Pandelímon**, then curls under the seemingly impregnable castle of **Agriosykiá**. From the saddle on the paved road overlooking the descent to Thólos (25min; also red-marked), a cairned route leads northwest to the citadel in twenty minutes. Head east a couple of curves along that paved road to the trailhead for **Áyios Séryis Bay**, Tílos's most pristine beach but also the hardest to reach (30min from the road).

Mikró Horió

The ghost village of **Mikró Horió**, whose 1200 inhabitants left for Livádhia during the 1950s, is less than an hour's walk west of the port, with some surviving path sections short cutting the road curves. Its only intact structures are churches (locked to protect their frescoes) and an old house restored as a small-hours **music bar** (July & Aug 9pm till the wee hours).

Megálo Horió

Tílos' capital, the village of **MEGÁLO HORIÓ**, lies 7km west of Livádhia along the main road. The only other significant settlement on the island, it enjoys sweeping views over the vast agricultural plain that stretches down to Éristos, and is overlooked in turn by a prominent **Knights' castle** (unrestricted access). Reaching the castle requires a stiff thirty-minute climb, which threads its way through a vast jumble of cisterns, house foundations and derelict chapels.

Museum

Main street • Closed indefinitely

A little **museum** – regrettably, closed at the time of writing – in the town hall displays the bones of midget elephants, found in the **Harkadhió cave** not far east in 1971. Such remains have been found on a number of Mediterranean islands, but Tílos' group may have been the last to survive, until as recently as 4000 BC.

Éristos beach

3km south of Megálo Horió

Long, pink-grey-sand **Éristos beach**, ranks among the island's finest, though swimmers have to cross a reef to reach open sea. The far south end, where the reef recedes, is nudist, as are the two secluded all-naturist coves at **Kókkino** beyond the headland (accessible by path from the obvious military pillbox).

ACCOMMODATION AND EATING

Eden Villas 500m north of Megálo Horió ☎ 22460 44094, ⓦ tilostravel.co.uk. Choice option run by Brits, this comfortable three-bedroom villa, with pool and wi-fi, is nicely located in the valley leading to Skáfi beach.

Available for extended stays year-round. **€200**
Eristos Beach Hotel Éristos ☎ 22460 44025, ⓦ eristos beachhotel.gr. Crisp modern complex, catering mainly to large package-tour groups, facing the large, barely developed beach at Éristos on the southwest, with lots of outdoor space, including a pleasant terrace and large pool. Studios sleeping two to four have large balconies, plus there are sizeable apartments suitable for four to six. **€60**
Kastro Megálo Horió ☎ 22460 44232. While the interior

of Megálo's only taverna can be a little gloomy, its patio has lovely long-range views, and the food is good, with meat and goat cheese from their own flock, and home-made *dolmádhes*. Daily lunch and dinner.
Mílios Apartments Megálo Horió ☎ 22460 44204. Attractive rooms and apartments set in pleasant flowery gardens in the heart of Megálo Horió, on the out-of-town road to Eristos Beach. All have balconies offering (distant) sea views. **€50**

The far northwest

The main road west of Megálo Horió hits the coast again at somewhat grim **ÁYIOS ANDÓNIOS**, which has an exposed, truncated beach and two tavernas. There's better, warm-water swimming at isolated, sandy **Pláka beach**, another 2km west, where people camp rough despite a total lack of facilities.

Ayíou Pandelímona monastery

Grounds daily 10am–7pm (Oct–April till 4pm), may close briefly at noon; monastery Sun only (same hours) • Free

The paved road ends 8km west of Megálo Horió at fortified **Ayíou Pandelímona monastery**, founded in the fifteenth century for the sake of its miraculous spring, still the best water on the island. A fitfully operating drinks café hosts the island's major **festival** of July 25–27. The monastery's tower-gate and oasis setting, high above the forbidding west coast, are its most memorable features, though a photogenic inner courtyard boasts a *votsalotó* surface, and the church a fine tesselated mosaic floor.

Níssyros

The volcanic island of **Níssyros** is unlike its neighbours in almost every respect. It's much lusher and greener than dry Tílos and Hálki to the south, blessed as it is with rich soil that nurtures a distinctive flora, and it supported a large agricultural population in ancient times. In contrast to long flat Kos to the north, Níssyros is round and tall, with the high walls of its central caldera rising abruptly from the shoreline around its entire perimeter. And Níssyros conceals a startling secret; behind those encircling hills, the interior of the island is **hollow**, centring on a huge crater floor that's dotted with still-steaming vents and cones.

For most visitors, the **volcano** is Níssyros' main attraction. It's easy enough to see it on a day-trip from Kos, so few bother to spend the night. That's a shame, because it's a genuinely lovely island, very short on beaches but abounding in spectacular scenery. The port and sole large town, **Mandhráki** on the northwest coast, is an appealing tight-knit community with some fine ancient ruins, while two delightful villages, Emboriós and Nikiá, straddle the crater ridge.

These days, much of the island's income is derived from the offshore islet of **Yialí**, a vast lump of pumice, all too clearly visible just north of Mandhráki, that's slowly being quarried away. Substantial concession fees have given the islanders economic security.

Níssyros also offers good **walking**, on trails that lead through a countryside studded with oak and terebinth; pigs gorge themselves on the abundant acorns, and pork figures prominently on menus.

ARRIVAL AND DEPARTURE

NÍSSYROS

By ferry Ferries moor at a concrete jetty a few hundred metres east of Mandhráki, out of sight of town. Book tickets with either Dhiakomihalis (☎ 22420 31459) or Kendris

(☎ 22420 31227).
Destinations Astypálea (1 weekly; 5hr 30min); Hálki (2–3 weekly; 1hr 40min); Kálymnos (2 weekly; 2hr 50min);

Kastellórizo (2 weekly; 8hr 30min); Kos Kardamena (4 weekly; 40min); Kos Town (8 weekly; 1hr–1hr 40min); Pireás (2 weekly; 17hr 30min); Rhodes (4–5 weekly; 3hr 10min–4hr 45min); Sými (3 weekly; 3–4hr); Tílos (4–5 weekly; 50min).

GETTING AROUND

By bus Buses from the jetty head up to six times daily to Emboriós and Nikiá, via Pálli.

By taxi For a fixed-rate taxi service, call ☎ 22420 31460.

By car and scooter Rental outlets include Manos K on Mandhráki harbour (☎ 22420 31029), and Dhiakomihalis in town (☎ 22420 31459).

By coach Several coach trips daily set off from the jetty to visit the volcano. English-run Enetikon Travel, nearby on the road into town (☎ 22420 31180), are typical in offering €8 round trips (1hr 45min) every morning from 10.30am onwards.

Mandhráki

The ancient harbour of **MANDHRÁKI**, the capital of Níssyros, silted up centuries ago, creating a fertile patch that now serves as the *kámbos* (community orchard), surrounded in turn by the modern town. Nonetheless, this remains the island's sole ferry port – boats pull in at a concrete jetty to the east, out of sight of the centre. Mandhráki's a nice little place, stretching along the seashore slightly further than appears at first glance. Behind the pedestrianized waterfront promenade, to some extent overwhelmed by poor tavernas and souvenir stores aimed at day-trippers, the tangled narrow lanes are lined with whitewashed houses, whose brightly painted balconies and shutters are mandated by law. The ensemble is punctuated by appealing little squares, and offers repeated glimpses of fruit trees to one side, and blue sea to the other.

5

At its western end, Mandhráki comes to an abrupt halt at a low bluff that's topped by the stout walls of a **Knights' castle**. Though records have been lost, it's known that the Knights Hospitaller occupied Níssyros from 1314 until 1522, and the island is thought to have reached its heyday around 1400. You can't access any more of the castle itself than the corner staircase and gateway that leads to the little **Panayía Spilianí monastery** (generally open daylight hours).

Langadháki, the district immediately below the castle, was badly hit by earthquakes in the 1990s, but little damage is now visible. At sea level, an attractive mosaic footpath leads further west around the headland to reach the short, black-rock beach of **Hokhláki**, which is seldom suitable for swimming.

Archeological Museum

A few blocks back from the sea on the main lane • Tues–Sun 8.30am–3pm • €2 • ☎ 22420 31588

Níssyros's modern **Archeological Museum** holds assorted treasures from the island's past. The main floor focuses on the pre-Christian era, starting with six-thousand-year-old artefacts created using obsidian from nearby Yialí. Ceramic pieces range from delicate winged figurines of Eros, dating from 350 BC but closely conforming to modern depictions of angels, to a colossal funerary *pithos* (urn) from the sixth century BC. Stelae in the downstairs galleries reveal a Christian presence on the island in the third century.

Paleókastro

Unrestricted access • Walk up the well-signposted path from beneath the cliffs at the west end of Mandhráki waterfront for roughly 20min; once you meet a cement road – also accessible by a much more circuitous drive up from town – turn right and you'll see the castle

The hugely impressive **Paleókastro** is a mighty ancient fortress that's one of the most underrated ancient sites in Greece. On its way up to the castle, the path through the fields passes numerous ancient stairways and ruins. This hilltop was occupied from the eighth century BC onwards; around four centuries later, **Mausolus of Halicarnassus**, the Persian satrap who left us the word "mausoleum", enclosed its inland slopes within 3m-thick walls – the cliffs on the seaward side already formed a natural boundary. If you think of ancient Greek ruins as all graceful white marble columns, prepare to see something different – much older and vaster. Slotted seamlessly together, the colossal trapezoid blocks are reminiscent of Inca masonry. Only the barest outlines of the buildings within the enclosure survive, but visitors can clamber onto the **ramparts** by means of broad staircases to either side of the still-intact **gateway**.

ACCOMMODATION   MANDHRÁKI

Haritos ☎ 22420 31322. Small hotel, a short walk from the ferry landing; head left along the coast road rather than towards town. Its eleven rooms have marble-trimmed baths and veneer floors, and the seafront across the road has a terrace restaurant and a hot-spring pool. Limited English spoken. Open year-round. **€50**

Porfyris ☎ 22420 31376, ⓦ porfyrishotel.gr. Large, somewhat old-fashioned hotel, well back from the sea in the town centre in a good location overlooking the common orchards. Most of the 38 spruce a/c rooms have sea views from private balconies and terraces, and there's a large seawater pool and breakfast (included) is served on the terrace. **€40**

Romantzo ☎ 22420 31340, ⓦ nisyros-romantzo.gr. Good-value family-run hotel, uphill to the left of the ferry

jetty out of sight of the town, with simple but comfortable a/c en-suite rooms and apartments. While the rooms themselves have rear-view windows, all benefit from the broad, shared and pleasant sea-view terrace. **€30**

★Ta Liotridia ☎ 22420 31580, ⓔ info@nisyros-taliotridin.com. Two incongruously gorgeous suites (sleeping up to four), above a rough-and-ready bar just metres from the sea on the oceanfront footpath in the centre of town. Exposed stone walls incorporating lava boulders, fine wooden furnishings and head-on sea views. **€80**

Xenon Polyvotis ☎ 22420 31011. Municipally owned hotel, on the quayside facing the ferry port; its en-suite rooms are large yet unremarkable, but there's no faulting the sea views. Breakfast included. May–Oct. **€40**

5

EATING AND DRINKING

Gleca Onera ☎ 22420 31700. Wonderful cake shop, with outdoor seating, a short walk from Platía Ilikiomenis. The owner, Anna, offers all manner of desserts and ice creams such as her home-made chocolate pie and cream-and-jelly cake. A popular choice to stop and indulge at following a good meal in town. Daily all day till 9pm.

Irini ☎ 22420 31365. Lively restaurant, in busy little tree-shaded Platía Ilikiomenis, inland at the west end of town, offering hearty traditional dishes like aubergine and mince, or pepper stuffed with rice for €6–8. In truth, the food isn't exceptional, but it's a convivial and involving place to spend an evening, plus Irini herself is incredibly hospitable. Daily lunch and dinner.

Kali Katsou Cheap and cheerful local specialities served at a place poised immediately above the water on the quayside: seafood such as mussels or squid as well as tasty island sausages for just €6. Daily lunch and dinner.

Kleanthis ☎ 22420 31484. The best seafood restaurant along the waterfront, with bright blue tables and chairs set out on the quayside. Tasty *pittiá* (chickpea croquettes) and other mezes, followed by fish dishes ranging from fried shrimps for €8 up to stuffed squid with cheese or swordfish for €16. Daily lunch and dinner.

Proveza ☎ 22420 31618, ⓦ proveza.net. Lively café-bar with extensive comfortable seating on the seafront promenade near *Ta Liotridia*. Besides being great for a sunset drink, with an appropriate soundtrack, it also offers free wi-fi and a row of internet-access computers indoors. Daily 11am–late.

Taverna Salonikios ☎ 22420 31371. Situated along the waterfront, this taverna offers a slightly more ambitious menu than its competitors, with dishes such as *kondosoúvli* for €8. Mezes such as fried courgette flower with Níssyros cheese and spicy melted fondue go for €5. Daily 9am–late.

To Kazanario ☎ 6972 240 556. A delightful ouzeri, with basement and garden seating, hidden in a small square opposite *Pali* bakery. The menu is meticulously written in Greek and English in a small textbook. Expect dishes such as grilled meat, fresh fish – caught that morning by the fisherman owner – and mushrooms stuffed with feta. No *mezédhes* over €8. Daily 7pm–midnight.

The coast

Níssyros is almost entirely devoid of **beaches**, and only a small proportion of its coast – along the north and northwest shoreline – is even accessible to visitors. While the coast road east from Mandhráki peters out after barely 10km, it does make a pretty **drive** – and you'll have to come this way anyway if you're heading for the volcano. The largest structures en route are a couple of huge abandoned spas, dating back to the Italian era.

Pálli

Four kilometres east of Mandhráki is **PÁLLI**, a fishing village turned low-key resort that can be a welcome retreat when Mandhráki fills with trippers. All summer, the little harbour here is busy enough with pleasure boats – which can't moor at Mandhráki – to support several tavernas. Pálli also has an excellent **bakery**, cranking out tasty brown bread and pies. A reasonable tamarisk-shaded **beach** of reddish-grey sand, kept well groomed, extends east to the derelict Pantelídhi spa, behind which the little grotto-chapel of **Panayía Thermianí** is tucked inside the vaulted remains of a Roman baths complex.

Liés and Pahiá Ámmos

If you keep going east beyond Pálli, along an initially bleak stretch of shore, you'll reach the pleasant cove of **Liés**, home to the summer-only *Oasis* snack-bar. The paved road ends at a car park a little further on, a spot that can also be reached in summer by taxi-boats from Mandhráki. There's a grey-sand beach right here, while another fifteen minutes by trail over the headland brings you to the idyllic, 300m expanse of **Pahiá Ámmos**, where the grey-pink sand is heaped in dunes, there's limited shade at the far end and a large colony of rough campers and naturists congregate in summer.

ACCOMMODATION AND EATING   THE COAST

Ellinis Pálli **☎** 22420 31397. This long-established taverna is the best in Pálli, serving spit-roasted meat by night and grilled fish in season, all at reasonable prices, and offering a handful of simple en-suite, a/c rooms upstairs (€25). Open daily lunch till late.

★ Limenari Limenari valley **☎** 22420 310233. Excellent traditional cooking, in an attractive location just below the main road, 1km west of Pálli, halfway down a terraced

valley towards its little namesake bay. Fair prices (around €12 each) for big portions of home-style food. Daily lunch and dinner.
Mammis Apartments Pálli ☎22420 31453. A dozen

tasteful self-contained a/c apartments, capable of sleeping four and equipped with large sea-view balconies and their own separate entrances, perched amid hillside gardens a short walk west of Pálli. **€40**

The interior

If you've come to Níssyros to see the **volcano**, you're already there – the whole island is the volcano. Beyond and behind the steep slopes that climb from the shoreline, the entire centre of the island consists of a vast bowl-shaped depression. The hills end in a slender ridge that's the rim of the caldera, meaning that the two hilltop villages that survive, **Emboriós** and **Nikiá**, are long thin strips that enjoy stupendous views both out to sea and down into the maw. The interior is etched almost in its entirety with ancient agricultural terraces, mostly long abandoned but giving a very real sense of the much greater population in antiquity. A side road just beyond Emboriós offers the only road access, and continues south to the craters at the far end.

Emboriós

The road up from Pálli winds first past the village of **EMBORIÓS**. As is obvious from the copious ruins that stretch high above the current village centre, the population here once numbered in the thousands; in winter these days it dwindles to just twenty. It's a gorgeous spot though, which is being bought up and restored by Athenians and foreigners. New owners often discover natural volcanic saunas in the basements of the crumbling houses; at the outskirts of the village there's a signposted public **steam bath** (unrestricted access) in a grotto, its entrance outlined in white paint. One can hike down to the caldera floor from Emboriós; a trail drops from behind the little platía, and it's another fifteen-minute walk to the craters.

Some 3km south of Emboriós, a paved drive leads down from the main road to **Panayía Kyrá**, the island's oldest and most venerable monastery, worth a stop for its enchanting, arcaded festival courtyard as much as its church.

HIKING ON NÍSSYROS ISLAND

Níssyros is a fabulous destination for **hikers**, with enticing **trails** to suit all abilities. The one drawback is that hiking to and from the volcano from Mandhráki is for most walkers too much to attempt in a single day. It's not so much the distance that's the problem as the fact that you have to climb back out of the island interior on your way home.

VOLCANO TO MANDHRÁKI

About 1km north of the volcano admission booth, a clear, crudely marked path climbs to a pass, then maintains altitude along the north flank of **Káto Lákki** gulch, emerging after an hour and a half at the important monastery of **Evangelístra**, with its giant terebinth tree just outside. Beyond Evangelístra, you have to walk about 1km on the paved access road before the old path kicks in for the final half hour down to Mandhráki. Look sharp at curves to find the old walled-in path. At first it just short cuts the road, then for quite a long stretch it loops above the port well away from the road, before finally curling around to emerge above the local school.

NIKIÁ TO EMBORIÓS

Hiking from **Nikiá to Emboriós** takes just under an hour and a half, with a short stretch of road-walking towards the end. Descend from Nikiá towards the volcano and bear right towards Theológos monastery, then take the left fork by the wooden gate before reaching it. The path ambles along through neglected terraces, without much altitude change, occasionally obstructed by debris and vegetation. You eventually emerge after just under an hour by some utility poles on the modern Emboriós–Nikiá road. Follow the road from there for about 1km (15min) to the turn-off for Lakkí, where the onward trail continues conspicuously uphill into Emboriós.

5

The volcano

Generally unrestricted access, though occasionally a ticket booth charges €2.50 admission • A steady procession of coach trips from Mandhráki (see p.308) usually keeps the area busy between 11am and 3pm; to enjoy it in solitude, make your own way up early or late in the day – either rent a vehicle or hike there (see box, p.311)

What's loosely referred to as being the "**volcano**" is the eerie conglomeration of cinder cones and deep craters at the far southern end of the summit caldera, reached by a single road that drops down beyond Emboriós. Although the volcano is dormant, and you won't therefore see fiery eruptions or flowing lava, it's disconcertingly alive, with sulphurous steam sprouting from holes and fissures on all sides. There's a snack-bar here, open at peak times only.

As soon as you follow the short trail from the road's-end car park to the fenced overlook, you realize that while the main crater – officially named **Stéfanos** – may look small from a distance, close up it's a massive, hissing, stinking pit. Its striated walls, yellow with sulphur, drop straight down 40m to a flat stained floor that's pockmarked with bubbling fumaroles. You can venture down there via an easy trail that winds along a timeworn groove in the crater wall. Don't get too close to the boiling mud-pots, which sound as though there's a huge cauldron bubbling away beneath you. In legend, this is the groaning of the titan Polyvotis, crushed by Poseidon under a huge rock torn from Kos.

The hillside immediately west holds several steep-sided **cones**, accessible via an obvious and undemanding trail. Climbing up lets you escape the crowds, and also offers a greater thrill of discovery. It seems a shame to reveal what awaits you at the **top**, but rest assured it's worth it.

Nikiá

The village of **NIKIÁ**, overlooking the caldera from high on its southeastern rim, is a gorgeous little place that should figure on any island itinerary. Its spectacular location, 14km from Mandhráki, enjoys panoramic views out to Tílos as well as across the volcano. Tiny lanes lead from the bus turnaround at road's end to railed volcano viewpoints as well as to the diminutive, engagingly round central platía called Pórta. Paved in pebble mosaic, ringed by stone seating for folk dances, and facing a pretty little church, it's all so dazzlingly white that it's hard to keep your eyes open.

A 45-minute **trail** descends from the end of the road to the crater floor. A few minutes downhill, detour briefly to the eyrie-like monastery of **Áyios Ioánnis Theológos**, whose grounds come to life at the September 25–26 evening festival.

EATING AND DRINKING   THE INTERIOR

★**Andriotis** Nikiá ☎ 22420 31027. The only taverna in Nikiá, at the village entrance, with huge views out over the sea, serves a good menu of meaty €6 specials, including rabbit or chicken stews, and succulent chocolatey desserts. Summer daily lunch and dinner.

Apyria Emboriós ☎ 22420 31377. Excellent little taverna, with a breezy indoor dining room and tables on the platía by the church in peak season, or crammed into a tiny alleyway when it's less busy. Delicious local food at

great prices (around €13 a head), including *kondosoúvli* in summer. The friendly owner is also a beekeeper; be sure to sample fresh honey if you're here in July. Daily lunch (Sun only in winter) and dinner.

Porta Pangiotis Nikiá ☎ 22420 31285. This welcoming village café, one of a matching pair on Nikiá's tiny, delightful circular platía, is an irresistible spot to pause for a snack, juice or coffee. Daily 10am–8pm.

Kos

After Rhodes, **Kos** ranks second among the Dodecanese islands for both size and visitor numbers. Here too, the harbour in **Kos Town** is guarded by an imposing **castle** of the Knights of St John, the streets are lined with Italian-built public buildings, and minarets and palm trees punctuate extensive Hellenistic and Roman remains. And while its interior mostly lacks the wild beauty of that of Rhodes, Kos is the most **fertile** island in the archipelago, blessed with rich soil and abundant groundwater.

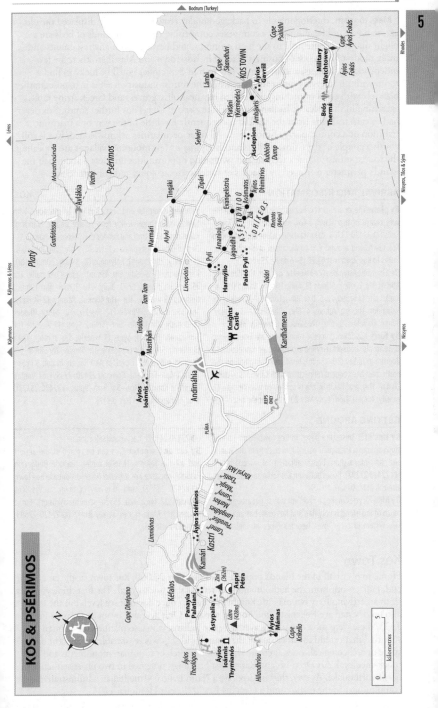

KOS & PSÉRIMOS

0 ____ 5
kilometres

5

Mass tourism, catering mainly to package-holiday crowds, has largely displaced the old agrarian way of life; all-inclusive complexes comprising tens of thousands of beds are a blight that contribute little to the local economy, and have forced many restaurants and more modest hotels out of business. Except in Kos Town and Mastihári, there are few independent travellers, and from mid-July to mid-September you'll be lucky to find a room without reserving far in advance, while the tourist industry itself is juxtaposed rather bizarrely with cows munching amid baled hay near olive groves, and Greek Army tanks exercising in the volcanic badlands around the airport. Like Tílos further south, Kos never had to earn its living from the sea and consequently has little in the way of a maritime tradition or a contemporary fishing fleet. All these peculiarities acknowledged, Kos is still worth a couple of days' time while island-hopping: its few **mountain villages** are appealing, the tourist infrastructure excellent and **swimming** opportunities limitless – about half the island's perimeter is fringed by beaches of various sizes, colours and consistencies.

ARRIVAL AND INFORMATION   KOS

By plane The local airport is just outside Andimahía, in the very centre of the island, 24km southwest of Kos Town. Taxis (☎ 22420 23333, ⓦ kostaxi.eu) charge around €40 to Kos Town, and around €20 to Mastihári or Kardhámena. Buses to Kos Town cost €3.20 (4–6 daily; 25min).
Destinations Astypálea (2–3 weekly; via Leros 1hr 45min, via Athens 3hr 20min); Athens (3 daily; 50min); Iráklio (Heraklion), Crete (3 weekly; 2, 5, 8 or 10hr); Léros (2–3 weekly; via Kalymnos 1hr, via Athens 4–6hr); Rhodes (2–3 weekly; 30min, via Athens 3–5hr); Thessaloníki (2 weekly; 3hr).
By ferry Kos Town domestic connections are listed below; there are also frequent ferry and excursion-boat connections to Bodrum in Turkey (30–45min). In addition, Mastihári on the north coast has frequent connections with Kálymnos (6 daily; 20min–1hr), and Kardhámena is connected with Níssyros (2 weekly; 40min). From early May 2015 and for the rest of the

summer season (till end Sept), Kos will be connected with Samos via a thrice-weekly ferry service via the islands of Kalymnos, Leros, Lipsi and Patmos (ferry times unknown).
Destinations Astypálea (1 weekly; 4hr 30min); Hálki (2 weekly; 2hr 45min); Kálymnos (3–5 daily; 30min–1hr); Kastellórizo (1 weekly; 9hr 45min); Léros (1–2 daily; 1hr 25min–3hr); Lipsí (2–3 daily; 2hr 10min–4hr 10min); Níssyros (8 weekly; 1hr–1hr 40min); Pátmos (2–4 daily; 1hr 35min–5hr); Pireás (12 weekly; 10–14hr); Rhodes (1–5 daily; 2hr 10min–6hr 15min); Sými (11 weekly; 1hr 30min–4hr 50min); Syros (3 weekly; 5hr 30min); Thíra (3 weekly; 5hr); Tílos (2 weekly; 1hr 50min–2hr 50min).
Tourist office Kos Travel, at Akti Kountouriotou 5 in Kos Town (Mon–Fri 9am–8pm; ☎ 22420 22359) or Voula's Travel, at Korai 3 (Mon–Sat 9am–9pm; ☎ 22420 28477), near *Afendoulis* hotel (see p.317).

GETTING AROUND

By bus KTEL buses are based in Kos Town, with several stops around a triangular park 400m back from the water, and an information booth adjacent at Kleopátras 7 (☎ 22420 22292). Buses between Kos Town and the airport also call at Mastihári.
By bike Bicycles make an excellent way to get around Kos; much of the island is very flat, and Kos Town has an extensive system of cycle lanes. George's Bikes, at Spetson 48

(☎ 22420 24157), has a good selection.
By car and scooter Cars can be rented at the airport and all the resorts. Helpful outlets include Budget in Psalídhi, opposite *Kos Imperial Hotel* just outside Kos Town (☎ 22420 28882), and AutoWay in town, at Vassiléos Yeoryíou 22 (☎ 22420 25326, ⓦ autowaykos.gr). For a scooter, try Moto Harley at Kanári 42 (☎ 22420 27693, ⓦ moto-harley.nl).

Kos Town

Home to over half of the island's population of just over 28,000, **Kos Town**, at the far eastern end, radiates out from the harbour and feels remarkably uncluttered. The first thing you see from an arriving ferry is a majestic **Knights' castle**, for once down at sea level, but the town also holds extensive **Hellenistic** and **Roman** remains. Only revealed by an earthquake in 1933, these were subsequently excavated by the Italians, who also planned the "garden suburbs" that extend to either side of the central grid. Elsewhere, sizeable expanses of open space or archeological zones alternate with a hotchpotch of Ottoman monuments and later mock-medieval, Art Deco-ish and Rationalist buildings, designed in two phases either side of the earthquake. As ever, they incorporate a "Foro Italico" – the Italian administrative complex next to the castle – and a Casa del Fascio (Fascist Headquarters).

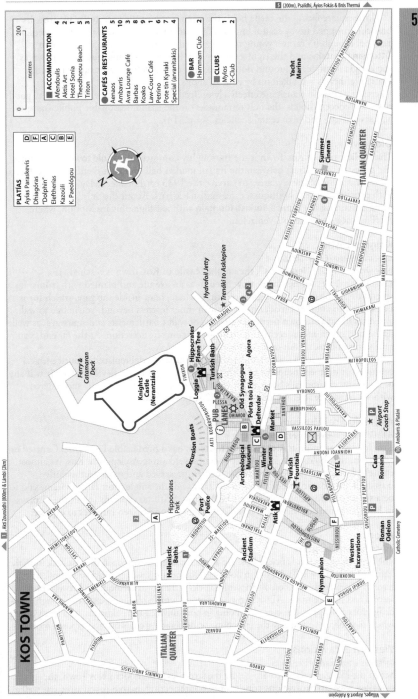

KOS TOWN

5 (200m), Psalidhi, Áyios Fokás & Brós Thermá

PLATIÁS
Ayías Paraskevís	D
Dhiagóras	F
"Dolphin"	A
Eleftherías	C
Kazoúli	B
K. Paeológou	E

ACCOMMODATION
Afendoulis	4
Aktis Art	2
Hotel Sonia	1
Theodhorou Beach	5
Triton	3

CAFÉS & RESTAURANTS
Aenaos	5
Ambavris	10
Avra Lounge Café	3
Barbas	8
Koako	9
Law-Court Café	1
Petrino	6
Pote tin Kyriaki	7
Special (arvanitakis)	4

BAR
Hammam Club	2

CLUBS
Mylos	1
X-Club	2

Yacht
Marina

ITALIAN QUARTER

Summer
Cinema

Ferry &
Catamaran
Dock

Knights'
Castle
(Nerantziás)

Hydrofoil Jetty

★ Trendki to Asklepion

Hippocrates'
Plane Tree

Turkish Bath

Old Synagogue

Agora

Loggia

Pórta toú Fórou

Defterdar

PUB
LANES

Excursion Boats

Market

Archeological
Museum

Winter
Cinema

Hippocrates
Park

Port
Police

Turkish
Fountain

KTEL

Casa
Romana

Airport
Coach Stop

Hellenistic
Baths

Ancient
Stadium

Atik

Nymphaion

Western
Excavations

Roman
Odeion

ITALIAN
QUARTER

1 Aktí Zouroúdhi (800m) & Limbi (2km)

1 Aktí Zouroúdhi (800m) & Limbi (2km)

Catholic Cemetery

10 Ambavris & Platáni

Villages, Airport & Asklepion

5

A little square facing the castle holds the riven trunk of **Hippocrates' plane tree**, its branches propped up by scaffolding; at 700 years of age, it's one of the oldest trees in Europe, though it's far too young to have seen the great healer. Adjacent are two **Ottoman fountains** and the eighteenth-century **Hassan Pasha mosque**, also known as the Loggia Mosque; its ground floor – like that of the **Defterdar mosque** on central Platía Eleftherías – is taken up by rows of shops.

Ferry travellers in transit are effectively obliged to stay in Kos Town. It's a pretty good base, with decent hotels, the best restaurants on the island, reasonable public transport, and several car- and bike-rental agencies (see p.314).

Old town

The liveliest part of Kos Town is the thoroughly commercialized **old town**, which lines the pedestrianized street between the Italian market hall on Platía Eleftherías and Platía Dhiagóras. One of the few areas to survive the 1933 earthquake, today it's crammed with expensive tourist boutiques, cafés and snack-bars. About the only genuinely old thing remaining is a capped **Turkish fountain** with a calligraphic inscription, where Apéllou meets Eleftheríou Venizélou.

Knights' castle

Tues–Sun 9am–3pm • €3 • ☎ 22420 27927

Known locally as "**Nerantziás**", the **knights' castle** in Kos Town is reached via a causeway over its former moat, now filled in as an avenue and planted with palms. It's a splendid, tumbledown, overgrown old ruin, where, once inside the gate, which turns out to lead to another broader moat with an inner fortress beyond, you're free to walk and stumble at your own peril over all sorts of walls, battlements and stairways, as well as the odd much more recent and unattractive concrete accretion. At the far end, you find yourself looking out over the ferry quays.

Built in stages between 1450 and 1514, the **double citadel** replaced a fourteenth-century fort deemed incapable of withstanding advances in medieval artillery. Few if any of the many cannonballs lying about were ever fired in anger; the castle surrendered without resistance after the marathon 1522 siege of Rhodes.

Archeological Museum

Platía Eleftherías • Temporarily closed for renovations

Kos Town's Italian-built **Archeological Museum** has a predictable Latin bias. Centred on an atrium that holds a mosaic of Hippocrates welcoming Asclepios to Kos, it's almost entirely devoted to **statuary**, of which the best preserved and most prominently displayed are Roman rather than Greek. That said, the single most famous item, said to be a statue of Hippocrates, is indeed Hellenistic. With no captions to put the displays in historical context, the whole thing only takes around fifteen minutes to explore.

Agora

Unrestricted access in daylight hours

The largest single relic of ancient Kos, the **agora**, occupies a huge open site just back from the harbour. The man who laid it out in 366 BC, Hippodamus, was credited by Aristotle as having "invented the division of cities into blocks". Thanks to **earthquakes** between the second and sixth centuries AD, it's now a confusing jumble of ruins. Scattered through a delightful public park, however, abounding in bougainvillea and palmettos, it's a lovely area in which to stroll, as you admire the crumbling walls, standing columns, and exposed mosaics.

Western excavations

Unrestricted access in daylight hours

Set in pit-like gardens up to 4m below the street level of modern Kos Town, the so-called **western excavations** consist of two intersecting marble-paved streets as well as the Xystos or colonnade of a covered running track. Crumbling plastic canopies at either end of the L-shaped complex shelter **floor mosaics**.

Across Grigoríou toú Pémptou to the south is a small, restored Roman-era **odeion**, which is capable of seating 750 spectators in 14 rows, and was built on the site of a similar Greek theatre.

ACCOMMODATION   KOS TOWN

★**Afendoulis** Evrypýlou 1 ☎ 22420 25321, ⓦ afendoulis hotel.com. Somewhat dated balconied en-suite rooms – including a few family quads – with fridges, a/c and wi-fi, yet all at excellent prices. Alexis Zikas, brother Ippokrates and wife Dionysia offer real personal service, ensuring a loyal repeat clientele; top-quality breakfast (included) with home-made preserves up to midday. Credit cards accepted. Mid-March to mid-Nov. **€40**

Aktis Art Vassiléos Yeoryíou 7 ☎ 22420 47200, ⓦ kosaktis.gr. Designer hotel whose futuristic standard doubles or suites, in brown, grey and beige, all face the water. Bathrooms are naturally lit and have butler sinks. There's wi-fi, gym, conference area, seaside bar and affiliated restaurant. All year. **€130**

Hotel Sonia Irodhótou 9, at Omírou ☎ 22420 28798, ⓦ hotelsonia.gr. Popular, friendly little hotel, across from the agora and formerly known as *Pension Alexis*. Its eleven wood-floored rooms have been thoroughly renovated with en-suite bathrooms, a/c and wi-fi; there's also a pleasant courtyard and bar. Run by the sister and niece of Alexis of the *Afendoulis* (see above). May–Oct. **€40**

Theodhorou Beach 1200m from the centre, towards Psalídhi ☎ 22420 22280, ⓦ theodorouhotel.com. Generous-sized units, including suites and a wing of self-catering studios, with disabled access. A leafy environment includes a lawn pool at the back and a small "private" beach with the *Nostos* day-and-night café-bar. A good choice if travelling as a family. **€80**

Triton Vassiléos Yeoryíou 4 ☎ 22420 20040, ⓦ triton -hotel.gr. Moderately upmarket, town-centre seafront hotel, part of a small local chain catering to package groups. Some of the veneered-floored rooms, in neutral decor and with somewhat small bathrooms, have sea views; free wi-fi. The ground-floor *Avanti* Italian restaurant and breakfast café is popular. **€80**

EATING AND DRINKING

RESTAURANTS

★**Ambavris** Vourina ☎ 22420 25696, ⓦ ampavris.gr. Top-notch restaurant, 500m south of the edge of town, in the eponymous suburb village. Skip the English-only à la carte menu, take the hint about mezédhes and let the house bring on their best. This changes seasonally but won't much exceed €25 (drink extra) for six plates – typically *pinigoúri*, *pikhtí* (brawn), little fish, spicy *loukánika*, stuffed squash flowers and *fáva*. May–Oct daily 5.30pm–late.

Koako Vassilios Yeoryíou 22 ☎ 22420 25645. This Spartan-looking place, with a crisp minimalist terrace just steps from the sea at the south end of Kos Town, is a versatile all-rounder, handling grilled meat and fish, mezédhes and a few daily *mayireftá* with equal aplomb – most priced below €10 – without the usual multinational flags and photo-menus. Daily lunch and dinner.

Petrino Platía Theológou 1 ☎ 22420 27251, ⓦ petrino -kos.gr. Elegant garden-set place with a menu of fish, shellfish, meat and the local hard cheese. Almost no meze costs over €10, though share a few plates and the bill mounts up. Children's menu offered. Two cosy indoor salons allow for year-round operation. Book ahead for large groups. Daily 11am–4pm & 6pm–late.

★**Pote tin Kyriaki** Pissándhrou 9 ☎ 22420 27872. Kos's sole genuine ouzerí, whose creatively assembled menu (painstakingly written out in school exercise books) has delights such as shrimps, fried mussels, *gávros*, *monastiriakí* (Cretan "monk's" salad), as well as grilled chops and *loukánika*. Look out for the couscous-like *pinigoúri*, served with pork, for €4. Summer Mon–Sat dinner only; winter Thurs–Sat lunch and dinner.

CAFÉS

Aenaos Platía Eleftherías ☎ 22420 26044. Join the largely local crowd at this café under the Defterdar mosque, and people-watch while refilling your Greek coffee from the traditional *bríki* used to brew it. They also serve a range of teas and flavoured hot chocolates. Daily 9am–late.

Avra Lounge Café Vassiléos Yeoryíou 5 ☎ 22420 27354. Beachside café set in colonial Italian building near Aktis Art (see above). Well-priced menu offering breakfasts, salads, pastas and snacks. Its own private beach for clients becomes a bar-restaurant at night. Free wi-fi. Daily 8am–4am.

Law-Court Café Finikon. Some of the cheapest and best-brewed coffees in Kos are available (along with cold drinks) under the arches at the rear of the courthouse, with a mostly civil-servant clientele, a few paces from Hippocrates' plane tree. There's no sign outside. Daily 8am–8pm.

★**Special (Arvanitakis)** Vassiléos Yeoryíou ☎ 22420 22087. This tiny hole-in-the-wall pastry and cake shop, right by the sea, also serves dynamite *gelato* and freshly squeezed orange juice. The a/c interior makes it a refreshing place to stop for a while. Small area for seating outside. Daily 10am–7pm.

5

NIGHTLIFE AND ENTERTAINMENT

Kos Town has a hyperactive nightlife. Visitors from all over the island congregate each night in the so-called "Pub Lanes", Nafklírou and Dhiákou, filled with an ever-changing array of generally mediocre bars and clubs. There are newer, better nightlife areas around Platía Dhiagóra (mostly Greeks) and out at Aktí Zouroúdhi towards Lambi.

Hammam Club Platía Dhiagóra ☎22420 21444. The most stable and classy music bar in town, installed in a former Turkish bath that still has its original oriental decor. Outdoor seating with chill-out sofas, until a midnight noise curfew moves everyone indoors. Daily 6pm–late.

Mylos Aktí Zouroúdhi ☎22420 23235. Sprawling around an old seafront windmill, with some tables out on Lambi beach, *Mylos* is Kos Town's top day-and-night-bar, with both live music and DJs. Daily noon–late.

X Club Kanari 2 ☎22420 22592. Beyond its large and very shiny front terrace on the west side of the inner port, this cavernous club is still among the hottest on the island, noted for its light shows. Daily 8pm–late.

Asklepion

4km west of Kos Town • Tues–Sun: May–Oct 8am–6pm; Nov–April 8.30am–2.30pm • €3 • ☎2242 028763

Native son **Hippocrates** is justly celebrated on Kos; not only does he have a tree, a street, a park, a statue and an international medical institute named after him, but his purported **Asklepion**, one of three in Greece, is a major attraction.

Although in fact founded just after Hippocrates' death, the methods used and taught at the Asklepion were probably his. Both a sanctuary of Asclepios (god of healing, son of Apollo) and a renowned curative centre, its magnificent setting on three artificial terraces overlooking Anatolia reflects early concern with the therapeutic environment. Little now remains standing, owing to periodic earthquakes and the Knights filching masonry to build their castle. The **lower terrace** never held many buildings, and was instead the venue for the observance of the Asclepieia – quadrennial athletic/musical competitions in honour of the god. Sacrifices to Asclepios were conducted at an **altar**, the oldest structure here, whose foundations are found near the middle of the **second terrace**. Just east are the Corinthian columns of a second-century AD **Roman temple**, partially re-erected by nationalistic Italians. A monumental staircase leads from the altar to a second-century BC **Doric temple** of Asclepios on the **highest terrace**, the last and grandest of the deity's local shrines.

The east

The shoreline of the **eastern** half of Kos, in both directions from Kos Town, is fringed with good **beaches**, albeit interspersed with marshlands. The best, around Cape Psalídhi to the east and Lámbi, Tingáki and Marmári to the southwest, have attracted resort development, but with a bike especially (thanks to the coastal bike paths) it's usually possible to find a stretch of sand to yourself. Inland, the rugged **hills** cradle some delightful villages, though sadly many are now empty.

HIPPOCRATES

Hippocrates (c.460–370 BC) is generally regarded as the father of scientific medicine, even if the Hippocratic oath, much altered from its original form, may well have nothing to do with him. Hippocrates was certainly born on Kos, probably at Astypalia near present-day Kéfalos, but otherwise confirmed details of his life are few. A great physician who travelled throughout the Classical Greek world, he spent at least part of his career teaching and practising on his native island. Numerous medical writings have been attributed to Hippocrates; *Airs, Waters and Places*, a treatise on the importance of environment on health, is generally thought to be his, but others are reckoned to be a compilation found in a medical library in Alexandria during the second century BC. His emphasis on good air and water, and the holistic approach of ancient Greek medicine, now seem positively contemporary.

5

Bros Thermá

East of Kos Town, beyond the huge hotels of Cape Psalídhi, the paved coast road ends after 12km. A dirt track continues for the final kilometre to the massively popular **hot springs** known as **Bros Thermá**. Best experienced at sunset or on moonlit nights, they issue from a grotto and flow through a trench into a shoreline pool formed by boulders, heating the seawater to an enjoyable temperature.

Tingáki and Marmári

Heading for either resort from Kos Town, especially by bike, the nicest and safest route is the minor road from the southwest corner of town

The coast west of Kos Town is home to the twin beach resorts of **Tingáki** and **Marmári**. There's almost always a breeze along this stretch, which makes it popular with windsurfers, while the profiles of Kálymnos, Psérimos and Turkey's Bodrum peninsula all make for spectacular offshore scenery.

Tingáki

A favourite with British travellers, **TINGÁKI** is 12km west of the harbour. Its long narrow beach of white sand improves, and becomes more separated from the frontage road, the further southwest you go. Thanks to the island of Psérimos just offshore, waves tend to stay small, and the warm shallow waters are ideal for children. There's little accommodation near the beach itself, though medium-sized hotels and studios are scattered amid the fields and cow pastures inland.

Marmári

MARMÁRI lies another 3km along, beyond the **Alykí** salt marsh, which retains water – and throngs of migratory birds, including flamingos – until June after a wet winter. Marmári has a smaller built-up area than Tingáki, and the beach is broader, especially to the west where it forms little dunes.

The Asfendhioú villages

Accessible via the curvy side road from Zipári, 8km from Kos Town; an inconspicuous minor road to Lagoúdhi; or by the shorter access road for Pylí

The **inland villages of Mount Dhíkeos**, a handful of settlements collectively referred to as **Asfendhioú**, nestle amid the island's only natural forest. Together, these communities give a good idea of what Kos looked like before tourism arrived, and all have been severely depopulated by the mad rush to the coast.

Ziá

There's precious little left of the original village of **ZIÁ**, 7km inland from Tingáki, which now holds barely a dozen resident families. Instead, its heavily commercialized main street and spectacular sunsets make it the target of dozens of tour buses daily, and the general tattiness seems to increase year on year.

Pylí

Both the contemporary village of **Pylí** and the separate ruins of the medieval town can be reached via the road through Lagoúdhi and Amanioú, or from beside the duck-patrolled Linopótis pond on the main island trunk road. Apart from its giant, lion-spouted cistern-fountain (the *piyí*), Pylí's other attraction is the **Harmýlio** ("Tomb of Harmylos"), a fenced-off, subterranean, niched vault that was probably a Hellenistic family tomb.

Paleó Pylí

Paleó Pylí (medieval Pylí), 3km southeast of its modern descendant, was the Byzantine capital of Kos. It's an absolutely wonderful spot, perched on what's now a very isolated peak but still well below the crest of the island's central ridge. Opposite the end of the

5

paved road up, a stair-path leads within fifteen minutes to the roof of the fort. En route you pass the remains of the abandoned town tumbling southwards down the slope.

ACCOMMODATION   THE EAST

Grecotel Kos Imperial Psalídhi ☎ 22420 58000, ⓦ grecotel.com. An all-inclusive designed for large package-holiday groups, this garden complex has a tropical river novelty pool and spa, where standard doubles and bungalows are spacious, tastefully decorated and come with sound systems. **€170**

Michals Apartments Studios Psalídhi ☎ 22420 23829, ⓦ michalisapartments.gr. Situated 1km from the marina and 3km from Kos Town, this welcoming and attentive Greek-Australian family run a superb outfit of twenty large studios and one- and two- bedroomed a/c apartments. There's a pool, gym and free wi-fi. **€45**

EATING AND DRINKING

★**Ambeli** Tingáki ☎ 22420 69682. The "Vineyard" is a great local taverna, in a rural setting 2.5km east of the main beachfront crossroads. Pleasant seating indoors and out, and dishes including *pinigoúri, bekrí mezé, pikhtí* (brawn), *yaprákia* (the local *dolmádhes*) and *arnáki ambelourgoú*, washed down with wine from their own vineyard. From €15 per head. Book ahead in peak season. May–Oct daily lunch and dinner; Nov–April Fri & Sat dinner only, Sun lunch only.

Iy Palia Piyi Pylí ☎ 22420 41510. Excellent taverna, in a superb setting beside a fountain fed by a natural

year-round spring in the upper part of Pylí, 100m west of the partly pedestrianized square and church. Inexpensive *soutzoukákia* grilled with onions, home-made tzatzíki, fried-vegetable mezédhes and local sweet red wine. Daily lunch and dinner.

★**Oromedon** Ziá ☎ 22420 69983, ⓦ pragmata.info /Oromedon_gb.htm. The best of Ziá's dozen tavernas, this Greek-patronized place serves good *pinigoúri*, mushrooms and local sausage on a roof terrace. Bill Clinton, the Greek president and Turkey's former president have all eaten here. May–Oct daily lunch and dinner.

The west

Near the desolate centre of the island, well sown with military installations, a pair of giant, adjacent roundabouts by the airport funnels traffic northwest towards **Mastihári**, northeast back towards town, southwest towards **Kéfalos** and southeast to **Kardhámena**. Most visitors are bound for the south-coast **beaches**, reached from the Kéfalos-bound turning.

Mastihári

The least "packaged" and least expensive of the north-shore resorts, **MASTIHÁRI**, 8km north of the airport, has a shortish, broad beach extending southwest, with less frequented dunes (and no sunbeds) towards the far end. Ferries and excursion boats from Kálymnos (see p.327) moor close to the centre, which has the feel of a genuine town.

Kardhámena

KARDHÁMENA, 31km from Kos Town and 8km southeast of the airport, is the island's largest package resort after the capital itself. In summer, locals are vastly outnumbered by boozing-and-bonking visitors, predominantly young Brits. A beach stretches to either side – sandier to the southwest, intermittently reefy and hemmed in by a road towards the northeast – but runaway development has banished any redeeming qualities the place might have had. The main reason anyone not staying here would bother to visit is to catch a boat to Níssyros (see p.307).

South-coast beaches

The coastline west of Kardhámena boasts a series of scenic and secluded **south-facing beaches**. Though each has a fanciful English name, they form essentially one long stretch at the base of a cliff, accessed by successive footpaths down from the main road. As the prevailing wind on the island is usually from the north, the water as a rule is gloriously calm.

5

The longest, broadest and wildest of the beaches, "**Magic**", officially Polémi, has a proper taverna above the car park, no jet skis and a nudist zone ("**Exotic**") at its eastern end. "**Sunny**", signposted as Psilós Gremmós and easily walkable from "Magic", has another taverna and jet skis; **Langádhes** is the cleanest and most picturesque, with junipers tumbling off its dunes and more jet skis. "**Paradise**", alias "**Bubble Beach**" because of volcanic gas-vents in the tidal zone, is small and oversubscribed, with wall-to-wall sunbeds and a large restaurant just above. Jet ski-free "**Camel**" (Kamíla) is the shortest and loneliest, protected by the steep, unpaved drive which runs in past its hillside taverna; the shore here is pure, fine sand, with good snorkelling to either side.

Kamári

The westernmost resort on Kos, **KAMÁRI**, comes just before the high headland at the island's western tip, and is essentially the shoreline annexe of the old town of Kéfalos. More popular with families and older visitors than Kardhámena, Kamári may look from the main road like a long and rather dispiriting strip, but the beach itself is good.

There's also a very lovely spot at its western end, 3km from the centre, where the tiny **Kastrí** islet, topped by a little chapel, stands just off the **Áyios Stéfanos** headland. A public access road, close to an abandoned Club Med, leads down to beaches either side of a small peninsula, crowned with the remains of two triple-aisled, sixth-century **basilicas**.

The far west

The village of **KÉFALOS**, 43km from Kos Town, covers a bluff looking down the length of the island. Aside from some lively **cafés** at the south end, it's a dull little place, mainly of note as a staging point for expeditions into the rugged **peninsula** that terminates at **Cape Kríkello**.

The main highlights of a visit there, along the ridge road south, include **Panayía Palatianí** Byzantine church amid the ruins of a larger ancient temple, 1km beyond the village, and the Classical theatre (unrestricted access) and Hellenistic temple of **ancient Astypalia**, 500m further via the side path starting from an unlocked gate. A paved road west just beyond Astypalia leads to windy **Áyios Theológos beach**, 7km from Kéfalos.

ACCOMMODATION AND EATING   THE WEST

Ayios Theologos Taverna Ayios Theológos ☏6974 503 556. High-quality taverna, at the far western tip of the island, from where you can witness incredible sunsets. A vast selection of fresh home-grown produce brings in the crowds at weekends. Expect roughly €10–12 per person. Lunch and dinner: summer daily, winter Sat & Sun.

Grand Café Kamári ☏22420 71290. Large and very comfortable café, at the point where Kamári beach briefly disappears and the sea laps directly against the road. As well as drinks, they serve top-quality pastries and sweets

from the adjoining bakery. All day: summer daily, winter Sat & Sun.

Kali Kardia Mastihári ☏22420 59289. Reliable taverna, facing the ferry jetty, that's good for fresh fish and mezédhes as well as standards like *stifádho*, plus great desserts. Almost all mains cost €8–10. Daily all day.

Panorama Studios Mastihári ☏22420 59019, ⊕kos panorama.eu. Simple studio apartments with a/c, kitchenettes and sea-view balconies, above a nice little restaurant just steps from the beach. **€60**

Psérimos

Were it not so close to Kos and Kálymnos, the little island of **PSÉRIMOS**, filled with remote beaches, might be idyllic. Throughout the season, so many excursion boats arrive that they've had to build a second jetty at little **AVLÁKIA** port. In midsummer, day-trippers blanket the main sandy beach that curves in front of Avlákia's thirty-odd houses and huge communal olive grove; even during May or late September you're guaranteed at least eighty outsiders daily (versus a permanent population of 25). Three other **beaches** are within easy reach: the clean sand-and-gravel strand at **Vathý** is a well-marked, thirty-minute walk east, starting from behind the *Taverna Iy Psérimos*. It takes 45 minutes of walking north along the main trans-island track to get to grubbier **Marathoúnda**, composed of pebbles. Best of all is **Grafiótissa**, a 300m-long beach of near-Caribbean quality half an hour's walk west of town.

ARRIVAL AND DEPARTURE	PSÉRIMOS

BY FERRY

From Kálymnos To spend the entire day on Psérimos, you'll have to take a day-trip from Póthia on Kálymnos; boats usually leave at 9.30am daily, and return at 5–6pm.

From Kos Boats from Kos Town operate triangle tours to Platý islet and somewhere on Kálymnos with only a brief stop on Psérimos.

ACCOMMODATION AND EATING

AVLÁKIA

Manola ☎ 22430 51540. Four reasonable studios, most with sea views and some with a/c, facing a very broad segment of the beach from its eastern end. €̲2̲5̲

Taverna Manola ☎ 22430 51540. Although it looks more like a bar, and stays open late as the island's main social hub, this beachfront taverna, run by the same

management as *Studios Kalliston*, serves good Greek standards and fresh seafood for around €10 a head. Daily 9am–late.

Tripolitis ☎ 22430 23196. Six simple en-suite studio apartments, three of which have sea views, upstairs from English-speaking *Anna's* café/snack-bar and directly across from the beach. May–Oct. €̲4̲0̲

Astypálea

Geographically, historically and architecturally, **Astypálea** really belongs to the Cyclades – on a clear day you can see Anáfi or Amorgós far more easily than any of the other Dodecanese. Its inhabitants are descended from colonists brought from the Cyclades during the fifteenth century, after pirate raids had left the island depopulated, and

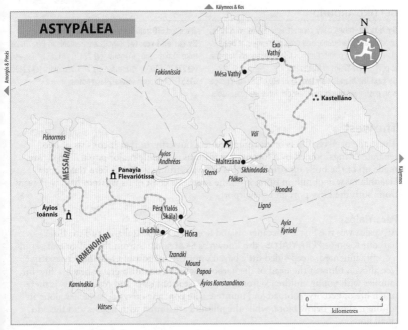

5

supposedly Astypálea was only reassigned to the Ottomans after the Greek Revolution because the Great Powers had such a poor map at the 1830 and 1832 peace conferences.

Astypálea's main visitor attractions include a beautiful old **citadel** – not just the castle itself, but also the whitewashed village of **Hóra** beneath it – as well as several good, easily accessible **beaches**. The island may not immediately strike you as especially beautiful: many beaches along its heavily indented coastline have reef underfoot and periodic seaweed, while the windswept heights are covered in thornbush or dwarf juniper. Hundreds of sheep and goats manage to survive, while citrus groves and vegetable patches in the valleys signal a relative abundance of water. Besides the excellent local **cheese**, Astypálea is renowned for its **honey**, **fish** and **lobster**.

There is no **package tourism** on Astypálea, and its remoteness discourages casual trade. During the short, intense **midsummer season** (mid-July to early Sept), however, visitors vastly outnumber the 1500 permanent inhabitants. The one real drawback is that **transport** connections (see below) are so poor.

ARRIVAL AND INFORMATION   ASTYPÁLEA

By air Astypálea's tiny airport, 8km northeast of Hóra and Péra Yialós, has infrequent connections to Athens (1 weekly) and to Léros, Kos and Rhodes, all on the same plane (2–3 weekly). Many hotels will pick up and drop off guests, and buses and taxis are available (see below).

By ferry Astypálea's main ferry port, at Áyios Andhréas, 7km north of Péra Yialós, is extremely inconvenient. There are no facilities whatsoever, and almost all boats arrive and depart in the dead of night. In addition to the destinations listed below, just one boat, the *Nissos Kalymnos*, calls in at Péra Yialós, with connections to Kálymnos only (3 weekly; 2hr 45min). Ferry tickets can be bought in Péra Yialós from

Astypalea Tours (☎ 22430 61571) and Paradise (☎ 22430 61224).

Destinations Amorgós (2 weekly; 1hr 25min); Dhonoússa (3 weekly; 2hr 20min); Kálymnos (1 weekly; 2hr 15min; Kastellórizo (1 weekly; 15hr 10min); Kos (1 weekly; 3hr 35min); Náxos (3 weekly; 3hr 45min); Páros (3 weekly; 5hr); Pireás (4 weekly; 9hr 45min–11hr 35min); Rhodes (1 weekly; 9hr 10min); Sými (1 weekly; 8hr 25min); Tílos (1 weekly; 6hr 35min).

Tourist office There's an information office in one of the windmills at the approach to Hóra (June–Sept daily 6–9pm; ☎ 22430 61412, ⓦ astypalia.gr).

GETTING AROUND

By bus Ten buses daily connect Péra Yialós with Hóra, Livádhia and Maltezána, and drop passengers at beaches along the way. A connecting bus takes passengers from the airport to Péra Yialós or Maltezána.

By taxi The island's only taxi (☎ 22430 61087) can't cope with passenger numbers in season. Fares are reasonable,

at around €10 from the airport to Péra Yialós.

By car and scooter Rentals are available in Péra Yialós from Lakis and Manolis (☎ 22430 61263), Tomaso (☎ 22430 61000, ⓦ tomaso.gr) and Vergoulis (☎ 22430 61351), or through several island hotels.

The west

The shape of Astypálea is often compared to a butterfly, in that it consists of two separate "wings" joined by a low narrow isthmus. The only major population centre, made up of the built-up strip that joins the waterfront villages of **Péra Yialós** and **Livádhia** by way of hilltop **Hóra**, is on the southeast coast of its **western** half, well away from both the ferry port and the airport.

Péra Yialós

Astypálea was the first Dodecanese island occupied by the Italians, and the little harbour town of **PÉRA YIALÓS**, also known as **SKÁLA**, dates from the Italian era. Set in a deeply indented, steep-sided little bay, it's not where most inter-island ferries arrive (see above). Only at the head of the harbour, where a broadish gravel beach – fine for families with young children – fronts a row of seafront cafés and restaurants, is there much life or activity. A broad and uninteresting concrete quayside stretches along its southern shore, below Hóra, while the hillsides are dotted with houses and the odd small hotel.

5

Archeological Museum

Tues–Sun: June–Sept 9am–1pm & 6–8.30pm; Oct–May 8.30am–2.30pm • Free • ☎ 2243 061 500

Just back from the waterfront in the centre of Péra Yialós, the local **Archeological Museum** consists of a single room. Many of its local finds, spanning the Bronze Age to medieval times, are little more than fragments, but it does hold impressive goblets and vases unearthed from two Mycenaean tombs.

Hóra

The delightful, very photogenic ensemble of **HÓRA**, accessible by road as well as steep stair-paths from Péra Yialós, neatly caps a high headland. Beneath the grey walls of the hilltop castle, the village itself is comprised of dazzling bright houses – many restored as holiday homes – threaded along intriguing narrow alleyways. The main approach road is lined with eight picturesque orange-roofed **windmills**.

Kástro

Unrestricted access • Free

Astypálea's thirteenth-century **kástro**, among the finest in the Aegean, was erected not by the Knights of St John, but by the Venetian Quirini clan, and modified by the Ottomans after 1537. Rather than purpose-built battlements, its unique "walls" consisted instead of the stacked-up frontages of private houses. Until well into the twentieth century, more than three hundred people lived inside, but depopulation and a severe 1956 earthquake combined to leave only a shell. Reached via a brightly whitewashed passageway beneath its main church of **Evangelístria Kastrianí**, the interior has been laid out with new pathways.

Livádhia

The little resort village of **LIVÁDHIA** occupies the next bay along from Hóra. A long, straight and pleasant **beach**, albeit scruffy with dried vegetation, lines the waterfront, fringed by cafés, restaurants and low-key hotels. You can walk there from Hóra in fifteen minutes; be sure to take the road that drops down to the sea just beyond the *Pylaia Boutique Hotel* (see p.326). If you simply go down to the beach you won't realize quite how far this fertile valley stretches inland.

Beyond Livádhia

When the beach at Livádhia is too busy, press on southwest for fifteen minutes on foot to reach the three small fine-pebble coves at **Tzanáki**. Beyond these is **Papoú**, an 80m fine-gravel strand accessible overland by a horrifically steep side track, and then a final path approach around a fenced-off farm.

The third large bay beyond Livádhia, **Áyios Konstandínos**, is a partly shaded, sand-and-gravel cove with a good seasonal taverna. Further afield are the lonely beaches of **Vátses** and **Kaminákia**, which are visited by a seasonal excursion boat from Péra Yialós. By land, **Vátses** has the easier dirt road and is 25 minutes by scooter from Livádhia; sandy, with a basic *kantína*, it's often windy. The track to **Kaminákia**, 8.5km from Livádhia, is rough and steep for the final 2km – best to go in a jeep – but the sheltered, clean and scenic cove, Astypálea's best, repays the effort.

ACCOMMODATION   THE WEST

PÉRA YIALÓS

Akti Rooms ☎ 22430 61114, ⓦ aktirooms.gr. Rather faded hotel in a beautiful hillside location near the Thalassa, offering cheap but minimally equipped rooms, not all with sea views, above a gorgeous terrace restaurant. Mid-April to mid-Oct. **45**

Hotel Thalassa ☎ 22430 59840, ⓦ stampalia.gr. The best accommodation in Péra Yialós, spilling down the hillside across from the castle, where the first access road down to the harbour drops from the coastal road. It consists entirely of very comfortable suites and studios, with fabulous views but no direct access to the sea. **€115**

HÓRA

Kalderimi ☎ 22430 59843, ⓦ kalderimi.gr. Smart modern complex, just beyond the *Pylaia Boutique Hotel* (see p.326) on

5

the road out of Hóra, where the eleven impeccably appointed mock-traditional a/c cottages (some large enough for families) hold all the lastest electronic gadgets. €140

Kallichoron Studios ☎ 22430 61934, ⓦ astypalea .com. Tasteful, upscale studios and one-bed apartments, close to the windmills at the edge of Hóra at the start of the road to Livádhia, all with flagstoned terrace and magnificent views of the citadel. Breakfast included. €120

Pylaia Boutique Hotel ☎ 22430 61070, ⓦ pylaiahotel .gr. Rather sumptuous new hotel, spilling down the hillside 200m out of Hóra towards Livádhia, with friendly young management. Slightly too large to be really "boutique", it holds 25 spacious, stylish rooms and suites, most with outdoor space and great views, plus a pool and summer-only rooftop restaurant. Breakfast included. €100

★ **Studios Kilindra** ☎ 22430 61131, ⓦ astipalea.com .gr. Plush studios and galleried maisonettes, on the quiet west slope of Hóra, with a swimming pool and good breakfasts – units accommodate two to three people. April–Dec. €150

EATING AND DRINKING

PÉRA YIALÓS

Akroyiali ☎ 22430 61863. While the food here is pretty good, with a wide range of mezhédes and tasty cheese dishes from roughly €7, the prime reason this beachfront taverna is so full every night is its unbeatable setting, with tables spreading out onto the sand. Daily lunch and dinner.

Australia ☎ 22430 61275. Dependable, long-established favourite, beneath a hotel of the same name, just back from the waterfront, with delicious seafood, and superbly prepared home-grown vegetable dishes. April–Nov daily lunch and dinner.

Dapia Café ☎ 22430 61590. The pick of the waterfront cafés, with a large well-shaded terrace overlooking the harbour and free wi-fi. Good for full breakfasts, crêpes, juices and infusions, as well as sunset drinks. Daily 10am–late.

★ **Maïstrali** ☎ 22430 61691. Welcoming, high-quality restaurant, with oblique sea views from the corner of the harbour. As well as rich stews like rabbit with tomato or chicken with yoghurt and mustard (under €10), they also serve seafood dishes like lobster, scaly fish or shrimp saganaki. Daily lunch and dinner.

HÓRA

Barbarossa ☎ 22430 61577. The only serious taverna

LIVÁDHIA

Maganas ☎ 22430 61468, ⓦ maganas.gr. Small, neat hotel, directly across from the beach on the frontage road, where the eight studios have a/c, kitchenettes and even tiny washing machines. €60

Mouras Studios ☎ 6972 453 571, ⓔ mourass@otenet .gr. Very nice little set of individual rental units, right by the beach, each with its own kitchen and balcony, and arranged around a courtyard. Reserve ahead for best rates. €50

To Yerani Studios ☎ 22430 61484, ⓔ gerani72 @hotmail.com. Ten nicely maintained and very comfortable marble-floored studios, with kitchens and little terraces facing flower-filled gardens, a short walk from the sea behind the village's best taverna. May–Oct. €60

Venetos Studios ☎ 22430 61490, ⓦ venetosstudios .gr. Several buildings scattered inland from the beach in a pleasant orchard at the base of the westerly hillside, containing well-furnished studios and apartments of varying sizes. May–Sept. €60

in Hóra, just as the main street starts to climb towards the kástro. Popular for its warm, pleasant interior and welcoming terrace, it serves hearty but generally unexceptional food, with rich meaty dishes like chicken with okra for €7.50 as well as more substantial seafood; the salads are disappointing. Daily noon–midnight.

LIVÁDHIA

Astropelos ☎ 22430 61473. With its large shaded patio, this beachside taverna is a great place to linger over vegetable dishes like stuffed tomatoes, but the seafood can be expensive. Expect to pay in the region of €13–15 per head. June–Sept daily 11am–late.

★ **To Yerani** ☎ 22430 61484. Livádhia's best food, set inland from the little bridge in the middle of the beach, but still enjoying sea views from its large tiled terrace. Home-cooked specialities range from delicious courgette flowers with cheese (€4) or moussaká (€6) to large meat grills. May–Oct daily 11am–late.

KAMINÁKIA

Linda ☎ 6972 129 088. Well-run beach taverna, which as well as offering honest, rustic fare (salads, fresh fish and a dish of the day for around €7), oversees a handful of sunbeds. Late June to early Sept daily noon–6pm.

The east

Astypálea's wilder and less populated **eastern** half is home to the island's airport and a small resort, **Maltezána**, but little else. Apart from a couple of south-coast beaches, the only day-trip worth making over here is the bumpy but spectacular drive out to the huge bay at **Mésa Vathý**.

Stenó and Plákes

Two good but isolated beaches stand on the southern shore of Astypálea's slender central isthmus. At **Stenó** (meaning "narrow", in reference to the isthmus), inviting turquoise shallows stretch away from a sandy shore. There's only limited shade, courtesy of a few tamarisks, but a *kantína* opens up in high summer.

Another kilometre east, the much quieter beach at **Plákes** has no facilities and can only be accessed by walking a few hundred metres down from the main road. It's at the end of the airport runways, but with barely a plane a day that's no problem.

Maltezána

The little resort of **MALTEZÁNA**, Astypálea's second-largest settlement, is 9km northeast of Péra Yialós, under 1km from the airport. Its official name is **ANÁLIPSI**, but it's universally known by the nickname it acquired thanks to medieval Maltese pirates. It's a nice enough spot, with a narrow, exposed, packed-sand beach, a small fishing port at its eastern end, and a good view south to islets.

ACCOMMODATION AND EATING   **MALTEZÁNA**

Analipsi ☎ 22430 61446. Maltezána's best taverna, also known as *Ilias-Irini's*, is a tranquil little space facing the jetty that doubles as the fishermen's *kafenío*. The food – fried squid, bean soup – is simple but wholesome; confirm prices and portion size of the often frozen seafood. Feb–Dec daily 11am–9pm.

Maltezana Beach ☎ 22430 61558, ⒲ maltezanabeach .gr. Astypálea's largest hotel, with 48 large, well-appointed bungalow-rooms – five of which are family-sized apartments – plus a pool and on-site restaurant. Easter–early Sept. **€100**

Villa Barbara ☎ 22430 61448. A dozen very spruce blue-and-white studios, set a short way back from the beach, all with kitchen and balcony and sleeping two to three. Mid-May to Sept. **€50**

Mésa Vathý

Although the main road turns to dirt east of Maltezána, it remains just about passable in an ordinary car, and snakes its way onwards across the exposed hillsides all the way to **MÉSA VATHÝ**, at the head of an utterly magnificent west-facing bay 23km out from Hóra. Much the best way to arrive at this sleepy fishing hamlet would be by boat; it's a popular anchorage for pleasure yachts in summer. There's no town, just one little taverna; walk onwards from the end of the road to reach a small beach.

Kálymnos

Despite its size and beauty, the island of **KÁLYMNOS** has long been overshadowed by Kos. Kálymnos fought in the Trojan War as a vassal of its southern neighbour, and to this day its tourist industry remains largely dependent on the overspill – and the airport – of Kos. In most respects, however, the islands are very different. Kálymnos is much more mountainous, consisting of three high limestone ridges that fan away from the continuous rugged cliffs of its west coast, to create two long sloping valleys that hold most of its settlements and agricultural land.

5

The island's capital and largest town, the busy port of **Póthia**, faces Kos from the midpoint of its southern shoreline. Most visitors head instead for the west coast, where a handful of small resorts have struggled to survive the collapse of a short-lived experiment in mass tourism. The pick of the pack, **Myrtiés**, stands close to some attractive little beaches. This craggy shoreline has found deserved fame among **climbers** and **hikers**, who keep businesses ticking along in the cooler spring and autumn months. For a beach holiday, you'd do better to head for the separate islet of **Télendhos** (a spectacular sight at sunset), or further north up the coast to **Emboriós**.

The prosperity of Kálymnos traditionally rested on its **sponge industry** (see box below), but blights have now wiped out almost all of the eastern Mediterranean's sponges. Only a few boats of the island's thirty-strong fleet remain in use, and most of the sponges sold behind the harbour are imported from Asia and the Caribbean.

ARRIVAL AND INFORMATION — KÁLYMNOS

By air Kálymnos's small airport, 6km northwest of Póthia, is served only by a few Olympic/Aegean Air flights.

Destinations Athens (1–2 daily; 1hr); Rhodes (3 weekly; via Kos 1hr 10min, via Athens 2hr 35min).

By ferry You can buy ferry tickets from Magos Tours (T 22430 28777) and Mahias Travel (T 22430 22909), both based in Póthia. The following schedules are from Póthia; there are also frequent ferries to Télendhos from Myrtiés (see above).

Detinations Agathoníssi (4 weekly; 2hr 15min–5hr 30min); Arkioi (3 weekly; 4hr 20min); Astypálea (3 weekly; 2hr 15min–2hr 45min); Kastelórizo (2 weekly; 10hr 15min–13hr); Kos (Kos Town 1–3 daily; 30min–1hr; Mastihari 8 daily; 20min–1hr); Léros (1–2 daily; 50min–1hr 20min); Lipsi (1–2 daily; 1hr 20min); Níssyros (2 weekly; 2hr 50min); Pátmos (1–2 daily; 1hr 40min–3hr 25min); Pireás (3 weekly; 9hr 40min–14hr 10min); Psérimos (1 daily; 20min); Rhodes (1–2 daily; 2hr 40min–8hr 15min); Sámos (3 weekly; 2hr 50min–6hr 50min); Sými (7 weekly; 2hr 10min–6hr 20min); Tílos (2 weekly; 4hr 20min).

Tourist office The municipal tourist office faces the ferry jetty in Póthia (Mon–Fri 8am–3pm; T 22430 50956, W kalymnosinfo.com).

SPONGES AND SPONGE DIVING

Sponges are colonies of microscopic marine organisms that excrete a fibrous skeleton. The living sponges that can be seen throughout the Aegean as black, melon-sized blobs, anchored to rocks in three to ten metres of water, are mostly "wild" sponges, impossible to clean or shape with shears. Kalymnian divers seek out "tame" sponges, which are much softer, more pliable, and dwell thirty to forty metres deep.

Sponge fishers were originally **free divers**; weighted with a rock, they'd collect sponges from the seabed on a single breath before being hauled back up to the surface. Starting in the late nineteenth century, however, divers were fitted with heavy, insulated suits (*skáfandhro*). Breathing through an air-feed line connected to compressors aboard the factory boats, they could now attain depths of up to 70m. However, this resulted in the first cases of the "bends". When divers came up too quickly, the dissolved air in their bloodstream bubbled out of solution – with catastrophic results. Roughly half of those early pioneers would leave with the fleets in spring but fail to return in autumn. Some were buried at sea, others, it's said, buried alive, up to their necks in hot sand, to provide slight relief from the excruciating pain of nitrogen bubbles in the joints.

By the time the malady became understood, during World War I, thousands of Kalymnians had died, with many survivors paralysed, deaf or blind. Even though the *skáfandhro* was banned elsewhere as the obvious culprit, it remained in use here until after World War II. After the first **decompression chambers** and diving schools reached Greece, in the 1950s, the seabed was stripped with ruthless efficiency, and the sponge fleets forced to hunt further from home.

Even the "tame" sponge is unusable until processed. The smelly organic matter and external membrane is thrashed out of them, traditionally by being trodden on the boat deck, and then they're tossed for a day or so in a vat of hot seawater. Visitors to Póthia's remaining handful of **workshops** can still watch the sponge vats spin; in the old days, the divers simply made a "necklace" of their catch and trailed it in the sea behind the boat.

To suit modern tastes, some sponges are bleached to a pale yellow colour with nitric acid. That weakens the fibres, however, so it's best to buy the more durable, natural-brown ones.

GETTING AROUND

By bus Buses to the west-coast resorts (9 daily in season; 30min), and also northwest to Emboriós (2 daily; 50min) and east to Vathýs (3 daily; 30min), run from two terminals beside the municipal "palace".

By taxi Shared taxis, available at Platía Kyprou, cost less than normal taxis, at roughly €5.

By car and scooter Car rental outlets along Póthia quay include the recommended Auto Market (☎ 22430 51780, ⓦ kalymnoscars.gr), while for scooters check out Kostas (☎ 22430 50110), very close to the tourist office.

Póthia

The long curving waterfront of **PÓTHIA**, Kálymnos's main town and port, may not be architecturally distinguished, but arranged around a huge curving bay it looks fabulous at sunset. The town itself remains vibrant year-round, even if it's not really a tourist destination in its own right. With its houses marching up the valley inland or arrayed in tiers along the surrounding hillsides, it forms a natural amphitheatre that readily fills with noise, whether from souped-up motorbikes or summer sound systems. As well as the usual Italian-era "palace", at the centre of the bay, Póthia also boasts backstreets lined with elegant **Neoclassical houses**, painted the traditional pink or ochre.

Sprawled to either side of the road to the west coast, the built-up area of Póthia stretches northwest up the valley to the suburb of **Mýli**. The whitewashed battlements of the Knights' **Kástro Khryssoheriás** (unrestricted access), 1.2km along, offer wonderful views over town towards Kos. Another 1.5km up is the former island capital, **Hóra**, which is still a large, busy village.

Archeological Museum of Kálymnos
Temporarily closed for restoration

Tucked away in an unremarkable and hard to find new building on Póthia's western hillside, the **Archeological Museum of Kálymnos** provides an excellent overview of local history. Everything is beautifully displayed, with very helpful captions in both Greek and English, and many of its artefacts are quite stunning. Its greatest treasures, discovered underwater during the 1990s, are a larger-than-life cast bronze figure of a woman draped in a chiton, thought to date from the second century BC, and the well-preserved bronze head of a ruler, which may have formed part of a colossal equestrian statue.

Municipal Nautical and Folklore Museum
Daily 10am–1pm • €2 • ☎ 2243 051361

Kálymnos's **Municipal Nautical and Folklore Museum**, very near the ferry port on the seaward side of Khristós cathedral, focuses on the sponge fishing past. A large photo shows Póthia in the 1880s, with no quay, jetty, roads or sumptuous mansions, and with most of the population still up in Hóra. You can also see horribly primitive divers' breathing apparatuses, and "cages" designed to keep propellers from cutting air lines.

Péra Kástro
Hóra • Dawn–dusk • Free • Access via a steep stair-path that climbs from the eastern edge of the village

The thirteenth-century Byzantine citadel-town of **Péra Kástro**, a magnificent fortified enclave atop the impressive crag that towers over Hóra, originally served as a refuge from seaborne raiders. Appropriated by the Knights of St John, it remained inhabited until the late 1700s.

Once you've passed through the massive gate and perimeter walls, you're faced with yet more stiff climbing, now through a jumble of overgrown ruins, tumbled stonework, and wild flowers, interspersed with the odd paved walkway. The views are tremendous, but the true highlights are the nine scattered **medieval chapels**, the only complete buildings to survive. Re-roofed and freshly whitewashed, several still have faded frescoes.

5

ACCOMMODATION

PÓTHIA

Evanik Enoria Kalamiotissa ☎ 22430 22057, ⓦ evanik -hotel.gr. Situated on the noisy main thoroughfare, these 28 plain, en-suite and a/c functional rooms all offer a balcony and free wi-fi. Rooms at the back are considerably quieter. **€60**

Hotel Panorama Amoudhára ☎ 22430 23138, ⓦ panorama-kalymnos.gr. Simple, well-kept hotel, high on the hillside west of the harbour, where all thirteen en-suite rooms have a/c, wi-fi and balconies overlooking the port. There's also a pleasant breakfast (included) salon. **€40**

★ **Villa Melina** Enoria Evangelístria ☎ 22430 22682, ⓦ villa-melina.com. Póthia's quietest and most elegant hotel, set in attractive gardens near the Archeological Museum, just inland from the eastern side of the port. The pink, century-old Italianate villa holds seven high-ceilinged, insect-screened, wood-floored rooms while a further thirteen studios and apartments, sleeping up to six, are laid out around the large swimming pool behind. There's a friendly and very helpful family atmosphere. **€50**

EATING AND DRINKING

Kafenes Khristós ☎ 22430 28727. This pavement café, close to the county "palace" in the centre of the harbour, is always full thanks to its generous, tasty salads, seafood, local goat cheese and bulk wine. Be sure to try the €6 "crab balls". Daily 8am–late.

O Stukas ☎ 6970 802 346. This traditional taverna and ouzerí, located along the harbour by the Town Hall, is popular with tourists and locals alike. Individual meze dishes don't go past €6, while regular special offers include salad, fish or grilled meat dish and dessert for €9. Daily lunch and dinner.

Taverna Pandelis Áyios Nikólaos ☎ 22430 51508. Large but inconspicuous restaurant, tucked into a cul-de-sac behind the waterfront *Olympic Hotel*. Dependably good meat and fish grills (around €8) – ask for the daily catch – as well as mezédhes. Daily lunch and dinner.

Zaharoplastio O Mihalaras Áyios Nikólaos. This wonderful local cake shop, a must for any fan of Greek sweetmeats, has two premises in Póthia. The traditional original is on the harbourfront close to the "palace", while there's a modern annexe near the ferry jetty. Daily 8am–6pm.

Vathýs and Rína

Ten kilometres northeast of Póthia, and accessed via an initially dispiriting coastal road, the long, fertile valley known as **VATHÝS** is Kálymnos' agricultural heartland. Its orange and tangerine groves make a startling contrast to the mineral greys and ochres of the surrounding hills, but visitors only pass this way to visit the fjord port of **RÍNA** at its southeastern end. Set at the end of a long slender inlet, Rína remains a popular stopover with yachties, and can also be reached by taxi-boats from Póthia. It's a very scenic spot, with tiny little Christian basilicas perched on the cliffs to either side, while the total lack of a beach keeps the crowds down. This safe anchorage has been in use since Neolithic times; several caves show signs of ancient occupation.

ACCOMMODATION AND EATING

VATHÝS AND RÍNA

Galini Hotel Restaurant Rína ☎ 22430 31241. Of the three similar, largely open-air seafood restaurants clustered around the harbour at Rína, only the friendly

Galina also doubles as a hotel, charging bargain B&B rates for its clean, simple sea-view rooms. Limited English spoken. **€30**

Northern Kálymnos

Fringed with wild flowers, and backed by mighty cliffs, Northern Kálymnos is great **hiking** and **climbing** territory. **Emboriós** at the road's end makes a great overnight stop, or you can simply complete a round-island car or scooter tour by heading inland from **Aryinónda**, further south, and making your way back to Póthia via Vathýs (see above).

Aryinónda to Emboriós

ARYINÓNDA itself, 5km beyond Massoúri at the head of its own deeply indented bay, has a clean pebble beach, plus a couple of small tavernas. Keep heading north along the west coast from here to find several more splendid, isolated beaches, including **Áyios Nikólaos** and **Kalamiés**. The village of **EMBORIÓS**, at the end of the bus line 20km out from Póthia, is a pretty little spot that offers a reasonable gravel-and-sand beach, and a scattering of apartments and tavernas. The little jetty in the middle is served by excursion boats from Myrtiés, which only run when demand is high enough.

A hundred metres beyond Emboriós, reached by a detour inland of the church, the next cove along holds the similar, goat-patrolled **Asprokykliá beach**. Follow the rough dirt track above Asprokykliá to the isthmus by the fish farm, then walk fifteen minutes north on path and track to reach **Aptíki**, a smallish but perfectly formed pea-gravel cove.

Paliónissos and around

From Skália, 1km or so southeast of Emboriós, a newly paved road – signposted only in Greek – switchbacks up the west flank of the island and back down the other side. A steep but safe 5km drive, it stops short of the eastern shoreline, leaving visitors to walk the final couple of hundred metres along a rough track.

Set at the head of another extravagantly indented fjord-like bay, the yacht anchorage of **Paliónissos** is more usually reached by excursion boats from Rína (see opposite). It boasts an ample crescent of shingle beach, with a taverna to either side.

ACCOMMODATION AND EATING　　　　　　　　　　　　　　　　**NORTHERN KÁLYMNOS**

Note that due to the lack of British tourists on Kálymnos, owners of smaller places outside Póthia rarely speak English.

★**Harry's Paradise** Emboriós ☎ 22430 40062, ⦿harrys -paradise.gr. This lovely taverna, set behind gorgeous flower-filled gardens a short walk from the beach, serves delicious home-cooked traditional food for all meals, using produce from their own fields. Their small hotel annexe alongside offers six great-value a/c en-suite apartments, each individually themed and equipped with a kitchenette and balcony (€45). Expect eggs from their neighbour's poultry and home-made marmalades for breakfast (included in apartment rates). April–Nov daily 9am–late.

The west coast

The mountainous headland that fills Kálymnos's southwest corner is largely inaccessible to visitors. From the moment the island's **west coast** can be reached by road, however, the shoreline is lined by a succession of small beach communities. Although several set out to turn themselves into beach resorts around the turn of the millennium, only **Myrtiés** and **Massoúri** have thrived enough to make worthwhile bases.

Myrtiés to Armeós

Beach tourism on Kálymnos is most heavily concentrated in the twin resorts of **MYRTIÉS** and **MASSOÚRI**. Occupying neighbouring coves that start 8km northwest of Póthia, they face across to towering Télendhos islet (see p.332), and enjoy dramatic **sunsets**.

They're easy enough to reach on the island's main road, though once it's crossed the island to Pánormos, the road has to climb the Kamári pass before it can zigzag back down to the sea. A lengthy one-way loop then leads drivers through the two resorts. There's no significant gap in the commercial strip of restaurants and hotels that runs through them both, 50m up from the beach, and neither has a historic core or town centre.

The narrow, pebbly **beach** at Myrtiés has a marina at its southern end and the small concrete jetty used by the Télendhos ferries in the middle. The beach at Massoúri, ten minutes' walk north, is broader and sandier; the largest and liveliest on the island, it has a noisy beach-bar vibe in summer. There's also an all-sand beach at **Melitsáhas** cove, 500m south of Myrtiés, but its surroundings have become very run-down; don't reckon on staying there.

Another kilometre north of Massoúri, the coastal village of **Armeós** is the terminus for most local buses. In low season especially, it tends to be dominated by European **rock-climbers**. Several popular cliffs soar overhead – look for the route-inscribed columns at their base – and various businesses cater to climbers' needs.

5

ACCOMMODATION THE WEST COAST

★**Acroyali** Myrtiés ☎ 22430 47521 or ☎ 21036 22688, ⓦacroyali.gr. Six clean, well-designed apartments, right on the beach, with unfussy furnishings and spacious sea-view balconies. Each sleeps two adults and two children; book well in advance. There's also an on-site restaurant. April–Nov. **€45**

Continental Hotel Massouri ☎ 22430 47331, ⓦcontinental-hotel.gr. A rather impersonal package style hotel, but there's no beating the location – all 33 rooms offer balconies with either mountain or sea view. Breakfast (included) is taken on the terrace around the pool, and there's access to a tiny pebbled beach. Open all year. **€60**

Hotel Atlantis Myrtiés ☎ 22430 47497, ⓦatlantis -kalymnos.gr. Located in Myrtiés Bay, this hotel has eighteen pleasant and well-located studios and apartments, complete with living room, kitchen and panoramic-view balconies looking across to the island of Télendhos. April–Oct. **€50**

Hotel Philoxenia Armeós ☎ 22430 59310, ⓦphiloxenia -kalymnos.com. Simple but good-value hotel, in prime climbing territory at the foot of the roadside hills, a 10min walk north of Massoúri. Plain clean rooms with large balconies, plus a nice pool with snack-bar; ask in advance if you want dinner. May–Oct. **€50**

EATING AND DRINKING

Kokkinidis Massoúri ☎ 22430 47202. Terrace restaurant, perched just above the main road in the centre of Massoúri, with nice views and a good menu of Greek and Mediterranean dishes, including a whole roast chicken for two at €15. Daily lunch and dinner.

To Steki tis Fanis Linária ☎ 22430 47317. Friendly family restaurant, in an old mansion on the hillside overlooking Linária beach. Local specialities such as *mermizéli*

(salad of greens, *kopanistí* and barley rusks) and ample tasty vegetarian starters, but quality of the mains (from €8) can vary. May–Oct, dinner only.

Tsopanakos Armeós ☎ 22430 47929. This friendly meat specialist is the best old-school taverna to survive on the west coast. Whether on the lovely terrace in summer, or in the cosy indoor dining room in winter, feast on fresh meat and cheese dishes from island-grazed goats. Daily noon–9pm.

Télendhos

The towering pyramid-shaped islet of **TÉLENDHOS**, silhouetted at sunset a few hundred metres west of Myrtiés, was severed from Kálymnos by a cataclysmic earthquake in 554 AD. **Car-free**, home to a mere handful of year-round inhabitants, and blissfully tranquil, it's the single most compelling destination for Kálymnos visitors, and the short row of hotels and restaurants on its east-facing shore makes it a great place to spend a few nights. It's said that somewhere far below the narrow straits between Myrtiés and Télendhos, an ancient town lies submerged.

Beaches

It only takes a few minutes to explore the little built-up strip that stretches in both directions from the boat landing. A narrow **beach** of reasonable sand runs along the straight seafront, and the calm shallow water is ideal for kids. Kayaks and beach toys are available for rent, while tousled tamarisks provide shade.

To find a more secluded beach, simply keep walking. A few hundred metres north – head right from the boat landing, and keep going after the paved coastal roadway peters out to become a dirt path – is the nudist **Paradise** beach, which is peaceful and sheltered, but at its best in the morning, before the sun disappears for good behind the mountain. A ten-minute walk southwest of the village, following a footpath over the ridge, will bring you to the pebble beach at **Hokhlakás**, a scenic but more exposed spot where the sea tends to be much rougher.

HIKING ON TÉLENDHOS

Setting out to **hike** right round Télendhos would be a mistake; it's a long and exposed walk with little reward. Devote an hour or two, however, to investigating the islet's **southwest corner**, a little low-lying afterthought. Follow the footpaths through the woods, signed to "Early Christian Necropolis", and in addition to some intact arched sixth-century tombs you'll come to a perfectly sheltered sandy cove that's ideal for swimming and snorkelling.

Áyios Vassílios and Ayía Triádha

While all the shoreline buildings are of modern construction, abundant ruins are scattered slightly further afield. Closest to the village, north of the boat landing, a seafront field holds the ruined outline of the thirteenth-century monastery of **Áyios Vassílios**. On the hillside immediately above Hokhlakás is **Ayía Triádha**, originally an enormous basilica, though now just a few stones survive. Further up the slopes, wherever you look, giant Cyclopean caves burrow deep into the foot of the central massif.

ARRIVAL AND DEPARTURE

By boat Regular boat-buses shuttle between Myrtiés, on Kálymnos, and Télendhos (8am–midnight every 30min; €2).

ACCOMMODATION — TÉLENDHOS

Hotel Porto Potha ⓣ22430 47321, ⓦtelendoshotel.gr. Friendly hotel on the hillside just north of *On The Rocks* (see below), with twelve comfortable and spacious guest rooms, eight self-catering studios alongside, and a large pool, plus what amounts to a private beach. Special offers for hikers and climbers in low season. April to mid-Oct. **€45**

On the Rocks ⓣ22430 48260, ⓦotr.telendos.com. Three superbly appointed en-suite rooms, with balconies and sea views, above the beachfront restaurant 200m north of the ferry jetty (see above). Breakfast (included) – and kayaks – available. The same friendly owners also rent a studio near Hokhlakás beach, which has double-glazing, kitchen and bug screens. Free boat connection from Mastihári on Kos. April–Nov. **€50**

Zorba's ⓣ22430 48660. Very simple en-suite rooms at bargain prices, above a reasonable taverna a short walk south from the ferry jetty. **€30**

EATING AND DRINKING

Barba Stathis ⓣ22430 47953, ⓦbarba-stathis.gr. Also known as *Tassia's*, this welcoming place is just behind *Zorba's* (see above) en route to Hokhlakás. BBQ every night, and daily specials like *moussaká* with home-made cream or fresh-made *dolmádhes*. Mains from €8. Daily 11am–late.

On the Rocks ⓣ22430 48260, ⓦotr.telendos.com. Very pleasant restaurant, with a shaded patio overlooking the beach not far north of the ferry jetty, and run by a very friendly Greek-Australian family. A full menu of fresh fish and meat dishes, typically costing around €10, plus pizzas and burgers, Greek specialities, and lovely home-made desserts. Wednesday night is Greek barbecue, with music and dancing. It also holds a lively bar. Daily 9am–late.

Plaka Next door to, and slightly cheaper than, *On the Rocks* (see above), this large vine-covered terrace, poised just above the beach, is a great place to enjoy inexpensive local dishes such as goat with tomato sauce, or fresh octopus, for under €10. Daily lunch and dinner.

Léros

As the island of **LÉROS** is indented with deep, sheltered bays, lined with little settlements, it doesn't have an obvious "capital". Ferries arrive at both **Lakkí** on the west coast and **Ayía Marína** on the east, but neither is recommended as a place to stay. Instead visitors congregate in the resorts of **Pandélli** and **Álinda**, and in more refined **Plátanos** up on the hillside. While Léros can be very attractive, however, it doesn't have spectacular **beaches**, so tourism remains relatively low-key.

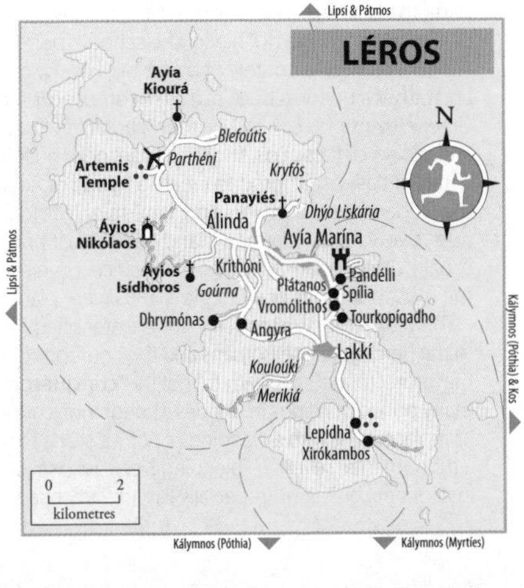

The island still bears traces of the **Battle of Léros** of November 1943, when German paratroops displaced a Commonwealth division that had occupied Léros following the Italian

5

capitulation. Bomb nose cones and shell casings turn up as gaily painted garden ornaments, or serve as gateposts. After the war, the local economy relied on prisons and sanatoria in former Italian military buildings. During the civil war and the later junta, leftists were confined to a notorious **detention centre** at Parthéni, while **hospitals** warehoused intractable psychiatric cases and mentally handicapped children. In 1989, a major scandal exposed conditions in the asylums; most wards were eventually closed.

ARRIVAL AND DEPARTURE   LÉROS

By air The tiny airport is near the island's northern tip. Destinations Astypálea (2 weekly; 25min); Athens (1 daily; 1hr); Kálymnos (2 weekly; 20min); Kos (2 weekly; via Kálymnos 1hr 45min; via Athens 3hr 15min); Rhodes (2 weekly; 4–5hr).

By ferry Large ferries and the *Dodekanisos Pride* catamaran arrive at Lakkí; smaller ferries and the *Dodekanisos Express* arrive at Ayía Marína. You can book tickets with Aegean Travel, 9 King George Ave, in Lakkí

(☎22470 26000, ⓦaegeantravel.gr) and Kastis Travel, in Ayía Marína (☎22470 22140).
Destinations Agathoníssi (4 weekly; 1hr 10min–4hr); Arkí (5 weekly; 2hr 50min); Kálymnos (1–2 daily; 45min–1hr 15min); Kos (1–3 daily; 1hr 25min–3hr); Lipsí (2–3 daily; 20min–1hr); Pátmos (2–4 daily; 40min–1hr 55min); Pireás (3 weekly; 9–11hr); Rhodes (1–2 daily; 4hr–5hr 15min); Samos (3 weekly; 1hr 55min–5hr 20min); Sými (6 weekly; 3hr 10min–5hr 50min); Syros (2–3 weekly; 5hr 30min).

GETTING AROUND

By bus Regular buses from the main taxi rank in Platanós run north via Ayía Marína, Álinda and the airport to Parthéni, and south to Lakkí and Xirókambos.
By car and scooter Take care if you rent a scooter – Lerian

roads are particularly narrow, potholed and gravel-strewn, and the low-slung, fat-tyred bikes on offer don't cope well. Try Motoland (Pandélli, ☎22470 24103; Álinda, ☎22470 24584) or Rent A Car Léros (Lakkí, ☎22470 22330).

Lakkí and around

Set in a hugely indented bay on Léros's southwest coast, the unusual town of **LAKKÍ** is the arrival port for all the island's large **ferries**. Built in the 1930s as a model town to house

---

ITALIAN ARCHITECTURE IN THE DODECANESE

The architectural heritage left by the Italian domination in the Dodecanese has only recently begun to be appreciated. Many structures had been allowed to deteriorate, if not abandoned, by Greeks who would rather forget the entire Italian legacy.

Although the buildings are often dubbed "Art Deco", and some contain elements of that style, most are properly classed as **Rationalist** (or in the case of Léros, **Stream Line Modern**). They drew on various post-World War I architectural, artistic and political trends across Europe, particularly Novecento (a sort of Neoclassicism), the collectivist ideologies of the time, and the paintings of Giorgio di Chirico. The school's purest expressions tended to have grid-arrays of windows (or walls entirely of glass); tall, narrow ground-level arcades; rounded-off bulwarks; and either a uniform brick surface or grooved/patterned concrete. As well as in Italy and Greece, examples can still be found as far afield as Moscow or London (underground stations and blocks of flats), Los Angeles (apartment buildings) and Ethiopia (cinemas).

Italy initially attempted to create a hybrid of Rationalist style and local vernacular elements in the Dodecanese, both real and semi-mythical, to evoke a supposed generic "Mediterranean-ness". Every Italian-claimed island had at least one specimen in this **"protectorate"** style, usually the gendarme station, post office, covered market or governor's mansion, but only on the most populous or strategic islands were plans drawn up for sweeping urban re-ordering.

The years from 1936 to 1941 saw an intensified Fascist imperial ideology, an increased reference to the heritage of the Romans and their purported successors the Knights, and the replacement of the "protectorate" style with that of the **"conqueror"**. This involved **"purification"**, the stripping of many public buildings in Rhodes (though not, curiously, in Kos) of their orientalist ornamentation, its replacement with a cladding of porous stone to match medieval buildings in the old town, plus a monumental severity – blending Neoclassicism and modernism – and rigid symmetry to match institutional buildings (especially Fascist Party headquarters) and public squares across Italy.

7500 civilian dependants of an adjacent Italian naval base, it's now an incongruous under-populated relic. Sweeping boulevards, out of all proportion to the traffic they ever see, are lined with Stream Line Modern edifices (see box opposite) including a round-fronted cinema, but the entire seafront tends to be devoid of life even in high season. It does have a handful of hotels and restaurants, but none worth recommending.

Lakkí's nearest approximation to a beach, sand-and-gravel **Kouloúki**, 500m west, has ample trees for shade and supports a seasonal taverna. A kilometre or so beyond is **Merikiá**, which is a little nicer, and has two tavernas.

War Museum

Merikiá · Daily 9.30am–1.30pm · €3 · ☎ 22470 22109

An interesting little **War Museum**, set in two long arched tunnels that burrow deep into the hillside close to Merikiá beach, 2km west of Lakkí, commemorates the 1943 Battle of Léros. Part of an enormous Italian-built subterranean complex, the tunnels are crammed with barely labelled World War II documents, models, machine guns and assorted military hardware. To make sense of it all, head first to the far end and watch the archival footage.

Xirókambos

The fishing port of **XIRÓKAMBOS**, 5km south of Lakkí, is served by regular *kaïki* from Myrtiés on Kálymnos. It's a pretty spot, and many visitors swim, but the beach itself is unremarkable, though it does improve as you head west.

In the hillside village of **LEPÍDHA**, 1km short of Xirókambos, a side turning north of the island's campsite leads up to a tiny **acropolis**. Behind the modern summit chapel, you can admire stretches of restored ancient masonry, while the views across to Kálymnos are superb.

ACCOMMODATION AND EATING | XIRÓKAMBOS

Hotel Efstathia ☎ 22470 24099. Studio apartments set 50m back from the beach, with huge, well-furnished doubles with rather basic bathrooms as well as family apartments facing a large pool. **€40**

To Aloni ☎ 22470 26048. Xirókambos's best waterfront taverna, right where the road meets the sea. Enjoy *mayireftá*, *souvláki* and barbecued meats as well as fish, at beachside tables shaded by jacarandas, for roughly €10 per head. Daily 11am–9pm.

Plátanos, Pandélli and around

Five kilometres north of Lakkí, across the island, a continuous built-up strip climbing across a low ridge to connect two east-coast bays nominally consists of three distinct villages. On the shore of the northern bay, **Ayía Marína** stretches along a quayside used by smaller inter-island ferries (see opposite). Immediately above it, older **Plátanos** stands beneath a Knight's castle, while on the bay to the south is **Pandélli**, a busy but attractive little resort.

Plátanos

A 1min taxi ride or 5min walk up from the ferry dock

Draped over the saddle between Ayía Marína and Pandélli, **PLÁTANOS** is a residential community full of fine Neoclassical and vernacular houses. It's a good central base for exploring the island, but short on restaurants or nightlife.

Kástro

Daily: May–Oct 8.30am–1pm and 4–8pm; Nov–April 8.30am–12.30pm · €1

Atop the mighty headland northeast of Plátanos, Léros' **kástro** overlooks virtually the entire island – which was of course why the Knights sited a castle up here. Reach it

5

either via a steep stair-path from the central square, or along a zigzagging road that starts its climb 100m back from the beach in Pandélli.

Although the castle's walls and staircases have been stabilized and/or restored, there's little to see; the reason to come is to enjoy the stupendous views from the battlements, especially dramatic at sunset.

Archeological Museum

July–Sept Mon–Sat 9am–2.30pm • €2 • ☎ 22470 24775

Léros's **Archeological Museum**, a short way down towards Ayía Marína, is little more than a single room. Its few artefacts are, however, well laid out, with a good explanation of where each was found, and a clear account of Lerian history.

Pandélli

Ten minutes' walk down from Plátanos, the former fishing village of **PANDÉLLI** has been transformed into a smart, rather upscale but still very pleasant little resort. In summer, there's little room on its small but reef-free, pea-gravel **beach** for anyone other than guests at its beachfront hotels, but it has a good crop of cafés and tavernas. A short way east around the bay, a long cement jetty still serves local fishermen rather than yachts, which in high season must anchor offshore.

Southern beaches

Sadly, the prominent coastal footpath that heads south from Pandélli peters out as soon as it curves out of sight. To reach **VROMÓLITHOS**, 1km south, pedestrians and drivers alike have to follow a higher road, through the village of Spília.

Although the **beach** at Vromólithos is usually less crowded than Pandélli, it's no place to linger, consisting of a long narrow strip of exposed gravel squashed up against the high walls of beachfront properties. The sea is clean, but you have to cross rock seabed at most points to reach deeper water. There's a more secluded, sandier cove southeast towards **Tourkopígadho**, and an even better duo at the end of the side road to **Aï Yiórgi**.

ACCOMMODATION   PLÁTANOS, PANDÉLLI AND AROUND

Castelo Beach Pandélli beach ☎ 22470 23030, ⓦ castelo .gr. With its castellated tiers dominating the west end of Pandélli beach, this hotel is an eyesore, but once you're inside – whether in the spacious en-suite rooms, many of which have four-poster beds, or in the terrace café, perched just above water – it's a great place to take it easy. **€85**

★**Maison des Couleurs** Plátanos ☎ 22470 23341, ⓦ maisondescouleurs.com. This gorgeous Italianate mansion, tucked up on the hillside just a few steps from the centre of Plátanos, holds five irresistibly stylish suites, each decorated in a different colour and featuring antique furnishings such as four-poster beds or clawfoot tubs. Charming and very helpful hosts, and superb breakfasts (included) out on the terrace. **€80**

Panteli Beach Studios Pandélli beach ☎ 22470

26450, ⓦ panteli-beach.gr. Dutch-owned complex of very tasteful and comfortable studios and apartments, all with balcony or terrace. There's no pool, but it opens directly onto the beach. **€50**

Pension Kavos Pandélli beach ☎ 22470 23247. Family-run studios, at the east end of the harbour by the fishing jetty, offering ten good-sized, airy terraced a/c rooms with sea-view balconies. They also rent out a large house accommodating four to five people. **€45**

★**Windmills/Anemomyli** Pandélli ☎ 6936 932 619, ⓦ leroswindmills.com. Lovely little B&B complex, poised above Pandélli on the road up to the castle, and consisting of two galleried windmill apartments and a long cottage, all with stone floors and great views from rear terraces. May–Oct. **€100**

EATING AND DRINKING

★**Mezedhopolio O Dimitris O Karaflas** Spília ☎ 22470 25626. One of the best-sited ouzerís on the island, adjoining the *Hotel Rodon* up in Spília, between Pandélli and Vromólithos. Ample portions of delicacies such as chunky local sausages, onion rings and *floyéres* (crispy rolls stuffed with cheese and sometimes ham) or

dairy-based dips like *galotýri*. Daily lunch and dinner.

★**Mylos** Ayía Marína ☎ 22470 24894. Excellent restaurant, with a romantic setting by the wave-lapped windmill at the western edge of Ayía Marína. The menu has a strong Italian leaning, featuring risotto and panacotta as well as specialities like expertly home-made *garidhopílafo* (shrimp-rice; €12), grilled *mastéllo* cheese, seasonal fresh fish, and *kolokythokeftédhes* (courgette patties). Book ahead in summer. March–Sept daily lunch and dinner.

View Café/Bar Apittiki ☎ 6906 454 664. Situated on the hillside just before the castle, this newly opened café/restaurant is in a prime location by the windmills, overlooking virtually the whole island. The flowered terraced garden makes it an ideal place to enjoy a drink or meal.

Pasta dishes for €6 and sweet delicacies home-made by the owner's family. May–Oct daily 8am–late.

Zorba's Pandélli beach ☎ 22470 22027. Pandélli's best seafront restaurant, with tables on the beach itself, as well as on a long terrace. The food is consistently good, with grills for €8 and steak or fish for €12–15 – choose your own fish in the kitchen – but service can be slow at peak times. Reserve ahead in summer. Daily lunch and dinner.

NIGHTLIFE

Café del Mar Vromólithos ☎ 22470 24766. Stylish, laidback bar, nestling along a shelf in the hillside just above the north end of Vromólithos beach. Very relaxing in the daytime, but it hots up at night. Daily noon–late.

Enallaktiko Ayía Marína ☎ 22470 25746. As well as offering a handful of tables right on the quayside, this friendly local café also offers computer terminals with

internet. Daily 10am–midnight.

Savana Pandélli beach ⓦ savanabar-leros.com. Long-standing and very civilized English-Danish bar at the far end of the port, which despite its shaded seafront terrace retains a laidback rural feel. The perfect spot for a late-night musical nightcap (request your favourites); things get going from 10pm nightly. Daily noon–late.

Álinda and around

ÁLINDA, 3km northwest around the bay from Ayía Marína, is the longest-established resort on Léros, with development fringing a long, narrow strip of pea-gravel beach. It's also the first area to open in spring and the last to shut in autumn.

Historical and Folklore Museum

Álinda • May–Sept Tues–Sun 10am–12pm • €3 • ☎ 22470 25040

Housed in a castle-like seafront mansion, the island's **Historical and Folklore Museum** concentrates on the Battle of Léros. Displays include relics from the sunken *Queen Olga*, a wheel from a Junkers bomber, and a stove made from a bomb casing. There's also a grisly mocked-up clinic (mostly gynaecological tools), assorted rural implements, costumes and antiques.

Beaches

Beaches near Álinda include **Krithóni**, 1.5km south, where its pretty cove gets very crowded in summer. Several more gravelly inlets lie alongside the road that curves around the bay further north, collectively known as **Dhýo Liskária**. From the dead end of the road, a 25-minute scramble north on a faint path brings you to pebbly **Kryfós** cove.

ACCOMMODATION AND EATING	ÁLINDA AND AROUND

★**Archontiko Angelou** Álinda ☎ 6944 968 182, ⓦ hotel-angelou-leros.com. Grand, marvellously atmospheric if slightly faded Italianate villa, a few hundred metres inland from the beach. Nine pretty and very different rooms, with Victorian bath fittings, beamed ceilings and antique furnishings; two have balconies with views of the lovely gardens. The healthy gluten-free breakfast is extra. Open most of the year – check for winter opening dates. **€80**

Hotel Alinda Álinda ☎ 22470 23266. Very friendly family-run hotel, also known as *Xenonas Mavrakis*, set just back from the middle of Álinda beach behind the good eponymous taverna, and offering good-value well-kept a/c rooms with fridges. **€60**

Hotel Papafotis Álinda ☎ 22470 22247, ⓦ apartments-studios-leros.com. A father-and-daughter run establishment, *Papafotis* offers fifteen rooms and studios (sleeping up to four), all with balconies or terrace. Simple, quiet, clean rooms, a 5min walk back from the beach, with wi-fi and a/c. **€30**

★**Nefeli Hotel** Krithóni ☎ 22470 24611, ⓦ nefeli-hotels-leros.com. Modern terraced bungalow complex between Ayía Marina and Álinda offering 24 individually styled a/c rooms and units, tastefully designed in a traditional style, all surrounding a gorgeous, well-tended garden/bar. Take local produce-based breakfast (included) in the garden room and expect very attentive service from the management. They have a sister hotel also in Lipsi. **€65**

5

To Arhontike Partheni ☎ 22470 24578. Directly opposite the tiny airport, near the marina, this taverna offers good, wholesome Greek dishes freshly prepared such as *biftéki* in tomato sauce and lamb dishes, plus hearty salads. Expect to pay roughly €7 per person. Worth the effort to drive out to, even if you don't have a flight to catch. Peak daily 7pm–late, off-peak varies.

Vareladiko Dhýo Liskária ☎ 22470 23726. The last beachfront taverna you come to, at road's end east of Álinda, where the owners have playfully painted walls and the hillside itself to make it look like a hotel, but all the "rooms" are just facades. As a restaurant, with seaside seating, it's adequate, with inexpensive options like meatballs or mussels for just €6–7. Daily lunch and dinner.

Goúrna and Dhrymónas

The best beach on Léros's west coast is **Goúrna**, at the head of a large bay 2km southwest of Álinda or 3km north of Lakkí. It's the longest sandy beach on the island, hard-packed and gently shelving, if wind-buffeted and somewhat scruffy. A road along the southern shore of the bay ends beside a jetty at little **Dhrymónas**.

Gourna Taverna Goúrna ☎ 22470 25120. Friendly taverna, with sunbed rental, slap in the middle of Goúrna beach. Grills include chicken on a spit, wild fish and tasty mezédhes for €8. Summer daily noon–7pm.

Ouzerí Sotos Dhrymónas ☎ 22470 24546. This quayside restaurant is so close to the sea that they plant some tables right in the water. Very good food at good prices, with mezédhes at €2–4, unusual shellfish for €8–10, and fresh fish daily courtesy of owner Sotos himself. May–Oct daily lunch and dinner.

Psilalonia Dhrymónas ☎ 22470 25283, ⓦ psilalonia .com. Lovely French-owned little B&B, up on the hillside above the far end of the bay at Dhrymónas (turn left at the little chapel where the coast road stops). Three pleasant en-suite rooms, set in a row with fabulous views of the bay. Feb–Nov, except Easter. **€60**

Pátmos

Arguably the most beautiful and certainly the best known of the smaller Dodecanese, **PÁTMOS** has a distinctive, immediately palpable atmosphere. It was in a cave here that St John the Divine (known in Greek as *O Theológos*, "The Theologian", and author of one of the four Gospels) set down the **Book of Revelation**, the final book of the New Testament. The huge fortified **monastery** that honours him remains the island's dominant feature; its monks owned all of Pátmos until the eighteenth century, and their influence remains strong.

For those visitors not motivated by religion, Pátmos's greatest strength is its **beaches**. With so many attractive strands, you can usually escape the crowds even in high season, though you may need a vehicle to do so. **Day-trippers** exceed overnighters, thanks in part to the island's lack of an airport, and Pátmos feels a different place once the last excursion boat has left after sunset. Among those staying, no single nationality predominates, lending Pátmos a **cosmopolitan** feel almost unique in the Dodecanese. The steady clientele can be very **posh** indeed, with assorted royal and ex-royal families among repeat visitors.

By ferry All ferries arrive in the heart of Skála.
Destinations Agathonisi (3 weekly; 1hr 50min–2hr 50min); Arkí (3 weekly; 40min); Kálymnos (2–3 daily; 1hr 35min–4hr); Kos (1–3 daily; 1hr 35min–5hr); Léros (2–4 daily; 40min–1hr 55min); Lipsi (1–3 daily; 25–50min); Pireás (4 weekly; 8hr 10min); Rhodes (1–3 daily; 4hr 45min–9hr 45min); Samos (3 weekly; 1hr–3hr 10min); Sými (6 weekly; 4hr–8hr); Syros (2 weekly; 4hr).

Travel agencies Astoria Travel (☎ 22470 31205, ⓦ astoriatravel.com) and Apollon Travel (☎ 22470 31324), both on Skála's main waterfront street.
Tourist office Pátmos has no tourist office, though ⓦ patmos-island.com and ⓦ patmosweb.gr are useful. The Orthodox Culture and Information Center facing the ferry landing (Mon, Tues, Thurs & Fri 9am–1pm & 6–9pm, Sat & Sun 6–9pm) aims to make visitors aware of the island's religious sites, and posts current opening hours.

5

GETTING AROUND

By bus Island buses leave from the quayside to Hóra (7 daily; 25min), Gríkou (4 daily; 25min) and Kámbos (3 daily; 25min). Flat fare €1.50. Amusingly, journey times may vary according to how many goats are on the road or if the driver stops to have a chat.

By car and scooter Numerous outfits, including Tom & Gerry (☎ 22470 31357) and Patmos Rent-a-Car (☎ 22470 32203). Expect difficulties finding a car in high season.

By excursion boat Boats to Psilí Ámmos and Arkí/Maráthi leave the quayside from 9.30–10am (10.10–11am to Léros and Lipsí depending on day/season).

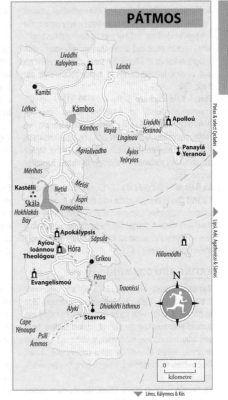

PÁTMOS

Pireás & select Cyclades

Lipsí, Arkí, Agathonísi & Samos

Léros, Kálymnos & Kós

Skála

Home to most of Pátmos's 3200 official residents, **SKÁLA** seems initially to contradict any solemn image of the island; the commercial district with its gift boutiques is incongruously sophisticated for such a small town. During peak season, the quay and inland lanes throng with trippers, and visitors still tend to arrive after dark, including those from the huge, humming cruisers that weigh anchor around midnight. Skála becomes a ghost town in winter (which here means by early October), when most shops and restaurants close.

Given time, Skála reveals more enticing corners in the residential fringes to its east and west, where vernacular mansions hem in pedestrian lanes creeping up the hillsides. At the summit of the westerly rise, **Kastélli**, you'll find an ancient acropolis, inside which is a more recently built chapel. An easy ten-minute walk southwest across the flat isthmus, starting from the central market street, brings you to pebbly **Hokhlakás Bay** on the island's west coast. More of a quiet seafront suburb than a beach, it enjoys wonderful sunset views.

ACCOMMODATION

SKÁLA

Asteri Near Mérihas cove, Nétia ☎ 22470 32465, ⓦ asteripatmos.gr. The best option in Nétia, set in spacious grounds on a knoll overlooking the bay, just under a 10min walk from the ferry. Simply furnished en-suite rooms of varying sizes, with sea-view balconies; many have a/c, two have wheelchair access. Breakfasts (included) feature own-grown produce and are available outdoors. **€40**

Australis Nétia ☎ 22470 32284, ⓦ patmosaustralis.gr. Very friendly, somewhat spartan en-suite hotel, owned by a helpful Greek-Australian family; an affiliated scooter-rental business with Tom & Gerry saves you traipsing into town. Units in the better-standard apartment annexe accommodate up to six. Breakfast included. **€45**

Blue Bay Skala ☎ 22470 31165, ⓦ bluebaypatmos.gr. Multitiered Australian-Greek-run hotel on the hillside just above the sea, a short walk south from the jetty just out of sight of Skála. There's no beach, but all the a/c en-suite rooms have substantial sea-view balconies, and there's a small internet café. Credit cards accepted for stays of over two days. Breakfast included. **€60**

Captain's House Konsoláto ☎ 22470 31793, ⓦ captains-house.gr. A hotel (not a house), with 17 a/c rooms, moments from the jetty and facing a tiny beach dotted with café tables. The quiet rooms in the rear wing overlook a fair-sized pool and shady terrace. Friendly management, nice furnishings and on-site car rental. **€45**

5

Hellenis Netiá ☎ 22470 31275, ⓦ hotelhellinispatmos .gr. This whitewashed forty-room hotel is very close to the sea path and just north of a new yacht marina. It has bright, airy common areas and better-than-average rooms with fridges, balconies and baths. The same management rents out six superior apartments in contemporary style out back. **€90**

Hotel Villa Zacharo Skála ☎ 22470 31529, ⓦ villa -zacharo.gr. Quietly set, small ten-roomed family-run hotel on the road to Hóra. The lovely front garden, a/c, free lobby tea/coffee facilities, freshly prepared breakfasts using local produce (included) and the attentive service offset the tiny bathrooms and simply furnished, balconied rooms. **€35**

Le Balcon Hellas ☎ 22470 32713, ⓦ www.lebalcon.gr. Located 1km from Skála on the road to Grikos, these ten a/c apartments/studios (some as large as 50sq m) all offer their own distinct design. Simply furnished, with a cosy feel, all offer sea views with terrace or balcony. Seven-night minimum (negotiable). **€65**

★**Porto Scoutari** Melóï hillside ☎ 22470 33124, ⓦ portoscoutari.com. Although slightly far from the main town, this is deservedly Pátmos's premier hotel, with a bungalow complex overlooking the beach and islets. The common areas and spacious accommodation units are arrayed around a large pool and small spa. Owner Elina Scoutari and her staff go out of their way to make you feel at home. Breakfast included. **€70**

Skala Hotel Skála ☎ 22470 31343, ⓦ skalahotel.gr. Smart, large, bougainvillea-drenched hotel, set a short way back from the quayside in the heart of the village, and accessed via a flowery gateway-gazebo. The 78 comfortable renovated rooms have sea-view balconies, and there's a large pool. **€85**

Studios Mathios Sápsila beach ☎ 22470 32583, ⓦ mathiosapartments.gr. Superior rural accommodation, ranging from small studios to an entire house, beside an unremarkable beach 2km southeast of Skála, with creative decor and extensive gardens. Owners Iakoumina and Theologos are exceptionally welcoming. **€45**

EATING AND DRINKING

Benetos Sápsila beach ☎ 22470 33089, ⓦ benetos restaurant.com. High-class Mediterranean fusion, 2km southeast of Skála, with idyllic conservatory seating and a menu encompassing the likes of smoked sardine, bean and salmon croustade, *astakomakaronádha* and decadent desserts; budget €35–40 for three courses plus drinks. Reservations recommended. June to early Oct Tues–Sun from 7.30pm–late.

La Strada Skála ☎ 22470 34188. Quality outfit, facing Theológos town beach a short walk along the quayside from the excursion boats, featuring above average Italian food (freshly made pastas, fish of the day) and dishes such as artichoke gratin for around €15 per person. As well as the enticing tables on the beach itself, seating is on the terrace with sea view. Daily 7pm–late.

Ostria Skála ☎ 22470 33254. The food tends to be run-of-the-mill at this central, mid-priced, year-round ouzerí,

facing the excursion-boat quay, but – late ferry arrivals take note – it's the only place serving after 11pm. Mezédhes from €7. Daily 10am–late.

To Hiliomodhi Skála ☎ 22470 34080. Cheap and crowded ouzerí, a few metres from the waterfront at the start of the road to Hóra, which offers vegetarian mezédhes (typically €3) and seafood delicacies such as limpets (served live) or grilled octopus (€7.50), plus decent *hýma* wine from Mégara. There's outdoor seating at the back, in an unremarkable pedestrian lane. Daily noon–late.

★**Vegghera** Skála ☎ 22470 32988, ⓦ patmosweb.gr /vegghera.htm. The best all-rounder, opposite the yacht marina, with flawlessly presented stuffed scorpion fish, vegetarian or seafood salads and superb desserts; bills of €40–45 per head (food only). It's the last place you come to as you walk north from the port. Reservations recommended. Easter–early Sept daily 7.30pm–late.

NIGHTLIFE

Art Café Skála ☎ 22470 33092. Bohemian-style café next to Patmos Rent-a-Car, on the harbour where owner Katerina makes cocktails, desserts and smoothies such as Baileys and crème de menthe. Sit inside at the bar, or on one of two roof terraces overlooking the harbour and monastery of St John. Listen to jazz, blues, rock, old classics, or sometimes live music. Daily 7pm–late.

Café Arion Skála ☎ 22470 31595. This appealing wood-panelled, barn-like place, in the centre of the quayside, is Pátmos's most durable café-bar; all sorts sit outside, dance inside or prop up the long bar. Daily 9am–late.

Ginger Bar Skála ☎ 22470 31009. This small, brightly furnished place along the main strip of bars plays the latest tunes, offers regular DJ and live performances and attracts a slightly younger, Greek crowd. Outside seating at the mosaic tables is a great place to people watch. Daily noon–late.

Koukoumavla Konsoláta ☎ 22470 32325. The "Owl" is a perennially popular, hippy-ish bar near the foot of the main road up to Hóra. Run by a friendly Italian-Greek couple, it has garden seating, wacky decor and live music, and sells crafts as well as snacks and drinks. Daily noon–late.

Apokálypsis monastery

Daily 8am–1.30pm, also Tues, Thurs & Sun 4–6pm • €2

A ten-minute walk up the hill from Skála, halfway to Hóra, the **Apokálypsis monastery** is built around the cave where St John heard the voice of God issuing from a cleft in the rock, and where he sat dictating to his disciple Prohoros. The cave itself, of course, was once open to the elements, but it's now enclosed within an eleventh-century **chapel**. In a recess in the rock, the place where the saint is said to have rested his head at night is fenced off and outlined in beaten silver. Only if you come first thing in the morning, before the cacophonous tour groups arrive, can you hope to get a sense of the contemplative peace that inspired St John.

Ayíou Ioánnou Theológou monastery

Daily 8am–1.30pm, also Tues, Thurs & Sun 4–6pm • Free, museum €6

In 1088, the soldier-cleric **Ioannis "The Blessed" Khristodhoulos** (1021–93) was granted title to Pátmos by Byzantine emperor Alexios Komnenos. Within three years, he and his followers had completed most of what's now **Ayíou Ioánnou Theológou monastery**. Enclosed within its stout hilltop walls, a warren of courtyards, chapels, stairways, arcades, and roof terraces offers a rare glimpse of a Patmian interior. In antiquity, this site held a temple of Artemis, marble columns from which were incorporated here and there in the monastery.

As most of the complex is closed to outsiders – it remains home to a community of around a dozen monks – few visitors spend more than half an hour up here. The diminutive flower-bedecked courtyard just inside the gate opens onto the church itself, where frescoes depict the Apocalypse. Off to one side, the **museum** has a magnificent array of religious treasures, including medieval icons of the Cretan school, and several later donations from Russia. Pride of place among the ancient manuscripts goes to the original chrysobull (edict) signed by Emperor Alexios Komnenos in the eleventh century, granting the island to Khristodhoulos.

SAINT JOHN ON PÁTMOS

Pátmos has been intimately associated with Christianity since **John the Evangelist** – later John the Divine – was exiled here from Ephesus by emperor Domitian in about 95 AD. John is said to have written his **Gospel** on Pátmos, but his sojourn is better remembered for the otherworldly voice that he heard coming from a cleft in the ceiling of his hillside grotto, which bid him to set down his words in writing. By the time John was allowed to return home, that disturbing finale to the New Testament, the **Book of Revelation** (aka the Apocalypse), had been disseminated as a pastoral letter to the Seven Churches of Asia Minor.

Revelation followed the standard Judeo-Christian tradition of apocalyptic books, with titanic battles in heaven and on earth, supernatural visions, plus lurid descriptions of the fates awaiting the saved and the damned following the **Last Judgement**. Open to widely different interpretations, Revelation was being wielded as a rhetorical and theological weapon within a century of appearing. Its vivid imagery lent itself to depiction in frescoes adorning the refectories of Byzantine monasteries and the narthexes of Orthodox churches, conveying a salutary message to illiterate medieval parishioners.

John also combated paganism on Pátmos, in the person of an evil wizard, **Kynops**, who challenged him to a duel of miracles. As the magician's stock trick involved retrieving effigies of the deceased from the seabed, John responded by petrifying Kynops while he was under water. A buoy just off Theológos beach in Skála today marks the relevant submerged rock.

Forever after in the Orthodox world, heights amid desolate and especially **volcanic topography** have become associated with John. Pátmos, with its eerie landscape of igneous outcrops, is an excellent example, as is Níssyros, where one of the saint's monasteries overlooks the volcano's caldera.

5

HÓRA FESTIVALS

The best dates to visit Hóra, besides the Easter observances, are September 25–26 for the **Feast of John the Theologian** and October 20–21 for the **Feast of Khristodhoulos**, both of which feature solemn liturgies and processions. The annual **Festival of Religious Music** (late Aug/early Sept) is held in the grounds of the Apokálypsis monastery (see p.341).

Hóra

St John's promise of shelter from pirates spurred the growth of **HÓRA** outside the stout fortifications of the monastery. A magnificent ensemble, it remains architecturally homogeneous, its cobbled lanes sheltering shipowners' mansions from the island's seventeenth- to eighteenth-century heyday. High, windowless walls and imposing wooden doors betray nothing of the painted ceilings, *votsalotó* terraces, flagstone kitchens and carved furniture inside. Inevitably, touristic tattiness disfigures the main approaches to the monastery, but by night, when the ramparts are startlingly floodlit, it's hard to think of a more beautiful Dodecanesian village. Neither should you miss the view from **Platía Lótza**, particularly at dawn or dusk.

Numerous "minor" churches and monasteries around Hóra contain beautiful icons and examples of local woodcarving; almost all are locked to prevent thefts, but key-keepers generally live nearby. Among the best are the church of **Dhiasózousa**; the convent of **Zoödhóhou Piyís** (daily except Sat 9am–noon), and the convent of **Evangelismoú**, at the edge of Hóra (daily 9–11am).

ARRIVAL AND INFORMATION
HÓRA

By bus Seven buses from Skála serve Hóra daily (7.30am–7.30pm; roughly 35min).

On foot The 40min walk from Skála to Hóra follows a beautiful old cobbled path. Don't try it in the full heat of the day, and whatever you do, don't walk up the much longer, switchbacking main road. To find the path, head through Skála towards Hokhlakás, then turn left onto a lane that leads uphill to the main road – you'll see the cobbles ahead of you.

ACCOMMODATION AND EATING

★**Archontariki** Hóra ☎ 22470 29368, ⊛ archontariki -patmos.gr. Gorgeous B&B, concealed behind high walls in a traditional village house that's been beautifully converted to create four exquisitely furnished, exceptionally comfortable suites and one double. As well as the lovely central courtyard, there's a garden and roof terrace; rates include a superb breakfast. Easter–Sept. **€200**

Loza Platía Loza, Hóra ☎ 22470 32405. Nicely positioned café/restaurant just below the eponymous platía, close to the main road, where the broad terrace offers sweeping views, and as well as hot and alcoholic drinks you can get mezédhes for €7–8, salads and pasta dishes for under €10, and pricier steaks. Daily all day.

Pantheon Hóra ☎ 22470 31226. The village's most authentic restaurant, at the start of the monastery approach. Good atmosphere and music, a lovely old interior or terrace views over the village and friendly management offset somewhat run-of-the-mill, pricey mezédhes, starting from the €10 mark. April–Dec daily all day.

The rest of the island

Pátmos's **best beaches** are concentrated north of Skála, tucked into the startling eastern shoreline, and accessible from side roads off the main road. Most of the island's west-facing bays are unuseable, owing to the prevailing wind and washed-up debris.

Gríkou and Pétra

Not far south of uninspiring Sapsila beach, roads converge at the sandiest part of **Gríkou**. The beach itself, far from the island's best, forms a narrow strip of hard-packed sand, yielding to sand and gravel, then large pebbles at **Pétra** immediately south. It's not possible to drive any further south along the coast.

5

Melóï and Agriolívadho

A couple of kilometres northeast of Skála, the large crescent beach at **Melóï** is handy and quite appealing, with tamarisks behind the slender belt of sand, and good snorkelling offshore. It's accessible by road at its southern end, which is home to a taverna. North of Melóï, **Agriolívadho** (Agriolivádhi) is another attractive sheltered bay. Most of the beach is pebbly gravel, but there's a reasonable amount of sand at its broad centre.

Kámbos

Hilltop **KÁMBOS**, 4km north of Skála, is the island's only other real village. Originally built to house the wives and children of lay workers at the monastery, it's surrounded by scattered farms.

Kámbos **beach**, 600m downhill to the east, is a strong contender for the best beach on the island, although it fills with local children in summer. Too deeply indented to be seen from the rest of Pátmos, it offers peaceful sheltered swimming, along with plentiful sunbeds, two tavernas, and beach toys to rent.

Beyond Kámbos

A succession of less busy coves lies **east** of Kámbos. **Vayiá** is a little bay where a few trees overhang a beach of pebbles and coarse sand, there's a snack-bar, and the sea is a particularly enticing shade of turquoise. The double bay at **Lingínou** can only be reached on foot, but has a *kantína*. **Livádhi Yeranoú** is a long stretch of mingled sand and gravel, shaded by tamarisks, and with a delightful islet offshore as a target for swimmers.

ACCOMMODATION | THE REST OF PÁTMOS

Patmos Aktis Gríkou Beach ☎ 22470 32800, ✉ patmos asktis.gr. As a style statement, this very upscale, dazzling white 56-room luxury hotel is incongruous for Pátmos, but there's no disputing the opulence of its rooms, spa and restaurant. The same management has also taken over and renovated the cheaper *Silver Beach* hotel nearby, bookable via the same website. April–Sept. **€150**

EATING AND DRINKING

★**Ktima Petra** Petra beach ☎ 22470 33207. The best rural taverna on Pátmos, set back slightly behind the trees at the north end of Petra beach, with its own large greenhouse. Lush salads, home-made *dolmádhes*, carefully cooked *mayireftá*, plus grills after dark; little on the menu costs over €10. Reservations advised in summer. Easter–Oct daily 1–10pm.

Lambi Lámbi Bay ☎ 22470 31490. Lovely little seafront taverna, founded in 1958, where the roof is held up by elderly tamarisk trees, and some tables are on the beach itself. The fish is recommended; the menu is very brief off-season. Easter to mid-Oct daily noon–8pm.

Livádhi Yeranou Taverna Livádhi Yeranoú beach ☎ 22470 32046. Good-value taverna, just short of the beach, with a nice terrace and a reasonable menu of seafood, chops, tzatzíki, *hórta* and salads from €6. May–Nov daily noon–late.

Tarsanas Patmos Marine boatyard, Dhiakoftí isthmus. The boatyard near the southern tip of the island might not seem the obvious place to find a smart, good-value taverna, but *Tarsanas* is a favourite (all-year) "power lunch" spot for locals. Mountainous salads, quiche-like *píttes* and Greek standards; the nicest tables are in a permanently grounded boat. Daily lunch and dinner.

★**Taverna Panagos** Kámbos Square ☎ 22470 31076. Opposite the town square and church, this good-value family-run taverna, popular with tourists and locals, offers new dishes of the day such as coq au vin, aubergine stuffed with cheese and rabbit stew as well as salads and mezédhes. No main dish over €9. Daily noon–late.

Lipsí

The largest, most interesting and most populated of the islets north and east of Pátmos, **LIPSÍ** also has the most significant tourist trade. Out of season, the island still provides an idyllic halt, its sleepy pace almost making plausible a dubious link with **Calypso**, the nymph who held Odysseus in thrall. Once a dependency of the monastery on Pátmos,

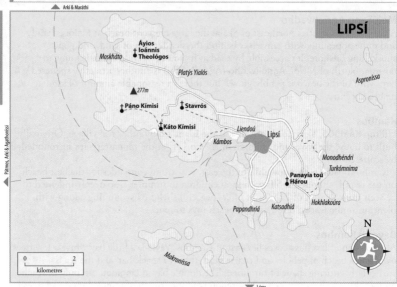

Lipsí is still conspicuously sown with blue-domed churches. Deep wells water small farms and vineyards, but there's only one flowing spring, and although plenty of livestock can be seen, the non-tourist economy is far from thriving.

ARRIVAL AND DEPARTURE LIPSÍ

By ferry The island's port is in Lipsi Village. Lipsi Bookings (☏ 22470 41382), tucked away in the central square (Mon–Fri 10am–2pm) or the public ticket office (☏ 22470 41250) near the jetty open one hour before ferry arrivals. Destinations Agathoníssi (3 weekly; 2hr 45min); Arkí (3 weekly; 1hr 35min); Kálymnos (1–2 daily; 1hr 20min–2hr

50min); Kos (1–2 daily; 1hr 40min–4hr 10min); Léros (2–3 daily; 25min–1hr 5min); Pátmos (2–3 daily; 20min); Pireás (1 weekly; 9hr 45min); Rhodes (1 daily; 5hr 10min–8hr 20min); Samos (3 weekly; 1hr 30min–4hr 5min); Sými (1 weekly; 4hr 20min–7hr).

GETTING AROUND

By bus All buses start from the Park (the central square) every 20min in season (10.30am–5.55pm) and go to the various beaches. Easy to flag down en-route. Flat fare €1.
By taxi Gorgos (☏ 6942 409 679) and Mikalis (☏ 6942 409

677) are the two taxi drivers on the island. Most fares to the harbour cost €4.
By scooter Studio Poseidon (☏ 22470 41130; see opposite) rents scooters. There's no car hire available on Lipsí.

Lipsí Village and around

Lipsí's only significant population centre, known as **LIPSÍ VILLAGE**, stretches around its large south-facing harbour. From the ferry jetty at its northwestern extremity, the hilltop centre of town is a 600m walk.

Beaches

None of the **beaches** is more than an hour's walk from the port. The closest, and sandiest, are crowded **Liendoú** and **Kámbos**, but many prefer attractive **Katsadhiá** (sand) and **Papandhriá** (coarse sand-and-gravel), adjacent coves 2km south of the port. Another paved road leads 4km west from town to protected **Platýs Yialós**, a shallow, sandy bay, continuing to sumpy Moskháto fjord (no beach). To reach the isolated east-coast beaches, which lack facilities, rent a **scooter** at the port (see above). **Hokhlakoúra** consists

5

MIRACLE OF LIPSÍ

Flowers on the icon of the church of Theochari are said to blossom only on **22 August**, the day of the **Miracle of Lipsí**, when the event is celebrated around the whole island with parties and traditional dancing until the early hours.

of coarse shingle (finer pebbles at mid-strand); nearby **Turkómnima** is sandy and much shadier, if mercilessly exposed to the *meltémi*.

ACCOMMODATION   LIPSÍ VILLAGE

Returning regulars make showing up to Lipsí in peak season without reservations unwise.

Aphroditi ☎ 22470 41000, ⊛ hotel-aphroditi.com. Complex of large, tiled-floor studios and apartments, some with kitchens and living room, set slightly back across the road from Liendoú beach. May–Sept. Breakfast included. **€60**

Filoxenia Studios ☎ 22470 41339. Set back away from the harbour, these thirteen ground-floor a/c studios are designed to a high standard, with iron double beds, some of which are four poster. Within easy walking distance of the town and harbour. **€30**

Galini Apartments ☎ 22470 41212. The first building you see on disembarking, right above the ferry jetty, is a prime budget choice in all respects, run by the hospitable

Matsouris family. Units have kitchens and balconies. Nikos sometimes takes guests fishing on request. **€40**

Studio Akrogiali ☎ 6947 218 842. This place offers three en-suites with harbour-view terrace, and the tastefully decorated and clean, fresh rooms in pastel hues with rounded corners make up for the slightly small bathrooms. May–Sept. **€35**

★**Studio Poseidon** ☎ 22470 41130, ⊛ lipsiposeidon .gr. Impeccable, roomy, modern studios with large balconies, 150m from the jetty, as well as a one-bedroom apartment. The decor may be IKEA-on-steroids, but they've thought of everything. **€45**

EATING AND DRINKING

Café du Moulin ☎ 22470 41316. The main daytime hub for travellers and locals, in the central square. Hearty lashings of *mayireftá* at shaded tables, as well as inexpensive breakfasts for roughly €4. Daily 8am–late.

Karnayio ☎ 22470 41422. This good-value restaurant, adjoining a blue-domed church on the far side of the bay, serves hefty salads and ample helpings of *mayireftá* such as pork with celery and carrots. Most dishes under €10. Daily lunch and dinner.

★**Manolis Tastes** ☎ 22470 41065, ⊛ manolistastes .com. Behind the main square, this restaurant and grill house is popular with tourists and locals alike. Outdoor seating and most produce, including the meat, comes from

Manolis' land. Expect dishes such as pork with plums (€9) and mezédhes such as mushrooms stuffed with local cheese (€6). Book ahead in July & Aug. Daily 10am–4pm & 5.30pm–late.

★**To Pefko** ☎ 22470 41404. Overlooking the main jetty, this restaurant serves classic Greek cuisine, strong on baked aubergine recipes and lamb-based hotpots like *ambelourgoú* (from €7) and with efficient service. May–late Sept daily lunch and dinner.

Yiannis ☎ 22470 41395. Brightly decorated taverna very near the jetty, next to *Studio Akrogiali* (see above). Good as your first-night option, with dishes such as mussels in white wine for €7. May–Oct daily lunch and dinner.

NIGHTLIFE

★**Dilaila** Katsadhiá ☎ 22470 41041. Garden-set beachfront taverna-café overlooking the strand at Katsadhiá. While pricier than the island norm, it's worth it for such delights as salad with bits of local cheese, chunky aubergine dip or *fáva* and marinated fish dishes. From

11pm until 4am it hots up as a late-night music bar. June to mid-Sept noon till very late indeed.

The Rock Lipsí's longest-lasting bar, right by the port, with a congenial crowd, boulder-like host Babis and good tunes. Daily 6pm–late.

Arkí and Maráthi

Roughly two-thirds the size of Lipsí, **ARKÍ** is a far more primitive island, lacking proper shops or a coherent village. A mere fifty or so inhabitants eke out a living, mostly fishing or goat/sheep-herding, though servicing yachts attracted by the superb

5

anchorage at Avgoústa Bay – named for the half-ruined Hellenistic/Byzantine **Avgoustínis fortress** overhead – is also important.

Excursion-boat clients swim at the "Blue Lagoon" of **Tiganákia** at the southeast tip, but other **beaches** on Arkí take some finding. The more obvious are the carefully nurtured sandy cove at **Pateliá**, by the outer jetty, and tiny **Limnári** pebble bay (fitting five bathers at a pinch) on the northeast coast, a 25-minute walk away via the highest house in the settlement.

Arkí's nearest large, sandy, tamarisk-shaded beach is a ten-minute boat trip away on **MARÁTHI**, the only inhabited islet (permanent population 3) of the mini-archipelago around Arkí.

ARRIVAL AND DEPARTURE

ARKÍ AND MARÁTHI

By ferry Ferries dock at the jetty on Arkí. Boats to Maráthi run roughly three times a week from Arki (10min); alternatively, take the daily excursion boat from Patmos to Maráthi (1hr 5min).

Destinations from Arkí; Agathoníssi (3 weekly; 1hr); Kálymnos (4 weekly; 5hr 15min); Lipsí (2 weekly; 2hr); Léros (3 weekly; 3hr 20min); Pátmos (3 weekly; 55min); Samos (3 weekly; 2hr 20min).

ACCOMMODATION AND EATING

ARKÍ

Nikolas ☎ 22470 32477. Friendly taverna on the flagstoned harbourside platía, where a mother/son team serve home-made puddings and *mayireftá* such as peppers with goat's cheese for roughly €10 per head. Daily lunch till late.

O Trypas ☎ 22470 32230. Also known as *Tou Manoli*, this waterfront taverna is renowned for its very decent fish meals and mezédhes. It also offers mock-trad, stone-floored rental units just up the hillside and doubles as the island's most happening music bar. Daily 1pm–late.

MARÁTHI

Pantelis ☎ 22470 32609, ⓦ marathi-island.gr. The most elaborate and "resort"-like establishment on Maráthi. The beachfront tables outside make a perfect venue to enjoy local free-range goat, fresh-caught fish, or vegetables from the adjacent garden, while the rooms are spacious, airy and tastefully furnished. May–Oct. €45

Piratis ☎ 22470 31580 or ☎ 6973 962 462, ⓦ marathi -island.com. Ten simple, adequate a/c en-suite rooms and a full-service taverna with waterside seating and a menu of home-baked classics as well as fresh fish. Barefoot proprietor Mihalis emphasizes his comic-book-pirate persona with a Jolly Roger flag and speedboat named *Piratis*. €35

Agathoníssi

The small, steep-sided, waterless islet of **AGATHONÍSSI** is too remote – closer to Turkey than Pátmos, in fact – to be a popular day-trip target. Intrepid Greeks and Italians form its main tourist clientele, along with yachts attracted by excellent anchorage. Even though the *Nissos Kalymnos* (and a summer catamaran) appear regularly, schedules mean you should count on staying at least two days.

Despite the lack of springs, the island is greener and more fertile than apparent from the sea; lentisk, carob and scrub oak on the heights overlook two arable plains in the west. Fewer than a hundred people live here full time, but they make a go of stock-raising or fishing (or rather, fish-farming), and few dwellings are abandoned or neglected.

Most of the population lives in **Megálo Horió** hamlet, just visible on the ridge above the harbour hamlet of **ÁYIOS YEÓRYIOS** and at eye level with tiny **Mikró Horió** opposite. Except for a small shop and two café-restaurants working peak-season nights only in Megálo Horió, all amenities are in the port.

With no rental scooters, exploring involves **walking** along the cement-road network, or following a very few tracks and paths – bring plenty of water. If you won't swim at the port, home to the largest sandy **beach**, hike ten minutes southwest to shingle-gravel **Spiliás**, or continue another quarter-hour by path over the ridge to **Gaïdhourávlakos**, another gravel cove. Bays in the east, all reached by paved roads, include tiny **Póros** (45min walk from the harbour), fine sand with lentisk-tree shade at the back; **Thóli**

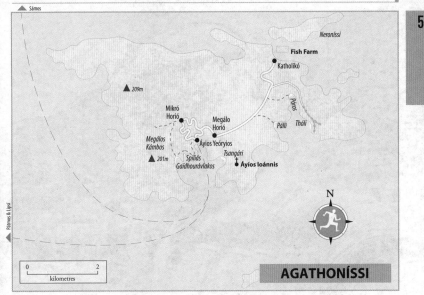

(25min further) in the far southeast, with good snorkelling and some morning shade; and **Pálli** across the same bay, a small but pristine fine-pebble cove reached by a fifteen-minute walk down from the trans-island road.

ARRIVAL AND DEPARTURE

AGATHONÍSSI

By ferry Ferries dock at Áyios Yeóryios.
Destinations Arkí (3 weekly; 1hr); Kálymnos (4 weekly; 1hr 50min–6hr 35min); Lipsí (4 weekly; 35min–3hr 20min); Léros (4 weekly; 35min–4hr 40min); Pátmos (3 weekly; 2hr 15min); Samos (3 weekly; 1hr 5min).

ACCOMMODATION AND EATING

Rooms Maria Kamitsi ☎ 22470 29065 or ☎ 6932 575 121. Thirteen pleasant a/c rooms at the centre of the beach, by the small port, sharing use of a kitchen and fridges, with a vine-covered patio outside. **€40**

Seagull ☎ 22470 29062. Central taverna, close to the yacht moorings, where the romantic waterside tables are filled every night for a full menu of baked and grilled dishes from €6. Daily lunch and dinner.

To Agnanti ☎ 22470 29019 or ☎ 6974 814 013. Good-value rooms, the newest on the island, above the popular *Memento Bar*, which has a wooden deck reaching out over the water. **€50**

The East and North Aegean

FISHERMAN, IKARÍA

The East and North Aegean

The seven substantial islands and four minor islets scattered off the Aegean coast of Asia Minor form a rather arbitrary archipelago. While there are similarities in architecture and landscape, the strong individual character of each island is far more striking and thus they do not form an immediately recognizable group, and neither are they all connected with each other by ferries. What they do have in common, with the possible exception of Sámos and Thássos, is that they receive fewer visitors than other island groups and so generally provide a more authentic Greek atmosphere. Yet the existence of magnificent beaches, dramatic mountain scenery, interesting sights and ample facilities makes them a highly attractive region of Greece to explore.

Verdant **Sámos** ranks as the most visited island of the group but, once you leave its crowded resorts behind, it has some of the finest scenery. Quirky **Ikaría** to the west remains relatively unspoilt, if a minority choice, and nearby **Foúrni** is (except in high summer) a haven for determined solitaries, as are the Híos satellites **Psará** and **Inoússes**. **Híos** proper offers far more cultural interest than its neighbours to the south, but far fewer tourist facilities. **Lésvos** may not impress initially, though once you get a feel for its old-fashioned Anatolian ambience you may find it hard to leave. By contrast, few foreigners visit **Áyios Efstrátios**, and for good reason, though **Límnos** to the north is much busier, particularly in its western half. The two islands in the far north are relatively isolated and easier to visit from northern Greece, which administers them: **Samothráki** has one of the most dramatic seaward approaches of any Greek island, and one of the more important ancient sites, while **Thássos** is more varied, with sandy beaches, mountain villages and minor archeological sites.

Brief history

Despite their proximity to modern Turkey, only Lésvos, Límnos and Híos bear significant signs of an **Ottoman** heritage, in the form of old mosques, hammams and fountains, plus some domestic architecture betraying obvious influences from Constantinople, Macedonia and further north in the Balkans. The limited degree of this heritage has in the past been duly referred to by Greece in an intermittent **propaganda war** with Turkey over the sovereignty of these far-flung outposts – as well as the disputed boundary between them and the Turkish mainland. Ironically, this friction gave these long-neglected islands a new lease of life from the 1960s onward, insomuch as their sudden **strategic importance** prompted infrastructure improvements to support garrisoning, and gave a mild spur to local economies, engaged in providing goods and services to soldiers, something predating the advent of tourism. Yet the region has remained one of the **poorest regions** in western Europe. Tensions with Turkey were periodically aggravated by disagreements over suspected undersea oil

MÓLYVOS, LÉSVOS

Highlights

❶ Vathý, Sámos The two-wing archeological museum is among the best in the islands, while there are atmospheric tavernas in the upper town of Áno Póli. **See p.355**

❷ Foúrni This small fishing island offers numerous deserted coves, a surprisingly lively port and a lovely main street lined with mulberry trees. **See p.365**

❸ Ikaría Western Ikaría has superb beaches and you can participate in the idiosyncratic nocturnal lifestyle of the Ráhes villages. **See p.368**

❹ Southern Híos The architecturally unique mastihohoriá (mastic villages) have a distinct Middle Eastern feel. **See p.380**

❺ Mólyvos, northern Lésvos This castle-crowned resort village is undoubtedly the most beautiful on the island, perhaps in the whole island group. **See p.401**

❻ Límnos villages Atmospheric basalt-built villages with lively central tavernas and great local wines to sample. **See p.404**

❼ Sanctuary of the Great Gods, Samothráki With Mount Fengári as a backdrop, the remote Sanctuary of the Great Gods is blessed with a natural grandeur. **See p.411**

❽ Alykí, Thássos A beautifully situated resort, with fine beaches flanked by ancient and Byzantine archeological sites. **See p.419**

HIGHLIGHTS ARE MARKED ON THE MAP ON P.352

THE EAST & NORTH AEGEAN

Kavála
Keramotí
Alexandhroúpoli

TURKEY

0   50
kilometres

Liménas
Skála
Prínou   *Thássos*
Limenária **8**

Kamariótissa **7**
Hóra   *Samothráki*

N

Gökçeada

Çanakkale

Límnos

6

Mýrina
Kondiás   Moúdhros

Bozcaada

HIGHLIGHTS

1. Vathý, Sámos
2. Foúrni
3. Ikaría
4. Southern Híos
5. Mólyvos, northern Lésvos
6. Límnos villages
7. Sanctuary of the Great Gods, Samothráki
8. Alykí, Thássos

Ay. Efstrátios

Mólyvos **5**
Ayvalık

Sígri
Eressós   **TURKEY**

Polikhnítos
Ayiássos   Mytilíni

Thessaloníki

Níymi
Skýros

A E G E A N
S E A   *Lésvos*
Plomári

Psará

Mármaro   *Inoússes*
Inoússes

Volissós
Híos
Híos

Çeşme

Mestá   **4**
Pyrgí

Izmir

Rafína
Ándhros

Lávrio

Píreás

Tinos

Mýkonos

Sýros

Efes
(Ephesus)

Kuşadası

Karlóvassi   **1**
Vathý

Áy. Kírykos
Évdhilos   **2**   Pythagório

Ikaría   **3**   *Foúrni*   *Sámos*

Pátmos   *Arkí*   *Agathoníssi*

deposits in the straits between the islands and Anatolia. The Turks also persistently demanded that Límnos, astride the sea lanes to the Dardanelles, be demilitarized, and since the millennium Greece has finally complied, with garrisons also much reduced on Sámos and Lésvos, as part of the increasing **détente** between the traditional enemies. Indeed, **Turkish tourists** on some of the islands now outnumber Greek conscripts.

Sámos

6

Lush, seductive and shaped like a pregnant guppy, **Sámos** seems to swim away from Asia Minor, to which the island was joined until Ice Age cataclysms sundered it from Mount Mykáli (Mycale) on the Turkish mainland. The resulting 2.5km **strait** provides the narrowest maritime distance between Greece and Turkey, except at Kastellórizo. In its variety of mountainous terrain, beaches and vegetation, Sámos has the feel of a much larger island, and despite recent development and wildfires taking their toll, it remains indisputably among the most beautiful in the Aegean.

Brief history

Sámos was during the Archaic era among the **wealthiest** islands in the Aegean and, under the patronage of tyrant Polykrates, home to a thriving intellectual community that included Epicurus, Pythagoras, Aristarcus and Aesop. Decline set in when Classical Athens rose, though Sámos' status improved in Byzantine times when it formed its own imperial administrative district. Late in the fifteenth century, the ruling Genoese **abandoned** the island to the mercies of pirates and Sámos remained almost uninhabited until 1562, when it was repopulated with Greek Orthodox settlers from various corners of the empire.

The new Samians **fought** fiercely for independence during the **1820s**, but despite notable land and sea victories against the Turks, the Great Powers handed the island back to the Ottomans in 1830, with the consoling proviso that it be semi-autonomous, ruled by an appointed Christian prince. This period, known as the **Iyimonía** (Hegemony), was marked by a renaissance in fortunes, courtesy of the hemp, leather-tanning and (especially) tobacco trades. However, union with Greece in 1912, an influx of refugees from Asia Minor in 1923 and the ravages of a bitter World War II occupation followed by mass emigration effectively reversed this recovery until tourism took over during the 1980s.

ARRIVAL AND DEPARTURE
SÁMOS

By plane Sámos' airport lies 14km southwest of Vathý and 3km west of Pythagório. A new airport bus service links up with most domestic but not international charter flights; taxi fares to all points are posted on placards, and in high summer taxis to the airport or ferry docks should be booked in advance. There are flights on Aegean/Olympic, Sky Express and Astra to the destinations listed below (frequencies are for June–Oct).
Destinations Athens (3–4 daily; 50min–1hr 20min); Híos (1 weekly; 30min); Iráklio (Heraklion), Crete (2 weekly; 1hr); Lésvos (2 weekly; 45min); Límnos (2 weekly; 1hr 40min–2hr 20min); Rhodes (1 daily; 45min); Thessaloníki (1 daily; 1hr 10min).
By ferry/hydrofoil There are three ferry ports: Karlóvassi in the west, plus Vathý and Pythagório in the east, making the island a major travel hub. All ferries between Pireás and Sámos call at both Karlóvassi and Vathý, while those from the northeast Aegean call at one or the other. Small boats to Kuşadası in Turkey depart mostly from Vathý, while

Karlóvassi has a small ferry to Foúrni and Ikaría. Pythagório offers ferry connections to the Dodecanese islands. Below is a summary of destinations and summer frequencies.
Destinations from Karlóvassi Áyios Kírykos, Ikaría (1–2 daily; 2hr); Évdhilos, Ikaría (3 weekly; 2hr); Foúrni (1–2 daily; 1hr 30min–2hr 30min); Híos (1 weekly; 4hr); Kavála (1 weekly; 18hr 30min–19hr 30min); Lésvos (1 weekly; 6hr 30min); Límnos (1 weekly; 11hr 30min–13hr); Mýkonos (5 weekly; 5hr–5hr 30min); Pireás (1–2 daily; 11–12hr); Sýros (5 weekly; 6hr–6hr 30min).
Destinations from Pythagório Agathónissi (3 weekly; 4hr); Lipsí (3 weeky; 4hr 30min); Léros (3 weekly; 5hr 30min); Kálymnos (3 weekly; 6hr 45min); Kos (3 weekly; 3hr 45min); Kuşadası, Turkey (2 weekly; 2hr); Pátmos (3 weekly; 3hr 30min).
Destinations from Vathý Áyios Kírykos, Ikaría (6 weekly; 3hr); Évdhilos, Ikaría (3 weekly; 3hr); Foúrni (3 weekly; 2hr); Híos (2 weekly; 3hr 30min); Kavála (1 weekly; 18–19hr); Kuşadası, Turkey (1–2 daily; 1hr 30min); Lésvos

6

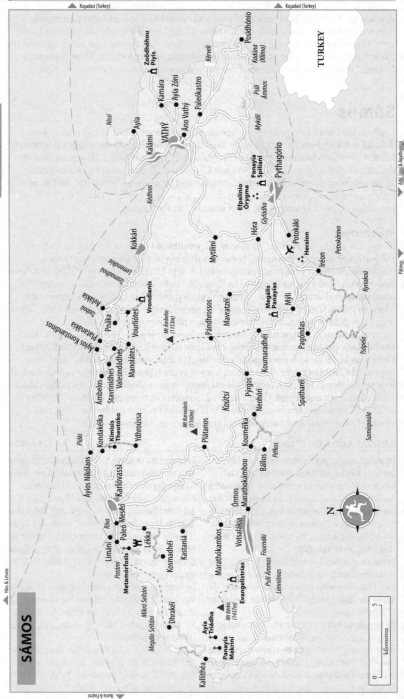

SÁMOS

TURKEY

Kuşadasi (Turkey)

Kuşadasi (Turkey)

Posidhónio

Kádara (Klíma)

Kérveli

Zoödhóhou Piyís

Kamára

Ayía Zóni

Áno Vathý

Paleókastro

Nissí

Ayía

Kalámi

VATHÝ

Psilí Ámmos

Mýkáli

Kédhros

Panayía Spilianí

Pythagório

Kokkári

Áyios Konstandínos

Lemonákia

Tzamadoú

Tzaboú

Efpalínio Órygma

Glyfádha

Potokáki

Petrokáravo

Hóra

Mytilíni

Heraíon

Iréon

Vrondianís

Mt Ámbelos (1153m)

Avláki

Pnáka

Pándhrossos

Mavratzeí

Megális Panayías

Mýli

Kyriakoú

Tsópela

Manoláltes

Voúrliótes

Ambelos

Stavrinídhes Valeondádhes

Pagóndas

Koumaradhéi

Pándhrossos

Samopoúla

Kondakéíka

Kímisis Theotóko

Mt Karvoúnis (1160m)

Pýrgos

Neohóri

Spatharéí

Ýdhroússa

Áyios Nikólaos

Karlóvassi

Platános

Koútsi

Koumeíka

Pídki

Paleó Meséo

Riva

Límáni

Lékka

Metamórfosis

Bállos

Péfkos

Mt Kerkís (1437m)

Ormos Marathokámbou

Votsalákia

Kosmadhéi

Kastaniá

Marathókambos,

Potámi

Mikró Seitáni

Megálo Seitáni

Dhrakéi

Ayía Triádha

Panayía Makríni

Kallithéa

Evangelístrias

Psilí Ámmos

Limniónas

Foúrndki

0   5

kilometres

N

Híos & Lésvos

Ikaría & Foúrni

Ikaría & Foúrni

Áyii Dhéka & Agathoníssi

Pátmos

(2 weekly; 6hr); Límnos (1 weekly; 11hr 30min–13hr); Mýkonos (5 weekly; 5hr–5hr 30min); Pireás (1–2 daily; 11–12hr); Sýros (5 weekly; 6hr–6hr 30min); Thessaloníki (1 weekly; 24hr).

Travel agents The most comprehensive island-wide travel agents, represented in all three ports and some resorts, are By Ship (☎ 22730 22116, ⓦ byshiptravel.gr) and ITSA (☎ 22730 23605, ⓦ itsatravelsamos.gr).

GETTING AROUND

By bus The KTEL service is good between Pythagório and Vathý, with eleven services on weekdays, nine on Sat and four on Sun, and fair on the Vathý–Kokkári–Karlóvassi route, with six weekday services, five on Sat and three on Sun, but poor for other destinations.

By car or motorbike Of the myriad scooter- and car-rental agencies dotted around the island, two to try are Aramis (☎ 22730 23253, ⓦ samos-rentacar.com), with branches island-wide, and Auto Union (☎ 22730 27444, ⓦ autounion.gr) at Themistoklí Sofoúli 79 in Vathý, which negotiates good long-term rates and will deliver cars to the airport.

By kaïki There are several weekly *kaïki* day-trips (10am–4pm; from €25–30) from Órmos Marathokámbou to the nearby islet of Samiopoúla and inaccessible parts of the south coast.

Vathý

Lining the steep northeastern shore of a deep bay, beachless **VATHÝ** (often confusingly referred to as "Sámos") is a busy provincial town which grew from a minor anchorage after 1830, when it replaced Hóra as the island's capital. It's an unlikely, rather ungraceful resort and holds little of interest aside from an excellent museum, some Neoclassical mansions and the hillside suburb of **Áno Vathý**.

Archeological Museum

Off the central park • Tues–Sun 8am–3pm • €3 • ☎ 22730 27469

The only real must is the excellent **Archeological Museum**, set behind the small central park beside the nineteenth-century town hall. The collections are housed in both the old Paschalion building and a modern wing just opposite, constructed for the star exhibit: a majestic, 5m-tall **kouros** discovered out at the Heraion sanctuary. The largest freestanding effigy surviving from ancient Greece, this *kouros* was dedicated to Apollo, but found next to a devotional mirror to Mut (the Egyptian equivalent of Hera) from a Nile workshop.

In the Paschalion, more votive offerings of **Egyptian** design – a hippo, a dancer in Nilotic dress, Horus-as-Falcon, an Osiris figurine – provide evidence of trade and pilgrimage links between Sámos and the Nile valley going back to the eighth century BC. The **Mesopotamian** and **Anatolian** origins of other artworks confirm an exotic trend, most tellingly in a case full of ivory miniatures: Perseus and Medusa in relief; a kneeling, perfectly formed mini-*kouros*; a pouncing lion; and a bull's-head drinking horn. The most famous local artefacts are numerous bronze **griffin-heads**, for which Sámos was the major centre of production in the seventh century BC; they were mounted on the edge of cauldrons to ward off evil spirits.

Áno Vathý

The best inland target on foot, a twenty-minute walk south from town and 150m above sea level, is the atmospheric hill village of **ÁNO VATHÝ**, a nominally protected but increasingly threatened community of tottering, canal-tile-roofed houses: some buildings are being replaced by bad-taste blocks of flats, others are being defaced with aluminium windows and modern tiles. The best of several venerable **churches** is quadruple-domed Aï Yannáki, in the vale separating the village's two hillside neighbourhoods.

ARRIVAL AND INFORMATION VATHÝ

By ferry Most ferries dock at the new port over 1km west of town, although boats to Turkey still use the old dock at the north end of the seafront.

By bus Buses stop at the KTEL depot (☎ 22730 27262) on the front, just south of the centre.

By taxi The taxi rank is in the middle of the seafront (☎ 22730 28404).

By car Details of car rental around the island are given above (see above). The southern seafront is the only area for free parking.

Tourist office The minimally helpful tourist office is at Themistoklí Sofoúli 107 (May–Oct Mon–Fri 9am–3pm; ☎ 22730 28582).

ACCOMMODATION

Emily Cnr of Grámmou and 11 Noemvríou, Katsoúni ☎ 22730 24691, ⓦ emilyhotel.gr. Small, well-run two-star hotel with cheerful and comfortable rooms – there's even wall art – and a roof garden. Breakfast included. March–Nov. **€50**

Ino Village Kalámi ☎ 22730 23241, ⓦ inovillagehotel .com. Surprisingly affordable three-star hotel about 1.5km north of the ferry dock, with views from most of its large, well-appointed rooms, a big pool and a decent on-site restaurant. Breakfast included. **€65**

Pythagoras Kalistrátou 12 ☎ 22730 28422, ⓦ pythagorashotel.com. This medium-sized hotel, around 600m north of the ferry dock, provides the best value in town with its basic but adequate rooms. There's a friendly bar-restaurant area. **€25**

Samos City Hotel Themistokli Soufoúli 11 ☎ 22730 28377, ⓦ samoshotel.gr. Refurbished behemoth by the ferry dock that's a firm favourite despite the rooms being rather small. Double-glazing against traffic noise, rooftop pool-terrace and popular café out front. Rudimentary breakfast included. **€60**

EATING AND NIGHTLIFE

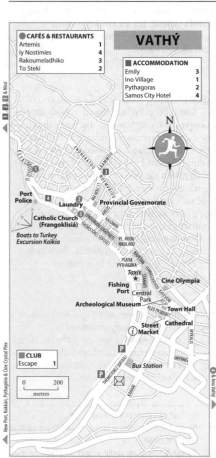

CAFÉS & RESTAURANTS
Artemis	1
Iy Nostimies	4
Rakoumeladhiko	3
To Steki	2

VATHÝ

ACCOMMODATION
Emily	3
Ino Village	1
Pythagoras	2
Samos City Hotel	4

CLUB
Escape	1

Vathý's perennial **nightlife** venue is a "strip" at the start of Kefalopoúlou north of the jetty, with annually changing bars that boast sea-view terraces.

★**Artemis** Kefalopoúlou 4 ☎ 22730 23639. Excellent, affordable seafood and starters like *fáva*, *hórta* and *seláhi* as well as the usual mains for under €10. Good bulk *robóla* wine from the hill villages. Pleasant indoor and outdoor seating. Mon–Sat 11am–1am.

Escape Kefalopoúlou 9 ☎ 22730 28345. The most durable of the many clubs in the area that plays a fairly standard mixture of foreign and Greek disco favourites. Pleasant outdoor terrace and a/c dancefloor within. Daily 9pm–late.

Iy Nostimies tis Ouranias Áno Vathý ☎ 22730 22488. Popular *inomayirío*, next to the school, which features grilled chops and mackerel in summer and more imaginative items at other times, mostly under €10. Try their *bouyiourdí* (pepper-and-cheese hotpot) year-round. Mon–Sat noon–late.

Rakoumeladhiko Lykoúrgou Logothéti ☎ 22730 27965. This *mezedhopolío*, tucked down an alleyway, serves a range of tasty mezédhes for €5–7. The atmosphere is especially enjoyable for the live music evenings on Tues & Thurs. Daily 10am–1am.

To Steki In the shopping centre behind the seafront Catholic church ☎ 22730 23580. Family-run *inomayirío* that's tops for dishes like bean soup at lunch; also good fish like *gávros* for €6 and decent bulk wine. Daily 11am–1am.

ENTERTAINMENT

Cinemas Plushly fitted Cine Olympia, inland on Yimnasiárhou Katevéni, offers a variable programme of films, in competition with newer Crystal Plex at the head of the bay (mostly action films).

Around Vathý

Around 5km east of Vathý, the ridgetop **Zoödhóhou Piyís convent** (8am–2pm & 5–8pm) is accessible on a climbing zigzag road from Kamára, 3km east of Vathý, and gives superb views across the end of the island to Turkey. The dome of its *katholikón*, where the nuns' chanting is excellent, is held up by four ancient columns from Miletus in Asia Minor.

Some modest **beaches** around Vathý compensate for lack of same in the capital. Striking **Kérveli Bay**, 8km southeast of Vathý via the attractive inland village of **Paleókastro**, has a small but popular pebble beach and a fine taverna just inland. On the far southeast coast of the island, almost within spitting distance of Turkey and accessed from a turning 1km west of Paleókastro, lie the reasonable beaches of **Mykáli** and **Psilí Ámmos**, both with a mostly mediocre range of facilities.

6

ACCOMMODATION AND EATING · AROUND VATHÝ

★ **ly Kryfí Folia** 300m uphill from Kérveli Bay ☎ 22730 25905. This secluded oasis with terraced seating offers simple but sustaining standards such as *kalamári* rings, the best lamb chops on Sámos for €9 and roast goat, which you can call to preorder. May to early Oct daily 11am–1am.

Kerveli Village Kérveli Bay ☎ 22730 23006, ⓦ kerveli .gr. One of the best hotels in eastern Sámos, located above the approach road to the beach, with sympathetic architecture, on-site car rental, pool, tennis court and private lido. April–Oct. **€65**

Psili Ammos Psilí Ámmos ☎ 22730 28301, ⓦ psili -ammos.gr. You can expect excellent service, as well as good seafood, salads and meat grills for €10 or less at this taverna on the far right as you face the sea. May–Oct daily 9am–midnight.

★ **Triandafyllos** Paleókastro ☎ 22730 27860. Excellent seafood, such as *yialisterés* for €8 and tuna steaks, is available at this taverna on the village square with unusually chic decor inside and ample outdoor seating. Daily 11am–1am.

Zefiros Beach Mykáli ☎ 22730 28532, ⓦ zefirosbeach .gr. Decent resort hotel with pleasant rooms, right behind the beach. Good for families, as it has ample watersports facilities off its patch of beach. May–Oct. **€55**

Pythagório

Originally called Tigani ("frying pan"), a reference to its reputation as a heat trap, the island's premier resort, **PYTHAGÓRIO**, was renamed in 1955 to honour Pythagoras, ancient mathematician, philosopher and initiator of a rather subversive cult. Sixth-century BC tyrant Polykrates had his capital here, whose sporadic excavation has made modern Pythagório expand northeast and uphill. The village core of cobbled lanes and stone-walled mansions abuts a cosy **harbour**, fitting almost perfectly into the confines of Polykrates' ancient jetty, traces of which are still visible, but today devoted almost entirely to pleasure craft and overpriced café-bars. There are, however, several worthwhile sights in the vicinity.

Archeological Museum

On the main road from Vathý · Tues–Sun 8am–3pm · €4 · ☎ 22730 62811

Pythagório's splendid **Archeological Museum** has a number of fascinating and well-labelled exhibits laid out over two floors. Star billing on the ground floor goes to the stunning collection of **gold coins** from a jar found by a Dutch archeologist at the west end of the island, plus there's a substantial number of votary objects and some Greek, Hellenistic and Roman statuary. Upstairs is the home for larger statues, such as the Roman Emperor Trajan and a fine *kouros* from 540–530 BC, but the most interesting display is on the subject of **ancient Greek dwellings**. There's also an unlabelled **hoard of gold byzants**, some of more than three hundred imperial coins from the fifth to seventh centuries AD – one of the largest such troves ever discovered.

The castle and around

Sámos' most complete **castle**, the nineteenth-century *pýrgos* of local chieftain Lykourgos Logothetis, overlooks both town and the shoreline where he, together with a certain "Kapetan Stamatis" and Admiral Kanaris, oversaw decisive naval and land victories against the Turks in the summer of 1824. The final battle was won on Transfiguration Day (Aug 6 – thus the dedication of the **church** by the castle); an annual fireworks show commemorates the triumph. Also next to the castle are the remains of an early **Christian basilica**, occupying the grounds of a slightly larger Roman villa.

Efpalínio Órygma

1km northwest of Pythagório • Tues–Sun: June–Sept 8am–8pm; Oct–May 8.30am–3pm • €4 • ☎ 22730 62813

The well-signposted **Efpalínio Órygma** is a 1036m aqueduct bored through the mountain just north of Pythagório. Designed by one Eupalinos of Mégara, and built by slave labour at the behest of Polykrates, it guaranteed the ancient town a siege-proof water supply, and remained in use until late Byzantine times. Even though the work crews started digging from opposite sides of the mountain, the horizontal deviation from true about halfway along – 8m – is remarkably slight, and the vertical error nil: a tribute to the competence of ancient surveyors. Unfortunately, the tunnel was closed for extensive restoration at the time of writing.

Panayía Spilianí

800m northwest of Pythagório • Cave open daylight hours • Free

On the way up to the Efpalínio Órygma is the well-marked turning for the monastery of **Panayía Spilianí**. The monastery itself, now bereft of nuns or monks, has been insensitively restored and the grounds are crammed with souvenir kiosks, but behind the courtyard the *raison d'être* of the place is still magnificent: a cool, illuminated, hundred-metre **cave**, at the drippy end of which is a subterranean shrine to the Virgin. This was supposedly the residence of the ancient oracular priestess Phyto, and a hiding place from medieval pirates.

Potokáki

The local, variable **beach** stretches several kilometres west of the Logothetis castle, punctuated part-way along by the end of the airport runway and the cluster of nondescript hotels known as **POTOKÁKI**. Although you'll have to contend with the hotel crowds and low-flying jets, the western end of the sand-and-pebble beach is well groomed, the water clean and sports available.

ARRIVAL AND ACTIVITIES   PYTHAGÓRIO

By ferry Ferries dock at the jetty towards the western end of the seafront.

By bus The main bus stop for buses from Vathý is beside the main inland T-junction.

By car Street parking is impossible but there are free car parks near the main T-junction just west of the town beach.

Diving Samos Dive Centre, at K. Kanári 1 (☎ 6972 997 645, ⓦ samosdiving.com), offers scuba diving.

ACCOMMODATION AND EATING

Doryssa Seaside Resort Potokáki beach ☎ 22730 61360, ⓦ doryssa-bay.gr. Huge complex including a hotel wing with Philippe Starck-ish rooms and a meticulously concocted fake village; each cosy bungalow is unique and there's even a platía with a pricey café. April to mid-Oct. **€150**

Faros ☎ 22730 62464. The best of the bunch stretching along from the harbour, where you can get basic seafood and small fish for well under €10. May–Oct daily 10am–1am.

Pension Dryoussa 2 blocks inland from the town beach ☎ 22730 61826, ⓦ dryoussa.gr. Friendly and picturesque guesthouse, with eight cosy, traditionally decorated rooms, most with small balconies. March–Nov. **€35**

Polyxeni On the western seafront ☎ 22730 61530. Bright yellow hotel right in the thick of the harbour action, with simple but clean and cosy rooms, most offering sea views. April–Oct. **€35**

To Magazaki Pou Legame On the square of Mytilinií village, 7km northwest ☎ 22730 51264, ⓦ tomagazaki poulegame.gr. Shaded by giant palms, this traditional taverna does fine lamb chops for €24/kilo and Turkish-style *melitzanosaláta*. Daily 11am–1am.

NIGHTLIFE AND ENTERTAINMENT

Amadeus 20m inland from the western seafront ☎ 22730 62290. Popular and enduring club that showcases quality live Greek acts followed by recorded hits. Tues–Sun 9pm–late.

Rex On the outskirts of Mytilinií village, 7km northwest ☎ 22730 51236. The Rex is one of the best-maintained outdoor cinemas on the islands, screening quality first-run films, with free *loukoumádhes* (sweet fritters) and cheap pizza at intermission. Late May to mid-Sept.

Seaside Poros Far west end of Potokáki beach ☎ 22730 27823. Smart new beach bar with a vast wooden deck and free sunbeds for patrons. Lots of cocktails, other drinks and snacks, accompanied by rock and disco sounds. Daily 10am–midnight (later in high season).

Heraion

5km west of Pythagório • Tues–Sun 8am–3pm • €3 • ☎ 22730 62811

Under layers of alluvial mud, plus today's runway, lies the processional Sacred Way joining ancient Samos with the **Heraion**, a massive shrine of the **Mother Goddess**. Much touted in tourist literature, this assumes humbler dimensions – one surviving column and low foundations – upon approach. Yet once inside the precinct you sense the former grandeur of the temple, never completed owing to Polykrates' untimely death at the hands of the Persians. The site chosen, near the mouth of the still-active Imvrassós stream, was Hera's legendary birthplace and site of her trysts with Zeus; in the far corner of the fenced-in zone you can tread a large, exposed patch of the Sacred Way.

Iréon

Modern **IRÉON**, barely a kilometre west of the ancient site, has a coarse-shingle beach and is at first glance a nondescript, grid-plan resort. Nonetheless its characterful pedestrianized waterfront remains popular: there are much better **tavernas** than at Pythagório, and after dark it has a more relaxed feel. The restaurants along the shore are especially busy on summer nights around the **full moon**, when Iréon is the best spot on the island to watch it rise out of the sea.

ACCOMMODATION AND EATING   IRÉON

Aegeon (Markos) Halfway along the seafront ☎ 22730 95271. Probably the most accomplished and Greek-patronized taverna, with fresh wild fish for €30–40/kilo and good starters like potato salad and mushroom soufflé. Book ahead on full moon nights. April–Oct daily 11am–2am.

★**Cohyli** One block back from the western seafront ☎ 22730 95282, ⓦ hotel-cohyli.com. The hotel rooms are simple but great value, especially during high season, while the courtyard taverna is a star, offering delights such as urchins, cockles and octopus salad for under €10 in the shady courtyard. Live music twice a week in season. Summer daily 10am–late and some winter weekends. **€40**

Glaros Two-thirds of the way west along the seafront ☎ 22730 95457. Cult place where the atmosphere and prices are excellent. Home-cooked delights include fish soup and okra, alongside standard grills, salads, fried vegetables and barrelled wine. May–Oct daily noon–1am.

Southern Sámos

Since island bus routes rarely pass through or near the following places, you really need your own vehicle to explore them. Three Samian "**pottery villages**" specialize, in addition to the usual wares, in the *Koúpa toú Pythagóra* or "Pythagorean cup", supposedly designed by the sage to leak over the user's lap if they were overfilled. Many of the **beaches** in this area are among the most deserted on the island, although it's not worth the effort and time involved in getting to the most remote.

Pottery villages

The biggest concentration of retail outlets is at **KOUMARADHÉΪ**, about 7km west of Hóra, along a route dotted with the odd spot to stop for refreshment and sweeping views. From the village you can descend to the sixteenth-century monastery of **Megális Panayías** (Mon–Sat 10am–1pm & 5.30–8pm; free), containing some recently cleaned frescoes, then carry on to **PAGÓNDAS**, a large hillside community with an unusual communal fountain house on the southerly hillside. From there, a scenic road curls 15km around the deforested hillside to **PÝRGOS**, at the head of a ravine draining southwest and the centre of Samian honey production.

Kouméïka and Bállos

6

The western reaches of the southern Samian shoreline are approached via handsome **KOUMÉÏKA**, which has a massive inscribed marble fountain and a pair of *kafenía*-snack-bars on its photogenic square. Below extends the long pebbly bay at **Bállos**, with sand and rock overhangs at the far east end. Bállos itself offers several places to stay and a few tavernas, all on the shore road.

From Kouméïka, the paved side road going west just before the village is a very useful short cut for travelling towards Órmos Marathokámbou (see p.364) and beyond.

Plátanos

From the main road between the south coast and Karlóvassi, it's worth detouring up to **PLÁTANOS**, on the flanks of Mount Karvoúnis; at 520m this is one of Sámos' highest villages, with sweeping views west and south. The name comes from the three stout plane trees (*plátanos* in Greek) on its platía, whose spring water in the arcaded fountain-house is immortalized in one of the most popular Samian folk songs. The only special sight is the double-naved thirteenth-century **church of Kímisis Theotókou** (key at house opposite west entrance) in the village centre.

ACCOMMODATION AND EATING — SOUTHERN SÁMOS

Amfilissos One block behind Bállos seafront ⊕ 22730 31669, ⓦ amfilissos.gr. Friendly medium-sized hotel, with functional, adequately furnished rooms, some with sea-view balconies, set behind a nicely landscaped courtyard. Late May to Sept. €35

Enalion Bállos beach ⊕ 22730 36444, ⓦ enalionsamos.gr. The name means "on the sea", and this small white block of fully equipped studios overlooks the beach. Its taverna, *Akrogiali*, does good fish and other items, mostly under €10. April–Oct roughly 10am–midnight. €40

Esperos Far eastern end of Bállos beach ⊕ 22730 36451. Restaurant with small but eclectic menu of mezédhes and fish like *tsipoúra* for €9. Also a relaxed beach bar serving great fruit smoothies. May to early Oct 9am–1am.

★ **Koutouki tou Barba Dhimitri** Central square, Pýrgos ⊕ 22730 41060. A good range of vegetarian mezédhes, as well as the usual meaty grills, in a surprisingly chic environment for such a remote village. Daily 11am–1am.

Leon Central square, Plátanos ⊕ 22730 39215. Great taverna, popular with the locals, where you can feast on goat in red sauce, *kondosoúvli* or *kokorétsi* for well under €10. Live folk music some nights. Daily noon–late.

Kokkári

KOKKÁRI, on Sámos' north coast, is the island's second major tourist centre. The town's coastal profile, covering two knolls behind mirror-image headlands called Dhídhymi ("Twins"), remains unchanged but its identity has been altered by inland expansion across old vineyards and along the west beach. The quaint harbour area is a lively place to hang out, but since the coarse-pebble **beaches** here are buffeted by near-constant winds, locals have made a virtue of necessity by developing the place as a successful **windsurfing** resort.

INFORMATION AND ACTIVITIES — KOKKÁRI

Tourist office. The helpful tourist office is on the main street heading inland (May–Sept Mon–Sat 8.30am–1.30pm plus Mon, Wed & Sat 7–9pm; ⊕ 22730 92333).

Windsurfing A windsurfing school thrives just west of town (⊕ 22730 92102, ⓦ samoswindsurfing.gr).

ACCOMMODATION AND EATING

Athena Hotel Opposite western beach ⊕ 22730 92030, ⓦ hotelathena-samos.gr. The modern, comfortable rooms are spread over three buildings, set in beautifully landscaped grounds with a large pool. Very helpful Greek-American owner and buffet breakfast included. April–Oct. **€55**

Cavos On the fishing harbour ☎22730 92436. This perennially popular place, run by a Greek-German couple, cranks out breakfast, snacks, coffees and cocktails according to the time of day, though the music can be rather middle-of-the-road. April–Oct daily 8am–late.

Girasole On western beach ☎22730 92037. Bright yellow Italian restaurant, serving authentic pizza, pasta and other classic dishes in the €10–15 range. Chic decor and comfy seating too. May–Oct daily noon–1am.

Sunrise Beach Hotel Behind eastern beach ☎22730 92447, ⓦsunrisebeach.gr. Perched on a green knoll above the beach, this upmarket hotel offers airy, spacious rooms, all with sea-view balconies. Buffet breakfast included. April–Oct. **€80**

★**Tarsanas** 100m down lane from western beach ☎22730 92337. Wonderful terrazzo-floored 1980s throwback doing pizzas, a couple of dishes of the day, like *briám* or *dolmádhes*, for €5–6, and their own dynamite red wine. Daily: June–Sept 11am–late, Oct–May 8pm–2am.

Tsamadou Middle of western beach ☎22730 92314, ⓦtsamadou.com. Friendly English-run place whose simple a/c rooms have fridges. Malaysian food is available in the garden conservatory for around €10. April–Oct. **€42**

The north coast

The closest sheltered **beaches** to Kokkári are about thirty minutes' walk west, fully carpeted with sunbeds and permanently anchored umbrellas. The further you move away from the resort, however, the wilder and quieter the strands become and the less-touristed the settlements.

Lemonákia and Tzamadhoú

The first beach west of Kokkári, **Lemonákia**, is a bit close to the road, so it's better to carry on 1km to the graceful crescent of **Tzamadhoú**. It can only be accessed by a path, and the eastern third of the beach, made up of saucer-shaped pebbles, is a well-established gay-friendly nudist zone.

Avlákia and Tzaboú

AVLÁKIA, 3km west of Tzamadhoú, is a quiet shoreline hamlet with an excellent taverna and some of the best views on the island. The nearest beach, 2km further west with a steep lane down, is **Tzaboú**, probably the most scenic north-coast beach with its rock formations but mercilessly buffeted by the prevailing wind most days – and the snack-bar tries to charge €6 for parking. There's a nudist annexe, with separate path access from Avlákia, off to the right.

Áyios Konstandínos

Platanákia, the next settlement west of Tzaboú and essentially a handful of buildings at a bridge by the turning for Manolátes, is actually the eastern quarter of **ÁYIOS KONSTANDÍNOS**, whose surf-pounded esplanade has been prettified. However, there are no significant beaches within walking distance, so the collection of mostly warm-toned stone buildings constitutes a peaceful alternative to Kokkári.

Áyios Nikólaos

West of Áyios Konstandínos the mountains hem the road in against the sea, and the terrain doesn't relent until **ÁYIOS NIKÓLAOS**, which is the tiny seaside annexe of more traditional **Kondakéïka**. A passable pebble beach, **Piáki**, lies ten minutes' walk east past the last studio units.

Kímisis Theotókou

2.5km inland from Kondakéïka along a partly paved road (signposted) • Unrestricted access

The Byzantine church of **Kímisis Theotókou** (left unlocked) is the second oldest and most artistically noteworthy on Sámos. Dating from the late twelfth/early thirteenth century, it has extensive frescoes contemporary with the building. The deceptively simple exterior gives little hint of the glorious barrel-vaulted interior, its decoration still vivid except where damp has blurred the images.

6

LEMONÁKIA AND TZAMADHOÚ

Arion 600m inland from Lemonákia beach ☎ 22370 92020, ⓦ arion-hotel.gr. This well-designed bungalow/hotel complex on a flattish patch of hillside has dazzlingly white, minimalist rooms and a large pool. Breakfast included. May–Oct. **€90**

★**Armonia Bay** Tzamadhoú ☎ 22730 92279, ⓦ armoniabay.gr. This hotel directly above the beach has tastefully decorated and sizeable rooms with marble-clad baths, as well as a fine pool and pleasant common areas. Good value. April–Oct. **€105**

AVLÁKIA AND TZABOÚ

To Delfini Central Avlákia ☎ 22730 94279. Kyra Alexandra is the heart and soul of this welcoming traditional taverna, which is strong on fresh little fish for €7–8, *hórta* and chips. May–Oct daily 10am–1am.

ÁYIOS KONSTANDÍNOS

Aeolos Far west end of the seafront ☎ 22730 94021. Terrific fish or grilled meat and a few daily oven dishes for €5–8, served at tables adjoining a tiny pebble cove. May–Sept daily noon–midnight.

Daphne 500m inland from the village ☎ 22730 94003, ⓦ daphne-hotel.gr. Set against a leafy backdrop on a hill, this good-value hotel has smart but compact rooms with baths and great views. Swimming pool and pool tables. Breakfast included. May–Oct. **€45**

To Kyma Central seafront ☎ 22730 94251. Numerous potted plants lend a garden feel to this taverna, which serves a wide range of meaty and fishy mains for €7–10. April to early Oct daily 10am–midnight.

Villa Agios Konstantinos On road to Platanákia ☎ 22730 94000, ⓦ hotelagios.gr. Attractive two-storey building on the street linking Platanákia to the sea, with a red-tile roof. Its sea-facing rooms are all well equipped and have small balconies. April–Oct. **€40**

ÁYIOS NIKÓLAOS

To Arhondospito Kondakéïka village centre ☎ 22730 38072. Popular with students, this convivial ouzerí-cum-taverna rustles up standard grills, some oven dishes and plenty of *mezédhes*, all for well under €10. Daily 11am–late.

Villa Eva ☎ 22730 30020, ⓦ villaeva-samos.gr. This hotel set in lush grounds, signposted downhill from the main coastal road, is also a thriving New Age retreat centre, with reiki, yoga and Sufi seminars. Breakfast, jacuzzi and exercise session included. May–Oct. **€65**

Northern hill villages

Inland between Kokkári and Kondakéïka, an idyllic landscape of pine, cypress and orchards is overawed by dramatic mountains. Despite bulldozer vandalism, some of the trail system linking the various **hill villages** is still intact, and walkers can return to the main highway to catch a bus back to base. Those with transport should leave it at Vourliótes and execute a **three-hour loop** via Manolátes, north and down to Aïdhónia, then back up east to your starting point. There is some waymarking, and the final stretch of trail has been rehabilitated.

Vourliótes

VOURLIÓTES, the closest sizeable village to Kokkári, has beaked chimneys and brightly painted shutters sprouting from its typical tile-roofed houses. But restaurateur greed has ruined the formerly photogenic central square by chopping down old mulberries and cramming in more tables. A detour from the road up to tiny **Pnaká**, bisected by a picturesque rivulet, is also rewarding.

Manolátes

MANOLÁTES, an hour-plus walk uphill from Vourliótes via a deep river canyon or accessed by a separate link road from the coast, has several excellent and authentic tavernas. The two high-quality *raku* ceramic workshops are anything but cheap though.

AAA Manolátes ☎ 22730 94472. Central taverna offering grilled *mastéllo*, an idiosyncratic version of aubergine *imám* and meat dishes such as fried liver for €7. March–Nov daily 11am–2am, some winter weekends from 8pm.

Galazio Pigadhi Vourliótes ☎ 22730 93480. Good spot for rabbit stew, *soutzoukákia* and aubergine dishes at limited pavement seating under a kangaroo vine up beyond the platía. Special €9.80 meze deal for two. Daily

noon–3pm & 6pm–midnight.
ly Pera Vrysi Vourliótes ☎ 22730 93277. This taverna at
the village entrance offers a huge range of well-priced,
imaginative mezédhes like spinach croquettes or chicken
livers, as well as local *robóla* wine. March–Nov daily
noon–1am.
★**Kallisti** Manolátes ☎ 22730 94661. Excellent roast
goat, courgette pie, grills and some small fish are all

available for a maximum of €8.50 at this great taverna, as
is fine barrelled wine. Warm welcome assured too. Daily
11am–1am.
★**Pnaka** Pnaká ☎ 22730 93297. Traditional
mezedhopolío revitalized by youthful owners, in a lovely
shady setting, where you can enjoy mezédhes like *bouréki*
and *bekrí mezé* or more substantial dishes for €8 at most.
March–Nov daily 11am–1am.

Karlóvassi and the northwest coast

KARLÓVASSI, 31km west of Vathý and Sámos' second town, is sleepier and more
old-fashioned than the capital, despite having roughly the same population. It's a useful
base for enjoying northwestern Sámos' excellent **beaches** or taking a number of
rewarding **walks**, though relatively few foreigners stay here. The town divides into five
straggly neighbourhoods: **Néo**, well inland, whose growth was spurred by the influx of
post-1923 refugees; **Meséo**, across the usually dry riverbed, tilting appealingly off a
knoll and then blending to the west with the shoreline district of **Ríva**; picturesque
Paleó (or **Áno**) lies further west, its hundred or so houses draped either side of a leafy
ravine; while below it is **Limáni**, the small harbour district. Most tourists stay at or near
Limáni, which has more facilities. The **port** itself is an appealing place with a working
boatyard at the west end.

Ríva

On the 1km-long street linking Meséo's Platía 8-Maïoú to **Ríva** stands a huge,
early twentieth-century **church**, topped with twin belfries and a blue-and-white
dome, typical of those that dot the coastal plain here. Ríva itself is something of
a ghost town, with derelict stone-built warehouses, tanneries and mansions,
reminders of the defunct leather industry that flourished here until the 1960s. The
epoch is immortalized in the modern **Tannery Museum** (Tues–Sat 9am–1pm; free;
☎ 22730 79137), which has informative displays on the industry, as well as on
tobacco production.

Potámi and around

The closest decent **beach** to Karlóvassi is **Potámi**, forty minutes' walk away via the coast
road from Limáni or an hour by a more scenic, high trail from Paleó. This broad arc of
sand and pebbles is presided over on the east by the striking modernist clifftop chapel
of Áyios Nikólaos from 1971. A streamside path leads twenty minutes inland from
Potámi, past the eleventh-century church of **Metamórfosis** – the oldest on Sámos – to
a point where the river disappears into a small gorge. Just above the Metamórfosis
church, a clear if precipitous path leads up to the remains of a small, contemporaneous
Byzantine fortress.

Mikró Seïtáni and Megálo Seïtáni

A couple of daily water-taxi services run in peak season from Karlóvassi port to both beaches

The coast west of Potámi ranks among the most beautiful and unspoilt on Sámos; since
the early 1980s it has served as a protected refuge for the rare **monk seal**, still glimpsed
occasionally by lucky hikers or bathers. Some twenty minutes along the dirt track at
the west end of Potámi Bay takes you to the well-marked side trail running parallel to
the water. After twenty minutes more you'll arrive at **Mikró Seïtáni**, a small pebble cove
guarded by sculpted rock walls. A full hour's walk from the trailhead, through olive
terraces, brings you to **Megálo Seïtáni**, the island's finest sand beach, at the mouth of
the intimidating Kakopérato gorge. Bring food, water and something to shade yourself,
though a swimsuit is optional.

6

ARRIVAL AND DEPARTURE

By ferry Karlóvassi's dock is an inconvenient 3km from the centre. Buses to town are infrequent but often do meet boats.

KARLÓVASSI AND THE NORTHWEST COAST

By bus Most buses call at multiple stops along the seafront before terminating near the port.

ACCOMMODATION AND EATING

★**Hippy's** Potámi beach ☎ 22730 33796, ⓦ hippys.gr. Laidback beach bar, set behind a sunflower garden, with a distinct Indian vibe. It does a limited breakfast and meals menu, plus ample coffee and cocktails. Regular parties and musical events. June to early Sept 10am–late.

ly Platia Platía 8-Maïoú, Meséo ☎ 22730 34600. Busy with locals at lunchtime thanks to plentiful traditional *mayireftá* and a few grills, mostly under €8 and served up speedily, though quality varies. Daily 11am–midnight.

O Dionysos Platía 8-Maïoú, Meséo ☎ 22730 30120. Offers creative dishes such as asparagus in mushroom sauce and richly cooked meat dishes for €10 and upwards. Pleasant indoor and outdoor seating, plus a wine list aspiring to Athenian sophistication. Mon–Sat 11am–1am.

Samaina Inn Limáni ☎ 22730 30400, ⓦ samaina hotels.gr. Fairly luxurious hotel near the old harbour, offering rooms with sea-facing balconies. The cheaper nearby sister hotel *Samaina Port* was under renovation at the time of writing. Breakfast included. April–Oct. **€64**

Southwestern beach resorts

The southwestern coast of Sámos boasts some of the island's best beaches, stretching in an almost unbroken line between Órmos Marathokámbou and Limniónas. These strands also offer a range of amenities.

Órmos Marathokámbou

The port of Marathókambos, **ÓRMOS MARATHOKÁMBOU**, 18km from Karlóvassi, has become something of a resort, though with ample character in its backstreets. Otherwise, the main focus of attention is the pedestrianized quay, home to several **tavernas** and starting point for excursion boats to the island of Samiopoúla and along the coast.

Votsalákia and Fournáki

Two kilometres west of Órmos is **VOTSALÁKIA** (signposted as "Kámbos"), Sámos' most family-pitched resort, straggling a further 2km behind the island's longest beach. The presence of Mount Kérkis (see opposite) looming overhead rarely fails to impress too. Just to the west, **Fournáki**, the collective name for a series of sand-and-pebble **coves** backed by low cliffs, is usually less crowded.

Psilí Ámmos and Limniónas

Three kilometres west of Votsalákia, you reach 600m-long **Psilí Ámmos**, not to be confused with its namesake beach in southeastern Sámos. The sea shelves ridiculously gently here – 100m out you're still just knee-deep – but that makes it ideal for families with young children. Access to **Limniónas**, a smaller but superior cove 2km west from Psilí Ámmos, passes the *Limnionas Bay Village Hotel*. Yachts and *kaïkia* occasionally call at the protected bay, which offers decent swimming at the east end, away from a rock shelf in the middle.

ACCOMMODATION AND EATING

Aspres Fournáki ☎ 22730 31662, ⓔ aspres.rooms @gmail.com. Attractive range of dazzling blue and white units differing in size and arranged round a central pool. May–Sept. **€35**

ly Trata Eastern end of Órmos Marathokámbou ☎ 6986 870 339. The most authentic taverna in the resort specializes in fresh local fish, such as swordfish for €8 per portion, but also does oven dishes for €5–6. April–Oct daily 10am–1am.

SOUTHWESTERN BEACH RESORTS

Limnionas Bay Village Limniónas ☎ 22730 37057, ⓦ hotel-limnionas-bay-village.co.uk. Large rather characterless resort right behind the bay with tiered units arrayed around a garden full of olive trees and a decent pool. Breakfast included. May–Oct. **€55**

★**Loukoullos** Fournáki ☎ 22730 37147. This welcoming restaurant with a lovely courtyard and separate bar overlooking the first cove is better in the evening, when the full range of delicious *mayireftá* and

---

CLIMBING MOUNT KÉRKIS

The classic **route up Mount Kérkis** begins from **Votsalákia**, along the paved but narrow lane leading inland towards the uninhabited Evangelistrías convent. After a 45-minute walk through olive groves, the path begins, more or less following power lines up to the convent, from which a paint-marked **trail** continues even more steeply up to the peak. The views are tremendous, though the climb itself is humdrum once you're out of the trees. About an hour before the top there's a chapel with an attached cottage for sheltering in emergencies, and just beyond, a welcome spring. All told, it's a seven-hour return outing from Votsalákia, not counting rest stops.

6

home-grown veg dishes is available for €5–8. May–Sept daily noon–midnight.

★ **Sirena Residence & Spa** 300m inland from Órmos Marathokámbou ☎ 22730 31035, ⊛ sirena.gr. One of the island's newest and smartest resorts, with a range of luxury studios and apartments and health facilities; spa treatments €15–85. Breakfast included. Easter to late Oct. **€80**

Mount Kérkis and around

A limestone/volcanic oddity in a predominantly schist landscape, **Mount Kérkis** (Kerketévs) – the Aegean's second-highest summit after Mount Sáos on Samothráki – attracts legends and speculation as easily as the cloud pennants that usually wreath it. Hermits colonized and sanctified the mountain's many caves in Byzantine times; resistance guerrillas controlled it during World War II; and mariners still regard it with superstitious awe, especially when mysterious lights – presumed to be the spirits of the departed hermits, or the aura of some forgotten holy icon – are glimpsed at night near the cave mouths. Gazing up from a supine seaside position, you may be inspired to **climb the peak** (see box above), though less ambitious walkers might want to **circle the mountain's flank**, first by vehicle and then by foot. The road beyond Limniónas through **Kallithéa** is paved all the way to **Dhrakéï**.

Dhrakéï, Kallithéa and around

During school term a vehicle leaves Karlóvassi (Mon–Fri 1.20pm) bound for Kallithéa; during summer it only operates twice a week (Mon to Dhrakéï, Fri to Kallithéa)

DHRAKÉÏ is a minuscule, back-of-beyond village with views across to Ikaría. A lovely trail – minimally disrupted by a track – descends ninety minutes through forest to **Megálo Seïtáni** (see p.363) from where it's easy to continue on to Karlóvassi within another two-and-a-half hours. People climbing up from Seïtáni must either retrace their steps, summon a taxi or stay at a few unofficial **rooms** establishments in Dhrakéï.

From **Kallithéa**, a small village 7km southwest of Dhrakéï with just a simple grill on its tiny square, a newer track (from beside the cemetery) and an older trail both lead up within 45 minutes to a spring, rural chapel and plane tree on the west flank of Kérkis, with path-only continuation for another thirty minutes to a pair of faintly frescoed cave-churches. **Panayía Makriní** stands at the mouth of a high, wide but shallow grotto, whose balcony affords terrific views. By contrast, **Ayía Triádha**, a ten-minute scramble overhead, has most of its structure made up of cave wall; just adjacent, another long, narrow, volcanic cavern can be explored with a torch some hundred metres into the mountain.

Foúrni

The straits between Sámos and Ikaría are speckled with a mini-archipelago – once haunted by pirates from various corners of the Mediterranean – of which only two are inhabited. Of these, the largest of the group, **FOÚRNI**, has a growing reputation as a great hideaway, while its little sister **Thýmena** to the west has minimal facilities. Unlike so many small Greek islands, Foúrni has a stable population (around 1600), as it is home to a huge fishing fleet and one of the more thriving boatyards in the Aegean.

Apart from remote **Khrysomiliá** hamlet in the north, reached by the island's longest (18km) road, Foúrni's inhabitants are concentrated in the **port** and **Kambí** hamlet just south.

6 The port

The **port** community is larger than it seems from the sea, with a friendly ambience reminiscent of 1970s Greece; the historical pirate connection is reflected in the municipality's official name, Foúrni Korseón ("Fourni of the Corsairs"). The main **market street**, field-stoned and mulberry-shaded, runs 200m inland from the seafront and culminates scenically at a little **platía** with two giant plane trees and a Hellenistic sarcophagus found in a nearby field.

Southern Foúrni

From the primary school near the port, it's a fifteen-minute walk south on a flagstone lane, then over the restored windmill ridge, to **KAMBÍ**, a scattered community overlooking a pair of sandy, tamarisk-shaded coves.

A path system starting at Kambí's last house continues south around the headland to other, more secluded **bays** of varying sizes and beach consistencies. These are also favourite anchorages for passing yachts, but unlike Kambí they have substantial summer communities of rough campers and naturists. In order of appearance they are sand-and-pebble **Áspa**, fifteen minutes along, with a tiny spring seeping from the rocks just before, **Pelekanía**, five minutes further, and equidistant **Elidháki** – both of these coarse pebble, the latter also with paved road access. The trail is slippery and steep just before Áspa so some may prefer to employ a taxi-boat service.

The side road serving Elidháki from the main island ridge-road also has an option for **Petrokopió** (Marmári) cove, named after its role as a quarry for ancient Ephesus in Asia Minor. The quarry itself, with obvious chisel marks and abandoned half-worked stones down by the shore, proves impressive; the beach is made of the same stone. The southernmost pebble and sand beach of **Vlyhádha** is easily accessible by steps from the end of the asphalt road.

Northern Foúrni

North from Foúrni harbour via steps, then path, are a pair of slightly sullied beaches. **Psilí Ámmos**, in front of a derelict fish-processing plant and equally defunct café at the end with tamarisks, is superior to **Kálamos** further along, which is dominated by a military watchpoint; both now have track access, while the former has a fishermen's jetty and beach bar. In the northeast of the island, **KAMÁRI** too has a beach. Without transport, it's possible to **walk** between town and Kamári on the old *kalderími*, which goes via the ridgetop monastery of Panayía. Isolated and somewhat unfriendly **Khrysomiliá** in the far north, however, is of very limited appeal.

Thýmena

Just a short boat ride west of Foúrni, the small but mountainous island of **THÝMENA** is part of Foúrni's municipality, as it has little over a hundred inhabitants. These mostly reside in the village that climbs sharply up the hill from the dock. A stiff twenty minute hike across a ridge to the southwest leads to a splendid sandy beach with the island's only taverna and rooms operation.

6

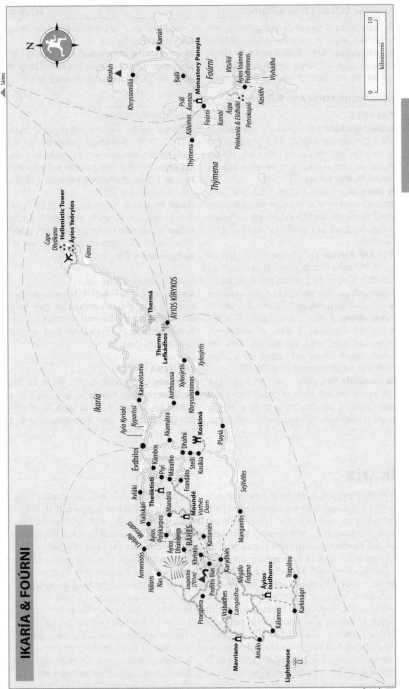

IKARÍA & FOÚRNI

Samos ▲

Syros & Mýkonos ▲

0 — 10 kilometres

N

Fourni
Kamári
Khryssomiliá
Kórakas ▲
Pili
Kálamos   Ammos
Kambi
Thýmena
Thýmena
Monastory Panayía
Balli
Aspa
Ayios Ioánnis   Vitsiliá
Pelekania & Eliáki   Pródhromos
Petrokopió   Kasídhi   Vlyhádha

Cape Dhrákano
Hellenistic Tower
Ayios Yeóryios
Fáros ✈
Thermá
Thermá   AYIOS KIRYKOS
Thermá Lefkádhos

Ikaría

Karavóstamo   Xylosýrtis
Arethoússa   Xylosýrtis
Akámatra   Xylosóstomos
Ayia Kyriakí   Khryssóstomos
Kyparíssi   Koskiná
Évdhilos   Dháfni
Kámbos   Plaýiá
Piýi   Stelli
Theóktisti   Maratho
Avláki   Frandáto   Kosíkia
Yialiskári   Mandhriá
Lividhi   Moundé
Ayios   Polýkarpos   Vathés   Seyhelles
Armenistís   Dhíantros   Dam
Hálaris   RAHES   Kastaniés   Manganítis
Nas   Ayios   Khristós
Proespéra   Dhíantros
Loupstra   Profítis Ilías
(701m)
Longádha   Ayios Isídhoros
Vrakádhes   Megálo   Isídhoros
Frágma
Mavriano   Longádha
Amálo   Kálamos   Karkinágri
Lighthouse   Trapalou

ARRIVAL AND GETTING AROUND

FOÚRNI

By ferry Foúrni is surprisingly well connected, with services to its neighbours, a couple of Cyclades and Pireás. Destinations Áyios Kírykos, Ikaría (8 weekly; 1hr 15min); Karlóvassi, Sámos (1–2 daily; 1–3hr); Mýkonos (3 weekly; 4hr–4hr 30min); Pireás (3 weekly; 10–11hr); Sýros

(3 weekly; 5hr–5hr 30min); Thýmena (1–2 daily; 20min); Vathý, Sámos (3 weekly; 2hr).

By car or scooter Although much of the island is walkable, you can rent a car or scooter from seafront Escape at the port (☎ 22750 51514, ✉ gbikes@hotmail.com).

ACCOMMODATION AND EATING

THE PORT

Archipelagos Hotel Northern end of seafront ☎ 22750 51250, ⊚ archipelagoshotel.gr. This smart modern hotel by the fishing port offers quality fittings in its eighteen doubles and suites, as well as an on-site restaurant during summer. Breakfast included. **€40**

Iy Drosia Main square ☎ 22750 51678. With tables crowded beneath one of the huge plane trees on the inland square, this traditional *kafenío* doubles up as a restaurant, serving the island's best *souvláki* for around €2. Daily 8am–late.

★**Iy Kali Kardhia** Just off main square ☎ 22750 51217. The aroma from the superb €8 *kondosoúvli* and *kokorétsi* rotating on the huge spits outside this place is tempting enough. Some *mayireftá*, fresh salads and decent wine complete the picture. April–Oct daily 7pm–late.

Patras Rooms Central seafront ☎ 22750 51268, ⊚ fourni-patrasrooms.gr. A choice of wood-floored, antique-bed rooms, some with balconies above the owner's laidback café-bar, and fourteen superb hillside apartments, in a tiered complex. April–Oct. **€25**

Ta Tsirnikakia Main market street ☎ 22750 51670. This popular spot with plenty of outdoor seating serves decent *mayireftá* and succulent roasts for under €10, as well as delights like stuffed courgettes in *avgolémono*. Daily noon–1am.

SOUTHERN FOÚRNI

O Yiorgos Behind southern end of Kambí beach ☎ 22750 51025, ✉ kikikampi@yahoo.com. The old couple here provide inexpensive fish plates, Ikarian *soúfiko* (ratatouille) and other oven dishes for well under €10. There are a couple of ultra-cheap rooms too. April–Oct daily noon–midnight. **€20**

Studio Rena North side of Kambí ☎ 22750 51364, ⊚ studio-rena.com. Stacked in three tiers on Kambí's northern hillside, these comfortable apartments, painted island blue and white, offer fully equipped kitchens and sea-view balconies. **€25**

NORTHERN FOÚRNI

Almyra Kamári beach ☎ 6979 141 653. The most accomplished out-of-town taverna on the island rustles up a range of fish at standard prices and various *mezédhes* for €3–6, with seating right on the beach or in a courtyard. May–Oct 1am–1am.

THÝMENA

O Kottaras On the beach ☎ 22750 32797. The only proper taverna on the island serves up a limited menu of fresh fish, *kalamári*, grills and salads for no more than €8. There are also three simple rooms. June–Sept 10am–11pm. **€25**

Ikaría

IKARÍA, a narrow, windswept landmass between Sámos and Mýkonos, is comparatively little visited and sadly underestimated by many people. The name supposedly derives from Icarus, who in legend fell into the sea just offshore after the wax bindings on his wings melted. For years the only substantial tourism was generated by a few **hot springs** on the southeast coast; since the early 1990s, however, tourist facilities of some quantity and quality have sprung up in and around **Armenistís**, the only resort of note.

Ikaría, along with Thessaly, Lésvos and the Ionian islands, has traditionally been one of the **Greek left**'s strongholds. This dates from long periods of right-wing domination in Greece, when, as in Byzantine times, the island was used as a place of **exile** for political dissidents, particularly communists, who from 1946 to 1949 outnumbered native islanders. This house-arrest policy backfired, with the transportees (including Mikis Theodhorakis in 1946–47) favourably impressing their hosts as the most noble figures they had ever encountered, worthy of emulation. Earlier in the twentieth century, many Ikarians had emigrated to North America and, ironically, their capitalist remittances kept the island going for decades. Yet anti-establishment attitudes still predominate and local pride dictates that outside opinion matters little. Thus many

Ikarians exhibit a lack of obsequiousness and a studied **eccentricity**, which is rather endearing, though some find it initially offputting. On the other hand, this leads to the island hosting some of the most musically authentic and rowdy *paniyíria* in Greece, especially in late summer.

Except for forested portions in the northwest, it's not a strikingly beautiful island, with most of the landscape being scrub-covered granite and schist put to use as building material. The mostly desolate south coast is overawed by steep cliffs, while the less sheer north face is furrowed by deep canyons creating hairpin road-bends extreme even by Greek-island standards.

6

ARRIVAL AND DEPARTURE
IKARÍA

By plane Ikaría airport, which can only handle small domestic planes, is around 12km northeast of Áyios Kírykos, the island capital.
Destinations Athens (1–2 daily; 50min); Iráklio (Heraklion), Crete (3 weekly; 45min); Lésvos (1 weekly; 1hr 50min); Límnos (6 weekly; 50min); Thessaloníki (6 weekly; 2hr).
By ferry Ikaría lies on the main Pireás–Sámos route and ferries alternate between calling at Áyios Kírykos, on the south coast, and Évdhilos on the north. Áyios Kírykos also has a weekly service on the northeast Aegean route to Kavála, as well as a small seasonal boat to Foúrni and Karlóvassi on Sámos.
Destinations from Áyios Kírykos Foúrni (8 weekly; 1hr); Híos (1 weekly; 5hr); Karlóvassi, Sámos (8 weekly; 1hr 30min–2hr); Kavála (1 weekly; 21hr); Lésvos (1 weekly; 7hr 30min); Límnos (2 weekly; 14hr); Mýkonos (3 weekly; 3hr); Pireás (3 weekly; 9hr–9hr 30min); Sýros (3 weekly; 4hr 30min); Vathý, Sámos (3 weekly; 2hr 30min–3hr).
Destinations from Évdhilos Karlóvassi, Sámos (3 weekly; 2hr); Mýkonos (3 weekly; 2hr 30min); Pireás (3 weekly; 8hr 30min–9hr); Sýros (3 weekly; 4hr); Vathý, Sámos (3 weekly; 2hr 30min).

GETTING AROUND

By bus There are one to two cross-island bus services between Áyios Kírykos, Évdhilos and Armenistís, with occasional erratic onward services to Khrístos. Unfortunately, the most reliable year-round service usually leaves Áyios Kírykos early morning and does not link with ferry arrivals. There's a frequent local bus from Áyios Kírykos to Thérma.
By car or motorbike Aventura (☎22750 31140;
@aventura@otenet.gr) and Dolihi Tours (☎22750 71122; @dolichi@otenet.gr) are the most prominent rental agencies, with branches in Armenistís, Évdhilos and Áyios Kírykos.
By taxi Taxis can be elusive and are best booked through a travel agent; a cross-island trip costs at least €50.
Hitching Note that hitching is a common and safe practice on this unconventional island.

Áyios Kírykos and around

The south-coast port and capital of **ÁYIOS KÍRYKOS** has little to detain foreign tourists, at least until the modest archeological museum reopens (which it may have done by the time you read this). The spa of **Thérma**, just over 1km northeast of the port, saw its heyday in the 1960s, and now relies on a mostly elderly clientele from July to early October. Of more general interest is the *spílio* or **natural sauna** on the shore (8am–8pm; €4.50), co-housed with plunge pools under the cave roof. Other good bets for informal soaks are the seaside, open-air pool (35–40°C) of the **Asklipioú hot springs**, reached by steps down from the Áyios Kírykos courthouse, or better still the natural, shoreline hot springs at **Thérma Lefkádhos**, 2km southwest of Áyios Kírykos, where 50–58°C water mixes with the sea to a pleasant temperature inside a ring of giant volcanic boulders. A further 3km brings you to another pleasant cove, below the small hamlet of **Xylosýrti**.

Fáros and around

The longest **beach** on the south coast is at **Fáros**, 12km northeast of Áyios Kírykos along a good road which also serves the airport. A colony of summer cottages shelters under tamarisks along the sand-and-gravel strand, with a reefy zone to cross before deep water. From a signposted point just inland from Fáros beach, a dirt track leads 2km to the trailhead for the round **Hellenistic watchtower** at **Cape Dhrákano**, much the oldest and most impressive ancient ruin on the island (closed long term for restoration). Right below this to the north, perfectly sheltered in most weathers, is a fantasy-image sand **beach**, with assorted rocks and islets off the cape-tip for contrast.

6

ACCOMMODATION — ÁYIOS KÍRYKOS AND AROUND

★Agriolykos Pension On the eastern bluff, Thérma 22750 22433, agriolykos.gr. Wonderful and welcoming place with original artwork, delightfully decorated rooms, use of kitchen, extensive shady grounds and direct access to a hidden cove. Breakfast included. April–Oct. €40

Akti Above the eastern quay, Áyios Kírykos 22750 23905, pensionakti.gr. Pleasant spot on a knoll above the harbour, with comfy a/c rooms, fluent English-speaking management and views of Foúrni from the café-garden. €35

Evon's Rooms Fáros beach 22750 32580, evonsrooms.com. Attractively appointed and well-equipped a/c rooms, especially the pricier galleried top-floor units. Right on the beach, with a pleasantly landscaped garden and private parking. €40

Marina Hotel Above western end of Thérma 22750 22188, marina-hotel.gr. All the rooms at this friendly little hotel, just above the end of the bay, have fridges, a/c and either balconies or verandas. June–Oct. €40

Pension Ikaria Central seafront, Áyios Kírykos 22750 22108, gmoulas@chi.forthnet.gr. Compact but cosy a/c rooms with small balconies, some above a seafront café. The entrance is on the first parallel street behind the front. €25

EATING

Arodhou Xylosýrti beach 22750 22700. This taverna on the shore, next to Ayía Paraskeví church, does excellent mezédhes and a full selection of meat and fish grills for €10 or under. Daily 2.30pm–midnight, closed Mon Oct–May.

Avra Western seafront, Thérma 22750 23805. The best of the handful of mostly fish tavernas set back from the beach, offering a number of seafood dishes for under €10, as well as baked items and fine wine. April–Oct daily 10am–midnight.

★Iy Klimataria 2 blocks back from seafront, Áyios Kírykos 22750 23686. With tables tucked on a pedestrianized alley beneath climbing vines, this old favourite does various salads, dips and grills for €6–9 and the odd oven dish, plus fine barrelled wine. April–Oct daily 11am–midnight.

Stou Tsouri Central seafront, Áyios Kírykos 22750 22473. Simple taverna serving up tasty baked dishes like okra, artichokes and stuffed fish for €6 each, plus the usual grilled meat and fish. May–Oct daily 11am–midnight.

SHOPPING

Studio Pelagos 1 block back from seafront, Áyios Kírykos 6972 845 546, studio-pelagos.com. You might want to take a peek or purchase one of the unique hand-painted marbles at this gallery, a block back from the seafront square. July–Sept daily 11am–2pm & 7–10pm.

Évdhilos and around

The north-coast port of **ÉVDHILOS** is the island's second town, with most of its facilities packed around the picturesque fishing harbour, separated by a headland from the busy port. Barely 1km west, the tiny hamlet of **Fýtema** offers better dining options. There are some decent beaches and places of interest in the villages around Évdhilos.

The twisting, 37km road from Áyios Kírykos, on the south coast, to Évdhilos is one of the most hair-raising in the islands, especially as a passenger, and Ikaría's longitudinal ridge often wears a streamer of cloud, even when the rest of the Aegean is clear. So it comes as quite a relief when you reach the north coast at the pleasant fishing village of **Karavóstamo**, 8km short of Évdhilos.

Kámbos

KÁMBOS, 1.5km west of Fýtema, offers a small hilltop **museum** (Tues–Sun 8.30am–3pm; €2; 22750 31300) with finds from nearby ancient Oinoe; the twelfth-century church of **Ayía Iríni** stands adjacent, with column stumps and mosaic patches of a fourth-century basilica defining the entry courtyard. Lower down still are the sparse ruins of a **Byzantine palace** used to house exiled nobles, signposted as "odeion", which earlier structure it encloses. An unmarked track below the palace leads to a 250m-long sandy **beach** with sunbeds and refreshments available.

Monastery of Theóktisti

4km west of Kámbos

Ikaría's outstanding medieval monument is the **monastery of Theóktisti**, 4km up from Kámbos along a twisty road (and an easier 3km road from the cute coastal village of Avláki). The monastery looks over pines to the coast from its perch under a chaos of slanted granite slabs, under one of which is tucked the much-photographed chapel of Theoskepastí. The *katholikón* features damaged but worthwhile frescoes dated to 1688.

ACCOMMODATION AND EATING

ÉVDHILOS AND AROUND **6**

Atheras On hill behind harbour, Évdhilos ☎ 22750 31434, ⓦ atheras-kerame.gr. The best of the three hotels in town offers smart modern rooms arranged around a pool. The sister hotel, *Kerame*, overlooking the eponymous beach has some slightly smarter apartments. April–Oct. **€40**

Coralli On the west quay, Évdhilos ☎ 22750 31924. This is a good place to feast on large portions of inexpensive oven-cooked meat, such as goat done as *yiouvétsi* or *kokkinistó* for around €8, plus ample salads, dips and so on. April–Oct daily 1pm–midnight.

★**Karimalis Winery** Piyí, 5km southwest of Évdhilos ☎ 22750 31151, ⓦ ikarianwine.gr. Several luxuriously restored ancient, family-sized cottages make for perhaps the classiest accommodation on the island. Breakfast and port/airport transfer included. Meals and cooking courses also offered. May–Sept. **€70**

★**Mandouvala** Karavóstamo ☎ 22750 61204. With a delightful patio set above wave-lapped schist rock, this popular taverna at the far right of the seafront provides a range of fish, mezédhes and veg delights such as local *soúfiko* (ratatouille) for under €10. May–Oct daily noon–midnight.

★**Mezedopolio tou Ilia** 300m up Theóktisti road, Avláki ☎ 22750 71009. The only real ouzerí on the north coast, with classy slate tables and fantastic sea views from the courtyard. Delightful mezédhes, all for €3–6, plus organic veg and home-made wine. June–Sept daily noon–1am; Oct–May Fri–Sun noon–1am.

Popi's Main coast road, Fýtema ☎ 22750 31928. Run by legendary leftist Popi, this place serves various pies and main courses like €9 cuttlefish in wine sauce which can be enjoyed on the shady terrace. May–Oct daily 11am–1am.

Armenistís and around

Most visitors congregate at **ARMENISTÍS**, 51km from Áyios Kírykos via Évdhilos, and for good reason: this little resort lies below Ikaría's greatest, if slightly fire-diminished, forest, with two enormous sandy **beaches** battered by seasonal surf – **Livádhi** and **Messaktí** – five and fifteen minutes' walk east respectively, the latter with several reed-roofed *kantínas*. The sea between here and Mýkonos is the windiest patch in the Aegean, generating a fairly consistent summer surf. The waves, which attract Athenian body-boarders, are complicated by strong lateral currents, and regular summer drownings have (at Livádhi) prompted a lifeguard service and a string of safety buoys.

Armenistís itself is spectacularly set, facing northeast along the length of Ikaría towards sun- and moonrise, with Mount Kérkis on Sámos visible on a clear day. A dwindling proportion of older, schist-roofed houses and ex-warehouses, plus boats hauled up in a central sandy cove, lend the place the air of a Cornish fishing village, though in fact it started out as a smuggler's depot, with warehouses but no dwellings. Just east of Messaktí, the fishing settlement of **Yialiskári** offers alternative facilities and looks out past pines to a picturesque jetty church.

ACCOMMODATION

ARMENISTÍS AND AROUND

★**Daidalos** Western edge of Armenistís ☎ 22750 71390, ⓦ daidaloshotel.gr. This smart place has a distinct artistic flavour, with a blob-shaped pool, unusually appointed rooms and a shady breakfast terrace. Breakfast included. May–Oct. **€55**

Erofili Beach Above Livádhi beach ☎ 22750 71058, ⓦ erofili.gr. Considered the island's best hotel, though the common area and pool, perched dramatically over the beach, impress more than the rooms. Breakfast included. April–Oct. **€80**

Valeta Apartments Central Armenistís ☎ 22750 71252, ⓦ valeta.gr. The attractive and comfortable studios and quads here above the harbour offer a comparable standard and setting to the hotels, at better rates. May–Oct. **€40**

6

WALKING IN WESTERN IKARÍA

Although bulldozers and forest fires have reduced the number of attractive possibilities, **walking** between Ráhes and both coasts on old paths is a favourite visitor activity. A locally produced, accurate map-guide, *The Round of Ráhes on Foot*, shows most asphalt roads, tracks and trails in the west of the island, as well as a **loop-hike** taking in the best of the Ráhes villages. The well-marked route sticks partly to surviving paths; the authors suggest a full day for the circuit, with ample rests, though total walking time won't exceed six hours. The highlight is the section from **Khristós to Kastaniés**, which takes in the **Hárakos ravine** with its Spanédhon watermill.

Those wishing to traverse across Ikaría are best advised to keep on a "Round of Ráhes" sub-route from Khristós to Karydhiés, from where a historic path crosses the lunar Ammoudhiá uplands before dropping spectacularly southeast to Managanítis on the south coast, a generous half-day's outing from Armenistís.

EATING AND NIGHTLIFE

Casmir Livádhi beach. One of the island's most enduring clubs acts as a beach bar during the day and pumps out foreign and Greek hits by night. June–Sept daily 11am–late.

★**Kiallaris (aka tis Eleftherias)** Central seafront, Yialiskári ☏ 22750 71227. Top place for well-executed *mayireftá* and the freshest fish, all caught locally. Especially good for its €7 fish soup and *melitzanosaláta*. May to early Oct daily 11am–2am.

Paradhosiaka Glyka (Kioulanis) Road to Armenistís harbour ☏ 22750 71150. On the road down to the harbour, this is one of the Aegean's star *zaharoplastía*, featuring addictive *karydhópita* (walnut cake) with goat's-milk, mastic-flavoured ice cream and other sweet delights. May–Oct daily 8am–1am; reduced winter hours.

★**Paskhalia** Road to Armenistís harbour ☏ 22750 71302. With a few simple rooms above, this extremely friendly taverna has a sea-view terrace, where you can enjoy tasty home-cooking such as rabbit *stifádho* and roast lamb for around €8. Great barrelled wine too. April–Oct daily 8am–1am.

Nas

Three kilometres west of Armenistís, **NAS**, a lush river canyon ending at a deceptively sheltered sand-and-pebble beach, remains a rather hippyish hangout. Although it is no longer a naturist's paradise, in many ways it is the most delightful spot on the island. The little bay is almost completely enclosed by weirdly sculpted rock formations, but again it's unwise to swim outside the cove's natural limits – marked here with a line of buoys. The crumbling foundations of the fifth-century BC temple of **Artemis Tavropoleio** ("Artemis in Bull-Headdress") overlook the permanent deep pool at the mouth of the river.

ACCOMMODATION AND EATING   NAS

Artemis West cliff ☏ 22750 71485, ⊛ artemis-studio .ikaria.gr. With rooms overlooking the river canyon, this rambling place provides great-value, comfortable and well-appointed accommodation, as well as some snacks and larger meals. May–Sept. €30

★**O Nas** West cliff ☏ 22750 71486. With a huge terrace on the cliff that has the best bay views, this place offers pasta, grills and oven-baked dishes for €8–10, plus there's a good bakery. May–Sept daily noon–midnight.

Thea East cliff ☏ 22750 71491, ⊛ theasinn.com. On the east cliff, this long-standing favourite has lots of vegetarian options like *soufikó* and pumpkin-filled *pítta*. Also has a few basic rooms. May–Oct daily 9am–1am (from noon in late July & Aug); Nov–April weekends 9am–1am. €25

The Ráhes villages

Armenistís was originally the port of four inland hamlets – Áyios Dhimítrios, Áyios Polýkarpos, Kastaniés and Khristós – collectively known as **Ráhes**. Curiously, these already served as "hill station" resorts during the 1920s and 1930s, with three hotels, since long-gone, and the only tourism on the island. Despite the modern, paved access

roads through the pines, the settlements retain a certain Shangri-La quality, with older residents speaking a positively Homeric dialect.

On an island not short of foibles, these villages are particularly strange in that most locals sleep until 11am or so, move around until about 4pm, then have another nap until 8pm, whereupon they rise and spend most of the night shopping, eating and drinking, in particular excellent home-brewed **wine** traditionally kept in goatskins.

EATING AND DRINKING	THE RÁHES VILLAGES
Kapilio Central Khristós ☎ 22750 41517. Right in the main pedestrian zone, this good, inexpensive carnivorous supper option serves mainly grills for around €6–8, with the odd dish from the oven and some simple salads. Daily 6pm–4am.	eponymous plane tree, this local favourite is renowned for its *mayireftá*, like beef in wine sauce and *moussaká* for €7–8. Daily 5pm–4am.
Platanos Main square, Áyios Dhimítrios ☎ 22750 41472. Underneath the deep shade of the platia's	**Ydrohöos** Main square, Áyios Dhimítrios ☎ 22750 41526. Typically offbeat art café on the square, which has a relaxed atmosphere and showcases frequent live rock, jazz, techno or Latin bands. Wed–Sun 5pm–4am.

The south coast

The well-paved route south from Évdhilos via Akamátra crosses the island watershed before dropping steadily towards the **south coast**; with your own vehicle this is a quicker and much less curvy way back to Áyios Kírykos compared to going via Karavóstomo. It's an eminently scenic route worth taking for its own sake, the narrow road threading corniche-like through oaks at the pass, and then olives at **Playiá** village on the steep southern slope of the island. Out to sea the islands of Pátmos and Dhonoússa are generally visible, and on really clear days Náxos and Amorgós as well. The principal potential detour, 2km past the castle turning, is the road right (west) to the secluded pebble beach of **Seÿhélles** ("Seychelles"), the best on this generally inhospitable coast, with the final approach by ten-minute hike.

With your own transport, you can visit several villages at the southwest tip of the island. **Vrahádhes** enjoys a natural-balcony setting, while a sharp drop below it, the impact of the empty convent of **Mavrianoú** lies mostly in its setting amid gardens overlooking the sea. Nearby **Langádha** is not actually a village but a lush hidden valley. Note that facilities are scarce over the whole south-coast area, with just the odd erratically opening *kafenío* or seasonal taverna providing refreshment.

Híos

"Craggy Híos", as **Homer** aptly described his putative birthplace, has a turbulent history and a strong identity. This large island has always been prosperous: in medieval times through the export of **mastic resin** – a trade controlled by Genoese overlords between 1346 and 1566 – and later by the Ottomans, who dubbed the place Sakız Adası ("Resin Island"). Since union with Greece in 1912, several shipping dynasties have emerged here, continuing to generate wealth, and someone in almost every family still spends time in the merchant navy.

Unfortunately, the island has suffered more than its share of **catastrophes** since the 1800s. The Ottomans perpetrated their most infamous, if not their worst, anti-revolutionary atrocity here in March 1822, massacring thirty thousand Hiots and enslaving or exiling even more. In 1881 much of Híos was destroyed by a violent earthquake, and throughout the 1980s the island's natural beauty was compromised by devastating forest fires, compounding the effect of generations of tree-felling by boat-builders.

Until the late 1980s, the more powerful ship-owning dynasts, local government and the military authorities discouraged **tourism** and even now it is concentrated mostly in the capital or the nearby beach resorts of Karfás and Ayía Ermióni. Despite this, various foreigners have discovered a Híos beyond its rather daunting port capital: fascinating **villages**, important **Byzantine monuments** and a respectable, if remote, complement of **beaches**. English is widely spoken courtesy of numerous returned Greek-Americans and Greek-Canadians.

ARRIVAL AND DEPARTURE

HÍOS

6

By plane The airport is 3km south of Híos Town harbour. Frequencies given below for the following destinations are for June–Oct.

Destinations Athens (4–5 daily; 45–50min); Iráklio (Heraklion), Crete (2 weekly; 2hr 30min–3hr 5min); Lésvos (2 weekly; 30min); Límnos (2 weekly; 1hr 40min); Rhodes

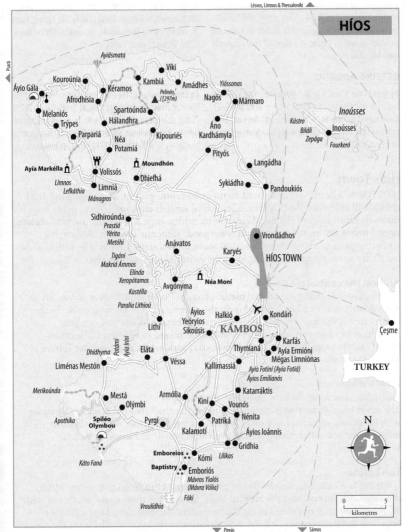

6

DAY-TRIPS FROM HÍOS

The most popular seasonal **boat excursions** from the main port of Híos Town are to the nearby satellite island of Inoússes (see p.385) and to the Turkish coast. Trips to **Inoússes** usually depart on Sunday at 9am, returning by 5pm at a cost of €20. The longer excursions to Turkey leave daily at 8am for the port of **Çeşme**, where an optional bus transfer takes you to the city of Izmir, returning by 7pm. The cost is €25, plus €15 for Izmir; Kanaris Tours at Leofóros Egéou 12 (☎ 22710 42490, ⓦ kanaristours.gr) sell tickets for both.

(2 weekly; 1hr–1hr 45min); Sámos (1 weekly; 35min); Thessaloníki (4 weekly; 1hr).

By ferry Híos is the only stop on the daily superfast service between Pireás and Lésvos and is also on the much slower northern mainland to Sámos/Ikaría route, while smaller boats connect it with the satellite islands of Psará and Inoússes, as well as Çeşme in Turkey. All boats currently leave from Híos Town.

Destinations Áyios Kírykos, Ikaría (1 weekly; 5hr); Çeşme (1–2 daily; 30–45min); Inoússes (1–2 daily; 30min); Karlóvassi, Sámos (1 weekly; 4hr); Kavála (2 weekly; 16hr); Lésvos (1–2 daily; 2hr 30min–3hr); Límnos (2–3 weekly; 8hr 15min–12hr 30min); Pireás (1 daily; 6hr 30min); Psará (6 weekly; 3hr); Thessaloníki (1 weekly; 19hr 45min); Vathý, Sámos (1 weekly; 4hr).

GETTING AROUND

By bus While services to the major destinations in the south run quite frequently (Mon–Sat 3–5 daily, Sun 1–2), those bound for the north are much less frequent (1–4 daily) and the northwest is especially poorly served, with no schedules on Sun.

By car or scooter Of the many rental agencies around the island, the best are Vassilakis/Reliable Rent a Car (☎ 22710 29300, ⓦ rentacar-chios.com), with branches at Evyenías Handhrí 3 in Híos Town, Karfás and Mégas Limniónas; for a scooter try NK in Karfás (☎ 22710 31461, ⓦ kovas.gr).

Híos Town

HÍOS TOWN, a brash, concrete-laced commercial centre with little predating the 1881 quake, will come as a shock after modest island capitals elsewhere. Yet in many ways it's the most satisfactory of the east Aegean ports, with a large and fascinating **marketplace**, several **museums**, an **old quarter** and some good, authentic **tavernas**. Although a sprawling place of about thirty thousand souls, most things of interest lie within a few hundred metres of the water, fringed by the coast road, Leofóros Egéou.

Around the central platía

The town's small triangular central **platía**, officially Plastíra but known universally as **Vounakíou**, lies only a block inland from the seafront, up by the main dock. To the south extends the marvellously lively tradesmen's **bazaar**, where you can find everything from parrots to cast-iron woodstoves. Inland to the west is the urban sprawl's single lung, the attractively lush central **park**, whose most notable feature is an Ottoman fountain.

Byzantine Museum

Kanári 12, Platía Vounakíou • Tues–Sun 8.30am–3pm • €2 • ☎ 22710 26866

The refurbished **Byzantine Museum**, occupying the renovated old **Mecidiye Mosque** with its leaning minaret, has a small but interesting collection, with sections on religious and secular architecture, some splendid murals and icons, as well as various ceramics.

The kástro

Until the 1881 earthquake, the Byzantine-Genoese **kástro** stood completely intact; thereafter developers razed the seaward walls, filled in the moat to the south and sold off the real estate thus created along the waterfront. Nevertheless, large sections of imposing ramparts remain and the most dramatic entry to the citadel is via the

Porta Maggiora behind the town hall. Much of the interior is inhabited and the most rewarding sight is the newly restored Turkish hammam (Tues–Sun 9am–3pm; free) in the far northeast corner.

Maritime Museum

Stefánou Tsoúri 20 • Mon–Sat 10am–2pm • Free • ☎ 22710 44139, ⓦ chiosnauticalmuseum.gr

The **Maritime Museum** consists principally of model ships and nautical oil paintings, all rather overshadowed by the mansion containing them. In the foyer are enshrined the knife and glass-globe grenade of Admiral Kanaris, who partly avenged the 1822 massacre by ramming and sinking the Ottoman fleet's flagship, thus dispatching Admiral Kara Ali, architect of the atrocities.

Argenti Folklore Museum

Koraï 2 • Mon–Thurs 7.30am–2pm, Fri 7.30am–2pm & 5–8pm, Sat 9am–2pm • €2 • ☎ 22710 44246, ⓦ koraeslibrary.gr

The central **Argenti Folklore Museum**, on the top floor of the Koraïs Library, features ponderous genealogical portraits of the endowing family, an adjoining wing of costumes and rural impedimenta, plus multiple replicas of Delacroix's *Massacre at Hios*, a painting which did much to arouse sympathy for the cause of Greek independence.

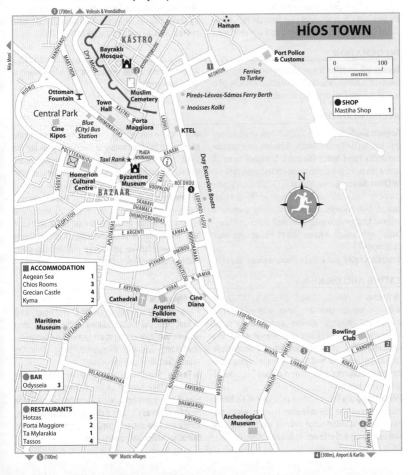

6

Archeological Museum

Mihálon 10 · Tues–Sun 8.30am–4pm · €2 · ☎ 22710 44239

The **Archeological Museum** has a wide-ranging, well-lit collection from Neolithic to Roman times. Highlights include limestone column bases from the Apollo temple at Faná in the shape of lions' claws; numerous statuettes and reliefs of Cybele (an Asiatic goddess especially honoured here); Archaic faience miniatures from Emborió in the shape of a cat, a hawk and a flautist; a terracotta dwarf riding a boar; and figurines (some with articulated limbs) of *hierodouloi* or sacred prostitutes, presumably from an Aphrodite shrine. Most famous is an inscribed edict of Alexander the Great from 322 BC, setting out relations between himself and the Hiots.

ARRIVAL AND GETTING AROUND   HÍOS TOWN

By air The poky airport lies 3km south of the capital at Kondári, a €5 taxi-ride away; otherwise any blue urban bus on the Híos Town–Karfás route should pass the stop opposite the airport.

By ferry Ferry agents cluster along the north end of waterfront Egéou and its continuation Neoríon.

By bus Blue city buses radiate out from the terminal on the north side of Híos Town's central park and serve some nearby beaches, principally Vrondhádhos and Karfás, but also as far as Ayía Ermióni. For anywhere further afield, long-distance KTEL buses leave from just behind the passenger waiting room on seafront Egéou.

By car or motorbike Parking in town is possible only on the southern fringes and in the moat west of the kástro.

By taxi For shorter distances around the capital, the main taxi rank is on the central platía (☎ 22710 41111).

INFORMATION

Tourist information The town's tourist office at Kanári 18 (Mon–Fri 7.30am–3pm; ☎ 22710 44389, ⓦ chioscity.gr) is one of the most efficient and friendliest in the Aegean.

A good general online resource for the whole island is ⓦ chiosonline.gr.

ACCOMMODATION

Aegean Sea Neoríon 33 ☎ 22710 81104, ⓦ aegeansea hotel.gr. Not the prettiest location but ultra-convenient for awkwardly timed ferries. The smart, functional rooms all have a private PC and there's an on-site restaurant. **€50**

★Chios Rooms Egéou 110 ☎ 22710 20198, ⓦ chios rooms.gr. Don and Dina's lovingly restored tile- or wood-floored, high-ceilinged rooms are relatively quiet for a seafront location. Some en suite; best is the penthouse "suite" with private terrace. Shared kitchen and book exchange. **€25**

Grecian Castle Bélla Vísta shore avenue ☎ 22710

44740, ⓦ greciancastle.gr. Converted factory towards the airport with lovely grounds and a sea-view pool, but smallish main-wing rooms, despite their marble floors, wood ceilings and bug screens, are inferior to the rear "villa" suites. Breakfast included. **€110**

★Kyma Evyenías Handhrí ☎ 22710 44500, ⊜ kyma @chi.forthnet.gr. Rooms of varying sizes in a Neoclassical mansion, with huge terraces on the sea-facing side; most have new handmade wood-and-leather furniture. Owner Theo's knowledgeable service really makes the place. Lavish breakfast included. **€65**

EATING AND DRINKING

★Hotzas Yeoryíou Kondhýli 3 ☎ 22710 42787. Oldest and most popular taverna in town, with an old-style interior and delightful summer garden. Menu varies seasonally, but expect a mix of vegetarian dishes and *lahanodolmádhes*, sausages, baby fish and *mydhopílafo* (rice and mussels), all well under €10 and accompanied by excellent barrelled wine. Mon–Sat 7pm–late; closed late May to late June.

Porta Maggiore Platía Kástrou ☎ 22710 44542. Worth visiting as much for the atmospheric setting within the kástro as the standard range of Greek and Italian dishes that cost mainly €10 or under. Daily noon–1am.

Ta Mylarakia Tambákika district ☎ 22710 40412. A large seafood selection at mostly €10–15, every kind of Hiot ouzo and limited seating at the island's most romantic waterside setting at the four restored windmills. Reservations advisable in summer. Daily: April–Oct 11am–2am; Nov–May 8pm–1am.

★Tassos Stávrou Livanoú 8, Bélla Vísta district ☎ 22710 27542. Good place for creative salads, delicious bean dishes, *dolmádhes*, snails, a strong line in seafood and meat for as low as €5.50, as well as decent barrelled wine. There's sea-view summer garden seating and a heated gazebo for winter. Daily noon–1am.

NIGHTLIFE AND ENTERTAINMENT

Some 1400 local university students help keep things lively, especially along the waterfront between the two "kinks" in Egéou. Shooting **pool** is big here; many bars have several tables.

Bowling Club Leofóros Egéou 120 ☎ 22710 28517. This popular bar has a multitude of pool tables and seven bowling alleys as well. Daily 10am–late.

Cine Kipos Corner of central park. Film fans are well served by Cine Kipos, with quality/art-house first-run screenings. Late June to early Sept.

Homerion Cultural Centre Iroón Polytekhníou 5 ☎ 22710 44391, ⊛ homerion.gr. This large events hall on

the south side of the park hosts changing exhibitions, and big-name acts, including some foreign ones, often come here after Athens concerts. Hours vary.

★**Odysseia** Leofóros Egéou 102 ☎ 22710 20585. Modern, tastefully decorated bar with good live music most nights. It also does tasty mezédhes and the full range of Hiot ouzo and beer from the local brewery. Daily 10am–late.

SHOPPING

Mastiha Shop Egéou 36 ☎ 22710 81600, ⊛ mastiha shop.com. Home base of a chain with nine branches in Greece plus others in New York, Paris and even Jeddah.

Sells all things mastic from chewing gum to shower gel. Daily: July–Sept 8.30am–midnight; Oct–June 8.30am–10pm.

Around Híos Town

North of Híos Town, **VRONDÁDHOS** is an elongated coastal suburb that's a favourite residence of the many local seafarers. Homer is alleged to have lived and taught here, and in terraced parkland just above the little fishing port and pebble beach you can visit his purported lectern, more likely an ancient altar of Cybele.

The locals swim at the tiny pebble coves near here or from the grubby town beach in Bélla Vísta, but really the closest decent bathing option is at **Karfás**, 7km south beyond the airport. However, as most large Hiot resort hotels are planted here, the 500m-long beach itself, sandy only at the south end, has limited appeal. The nearby inland village of **Thymianá** offers a more authentic atmosphere and better dining options.

Some 2km further along the coast from Karfás, **Ayía Ermióni** is a fishing anchorage, adjoining the next proper beach at **Mégas Limniónas**, a few hundred metres further on, smaller than Karfás but more scenic, with low cliffs as a backdrop. Some 4km further south is the turning for **Ayía Fotiní**, also known as Ayía Fotiá, a 600m pebble **beach** with exceptionally clean water. Cars are excluded from the shore area and the pedestrian esplanade is lined with various rooms and tavernas. Five kilometres further south, back via the main road, the small fishing village of **Katarráktis** is a pleasant spot where locals in the know go to eat.

ACCOMMODATION   AROUND HÍOS TOWN

Apartments Iro On seafront beside the access road, Ayía Fotiní ☎ 22710 30226, ✉ hroapartaments@gmail.com. Large self-catering studios, with sea views from the balconies, all nicely furnished. Dedicated parking. April–Oct. **€25**

Karatzas Northern end of seafront, Karfás ☎ 22710 31221, ⊛ karatzaschios.com. Typically compact but decent-value rooms above a large courtyard taverna, which offers pricey fish but much more reasonable meat dishes for €7–8. April–Oct. **€45**

Mavrokordatiko 1.5km south of the airport ☎ 22710 32900, ⊛ mavrokordatiko.com. With enormous wood-panelled rooms and spacious communal areas, including a fine café-restaurant, this renovated mansion oozes atmosphere. Breakfast included. **€65**

Sun Rooms Studios Off the southern end of Mégas Limniónas ☎ 22710 33351, ⊛ sunrooms.gr. Neat modern block with clean, compact rooms and artistic touches provided by the friendly owner herself. April–Oct. **€30**

EATING

Ankyra Central Mégas Limniónas beach ☎ 22710 32178. All-round reliable *psarotaverna*, serving fish of all categories from €35/kilo and an accompanying range of meat, veg and salads, as well as a fine ouzo selection.

May–Oct daily 11am–midnight.

Asterias Above the harbour, Katarráktis ☎ 22710 61428. Spacious taverna that offers a wide menu of starters, plus grills, the cheaper fish and pizza for €7–10.

April–Oct daily 11am–1am.

Iy Apolafsi Above the harbour, Ayía Ermióni ☎ 22710 31359. The huge terrace perched on a bluff makes a fine location for fresh fish from €40/kilo and cheaper meat and veg options. April–Oct daily 11am–1am.

Psarokokkalo On seafront beside the access road, Ayía Fotiní ☎ 22710 51596. Easily the best taverna in the resort, providing tasty mezédhes, *souvláki*, pizza, fish and other seafood delights, mostly under €10. Easter–Oct daily 8.30am–late.

The mastihohoriá

Besides olive groves, southern Híos' gently rolling countryside is home to the **mastic bush**, and the twenty or so **mastihohoriá**, or **mastic villages** (see box below). Since the decline of the mastic trade, the *mastihohoriá* live mainly off their tangerines, apricots and olives, though the villages, the only settlements on Híos spared by the Ottomans in 1822, retain their architectural uniqueness; they were designed by the Genoese but have a distinctly Middle Eastern feel. The basic plan involves a rectangular warren of tall houses, with the outer row doubling as perimeter fortification, and breached by a limited number of gateways. More recent additions, whether in traditional architectural style or not, straggle outside the original defences. Of the surviving villages, three stand out: **Pyrgí**, **Olýmbi** and **Mestá**.

Pyrgí

PYRGÍ, 25km south of Híos Town, is the most colourful of the *mastihohoriá*, its houses elaborately embossed with *xystá*, patterns cut into whitewash to reveal a layer of black volcanic sand underneath; in autumn, strings of sun-drying tomatoes add a further splash of colour. On the northeast corner of the central square the twelfth-century Byzantine church of **Áyii Apóstoli** (erratic hours), embellished with much later frescoes, is tucked under an arcade.

Olýmbi and around

OLÝMBI, 7km west of Pyrgí along the same bus route, is one of the less-visited mastic villages but not devoid of interest. The characteristic **tower-keep**, which at Pyrgí stands half-inhabited away from the modernized main square, here looms bang in the middle of the platía.

The Spiléo Olýmbou cave

6km southwest of Olýmbi • Tues–Sun: June–Aug 10am–8pm; Sept 11am–6pm • Admission every 30min; guided tours last 20–25min • €5

From Olýmbi, a paved road leads to the well-signed cave of **Spiléo Olýmbou**, near the hamlet of Sykiá. For years it was just a hole in the ground where villagers disposed of

---

MASTIC MASTICATION

The **mastic bush** (*Pistacia lentisca*) is found across much of Aegean Greece, but only in southern Híos – pruned to an umbrella shape to facilitate harvesting – does it produce **aromatic resin** of any quality or quantity, scraped from incisions made on the trunk during summer. For centuries it was used as a base for paints, cosmetics and the chewable jelly beans that became an addictive staple in Ottoman harems. Indeed, the interruption of the flow of mastic from Híos to Istanbul by the revolt of spring 1822 was a main cause of the brutal Ottoman reaction. The wealth engendered by the **mastic trade** supported twenty *mastihohoriá* (mastic villages) from the time the Genoese set up a monopoly in the substance during the fourteenth century, but the demise of imperial Turkey and the development of petroleum-based products knocked the bottom out of the mastic market.

Now it's just a curiosity, to be chewed – try the sweetened Elma-brand gum – or drunk as *mastíha* liqueur. It has had medicinal applications since ancient times; contemporary advocates claim that mastic boosts the immune system and thins the blood. High-end cosmetics, toothpaste and mouthwash are now sold at the Mastiha Shop in Híos Town (see p.379).

dead animals, but since 1985 it has been regularly explored by speleologists. The cavern, with a constant temperature of 18°C, evolved in two phases between 150 million and 50 million years ago, and has a maximum depth of 57m (though tours only visit the top 30m). Its formations, with fanciful names like Chinese Forest, Medusa and Organ Pipes, are among the most beautiful in the Mediterranean.

Mestá

Sombre, monochrome **MESTÁ**, 4km west of Olýmbi, is considered the finest of the mastic villages; despite having more snack-bars and trinket shops than strictly necessary, it remains just the right side of twee. From its main square, dominated by the **church of the Taxiárhis** with its two icons of the Archangel – one dressed in Byzantine robes, the other in Genoese armour – a maze of dim lanes with anti-seismic tunnels leads off in all directions. Most streets end in blind alleys, except those leading to the six portals; the northeast one still has its original iron gate.

<table>
<tr><td>**ACCOMMODATION AND EATING**</td><td style="text-align:right">**THE MASTIHOHORIÁ**</td></tr>
</table>

Tourist facilities are relatively sparse in the mastic villages. Apart from the establishments listed below, you will find a smattering of cafés, the odd tiny taverna and some signs for private rooms, usually available on spec.

Chrysanthi Apartments Olýmbi ☎ 22710 76196, ⓦ chrysanthi.gr. Three units suitable for two to five people near the central platía – nicely furnished with smart kitchens – retaining many original features such as stone alcoves. €55
★**Medieval Castle Suites** Mestá ☎ 22710 76345, ⓦ mcsuites.gr. Superbly refurbished medieval mansion on a lane just off the main square, with much of the original stone exterior, yet lavishly furnished and equipped with

all modern facilities inside. Special online deals available. Easter–Oct. €75
★**Mesaionas (Kyra Dhespina)** Mestá ☎ 22710 76050. Excellent home-cooked dishes, such as stewed octopus, *moussaká* and various veg in sauces for well under €10 each, served on the square. The welcoming owner can put you in touch with places offering rooms. Daily 11am–midnight.

The mastic coast

The most popular **beaches** at the southern end of Híos are in the vicinity of **Emboriós**, tucked in the southeast corner. Over on the southwest coast, the closest good, protected beach to Mestá lies 4.7km southwest at **Apothíka**. Others, east of ugly but functional **Liménas Mestón** port, include **Dhídhyma**, 4km away, a double cove guarded by an islet; **Potámi**, with a namesake stream feeding it; and less scenic **Ayía Iríni**, 8km distant, with a reliably open taverna.

Emboriós and around

EMBORIÓS, an almost landlocked harbour, is 6km southeast of Pyrgí. Ancient **Emboreios**, on the hill to the northeast, has been rehabilitated as an "archeological park" (Tues–Sun 8am–3pm; free). Down in modern Emboriós a cruciform early Christian **baptistry** is signposted in a field just inland; it's protected by a later, round structure, which remains locked, but everything's visible through the grating.

For **swimming**, follow the road a short way south from Emboriós to an oversubscribed car park and the beach of **Mávros Yialós**, better known as Mávra Vólia, then continue by flagstoned walkway over the headland to more dramatic **Fóki**. Twice as long and backed by impressive cliffs, this pebble strip of purple-grey volcanic stones is part nudist. If you want sand and more amenities go to **Kómi**, 3km northeast of Emboriós, which is the main (albeit low-key) resort for the area. A further 2km east of Kómi, **Lílikas** beach is even quieter and more picturesque.

<table>
<tr><td>**ACCOMMODATION AND EATING**</td><td style="text-align:right">**THE MASTIC COAST**</td></tr>
</table>

Emporios Bay 50m back from harbour, Emboriós ☎ 22710 71228. This smart modern hotel is a decent bet, with

its rooms and larger apartments painted in vibrant colours and nicely furnished. Breakfast included. April–Oct. €40

6

Nostalgia Western end of Kómi beach ☎ 22710 70070. Good all-round taverna behind the northern end of the beach, specializing in grilled fish and meat for under €10 but also offering a line in veg dishes and some decent barrelled wine. April to mid-Oct daily noon–2am.

★ **Notos** Western end of Lílikas beach ☎ 22710 71542. This popular place combines a courtyard ouzerí, which serves lots of mezédhes around €5 and main dishes such as pork in cream sauce for €10, with a laidback beach bar on the lower level. Mid-May to Oct 10am–late.

Porto Emborios Emboriós ☎ 22710 71306. The best of the four tavernas clustered around the harbour offers good seafood at fair prices, a range of salads and dips, plus home-made desserts. March–Oct daily 10am–1am.

Central Híos

The inland portion of Híos extending west and southwest from Híos Town matches the south in terms of interesting **monuments**, and good roads make touring under your own steam an easy matter. The flat **Kámbos** leads to more mountainous terrain to the west and north.

The Kámbos

The **Kámbos**, a vast fertile plain carpeted with citrus groves, extends southwest from Híos Town almost as far as the village of Halkió. The district was originally settled by the Genoese during the fourteenth century, and remained a preserve of the local aristocracy until 1822. Exploring by two-wheeler may be less frustrating than going by car, since the web of narrow, poorly marked lanes sandwiched between high walls guarantees disorientation and frequent backtracking. Behind the walls you catch fleeting glimpses of ornate old mansions built from locally quarried sandstone, whose courtyards are paved in pebbles or alternating light and dark tiles.

Néa Moní

15km west of Híos Town • Daily: summer 7am–8pm; winter 8.30am–3pm • ☎ 22710 79391, ⓦ neamoni.gr

Almost exactly in the middle of the island, the monastery of **Néa Moní** was founded by the Byzantine emperor Constantine Monomahos IX ("The Dueller") in 1042 on the spot where a wonder-working **icon** had been discovered. It ranks among the most important monuments on any of the Greek islands; the mosaics, together with those of Dhafní and Ósios Loukás on the mainland, are the finest surviving art of their era in Greece, and the setting – high in partly forested mountains – is equally memorable. Once a powerful community of six hundred monks, Néa Moní was pillaged in 1822 and most of its residents, including 3500 civilians sheltering here, were put to the sword. The 1881 tremor caused comprehensive damage, wrecking many of its outbuildings, while exactly a century later a forest fire threatened to engulf the place until the resident icon was paraded along the perimeter wall, miraculously repelling the flames.

The chapel and museum

Museum: Tues–Sun 8am–1pm • €2

Just inside the **main gate** stands a **chapel/ossuary** containing some of the bones of the 1822 victims; axe-clefts in children's skulls attest to the savagery of the attackers. The restored *katholikón* has a cupola resting on an octagonal drum, a design seen elsewhere only in Cyprus; the famous **mosaics** within have now been restored to their former glory. The narthex contains portrayals of various local saints sandwiched between *Christ Washing the Disciples' Feet* and the *Betrayal*, in which Judas's kiss has unfortunately been obliterated, but Peter is clearly visible lopping off the ear of the high priest's servant. The **museum**, located in the group of buildings behind the chapel, contains an interesting display of ecclesiastical paraphernalia and garments.

Avgónyma

Some 5km west of Néa Moní sits **AVGÓNYMA**, a cluster of dwellings on a knoll over-looking the coast; the name means "Clutch of Eggs", an apt description when viewed from the ridge above. Since the 1980s, the place has been restored as a summer haven by descendants of the original villagers, though the permanent population is fewer than ten.

ACCOMMODATION AND EATING

★ **Arhondiko Perleas** 3km southwest of the airport, Kámbos ☎ 22710 32217, ⊛ perleas.gr. Set in a huge organic citrus ranch, this extremely classy converted mansion boasts dark wood interiors and original artwork, as well as lavish furnishings. Gourmet breakfast included. **€100**

0 Pyrgos Central square, Avgónyma ☎ 22710 42175, ⊛ chiospyrgosrooms.gr. In an attractive arcaded mansion

on the main square, with ample courtyard seating, this taverna run by Greek-Americans offers both oven-cooked dishes and grills for €10 or less. There are some simple but adequate rooms too. Daily roughly 11am–midnight. **€40**

Spitakia Avgónyma ☎ 22710 20513, ⊛ spitakia.gr. A cluster of small stone cottages sleeping up to five people, plus some rooms, all lovingly restored and tastefully decorated, with good heating for the winter months. **€50**

The west coast

The central section of the island's **west coast** offers a couple of picturesque villages and some not too crowded beaches, given that they are so easily accessible from Híos Town by way of Avgónyma, from where the main road descends 6km to the sea in well-graded loops.

Tigáni and Makriá Ámmos

On the northern stretch of the central west coast, bypass Elínda, alluring from afar but rocky and often murky up close, in favour of the more secluded coves to either side of Metóhi – best of these are **Tigáni** and **Makriá Ámmos**, the latter nudist.

Lithí and Paralía Lithioú

Friendly **LITHÍ** village perches on a forested ledge overlooking the sea towards the southern end of the central west coast. You can eat here but most visitors head 2km downhill to **Paralía Lithioú**, a popular weekend target of Hiot townies thanks to its large but hard-packed, windswept beach.

Véssa

Some 5km south of Lithí, valley-bottom **VÉSSA** is an unsung gem: more open and less casbah-like than Mestá or Pyrgí, but still homogeneous, its tawny buildings are arrayed in a vast grid punctuated by numerous belfries and arcaded passages.

ACCOMMODATION AND EATING

Almyriki Apartments Paralía Lithioú ☎ 22710 73124, ⊛ almiriki.gr. Smart new complex behind the middle of the beach, with well-appointed rooms sporting modern furniture, LCD TVs and fridges. Chic café-bar on site too. April–Oct. **€85**

To Akroyiali Paralía Lithioú ☎ 22710 73286. The best of the handful of tavernas here, behind the beach's north end, providing fresh fish, a variety of seafood, simple grilled meat for €6–8 and some tasty mezédhes. May–Sept daily 11am–1am.

Northern Híos

Northern Híos never really recovered from the 1822 massacre, and between Pityós and Volissós the forest's recovery from 1980s **fires** has been partly reversed by a bad 2007 blaze. Most villages usually lie deserted, with about a third of the former population living in Híos Town, returning occasionally for major festivals or to tend smallholdings; others, based in Athens or North America, visit their ancestral homes for just a few midsummer weeks.

Langádha and around

Some 16km north of Híos Town, **LANGÁDHA** is probably the first point on the eastern coast road you'd be tempted to stop, though there is no proper beach nearby. Set at the

6

mouth of a deep valley, this attractive little harbour settlement looks across its bay to a pine grove, and beyond to Turkey.

Just beyond Langádha a side road leads 5km up and inland to **Pityós**, an oasis in a mountain pass presided over by a small, round castle; continuing 4km further brings you to a junction that allows quick access to the west of the island.

Mármaro and around

Káto Kardhámyla, 37km out of Híos Town, is the island's second town. Better known as **MÁRMARO**, it's positioned at the edge of a fertile plain rimmed by mountains, which comes as welcome relief from the craggy coastline. However, there is little to attract casual visitors other than some Neoclassical architecture; the mercilessly exposed port is strictly businesslike and offers only a limited range of tourist facilities and a mediocre beach. Swimming is much more enjoyable at the pebble bay of **Nagós**, 5km west, or at **Yióssonas**, a much longer and rockier beach, 1km further on.

Volissós and around

VOLISSÓS, 42km from Híos Town, was once the market town for a dozen remote hill villages beyond. The buildings around the main square are mostly modern but a host of old stone houses still curl appealingly beneath a crumbling hilltop Byzantine-Genoese **fort**. These upper quarters, known as **Pýrgos**, are in the grip of a restoration mania, mostly in good taste, with ruins changing hands for stratospheric prices and usually being turned into quality accommodation.

Beaches around Volissós

LIMNIÁ (or Limiá), the port of Volissós, lies 2km south of town, bracketed by the local beaches. A 1.5km drive or walk southeast over the headland brings you to **Mánagros**, a seemingly endless sand-and-pebble beach. More intimate, sandy **Lefkáthia** lies just a ten-minute stroll along the cement drive over the headland north of the harbour.

Límnos, the next protected cove 400m east of Lefkáthia, can also be accessed by a direct road from Volissós. **Ayía Markélla**, 5km further northwest of Límnos, has another long beach, fronting the eponymous, barracks-like pilgrimage **monastery** of Híos' patron saint (festival on July 22).

Monastery of Moundhón

Just outside Dhiefhá village, 2km north of the main Hios Town–Volissós road • For access, seek out the warden, Yiorgos Fokas, in Dhiefhá (☎ 22740 22011)

The engagingly set sixteenth-century **monastery of Moundhón** was second in rank to Néa Moní before its partial destruction in 1822. Best of the naive interior frescoes of the (locked) church is one depicting the *Ouranódhromos Klímax* ("Stairway to Heaven", not to be confused with Led Zeppelin's): a trial-by-ascent, in which ungodly priests are beset by demons hurling them into the mouth of a great serpent symbolizing the Devil, while the righteous clergy are assisted upwards by angels.

ACCOMMODATION AND EATING   **NORTHERN HÍOS**

LANGÁDHA AND AROUND

★**Makellos** Pityós ☎ 22720 23364. Renowned all over the island for its splendid home-style lamb and beef dishes, as well as the likes of rabbit and free-range rooster, all €10 and under. Great barrelled wine too. May–Sept daily noon–1am; Oct–April most weekends same hours.

T'Ayeri On the harbour, Langádha ☎ 22710 74813. The cheapest and most traditional taverna here, serving a combination of small fish and excellent *mayireftá* for €7–8,

as well as very palatable barrelled wine. April–Oct daily noon–2am; Nov–March Fri–Sun same hours.

MÁRMARO AND AROUND

Hotel Kardamyla Central Mármaro ☎ 22720 23353. Co-managed with Híos Town's *Hotel Kyma*, this friendly central hotel offers spacious, fan-equipped rooms and a few suites, all pleasantly furnished and some with sea views. The restaurant is good too. Breakfast included. June–Sept. €75

Thalasses Northern seafront, Mármaro ☎ 22720 23888. Slightly upmarket but still good value, this *psarotavérna* specializes in fresh fish and seafood, with delights such as crab and octopus salads for around €6–7. Daily noon–2am.

VOLISSÓS AND AROUND

Aigiali Beach end of the access road, Límnos ☎ 22740 21856, ⓦ aigiali.gr. Attractive, comfortably furnished apartments with well-equipped kitchens and sea-view balconies in a sturdy modern stone building. The café does great sweets too. May–Sept. **€40**

★ **Fabrika** Just behind main square, Volissós ☎ 22740 22045. This converted factory, which also has six pleasant rooms, does superb *kondosoúvli* and *kokorétsi* for around €8, as well as a range of daily-changing oven-baked dishes. Seating in the attractive interior or leafy courtyard. Daily noon–2am. **€35**

Limnos Near access road, Límnos ☎ 22740 22122. Good all-round beachside taverna that dishes up fish grills and specials like *kókoras krasáto* for €7, as well as delicious *mezédhes* and highly drinkable wine. May to mid-Oct daily 10am–midnight.

★ **Moneos A & B/Theias** Pýrgos district, Volissós ☎ 22740 21421, ⓦ volissostravel.gr. Five apartments in two skilfully converted stone houses – all have terraces, fully equipped kitchens and features such as tree trunks upholding sleeping lofts, reflecting proprietress Stella's background as a sculptor. **€50**

Mavro Provato Main square, Volissós ☎ 22740 22116. Delightful café, which does quality coffees, juices and cocktails, as well as good salads, risotto and a few items like burgers for €7.80. Daily 8am–midnight.

Ta Petrina Pýrgos district, Volissós ☎ 22740 21228, ⓦ tapetrina.gr. Half a dozen unique properties, expertly renovated by the British co-owners. They vary in size and character from a tiny stone house to a converted church. **€75**

Inoússes

INOÚSSES, the closer and more easily accessible of Hios' two satellite islands, has a permanent population of about three hundred, less than half its 1930s figure. For generations this islet, first settled around 1750 by Hiot shepherds, provided Greece with many of its wealthiest **shipping families**: various members of the Livanos, Lemos and Pateras clans were born here.

Inoússes town

Two church-tipped, privately owned islets guard the unusually well-protected harbour of **INOÚSSES TOWN**, which is surprisingly large, draped over hillsides enclosing a ravine. Its illustrious maritime connections help explain the presence of large villas and visiting summer gin-palaces in an otherwise sleepy Greek backwater. Near the quay, the island's only specific sight, the impressive **Marine Museum** (daily 8am–2pm; €1.50; ☎ 22710 55182), also has a nautical theme and was endowed by various shipping magnates. At the west end of the quay, the bigwigs have also funded a nautical academy, which trains future members of the merchant navy.

Around the island

The southern slope of this tranquil island is surprisingly green and well tended; there are no springs, so water comes from a mix of fresh and brackish wells, as well as a reservoir. The sea is extremely clean and calm on the sheltered southerly shore; among its beaches, choose from **Zepága**, **Biláli** or **Kástro**, respectively five, twenty and thirty minutes' walk west of the port. More secluded **Fourkeró** (or Farkeró) lies 25 minutes east.

ARRIVAL AND DEPARTURE   INOÚSSES

By ferry Inoússes can be reached from Híos Town either on a day-trip (see box, p.376) or on the daily ferry (1hr), which departs from Híos in the afternoon and returns in the morning (reduced service in winter).

ACCOMMODATION AND EATING

Naftikos Omilos Near the jetty ☎ 22710 55596. This yachtie hangout provides a steady stream of coffee and snacks during the day before morphing into a fairly lively bar by night, as the music volume ramps up. May–Sept daily 9am–2am.

Oinousses Studios Above the harbour ☎ 22710 55255, ✉ oinoussesstudios@gmail.com. Smart modern apartments with fully equipped kitchens and large balconies facing the sea. May–Sept. €35

Pateronisso Beside the jetty ☎ 22710 55311. The best of the small bunch of tavernas dotted on or around the seafront.

All the usual fish, meat and salad staples are available at mostly under €10. June–Sept daily 8am–midnight.

Thalassoporos On the town's main easterly lane ☎ 22710 55475. This modest establishment is the island's only bona fide hotel, with small and basic but very clean rooms, mostly affording sea views. May–Sept. €45

Psará

Remote **Psará** lies a good 20km west of the northwest tip of Híos and is too far from it to be visited on a day-trip. The birthplace of revolutionary war hero Admiral Konstandinos Kanaris, the island devoted its merchant fleets – the third largest in 1820s Greece – to the cause of independence, and paid dearly for it. Vexed beyond endurance, the Turks landed overwhelming forces in 1824 to stamp out this nest of resistance. Perhaps three thousand of the thirty thousand inhabitants escaped in small boats to be rescued by a French fleet, but the majority retreated to a hilltop powder magazine, blowing it and themselves up rather than surrender. Today, it's a sad, bleak place fully living up to its name ("the mottled things" in ancient Greek), never really having recovered from the holocaust. The official population now barely exceeds four hundred, and, despite some revitalization since the 1980s, it has never seen a tourist boom.

The harbour

Since few buildings in the east-facing harbour community predate the twentieth century, a strange hotchpotch of ecclesiastical and secular architecture greets you on disembarking. There's a distinctly southern feel, more like the Dodecanese or the Cyclades, and some peculiar churches, no two alike in style.

Around the island

Psará's **beaches** are decent, improving the further northeast you walk from the port. You quickly pass **Káto Yialós**, **Katsoúni** and **Lazarétto** with its off-putting power station, before reaching **Lákka** ("narrow ravine"), fifteen minutes along, apparently named after its grooved rock formations. **Límnos**, 25 minutes from the port along the coastal path, is big and attractive, but there's no reliable taverna here, or indeed at any of the beaches.

The only other thing to do on Psará is to follow the paved road north across the island to **Kímisis (Assumption) monastery**. Uninhabited since the 1970s, it comes to life only in early August, when its revered icon is carried in ceremonial procession to town and back on the eve of August 5.

ARRIVAL AND DEPARTURE   PSARÁ

By ferry Psará has decent ferry links with Híos Town (6 weekly; 3hr); frequencies drop drastically off season.

ACCOMMODATION

Kato Gialos Apartments Behind Káto Yialós beach ☎ 22740 61178. A mixture of spotless rooms and larger apartments with kitchen facilities, all with sea views and only a minute from the water. June–Sept. €50

Psara Studios At the back of the harbour village ☎ 22740 61180. The rooms here are large and furnished well enough, and have functional kitchenettes, plus there's a pleasant garden fringed with palms. May–Sept. €45

EATING

Iliovasilema Behind Káto Yialós beach ☎ 22740 61121. Sunset is the best time to dine here on seafood delights such as fried *kalamári* or octopus with aubergines

for €10 or less. A friendly welcome is guaranteed. June–Sept daily 11am–midnight.

★**Spitalia** Behind Katsoúnis beach ☎ 22740 61376.

Located in a restored medieval hospital, this great taverna comes up with specialities such as stuffed goat and other home-style dishes for €7–9, plus grills, salads and good wine. May–Sept daily 11am–1am.

Ta Delfinia In the middle of the harbour ☎ 22740 61352. Probably the top place for simply but expertly grilled fish and seafood, such as lobster, *tsipoúra* and *barboúni*. Also does various *pikilíes* from €8. May–Oct daily 7am–1am.

Lésvos

LÉSVOS (Mytilíni), the third-largest Greek island after Crete and Évvia, is the birthplace of the ancient bards Sappho, Aesop, Arion and – more recently – primitive artist Theophilos and Nobel Laureate poet Odysseus Elytis. Despite these **artistic associations**, the island is not at first sight particularly beautiful or interesting: much of the landscape is rocky, volcanic terrain, encompassing vast grain fields, scrubland and saltpans. But there are also oak and pine forests as well as endless olive groves, some more than five centuries old. With its balmy climate and suggestive contours, Lésvos tends to grow on you with prolonged exposure. Lovers of medieval and Ottoman **architecture** certainly won't be disappointed, and castles survive at Mytilíni Town, Mólyvos, Eressós, Sígri and near Ándissa.

Social and political **idiosyncrasies** add to the island's appeal: unsurprisingly, as the country's major producer of ouzo, Lésvos has the highest alcoholism rate in Greece. There is a tendency to **vote communist** (with usually at least one Red MP in office), a legacy of Ottoman-era quasi-feudalism, 1880s conflicts between small and large olive producers and further disruption occasioned by the arrival of many refugees. Breeding livestock, especially horses, remains important, and organic production has been embraced enthusiastically as a way of making Lésvos' agricultural products more competitive.

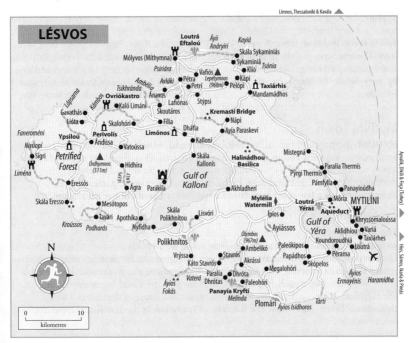

Historically, the olive plantations, ouzo distilleries, animal husbandry and fishing industry supported those who chose not to emigrate, but when these enterprises stalled in the 1980s, **tourism** made appreciable inroads. However, it still accounts for only around ten percent of the local economy: there are few large hotels outside the capital, Skála Kalloní or Mólyvos, and visitor numbers continue to decline, except for a mini-boom in Turkish weekenders.

Brief history

6

In antiquity, Lésvos' importance lay in its artistic and commercial connections rather than in historical events: being on the trade route to Asia Minor, it always attracted merchants and became quite wealthy during **Roman times**. During the late fourteenth century, Lésvos was given as a dowry to a Genoese prince of the Gattilusi clan following his marriage to the sister of one of the last Byzantine emperors – it's from this period that most of its castles remain. The first two centuries of **Ottoman rule** were particularly harsh, with much of the Orthodox population sold into slavery or deported to the imperial capital – replaced by more tractable Muslim colonists, who populated even rural areas – and most physical evidence of the Genoese or Byzantine period demolished. Out in the countryside, Turks and Greeks got along, relatively speaking, right up until 1923; the Ottoman authorities favoured Greek *kahayiádhes* (overseers) to keep the peons in line. However, large numbers of the lower social classes, oppressed by the pashas and their Greek lackeys, fled across to Asia Minor during the nineteenth century, only to return again after the exchange of populations.

ARRIVAL AND GETTING AROUND LÉSVOS

Public **buses** run once or twice daily to most major towns and resorts, but Lesvos' sheer size makes day-trips from the capital impractical. Even with a **car** or **motorbike**, it's better to choose a base and tour locally from there.

By plane There are services (frequencies for June–Oct) to Athens (3–4 daily; 50min–1hr); Híos (2 weekly, 30min); Ikaría (1 weekly; 1hr 50min); Límnos (5 weekly; 40min); Rhodes (2 weekly; 50min–1hr 10min); Sámos (2 weekly; 45min); Thessaloníki (5 weekly; 55min).

By ferry Despite the island's size, all ferries dock in Mytilíni.

Destinations Ayvalık, Turkey (May–Oct daily, winter sporadic; 1hr 20min); Dikili, Turkey (May–Oct daily, winter sporadic; 1hr 30min); Foça, Turkey (May–Oct 4 weekly; 1hr); Híos (1–2 daily; 2–3hr); Ikaría (1 weekly; 7hr 30min); Kavála (2 weekly; 12–13hr); Límnos (2–3 weekly; 6hr 30min–7hr); Pireás (1–2 daily; 8hr 30min–9hr); Sámos (3 weekly; 7hr); Thessaloníki (1 weekly; 14hr 30min–15hr).

Mytilíni Town

MYTILÍNI, the port and capital, sprawls between and around two bays divided by a fortified promontory, and in Greek fashion often doubles as the name of the island. Many visitors are put off by the combination of urban bustle and, in the humbler northern districts, slight seediness. However, several diversions, particularly the marketplace and a few museums within a few minutes' walk of the waterfront, can occupy you for a few hours.

The fortress

Just north of port • Tues–Sun 8.30am–3pm; sometimes later in summer • €2 • ☎ 22510 27970

On the promontory sits the Byzantine-Genoese-Ottoman **fortress**, its mixed pedigree reflected in the Ottoman inscription immediately above the Byzantine double eagle at the southern outer gate. Inside you can make out the variably preserved ruins of the Gattilusi palace, a Turkish *medresse* (Koranic academy), a dervish cell and a Byzantine cistern. Just below the fortress, at **Tsamákia**, is the mediocre, fee-entry town "beach".

The bazaar area

Inland, the town skyline is dominated in turn by the Germanic-Gothic belfry spire of **Áyios Athanásios cathedral** and the mammary dome of **Áyios Therápon**, both expressions of the post-Baroque taste of the nineteenth-century Ottoman Greek bourgeoisie. The interior decor of Áyios Therápon in particular seems more appropriate to an opera house than a church, with gilt aplenty in the vaulting and ornate column capitals. They stand more or less at opposite ends of the **bazaar**, whose main street, Ermoú, links the town centre with the little-used north harbour of **Epáno Skála**.

The old town

Between the bazaar and Epáno Skála, Ermoú passes various expensive antique shops near the roofless, derelict **Yéni Tzamí** at the heart of the old Muslim quarter, just a few steps east of a superb, beautifully restored Turkish **hammam**, which unfortunately – like the mosque – is closed unless a special exhibition is being held. Between Ermoú

6

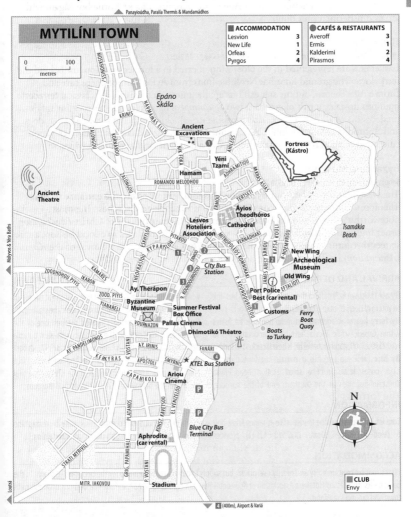

■ ACCOMMODATION	
Lesvion	3
New Life	1
Orfeas	2
Pyrgos	4

● CAFÉS & RESTAURANTS	
Averoff	3
Ermis	1
Kalderimi	2
Pirasmos	4

■ CLUB	
Envy	1

and the castle lies a maze of atmospheric lanes lined with *belle époque* mansions and humbler vernacular dwellings.

Archeological Museum

Mytilíni's excellent **Archeological Museum**, the town's only real must-see, is housed in two separate galleries, a few hundred metres apart. If you only have time to visit one of them, the old wing is more rewarding.

6

The new wing

8-Noemvríou • Tues–Sun 8.30am–3pm • €3 (includes the old wing) • ☎ 22510 40223

The **newer wing** is devoted to finds from wealthy Roman Mytilene, in particular three rooms of well-displayed **mosaics** from second/third-century AD villas. Highlights include a crude but engaging scene of Orpheus charming all manner of beasts and birds, two fishermen surrounded by clearly recognizable (and edible) sea creatures, and the arrival of baby Telephos, son of Auge and Hercules, in a seaborne box, again with amazed fishermen presiding.

The old wing

Eftalióti 7 • Tues–Sun 8.30am–3pm (includes the new wing) • €3 • ☎ 22510 28032

Earlier eras are represented in the **older wing**, located in a former mansion just behind the ferry dock. The ground floor has Neolithic finds from Áyios Vartholoméos cave and Bronze Age Thermí, but the star exhibits are the minutely detailed late Classical **terracotta figurines** upstairs: a pair of acrobats, two *kourotrophoi* figures (goddesses suckling infants, predecessors of all Byzantine *Galaktotrofoússa* icons), children playing with a ball or dogs, and Aphrodite riding a dolphin. A rear annexe contains stone-cut inscriptions of various edicts and treaties, plus a Roman sculpture of a drunken satyr asleep on a wineskin.

Byzantine Museum

Aríonos • Mon–Sat 9am–1pm • €2 • ☎ 22510 28916

The well-lit and well-laid-out **Byzantine Museum**, just opposite the entrance to Áyios Therápon, contains various icons rescued from rural island churches. The most noteworthy exhibit, and the oldest, is a fourteenth-century icon of Christ *Pandokrátor*; other highlights include a sultanic *firmáni* or grant of privileges to a local bishop, a rare sixteenth-century three-dimensional icon of *The Crucifixion* and a canvas of the *Kímisis* (*Assumption*) by Theophilos (see box, p.392).

ARRIVAL AND DEPARTURE | MYTILÍNI TOWN

By air The town is 7km from the airport; there's no bus link so you may need to take a taxi (€10).

By ferry Nearly all agencies can make bookings for ferries within Greece, while Picolo Travel at Koundouriótou 73a (☎ 22510 27000, ☎ picolotravel.gr) is best for tickets to Turkey.

By bus There are two bus terminals: the long-distance KTEL buses leave from a small station near Platía Konstandinopóleos at the southern end of the harbour,

while the blue town buses depart from a stand at the top of the harbour, or the dedicated terminal near the stadium.

By car Car rental can be arranged through one of the franchises dotted around the harbour, such as reputable Best at Koundouriótou 87–89 (☎ 22510 37337, ☎ best -rentacar.com). Drivers should use the enormous free public car park a few blocks south of the KTEL or the oval plaza near the new wing of the Archeological Museum.

INFORMATION

Tourist information The tourist office at James Aristárhou 6 (Mon–Fri 8am–2.30pm; ☎ 22510 42511) provides

excellent town and island maps, plus other brochures. The website ☎ lesvos.com is highly useful and entertaining.

ACCOMMODATION

Waterfront **hotels** are noisy and mostly overpriced, but supply usually exceeds demand for the better-value rooms in the backstreets. The Lesvos Hoteliers Association at Koundouriótou 47a (☎ 22510 41787, ☎ filoxenia.net) can book rooms in town and around the island.

Lesvion Koundouriótou 27A **☎**22510 28177, **ⓦ**lesvion
.gr. This smart mid-quay hotel is the most reasonably
priced of those on the front, with compact but comfy
rooms. Choose between a noisier harbour view or a room
at the back. **€42**

★**New Life** Olýmbou, cul-de-sac off Ermoú **☎**22510
23400, **ⓦ**new-life.gr. Moderate-sized, snug en-suite
rooms (some a/c) with polished wood floors, in an old
eccentrically decorated mansion with a garden. Great value
and very popular. **€30**

Orfeas Katsakoúli 3 **☎**22510 28523, **ⓦ**orfeas-hotel
.com. Probably the quietest of the town hotels, this well-
restored nineteenth-century building has somewhat small
a/c doubles with cheerfully hued modern furnishings.
Some balconies; lift; breakfast included. **€45**

Pyrgos Eleftheríou Venizélou 49 **☎**22510 25069,
ⓦpyrgoshotel.gr. Premier in-town restoration, with
utterly over-the-top kitsch decor in the common areas.
Most rooms have a balcony, some have bath tubs and there
are three round units in the tower itself. **€90**

EATING AND NIGHTLIFE

Averoff Koundouriótou 33 **☎**22510 22180. Its handy
location on the west quay makes this old-fashioned
estiatório a popular venue for *mayireftá* (including early-
morning *patsás*). Most dishes €5–8. Daily 6am–11pm.

Envy Koundouriótou 78 **☎**6976 214 947. The most
happening club, whose cutting-edge sounds carry on
through till dawn, while the rest of the day it's a decent
spot for quality coffee, snacks and sweets. Daily
10am–late.

★**Ermis** Ermoú, Epáno Skála **☎**22510 26232. This is the
best-value, and friendliest, of the ouzerís in this district.
Belle époque decor (panelled ceiling, giant mirrors,

faded oil paintings) inside and a pleasant courtyard. Daily
noon–2am.

Kalderimi Thássou 2 **☎**22510 46577. One of the few
surviving bazaar ouzerís, occupying three picturesque
buildings with seating under the shade of vines; the food is
abundant if a bit plainly presented. Mon–Sat 11am–2am,
Sun 11am–4pm.

Pirasmos Fanári quay **☎**22510 54970. Better value
than the fish tavernas surrounding it, this unpretentious
grill house specializes in delicious meat such as *kondosoúvli*
and *kokorétsi*, as well as simple salads and starters. Daily
1pm–1am.

ENTERTAINMENT

Cinemas The summer cinema, Pallas, is on Vournázon near the park; the winter cinema, Arion, is near the KTEL.

Around Mytilíni

The road heading **north** from Mytilíni towards Mandamádhos follows a rather
nondescript coastline, but offers startling views across the straits to Turkey. South of
the capital, there are two fine museums at **Variá** and a couple of decent beaches further
down the peninsula.

Paralía Thermís

Just 500m beyond Pýrgi Thermís, at **PARALÍA THERMÍS**, the Roman/Byzantine
hammam has been allowed to decay in favour of an ugly, sterile modern facility
adjacent, though it still supplies the hot water, and you can stick your head in to
admire the vaulted brickwork. At 12km, you're a bit far from town and the beach is
rather scrappy, but there is a decent accommodation option here.

Loutrá Yéras

8km along the main road to Kalloní • Baths daily: April–May & Oct 8am–6pm; June–Sept 8am–7pm; Nov–March 9am–5pm • €3 •
☎22510 41503

For a lovely warm bath near Mytilíni, make for **Loutrá Yéras**: these **public baths** are just
the thing if you've spent a sleepless night on a ferry. Two ornate spouts feed 38°C water
to marble-lined pools in vaulted chambers, there are separate facilities for men and
women (the ladies' pool is a tad smaller but has lovely masonry), and skinny-dipping is,
unexpectedly in prudish Greece, obligatory.

If you take the more northerly route via Mória to Loutrá Yéras, you will pass close
by the impressive remains of a second-century **Roman aqueduct**, signposted down a
fertile valley.

Variá

Variá is accessible by hourly buses from Mytilíni (around 15min)

The most rewarding sights to be visited near Mytilíni are a pair of museums at **VARIÁ**, 5km south of town, which between them hold much of the island's artistic legacy.

Theophilos Museum

Signposted inland from coastal road • Mon–Fri 9am–2pm • €3 • ☎ 22510 41644

The **Theophilos Museum** honours the painter (see box below), born here in 1873, with four rooms of wonderful, little-known compositions commissioned by his patron Thériade (see below) during the years immediately preceding Theophilos' death. A wealth of detail is evident in elegiac scenes of fishing, reaping, olive-picking and baking from the pastoral Lésvos which Theophilos obviously knew best. The *Sheikh-ul-Islam* with his hubble-bubble (Room 2) seems drawn from life, as does a highly secular Madonna merely titled *Mother with Child* (also Room 2). But in the museum's scenes of classical landscapes and episodes from wars historical and contemporary Theophilos seems on shakier ground.

Thériade Museum

Signposted inland from coastal road • The museum was closed for restoration at the time of writing

Next door to the Theophilos Museum, the imposing **Thériade Museum** is the legacy of another native son, Stratis Eleftheriades (1897–1983). Leaving the island aged 18 for Paris, he Gallicized his name to Thériade and eventually became a renowned avant-garde art publisher, enlisting some of the leading artists of the twentieth century in his ventures. The displays comprise two floors of lithographs, engravings, ink drawings, wood-block prints and watercolours by the likes of Picasso, Matisse, Le Corbusier and others: an astonishing collection for a relatively remote Aegean island.

South of Variá

Heading **south** beyond the airport and Krátigos village, the paved road loops around the peninsula to **Haramídha**, 14km from town and the closest decent (pebble) **beach**; the eastern bay has a few tavernas. **Áyios Ermoyénis**, 3km west and directly accessible from Mytilíni via Loutrá village, is more scenic and sandy. The patron saint's chapel perches on the cliff separating two small, sandy coves from a larger, less useable easterly bay accessed by a separate track.

THEOPHILOS HADZIMIHAÏL: THE ROUSSEAU OF GREECE?

The "naïve" painter **Theophilos Hadzimihaïl** (1873–1934) was born and died in Mytilíni Town, and both his eccentricities and talents were remarkable from an early age. After wandering across the country from Pílio to Athens and the Peloponnese, Theophilos became one of *belle époque* Greece's prize eccentrics, dressing up as Alexander the Great or various revolutionary war heroes, complete with pom-pommed shoes and pleated skirt. Theophilos was ill and living as a recluse in severely reduced circumstances back on Lésvos when he was introduced to Thériade in 1919; the latter, virtually alone among critics of the time, recognized his peculiar genius and ensured that Theophilos was supported both morally and materially for the rest of his life.

With their childlike perspective, vivid colour scheme and idealized mythical and rural subjects, Theophilos' **works** are unmistakeable. Relatively few of his works survive today, because he executed commissions for a pittance on ephemeral surfaces such as *kafenío* counters, horsecarts, or the walls of long-vanished houses. Facile comparisons are often made between Theophilos and **Henri Rousseau**, the roughly contemporaneous French "primitive" painter. Unlike "Le Douanier", however, Theophilos followed no other profession, eking out a precarious living from his art alone. And while Rousseau revelled in exoticism, Theophilos' work was principally and profoundly rooted in Greek mythology, history and daily life.

ACCOMMODATION AND EATING   **AROUND MYTILÍNI**

Loriet/Laureate Variá, 4km south of Mytilíni ☎ 22510 43111, ⓦ loriet-hotel.com. A nineteenth-century mansion with modern wings, gardens, fine restaurant and 25m saltwater pool. Rooms vary from blandly modern, marble-trimmed studios to massive suites with retro decor and big bathrooms. **€50**

★ **Theodora Glava** Haramídha ☎ 22510 91420. Legendary Theodora lovingly serves up a great range

vegetarian and seafood mezédhes, such as *louloudhákia* (stuffed courgette flowers) for €5, plus more substantial meat and fish items. May to early Oct daily 11am–1am.

★ **Votsala** Paralía Thermís ☎ 22510 71231, ⓦ votsala hotel.com. This comfortable and relaxing place offers watersports off the beach and well-tended gardens. It prides itself on having no TV in the rooms and no "Greek nights" or disco. April–Oct. **€56**

6

Southern Lésvos

Southern Lésvos is indented by two great inlets, the gulfs of **Kalloní** and **Yéra**, the first curving in a northeasterly direction, the latter northwesterly, creating a fan-shaped peninsula at the heart of which looms 967m **Mount Ólymbos**. Both shallow gulfs are landlocked by very narrow outlets to the open sea, which don't – and probably never will – have bridges spanning them. This is the most verdant and productive olive-oil territory on Lésvos, and stacks of pressing-mills stab the skyline.

Pérama

A regular kaïki service (no cars) links Pérama with Koundoroudhiá, which has a blue city bus service to/from Mytilíni

PÉRAMA, disused olive-oil warehouses dotting its oddly attractive townscape, is one of the larger places on the Gulf of Yéra. Although it feels rather forlorn and end-of-the-road, it is easily accessible by public transport from Mytilíni and offers great eating.

Plomári and around

Due south of Mount Ólymbos, at the edge of the "fan", **PLOMÁRI** is the only sizeable coastal settlement hereabouts, and indeed the second-largest municipality on Lésvos. It presents an unlikely juxtaposition of scenic appeal and its famous ouzo industry, courtesy of several local **distilleries**. Despite a resounding lack of good beaches within walking distance, Plomári is popular with Scandinavian tourists; most actually stay at **Áyios Isídhoros**, 3km east.

Varvayianni Distillery

1km east of centre • May–Oct Mon–Fri 9am–7pm, Sat 9am–1pm; Nov–April Mon–Fri 8am–4pm • Free • ☎ 22520 32741, ⓦ barbayanni-ouzo.com

The largest and oldest of Plomári distilleries, **Varvayianni**, offers free tours and tasting, plus a fascinating display of old alembics, presses, storage jars and archival material. Best venues for a tipple afterwards are the old *kafenía* on central Platía Beniamín.

Melínda

Melínda, a 700m sand-and-shingle beach at the mouth of a canyon lush with olive trees, lies 6km west of Plomári by paved road. It's an alluring place, with sweeping views west towards the Vaterá coast and the cape of Áyios Fokás, and south (in clear conditions) to northern Híos, Psará and the Turkish Karaburun peninsula.

Panayía Kryftí hot springs

One of the best excursions beyond Melínda is to the **Panayía Kryftí hot springs**. From the first curve of the paved road up to Paleohóri, a dirt track goes 2.8km to a dead end with parking space, with the final 400m on a downhill path to the little chapel just above a protected inlet. On the far side of this you'll see a rectangular cement tank, just big enough for two people, containing water at a pleasant 37–38°C.

6

Ayiássos and around

AYIÁSSOS, 26km from Mytilíni, nestled in a remote, wooded valley under the crest of Mount Ólymbos, is the most beautiful hill town on Lésvos, its narrow cobbled streets lined by ranks of tiled-roof houses, built in part from proceeds of the trade in *tsoupiá* (olive sacks). On the usual, northerly approach, there's no hint of the enormous village until you see huge knots of parked cars at the southern edge of town. Most visitors proceed past endless ranks of kitsch wooden and ceramic souvenirs or carved "Byzantine" furniture, aimed mostly at Greeks, and the central church of the **Panayía Vrefokratoússa** – built in the twelfth century to house an icon supposedly painted by the Evangelist Luke – to the old bazaar. With such a venerable icon as a focus, the local August 15 *paniyíri* is one of the liveliest on Lésvos.

Mount Ólymbos

From the southern side of Ayiássos, keen walkers can follow a network of marked paths and tracks for three hours to the **Ólymbos summit**. Approaching from Plomári, there's asphalt road and public transport only up to Megalohóri, with a good dirt surface thereafter up to some air-force radar balls, where paving resumes. Dense woods of oak and chestnut take over from the recovering pine growth beyond the first main ridge.

Mylélia watermill

6km northeast of Ayiássos, signposted along a track near the turning for Ípio • Daily 9am–6pm • ⓦ mylelia.gr

Mylélia means "place of the mills", and there were once several hereabouts – the **Mylélia watermill** is the last survivor, restored to working order in the 1990s. The keeper will show you the millrace and paddle-wheel, as well as the flour making its spasmodic exit, after which you can browse the gourmet pastas and other products at the shop, including cheeses, jams, vinegar and salted fish. They also do cooking courses.

Polikhnítos and around

The largest settlement in the southwestern part of southern Lésvos is **POLIKHNÍTOS**, a rather dull, workaday rural centre. It is, however, the point of access to magnificent **Vaterá** beach, the seaside villages of **Skála Polikhnítou** and **Nifídha**, each with its own smaller beach, and the Natural History Museum of **Vrýssa**.

Natural History Museum, Vrýssa

Centre of village • May & June daily 9.30am–3.30pm; July–Sept daily 9.30am–3pm & 4–8pm; Oct–April Wed–Sun 9.30am–3.30pm • €2 • ⓣ 22520 61890

Vrýssa, 4km south of Polikhnítos, has a mildly diverting **Natural History Museum** documenting local paleontological finds. In 1997 Athenian paleontologist Michael Dermitzakis confirmed what farmers unearthing bones had long suspected when he pronounced the area a treasure-trove of **fossils**, including those of two-million-year-old gigantic horses, mastodons, monkeys and tortoises the size of a Volkswagen Beetle. Until twenty thousand years ago, Lésvos (like all other east Aegean islands) was joined to the Asian mainland, and the gulf of Vaterá was a subtropical freshwater lake; the animals in question came to drink, died nearby and were trapped and preserved by successive volcanic flows.

Vaterá and around

Vaterá, 9km south of Polikhnítos, is a 7km-long sand **beach**, backed by vegetated hills; the sea here is delightfully calm and clean, the strand itself perhaps the best on Lésvos. Development, mostly seasonal villas and apartments for locals, straggles for several kilometres to either side of the central T-junction but is nicely spread out, so the strip does not feel overtly commercialized.

Some 3km west at the cape of **Áyios Fokás** only the foundations remain of a temple of Dionysos and a superimposed early Christian basilica. The little tamarisk-shaded anchorage here has a superb taverna.

POLIKHNÍTOS SPA

If you're after a hot bath, head for the vaulted, well-restored **Polikhnítos Spa** complex (Mon–Sat 2–8pm, Sun 10am–8pm; €4; ☎ 22520 41229, ⊛ hotsprings.gr) 1.5km east of the town of **Polikhnítos**; there are separate, warm-hued chambers for each sex. The water actually gushes out at temperatures up to 87°C, so needs to be tempered with cold.

ACCOMMODATION AND EATING   **SOUTHERN LÉSVOS**

6

PÉRAMA

★**Balouhanas** ☎ 22510 51948. The northernmost establishment on the front, with a wooden, cane-roofed deck jutting out over the water. Seafood is a strong point, whether grilled or as €6 croquettes, as are regional mezédhes and home-made desserts. Daily 11am–1am.

PLOMÁRI AND AROUND

Maria's Sea end of access road, Melinda ☎ 22520 93239. The restaurant here is excellent, serving a range of fish, meat and mezédhes, all under €10, while the rooms are simple but extremely cheap. May–Oct daily 9am–midnight. **€25**

Melinda Studios Just west of access road, Melinda ☎ 22520 93282, ✉ melindastudios@gmail.com. This small pension has clean, bright studios with small kitchenettes and sea-facing balconies. May–Sept. **€30**

Pebble Beach Áyios Isídhoros ☎ 22520 31651, ⊛ pebble beach-hotel.com. Many of the rooms here, which are adequate in size and comfort, overlook a slightly reefy section of beach. Breakfast included. May–Oct. **€45**

Pension Leda 2 Near Platía Beniamín, Plomári ☎ 22520 32507, ⊛ leda.gr. Cosy, traditionally decorated rooms in an old house, run by an affable olive-oil producer. The original mansion next door is now only used for overspill. **€25**

★**Taverna tou Panai** 800m north of Áyios Isídhoros ☎ 22520 31920. Set in an olive grove, this rustic taverna serves fine meat, seafood and mayireftá dishes for €6–8 to a mostly Greek clientele. Most produce is home-grown and organic. Daily 10am–late.

AYIÁSSOS

Dhouladhellis Near the fork at the southern end of town ☎ 22520 22236. Friendly family taverna with a huge courtyard, serving various soups, meat dishes for €6–7 and plenty of glyká koutalioú. March–Nov daily 9am–midnight.

Ouzerí To Stavri Stavrí district ☎ 22520 22936. This quirky little place on the upper north side of town offers a warm welcome and great home-style mezédhes such as cheese croquettes and octopus in vinegar for €4–6. Daily 11am–late.

POLIKHNÍTOS AND AROUND

★**Akrotiri/Angelerou** Áyios Fokás ☎ 22520 61465. Top-notch little taverna, specializing in seafood delights such as shrimp salad, fish soup or sardhélles Kallonís, plus starters like cheese croquettes. All cost well under €10 and can be washed down with aromatic wine. April–Oct daily noon–1am.

★**Aphrodite Beach** Towards eastern end, Vaterá ☎ 22520 61288, ⊛ aphroditehotel.gr. Sparkling blue-and-white complex of comfortable units with a/c, fridges and small balconies. The extremely welcoming family restaurant features tasty dishes like lamb, briám, very palatable wine and occasional live music sessions. Buffet breakfast optional. May to early Oct 9am–1am. **€30**

Kalamakia Towards eastern end, Vaterá ☎ 22520 61270. Principally a taverna specializing in superb home cooking such as fish in tomato sauce and stuffed chicken patties, there are also some smart rooms and apartments at the back. Daily 9am–late. **€25**

O Grigoris Nifídha ☎ 22520 41838. Good seafront psarotavérna with the usual range of fish from €35/kilo and seafood, backed up by some salads and veg dishes. March–June & mid-Sept to Nov Fri–Sun noon–1am; July to mid-Sept daily noon–1am.

Western Lésvos

The area from the Gulf of Kalloní to the island's west coast is a mostly treeless, craggy region whose fertile valleys offer a sharp contrast to the bare ridges. River mouths form little oases behind a handful of **beach resorts** like Skála Kallonís, Sígri and Skála Eressoú. A few **monasteries** along the road west of Kalloní, plus the occasional striking **inland village**, provide monumental interest.

Ayía Paraskeví and around

A rewarding detour en route to Kalloní is to **AYÍA PARASKEVÍ** village, midway between two important and photogenic monuments from diverse eras: the paleo-Christian, three-aisled basilica of **Halinádhou**, its dozen basalt columns amid pine-and-olive scenery, and the large medieval bridge of **Kremastí**, the largest and best preserved such in the east Aegean, 3km west of Ayía Paraskeví.

Museum of Industrial Olive Oil Production in Lésvos

Southern outskirts of Ayía Paraskeví · Daily except Tues: March to mid-Oct 10am–6pm; mid-Oct to Feb 10am–5pm · €3 · ☎ 22530 32300, Ⓦ piop.gr

The eminently worthwhile **Museum of Industrial Olive Oil Production in Lésvos** (Mousío Viomihanikís Elaeouryías Lésvou) is housed in a restored communal olive mill. The mill, built by public subscription in the 1920s, only ceased working under the junta; the industrial machinery has been lovingly refurbished and its function explained, while former outbuildings and warehouses are used as venues for secondary exhibits and short explanatory films.

Kalloní and around

KALLONÍ is a lively agricultural and market town in the middle of the island. Some 3km south lies the town's seaside package resort, **Skála Kallonís**, backing a long, sandy but absurdly shallow beach on the lake-like gulf whose water can be turbid. It's mainly distinguished as a **bird-watching** centre during the nesting season (March–May) in the adjacent salt marshes. The local speciality is the gulf's celebrated, plankton-nurtured **sardines**, best eaten fresh-grilled from August to October, although they're available salt-cured all year round.

ACCOMMODATION AND EATING   KALLONÍ AND AROUND

Aegeon Kalloní ☎ 22530 22398, Ⓦ aegeon-lesvos.gr. Set in a leafy garden, with above-average furnishings for its class, a large pool and friendly owners, this is the best option among the hotels grouped on the west side of town. **€45**

Medousa Skála Kallonís ☎ 6972 201 813. Top restaurant for sardines done Kalloní style and other super-fresh fish and seafood, much of it under €10. Pleasant location in a renovated stone house on the seafront. April–Oct daily 10am–1am.

Limónos monastery

4km west of Kalloní · Museum daily 9.30am–6.30pm, may close 3pm off season · €2

West of Kalloní, the road winds uphill to **Limónos monastery**, founded in 1527 by the monk Ignatios, whose cell is maintained in the surviving medieval north wing. It's a rambling, three-storey complex around a vast, plant-filled courtyard, home to just a handful of monks and lay workers. The *katholikón*, with its ornate carved-wood ceiling and archways, is traditionally off limits to women; a sacred spring flows from below the south foundation wall. Only the ground-floor **ecclesiastical museum** is currently functioning, with the more interesting ethnographic gallery upstairs still closed.

Hídhira

Seven kilometres south of the beautiful settlement of **Vatoússa**, which boasts a classic plane-shaded square and some fine architecture, stands the hilltop village of **HÍDHIRA**, with a fine winery and interesting museum. The village is a dead end unless you have a jeep capable of continuing across the rough track to Eressós by way of Ágra.

Methymneos Winery

Just below the entrance to Hídhira · Aug–Sept Tues–Sun 10am–2pm, otherwise by appointment · ☎ 6972 085 371, Ⓦ methymneos.gr

The **Methymneos Winery** has successfully revived the local ancient grape variety, decimated by phylloxera some decades ago. Because of the altitude (300m) and sulphur-rich soil (you're in a volcanic caldera), their velvety, high-alcohol, oak-aged red can be produced organically; 2007 saw the introduction of bottled white wines. Proprietor Ioannis Lambrou offers a highly worthwhile free twenty-minute **tour** of the state-of-the-art premises in English.

> ## THE OLIVES OF LÉSVOS
> No other Greek island is as dominated by **olive production** as Lésvos, which is blanketed by approximately eleven million olive trees. Most of these vast groves date from after a lethal frost in 1851, though a few hardy survivors are thought to be over five hundred years old. During the first three centuries after the Ottoman conquest, production of olive oil was a monopoly of the ruling pasha, but following eighteenth-century reforms in the Ottoman Empire, extensive tracts of Lésvos (and thus the lucrative oil trade) passed into the hands of the new Greek bourgeoisie, who greatly expanded the industry.

6

Digital Art Museum of George Jakobides

Centre of village • Tues–Sun: July & Aug 9am–7pm; Sept–June 9am–5pm • €2 • ☎ 22530 51128, ⓦ jakobides-digital-museum.gr

The fancy name of the **Digital Art Museum of George Jakobides** is a slight misnomer in that it is not about anything hi-tech and the artist to whom it is dedicated, a native of Hídhira who lived from 1853 to 1932, predated the computer age. Yet the short digital film and copies of seven of his most famous works, such as *Children's Concert* and *Naughty Grandson*, are worth a peep.

Monastery of Perivolís

8km west of Vatoússa • Daily 10am–1pm & 5–6pm • Donation • No photos

From the main road, a short track leads down to the thirteenth-century monastery of **Perivolís**, built amid a riverside orchard (*perivóli*), which has fine if damp-damaged sixteenth-century frescoes in the narthex. An apocalyptic panel worthy of Bosch (*The Earth and Sea Yield up their Dead*) shows the Whore of Babylon riding her chimera and assorted sea monsters disgorging their victims; just to the right, towards the main door, the Three Magi are depicted approaching the Virgin enthroned with the Christ Child. On the north side there's a highly unusual iconography of Abraham, the Virgin, and the penitent thief of Calvary in paradise, with the four heavenly rivers gushing forth under their feet; just right are assembled the Hebrew kings of the Old Testament.

Ándissa and around

ÁNDISSA, 11km west of Vatoússa, nestles under this parched region's only substantial pine grove; at the edge of the village a sign implores you to "Come Visit Our Square", not a bad idea for the sake of a handful of refreshment options sheltering under three sizeable plane trees.

Gavathás and around

Directly below Ándissa a paved road leads 6km north to **GAVATHÁS**, a village with a shortish, partly protected **beach** and a few places to eat and stay. A side road leads one headland east to huge, dune-dominated, surf-battered **Kámbos** beach, which you may well have to yourself, even in August.

ACCOMMODATION AND EATING	**ÁNDISSA AND AROUND**
Paradise Gavathás ☎ 22530 56376. This pension-cum-restaurant, 300m back from the seafront, has simple but adequate rooms and serves good fish and locally grown vegetables. May–Sept. **€30** ★**Pedhinon** Ándissa ☎ 22530 56106. The village's	oldest and best taverna, shaded by the largest plane tree, is very friendly and rustles up excellent *mayireftá*, such as lamb fricassee and okra. You may even run into local octogenarian poet Panayiótis Petréllis. Daily 10am–midnight.

Monastery of Ypsiloú

3km west of Ándissa • Museum daily 8.30am–3pm • Donation

Two kilometres west of Ándissa there's an important junction. Keeping straight leads you past the still-functioning, double-gated monastery of **Ypsiloú**, founded in 1101 atop an outrider of extinct Órdhymnos volcano. The *katholikón*, tucked in one corner of a large, irregular courtyard, has a fine wood-lattice ceiling but has had its frescoes repainted to detrimental effect. Exhibits in the upstairs **museum** encompass a fine collection of *epitáfios* (Good Friday) shrouds, ancient manuscripts, portable icons and – oddest of all – a *Deposition* painted in Renaissance style by a sixteenth-century Turk.

The petrified forest

5km south of the main Ándissa–Sígrí road • Daily: June–Sept 8am–sunset; Oct–May 8am–4pm • €2

To the west of Ypsilóu begins the 5km side road to the main concentration of Lésvos' overrated **petrified forest**, a fenced-in "reserve" toured along 3km of walkways. For once, contemporary Greek arsonists cannot be blamed for the state of the trees, created by the combined action of volcanic ash from Órdhymnos and hot springs some fifteen to twenty million years ago. The mostly horizontal sequoia trunks average 1m or less in length, save for a few poster-worthy exceptions; there's another more accessible (and free) cluster south of Sígri.

Sígri

SÍGRI, near the western tip of Lésvos, has an appropriately end-of-the-line feel; its bay is guarded both by an Ottoman castle and the long island of **Nissiopí**, which protects the place somewhat from prevailing winds. The eighteenth-century **castle**, built atop an earlier one, sports the reigning sultan's monogram over the entrance, something rarely seen outside İstanbul, evidence of the high regard in which this strategic port with a good water supply was held. The odd-looking church of **Ayía Triádha** is in fact a converted **mosque**, with a huge water cistern taking up the ground floor; this supplied, among other things, the half-ruined **hammam** just south.

Natural History Museum of the Lésvos Petrified Forest

Centre of village • July–Sept Mon–Sat 8am–6pm, Sun 9am–6pm; Oct–June Mon–Sat 9am–5pm, Sun 10am–5pm • €5 • ☎ 22530 54434, ⓦ lesvosmuseum.gr

At the top of town stands the well-executed but overpriced **Natural History Museum of the Lésvos Petrified Forest**, which covers pan-Aegean geology with samples and maps (including, ominously, seismic patterns), as well as the expected quota of petrified logs and plant fossils from when the surrounding hills were far more vegetated.

The beaches

The nearest of several **beaches**, south of the castle headland, is somewhat narrow but is the only one with amenities. The far superior strand of **Faneroméni** lies 3.5km north by a coastal dirt track from the northern outskirts of town. A shorter but equally good beach, **Liména**, can be found 2km south of Sígri at another creek mouth, just off the rough, one-lane, 15km track to Eressós, passable with care in an ordinary car, in 35 minutes.

ACCOMMODATION AND EATING   SÍGRI

Cavo d'Oro (no sign) ☎ 22530 54221. The only taverna on the harbour itself is a classic for lobster and scaly fish from €40/kilo, far better than the restaurants around the nearby platía. Daily 11am–2am.

Pyrgospito/Towerhouse 500m east of the village ☎ 22530 22909, ⓦ lesvos-towerhouse.gr. Four spacious antique-furnished apartments in a *belle époque* folly, set on a landscaped hillside setting, with a pool. May–Oct. **€65**

Skála Eressoú

Most visitors to western Lésvos park themselves at **SKÁLA ERESSOÚ**, reached via a southerly turning between Ándissa and Ypsilóu. Its 3km dark-coloured **beach** almost rivals Vatera's as the best on the island. Behind stretches the largest and most attractive agricultural plain on Lésvos, a welcome green contrast to the volcanic ridges above.

There's not much to central Skála – just a roughly rectangular grid of perhaps five streets by twelve, angling up to the oldest cottages on the slope of Vígla hill above the

6

SAPPHIC AND MYSTIC SKÁLA

Through its obvious associations with **Sappho** (see below), Skála Eressoú has for decades been a magnet for lesbians from all over the globe. Various events take place here, most notably the **International Eressos Women's Festival** in September (⊛womensfestival.eu). Every day except Sunday from June to late September, barring bad weather conditions, the **Skala Women's Rock Group** hold a swim from beside the *Zorba The Buddha* café (see below) to the islet in the middle of the bay and back. This social and non-competitive event is open to women of any sexual orientation.

As evidenced by the name of the café, there is also a perceptible Eastern mystical influence in the village, largely due to the presence of the Osho Afroz Meditation Center (⊛oshoafroz.com) 3km inland. Consequently, as well as the centre's programmes, there are various yoga, meditation and healing sessions available in Skála. Together, the female and spiritual energies create a unique resort.

east end of the beach. The waterfront pedestrian lane is divided midway by a café-lined, circular platía with a bust of **Theophrastos**. This renowned botanist hailed from **ancient Eressós** atop Vígla hill – what little remains of the citadel wall is still visible from a distance, and the views reward a scramble up. An even more famous native of ancient Eressós, honoured by a stylized statue on the platía, was **Sappho** (c.615–562 BC), poet and reputed lesbian. There are thus always conspicuous numbers of gay women about, particularly in the women-only clothing-optional zone of the **beach** west of the river mouth, also home to a small community of terrapins.

ACCOMMODATION

SKÁLA ERESSOÚ

For **accommodation**, at busy times it's wise to entrust the search to Sappho Travel (☎22530 52202, ⊛sapphotravel.com) who can arrange something to suit your needs; they also rent out cars.

Iy Galini Three blocks inland ☎22530 53138, ⊛hotel-galinos.gr. This welcoming, slightly old-fashioned hotel with a colourful yard outside has cosy, spotlessly clean rooms with little balconies. Wi-fi in lobby. Breakfast included. **€40**

Sappho Hotel Western seafront ☎22530 53233, ⊛sappho-hotel.com. With decent-sized rooms and a pleasant ground-floor snack-bar, this hotel has been spruced up to attract allcomers, having dropped its previous women-only policy. **€50**

EATING AND NIGHTLIFE

With about seven clubs/bars to choose from in peak season, local **nightlife** is the best on the island and all are gay-friendly. There's also a central, open-air **cinema** (July to early Sept), predictably named after the ancient poet, several blocks inland.

Aigaio Just west of seafront square ☎22530 53808. The best traditional restaurant for baked veg and meat dishes in the €6–8 range, plus fish at market rates. April–Oct daily 10am–1am.

Ioannis & Gabi A block back from the eastern seafront ☎22530 53272. Run by a Greek-Austrian couple, this garden taverna is a delightful spot to sample simple home-style cooking with a range of meat, fish and vegetarian dishes for €10 or less. May–Oct daily noon–midnight.

Parasol Eastern seafront ☎22530 52020. Ethnic sounds abound and exotic cocktails flow at one of the resort's most enduring café-cum-bars, with an attractive central sea-front location under a thatched bamboo roof. May to early Oct daily 10am–late.

★Zorba The Buddha Eastern seafront ☎22530 53777. Colourful and convivial café-cum-restaurant, with an eastern vibe and a spacious wooden deck where you can enjoy quality teas, juices, ice creams and daily specials like lamb wrapped in vine leaves for €6–8. May–Sept daily 9am–2am.

Northern Lésvos

The northern part of Lésvos is largely fertile and green countryside stippled with poplars and blanketed by olive groves. Occupying the prime position on a promontory in the middle of the coast is one of the northeast Aegean's most attractive resorts,

Mólyvos, whose castle's cockscomb silhouette is visible for many kilometres around. On either side of it, a number of **coastal resorts** offer superior bathing.

Mólyvos (Míthymna)

MÓLYVOS (officially Míthymna after its ancient predecessor), 61km from Mytilíni, is the island's most beautiful village, with tiers of sturdy, red-tiled houses, some standing with their rear walls defensively towards the sea, mounting the slopes between the picturesque harbour and the Byzantine-Genoese **castle**. A score of weathered Turkish fountains, a mosque and hammam grace flower-fragrant, cobbled alleyways, reflecting the fact that before 1923 Muslims constituted more than a third of the local population and owned many of the finest dwellings.

Modern dwellings and hotels have been banned from the old core, but this hasn't prevented a steady drain of all authentic life from the upper **bazaar**; perhaps four or five "ordinary" shops ply their trade among souvenir shops vastly surplus to requirements. The shingly **town beach** is mediocre, improving considerably as you head towards the sandy southern end of the bay, called **Psiriára**.

The castle
Daily 8.30am–3pm • €2

The imposing ramparts of the **Byzantine castle** of Mólyvos, later repaired by Genoan Francesco Gattelusi, are visible from many kilometres around. Sections can now be accessed from the inside, affording splendid views of the harbour and beyond. Entrance is via the impressive main gate, through which a set of steps leads up to the largely open interior, where a wooden **amphitheatre** is used for occasional summer performances.

ARRIVAL AND GETTING AROUND   MÓLYVOS (MÍTHYMNA)

By bus or taxi The bus stop and taxi rank are at the southeast edge of town.

By car or motorbike There are numerous motorbike and car rental places near the tourist office, including Kosmos

(☎ 22530 71710) and Best (☎ 22530 72145), both offering the option of pick-up here and drop-off in Mytilíni or the airport. The main car park is at the southeast edge of town; there are further car parks above the port and up by the castle.

INFORMATION

Tourist office The municipal tourist office, near the main junction on the south side of town, keeps lists of rented rooms but actual opening hours are erratic (May–Oct

Mon–Sat roughly 10am–5pm; ☎ 22530 71347, ⓦ mithymna.gr).

ACCOMMODATION

Delfinia 1km south of town ☎ 22530 71315, ⓦ hotel delfinia.com. Luxury resort hotel set in 87 acres of greenery, with rooms and bungalows, a castle-view pool, tennis courts and direct access to Psiriára beach. Breakfast included. €70

Hermes On the main town beach ☎ 22530 71250, ⓦ hermeshotel-molivos.com. Single-storey hotel with variable, marble-floored rooms, all fitted with bright contemporary furnishings and set in quite lush grounds. Breakfast included. May–Oct. €50

Molyvos I On the main town beach ☎ 22530 71496,

ⓦ molyvos-hotels.com. Modern block with large balconied and comfortably furnished rooms. Complimentary breakfast served on the flagstoned terrace under the palms. Sister *Molyvos II* is nearby Eftaloú beach. April–Oct. €55

★ **Sun Rise** 2km east of town ☎ 22530 71713, ⓦ sunrisehotel-lesvos.com. High-class hotel that sprawls in startling white tiers over a hillside. The rooms come in varying sizes but all are well appointed. Two pools, tennis courts, gym, sauna and classy restaurant. Breakfast included. April–Oct. €65

EATING AND NIGHTLIFE

Apart from a selection of lively bars, there's also an outdoor **cinema** (June–Sept) next to the taxi rank.

★ **The Captain's Table** On the harbour ☎ 22530 71241. Having reinvented itself in more ouzerí style after complete destruction in a 2014 fire, this enduring spot still

produces excellent mezédhes and main courses, mostly under €10. May–Oct daily noon–2am.

Molly's Bar On the road down to the harbour ☎ 22530

71772. Popular hangout, with taped music at a conversational level during the day and louder music videos by night. The cosy balcony has atmospheric harbour views. May–Oct daily 10am–late.

Orizontas On the main town beach ☎ 22530 71861. Comfortably the best of the beachside tavernas, with a simple but adequate menu of starters, dips and main courses such as *mýdhia saganáki* for €8. May–Oct daily 9am–1am.

Oxy 2km west of town ☎ 6946 506 178. Massive new club with a swimming pool, state-of-the-art light show and sound system, pumping out the latest techno and dance hits. Tues–Fri 6pm–late, Sat & Sun 1pm–late.

To Ouzadhiko tou Baboukou On the south quay ☎ 22530 71776. This joint has an impressive array of ouzos, a bohemian atmosphere and competent renditions of the usual mezédhes, mostly €6–8. Daily 11am–1am.

Around Mólyvos

West of Mólyvos there's a string of decent beaches with varying degrees of commercialization, most rampant at **Pétra**. To the east, coastal development is more measured, with some appealing beaches and yet another spa. Inland and southeast, the main paved road via Vafiós curves around 968m, poplar-tufted **Mount Lepétymnos**. You can complete a scenic loop of the mountain via Kápi and Ypsilométopo on its southern flank.

Pétra

Given the limited space in Mólyvos, many package companies operate mostly in **PÉTRA**, 5km due south. The modern outskirts sprawl untidily behind its broad, sandy beach, but two attractive nuclei of old stone houses, some with Levantine-style balconies overhanging the street, extend back from the part-pedestrianized seafront square. Pétra takes its name from the giant, unmissable rock monolith inland, enhanced by the eighteenth-century church of the **Panayía Glykofiloússa**, reached via 114 rock-hewn steps. Other local attractions include the sixteenth-century church of **Áyios Nikólaos**, with three phases of well-preserved frescoes up to 1721, and the intricately decorated **Vareltzídhena mansion** (Tues–Sun 8am–3pm; free).

Ánaxos

ÁNAXOS, 3km south of Pétra, is a higgledy-piggledy package resort fringing by far the cleanest **beach** and seawater in the area: 1km of sand well sown with sunbeds and a handful of tavernas. From anywhere along here you enjoy beautiful sunsets between and beyond three offshore islets.

Loutrá Eftaloú

5km east of Mólyvos • Daily: May & Oct 9am–1pm & 3–7pm; June–Sept 10am–2pm & 4–8pm; Nov–April variable access • €3.50 for group pool

The **Loutrá Eftaloú** thermal baths are east of Mólyvos, just beyond the end of the paved road. Patronize the hot pool under the Ottoman-era domed structure, rather than the sterile modern tub-rooms. The spa is well looked after, with the water mixed up to a toasty 43°C, so you'll need to cool down regularly; outside stretches the long, good pebble beach of **Áyii Anáryiri**, broken up by little headlands, with the two remotest coves nudist.

Sykaminiá

The exquisite hill village of **SYKAMINIÁ** (Sykamiá, Skamniá), just under 10km from Mólyvos, is the birthplace in 1892 of novelist **Stratis Myrivilis**. One of the imposing basalt-built houses below the platía, from which there are views north to Turkey, is marked as his childhood home.

Skála Sykaminiás

A marked trail short cuts the twisting road from just east of Sykaminiá down to **SKÁLA SYKAMINIÁS**, easily the most picturesque fishing port on Lésvos. Myrivilis used it as the setting for his best-known work, *The Mermaid Madonna*, and the tiny rock-top **chapel** at the end of the jetty will be instantly recognizable to anyone who has read the book. The only local **beach** is the one of Kayiá 1.5km east, which has a pebble-on-sand base.

Klió and Tsónia

Some 5km east from upper Sykaminiá is **KLIÓ**, whose single main street leads down to a platía with a plane tree, fountain and more views across to Turkey. The village is set attractively on a slope, down which a wide, paved road descends 6km to **Tsónia** beach, 600m of beautiful pink volcanic sand.

ACCOMMODATION AND EATING

PÉTRA

Hotel Michaelia Southern seafront ☎ 22530 41731. Good-value hotel with smart if slightly cramped rooms, most with balconies facing the sunset. Decent buffet breakfast included. May–Sept. €45

Mermaid Far north end of the seafront ☎ 22530 41275. This all-round taverna provides heaps of inexpensive small and more upscale fish from €40/kilo, as well as some meat dishes and a variety of starters. April to mid-Oct daily 9am–1am.

★**Women's Agricultural Tourism Cooperative** Central seafront ☎ 22530 41238, ⓦ lesvos-travel.com /womens-cooperative. The cooperative arranges rooms or studios in scattered premises from its rooftop restaurant, which serves up tasty grills and *mayireftá* for €7–8. Proceeds go to the organization's efforts. Daily 10am–midnight. €30

ÁNAXOS

Klimataria Northern end of beach ☎ 22530 41864. Tucked under a cliff, the best local restaurant has a large shady courtyard, where you can enjoy healthy portions of fresh fish, meat and salads. Most items under €10. Mid-May to Sept daily 11am–midnight.

LOUTRÁ EFTALOÚ

Iy Eftalou Behind beach ☎ 22530 71649. The nearest location to the spa to grab a snack or fuller meal, with a shady courtyard, where large meat grills, fish and *mayireftá* cost €10 or under. April–Oct daily 9am–midnight.

AROUND MÓLYVOS

Khrysi Akti 300m east of main beach ☎ 22530 71879. Typical taverna-plus-rooms combo in the converted old spa-patrons' inn. The en-suite rooms are quite small but cost the same all season, while the menu offers a mixture of grills and the odd oven-baked dish for €7–9. May–Sept 9am–midnight. €35

SKÁLA SYKAMINIÁS

Anemoessa By the harbour chapel ☎ 22530 55360. This place has the local edge quality-wise, with imaginative starters like stuffed squash blossoms complementing fresh fish, much of which costs €10–14. April–Oct daily noon–1am, plus some winter weekends (Fri–Sun) same hours.

★**Gorgona** Near the harbour ☎ 22530 55301, ⓦ gorgonahotel.gr. Small hotel run by a friendly old couple, whose simple but clean rooms have wraparound balconies. There's a shaded terrace for the complimentary breakfast and meals are available too. May–Sept. €35

Iy Mouria tou Myrivili ☎ 22530 55319. Picturesque taverna named after the mulberry tree in which Myrivilis used to sleep on hot summer nights. You can tuck into a standard range of mezédhes, salads, meat and seafood dishes, such as octopus in wine sauce for €9. May–Oct daily 11am–1am.

KLIÓ AND TSÓNIA

Iy Apolafsi Near access road, Tsónia ☎ 22530 93700. Homely family taverna, which provides a good range of starters, grills and some *mayireftá* like *exohikó* for €6–8. May–Sept daily 10am–midnight.

Áyios Efstrátios

Áyios Efstrátios (Aï Strátis) is one of the quietest and loneliest islands in the Aegean, with a registered population of under four hundred, only half of whom live here all year round. It was only permanently settled during the sixteenth century, and land is still largely owned by three monasteries on Mount Áthos. Historically, the only outsiders to visit were those compelled to do so – political prisoners were exiled here both during the 1930s and the civil war years.

Áyios Efstrátios village

ÁYIOS EFSTRÁTIOS village – the island's only habitation – is among the ugliest in Greece. Devastation caused by an earthquake on February 20, 1968, which killed 22 and injured hundreds, was compounded by the reconstruction plan conducted by a junta-linked company, who bulldozed even those structures that could have been repaired. From the hillside, some two dozen surviving houses of the old village overlook grim rows of prefabs, a sad monument to the corruption of the junta years.

Architecture apart, Áyios Efstrátios still functions as a traditional fishing and farming community, with the prefabs set at the mouth of a wooded stream valley draining to the sandy harbour beach. There are scant tourist amenities.

Around the island

6

Beyond the village – there are few vehicles and no paved roads – the hilly **landscape**, dotted with a surprising number of oak trees, is deserted apart from rabbits, sheep and the occasional shepherd. **Alonítsi**, on the north coast – ninety minutes' walk from the port following a track due east and over a low ridge – is the island's best **beach**, a 1.5km stretch of sand with rolling breakers and views across to Límnos. South of the harbour lies a series of grey-sand beaches, most with wells and drinkable water, accessible by roundabout tracks. **Áyios Dhimítrios**, an hour-plus distant, and **Lidharió**, ninety minutes away at the end of a wooded valley, are the most popular.

ARRIVAL AND DEPARTURE   ÁYIOS EFSTRÁTIOS

By ferry There are ferry connections with Lávrio (4 weekly; 8hr 30min), Límnos (4 weekly; 1hr 30min) and Kavála

(4 weekly; 5hr). You can also visit from Límnos on one of the overpriced day-trips (2 weekly; €35 return).

ACCOMMODATION AND EATING

Veranda ✆ 6947 050 153. The best of the island's handful of tavernas, near the port, has super-fresh though rather pricey fish and seafood, plus a limited range of salads and starters. June–Sept daily noon–midnight.

Xenonas Aï-Stratis ✆ 22540 93372. The only bona fide pension on the island (otherwise just look for rooms signs) offers cosy and comfortable lodgings on the north side of the village. May–Sept. €45

Límnos

Bucolic **Límnos** is a sizeable agricultural and military island that has become positively trendy of late: there are upscale souvenir shops, old village houses restored by mainlanders as seasonal retreats and music bars during summer at nearly every beach. For all that, the island's remoteness and peculiar ferry schedules protected it until the mid-1990s from most aspects of the holiday trade, and conventional tourism was late in coming because hoteliers lived primarily off the visiting relatives of the numerous soldiers stationed here. Most summer visitors are still Greek, particularly from Thessaloníki, though some Brits and other Europeans now arrive by charter flights.

The island was often the focus of **disputes** between the Greek and Turkish governments, with frequent posturing over invaded airspace, although the detente of recent years has seen such incidences cease. As a result, Límnos' **garrison** of 25,000 soldiers – at the nadir of Greco-Turkish relations during the 1970s and 1980s – is now down to not much over five thousand, and set to fall further with the closure of more bases.

The **bays** of **Bourniá** and **Moúdhros**, the latter one of the largest natural harbours in the Aegean, divide Límnos almost in two. The **west** of the island is dramatically hilly, with abundant basalt put to good use as street cobbles and house masonry. The **east** is low-lying and speckled with seasonal salt marshes where it's not occupied by cattle, combine harvesters and vast corn fields. There are numerous sandy **beaches** around the coast – mostly gently shelving – and it's easy to find a stretch to yourself.

Like most volcanic islands, Límnos produces excellent **wine** – good dry white, rosé and retsina – plus ouzo. The Limnians proudly tout an abundance of **natural food products**, including thyme honey and sheep's cheese, and indeed the population is almost self-sufficient in foodstuffs.

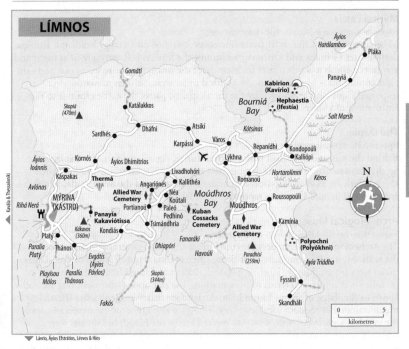

LÍMNOS

Lávrio, Áyios Efstrátios, Lésvos & Híos

ARRIVAL AND DEPARTURE

LÍMNOS

By plane The airport lies 18km east of Mýrina, almost at the geographic centre of the island; a few taxis always linger outside, there being no shuttle bus into town, and cost at least €25. Frequencies below are for June–Oct.

Destinations Athens (1–2 daily; 50min); Híos (2 weekly; 1hr 40min); Ikaría (1 daily; 50min); Lésvos (5 weekly; 40min); Rhodes (4 weekly; 2hr 15min–3hr); Sámos (2 weekly; 1hr 55min–2hr 30min); Thessaloníki (9 weekly; 40min).

By ferry Límnos is on two ferry routes, the one from Lávrio to Kavála and from the northern mainland ports down through the eastern Aegean.

Destinations Áyios Efstrátios (4 weekly; 1hr 30min); Híos (2–3 weekly; 8hr 15min–12hr 30min); Ikaría (2 weekly; 14hr); Kavála (6 weekly; 4hr–4hr 30min); Lávrio (4 weekly; 9hr 30min); Lésvos (3 weekly; 6hr 30min); Sámos (2–3 weekly; 14–15hr); Thessaloníki (1 weekly; 8hr 30min).

GETTING AROUND

By bus Buses are fairly infrequent on Límnos, with only afternoon departures from Mýrina to many of the more distant villages and 1–2 daily to those nearer the capital.

By car or scooter A vehicle is required for touring; a scooter is quite sufficient for the more touristed western third of the island, although a car is preferable to reach the east of the island.

Mýrina

MÝRINA (aka Kástro), the port-capital on the west coast, has the ethos of a provincial market town rather than of a resort. With about five thousand inhabitants, it's pleasantly low-key, if not especially picturesque, apart from a core neighbourhood of old stone houses dating from the Ottoman era, and the ornate Neoclassical mansions backing **Romeïkós Yialós**, the town's beach-lined esplanade. Shops and amenities are mostly found along Kydhá and its continuation Karatzá – which meanders north from the harbour to Romeïkós Yialós – or Garoufalídhi, its perpendicular offshoot, roughly halfway along.

Mýrina castle
Between the town harbour and Romeïkós Yialós • Unrestricted access

Mýrina's main attraction is its Byzantine **castle**, perched on a craggy headland. Ruinous despite later Genoese and Ottoman additions, the fortress is flatteringly lit at night and warrants a climb towards sunset for views over the town, the entire west coast and – in clear conditions – Mount Áthos, 35 nautical miles west. Skittish miniature deer, imported from Rhodes and fed by the municipality, patrol the castle grounds to the amusement of visitors.

6

The Dápia
In park behind hospital • Unrestricted access

Behind the hospital in a small park is a diminutive, signposted fort, the **Dápia**, built by the Russian Orloff brothers during their abortive 1770 invasion. The fort failed spectacularly in its avowed purpose to besiege and bombard the main castle, as did the entire rebellion, and Ottoman reprisals on the island were severe.

Archeological Museum
Romeïkós Yialós • Tues–Sun 8.30am–3pm • €2 • ☎ 22540 22900

The **Archeological Museum** occupies the former Ottoman governor's mansion on the seafront, not far from the site of Bronze Age **Mýrina**. Finds from all of the island's major sites are assiduously labelled in Greek, Italian and English, and the entire premises is exemplary in terms of presentation. The star upper-storey exhibits are votive lamps in the shape of sirens, found in an Archaic sanctuary at Hephaestia (Ifestía), much imitated in modern local jewellery. There are also numerous representations of the goddess Cybele/Artemis, who was revered across the island; her shrines were typically situated near a fauna-rich river mouth – on Límnos at Avlónas, now inside the grounds of the *Porto Myrina* resort. An entire room is devoted to metalwork, featuring impressive gold jewellery and bronze objects, both practical (cheese graters, door-knockers) and whimsical-naturalistic (a snail, a vulture).

Town beaches

As town beaches go, **Romeïkós Yialós** and **Néa Mádhitos** (ex-Toúrkikos Yialós), its counterpart to the southeast of the harbour, are not bad. **Rihá Nerá**, the next bay north of Romeïkós Yialós, is even better – shallow as the name suggests ("shallow waters") and well attended by families, with watersports on offer.

ARRIVAL AND INFORMATION   MÝRINA

By bus The bus station is on Platía Eleftheríou Venizélou, at the north end of Kydhá.

By ferry The new jetty is on the far side of the bay. The most efficient agency for tickets is Sunflight on Platía Eleftheríou Venizélou (☎ 22540 29571).

By car or motorbike Petrides Travel at Karatzá 118 (☎ 22540 29550, ⓦ petridestravel.gr), which also has a branch at the airport, is the best local company for car rental, while Rent a Moto (☎ 22540 25419), on the north side of town at Leofóros Dhimokratías 89, has good rates on two-wheelers.

Tourist information There is no official tourist office but a useful site is ⓦ limnosisland.gr.

ACCOMMODATION

Apollo Pavilion Frýnis ☎ 22540 23712, ⓦ apollo pavilion.gr. In a peaceful cul-de-sac about halfway along Garoufalídhou, this mock classical hotel offers three-bed a/c studios with TV and mini-kitchen. Most have balconies, with castle or mountain views. **€55**

Arhondiko Cnr of Sakhtoúri and Filellínon, Romeïkós Yialós ☎ 22540 29800, ⓦ arxontikohotel.gr. Límnos' first hotel, this 1851-built mansion has three floors of small-to-medium-sized wood-trimmed rooms with all mod cons but no balconies. There's a pleasant ground-floor bar/breakfast lounge. **€70**

Hotel Lemnos Limáni Mýrinas ☎ 22540 22153, ⓔ lemnos-hotel@yahoo.gr. Standard 1960s-style hotel with average-sized, simply decorated rooms, but the balconies overlooking the fishing harbour and price make it good value. **€35**

Ifestos Ethnikís Andístasis 17, Andhróni ☎22540 24960, ⓦ ifestoshotel.gr. Quiet, professionally run two-star hotel with pleasant common areas. Slightly small rooms have a/c, fridges, balconies and a mix of sea or hill views. Breakfast included. **€60**

EATING AND NIGHTLIFE

Karagiozis Romeïkós Yialós 32, ☎ 22540 24055. The most established watering hole on the island transforms from laidback café by day to buzzing bar by night, which sometimes holds theme parties or hosts live bands. Daily 11am–late.

Kosmos Romeïkós Yialós ☎22540 22050. The most reasonable of the establishments on this popular but mostly overpriced strip offers fresh fish from €45/kilo, a range of mezédhes and glorious sunsets across Mt Áthos. April–Oct daily noon–1am.

★ **O Platanos** Kydhá ☎ 22540 22070. Excellent if rather oily *mayireftá* such as *papoutsáki* for €6–7 and highly quaffable aromatic Limniot wine draw big crowds to the atmospheric little square beneath two plane trees. Daily 11am–6pm, until midnight June–Sept.

Western Límnos

Nearly all the tourist amenities are concentrated in the western third of the island, mostly in and around the coastal stretch between Mýrina and the vast Moúdhros Bay. This area includes many of the best **beaches** and most picturesque inland **villages**.

Coast north of Mýrina

Beyond Mýrina's respectable town beaches, the closest good sand lies 3km north at **Avlónas**, unspoilt except for the local power plant a short way inland. Just beyond, the road splits: the right-hand turning wends its way through **Káspakas**, its north-facing houses in neat tiers and a potable spring on its platía, before plunging down to **Áyios Ioánnis**, also reached directly by the left-hand bypass from the capital. The furthest of its three **beaches** is the most pleasant, a curved cove punctuated by a tiny fishing harbour and offshore islet named Vampire Island.

Thérma

6km northeast of Mýrina • Daily 10am–2pm & 5–9pm • ⓦ thermaspa.gr

The old Ottoman baths at **Thérma**, complete with calligraphic plaques, have been restored as a contemporary health spa, with a range of expensive treatments available – or you can just relax in the outdoor bath (€8), an indoor tub (€10) or the sauna (€20). Unusually for a hot spring, the water is non-sulphurous and is the tastiest on the island, so there is always a knot of cars parked nearby under the trees while their owners fill jerry cans with warm water from a **public fountain**, which has a bilingual Greek/Ottoman Turkish inscription.

Chapel of Panayía Kakaviótissa

3km south of Thérma

Just south of Thérma is the iconic poster image of Límnos: the **chapel of Panayía Kakaviótissa**, tucked into a volcanic cave on the flank of Mt Kákavos (360m). The location is more impressive than the simple collection of icons and brasswork inside.

Sardhés

Some 7km north of Thérma, **SARDHÉS** is the highest village on the island, with wonderfully broody sunsets and a celebrated central taverna. The handsome local houses are typical of mountain villages on Límnos in having an external staircase up to the first floor, as the ground floor was used for animals.

Gomáti

Beyond Sardhés and 5km below Katálakkos lies the spectacular, well-signposted **dune** environment at **Gomáti**, one of the largest such in Greece. There are two zones, reached by separate dirt tracks: one at a river mouth, with a bird-rich marsh, and the other to the northwest, with a beach bar and sunbeds. The latter portion especially is a popular outing.

6

Platý

PLATÝ, 2km southeast of Mýrina, has had its traditional profile somewhat compromised by modern villa construction, but it does have two nocturnal tavernas. The long sandy **beach**, 700m below, is popular, with non-motorized **watersports** available at the south end through Babis, below the *Lemnos Village* complex.

Thános and its beaches

THÁNOS has more architectural character than smaller Platý, 2km southeast. **Paralía Thánou**, 1.5km below, is among the most scenic of southwestern beaches, flanked by volcanic crags and looking out to Áyios Efstrátios island. Beyond Thános, the road curls over to the enormous beach at **Evgátis** (**Áyios Pávlos**), reckoned the island's best, with more igneous pinnacles for definition and Áyios Efstrátios on the horizon.

Kondiás and around

Eleven kilometres east of Mýrina, **KONDIÁS** is the island's third-largest settlement, cradled between hills tufted with Límnos' biggest pine forest. Stone-built, often elaborate houses combine with the setting to make Kondiás an attractive inland village, a fact not lost on the Greeks and foreigners restoring those houses with varying degrees of taste. Cultural interest is lent by two almost adjacent galleries: the imposing **Contemporary Balkan Art Gallery** (Tues–Sun 10am–2pm & 7–9pm; €2; ☎ 22540 51425, ⓦpinakothikikondia.gr), which features works by prominent painters from across the Balkans, especially Bulgarian Svetlin Russev, while Ukrainian artist Ludmilla Christinitz-Papayiannidhou displays her vibrant works in a colourful garden studio. **Tsimándhria**, 2.5km further east, has better dining options.

ACCOMMODATION AND EATING   WESTERN LÍMNOS

COAST NORTH OF MÝRINA

Aï Yiannis At the end of the first beach, Áyios Ioánnis ☎ 22540 61669. Featuring seating in the shade of piled-up volcanic boulders, this modest *psarotavérna* has fresh fish for under €10/portion. June–Aug daily 11am–midnight.

Aliotida Apartments Behind the third beach, Áyios Ioánnis ☎ 22540 24406, ⓦaliotida-apartments.gr. Bright, well-furnished studios with kitchenettes, tastefully designed amid nicely landscaped grounds. May–Sept. **€35**

SARDHÉS

★**Man-Tella** Village centre ☎ 22540 61349. Portions of rural delights such as rabbit *stifádho* and village rooster are huge and cost around €7–8, the local barrelled wine is superb and the location in the vine-trellised courtyard is atmospheric. Daily noon–1am.

PLATÝ

Grigoris Centre of beach ☎ 22540 22715. With its huge shady courtyard within earshot of the waves, this taverna does good four-course meal deals from €10, including tasty roast lamb or grilled fish. April–Oct 10am–1am.

★**O Sozos** Just off the main platía ☎ 22540 25085. Local favourite serving up huge portions of succulent *kondosoúvli* and *kokorétsi*, salads and a few *mayireftá* like *dolmádhes*, all well under €10, as well as good *tsípouro* and local barrelled wine. Daily noon–late.

Studios Magda 100m back from the beach ☎ 22540 25370, ✉ studiosmagdalimnos@hotmail.com. This block of modern studios is well designed, with moderate-sized, comfortable rooms and friendly management. May–Sept. **€35**

★**Villa Afroditi** 200m back from the beach ☎ 22540 23141, ⓦafroditi-villa.gr. With splendid topiary, welcoming owners, pleasant pool bar and mixture of spotless doubles and studios, this is one of the best resorts on Límnos. Free port pick-up and buffet breakfast included. New block of larger apartments available too. Mid-May to early Oct. **€65**

THÁNOS AND ITS BEACHES

Evgatis Hotel Opposite side of main road from beach, Evgátis ☎ 22540 51700. Functional hotel with decent rooms and smarter apartments next door and a full-service taverna serving home-cooked food. May–Oct. **€35**

Petradi Studios East end of beach, Paralía Thánou ☎ 22540 29905, ⓦ petradistudios.gr. Modern but tastefully designed two-storey building, warm ochre in colour, with spacious and comfortable rooms. There's a pleasant, relaxed beach bar on the premises. May–Sept. **€30**

Yiannakaros Centre of beach, Paralía Thánou ☎ 22540 22787. Reliable taverna that covers all the bases, with simple fish and some meat dishes for €6–8 and a fair range of starters and salads. May to late Sept daily noon–midnight.

KONDIÁS AND AROUND
O Hristos (aka Iy Kali Kardhia) Central square, Tsimándhria ☎22540 51278. Old-favourite taverna that dishes up cheap, salubrious grills and a few seafood dishes for €5–8, plus great dips, salads and wine. Daily 10am–midnight.

Eastern Límnos

The shores of **Moúdhros Bay**, glimpsed south of the trans-island road, are muddy and best avoided by serious bathers. The bay itself enjoyed strategic importance during World War I, culminating in Allied acceptance of the Ottoman surrender aboard the anchored British warship HMS *Agamemnon* on October 30, 1918. The huge chunk of Límnos east of the bay is little visited but offers some deserted **beaches** and interesting reminders of the island's recent and more distant past.

Moúdhros

MOÚDHROS, the second-largest town on Límnos, is rather a dreary place, with only the wonderfully kitsch, two-belfried **Evangelismós church** to recommend it. The closest decent beaches are at **Havoúli**, 4km south by dirt track, and **Fanaráki**, 4km west, but both have muddy sand and don't really face the open sea. Until recently Moúdhros was quite literally a God-forsaken place, owing to an incident late in Ottoman rule. Certain locals killed some Muslims and threw them down a well on property belonging to the Athonite monastery of Koutloumousioú; the Ottoman authorities, holding the monks responsible, slaughtered any Koutloumousiot brethren they found on the island and set the local monastery alight. Two monks managed to escape to Áthos, where every August 23 until 2000 a curse was chanted, condemning Moúdhros's inhabitants to "never sleep again".

Polyochni (Polyókhni) and around

Traces of the most advanced Neolithic Aegean civilization have been unearthed at **Polyochni (Polyókhni)**, 10km east of Moúdhros, on a bluff overlooking a long, narrow beach. Since 1930, Italian excavations have uncovered five layers of settlement, the oldest from late in the fourth millennium BC, predating Troy on the Turkish coast opposite. The town met a sudden, violent end from war or earthquake in about 2100 BC. The **ruins** at the site (Tues–Sun 8am–3pm; free; ☎22540 91249) are well labelled but mostly of specialist interest, though a small, well-presented **museum** behind the entrance helps bring the place to life.

The only really decent beach in the area is **Ayía Triádha**, accessed off the Polyókhni road, with blonde sand heaped in dunes.

Kótsinas

Some 10km north of Moúdhros, reached via Repanídhri, is the hard-packed beach at **KÓTSINAS**, which is set in the protected western limb of Bourniá Bay. The nearby anchorage offers two busy, seafood-strong tavernas. On a knoll overlooking the jetty stands a corroded, sword-brandishing statue of **Maroula**, a Genoese-era heroine who briefly delayed the Ottoman conquest, and a large church of **Zoödhóhou Piyís** ("the Life-Giving Spring"), where you can see intriguing kitsch icons, a vaulted wooden ceiling and antique floor tiles. Out front, 63 steps lead down through an illuminated tunnel in the rock to the potable (if slightly mineral) spring in question, oozing into a cool, vaulted chamber.

Kerós beach

Kalliópi, 8km northeast of Moúdhros via attractive Kondopoúli, is a pleasant little village, giving direct access to **Kéros beach**, a 1.5km stretch of sand with dunes and a small pine grove, plus shallow water. It remains popular despite being exposed and often dirty, and attracts plenty of windsurfers and foreigners with campervans.

6

THE WAR CEMETERIES

About 800m along the Roussopoúli road from Moúdhros is an unlocked **Allied military cemetery** maintained by the Commonwealth War Graves Commission, its neat lawns and rows of white headstones incongruous in such parched surroundings. During 1915, Moúdhros Bay was the principal staging area for the disastrous Gallipoli campaign. Of approximately 36,000 Allied dead, 887 are buried here – mainly battle casualties, who died after having been evacuated to the base hospital at Moúdhros. Though the deceased are mostly British, there is also a French cenotaph, and – speaking volumes about imperial sociology – a mass "Musalman" grave for Egyptian and Indian troops in one corner, with a Koranic inscription.

There are more graves at another immaculately maintained cemetery behind the hilltop church in **Portianoú**, a little over 1km from the west side of Moúdhros Bay. Among the 348 buried here are two Canadian nurses, three Egyptian labourers and three Maori soldiers. East of Portianoú and Paleó Pedhinó, signposted on a headland, lies the last and strangest of Límnos' military cemeteries: about forty 1920–21 graves of **Kuban Cossacks**, White Army refugees from the Russian civil war.

Hephaestia

4.5km from Kondopoúli • Tues–Sun 8am–3pm • Free

Reached via a rough, signposted track from Kondopoúli, the ancient site of **Hephaestia** (present-day Ifestía) offers an admirably reconstructed **theatre** overlooking its former harbour. The name comes from the god Hephaestos, rescued and revered by the ancient Limnians after he crash-landed on the island, hurled from Mt Olympos by Hera.

Kabirion

4km north of main road to Pláka • Tues–Sun 8am–3pm • Free

More evocative than Hephaesia is **Kabirion**, also signposted as "Kabeiroi" (modern Kavírion), on the opposite shore of Tigáni Bay and accessed by a paved road. The **ruins** are of a sanctuary connected with the cult of the Samothracian Kabiroi (see box, p.412), though the site here is probably older. Little survives other than eleven column stumps staking out a *stoa*, behind the *telestirio* or shrine where the cult mysteries took place. A nearby **sea grotto** has been identified as the Homeric Spiliá toú Filoktíti, where Trojan war hero Philoktetes was abandoned by his comrades-in-arms until his stinking, gangrenous leg had healed by application of *límnia yí*, a poultice of volcanic mud still prized on the island. Access to the cave is via steps leading down from the caretaker's shelter, though final access through the narrower of the two entrances involves some wading.

ACCOMMODATION AND EATING   **EASTERN LÍMNOS**

Keros Village end of Kéros beach road, Kalliópi ☎ 22540 41059. One of the few accommodation options in the far east of Límnos, this place has a small garden restaurant. Pleasant rooms with balconies but very remote.

June to mid-Sept. **€30**

To Mourayio Kótsinas ☎ 22540 41065. Easily the best of the three tavernas here, serving well-executed fish, meat and veg dishes for €7–9. Daily noon–midnight.

Samothráki

SAMOTHRÁKI (Samothrace) has one of the most dramatic profiles of all the Greek islands, second only to Thíra (Santorini): its dark mass of granite rises abruptly from the sea, culminating in the 1611m **Mount Fengári**. Seafarers have always been guided by its imposing outline, clearly visible from the mainland, and its summit provided a vantage point for Poseidon to watch over the siege of Troy. Landing is subject to the notoriously unpredictable weather, but that did not deter pilgrims who, for hundreds of years in antiquity, journeyed to the island to visit the **Sanctuary of the Great Gods** and were initiated into its mysteries. The sanctuary remains the main archeological attraction of the island, which, too remote for most tourists, combines earthy simplicity with natural grandeur. The tourist season is relatively short – essentially (late) July and August – but you will find some facilities open as early as Easter and one or two all year round.

Kamariótissa

Ferries dock at the dull village of **KAMARIÓTISSA**. While you're unlikely to want to spend much time here, it does make a convenient base, as some of Samothráki's best hotels lie along or just behind the tree-lined seafront and various rooms for rent can be found in the maze of streets behind; unlike most places these days, owners often meet incoming vessels.

Hóra

HÓRA, also known as **Samothráki**, is the island's capital. Far larger than the portion visible from out at sea would suggest, it's an attractive town of Thracian-style stone houses, some whitewashed, clustered around a hollow in the western flanks of Mount Fengári. It is dominated by the Genoese **Gateluzzi fort**, of which little survives other than the gateway. Half an hour or so can be whiled away at the charming **Folklore Museum** (late May to late Sept daily 9am–2pm & 6–10pm; €1; ☎22510 41227), which contains a motley collection of clothing, domestic items and miscellany.

The Sanctuary of the Great Gods

Paleópoli, 6km northeast from Kamariótissa and 3km directly north from Hóra • Daily 8.30am–3pm; museum Tues–Sun only • €3 combined ticket • ☎ 22510 41474

Hidden in a stony but thickly wooded ravine between the tiny hamlet of **Paleópoli** and the plunging northwestern ridge of Mount Fengári lie the remains of the **Sanctuary of the Great Gods**. From the late Bronze Age (around the eighth century BC) until the early Byzantine era (fifth century AD), the mysteries and sacrifices of the cult of the Great Gods (see box, p.412) were performed on Samothráki, in ancient Thracian, until the second century BC. Little is known of this dialect except that it was a very old

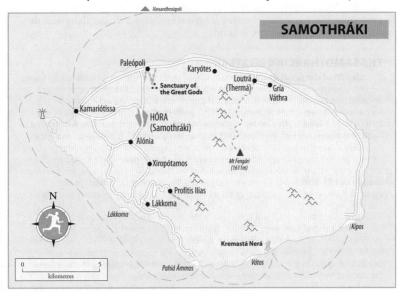

Indo-European tongue, related to and eventually replaced by ancient Greek. The spiritual focus of the northern Aegean, the importance of the island's rituals was second only to the Mysteries of Eleusis in all the ancient world. The well-labelled site strongly evokes its proud past while commanding views of the mountains and the sea.

Archeological Museum

For an explanatory introduction, it is best first to visit the **Archeological Museum**, whose exhibits span all eras of habitation, from the Archaic to the Byzantine. Highlights include a frieze of dancing girls from the propylaion of the Temenos, entablatures from different buildings, and Roman votive offerings such as coloured glass vials from the necropolis of the ancient town east of the sanctuary. You can also see a reproduction of the exquisitely sculpted marble statue, the *Winged Victory of Samothrace*, which once stood breasting the wind at the prow of a marble ship in the Nymphaeum. Discovered in 1863 by a French diplomat to the Sublime Porte, it was carried off to the Louvre, where it remains a major draw.

The Anaktoron and Arsinoeion

The **Anaktoron**, or hall of initiation for the first level of the mysteries, dates in its present form from Roman times. Its inner sanctum was marked by a warning stele, now in the museum, and at the southeast corner you can make out the **Priestly Quarters**, an antechamber where candidates for initiation donned white gowns. Next to it is the **Arsinoeion**, the largest circular ancient building known in Greece, used for libations and sacrifices. Within its rotunda are the fourth-century BC walls of a double precinct where a rock altar, the earliest preserved ruin on the site, has been uncovered.

The Temenos and Hieron

A little further south, on the same side of the path, you come to the **Temenos**, a rectangular area open to the sky where the feasting probably took place, and, edging its rear corner, the conspicuous **Hieron**, the site's most immediately impressive structure. Five columns and an architrave of the facade of this large Doric edifice, which hosted the higher level of initiation, have been re-erected; dating in part from the fourth century BC, it was heavily restored in Roman times. The stone steps have been replaced by modern blocks, but Roman benches for spectators remain *in situ*, along with the sacred stones where confession was heard.

THE SAMOTHRACIAN MYSTERIES

The **religion of the Great Gods** revolved around a hierarchy of ancient Thracian fertility figures: the Great Mother Axieros; a subordinate male deity known as Kadmilos; and the potent and ominous twin demons the Kabiroi, originally the local heroes Dardanos and Aeton. When the Aeolian colonists arrived (traditionally c.700 BC) they simply merged the resident deities with their own – the Great Mother became Cybele, while her consort Hermes and the Kabiroi were fused interchangeably with the *Dioskouroi* Castor and Pollux, patrons of seafarers. Around the nucleus of a sacred precinct the newcomers made the beginnings of what is now the sanctuary.

Despite their long observance, the mysteries of the cult were never explicitly recorded, since ancient writers feared incurring the wrath of the Kabiroi (who could reputedly brew up sudden, deadly storms), but it has been established that two levels of **initiation** were involved. Both ceremonies, in direct opposition to the elitism of Eleusis, were open to all, including women and slaves. The lower level of initiation, or *myesis*, may, as is speculated at Eleusis, have involved a ritual simulation of the life, death and rebirth cycle; in any case, it's known that it ended with joyous feasting, and it can be conjectured, since so many clay torches have been found, that it took place at night. The higher level of initiation, or *epopteia*, carried the unusual requirement of a moral standard – the connection of theology with morality, so strong in the later Judeo-Christian tradition, was rarely made by the early Greeks. This second level involved a full confession followed by absolution and baptism in bull's blood.

The Nymphaeum (Fountain) of Nike and around

To the west of the path you can just discern the outline of the **theatre**, while just above it, tucked under the ridge, is the **Nymphaeum (Fountain) of Nike**, over which the *Winged Victory* used to preside. West of the theatre, occupying a high terrace, are remains of the main **stoa**; immediately north of this is an elaborate medieval fortification made entirely of antique material.

Loutrá and the far east

With its running streams, giant plane trees and namesake hot springs, **LOUTRÁ** (aka **Thermá**), 6km east of Paleópoli, is a pleasant enough place to stay, although in late July and August it gets packed, mainly with an incongruous mixture of foreign hippies and elderly Greeks, here to take the sulphurous waters. Far more appealing than the grim **baths** themselves (June–Oct daily 7–10.45am & 4–7.45pm; €3; ☎ 22510 98229) are the low waterfalls and rock pools of **Gría Váthra**, which are signposted 1.5km up the paved side road leading east from the main Thermá access drive. Loutrá is ghostly quiet for most of the year and its miniature harbour, built as an alternative to Kamariótissa, is never used at all.

Beaches on Samothráki's north shore are mostly clean but uniformly pebbly and exposed. Some 15km from Loutrá along a corniche road that deteriorates noticeably towards the end is **Kípos beach**, a long strand facing the Turkish island of Gökçeada (Ímvros to the Greeks) and backed by open pasture and picturesque crags. The water is clean and there's a rock overhang for shelter at one end, plus a spring but no other facilities.

The south coast

The warmer south flank of the island, its fertile farmland dotted with olive groves, boasts fine views out to sea – as far as Gökçeada on a clear day. On the way south, beyond sleepy **Lákkoma**, the attractive hill village of **Profítis Ilías** is worth the brief detour.

From Lákkoma itself, it's less than 2km down to the eponymous **beach**. A further 6km east lies **Pahiá Ámmos**, a long, clean beach with a solitary taverna for sustenance, which does good business with the big summer crowds who also arrive by excursion *kaïkia*. These continue east to **Vátos**, a secluded nudist beach, the **Kremastá Nerá** coastal waterfalls and finally round to Kípos beach (see above).

ARRIVAL AND GETTING AROUND SAMOTHRÁKI

By ferry The only current connection with Samothráki is the ferry from Alexandhroúpoli (2hr 30min; ☎ 25510 38503, ⓦ saos.gr); frequency varies from 2–3 daily in July & Aug to 4–5 weekly in winter.

By kaïki In peak season 1–2 daily excursions run from Kamariótissa to the south-coast beaches. There is also an anticlockwise boat trip round the island from the dock at Loutrá (mid-July to early Sept daily noon–6pm; €20; ☎ 6974 062 054).

By bus There are plenty of buses from Kamariótissa along the north coast to Loutrá (6–7 daily; 20min) and

inland to Hóra (5–6 daily; 10min) in season, though far fewer in winter.

By car or motorbike You can only get to the south and far east of the island with your own transport. The best places to rent wheels are Niki Tours (☎ 25510 41465, ⓔ niki_tours@hotmail.com) and Kyrkos car rental (☎ 25510 41628, ⓔ akis1kirkos@gmail.com), both on the seafront at Kamariótissa; best book in advance in high season, as supply is short. The only fuelling station on the entire island is 1km above the port, en route to Hóra.

ACCOMMODATION AND EATING

KAMARIÓTISSA

Aeolos Behind northeastern seafront ☎ 25510 41595, ⓦ hotelaiolos.gr. Reasonably well-maintained hotel with a large pool and quiet, spacious rooms. There are good half-board deals in the low season. June–Sept. **€40**

Iy Klimataria Towards northeast end of seafront ☎ 25510 41535. With a huge summer terrace, this enduring taverna serves dishes like fried aubergines, oven-baked goat and *soutsoukákia*, all well under €10, plus palatable barrelled wine. June–Sept daily noon–2am.

6

CLIMBING THE MOON

Loutrá is the prime base for the tough six-hour **climb** up the 1611m **Mount Fengári** (known to the ancients as **Sáos**, a name found on some maps to this day), the highest peak in the Aegean islands; the **path** starts at the top of the village, beside a concrete water tank and a huge plane tree. Tell your accommodation proprietors that you're going. Fengári is Greek for "**moon**" and, according to legend, if you reach the top on the night of a full moon your wish will come true – most of those foolhardy enough to attempt this will just hope to get back down safely.

Niki Beach Hotel 500m northeast of centre ⊤25510 41545, Ⓦnikibeach.gr. Newest and smartest hotel near the port, right on the coast, with swish lobby, stylishly furnished rooms, plus a pool and bar. May–Oct. €50

HÓRA

★**1900** ⊤25510 41222. Boasting a lovely vine-shaded terrace with stunning views of the kástro and the valley below, this friendly taverna serves stuffed goat for €8 and spicy aubergines. Mid-May to mid-Sept daily noon–1am.

THE SANCTUARY OF THE GREAT GODS

Samothraki Village Paleópoli ⊤25510 42300, Ⓦsamothrakivillage.gr. Smart new resort, handily placed for the Sanctuary of the Great Gods, with manicured grounds, neatly furnished rooms, two pools and a bar-restaurant. €50

LOUTRÁ AND THE FAR EAST

Camping Voradhes 3km east of the village ⊤25510 98258. The island's prime municipal campsite has hot-water showers, electricity, a minimarket, restaurant and bar. July & Aug. €11

O Paradhisos Village centre ⊤6975 775 997. This place has the advantage of the village's best location, up under the plane trees. The traditional cuisine for €8 or less and barrelled wine also hit the spot. Mid-May to mid-Sept daily noon–1am.

Parselia Studios Northwest edge of village ⊤25510 98318, Ⓦsamothraki-studios.gr. Attractive rustic studios in a peaceful wooded setting. Each cosy unit has its own yard or balcony. May–Sept. €30

★**To Perivoli T'Ouranou** On the lane to Gría Váthra ⊤25510 98313. "Heaven's Orchard" aptly describes this leafy taverna. Various dips, types of *saganáki* and €7–8 spaghetti dishes supplement the usual grills and salads. Regular live traditional music. June to mid-Oct daily 11am–2am.

THE SOUTH COAST

Delfini West end of beach, Pahiá Ámmos ⊤25510 94235. Classic taverna-cum-rooms enterprise, whose rooms are fairly basic but habitable enough. The taverna is a friendly hangout with a decent range of staples for well under €10. May–Sept. €25

Paradisos Profítis Ilías ⊤25510 95267. Atmospheric rustic taverna, with a lovely terrace facing sunsets over Thássos. The house speciality is a selection of meats such as lamb, goat and *kondosoúvli* roast on the spit for €7–8, accompanied by fiery *tsípouro* or soothing wine. June to mid-Sept daily 10am–2am.

To Akroyiali Lákkoma beach ⊤25510 95123. Simple but clean rooms with sea-view balconies are available above a friendly taverna, which serves fresh fish from €35/kilo, some meat and a standard menu of mezédhes and salads. June–Sept. €30

Thássos

Just 12km from the mainland, **Thássos** has long been a popular resort island for northern Greeks, and since the early 1990s has also attracted a cosmopolitan mix of tourists, particularly Germans and Scandinavians on packages, as well as an increasing number of people from eastern Europe. They are all entertained by vast numbers of *bouzoúkia* (music halls) and music tavernas, while nature-lovers can find some areas of outstanding beauty, especially inland. Moreover, the island's traditional industries have managed to survive the onslaught of modernity. The elite of Thássos still make a substantial living from the pure-white **marble** that constitutes two-thirds of the landmass, found only here and quarried at dozens of sites in the hills between Liménas and Panayía. Olives, especially the oil, honey, nuts and fruit (often sold candied) are also important products. The spirit *tsípouro*, rather than wine, is the main local tipple; pear extract, onions or spices like cinnamon and anise are added to home-made batches.

Brief history

Inhabited since the Stone Age, Thássos was settled by Parians in the seventh century BC, attracted by **gold** deposits between modern Limónas and Kínyra. Buoyed by revenues from these, and from **silver** mines under Thassian control on the mainland opposite, the ancient city-state here became the seat of a medium-sized seafaring empire. Commercial acumen did not spell military invincibility, however; the Persians under Darius swept the Thassian fleets from the seas in 492 BC, and in 462 BC Athens permanently deprived Thássos of its autonomy after a three-year siege. The main port continued to thrive into Roman times, but lapsed into Byzantine and medieval obscurity.

6

ARRIVAL AND GETTING AROUND   THÁSSOS

By ferry/hydrofoil Kavála-based ferries (2–5 daily; 1hr 15min) arrive at Skála Prínou, in the northwest of the island. Ferries to the island capital, Limónas (8–12 daily; 40min), leave from Keramotí on the mainland opposite.

By bus The service is fairly good, with frequent buses from Limónas to Panayía and Skála Potamiás (6–8 daily;

15–20min), Limenária (6 daily; 45min), Theológos (5 daily; 1hr) and Alykí (3 daily; 30min).

By car or motorbike Thássos is small enough to circumnavigate in one full day by rented motorbike or car. Car rental is offered by the major international chains and local Potos Car Rentals (☎ 25930 23969, ⊕ rentacarpotos.gr),

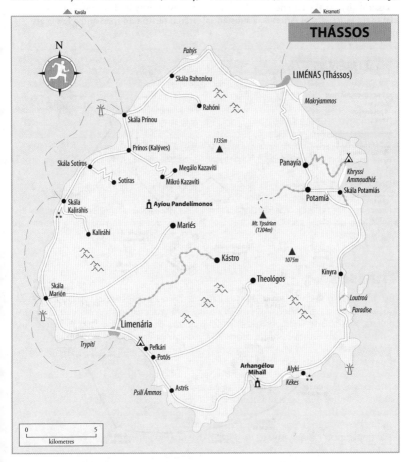

with seven branches around the island; try bargaining in the shoulder seasons.

Water-taxi In peak season there are 2 daily services from Liménas to Khryssí Ammoudhía via intermediate coves.

Liménas

Largely modern **LIMÉNAS** (also signposted as Limín or Thássos) is the island's capital, though not the only port. Although it's often plagued with surprisingly clogged traffic, it is partly redeemed by its picturesque fishing harbour and the impressive remains of the **ancient city**. Thanks to its mineral wealth and safe harbour, ancient Thássos prospered from Classical to Roman times. There are substantial remains which appear above and below the streets, plus a fine archeological museum. Thássos hosts a **summer festival** (ⓦthassos -festival.gr), with performances of anything from jazz to comedy at the Hellenistic theatre.

The agora

Just back from fishing harbour • Unrestricted access

The largest excavated area is the **agora**; the grassy site is fenced but not usually locked, and is most enjoyably seen towards dusk. Two Roman *stoas* are prominent, but you can also make out shops, monuments, passageways and sanctuaries from the remodelled Classical city. At the far end, a fifth-century BC passageway leads through to an elaborate sanctuary of Artemis, a substantial stretch of Roman road and a few seats of the *odeion*.

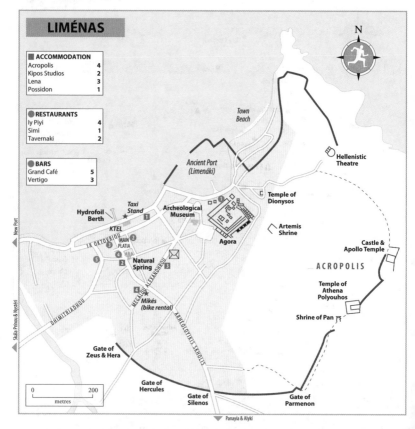

LIMÉNAS

N

ACCOMMODATION
Acropolis	4
Kipos Studios	2
Lena	3
Possidon	1

RESTAURANTS
Iy Piyi	4
Simi	1
Tavernaki	2

BARS
| Grand Café | 5 |
| Vertigo | 3 |

Town Beach

Ancient Port (Limenáki)

Hellenistic Theatre

Temple of Dionysos

Hydrofoil Berth

Taxi Stand

Archeological Museum

Artemis Shrine

KTEL

18 OKTOVRIOU MAIN PLATIA

Agora

Castle & Apollo Temple

Natural Spring

MEGALOU ALEXANDROU

ARHEOLOYIKIS SKROLIS

ACROPOLIS

Temple of Athena Polyouhos

Mikés (bike rental)

Shrine of Pan

DHIMITRIADHROU

New Port

Skála Prínou & Nystéri

Gate of Zeus & Hera

Gate of Hercules

Gate of Silenos

Gate of Parmenon

0   200
metres

Panayía & Alykí

Archeological Museum

Next to agora • Tues–Sun 8.30am–3pm • €2 • ☎ 25930 22180

The renovated **Archeological Museum**, close to the agora, contains small but absorbing displays on prehistoric finds, archeological methods and ancient games. Pride of place goes to the 4m-tall, seventh-century BC *kouros* carrying a ram, found on the acropolis. The courtyard contains some impressive sarcophagi and statuary.

Other ancient remains

From a **temple of Dionysos** behind the fishing port, a path curls up to a **Hellenistic theatre**, fabulously positioned above a broad sweep of sea. Sadly, it's only open for performances of the summer festival. From just before the theatre, the trail winds on the right up to the **acropolis**, where a Venetian-Byzantine-Genoese fort arose between the thirteenth and fifteenth centuries, constructed from recycled masonry of an Apollo temple. You can continue, following the remains of a massive circuit of fifth-century walls, to a high terrace supporting the foundations of the **Athena Polyouhos** (Athena Patroness of the City) temple, with Cyclopean walls.

From the temple's southern end, a short path leads to a cavity in the rock outcrop that was a **shrine of Pan**, shown in faint relief playing his pipes. Following the path to the left around the summit brings you to a precipitous rock-hewn stairway with a metal handrail, which provided a discreet escape route to the **Gate of Parmenon**, the only gate in the fortifications to have retained its lintel. From here a track, then a paved lane, descend through the southerly neighbourhoods of the modern town, completing a satisfying one-hour circuit. All of these remains offer unrestricted access.

ARRIVAL AND GETTING AROUND   LIMÉNAS

By bus Buses operate from the KTEL office (☎ 25930 22162), halfway along the seafront.

By ferry Ferries from Keramotí dock towards the west end of the seafront at the New Port.

By taxi The taxi rank is just in front of the KTEL office.

By bike or car Bikes can be rented from Mike's (☎ 25930 71820), opposite the *Acropolis* hotel. Car rental is also available (see p.415).

Services There is no official tourist office. Thassos Tours (☎ 25930 22546, ⓦ thassostours.gr) provide various services.

ACCOMMODATION

Acropolis Arheoloyikís Skholís 59 ☎ 25930 22488, ⓦ acropolis-hotel.com. Occupying a fine traditional house with flagstone floors, comfortable rooms decorated in traditional style and a rear garden-bar. Breakfast included. **€50**

Kipos Studios Cul-de-sac off Arheoloyikís Skholís ☎ 25930 22469, ⓦ kipos.gr. Attractive building with cool lower-ground-floor doubles and galleried apartments holding up to five upstairs, plus a small pool in the garden. Late May–Sept. **€30**

★**Lena** Megálou Aléxandhrou ☎ 25930 22933, ⓔ hotel_lena@hotmail.com. The best-value budget hotel in town, with compact but clean and comfy rooms; run by a welcoming Greek-American family and young British in-law. May–Oct. **€30**

Possidon Central seafront ☎ 25930 22690, ⓦ thassos -possidon.com. Unattractive concrete block which greatly improves inside, with a spacious lobby café and nicely refurbished rooms, decorated in bright hues. **€45**

EATING AND DRINKING

Iy Piyi Southwest corner of main square ☎ 25930 22941. Classic *estiatório* with a small terrace, which is a dependable favourite for meaty *mayireftá* at only €6–7. April–Oct daily 7pm–midnight.

★**Simi** Behind ancient port ☎ 25930 22517, ⓦ thassos restaurant.gr. Recently spruced up with a bright modern interior and pleasant courtyard, this taverna has a full

menu of fish, meat and mezédhes, mostly costing €4–12, along with memorably good wine. Daily noon–1am.

Tavernaki Northeast corner of main square ☎ 25930 23181. Friendly and traditional taverna with tables lining the alley outside, where you can feast on succulent grills and saucy *mayireftá* for under €10, a bit more for most fish. Daily 10am–1am.

NIGHTLIFE

Grand Café Dhimitriádhou ☎ 6948 573 947. Just about the hippest venue in town, with trendy decor and a bohemian vibe, featuring jazz and techno sounds. Quality coffees, cocktails and the odd snack are served. Daily 10am–late.

Vertigo Corner of seafront and Arheoloyikís Skholís ☎6943 097 717. Popular with trendy young Greeks and assorted tourists for its rocking ambience, with touches of

more dance sounds as the evening draws on. Plenty of shots downed every night. Daily 10am–4am.

The east coast

The busy **east coast** between Liménas and Alykí, occupying roughly a third of the clockwise circuit of the island – the logical way to conduct an island tour if you want to maximize the sun's presence on the beaches – contains many of the more attractive coves and best alternative bases to the capital.

Panayía

The first place worthy of a halt southeast from Liménas is **PANAYÍA**, the attractive hillside village overlooking Potamiá Bay. It's a large, thriving place where life revolves around the central square with its huge plane trees, fountain and slate-roofed houses. Up above the village towers the island's highest peak, **Mount Ypsárion**.

Potamiá

POTAMIÁ, much lower than Panayía in the river valley, is far less prepossessing – with modern red tiles instead of slates on the roofs – though it has a lively winter carnival. It also offers the modest **Polygnotos Vayis Museum** (May–Oct Tues–Sat 9.30am–12.30pm & 6–9pm, Sun 10am–12.30pm; €2; ☎25930 61400), devoted to the locally born sculptor; though Vayis emigrated to America when young, he bequeathed most of his works to the Greek state.

Skála Potamiás and Khryssí Ammoudhiá

The road from Potamiá towards the coast is lined with rooms for rent and apartment-type accommodation. A side road some 12km from Liménas takes you down to **SKÁLA POTAMIÁS**, at the southern end of the bay. From the harbourfront a road off to the left brings you to sand dunes extending all the way to the far northern end of the bay.

The north end of Skála Potamiás beach, **Khryssí Ammoudhiá** – often anglicized to "**Golden Beach**" for the benefit of tourists – is quite built-up but is preferable to the southern end in the quality of both sand and sea; it can also be approached by a direct road that spirals for 5km down from Panayía.

Kínyra and its beaches

The dispersed hamlet of **KÍNYRA**, some 24km south of Liménas, marks the start of the burnt zone which overlooks it, though recovery is under way. Although not having much to recommend it per se, Kínyra is convenient for the superior **beaches** of Loutroú (1km south) and partly nudist Paradise (3km along) – officially called Makrýammos Kinýron – both of which can be reached down poorly signposted dirt tracks. The latter ranks as the most scenic of all Thassian beaches.

ACCOMMODATION AND EATING   **THE EAST COAST**

PANAYÍA

★**Hotel Thassos Inn** Tris Piyés district near the Kímisis church ☎25930 61612, ⓦthassosinn.gr. Affording superb views over the rooftops, this hotel's bright yellow walls mirror the colour of the mature carp in its fishpond. The rooms are fine and the terrace cafeteria very relaxing. April–Oct. **€30**

Iy Thea Southeast edge of town en route to Potamiá ☎25930 61265. Excellent *psistariá* with fine views from the terrace, where you can enjoy simple but succulent grills for €6–8 and aromatic local wine. Daily noon–midnight.

SKÁLA POTAMIÁS

Eric's On main road 400m inland ☎25930 61554, ⓦerics.gr. So called after the owner who advertises his resemblance to footballer Eric Cantona widely. The rooms and studios are spotless, and there are Premiership matches on satellite TV and a swimming pool with bar. **€40**

Hera Just inland from far south end of beach ☎25930 61467, ⓦhotel-hera.gr. This four-storey cream-coloured building contains neat rooms and larger studios, set behind a small, well-tended garden. June–Sept. **€45**

Theagenis On harbour ☎ 25930 61481. Popular local taverna by the fishing harbour, which serves some oven-baked meat and veg dishes, grilled meat and fish, all under €10, plus decent wine. May–Oct daily 10am–midnight.

KHRYSSÍ AMMOUDHIÁ

Camping Golden Beach On beach ☎ 25930 61472, ⓦ camping-goldenbeach.gr. The only official campsite on this side of the island has plenty of shaded pitches, clean baths and laundry facilities and a minimarket. May to mid-Oct. **€12.70**

Enavlion On main road ☎ 25930 58222, ⓦ enavlionhotel .com. Cream-and-pastel-blue mock-Classical hotel, somewhat resembling a wedding cake. Still, the rooms are luxurious, with all mod cons. Breakfast included. Late April–Sept. **€65**

Golden Sand On beach ☎ 25930 61771, ⓦ hotel -goldensand.gr. Backing onto the sand after which it is named, this mid-sized resort hotel has smart rooms, most with sea-facing balconies, and a café-bar. April–Oct. **€55**

Sotiris On beach ☎ 25930 61478. Best of the tavernas dotted along the strand, serving a large selection of mezédhes such as crab salad and small cheese pies for €3–5, plus more substantial grilled fish and meat courses. May–Sept daily noon–1am.

KÍNYRA AND ITS BEACHES

Agorastos On main road behind village ☎ 25930 41225, ⓦ agorastos-thassos.gr. Colourful pension with a leafy terraced garden and cosy, well-furnished rooms, plus a small on-site taverna. April–Oct. **€30**

Paradise Beach South of Kínyra ☎ 25930 41248. Pleasant daytime restaurant on the eponymous beach, serving filling breakfasts, good coffee and a full menu with meat dishes for €8–12. May–Oct daily 8am–10pm.

Studios Niki 3km south of Kínyra ☎ 25930 25930, ⓦ studios-niki.gr. Sparking white building just below the main road, whose smart rooms have balconies overlooking Paradise beach. May–Sept. **€35**

Southern Thássos

The south-facing coast of Thássos has the balance of the island's best beaches, starting with the prettiest resort, in the shape of **Alykí**. In the southwest corner, by way of contrast, **Limenária** is rather dull and functional, although its greater local population means it has more authentic dining choices.

Alykí and around

ALYKÍ hamlet, 35km from Liménas and just below the main road, faces a perfect double bay which almost pinches off a headland. Uniquely, it retains its original whitewashed, slate-roofed architecture, since the presence of extensive antiquities here has led to a ban on any modern construction. Those **ruins** include an ancient temple to an unknown deity, and two exquisite early Christian basilicas out on the headland, with a few columns re-erected.

Of the **beaches**, the sand-and-pebble west bay gets oversubscribed in peak season, though you can always head off to the less crowded, rocky east cove, or snorkel in the crystal-clear waters off the marble formations on the headland's far side. Alternatively, head for secluded **Kékes** beach, in a pine grove 1km further southwest.

Convent of Arhangélou Miháïl

5km southwest of Alykí • Open during daylight hours

The **convent of Arhangélou Miháïl** clings spectacularly to a cliff on the seaward side of the road. Though founded in the twelfth century above the spot where a spring had gushed forth, the convent has been hideously renovated by the nuns, resident here since 1974. A dependency of Filothéou on Mount Áthos, its prize relic is a purported nail from the Crucifixion.

Potós and around

Just 1km west of the island's southern tip is a good but crowded beach, **Psilí Ámmos**, with watersports on offer. A few kilometres further, **POTÓS** is the island's prime German-speaking package venue, its centre claustrophobically dense, with the few non-block-booked rooms overlooking cramped alleys. Although the kilometre-long beach is decent enough, there is little to warrant lingering here. **Pefkári**, with its manicured beach and namesake pine grove, 1km west, is essentially an annexe of Potós, with a few mid-range places to stay and better eating options.

Limenária and around

LIMENÁRIA, the island's second town, was built to house German mining executives brought in by the Ottomans between 1890 and 1905. Their remaining mansions, scattered on the slopes above the harbour, lend some character, but despite attempts at embellishing the waterfront, it's not the most attractive place on Thássos.

The nearest good beach is **Trypití**, a couple of kilometres west – turn left into the pines at the start of a curve right. The broad, 800m-long strand is rather marred by the massed ranks of umbrellas and sun loungers for rent. The cleft to which the name refers (literally "pierced" in Greek) is a slender tunnel through the headland at the west end of the beach, leading to a tiny three-boat anchorage.

ACCOMMODATION AND EATING   SOUTHERN THÁSSOS

ALYKÍ AND AROUND

Beautiful Alice Village centre ☎ 25930 31574. The oldest taverna in the village, with a lovely terrace, where you can choose from a bewildering array of reasonably priced seafood and fish, including sardines cooked in four different ways for €7–9. May–Oct daily 11am–1am.

Skidhia On Kékes beach, 3km south of Alykí ☎ 25930 31528, ⓦ kekesbeach.gr. This traditional seaside taverna, which serves good seafood and grills, has a set of simple but adequate bungalow-style rooms. May–Sept 9am–midnight. **€30**

POTÓS AND AROUND

Camping Pefkari Beach Pefkári ☎ 25930 51190, ⓦ camping-pefkari.gr. With its attractive wooded location and clean facilities, this is undoubtedly the best campsite on Thássos. May–Sept. **€13**

Thassos Pefkári ☎ 25930 51596, ⓦ hotel-thassos.gr. Accomplished resort hotel just behind the beach with refreshingly colourful and contemporary decor, from its spacious lobby to the well-appointed rooms. Pool, tennis

and watersports available too. Breakfast included. **€60**

LIMENÁRIA AND AROUND

Mouragio On seafront ☎ 25930 51178. The most authentic of the seafront tavernas, serving a mixture of tasty oven-baked items for €5–7 and grilled meat or fish, while its *Street Café* behind is a colourful hangout. Mid-April to mid-Oct daily noon–1am.

Must On seafront ☎ 25930 34795. Hip bar with imaginative decorations and a surprisingly cutting-edge line in both rock and dance sounds, plus the usual battery of beers and spirits. May–Sept daily noon–late.

Sgouridis One block back from seafront ☎ 25930 51241, ⓦ hotelsgouridis.gr. This artfully refurbished hotel, with vines creeping up the exterior, has nicely furnished if rather cramped rooms. April to mid-Oct. **€35**

★ **To Limani** On harbour ☎ 25930 52790. This old-style *tsipourádhiko* is the preferred gathering place for the savvy locals, who accompany the fiery spirit with freshly caught fish from the adjacent sea (from €8 per portion). Daily 11am–midnight.

The west coast

The **western coast**, between Limenária and Liménas, is Thassós' most exposed and scenically least impressive, and the various *skáles* (harbours) such as Skála Kaliráhis and Skála Sotíros – originally the ports for namesake inland villages – are bleak, straggly and windy. **SKÁLA MARIÓN**, 13km from Limenária, is the exception: an attractive little bay, with fishing boats hauled up on the sandy foreshore, and the admittedly modern low-rise village arrayed in a U-shape all around with two fine **beaches** on either side.

SKÁLA PRÍNOU has little to recommend it, other than ferry connections to Kavála. **SKÁLA RAHONÍOU**, between here and Liménas, has a smattering of facilities, as well as proximity to **Pahýs beach**, 9km short of Liménas, by far the best strand on the northwest coast. Narrow dirt tracks lead past various tavernas through surviving pines to the sand, partly shaded in the morning.

ACCOMMODATION AND EATING   THE WEST COAST

Brian's Restaurant 500m east of the port, Skála Prínou ☎ 25930 71445. Located in a huge new building, this all-round taverna does daily specials for €8–10 and a wide standard menu. It also hosts

live music every Sat night in season. May–Sept daily 10am–1am.

★ **Pefkospilia** Pahýs beach, Skála Rahoníou ☎ 25930 81051. One of the oldest and most picturesque tavernas on the island, where great traditional cuisine costs well under €10 and is served outside the tiny whitewashed building, almost hidden by firs, as the name ("Fir cave") suggests. May–Sept daily noon–1am.

Pension Dimitris On hilltop behind port, Skála Maríon ☎ 6944 505 064, ⓦ pension-dimitris.gr. Attractively designed modern building offering smart rooms, a communal kitchen and optional breakfast for a small extra charge. May to mid-Oct. €30

Ploumis On beach, Skála Rahoníou ☎ 25930 81442. This café-taverna provides everything from breakfast through light snacks to full-blown meals of freshly grilled fish, seafood and meat for around €10. Good for sunsets especially. May to mid-Oct daily 9am–midnight.

6

The interior

Few people get around to exploring inland Thássos – with the post-fire scrub still struggling to revive, it's not always rewarding – but there are several worthwhile excursions to or around the **hill villages**, which, as usual, portray a very different lifestyle to the coastal resorts.

Theológos

THEOLÓGOS, 10km along a well-surfaced but poorly signposted road from Potós, was founded in the sixteenth century by refugees from Constantinople and became the island's capital under the Ottomans. Its houses, most with oversized chimneys and slate roofs, straggle in long tiers to either side of the main street, surrounded by generous kitchen gardens or walled courtyards. A stroll along the single high street, with its couple of *kafenía*, a soldiers' bar, a sandal-maker and traditional bakery, is rewarding.

Kástro

KÁSTRO is the most naturally protected of the island's anti-pirate redoubts: thirty ancient houses and a church surround a rocky pinnacle, fortified by the Byzantines and the Genoese, which has a sheer drop on three sides. Summer occupation by shepherds is becoming the norm after total abandonment in the nineteenth century, when mining jobs at Limenária proved irresistible. Despite its proximity to Theológos as the crow flies, there's no straightforward route to it; especially with a car, it's best to descend to Potós before heading up a rough, 17km dirt track from Limenária.

Sotíras

SOTÍRAS, a steep 3.5km up from Skála Sotíros, is the only interior village with an unobstructed view of sunset over the Aegean, and is thus popular with foreigners, who've bought up about half of the houses for restoration. On the ridge opposite are exploratory shafts left by the miners, whose ruined lodge looms above the church.

The Kazavíti villages

From Prínos (Kalýves) on the coast road, it's a 6km journey inland to the **Kazavíti villages**, which are shrouded in greenery that escaped the fires; they're signposted, albeit poorly, and mapped officially as Megálo and Mikró Prínos but still universally known by their Ottoman name. **MIKRÓ KAZAVÍTI** marks the start of the track for **MEGÁLO KAZAVÍTI**, where the magnificent platía is one of the prettiest spots on the whole island.

EATING AND DRINKING	THE INTERIOR

★**Kleoniki/Tou Iatrou** Theológos village centre ☎ 25930 31000. This excellent traditional taverna is at its best in the evening when the roasting spits, loaded with goat and suckling pig for around €7–8, start turning. Great barrelled wine too. Daily noon–1am.

★**Opos Palia** Main square, Sotíras ☎ 6979 635 703. Wonderfully re-created old-style village *mezedhopolío* below the old fountain, serving original recipes for dishes such as octopus in tomato sauce, *strapatsádha* and *bekri mezé* for €6–9. Daily noon–midnight, except occasional winter closing.

The Sporades and Évvia

VIEW FROM ALÓNISSOS

The Sporades and Évvia

The Sporades lie close off Greece's eastern coast, their hilly terrain betraying their status as extensions of Mount Pílio, right opposite on the mainland. The three northern islands, Skiáthos, Skópelos and Alónissos, are archetypal Aegean holiday venues, with wonderful beaches, lush vegetation and transparent sea; they're all packed out in midsummer and close down almost entirely from October to April. Skýros, the fourth inhabited member of the group, lies well southeast, and is much more closely connected – both physically and historically – to Évvia than to its fellow Sporades. These two have less obvious attractions and far fewer visitors.

Skiáthos, thanks to its international airport and extraordinary number of sandy beaches, is the busiest of the islands, though **Skópelos**, with its *Mamma Mia!* connections, extensive pine forests and idyllic pebble bays, is catching up fast. **Alónissos**, much quieter, more remote and less developed, lies at the heart of a National Marine Park, attracting more nature lovers than night owls. Traditional **Skýros** sees fewer foreign visitors, partly because it's much harder to reach, though plenty of domestic tourism means no shortage of facilities. Between Skýros and the mainland, **Évvia** (classical Euboea) extends for nearly 200km alongside central Greece. Although in spots one of the most dramatic Greek islands, with forested mountains and rugged stretches of little-developed coast, its sheer size and proximity to the mainland means that it rarely has much of an island feel; mainlanders have holiday homes around numerous seaside resorts, but foreigners are very thin on the ground.

An indented coastline full of bays and coves to moor in, relatively steady winds and the clear waters of the National Marine Park, also make the northern Sporades, rightly, a magnet for **yacht flotillas** and charters. Many companies have bases in Skiáthos, in particular.

ARRIVAL AND DEPARTURE
THE SPORADES AND ÉVVIA

By plane Skiáthos airport receives regular international charters from across Europe as well as daily scheduled domestic flights. There are also international charters to Vólos on the nearby mainland (see p.76), while Skýros sees half a dozen flights a week from Athens and Thessaloníki.

By ferry Frequent ferries, fast cats and hydrofoils run from Vólos (see p.76) and Áyios Konstandínos (see p.70) to Skiáthos, Skópelos and Alónissos; in summer there's also a twice-weekly connection to Mandoúdhi in northern Évvia.

Skýros is accessed from the port of Kými on Évvia (see p.451), where ferries connect with buses from Athens. Two or three times a week in midsummer, this same ferry runs between Kými and Alónissos and Skópelos. For Évvia, local ferries shuttle from various strategic points on the mainland.

By bus and train Évvia is joined to central Greece by two bridges. Buses from Athens run to various points on the island, and there are trains to the island capital, Halkídha.

Skiáthos

Undulating green countryside, some fine rural monasteries and a labyrinthine old town notwithstanding, the real business of **Skiáthos** is **beaches**: by far the best, if also the busiest, in the Sporades. There are over fifty strands (plus a few more on satellite islets),

SKÓPELOS TOWN

Highlights

❶ Lalária beach, Skiáthos Glistening white pebbles and turquoise waters, backed by steep cliffs and a natural rock arch, form a photogenic contrast to the island's other, mostly sandy, bays. See p.429

❷ Skópelos Town Old-fashioned shops, ornate balconies, domed churches and atmospheric passageways make this one of the most alluring island towns in Greece. See p.431

❸ National Marine Park of Alónissos-Northern Sporades Spend a day – or longer – on a boat exploring the islets of this pristine reserve, with their wildlife, monasteries and secluded bays. See p.442

❹ Skýros An outrageously pagan carnival, a striking hillside Hóra and traditional interiors are all found on one of the least spoiled islands in the Aegean. See p.442

❺ Dhimosári Gorge, southern Évvia Traverse the wildest corner of the island on a mostly cobbled path descending from Mount Óhi. See p.454

❻ Paralía Áyíou Nikoláou, northern Évvia The journey to this beautiful cove beach with an excellent taverna is half the point, via sinuous mountain roads through verdant pine forests. See p.455

HIGHLIGHTS ARE MARKED ON THE MAP ON P.426

most with fine, pale sand, but still barely enough room for the legions of visitors; Italians and Greeks in summer, Brits and Scandinavians in spring and autumn. The main road along the south and southeast coasts serves an almost unbroken line of villas, hotels, minimarkets and restaurants; although they've not impinged much on Skiáthos' natural beauty, they make it difficult to find anything particularly Greek here. But by **hiking** or using a **4WD vehicle**, you can find relative solitude, refreshing vistas and charming medieval monuments in the island's north.

ARRIVAL AND DEPARTURE   SKIÁTHOS

BY PLANE

As well as international charters, there are regular Olympic flights to Athens (ⓦ olympicair.com) and Sky Express (ⓦ www.skyexpress.gr) operate a seasonal service to Thessaloníki via Skýros. Skiáthos airport is a tourist attraction in itself; built on reclaimed land less than 2km east of Skiáthos Town, it has an extremely short runway, and planes come in incredibly low over the harbour. Every Fri, the busiest day for charters, hundreds of people gather by the road at the end of the runway where landing planes pass just a few

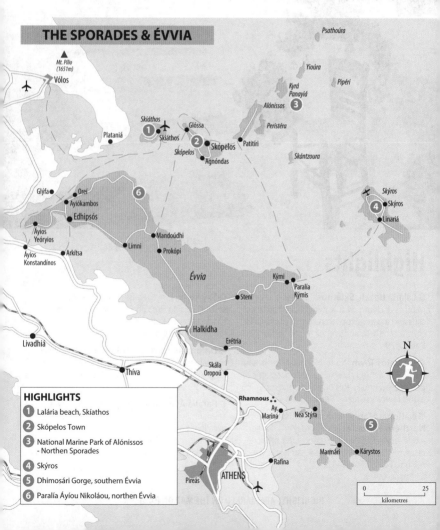

THE SPORADES & ÉVVIA

HIGHLIGHTS

1. Lalária beach, Skiáthos
2. Skópelos Town
3. National Marine Park of Alónissos - Northen Sporades
4. Skýros
5. Dhimosári Gorge, southern Évvia
6. Paralía Áyíou Nikoláou, northen Évvia

0   25
kilometres

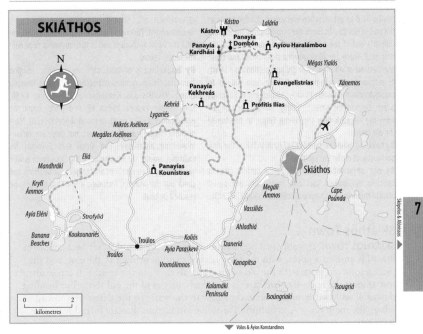

metres overhead, and the jet blast from those taking off can knock you over; check it out on YouTube.

Destinations Athens (April–Oct 1 daily, otherwise 2 weekly; 45min); Thessaloníki (summer 3 weekly; 1hr 45min) via Skýros (35min).

BY FERRY

Ferries dock at the new port right in the centre of Skiáthos Town, virtually opposite the bottom of the main street, Papadhiamándi. In summer, Hellenic Seaways fast catamarans and ferries (w hsw.gr), Aegean Flying Dolphins hydrofoils (w aegeanflyingdolphins.gr) and the ANES ferry *Proteus* (w anes.gr) connect Skiáthos Town with Vólos and Áyios Konstandínos on the mainland, and with Skópelos and Alónissos. The *Proteus* also goes to Mandoúdhi in northern Évvia twice a week. The rest of the year, Hellenic Seaways and ANES offer a reduced service of ferries or fast cats to Vólos, Skópelos and Alónissos. It is always a good idea to prebook for the hydrofoils and cats here; when a plane arrives they can be packed.

Tickets and agencies There are ticket booths on the Skiáthos Town dock at busy times; otherwise the Hellenic Seaways agent (daily 7am–10pm; ☎ 24270 22209) is directly opposite the jetty at the base of Papadhiamándi; Aegean Flying Dolphins and ANES are handled by Heliotropio Travel/Aegean Car Rental (daily 7.30am–late; ☎ 24270 22430), facing the harbour immediately north of here, with a branch office under the seafront *Hotel Akti*.

Destinations Alónissos (summer 4–7 daily, winter 3 daily; 1hr–2hr 40min); Áyios Konstandínos (summer 3 daily; 1hr 20min–2hr 40min); Mandoúdhi (Évvia; summer 2 weekly; 2hr 20min); Skópelos (summer 4–8 daily, winter 3 daily; 35min–1hr 40min); Vólos (summer 4 daily, winter 3 daily; 1hr 15min–2hr 45min).

INFORMATION

Tourist information There is no tourist office on the island, but w skiathos.gr is useful and has extensive accommodation listings.

Services In Skiáthos Town, the National Bank is on Papadhiamándi, and there are numerous others nearby and around the harbour, many with ATMs. The post office is also on Papadhiamándi.

GETTING AROUND

By bus A superb bus service (€2) runs along Skiáthos' coast road, from town to Koukounariés at the western end of the island, daily from 7am to 12.30am, with departures every 20min, more frequently at the busiest periods; the entire run takes about 30min most of the time, much longer in Aug when traffic is chaotic. Despite the number of buses, it can be hard to get on when everyone is coming home at the end of the day. In town, the terminus is at the eastern (airport) end of the new port, with further stops on the ring road. There are 26 numbered stops in all, and these numbers are often used when giving directions to a beach or restaurant. In summer, small buses also run up to Evangelistrías monastery (8 daily; 15min) and to Xánemos beach, beyond the airport (5 daily; 20min); they depart from the car park near the Health Centre at the top of the old town.

By taxi The main taxi rank (☎ 24270 24461) is at the new port just east of the ferry jetties.

By car or scooter Numerous rental outlets offering bicycles, motorbikes, cars and motorboats are based around the new port; Aegean Car Rental (☎ 24270 22430, ⓦ aegeancars.gr), virtually opposite the ferries, is recommended. Parking in town is impossible, except out past the yacht anchorage and at the southwest edge near the health centre.

By boat Dozens of boat trips are on offer, ranging from shuttles to numerous beaches (including Tsougriá island, Vassiliás and Kanapítsa, all 10–15min, €2.50; Koukounariés express, 15min, €5) to day-trips round the island (around €15 a head) or round Skópelos (€20). Most of these depart from the old port, but there are various interesting alternatives, on small sailing yachts for example, around the new harbour. The island tour is well worth doing – an excellent way to get your bearings and check out the beaches, including a few that can only be reached by boat.

Skiáthos Town

SKIÁTHOS TOWN, the only real population centre on the island, is set on a couple of low hills around a point, with the ferry harbour and new town to the east, and the picturesque old port, with the old town rising above it, in the west. You can easily get lost among the maze-like backstreets and shady platíes of the old town, but heading downhill will swiftly bring you back, either to the water or the flatter new town, where the main drag, Alexándhrou Papadhiamándi, runs directly inland from the ferry jetties.

Alexándros Papadiamántis Museum

Just off Alexándhrou Papadhiamándi • Daily 9.30am–1.30pm & 5.30–8.30pm • €1.50 • ☎ 24270 23843

There are few specific sights in Skiáthos, though the **Alexándros Papadiamántis Museum**, housed in the nineteenth-century home of one of Greece's best-known writers, is worth a look. The upper storey – basically two tiny rooms – has been maintained as it was when the writer, who plainly enjoyed a remarkably ascetic lifestyle, lived (and died) here. The ground floor operates as a bookshop-cum-exhibition area.

Boúrtzi

The peninsula that separates the two harbours, the **Boúrtzi**, makes for an enjoyable stroll. Surrounded by crumbling defences and a few rusty cannon – there was a castle in this obvious defensive position from at least the thirteenth century – it is today a peaceful setting for occasional **exhibitions**, a **café** with great views, and an open-air municipal **theatre**, with regular summertime music and drama performances.

The rest of the island

Skiáthos' **south coast** is lined with beach after beach after beach, almost all of them easily accessible on the bus. If you want to explore the mountainous area north of town, though, or get to the **north coast** beaches, you'll need to have your own transport or be prepared for some very hot hiking. Be warned that a 50cc moped simply won't make it up some of the exceptionally steep tracks, especially around Kástro. Thanks to the humid climate and springs fed from the mainland, the **interior** is exceptionally green, thick with pine, lentisk, holm oak, heather and arbutus even where (as is all too common) it has been ravaged by forest fires over the years. There are plenty of villas and tourist facilities on the coast, and chapels and farms in the interior, but only **Troúlos** (with another excellent beach) really counts as a village, and even that a tiny one.

Evangelistrías monastery

Monastery Daily 10am–sunset • Free • **Museum** Daily 10am–2pm • €2 • From town, you can drive here in 10min, or walk it in just over an hour; the path takes various short cuts from the road, mostly well signed, starting out from the ring road close to bus stop 2

It was at the eighteenth-century **Evangelistrías monastery**, in a beautiful and much-revered spot and the scene of major pilgrimages at Easter and on August 15, that the modern Greek flag was first unfurled in 1807. Inside it's alive with the sound of caged songbirds, and there's a shop selling local wine and preserves. You can also visit an eclectic **museum** comprised of ecclesiastical and rural-folklore

---

SKIÁTHOS' TOP TEN BEACHES

Although almost all the island's **beaches** are sandy, some of them are very narrow. On the south coast, every one will have loungers and at least one bar or taverna which often pumps out loud music; most have watersports too. If you want to get away from it all, the harder to reach sands on the north coast offer more chance of escape. These (listed clockwise from town) are our favourites:

Tsougriá An islet in the bay opposite Skiáthos Town, with excursion boats shuttling back and forth from the old port three or four times daily. A favourite of locals, it has two spectacular sand beaches, each with a taverna.

Vromólimnos The prettiest of the beaches on the Kalamáki peninsula, fine-sand Vromólimnos is a bit of a walk from bus stop 13, and hence a little quieter than many south-coast sands. It still has a couple of cafés from which to enjoy the sunset views, though, and a busy waterski operation.

Koukounariés Huge stretch of sand at the end of the bus route which is arguably the island's finest beach, and certainly one of its busiest. Wooden walkways traverse the sand to a series of *kantínas*, there's a harbour for excursion boats and every imaginable form of watersport including snorkelling and diving with Skiathos Diving, one of the island's best outfits (𝐓 6977 081 444, 𝐰 skiathosdiving.gr). Behind the beach, a small salt lake, Strofyliá, sits in the midst of a grove of pine trees – all of it a protected reserve. There's horseriding, too, in the forested dunes to the north, with Skiathos Riding Centre (𝐓 24270 49548).

Big Banana Reached by a short track over the headland from bus stop 26 at Koukounariés, Big Banana is announced before you arrive by the thumping bass tracks from three competing beach bars. It's beautifully sandy but absolutely packed, with a young crowd and a clubbing atmosphere, plus ski boats, kayaks, pedaloes and more.

Small Banana In the next cove beyond Big Banana, this beach is almost entirely nudist yet still thoroughly commercialized, with a café and loungers occupying almost every centimetre. Like its neighbour, it is named not for any appendages on display but for its perfect yellow crescent of sand.

Ayía Eléni About 600m from bus stop 25 in Koukounariés, Ayía Eléni is a stunning, broad, sandy beach looking west towards the mountainous mainland. It is bigger and more family-oriented than the neighbouring Banana beaches, with a couple of beach bars and pedaloes and kayaks to rent.

Mandhráki Dunes and a protected pine forest back Mandhráki, a sandy beach with views of Mount Pílio and an exceptionally friendly snack-bar serving *souvláki*, salads and omelettes. One of the island's least developed, it is accessed either by a walking path from bus stop 23 in Koukounariés, or a driveable track that follows the coast round past Ayía Eléni beach.

Megálos Asélinos From Troúlos village, a side road leads 3.5km north through a lush valley to Megálos Asélinos, a large and exposed beach of gritty sand. There's a big taverna where many excursion boats stop for lunch, but it's a lovely, unspoilt spot at the end of the day when they've all headed home.

Kástro In a small cove set steeply below Kástro (see p.430), this beach can be very crowded in the middle of the day when the tour boats arrive, but is delightful early or late – though it loses the sun early. There's a wonderfully ramshackle snack-bar with a shower of cold river water.

Laláïa This famous beach, nestling near the northernmost point of Skiáthos, is only accessible by taxi- or excursion-boat from town. With steep cliffs rising behind a white-pebble shore and an artistic natural arch, it's undeniably beautiful; three sea-grottoes just east rate a stop on most round-the-island trips.

galleries plus a vast collection of documents, posters and photos from the independence struggle and Balkan wars.

Below the monastery, another signed **path** leads north, past restored **Ayíou Haralámbou** monastery, full of cats and chickens kept by the caretaker, and on past **Panayía Dombón** chapel and then to **Panayía Kardhási** on the way to Kástro.

Kástro

Daily sunrise–sunset • Free

Kástro, occupying a windswept headland at the northernmost tip of Skiáthos, was the island's main population centre throughout the Middle Ages. The **fortified settlement**, established for security from pirate raids, thrived under Byzantine, Venetian and Turkish control until its abandonment around 1830, when the new Greek state stamped hard on piracy, and the population left to build the modern capital. Most of the buildings were dismantled and the materials reused elsewhere, so all that's left now are the remains of the **defences**, half a dozen **churches** (there were once twenty) and a **mosque**. You enter the rocky outcrop across a narrow, stone ridge – a superb natural defence once enhanced by walls and a drawbridge. Inside, the remains are beautifully maintained and well signed; there's fresh spring water and tables where you can picnic.

If you come by boat you're unlikely to escape the crowds; driving or walking involves an exceptionally steep, narrow cobbled track, but does give the chance to arrive early or late, and perhaps get the place to yourself.

ACCOMMODATION   SKIÁTHOS

Much of the accommodation on Skiáthos, especially villas and places out of town with pools, is block-booked by package companies; in Skiáthos Town, there are dozens of little pensions and small rooms places scattered throughout the backstreets. You may find it easier to check the island's website (ⓦ skiathos.gr) or go through a local agent. There are also two local room-owners' association kiosks on the quayside (ⓣ 24270 22990/21488) who operate long hours in high season. Everywhere is heavily booked in Aug when rates may double; there are plenty of bargains out of season.

SKIÁTHOS TOWN

Bourtzi Moraïtou 8 ⓣ 24270 21304, ⓦ hotelbourtzi.gr. Boutique hotel just off Papadhiamándi, with designer decor and a courtyard pool; rooms boast marble floors, flat-screen TVs and all mod cons. Impressive, though the atmosphere is more business than island. **€175**

Pension Margarita Ayíou Nikoláou 23 ⓣ 24270 21288, ⓦ pensionmargarita.gr. High on the hill above the new harbour, close to the much-signed *Windmill* restaurant, *Margarita* is a traditional rooms place, simply furnished but good value, with a/c and fridge. There are great views from the front rooms and from the roof terrace, where you can enjoy breakfast or coffee made in the well-equipped communal kitchen. The helpful owner often meets arriving ferries, and will pick up or drop off at the airport. **€45**

Pension Nikolas Evangelistrías ⓣ 24270 23062, ⓦ nikolaspension.gr. Very central place, off Papadhia-mándi, close to the port, in two buildings facing each other across an internal courtyard, tucked away from the street so reasonably quiet. The simple rooms all have a/c, fridge and TV, with balconies overlooking the courtyard. **€70**

VROMÓLIMNOS

★ **Skiathos Holidays** ⓣ 24270 21597, ⓦ skiathos -holidays.com. This group of elegant modern studios, apartments and villas is set in a great location, in a garden behind the beach. All options have cooking facilities of some sort and good modern bathrooms, plus there's a garden bar. **€90**

KOUKOUNARIÉS

Mandraki Village ⓣ 24270 49301, ⓦ mandraki -skiathos.gr. Delightful garden complex near the lake, at bus stop 23, set in spacious grounds with a pool. Rooms are tasteful, modern and pastel-coloured; family quads and junior suites (worth the small price difference) are also available, all very well equipped. **€140**

EATING AND DRINKING

By Greek standards – just about any standards in fact – eating in Skiáthos is expensive. The best places also get very busy, so booking is advisable.

SKIÁTHOS TOWN

Alexandhros Old town backstreets ☎ 24270 22431. Traditional Greek old-town restaurant, signposted from Platía Trión Ierarhón but still hard to find, packed every night thanks to some of the lowest prices in town. There's live Greek music most nights. Service can suffer from the crowds, and book or be prepared to wait. Daily, evenings only.

★**Amfiliki** Opposite old-town health centre ☎ 24270 22839, ⓦ amfiliki.gr. Walk through what seems an ordinary house, up on the west side of the old town, past the kitchen, and you'll find a gorgeous terrace, high above the sea. They serve all the standard taverna recipes here, skilfully prepared – and excellent seafood dishes like octopus *stifádho* (onion and tomato stew; €13.50), fish fillet with spicy tomato sauce (€15) or mussel pilaf (€8). Just forty seats overlooking the sea, so book to be sure of the view (or come for breakfast). They also have some very simple rooms to rent (€45). Daily all day.

Bakaliko Club strip ☎ 24270 24024. The best of the restaurants in the club strip (the coast road beyond the new harbour), with mock decor of a traditional Greek grocer's, unimprovable seating on a deck over the water and decently priced, Turkish-influenced food (*taş* kebab at €8.80, for example, or Smyrnian meat balls, €8.60); live acoustic Greek music some nights. Daily, evenings only.

La Cucina di Maria Up the steps from the old port ☎ 24270 24168. Excellent pizza, pasta and creative salads are served at this restaurant behind Trís Ierárhes church. Check out the menus handwritten in old accounting books and the eclectic decor inside, though in summer you might prefer to sit out on the balcony, or down in the courtyard. The downside is price; simple pasta and pizza dishes start from

around €12, though portions are large. Daily from 6pm.

Kouzina Old harbour ☎ 24270 21912. A bit more interesting than the others crowded round the old harbour, *Kouzina* offers a modern take on a traditional Greek taverna, with appetizing mains from around €9. Take a look in the kitchen at the day's specials. Daily 1pm till late.

Mesoyia Old town backstreets ☎ 24270 21440. Cheap-and-cheerful outfit (though still around €40 for two, with house wine) featuring the usual grilled and *mayireftá* suspects, plus daily changing seafood, such as prawn *yiouvétsi* (casserole with pasta). Tables are out on the lane in summer (they can usually squeeze in one more when busy); indoors during the cooler months. Daily, evenings only.

PROFÍTIS ILÍAS

Platanos 4km from Skiáthos Town ☎ 6932 413 539, ⓦ platanos-restaurant.net. Close to the island's highest point, *Platanos* has fabulous views over town and towards Skópelos and Évvia. The food is almost beside the point, but there's a decent taverna menu, plus breakfast, omelettes, sandwiches or simply coffee and baklává; it's wise to book if you want a decent view in the evening. Daily 10.30am–11pm.

KOLIÓS

Infinity Blue Koliós Bay ☎ 24270 49750, ⓦ infinity blue.gr. Hop off at bus stop 15 to get to *Infinity Blue*, with its lovely vistas from a romantic, hillside setting. The restaurant has a Greek/Mediterranean menu and a more refined ambience than most, with proper linen and wine glasses. Fine steaks for around €19, plus pasta, risotto and plenty of Greek dishes for €11–15. Daily, evenings only.

NIGHTLIFE AND ENTERTAINMENT

SKIÁTHOS TOWN

There are plenty of bars and pubs on Papadhiamándi and the nearby old-town backstreets, but the coolest places are overlooking the old port or out on the "club strip" at the start of the coast road beyond the yacht marina.

Attikon Papadhiamándi ☎ 6972 706 305, ⓦ on.fb.me /UmF4UQ. This summer open-air cinema, at the bottom of Papadhiamándi by the museum, has been showing *Mamma Mia!* at least three times a week since the film's release. Summer; film times vary.

BBC Club strip ☎ 6980 990 741. Club-strip venues seem to be annually changeable, and operate only in July and Aug, but *BBC* is bigger and longer-lived than most: a

riotous crowd inside and a deck jutting out over the shallows to chill out on. Summer Fri–Sun and some weeknights 11pm–late.

Kentavros Mitropolítou Ananíou ☎ 24270 22980. An evergreen, much-loved rock, jazz and blues bar right in the centre of town, just a few paces from the new harbour, near the Papadiamántis Museum. Daily 9.30pm–4am.

Rock'n'Roll Old port ☎ 24270 22944, ⓦ skiathos -rocknroll.gr. The busiest of four neighbouring, essentially identical bars on the steps leading up to Platía Trión Ierarhón, *Rock'n'Roll* has outdoor seating with bean bags and scatter cushions; inside a DJ serves up mainstream rock, Latin and dance music. Daily 7pm–4am.

Skópelos

SKÓPELOS is bigger and more rugged than Skiáthos, and its concessions to tourism are lower-key and in better taste, despite a boom in recent years fuelled by the filming here of *Mamma Mia!*. Much of the countryside, especially the southwest coast, really is as spectacular as it appears in the movie, with a series of pretty cove beaches backed by extensive pine forests as well as olive groves and orchards of plums (**prunes** are a local speciality), apricots, pears and almonds. **Skópelos Town (Hóra)** and **Glóssa**, the two main towns, are among the prettiest in the Sporades.

ARRIVAL AND DEPARTURE SKÓPELOS

BY FERRY

In summer, Hellenic Seaways fast catamarans and ferries (Ⓦ hsw.gr), Aegean Flying Dolphins hydrofoils (Ⓦ aegean flyingdolphins.gr) and the ANES ferry *Proteus* (Ⓦ anes.gr) run regularly to Alónissos, and to Skiáthos and the mainland. Some call at Loutráki, the port for Glóssa (and known as Glóssa on ferry and hydrofoil schedules), as well as Skópelos Town. Also in summer, Skyros Shipping (Ⓦ sne.gr) ply twice a week to Kými on Évvia, via Alónissos, and from there on to Skýros, while the *Proteus* also goes from Glóssa to Mandoúdhi in northern Évvia twice a week. The rest of the year Hellenic Seaways and ANES offer three daily ferries or fast cats to Alónissos, and to Skiáthos and Vólos, most calling at both of the island's ports. Hydrofoil and fast cat connections to flights in Skiáthos can be very busy: try to book in advance.

Tickets and agencies There are ticket booths on the dock in Skópelos Town at busy times; otherwise the Hellenic Seaways agent (daily 6.30–7.15am & 9am–9pm; ☎ 24270 22767) is directly opposite the harbour gate, and Aegean Flying Dolphins, ANES and Skyros Shipping are handled by Lemonis Travel (daily 9am–10pm; ☎ 24270 22363), by the National Bank, on the far side of the harbour close to the old port. The harbour agent in Loutráki is Triandafyllou (☎ 24240 33435).

Destinations Alónissos (summer 4–7 daily; 20–35mins); Áyios Konstandínos (summer 3 daily; 2hr 5min–4hr 15min); Kými, Évvia (summer 2 weekly; 3hr 5min); Mandoúdhi, Évvia (from Glóssa only; summer 2 weekly; 1hr 30min); Skiáthos (summer 4–8 daily; 35min–1hr 35min); Skýros (summer 2 weekly; 6hr 15min); Vólos (summer 4 daily, winter 3 daily; 2hr–4hr 25min).

INFORMATION

Tourist information There's no tourist office on the island, but useful sites include Ⓦ skopelosweb.gr, Ⓦ skopelos.com and Ⓦ skopelos.net.

Internet Cafés all along the front have wi-fi; Blue Sea, the very last place at the northern (old port) end of the harbour, is a large internet café.

Services Several banks with ATMs are on the quayside in Skópelos Town; the post office is on Dhoulídhi, just off Platía Plátanos ("Souvláki Square"), which lies directly up from the ferry harbour.

Newspapers English-language newspapers are sold at a shop just off Souvláki Square.

GETTING AROUND

By bus Services run from Skópelos Town across to the island's south coast and then along the south and west coast past all the major beaches; in summer at least a dozen buses a day go via Stáfylos as far as Kastáni – half of them continue to Glóssa and Loutráki. The bus stop is on the seafront by the ferry dock in Hóra.

By car and scooter There are numerous car and scooter rental outlets near the ferry dock in Hóra, around the corner of the coast road and the main road heading inland, and along this inland road; they include Magic (☎ 22420 23250, Ⓦ skopelos.net/magiccars) and Maxi

(☎ 24240 24380, Ⓦ maxiautos.gr).

By taxi The central taxi stand is to the left as you leave the ferry dock in Hóra.

By bike Skópelos Cycling (Mon–Sat 10am–2pm & 6.30–9.30pm; ☎ 22420 22398), with a small shop by the back of the old olive factory, rents out high-quality bikes.

Boat trips A huge variety of boat trips is on offer around the harbour, at prices ranging from around €10 for a return shuttle to Glystéri beach to €30 for a trip to Alónissos; island circuits, many of them *Mamma Mia!* themed, go for around €20.

Skópelos Town and around

SKÓPELOS TOWN (Hóra) pours off a hill on the west flank of a wide, oval bay: a cascade of handsome mansions and slate-domed churches below the ruined Venetian **kástro**. Away from the waterside commercial strip, the town is endearingly time-warped – indeed among the most unspoilt in the islands – with wonderfully idiosyncratic shops of a sort long vanished elsewhere, and vernacular domestic architecture unadulterated with tasteless monstrosities. There are also a couple of **museums**, hard to find in the labyrinthine backstreets.

Folklore Museum

June–Sept Mon–Sat 10am–2pm & 7–10pm • €3 •
☎ 24240 23494

The **Folklore Museum** contains a fine
local collection of weaving, embroidery
and costumes, mostly from the late
nineteenth and early twentieth
centuries, with detailed panels
explaining local customs and the
religious calendar.

Old Skopelitian Mansion Museum

Tues–Sun 10am–2pm & 6–9pm • €3 • ☎ 2424 0 22940

The **Old Skopelitian Mansion Museum**,
also known as the Vakratsa Museum,
was the former home of the island's
doctor – subsequently occupied by his
three daughters, all spinsters and all

doctors. Left to the town by the last surviving daughter, it is displayed much as it was
when they lived here; a comfortable, bourgeois home full of everyday items, furniture,
clothing and books.

Beaches

The town **beach** doesn't amount to much, but there are a couple of excellent
alternatives very close by: towards **Stáfylos** is a busy road around which cluster many
accommodation options; north to **Glystéri** is less populated.

Stáfylos

4km from Hóra • First stop on the bus route round the south coast

Stáfylos is the closest decent beach to Hóra, though it gets very crowded in season.
There's a noisy beach bar, so if it's peace you're after, walk to the end of the beach and
climb over the headland to larger, more scenic, sand-and-fine-gravel **Velanió**, where
there's a summer-only *kantína* and a bit of a nudist scene.

Agnóndas and Limnonári

The beautiful bay of **AGNÓNDAS** has very much the feel of traditional old Greece, with
yachts moored and a pretty fishing harbour where the water laps right up to the tables
of several tavernas. There's not much of a beach, though, so for that follow the side
road to **Limnonári**, about 1km west, for 300m of white sand in a steep-sided bay.

Glystéri

Less than 4km northwest of Skópelos Town • Small boats run several times a day (€5 return) in summer from the harbour in Skópelos Town

Glystéri is a small sand-and-pebble beach at the base of an almost completely enclosed
bay. Plenty of people brave the narrow, steep road and many more arrive by shuttle
boat, so it can get busy.

ACCOMMODATION   SKÓPELOS TOWN AND AROUND

There are numerous rooms for rent in the backstreets of Skópelos Town, as well as entire houses, but in high season
everything is very booked up. In midsummer a Rooms Association office (☎ 24240 24567) opens in the lane leading up to
Souvláki Square; a wider choice, including apartments and hotels across the island, can be arranged through helpful Madro
Travel, by the old port (☎ 24240 22145, ✪ madrotravel.com), or check the useful island websites (see opposite). Aug prices
can be double those for the rest of the year. Most of these places will pick you up from the harbour if you let them know
which ferry you're on.

Georgios L Old port ☎ 24240 24625, ⓦ georgios .skopelos-hotels.gr. The last building at the northern end of the harbour, above the *Blue Sea* café, houses this small hotel with basic, old-fashioned, stone-floored rooms with a/c and TV; those at the front have great views. **€45**

★Mando Stáfylos ☎ 24240 23917, ⓦ skopelosweb.gr /en/studios/mando. Among the best accommodation on the island, *Mando* is very friendly and quiet with stone-floored, a/c rooms (plus new superior rooms and a villa) set among manicured lawns where steps lead down to a private swimming platform. There are fridges and tea- and coffee-making equipment in the rooms, plus an outdoor communal kitchen area. **€60**

Milos Studios Kástro ☎ 24240 24034, ⓦ skopelosweb .gr/en/studios/milos. White-painted studios and apartments behind the kástro (all the way round the ring road, or a steep climb up from the harbour) with flagstone floors and mini kitchens. They enjoy great views towards Alónissos. **€45**

Pension Kir Sotos Harbourfront ☎ 24240 22549, ⓦ skopelos.net/sotos. A rambling old house, set back from the middle of the harbour behind the giant plane trees, whose wood-floored, a/c, en-suite rooms are justifiably a favourite budget option, though perhaps due for a revamp. Go for the quieter rear units, especially no. 4, with its fireplace. There's a communal kitchen and sunny courtyards. **€30**

Skopelos Village Town Beach ☎ 24240 22517, ⓦ skopelosvillagehotel.com. Self-catering complex, 600m east around the bay, with luxurious studios and suites set among landscaped grounds with two pools and a restaurant. The "Seabreeze" studios are worth the extra for their modern design and sleek bathrooms, though it's only good value if you get an off-season deal. **€125**

Sofia's Garden Studios Old town ☎ 6937 039 332. In the heart of the old town, hidden in the backstreets above Souvláki Square, *Sofia's* has three storeys of studios tucked away in a lovely garden setting. Simple but comfy, with wi-fi. **€35**

★Thea Home Ring road ☎ 24240 22859, ⓦ theahome hotel.com. Lovely rooms (some pretty small) and a family apartment are set in the old house, all with fridge, a/c and sweeping views from the top of the town; modern studios and a pool are immediately below. Bikes are available (free) and there's an excellent home-made breakfast (extra). **€55**

EATING AND DRINKING

The seafront is lined with cafés and tavernas, the best of which are up at the old port end; for something rather more modest, aptly nicknamed Souvláki Square is packed with decent fast-food outfits.

Gorgones Old town ☎ 24240 24709. Popular place in town (beside the well-signed *Oionos Blue Bar*), with tables in a stepped alley, garden courtyard and on indoor space. There's a short menu of good Greek food at fair prices (Skopelos cheese pie €4.50, spit-roasted pork €7.50), though occasionally erratic service. Daily lunch and dinner.

Kymata Old port ☎ 24240 22381, ⓦ skopelitissa.com. About the oldest taverna on Skópelos and practically the last on the harbour, this is a shrine of quality traditional cooking such as *papoutsákia* (€6) or veal *yiouvétsi* (casserole with pasta; €10), much of which can be inspected in the kitchen. Daily lunch and dinner.

★Kyratso's Kitchen Old port ☎ 24240 23184. Named after Kyratso, the matriarch of the family who presides over the kitchen, this is a wonderful traditional taverna (relocated from Glystéri beach), where the daily specials are proudly displayed in the kitchen. Simple dishes like goat with fresh tomato (€13) or pork with prunes (€11) are best, or try the speciality, black fish. There's live music every evening from 7pm. Daily lunch and dinner.

Limnonari Taverna Limnonári ☎ 24240 23046, ⓦ skopelos.net/limnonarirooms. An excellent taverna serving plain but delicious food, such as a rich goat *kokkinísto* (slow cooked in a rich tomato sauce; €10) and delicious local spiral *tyrópittes* (cheese pastries). There are pleasant rooms too, also simple and mostly with inland views (€35). Daily all day.

★Pavlos Agnóndas ☎ 24240 22409. The most popular of the simple harbourside tavernas here, *Pavlos* is an unpretentious place with fair prices for fish and plenty of well-prepared Greek dishes (mains €7.50–9), plus decent house wine. Daily lunch and dinner.

WALKING ON SKÓPELOS

Away from the main roads there's plenty of **walking** on Skópelos. Long-time resident Heather Parsons battles to maintain paths and leads spring/autumn walks along what remains (☎ 6945 249 328, ⓦ skopelos-walks.com), as well as publishing a hiking guide, *Skopelos Trails*. Among the better walks are those east of Skópelos Town, where three historic **monasteries**, Metamórfosis, Evangelistrías and Prodhrómou (all open daily roughly 8am–1pm & 5–8pm), stand on the slopes of Mount Paloúki. Near Glóssa, there's a beautiful 45-minute trail to the renovated village of **Palió Klíma**, via the island's oldest settlement, **Athéato** (Mahalás), which is slowly being restored by outsiders, and the foreigner-owned hamlet of **Áyii Anáryiri**.

Perivoli Old town ☎ 24240 23758. A beautiful spot in the garden courtyard of an old house, up an alley just above Souvláki Square. The Greek/Mediterranean menu includes pasta and risotto as well as inventive Greek dishes like rolled pork with apple and plum in wine sauce (€11) or stuffed courgette (€7.50) – plus a selection of wines by the glass. Daily from 7.30pm.

Zoupa Old Olive Factory ☎ 24240 24494. Classy, modern Greek place in the Old Olive Factory area, where there's also a good Italian restaurant, and pizza/burger takeaway. Starters include the likes of tzatzíki with lemon and wild fennel (€4.80); mains from *moussaká* (€8.50) and meatballs to goat *yiouvétsi* (casserole with pasta). Daily 7pm–12.30am.

NIGHTLIFE

Anatoli Kástro ☎ 24240 22851. Veteran rembétika musician Yiorgos Xintaris performs at this tumbledown place on top of the kástro, where there's live music nightly from late June to early Sept. They also serve food, and by day there's a café with incomparable views. Daily 10am–late.

Bardon Old Olive Factory, harbour ☎ 24240 24494. This elegant lounge bar is set in a food-and-nightlife complex which occupies a restored industrial area directly opposite the harbour car park. There are cocktails, dance music and occasional live bands. Daily 8pm–3am.

Merkourio (Mercurius) Between Souvláki Square and the Folklore Museum ☎ 24240 24593. Just up from the ferry jetty, this cool bar has views over the harbour action. Cocktails are served on candlelit terraces, to a soft-rock and Latin soundtrack; also open during the day for breakfast and coffee. Daily 10am–2am.

Oionos Blue Bar Old town ☎ 6942 406 136. Small, often crowded bar in an old house, well signed inland from the centre of the harbour, with a jazz, blues and world-music playlist, plus a staggering variety of imported beers and whiskies. Daily 10am–2am.

Around the island

Many of the island's best, and certainly the most accessible, **beaches** lie just off the main road and bus route, which heads south across the island from Hóra and then up the west coast to Glóssa. The island's **northeast coast** is harder to reach, with just a couple of paved roads from Glóssa to Perivolioú or Áyios Ioánnis Kastrí.

Pánormos

PÁNORMOS is the biggest resort outside Skópelos Town, though still very understated and low-key. An extensive pebble beach lines the expansive bay, with plenty of tavernas (most offering free loungers for customers), shops and rooms. Adjoining **Blo** inlet is a beautiful, quiet anchorage, though there's no beach here.

Miliá and the Mamma Mia! beaches

The wide-open spaces of **Miliá**, immediately beyond Pánormos, comprise two 400m sweeps of grey sand and pebbles opposite Dhassía islet, divided by a headland with a sometimes obtrusively noisy beach bar at the south cove. Having found fame as the *Mamma Mia!* beach, **Kastáni**, almost adjacent to Miliá, has become very crowded, with a big beach bar pumping out dance music. Nonetheless, it's a beautiful place, with fine sand and crystal-clear water. Beyond unattractive **Élios** (**Néo Klíma**), isolated **Armenópetra** boasts two spectacular beaches either side of a point. There's no shade and no facilities, but great views of Glossá on the hillside above.

Glóssa

Skópelos' second town, **GLÓSSA**, 26km from Hóra near the northwest tip of the island, is spectacularly arrayed in stepped, hillside tiers, high above the coast. A traditional, rural place where many of the houses have overhanging balconies and lush gardens, it is explored along narrow, steep, mostly **car-free lanes** (there's an unsigned car park behind the church on the main road), with breathtaking **views** around almost every corner. Apart from wandering the photogenic alleys and visiting the excellent tavernas, there's not a great deal to do here, and the only official accommodation in town is in rented houses (rarely available locally); there is a small **Folklore Museum** just above the main square, though (10am–2.30pm & 5.30–9pm, Thurs 10am–2.30pm only, closed Mon; free).

Loutráki

LOUTRÁKI, some 3km steeply down a serpentine road from Glóssa (or on foot by a shorter, well-signed *kalderími*), is a pretty little place with views of Skiáthos. The port of the larger town, it has a line of cafés and tavernas around the ferry dock, an archeological kiosk with information on local sites and island history, lots of **yachts** at anchor and a narrow pebble beach.

Perivolioú

A narrow, winding road through mature pine forest leads to beautiful little **Perivolioú** beach, some 7km from Glóssa and close to the island's northern tip. There's ice-clear water and no development at all at this sandy cove, nor at nearby **Hondroyiórgis** beach, reached along a driveable track. Continue on this track, and you'll join the road down to Áyios Ioánnis Kastrí.

Áyios Ioánnis Kastrí

The tiny sand cove at **Áyios Ioánnis Kastrí** is one of the busiest on the island, thanks to its position at the base of the *Mamma Mia!* wedding chapel. Perched on a rock monolith (105 steps lead up), the chapel is almost ridiculously photogenic, and attracts tour boats from Skiáthos as well as being an essential halt on the round-island trip. Late afternoon, when they've all left, is generally the quietest time. There's an excellent **snack-bar** (summer daily 10am–sunset) here, where they serve a mean Greek salad.

ACTIVITIES

AROUND THE ISLAND

Watersports There are ski boats offering all the usual rides at Pánormos, Miliá and Kastáni. In Pánormos, you can rent motorboats (☏ 24240 24788, ⓦ holidayislands .com/boathire) to explore the surrounding bays, while

there's an excellent kayaking outfit, Kayaking Skopelos (☏ 6983 211 298, ⓦ aegeanescapes.com/sea-kayaking -skopelos), based in Glóssa, which offers day-trips and longer expeditions.

ACCOMMODATION AND EATING

Adrina Beach Hotel Between Pánormos and Miliá ☏ 24240 23371, ⓦ adrina.gr. Beautiful, ivy-clad, four-star bungalow complex tumbling down a hillside to its own private beach. Wonderful sea views from the rooms and duplex maisonettes, plus there's a seawater pool and taverna. Adjacent is the still more glamorous, five-star *Adrina Resort & Spa*, with the same management and contact details. **€100**

★ **Agnanti** Glóssa ☏ 24240 33606, ⓦ agnanti.com.gr. Traditional taverna, well signposted in the heart of the old town, with upmarket takes on traditional recipes – pork with prunes or *hortokeftédhes* (vegetable croquettes) – served indoors and on a terrace with spectacular views. Only marginally pricier than average, and well worth it. Daily lunch and dinner.

Milia Apartments Miliá ☏ 24242 23998, ⓦ milia apartments.com. Modern complex with double and triple

studios and duplex quad apartments; breakfast is available on the terrace, and there's a decent taverna nearby. Before the crowds arrive, you have your own private beach. **€60**

Selenunda Hotel Loutráki ☏ 24240 34073, ⓦ hotel selenunda.com. High above the harbour at Loutráki, the peaceful *Selenunda* has stunning views from every room. All the tile-floor rooms come with a/c, TV and kitchenette, and bigger family apartments are available. Steps lead down to the waterfront, but with luggage you may want to call to be picked up. **€40**

To Steki tou Mastora Glóssa ☏ 24240 33563. Café-restaurant by the church on the main road in Glóssa, with wonderful views of Loutráki, Skiáthos and the mainland. It does a brisk trade in coffee and sandwiches as well as charcoal-grilled meats, including whole roast lamb or goat on the spit (midsummer daily, off-season weekends only). Daily all day.

Alónissos

ALÓNISSOS is the largest and only permanently inhabited member of a mini-archipelago at the east end of the Sporades. It's more rugged and wild than its neighbours, but no less green; pine forest, olive groves and fruit orchards cover the southern half, while a dense maquis of arbutus, heather, kermes oak and lentisk cloaks the north. In part thanks to its marine park status (see p.442), some of Greece's cleanest sea surrounds Alónissos – the **beaches** rarely match those of Skópelos or Skiáthos for sand or scenery, but the white pebbles on most of them further enhance the impression of gin-clear water. Remoteness and limited ferry connections mean that Alónissos attracts **fewer visitors** than its neighbours. There is, however, a significant British and Italian presence (the latter mostly in all-inclusive hotels), while Greeks descend in force all summer.

ARRIVAL AND DEPARTURE
ALÓNISSOS

BY FERRY

All ferries to Alónissos dock at the harbour in Patitíri. In summer, Hellenic Seaways fast catamarans and ferries (whsw.gr), Aegean Flying Dolphins hydrofoils (waegean flyingdolphins.gr) and the ANES ferry *Proteus* (wanes.gr) run regular daily services to Skópelos, Skiáthos and the mainland. Also in season, Skyros Shipping (wsne.gr) go twice a week to Kými on Évvia and from there on to Skýros. The rest of the year Hellenic Seaways and ANES offer three daily ferries or fast cats to Skópelos, Skiáthos and Vólos. Hydrofoil and fast cat connections to or from flights in Skiáthos can be very busy: try to book in advance.

Operators and tickets The Hellenic Seaways agent is Vlaikos Travel (☎ 24240 65220), under the *Alkyon Hotel* on the Patitíri harbourfront at the bottom of the eastern (right-hand facing from the sea) street heading inland; Aegean Flying Dolphins is handled by Albedo Travel (☎ 24240 65804, walonissosholidays.com), at the bottom of the western (left-hand) street, and ANES and Skyros Shipping by Alonnisos Travel (☎ 24240 66000, walonnisos travel.gr), between the two.

Destinations Áyios Konstandínos (summer 3 daily; 2hr 25min–5hr 5min); Kými, Évvia (2 weekly; 2hr 20min); Skiáthos (summer 4–6 daily, winter 3 daily; 1hr–2hr

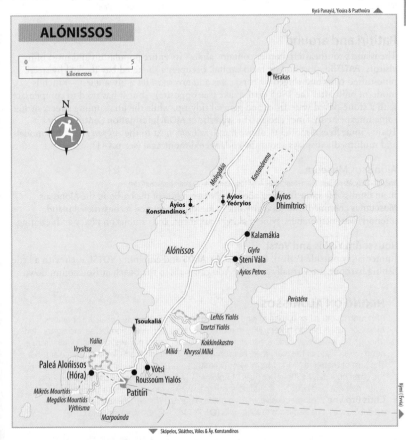

30min); Skópelos (summer 4–6 daily; winter 3 daily; 20–30min); Skýros (2 weekly; 5hr 30min); Vólos (summer 3–4 daily, winter 3 daily; 2hr 20min–5hr 15min).

INFORMATION

Services There's a bank with an ATM and a post office on the eastern shopping street leading up from the harbour in Patitíri.

Tourist information Alónissos lacks a tourist information office. Useful local websites include ⓦ alonissosholidays .com, ⓦ alonissostravel.gr and ⓦ ivicourt.com.

Newspapers English-language newspapers are sold near the bottom of the western shopping street in Patitíri.

GETTING AROUND

By bus There are just two bus routes on Alónissos: from Patitíri up to Hóra (daily 9am–2pm & 5pm–midnight roughly hourly, more in early evening; €1.60) and to Stení Vála (3 daily; €1.70). In Patitíri the bus stop is on the harbour at the bottom of the eastern inland street; tickets cannot be bought on the bus, so get them from the *Avra Café*, opposite the stop, or from shops in Hóra or Stení Vála. In high season Alonissos Transport, with a harbourfront booth, offers return trips to the beaches at Khryssí Miliá and around during the day, and to Hóra in the evening.

By taxi The taxi stand in Patitíri is on the harbour opposite the bus stand.

By car and scooter There are numerous car and scooter rental outlets near the harbour, including Albedo Travel (see p.437) and others in the inland street immediately beyond it.

Boat trips and excursions Various boat trips are on offer around the harbour; the best marine park (see p.442) tours cost around €40 a head (including lunch and drinks), but check their itineraries, as some don't go far in; walking (see box below), diving, sea-kayak excursions and more can be arranged through Albedo Travel.

Patitíri and around

The island's southeastern corner contains almost its entire population and most of its visitors. **PATITÍRI**, port and de facto capital, occupies a sheltered bay flanked by steep, pine-tufted cliffs and ringed by bars, cafés and tavernas. It's a bit soulless – much is modern, built after the 1965 earthquake (see opposite) – but it has tried to compensate with a stone-paved waterfront and general tidy-up, while the unassuming streets shelter some unexpectedly fancy shops. The waterfront **MOM Information Centre** (daily 10am–5pm; free; ⓦmom.gr), above the *Avra Café*, next to the *Alkyon Hotel*, has models and multimedia displays about the endangered **monk seal** (see p.441).

Alonissos Museum

Harbour • Daily: May & Sept 11am–6pm; June–Aug 11am–8pm • €4 • ⓦ alonissosmuseum.com

In an unmissable stone building above the western side of the harbour, the **Alonissos Museum** is crammed with local artwork, traditional costumes, reconstructed island interiors, war memorabilia, wine-making equipment, and exhibits on piracy and seafaring.

Roussoúm Yialós and Vótsi

Immediately outside Patitíri, **ROUSSOÚM YIALÓS** and adjoining **VÓTSI**, each with a little fishing harbour, are virtually suburbs. You can walk to the **beach** at Roussoúm, down

---

HIKING ON ALÓNISSOS

Although its often harsh, rugged landscape might suggest otherwise, of all the Sporades, Alónissos caters best to **hikers**. Fifteen routes have been surveyed, numbered and signposted (though signs and waymarks are starting to deteriorate): many provide just short walks from a beach to a village or the main road, but some can be combined to make meaty circular treks. The best of these are trail #11 from Áyios Dhimítrios, up the Kastanórema and then back along the coast on #15 (2hr 30min), or trails #13 plus #12, Melegákia to Áyios Konstandínos and Áyios Yeóryios (just over 2hr, including some road walking to return to start). Island resident **Chris Browne**'s comprehensive walking guide, *Alonissos Through the Souls of Your Feet*, is available locally; he also leads guided treks (ⓟ6979 162 443, ⓦalonissoswalks.co.uk).

steps from town, which is considerably more pleasant than swimming in Patitíri itself. Both offer pleasant, good-value rooms and tavernas.

Hóra

HÓRA (Paleá Alónissos), the island's original settlement, was severely damaged by a Sporades-wide earthquake in March 1965, after which most of the reluctant population was compulsorily moved to Patitíri; the issue was essentially forced in 1977 by the school's closure and cutting off of electricity. Outsiders later acquired the abandoned houses for virtually nothing and restored them in variable taste; only a few locals still live here, which gives the village a very twee, un-Greek atmosphere, abetted by multiple knick-knack and crafts shops. But it's stunningly picturesque, with great views as far as Mount Áthos in clear conditions. For much of the year, and indeed for much of most days, there are more hedgehogs than people about; the place only really comes to life – noisily so – on midsummer evenings. As an alternative to the bus ride, you can walk up on a well-preserved *kalderími*, or footpath (45min uphill, 30min down), signposted off Patitíri's western inland street, almost at the edge of town.

Southern beaches

Numerous small cove beaches surround Alónissos' southern tip. Closest to Patitíri is **Výthisma** – less than 1km down a track off the road to **Marpoúnda** beach (monopolized by an all-inclusive Italian complex) and then a scramble down into the cove. Look out for the latest signs, as the paths down are regularly washed out. The grey sand-and-pebble beach is pretty, and part nudist, but without facilities or shade. **Megálos Mourtiás** is just a short swim further round, and there is a path which continues that way, but most people get here on the steep paved road from Hóra. With bright white pebbles and two tavernas, it's a complete contrast; crowded and noisy. **Mikrós Mourtiás**, just west, is served by a well-maintained footpath from Hóra (#1), or you can get most of the way down on a driveable dirt track. Another enclosed cove, it has graffiti proclaiming it a nudist beach – though in practice it doesn't seem to be. Immediately north of Hóra, visible tucked into their respective finger-like inlets, are compact **Vrysítsa** and **Yiália** (with a picturesque windmill), both of which have more sand than pebbles, but no facilities.

ACCOMMODATION — PATITÍRI AND AROUND

Most Alónissos accommodation is in Patitíri or immediately around; you may be approached with offers as you disembark at the port. Albedo Travel (☎ 24240 65804, ⓦ albedotravel.com) handles hotels, studios and villas across the island, while the local room-owners' association booth (☎ 24240 66188, ⓦ alonissos-rooms.gr), on the waterfront, can also find you a room. Most places will offer transport up the steep streets.

PATITÍRI

Ikion Eco Hotel High up on the eastern side of town, behind the Town Hall ☎ 24240 66360, ⓦ ikion.com. Newly renovated in boutique style, the *Ikion* has been classily done up in shades of cream and white. Standard rooms are fairly small, but some have great views, and there are also suites and junior suites, some with kitchenette. Breakfast included. **€85**

Nereides Hotel Paliohorafína, above the western edge of town ☎ 24240 65643, ⓦ nereides.gr. This pleasant hotel complex offers stunning views, a small pool, and rooms, studios and family apartments with free wi-fi, flat-screen TVs, modern wooden furniture, and quality bathrooms. Very good deals out of season. Breakfast included. **€80**

Paradise Hotel Above the eastern side of the harbour, overlooking Roussoúm ☎ 24240 65213, ⓦ paradise-hotel.gr. Two-star hotel which boasts a pool, bar and exceptionally friendly welcome. Plain rooms have a/c and balcony but no TV; many have views over the bay. Breakfast included. **€70**

HÓRA

Elma's Houses Upper part of the village ☎ 24240 66108, ⓦ elmashouses.com. Two exquisitely restored studios (a one-bed and a two-bed) and two houses, which accommodate up to four people, beautifully furnished from the owner's Gorgona antique shop. Upmarket, but worth it. **€75**

Fantasia House Off the main square at the bottom of the village ☎ 24240 65186. Beamed ceilings and a terrace with amazing views to the south and east are the big attractions of these simple, a/c rooms. **€60**

Konstantina Studios Lower part of the village ☎ 24240 66165, ⊛ konstantinastudios.gr. This renovated building, past *Fantasia House*, has eight fully equipped studios and one apartment, all of which enjoy exceptional views. There's a lovely garden, wi-fi, and a home-made breakfast is included. **€85**

VÓTSI

Pension Oniro Overlooking the harbour ☎ 24240 65368, ⊛ pension-oniro.gr. Pleasant rooms and studios whose balconies have fine views down over Vótsi and out to sea. All have a/c and TV, plus there are kitchenettes in the studios. Expect a very friendly welcome. **€55**

EATING AND DRINKING

Though there's no shortage of **places to eat** in Patitíri, only a couple stand out from the crowd. **Nightlife** here consists of a few music bars over on the western side of the harbour, below the museum. There's generally better, if pricier, food, and more night-time activity, up in Hóra. Hóra's main street is lined with restaurants, mostly with wonderful views, but few that are good value or particularly high quality. Locals and those in the know tend to eat further down, or in the backstreets.

PATITÍRI

Archipelagos Waterfront ☎ 24240 65031. The waterfront restaurants are generally nothing special; an exception, popular with locals, is *Archipelagos*, at the bottom of the western street, with good mezédhes, fish and traditional Greek cooking – plus excellent home-made chips. Daily lunch and dinner.

Helios On a terrace overlooking the harbour ☎ 24240 65667. *Helios* offers great harbour views, cocktails at night, and a menu with some alternative flavours, such as chicken stir-fry or pork with prunes (both €10), as well as pasta, quesadillas and omelettes. Occasional live music, and worth booking if you want the view in the evening. Daily noon–late.

To Kamaki On the eastern street, 150m from the waterfront ☎ 24240 65245. Authentic, welcoming ouzerí where portions are not huge, but the seafood-heavy menu encompasses unusual dishes like crab croquettes, skate and *tsitsírava* shoots. Meze €4–5, mains €7.50–9. Live Greek music Tues, Thurs & Sat from 9pm. Dinner daily, plus lunch Sat & Sun.

HÓRA

Astrofeyia Near the lower square ☎ 24240 65182. Unusual (for Greece) dishes like chicken curry or chilli con carne (each €10) as well as vegetarian options and more ambitious offerings such as shrimp millefeuille, all served on a terrace with a friendly welcome and great view. Daily 7pm–midnight.

★**Hayiati** At the end of the main street ☎ 24240 66244, ⊛ hayiati.com. *Hayiati* has probably the best view in Hóra (which is saying something); an unbeatable setting to sip coffee and try traditional sweets like *kazandibí* (Turkish-style milk pudding). Later it transforms to a piano bar with live easy-listening music nightly. Cocktail prices are steep, but otherwise not too bad considering the location, though it can be very busy. Daily all day.

Peri Orexeos On the lower square by the bus stop ☎ 24240 66421. Not a very glamorous setting, but the food here is a great deal better than you might guess from the fast-food style menu, and prices are some of the lowest in Hóra. You can get snacks, sandwiches and burgers as well as Greek standards, but also delicious, innovative salads and dishes like honey-and-lemon pork belly, or paella-like fried rice with tuna. Daily noon–11.30pm.

Northern Alónissos

A single road runs **northeast** from Patitíri up the spine of the island, giving access to **beaches** which are almost exclusively on the **east coast**. There are great views across to the substantial islet of Peristéra (see p.442) much of the way, and many of the marked hiking trails (see box, p.438) start from the road.

Tsoukaliá

The first turning on the northbound road heads westwards to **Tsoukaliá**, a scruffy cove signed as an archeological site; there was an ancient kiln here, and pottery continued to be made until recently, so thousands upon thousands of potsherds are strewn across the closed, fenced site and beach.

East-coast beaches

First of the **east-coast beaches** are Miliá and Khryssí Miliá: the former is busy, with white pebbles, piney cliffs and a *kantína*; the latter sandy, shallow (ideal for kids) and hence very busy, with loungers, taverna and beach bars. Next up is scenic **Kokkinókastro**, named for the red-rock cliffs which overlook it. Pebbles on a red-sand base extend both sides of a promontory, and there's a seasonal bar. Another road leads to **Leftós Yialós** and **Tzórtzi Yialós**: the pretty white-pebble beach at Leftós, with its tavernas and loud beach bars, attracts plenty of day-trip boats; Tzórtzi is smaller and less attractive, but much quieter.

STENÍ VÁLA is the biggest settlement away from the island's southern corner, though still barely a village. There are plenty of rooms, while the harbourfront shops and tavernas attract yachts and day-trip boats. A long pebble beach – **Glýfa** – lies immediately north, and a better, partly sandy one, **Áyios Pétros**, is a ten-minute walk south. **KALAMÁKIA**, the next hamlet north, has no beach but does have a timeless fishing-port feel and some great waterfront tavernas. At **Áyios Dhimítrios**, the final beach easily accessible by road, brilliantly white pebbles stretch around both sides of a narrow point; the south-facing side has loungers and a couple of café/bars, while the other is quite undeveloped. **Yérakas**, almost at the island's northern tip, is the end of the road and feels like it; there's a tiny fishing harbour in the deep bay and a dirty-white pebble beach where a snack truck parks in summer – the water, however, is spectacularly clean and clear.

ACTIVITIES   NORTHERN ALÓNISSOS

7

Scuba diving There's a good diving outfit, Ikion Diving (☎ 24240 65158, ⓦ ikiondiving.gr), at Stení Vála.

ACCOMMODATION AND EATING

4 Epohes Stení Vála ☎ 24240 66101, ⓦ 4epoches .com.gr. The *4 Epohes* (*4 Seasons*) is a pretty new studio complex set around a good-sized pool just above Stení Vála; very comfortable, modern, well-equipped rooms, and a roof-garden bar with live music every Thurs. **€60**

Eleonas Leftós Yialós ☎ 24240 66066, ⓦ eleonas -alonissos.gr. Set in an olive grove immediately behind the beach, this is the better of the popular tavernas at Leftós Yialós. Alónissos pies are their speciality, from excellent plain cheese (€8) to more exotic octopus and goat varieties (€12). Prices are relatively high but portions big – a single

pie and a salad makes a substantial lunch for two. Daily lunch and dinner.

Margarita Kalamákia ☎ 24240 65738. The best of four tavernas lined up along the quayside, each with its own fishing boat, *Margarita* serves excellent fish and mezédhes. They also have simple a/c rooms at the back (€40). Daily lunch and dinner.

Milia Bay Hotel Apartments Miliá ☎ 24240 66032, ⓦ milia-bay.gr. In a great position above Miliá beach and in a handy location for town, these modern studios and apartments have views out to sea over the landscaped grounds. There's a pool and pool-bar. **€90**

THE MEDITERRANEAN MONK SEAL

The **Mediterranean monk seal** (*Monachus monachus*) has the dubious distinction of being the most endangered European mammal. Fewer than six hundred survive, around half of them in Greek waters, of which fifty or more inhabit this part of the northern Sporades; the rest are mainly off the Turkish coast or around islands off the coast of West Africa.

Females have one **pup** about every two years, which can live for 45 years. As **adults**, they can grow to 2m in length and weigh over 200kg. Formerly, pups were reared in the open, but disturbance by man led to whelping seals retreating to isolated sea caves with partly submerged entrances. Without spending weeks on a local boat, your chances of seeing a seal are slim (marine-park cruises are far more likely to spot dolphins); if seals are spotted (usually dozing on the shore or swimming in the open sea), keep a deferential distance.

Monk seals can swim 200km a day in search of food – and compete with fishermen in the overfished Aegean, often destroying nets. Until recently, fishermen routinely killed seals; this occasionally still happens, but the establishment of the **National Marine Park of Alónissos-Northern Sporades** has helped by banning September–November fishing northeast of Alónissos and prohibiting it altogether within 1.5 nautical miles of Pipéri. These measures have won local support through the efforts of the **Hellenic Society for the Protection of the Monk Seal** (ⓦ mom.gr; see p.438), even among Sporadean fishermen, who realize that the restrictions should help restore local fish stocks. The society has reared several abandoned seal pups (bad weather often separates them from their mothers), who are subsequently released in the sea around Alónissos.

Sossinola Sténi Vála ☎ 24240 65776, ⓦ sossinola.gr. Harbourfront taverna that also has modern, a/c studios and two-room apartments, with balconies looking out over the harbour or out to sea (€40). Plenty of fish on the menu, plus Alónissos pies and a meaty goat in tomato sauce. Daily lunch and dinner.

National Marine Park of Alónissos-Northern Sporades

ⓦ www.alonissos-park.gr

Founded in 1992, the **National Marine Park** protects monk seals, dolphins, wild goats and rare seabirds in an area encompassing Alónissos plus a dozen **islets** speckling the Aegean to the east. None of these (save one) has any permanent population, but a few can be visited by excursion boats (see p.438), weather permitting. **Pipéri** islet forms the core zone of the park – an off-limits seabird and monk-seal refuge, approachable only by government-authorized scientists. **Peristéra**, opposite Alónissos, is uninhabited, though some Alonissans cross to tend olive groves in the south; it's little visited by excursion craft except for a brief swim-stop at the end of a cruise. Well-watered **Kyrá Panayiá**, the next islet out, has a tenth-century monastery whose old bakery and wine/olive presses, restored in the 1990s, are maintained by one farmer-monk. Nearby **Yioúra** has a stalactite cave which mythically sheltered Homer's Cyclops, plus the main wild-goat population, but you won't see either as *kaïkia* must keep 400m clear of the shore. Tiny, northernmost **Psathoúra** is dominated by its powerful lighthouse, the tallest in the Aegean; some excursions stop for a swim at a pristine, white-sand beach.

Skýros

Despite its natural beauty, **SKÝROS** has a relatively low profile. There are few major sites or resorts, and access, wherever you're coming from, is awkward. Those in the know, however, realize it's worth the effort, and there are increasing numbers of trendy Athenians and Thessalonians taking advantage of domestic flights – and making Skýros Town a much more cosmopolitan place than you might expect – plus steadily growing international tourism. The New Age **Skyros Centre**, pitched mostly at Brits, has also effectively publicized the place. There are plenty of **beaches**, but few that can

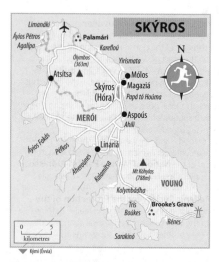

rival the sand of Skiáthos or film-set scenery of Skópelos. There's also a substantial **air-force presence** around the airport in the north, and a big **naval base** in the south; almost all the accommodation and tourist facilities cluster around Skýros Town in the centre of the island.

A position bang in the centre of the Aegean has guaranteed the island a busy **history**: it was occupied from prehistory, with a truly impressive Bronze Age settlement currently being excavated, was a vital Athenian outpost in the Classical era, and an equally important naval base for the Byzantines and under Venetian and Turkish rule, when it was a crucial staging post on the sea lanes to Constantinople.

SNORKELLING NEAR LALÁRIA BEACH, SKIÁTHOS (P.424) >

CARNIVAL ON SKÝROS

Skýros has a particularly outrageous *apokriátika* (pre-Lenten) **carnival**, featuring its famous **goat dance**, performed by groups of masked revellers in the streets of Hóra. The leaders of each troupe are the **yéri**, menacing figures (usually men but sometimes sturdy women) dressed in goat-pelt capes, weighed down by huge garlands of sheep bells, their faces concealed by kid-skin masks, and brandishing shepherds' crooks. Accompanying them are their "brides", men in drag known as **korélles** (maidens), and **frángi** (maskers in assorted "Western" garb). When two such groups meet, the *yéri* compete to see who can ring their bells longest and loudest with arduous body movements, or even get into brawls using their crooks as cudgels.

These rites take place on each of the four weekends before **Clean Monday** (see p.43), but the final one is more for the benefit of tourists, both Greek and foreign. The Skyrians are less exhausted and really let their (goat) hair down for each other during the preceding three weeks. Most local hotels open for the duration, and you have to book rooms well in advance.

ARRIVAL AND DEPARTURE

SKÝROS

By plane Aegean (ⓦ aegeanair.com) connects Skýros with Athens, and Sky Express (ⓦ www.skyexpress.gr) operates flights in summer to and from Skiáthos and Thessaloníki. The airport is about 10km from town; some Aegean flights are met by a bus, but normally you'll have to take a taxi or rent a car – a Pegasus car rental booth opens at flight times (see below).
Destinations Athens (2–4 weekly; 40min); Skiáthos (summer 3 weekly; 35min); Thessaloníki (summer 3 weekly; 45min).

By ferry Skyros Shipping (ⓦ sne.gr) sail daily from Kými, on Évvia (see p.451), to Linariá, Skýros' port. The ferry leaves Kými every evening, returning from Skýros early in the morning (afternoon on Sun). To get to Kými there are

direct KTEL buses from Athens' Liossíon bus station, with early-afternoon departures connecting with the ferry.
Destinations Alónissos (July & Aug 2 weekly; 5hr 20min); Kými, Évvia (daily, more in summer, especially weekends; 1hr 40min); Skópelos (July & Aug 2 weekly; 6hr).

Agents and tickets Skyros Travel (ⓣ 22220 91600, ⓦ skyrostravel.com), about 100m above the platía on the main street in Skýros Town, is the local agent for both plane and ferry tickets (daily 9.30am–1pm & 6.30–9pm; timetables and other useful info displayed outside); they also have a ticket office in Linariá that opens an hour before departures and can arrange taxi or minibus transfers between Kými and Athens airport.

INFORMATION

Tourist information The Visit Skyros website (ⓦ visit-skyros.gr) has impressive interactive mapping.
Services The post office and National Bank (with ATM) are on the platía in Skýros Town, and there's a further ATM

higher up the main street; the most reliable internet café is U, also on the main street.
Newspapers English-language newspapers are sold from a hut opposite the platía in Skýros Town.

GETTING AROUND

By bus Buses run three times daily between Skýros Town and Linariá (€1.60), connecting with the ferries; in town the bus stop is near the bottom of the main street, by the school. In summer the buses also go to Magaziá and Mólos.
By taxi There are plenty of taxis (ⓣ 22220 91666) to meet the ferries, with taxi stands by the main square in town,

and close to the bus stop.
By car and scooter Skyros Travel (see above) rent cars (trading as Pegasus; ⓣ 22220 91600, ⓦ skyrosrentacar.com), or you can get scooters from several places including Vagios (ⓣ 22220 92957), in a side street just below the main square in town.

Skýros Town and around

Once through the rather scruffy outskirts, **SKÝROS TOWN** (**Hóra**) is a beautiful place, its Cycladic-style white, flat-roofed, red-tiled houses clinging to the inland slope of a pinnacle rising precipitously from the coast. In legend, King Lykomedes raised the young Achilles in his palace here, and also pushed Theseus to his death from the summit. A single main street leads up to a central platía; beyond that, cobbled and increasingly narrow and **traffic-free**, lies a 150m stretch lined with almost everything you'll need – shops, many of them selling classy jewellery, crafts and antiques, restaurants, banks and sophisticated bars. Wander off the main street and the place is suddenly bigger than it first seemed. There are always fascinating glimpses – covered passageways, churches and front doors open to reveal **traditional house interiors** with gleaming copperware, antique embroideries and the proud local crafts of painted ceramics and elaborately carved wooden furniture.

Kástro

The Byzantine-Venetian **kástro** atop the ancient **acropolis** above town is a very steep climb, so unless you're interested in seeing the picturesque old quarter along the way, you may want to check that it is open following reconstruction – it was badly damaged by an earthquake in 2001. Even from outside, there are great views; inside is the Byzantine **monastery of Áyios Yeóryios**.

Rupert Brooke memorial

On the northern edge of town • ⓦ rupertbrookeonskyros.com • Follow the main street uphill and take the signed left fork, or walk up steps from Magaziá

The British poet Rupert Brooke is always associated with Skýros, though in fact he spent only a few days here, arriving as a **naval officer** off the south of the island on April 17, 1915, and dying six days later of blood poisoning on a French hospital ship. He lies buried in an olive grove above the bay of Trís Boúkes (see p.448). The **Rupert Brooke memorial** comprises a nude bronze statue of "Immortal Poetry", in a quiet square with wonderful seaward views.

Archeological Museum

Below the Rupert Brooke memorial • Tues–Sun 8am–3pm • €2 • ☎ 22220 91327

Skýros' two-room **Archeological Museum** is far better than you might expect, with the added bonus of a lovely setting above the sea. The highlights are early Bronze Age pottery, obsidian axe-heads and stone blades and tools from Palamári (see p.447); later artefacts include a Geometric-era ceramic rhyton (drinking vessel) in the form of a Skyrian pony, and a vase with eight ducks being beset by snakes. There's also a side room in the form of a traditional Skyrian house, with carved wooden screen and furniture.

Manos Faltaïts Museum

Below the Rupert Brooke memorial • Daily 10am–2pm & 6–9pm • €2 • ⓦ faltaits.gr

An early nineteenth-century mansion built over a bastion in the ancient walls houses the eccentric **Manos Faltaïts Museum**, in the family home of a prolific local painter. Along with his own works, it's an Aladdin's cave of local history and folklore, with traditional furnishings and costumes, curios and books.

Magaziá and Mólos

Immediately below Skýros Town, reached by a direct stairway or more roundabout roads, is the beach hamlet of **MAGAZIÁ**. From here, a long sandy beach, the island's best, extends to **MÓLOS**; these days the two are pretty much joined by low-key, low-rise development – much of the island's **accommodation** is down here, along with plenty of **restaurants** and a couple of lively beach **bars**. Around the point beyond Mólos, a much more exposed beach is punctuated by rock outcrops whose weird, squared-off shapes are the result of Roman (and later) quarrying rather than natural erosion; one monolith, by the cape with its snack-bar/windmill, has a **rock-hewn chapel** inside.

Linariá and around

Excursions to Sarakinó €30 including lunch

LINARIÁ, where the ferries dock, is a pleasant enough place, with plenty of options for eating and drinking if you're waiting for a boat, but little reason to stay. In high season, **excursion boats** offer trips to the islet of **Sarakinó**, with its white-sand beach, stopping at various sea caves en route. Should you want to stay around here, go to the next little bay, **Aheroúnes**, a peaceful spot with a much better beach, and only about fifteen minutes' walk away.

ACCOMMODATION
SKÝROS TOWN AND AROUND

SKÝROS TOWN

★ **Nefeli** On the main road as you enter town ☎ 22220 91964, ⓦ skyros-nefeli.gr. The island's plushest hotel has a range of lovely designer rooms, studios and apartments, arrayed around a large saltwater pool. Breakfast (included) is served on an outdoor terrace, and there's free wi-fi in the lobby. **€100**

Pension Nicolas On the southern edge of town ☎ 22220 91778, ⓦ nicolaspension.gr. In a quiet location, 5min walk out of town, this friendly establishment offers double and quad rooms; the latter have hand-carved traditional wooden sleeping platforms, and all have a/c and TVs. **€45**

MAGAZIÁ/MÓLOS

Angela Mólos ☎ 22220 91764, ⓦ angelahotelskyros .com. Large complex of two-storey rooms and studios, close to the beach at the northern end of Mólos, beyond the harbour, in extensive gardens around a pool. All with a/c, TV and fridge, and some with kitchenette. **€60**

Georgia Tsakami Magaziá ☎ 22220 91357,

ⓦ georgiashouse.gr. Simple, old-fashioned rooms with fridge and electric ring, in a great position directly behind the beach. Most have private balcony at the back, and there's a communal terrace at the front. **€35**

★ **Perigiali** Magaziá ☎ 22220 92075, ⓦ perigiali.com. Sparkling new rooms, studios and family apartments around a good-sized pool, in a narrow lane behind the beach at the southern end of Magaziá. A few options have sea views, though most look over the gardens, and there are a few simpler, cheaper rooms in the original wing; all have a/c, wi-fi and cooking facilities. **€80**

LINARIÁ/AHEROÚNES

King Lykomides Linariá ☎ 22220 93249, ⓦ lykomides .gr. Spotless *dhomátia* with wooden-shuttered balconies overlooking the harbour; all have fridge, a/c and TV, and some include basic cooking facilities. **€50**

Pegasus Aheroúnes ☎ 22220 93442, ⓦ skyrosvillas .com. A variety of studios and apartments, most with good views, in a tranquil spot behind the beach. All come with kitchenette, a/c, TV and a friendly welcome. **€50**

EATING, DRINKING AND NIGHTLIFE

SKÝROS TOWN

Akamatra Main square ☎ 22220 29029. Large, fancy bar on two floors, with leather seating and terraces overlooking both the platía and street. Open during the day for coffee, and till the early hours for regular DJ events. Daily 10am–2am.

Maryetis Main street ☎ 22220 91311. Much the most popular place in town, certainly among tourists, with only a few tables on a terrace (opposite Skyros Travel), so you may well have to wait. Simple Greek oven dishes and grilled meat or fish at reasonable prices (mains €7–9) are the attraction, washed down with decent house wine. Daily lunch and dinner.

★ **O Pappous ki Ego** Near the top of the main street ☎ 22220 93200. "My Grandfather and I" serves traditional Skyrian dishes such as fried bread with Skyrian cheese (actually more like a giant cheese pie), cuttlefish with fennel, and excellent meatballs with ouzo; mostly smaller, meze-style dishes (€5–8, with a few mains for around €10). It's designed to be reminiscent of a traditional village store, and classier than your average Greek taverna. Daily from 7pm.

MAGAZIÁ/MÓLOS

Asterias Mólos ☎ 22220 93008. Excellent restaurant on the waterfront platía with a pretty beachfront terrace and

sunbeds below for customer use. There's no printed menu – usually a good sign – just half a dozen daily specials reeled off by the waiter, plus the usual salads and sides. Daily lunch and dinner.

★ **Ιy Istories tou Barba** Mólos ☎ 22220 91453. In a lovely setting, with blue chairs on a blue terrace above the Magaziá end of Mólos beach, this restaurant offers traditional and interesting food such as crab salad, fish soup and seafood spaghetti. The atmosphere matches, with black-and-white photos of old island life stuck in the menu. Starters €5–8, mains €6–9. Daily 1pm–midnight.

Juicy Beach Bar Magaziá ☎ 22220 93337. Beach bar with loungers, umbrellas and watersports, plus a terrace with food (sandwiches, crêpes, pasta), juices and smoothies, free wi-fi and a bar. Quiet music by day, cranked up at night with summer events such as a full-moon party. Daily breakfast till the early hours.

Stefanos Magaziá ☎ 22220 91272. Attractive, traditional taverna with wooden tables on a terrace hanging out over the sand at the southern end of Magaziá beach. Standard dishes such as *stifádho* (€9) or lamb with potatoes (€7.50) are deliciously prepared. Daily all day.

Thalassa Mólos beach ☎ 22220 92044. Beach bar by day (with wi-fi, sunbeds, bar and snacks), cocktail bar and club at night, when there's a huge dance space, though that only really gets busy in Aug. Daily 9am–3am.

LINARIÁ

Kavos ☎22220 93213. All-day bar tumbling down a rocky cliff on a series of terraces, with steps down to a private swimming area below. Quiet daytime sounds are turned up loud to greet the evening ferry; there's wi-fi, drinks and light meals, plus late-night revelry in mid-season. Daily 10am–late.

Psariotis ☎22220 93250. Probably the best of the tavernas around Linariá's harbour, *Psariotis* has its own boat to catch fish, which is marginally less expensive than elsewhere (€12 for most fish dishes). They also do a good fish soup, plus plenty of standard Greek dishes at regular prices (*moussaká* €6). Daily lunch and dinner.

Merói

A single paved road loops around Skyros's northern half, **Merói**. Heading anticlockwise from Hóra, the first possible stop is at secluded **Kareflóu** beach, 1.5km down a poorly signed rough track. Sandy and extensive, it's also exposed and has no facilities at all.

Palamári

Mon–Fri 7.30am–2.30pm • Free

The early Bronze Age settlement of **Palamári**, inhabited from around 2800 to 1600 BC, and then lost for 3500 years, is set on the ridge of a low cape at the northeastern edge of the island, above a beach and a river which once formed a lagoon and natural harbour. The site, still being excavated, is extraordinary: you can make out the houses, streets, drainage and walls of a well-organized and powerfully **fortified city**, which must have been at the heart of Aegean trading in the Minoan era. Informative signage and a small exhibition fill in the background.

Atsítsa and around

Past the airport at the island's northern tip, the west coast is infinitely greener, heavily forested in pine. Around 2.5km of rough track leads to a couple of the island's most scenic and remote beaches: nudist **Áyios Pétros**, more respectable **Limanáki**, right by the airport almost at the end of the runway, and still more isolated **Agalípa**. **Atsítsa** itself is well-known as the home of the **Skyros Centre** (🌐skyros.com), and the attractive, pine-fringed bay here is sheltered by an islet and has lovely clear water for swimming, but not much of a beach.

Beyond Atsítsa, you can head back across the centre of the island on a good dirt road through the woods, or carry on around the coast, through an area devastated by forest fire in 2007 and still characterized by charred stumps. **Áyios Fokás**, in the heart of this area, is a quiet beach that makes a great lunch spot; and the descent through woods to deeply indented **Péfkos**, the best of the southwest-coast bays with a fine, long, sandy beach, offers spectacular views.

EATING AND DRINKING   MERÓI

Perasma Near Palamári ☎22220 92911. Excellent, reasonably priced taverna at the junction of the airport road not far from Palamári; apparently in the middle of nowhere, but with plenty of custom from local air-force families. The family-style cooking is based on local produce, much of it organic and produced in the taverna's own fields,

served beneath a shady awning. Daily lunch and dinner.

Taverna tis Kyra Kalis Áyios Fokás. A wonderfully out-of-the-way lunch spot, with octopus and sardines thrown on a charcoal grill on the beach and simple Greek home-style cooking. Lush vines and pot plants compensate for the burnt slopes roundabout. Daily lunch and dinner.

Vounó

South of Skýros Town, you turn off at **Aspoús**, where there's a decent grey-sand beach, to reach **Vounó**. Much of this southern half of the island, especially as you ascend **Mount Kóhylas**, is almost eerily barren, home only to goats and a few stunted trees, but it's here also – high on the mountain – that you're most likely to see wild Skyrian horses and other **wildlife**, including abundant Eleonora's falcon. En route there's a narrow pebble strand at **Kalamítsa**, and a slightly better beach at **Kolymbádha**.

SKYRIAN HORSES

Skýros has a race of **native pony**, related to the breeds found on Exmoor and Dartmoor in the UK. They are thought to be the diminutive steeds depicted in the Parthenon frieze; according to legend, Achilles went off to fight at Troy mounted on a chestnut specimen. In more recent times they were used for summer threshing; communally owned, they were left to graze wild ten months of the year on Vounó, from where each family rounded up the ponies they needed. Currently only about 150 individuals survive, and the breed is **threatened** by the decline of local agriculture, indifference and cross-breeding. To be classed as a true Skyrian pony, the animal must be 98–115cm in height, and 130cm maximum from shoulder to tail. They're elusive in the wild, but you can see (and ride) them at the centre opposite *Mouries* restaurant in Vounó (see p.447).

Brooke's grave

Follow the turning to the naval base for just over 1km; it's in an olive grove off to the left of the road

The one sight down on the southern tip of the island (though it's tricky to spot) is Rupert **Brooke's grave** at **Trís Boúkes**, a simple marble tomb inscribed with his most famous poem, *The Soldier* ("If I should die, think only of this of me / That there's some corner of a foreign field / That is for ever England…").

EATING AND DRINKING   VOUNÓ

Mouries Fléa ☏ 22220 93555. A big, traditional taverna in this tiny hamlet on the road between Aspoús and Kalamítsa. They serve local lamb, goat and wine under the namesake mulberries; the kid in lemon sauce is great (€10). It's very popular at weekends when they often have live Greek music, and over the road they run a Skyrian Horse Centre, with riding and pony-and-trap rides. Daily lunch and dinner.

★**O Pappous ki Ego sti Thalassa** On the road approaching Kalamítsa ☏ 22220 93200. This is the original branch of *O Pappous ki Ego* (see p.446), but now the town one is open all year while this opens only in July and Aug, and busy weekends in spring and autumn. There are fine coastal views from the shaded terrace and the menu is similar to the town branch though at weekends there's spit-roast lamb and *kokorétsi* (mains €10). Daily lunch and dinner.

Évvia

The second-largest of the Greek islands after Crete, **ÉVVIA** (**Euboea**) – separated only by a narrow gulf from central Greece – often feels more like an extension of the mainland than an entity in its own right. At **Halkídha**, the old drawbridge spans a mere 40m channel where Évvia was mythically split from Attica and Thessaly by a blow from Poseidon's trident. Easy access from Athens means that in summer Évvia can seem merely a beach annexe for Athens and the mainland towns across the Gulf.

Nevertheless, Évvia is an island, often a very beautiful one, and in many ways its problems – long distances to cover, poor communications, few concessions to tourism – are also its greatest attractions, ensuring that it has remained out of the mainstream of tourism. Exceptionally **fertile**, Évvia has always been a quietly prosperous place that would manage pretty well even without visitors. The classical name, Euboea, means "rich in cattle", and throughout history it has been much coveted. Today **agriculture** still thrives, with plenty of local goat and lamb on the menu, along with highly rated local retsina.

Évvia divides naturally into three sections, with just a single road connecting the northern and southern parts to the centre. The **south** is mountainous, barren and rocky; highlights are low-key Kárystos and hiking the nearby mountains and gorges. The **centre**, with the sprawling island capital at Halkídha, is green, wealthy and busy with both industry and agriculture, but for visitors mainly a gateway, with the bridges at Halkídha and onward transport to Skýros from the easterly port of Kými. In the **north**, grain fields, olive groves and pine forest are surrounded by the bulk of the island's resorts, most dominated by Greek holiday homes.

ARRIVAL AND DEPARTURE

ÉVVIA

By ferry Ferries make the short crossing from the mainland to Évvia at various points all the way up the coast: from Ráfina to Marmári, Ayía Marína to Néa Stýra, Skála Oropoú to Erétria, Arkítsa to Edhipsós, Áyios Konstandínos to Áyios Yeóryios and Glýfa to Ayiókambos. Which you choose depends on where you are heading on Évvia; most run very frequently – details are given under the individual ports.

By car Two bridges link Évvia to the mainland, the old drawbridge right in the heart of Halkídha and a suspension bridge on the outskirts. If you are driving you can use these or any of the ferries (more expensive, but the mainland motorway is far faster than roads on the island if you're heading to the north or south).

GETTING AROUND

By bus and car Most places in Évvia can be reached by bus, but services tend to run just a couple of times a day, so if you hope to explore you'll really need a car. All the major rental companies have offices in Halkídha, and there are local operations in the resorts. If you're bringing a hire car from the mainland, tell the rental company.

Halkídha

Évvia's capital, **HALKÍDHA** (ancient Chalkis), has a population of over 100,000, making it one of the ten biggest cities in Greece. So it's not entirely surprising if it often has an urban feel, rather than an island one. Nonetheless, the centre is compact and easy to explore, and the busy waterfront thoroughly attractive. Right at the centre, beneath the drawbridge across the narrow **Évripos channel** to the mainland, the gulf-water swirls by like a river; every few hours the current reverses. Aristotle is said to have thrown himself into the waters in despair at his inability to understand what was happening; there is still no entirely satisfactory explanation for the capricious currents.

An impressive **fortress**, floodlit at night, protects Halkídha from the mainland side. Across the bridge, Odhós Kótsou heads directly uphill towards the centre through the old **Kástro** district, where a few relics of an older city survive. Chief of these is a handsome fifteenth-century

By bus KTEL buses run direct from Athens' Liossíon bus station to many destinations on Évvia including Halkídha (every 30min most of the day), Kárystos, Kými, Límni and Edhipsós. There are also buses from Athens to all of the mainland ports above.

By train Frequent trains connect Athens with Halkídha.

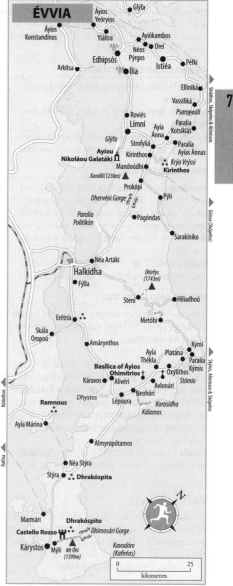

mosque (locked), now a warehouse of Byzantine artefacts, with an exceptionally ornate carved **Ottoman fountain** out front, and the nearby **old cathedral** (daily 7am–noon & 5.30–7.30pm; free) whose tower is visible from the mosque. Originally a Dominican priory, founded around 1250, it retains many original features. Off to the right further up Kótsou you'll find the **Folklore Museum** (Skalkóta 4; Wed–Sun 10am–1pm; Thurs also 6–8pm; €3; ☎ 22210 21817) housed in the old jail, with a jumbled collection of costumes, furniture and local traditions in a series of reconstructed rooms. Higher up still, then left on the main street, the **Archeological Museum** at Venizélou 13 (Tues–Sun 8am–3pm; €2; ☎ 22210 25131) offers a pleasant escape from the raucous surrounds; a tortoise roams the statuary in the shady garden, while inside there's a good display of finds from across the island.

ARRIVAL AND DEPARTURE   HALKÍDHA

By train The train station is very close to the bridge on the mainland side.
Destination Athens (at least 16 daily 5.30am–10.20pm; 1hr 25min).
By bus The KTEL bus station is almost 2km from the centre at Stíron 1, on the ring road at the southeastern edge of town; local buses will take you in to the market area, but it's much easier to use a taxi (about €5).
Destinations Athens (every 30min 5am–10pm; 1hr 15min); Edhipsós (1 daily; 2hr 30min); Erétria (15 daily; 30min); Kárystos (2 daily; 3hr); Kými (6 daily; 2hr); Límni (3 daily; 2hr).

ACCOMMODATION

Kentrikon Angéli Govíou 5 ☎ 22210 22375, ⊛ hotel -kentrikon.com. This rather forbidding nineteenth-century mansion, just up from the bridge, conceals unexpectedly modern a/c rooms which have wi-fi and satellite TV. No real views, so go for a quieter room at the back. **€50**
Kymata Liáska 1 ☎ 22210 74724, ⊛ kimata.com.gr. Simple, minimally furnished rooms above a busy main road overlooking the port; modern double glazing and a/c keep out most of the noise, and it's good value for the location. **€45**
Paliria Eleftheríou Venizélou 2 ☎ 22210 28002, ⊛ paliria-hotel.gr. Big, business-style three-star whose main attraction is the amazing view across the water, so be sure to get a room at the front; all have wi-fi and cable TV. Basic buffet breakfast included. **€60**

EATING AND DRINKING

A long line of cafés and restaurants extends along the waterfront to the north of the bridge; there are plenty of fancy seafood restaurants and elegant café-bars (most with wi-fi) but also a number of simpler places. Prices are lower inland towards the centre, though.

Apanemo Ethníkis Symfilíosis 78, Fanári ☎ 22210 22614. Very popular, decent-value seafood restaurant with tables on the beach; try the seafood pasta, or Évvia-style fish. It's a good 30min walk from the centre in a quiet suburb, just before the lighthouse at the far north end of the shoreline, so you may want to book, and/or take a taxi. Daily noon–midnight.
Paralia Voudoúri 10 ☎ 22210 87932. Long-established, old-fashioned, waterfront *psistariá*, serving up large portions of grilled meat at very reasonable prices (typically around €8 a large portion); salads and oven-baked dishes too. Daily lunch and dinner.
Tsaf Papanastasíou 3 ☎ 6948 180 857. An imposing stone building, off Platía Agorás near the top of Kótsou, houses this bustling ouzerí, with good fish and mezédhes (meze €4–8). It's popular with locals, hence busiest late in the evening. Tues–Sun dinner.

Central Évvia

The **coast road** southeast of Halkídha heads through industrial suburbs to a coastline of second homes, small hotels and beaches which make popular escapes from the city. At **Lépoura** it forks, to the right for the south of the island, left to curl around towards the east coast and **Kými**. Beyond Kými you can cut back across the mountainous heart of the island via **Metóhi** and **Stení**.

Erétria

Modern **ERÉTRIA** is a dull-looking resort on a grid plan; for most travellers its main asset is a ferry service across to Skála Oropoú (in Attica). The place deserves a closer look, though. For a start it boasts some of the best **beaches** on this stretch of coast, to the east of the harbour, and more importantly it preserves the remains of **Ancient Eretria**, the most impressive site on the island. Eretria was an important city from the eighth century BC to the sixth century AD, flourishing above all around 400 BC following the decline of Athens.

Archeological Museum

On the inland edge of town by the main road • Tues–Sun 8.30am–3pm • €2 • ☎ 22290 62206

First stop on your exploration should be the **Archeological Museum**, where you can pick up a leaflet with a map showing all the main sites around town. Among the museum's displays of ceramics, statues and jewellery, labelled mainly in Greek and French, the tenth-century BC Lefkandi Centaur stands out – a lovely piece and one of the earliest known examples of **figurative pottery**. There are also fascinating models of the ancient city.

House of Mosaics

It's worth crossing the road from the museum to see the overgrown West Gate and **theatre**, but of the other sites, many of them locked, the unarguable highlight is the **House of Mosaics**. Here, under a modern cover, four magnificent mosaic floors dating from around 370 BC have been preserved, vividly depicting animals and mythical scenes.

7

ARRIVAL AND DEPARTURE ERÉTRIA

By ferry Ferries shuttle the short crossing to Skála Oropoú every 30min in summer (7am–10pm; 25min; ☎ 22290 64990, or ☎ 22950 37270 in Skála Oropoú; ⓦ eretriaferries.blogspot.co.uk).

By bus Erétria is linked to Halkídha (15 daily; 30min) and there are frequent services from Athens to Skála Oropoú.

ACCOMMODATION

Eviana Beach Oníron ☎ 22290 62113, ⓦ evianabeach .gr. Smart hotel at the start of the beach road, right behind the beach, handy for town and with great sea views; all the rooms have a/c, TV, balcony and wi-fi, though they're not as fancy as the exterior might lead you to expect. **€65**

Kálamos

The most accessible of a number of beautiful coves on the west coast is **Kálamos**, about 7km down narrow lanes from Neohóri on the main road. This stretch of the main road is dotted with medieval remains – Byzantine chapels and watchtowers which gave warning of approaching pirates. Kálamos itself is a tiny but stunning cove enclosing a sandy **beach**, surrounded by half a dozen tavernas and rooms establishments. In August it's packed; the rest of the year often deserted.

ACCOMMODATION AND EATING KÁLAMOS

Tota Marinou ☎ 22230 41881. One of many simple rooms places right behind the beach, with a welcoming waterfront taverna too (daily lunch and dinner). **€40**

Kými

KÝMI consists of two parts: the ferry port, properly known as Paralía Kýmis, and the upper town, 4km up a spectacularly winding road. The port offers plenty of accommodation and a long row of harbourfront restaurants and cafés that might come in handy should you be waiting for a ferry, but the upper town is far more attractive, with great views towards Skýros from its lush, green hillside location.

Folklore Museum

Upper town • Daily: April–Oct 10am–1pm & 6–8.30pm; Nov–March 8.30am–3pm • €2 • ☎ 22220 22011

There's a small **Folklore Museum** with weaving and embroidery, costumes, rural implements and old photos recording the doings of Kymians both locally and in the US, home to a huge emigrant community. Among them was **Dr George Papanikolaou**, deviser of the "Pap" cervical smear test, who is honoured with a statue up on the platía.

ARRIVAL AND DEPARTURE   KÝMI

By bus Buses generally drop off in the upper town, except for those connecting with Skýros ferries.
Destinations Athens (5 daily; 4hr); Halkídha (6 daily; 2hr).
By ferry Skyros Shipping (☎ 22220 22020, ⏱ sne.gr) sail every evening to Linariá on Skýros, returning from Skýros

early in the morning. The ticket office is on the quayside; Athens buses connect with all the ferries.
Destinations Alónissos (summer 2 weekly; 2hr 20min); Skópelos (summer 2 weekly; 3hr 5min); Skýros (1 daily, more in summer, especially weekends; 1hr 40min).

Steni

At bustling Néa Artáki, 5km north of Halkídha, a side road leads east to **STENÍ**, a village-cum-hill-station at the foot of Mount Dhírfys, Évvia's highest summit where traces of snow survive till early summer. It's a beautiful place, cool in summer and full of rushing streams, and is striving to make itself something of a centre of **activity tourism**: there are marked hiking trails up the mountain, mountain-bike routes, and even a ski lift in winter. Steni also marks pretty much the halfway point of a wonderfully scenic **road link to Kými**, all paved except for a short section just outside Metóhi; Kými is 51km or an hour and 35 minutes' drive away (follow signposting for Metóhi if starting from Kými).

ACCOMMODATION AND EATING   STENÍ

Steni ☎ 22280 51221, ⏱ hotelsteni.gr. Cosy, welcoming hotel looking across at the village, with spectacular views from its sumptuous common areas and simple, comfortable if rather old rooms with modern bathrooms. **€50**
Vrahos ☎ 6938 582 162. Numerous tavernas specializing in meaty fare line the road as it passes through Steni, all popular for weekend outings, but there are more

options in the village itself. *O Vrahos*, on the village-centre platía, is an atmospheric place with firewood stacked outside and views of the village goings-on. The menu offers standard Greek fare and delicious barbecued meats – try the *kondosoúvli* (hunks of spit-roasted pork; €9). Daily lunch and dinner.

Southern Évvia

So narrow that you sometimes spot the sea on both sides, mountainous **southern Évvia** is often barren, bleak and windswept. The single road from the north is winding and tortuous – most people who come here arrive by ferry, and though Greeks have holiday homes in numerous coastal spots there's really just one attractive resort, at **Kárystos**.

Heading south by road, you'll pass what maps mark as **Lake Dhýstos**; these days it has been largely reclaimed as farmland, and there's barely any water. Atop conical Kastrí hill on the east shore are sparse fifth-century BC ruins of **ancient Dystos** and a medieval citadel. At **STÝRA**, 35km from Lépoura, three **dhrakóspita** ("dragon houses") are signposted and reachable by track. So named because only dragons were thought capable of installing the enormous masonry blocks, their origins and purpose remain obscure. The shore annexe of **NÉA STÝRA**, 3.5km downhill, is a locals' resort, pretty enough, but worth knowing about mainly for its handy ferry connection to Ayía Marína. Much the same is true of **MARMÁRI**, 20km south, except here the link is with Rafína. Both have plenty of food and accommodation should you be stuck waiting for a bus or ferry.

ARRIVAL AND DEPARTURE — SOUTHERN ÉVVIA

By ferry In high summer there are at least nine ferries daily shuttling between Néa Stýra and Ayía Marína (45min; information ☎22240 41533), and four to six a day linking Marmári and Rafína (1hr; information ☎22240 31222); around half that number run through the winter. Ferry tickets are sold on the quaysides.

By bus Most ferries in Marmári are met by a bus to Kárystos (4 daily). In Néa Stýra, unreliable buses (2 daily) stop on the main street, inland from the front. Connecting buses link Athens Mavrommatéon terminal with both Rafína (see p.74) and Ayía Marína.

Kárystos

KÁRYSTOS is a delightfully old-fashioned, thoroughly Greek resort, strung out along a broad bay flanked by good (if often windy) beaches. It's a quiet place – even in August, when thousands of Greeks descend, they're a fairly staid crowd – but its attractions grow on you; graceful Neoclassical buildings in the centre, endearingly old-fashioned shops and tavernas, and a magnificent setting. On the main town **beach**, west of the centre, there are beach bars, sunbeds and kayak rental; further out this way, and around the bay to the east, there are plenty of empty patches of sand.

Though a place of some importance in antiquity, mentioned by Homer and a rival of Athens, there's very little trace now of this history: only a fenced-in **Roman heroön** (mausoleum), a block from the water at the corner of Kotsíka and Sakhtoúri, and the thirteenth-century, waterfront **Boúrtzi** (locked except for special events), all that's left of once-extensive fortifications. Just uphill from this small Venetian tower, the tiny but well-explained **Archeological Museum of Karystos** (Tues–Sun 8.30am–3pm; €2; ☎22240 29218) displays statues, temple carvings and votive objects from the region.

ARRIVAL AND INFORMATION — KÁRYSTOS

By bus The bus stop is on Amerikís, to the east of the Town Hall, about three blocks in and one east from central Platía Amalías.

Destinations Halkídha (2 daily, 3hr); Marmári (4 daily, 30min); Néa Stýra (2 daily, 1hr).

Tourist information There's no tourist office, but helpful South Evia Tours at Platía Amalías 7 (daily 9am–11pm; ☎22240 26200, @eviatravel.gr) sells ferry tickets, rents cars and bikes, finds lodging, arranges excursions and also has a shop selling souvenirs, maps and foreign newspapers. Some useful websites are @southevia.gr and @in-karystos.gr.

Services The post office and ATMs lie within sight of Platía Amalías.

GETTING AROUND

By bike Karystos Bikes at the corner of Sakhtoúri and Platía Amalías (☎22240 26530, @karystosbikes.gr) rent out high-quality mountain bikes by the hour or day, and offer suggested routes.

By taxi There's a taxi office (☎22240 26500) on Platía Amalías.

ACCOMMODATION

★Galaxy Odysséos 1 ☎22240 22600, @galaxyhotelkaristos.com. Big old hotel at the western end of the waterfront with a friendly, family atmosphere. Unusually, the rooms have been upgraded before the communal areas, so it's better than it looks; get one with a view – it's excellent value. Breakfast included. **€45**

Karystion Kriezótou 3 ☎22240 22391, @karystion.gr. A lovely spot on a quiet, pine-covered promontory with direct access to the adjacent beach. The rather old-fashioned rooms are not quite what the modern exterior and public areas would lead you to expect, though. **€50**

EATING, DRINKING AND NIGHTLIFE

Seafront Kriezótou is lined with cafés and touristy tavernas, though you'll generally find better value away from the front. Theohári Kótsíka, one of the lanes leading inland from here to parallel Sakhtoúri, just to the west of the platía, has several *psistariés* and takeaway kebab places, as does I. Kótsika, between Platía Amalías and the Town Hall. There are also plenty of wonderful old-fashioned food stores, such as *Galaktopoleío Stani* (see p.454).

7

Aeriko West beach ☎ 22240 22365. Lounge bar behind the beach with a beach bar area on the sand; probably the best of a selection of bar/clubs behind the beach here. Live music and club nights in summer. Daily all day till late.

★**Cavo D'oro** Paródos Sakhtoúri ☎ 22240 22326. Despite the name, this is an absolutely traditional Greek taverna, always busy, serving the likes of cheese-stuffed peppers, home-made tzatzíki and goat in tomato sauce (€8). There's no menu, so choose from the bubbling pots or raw ingredients in the kitchen. You'll find it in the first alley off the waterfront west of the square. Noon–4.30pm & 7pm–late; closed Tues.

Galaktopoleío Stani Sakhtoúri. Just west of Platía Amalías, this dairy store sells virtually nothing but traditional home-made yoghurt and rice pudding. Hours vary.

Hovolo Kriezótou 118. Elegant café on the waterfront serving coffee and sweets by day, wine by the glass and beer at night; somewhat pricey, but offset by the delicious traditional snacks that come with each drink. Daily all day till late.

To Kyma Káto Aetós ☎ 22240 23365. Big seaside restaurant 2km east of town, with a terrace above the water and another further up. The seafood-heavy menu makes this place a popular weekend excursion for big parties, so it's safest to book. Fri–Sun lunch and dinner.

Mýli and the south-east

MÝLI, a lovely place full of rushing water, lies just 3km inland from Kárystos, and is a natural first stop on any trip east. The one real sight here is medieval **Castello Rosso** (**Kokkinókastro**), a twenty-minute climb above the village; seen from Kárystos, the castle looks amazingly well preserved, but up close it's ruinous, apart from an Orthodox **chapel** built over the water cistern. The sweeping views make the trip worthwhile, however.

Mount Óhi

Alpine club shelter ☎ 22240 22472 to get the keys

Mount Óhi (1399m), inland from Kárystos, is Évvia's third-highest peak and the focus of trails of sufficient quality to attract overseas trekkers. From Mýli, it's a three-hour-plus **hike** up the bare slopes of Óhi, mostly by a good path short cutting the road; about forty minutes along are various finished and half-finished cipollino marble **columns**, abandoned almost two thousand years ago. The Romans loved the greenish, veined material and extensively quarried southern Évvia, shipping the marble back to Italy. The path reaches an **alpine club shelter**, with spring water outside, just below the summit, and a **dhrakóspito** ("dragon house"), more impressive than the Stýra trio (see p.452), which seemingly sprouts from the mountainside.

Dhimosári Gorge

The one unmissable excursion in southern Évvia is the three-hour hike down the **Dhimosári Gorge**. The descent northeast from Mt Óhi, mostly in deep shade, past various springs and watermills, follows a path (often *kalderími*) as far as the farming hamlet of Lenoséi, then a track to **Kallianós** village, with another path just before the latter down to a beach. South Evia Tours (see p.453) organize a weekly guided trek here in summer as well as other walking trips; otherwise you'll have to arrange a taxi transfer back, or hitch.

Northern Évvia

Leaving Halkídha to the north, the main road snakes steeply over a forested ridge, with spectacular views back over the city and the narrow strait, and then down through the **Dhervéni Gorge**, gateway to Évvia's northwest.

ARRIVAL AND DEPARTURE   NORTHERN ÉVVIA

By ferry Ten or more ferries a day shuttle between Edhipsós and Arkítsa (45min; ☎ 22260 23330, ⓦ ferries edipsos.gr), and eight between Ayiókambos and Glýfa (25min; ☎ 22260 31680, ⓦ ferriesglyfa.gr); there are also more seasonal services from Áyios Konstandínos to Áyios Yeóryios (25min; ☎ 22260 33460). Tickets are sold on the quayside, and buses from Athens' Liossíon 260 terminal serve the mainland ports.

By bus Bus connections with Athens via the ferry are better than with Halkídha; Edhipsós has at least three daily to Athens (3hr), and just one to Halkídha (2hr 30min).

There are also at least a couple of buses a day from Athens, Halkídha and Edhipsós to Límni, Roviés and to Istiéa, the hub for north- and west-coast beaches.

Prokópi and the Church of St John the Russian

PROKÓPI, in a broad wooded upland where the road emerges from the gorge, is famous for its hideous 1960s pilgrimage **Church of St John the Russian**, actually a Ukrainian soldier captured by the Ottomans early in the eighteenth century and taken to central Anatolia, where he died. His mummified body began to work miracles, leading to canonization; the saint's relics were brought here in the 1923 population exchange (see p.539). A vast pilgrimage in late May sees people walking from Halkídha (and beyond) and camping all around the church.

Candili manor house

ⓦ candili.gr

The large **manor house** overlooking Prokópi is home to Philip Noel-Baker, a descendant of English Philhellene nobleman Edward Noel, a relative of Lady Byron, who bought the estate from the Turks in 1832 in order to support the new Greek state. The house now operates as **Candili**, a tranquil centre for conferences and courses (yoga, art, etc).

Límni and around

LÍMNI, a well-preserved Neoclassical town and sheltered port, with magnificent views west to the mainland, rivals Kárystos as the most characterful resort on Évvia. The main drawback is a lack of decent beaches, though there are plenty of pebble strands all around.

Immediately west of Límni, the hamlets of **Sipiádha** and **Khrónia** are virtually suburbs, each with good pebbly beaches and a choice of accommodation. **ROVIÉS**, 7km from Límni, is a bigger place, famous for its olives and with a picturesque, ruined medieval tower at its heart.

Folklore Museum

Límni • Tues–Sat 10am–1pm, Sun from 10.30am • €2 • ☎ 22270 31335

Behind Límni's waterfront is a maze of unnamed alleys; on one such is the little **Folklore Museum**. This traces the history of the place from Mycenaean times – ancient Elymnia was an important city in Euboea – to the twentieth century, with some wonderful old photos, and it's a fun visit, where you're likely to get a personal tour from the curator, who speaks little English.

Ayíou Nikoláou Galatáki

Daily: winter 9am–noon & 2–5pm; summer 9am–noon & 5–8pm • Free • Knock and wait for entry; strict clothing rules apply

Around 7km southeast of Límni, the beautiful monastery of **Ayíou Nikoláou Galatáki** perches on the wooded slopes of Mount Kandíli, overlooking the Evvian Gulf. Though much rebuilt since its original Byzantine foundation atop a temple of Poseidon, the convent retains a thirteenth-century anti-pirate tower and a crypt. One of the six nuns will show you **frescoes** dating from a sixteenth-century renovation. Especially vivid, on the right, is the *Entry of the Righteous into Paradise*: the virtuous ascend a perilous ladder to be crowned by angels and received by Christ, while the wicked miss the rungs and fall into the maw of Leviathan.

There are pebble-and-sand **beaches** scattered along the road to the monastery, and more that can only be reached on foot immediately below it.

ARRIVAL AND DEPARTURE	**LÍMNI AND AROUND**

By bus Buses stop on Límni's central waterfront near the bottom of the main street, Angéli Govioú. Tickets are sold at the nearby Kafenío Neon.

7

ACCOMMODATION

Dennis House Khrónia ☎ 22270 31787, ⓦ dennishotel
.gr. Apartment block in lush gardens, 500m out of the
village towards Límni, with its own bar and pizza restaurant;
simple studios and two-room apartments with a/c, TV and
great sea views. **€50**

★ **Eleonas** Roviés ☎ 22270 71619, ⓦ eleonashotel
.com. Classy, peaceful place in a secluded olive grove
outside town, with ground-floor a/c garden rooms or first-
floor ones with balconies. Set back some way from the sea,
but still with fine views. Good restaurant, where home-
made breakfast is included. **€80**

Graegos Studios Límni ☎ 22270 31117, ⓦ graegos
.com. Just four comfortable a/c studios, with well-equipped
kitchens, right at the eastern end of the waterfront. The
two at the front have fabulous big balconies with views of
the fishing port. **€70**

Kaminos Límni ☎ 22270 31640, ⓦ www.kaminoshotel
.com. On the waterfront a couple of kilometres south of Límni,
this stunning conversion of a magnetite processing factory
offers four modern suites, each with kitchenette and classy
modern furnishings. There's also a pool and an excellent retro-
industrial style restaurant in the old warehouse. **€125**

EATING AND DRINKING

7 Anemous Límni ☎ 22270 32121. Unexpectedly fancy,
though not overly expensive restaurant in a restored stone
building in a backstreet behind the eastern seafront.
Mediterranean menu includes pizza, pasta with salmon,
salads and a few grills served in a garden or (in winter)
inside by a roaring fire. Daily 6pm–midnight; Oct–May
closed Tues.

Lamoros Límni ☎ 22270 31351. Immaculate setting
with a waterfront terrace and steps down to the water in

an absolutely tranquil spot, 500m out of town, on the road
to the monastery. Food is the regular Greek taverna array,
with plenty of fish, cooked with care; mains €6.50–8.50.
Daily, evenings only.

Platanos Límni ☎ 22270 31686. Lovely taverna/
tsipourádhiko shaded by an ancient plane on the waterfront
in the heart of town. Simple dishes like sardines or kalamari
(€8) and a wide range of *ráki* and *tsipoúro* served with *pikilía*
(small selection €8, large €16). Daily lunch and dinner.

Edhipsós

EDHIPSÓS (aka **LOUTRÁ EDHIPSOÚ**, the baths of Edhipsós) is one of Greece's most
popular **spa** towns, with a line of grand hotels gracing the front and plenty of places to
eat and drink. The sulphurous **natural hot springs** here, with water gushing to the
surface at up to 75°C, were well known in antiquity, but reached their modern heyday
in the 1930s, when the likes of Winston Churchill and Greta Garbo took to the waters
here. Today, the place's faded glory is undergoing something of a revival. If your wallet
doesn't stretch to services at the *Thermae Sylla Spa* (see below), you can bathe for free
at the adjacent public **beach**, where geothermal water pours into an artificial set of
cascades. There are more free, open-air hot springs at **Ília**, 8km east, where the water is
channelled into ad hoc pits by shovel-wielding locals.

ARRIVAL AND DEPARTURE

EDHIPSÓS

By ferry Ferries arrive on the central seafront.
By bus The bus station is a couple of blocks south on
Thermopotámou, the main street inland from the waterfront.

Taxis The taxi stand (☎ 22260 23280) is directly opposite
where the ferry docks.

ACCOMMODATION

Kentrikon 25th Martíou 14 ☎ 22260 22302, ⓦ kentrikon
hotel.com. Friendly, newly restored hotel which is excellent
value given the facilities, which include comfortable modern
rooms, gym and indoor and outdoor spa pools. Breakfast
included. **€45**

Thermae Sylla Waterfront ☎ 22260 60100, ⓦ www

.thermaesylla.gr. Five-star complex at the northern end
of the seafront promenade that's by far the grandest of
the surviving hotels, with indoor and outdoor pools and
a spa with a huge variety of treatments, also available to
nonguests. **€175**

The north and west coasts

Beyond Edhipsós and round to the **west coast** stretches a string of small resorts, on
the whole consisting of long, exposed pebble beaches, backed by hamlets of second
homes and small hotels; if you want a quiet escape to old-fashioned Greece, there's
plenty to like here, though very little to do except when the Athenians turn up in

August. Between villages, the driving is often steep and winding, the scenery green and spectacular.

The cape immediately east of Edhipsós, off the main road, is particularly quiet and scenic, the venue of Greek family holidays and an incongruous Club Med. **ÁYIOS YEÓRYIOS** is the one coastal settlement of any size, with summer ferries from Áyios Konstandínos. On the main road, heading clockwise from Edhipsós, you come first to **AYIÓKAMBOS**, with regular **ferry** connections to Glýfa on the mainland. **NÉOS PÝRGOS** and **OREÍ**, next up, pretty much merge together into a single resort; the latter has good restaurants around its attractive harbour. **PÉFKI** is another small, pleasant resort with extensive, windswept beaches either side, good for kitesurfing (see below).

Beyond Péfki, the road mainly heads inland. **Paralía Áyíou Nikoláou**, signed from the village of **ELLINIKÁ**, is a lovely, sandy cove overlooked by tavernas and by a tiny white chapel on a little islet. At **Psaropoúli**, steeply below the town of **VASILIKÁ**, there's a vast, barely developed bay of grey sand and pebbles. **PARALÍA AYÍAS ÁNNAS**, by contrast, is a substantial resort on a couple of kilometres of brownish sand, with showers and loungers at the resort end, and plenty of empty space beyond. Finally, at the tiny hamlet of **KRÝA VRÝSSI**, there's a lovely brown-sand beach with the ruins of ancient **Kirinthos** at its southern end.

ACTIVITIES

Kitesurfing The winds at Péfki beach are exploited by the excellent kitesurfing school, Kites Guru (☎ 6977 245 438; ⓦ kitesguru.gr).

EATING

NORTH COAST

Paradeisos Paralía Áyíou Nikoláou ☎ 22260 42257. A wonderful space set among the pines on the point above the beach. In the setting the food is almost irrelevant, but it's good hearty Greek staples, with plenty of local veg. Daily lunch and dinner.

To Pirofani Néos Pýrgos ☎ 22260 71448. A good *psarotavérna* (seafood restaurant) overlooking the fishing harbour, serving all the usuals at waterfront tables and on a substantial roof terrace across the road. Daily lunch and dinner.

To Steki tis Yiannas Oreí ☎ 22260 71540. Excellent taverna with a lovely seaside setting by the harbour, serving fresh fish, octopus and calamari, plus daily oven-baked specials. Mains €7.50–12. Daily lunch and dinner.

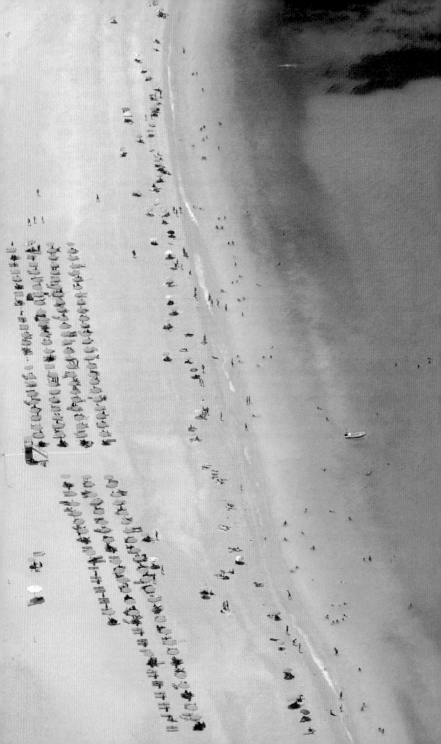

The Ionian islands

MYRTOS BEACH, KEFALONIÁ

The Ionian islands

The six core Ionian islands, which shepherd their satellites down the west coast of the mainland, float on the haze of the Ionian Sea. Their lush green contours, a result of heavy winter rains, come as a shock to those more used to the stark outlines of the Aegean. The west coasts of the larger islands also boast some of Greece's most picturesque cliff-backed beaches, whose sands are caressed by a band of milky turquoise water leading to the deeper azure sea.

Tourism is the dominant influence these days, as it has been for decades on **Corfu** (Kérkyra), which was one of the first Greek islands established on the package-holiday circuit, though the continuing downturn means it does not feel as swamped as in the past. And while parts of its coastline are among the few stretches in Greece with development to match the Spanish *costas*, the island is large enough to contain parts as beautiful as anywhere in the group. The southern half of **Zákynthos** (Zante) has also gone down the same tourist path, but elsewhere the island's pace is a lot less intense. Little **Paxí** lacks the water to support large-scale hotels and has limited facilities tucked into just three villages, which means it gets totally packed in season. The most rewarding trio for island-hopping are undoubtedly Kefaloniá, Itháki and **Lefkádha**. The latter is connected to the mainland by a causeway and iron drawbridge but still has quite a low-key straggle of tourist centres and only two major resorts, despite boasting some excellent beaches, strung along its stunning west coast. **Kefaloniá** offers a series of "real towns" and more stunning beaches, as well as a selection of worthwhile attractions, while **Itháki**, Odysseus's rugged home, is protected from a tourist influx by an absence of sand. Finally, although officially counted among the Ionians and constituting the seventh of the traditional *eptánisos* (heptanese or "seven islands"), rugged **Kýthira** is quite separate from the six main islands on several counts. It is geographically 200km removed and only accessible from the southern Poloponnese, it shares the drier and warmer climate of southern Greece, and it remains quite a touristic backwater.

Brief history

The Ionian islands were the Homeric realm of Odysseus, centred on Ithaca (modern Itháki), and here alone of all modern Greek territory the Ottomans never held sway – except on Lefkádha. After the fall of Byzantium, possession passed to the **Venetians**, and the islands became a keystone in Venice's maritime empire from 1386 until its collapse in 1797. Most of the population remained immune to the establishment of Italian as the official language and the arrival of Roman Catholicism, but Venetian influence remains evident in the architecture of the island capitals, despite damage from a series of earthquakes.

Corfu Town combination ticket p.463	**Lefkádha's summer festivals** p.486
The Ionian School of painting p.467	**Boat trips from Nydhrí** p.488
Mount Pandokrátor p.470	**Lover's leap** p.491
Boat trips from Paleokastrítsa p.475	**Odysseus sights around Vathý** p.502
Walking the Corfu Trail p.479	**Boat trips from Zákynthos Town** p.507
Walks around Lákka p.482	**Loggerhead turtles** p.509

THE LISTÓN, CORFU TOWN

Highlights

❶ **Corfu Town** Venetian fortresses, beautiful churches, fine museums and appealing Venetian architecture. **See p.463**

❷ **Longás beach, Corfu** Shaded till early afternoon and backed by sheer vertical red cliffs, this beach is an excellent hangout. **See p.476**

❸ **Andípaxi** Some of the Ionians' best swimming and snorkelling is on offer at the exquisite beaches of Paxí's little sister. **See p.483**

❹ **Lefkádha's west coast** Between Áï Nikítas and Pórto Katsíki lie some of the archipelago's finest and least crowded beaches. **See p.491**

❺ **Mount Énos, Kefaloniá** The highest point in the Ionians has stunning vistas of sea and distant land, plus a unique species of pine. **See p.496**

❻ **Melissáni Cave, Kefaloniá** Take a boat trip inside this once-enclosed underwater cave and see dappled sunlight on the water amid rock formations. **See p.499**

❼ **Itháki's Homeric sites** Relive the myths on Odysseus's island by visiting locations described by Homer. **See p.502**

❽ **Boat tour around Zákynthos** The best way to see the impressive coastline, including the Blue Caves and Shipwreck Bay, is to cruise from Zákynthos Town. **See p.507**

HIGHLIGHTS ARE MARKED ON THE MAP ON P.462

On Corfu, the Venetian legacy is mixed with that of the **British**, who imposed a military "protectorate" over the Ionian islands at the close of the Napoleonic Wars, before ceding the archipelago to Greece in 1864. There is, however, no question of the islanders' essential Greekness: the poet Dhionyssios Solomos, author of the national anthem, hailed from the Ionians, as did Nikos Mantzelos, who provided the music, and the first Greek president, Ioannis Kapodhistrias.

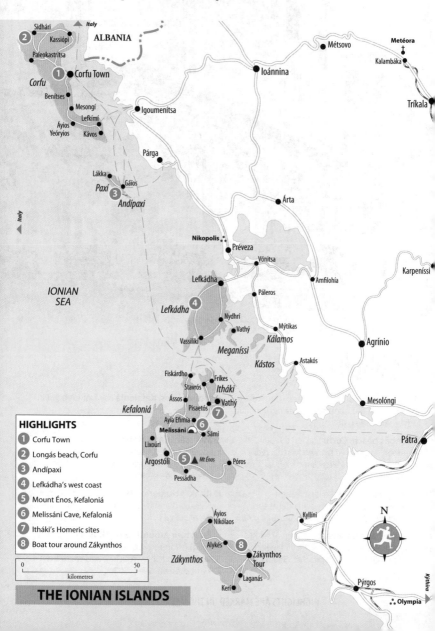

HIGHLIGHTS

1. Corfu Town
2. Longás beach, Corfu
3. Andípaxi
4. Lefkádha's west coast
5. Mount Énos, Kefaloniá
6. Melissáni Cave, Kefaloniá
7. Itháki's Homeric sites
8. Boat tour around Zákynthos

THE IONIAN ISLANDS

Corfu

Dangling between the heel of Italy and the west coast of mainland Greece, green, mountainous **CORFU (Kérkyra)** was one of the first Greek islands to attract mass tourism in the 1960s. Indiscriminate exploitation turned parts into eyesores but a surprising amount of the island still consists of olive groves, mountains or woodland. The majority of package holidays are based in the most developed resorts and unspoilt terrain is often only a few minutes' walk away.

Corfu is thought to have been the model for Prospero and Miranda's place of exile in Shakespeare's *The Tempest*, and was certainly known to **writers** such as Spenser, Milton and – more recently – Edward Lear and Henry Miller, as well as Gerald and Lawrence Durrell. Lawrence Durrell's *Prospero's Cell* evokes the island's "delectable landscape" still evident in some of its beaches, the best of the whole archipelago.

The staggering amount of **accommodation** on the island means that competition keeps prices down even in high season, at least in many resorts outside of Corfu Town. Prices at restaurants and in shops also tend to be a little lower than average for the Ionians.

ARRIVAL AND DEPARTURE CORFU

By plane Corfu's airport, 2km south of Corfu Town, receives seasonal charters and a few scheduled flights from different parts of northern Europe, as well as scheduled year-round and seasonal domestic services (see p.468).

By ferry and hydrofoil The vast majority of domestic services, all those to Italy and the hydrofoil to Albania run from Corfu Town (see p.468), although there are a few boats to the mainland from Lefkímmi.

GETTING AROUND

By bus Corfu's bus service radiates from the capital (see p.468). Island-wide services stop operating between 6 and 9pm, suburban ones between 9 and 10.30pm. Printed English timetables are available for both and can be picked up at the respective terminals.

By car or motorbike Many people rent vehicles to get around the island, and there are numerous international and local companies in Corfu Town (see p.468) and around the resorts.

Corfu Town

The capital, **CORFU TOWN**, has been one of the most elegant island capitals in the whole of Greece since it was spruced up for the EU summit in 1994. Although many of its finest buildings were destroyed by Nazi bombers in World War II, two massive forts, the sixteenth-century church of Áyios Spyrídhon and some buildings dating from French and British administrations remain intact. As the island's major port of entry by ferry or plane, Corfu Town can get packed in summer.

The city comprises a number of distinct areas. The **Historic Centre**, the area enclosed by the Old Port and the two forts, consists of several smaller districts: **Campiello**, the oldest, sits on the hill above the harbour; **Kofinéta** stretches towards the Spianádha (Esplanade); **Áyii Apóstoli** runs west of the Mitrópolis (Orthodox cathedral); while, tucked in beside the Néo Froúrio, is what remains of the old **Jewish quarter**. These districts and their tall, narrow alleys conceal some of Corfu's most beautiful architecture. The **New Town** comprises all the areas that surround the Historic Centre.

CORFU TOWN COMBINATION TICKET

There is a handy **combination ticket** that covers four of Corfu Town's main attractions: the Paleó Froúrio, Byzantine Museum, Archeological Museum and Asiatic Museum. The ticket costs €8 and is available at any of the four sights.

8

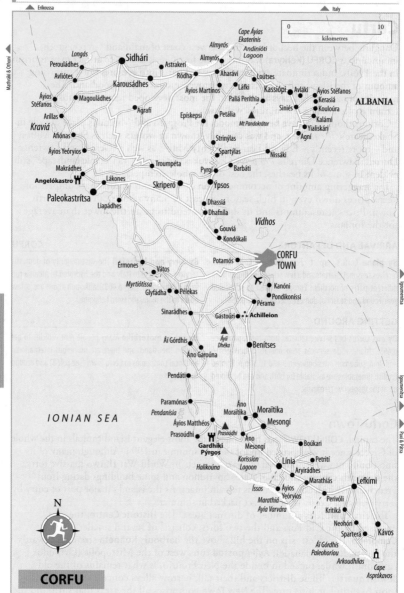

Historic Centre

The most obvious sights in the **Historic Centre** are the forts, the **Paleó Froúrio** and **Néo Froúrio**, whose designations (*paleó* – "old", *néo* – "new") are a little misleading, since what you see of the older structure was begun by the Byzantines in the mid-twelfth century, just a hundred years before the Venetians began work on the newer citadel. They have both been damaged and modified by various occupiers and besiegers – the last contribution was the Neoclassical shrine of St George, built by the British in the middle of Paleó Froúrio during the 1840s.

Néo Froúrio

Daily: April–Oct 9am–9pm (or sunset if earlier); Nov–March 8am–3pm • €3

Looming above Old Port's west side, the **Néo Froúrio** is the more architecturally interesting of Corfu Town's two forts. The entrance, at the back of the fort, gives onto cellars, dungeons and battlements, with excellent views over the town and bay; there's a small gallery and seasonal café at the summit.

Paleó Froúrio

April–Oct Mon–Sat 8am–8pm, Sun 8.30am–3pm; Nov–March daily 8.30am–2.30pm • €4 (or part of combination ticket) • T 26610 48310

The **Paleó Froúrio**, on the east town, is not as well preserved as the Néo Froúrio and contains some incongruous modern structures, but it has an interesting **Byzantine Museum** just inside the gate, and even more stunning views from the central Land Tower. It also hosts daily *son et lumière* shows.

The Listón and Spianádha

Just west of the Paleó Froúrio, the focus of town life is the **Listón**, an arcaded café-lined street built during the French occupation by the architect of the Rue de Rivoli in Paris, and the green **Spianádha** (Esplanade) it overlooks. The cricket pitch, still in use at the northern end of the Spianádha, is another British legacy, while at the southern end is the **Maitland Rotunda**, built to honour the first British High Commissioner of Corfu and the Ionian islands. The neighbouring statue of Ioannis Kapodhistrias celebrates the local hero and statesman (1776–1831) who led the diplomatic efforts for independence and was made Greece's first president in 1827.

8

Palace of SS Michael and George

Listón • **Asiatic Museum** Tues–Sun 8.30am–3.30pm • €3 (or part of combination ticket) • **Modern Art Gallery** Wed–Sun 9am–3pm • €4 • T 26610 30443, W matk.gr

At the far northern end of the Listón is the nineteenth-century **Palace of SS Michael and George**, a solidly British edifice built as the residence of their High Commissioner (one of whom was the future British prime minister William Gladstone) and later used as a palace by the Greek monarchy. The former state rooms house the **Asiatic Museum**, a must for aficionados of oriental culture. Amassed by Corfiot diplomat Gregorios Manos (1850–1929) and others, it includes Noh theatre masks, woodcuts, wood and brass statuettes, samurai weapons and artworks from Thailand, Korea and Tibet, as well as some exquisite garments and jewellery from Central Asia in the new Jason Deighton-Sartzetakis collection. The adjoining **Modern Art Gallery** holds a small collection of contemporary Greek art.

Byzantine Museum

Arseníou • Tues–Sun 8.30am–3pm • €2 (or part of combination ticket) • T 26610 38313

Up a short flight of steps on Arseníou, the **Byzantine Museum** is housed in the restored church of the Panayía Andivouniótissa. It houses church frescoes, sculptures and sections of mosaic floors from the ancient site of Paleópolis, just south of Corfu Town. There are also some pre-Christian artefacts, and a collection of icons dating from between the fifteenth and nineteenth centuries.

Solomos Museum

Theodhórou Mákri, off Arseníou • Mon–Fri 9.30am–1pm • €1 • T 26610 30674

This hidden **Solomos Museum** is dedicated to modern Greece's most famous nineteenth-century poet, **Dhionysios Solomos.** Born on Zákynthos, Solomos was

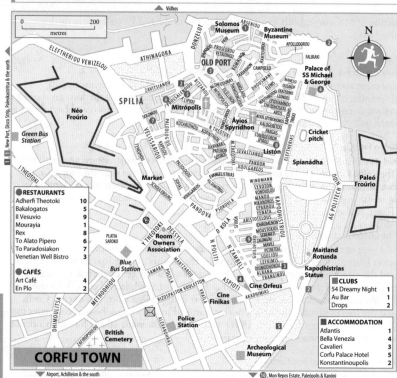

CORFU TOWN

author of the poem *Amnos stín Elefthería* ("Hymn to Liberty"), which was to become the Greek national anthem. He studied at Corfu's Ionian Academy and lived in a house on this site for much of his life.

Áyios Spyrídhon

Spyrídhonos • Daily 8am–9pm • Free

A block behind the Listón is the sixteenth-century church of **Áyios Spyrídhon**, whose maroon-domed campanile dominates the town. Here you will find the silver-encrusted coffin of the island's patron saint, **Spyrídhon** – Spyros in the diminutive – after whom seemingly half the male population is named. Four times a year (Palm Sunday and the following Sat, Aug 11 and the first Sun in Nov), to the accompaniment of much celebration and feasting, the relics are paraded through the town streets. Each of the days commemorates a miraculous deliverance of the island credited to the saint – twice from plague, once from a famine and, in the eighteenth century, from the Turks.

Mitrópolis

Platía Mitropóleos • Daily 8am–7pm • Free

After Áyios Spyrídhon, the next most important of the town's many churches, is the **Mitrópolis** (Orthodox cathedral), which is perched at the top of its own square opposite the Old Port. It also houses the remains of a saint, in this case St Theodora, the ninth-century wife of Emperor Theophilos. The building dates from 1577, and the plain exterior conceals a splendid iconostasis, as well as some fine icons, including a sixteenth-century image of *Saint George Slaying the Dragon*.

Vídhos

Hourly shuttle *kaïkia* run from the Old Port (daily 8am–1.30am; €2 return)

Vídhos, the wooded island visible from the Old Port, is a quieter day-trip destination than Vlahérna or Pondikoníssi (see p.468). It makes a particularly pleasant summer evening excursion, when there is live music at the municipal restaurant near the jetty.

New Town

There are a couple of noteworthy sights in the **New Town** which surrounds the Historic Centre. This area also encompasses much of Corfu Town's commercial heart, centred around busy **Platía Saróko**.

Archeological Museum

Braïla 1 • Closed until at least end 2015; previous operational hours Tues–Sun 8.30am–3pm • €3 (or part of combination ticket) • ☎ 26610 30680

At the time of writing, Corfu Town's **Archeological Museum** was undergoing extensive renovations and was not expected to reopen until at least the end of 2015. Entry details and some exhibits may change, but you can be sure it will still include the star attraction, a massive (17m) **Gorgon pediment** excavated from the Doric temple of Artemis at Paleópolis, just south of Corfu Town, as well as a fine range of neolithic and classical treasures.

British cemetery

Cnr of Zafiropoúlou and Kolokotróni • 24hr • Free

Just south of Platía Saróko, the well-maintained **British cemetery** features some elaborate civic and military memorials. It's a quiet green space away from the madness of Saróko and, in spring and early summer, comes alive with dozens of species of orchids and other exotic blooms.

The outskirts

Each of the sights on the sprawling **outskirts** of the city can easily be seen in a morning or afternoon, and you could conceivably cover several in one day. Mon Repos and the remains of Paleópolis are the most worthwhile sights at which to spend some time.

THE IONIAN SCHOOL OF PAINTING

The Ionian islands have a strong tradition of excellence in the fine arts, particularly iconography. Once occupied by the Venetians and later the British, the islands spent centuries more in touch with developments in western Europe than in the Ottoman empire.

Until the late seventeenth century, religious art in the Ionians, as elsewhere, was dominated by the stylistic purity and dignified austerity of the Cretan School. The founder of the **Ionian School of painting** is considered to be **Panayiotis Dhoxaras**, who was born in the Peloponnese in 1662 but, after studying in Venice and Rome, moved to Zákynthos and later lived and worked in Lefkádha and Corfu until his death in 1729. From his travels, Dhoxaras absorbed the spirit of Italian Renaissance art, and brought a greater degree of naturalism into iconography by showing his subjects, usually saints, in more human poses amid everyday surroundings. He is also credited with introducing the technique of **oil painting** into Greece in place of the older method of mixing pigments with egg yolk.

Dhoxaras' work was carried on by his son, **Nikolaos** (1710–1775), and over the next two centuries the tradition flourished through the skilled brushwork of a host of talented artists, such as Corfiot **Yioryios Khrysoloras** (1680–1762), Zakynthian **Nikolaos Kandounis** (1768–1834) and three generations of the Proselandis family, starting with **Pavlos Proselandis** (1784–1837).

Mon Repos estate and around

Estate Daily 8am–7.30pm · Free · **Paleópolis Museum** Daily 8.30am–3.30pm · €3 · ☎ 26610 41369

About 1.5km around the bay from the Rotunda and the Archeological Museum, tucked behind Mon Repos beach, the area centred on the **Mon Repos estate** contains the most accessible archeological remains on the island, collectively known as **Paleópolis**. Within the estate, thick woodland conceals two **Doric temples**, dedicated to Hera and Poseidon. The Neoclassical **Mon Repos villa**, built by British High Commissioner Frederic Adam in 1824 and handed over to Greece in 1864, is the birthplace of Britain's Prince Philip and has been converted into the **Paleópolis Museum**. As well as various archeological finds from the vicinity, including some fine sculpture, it contains previous residents' period furniture and temporary modern art exhibitions.

Other remains worth a peek outside the confines of the estate include the **Early Christian Basilica** (Tues–Sun 8.30am–3pm; free) opposite the entrance, the **Temple of Artemis** (open access; free), a few hundred metres west, and the eleventh-century church of **Áyii Iáson and Sosípater**, back towards the seafront on Náfsikas.

Vlahérna and Pondikoníssi

Bus #2 leaves Platía Saróko every 30min for Vlahérna convent; boats frequently leave Vlahérna dock for Pondikoníssi (€3 return)

The most famous excursion from Corfu Town is to the islets of **Vlahérna and Pondikoníssi**, 2km south of town below the hill of Kanóni, named after the single cannon trained out to sea atop it. Reached by a short causeway, the tiny, white convent of Vlahérna is one of the most photographed images on Corfu. Pondikoníssi, tufted by greenery from which peeks the small chapel of Panayía Vlahernón, is identified in legend with a ship from Odysseus's fleet, petrified by Poseidon in revenge for the blinding of his son Polyphemus.

Achilleion

Gastoúri, 6km south of Corfu Town · Daily 8am–7pm (Nov–April till 4pm) · €7 · ☎ 26610 56245, ⓦ achillion-corfu.gr · Bus #10

Just south of Corfu Town, past the resort sprawl of Pérama sits the bizarre **Achilleion**, a palace built in a mercifully unique blend of Teutonic and Neoclassical styles in 1890 by Elizabeth, Empress of Austria. Henry Miller considered it "the worst piece of gimcrackery" that he'd ever laid eyes on and thought it "would make an excellent museum for surrealistic art". The house is predictably grandiose but the **gardens** are pleasant to walk around and afford splendid views in all directions.

ARRIVAL
CORFU TOWN

By plane The airport is 2km south of the town centre. A dedicated bus connects with central Corfu Town 8 times daily, or you can flag down blue city buses #5 and #6 at the junction 500m north of the terminal. Taxis charge a rather steep €10 into town.

Domestic destinations Athens (4–5 daily; 1hr); Kefaloniá (summer 2–3 weekly; 1hr 20min); Préveza (summer 5 weekly; 30min); Thessaloníki (summer 4 weekly; 1hr); Zákynthos (summer 2–3 weekly; 2hr 5min).

By bus There are two bus terminals: the islandwide green bus service is based on Avramíou (also for Athens and Thessaloníki; ☎ 26610 28900, ⓦ ktelkerkyras.gr), and the suburban blue bus system, which also serves nearby resorts such as Benítses and Dhassiá, is based in Platía Saróko (☎ 26610 31595, ⓦ corfucitybus.com).

By ferry All vessels dock at the New Port (Néo Limáni), just west of the Néo Froúrio. The Old Port (Paleó Limáni), east of the New Port, is used only for day excursions. Most

of the ferry offices are on the main road opposite the New Port; if you're travelling to Italy, go to Igoumenítsa for more options as the number of ferries direct to Italy has been severely reduced. The port authority (domestic ☎ 26610 32655, international ☎ 26610 30481) can advise on services. There are buses that board the ferry from the New Port to Athens (3 daily; 9–10hr) and Thessaloníki (1–2 daily; 6–7hr); schedules are year-round. For the additional destinations below, frequencies given are for the summer season and are greatly reduced or nonexistent in winter.

Destinations Ancona (2 weekly; 14hr); Bari (2–3 weekly; 11hr); Brindisi (2–4 weekly; 6–8hr); Eríkoussa/Mathráki/Othoní (3 weekly; 2–4hr); Igoumenítsa (every 10–45min; 1hr 15min–2hr).

By hydrofoil Hydrofoils dock at the eastern end of the New Port and run for most of the tourist season.

Destinations Gáïos (Paxí; May–Oct 1–3 daily; 50min); Sarande (Albania; 1–2 daily; 30min).

By car Most of the international car rental chains have outlets at the airport and New Port. Among the more competitive local companies are Ionian Travel (**☎**26610 80444, **ⓦ**ioniantravel.gr), based in nearby Gouviá but happy to bring you a vehicle, or Sunrise (Ethnikís Andístasis 6, **☎**26610 44325, **ⓦ**corfusunrise.com).

By motorbike or scooter Motorbikes and scooters can be rented from Easy Rider, Venizélou 4 (**☎**26610 43026), or Atlantis, Xenofóndos Stratigoú 48 (**☎**26610 40580), both in the New Port.

ACCOMMODATION

Accommodation in Corfu Town is busy all year, and expensive for the island. The Room Owners' Association at D. Theotóki 2A (Mon–Fri 9am–1.30pm, plus summer Tues, Thurs & Fri 6–8pm; **☎**26610 26133, **ⓔ**oitkcrf@otenet.gr) can help find rooms.

Atlantis Xenofóndos Stratigoú 48 **☎**26610 35560, **ⓦ**atlantis-hotel-corfu.com. Large and spacious a/c hotel in the New Port; with its functional 1960s ambience, it rather lacks character, but the rooms are perfectly adequate. **€50**

★**Bella Venezia** Zambéli 4 **☎**26610 46500, **ⓦ**bella veneziahotel.com. Smart, yellow Neoclassical building which blends elegance with a cosy atmosphere. The sophisticated rooms are furnished and decorated in warm hues. Breakfast in the airy conservatory included. **€115**

Cavalieri Kapodhistríou 4 **☎**26610 39041, **ⓦ**cavalieri -hotel.com. Classy and large yet still welcoming, the lavishly decorated rooms in the *Cavalieri* have all mod cons

and some have great views, plus there's a rooftop bar open to nonresidents. Breakfast included. **€90**

Corfu Palace Hotel Leofóros Dhimokratías 2 **☎**26610 39485, **ⓦ**corfupalace.com. The most luxurious hotel on the island, with sweeping staircases up from the lobby, indoor and outdoor pools, landscaped gardens and well-appointed rooms, each with a marble bath. Breakfast included. **€230**

Konstantinoupolis Zavitsiánou 11 **☎**26610 48716, **ⓦ**konstantinoupolis.com.gr. A classy hotel in the Old Port with tasteful decoration and comfortable rooms, most with fine harbour views. Good discounts out of high season. **€62**

EATING AND DRINKING

RESTAURANTS

Adherfi Theotoki M. Athanassíou, Garítsa **☎**26610 45910. By far the best of the several establishments tucked behind the seafront park, this popular family taverna serves excellent mezédhes, meat and good-value fish dishes for €10 or less. March–Oct daily noon–2am.

Bakalogatos Alipíou 23 **☎**26613 01721. Deservedly popular modern restaurant in Spiliá which has a variety of veg and cheese mezédhes, meat and fish dishes for under €10, plus microbrewery beer and local wine. Daily 11am–2am.

Il Vesuvio Guildford 16 **☎**26610 21284. *Il Vesuvio* serves the town's most authentic Italian food, including fine antipasti and meat or seafood spaghetti dishes at around €10–15. Daily noon–1am.

Mourayia Arseníou 15–17 **☎**26610 33815. This unassuming, good-value ouzerí near the Byzantine Museum does a range of tasty mezédhes for €6–8, including sausage or seafood such as mussels and shrimp in exquisite sauces. It also boasts views of passing ferries and Vídhos island. March–Nov daily noon–midnight.

Rex Kapodhistríou 66 **☎**26610 39649. Rather pricey, owing to its location just behind the Listón, but this place has some of the best food in town, especially the delicious oven dishes, such as pork stuffed with plum and fig (€18). Daily 11am–1am.

★**To Alato Pipero** Dhoná 17 **☎**6942 263 873. This

ouzerí in Spiliá is one of the best new places that have sprung up; they serve a moderate range of delicious mezédhes, such as sausages and *saganáki* for mostly €4–6. Daily 8pm–2am.

To Paradosiakon Solomoú 20 **☎**26610 37578. This friendly Spiliá restaurant serves good inexpensive fresh food, especially home-style oven dishes such as *stifádho* (meat-and-onion stew) and *kokkinistó* (meat cooked in tomato sauce) for around €7–8. April–Oct daily 10.30am–midnight.

★**The Venetian Well** Platía Kremastí **☎**26615 50955, **ⓦ**venetianwell.gr. Tucked in a tiny square a few alleys north of the cathedral, this place has been totally renovated but still provides superb quality – at a price. Main dishes such as lamb shank run over €20, but compatible starters like courgette soup are often offered on the house. Easter–Oct daily 7pm–midnight.

CAFÉS

Art Café Gardens behind Palace of SS Michael and George. In a delightful verdant setting behind the Modern Art Gallery, this is a great relaxed spot to take in some refreshment in between sightseeing. Daily 9am–midnight.

En Plo Faliráki jetty **☎**26610 27000. This popular café boasts an unbeatably brilliant, breezy setting, with views of the Paleó Froúrio. A fine place for a preprandial ouzo or late-night brandy. Daily 10am–late.

8

NIGHTLIFE AND ENTERTAINMENT

There are some hip bars in town, usually full of young people, and a few remaining clubs on the "disco strip" of Ethnikís Andistáseos, a couple of kilometres north of town, past the New Port, though much of the action has shifted to the resorts.

CLUBS

54 Dreamy Nights Emborikó Kéndro, Ethnikís Andistáseos 54 ☎ 6940 645 436, ⓦ facebook.com /54dreamynights. This huge club has outstripped all its rivals in and around the Emborikó Kéndro shopping centre, with the latest sounds, a retractable roof and frequent fireworks. Daily 10pm–late.

Drops Leofóros Dhimokratías 14 ☎ 6944 912 947. This popular new place, perched above the yacht harbour with super views of the Old Fort, buzzes till the wee hours with the clink of glasses and the latest trendy sounds. Daily 8pm–late.

CINEMAS

Cine Finikas Akadhimías ☎ 26610 39768. Down the cul-de-sac extension of Akadhimías, the town's open-air summer cinema is a lovely place to take in a film. June–Sept, showings usually 9pm & 11pm.

Cine Orfeus Akadhimías, at Aspióti ☎ 26610 39768. Corfu's winter cinema has comfy seats and a big screen. Oct–May, times vary.

The northeast

The **northeast**, at least beyond the suburban resorts near Corfu Town, is the most typically Greek part of Corfu – it's mountainous, with a rocky coastline chopped into pebbly bays and coves, above wonderfully clear seas.

Dhassiá

Six kilometres from Corfu Town, the coastline begins to improve at **Dhafníla** and **DHASSIÁ**, set in adjacent wooded bays with pebbly beaches. The latter, the first worthwhile place to stop in this direction, is much larger and contains nearly all the area's facilities, including several **watersports** enterprises.

Ýpsos

ÝPSOS, 2km north of Dhassiá, can't really be recommended to anyone but hardened bar-hoppers, though it is home to a diving centre (see opposite). The thin

---

MOUNT PANDOKRÁTOR

Mount Pandokrátor, Corfu's highest mountain, is crowned by the moderately interesting **Pandokrátoras monastery**, whose main sanctuary, built in the seventeenth century, is open to visitors; nothing remains of the original buildings from three centuries earlier.

The most direct route from the south is signposted via Spartýlas and then the village of **Strinýlas**, a popular base for walkers and served by buses from Corfu Town. An alternative approach from the north coast goes via Loútses to the charming ghost village of **Paliá Períthia**, from where you are a steep 5km from the summit and can only climb any higher on foot or in a four-wheel drive. Apart from taking a quick peek at the crumbling remains of half a dozen churches, there is good eating in the village. The main westerly route ascends via **Láfki** to **Petália**, just south of which a paved road leads the final 5km east to the summit.

Anyone interested in walking the Pandokrátor paths is advised to get the **map** of the mountain by island-based cartographer Stephan Jaskulowski or one of Hilary Whitton-Paipeti's walking books, available from the better English-language bookshops in Corfu Town.

ACCOMMODATION AND EATING

★ **The Merchant's House** Paliá Períthia ☎ 26630 98444, ⓦ merchantshousecorfu.com. Superbly renovated old stone house, with warmly painted suites, which can sleep four, and stylish furniture. This boutique B&B offers comfort, great views and a fine breakfast. April–Oct. **€140**

★ **Old Perithia** Paliá Períthia ☎ 26630 98055. Worth climbing any mountain for, this traditional taverna is renowned for succulent goat and home-produced feta cheese. The views are splendid too, of course. Noon–midnight: May–Sept daily; Oct–April Sat & Sun.

pebble beach lies right beside the busy coast road, and the resort is generally
pretty tacky.

Barbáti

At **BARBÁTI**, 4km north of Ýpsos, you'll find the sandiest beach on this coast, though
its charm has been somewhat diminished recently by the construction of the
gargantuan *Riviera Barbati* apartment complex. The beach is a favourite with families,
and much accommodation is prebooked in advance.

Agní and Yialiskári

The first of a series of idyllic pebbly coves you encounter when travelling north from
largely missable Nissáki is **AGNÍ**, a favourite mooring spot for yachties, largely because
of its well-established reputation as something of a gourmet's paradise. The even more
scenic, facility-free bay of **Yialiskári** can be reached in ten minutes by a path from Agní.

Kalámi

KALÁMI, around 3km north of Agní, is somewhat commercialized, but the village is
still small and you can imagine how it would have looked in the year Lawrence Durrell
spent here on the eve of World War II. The **White House**, where Durrell wrote *Prospero's
Cell*, is now split in two: the ground floor is an excellent taverna (see p.472), while the
upper floor houses exclusive accommodation.

Kouloúra

The tiny harbour of **KOULOÚRA**, barely a kilometre north of Kalámi, has managed to
keep its charm intact, set at the edge of an unspoilt bay with nothing to distract from
the pine trees and *kaïkia* apart from its idyllically located taverna (see p.472).

8

Áyios Stéfanos

The most attractive resort on this stretch of coast, 3km down a lane from Siniés on the
main road, is **ÁYIOS STÉFANOS** (officially Áyios Stéfanos Sinión to distinguish it from
its namesake in northwest Corfu). The delightful bay bends almost at a right angle,
the northern section of which contains the beach, beyond the string of restaurants.

ARRIVAL AND GETTING AROUND   **THE NORTHEAST**

By bus Green buses between Corfu Town and Kassiópi serve all resorts, along with some blue suburban buses as far as Dhassiá.

By boat In Áyios Stéfanos, Giannis Boats (☎ 26630 81532, ⓦ giannisboats.gr) rents out vessels of varying sizes from €50/day.

ACTIVITIES

Diving Ýpsos beach is home to one of the island's major diving centres, Waterhoppers (☎ 26610 93867, ⓦ water hopperscorfu.gr).

Watersports Corfu Ski Club, the most established watersports outfit in Dhassiá (☎ 6942 852 188, ⓦ corfuskiclub .com), claims to be the world's first paragliding operator.

ACCOMMODATION

Kalami Tourist Services, based in the eponymous village, (☎ 26630 91062, ⓦ kalamibay.com) manage a range of properties in Kalámi and Agní.

DHASSIÁ

Dassia Beach/Dassia Margarita ☎ 26610 93224, ⓦ dassiahotels.gr. These two almost adjacent sister hotels are the best options on the beach itself, with large dining rooms and adequate balconied guest rooms. Breakfast included. April–Oct. **€50**

★**Dionysus Camping Village** ☎ 26610 91417,

ⓦ dionysuscamping.gr. At this, Corfu's top campsite, tents are pitched under terraced olive trees and there are also bungalow huts for rent, plus a pool, shop, bar and a restaurant. Camping **€15.30**, bungalow **€10** per person

BARBÁTI

Paradise ☎ 26630 91320, ⓦ corfu-paradise.gr. Up

above the main road and set amid a colourful tiered garden, this place offers decent-sized rooms that have balconies with bird's-eye sea views. April–Oct. **€40**

YIALISKÁRI

★ **Orchard Villas** ☎ 26610 99403, ⓦ theorchardvillas .com. Four superbly constructed luxury villas of varying sizes, perched on the hillside above a deserted beach.

All are beautifully furnished, fully equipped and have individual pools. They even have UK sockets. **€147**

ÁYIOS STÉFANOS

Kochili ☎ 26630 81522. This fine family taverna, which serves good home-style oven food and grills for €7–8, also has the only independently bookable rooms in the village, simply furnished but with lovely bay views. May–Oct. **€35**

EATING, DRINKING AND NIGHTLIFE

DHASSIÁ

EDEM ☎ 26630 93013, ⓦ edemclub.com. Corfu's prime beach nightclub draws revellers from far and wide. International DJs play cutting-edge techno, trance and other dance genres to a lively crowd. Also hosts occasional rock and other theme nights. May–Sept daily 9pm–late.

Karydia ☎ 26630 93562. A good restaurant on the main road, with a pleasant garden, serving well-prepared versions of Corfiot specialities such as *sofríto* (beef fried in garlic sauce) and *pastitsádha* (pasta-and-meat dish) for under €10, accompanied by decent barrelled wine. April–Oct daily 2pm–midnight.

AGNÍ

★ **Nikolas** ☎ 26630 91243, ⓦ agnibay.com. The oldest taverna of the excellent Agní trio. Superb home-style dishes (around €10–12) such as lamb *kléftiko* are served with a smile, and there are plenty of tasty *mezédhes* to choose from. April–Oct daily 9am–1am; Nov–March Fri–Sun noon–1am.

Toula's ☎ 26630 91350, ⓦ toulasagni.gr. Rather upmarket restaurant with a grand terrace, where the huge menu includes a range of home-made pies and even Black

Angus Argentinian steaks (upwards of €20). May–Sept 12.30–11pm.

KÁLAMI

White House ☎ 26630 91040, ⓦ corfu-kalami.gr. Located in the old Durrell house and recommended for its €12–20 specials (such as mussels and swordfish with garlic) but also good for simple grills, salads and a variety of *mezédhes*. Noon–1am: April–Oct daily; Nov–March Fri–Sun.

KOULOÚRA

Kouloura ☎ 26630 91253, ⓦ tavernakouloura.com. This taverna dates from 1960 and is deservedly popular for its romantic location right by the water and its excellent fresh fish at reasonable prices (from €8). April–Oct noon–midnight.

ÁYIOS STÉFANOS

★ **Fagopotion** ☎ 26630 82020. With a deck right on the quay, this place offers finely prepared seafood, dishes such as rabbit *stifádho* and unusual items such as *zogorítiki* (soufflé with four cheeses). Most main dishes €11–18. Noon–1am: April–Oct daily; Nov–May Fri–Sun.

The north coast

The north coast between **Kassiópi** and **Sidhári** is blessed with some of the island's best stretches of sand and, as a direct result, is also home to a few of Corfu's most crowded package-tourism resorts, which vary in degrees of development but still have plenty to offer the independent traveller.

Kassiópi

At the far east end of the north coast is **KASSIÓPI**, a fishing village that's been transformed into a major party resort. The Roman emperor Tiberius had a villa here, and the village's sixteenth-century Panayía Kassópitra church is said to stand on the site of a temple of Zeus once visited by Nero. Little of Kassiópi's past survives, apart from an abandoned Angevin *kástro* on the headland – most visitors come for the nightlife and the five **pebbly beaches**, the largest of which is **Kalamiónas**, close to the coast road.

Almyrós beach and around

Little-developed **Almyrós beach**, around 10km west along the marshy, overgrown coastline from Kassiópi, is one of the longest on the island, with only a few apartment buildings and one huge new resort dotted sporadically behind it. The **Andinióti lagoon**, a haven for birds and twitchers, backs Cape Ayías Ekaterínis to the east, which marks the northern end of the Corfu Trail (see box, p.479).

Aharávi

At the western end of Almyrós beach, the old village of **AHARÁVI** is tucked on the inland side of the busy main road in a quiet crescent. The village serves as a base for those seeking alternative routes up onto **Mount Pandokrátor** (see box, p.470). Roads to small hamlets such as Áyios Martínos and Láfki continue onto the mountain, and even a stroll up from the back of Aharávi will find you on the upper slopes in under an hour.

Ródha

RÓDHA, barely 3km west of Aharávi, has tipped over into overdevelopment, and is certainly not the place to come for a quiet time. The resort does, however, offer some handy facilities. "Old Ródha" is a small warren of alleys between the main road and the seafront, where you'll find the best restaurants and bars.

Sidhári

At the west end of the north coast, **SIDHÁRI** is totally dominated by British package tourists; its small but pretty town square, with a bandstand set in a small garden, is lost in a welter of restaurants, bars and shops. The **beach** is sandy but not terribly clean, and many people tend to head just west to the curious coves, walled by wind-carved sandstone cliffs, around the vaunted Canal d'Amour. Sidhári also has its own modest **water park** (€5; ⓦsidariwaterpark.com), a good place to keep the kids happy.

8

GETTING AROUND   THE NORTH COAST

By car or motorbike Vlasseros Travel (☎ 26630 95695) is Sidhári's biggest general tourist agency and handles car rental. In Ródha, Myron offers good rates for motorbike

rental (☎ 26630 63477).
By boat Voyager in Ródha (☎ 6932 908 173) has boat rental from €15/hr.

ACTIVITIES

Diving Kassiópi is home to one of the island's most reliable diving operations, Corfu Divers (☎ 26630 81218, ⓦ corfu -divers.com), which is partly British-run.

Horseriding Costas in Ródha offers horseriding (☎ 6944 160 011; €25/2hr), as does Vlasseros Travel in Sidhári (€15/ hr; see above).

ACCOMMODATION

KASSIÓPI

★**Kastro** ☎ 26630 81045, ⓦ kastrokassiopi.com. Overlooking the beach behind the castle, these smart a/c apartments have balconies with sweeping views, as does the attached restaurant, which does excellent fresh food. May to mid-Oct. **€45**
Panayiota Apartments ☎ 26630 81063, ⓦ panayota kassiopi.com. Bargain studios, quite small and simply furnished, one block behind Kalamíones beach on the west side of the castle's peninsula. April–Oct. **€35**

ALMYRÓS BEACH

Akti Anastasia ☎ 6977 972 280, ⓦ aktianastasia.gr. The ideal place for a peaceful escape, this squat rectangular

block sits on a grassy plot close to the quiet beach and has sea-facing balconies. May–Oct. **€40**

AHARÁVI

Dandolo ☎ 26630 63557, ⓦ dandolo.gr. Set in lush grounds on the edge of the old village, the refurbished complex contains fair-sized studios with well-equipped kitchens and verandas. April–Oct. **€45**

RÓDHA

Roda Camping ☎ 26630 93120, ⓦ rodacamping.gr. Around 2km east of the resort, one of the island's best campsites offers a plethora of amenities, including a pool, restaurant and minimarket. May–Sept. **€14**

EATING, DRINKING AND NIGHTLIFE

KASSIÓPI

Janis ☎ 26630 81082. Where Kalamíones beach meets the coast road, this huge taverna has an equally

extensive menu, or, for a splurge, you can choose a live lobster from the tank (€70/kg). April–Oct daily 9am–2am.

The Old School Taverna ☎ 26630 81211. Fish restaurant at the harbour, which offers deals like sea bass, salad and wine for €12, plus meat dishes and all the standard dips. May–Oct daily 11am–1am.

One For The Road ☎ 26630 99113. The liveliest of the cluster of bars around the only junction in the resort, *One For The Road* shows live football, plays a rock soundtrack and occasionally hosts live acts. April–Oct daily 11am–late.

AHARÁVI

★**Theritas** ☎ 26630 63527. This taverna in the old village is the most authentic in the area, serving good home-cooked dishes (€7–8) such as *sofríto*, grills and various starters as well as very palatable wine. May–Oct daily noon–1am.

Votsalakia ☎ 26630 63346. At the western end of the beach, this is the best seaside restaurant, serving fresh fish and seafood, from around €8, as well as the usual array of salads and mezédhes. May–Oct daily 10am–midnight.

RÓDHA

Dolphin ☎ 26630 63431. This seafront taverna in Old Ródha is the best place for fish or seafood (€8–12), which you can enjoy beside the waves that lap below the patio, accompanied by some good local barrelled wine. May–Oct daily 11am–1am.

SIDHÁRI

Kavvadias ☎ 26630 99032. Reliable taverna on the eastern stretch of beach, which dishes up all the Greek favourites and has the odd foray into Asian cuisine. Three-course specials are €7.50. April–Oct daily 10am–midnight.

Kohenoor ☎ 26630 95111. One of Corfu's best curry houses, on the road in from the east, serving a wide range of subcontinental favourites from tandoori to vindaloo for as little as €7–8. May–Sept daily 6pm–midnight.

Talk of the Town ☎ 26630 99113. Snazzy Brit-run bar, on the main strip, which features a variety of music, some live, and has a gourmet restaurant on one side of the premises. Open all year. Daily noon–late.

8 Corfu's satellite islands

Only three of Corfu's quintet of **Dhiapóndia islands**, scattered up to 20km off the northwest coast, are inhabited: Eríkoussa, Othoní and Mathráki. Each of them supports a tiny year-round community but they only really come alive in summer and even then the islands remain a relaxed backwater.

Flattish **Eríkoussa** is the sandiest and most visited of the three. There is an excellent golden sandy beach right by the harbour and quieter **Bragíni beach**, reached by a path across the wooded island interior. **OTHONÍ** is the largest island and has a handful of places to stay and eat in its port, **Ámmos**, which has two pebbly beaches. The village of **Horió** in the island's centre and sandy but deserted **Fýki Bay** are worth visiting if you stay. Hilly, densely forested and with the long, almost invariably deserted **Portéllo beach**, beautiful **MATHRÁKI** has the fewest inhabitants, though it is gradually gearing up towards visitors.

ARRIVAL AND DEPARTURE

CORFU'S SATELLITE ISLANDS

Day-trips Some travel agencies in the northern resorts offer day-trips just to Eríkoussa, while a trip taking in all three islands from Sidhári or Áyios Stéfanos is excellent value. Vlasseros Travel in Sidhári (see p.473) offer thrice weekly trips to Eríkoussa for €16, while on the west coast, day-trips run several times a week in season (€25 per person) from Áyios Stéfanos to all three islands.

By kaïkia and ferry You can travel independently between the islands on regular *kaïkia* from Sidhári; there are also passenger services on the Aspiotis lines *kaïki* (3–5 weekly; €10–12 return; ☎ 26630 41297, ⊕ aspiotislines. gr) from Áyios Stéfanos. The thrice-weekly ferry from Corfu Town (2–4hr) is the least efficient way to get there.

ACCOMMODATION, EATING AND DRINKING

Apart from the hotel listed below, on Othoni rooms are rented by local islanders such as Tassos Kassimis (☎ 26630 71700; €35) and Khristos Aryiros (☎ 26630 71652; €45), both based on Portéllo beach.

Erikousa Eríkoussa ☎ 26630 71110, ⊕ hotelerikousa .gr. Busy throughout the season by virtue of being the island's sole hotel, with simple but adequate rooms, *Erikousa* also boasts the only bona fide taverna. Breakfast

included. May–Sept. **€60**

Hotel Calypso Othoni ☎ 26630 72162. Some 200m east of the jetty, Othoni's only hotel has pleasant, comfortably furnished rooms with balconies plus a small bar. May–

BOAT TRIPS FROM PALEOKASTRÍTSA

From Paleokastrítsa's first beach, you can get a boat trip (€12/30min) to some nearby seawater caves, known as the **"blue grottoes"**, which is worth taking for the spectacular coastal views. Boats also serve as a taxi service to three neighbouring **beaches**, Áyia Triánda, Palatákia and Alípa, which all have snack-bars.

Sept. €40

La Locanda dei Sogni Othoní ☎ 26630 71640, ⓦ othoni.com. Quality but not unreasonably priced Italian restaurant, which does a line in authentic antipasti, pasta and pizza dishes for €10 or less, plus plenty of Greek items. They also rent out some rooms (€40). May–Sept daily

noon–1am.

Port Centre Mathráki. Good restaurant on the harbour that specializes in freshly caught fish at very decent prices, plus a few simple salads and mezédhes. Most dishes €5–8. Late May to Sept daily noon–midnight.

Paleokastrítsa

PALEOKASTRÍTSA, a sprawling village 23km west of Corfu Town, surrounded by dramatic hills and cliffs, has been identified as the Homeric city of Scheria, where Odysseus was washed ashore and escorted by Nausicaa to the palace of her father Alkinous, king of the Phaeacians. It's a stunning site, as you would expect, with a delightful centre, though it's one that's long been engulfed by tourism.

Beaches

The focal point of the village is the largest and least attractive of three **beaches**, home to sea-taxis and *kaïkia* (see box above). The second beach, to the right, is stony with clear water, but the best of the three is a small, unspoilt strand reached along the path by the *Astacos Taverna* (see below). Protected by cliffs, it's almost entirely undeveloped.

8

Corfu Aquarium

At the neck of the promontory • April–Oct daily 10am–8pm • €6 • ☎ 26630 41339, ⓦ corfuaquarium.com

The attractive log-and-stone structure of the **Corfu Aquarium** contains a comprehensive selection of local fish species, as well as lobster, squid and octopus. There is also a selection of exotic snakes and reptiles, which are enthusiastically presented by the staff.

Theotókou monastery

On the rocky bluff above the village • Daily 7am–1pm & 3–8pm • Free, donations welcome

The **Theotókou monastery** is believed to have been established in the thirteenth century. There's a **museum** here, resplendent with icons, jewelled bibles and other impedimenta of Greek Orthodox ritual, though the highlight is the **gardens**, from which there are spectacular coastal views.

Angelókastro

Around 6km north up the coast from Paleokastrítsa • June–Oct daily 8.30am–2pm • €2

Paleokastrítsa's ruined Byzantine castle, the **Angelókastro**, is only approachable by a path from the hamlet of **Kríni**. En route, there are a couple of outstanding spots around the village of **Makrádhes** for a snack or drink while you take in the whole vista of Paleokastrítsa's promontory. The **fortress** itself has been partially restored for visitor safety and is worth the steep climb for the stunning, almost circular views of the surrounding sea and land from the battlements.

ACCOMMODATION AND EATING   PALEOKASTRÍTSA

Astacos Taverna ☎ 26630 41068, ⓦ astacos.biz. Highlights at this friendly taverna, just behind the second beach, include the lobster after which the restaurant is named (€70/kilo), or more pocket-friendly *moussaká*. There are also some well-appointed studios just behind (€45). May–Sept daily 9am–late.

Dolphin Snackbar ☎ 26630 41035. Just down some steps from the main road and above Alípa beach, the simple rooms here are adequate, with easy beach access. The terrific Greek food on offer, such as garlic swordfish, is more substantial than the name suggests, and you can fill up for under €10. April–Oct daily 8.30am–midnight. **€35**

Paleo Camping ☎ 26630 41204, ⓦ campingpaleo kastritsa.com. Just off the main road, almost a 30min walk from the centre, this campsite has good facilities, shady if slightly cramped tent pitches and a mini-market. May–Sept. **€11.90**

Vrahos ☎ 26630 41128. This upmarket taverna, opposite the aquarium, with starched tablecloths and rather stiff service, offers pricey top-of-the-range fish, Italian cuisine and some unusual dishes like artichokes. Most mains €10–15. April to mid-Oct daily noon–1am.

The northwest coast

The northwest conceals some of the island's most dramatic coastal scenery, with violent interior mountainscapes jutting out of the verdant countryside. North of Paleokastrítsa, the densely olive-clad hills conceal good sandy beaches, such as **Áyios Yeóryios** and **Áyios Stéfanos**.

GETTING AROUND	THE NORTHWEST COAST

By bus Public transport between west coast resorts is difficult: virtually all buses ply routes from Corfu Town to single destinations and rarely link resorts.

Áyios Yeóryios

Like many of the west-coast resorts, **ÁYIOS YEÓRYIOS**, around 9km north of Paleokastrítsa, isn't actually based around a village, though it is sometimes referred to as Áyios Yeóryios Pagón after the inland village of Payí to avoid confusion with its southern namesake. The resort has developed in response to the popularity of the large sandy bay, and it's a major **windsurfing** centre, especially towards the northern end, where boats can also be rented.

Afiónas

The village of **AFIÓNAS**, perched high above the north end of Áyios Yeóryios bay, has been suggested as the likely site of **King Alkinous' castle** – there are vestigial Neolithic remains outside the village – and the walk up to the lighthouse on Cape Aríllas affords excellent views over Áyios Yeóryios and Aríllas Bay to the north.

Áyios Stéfanos

The northernmost of the west coast's resorts, **ÁYIOS STÉFANOS** is low-key, popular with families and a quiet base from which to explore the northwest and the Dhiapóndia islands (see p.474), visible on the horizon. The small harbour lies a good kilometre south of the long sandy beach.

Avliótes and around

In the northwest corner of Corfu stands **AVLIÓTES**, a handsome hill town with the odd *kafenío* and tavernas but few concessions to tourism. The town is useful for its accessibility to the small, quiet village of **Perouládhes** in the very northwest and stunning **Longás beach** below, bordered by vertical reddish layer-cake cliffs that make for shady mornings.

ACCOMMODATION, EATING AND DRINKING	THE NORTHWEST COAST

ÁYIOS YEÓRYIOS

★ **Ostrako** ☎ 26630 96028. This gaily painted taverna has a terrace overlooking the southern end of the beach, and it's unbeatable for seafood such as squid and octopus for less than €10. The eclectic recorded folk music helps create a pleasant atmosphere. May–Oct daily 11am–1am.

Pension Vrahos ☎ 26630 96366, ⓦ pension-vrachos .com. At the far northern end of the beach, under the eponymous cliff, this pension offers bright, good-value rooms in the building behind its taverna, which serves Greek and international cuisine. May–Oct. **€40**

AFIÓNAS

Panorama ☎ 26630 51846, ⓦ panoramacorfu.com. Friendly family restaurant on the west side of the village which serves tasty meals made from organic produce for

€7–9 and has great views from its terrace; it also has some good-value rooms (€30) and apartments (4-person €55). May–Sept daily 10am–1am.

ÁYIOS STÉFANOS

Nafsika ☎ 26630 51051, ⓦ nafsikahotel.com. Located behind the southern strip of beach, the resort's oldest hotel has comfy rooms, a popular restaurant and gardens with a pool and bar. April–Oct. **€60**

★❶ Manthos ☎ 26630 52197. The oldest taverna, behind the southern beach, is still the best, and serves Corfiot specialities such as *sofríto* and *pastitsádha* for around €8. Ask the venerable owner to show you his memorabilia. There's music and dance every Sat. May–Oct daily noon–1am.

AVLIÓTES AND AROUND

Panorama Longás beach ☎ 26630 51846. The taverna's name gives the game away – perched on the cliff above the beach, its garden terrace is a great spot for a sunset dinner or cocktail at the attached *7th Heaven Café*. Most main dishes €8–10. May–Sept daily 11am–midnight.

Central Corfu

Much of **central Corfu** is occupied by the **plain of Rópa**, whose fertile landscape backs onto some of the best beaches on the west coast, such as delightful **Myrtiótissa**, as well as the island's only mountain resort, **Pélekas** – all a quick bus ride across the island from Corfu Town. The only place of note on the central east coast is **Benítses**.

Érmones and around

ÉRMONES, around 15km south of Paleokastrítsa by road, is one of the busiest resorts on the island, its lush green bay backed by the mountains above the Rópa River but rather marred by the ugly tiered *Ermones Beach Hotel* and its private funicular.

Myrtiótissa

Far preferable to the gravelly sand of Érmones is the idyllic strand of **MYRTIÓTISSA**, about 3km south. In *Prospero's Cell*, Lawrence Durrell described Myrtiótissa as "perhaps the loveliest beach in the world"; it was for years a well-guarded secret but is now a firm favourite, especially with nudists, and gets so busy in summer that it supports three *kantínas*, meaning it's at its best well out of high season. Above the north end of the beach is the tiny, whitewashed **Myrtiótissa monastery**, dedicated to Our Lady of the Myrtles.

Pélekas

PÉLEKAS, inland and 5km southeast of Érmones, has long been popular for its views – the **Kaiser's Throne** viewing tower, just above the town, was Wilhelm II's favourite spot on the island. On the small square, the **Odhiyítria church**, renovated in 1884, is worth a peek. Pélekas' sandy **beach** is reached down a short path, though sadly it's been rather spoilt by the monstrous *Pelekas Beach* hotel that now looms over it.

Sinarádhes

The inland area around Pélekas holds some of Corfu's most traditional villages. This atmosphere of days gone by is best reflected in **SINARÁDHES**, around 4km away, which houses the **Folklore Museum of Central Corfu** (Tues–Sun 9.30am–2pm; €2; ☎ 26610 54962) in an authentic village house, complete with original furniture and full of articles and utensils that once formed an intrinsic part of daily rural life.

Áï Górdhis

Around 7km south of Pélekas, **ÁÏ GÓRDHIS** is one of the major party beaches on the island, largely because of the activities organized by the startling *Pink Palace* complex (see p.478), which dominates the resort.

Áyii Dhéka

Inland from Áï Górdhis is the south's largest prominence, the humpback of **Áyii Dhéka** (576m), reached by path from the hamlet of Áno Garoúna; it is the island's second-largest mountain after Pandokrátor. The lower slopes are wooded, and it's possible to glimpse buzzards wheeling on thermals over the higher slopes. The monks at the tiny monastery just below the summit lovingly tend a bountiful orchard.

Áyios Matthéos

In south-central Corfu, the town of **ÁYIOS MATTHÉOS**, 3km inland, is still chiefly an agricultural centre, although a number of *kafenía* and tavernas offer a warm welcome to passers-by. On the other side of Mount Prasoúdhi, 2km by road, is the **Gardhíki Pýrgos**, the ruins of a thirteenth-century castle built in this unlikely lowland setting by the despots of Epirus.

Benítses

South of Corfu Town on the east coast, there's nothing to recommend before **BENÍTSES**, a once-notorious bonking-and-boozing resort, whose old centre at the north end has long since reverted to a quiet bougainvillea-splashed Greek village, popular with eastern Europeans. There are a couple of minor attractions, namely the modest ruins of a **Roman bathhouse** at the back of the village and the small but impressive **Shell Museum** (daily: March–May & Oct 10am–6pm; June–Sept 9am–8pm; €4; ☎ 26610 72227).

ACCOMMODATION, EATING AND DRINKING   **CENTRAL CORFU**

ÉRMONES

Nafsica ☎ 26610 94911. Perched just above the southern end of the beach, with a huge terrace, *Nafsica* provides good, filling *mezédhes* and main courses of both meat and fish for under €10. April–Oct daily 11am–1am.

Philoxenia ☎ 26610 94091, ⊛ hotelphiloxenia.gr. Far better value than the *Ermones Beach Hotel*, this spacious modern hotel on the south side of the creek has two pools and a bar, and all the rooms face the sea. May to mid-Oct. **€70**

MYRTIÓTISSA

★**Myrtia** ☎ 26610 94113, ✉ sks_mirtia@hotmail.com. Just before the path down to the beach lies this delightful taverna with an olive-shaded garden, where they serve tasty home-style cooking for €6–9 and offer a few simple but clean and cosy rooms (€45). May–Oct daily noon–midnight.

PÉLEKAS

Pension Paradise ☎ 26610 94530, ⊛ paradisepelekas .com. Located on the road in from Vátos, this ochre-tinted year-round *pension* run by a friendly old couple has simple homely rooms at bargain rates. **€25**

★**Pink Panther** ☎ 26610 94360. There are quite a few imaginative dishes on the menu here, with a refreshing array of peppery sauces, all at under €10, which can be enjoyed along with a glass or two of aromatic local wine

while gazing at the splendid view from the lofty terrace. Easter–Oct daily 11am–1am.

AÏ GÓRDHIS

★**Elena's** ☎ 26610 53210, ⊛ elenasapartments.com. A variety of rooms and apartments in the village is available through this seafront taverna, which is painted marine blue and white and serves excellent home-style cuisine at low prices, such as beef in mustard sauce for €8.50. April–Oct. **€30**

Pink Palace ☎ 26610 53103, ⊛ thepinkpalace.com. Legendary year-round backpackers' haunt, with pools, games courts, internet access, restaurants, a shop and a disco. Apart from the dorms which sleep five or six, there are compact singles and doubles. Rates include breakfast and an evening buffet. Dorm **€19**, double **€44**

BENÍTSES

Benitses Arches ☎ 26610 72113, ⊛ hotelbenitses arches.com. Pleasant bougainvillea-adorned hotel, with quiet rooms set a couple of blocks back from the main road. April–Oct. **€50**

O Paxinos ☎ 26610 72339. Intimate taverna in the old village, specializing in Corfiot dishes such as *sofrito* and *pastitsádha*, not cheap at €12 a pop but expertly prepared and washed down with fine barrelled wine. Daily noon–1am.

Southern Corfu

Corfu's **southwest coast** offers perhaps the island's finest stretches of sand, from the peaceful **Korissíon lagoon** on down, almost unbroken to the island's tip. On the east side, there is a mixture of resorts, ranging from peaceful enclaves like **Boúkari** to the full-on party antics of **Kávos**, accessible via Corfu's second-largest settlement, traditional **Lefkími**.

Moraïtika and Áno Moraïtika

On the east coast, roughly 20km south of the capital, the first real development after Benítses is **MORAÏTIKA**, whose main street is an ugly strip of bars, restaurants and shops, but its beach is the best between Corfu Town and Kávos. The original village, **ÁNO MORAÏTIKA**, is signposted a few minutes' hike up the steep lanes inland and is virtually unspoilt, its tiny houses and alleys practically drowning in dazzling bougainvillea. The resort has become very popular with eastern Europeans.

Mesongí

Commencing barely a hundred metres on from the Moraïtika seafront and separated only by the Mesongí River, **MESONGÍ** continues this stretch of package-tour-oriented coast but is noticeably quieter and has a range of accommodation deals.

Boúkari and around

BOÚKARI, linked to Mesongí by a quiet road that follows the seashore for about 3km, often only a few feet above it, comprises little more than a handful of tavernas, a shop and a few small, family-run hotels. It's out of the way, so is an idyllic little strip of **unspoilt coast** for anyone looking to relax. It is also handily placed for the wooded region inland around **Aryirádhes**, rarely visited by tourists and perfect for quiet walks.

Petrití and around

Four kilometres south of Boúkari, the village of **PETRITÍ**, only created in the 1970s when geologists discovered the hill village of Korakádhes was sliding downwards, fronts onto a small but busy harbour. It is mercifully free of noise and commerce, with a beach of rock, mud and sand set among low olive-covered hills. Barely 2km south of Petrití are the picturesque rocky coves of **Nótos beach**, which are little visited.

Korissíon lagoon and around

Over on the southwest coast, one of the island's most distinctive geographical features is the **Korissíon lagoon**, home to turtles, tortoises, lizards and numerous indigenous and migratory birds. Its northern section, which is over 5km long and 1km wide at its centre, is separated from the sea by the dunes of **Halikoúna beach**, an idyllic spot for swimming and rough camping, while more touristic **Íssos beach** borders the southern end.

WALKING THE CORFU TRAIL

The **Corfu Trail**, 200km in length and open since 2001, covers the whole island from **Cape Asprókavos** in the south to Áyios Spyrídhon beach, next to **Cape Ayías Ekaterínis** in the far north. The route avoids roads as much as possible and takes walkers across a variety of terrain – from beaches to the highest peaks – passing by Lefkími, Korissíon lagoon, Áyii Dhéka, Pélekas, Myrtiótissa, Paleokastrítsa, Áyios Yeóryios Pagón, Spartýlas and Mount Pandokrátor.

Paths along the entire route are **waymarked** with yellow aluminium signs. As usual, ramblers are advised to wear headgear and stout footwear and carry ample water and provisions, as well as all-weather kit in all but the high summer months. It is reckoned that strong walkers can cover the route in ten days.

Those interested in attempting all or part of the trail should pick up Hilary Whitton Paipeti's excellent *Companion Guide to the Corfu Trail* (ⓦ corfutrailguide.com; €10), which contains detailed **maps** and descriptions of the route, divided into ten daily sections. A proportion of the profits goes towards maintenance of the trail, and anyone using the trail is asked to contribute €3 for the same reason. You can also log on to ⓦ travelling.gr/corfutrail for information on organized walking packages including accommodation.

Áyios Yeóryios, Marathiá and Ayía Varvára

Far pleasanter than **Áyios Yeóryios**, the main Brit-dominated but rather brash resorts on the coast south of the Korissíon lagoon are **MARATHIÁ** and **AYÍA VARVÁRA**, both essentially forming a single resort further southeast along the same continuous strand. They are separated only by a stream that you can easily cross on the beach but each settlement must be approached by different roads. The most direct route to Marathiá beach is signposted from the tiny village of **Marathiás**, a couple of kilometres southeast of Aryirádhes on the main road, while Ayía Varvára is signposted from the village of Perivóli further south.

Lefkími

Anyone interested in how a Greek town works away from the bustle of tourism shouldn't miss **LEFKÍMI**, towards the island's southern tip. The second-largest settlement after Corfu Town, it's the administrative centre for the south of the island as well as the alternative ferry port for Igoumenítsa. The town has some fine architecture including several striking churches: **Áyii Anáryiri**, with a huge double belfry, **Áyios Theódhoros**, on a mound above a small square, and **Áyios Arsénios**, with a vast orange dome that can be seen for miles.

Kávos

There are no ambiguities in **KÁVOS**, 6km south of Lefkími: either you like 24-hour drinking, clubbing, bungee-jumping, go-karts and chips with almost everything, or you should avoid the resort altogether. As numbers have dropped in recent years, unbelievable accommodation bargains can be had, should you choose to stay.

8

South of Kávos

Beyond the limits of Kávos, where few visitors stray, a path leaving the road south to the hamlet of Sparterá heads through unspoilt countryside; after around thirty minutes of walking it reaches the cliffs of **Cape Asprókavos** and the crumbling **monastery of Arkoudhílas**. The cape looks out over the straits to Paxí, and down over deserted **Arkoudhílas beach**, which can be reached from Sparterá, a pleasant village 5km by road but only 3km by the signed path from Kávos. Even wilder is **Aï Górdhis Paleohoríou beach**, 3km further on from Sparterá, one of the least visited on the island and not to be confused with the eponymous beach further north. A municipal café provides the only refreshment. The Cape is also the southern starting point for the **Corfu Trail** (see box, p.479).

ARRIVAL AND DEPARTURE   SOUTHERN CORFU

By ferry Lefkími has a year-round ferry connection to Igoumenítsa (4–6 daily; 40min).

By bus Lefkími is on the frequent bus route from Corfu Town to Kávos (10 Mon–Fri, 8 Sat, 2 Sun; 1hr 20min).

ACCOMMODATION, EATING AND DRINKING

MORAÏTIKA AND ÁNO MORAÏTIKA

Bella Vista Áno Moraïtika ☏ 26610 75460. The menu here is fairly basic but wholesome, with grills for €7–8 and fresh salads, but the place justifies its name with a lovely garden, sea views and breezes. March–Nov daily noon–midnight.

Charlie's Bar Moraïtika. The village's oldest bar, which opened in 1939, is a meeting place for locals and tourists alike, with a central location on the main road. Light snacks are available and the music consists of old pop favourites. Daily noon–late.

Firefly Moraïtika ☏ 26610 75850, ⓦ fireflyhotel.eu. On one of the northernmost lanes down to the beach, this taverna has a good range of meat, fish, salads and dips (all well under €10) plus it rents out whatever rooms are not booked by Romanian tour operators (€30). May–Sept daily 11am–late.

MESONGÍ

Hotel Gemini ☏ 26610 75221, ⓦ geminihotel.gr. This rather elegant hotel boasts a large pool and manicured gardens, plus sizeable en-suite rooms with balconies. Breakfast included. May–Sept. €60

Spiros on the Beach ☏ 26610 75285. Beachfront restaurant with two premises 20m apart, good for tasty €8 fish soup plus other offerings from the deep, plus various carnivorous or vegetarian options. May to mid-Oct daily 11am–2am.

BOÚKARI

★**Boukari Beach** ☎26620 51791, ⓦboukaribeach .gr. Right on the sea, 1km north of Boúkari's harbour, is one of Corfu's best tavernas. It offers delicious home cooking, fresh fish and live lobster from €40/60 per kilo. The friendly family also run the smart and comfortable *Penelopi* and *Villa Alexandra,* with huge self-catering suites (€45). Breakfast included. April–Nov daily 9am–late.

PETRITÍ AND AROUND

★**Panorama Villas** Nótos beach ☎26620 51707, ⓦpanoramacorfu.gr. A wonderfully friendly haven worth making the detour to, whether to stay at (€40) or for its fine shady restaurant, renowned for its excellent home cooking, such as *moussaká* for €7. Breakfast included. April–Oct daily 10am–midnight.

Pension Egrypos Petrití ☎26620 51949, ⓦegrypos .gr. About 200m back from the harbour, this pleasantly landscaped complex has a pool, bar and a restaurant. The rooms are smart, modern and fully equipped. Breakfast included. May to mid-Oct. €50

Stamatis Petrití ☎26620 51920. The best of the bunch clustered around the harbour, this year-round local taverna rustles up goodies like mussels and small fish for around €7–8. Daily noon–1am.

ÁYIOS YEÓRYIOS, MARATHIÁ AND AYÍA VARVÁRA

Akroama Marathiá ☎26620 52736. Good family-run taverna with treats like swordfish and local sausage for €7–8, which can be enjoyed from the low-lying cliff terrace. They also rent some comfortable rooms (€30). May–Sept daily 11am–1am.

Family Studios Marathiá ☎26620 51192, ⓦfamily-studios.com. This homely family-run complex has some spanking new studios and the excellent *Perfect Ten* taverna stretching back from the lively seafront *Bright Blue* beach bar. May–Sept. €35

LEFKÍMI

Cheeky Face ☎26620 22627. The old couple who run this simple year-round *estiatório*, by the bridge over the canal in the lower part of town, provide inexpensive staples such as *pastítsio* for €6.50 and a few equally basic rooms upstairs (€35). Daily 10am–11pm.

KÁVOS

Future ☎01772 923989, ⓦfutureatlantiskavos.com. The most lively club of the dozens that line the main drag, with imported north European DJs, state-of-the-art sound-and-light systems, shots galore and a constant parade of the scantily clad. May–Oct daily 10pm–late.

8

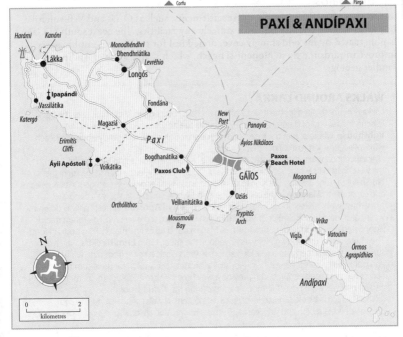

PAXÍ & ANDÍPAXI

Paxí and Andípaxi

Unusually verdant and still largely unspoilt, **PAXÍ (Paxos)** has established a firm niche in Greece's tourist hierarchy, despite being the smallest of the main Ionian islands at barely 12km by 4km, with only mediocre beaches and no historical sites. Yet it has become so popular that it is best avoided in high season. It's a particular favourite of yachting flotillas, whose spending habits have brought the island an upmarket reputation and made it just about the most expensive place to visit in the Ionian islands. The capital, **Gáïos**, is quite cosmopolitan, with delis and boutiques, but northerly **Lákka** and tiny **Longós** are where hard-core Paxophiles head, while by far the best swimming is at Paxí's little sister island, **Andípaxi**.

Gáïos

The island's capital, **GÁÏOS**, is a pleasant town built around a small square in the middle of an elongated seafront overlooking two islands, Áyios Nikólaos and Panayía. Nearly all the town's facilities are to be found on the seafront or within little over 100m of it.

Folk Museum

Seafront • June to mid-Sept daily 10am–2pm & 7–11pm • €2

Gáïos' only museum, the **Folk Museum**, is housed in an old school building on the seafront about 200m south of the main square. One room is set up as an eighteenth-century bedroom with some period furniture and costumes. Other items on display from different epochs include kitchen implements, musical instruments, china, stationery and guns.

Around Gáïos

Inland are some of the island's oldest settlements, such as Oziás and Vellianitátika, in prime walking country but with scarcely any facilities. The **coast south** of Gáïos is punctuated by the odd shingly cove, none ideal for swimming, until matters improve towards the tip at **Mogoníssi beach**, which shares some of Andípaxi's sandier geology.

WALKS AROUND LÁKKA

Lákka is perfectly sited for the finest walking on Paxí. For a simple, short hike, take the track leaving the far end of Harámi beach. This mounts the headland and leads on to the **lighthouse**, where a goat track descends through tough scrub to a sandy open-sea beach with rollers best left to confident swimmers.

Another good walking route heads west into the hills above the village to **Vassilátika**, high on the west-coast cliffs, which has stunning views out to sea. From here, the path to the left of the blue-painted stone archway leads on to the most dramatic cliff-edge views (vertigo sufferers beware) and continues to **Magaziá** in the centre of the island, where you can flag down a bus or taxi.

The best **walk** on Paxí, however, is to the church at **Áyii Apóstoli**, almost halfway down the west coast, next to the hamlet of **Voïkátika**, which has a decent taverna. The rough track is signposted a few hundred metres south of Magaziá, and takes less than half an hour on foot. The church and surrounding vineyards overlook the sheer 150m **Erimítis cliffs**, which at sunset are transformed into a seaside version of Ayers Rock, turning from dirty white to pink and gold and brown. If you visit Áyii Apóstoli at sunset, take a torch for the return trip. The *Sunset* bar, next to the church, can provide a welcome drink to augment the natural splendour and sometimes even hosts full-moon parties during the warmer months.

Noel Rochford's **book**, *Landscapes of Paxos*, lists dozens of walks on the island; this and cartographers Elizabeth and Ian Bleasdale's *Paxos Walking Map* are on sale in most travel agencies.

Longós and around

LONGÓS is the prettiest village on the island, though it's dominated by the upmarket villa crowd. Its scruffy beach is favoured by local grannies for the sulphur springs, so most people swim off **Levrehió beach** in the next bay south. Longós is at the bottom of a steep winding hill, which makes **walking** a bit of a chore, but the short circuit around neighbouring **Dhendhriátika** provides spectacular views and allows access to the small but excellent **Monodhéndhri beach**. You can also walk to **Fondána** and the former capital of **Magaziá**, back on the main road.

Lákka and around

Buses run 3–4 times Mon–Sat between Gáïos and Lákka (20min), and most divert through Longós

Approached from the south, **LÁKKA** is an unprepossessing jumble of buildings, but once in its maze of alleys and neo-Venetian buildings or on the quay with views of distant Corfu, you do get a sense of its charm. Lákka's two **beaches**, Harámi and Kanóni, are none too brilliant for swimming or sunbathing, but there's a sense of community about the place and overall it's the best spot to hang out on the island, with plenty of great dining and local walking.

Andípaxi

Frequent seasonal *kaḯkia* shuttle between Gáïos and Andípaxi (€10 return); the glass-bottomed boat from Gáïos to Andípaxi (€15 return) also takes you to its sea stacks and caves

Less than 2km south, Paxí's tiny sibling **ANDÍPAXI** has scarcely any accommodation and no facilities beyond several beach tavernas open during the daytime in season. Andípaxi's sandy, blue-water coves have been compared with the Caribbean, but you'll have to share them with *kaḯkia* and sea taxis from all three villages on Paxí, plus larger craft from Corfu and the mainland resorts.

Boats basically deposit you either at the sandy **Vríka beach** or the longer pebble beach of **Vatoúmi**, although quieter bays are accessible to the south. Paths also lead inland to connect the handful of homes and the southerly lighthouse, but there are no beaches of any size on Andípaxi's western coastline and thick thorny scrub makes access difficult.

8

ARRIVAL AND DEPARTURE

PAXÍ AND ANDÍPAXI

By ferry/hydrofoil Both ferries and hydrofoils dock at the new port of Gáïos on Paxí, 1km north of the town centre. Tickets are available at travel agencies around the island and booths at the dock prior to departure.

Destinations Corfu Town (hydrofoil; May–Sept 1–3 daily; 50min); Igoumenítsa (summer 1–2 daily, less frequently in winter; 1hr).

ACCOMMODATION, EATING, DRINKING AND NIGHTLIFE

As there are only three bona fide hotels and much of the accommodation on Paxí is booked by foreign tour companies, rooms and villas are best **arranged in advance** through one of the island's travel agencies: Gáïos Travel (☎ 26620 32033, ⓦ gaiostravel.co.uk) and Bouas Tours (☎ 26620 32401, ⓦ bouastours.gr), both on the capital's seafront; or Routsis (☎ 26620 31807, ⓦ routsis-holidays.com) and British-owned Planos Holidays (☎ 26620 31744 or UK ☎ +44 1373 814200, ⓦ planos.co.uk), both based in Lákka, for northern Paxí.

GÁÏOS

Dodos ☎ 26620 32265, ⓦ dodos-paxos.blogspot.co.uk. Set in a garden inland from the Anemoyiannis statue towards the southern end of the seafront, this old favourite has a full range of mezédhes and main courses, mostly under €10. May to early Oct daily noon–midnight.

★**Genesis** ☎ 26620 32495. Convivial, brightly decorated taverna-cum-café, by far the best of the seafront establishments, right opposite the Anemoyiannis statue, serving great wine and home-cooked dishes, such as several types of *stifádho* including octopus for €8–10. May–Oct daily 10am–1am.

★**Paxos Beach Hotel** ☎ 26620 32211, ⓦ paxos beachhotel.gr. Attractive en-suite bungalows with balconies on a hillside above a pebbly beach 2km south of town; amenities include a saltwater pool, yoga studio, tennis court and mini-golf. Free shuttle bus. Breakfast included. May–Oct. **€110**

Paxos Club ☎ 26620 32450, ⓦ paxosclub.gr. Nearly 2km inland from Gáïos, this luxury resort set in lavish gardens offers large, well-furnished rooms and suites with kitchens, as well as a classy restaurant, pool and bar. Breakfast included. May–Sept. **€130**

Phoenix Disco ☎ 26620 32210. On a hill overlooking the bay, with a large outdoor dancefloor and the usual mix of foreign and Greek disco hits. The island's premier nightclub. June–Sept daily 10pm–late.

LONGÓS

O Gios ☎ 26620 31735. A simple and cheap taverna in the middle of the harbour, where you can get great grills for €6–7, the odd oven dish and some basic salads and dips. June–Sept daily noon–midnight.

★ **Vassilis** ☎ 26620 30062. Friendly port-side restaurant, where the bus has to squeeze past the pavement tables. Terrific seafood dishes, such as corals of sea urchins for €12.90, and tasty starters, outlined on a memorable newspaper-style menu. May–Oct daily 11am–1am.

LÁKKA

★ **Alexandros** Platía Edward Kennedy ☎ 26620 30045. Very friendly taverna tucked in the southwest corner of the village, great for fresh fish, *gourounópoulo*, creamed mushrooms and pork roll (mains €10). May–Oct

daily 1pm–1am.

Amfitriti Hotel ☎ 26620 30011, ⓦ amfitritihotel.gr. Hidden among olive groves behind Harámi beach, the least expensive of Paxí's three hotels offers comfortable rooms with private balconies and kitchenettes. May–Oct. **€70**

Harbour Lights ☎ 26620 31412. This perennially favourite bar in the middle of the harbour is most likely to stay open the longest hours. There's a good range of drinks and mostly well-known pop and rock sounds. May–Oct daily noon–late.

La Rosa di Paxos ☎ 26620 31471. Slightly upmarket seafront restaurant, which does good risottos and ravioli for €10–15, a variety of salads and some more standard Greek favourites. Mid-May to mid-Oct daily noon–1am.

ANDÍPAXI

Bella Vista Vatoúmi beach ☎ 26620 31766. Perched on a cliff overlooking the cove, this taverna justifies its name and also dishes up fresh fish and meat grills for under €10, plus a suitable range of salads and mezédhes. June–Sept daily noon–6pm.

Spiros Vríka beach ☎ 26620 31172. The oldest taverna on the island has great grilled and oven food. They can also arrange self-catering accommodation up in Vígla, Andípaxi's settlement, on a weekly basis. Late May to mid-Sept daily 11am–7pm.

Lefkádha

LEFKÁDHA (Lefkás) is an oddity, which is exactly why it is some people's favourite Ionian island. Connected to the mainland by a long causeway through lagoons and a 30m pontoon bridge, Lefkádha was long an important strategic base. As you approach the causeway, you'll pass a series of fortresses which climax in the fourteenth-century castle of **Santa Maura** – the Venetian name for the island. These defences were too close to the mainland to avoid an Ottoman tenure, which began in 1479, but the Venetians wrested back control a couple of centuries later. They were in turn overthrown by Napoleon in 1797 and then the British took over as Ionian protectors in 1810, until reunification with Greece in 1864.

The whiteness of its **rock strata** – *lefkás* has the same root as *lefkós*, "white" – is apparent on its partly bare ridges. While the marshes and boggy inlets on the east coast can lead to a mosquito problem, the island is a fertile place – it supports cypresses, olive groves and vineyards, particularly on the western slopes. The rugged **west coast**, however, is the star attraction and boasts some of the finest beaches in the archipelago.

ARRIVAL AND INFORMATION LEFKÁDHA

By plane Lefkádha itself does not have an airport but is less than 20km from the one at Préveza. There is no airport bus, but KTEL services from Préveza stop at the terminal entrance and taxis are readily available.

Domestic destinations Athens (1–2 daily; 50min); Corfu (summer 5 weekly; 30min), Kefaloniá (summer 3 weekly; 30min); Zákynthos (summer 3 weekly; 1hr 15min).

By bus The new bus station is out past the marina, around

1km from the centre of Lefkádha Town (☎ 26450 22364, ⓦ ktel-lefkadas.gr).

Destinations Athens (5 daily; 5hr 30min); Igoumenítsa (1 daily; 3hr); Pátra (2 weekly; 3hr); Préveza (6 Mon–Sat, 2 Sun; 30min); Thessaloníki (1 daily; 7hr).

By ferry Apart from the shuttle ferry from Nydhrí to Meganíssi (see p.491), the only ferries departing from Lefkádha now leave from Vassilikí; the summer schedules

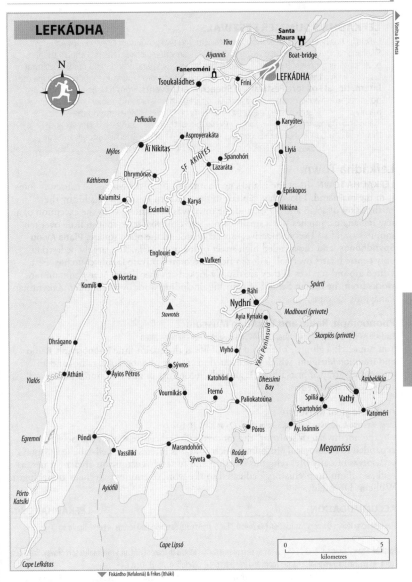

Voïtza & Préveza

LEFKÁDHA

Santa Maura

Yíra

Aïyannis

Boat-bridge

Faneroméni

Tsoukaládhes

Fríni

LEFKÁDHA

Karyótes

Pefkoúlia

Asproyerakáta

Mýlos

Áï Nikítas

Liyiá

SF AKIÓTES

Spanohóri

Lazaráta

Dhrymónas

Káthisma

Kalamítsi

Karyá

Epískopos

Exánthia

Nikiána

Englouvi

Vafkerí

Komíli

Hortáta

Spárti

Ráhi

Nydhrí

Stavrotós

Ayía Kyriakí

Madhoúri (private)

Skorpiós (private)

Dhrágano

Vlyhó

Yení Peninsula

Yialós

Atháni

Áyios Pétros

Sývros

Katohóri

Dhessími Bay

Ambelákia

Vournikás

Fternó

Paliokatoúna

Spiliá

Vathý

Spartohóri

Katoméri

Póros

Ay. Ioánnis

Egremní

Póndi

Marandohóri

Roúda Bay

Meganíssi

Vassilikí

Sývota

Pórto Katsíki

Ayiófili

Cape Lipsó

0   kilometres   5

Cape Lefkátas

Fiskárdho (Kefaloniá) & Fríkes (Itháki)

8

below are reduced drastically in the low season.
Destinations Fiskárdho (Kefaloniá; summer 1–2 daily;
1hr); Fríkes (Itháki; summer 1 daily; 1hr 30min).

Information There is no tourist office on Lefkádha, but
for further information you can check out ⓦ lefkasgreece
.com, the most comprehensive site on the island.

GETTING AROUND

By bus There are services from Lefkádha Town to almost every
village on the island, with frequent daily schedules to Nydhrí,
Vassilikí and Áyios Nikítas/Káthisma, especially in summer.
By car or motorbike The best outlet for car and

motorbike rental in the capital is Santas (☏ 26450 25250,
ⓦ ilovesantas.gr), next to the *Ionian Star* hotel. There are
numerous other rental agencies throughout the island,
especially Nydhrí, Vassilikí and Áyios Nikítas.

LEFKÁDHA'S SUMMER FESTIVALS

Lefkádha has been home to various literati including two prominent Greek poets, Angelos Sikelianos and Aristotelis Valaoritis, and the American writer Lafcadio Hearn. Fittingly then, each summer for over fifty years, Lefkádha has hosted two parallel and wide-ranging cultural festivals, which these days attract performers and visitors from around the world. These are the **International Folklore Festival** and **Speech & Arts Events**. From June to September, troupes come from eastern and western Europe, South America and elsewhere, performing mainly at Santa Maura castle near Lefkádha Town, but also in villages around the island. The island and mainland Greece respond with troupes of their own musicians, dancers and theatrical companies. For details, contact ☏ 26450 26711 or see ⊕ lefkasculturalcenter.gr.

Lefkádha Town

LEFKÁDHA TOWN sits at the island's northernmost tip, right where the causeway joins it to the mainland. Like other capitals in the southern Ionian, it was hit by the earthquakes of 1948 and 1953, and the town was devastated, with the exception of a few Italianate churches. It's a small town – you can cross it on foot in little over ten minutes – and still very attractive, especially around the main square, **Platía Ayíou Spyridhónos**, and the arcaded high street of Ioánnou Méla. The largely pedestrian-only centre boasts over half a dozen richly decorated private family **churches**, best visited around services as they are usually locked at other times. Many contain rare works from the Ionian School of painting, including work by its founder, Zakynthian Panayiotis Doxaras.

Phonograph, Radio and Tradition Museum

Panayióti Políti 1–3 • May–Oct daily 10am–2pm & 7pm–midnight • Free • ☏ 26450 21088

You can catch a glimpse of the old way of life at the quaint little **Phonograph, Radio and Tradition Museum**, which is dedicated to antique phonographs, radios and an astounding array of bric-a-brac. It also sells recordings of rare traditional music and a few assorted souvenirs.

Archeological Museum

Cnr of Sikelianoú & Svorónou • Tues–Sun 8.30am–3pm • €2 • ☏ 26450 21635

On the northwestern seafront, the modern cultural centre houses the newly expanded **Archeological Museum**, which contains interesting, well-labelled displays on aspects of daily life, religious worship and funerary customs in ancient times, as well as a room on prehistory dedicated to the work of eminent German archeologist Wilhelm Dörpfeld.

ACCOMMODATION   **LEFKÁDHA TOWN**

The Lefkádha Room Owners Association (☏ 26450 21266; from €30) can help find rooms in Lefkádha Town.

Ionian Star Panágou 2 ☏ 26450 24672, ⊕ ionion-star .com. As well as its own pool, a games room and free internet access for guests, the island's top hotel has comfortable spacious rooms, many with sea-view balconies. Breakfast included. **€55**

Nirikos Ayías Mávras ☏ 26450 24132, ⊕ nirikos.gr. This fairly standard four-storey block contains quite spacious rooms that are stylish in a minimalist sort of way. Breakfast included. April–Oct. **€45**

Pension Pirofani Dörpfeld ☏ 26450 25844, ⊕ pirofani pansion@yahoo.gr. This smallish *pension*, just on the sea side of the main square, boasts a smart new reception and comfortable rooms, decorated in a snazzy modern fashion. May–Oct. **€50**

EATING AND DRINKING

Burano Golémi ☏ 26450 26025. Smart *mezedhopolío* on the seafront almost opposite the marina, which has candlelit tables within, as well as pavement seating to enjoy the wide range of items available (mostly €5–8).

May–Oct daily noon–1am.

Eftyhia Alley just off Dörpfeld ☎26450 24811. A fine little old-fashioned *estiatório* where you can make your choice from the mostly baked delights, such as the €7 stuffed marrow, once you've perused the glass window in the kitchen. April–Oct daily, plus occasional winter days 11am–11pm.

Ev Zin Filarmonikís 8 ☎6974 641 160. Self-proclaimed "soul food place" with a slightly bohemian atmosphere,

imaginative decor and unusual dishes such as Tex-Mex, risotto and Roquefort steak for €14. April–Oct daily noon–1am.

★**Regantos** Dhimárhou Venióti ☎26450 22855. Well-established local favourite that serves a delicious array of meat like stuffed pork, fish and starters such as baked octopus, all around €7–9. Often has live Lefkadan *kantádhes* (folk ballads). Feb–Nov daily 7pm–2am.

NIGHTLIFE AND ENTERTAINMENT

Cäsbäh Platía Ayíou Spyridhónos ☎26450 25486. One of the most enduring café-bars in town, which echoes its name by playing some ethnic sounds and having touches of eastern decor. Daily 11am–late.

Coconut Sikelianoú ☎26450 23341. Airy and relaxed café on the seafront west of the bridge, which turns into a

lively club as the night wears on. Sip a cocktail or down shots to the latest dance tunes. May–Oct noon–late.

Eleni Faneroménis 51 ☎26450 24550. The town's outdoor cinema has two showings of mostly English films. Programmes change daily. May to mid-Oct daily from 9pm.

Around Lefkádha Town

Lefkádha has the best swimming options close to town of any Ionian capital, thanks to the sandy lagoon borders at **Yíra** and **Aïyánnis**. Inland, there is also the attractive **Faneroméni monastery** and there are some traditional mountain villages centred around **Karyá**.

Yíra and Aïyánnis

There is a decent and lengthy shingle-and-sand beach west of the lagoon at **YÍRA**, a thirty-minute walk from the centre of Lefkádha Town. Roughly 4km long, the beach is often virtually deserted even in high season. Its western extension, **AÏYÁNNIS**, is a popular yet relaxed spot with several restaurants.

Faneroméni monastery

Fríni · Daily 8am–2pm & 4–8pm · Free

The uninhabited **Faneroméni monastery** is reached by any of the west-coast buses or by a steep 45-minute hike on foot from town through the hamlet of Fríni. There's a small museum and chapel, and an ox's yoke and hammer, used when Nazi occupiers forbade the use of bells.

Karyá and the interior

The island's **interior** offers imposing mountainscapes and excellent walking between villages only a few kilometres apart. **KARYÁ** is at the centre of the interior, and offers some rooms. This is the centre of the island's lace and weaving industry, with the small but fascinating **Folklore Museum** set in a former lacemaker's home (April–Oct daily 9am–9pm; €3; ☎26450 41590). The historic and scenic villages of **Vafkerí** and **Englouví** are within striking distance, with the west-coast hamlets of **Dhrymónas** and **Exánthia** a hike over the hills.

ACCOMMODATION AND EATING	AROUND LEFKÁDHA TOWN

Club Milos Yíra ☎26450 21332, ⓦmilosbeach.gr. Spreading out around their long-established club in a disused windmill on the beach, this is now a fully fledged windsurfing and kitesurfing resort with a variety of studios. May–Sept. €70

Ta Platania Karyá ☎26450 41247. The best of the trio of tavernas that fringe the beautiful plane-shaded square,

here they dish up ample portions of mostly meat dishes such as *frigadhéli* for around €5–7. Daily 11am–1am.

Tilegraphos Aïyánnis ☎26450 24881, ⓦtilegrafos.eu. With a shady elongated garden, this restaurant serves a decent range of *mezédhes* and seafood, mostly under €10. There is also a nice yellow block of simple but comfy rooms (€40). May–Oct daily 9am–late.

8

BOAT TRIPS FROM NYDHRÍ

Nydhrí is the base for myriad **boat trips** around the nearby **satellite islands** and further afield to **Itháki** and **Kefalloniá**. The boats line up along the quay each morning, ready for departure between 9 and 10am, and return late afternoon. Tickets are around €12 per person for the local trips, €20–25 for the longer distances. Most craft to the nearby islets are interchangeable: small fibreglass *kaïkia*, with bars and toilets, and open seating areas on the top deck or aft. Where they do differ, however, is in their itinerary – some will take in the sea caves of Meganíssi and others not, so it's advisable to check.

The east coast

Anchored by the island's busiest resort of **Nydhrí**, Lefkádha's east coast is the most accessible and most developed part of the island, much more so, in fact, than the nearby mainland coast. The beaches are mostly shingly and unspectacular, with the exception of **Dhessími** and **Rouda** bays, until you reach the long strand on the bay of **Vassilikí**.

Northeast coast

The stretch of the **northeast coast** between the capital and Nydhrí is a rather unprepossessing sprawl of seaside villages linked by almost unbroken development. Unless you choose to camp at **Karyótes**, there's little point stopping before the small fishing port of **Liyiá**. Further on lies **Nikiána**, another reasonably picturesque fishing village. Beaches all along this part of the coast tend to be pebbly and small.

Nydhrí

Most package travellers will find themselves in **NYDHRÍ**, the island's biggest resort by far and also the jumping-off point for Meganíssi (see p.491). It's an average resort but has a lovely setting and a reasonable pebble beach which offers watersports.

Dhessími Bay and Roúda Bay

Just south of Nydhrí, beyond somnolent **Vlyhó**, the neck of the Yéni peninsula to the east joins the main body of the island. Across this thin but steep strip of land, sizeable **Dhessími Bay** is perhaps the prettiest spot on the whole east coast, carved out by deep pine-ridged promontories. Just south of the quiet village of **Póros** is the increasingly busy beach resort of **Roúda Bay**, officially Mikrós Yialós, some 10km from Nydhrí.

Sývota

Around 14km south of Nydhrí, the fjord-like inlet of **SÝVOTA**, 2km down a steep hill from the main road, cuts a deep gash into the coastline. This is one of the most popular stops for yachting flotillas. There's no beach except for a remote cove, but there are some fine tavernas which mostly specialize in fish.

Vassilikí, Póndi and around

Around 5km due west of Sývota but longer by the winding road, **VASSILIKÍ**, the island's premier **watersports resort**, lies at the east end of a huge bay, cut off from the rest of the east coast by the barren peninsula of Cape Lipsó. Winds in the bay draw vast numbers of windsurfers, with light morning breezes for learners and tough afternoon blasts for advanced surfers.

The **beach** at Vassilikí is stony and poor but improves 1km west at tiny **Póndi**. Most non-windsurfers, however, use the daily *kaïki* trips to superior beaches on the sandy west coast (see p.491).

8

ACTIVITIES

Windsurfing In Vassilikí: the largest of the three beach windsurf centres, British-run Club Vassiliki (☎ 26450 31588, ⊛ clubvass.com) offers all-in windsurfing tuition

THE EAST COAST

and accommodation deals; Wildwind is another UK-based operation (☎ 6979 110 665, ⊛ wildwind.co.uk).

ACCOMMODATION, EATING AND DRINKING

NORTHEAST COAST

Camping Kariotes Beach Karyótes ☎ 26450 71103, ⊛ campingkariotes.com. The nearest campsite to Lefkádha Town has shady pitches, a small shop and a nice pool – handy, as the local beach is poor. May–Oct. **€14**

Pantazis Nikiána ☎ 26450 71211. ⊛ pantazis-studios .gr. This is a good fish restaurant, with fresh fish from €45 per kilo, at the south end of the small curved beach, and it also has simple rooms to let in a row of adjoining bungalows at the back (€40). May–Sept 11am–late.

NYDHRÍ

The Barrel ☎ 26450 92906. At the northern end of the busy quayside, this restaurant has a huge patio, where you can enjoy a wide range of mezédhes and main courses from €7 for the basics up to €15 for steak in cream sauce. April–Oct 11am–1am.

★ **Ionian Paradise** ☎ 26450 92268, ⊛ ionianparadise .gr. The rooms at this hotel complex, set in a lush garden only a minute along the Ráhi turning from the main road, have been recently refurbished with smart furniture and kitchenettes. May–Oct. **€35**

DHESSÍMI BAY / ROÚDA BAY

Camping Santa Maura Dhessími Bay ☎ 26450 95007, ⊛ campingsantamaura.com. This is marginally the better of the two huge campsites that dominate the olive groves behind Dhessími Bay. April–Oct. **€13.50**

Pirofani Dhessími Bay ☎ 26450 95700. This beach taverna in between the two Dhessími Bay campsites is very good, dishing up exquisite mezédhes such as octopus in wine sauce and *koloukythopittákia* (little courgette pies), mostly under €10. May to mid-Oct daily 11am–midnight.

Póros Beach Camping Roúda Bay ☎ 26450 95452, ⊛ porosbeach.com.gr. One of the smartest campsites in the archipelago, with a bar, post office, shop, pool, vehicle rental and forty spanking new studios. May–Oct. Camping **€15**, studios **€40**

★ **Rouda Bay** Roúda Bay ☎ 26450 95634, ⊛ roudabay .gr. Taverna-cum-studios venture right opposite the beach.

The food includes excellent home-cooked dishes for €10 or less and the accommodation is in luxurious and spacious suites. Breakfast included. May–Oct. **€70**

SÝVOTA

Asterida Apartments ☎ 26450 23548, ⊛ asterida.gr. Just above the middle of the harbour, these delightful studios and apartments all have fully equipped kitchens and bay views. May–Sept. **€45**

★ **Palia Apothiki** ☎ 26450 31895. At this, by far the most attractive of Sývota's tavernas, located in an old store-house as the name indicates, they serve unique dishes such as giant shrimps wrapped in bacon (€12). May–Oct daily 11am–midnight.

VASSILIKÍ, PÓNDI AND AROUND

Akroyiali Póndi ☎ 26450 31569. A welcoming old couple run this taverna, which has a beachside setting and offers delights such as garlic prawns and steak Diane for €10, as well as fine barrelled wine. May–Oct daily 11am–1am.

Grand Nefeli Póndi ☎ 26450 31378, ⊛ grandnefeli .com. Right on the beach, this smart block has comfortably furnished rooms, many with sea-view balconies, and some luxury suites. They can arrange windsurfing lessons. Breakfast included. May to mid-Oct. **€60**

Pension Holidays Vassilikí ☎ 26450 31011, ⊛ pensionholidays@hotmail.com. Round the corner from the ferry dock, this remains the best-value option in Vassilikí, with a/c and TV in all the cosy rooms. May–Oct. **€30**

Vangelaras Vassilikí ☎ 26450 31224. Well-established taverna on the eastern quay, which offers the most authentic selection of Greek cuisine (for €7–10) in the resort and a variety of wines, as well as a pleasant ambience. April–Oct daily 11am–1am.

Volero Club Vassilikí ☎ 26450 31859. The resort's liveliest club, a short way back from the seafront, provides post-windsurfing dancefloor frolics to the predominantly young crowd that spend the summer here. May–Sept daily 7pm–late.

Lefkádha's satellites

Lefkádha has four satellite islands clustered off its east coast, although only one, **Meganíssi**, the largest and most interesting, is accessible. **Skorpiós**, owned by the Onassis family, fields armed guards to deter visitors. **Madhourí**, owned by the family of poet Nanos Valaoritis, is private and similarly off limits, while tiny **Spárti** is a large scrub-covered rock. Day-trips from Nydhrí skirt all three islands (see box, p.488), and some stop to allow swimming in coves. Though officially a dependency of Lefkádha, the more remote island of **Kálamos** is only accessible from the mainland.

Meganíssi

Ferries run from Nydhrí (7 daily; 20min)

Meganíssi is a sizeable island with a decent number of facilities and a magical, if somewhat bleak and scrubby, landscape. The locals – many returned émigrés from Australia – live from farming and fishing and are genuinely welcoming. There are actually two **ports**, the main one of **Vathý** in the north, and **Spiliá** on the west coast, ten minutes' steep walk below **Spartohóri**, an immaculate village with whitewashed buildings and an abundance of bougainvillea. The walk between the two docks takes little over an hour, by way of the attractive inland village of **Katoméri**. From here, paths lead from Katoméri to remote beaches including popular **Ambelákia**.

ACCOMMODATION, EATING AND DRINKING

MEGANÍSSI

Esperides Resort Hotel Spartohóri ⊙ 26450 22170, ⓦ esperides-resort.gr. The island's poshest resort sits atop a headland 500m from the village and offers splendidly stylish rooms, as well as a pool, two jacuzzis and two bar-restaurants. May–Sept. **€90**

Meganissi Katoméri ⊙ 26450 51240. The island's longest-established hotel is a relaxed place with

decent-sized, comfortable rooms, a restaurant and pool, and is handily located for exploring. May–Sept. **€45**

Rose Garden Vathý ⊙ 26450 51216. A popular place tucked into the corner of the square and seafront, where you can get good fresh fish or a few meat or veg options from the oven, mostly €7–9. There is also a small block of rooms (€40). May–Sept daily noon–midnight.

The west coast

Lefkádha's **west coast** vies with anywhere in Greece in its display of coastal scenery at its most dramatic. On both sides of **Áï Nikítas**, the only real resort, mountainous roads rise and descend from the sea, offering tantalizing glimpses of the stunning sandy beaches, sandwiched between imposing cliffs and turquoise lapping waves.

Áï Nikítas and around

Jammed into a picturesque gorge 12km southwest of Lefkádha Town is **ÁÏ NIKÍTAS**, the prettiest resort on Lefkádha, a jumble of lanes and small wooden buildings. To add to its appeal, the village itself is now a pedestrian zone, at least in theory. Sea taxis (€4 one way) ply between Áï Nikítas and **Mýlos beach**, the delightful cove just round the southern promontory. A couple of kilometres back north is sand-and-pebble **Pefkoúlia beach**, which is one of the longest on the island.

> ### LOVER'S LEAP
>
> Fourteen kilometres south along the main road from Atháni, barren **Cape Lefkátas** drops abruptly 75m into the sea. **Byron's Childe Harold** sailed past this point, and "saw the evening star above, Leucadia's far projecting rock of woe: And hail'd the last resort of fruitless love". The fruitless love is a reference to Sappho, who in accordance with the ancient legend that you could cure yourself of unrequited love by leaping into these waters, leapt – and died. In her honour, the locals termed the place **Kávos tis Kyrás** ("lady's cape"), and her act was imitated by the lovelorn youths of Lefkádha for centuries afterwards. And not just by the lovelorn, for the act (known as *katapondismós*) was performed annually by scapegoats – always a criminal or a lunatic – selected by priests from the Apollo temple whose sparse ruins lie close by. This **purification rite** continued into the Roman era, when it degenerated into little more than a fashionable stunt by decadent youth. These days, in a more controlled modern re-enactment, Greek hang-gliders hold a tournament from the cliffs every July.

Káthisma beach

A 45min walk or a short (under 10min, several daily in season) bus ride from Áï Nikítas

The most popular beach on the coast, **Káthisma**, is a shadeless kilometre of fine sand, which becomes nudist and a lot less crowded beyond the large jutting rocks halfway along. Freelance camping still goes on at this end too.

Atháni and around

South of Kalamítsi, past the hamlets of Hortáta and Komíli, the landscape becomes almost primeval. At 38km from Lefkádha Town, **ATHÁNI** is the island's most remote spot to stay. Three of the Ionian's choicest **beaches** are accessible from Atháni: the nearest, reached by a 4km paved road, is **Yialós**, followed by **Egremní**, down a steep incline unpaved for the last 2km. Further south, an asphalted road leads to the dramatic and popular twin beach of **Pórto Katsíki**.

ACCOMMODATION, EATING AND DRINKING

THE WEST COAST

ÁÏ NIKÍTAS AND AROUND

Captain's Corner Áï Nikítas ☎ 26450 97493. Near the beach, this is the liveliest drinking venue in the village, with a pub-style atmosphere, a decent selection of drinks, snacks and mostly rock tunes. May to mid-Oct daily 10am–late.

Deck Pefkoúlia beach ☎ 26450 97070. Buzzing café-restaurant halfway along the huge beach, with a selection of coffees and cocktails, plus sandwiches, salads and other light meals to choose from for €4–8. They also rent out some well-equipped studios (€45). May–Sept daily 9am–late.

Klimataria Áï Nikítas ☎ 26450 97383. This place, halfway along the main street and with a leafy courtyard, serves good traditional cuisine, including favourites like *pastítsio* for €7–8. May–Sept daily noon–1am.

O Lefteris Áï Nikítas ☎ 26450 97495. Simple grilled fish and meat dishes for €7–8, accompanied by the expected choice of salads, dips and starters, and washed down with quaffable local wine. May to mid-Oct daily 11am–midnight.

★Pension Ostria Áï Nikítas ☎ 26450 97483. Set in a beautiful blue-and-white building above the village, this *pension* is decorated in a mix of beachcomber and ecclesiastical styles, with compact but comfortable rooms and a snack-bar with terrace. Breakfast included. May–Oct. **€75**

KÁTHISMA BEACH

Club Copla ☎ 26450 29411, ⓦcopla.gr. This beach bar-cum-club has long established itself as a favourite with the night-time crowd; they hold regular parties and raves to a techno soundtrack. May–Sept daily 11am–late.

Kathisma ☎ 26450 97050, ⓦkathisma.com. Vast taverna at the north end of the beach, with an equally extensive menu of Greek staples for €7–10 and some smart apartments (€50). May–Oct daily 10am–midnight.

ATHÁNI AND AROUND

★Lygos Hortáta ☎ 26450 71716, ⓦamadryades -villas.gr. Good local taverna serving up simple home recipes such as *moussaká* or *briám* for €6–8, expertly cooked and accompanied by inexpensive barrelled wine. Nicely designed stone villas available too (€60). May–Sept daily 11am–midnight.

★Panorama Atháni ☎ 26450 33291, ⓦpanorama -athani.com. One of the most welcoming tavernas on the island, where you can enjoy excellent fresh local dishes for €6–9 while gazing towards the distant sea from the terrace. Great-value rooms also available (€30). May–Oct daily 10am–midnight.

★Serenity Atháni ☎ 26450 33639, ⓦserenity-th .com. Run by two Israeli women, this wonderful retreat and health spa is beautifully constructed in stone on the hillside 500m south of the village. The five rooms are decorated in ethnic style, and there are chill-out tents and an infinity pool. May–Oct. **€100**

Kefaloniá

KEFALONIÁ (also known in English as Cephalonia) is the largest of the Ionian islands, a place that has real towns as well as resorts. Like its neighbours, Kefaloniá was overrun by Italians and Germans in **World War II**; the "handover" after Italy's capitulation in 1943 led to the massacre of over five thousand Italian troops on the island by invading German forces, as chronicled by Louis de Bernières in his novel, *Captain Corelli's Mandolin* (see p.560). Virtually all of its towns and villages were

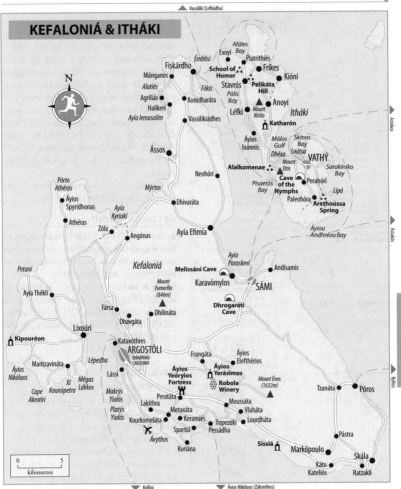

levelled in the **1953 earthquake**, and these masterpieces of Venetian architecture had been the one touch of elegance in a severe, mountainous landscape. Seismic events are still a regular phenomenon – the strong quake of January 2014 caused severe damage on the Lixoúri Peninsula and in Argostóli, but mercifully no loss of life.

Until the late 1980s, the island paid scant regard to **tourism**; perhaps this was partly due to a feeling that Kefaloniá could not be easily marketed. A more likely explanation, however, for the island's late emergence on the Greek tourist scene is the Kefalonians' legendary reputation for insular pride and stubbornness, plus a good measure of eccentricity. There are, however, definite attractions here, with some **beaches** as good as any in Greece and the fine local wines of Robola. Moreover, the island seems able to soak up a lot of people without feeling at all crowded, and the magnificent scenery speaks for itself.

ARRIVAL AND DEPARTURE
KEFALONIÁ

By plane Kefaloniá airport lies 7km south of Argostóli. Domestic destinations Athens (2 daily; 1hr); Corfu (summer 3 weekly; 1hr 20min), Préveza (summer 3 weekly; 30min) and Zákynthos (summer 3 weekly; 25min).

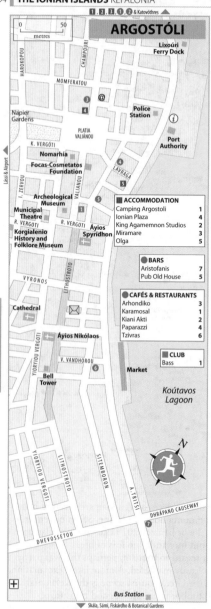

By ferry Kefaloniá has three ports that provide ferry connections with neighbouring islands and the mainland. Below are summer schedules, most of which are reduced drastically in winter; any services that stop altogether are indicated by months of operation. Be warned that there are no bus services at Pessádha or Áyios Nikólaos (on Zákynthos) ports. You'll have to hitch or take an expensive taxi in most cases.

Destinations Astakós (from Sámi, 2 daily; 2hr 30min); Áyios Nikólaos, Zákynthos (from Pessádha, 2 daily May–Sept; 1hr 30min); Kyllíni (from Póros, 5–7 daily; 1hr 15min); Pisaetós, Itháki (from Sámi, 2–3 daily; 40min).

By bus Buses run from Argostóli to Athens via Póros (2–3 daily; 7hr) and via Pátra (1 daily; 4hr).

GETTING AROUND

By bus Kefaloniá's basic KTEL bus network radiates out from Argostóli (see opposite). There are two or three services to all the main island destinations Mon–Fri, one or two on Sat but no buses on Sun.

By car or motorbike The reliable Sunbird agency (☎ 26710 23723, ⓦ sunbird.gr) has outlets all over the island, but Etam (☎ 26710 25651, ⓦ etamtravel.gr) and CBR (☎ 26710 22770, ⓦ cbr-rentacar.com) offer more competitive prices.

Argostóli

ARGOSTÓLI, Kefaloniá's capital, is a large and thriving town – virtually a city – with a marvellous position on a bay within a bay. The causeway connecting the two sides of the inner bay, known as Dhrápano owing to its sickle shape, was initially constructed by the British in 1813 and is now closed to traffic. The town was totally rebuilt after the 1953 earthquake, but has an enjoyable atmosphere that remains defiantly Greek, especially during the evening *vólta* around **Platía Valianou** (formerly Platía Metaxá) – the nerve centre of town – and along the pedestrianized **Lithóstroto**, the main shopping street which runs parallel to the seafront.

Korgialenio History and Folklore Museum
Ilía Zervoú 12 · Mon–Sat 9am–2pm · €3 · ☎ 26710 28835, ⓦ corgialenios.gr

The **Korgialenio History and Folklore Museum**, behind the Municipal Theatre, has a rich collection of local religious and cultural artefacts including photographs taken before and after the 1953 earthquake. At the time of writing it was closed due to staffing difficulties.

Focas-Cosmetatos Foundation
Valiánou 1 • Mon–Sat 9.30am–12.30pm, plus June–Sept 7–9.30pm • €3 • ☎ 26710 26595

Insight into how the island's nobility used to live can be gained from a visit to the **Focas-Cosmetatos Foundation**, opposite the provincial government building. It contains elegant furniture and a collection of lithographs and paintings including works by nineteenth-century British artists Joseph Cartwright and Edward Lear.

Archeological Museum
Y. Vergóti • Tues–Sun 8.30am–3pm • €3 • ☎ 26710 28300

The refurbished **Archeological Museum** has a sizeable collection of pottery, jewellery, funerary relics and statuary from prehistoric, through Mycenaean to late Classical times. Unfortunately, it suffered extensive damage in the 2014 earthquake and was closed indefinitely at the time of writing.

Botanical Gardens
2km south of the town centre • Tues–Sat 9am–2.30pm • Free • ☎ 26710 26595

The pleasantly relaxing **Botanical Gardens** have been transformed under the stewardship of the Focas-Cosmetatos Foundation into a diverse collection of the island's flora, arranged in a natural fashion with a stream running through the middle.

ARRIVAL AND INFORMATION ARGOSTÓLI

By plane The airport is 7km south of Argostóli. There are no airport buses, so taxis (at least €15) are the only way into town.

By bus The KTEL bus station (☎ 26710 22276, ⓦ ktel kefallonias.gr) is 100m south of the Dhrápano causeway in the south of town.

Destinations Fiskárdho (Mon–Sat 1–2 daily; 1hr 45min); Lássi (summer at least hourly; 30min); Póros (Mon–Sat 2 daily; 1hr); Sámi (Mon–Sat 4 daily; 45min); Skála (Mon–Sat 2 daily; 1hr)

By ferry There are frequent flat-bottomed boats to Lixoúri (Mon–Sat every 30min, Sun hourly; 20min).

Tourist office Andoníou Trítsi, at the north end of the seafront next to the port authority (Mon–Fri 7am–3pm; ☎ 26710 22248).

ACCOMMODATION

The Kefalonia & Ithaca Federation of Lodgings (☎ 26710 29109, ⓦ kefalonia-ithaca.gr) can arrange rooms in Argostóli and around the island, as can travel agencies such as Ainos Travel (☎ 26710 22333, ⓦ ainostravel.gr).

Camping Argostoli 2km north of town ☎ 26710 23487, ⓦ camping-argostoli.gr. Although it's inconveniently out of town, just beyond the Katavóthres sea mills, this campsite has decent facilities including a minimarket. May–Sept. **€15**

★**Ionian Plaza** Platía Valiánou ☎ 26710 25581, ⓦ ionianplaza.com. One of the ritziest hotels on the island and surprisingly reasonable for what it is – designer decor throughout, from the lobby up to the chic bathroom fixtures. Breakfast included. **€60**

King Agamemnon Studios A. Metaxá ☎ 26710 24260, ⓔ kathya@europe.com. Basic modern studios with kitchenettes, in a brightly painted block north of the Lixoúri ferry dock, all with a/c and TV, some with sea-facing balconies. **€30**

Miramare A. Metaxá 2 ☎ 26710 25511, ⓔ miramare hotelargostoli@gmail.com. Reasonably smart and nicely furnished hotel, north of the Lixoúri ferry dock, offering several seafront rooms with balconies. **€35**

EATING, DRINKING AND NIGHTLIFE

RESTAURANTS
★**Arhondiko** Rizospastón 5 ☎ 26710 27213. Classy stone building with a small patio out front, where the friendly proprietress serves tasty dishes such as *exohikó*, *strapatsádha* and *biftéki* in Roquefort sauce, mostly for under €10. Daily noon–1am.

Karamosal A. Trítsi ☎ 26710 28590. Good ouzerí, with an artistic touch to the bright decor and a fair bit of imagination in the preparation of the mezédhes, which include cheese croquettes, pickled anchovies, meatballs and various veg options for €3–6. Daily noon–1am.

★**Kiani Akti** A. Trítsi ☎ 26710 26680. Unmissable dining experience on a large wooden deck jutting out over the water by the cruise-ship dock, about 400m north of Platía Valianou. Specializes in seafood such as razor clams in mustard sauce and shrimps in ouzo for around €10–12.

Daily 1pm–2am.

Paparazzi Lavrága 2 ☎ 26710 22631. Just southeast of Platía Valiánou, this Italian-run restaurant serves delights such as prosciutto with melon and veal stuffed with ham and mozzarella in a mushroom sauce for €10–16. May–Oct daily 7.30pm–1am.

Tzivras V. Vandhórou 1. A classic daytime-only *estiatório* with an impressive range of staples from the oven, including a lot of vegetarian options such as *briám*, helpings of which tend to be large and all cost well under €10. Daily 10am–5pm.

CAFÉS, BARS AND CLUBS

Aristofanis A. Trítsi ☎ 26710 28012. Right by the Dhrápano bridge, this simple old-style *kafenío* might have a limited repertoire of coffee and basic booze but it enjoys one of the best locations in town, ideal for some gentle people-watching. Daily 8am–midnight.

Bass P. Valiánou ☎ 26710 25020, ⓦ bassclub.gr. Opposite the archeological museum, this is the town's main late-night indoor club, whose hi-tech interior shakes to the latest vibes of various dance genres and hosts occasional live acts. Daily 10pm–late.

★**Pub Old House** A. Yerasímou 7 ☎ 26710 23532. Boasting a new modern premises, the most relaxed and welcoming hangout on the island is a great place to have a drink on the patio or unwind indoors to an eclectic range of (mostly) rock sounds. Daily 11am–late.

Livathó peninsula

The bulge of land southeast of Argostóli known as the **Livathó peninsula** is a patchwork of small villages and agricultural land bordered by some attractive coastline. Many package travellers will find themselves staying in **Lássi**, a short bus ride or half-hour walk from town. The only other reason you might come to this corner of the island is for the summer ferry link with Zákynthos from **Pessádha** (see.p.494).

Áyios Yeóryios

The best inland excursion from Argostóli is to **ÁYIOS YEÓRYIOS**, the medieval Venetian capital of the island, 7km southeast of Argostóli but not connected by public transport. The old town here supported a population of fifteen thousand until its destruction by an earthquake in the seventeenth century: substantial ruins of its **castle** (Tues–Sun 8.30am–3pm; free) can be visited on the hill above the modern village of Peratáta, a steep 1km walk below on the main southeast bus routes.

Mount Énos and around

At 15km from a point halfway along the Argostóli–Sámi road, **Mount Énos** isn't really a walking option, but roads nearly reach the official 1632m summit. The mountain has been declared a **national park**, to protect the *Abies cephalonica* firs named after the island, which clothe the slopes. There are absolutely no facilities on or up to the mountain, but the **views** from the highest point in the Ionian islands out over Kefaloniá's neighbours and the mainland are wonderful. At any time other than summer, watch the weather, which can deteriorate with terrifying speed.

Áyios Yerásimos monastery and Robola winery

Monastery Daily 9am–1pm & 4–8pm • Free • **Winery** April–Oct daily 7am–8.30pm; Nov–March Mon–Fri 7am–3pm • Free • ⓦ robola.gr

If you're coming from Argostóli and heading for Mount Énos, there's a doubly rewarding detour via a turning on the right (not far west of the mountain) towards Frangáta. First, there's the huge and lively **Áyios Yerásimos monastery**, which hosts two of the island's most important festivals (Aug 15 and Oct 20); the most interesting feature is the double cave beneath the back of the sanctuary, where the eponymous saint meditated for lengthy periods. Right behind the monastery is the **Robola winery**, which offers a free self-guided tour and generous wine tasting.

Lixoúri and its peninsula

Ferries run from Argostóli to Lixoúri till well after midnight (summer Mon–Sat every 30min, Sun hourly; winter hourly; 20min)

Across the water from Argostóli, the town of **LIXOÚRI** was flattened by successive **earthquakes** and hasn't risen much above two storeys since – a wise decision which has kept damage to manageable levels, most recently in January 2014. It's a little drab but has good restaurants, quiet hotels and is favoured by those who want to explore the eerie quake-scapes left in the south and the barren north of the peninsula.

Beaches around Lixoúri

Xi and Mégas Lákkos are served by buses from Lixoúri (2–3 daily; 15–20min)

Lixoúri's nearest beach, a 2km walk south, is **Lépedha**, composed of rich-red sand and backed by low cliffs, as are **Xi** and **Mégas Lákkos** (the name means "big hole") beaches, both of which have good facilities. Around 4km southwest lies the quieter beach at **Kounópetra**, site of a curious rock formation. Until the 1953 earthquake, this "rocking stone" (as the name signifies in Greek) had a strange rhythmic movement that could be measured by placing a knife into a gap between the rock and its base. However, after the quake, the rock became motionless. Some 2km further west, in an area known as Vátsa, the last beach of any size on the southern tip of the peninsula is sandy **Áyios Nikólaos**, a very quiet and scenic strand.

The western coast

Those with transport can strike out for the rugged western coast of the peninsula. First you can visit the monastery at **Kipouréon** (daily 8am–6pm; free), now home to just a single aged monk, before heading north to the spectacular beach at **Petaní**, one of the best in the Ionians. Tucked in the fold of the **Áyios Spyrídhonas** inlet further north is the beach of **Pórto Athéras**, which serves the traditional village of Athéras a short way inland and is another fine strip of sand with shallow water.

ACCOMMODATION AND EATING   LIXOÚRI AND ITS PENINSULA

★**Akrogiali** Lixoúri ☎26710 92613. Wonderful unpretentious taverna on the seafront, which draws admirers from all over the island for its excellent and inexpensive grilled and baked meat, fish and seafood, mostly well under €10. Daily noon–1am.

La Cité Lixoúri ☎26710 92701, ⓦlacitehotellixouri.gr. Four blocks back from the seafront, this great-value hotel has a uniquely shaped pool in its exotic garden, while the rooms are spacious and colourfully furnished. April–Oct. **€50**

O Yialós Pórto Athéras ☎26710 69315. Set at the back of the beach, this good all-round taverna serves mostly grills for €7–8. Their garden acts as home for families with camper vans and can be used for camping. May–Sept

daily noon–1am.

★**Spiaggia** Áyios Nikólaos ☎697 76 31 053, ⓦvatsa .gr. Atmospheric restaurant with an attractive wood-and-bamboo deck, where you can tuck into excellent pasta, seaweed salad and seafood for around €10. There are four well-equipped chalets and two luxury villas behind (€75). May–Oct daily 11am–late.

★**Xouras** Petaní ☎26710 97458, ✉petanoi@gmail .com. By far the better of the two tavernas here, where the friendly Greek-American owner Dina serves a fine selection of grills, salads and some oven-cooked dishes, all under €10. There are comfortable studios attached too (€45). May–Oct daily 9am–midnight.

Southeast Kefaloniá

Southeast Kefaloniá contains some fine beaches and much of the island's package tourism, from smaller resorts such as **Lourdháta** and **Káto Kateliós** east via the busiest foreign enclave of **Skála** to the port resort of **Póros**. One or two of the villages strung along the main Argostóli–Póros road, which follows the southern contours of Mt Énos, are also worth a brief halt, especially **Markópoulo**.

Lourdháta and Trapezáki

From the pleasant village of Vlaháta, around 15km east of Argostóli, a couple of turnings bear 2km down the mountainside to **LOURDHÁTA**, which has a kilometre-long shingle beach, mixed with imported sand. Another fine beach, reached by a turning from Moussáta, 2km west of Vlaháta, is **Trapezáki**, a relatively slim but appealing strand with just one restaurant by the small jetty.

Markópoulo

The inland village of **MARKÓPOULO** witnesses a bizarre snake-handling ritual every year on August 15, on the occasion of the **Assumption of the Virgin Festival**, when a swarm of harmless snakes "appears" in commemoration of a legend that the nuns of the former convent here prayed to be turned into snakes to avoid an attack by pirates. The **church** at which the ritual is enacted is well worth visiting at any time of year.

Káto Kateliós and around

Some of the finest sandy beaches on the island are to be found around the growing micro-resort of **KÁTO KATELIÓS**, which already has a couple of hotels, and below the village of **Ratzaklí**, just before the resort of Skála. The coast around Káto Kateliós is also Kefaloniá's key breeding ground for the loggerhead **turtle** (see p.509); camping on the nearby beaches is therefore prohibited.

Skála

SKÁLA is a low-rise, mostly package resort with little independent accommodation, set among handsome pines above a few kilometres of good sandy beach. A **Roman villa** (daily 10am–2pm & 5–8pm, longer hours in summer; free) and some mosaics were excavated here in the 1950s, on the western edge of the village, and are open to the public.

Póros

Connected to Skála by a lovely 12km coastal route that at times seems to skim across the shallow sea, **PÓROS** was one of the island's earliest resorts, though it has now certainly seen better days. The town's small huddle of hotels and apartment blocks is not enhanced by a scruffy seafront and thin pebbly beach. Póros is actually made up of **two bays**: the northern one, where most tourists are based, and the harbour bay, a few minutes over the headland, with connections to Kyllíni on the Peloponnesian coast.

ACCOMMODATION, EATING AND DRINKING · SOUTHEAST KEFALONIÁ

LOURDHÁTA AND TRAPEZÁKI

Christina Studios Lourdháta ☎ 26710 31130, ⓦ christinastudio.gr. Fully equipped kitchen-studios with side views to the sea are available at this lovely building set into the lush vegetation behind the beach. May–Oct. **€40**

★ **Denis** Trapezáki ☎ 26710 31454. This friendly taverna does not abuse its monopoly. Instead, it maintains a fine level of quality in the typical Greek menu of grills for €7–8 with salads and dips, plus good service, even when especially busy around lunchtime. May–Oct daily 11am–11pm.

★ **Lorraine's Magic Hill** Lourdháta ☎ 26710 31605, ⓦ lorrainesmagichilllourdas.com. With a lovely airy terrace, on the hill just behind the beach, this relaxed joint serves a wide range of home produce, including tender calves' liver and succulent goat for €10 or less. Also does cocktails in its alter ego as a bar. May–Oct daily noon–late.

Trapezaki Bay Hotel Trapezáki ☎ 26710 31503, ⓦ trapezakibayhotel.com. This luxury hotel 500m uphill from the beach offers all mod cons, plus a spa and beauty treatments. The fixed price all summer means good value in peak season and the rate includes airport transfer and breakfast. May–Oct. **€115**

KÁTO KATELIÓS

Blue Sea ☎ 26710 81122. Seafront taverna renowned for the freshness and quality of its fish, which goes from €50 per kilo, and lobster (€70/kg). Also does the usual accompanying dishes, plus pizza and pasta. May–Oct daily 11am–1am.

Cozy ☎ 26710 81031. This little bar with a fitting name, at the west end of the seafront, is the prime drinking location in the area, where you can enjoy a beer or cocktail to the accompaniment of some laidback summer sounds. Mid-May to Oct daily 10am–late.

Maria's ☎ 26710 81765. Located at the western end of the seafront, this ouzerí-cum-taverna offers a wide selection of dishes such as stuffed pork or baked swordfish for around €8. May–Oct daily noon–1am.

Odyssia ☎ 26710 81615, ⓦ odyssia-apartments.gr. These smart and comfortable apartments, run by a welcoming family, enjoy a convenient and quiet location behind the east end of the harbour. May–Oct. **€40**

SKÁLA

★**Captain's House** ☎26710 83389, ⊛www
.captainshouse.net. On the road parallel to the main street
to the east, *Captain's House* offers warmly decorated rooms
and studios, plus a cute little bar outside. April–Oct. **€40**

Paspalis ☎26710 83140. This well-established beachside favourite serves fish and home-cooked meat and
vegetable dishes, mostly under €10. Especially popular
during the day, as it has a pool for patrons. May–Oct daily
11am–midnight.

Ta Pitharia ☎26710 83567. The best taverna in the village
provides a range of mezédhes, oven dishes and roasts like

kondosoúvli (spit-roasted pork) for under €10, or you can go
for a massive €18 steak. May–Oct daily 10am–1am.

PÓROS

Fotis Family ☎26710 72972. Tucked into the rocky
corner of the northern bay, this taverna serves an array of
grilled meat and fish in the €7–10 range, plus plenty of
salads and mezédhes. April–Oct daily 11am–midnight.

Santa Irina ☎26740 72017, ✉maki@otenet.gr. By the
crossroads inland, this medium-sized *pension* has basic but
clean rooms offered at superb value. Breakfast included.
Mid-May to Sept. **€30**

Sámi and around

Most boats to the island dock at the large and functional port town of **SÁMI**, near the
south end of the Itháki straits, more or less on the site of **ancient Sami**. This was the
capital of the island in Homeric times, when Kefaloniá was part of Ithaca's maritime
kingdom. Ironically, today the administrative hierarchy is reversed, with Itháki considered
the backwater. In more recent times, Sámi was used as the set for much of the filming of
Captain Corelli's Mandolin (see p.560). The long sandy beach that stretches round the bay
to the village of **Karavómylos** is perfectly adequate, but 2km further east, beyond ancient
Sami, lies a more dramatic pebble beach, **Andísamis**, set in a stunning curved bay.

Dhrogaráti Cave

5km southwest of Sámi • April–Oct daily 9am–8pm • €4

Signposted just off the Sámi–Argostóli road lies a very impressive stalagmite-bedecked
chamber, known as the **Dhrogaráti Cave**. The cave, which reaches a depth of 60m and
was discovered over 300 years ago, is occasionally used for concerts thanks to its
marvellous acoustics.

Melissáni Cave

3km northwest of Sámi • Daily 8am–7pm • €7

The **Melissáni Cave**, on the road north from Sámi, is partly submerged in brackish
water, which, amazingly, emerges from an underground fault extending the whole way
underneath the island to a point near Argostóli. At that point, known as Katavóthres,
the sea gushes endlessly into a **subterranean channel** – the fact that the water ends up
in the cave has been shown with fluorescent tracer dye. The beautiful textures and
shades created by the light pouring through the collapsed roof of the cave make the
short boat excursion into it a must.

Ayía Efimía

9km north of Sámi

AYÍA EFIMÍA, reachable from Sámi via a scenic coastal drive that includes coves such as
Ayía Paraskeví, is a small fishing harbour popular with package operators, yet with no
major developments. Its main drawback is its beaches, or lack thereof – the largest,
absurdly named Paradise beach, is a pathetic 20m of shingle. It is, however, home to
one of the island's few **scuba-diving** enterprises (see p.500).

ARRIVAL AND GETTING AROUND	SÁMI AND AROUND
By ferry The dock is towards the southern end of the long seafront. **By bus** Island buses congregate outside the KTEL office about 100m from the dock.	**By car and motorbike** The seafront Sami Center (☎26740 22254) rents out motorbikes at fair rates, and Island (☎26740 23084, ✉islecars@otenet.gr) is a reliable local car rental company.

8

ACTIVITIES

Diving The Aquatic Scuba Diving Club in Ayía Efimía (☎ 26740 62006, 𝕨 aquatic.gr) is the island's premier scuba-diving outfit. It runs courses, does wreck diving and offers introductory dives.

ACCOMMODATION, EATING AND DRINKING

SÁMI

Akrogiali ☎ 26740 22494. At the far northern end of the seafront, this family taverna has seating right above the beach and offers a range of the cheaper fish and meat dishes for around €7–8. May–Sept daily noon–midnight.

★ **Camping Karavomilos Beach** Karavómylos ☎ 26740 22480, 𝕨 camping-karavomilos.gr. Just 1km along the beach from Sámi, the better of the island's two campsites has over three hundred well-shaded spaces, a taverna, shop and bar. May–Oct. **€19**

Melissani ☎ 26740 22464, 𝕨 melissanihotel.gr. Up a couple of blocks behind the main dock, this slightly old-fashioned but welcoming hotel has cosy, great-value rooms, many with good views from their balconies. May–Sept. **€25**

Mermaid ☎ 26740 22202. With a decent selection of vegetable and meat dishes, including the famous local meat pie for €9, this is the best of the central bunch of portside tavernas. April–Oct daily 11am–2am.

Staggia Studios ☎ 26740 22706, 𝕨 sami-kefalonia .gr. Cosy studios and larger apartments in a building with a leafy courtyard, tucked in the backstreets. May–Oct. **€55**

AYÍA EFIMÍA

Amalia ☎ 26740 61088. Round the headland past the harbour, this is the place for moderately priced island cuisine such as small fried fish and local sausage (€7–8). May–Sept daily noon–1am.

Captain Corelli's ☎ 26740 61955. Predictably renamed after the film crew and cast who spent hours unwinding here, this café-restaurant is nonetheless a good spot right on the harbour for a refreshing drink or light snack. April–Oct daily 8am–2am.

Odyssey ☎ 26740 61089, 𝕨 hotelodyssey.gr. Round the headland from the harbour, this spanking hotel has spacious modern rooms and offers a restaurant, bar, spa and huge pool. April–Oct. **€50**

Spiros ☎ 26740 61739. A wide range of specials such as lamb *kléftiko* and beef ragout with yoghurt sauce can be enjoyed for under €10 at this taverna that's halfway along the harbour. May–Sept daily noon–1am.

Northern Kefaloniá

Northern Kefaloniá offers some splendid beaches, an architecturally attractive village in **Fiskárdho**, and some amazing coastal scenery. Indeed, the northern half of the road between Argostóli and Fiskárdho, starting at the point where a side road peels off to the long sandy beach of **Ayía Kyriakí**, is the most spectacular ride in the Ionian archipelago.

Mýrtos beach and around

Four kilometres by paved road below the main north–south artery, stunningly photogenic **Mýrtos** is regarded by many as the most dramatic beach in the Ionian islands – a splendid strip of pure-white sand and pebbles. Sadly, it has no natural shade for most of the day and gets mighty crowded in high season, with just a couple of seasonal snack-shacks for refreshment. Back at the crossroads, the small settlement of **Dhivaráta** has the nearest amenities to Mýrtos.

Ássos

Six kilometres beyond Dhivaráta, as you head north from Argostóli, is the turning for the atmospheric village of **ÁSSOS**, clinging to a small isthmus between the island and a huge hill crowned by a ruined fort. It can get a little claustrophobic, but there's nowhere else quite like it in the Ionians. Ássos has a small pebble beach and three tavernas on a plane-shaded village square backed by mansions, mostly now restored after being ruined in the 1953 quake.

Fiskárdho

FISKÁRDHO, on the northernmost tip of the island, sits on a bed of limestone that buffered it against the worst of the quakes. Two **lighthouses**, Venetian and Victorian, guard the bay, and the headland ruins are believed to be from a twelfth-century chapel begun by Norman invader Robert Guiscard, who gave the place its name. The nineteenth-century harbour frontage is occupied by chic restaurants and boutiques.

Environmental and Nautical Museum

Summer Mon–Fri 10am–6pm, Sun till 2pm · Donation · ☎ 26740 41182

Fiskárdho has an **Environmental and Nautical Museum** housed in a renovated Neoclassical mansion on the hill behind the village. The volunteers who curate it conduct valuable ecological research and can also arrange **scuba diving**.

Around Fiskárdho

There are two good pebble beaches close to Fiskárdho – **Émblisi** 1km back out of town and **Fókis** just to the south – and a nature trail on the northern headland. It is worth making the effort to explore the coastal region west of **Mánganos: Alatiés** has a tiny beach tucked in between folds of impressive white volcanic rock, but the real gem is the small bay of **Ayía Ierousalím**, whose gravel-and-sand beach remains quiet even in August.

ACCOMMODATION, EATING AND DRINKING NORTHERN KEFALONIÁ

MÝRTOS BEACH AND AROUND

Mina Studios Dhivaráta ☎ 26740 61716, ✉ markela1 @hol.gr. Just above the main junction, these large and well-appointed studios with kitchenettes are the best accommodation close to Mýrtos beach. April–Oct. **€40**

ÁSSOS

Cosi's Inn ☎ 26740 51420, 🌐 cosisinn.gr. Brightly decorated, well-furnished and good-value rooms are the attraction at this pleasant hillside inn on the approach road to the centre. Breakfast included. April–Oct. **€45**

Kanakis Apartments ☎ 26740 51631, 🌐 kanakis apartments.gr. Very smart studios and spacious maisonettes which share a pool and are equipped with all mod cons. Only 100m from the heart of the village. April–Oct. **€55**

Nefeli ☎ 26740 51251. With its prime location on the quay beside the beach, this taverna does a nice line in seafood, mezédhes and salads. Most main courses around €9–12. April–Oct daily 10am–1am.

★**Platanos** Set just back from the seafront under a huge plane tree, hence the name, this place is good for grilled meat and fish, as well as oven food, mostly €10 and up. There's also a wide selection of salads and starters, plus aromatic local wine. April–Oct daily 11am– midnight.

FISKÁRDHO

Archontiko ☎ 26740 41342, 🌐 archontiko-fiskardo.gr. Beautiful traditional stone mansion that has been converted into luxurious rooms above and behind a harbourfront minimarket. The furniture is period style, but all the equipment, such as the TVs, is cutting edge. April– Oct. **€100**

Kastro Club ☎ 26740 41010. Up behind the main bypass road, the oldest club in northern Kefaloniá has tiered terraces and a big outdoor dancefloor. The isolated location allows the volume to be jacked up on the usual mix of international and Greek hits. July–Sept daily 10pm–late.

Lagoudera ☎ 26740 41275. With two premises, one on the harbour, the other just off the small square, *Lagoudera* specializes in tasty oven food for around €10 but also does grills and all the usual side dishes. April–Oct daily noon–2am.

Lord Falcon ☎ 26740 41072. One block back from the harbour, the Ionians' first Thai restaurant does a fine array of soups, stir-fries and red, green and Penang curries for around €10–12. May–Oct Mon–Sat 6.30pm–midnight, Sun 1–4.30pm.

★**Regina's** ☎ 26740 41125, 🌐 regina-studios.gr. Up by the car park, these friendly family-run studios are compact but great value. Some have balconies looking over the village to the bay, and there's a lovely courtyard. They can arrange motorboat rental too. April–Oct. **€40**

AROUND FISKÁRDHO

★**Odisseas** Ayía Ierousalím ☎ 26740 41133. The extremely friendly brother-sister-mum trio who run *Odisseas* serve up exquisite traditional dishes from free-range meat for under €10 and do a line in olive bread and other baked goodies, plus jams and preserves. They also allow camping on their grounds. April–Oct daily noon–midnight.

Itháki

Rugged **ITHÁKI**, Odysseus's legendary homeland, has yielded no substantial archeological discoveries, but it fits Homer's description to perfection: "There are no tracks, nor grasslands … it is a rocky severe island, unsuited for horses, but not so

ODYSSEUS SIGHTS AROUND VATHÝ

Three of the main **Odysseus** sights are just within walking distance of Vathý: the Arethoússa Spring, the Cave of the Nymphs and ancient Alalkomenae, although the last is best approached by **moped** or **taxi**.

ARETHOÚSSA SPRING

The walk to the **Arethoússa Spring** – allegedly the place where Eumaeus, Odysseus's faithful swineherd, brought his pigs to drink – is a three-hour round trip along a track signposted next to the seafront telecoms office. The unspoilt but shadeless landscape and sea views are magnificent but some of the inclines can be slippery.

Near the top of the lane leading to the spring path, a signpost points up to what is said to have been the **Cave of Eumaeus**. The route to the spring continues for a few hundred metres, and then branches off onto a narrow footpath through steep gorse-covered cliffs. Parts of the final downhill track involve scrambling across rock fields (follow the splashes of green paint), and care should be taken around the small but vertiginous ravine that houses the **spring**. The ravine sits below a crag known as **Kórax** (the raven), which matches Homer's description of the meeting between Odysseus and Eumaeus. In summer it's just a dribble of water.

THE CAVE OF THE NYMPHS

The **Cave of the Nymphs** (Marmarospíli) is about 2.5km up a rough but navigable road signposted on the brow of the hill above Dhéxa beach. The cave is atmospheric, but it's underwhelming compared to the caverns of neighbouring Kefaloniá and, these days, is illuminated by coloured lights. The claim that this is *The Odyssey*'s Cave of the Nymphs, where the returning Odysseus concealed the gifts given to him by King Alkinous, is enhanced by the proximity of **Dhéxa beach**.

ALALKOMENAE

Alalkomenae, Heinrich Schliemann's much-vaunted "Castle of Odysseus", is signposted on the Vathý–Pisaetós road, on the saddle between Dhéxa and Pisaetós, with views over both sides of the island. The actual site, however, some 300m uphill, is little more than foundations spread about in the gorse, and in fact the most likely contender for the site of Odysseus's castle is above the village of **Stavrós** (see p.504).

wretched, despite its small size. It is good for goats." Despite its proximity to Kefaloniá, relatively little tourist development has arrived to spoil the place. This is doubtless accounted for in part by a dearth of beaches beyond a few pebbly coves, though the island is good walking country, and indeed the interior, with its sites from **The Odyssey**, is the real attraction. In the scheme of modern Greek affairs, the island is a real backwater, and its inhabitants rather resentful that it is officially a subsection of Kefaloniá prefecture.

ARRIVAL AND DEPARTURE

ITHÁKI

By ferry For such a small island, Itháki, perhaps surprisingly, has three active ports. The following are summer schedules, which are often reduced drastically in winter; any services that stop altogether are denoted by months of operation.

Fríkes destinations Fiskárdho (Kefaloniá; May–Oct 4 weekly; 1hr); Vassilikí (Lefkádha; May–Oct 1 daily; 1hr 30min).

Pisaetós destinations Astakós (1–2 daily; 2hr 30min); Sámi (Kefaloniá; 2–3 daily; 40min).

Vathý destinations Astakós (1–2 daily; 1hr 30min); Pisaetós (1–2 daily; 1hr); Sámi (Kefaloniá; 1–2 daily; 1hr 45min).

GETTING AROUND

By bus There is effectively no public transport on the island, though you might be able to flag down the school bus during term.

By taxi Taxis are available, especially at Vathý's square.

By car and motorbike Cars and motorbikes can be rented through the two main travel agencies, based in Vathý, Polyctor Tours (☏ 26740 33120, ⓦ ithakiholidays.com) and Delas Tours (☏ 26740 32104, ⓔ delas@otenet.gr).

Vathý and around

Itháki's main port and capital is **VATHÝ**, enclosed by a bay within a bay so deep that few realize the mountains out "at sea" are actually the north of the island. This snug town is compact, relatively traffic-free and boasts the most idyllic seafront setting of all the Ionian capitals. Like its southerly neighbours, it was heavily damaged by the 1953 earthquake but some fine examples of pre-quake architecture remain. Vathý has a small **archeological museum** on Kalliníkou (Tues–Sun 8.30am–3pm; free; ☎26740 32200), a short block back from the quay. Near the corner of the quay behind the Agricultural Bank, there is also the moderately interesting **Folklore & Cultural Museum** (April–Oct Mon–Fri 10am–2pm & 7.30–9.30pm; €1).

Beaches around Vathý

There are two reasonable pebble **beaches** within fifteen minutes' walk of Vathý: **Dhéxa**, over the hill above the ferry quay, and tiny **Loútsa**, opposite it around the bay. The better beaches at **Sarakíniko** and **Skínos** are an hour's trek along paved roads leaving the opposite side of the bay. In season, daily *kaïkia* ply between the quay and remote coves.

Pisaetós

The harbour of **PISAETÓS**, around 5km west of Vathý via a steep route across the island's neck, has a fair-sized rocky beach that's all right for a pre-ferry swim and popular with local rod-and-line fishermen. Little goes on here except during the busy period around ferry arrivals, when a small canteen on the quay is the focus of activity.

8

INFORMATION
VATHÝ

Tourist information There is no tourist office in Vathý, but an excellent website on the island is ⓦ ithacagreece.com.

Services Vathý has a smattering of banks, a post office, police and a medical centre around the harbour.

ACCOMMODATION

The best source of rooms, studios or villas around the capital or all over the island are the two main quayside travel agencies (see opposite).

★ **Captain Yiannis** ☎26740 33311, ⓦ captainyiannis .com. Complete with tennis court and pool with bar, this great-value resort round the east side of the bay is spread over several blocks of modern rooms and apartments. Breakfast included. Mid-May to Sept. **€50**

Mentor ☎26740 32433, ⓦ hotelmentor.gr. The town's oldest hotel, in the southeast corner of the harbour, was refurbished a few years ago and its comfortable rooms have balconies either with direct or side views of the water. **€60**

Omirikon Residence ☎26740 33596, ⓦ omirikon hotel.com. Stylish boutique hotel, yet with a personal, family-run touch. All its rooms are classed as suites, and are spacious and well furnished with sea-view balconies. Breakfast included. May–Oct. **€75**

EATING AND DRINKING

O Nikos ☎26740 33039. Just off the square, this is a good old-fashioned *estiatório*, where you can feast on heaps of oven-baked goodies (€6–8), on show behind the glass panel within. Pavement seating in summer. Daily 11am–midnight.

Paliocaravo (aka Gregory's) ☎26740 32573. This place round the east side of the bay is popular for its lamb and fish, mostly €10 or less, with a good range of accompanying dishes and beverages, plus the occasional impromptu music session. April–Oct daily noon–1am.

★ **To Kohili** ☎26740 33565. By far the best of the half-dozen harbourside tavernas, serving a good range of mezédhes as well as tasty meat dishes such as lamb *kléftiko*, *yiouvétsi* and *soutzoukákia*, plus grills and pasta for under €10. Daily 11am–1am.

Northern Itháki

The main road out of Vathý continues across the isthmus and takes a spectacular route to the northern half of Itháki, which is based around **Stavrós**. This is excellent scooter country, and the close proximity of the settlements, small coves and Homeric interest also make it good rambling terrain. As with the rest of Itháki, there are only limited tourist facilities, concentrated mostly in **Fríkes** and **Kióni**.

Stavrós

STAVRÓS, the second-largest town on Itháki, is a steep 2km above the nearest beach at Pólis Bay. It's a pleasant enough town, with *kafenía* edging a small square dominated by a rather fierce statue of Odysseus.

Stavrós Museum

Off the road to Platrithriés • Tues–Sun 8.30am–3pm • Free

The tiny **Stavrós Museum** displays local archeological finds. Most of these come from the early Helladic site on the side of **Pelikáta Hill**, where remains of roads, walls and other structures have been suggested as the possible site of Odysseus's palace.

Anoyí

Some 5km southeast of Stavrós along a scenic mountain road is **ANOYÍ**, which translates roughly as "upper ground". Once the second-most important settlement on the island, it is almost deserted today. The centre of the village is dominated by a freestanding Venetian campanile, built to serve the church of the **Panayía**, which features heavily restored Byzantine frescoes. The church comes alive for the annual *paniyíri* on August 14, the eve of the Virgin's Assumption; at other times, enquire at the *kafenío* about access. In the surrounding countryside are some extremely strange rock formations, the biggest of which is the 8m-high Iraklis (Hercules) rock, just east of the village.

Monastery of Katharón

3km south of Anoyí • Free

The **monastery of Katharón** boasts stunning views down over Vathý and the south of the island. It houses an icon of the *Panayía* (Madonna), discovered by peasants clearing scrubland in the area. The monastery celebrates its festival on September 8 with services, processions and music.

Afáles Bay area

Local British expat Katrina (☎ 6975 928 240) offers expert guided rambles in the area

Afáles Bay, the largest cove on the entire island, with an unspoilt and little-visited pebble-and-sand beach, can be accessed by a track down from the outskirts of **Platrithriés**. This quiet yet rather spread-out village lies on the less direct westerly route from Stavrós to Fríkes, which first loops below the hill village of Exoyí. Just off the start of the road up to Exoyí, a signpost points about 1km along a rough track to the supposed **School of Homer**, where excavations still in progress have revealed extensive foundations, a well as ancient steps. The site is unfenced and well worth a detour for its views of Afáles Bay as much as the remains.

Fríkes

Wedged in a valley between two steep hills, **FRÍKES** was only settled in the sixteenth century and emigration in the nineteenth century almost emptied the place – as few as two hundred people live here today – but the protected harbour is a natural port. There are no beaches in the village, but plenty of good, if small, pebble **coves** a short walk away towards Kióni; it also offers superior **dining options** to its neighbour. When the ferries and their cargoes have departed, Fríkes falls quiet – this is its real charm.

Kióni

KIÓNI sits at a dead end 5km southeast of Fríkes. On the same geological base as the northern tip of Kefaloniá, it avoided the very worst of the 1953 earthquake and so retains some fine examples of pre-twentieth-century **architecture**. It's an extremely pretty village, wrapped around a tiny harbour, and tourism here is dominated by British blue-chip travel companies and visiting yachts. The bay has a small **beach**, 1km along its south side, a sand-and-pebble strand below a summer-only snack-bar.

ACCOMMODATION AND EATING | NORTHERN ITHÁKI

STAVRÓS

Margarita ☎ 26740 31229. This large, friendly *zaharoplastío* is a good place for a coffee, a refreshing drink or to sample the local sweet *ravaní*. Also has sport on TV. Daily 8am–11pm.

Polyphemus ☎ 26740 31596. With a lovely shady garden, this popular village restaurant is good for both grilled and oven dishes including fresh kalamari for €8 and a range of salads. May to early Oct 11.30am–2.30pm & 6.30–11pm.

FRÍKES

Frikes Bay Suites ☎ 6977 700 377, ✉ frikesbaysuites @gmail.com. These smart and airy new bayside apartments, very close to the harbour, are spacious and tastefully furnished in modern style. May–Oct. **€80**

Nostos ☎ 26740 31644, ⊛ hotelnostos-ithaki.gr. Around 100m from the seafront, this, the only conventional hotel in northern Itháki, has a pool in its relaxing grounds and smart, spacious rooms. Buffet breakfast included. May to mid-Oct. **€70**

★ **Rementzo** ☎ 26740 31719. In the corner of the quay, this friendly taverna offers a selection of fresh fish, baked meat and vegetable dishes, salads and pizza, plus good wine and ouzo (mains €5–10). April–Oct daily 10am–1am.

Ulysses ☎ 26740 31733. Specializing in succulent home-style cuisine for around €10, this popular restaurant in the middle of the seafront also provides plenty of snacks, sweets and beverages. May–Oct daily 11am–midnight.

KIÓNI

Calypso ☎ 26740 31066. Pleasant taverna in the middle of the tiny bay, which has imaginative dishes like pork with artichokes for €12 and some very drinkable aromatic wine. May–Oct daily noon–midnight.

Captain's Apartments ☎ 26740 31481, ⊛ captains -apartments.gr. Set up above the village, with sweeping views of the bay, these roomy apartments are decorated in warm rustic colours. May–Sept. **€50**

Maroudas Apartments ☎ 26740 31691, ✉ maroudas @greek-tourism.gr. Just a couple of blocks from the harbour, these compact, convenient and comfortable apartments offer modern amenities and a warm welcome. May–Sept. **€45**

Oasis ☎ 26740 31317. Harbourside taverna that offers the usual selection of fresh salads, some dips and a good choice of mainly grilled meat for under €10, and fish courses to suit all budgets. May–Sept daily noon–1am.

Zákynthos

ZÁKYNTHOS (Zante), southernmost of the six core Ionian islands, is divided between relative wilderness and indiscriminate commercialization. However, much of the island is still green and unspoilt, with only token pockets of tourism, and the main resorts seem to be reaching maximum growth without encroaching too much on the quieter parts. The island has **three distinct zones**: the barren, mountainous northwest; the fertile central plain; and the eastern and southern resort-filled coasts. The biggest resort is **Laganás**, on Laganás Bay in the south, a 24-hour party venue that doesn't stop for breath during the busy summer season. There are smaller, quieter resorts north and south of the capital, and the southerly Vassilikós peninsula has some of the best countryside and beaches, including exquisite **Yérakas**.

The island still produces fine **wines**, such as the white Popolaro, as well as sugar-shock-inducing *mandoláto* **nougat**, whose honey-sweetened form is best. Zákynthos is also the birthplace of **kantádhes**, the Italianate folk ballads which can be heard in tavernas in Zákynthos Town and elsewhere. In addition, the island harbours one of the key breeding sites of the endangered **loggerhead sea turtle** at Laganás Bay (see box, p.509).

8

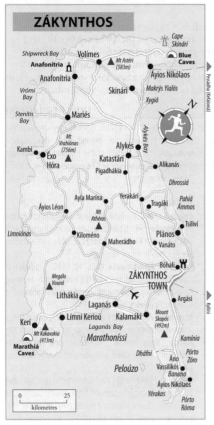

ZÁKYNTHOS

ARRIVAL AND DEPARTURE
ZÁKYNTHOS

By plane Zákynthos' airport is 4km southwest of the capital.

Domestic destinations Athens (1–2 daily; 55min); Corfu (summer 3 weekly; 2hr); Kefaloniá (summer 3 weekly; 25min); Préveza (summer 3 weekly; 1hr 15min).

By bus Buses from Zákynthos Town to the mainland destinations below are timed to connect with ferry sailings. You can board the bus at the station or by the ferry itself.

Destinations Athens (3 daily; 5hr); Pátra (3–4 daily; 2hr 30min); Thessaloníki (2 weekly; 9–10hr).

By ferry The island is well connected from Zákynthos Town year-round with Kyllíni on the Peloponnesian coast (5–7 daily; 1hr 30min) and has a seasonal ferry link with Pessádha on Kefaloniá (2 daily May–Sept; 1hr 30min) from the northern Áyios Nikólaos (aka Skinári).

GETTING AROUND

Town with frequent summer services to the busiest tourist resorts, especially Argási, Kalamáki and Laganás, but few or no buses to the far north or the west coast.

By cars and motorbike There are many rental outlets around the island, such as Eurosky (☎ 26950 26278, ⊛ eurosky.gr), whose head Zákynthos Town office is at Makrí 6, two blocks south of the main square. Diamond Cars, based at Sarakinádho and Tsiliví (☎ 26950 65155, ⊛ diamond-carrentals.gr), will bring a vehicle to wherever you are.

By taxi Taxis are widely available and can be called on ☎ 26950 48400.

By bus The local KTEL network radiates out from Zákynthos

Zákynthos Town

The town, like the island, is known as both **ZÁKYNTHOS** and Zante. This former "Venice of the East" (*Zante, Fior di Levante*, "Flower of the Levant", in an Italian jingle), rebuilt on the old plan after the 1953 earthquake, has bravely tried to re-create some of its style, though reinforced concrete can only do so much.

The town stretches beyond the length of the wide and busy harbour, its main section bookended by the grand **Platía Solomoú** at the north, and the church of **Áyios Dhionýsios**, patron saint of the island, at the south. Zákynthos is a working town with limited concessions to tourism, although there are sufficient facilities and it's the only place to stay if you want to see the island by public transport.

Áyios Dhionýsios

Southern end of seafront • **Church** Daily 8am–1pm & 5–10pm • Free • **Museum** Daily: May–Sept 8am–11pm; Oct–April 9am–noon & 5–8pm • €2

The church of **Áyios Dhionýsios** is well worth a visit for the dazzling giltwork and fine modern murals inside, which were completely repainted at the turn of the millennium. Behind the church there is also a **museum**, which has some fine paintings and icons.

Platía Solomoú

Platía Solomoú is named after the island's most famous son, the poet Dhionysios Solomos, the father of modernism in Greek literature, who was responsible for establishing demotic Greek (as opposed to the elitist *katharévousa* form) as a literary idiom. He is also the author of the lyrics to the national anthem, an excerpt from which adorns the statue of Liberty in the square.

Platía Solomoú is home to the town's **library**, which has a small collection of pre- and post-1953 quake photography, and the massive Byzantine Museum, sometimes referred to as the Zákynthos Museum. On the seaward corner of the square stands the squat restored church of **Áyios Nikólaos tou Mólou**, where the vestments of St Dhionysios are kept.

Byzantine Museum

Platía Solomoú • Tues–Sun 8.30am–3pm • €3 • ☎ 26950 42714

The **Byzantine Museum** is most notable for its collection of artworks from the **Ionian School** (see box, p.467), the region's post-Renaissance art movement, spearheaded by Zakynthian painter Panayiotis Doxaras. The movement was given impetus by Cretan refugees, unable to practise their art under Turkish rule. It also houses some secular painting and a fine model of the town before the 1953 earthquake. It was closed due to staffing problems at the time of writing.

Museum of D. Solomos and Eminent People of Zákynthos

Platía Ayíou Márkou • Daily 9am–2pm • €3 • ☎ 26950 48982

The impressive **Museum of D. Solomos and Eminent People of Zákynthos** is devoted to the life and work of Solomos and other Zakynthian luminaries. It shares its collection of manuscripts and personal effects with an eponymous museum on Corfu (see p.465), where Solomos spent most of his life. There are also plenty of photographs and paintings of notable islanders.

The kástro

Bóhali • Daily: June–Sept 8am–8pm; Oct–May 8.30am–3pm • €1.50

Zákynthos' massive **kástro** broods over the hamlet of Bóhali on its bluff above the town. The ruined **Venetian fort** has vestiges of dungeons, armouries and fortifications, plus stunning views in all directions. Its shady carpet of fallen pine needles makes it a great spot to relax or picnic.

ARRIVAL AND INFORMATION   **ZÁKYNTHOS TOWN**

By plane The airport is 4km southwest of town (see opposite).

By bus The bus station is inconveniently located nearly 2km up from the seafront, near the hospital (☎ 26950 22255, ⓦ ktel-zakynthos.gr). There are buses to mainland destinations and the main resorts (see opposite).

By ferry The ferry quay is at the southern end of the town's seafront (see opposite).

Tourist information The tourist police, in the main police station halfway along the seafront, can supply basic information and keep a list of accommodation (May–Oct daily 8am–10pm; ☎ 26950 24482).

BOAT TRIPS FROM ZÁKYNTHOS TOWN

At least ten pleasure craft offer **day-trips** around the island from the quay in Zákynthos Town (around €25). All take in sights such as the **Blue Caves** at Cape Skinári, and moor in **Tó Naváyio (Shipwreck Bay)** and at the Marathiá caves at **Cape Kerí** in the southwest. You might want to shop around for the trip with the most stops, as eight hours bobbing round the coast can become a bore. It's also worth checking that the operators actually take you into the caves. Additionally, there are shorter trips to **Kerí** and turtle-spotting in **Laganás Bay** for €15, including on one vessel with underwater seating. **Cavo Grosso** at Lombárdhou 22 (☎ 26950 48308, ⓦ cavogrosso.gr) offers a range of excursions.

ACCOMMODATION

The Room Owners Association (☎ 26950 49498) can be contacted for accommodation around town and all over the island. Some of the best hotels are in the quiet Repára district, just north of the centre.

Egli Loútzi ☎ 26950 28317. Smallish hotel whose entrance is just off the seafront, tucked in beside the gargantuan *Strada Marina*, though some of its clean, compact rooms face the harbour. €35

★**Palatino** Kolokotróni 10, Repára ☎ 26950 27780, ⓦ palatinohotel.gr. Classy and surprisingly good-value place, which has beautifully furnished rooms with all mod cons and ritzy common areas. Ample buffet breakfast included. €60

Plaza Kolokotróni 2, Repára ☎ 26950 45733, ⓦ plazazante.gr. Barely 50m from the town beach, this pleasant four-storey hotel has comfortable, modern rooms, some with sea-facing balconies, and a relaxing lobby café. Breakfast included. €55

EATING AND DRINKING

★**Malanos** Ayíou Athanasíou 38, Kípi ☎ 26950 45936. Off the Kalamáki road, this superb rustic taverna offers quality home-style cooking, as well as grills and ample fresh salads, mostly under €10. Live music on Fri & Sat, or nightly in high season. Daily 10am–4pm & 8pm–1am.

Varkarola Lombárdhou 78 ☎ 26950 26999. Nicely designed establishment that offers dishes such as soufflé and roast pork for €6–7, plus a €7.50 lunch menu. The best place in town to come for its nightly *kantádhes*. Daily 11am–2am.

Iy Thymalos Lombárdhou 78 ☎ 26950 26732. Huge seafront taverna with a nautical theme and pavement seating, where you can feast on imaginative prawn and crab salad, plenty of quality fish and some Cypriot dishes such as *seftaliá* (sausage without skin, bound by caul fat). Lunch menu deal for €7.50. March–Nov daily noon–2am.

Komis Bastoúni tou Ayíou ☎ 26950 26915. Across the quay from Áyios Dhionýsios, this upmarket favourite serves unusual seafood dishes like clams and urchins, mostly over €10, along with multiple *mezédhes* and good barrelled wine. Daily noon–2am.

NIGHTLIFE

Base Platía Ayíou Márkou ☎ 26950 42409. Perennially busy favourite, in a prime location, which plays an eclectic dance mix at night, while its daytime café mode is more prone to rock and ethnic sounds. Daily 11am–late.

Bliss 21 Maïou 23 ☎ 26950 22004. Trendy place with a chilled café-style space downstairs and a bar that often features live music upstairs. Genres vary from rock through jazz to Latin. Daily 10pm–late.

The Vassilikós peninsula

The busy southern end of Zákynthos' most noticeable feature is the **Vassilikós peninsula**, which points in somewhat phallic mimicry of Florida towards the Peloponnese. It is headed by the package resort of **Argási**, but its treasures really lie in the succession of sandy beaches, mostly on the eastern side, which culminate in the stunning strand of **Yérakas**.

Argási

Barely 4km south of Zákynthos Town, **ARGÁSI** is the busiest resort on this coast, sprawling for over a kilometre behind a beach that is scarcely a few feet wide in parts. Although the rest of the peninsula is far more appealing, it does offer a wide choice of facilities, including a popular concentration of clubs, and is a closer base for exploring the rest of the island.

The east coast

The first two coves south of Argási are **Kamínia** and the more scenic **Pórto Zóro**. The main road dips and dives along the east coast of the peninsula, with short access roads descending to these and other longer beaches further south, such as **Iónio** and **Banana**. Above these contiguous strands, the only real facilities away from the coast are to be found at the rather formless village of **Áno Vassilkós**.

Áyios Nikólaos

The coast ends up at **ÁYIOS NIKÓLAOS**, which has a good beach and lures day-trippers from Argási, Kalamáki and Laganás with a free bus service in season. It's a fast-emerging hamlet with a fair range of amenities; a ferry service leaves here for Kefaloniá (see p.496).

The west coast

At the very southwestern tip of the peninsula, **Yérakas** is the star attraction: a sublime crescent of golden sand. It's also a key loggerhead **turtle breeding ground**, and is therefore off limits between dusk and dawn, as well as being subject to strict rules on the number and placement of umbrellas. The excellent open-air **Turtle Information Centre** (ⓦearthseasky.org), about 200m in from the beach, provides interesting background on these and other sea creatures, some of which are on display in its recently acquired **aquarium** (free).

Further north along the rugged west coast of the peninsula, accessed by the only (partly unpaved) road which crosses it, is **Dháfni**, home to a couple of tavernas.

ACTIVITIES	THE VASSILIKÓS PENINSULA

Watersports St Nicholas Beach Watersports in Áyios Nikólaos (ⓣ6937 107 652) rents equipment for a range of activities including windsurfing, parasailing and scuba diving.

ACCOMMODATION, EATING AND NIGHTLIFE

ARGÁSI

Barrage ⓣ6932 452 020. One of the big outdoor clubs that line the road from Zákynthos Town into Argási, where well-known DJs play house, techno and other dance vibes to a crowd of gyrating bodies. May to mid-Oct daily 10pm–late.

Beer Academy ⓣ26950 43903. Up the main road that runs inland, this is a great place to come for cheap drinks, a game of pool and football or other sporting events on multiple screens. Decent bar food too. April–Oct daily 9pm–late.

Ethnic Grill House ⓣ6978 267 094. Nicely fitted out Greek–Australian joint, on the main strip, which can rustle up comfort food like liver and onions, as well as the usual grills, for €8–10. April–Oct daily 11am–1am.

Locanda ⓣ26950 45386, ⓦlocanda.gr. Smart seafront

8

LOGGERHEAD TURTLES

The Ionian islands harbour the Mediterranean's main concentration of **loggerhead sea turtles**, a sensitive species which is, unfortunately, under direct threat from the tourist industry. These creatures lay their eggs at night on sandy coves and, easily frightened by noise and lights, are therefore uneasy cohabitants with rough campers and late-night discos. Each year, many turtles fall prey to motorboat injuries, nests are destroyed by bikes and the newly hatched young die entangled in deckchairs and umbrellas left out at night.

The Greek government has passed laws designed to protect the loggerheads, including restrictions on camping at some beaches, but local economic interests tend to prefer a beach full of bodies to a sea full of turtles. On **Laganás**, nesting grounds are concentrated around the 14km bay, and Greek marine zoologists are in angry dispute with those involved in the tourist industry. The turtles' nesting ground just west of **Skála** on Kefaloniá is another important location, although numbers have dwindled to half their former strength and now only about eight hundred remain. Ultimately, the turtles' best hope for survival may rest in their potential draw as a unique tourist attraction in their own right.

While capitalists and environmentalists are still at, well, loggerheads, the **World Wide Fund for Nature** has issued guidelines for visitors:

• Don't use the beaches of Laganás and Yérakas **between sunset and sunrise**.
• Don't stick **umbrellas** in the sand in the marked nesting zones.
• Take your **rubbish** away with you – it can obstruct the turtles.
• Don't use **lights** near the beach at night – they can disturb the turtles, sometimes with fatal consequences.
• Don't take any **vehicle** onto the protected beaches.
• Don't **dig** up turtle nests – it's illegal.
• Don't pick up the **hatchlings** or carry them to the water.
• Don't use **speedboats** in Laganás Bay – a 9kph speed limit is in force.

hotel with a choice of standard doubles or larger studios, all with kitchenettes and balconies facing the sea or mountain. There's also a pool and bar. Breakfast included. April–Oct. **€50**

THE EAST COAST

★**Levantino Studios & Apartments** Kaminía ☎ 26950 35366, ⓦ levantino.gr. Well-equipped units of varying size, set in carefully manicured grounds at the back of the beach. They also have a snack-bar and free sunbeds with umbrellas. May–Oct. **€40**

Logos Áno Vassilkós ☎ 26950 35296, ⓦ logosbar.com. Legendary rustic club which occupies a large space in the pine woods, where night owls dance to a mixture of rock and disco sounds and sip exotic cocktails. June–Sept Mon, Wed, Fri & Sat 9pm–late.

Porto Zorro Pórto Zóro ☎ 26950 35304, ⓦ portozorro .gr. This good-value hotel, right on the eponymous beach, has decent-sized rooms whose stark white linen is tempered by the brown wood-panelling. The attached taverna offers a full menu. **€40**

Vasilikos Beach Áyios Nikólaos ☎ 26950 35325, ⓦ hotelvasilikosbeach.gr. Huge beach-resort complex that has a variety of rooms but also offers a pool, jacuzzi and watersports among its many amenities. Buffet breakfast included. May–Oct. **€50**

THE WEST COAST

Antonis Dháfni ☎ 26950 26989. Fine taverna-cum-bar, where you can have a full meal of fresh fish or home-cooked meat for under €10, a lighter snack or just sip a sunset cocktail. June–Sept daily 10am–10pm.

Gerakas Eco Villagers Yérakas ☎ 0871 711 5065 (UK), ⓦ relaxing-holidays.com. Thoughtfully constructed according to green principles, these spacious stone apartments make for a very comfortable as well as eco-conscious stay. May–Oct. **€50**

★**To Triodi** Yérakas ☎ 26950 35215. Excellent taverna with a leafy garden, great for fresh fish or well-prepared meat dishes (under €10), plus all the usual salads, dips and good local wine. May–Oct daily 11am–1am.

8 | Laganás Bay

The large sweep of **Laganás Bay**, anchored on the major party resort of **Laganás** itself, dominates southern Zákynthos. **Kalamáki** is another busy resort at the eastern end, while delightful **Límni Kerioú** in the southwest completes the picture. As the bay is also a prime home to the **loggerhead turtle**, there has long been an uneasy coexistence between mass tourism and conservation (see box, p.509).

Laganás

The majority of the hundreds of thousands of people who visit Zákynthos each year find themselves in **LAGANÁS**. Set amid the fine 9km beach that runs almost the entire length of the bay, it offers entertainments from watersports to ballooning, and even an occasional funfair. Beachfront **bars and restaurants** stretch for well over 1km, the bars and restaurants on the main drag another kilometre inland. Some stay open around the clock; others just play music at deafening volume until dawn. The competing video and music bars can make Laganás at night resemble the set of *Blade Runner*, but that's how its predominantly English visitors like it.

Kalamáki

Neighbouring Laganás to the east, **Kalamáki** has a better, much wider beach than its westerly neighbour and is altogether quieter, with a slightly more family-oriented feel. Even the bars are more laidback, although it does suffer from some airport noise.

Límni Kerioú

Límni Kerioú, at the southwestern end of Laganás Bay, has gradually evolved into a relaxing and picturesque resort, and has a couple of diving operations. It's reached by a turning that branches off the main road before it climbs up towards the west coast, after the hill village of **Lithákia**.

ACTIVITIES   **LAGANÁS BAY**

Diving Límni Kerioú is home to Diving Center Turtle Beach (☎ 26950 49424, ⓦ diving-center-turtle-beach.com).

Horseriding Nana's Horses (☎ 26950 23195), just outside Kalamáki, can arrange riding trips.

ACCOMMODATION, EATING, DRINKING AND NIGHTLIFE

LAGANÁS

Ionis Art Hotel ☎26950 51141, ⊕zante-ionis-hotel
.com. On the main drag towards the beach, one of the
few places not block-booked is this surprisingly classy
boutique hotel with tastefully designed rooms and a
huge pool. Breakfast included. If they're full try the local
Union of Room Owners (daily 8.30am–2pm & 5–8pm;
☎26950 51590), which has a range of accommodation.
May–Oct. **€75**

Rescue Club ☎26950 51612, ⊕rescueclub.net.
Proclaiming itself to be the biggest club on the island, this
place, in the middle of the main strip, has an outdoor bar
area and huge indoor dancefloor with top sound and
lighting equipment to enhance the nonstop dance
favourites. May–Oct daily 10pm–late.

★**Sarakina** ☎26950 51606. Best taverna in the area,
serving tasty dishes such as pork in wine sauce for around
€10 and featuring nightly *kantádhes*. There's a free minibus
to convey diners to its leafy location nearly 2km inland.
May–Oct daily 6pm–2am.

Zeros ⊕zerosclubzante.com. Massive club, on the main
strip, with state-of-the-art sound systems and top DJs, which
hosts various big events through the summer and regular
foam parties and other themes. May–Oct daily 9pm–late.

KALAMÁKI

Cave Club ☎26950 48278, ⊕cavebar.tripod.com. Set
into a real cave on the hillside above the village, with a
pleasantly leafy patio garden where you can enjoy a cocktail to
the mostly laidback rock sounds. May–Oct daily 9pm–3am.

Crystal Beach ☎26950 42788, ⊕crystalbeach.gr.

Large resort hotel, which has smart rooms for independent
as well as package holiday-makers, plus restaurant, bar,
pool and watersports on the beach. Breakfast included.
May–Oct. **€70**

Stani ☎26950 26374. Both branches of this well-
established taverna have extensive menus of Greek and
international dishes (under €10), although the one by the
beach is predictably busier during the day than the *Stani*
on the main strip. May–Oct daily 11am–1am.

LÍMNI KERIOÚ

Camping Tartaruga ☎26950 51967, ⊕tartaruga
-camping.com. Easily the best campsite on the island,
though reaching it requires a vehicle as it's on a remote stretch
of Laganás Bay below Lithákia. Shady pitches, a pebble beach
and minimarket are all to hand. May–Oct. **€11.80**

★**Pansion Limni** ☎26950 48716, ⊕pansionlimni
.com. Disarmingly friendly and great-value family guesthouse, with comfortable self-catering rooms and a shared
wraparound balcony that has sea views. Their wonderful
stone *Porto Tsi Ostrias pension* nearby has huge, beautifully
designed apartments. May–Oct. **€25**

Poseidon ☎26950 48708. Overlooking the bay from the
hill at the east end, *Poseidon* serves a variety of grilled meat
and fish, plus good daily specials. May–Oct daily
noon–1am.

Rock Café ☎26950 23401. Chilled-out joint with an airy
wooden balcony overlooking the beach, a well-stocked bar
and, as the name suggests, a decent line in rock sounds.
May–Oct daily noon–2am.

Western Zákynthos

At the far southwest end of Laganás Bay, the landscape ascends into the mountains
around **Kerí**, the first of a series of pretty villages along the sparsely inhabited **west coast**
which contain some of the island's best architecture, including some especially splendid
churches.

ARRIVAL AND DEPARTURE

By car and motorbike The bus system does not reach the wild western side of the island, so a rental car or sturdy
motorbike is required to get there.

Kerí

Hidden in a fold above the cliffs at the island's southernmost tip, the village of **KERÍ**
retains several pre-quake Venetian buildings including the **Panayía Kerioú** church; the
Virgin is said to have saved the island from marauding pirates by hiding it in a sea mist.
A road leads 1km on to the lighthouse, with spectacular views of the sea, rock arches
and stacks.

Maherádho

MAHERÁDHO boasts impressive pre-earthquake architecture set in beautiful arable
uplands, surrounded by olive and fruit groves. The church of **Ayía Mávra** has an

impressive freestanding campanile and, inside, a splendid carved iconostasis and icons. The town's major **festival** – one of the biggest on the island – is the saint's day, which falls on the first Sunday in June. The other notable church in town, that of the **Panayía**, commands breathtaking views over the central plain.

Kilioméno and around
KILIOMÉNO is the best place to see surviving pre-earthquake domestic architecture, in the form of the island's traditional two-storey houses. The town was originally named after its church, **Áyios Nikólaos**, whose impressive campanile, begun over a hundred years ago, still lacks a capped roof. The road from Kilioméno passes through the nondescript village of Áyios Léon, from where two turnings lead through fertile land and down a paved loop road to the impressive rocky coast at **Limniónas**, where there is a tiny bay.

Kambí
The tiny clifftop hamlet of **KAMBÍ** is popular with day-trippers who come to catch the sunset over the sea; there are extraordinary views to be had of the 300m-high cliffs and western horizon from Kambí's three clifftop tavernas.

Mariés and around
Set in a wooded green valley 5km north of Kambí, the tiny village of **MARIÉS** is the only other place with coastal access on this side of Zákynthos: a 7km track leading down to the rocky inlet of **Stenítis Bay**, where there's a taverna and yacht dock. Another steep road leads to the uninspiring **Vrómi Bay**, from where speedboats run trips to Shipwreck Bay (see p.514), while the main road continues north towards Volímes (see p.514).

ACCOMMODATION AND EATING	THE WEST COAST

KERÍ

Apelati ☏ 26950 43324, ✉ apelatidenia@gmail .com. Just off the main road before the incline east of the village, this farm-like taverna serves home-style dishes from fresh ingredients for well under €10 and has a few simple rustic rooms (€25). May–Oct 11am–midnight.

Lighthouse ☏ 26950 43384. Scenically situated taverna, 1km west of the village, where people flock for sunset dinners in the large and lush patio garden. The food is standard fare (€8–10), but the view unsurpassed. May–Sept daily noon–midnight.

KILIOMÉNO AND AROUND

★**Alitzerini** Kilioméno ☏ 26950 48552, ⊛ alitzerinoi .gr. Beautifully restored eighteenth-century stone house with a terrace and log fire indoors for winter. They serve traditional cuisine with a twist, such as the €10 speciality, *sfigadoúra* – beef in tomato sauce with cheese and red pepper. Occasional live music. 7pm–1am: May–Sept daily; Oct–April Sat & Sun; also some Sun lunches.

Porto Limnionas Limniónas, ☏ 6977 258 541. Perched on a rocky outcrop just above the tiny harbour, this *psarotavérna* is known for its high-quality if rather pricey fish at €50 per kilo minimum, and also has a huge selection of tasty mezédhes. May–Oct daily noon–11pm.

The northeast
The amalgamated resorts of **Tsiliví** and **Plános**, a few kilometres north of Zákynthos' capital, are the touristic epicentre of this part of the island. Further north, they give way to a series of tiny beaches, while picturesque villages punctuate the lush landscape inland. Beyond **Alykés**, as you approach the island's tip at **Cape Skinári**, the coast becomes more rugged, while the mountains inland hide the weaving centre of **Volímes**.

Tsiliví, Plános and around
North and inland from Zákynthos Town, the roads thread their way through luxuriantly fertile farmland, punctuated with tumulus-like hills. **TSILIVÍ**, 5km north of the capital, is the first beach resort here and is in effect one with the hamlet of **PLÁNOS**; the resultant conglomeration rivals Argási for development.

The beaches further along this stretch of coast become progressively quiet and more pleasant, and all have at least some accommodation and restaurants to choose from. Good choices include **Pahiá Ámmos** and **Dhrossiá**.

Alykés Bay

Alykés Bay, 12km north of Tsiliví, is a large sandy bay with lively surf and the northeast's two largest resorts. The first, **ALIKANÁS**, is a small but expanding village, and much of its accommodation is foreign-owned villa rentals. The second, **ALYKÉS**, named after the spooky saltpans behind the village, has the best beach north of the capital.

Makrýs Yialós and around

Tiny **Xygiá beach**, cut into a deep cove 4km north of Alykés, has sulphur springs flowing into the sea – follow the smell – which provide the odd sensation of swimming in a mix of cool and warm water. The next somewhat longer beach of **Makrýs Yialós** also makes for an extremely pleasant break on a tour of the north. Just to the north of Makrýs Yialós, you'll come to a pretty promontory with a small harbour, called **Mikró Nissáki**.

Áyios Nikólaos and around

Ferries to Pessádha on Kefaloniá run twice a day May–Sept (1hr 30min); there's no bus to either port

Just over 20km from Zákynthos Town is **ÁYIOS NIKÓLAOS**, known to locals as **Skinári** (after the nearby inland village) to avoid confusion with its namesake on the Vassilikós peninsula, which is a small working port with a daily summer ferry connection to Pessádha on Kefaloniá.

The Blue Caves

Boat trips €7.50; €15 combined with Shipwreck Bay

The **Blue Caves** are some of the more realistically named of the many contenders in Greece; ignore scams claiming that Áyios Nikólaos is the last place from which you can catch a boat. They're terrific for snorkelling, and when you go for a dip here your skin will appear bright blue. To reach them, follow the road as it snakes onwards from Áyios Nikólaos through a landscape of gorse bushes and dry-stone walls until it ends at the lighthouse of **Cape Skinári**, from below which the cheapest **boat trips** operate.

Katastári

Two kilometres inland from Alykés, **KATASTÁRI** is the largest settlement after the capital. Precisely because it's not geared towards tourism, it's the best place to see Zakynthian life as it's lived away from the usual racket. Its most impressive edifice is the huge rectangular church of Iperáyia Theotókos, with a twin belfry and small new amphitheatre for festival performances.

Pighadhákia

A couple of kilometres south of Katastári, the tiny hamlet of **PIGHADHÁKIA** is the unlikely setting for the **Vertzagio Cultural Museum** (March to early Nov daily 9am–2pm & 6–8pm except Sat; €3), which houses an interesting array of agricultural and folk artefacts. There is also the diminutive **Áyios Pandeléïmon** chapel, which has the unusual feature of a well, hidden beneath the altar.

Ayía Marína

AYÍA MARÍNA, a few kilometres southwest of Katastári, has a **church** with an impressive Baroque altar screen and a belfry that's being rebuilt from the remnants left after the 1953 earthquake. As in most Zákynthos churches, the bell tower stands detached, in Venetian fashion.

8

Helmi's Natural History Museum

Daily 9am–6pm (Nov–April till 2pm) • €2 • ⓦ museumhelmis.gr

In the upper part of the village is **Helmi's Natural History Museum** which displays plenty of stuffed birds and mammals, seashells and the largest ammonite found in Greece. You can also watch an informative film about turtles.

Volímes and around

Divided into three contiguous parts, **VOLÍMES** is the centre of the island's embroidery industry and numerous shops sell artefacts produced here. With your own transport, you could make it to the **Anafonítria monastery**, 3km south, thought to have been the cell of the island's patron saint, Dhionysios, whose festivals are celebrated on August 24 and December 17.

Shipwreck Bay

A paved road leads on from Volímes to the cliffs overlooking **Shipwreck Bay** (Tó Naváyio), with hair-raising views down to the shipwreck, a cargo ship which was mistaken for a drug-running vessel and run aground by the coastguard in the 1960s.

ACCOMMODATION AND EATING   THE NORTHEAST

TSILIVÍ

Anetis Hotel ☎ 26950 44590, ⓦ anetishotel.gr. Comfortable, good-value hotel with sizeable a/c rooms, many with sea-facing balconies overlooking the lively beach bar. April–Oct. €40

The Olive Tree ☎ 26950 62834. The best of the predictably touristy bunch, with a huge menu, including grilled meat and fish, a host of starters and perfectly acceptable wine by the kilo. May–Oct daily noon–1am.

Passage to Asia ☎ 26950 43788. One of the best oriental restaurants on the island, serving authentic-enough versions of both Indian and Chinese cuisine. Has meal deals for two people at around €20. May–Oct daily noon–midnight.

ALYKÉS BAY

Astoria ☎ 26950 83533, ⓦ astoriazante.com. Large but friendly seafront establishment with standard rooms, run by returnees from New York – hence the Statue of Liberty images and the like. Easter–Oct. €40

★**To Paradosiako** ☎ 26950 83412. On the main road coming in from the south, this restaurant lives up to its name, meaning "traditional", by appealing to locals. It has unusual dishes like swordfish in tarragon sauce for only €8.50. May–Oct daily 9am–1am.

MAKRÝS YIALÓS

Pilarinos ☎ 26950 31396. This good taverna on the flattish hillock behind the beach does a decent line in grills, fish and the usual accoutrements, mostly under €10, plus there's a makeshift campsite on the grounds. May–Oct daily 11am–midnight.

ÁYIOS NIKÓLAOS AND AROUND

★**Anemomilos** Cape Skinári ☎ 26950 31241, ⓦ potamitisbros.gr. Two expertly converted windmills make for a unique place to stay. There are also some more conventional rooms, a snack-bar, and the same family run the excellent *To Faros* taverna nearby. May–Oct. €50

Panorama Áyios Nikólaos ☎ 26950 31013, ⓔ panorama -apts@ath.forthnet.gr. These friendly studios are a good-value option if you are leaving on the morning ferry to Kefaloniá or want a northern base. Breakfast included. April–Oct. €30

PIGHADHÁKIA

★**Kaki Rahi** ☎ 26950 83670. Traditional family-run taverna, which serves tasty local cuisine from home-grown ingredients, its own barrelled wine and provides transport on its little train twice daily from Alykés. €12.50 including set mixed plate. Live music Sat evenings. May–Oct daily 11am–midnight.

Kýthira

Isolated at the foot of the Peloponnese, the island of **KÝTHIRA** traditionally belongs to the Ionian islands, and shares their history of **Venetian** and, later, **British** rule; under the former it was known as Cerigo. For the most part, similarities end there. The island architecture of whitewashed houses and flat roofs looks more like that of the Cyclades. The landscape is different, too: wild scrub- and gorse-covered hills, or moorland sliced by deep valleys and ravines. Though badly affected by **emigration** tourism has brought

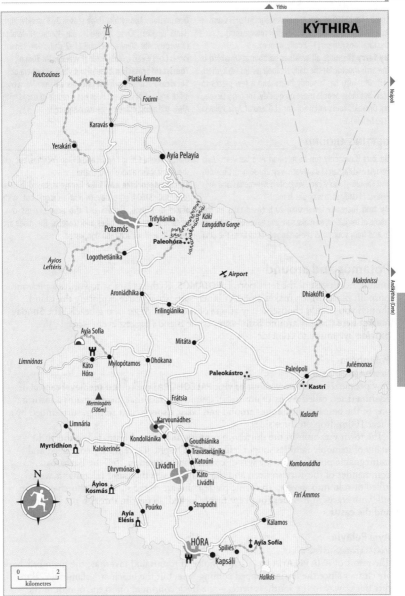

Yithio

KÝTHIRA

Routsoúnas

Platiá Ámmos

Foúrni

Karavás

Yerakári

Ayía Pelayía

Trifyliánika

Káki Langádha Gorge

Potamós

Paleohóra

Logothetiánika

Áyios Leftéris

Aroniádhika

✈ *Airport*

Makrónissi

Dhiakófti

Frilingiánika

Mitáta

Ayía Sofía

Limniónas

Káto Hóra

Mylopótamos

Dhókana

Paleokástro

Paleópoli

Avlémonas

Kastrí

▲ *Mermingáris (506m)*

Frátsia

Kaladhí

Limnária

Karvounádhes

Myrtidhíon

Kalokerinés

Kondoliánika

Goudhiánika

Travasariánika

Kombonádha

Dhrymónas

Livádhi

Katoúni

Áyios Kosmás 🛉

Káto Livádhi

Firí Ámmos

Poúrko

Strapódhi

Ayía Elésis 🛉

Kálamos

HÓRA

Spiliés

† **Ayía Sofía**

Kapsáli

Halkós

N

0   2
kilometres

Neápoli ▸

Andikýthira (Crete) ▸

8

some prosperity but most summer visitors are Greeks. For the few foreigners who reach Kýthira, it remains something of a refuge, with its undeveloped **beaches** a principal attraction.

ARRIVAL AND INFORMATION

KÝTHIRA

By air Kýthira's Alexander Onassis airport is deep in the interior, 8km southeast of Potamós (☎ 27360 33297).

Potamós has an Olympic Airways office (☎ 27360 33362), and you can also get flight tickets through Drakakis Tours at

Livadhi (☎ 27360 31160, ⌨ drakakistours.gr) or El Greco at Ayía Pelayía (☎ 27360 33903, ⌨ elgrecotours.com).
Destinations Athens (1–2 daily; 45min).

By ferry The huge all-weather harbour at Dhiakófti is the arrival point for the daily Neápoli ferries (⌨ kythera .gr). Dhiakófti has a sandy beach and a few places to stay, but most people move on quickly. For ferry tickets, try Drakakis Tours at Livadhi or El Greco at Ayía Pelayía (see below).

Destinations Andikýthira (high season 2–3 weekly; 2hr); Haniá (Chania), Crete 2 weekly; 3hr 40min); Kalamáta (1 weekly; 4hr 30min); Neápoli (1–2 daily; 1hr 15min); Pireás (2–3 weekly; 6hr); Ýithio (1 weekly; 2hr 30min).

Tourist information A useful website is ⌨ kythera.gr.

Services Potamós town has tavernas, a bank ATM, a post office and petrol stations. Hóra has a couple of banks with ATMs and a post office on the main square.

GETTING AROUND

By bus Buses only run in July and Aug between: Ayía Pelayía and Kapsáli (1 daily each way; 2hr 30min); Dhiakófti and Kapsáli (1 daily each way; 5hr); Avlémonas and Ayía Pelayía (1 daily each way; 3hr 30min).

By taxi There are fewer than 20 licensed taxis on the whole of the island, so make sure you have your transport to and from your hotel pre-arranged. Taxis from the port

charge around €25 to Kapsáli and €17 to Potamós, but you should establish a price beforehand.

By car, motorbike and bike Panayotis, based in Hóra (☎ 27360 31004, ⌨ panayotis-rent-a-car.gr) but with offices in Kapsáli, Livádhi and the airport, rents cars, motorbikes, mountain bikes and scooters. The roads are generally well surfaced and signposted.

Potamós and around

Inland, northwest of the ferry port, is **POTAMÓS**, Kýthira's largest town. It's a pleasant, unspoilt place, which makes a perfect lunch stop when you're exploring the island, though you should choose to stay at one of the towns on or near a beach. The **Sunday market** here (usually around 8am–4pm) is the island's biggest event – local cafés provide live music to coincide.

Paleohóra

About 3km east of Potamós

Few people seem to know about or visit **PALEOHÓRA**, the ruined **medieval capital** of Kýthira (then called Áyios Dhimítrios), despite the fact that these remains constitute one of the best Byzantine sites around and boast a spectacular setting, surrounded by a sheer 100m drop on three sides.

The town was built in the thirteenth century, and when Mystra fell to the Turks, many of its noble families sought refuge here. Despite its seemingly concealed and impregnable position, the site was discovered and **sacked** in 1537 by Barbarossa, commander of the Turkish fleet, and the island's seven thousand inhabitants were killed or sold into slavery. The principal remains are of the surviving **churches**, some still with traces of **frescoes** (but kept firmly locked, so peer in through the windows), and the **castle**.

Ayía Pelayía

About 4km northeast of Potamós

The resort of **AYÍA PELAYÍA** has a good choice of **rooms** and **tavernas**; the main beaches are cleaner since the ferries stopped coming here, but the beach at Kalamítsa, a 2km dirt track away to the south, is better – the track continues on to the mouth of the Káki Langádha gorge which offers excellent hiking.

Mylopótamos

Head south from Potamós for about 4km, then take the westbound turning for another couple of kilometres

It's worth taking the time to stop off at **MYLOPÓTAMOS**, a lovely traditional village and a shady oasis in summer, set in a wooded valley with a small stream. Follow the signs from the main square to find a series of old **watermills** and a small **waterfall**, hidden from view by lush vegetation where you can have a refreshing swim.

Ayía Sofía cave

July & Aug daily 11am–7pm; Sept Tues, Wed & Fri–Sun 11am–6pm • €5 (includes 30min guided tour) • A 30min signposted walk from Mylopótamos, or a short drive along a paved road off the Limniónas road • When the cave is closed, you can probably find a guide in Mylopótamos; ask around, giving a day's notice if possible

Most visitors come to Mylopótamos to see the **Ayía Sofía cave**, the largest and most impressive of a number of caverns on the island. The cave's entrance has been used as a **church** and has an iconostasis carved from the rock, with important Byzantine **frescoes** on it. Beyond, the cave system comprises a series of **chambers**, which reach 250m into the mountain, although the guided tour (in Greek and English) only takes in the more interesting outer chambers.

ACCOMMODATION AND EATING

POTAMÓS

Panaretos ☎ 27360 34290. Traditional, lively taverna that dominates the central square, with indoor seating in the main restaurant down below. Excellent home-made bread and juicy olives. Daily noon–midnight; Nov–March closed Sun eve.

AYÍA PELAYÍA

★**Kaleris** ☎ 27360 33461. The chef here specializes in inventive, original takes on a whole range of traditional dishes, such as "feta French fries". Expect about €15/person. April–Oct daily noon–midnight.

Moustakias ☎ 27360 33519. A classic seafood taverna, with port-side seating and very friendly service. Catch-of-the-day is always a good choice, along with whatever is in season – green beans, artichokes or courgettes. Live music

POTAMÓS AND AROUND

Sat eve. May–Oct daily 10am–11pm; Nov–March Sat & Sun 6pm–11pm.

★**Venardos** ☎ 27360 34100, ⓦ venardos-hotels.gr. Extensive hotel complex boasting hilltop views and located just a short walk from the beach. Rooms range from standard doubles to suites and studios, and facilities include a large pool, jacuzzi and sauna. You can organize hikes and excursions here too. Breakfast included. **€60**

MYLOPÓTAMOS

Plátanos ☎ 27360 33397. This shady café-taverna makes a pleasant stop for a freshly squeezed orange juice or a full meal, above the village's springs. About €12/person. Inside, there's an appealing music bar. Easter–Oct daily 9am–1am.

Kapsáli and the south

KAPSÁLI, on the **south coast**, is largely devoted to summer tourism – in fact, much of it closes down from September to June. Most savvy foreign visitors to Kýthira in summer stay here, and it's a popular port of call for yachts, particularly since it is sheltered from the strong north winds of summer. Set behind double-coved beaches and looked over by a **castle**, as well as the tiny white **monastery** of Áyios Ioánnis Éngremmos perched high on grey cliffs, it is certainly memorable.

Hóra

HÓRA (or Kýthira Town), the island's picturesque capital, is a steep 2km haul above Kapsáli, and is quite somnolent in comparison. It does enjoy an equally dramatic position, however, with its Cycladic-style houses tiered on the ridge leading to its very own Venetian **castle**. Below the castle are both the remains of older Byzantine walls and, in Mésa Voúrgo, numerous well-signed but securely locked Byzantine churches.

Hóra's castle

Daily 8am–7pm • Free

Hóra's castle is a must mostly for the breathtaking 360-degree **panorama** it affords over the entire area – on a clear enough day you can even see Crete. Access to the fortress is up a modern pathway, but, to the right of this, the original narrow tunnel entrance is still useable. Within the castle walls, most of the buildings are in ruins, except for the paired churches of Panayía Myrtidhiótissa and the smaller Panayía Orfaní (Catholic and Orthodox respectively, under the Venetian occupation). There are spectacular **views** down to Kapsáli and out to sea to the chunk of inaccessible islet known as **Avgó** (Egg), legendary **birthplace of Aphrodite**. On its cliffs grow the endemic yellow-flowered everlasting *sempreviva*, used locally for making small dried flower arrangements (which you see for sale in every shop), symbol of the goddess's eternal beauty.

ACCOMMODATION AND EATING   KAPSÁLI AND THE SOUTH

In high season, you must book ahead if you want accommodation in Kapsáli. Finding a hotel in Hóra is easier, since it's well away from the beach. Both towns have plenty of good places to eat.

KAPSÁLI

Hydragogio ☎ 27360 31065. This place, facing the water at the Hóra end of the beach, serves up good veggie options such as split peas with spinach, as well as seafood combinations such as stuffed peppers with shrimps. Main dishes average about €7. May–Sept daily noon–11pm.

Hýtra ☎ 27360 37200. Named after the island offshore, the Kettle (aka the Egg), where Aphrodite is said to have been born, this appealing harbourside taverna offers all the best of Greek traditional cookery – extraordinary stewed broad green beans in season – or satisfying eats such as burgers (€9), with beachfront seating. April–Oct daily 11am–11pm.

Porto Delfino ☎ 27360 319401 ⓦ portodelfino.gr. In a great location 500m from the beach and with both sea and kástro views, swimming pool, bar, garden and restaurant. May–Oct. €90

Vasili Spitia ☎ 27360 31125, ⓦ www.kythira bungalowsvasili.gr. Located on a hillside amid an old olive grove, this place offers comfortable rooms and studios, all with a/c, balconies and sea views. Breakfast included. June–Sept. €50

HÓRA

Belvedere ☎ 27360 31892. Overlooking both the castle and the twin bays of Kapsáli, the main draw here is the impressive terrace seating. Traditional Greek dishes, pies and pizzas for around €8. Daily noon–midnight.

Castello Apartments ☎ 27360 31869, ⓦ castelloapts -kythera.gr. This cheerful structure, on the Kapsáli side of town, is off the street, in a garden setting with great views all around. The nine self-catering rooms, studios and apartment are simple and some have balconies and views. €40

★ Margarita ☎ 27360 31711, ⓦ hotel-margarita .com. This beautiful, immaculately maintained 1840s house just below the main street offers wonderful views of the coast and the castle, and has very friendly and helpful staff. Buffet breakfast €10/person. Prices double in Aug. April–Oct. €50

Zorba's ☎ 27360 31655. By far the best value taverna in town – only €8–10 for a full meal, with grilled specialities such as *kondosoúvli* (a kind of chicken kebab), served on a beautiful terrace. Mon 7.30pm–midnight, Tues–Sun noon–midnight.

Avlémonas

The prettiest destination on the east coast is **Avlémonas**, on a rocky bay at the top of this coast. It's a small **fishing port** with an end-of-the-world feel as you approach from a distance. It becomes much more attractive once reached, and has a remarkable coordination of colour schemes throughout the village. There is a small **Venetian fortress** and little coves with some of the clearest water around, fine for **swimming**.

ACCOMMODATION AND EATING   AVLÉMONAS

Maryianní ☎ 27360 33316, ⓦ maryianni.gr. This bright, pleasantly landscaped complex is the closest one to the sea. Most rooms are fully self-catering and offer great views from private terraces. No breakfast. €70

Sotiris ☎ 27360 33722. This taverna, with seating overlooking the sparkling little cove, offers a wide selection of fresh, well-prepared and reasonably priced fish dishes (around €10). If you feel in a lavish mood, order their *astakomakaronádha* (lobster spaghetti). Daily noon–midnight.

Andikýthira

Thirteen kilometres to the south of Kýthira, the tiny, wind-blown 22-square-kilometre island of **ANDIKÝTHIRA** is linked to its bigger sister by a sporadic ferry service. Rocky and poor, and a site of political exile until 1964, the island only received electricity in 1984, but it has one remarkable claim to fame: the **Andikythera Mechanism**. Local attractions include good birdlife (a bird observatory has been built in the old school at

Lazianá) and flora, but it's not the place if you want company, with only 45 residents divided among a scattering of settlements – mainly in **Potamós**, the harbour, and **Sohória**, the village. Ferries permitting, the **festival of Áyios Mýron** is held here on August 17 – an annual reunion jamboree for the Andikytheran diaspora.

Recent excavation work above Xeropótamos has revealed the site of ancient **Aigila**, a 75-acre fortress city of the Hellenistic period. At the harbour below are the remains of one of ancient Greece's best-preserved warship slipways, a *neosoikos*, carved out of the rock. The organization Dig Kythera (ⓦkrg.org.au) can arrange volunteer excavation work either at Andikýthira or Kýthira.

ARRIVAL AND INFORMATION   ANDIKÝTHIRA

By ferry Andikýthira has, theoretically, a twice-weekly summer connection with Kýthira (2hr) on the Pireás–Kýthira–Kastélli (Crete) run, but landings are often impossible due to adverse weather.

Toursit information A useful online resource is ⓦantikythira.gr.

ACCOMMODATION AND EATING

You can camp in the open anywhere on the island. There are a couple of tavernas and a village shop at Sohória, but you'd be wise to bring plenty of supplies with you.

Antikythera Rooms Potamós ☎27360 33004, ⓦantikythera.gr. The only official accommodation on the island, this set of rooms with shared bathroom is run by the local community for free (donations only). June–Sept. Suggested donation per person €20

8

MINOAN VASES, IRÁKLIO MUSEUM

Contexts

History

The history of the Greek Islands is, broadly, the history of Greece, and it is that which follows. However, in the context of well over five thousand years of civilization on the islands, and of constant trade between them and the wider world, it is not surprising that individual islands have their own unique histories. What is consistent is that their position at the crossroads of Europe, Asia and Africa has made them a prize much fought over. The islanders have also played a full part in Greece's unparalleled impact on Western society in the fields of politics, philosophy, literature, science and art.

Prehistoric Greece: to 2100 BC

Evidence of human habitation in Greece goes back half a million years, as demonstrated by the skeleton of a **Neanderthal** youth in the **Petralóna Cave**, 50km east of the northern city of Thessaloníki, along with the earliest known site of a man-made fire in Europe.

Only very much later, about 40,000 years ago, did **Homo sapiens** make his first appearance in Greece after migrating out of Africa. At several sites in **Epirus** in northwest Greece (including some on what are now the Ionian islands, then attached to the mainland), Homo sapiens used tools and weapons of bone, wood and stone to gather wild plants and hunt. Even between 20,000 and 16,000 years ago, when the Ice Age was at its peak, **Stone Age man** continued to make a home in Greece, though only in around 10,000 BC did a considerably warmer climate set in and the glaciers retreat, raising sea levels and finally separating many of the islands from the mainland.

The Neolithic period

Agricultural communities first appeared in northern Greece around **6500 BC**. Whether agriculture developed indigenously or was introduced by migrants from Asia Minor is much debated: what is certain, however, is its revolutionary effect.

An assured supply of food enabled the Stone Age inhabitants of Greece to settle in fixed spots, building mud-brick houses on stone foundations. Though still reliant on stone implements, this new farming culture marked a significant break with the past, so a "new stone age" or **Neolithic period** is said to have begun. As the flint needed for weapons and tools was rare in Greece, mainlanders imported obsidian from the island of **Melos** (Mílos) in the southern Cyclades. The earliest **seaborne trade** known anywhere in the world, this clearly involved a mastery of building and handling boats, skills that were to define the Greek islanders throughout their history.

Cycladic culture and the beginnings of the Greek Bronze Age

Around **3000 BC** a new people settled in the **Cyclades**, probably from Asia Minor, bringing with them the latest metallurgical techniques. While continuing the old

c.40,000 BC	c.6500 BC	c.3000 BC	c.2100 BC
Stone Age Homo sapiens arrives in Greece.	Permanent communities and the world's earliest seaborne trade herald the Neolithic era.	In the Cycladic islands, a new people introduce striking new art forms. The dawn of the Bronze Age.	The Greek language is heard in Greece for the first time.

trade in obsidian, they also developed a **trade in tin** and were making prodigious voyages westwards as far as Spain by 2500 BC. The mining of **gold and silver** in the Cyclades may have dated from this period, too. Long before Crete or the Greek mainland, these new islanders became specialists in **jewellery-making**, **metalwork** and **stone-cutting**. From the abundant marble of the Cyclades, they sculpted statuettes, mostly of female figures. Slender, spare and geometric, these **Cycladic sculptures** are startlingly modern in appearance, and were exported widely, to Crete and mainland Greece.

In about 3000 BC, the introduction of bronze technology to the mainland, also from the Cyclades, marked the start of the **Bronze Age** in Greece. By **2500 BC** the widespread use of bronze had transformed farming and fighting throughout the Eastern Mediterranean and the Middle East. Because **tin** (which when alloyed with copper creates bronze) came from so far afield – in the east from the Caucasus, Persia and Afghanistan, in the west from Cornwall, Brittany, northwest Spain and northern Italy – the Aegean became an important trade route. Hence the burst of development that now took place along the eastern coast of **central Greece** and the **Peloponnese**, and on the **Aegean islands** which linked the Greek mainland to Asia Minor and the Middle East.

It is uncertain what **language** was spoken at this time, but one thing is clear: it was not yet Greek. Indeed, when **Greek-speaking people** did arrive on the mainland in about 2100 BC, their destructive impact paralysed its development for five hundred years, while the large and secure island of **Crete** – which they did not invade or settle – flourished and dominated the Aegean.

The coming of the Greeks

The destruction of numerous mainland sites in about **2100 BC**, followed by the appearance of a new style of pottery, has suggested to archeologists the violent arrival of a **new people**. They domesticated the horse, introduced the potter's wheel and possessed considerable metallurgical skills. These newcomers replaced the old religion centred on female fertility figures with **hilltop shrines**, thought to have been dedicated to the worship of male sky gods like Zeus. And with them came a new language, an early form of **Greek**, though they were obliged to adopt existing native words for such things as olives, figs, vines, wheat and the sea, suggesting that these new migrants or invaders may have come from distant inland steppes where they had been pastoral highlanders, not farmers, fishermen or sailors.

Minoan and Mycenaean civilizations: 2100–1100 BC

The history of the Aegean during the second millennium BC can be seen as a struggle between the **Mycenaean culture** of the Greek mainland and the **Minoan culture** of Crete. Situated halfway between mainland Greece and Egypt, Crete exploited the Bronze Age boom in trade to become the dominant power in the Aegean by the start of the second millennium BC. Its influence was felt throughout the islands and also on the mainland, where the Greek-speaking invaders were "Minoanized", gradually developing a culture known as Mycenaean (after Mycenae, a principal mainland Bronze Age site) that owed a lot to Crete.

c.2000 BC	c.1700 BC	c.1650 BC	c.1500 BC
On Crete, the great Minoan palaces are built.	Knossós and the other palaces are destroyed by earthquake, but rebuilt even more grandly.	Thíra (Santoríni) devastated by a massive volcanic explosion, whose effects spread across the region.	Mainland Mycenaeans gain control of Crete.

THE TROJAN WAR

For the Greeks, the story of the **Trojan War** was the central event in their early history, and in their minds Homer's **Iliad** was not just a poem of heroic deeds sung at noble courts, but the epic of their first great national adventure.

Excavations in the late nineteenth century by Heinrich Schliemann (see p.547) uncovered many Troys of several periods, but the layer known as **Troy VIIa** clearly suffered violent destruction in about 1220 BC. The Mycenaeans are the likeliest perpetrators, though the abduction of a Greek beauty called **Helen** would not have been the only reason they launched a thousand ships against the Trojans. Mycenaean prosperity greatly depended on trade with the Eastern Mediterranean, where increasingly unsettled conditions made it imperative that the Mycenaeans secure their lines of **trade and supply**. Troy commanded a strategic position overlooking the Hellespont, the narrow waterway (today called the Dardanelles) dividing Europe and Asia and linking the Aegean to the Black Sea, where it controlled important trade routes. Trade was especially important to island peoples, which is why so many were involved in the expedition: Ithaca, Rhodes, Kos, Symí, Évvia, Kálymnos and Crete all sent ships to Troy.

The capture of Troy was the last great success of the Mycenaeans, and perhaps for that reason it was long remembered in poetry and song. It inspired later generations of Greeks to dream of overseas expansion, culminating in the fourth century BC when Alexander the Great carried a copy of the *Iliad* as he marched across Asia.

Minoan Crete

Living on a large and fertile island with good natural harbours, the people of **Crete** raised sufficient crops and livestock to export surplus quantities of oil and wool. Among their most impressive tools, literally at the cutting edge of new technology, was a metre-long bronze saw that readily converted the forest-clad mountains into an ample source of **timber for ships**. Some timber was probably also exported, most likely to treeless Egypt, while metalwork, jewellery and pottery of superb Cretan craftsmanship were shipped to the mainland and beyond. **Kamares ware**, as Cretan pottery of this period is known, was especially valued; it has been found all along the Cretans' 875km-long maritime trade route to the East – on the Aegean islands of Rhodes and Sámos, on the coast of Asia Minor at Miletus, and in Syria and Egypt.

On Crete itself, Minoan power was concentrated on three vast **palace complexes** – at **Knossós**, **Phaestos** and **Malia**, all in the centre of the island. First built around 2000 BC, their similarity of plan and lack of defences suggest that some form of confederacy had replaced any regional rivalries on the island, while Minoan sea power induced a sense of security against foreign invasion. Crete's maritime supremacy was consolidated by a network of **colonies**, or close allies throughout the islands – most famously **Thíra** (Santoríni), but also Kýthira, Mílos, Náxos, Páros, Mikonós, Delos, Rhodes and others. On Crete, prosperity was not confined to the palace centres; the numerous remains of villas of the Minoan gentry, and of well-constructed villages, show that the wealth generated by the palaces was redistributed among the island's population. Following an **earthquake** around 1700 BC, the palaces at Knossós and Phaestos were rebuilt, and a more modest palace constructed at **Zakros** on the east coast. This activity coincided with an apparent centralization of power at Knossós, giving rise to a **Minoan golden age**.

c.1220 BC	c.1150 BC	c.1100 BC	900–700 BC
Trojan War, whose events are immortalized by Homer and enter the realm of myth.	The so-called Sea Peoples sweep across Greece, ushering in a new Dark Age.	The first iron tools and weapons begin to transform agriculture and warfare.	Geometric Period.

Mycenaean dominance

Suddenly, however, around **1500 BC**, the Mycenaeans gained control of the palace of Knossós and were soon in full possession of Crete. How this happened is unknown, but it probably marked the culmination of a growing rivalry between the Mycenaeans and the Minoans for control of the Aegean trade, which perhaps coincided with a **volcanic explosion** on the island of Thíra (Santoríni) and its consequent **tsunami**.

Greek now became the language of administration at Knossós and the other former Minoan palaces, as well as on the mainland – indeed this is the earliest moment that Greek language can definitely be identified, as the palace records on Crete are from now on written in a script known as **Linear B**, which when deciphered in 1953 was shown to be a form of Greek. Having wrested control of the Aegean trade from the Minoans, the **Mycenaeans** were dominant for another three hundred years. At the end of that period in about 1220 BC, they famously laid siege to, and destroyed, yet another rival, the city of **Troy**.

Yet within a generation the Mycenaean world was overwhelmed by a vast **migration** of northerners from somewhere beyond the Black Sea. Probably victims of a catastrophic change in climate that brought drought and famine to their homelands, these **Sea Peoples**, as the ancients called them, swept down through Asia Minor and the Middle East and also crossed the Mediterranean to Libya and Egypt, disrupting trade routes and destroying empires as they went. With the palace-based Bronze Age economies destroyed, the humbler **village-based economies** that replaced them lacked the wealth and the technological means to make a mark in the world. Greece was plunged into a Dark Age, and knowledge of the Minoan and Mycenaean civilizations slipped into dim memory.

The Dark Age and the rise of the city-state: 1150–491 BC

The poverty and isolation that characterized Greece for the next five hundred years did have one lasting effect: **emigration**. Greeks spread to the Dodecanese islands, to Cilicia along the south coast of **Asia Minor**, and to **Cyprus**, which became Greek-speaking. Later, around 1000 BC, they also settled in large numbers along the western coast of Asia Minor. Even in the Dark Age there were a few glimmers of light: **Athens**, for example, escaped the destruction that accompanied the fall of Mycenaean civilization and maintained trading links abroad. It became the route through which the **Iron Age** was introduced to mainland Greece with the importation of iron weapons, implements and technological know-how around 1100 BC.

A new cultural beginning was also made in the form of pottery painted in the **Geometric style**, a highly intricate and controlled design that would lie at the heart of later Greek architecture, sculpture and painting. But it was the **Phoenicians**, sailing from Sidon and Tyre in present-day Lebanon, who really re-established trading links between the Middle East and the Aegean world in the eighth century BC, and Greeks followed swiftly in their wake.

With wealth flowing in again, Greek civilization developed with remarkable rapidity; no other people achieved so much over the next few centuries. The institution most responsible for this extraordinary achievement, the **city-state** or **polis**, came into being at a time of rapidly growing populations, greater competition for land and resources, increasing productivity and wealth, expanding trade and more complex relationships

800–700 BC	776 BC	750–650 BC	c.725 BC
Revival of trade between Greece and the Middle East kick-starts an economic revival.	The first Olympic Games staged at Olympia.	Greeks colonize the Eastern Mediterranean, from Italy to Asia Minor.	The *Iliad* and *Odyssey*, hitherto retold as oral sagas, are set down in writing.

THE ILIAD AND THE ODYSSEY

The **Iliad** and the **Odyssey**, the oldest and greatest works in Greek literature, were the brilliant summation of five centuries of poetic tradition, first developed by nameless bards whose recitations were accompanied by music. Completed by 725 BC, they are far older than the *Pentateuch*, the first five books of the Old Testament, which achieved their finished form only around 400 BC. The whole Greek world knew the Homeric epics, and their influence upon the subsequent development of Greek literature, art and culture in general cannot be overstated. Few works, and probably none not used in worship, have had such a hold on a nation for so long.

The *Iliad* is the story of a few days' action in the tenth and final year of the Trojan War, which in its tales of heroic exploits recalls the golden age of the Mycenaeans. The *Odyssey* begins after the war and follows the adventures of Odysseus, who takes ten years to return to his island home of Ithaca (usually taken to be Itháki, in the Ionian islands) on the western side of Greece. The story of his voyages demonstrates the new Greek interest in the area around the Black Sea and in Italy and Sicily to the west. They are also a celebration of an emerging hellenic identity, of a national adventure encompassing both shores of the Aegean and beyond.

with neighbouring states. The birthplace of **democracy** and of equality before the law, the city-state became the Greek ideal, and by the early seventh century BC it had spread throughout Greece and wherever Greeks established colonies overseas, with important centres growing up throughout the islands.

Trade also acted as a cultural stimulus; contact with other peoples made the Greeks aware of what they shared among themselves, and led to the development of a **national sentiment**, notably expressed and fostered by the **panhellenic sanctuaries** that arose during the eighth century BC, of **Hera** and **Zeus** at **Olympia**, and of **Apollo** and **Artemis** on **Delos**, as well as the **oracles** of **Zeus** at **Dodona** and of **Apollo** at **Delphi**.

Expansion and colonization

Around 750 BC, Greeks began to found **colonies** in the Western Mediterranean – in **Sicily** and **southern Italy** especially – while a century later, around 650 BC, further colonies were established round the shores of the **Black Sea**. By the fifth century BC Greeks seemed to sit upon the shores of the entire world, in Plato's words like "frogs around a pond". The islands were vital staging points en route to the new colonies, and thrived on the trade they brought.

One impetus for expansion was competition between the Greeks and the Phoenicians over trade routes; but there was also rivalry among the Greek city-states themselves. **Chalkis**, **Eretria** and **Corinth** were the major colonizers in the west, while the **Ionian Greeks** were the chief colonizers around the Black Sea. When the Spartans needed more land, they conquered neighbouring Messenia in 710 BC, but generally land shortage drove Greeks overseas. Thus colonists were sent from Thera (Thíra) to found Cyrene in North Africa, and were forbidden to return on pain of death. Whatever the reason for their foundation, however, most colonies kept up close relations with their mother cities.

Democracy, tyranny and slavery

Meanwhile, at home in the city-states, political tensions were building between the **aristocratic rulers** and the **people**. A large class of farmers, merchants and the like was

700–480 BC	621 BC	c.620–570 BC	498 BC
Archaic period.	Draco's reforming "draconian" law code is published in Athens.	The literary zenith of Lésvos, where Sappho, one of the greatest poets of the ancient world, and Aesop both live.	Rebellious Ionian Greeks burn the city of Sardis, provoking a Persian invasion of Greece.

excluded from political life but forced to pay heavy taxes. The pressure led to numerous reforms and a gradual move towards **democracy**. Ironically, the transition was often hastened by **tyrants**. Despite the name – which simply means they seized power by force – many tyrants were in fact champions of the people, creating work, redistributing wealth and patronizing the arts. **Peisistratos**, tyrant of Athens during the sixth century BC, is perhaps the archetype. Successful and well-liked by his people, his populist rule ensured Athenian prosperity by gaining control of the route into the Black Sea. He also ordered that Homer's works be set down in their definitive form and performed regularly, and encouraged the theatrical festivals where Greek drama would be born.

City-states also flourished on islands throughout the Aegean, and they too had their tyrants and their artists. On **Lésvos**, for example, the poet **Sappho**, part of a long tradition of poetry on the island, was writing around the turn of the sixth century BC; some claim that her contemporary Aesop (of Fables fame) was also from Lésvos. Not long after their time, the island, along with other nearby territories, was captured by **Polycrates**, tyrant of **Sámos**, who built up his island's navy to establish himself as a regional power, at various times in alliance with the Egyptian pharaoh, the king of Persia and with Lygdamis, tyrant of **Náxos**. **Lygdamis**, in turn, was a close ally of Peisistratos.

Athens and the Golden Age: 490–431 BC

Democracy was a very long way from universal. The population of **Athens** and surrounding Attica amounted to some 400,000 people, of whom about 80,000 were slaves, 160,000 foreigners, and another 160,000 free-born Athenians. Out of this last category came the **citizens**, those who could vote and be elected to office, and their number amounted to no more than 45,000 adult men.

Yet if the powers of democracy were in the hands of the few, the energy, boldness and creative spirit that it released raised Athens to greatness. Throughout the **fifth century BC** the political, intellectual and artistic activity of the Greek world was centred on the city. In particular Athens was the patron of **drama**, both tragedy and comedy. Athenian tragedy always addressed the great issues of life and death and the relationship of man to the gods. And the Athenians themselves seemed to be conscious of living out a high drama as they fought battles, argued policy, raised temples and wrote plays that have decided the course and sensibility of Western civilization.

The Persian Wars

The wars between Greece and Persia began with a revolt against Persian rule by Ionian Greeks in Asia Minor. Athens and Eretria (on Évvia) gave them support, burning the city of Sardis in 498 BC. Provoked by their insolence, **Darius**, the Persian king, launched a punitive expedition. The **Persians'** unexpected repulse at **Marathon** in 490 BC persuaded Darius to hurl his full military might against Greece, to ensure its subjection once and for all to the Persian Empire.

After Darius died in 486 BC, his son **Xerxes** took over. In 483 BC, he began preparations that lasted two years and were on a fabulous scale. Bridges of boats were built across the Hellespont for Persia's vast imperial army to parade into Europe, and a canal was cut through the peninsular finger now occupied by the Mount Áthos monasteries, so that the Persian fleet could avoid storms while rounding the headlands of the Halkidhikí.

490 BC	**480 BC**	**480 BC**
After the Battle of Marathon, a runner is despatched to Athens to relay the good news; having run the first marathon, Pheidippides drops dead.	Greek defeat at the Battle of Thermopylae, scene of heroic Spartan defiance.	Persians sack and burn Athens.

Though the Greek historian **Herodotus** claimed that Xerxes' army held one million eight hundred thousand soldiers, his figure is probably a tenfold exaggeration. Even so, it was a massive force, an army of 46 nations, combined with a fleet of eight hundred triremes carrying almost as many sailors as there were soldiers in the army.

Despite their numerical superiority, the might of Asia was routed at sea off **Salamis** in 480 BC (see p.83). A significant part of the Greek fleet came from the islands: above all from Égina, then a major rival of Athens, but with ships from Náxos, Lefkádha, Styra on Évvia, Kýthnos, Kéa, Mílos, Sífnos and Sérifos (there were also ships from Rhodes and others in the Persian fleet). The following year the Persians were also defeated on land, at **Plataea**. Within a few days of that second battle came another naval victory at **Mycale**, off Sámos, where the battle was won when Xerxes' subject Ionians went over to their fellow Hellenes. Xerxes could do no more than return to Susa, his capital deep in Persia, leaving the entire Aegean free.

Despite occasional reversals, this sudden shift in the balance of power between East and West endured for the next 1500 years. Within 150 years, Alexander the Great achieved in Asia what Xerxes had failed to achieve in Europe, and the Persian Empire succumbed to a Greek conqueror.

The rise of the Athenian Empire: 478–431 BC

The first consequence of the Greek victory against the Persians was not, as might have been expected, the rise of **Sparta**, the pre-eminent Greek military power, whose soldiers had obediently sacrificed themselves at Thermopylae and won the final mainland battle at Plataea. Instead, many Greek city-states voluntarily placed themselves under the leadership of Athens.

This Aegean confederation was named the **Delian League**, after the island of **Delos** where the allies kept their treasury; it included cities on virtually every island in the Aegean, plus many on the eastern coast of Greece and western coast of Asia Minor. Its first task was to protect the Greeks of Asia Minor against a vengeful Xerxes. This was the opposite of the policy proposed by Sparta and its Peloponnesian allies, which called for the abandonment of Greek homes across the Aegean and the resettlement of Asian Greeks in northern Greece.

That typified the Spartan attitude throughout the Persian crisis, in which Sparta had shown no initiative and acted only at the last minute. Its policy was provincial, protecting its position in the Peloponnese rather than pursuing the wider interests of Greece. Thus over the coming decades Sparta lost prestige to Athens, which Themistocles had established as a maritime power and whose imperial potential was realized under Pericles.

This was the **Athenian golden age**, and indeed a golden age for all Greece. The fifty years following Salamis and Plataea witnessed an extraordinary flowering in architecture, sculpture, literature and philosophy whose influence is felt to this day. Greeks of the time recognized the historical importance of their experience and gave it realization through the creative impulse. Just as **Herodotus**, the "father of history", made the contest between Europe and Asia the theme of his great work, so **Aeschylus**, who fought at Marathon, made Xerxes the tragic subject of *The Persians* and thereby brought the art of drama to life. Indeed in the intoxicating Athenian atmosphere the warriors who turned back the Persian tide seemed to have fought in the same cause as

480 BC	480–323 BC	479 BC	447–438 BC
Naval victory at Salamis, involving fleets from many islands, marks the beginning of the end of the invasion.	Classical Period.	Persians defeated at the Battle of Plataea and are forced out of Greece.	Parthenon constructed, the symbol of Athens' Golden Age.

Homer's heroes at Troy. In thanksgiving and celebration the temples upon the Acropolis that the Persians had destroyed were rebuilt – most notably with the building of the **Parthenon**.

Yet Athens was still just one among numerous city-states, each ready to come together during a common danger but reasserting its sovereignty as the foreign threat receded. This was illustrated by the ten-year struggle from 461 BC onwards between Athens (and her island allies in the Delian League) and various **Peloponnesian states**, itself a warning of a yet greater war to come between Athens and Sparta. Perhaps 451 BC marks the fatal moment when Athens passed up the opportunity to create an institution more generous, and more inclusive, than the city-state. Instead Pericles (c.495–429 BC), Athens' greatest leader, supported the parochial and populist demand that **Athenian citizenship** should not be extended to its allies, thereby stoking up the flames of envy and foregoing the chance of creating a genuine and enduring Greek confederacy.

The decline of the city-state: 431–338 BC

The **Peloponnesian War** that began in **431 BC** was really a continuation of earlier conflicts between Athens and its principal commercial rivals, Corinth and Aegina (though technically a member of the Delian League, ancient Aegina – Égina – was also a jealous rival of Athens) and their various allies in the Peloponnese. Sparta had earlier stood aside, but by 432 BC when Corinth again agitated for war, the **Spartans** had become fearful of growing Athenian power.

The Athenian empire was built on trade, and the city was a great sea power, with 300 triremes. The members of Sparta's **Peloponnesian League**, meanwhile, had powerful armies but no significant navy (though from time to time various islands, particularly in the Dodecanese, would ally themselves with Sparta). Just as Themistocles had sought to fight the Persians by sea, so Pericles followed the same strategy against Sparta and its allies, avoiding major battles against superior land forces. Athens and Piraeus were protected by their walls, but the Peloponnesians and their allies were allowed to invade Attica with impunity nearly every year, and Thrace saw constant warfare. On the other hand the Peloponnesians lacked the sea power to carry the fighting into Asia Minor and the Aegean islands or to interfere with Athens' trade, while the Athenians used their maritime superiority to launch attacks against the coasts of the Peloponnese, the Ionian islands and the mouth of the Gulf of Corinth, hoping to detach members from the Peloponnesian League. So long as Athens remained in command of the sea, it had every reason to expect that it could wear down its enemies' resolve.

Pericles' death in 429 BC was an early blow to the Athenian cause. Although **Kleon**, his successor, is widely blamed for Athens' eventual defeat, after Pericles the city was in fact always divided into a peace party and a military one, unable to pursue a consistent policy. The final straw came in 415 BC, when a bold operation designed to win Sicily to the Athenian cause turned into a catastrophic debacle. Though not entirely defeated, Athens was never to be a major power again.

City-state rivalries

The Peloponnesian War left **Sparta** the supreme power in Greece, but those whom the Spartans had "liberated" swiftly realized that they had simply acquired a new and

431–415 BC	408 BC	399 BC	380 BC
Peloponnesian War marks the end of Athens' ascendancy.	Rhodes town founded.	Socrates tried and condemned to death for corrupting the minds of the youth of Athens.	Plato establishes his Academy in Athens.

THUCYDIDES: THE FIRST MODERN HISTORIAN

The writing of history began among the Greeks, first with **Herodotus**, then with Thucydides. Whereas Herodotus gives the impression that he prefers telling a good story, and that he still inhabits Homer's world of epic poetry, for **Thucydides** the paramount concern is to analyse events. In that sense Thucydides is the first modern historian; wherever possible he seeks out primary sources, and his concern is always with objectivity, detail and chronology. Not that there is anything dry about his writing; its vividness and insight make reading him as powerful an experience as watching a Greek drama.

Thucydides began writing his history at the outset of the **Peloponnesian War**, intending to give an account of its whole duration. For reasons unknown, however, he abruptly stopped writing in the twentieth year, though he is thought to have survived the war by a few years, living until about 400 BC. Born into a wealthy, conservative Athenian family around 455 BC, he was a democrat and an admirer of Pericles; his reconstruction of Pericles' speeches presents the most eloquent expression of the Athenian cause. But the exile of Thucydides from his city seven years into the war was the making of him as an historian. As he put it, "Associating with both sides, with the Peloponnesians quite as much as with the Athenians, because of my exile, I was thus enabled to watch quietly the course of events".

Thucydides was himself a military man, who understood war at first hand, hence his concern for method in his research and analysis in his writing – he intended his book to be useful to future generals and statesmen. For these reasons we have a better understanding of the Peloponnesian War than of any ancient conflict until Julius Caesar wrote his own first-hand accounts of his campaigns. And for these reasons too, Thucydides' history stands on a par with the greatest literature of ancient Greece.

---

inferior master, one that entirely lacked the style, the ability and the intelligence of Athens. Meanwhile Athens had lost its empire but not its trade, so its mercantile rivals faced no less competition than before. During the first decade of the fourth century, Athens managed to restore much of its naval power in the Aegean.

Adding to the intrigues between Persia, Athens and Sparta was a bewildering and unstable variety of alliances involving other Greek states. The most important of these was **Thebes**, which had been an ally of Sparta during the Peloponnesian War but came round to the Athenian side, and then for a spectacular moment under its brilliant general **Epaminondas** became the greatest power in Greece, in the process dealing Sparta a blow from which it never recovered. Theban supremacy did not survive the death of Epaminondas, however, and Greece subsequently found itself free for the first time in centuries from the dictates of Persia or any over-powerful Greek city-state. Exhausted and impoverished by almost continuous war, it was an opportunity for Greece to peacefully unite. But the political and moral significance of the city-state had by now eroded, and with the **rise of Macedonia** came the concept of an all-embracing kingship.

The Macedonian Empire

Despite its large size and population, **Macedonia** played little role in early Greek affairs. Many in Greece did not consider the Macedonians to be properly Greek; not in speech, culture or political system. They did not live in city-states, which Aristotle said was the mark of a civilized human being, but as a tribal people, led by a king, and were closer to

371 BC	359 BC	338 BC	336 BC
Sparta defeated by Thebes at the Battle of Leuctra.	Philip II becomes king of Macedonia.	Philip II's victory at Chaeronia unites Greece under Macedonian rule.	Alexander the Great succeeds his father, and within six years has conquered all of Persia.

BIG IDEAS: SOCRATES, PLATO AND ARISTOTLE

The Golden Age of Athens under Pericles, and the city-state rivalry after the Peloponnesian War, saw the **birth of Western philosophy** under the towering figures of Socrates, Plato and Aristotle.

SOCRATES (C.470–399 BC)

The son of an Athenian sculptor, **Socrates** was for a time a sculptor himself. Though he fought bravely for Athens as a hoplite in the Peloponnesian War, much earlier, in his twenties, he had turned to philosophy, which he practised in his own peculiar style. Promoting no philosophical position of his own, he asserted, ceaselessly, the supremacy of reason. Often this was done in the streets of Athens, buttonholing some self-regarding Athenian of the older generation, asking him questions, picking his answers to pieces, until he came up with a definition that held water or, more likely, the spluttering victim was reduced to confess his own **ignorance** before crowds of Socrates' mirthful young supporters.

By this "Socratic method" he asked for definitions of familiar concepts such as piety and justice; his technique was to expose the ignorance that hid behind people's use of such terms, while acknowledging his own similar ignorance. Indeed when the Delphic oracle proclaimed that no man was wiser than Socrates, he explained this by saying wisdom lies in knowing how little one really knows. Because he valued this question-and-answer process over settling on fixed conclusions, Socrates never wrote anything down. Yet his influence was pivotal; before his time philosophical enquiry concerned itself with speculations on how the natural world was formed and how it operates; afterwards it looked to the **analysis of concepts** and to **ethics**.

Socrates' method could be irritating, especially when he questioned conventional morality, and this, coupled with powerful friendships with unpopular oligarchs, led to a backlash. Having tried him for impiety and corrupting the young, and sentenced him to death, the city gave him the option of naming another penalty, probably expecting him to choose exile. Instead Socrates answered that if he was to get what he deserved, he should be maintained for life at public expense. At this the death penalty was confirmed, but even then it was not to be imposed for two months, with the tacit understanding that Socrates would escape. Instead Socrates argued that it was wrong for a citizen to disobey even an unjust law, and in the company of his friends he drank the cup of hemlock. "Such was the end," wrote Plato, "of our friend; of all the men of his time whom I have known, he was the wisest and justest and best."

PLATO (C.427–347 BC)

As a young man, **Plato** painted, composed music and wrote a tragedy, as well as being a student of Socrates. He intended a career in politics, where his connections would have ensured success, but Socrates' death made Plato decide that he could not serve a government that had committed such a crime, and instead his mission became to exalt the memory of his teacher. In Plato's writings, many of them **dialogues**, Socrates is frequently the leading participant, while at the **Academy** in Athens, which Plato founded, the Socratic question-and-answer method was the means of instruction.

the barbarians (such attitudes still rankle today, and inform some of the bitter debate over the name and status of the FYROM, the Former Yugoslav Republic of Macedonia).

Towards the middle of the fourth century, however, the power of Macedonia grew under the leadership of **Philip II**. Philip was determined to Hellenize his country; borrowing from Greek ways and institutions, he founded the city of **Pella** as his capital and lured teachers, artists and intellectuals to his court, among them **Aristotle** and **Euripides** (the latter originally from the island of Salamis). An admirer of Athens, Philip

335 BC	323 BC	c.300 BC	226 BC
Aristotle founds the Lyceum in Athens.	Death of Alexander.	Euclid's Elements published, its 13 volumes creating the basis of much of modern maths and science.	The vast statue known as the Colossus of Rhodes, one of the wonders of the Ancient World, collapses in an earthquake.

Plato's philosophy is elusive; he never sets out a system of doctrines, nor does he tell us which of his ideas are most basic, nor rank them in hierarchical order, nor show how they interrelate. Nevertheless, certain themes recur. He believed that men possess **immortal souls** separate from their mortal bodies. **Knowledge**, he believed, was the recollection of what our souls already know; we do not gain knowledge from experience, rather by using our reasoning capacity to draw more closely to the realm of our souls. The true objects of knowledge are not the transient, material things of this world, which are only reflections of a higher essence that Plato called **Forms** or **Ideas**. Forms are objects of pure thinking, cut off from our experience; but also Forms motivate us to grasp them, so that the reasoning part of us is drawn to Forms as a kind of mystic communion.

Plato's notion of a mystic union with a higher essence would play an important role in later religious thought. But more immediately his teachings at the Academy concerned themselves with logic, mathematics, astronomy and above all **political science**, for its purpose was to train a new ruling class. Prominent families sent him their sons to learn the arts of government. Plato taught that the best form of government was a constitutional monarchy, at its head a wise and just philosopher-king. Though it was a utopian vision, Plato's political philosophy helped prepare the intellectual ground for the acceptance of an absolutist solution to the increasing uncertainties of fourth-century BC Greece.

ARISTOTLE (384–322 BC)

Aristotle grew up in Pella, the capital of an increasingly powerful Macedonia, where his father had been appointed doctor to King Amyntas II; it is therefore not unlikely that Amyntas' son, the future Philip II, and Aristotle were boyhood friends. Aged seventeen, Aristotle was sent to Plato's Academy at Athens to continue his education, and he remained there, first as a student, then as a teacher, a faithful follower of Plato's ideas. His independent philosophy matured later, during the years he spent, again at Pella, as tutor to Alexander the Great, and later still, after 335 BC, when he founded his own school, the **Lyceum**, in Athens.

Aristotle came to reject Plato's dualism. He did not believe that the soul was of a substance separate from the body, rather that it was an aspect of the body. Instead of Plato's inward-looking view, Aristotle sought to explain the physical world and human society from the viewpoint of an outside observer. Essentially a **scientist** and a **realist**, he was bent on discovering the true rather than establishing the good, and he believed sense perception was the only means of human knowledge. His vast output covered many fields of knowledge – logic, metaphysics, ethics, politics, rhetoric, art, poetry, physiology, anatomy, biology, zoology, physics, astronomy and psychology. Everything could be measured, analysed and described, and he was the first to classify organisms into **genera and species**.

The exactitude of Aristotle's writings does not make them easy reading, and Plato has always enjoyed a wider appeal owing to his literary skill. All the same, Aristotle's influence on Western intellectual and scientific tradition has been enormous.

---

sought an alliance that would make them joint masters of the Greek world. But the Athenians opposed him, and he took matters into his own hands.

In **338 BC** Philip defeated the Theban and Athenian forces at **Chaeronia**, and effectively brought the whole of Greece including virtually all the islands (though not Crete) under one rule for the first time. His success was built on one of the most formidable fighting units the world has ever seen: the **Macedonian phalanx**. Armed with the *sarissa*, an eighteen-foot pike tapering from butt to tip, its infantrymen were

c.287	215–213 BC	200–197 BC	146 BC
Mathematician, inventor and scientist Archimedes is born on the Greek colony of Sicily.	First Macedonian War extends Roman influence in Greece.	Second Macedonian War, culminating in the Roman victory at Cynoscephalae.	Greece divided into Roman provinces.

trained to move across a battlefield with all the discipline of a parade ground drill. Instead of relying on a headlong charge, its effectiveness lay in manipulating the enemy line – seeking to open a gap through which the cavalry could make its decisive strike.

Alexander's conquests

After Chaeronia, Philip summoned the Greek states to Corinth, and announced his plans for a panhellenic conquest of the Persian Empire. But Philip was murdered two years later and his plans for an **Asian campaign** fell to his son **Alexander** – throughout which, it is said, he slept with the *Iliad* under his pillow.

In the East too there was an assassination, and in 335 BC the Persian throne passed to **Darius III**, namesake of the first and doomed to be the last king of his line. Using essentially his father's tactics, Alexander led his army through a series of astonishing victories, usually against greater numbers, until he reached the heart of the Persian Empire. Alexander crossed the Hellespont in May of **334 BC**, with thirty thousand foot soldiers and five thousand horses. By autumn all the Aegean coast of **Asia Minor** was his; twelve months later he stood on the banks of the Orontes River in **Syria**; in the winter of 332 BC **Egypt** hailed him as pharaoh; and by the spring of 330 BC the great Persian cities of **Babylon**, **Susa**, **Persepolis** and **Pasargadae** had fallen to him in rapid succession until, at **Ecbatana**, he found Darius in the dust, murdered by his own supporters. Alexander wrapped the corpse in his Macedonian cloak, and assumed the lordship of Asia.

Hellenistic Greece

No sooner had **Alexander** died at Babylon in 323 BC, aged 33, than Athens led an alliance of Greeks in a **war of liberation** against Macedonian rule. But the Macedonians had built up a formidable navy which inflicted heavy losses on the Athenian fleet. Unable to lift the Macedonian blockade of Piraeus, Athens surrendered and a pro-Macedonian government was installed. The episode marked the end of the city as a sea power and left it permanently weakened.

Greece was now irrevocably part of a new dominion, one that entirely altered the scale and orientation of the Greek world. Alexander's strategic vision had been to see the Mediterranean and the East as two halves of a greater whole. Opened to Greek settlement and enterprise, and united by Greek learning, language and culture, if not always by a single power, this **Hellenistic Empire** enormously increased international trade and created unprecedented prosperity.

Asked on his deathbed to whom he bequeathed his empire, Alexander replied "To the strongest". Forty years of warfare between his leading generals gave rise to three dynasties: the **Antigonid** in Macedonia, which ruled over mainland Greece, the Ionian islands and most of those in the western Aegean; the **Seleucid** which ultimately centred on Syria and Asia Minor, including most of the Dodecanese and eastern Aegean islands; and the **Ptolemaic** in Egypt, ruled from Alexandria, founded by Alexander himself, which in wealth and population, not to mention literature and science, soon outshone anything in Greece. **Rhodes** in particular was caught up in the battles between the dynasties, enduring a long and ultimately unsuccessful siege in 305 BC – the Colossus of Rhodes was constructed to commemorate the event and the island became one of the leading powers of the succeeding age.

86 BC	31 BC	49–52 AD
Romans, led by Sulla, sack Athens.	Defeat of Antony and Cleopatra at the Battle of Actium brings all of Greece and the Middle East under Roman sway.	St Paul lives and preaches in Corinth and Athens, first introducing Christianity to Greece.

Meanwhile, in the Western Mediterranean, **Rome** was a rising power. **Philip V** of Macedonia had agreed a treaty of mutual assistance against Rome with Hannibal. After Hannibal's defeat, Rome's legions marched eastwards, and routed Philip's army at **Cynoscephalae** in Thessaly in 197 BC.

Roman Greece: 146 BC–330 AD

Rome was initially well disposed towards Greece, which they regarded as the originator of much of their culture, and granted autonomy to the existing city-states. However, after a number of uprisings, the country was divided into **Roman provinces** from 146 BC.

During the first century BC Rome was riven by civil wars, many of whose climactic battlefields were in Greece: in 49 BC **Julius Caesar** defeated his rival Pompey at **Pharsalus** in Thessaly; in 42 BC Caesar's assassins were beaten by **Mark Antony** and **Octavian** at **Philippi** in Macedonia; and in 31 BC **Antony** and his Ptolemaic ally **Cleopatra** were routed by **Octavian** in a sea battle off **Actium**, just north of Lefkádha in western Greece. The latter effectively marked the birth of the **Roman Empire** – an empire that in its eastern half continued to speak Greek.

By the first century AD Greece had become a **tourist destination** for well-to-do Romans; they went to Athens and Rhodes to study literature and philosophy, and toured the country to see the temples with their paintings and sculpture. They also visited the by now thoroughly professional **Olympic Games**. When the emperor **Nero** came to Greece in AD 67, he entered the Games as a contestant; the judges prudently declared him the victor in every competition, even the chariot race, in which he was thrown and failed to finish.

Greece had an early taste of **Christian teaching** when **Saint Paul** came to preach in 49–52 AD. Brought before the Court of the Areopagus in Athens, he was asked to defend his talk of the death and resurrection of his foreign god, and dismissed as a crank. Paul then spent eighteen months in **Corinth**; he made some converts, but as his subsequent Epistles to the Corinthians show, their idea of Christianity often amounted to celebrating their salvation with carousing and fornication. His journeys also took him to Crete, and to other islands. In the last decades of the century, **Saint John the Divine**, who was proselytizing at Ephesus, was exiled by the Romans to Pátmos, where in a cave still shown to visitors today he is said to have written Revelation, the apocalyptic last book of the Bible.

Byzantine and medieval Greece: 330–1460 AD

The **Byzantine Empire** was founded in May 330 when the **emperor Constantine** declared Nova Roma (as he called the city of Byzantium – known today as Istanbul) the new capital of the Roman Empire. Founded on the banks of the Bosphorus by Greek colonists in the seventh century BC, Byzantium occupied a commanding point from where the entire trade between the Black Sea and the Mediterranean could be controlled. **Constantinople**, the city of Constantine, as it became popularly known, was perfectly positioned for the supreme strategic task confronting the empire: the defence of the Danube and the Euphrates frontiers. Moreover, the new capital stood astride the flow of goods and culture from the East, that part of the empire richest in economic resources, most densely populated and rife with intellectual and religious activity.

95 AD	**117–138**	**267**
St John the Divine is exiled to Pátmos, where he compiles the Bible's Book of Revelation.	The reign of Emperor Hadrian, a Hellenophile who left many monuments, above all his great library and triumphal arch in Athens.	Barbarians pillage Athens.

THE ORIGINS OF THE ORTHODOX CHURCH

The split between the Orthodox and Catholic churches is traditionally dated to the "**Great Schism**" of 1054, but in practice the Churches had been diverging for centuries, and arguably the final break came much later. The causes of the split were as much linguistic – following the division of the Roman Empire, the language of the Church in Rome was Latin, while in the East it was Greek – and political as they were doctrinal, though there were certainly significant theological differences. Chief among these were the **iconoclastic controversy** – over the use of images in worship – the use of leavened (in the East) or unleavened bread (in the West) in the liturgy, and the Roman adjustment of the Creed, in 1014, to include the word "filioque" (and the Son).

The final schism was precipitated by the pope's claim to **supremacy over the Church**. While the patriarch in Constantinople and other Orthodox leaders accepted the bishop of Rome as "first among equals", they were not prepared to accept his ultimate authority over all the Church – or his subsequent claims to infallibility. In 1054, papal legates went to Constantinople to press the patriarch, Michael Celaurius, to accept Rome's claims. When he refused, Cardinal Humbert, leader of the Latin contingent, excommunicated Celaurius, who responded by in turn excommunicating Humbert and his colleagues.

Any hope of reconciliation disappeared with the sacking of Constantinople during the Fourth Crusade, when Orthodox churches were looted by Catholic crusaders, and forcibly converted to Catholic worship, and by the centuries of separation which followed the fall of Constantinople, when much of the Orthodox East came under Ottoman rule.

The Christian empire

Constantine's other act with decisive consequences was to **legalize** and patronize the **Christian Church**. Here again Constantinople was important, for while Rome's pagan traditions could not yet be disturbed, the new capital was conceived as a Christian city. Within the century Christianity was established as the religion of state, with its liturgies (still in use in the Greek Orthodox Church), the Creed and the New Testament all in Greek.

In 391 emperor **Theodosius I** issued an edict banning all expressions of **paganism** throughout the empire. In Greece the mysteries at Eleusis ceased to be celebrated the following year, and in 395 the Olympic Games were suppressed, their athletic nudity an offence to Christianity. Around this time too the Delphic oracle fell silent. The conversion of pagan buildings to Christian use began in the fifth century. Under an imperial law of 435 the Parthenon and the Erechtheion on the Acropolis, the mausoleum of Galerius (the Rotunda) in Thessaloníki and other temples elsewhere became churches. Even this did not eradicate pagan teaching: philosophy and law continued to be taught at the Academy in Athens, founded by Plato in 385 BC, until prohibited by the emperor Justinian in 529.

In 395 the Roman Empire split into **Western and Eastern empires**, and in 476 **Rome fell** to the barbarians. As the Dark Ages settled on Western Europe, Byzantium inherited the sole mantle of the empire. Latin remained its official language, though after the reign of Justinian (527–565) the emperors joined the people in speaking and writing Greek.

Thessaloníki, the second city of the Byzantine Empire, was relatively close to Constantinople, yet even so the journey by land or sea took five or six days. The rest of Greece grew decidedly provincial, and conditions worsened sharply in the late sixth century when the country was devastated by **plague**. In Athens after 580 life almost

395	435	730
Roman Empire splits; Greece becomes part of the eastern, or Byzantine, empire; Olympic Games suppressed.	The Parthenon and other Greek temples converted to churches.	Icons and other images banned in the Orthodox Church for being idolatrous; the height of the iconoclastic controversy.

came to an end, as the remaining inhabitants withdrew to the Acropolis, while at Corinth the population removed itself entirely to the island of Égina. The islands, especially those of the eastern Aegean closer to Byzantium, perhaps suffered less, though as central authority broke down so the threat of **piracy** grew. Remnants of very **early Christian churches**, from the sixth and seventh centuries onward, are scattered widely across the islands.

The Crusades

In 1071 the **Byzantine army** was destroyed at **Manzikert**, a fortress town on the eastern frontier, by the **Seljuk Turks** who went on to occupy almost all Asia Minor. After the Byzantine emperor turned to the West for help, the Roman Catholic pope replied by launching the **First Crusade** in 1095. Together, the Crusaders and the Byzantines won a series of victories over the Seljuks in Asia Minor, but the Byzantines, wary of possible Crusader designs on the empire itself, were content to see their Latin allies from the West advance alone on Jerusalem, which they captured in 1099.

The worst fears of the Byzantines were borne out in 1204 when the **Fourth Crusade** attacked and sacked **Constantinople** itself. Greece and its islands were shared out and endlessly changed hands between Franks, Venetians and many others in a bewildering patchwork of feudal holdings; for the maritime empires of Venice and Genoa, the islands held special appeal. Amid this endless infighting in the West, a new Turkish dynasty, the **Ottomans**, emerged in the late thirteenth century. By 1400 they had conquered all of mainland Byzantine Greece except Thessaloníki and the Peloponnese. In 1452 they invaded the Peloponnese as a diversion to the main attack on **Constantinople**, which fell on May 23, 1453. In 1456 the Ottomans captured **Athens** from the Venetians and turned the Parthenon church into a mosque, and in 1460 they conquered the **Peloponnese**. **Trebizond** fell the following year, and the Byzantine Empire was no more.

The fates of the islands were more varied. **Crete** enjoyed a spectacular cultural renaissance after the fall of Constantinople as a stream of refugees arrived from the east. Though increasingly embattled, it held out as a Venetian-ruled outpost for over two hundred years, before Iráklio was finally surrendered in 1669. In the **Dodecanese**, meanwhile, Rhodes and Kos had been built up as formidable fortresses during the Crusades, home to the **Knights Hospitallers of St John**. The Knights held out until 1522 before Süleyman the Magnificent finally drove them out – the trigger for the last Venetian islands in the Aegean, **Évvia** and **Égina**, to succumb not much later. In the west, closer to Venice, **Corfu** and the other Ionian islands were occasionally fought over, but never submitted for long – they remained in Venetian hands through most of the Turkish occupation, passing to France in the eighteenth century when Napoleon conquered Venice.

Greece under Turkish occupation: 1460–1821

Although the Greeks refer to the Turkish occupation as *sklaviá* – "slavery" – in practice, in exchange for submitting to Muslim rule and paying tribute, the Greeks were free to pursue their religion and were left very much in charge of their own religious and civil affairs. The essence of the Turkish administration was **taxation**; collection was often farmed out to the leaders of the Greek communities, and some local magistrates profited sufficiently to exercise a dominant role not only within their own region but

824–961	1071	1095	1204
Arab occupation of Crete; a warning of things to come.	Byzantine army defeated by the Turks.	First Crusade drives back the Turks.	Fourth Crusade sacks Constantinople; many of the islands taken over by western European powers.

also in the Ottoman Empire at large. On the mainland and larger islands, the Ottomans controlled the towns and the plains but left the mountains almost entirely to the Greeks. The fate of smaller islands depended largely on their resources; where there were none, they saw little interference.

The other important institution within Greece was the **Orthodox Church**. The Church was wealthy and powerful; Greeks preferred to give their lands to the monasteries than have them occupied by the Turks, while the Muslims found it easier to work with the Church than to invent a new administration. Though often corrupt and venal, the Church did at least preserve the traditional faith and keep alive the written form of the Greek language, and it became the focus of Greek nationalism.

Western resistance

In 1570 Ottoman troops landed on **Cyprus**. Nicosia was swiftly captured, and 30,000 of its inhabitants slaughtered. Turkish brutality in Cyprus horrified Europe, and the **Holy League** was formed under the aegis of the pope. Spain and Genoa joined Venice in assembling a fleet led by Don John of Austria, the bastard son of the Spanish king, its lofty aim not only to retake the island but to recapture all Christian lands taken by the Ottomans. In the event, it was utterly ineffectual; no serious attempt was made even to launch an expedition to relieve Cyprus. Yet out of it something new arose – the first stirrings of **Philhellenism**, a desire to liberate the Greeks, whose ancient culture stood at the heart of Renaissance thought.

There was, too, the encouragement of a naval victory, when in 1571 Don John's fleet surprised and overwhelmingly defeated the much larger Ottoman fleet, at its winter quarters at **Lepanto** on the Gulf of Corinth in western Greece. Two hundred and sixty-six Ottoman vessels were sunk or captured, fifty thousand sailors died, and fifteen thousand Christian galley slaves were freed. Throughout Europe the news of Lepanto was received with extraordinary rejoicing; this was the first battle in which Europe had triumphed against the Ottomans, and its symbolic importance was profound. Militarily and politically, however, the Ottomans remained dominant. The fall of **Crete**, in 1669, marked the end of the last bastion of Byzantine culture.

Greek nationalist stirrings

During the eighteenth century the islanders of **Ýdhra** (Hydra), **Spétses** and **Psará** built up a Greek merchant fleet that traded throughout the Mediterranean, where thriving colonies of Greeks were established in many ports. The fleets were to form the basis of the Greek naval forces in the struggle for independence, and these islands produced many of the movement's early leaders. Greek merchant families were also well established, often in important administrative positions, throughout the Ottoman Empire.

These wealthier and more educated Greeks enjoyed greater than ever opportunities for advancement within the Ottoman system, while the Greek peasantry, unlike the empire's Muslim inhabitants, did not have to bear the burden of military service. Nevertheless the Greeks had their grievances against the Ottoman government, mostly concerning the arbitrary, unjust and oppressive system of taxation. Among the Greek peasantry it was primarily religion that set them against their Muslim neighbours – as much as one-fifth of the population – and their Ottoman overlords. Muslim leaders had long preached hatred of the infidel, a view reciprocated by the priests and bishops of the Orthodox Church.

1453	1571	1669	1715
Constantinople falls to the Ottoman Turks, followed by much of Greece.	Battle of Lepanto – the first significant military defeat for the Ottoman Empire.	Iráklio falls to the Ottomans – the end of a brutal 25-year conquest of Crete.	Tínos is finally taken by the Ottomans, the last of the Cyclades to succumb.

The War of Independence: 1821–32

The **ideology** behind the **War of Independence** came from the Greeks of the diaspora, particularly those merchant colonies in France, Italy, Austria and Russia who had absorbed new European ideas of nationalism and revolution. Around 1814, assorted such Greeks formed a secret society, the **Filikí Etería** (Friendly Society). Their sophisticated political concepts went uncomprehended by the peasantry, who assumed that the point of an uprising was to exterminate their religious adversaries. And so when war finally broke out in **spring 1821**, almost the entire settled **Muslim population of Greece** – farmers, merchants and officials – was **slaughtered** within weeks by roaming bands of Greek peasants armed with swords, guns, scythes and clubs. They were often led by Orthodox priests, and some of the earliest Greek revolutionary flags portrayed a cross over a severed Turkish head.

The war

While the Greeks fought to rid themselves of the Ottomans, their further aims differed widely. Landowners sought to reinforce their traditional privileges; the peasantry saw the struggle as a means towards land redistribution; and westernized Greeks were fighting for a modern nation-state. Remarkably, by the end of **1823** the Greeks appeared to have won their independence. Twice the sultan had sent armies into Greece; twice they had met with defeat. Greek guerrilla leaders, above all **Theodoros Kolokotronis** from the Peloponnese, had gained significant military victories early in the rebellion, which was joined by a thousand or so **European Philhellenes**, almost half of them German, though the most important was the English poet, **Lord Byron**.

But the situation was reversed in 1825, when the Peloponnese was invaded by formidable Egyptian forces loyal to the sultan. Thus far, aid for the Greek struggle had come neither from Orthodox Russia, nor from the Western powers of France and Britain, both wearied by the Napoleonic Wars and suspicious of a potentially anarchic new state. But the death of Lord Byron from a fever while training Greek forces at **Mesolóngi** in 1824 galvanized European public opinion. When Mesolóngi fell to the Ottomans in 1826, Britain, France and Russia finally agreed to seek autonomy for certain parts of Greece, and sent a combined fleet to put pressure on the sultan's army in the Peloponnese and the Turkish-Egyptian fleet harboured in Navaríno Bay. Events took over, and an "accidental" naval battle at **Navaríno** in October 1827 resulted in the destruction of almost the entire Ottoman fleet. The following spring, Russia itself declared war on the Ottomans, and Sultan Mahmud II was forced to accept the existence of an autonomous Greece.

At a series of conferences from 1830 to 1832, **Greek independence** was confirmed by the Western powers, and borders were drawn in 1832. These included just 800,000 of the six million Greeks living within the Ottoman Empire, and territories that were largely the poorest of the classical and Byzantine lands: **Attica**, the **Peloponnese** and the islands of the **Argo-Saronic**, the **Sporades** and the **Cyclades**. The rich agricultural belt of **Thessaly**, **Epirus** in the west and **Macedonia** in the north remained in Ottoman hands, as did the Dodecanese and Crete. Meanwhile after the Napoleonic Wars the **Ionian islands** had passed to British control.

1821	1825	1827	1826–28
Rebellion breaks out in various parts of the empire; much of Greece liberated.	Egyptian armies reconquer most of Greece.	Ottoman fleet destroyed at the Battle of Navaríno, encouraging Great Power intervention.	The first capital of independent Greece is on the island of Égina.

The emerging state: 1832–1939

Modern Greece began as a **republic**, with its first capital on the island of Égina. **Ioannis Kapodistrias**, the first president, a native of Corfu, concentrated his efforts on building a viable central authority. Almost inevitably he was assassinated, and perhaps equally inevitably the "Great Powers" – Britain, France and Germany – stepped in. They created a **monarchy**, setting a Bavarian prince, Otto (Otho), on the throne with a new capital at Athens. By 1834, Greece also had its own national, state-controlled **Orthodox Church**, independent from the Patriarchate in Constantinople; at the same time, two-thirds of the monasteries and convents were closed down.

Despite the granting of a constitution in 1844, **King Otto** proved autocratic and insensitive, filling official posts with fellow Germans and ignoring all claims by the landless peasantry for redistribution of the old estates. When he was forced from the country by a popular revolt in 1862, the Europeans produced a new prince, this time from Denmark. The accession of **George I** (1863–1913) was marked by Britain's decision to hand over the **Ionian islands** to Greece. During his reign, Greece's first roads and railways were built, its borders were extended, and land reform began in the Peloponnese.

The Great Idea and expansionist wars

From the start, Greek foreign policy was motivated by the **Megáli Idhéa** (Great Idea) of redeeming ethnically Greek populations outside the country and incorporating the old territories of Byzantium into the new kingdom. There was encouragement all around, as Ottoman control was under pressure across the Balkans.

In 1881, revolts broke out among the Greeks of **Crete**, **Thessaly** and **Epirus**, aided by guerrillas from Greece. Britain forced the Ottoman Empire to cede Thessaly and Arta to Greece, but Crete remained Ottoman. When Cretan Greeks set up an independent government in 1897, declaring *énosis* (union) with Greece, the Ottomans responded by invading the mainland and came within days of reaching Athens. The Great Powers came to the rescue by warning off the Turks and placing Crete under an international protectorate. Only in 1913 did **Crete** unite with Greece.

It was from Crete, nonetheless, that the most distinguished modern Greek statesman emerged: **Eleftherios Venizelos**, having led a civilian campaign for his island's liberation, was elected as Greek prime minister in 1910. Two years later he organized an alliance of Balkan powers to fight the **Balkan Wars** (1912–13), campaigns that saw the Ottomans virtually driven from Europe, and the Bulgarian competition bested in the culmination of a bitter, four-decade campaign for the hearts and minds of the **Macedonian** population. With Greek borders extended to include the **northeast Aegean islands**, **northern Thessaly**, **central Epirus** and parts of **Macedonia** (though not the Dodecanese, which had been seized by Italy in 1912), the Megáli Idhéa was approaching reality.

World War I

Division, however, appeared with the outbreak of **World War I**. Although Venizelos urged Greek entry on the Allied side, hoping to liberate Greeks in Thrace and Asia Minor, the new king, **Constantine I**, who was married to the German Kaiser's sister, imposed neutrality. Eventually Venizelos set up a revolutionary government in Thessaloníki, polarizing the country into a state of **civil war**. In 1917 Greek troops

1829	1832	1834	1864
Náfplio, on the mainland, becomes the official capital.	Cyclades become part of the new Greek state.	Capital transferred to Athens.	Control of the Ionian islands is granted to the Greek state.

entered the war to join the French, British and Serbians in the Macedonian campaign against Bulgaria and Germany. Upon the capitulation of Bulgaria and the Ottoman Empire, the Greeks occupied **Thrace**, and Venizelos presented demands at Versailles for predominantly Greek **Smyrna** (modern Izmir), on the Asia Minor coast, to become part of the Greek state.

The Katastrofí and its aftermath

The demand for Smyrna triggered one of the most disastrous episodes in modern Greek history, the so-called **Katastrofí** (Catastrophe). Venizelos was authorized to move forces into Smyrna in 1919, but a new Turkish nationalist movement was taking power under Mustafa Kemal, or **Atatürk**. After monarchist factions took over when Venizelos lost elections in 1920, the Allies withdrew support for the venture. Nevertheless the monarchists ordered Greek forces to advance upon Ankara, seeking to bring Atatürk to terms. The Greeks' **Anatolian campaign** ignominiously collapsed in summer 1922 when Turkish troops forced the Greeks back to the coast. As the Greek army hurriedly evacuated from **Smyrna**, the Turks moved in and **massacred** much of the **Armenian and Greek** population before burning most of the city to the ground.

For the Turks, this was the successful conclusion of what they call their War of Independence. The borders of modern Turkey, as they remain today, were established by the **1923 Treaty of Lausanne**, which also provided for the **exchange of religious minorities** in each country – in effect, the first large-scale regulated ethnic cleansing. Turkey was to accept 390,000 Muslims resident on Greek soil. Greece, with a population of under five million, was faced with the resettlement of over **1.3 million Christian refugees** from Asia Minor; significant numbers were settled across Macedonia, western Thrace, Epirus and in Athens, as well as on Límnos, Lésvos, Híos, Sámos, Évvia and Crete.

The Katastrofí had intense and far-reaching consequences. The bulk of the agricultural estates of **Thessaly** were finally redistributed, to Greek tenants and refugee farmers, and huge shanty towns grew into new quarters around **Athens**, **Pireás** and **Thessaloníki**, spurring the country's then almost nonexistent industry. Politically, reaction was even swifter. By September 1922, a group of Venizelist army officers "invited" King Constantine to abdicate and executed six of his ministers held most responsible for the debacle. Democracy was nominally restored with the proclamation of a **republic**, but for much of the next decade changes in government were brought about by factions within the armed forces. Meanwhile, among the urban refugee population, unions were being formed and the **Greek Communist Party (KKE)** was established.

The rise of Metaxás

In 1935 a plebiscite restored the king, **George II**, to the throne, and the next year he appointed **General Ioannis Metaxás** as prime minister. Metaxás had opposed the Anatolian campaign, but had little support in parliament, and when KKE-organized strikes broke out, the king dissolved parliament without setting a date for new elections. This blatantly unconstitutional move opened the way for five years of ruthless and at times absurd **dictatorship**. Metaxás proceeded to set up a state based on the fascist models of the era. Left-wing and trade-union opponents were imprisoned or forced into exile, a state youth movement and secret police were set up, and rigid censorship, extending even to passages of Thucydides, was imposed. But it was at least

1896	1912–13	1923
First modern Olympics are held in Athens.	Balkan Wars extend Greece's borders close to its modern extent; Crete also becomes part of the new nation.	Following a disastrous campaign against Turkey, over one million Christian refugees are resettled in Greece.

GREEK JEWS AND WORLD WAR II

Following the German invasion of Greece, Jews who lived in the Italian zone of occupation were initially no worse off than their fellow Greeks. But after Italy capitulated to the Allies in September 1943 and German troops took over from the Italians, the Jewish communities in Rhodes and Kos in the Dodecanese, as well as in Crete, Corfu, Vólos, Évvia and Zákynthos, were exposed to the full force of Nazi **racial doctrine**. The Germans applied their "final solution" in Greece during the spring and summer of 1944 with the deportation of virtually the entire Jewish population, about 80,000 in all, to extermination camps in Poland.

Greek Christians often went to extraordinary lengths to protect their persecuted countrymen. Thus when the Germans demanded the names of the Jews of Zákynthos prior to a roundup, Archbishop Khrysostomos and Mayor Loukas Karrer presented them with a roster of just two names – their own – and secretly oversaw the smuggling of all the island's 275 Jews to remote farms. Their audacious behaviour paid off, as every Zakynthian Jew survived the war. In Athens, the police chief and the archbishop arranged for false identity cards and baptismal certificates to be issued. Elsewhere, others were warned in good time of what fate the Germans had in store for them, and often took to the hills to join the partisans.

a Greek dictatorship, and while Metaxás was sympathetic to fascist organizational methods and economics, he utterly opposed German or Italian domination.

World War II and civil war: 1939–1950

When World War II broke out, the most immediate threat to Greece was **Italy**, which had invaded Albania in April. Even so, Metaxás hoped Greece could remain neutral, and when the Italians torpedoed the Greek cruiser *Elli* in Tínos harbour on August 15, 1940, they failed to provoke a response. **Mussolini**, however, was determined to have a war with Greece, and after accusing the Greeks of violating the Albanian frontier, he delivered an ultimatum on October 28, 1940, to which Metaxás famously if apocryphally answered "**ohi**" (no). Galvanized by the crisis, the Greeks not only drove the invading Italians out of Greece but managed to gain control over the long-coveted and predominantly Greek-populated area of northern Epirus in southern Albania. ("Ohi Day" is still celebrated as a national holiday.)

Mussolini's failure, however, only provoked Hitler into sending his own troops into Greece, while the British rushed an expeditionary force across the Mediterranean from Egypt. Within days of the **German invasion**, on April 6, 1941, the German army was pouring into central Greece. Outmanoeuvred by the enemy's highly mechanized forces and at the mercy of the Luftwaffe, resistance was soon broken. When the Germans occupied Crete in May, King George and his ministers fled to Egypt and set up a government-in-exile. Metaxás himself had died before the German invasion.

Occupation and resistance

The joint Italian-German-Bulgarian **occupation of Greece** was among the most bitter experiences of the European war. Nearly half a million Greek civilians starved to death over the winter of 1941–42, as all food was requisitioned to feed the occupying armies. In addition, entire villages throughout the mainland, but especially on Crete, were

1924	1935	1936–41	1941
Plebiscite abolishes the monarchy and establishes a republic.	Monarchy restored.	Fascist-style dictatorship of Ioánnis Metaxás.	German invasion rapidly overruns the country; mass starvation in the Greek cities in the winter.

burned at the least hint of resistance and nearly 130,000 civilians were slaughtered up to autumn 1944. In their northern sector, which included Thássos and Samothráki, the Bulgarians demolished ancient sites and churches to support any future bid to annex "Slavic" Macedonia.

No sooner had the Axis powers occupied Greece than a spontaneous resistance movement sprang up in the mountains. The National Popular Liberation Army, known by its initials **ELAS**, founded in September 1941, quickly grew to become the most effective resistance organization, working in tandem with **EAM**, the National Liberation Front. Communists formed the leadership of both organizations, but opposition to the occupation and disenchantment with the prewar political order ensured they won the support of many non-communists. By 1943 ELAS/EAM controlled most areas of the country, working with the British SOE (Special Operations Executive) against the occupiers.

But the Allies were already eyeing the shape of postwar Europe, and British prime minister **Winston Churchill** was determined that Greece should not fall into the communist sphere. Ignoring advice from British agents in Greece that ELAS/EAM were the only effective resistance group, and that the king and his government-in-exile had little support within the country, Churchill ordered that only right-wing groups like **EDES**, the National Republican Greek Army, should receive British money, intelligence and arms. In August 1943 a resistance delegation asked the Greek king, George, in Cairo, for a postwar coalition government in which EAM would hold the ministries of the interior, justice and war, and requested that the king himself not return to Greece without popular consent expressed through a plebiscite. Backed by Churchill, King George flatly rejected their demands.

Liberation and civil war

As the Germans began to withdraw from Greece in September 1944, most of the ELAS/EAM leadership agreed to join an interim government headed by the liberal anti-communist politician **George Papandreou**, and to place its forces under that government's control, which effectively meant under command of the British troops who landed in Greece that October. But many partisans felt they were losing their chance to impose a communist government and refused to lay down their arms. On December 3, 1944 the police fired on an EAM demonstration in Athens, killing at least sixteen. The following day, vicious **street fighting** broke out between members of the Greek Communist Party (KKE) and British troops which lasted throughout the month, until eleven thousand people were killed and large parts of Athens destroyed. In other large towns, ELAS rounded up its most influential and wealthy opponents and marched them out to rural areas in conditions that guaranteed their deaths.

After Papandreou resigned and the king agreed not to return without a plebiscite, a **ceasefire** was signed on February 12, 1945, and a new British-backed government agreed to institute democratic reforms. Many of these were not implemented, however. The army, police and civil service remained in right-wing hands, and while collaborators were often allowed to retain their positions, left-wing sympathizers were excluded. A KKE boycott of elections in March 1946 handed victory to the parties of the right, and a **rigged plebiscite** followed that brought the king back to Greece. Right-wing gangs now roamed the towns and countryside with impunity, and by the

1943	1944–49	1952	1959
Massacre of Italian troops on Kefalloniá by the Germans, following the island's "handover".	German withdrawal is promptly followed by the outbreak of bitter civil war.	New constitution establishes a parliamentary democracy, with king as Head of State.	Cyprus gains independence.

summer of 1946 eighty thousand leftists who had been associated with ELAS had taken to the mountains.

By 1947 guerrilla activity had again reached the scale of a **full civil war**, with ELAS reorganized into the Democratic Army of Greece (DSE). In the interim, King George had died and been succeeded by his brother Paul, while the Americans had taken over the British role and began implementing the Cold War **Truman Doctrine**, in which massive economic and military aid was given to an amenable Greek government. In the mountains American military advisors trained the initially woeful Greek army for campaigns against the DSE, while the cities saw mass arrests, courts martial and imprisonments. From their stronghold on the slopes of Mount Grámmos on the border of Greece and Albania, the partisans waged a losing guerrilla struggle. At the start of 1948 Stalin withdrew Soviet support, and in the autumn of 1949, after Tito closed the Yugoslav border, denying the partisans the last means of outside supplies, the remnants of the DSE retreated into Albania and the KKE admitted defeat by proclaiming a supposedly temporary suspension of the civil war. Also in 1948, the **Dodecanese** islands finally became an official part of the Greek state.

Reconstruction and dictatorship: 1950–74

After a decade of war that had shattered much of Greece's infrastructure (it is said that not one bridge was left standing by 1948), and had killed twelve percent of the 1940 population, it was a demoralized, shattered country that emerged into the Western political orbit of the 1950s. Greece was **American-dominated**, enlisted into the **Korean War** in 1950 and **NATO** not long after. The US embassy – still giving the orders – foisted an electoral system on the Greeks that ensured victory for the right for the next twelve years. Overt leftist activity was banned (though a "cover" party for communists was soon founded), and many of those who were not herded into political "re-education" camps or dispatched by firing squads, legal or vigilante, went into exile throughout Eastern Europe, to return only after 1974. The 1950s also saw the wholesale **depopulation of remote villages** and the virtual emptying of many of the smaller islands as migrants sought work in Australia, America and Western Europe, or the larger Greek cities.

Constantine Karamanlis and Cyprus

The American-backed right-wing **Greek Rally** party, led by **General Papagos**, won the first decisive post-civil-war elections in 1952. After the general's death, the party's leadership was taken over – and to an extent liberalized – by **Constantine Karamanlis**. Under his rule, stability of a kind was established and some economic advances registered, particularly after the revival of Greece's traditional German markets.

The main ongoing crisis in foreign policy was **Cyprus**, where Greek Cypriots demanding *énosis* (union) with Greece waged a long terrorist campaign against the British. Turkey adamantly opposed *énosis* and said that if Britain left Cyprus it should revert to Turkish rule. A 1959 compromise granted independence to the island and protection for its Turkish Cypriot minority but ruled out any union with Greece.

By 1961, unemployment, the Cyprus issue and the presence of US nuclear bases on Greek soil were changing the political climate, and when Karamanlis was again elected there was strong suspicion of intimidation and fraud carried out by right-wing

1964	1964	1967	1973
Release of the film *Zorba the Greek*, shot on Crete; its soundtrack goes on to grace (or blight) every Greek restaurant ever since.	King Constantine II succeeds his father, Paul.	Colonels' coup marks the start of seven years of repressive military rule.	Monarchy abolished and a republic declared.

elements and the army. After eighteen months of strikes and protest demonstrations, Karamanlis resigned and went into voluntary exile in Paris.

George Papandreou and the colonels

New elections in 1964 gave the **Centre Union Party**, headed by **George Papandreou**, an outright majority and a mandate for social and economic reform. The new government was the first to be controlled from outside the right since 1935, and in his first act as prime minister, Papandreou sought to heal the wounds of the civil war by **releasing political prisoners** and allowing exiles to return. When King Paul died in March and his son came to the throne as **Constantine II**, it seemed a new era had begun.

But soon **Cyprus** again took centre stage. Fighting between Turkish and Greek Cypriots broke out in 1963, and only the intervention of the United States in 1964 dissuaded Turkey from invading the island. In the mood of military confrontation between Greece and Turkey – both NATO members – Papandreou questioned Greece's role in the Western alliance, to the alarm of the Americans and the Greek right. When he moved to purge the army of disloyal officers, the army, with the support of the king, resisted.

Amid growing tension, elections were set for May 1967. It was a foregone conclusion that Papandreou's Centre Union Party would win, but **King Constantine**, disturbed by the party's leftward shift, was said to have briefed senior generals for a coup. True or not, the king, like almost everyone else in Greece, was caught by surprise when a group of unknown **colonels** staged their own **coup** on April 21, 1967. In December the king staged a counter-coup against the colonels, and when it failed he went into exile.

The junta announced itself as the "**Revival of Greek Orthodoxy**" against corrupting Western influences, not least long hair and miniskirts. Political activity was banned, independent trade unions were forbidden to recruit or meet, the press was so heavily censored that many papers stopped printing, and thousands of communists and others on the left were arrested, imprisoned and often tortured. Culturally, the colonels put an end to popular music and inflicted ludicrous censorship on literature and the theatre, including a ban on the production of classical tragedies. In 1973, chief colonel **Papadopoulos** abolished the monarchy and declared Greece a republic with himself as president.

Restoration of democracy

The colonels lasted for seven years. Opposition was voiced from the start by exiled Greeks in London, the US and Western Europe, but only in 1973 did demonstrations break out openly in Greece – the colonels' secret police had done too thorough a job of infiltrating domestic resistance groups and terrifying everyone else into docility. After students occupied the **Athens Polytechnic** on **November 17**, the ruling clique sent armoured vehicles to storm the gates. A still-undetermined number of students (estimates range from twenty to three hundred) were killed. Martial law was tightened and Colonel Papadopoulos was replaced by the even more noxious and reactionary **General Ioannides**, head of the secret police.

The end came within a year when the dictatorship embarked on a disastrous adventure in **Cyprus**. By attempting to topple the Makarios government, the junta provoked a **Turkish invasion** and occupation of forty percent of Cypriot territory. The army finally mutinied and **Constantine Karamanlis** was invited to return from Paris to resume office.

1974	1975	1981	1991
Greek-backed attempted coup in Cyprus leads to Turkish invasion and the division of the island.	New constitution provides for parliamentary government with president as Head of State.	Greece joins the EU.	Yugoslav Republic of Macedonia declares independence; Greece objects to use of the name Macedonia.

Karamanlis swiftly negotiated a ceasefire in Cyprus, and in November 1974 he and his **Néa Dhimokratía** (New Democracy) party were rewarded by a sizeable majority in elections. The chief opposition was the new Panhellenic Socialist Movement (PASOK), led by **Andreas Papandreou**, son of George.

Europe and a new Greece: 1974–2000

To Karamanlis's enduring credit, his New Democracy party oversaw an effective return to **democratic stability**, even legalizing the KKE (the Greek Communist Party) for the first time. Karamanlis also held a **referendum on the monarchy**, in which seventy percent of Greeks rejected the return of Constantine II. So a largely symbolic presidency was instituted instead, occupied by Karamanlis from 1980 to 1985, and again from 1990 to 1995. In 1981, Greece joined the **European Community**.

In the same year the socialist party, **PASOK**, and its leader **Andreas Papandreou** swept to power. The new era started with a bang as long overdue **social reforms** were enacted; peasant women were granted pensions; wages were indexed to the cost of living; civil marriage was introduced; family and property law was reformed in favour of wives and mothers; and equal rights legislation was passed. By the time PASOK was returned to power in 1985, it was apparent the promised economic bonanza was not happening: hit by low productivity, lack of investment (not helped by anti-capitalist rhetoric from the government) and world recession, unemployment rose, inflation hit 25 percent and the national debt soared.

In the event it was the European Community, once Papandreou's bête noire, which rescued him, with a huge loan on condition that an austerity programme was maintained. Forced to drop many of his populist policies, the increasingly autocratic Papandreou turned on his former left-wing allies. Combined with the collapse of Soviet rule in Eastern Europe, his own very public affair with an Olympic Airways hostess half his age, and a raft of economic scandals, PASOK's hold on power was not surprisingly, weakened. Since 1989, when New Democracy was elected once more, the two parties have exchanged power on a regular basis.

The 1990s were not easy, with an economy riven by unrest and division, and huge foreign policy headaches caused by the break-up of the former Yugoslavia and the ensuing wars on Greece's borders. Alone among NATO members, Greece was conspicuous for its open support of **Serbia**, ostentatiously supplying trucks to Belgrade via Bulgaria.

By the end of the 1990s, the economy was apparently stabilizing, with inflation consistently in single figures, and in 1997 national morale was further boosted with the award of the 2004 Olympic Games to Athens. In addition, a dramatic and unexpected change in Greece's always distrustful **relations with Turkey** came when a severe **earthquake** struck northern Athens on September 7, 1999, killing scores and rendering almost 100,000 homeless. Coming less than a month after a devastating earthquake in northwest Turkey, it spurred a thaw between the two historical rivals. Greeks donated massive amounts of blood and foodstuffs to the Turkish victims, and were the earliest foreign rescue teams to reach Turkey; in turn they saw Turkish disaster-relief squads among the first on the scene in Athens. Soon afterwards, foreign minister George Papandreou (son of Andreas, later Prime Minister) announced that Greece had dropped its opposition to EU financial aid to Turkey and that Greece would no longer oppose Turkish candidacy for the EU.

1999	2001	2004
Athens earthquake; rapprochement between Greece and Turkey.	Greece adopts the euro, consigning the drachma to history.	Athens Olympics pass off triumphantly and Greece's football team unexpectedly win Euro 2004 in Portugal.

IMMIGRATION – AND THE ALBANIAN INFLUX

Since 1990, **immigrants** to Greece have arrived in numbers estimated at **over a million**, a huge burden for a country of just over ten million citizens, creating a permanent economic underclass. The three largest groups are Albanians, Bulgarians and Romanians, followed by Poles, Pakistanis, Bangladeshis, Syrians, Filipinos, Ukrainians, Russians, Equatorial Africans, Kurds and Georgians. This constitutes a striking change for a traditionally homogeneous and parochial culture, with Athens at least becoming increasingly **multicultural**.

The Greek response has been decidedly mixed. While the Albanians, who make up roughly half the influx, have largely integrated and are not as reviled as they were originally, immigrants in general are blamed for all manner of social ills. For the first time, **crime** – especially burglary – is a significant issue. This has led to the first significant anti-immigration measures – as a member of the Schengen visa scheme, Greece sees itself once more as the first line of defence against the "barbarian hordes". More worryingly, there has been a significant increase in support for the utterly repugnant fascist party Golden Dawn, although their presence is less evident on the islands. However, the Aegean islands in particular do receive boatloads of immigrants and it is not uncommon to see them being transported under police guard on the ferries.

The twenty-first century: boom … and bust?

Greece entered the twenty-first century on a high; entry to the **eurozone** in 2001 was seen as hugely prestigious, while the **2004 Olympic Games** were considered a triumph and national pride was bolstered still further when no-hopers Greece surprisingly won the **Euro 2004 football championships**. EU funds and Olympic investment kick-started widespread infrastructure improvements, and the future seemed rosy. These ostensibly positive developments, however, turned out to be symptomatic of Greece's **problems**. Even at the time of entry to the euro, it was an open secret that the figures had been massaged to ensure Greece met the strict criteria – the extent of that fix only became apparent later. The Olympics had also incurred massive debts and a complete lack of legacy planning has left many venues to rot.

In December 2008, **rioting** broke out in Athens, provoked by the police shooting of a 15-year-old student. The weeks of unrest that followed were the first sign that the wider world had of Greece's deep-rooted troubles and impending **crisis**. When PASOK was returned to power in 2009, now led by **George Papandreou**, the extent of the economic problems began to be fully revealed, with a **national debt** of €262 billion and a deficit running at 12.7 percent of GDP (against a euro limit of 3 percent). As Greece's huge public sector, lax tax collection and allegedly widespread corruption came under scrutiny, government attempts to cut spending and increase revenue ran up against popular opposition and economic downturn.

Following Papandreou's resignation and a brief government of "national unity", a cross-party coalition led by New Democracy chief **Antonis Samaras** came to power after two elections in quick succession in summer 2012. They accepted the terms of fresh **EU bailouts** in exchange for even harsher **austerity measures**, but popular displeasure with continued hardships became evident with the victory of the new radical left party **SYRIZA**, who had come a narrow second in 2012, at the European elections in 2014. Led by charismatic young **Alexis Tsipras**, they oppose all EU-imposed bailout terms and are widely expected to win the next national elections in 2016. Whatever happens, Greece's economic future looks bleak for years to come.

2008	2012	2014
Rioting breaks out in Athens, bringing the country's economic crisis to world attention.	Uneasy New Democracy-led coalition agrees to bailout with imposed austerity measures.	Radical leftist coalition SYRIZA top European elections.

Archeology

Until the second half of the nineteenth century, archeology was a very hit-and-miss, treasure-hunting affair. The early students of antiquity went to Greece to draw and make plaster casts of the great masterpieces of Classical sculpture. Unfortunately, a number soon found it more convenient or more profitable to remove objects wholesale, and might be better described as looters than scholars or archeologists.

Early excavations – and pillaging

The **British Society of Dilettanti** was one of the earliest promoters of Greek culture, financing expeditions to draw and publish antiquities. Founded in the 1730s as a reputedly drunken club for young aristocrats who had completed the Grand Tour and fancied themselves arbiters of taste, its leading spirit was **Sir Francis Dashwood**, a notorious rake who also founded the infamous Hellfire Club. Nevertheless, the society was the first body organized to sponsor systematic research into Greek antiquities, though it was initially most interested in Italy, as Greece was then still a backwater of the Ottoman Empire.

In the 1740s, two young artists, **James Stuart** and **Nicholas Revett**, formed a plan to produce a scholarly record of ancient Greek buildings. With the support of the society they spent three years in Greece, principally in and around Athens, drawing and measuring the antiquities. The publication of their exquisite illustrations and the 1764 publication of **Johann Winckelmann**'s *History of Art*, in which the **Parthenon** and its sculptures were exalted as the eternal standard by which beauty should be measured, gave an enormous boost to the study (and popularity) of Greek sculpture and architecture; many European Neoclassical town and country houses date from this period.

While most of the early excavations were carried out on the mainland, in 1811, a party of English and German travellers, including the architect **C.R. Cockerell**, uncovered the **Temple of Aphaea** on **Égina** and shipped away the pediments. They auctioned off the marbles for £6000 to Prince Ludwig of Bavaria, and, inspired by this success, returned to Greece for further finds. This was a huge sum for the time but their work was also pioneering archeology for the period. Besides, removing the finds was hardly surprising: Greece, after all, was not yet a state and had no public museum; antiquities discovered were sold by their finders – if they recognized their value.

The new nation

The Greek War of Independence (1821–28) and the establishment of a modern Greek nation changed all this. As a result of the selection of Prince Otto of Bavaria as the first king of modern Greece in 1832, the **Germans**, whose education system stressed classical learning, were in the forefront of archeological activity. One dominant Teutonic figure during the early years of the new state was **Ludwig Ross**, who in 1834 began supervising the excavation and restoration of the **Acropolis**. Dismantling the accretion of Byzantine, Frankish and Turkish fortifications, and reconstructing Classical originals, began the following year. The Greeks themselves had begun to focus on their ancient past when the first stirrings of the independence movement were felt. In 1813 the **Philomuse Society** was formed, aiming to uncover and collect antiquities, publish books and assist students and foreign philhellenes. In 1829 an orphanage on the island of Égina became the first **Greek archeological museum**.

In 1837 the **Greek Archeological Society** was founded "for the discovery, recovery and restoration of antiquities in Greece" under the auspices of **Kyriakos Pittakis**, who played a major role in the attempt to convince Greeks of the importance of their heritage at a time when antiquities were still being looted or burned for lime.

The great Germans: Curtius and Schliemann

Although King Otto was deposed in 1862 in favour of a Danish prince, Germans remained in the forefront of Greek archeology in the 1870s. Two men dominated the scene: Heinrich Schliemann and Ernst Curtius.

Curtius was a traditional classical scholar. He had come to Athens originally as tutor to King Otto's family and in 1874 returned to Greece to secure permission to excavate at **Olympia**. He set up a **German Archeological Institute** in Athens and negotiated the **Olympia Convention**, under the terms of which the Germans were to pay for and have total control of the dig; all finds were to remain in Greece, though the excavators could make copies and casts; and all finds were to be published simultaneously in Greek and German.

This was an enormously important agreement, which almost certainly prevented the treasures of Olympia and Mycenae following those of Troy to a German museum. But other Europeans were still in acquisitive mode: **French consuls**, for example, had been instructed to buy any "available" local antiquities in Greece and Asia Minor, and had picked up the Louvre's great treasures from separate islands, the **Venus de Milo** and **Winged Victory of Samothrace**, in 1820 and 1863 respectively.

While Curtius was digging at Olympia, a man who represented everything that was anathema to orthodox classical scholarship was standing archeology on its head. **Heinrich Schliemann**, who had amassed a private fortune through various Midas-like enterprises, had embarked on the **search for Troy** and the vindication of his lifelong belief in the truth of Homer's tales of prehistoric cities and heroes. Schliemann's work, almost all carried out on the Greek and Turkish mainland in the face of continuous academic obstruction, revolutionized archeology and broadened the knowledge of Greek history and civilization by a thousand years. Although some of his results have been shown to have been deliberately falsified in the sacrifice of truth to beauty, his achievement remains enormous.

Evans and Knossos

The early twentieth century saw the domination of Greek archeology by an Englishman, **Sir Arthur Evans**. An egotistical maverick like Schliemann, he too was independently wealthy, with a brilliantly successful career behind him when he started his great work and recovered another millennium for Greek history. Evans excavated what he called the "Palace of Minos" at **Knossós** on **Crete**, discovering one of the oldest and most sophisticated of Mediterranean societies, which he christened Minoan.

The son of a distinguished antiquarian and collector, Evans read history at Oxford and travelled whenever he could. It was in 1893, while in Athens, that his attention was drawn to Crete. In a vendor's stall he came upon some small drilled stones with tiny engravings in a hitherto unknown script; he was told they came from Crete. He had seen Schliemann's finds from Mycenae and had been fascinated by this prehistoric culture. Crete, the crossroads of the Mediterranean, seemed a good place to look for more.

Evans visited Crete in 1894 and headed for the legendary site of Knossós, which had earlier attracted the attention of Schliemann (who had been unable to agree a price with the Turkish owners of the land) and where a Cretan, appropriately called Minos, had already done some impromptu digging, revealing massive walls and a storeroom filled with jars. Evans succeeded in buying the site and in March 1900 began

TOP TEN ARCHEOLOGICAL SITES

In a country with such a wealth of ancient remains as Greece, it's hard to pick out a definitive list of highlights, but here are some of the most famous and unmissable sites on the islands, along with a few of the more obscure but equally worthy ones.

Temple of Aphaea, Égina A wonderfully complete temple, in a hilltop island setting with views of Athens (see p.87).

Delos Guarded by majestic stone lions, the treasury of the Athenian Empire occupied the entire island (see p.147).

Akrotíri, Santoríni Newly re-opened, the remains of the Minoan outpost on Santoríni, long buried under lava, are astonishing, their setting unique (see p.195).

Knossós, Crete The part-reconstructed Minoan palace contains some beautiful ancient frescoes (see p.211).

Festós, Crete The second of the great Minoan palaces, with fewer crowds and glorious views (see p.215).

Líndhos, Rhodes The splendid ancient acropolis contains remains from prehistoric to medieval times (see p.278).

Sanctuary of the Great Gods, Samothráki An idyllically located site that was a major centre of an ancient mystery cult (see p.411).

Ancient Thassos, Thássos The lush agora in the modern town centre is overlooked by various temples on the hill behind (see p.416).

Palamári, Skýros If only as evidence that new discoveries can still be made, Palamári, a fortified Bronze Age settlement at the heart of the Aegean, is extraordinary (see p.447).

Paleopolis, Corfu Relatively few people visit this scattering of temples and basilicas in the suburbs of Corfu Town (see p.468).

excavations. Within a few days, evidence of a great complex building was revealed, along with artefacts that indicated an astonishing cultural sophistication. The huge team of diggers unearthed elegant courtyards and verandas, colourful wall-paintings, pottery, jewellery and sealstones – the wealth of a civilization which dominated the eastern Mediterranean 4000 years ago.

Evans continued to excavate at Knossós for the next thirty years, during which time he established, on the basis of changes in the pottery styles, the **system of dating** that remains in use today for classifying **Greek prehistory**: Early, Middle and Late Minoan (Mycenaean on the mainland). Like Schliemann, Evans attracted criticism and controversy for his methods – most notably his decision speculatively to reconstruct parts of the palace in reinforced concrete – and for many of his interpretations. Nevertheless, his discoveries and his dedication put him near the pinnacle of Greek archeology.

Into the twentieth century: the foreign institutes

In 1924 Evans gave the **British School at Athens** the site of **Knossós** along with his on-site residence, the Villa Ariadne, and all other lands within his possession on Crete (it was only in 1952 that Knossós became the property of the Greek state). At the time the British School was one of several foreign archeological institutes in Greece; founded in 1886, it had been preceded by the **French School**, the **German Institute** and the **American School**.

Greek archeology owes much to the work and relative wealth of these foreign schools and others that would follow. They have been responsible for the excavation of many of the most famous sites in Greece: the **Heraion** on **Sámos** (German); the sacred island of **Delos** (French); sites on **Kos** (Italian) and in central **Crete** (Italian, American, British); and **Samothráki** (American), to name but a few.

The years between the two world wars saw an expansion of excavation and scholarship, most markedly concerning the prehistoric civilizations. Having been shown by Schliemann and Evans what to look for, a new generation of archeologists was uncovering numerous **prehistoric sites** on the mainland and Crete, and its members were spending proportionately more time studying and interpreting their finds.

One of the giants of this era was **Alan Wace** who, while director of the British School at Athens from 1913 to 1923, conducted excavations at **Mycenae** and proposed a new chronology for prehistoric Greece, which put him in direct conflict with Arthur Evans. Evans believed that the mainland citadels had been ruled by Cretan overlords, whereas Wace was convinced of an independent Mycenaean cultural and political development. Wace was finally vindicated after Evans's death, when in the 1950s it emerged that Mycenaean Greeks had conquered the Minoans in approximately 1450 BC.

Classical archeology was not forgotten in the flush of excitement over the Mycenaeans and Minoans. The period between the wars saw the continuation of excavation at most established sites, and many new discoveries, among them the sanctuary of **Asklepios** and its elegant Roman buildings on **Kos**, excavated by the Italians from 1935 to 1943.

More recent excavations

A number of postwar excavations were as exciting as any in the past. In 1961 the fourth great **Minoan palace** (following the unearthing of Knossós, Festós and Mália) was uncovered by torrential rains at the extreme eastern tip of the island of Crete at **Káto Zákros** and cleared by Cretan archeologist **Nikolaos Platon**. Its harbour is now thought to have been the Minoans' main gateway port to and from southwest Asia and Africa, and many of the artefacts discovered in the palace storerooms – bronze ingots from Cyprus, elephants' tusks from Syria, stone vases from Egypt – seem to confirm this. Greek teams have found more Minoan palaces at **Arhánes** and **Galatás**, and possibly at **Haniá** in the west and **Petrás** and **Palékastro** in the east of the island. Challenging previous orthodoxy, many of the next generation of scholars believed that these were ceremonial buildings and not the seats of dynastic authority, as Evans proposed. American excavations at **Kommós**, in southern Crete, have uncovered another gateway site with an important harbour of the Minoan and Mycenaean periods.

At **Akrotíri** on the island of **Santoríni** (Thíra), **Spyros Marinatos** revealed, in 1967, a Minoan-era site that had been buried by volcanic explosion sometime between 1650 and 1550 BC – scientists (using carbon dating evidence) and archeologists (relying on dating of discovered artefacts) are still deliberating its exact date. Its buildings were two or three storeys high, and superbly frescoed. Marinatos was later tragically killed while at work on the site when he fell off a wall, and is now buried there.

As of the beginning of this century, the various foreign schools are still at work in the field, recently joined by the Australian, Austrian, Belgian, Canadian, Danish, Dutch, Finnish, Georgian, Irish, Norwegian, Spanish, Swedish and Swiss, along with Greek universities and the 25 *ephorates*, or inspectorates, of Prehistoric and Classical Antiquities. The emphasis today, however, is as concerned with **conserving and protecting** what has been revealed as unearthing new finds. All too often newly discovered sites have been inadequately fenced off or protected, and a combination of the elements, greedy developers and malicious trespassers – sometimes all three – has caused much damage and deterioration. On a happier note, unexpected new discoveries are still being made, such as the Bronze Age fortified port of **Palamári** (see p.447) on **Skýros**.

Wildlife

For anyone who has seen Greece only at the height of summer with its brown parched hillsides and desert-like ambience, the richness of the wildlife – in particular the flora – may come as a surprise. As winter warms into spring, the countryside transforms itself from green to a mosaic of coloured flowers, which attract a plethora of insect life, followed by birds. Isolated islands and remote areas like Crete's White Mountains have had many thousands of years to develop their own individual species. Overall, Greece has around six thousand species of native flowering plants – nearly four times that of Britain, over the same land area. Many are unique to Greece, and make up about a third of Europe's endemic plants.

Plants

Whereas in temperate northern Europe plants flower from spring until autumn, the arid summers of Greece confine the main **flowering period** to the spring, before temperatures become too high and groundwater scarce. In Rhodes and eastern Crete, spring arrives in early March, and then travels progressively westwards and northwards. Rhodes and Kárpathos are at their best in March, western Crete in early April, the eastern Aegean mid- to late April, and the Ionian islands in early May, though a cold dry winter can cause several weeks' delay. In the high mountains the floral spring arrives in the chronological summer, with the alpine zones of central and western Crete in full flower in June and July.

The delicate flowers of early spring – orchids, fritillaries, anemones, cyclamen, tulips and small bulbs – are replaced as the season progresses by more robust shrubs, tall perennials and abundant annuals, but many of these close down completely for the fierce **summer**. A few tough plants, like shrubby thyme and savory, continue to flower through the heat and act as magnets for butterflies.

Once the worst heat is over, and the first showers of **autumn** arrive, so does a second "spring", on a much smaller scale but no less welcome after the brown drabness of summer. Squills, autumn cyclamen, crocus and other small bulbs all come into bloom, while the seeds start to germinate for the following year's crop of annuals. By the new year, early spring bulbs and orchids start to flower in the south.

Coastal species

Plants on the **beach** grow in a difficult environment: fresh water is scarce, salt is in excess, and dehydrating winds are often very strong. Feathery **tamarisk** trees are adept at surviving this habitat, and consequently are often planted to provide shade. On hot days or nights you may see or feel them sweating away surplus saltwater from their foliage.

THE FIRST NATURALISTS

Despite an often negative attitude to wildlife, Greece was probably the first place in the world where it was an object of study. **Theophrastos** (372–287 BC) from Lésvos was the first recorded botanist and a systematic collector of general information on plants, while his contemporary, **Aristotle**, studied the animal world. During the first century AD the distinguished physician **Dioscorides** compiled a herbal study that remained a standard work for over a thousand years.

TOURISM AND THREATS TO WILDLIFE

Since the 1970s, tourist developments have ribboned along island **coastlines**, sweeping away both agricultural plots and wildlife havens as they do so. These expanding resorts increase local employment, often attracting inland workers to the coast; the generation that would once have herded sheep on remote hillsides now works in tourist bars and tavernas. Consequently, the pressure of domestic animal grazing, particularly in the larger islands, has been significantly reduced, allowing the regeneration of tree seedlings; Crete, for example, has more woodland now than at any time in the last five centuries. However, **forest fires** remain a threat everywhere; the trees may well regenerate eventually, but by then the complex shade-dependent ecology is irrecoverably lost.

Meadow and hill plants

Arable fields can be rich with colourful weeds, and small, unploughed **meadows** may be equally colourful, with slower-growing plants such as orchids in extraordinary quantities. The rocky earth makes cultivation on some hillsides difficult and impractical, so agriculture is often abandoned and areas regenerate to a rich mixture of shrubs and perennials – known as **garigue**. With time, a few good wet winters and in the absence of grazing, some shrubs will develop into small trees, intermixed with tough climbers – the much denser **maquis** vegetation. The colour yellow often predominates in early spring, followed by the blues, pinks and purples of bee-pollinated plants. An abundance of the pink and white of *Cistus* rockroses is usually indicative of an earlier fire, since they are primary recolonizers. A third vegetation type is **phrygana** – smaller, frequently aromatic or spiny shrubs, often with a narrow strip of bare ground between each hedgehog-like bush. Many aromatic herbs such as lavender, rosemary, savory, sage and thyme are native to these areas.

Orchids

Nearly 140 species of **orchid** are believed to occur in the Greek islands; their complexity blurs species' boundaries and keeps botanists in a state of taxonomic flux. In particular, the *Ophrys* bee and spider orchids have adapted themselves, through subtleties of lip colour and false scents, to seduce small male wasps. These insects mistake the flowers for a potential mate, and unintentionally assist the plant's pollination. Though all species are officially protected, many are still picked.

Mountains and gorge plants

The **limestone peaks** of islands such as Corfu, Kefaloniá, Crete, Rhodes, Sámos and Thássos hold rich collections of attractive **rock plants**, flowers whose nearest relatives may be from the Balkan Alps or the Turkish mountains. **Gorges** are another spectacular habitat, particularly rich in Crete. Their inaccessible cliffs act as refuges for plants that cannot survive the grazing, competition or more extreme climates of open areas. Many of Greece's endemic plants are confined to cliffs, gorges or mountains.

Birds

Migratory species that have wintered in East Africa move north, through the eastern Mediterranean, from around **mid-March to mid-May**. Some stop in Greece to breed; others move on into the rest of Europe. The southern islands are the first landfall after a long sea crossing, and smaller birds recuperate for a few days before moving on. Larger birds such as storks and ibis often fly very high, and binoculars are needed to spot them as they pass over. In autumn birds return, but usually in more scattered numbers.

Larger raptors occur in remoter areas, preferring mountain gorges and cliffs. Buzzards are the most abundant, and often mistaken by optimistic birdwatchers for the rarer, shyer eagles. Griffon vultures, however, are quite unmistakeable, soaring on broad,

TOP FIVE WILDLIFE SPOTS

Samariá Gorge Crete's most famous ravine hides some of Greece's rarest plants, though other nearby gorges feel far wilder. See p.253

Petaloúdhes, Rhodes A delightful canyon here is home to thousands of tiger moths during summer. See p.283

Korissíon Lagoon, Corfu This serene patch of water bordered by sand dunes hosts various waterfowl. See p.479

Mount Énos, Kefaloniá The highest point in the Ionians is home to much flora, including its own species of fir. See p.496

Laganás Bay, Zákynthos Though much of it is touristic, this bay is still a prime breeding ground for the loggerhead turtle. See p.510

straight-edged wings, whereas the lammergeier (bearded vulture) is a state-of-the-art flying machine with narrower, swept wings, seen over mountaintops by the lucky few; the remaining nine or ten pairs in Crete are now the Balkan's largest breeding population.

In areas of **wetland** that remain undrained and undisturbed, such as salt marshes, coastal lagoons, estuaries and freshwater ponds, ospreys, egrets, ibis, spoonbills, storks, pelicans and many waders can be seen feeding. Flamingos sometimes occur, as lone individuals or small flocks, particularly in the eastern Aegean saltpans between December and May.

Mammals

The islands' small **mammal** population ranges from rodents and shrews to hedgehogs and hares, and the dark-red Persian squirrel on Lésvos. Medium-sized mammals include badgers, foxes and the persecuted golden jackal, but the commonest is the ferret-like stone (or beech) marten, named for its habit of decorating stones with its droppings to mark territory.

Occasionally seen running wild in Crete's White Mountains, but more often as a zoo attraction, is an endemic ibex, known as the *agrími* or *krí-krí*. Formerly in danger of extinction, a colony of them was established on the offshore islet of Dhía, where they thrived, exterminating the rare local flora.

Marine mammals include dolphins, spotted as you travel between islands; monk seals, especially around Alónissos; and even whales in the waters off southwest Crete.

Reptiles and amphibians

Reptiles, the commonest of which are **lizards**, flourish in the hot dry summers of Greece. Most of these are small, agile and wary, rarely staying around for closer inspection. Nocturnal **geckos** are large-eyed, short-tailed lizards. Their spreading toes have claws and ingenious adhesive pads, allowing them to cross house walls and ceilings in their search for insects, including mosquitoes. The rare **chameleon** is a swivel-eyed inhabitant of eastern Crete and some eastern Aegean islands such as Sámos, though its ability to blend into its surroundings makes it exceptionally hard to spot.

Once collected for the pet trade, **tortoises** can be found on some islands; usually their noisy progress through hillside scrub vegetation is the first signal of their presence, as they spend their often long lives grazing the vegetation. Closely related **terrapins** are more streamlined, freshwater tortoises which love to bask on waterside mud by streams or ponds. Usually seen only as they disappear under water, their numbers have recently declined steeply on many islands.

Sea turtles occur mostly in the Ionian Sea, but can be seen in the Aegean too. The least rare are the loggerhead turtles (*Caretta caretta*), which nest on Zákynthos and Kefaloniá, and occasionally in Crete. Their nesting grounds are disappearing under tourist resorts, although they are a protected endangered species (see box, p.509).

By contrast, **snakes** are abundant in Greece and many islands; most are shy and non-venomous. Several species, including the Ottoman viper, the nose-horned viper and the localized Cycladic lebetina viper, do have a venomous bite, though they are not usually aggressive; they are adder-like and often have a very distinct, dark zigzag stripe down the back. Leave snakes alone, and they will do the same for you, but if bitten, seek immediate treatment. Most are not only completely harmless to humans, but beneficial since they keep down populations of pests such as rats and mice.

Frogs and toads are the commonest and most obvious amphibians, particularly during the spring breeding season. Frogs prefer the wettest places, and the robust marsh frog revels in artificial water-storage ponds, whose concrete sides magnify their croaking impressively. Tree frogs are tiny emerald green jewels, with huge and strident voices at night, and can sometimes be found in quantity on the leaves of waterside oleanders.

Insects

Greece teems with insects: some pester, like flies and mosquitoes, but most are harmless to humans. From spring through to autumn, the islands are full of **butterflies**. Swallowtail species are named for the drawn-out corners of the hindwings, in shades of cream and yellow, with black and blue markings. The unrelated, robust brown-and-orange pasha is Europe's largest butterfly. Tiger moths, with their black-and-white forewings and startling bright orange hindwings, are the "butterflies" occurring in huge quantity in sheltered sites of islands such as Rhodes, Níssyros and Páros.

Other insects include the camouflaged **praying mantis**, whose powerful forelegs are held in a position of supplication until another insect comes within reach. The females are notorious for eating the males during mating. Corfu is famous for its extraordinary **fireflies**, which flutter in quantities across meadows and marshes on May nights, speckling the darkness with bursts of cold light to attract partners; look carefully in nearby hedges, and you may spot the less flashy, more sedentary and more widespread glow-worm.

FLORA AND FAUNA FIELD GUIDES

FLOWERS

Christopher Grey-Wilson and Marjorie Blamey *Wild Flowers of the Mediterranean.* Comprehensive field guide, with coloured drawings; recent and taxonomically reasonably up to date.

John Fielding and Nicholas Turland *Flowers of Crete.* Coffee-table volume with 1900 coloured photos of the Cretan flora, much of which is also widespread in Greece.

Karl Peter Buttler *Orchids of Britain and Europe.* A comprehensive, though now rather dated guide, published in 1991. Pierre Delforge's Collins guide, with the same title, was more up to date, but is now out of print.

BIRDS

George Handrinos and T. Akriotis *The Birds of Greece (o/p).* A comprehensive guide that includes island birdlife.

Lars Jonsson et al *Collins Bird Guide.* The ornithologist's choice for the best coverage of Greek birds (it covers the whole of Europe), with excellent descriptions and illustrations.

MAMMALS

MacDonald and Barrett *Mammals of Britain and Europe (o/p).* The best field guide on its subject, sadly now hard to find.

REPTILES

Arnold, Burton and Ovenden *Reptiles and Amphibians of Britain and Europe.* An excellent guide, though it excludes the Dodecanese and east Aegean islands.

INSECTS

Michael Chinery *Insects of Britain and Western Europe.* Although Greece is outside the geographical scope of the guide, it provides generic identifications for many of the insects you might see there.

Tom Tolman and Richard Lewington *Collins Butterfly Guide.* A thorough and detailed field guide that illustrates most of the species seen in Greece.

MARINE LIFE

W. Luther and K. Fiedler *Field Guide to the Mediterranean Sea Shore (o/p).* Very thorough, if now very old; includes most Greek shallow-water species.

Music

Music is ubiquitous in modern Greek culture; even the most indifferent visitor can't fail to notice it in tavernas and other public spaces. Like so many aspects of the country, it amalgamates "native" and eastern styles, with occasional contributions from points west, and flourishes alongside and often in preference to Western pop. Music and dance form an integral part of weddings, betrothals, baptisms, elections, saints' days and name-days.

Don't be shy about asking people where you can hear *ta paradhosiaká* (traditional music); a few words of Greek go a long way towards inclining locals to help foreign travellers. Learn the Greek names of the instruments you would like to hear, or find someone to translate for you. Once it's clear that you're a budding *meraklís* (untranslatable, but roughly, aficionado), people will be flattered by the respect paid to "real" music, and doors will open for you.

Island styles

Island musical **traditions** are wonderfully **diverse**, so only a general overview will be attempted here. Each archipelago has its dances, songs and customs which vary between islands and even between towns on the same island. Different dances go by the same name from place to place, while different lyrics are set to many of the same melodies and vice versa. The same tune can be played so idiosyncratically between neighbouring island groups as to be barely recognizable to an outsider. Compared to Western styles, Aegean music is more circuitous than linear, as would be expected from its Byzantine origins and later Ottoman influences. Although transcriptions exist, and there are some who teach with written notes, most folk pieces are learned by ear.

Traditional island folk songs – *nisiótika* – feature melodies which, like much folk music the world over, rely heavily on the pentatonic scale. Lyrics, especially on smaller islands, touch on the perils of the sea, exile and (in a society where long separations and arranged marriages were the norm) thwarted love. In Crete, **rhyming couplets** called *mantinádhes* are sung in alternation with instrumental interludes; similar satirical couplets are found in the Dodecanese (such as *pismatiká* on Kálymnos), while on Náxos such couplets are called *kotsákia*, and the short repeating melody to which they are set is called a *kotsátos*. Singers improvise such rhymed couplets on the spot, thinking up new lines during the short instrumental breaks and coming in again when ready with new lines. These often tease the wedding couple, praise the in-laws, lament the

---

WEDDINGS AND RELIGIOUS MUSIC

Many pieces, which vary from island to island, are specifically associated with **weddings**. Some are processional songs/tunes (*patinádhes*), sung/played while going to fetch the bride from her home, or as the wedding couple leave the church, plus there are specific dances associated with different stages of the wedding ritual. It was common in the past for the music and dancing that followed a wedding to last for up to three days – nowadays overnight into the next day is more common. Some songs are heard only at **Carnival time**, accompanied by the wearing of animal skins or costumes and, in places such as Skýros, by the shaking of large goat bells roped together. Such rituals, widespread across Europe, date back to pre-Christian times. Music also accompanies informal, unpublicized **private gatherings** in homes, *kafenía* and tavernas with facilities for musicians and patrons.

loss of a community member or chide a politician. There are also "set" couplets, sometimes mixed in with newly improvised material.

The **Sporades** – linked in many cultural ways to the Magnesian peninsula opposite – never had a *nisiótika* tradition, according to Yiorgos Xintaris, owner/main soloist of a successful rembétika (urban underground music) ouzerí on Skópelos. The soundtrack of his mid-twentieth-century youth was not only rembétika but *laïká* (popular songs), operatic arias and tangos.

Alone of all modern Greek territory, the **Ionian islands** were never occupied by the Ottomans, but instead by the Venetians, and thus have a predominantly Western musical tradition. The indigenous song form is both Italianate in names (*kantádhes, ariétes, arékia*), instrumentation (guitar and mandolin – as in Captain Corelli's) and vocals (harmonized choir). Style and nomenclature differ subtly between the various islands: the equivalent of *ariétes* on Kefaloniá is known as *arékia* on Zákynthos. All of the Ionians, especially Corfu, have a tradition of formal musical instruction and excellence.

The **rizítika** of Crete, slow elegies for historic events and personages with a bare minimum of instrumentation, are confined to the foothill villages of the Lefká Óri (White Mountains); over six hundred bodies of lyrics have been collected, but it's claimed that there are only 34 distinct melodies. Also Cretan are *tragoúdhia tís strátas* or travelling songs, sung a capella in pre-motor-car days to ease the boredom of long journeys between villages.

Many songs (except for the slow table songs, or *epitrapézia*, of which Cretan *rizítika* are a type) are in **dance rhythm**, with a vital interaction between dancers and musicians/singers. Dancers and listeners may also join in the song (solo or as a chorus), or even initiate verses. It is customary for the lead dancer to tip the musicians, often requesting a particular tune and/or dance rhythm for his party to dance to. Fairly similar dances for couples are called *soústa* in Crete but *bállos* across the rest of the Aegean. The *pendozális* of Crete ("five-step", *zála* being Cretan dialect for step) is an easy, slow-starting dance for all abilities, though the *pidhiktós* "jumping" dance requires more acrobatic ability.

The instruments

The violin (**violí** in Greek) supposedly appeared in Greece during the seventeenth century, migrating from Western Europe (followed some decades later by the clarinet, which feature mainly in mainland Greek music). Although the violin is also played on the Greek mainland, it is the principal melody instrument of the Aegean islands, with the striking exceptions of Crete, Kárpathos, Kássos and Hálki in the southern Aegean, where two kinds of *lýra* prevail (see p.556). The violin bridge may be sanded in Greece to a less highly arched form than that used for Western classical music (this is also done in Western folk traditions). An alternative **tuning** known as "*álla Toúrka*", more widespread in the past, is still used by some musicians on certain islands (eg Sífnos, Kýthnos and Kos). From high to low, its string values are D, A, D and G, with a fourth between the two higher-pitched strings instead of the typical all-fifths arrangement. The lowered high string is slacker and "sweeter", and the violin's tonality altered by the modified tuning.

Playing **styles** vary widely within island groups, or even between villages, but Greek violin technique differs radically from both classical and Western folk styles. Modes (related to both the Byzantine and Ottoman musical systems) are used rather than Western scales, there's a range of ornamentation techniques, and, in some places, unmetered solos (called *taxímia*) based upon the mode of the melody and subject to modulation into other modes. Idiosyncratic violin styles are still found on Sífnos or Kýthnos in the Cyclades, and on Kálymnos or Kos in the Dodecanese, with a few of the finest old-style performers only fairly recently deceased (eg Andonis Xanthakis and Andonis Mougadhis Komis in Sífnos). Bowing patterns in these places can be swift and angular, resulting in a more "fiddle"-like sound than styles that rely on smoother, longer bow-strokes.

The **laoúto** is a member of a family of instruments generally referred to as long-necked lutes. It has a fat, gourd-like back like the oud (*oúti* in Greek, *al-ud* in Arabic) from which the *laoúto* (and lute) derives its name and basic form, but a long fretted neck (the oud has a short, unfretted one) and four sets of double metal strings (the oud has gut ones). The Greek *laoúto* is tuned in fifths (C, G, D, A from lowest to highest), but the G actually has the lowest pitch, since the C is anomalously tuned a fourth higher than the G. On Sífnos and Kýthnos the heavier of the lowest-pitched doublet is removed to accentuate the treble, and make the *laoúto*'s sound less "thunderous".

In most of the Aegean, the *laoúto* is played with the *violí* or *lýra* and sometimes also with the island bagpipe, the *tsamboúna* (see below). Typical duos are *violí/laoúto* in the Cyclades or *lýra/laoúto* in Crete and the Dodecanese. In north Aegean islands (such as Lésvos and Samothráki) the *laoúto* may be played with violin and *sandoúri* or even in large ensembles which include brass instruments and accordion. In the hands of a competent player, the *laoúto* doesn't merely "accompany" a *violí* or *lýra*, but forms part of a true duo by virtue of well-chosen rhythmic patterns and melodic phrases in chime-like tones.

The **sandoúri** is a member of the zither family, resembling the hammered dulcimer and played with the *violí* (or *violí* plus *laoúto*) in many of the Dodecanese and also the northeast Aegean islands, where it may also appear in much larger ensembles. It entered these island groups from nearby Asia Minor, especially after 1923 when it was (re)introduced by refugees, especially on Lésvos. The *sandoúri* plays both chords and melody, as well as introductory *taxímia*. While at times only basic chords are played to complement the violin, it can fill in with arpeggios, scale runs or melodic tags, and occasionally serves as a solo instrument, especially on Lésvos.

The term **lýra** refers to a family of small, pear- or bottle-shaped instruments which are held upright on the player's thigh with strings facing forward and bowed with the palm facing away from the body. Greek-island types are pear-shaped and have three metal strings, with notes played by pressing the fingernails laterally against the strings. The **Dodecanesian lýra** has a loose bow which can touch all three gut strings (the middle one a drone) simultaneously, making double chords possible; the bow in some cases has little bells on it which provide rhythmic accompaniment. Its tonal range matches that of the *tsamboúna* played in the Dodecanese and can be played alone, with *laoúto*, with *tsamboúna*, or both of these together, often accompanying vocalists. The **Cretan lýra** is a relatively modern instrument, having supplanted the Dodecanesian type which was used on Crete before the 1930s. The contemporary *lýra* is larger and fatter, lacks a drone string and is tuned lower and in successive fifths, thus extending the melodic range by a fifth beyond that of the older instrument. A fingerboard was added to make fingering easier, as well as a longer, narrow neck, and a modern violin bow replaced the older, more convex bow. Yet despite all these violin-like innovations, the *lýra* retains a very different tonal quality; even a skilled violinist can never entirely imitate its sound.

The **tsamboúna** (in Crete, *askomandoúra*) is a Greek-island bagpipe made of goatskin, with no drone and a double chanter made of calamus reed. The left side of the chanter never varies, having five holes which allow an incomplete diatonic scale from "do" to "fa". The right chanter is of three types, with anywhere from two to five holes depending on the locale. In the Dodecanese this bagpipe may be played alone, with another *tsamboúna*, or with a *laoúto* and *lýra*; many songs are accompanied by these various combinations. In the Cyclades (and formerly Híos) the *tsamboúna* is (or was) played with a **toumbáki** or two-headed drum, only one side of which is struck with two wooden (or bone) drumsticks. It is suspended to one side of the player's torso by a strap. The *tsamboúna* and *toumbáki* are quintessential shepherds' instruments, their skins taken from their flocks. Along with the *lýra*, they are the oldest of the instruments played on the islands, though rare now except in some of the places mentioned above. On Náxos the *tsamboúna-toumbáki* duo is still heard during the pre-Lenten Carnival.

Accordion, clarinet, guitar and *bouzoúki*, all **imported** from the Greek mainland or urban traditions, are sometimes played along with the more traditional instruments on the islands.

Discography

The following CDs are among the best available for the island genres detailed above: ★ denotes a particularly strong recommendation. Unless otherwise specified, all are Greek pressings. Athens has numerous good Greek CD stores. Online, you'll find some of our choices at Amazon, but far more at Thessaloníki-based Studio 52 (ⓦwww .studio52.gr), which operates a worldwide online order service, and at Athens-based Xylouris (ⓦxilouris.gr).

COLLECTIONS

★**Avthentika Nisiotika tou Peninda** (Lyra CD 0168). Good Cretan and Dodecanesian material recorded during the 1950s, from the collection of the late Ted Petrides, musician and dance master.

Ellines Akrites (FM Records). FM's folk pressings are generally to be approached with caution, but Vol. 1 of this 12-CD series (FM 801, "Híos, Mytilíni, Sámos, Ikaría"), Vol. 2 (FM 802, "Límnos, Samothráki, Ímvros, Ténedhos") and Vol. 9 ("Pátmos, Kálymnos, Léros, Kos, Astypálea") feature excellent local musicians (*violí/lýra*) and singers such as Stratis Rallis of Lésvos, as well as violinist Kyriakos Gouvendas of Thessaloníki and the late Gavriel Yiallizis of Kos.

Kalimera Theia – Samothrakiki Skopi ke Tragoudia/Good Morning Auntie – Tunes and Songs of Samothraki (Arheio Ellinikis Musikis-AEM 014). The local repertoire from this north Aegean island, as well as pieces from neighbouring islands and Asia Minor.

★**Tis Kritis ta Polytima** (MBI 7056). Double box-set showcasing the best Cretan talent since the 1980s by Lyra/MBI artists, all the more valuable given that many of the source discs are now out of circulation. Mostly big names whom you're likely to see in concert: Vasilis Skhoulas, Yiorgo Xylouris, Lizeta Kalimeri, Psarantonis. Avoid the inferior single-disc offering.

Tis Lerou ta Tragoudhia/Songs of Leros (Politistikós ké Morfotikós Sýllogos Néon Lérou/Instructive & Cultural Lerian Youth Society), double CD produced by Music Folklore Archive. Live field recordings from 1996–98 of Lerian musicians and singers; *violí*, *sandoúri*, *laoúto* and bagpipes in various combinations, plus unaccompanied singing.

★**Lesvos Aiolis: Tragoudhia ke Hori tis Lesvou/ Songs & Dances of Lesvos** (Panepistimiakés Ekdhóseis Krítis/University Press of Crete, double CD 9/10). Two decades (1974–96) of field recordings of this island's last traditional music, a labour of love supervised by musicologist Nikos Dhionysopoulos. Expensive, but the quality and uniqueness of the instrumental festival tunes and dances especially, and the illustrated booklet, merit the expense (typically around €30).

Lesvos: Mousika Stavrodhromia sto Egeo/Musical Crossroads of the Aegean (University of the Aegean). Pricey five-CD set with an accompanying fat, illustrated booklet. Everything from originally Asia Minor music to carols and wedding songs.

★**Iy Protomastores, 1920–1955** (Aerakis; 10-CD set). Some of the artists on this massive retrospective of early Cretan recordings are a bit arcane, but the following four standout discs justify the price tag: Disc 1, Baxevanis, on *lýra* with small orchestra; Disc 4, Stelios Fousalieris, last master of the *voúlgari*, knowledge of which died with him; Disc 5, Yiannis Demirtzoyiannis, guitarist and epic singer; and Disc 6, Yiorgis Kousourelis, melodic *laoúto*.

Samos: Iy Musiki Mas Paradhosi, Tragoudhi kai Skopi tis Samou (Culture Music CM 117). Superb archival material collected by Dhinitris Zahariou, that takes you way beyond the hackneyed island standard "Samiotissa".

Skopi tis Kalymnou/Kalymnian Folk Music (Lýkio tón Ellinídhon E2-276-97). Double CD with excellent notes and song translations. Traditional Kalymnian repertoire and native musicians featuring Mikes Tsounias on violin, his grandson playing unison violin on some pieces, plus *tsamboúna* accompaniment.

Songs of… (Society for the Dissemination of National Music, Greece). A thirty-disc-plus series of field recordings from the 1950s–70s, each covering traditional music of one region or type. Lyrics in English, all available in CD form, especially at the Museum of Greek Popular Instruments in Athens. The best island discs, besides *Amorgos, Kythnos and Sifnos* (SDNM105), are:

Songs of Kassos and Karpathos (SDNM 103). The Kárpathos side is unremittingly poignant (or monotonous, depending on your tastes), enlivened by passages on the *tsamboúna*. You'll still hear material like this at Ólymbos festivals. The Kássos side is more sweetly melodic, closer to Crete musically and geographically.

Songs of Rhodes, Chalki and Symi (SDNM 104). The pieces from Sými are the most accessible, while those from Rhodes and Hálki show Cretan influence. All material was recorded in the early 1970s; you're unlikely to hear similar pieces today, though Sými retains the instrumentation (*violí*, *sandoúri*) heard here.

★**Songs of Mytilene and Chios** (SDNM 110), **Songs of Mytilene and Asia Minor** (SDNM 125). The Mytilene (Lésvos) sides are the highlight of each of these discs, including sublime instrumental and vocal pieces from the mid-1970s. Most selections are from the south of the island, particularly Ayiássos, where a tradition of live festival music was – and still is – strong.

Songs of Ikaria & Samos (SDNM 128). Much older material, from the 1950s; even then it was obvious that indigenous styles were dying out, as there is extensive reliance on cover versions of songs common to all the east Aegean and Anatolian refugee communities, and the music – mostly choral with string accompaniment – is executed by the SDNM house band of the time, directed by Simon Karas. The Ikarian side is more distinctive, though marred by an irritating voice-over.

Songs of the North and East Aegean (SDNM CD7). Features music of Límnos, Thássos, Samothráki, Lésvos and Híos including local dances (*pyrgoúsikos*, *kehayiádhikos*) using local musicians recorded during the early 1970s.

★**Thalassa Thymisou/Sea of Memories: Tragoudhia ke Skopi apo tis Inousses** (Navtikó Mousío Inoussón-En Khordais CD 1801/1802). The result of a "field trip" by the En Khordais traditional music school of Thessaloníki to Inoússes, a small islet northeast of Híos, to rescue vanishing material with the help of the islanders' long memories; the result is superb, a mix of live sessions in Inoussan tavernas and some studio recordings. Thorough, intelligent notes, but no lyrics translations.

Tragoudhia ke Skopi tis Patmou/Songs and Melodies of Patmos (Politistikón Ídhryma Dhodhekanísou 201). Live 1995 field recordings of well-edited pieces, as raw but compelling as you'd hear them at an old-time festival. Local singers and instrumentalists on *violí*, *tsamboúna* and *sandoúri*.

INDIVIDUAL ARTISTS/GROUPS

Anna Karabesini & Efi Sarri CD reissues from old LPs: *Yialo Yialo Piyeno* (Lyra 0102067), *Tis Thalassas* (Lyra 10777) and *Ena Glenti* (Lyra 10717). Two singing sisters from the island of Kos, who were for the Dodecanese what the Konitopoulos family (see next entry) was for the Cyclades; that they performed only for private gatherings added to their cachet.

Irini Konitopoulou-Legaki *Athanata Nisiotika 1* (Tzina-Astir 1020). A 1978 warhorse, beloved of bus drivers across the islands. *Anefala Thalassina* (Lyra 4693) from 1993 is far less commercial than the usual Konitopoulous-clan offerings and one of the finest recordings from Náxos, featuring Naxian *lautiéris* Dhimitris Fyroyenis and Yiannis Zevgolis, one of the last old-style violinists. Then aged 61, Irini sung her heart out in a richer, deeper voice than she was known for on club stages.

★**Argyris Kounadis** *Kefalonitikes Arietes* (Philips 526 492-2). Sweet without being syrupy, this is one of the very few still in-print collections of traditional vocal music from Kefaloniá (indeed from any of the Ionians); largely songs composed by Kounadis.

★**Nikos Oikonomidis** *Perasma stin Amorgo/Passage to Amorgos* (Keros Music CD 101). A native of Skhinoússa islet, violinist and *lautiéris* Oikonomidis plays and sings traditional pieces from nearby Amorgós on this 2001 recording, with guest appearances by Yiasemi Saragoudha, wife of the great oudist, and folklorist Domna Samiou. His latest (2006) outing, *Antikeri*, is all-acoustic, with Oikonomidis' own compositions and lyrics.

★**Andonis Xylouris (Psarantonis)** *Palio Krasi In'ïy Skepsi Mou* and *Idheon Antron* (both Lyra MBI). Psarantonis – shunned by other Cretan musicians as too "out there" – has an idiosyncratically spare and percussive *lýra* style, but here unusual instruments are well integrated into a densely textured whole. Daughter Niki, now a star in her own right, executes a gorgeous rendition of "Meraklídhiko Poulí" on *Idheon Antron*, and also proves a highlight of Psarantonis's 2008 *Mountain Rebels* (Network/Raki 495123), especially on "Kimáte o Ílios sta Vouná" and "Neraïdhas Yié", with brothers Yiorgos and Lambis on *laoúto* and oud respectively.

Nikos Xylouris *O Arkhangelos tis Kritis, 1958–1968* (MBI 10376); *Ta Khronia stin Kriti* (2CD, MBI 10677/78). The best two retrospectives of the sweet-voiced Cretan singer (Andonis' brother), in traditional mode, with copious notes; the first covers his initial decade of recordings before he became a noted *éntekhno* (art music) star, with self-accompaniment on the *lýra*.

★**Ziyia** (now reformed as **Edessa**). Fine arrangements and singing, by a five-member American group who simply run rings around most native-Greek session musicians. Their first outing, *From the Mountains to the Islands* (AgaRhythm, 1992), has more island music than *Travels with Karaghiozis* (AgaRhythm, 1995), which does, however, include a lovely song from Kálymnos. Their latest, *Regional Music of Greece* (2014) is equally good. All are available through ⓦ ziyia.com.

Books

The best books in this selection are marked by a ★ symbol; titles currently out of print are indicated as "o/p". Recommended specialist Greek booksellers include, in the UK, the Hellenic Bookservice (⊚hellenicbookservice.com) and, in Canada, Kalamos Books (⊚kalamosbooks.com).

TRAVEL/IMPRESSIONS

James Theodore Bent *Aegean Islands: The Cyclades, or Life Among the Insular Greeks.* Originally published in 1881, this remains an authoritative account of Greek island customs and folklore, gleaned from a long winter's travel in the archipelago.

Michael Carroll *An Island in Greece: On the Shores of Skopelos* (aka The Gates of the Wind). A 1960s account of Skópelos and the surrounding islands. Carroll arrived by boat, was essentially adopted by a leading local family, and still lives there today.

Charmian Clift *Mermaid Singing* (o/p). Clift and family's experiences living on 1950s Kálymnos – among the first postwar expats to do so. Her *Peel Me a Lotus*, about a subsequent sojourn on Ýdhra, may also appeal, and is often co-bound with *Mermaid Singing*.

Charles Cockerell *Travels in Greece.* Cockerell arrived in Greece in 1810, stayed four years, engaged in archeological pillaging typical of the era – which he recounts with extraordinary insouciance – and had more adventures on islands and mainland than he bargained for.

★**Gerald Durrell** *My Family and Other Animals.* Delightful evocation of Durrell's 1930s childhood on Corfu, where his family settled, and where he developed a passion for the island's fauna while elder brother Lawrence entertained Henry Miller and others.

Lawrence Durrell *Prospero's Cell* and *Reflections on a Marine Venus.* The former constitutes Durrell's Corfu memoirs, from his time there as World War II loomed. *Marine Venus* recounts his 1945–47 colonial-administrator experiences of Rhodes and other Dodecanese islands.

Peter Hemming *Oil Paint and Greece.* Entertaining diary-style account of island life by an English artist who went to live on Kefaloniá for six months and ended up staying over six years.

★ **Roger Jinkinson** *Tales from a Greek Island* and *More Tales from a Greek Island.* Tales, long and short, set in and around Dhiafáni, Kárpathos (identified cryptically as "The Village"), by turns poignant, revisionist about World War II heroics or blackly funny. The We (The Villagers, among whom part-time resident Jinkinson counts himself) vs. Them (tourists) tone can grate, but he's been there and done it, with special insight into the mysterious craft of Aegean fishing.

★ **Elias Kulukundis** *The Feasts of Memory: Stories of a Greek Family.* A journey back through time and genealogy by a diaspora Greek two generations removed from Kássos, poorest of the Dodecanese. A re-release, with an extra chapter, of his 1967 classic *Journey to a Greek Island*.

Edward Lear *The Corfu Years* and *The Cretan Journal.* Highly entertaining journals from the 1840s and 1850s, beautifully illustrated with watercolours and sketches.

John Lucas *92 Acharnon Street.* Beautifully told tale of a British poet who moves to Athens in the mid-Eighties to teach literature, and gets hooked – not on the glories of the ancients, but on modern Greece, specifically its poets, tavernas, politics and foibles; plenty on Égina, his preferred island retreat, as well.

★ **Willard Manus** *This Way to Paradise: Dancing on the Tables.* American expat's memoir of nearly four decades in Líndhos, Rhodes, beginning long before its submersion in tourism. Wonderful period detail, including bohemian excesses and cameos from such as S.J. Perelman, Germaine Greer and Martha Gellhorn.

Henry Miller *The Colossus of Maroussi.* Corfu, Crete, Athens and the soul of Greece in 1939, with Miller completely in his element; funny, sensual and transporting.

Jim Potts *The Ionian Islands and Epirus.* An erudite ramble through the Ionian Islands, touching on history, popular culture and their vital relation to the mainland opposite.

Dilys Powell *The Villa Ariadne.* A 1950s account of the British in Crete, from Arthur Evans to Patrick Leigh Fermor, viewed through the prism of the villa at Knossós which hosted all of them. Brings early archeological work to life, but rather syrupy style.

Tom Stone *The Summer of My Greek Taverna.* Enjoyable cautionary tale for those fantasizing about a new life in the Aegean sun. Moving to Pátmos in the early 1980s, Stone tries to mix friendship and business at a beach taverna, with predictable (for onlookers anyway) results.

Richard Stoneman, ed *A Literary Companion to Travel in Greece.* Ancient and medieval authors, plus Grand Tourists – an excellent selection.

Patricia Storace *Dinner with Persephone.* A New York poet, resident for a year in Athens (with forays to the provinces, including Corfu) puts the country's 1990s psyche on the couch. Storace has a sly humour and an interesting take on Greece's "imprisonment" in its imagined past.

John L. Tomkinson, ed *Travellers' Greece: Memories of an Enchanted Land*. Seventeenth- to nineteenth-century (mostly English) travellers' impressions of islands and mainland, ranging from the enraptured to the appalled; ideal for dipping into.

Sarah Wheeler *Evia: Travels on an Undiscovered Island*. Entertaining, re-issued chronicle of a five-month ramble through Évvia, juxtaposing meditations on culture and history with an open approach to nuns, goatherds or academics. The main quibble is her success in making the island seem more exotic than it really is.

FICTION

FOREIGN FICTION

★**Louis de Bernières** *Captain Corelli's Mandolin*. Set on Kefaloniá during the World War II occupation and aftermath, this accomplished 1994 tragi-comedy quickly acquired cult, then bestseller, status in the UK and US. But in Greece it provoked a scandal, once islanders, Greek Left intellectuals and surviving Italian partisans woke up to its virulent disparaging of ELAS. It seems the novel was based on the experiences of Amos Pampaloni, an artillery captain on Kefaloniá in 1942–44 who later joined ELAS, and who accused De Bernières of distorting the roles of both Italians and ELAS on the island. The Greek translation was abridged to avoid causing offence.

Meaghan Delahunt *To The Island*. Novel of an Australian woman travelling with her young son to Náxos, to meet the father she has never met, and encountering also his past, as a political activist tortured by the junta. Not your usual travelogue.

Oriana Fallaci *A Man* (o/p). Gripping tale of the junta years, based on the author's involvement with Alekos Panagoulis, the army officer who attempted to assassinate Colonel Papadopoulos in 1968 – and who himself died in mysterious circumstances in 1975.

★ **John Fowles** *The Magus*. Fowles' biggest and best tale of mystery and manipulation – plus Greek island life – based on his stay on Spétses as a teacher during the 1950s. A period piece that repays revisiting.

Victoria Hislop *The Island*. The former leper colony of Spinalonga forms the backdrop to *The Island*, a huge-selling novel about a young woman discovering her Cretan roots.

Evelyn Waugh *Officers and Gentlemen*. This second volume of Waugh's brilliant, acerbic wartime trilogy includes an account of the Battle of Crete and subsequent evacuation.

GREEK FICTION

★**Apostolos Doxiadis** *Uncle Petros and Goldbach's Conjecture*. Uncle Petros is the disgraced family black sheep, living reclusively in outer Athens; his nephew discovers that Petros had staked everything to solve a theorem unsolved for centuries. Math-phobes take heart; it's more a meditation on how best to spend life, and what really constitutes success.

Vangelis Hatziyannidis. Hatziyannidis' abiding obsessions – confinement, blackmail, abrupt disappearances – get a workout in his creepy debut novel *Four Walls*, set on an unspecified east Aegean isle, where a reclusive landowner takes in a fugitive woman who convinces him to revive his father's honey trade – with unexpected consequences. His next novel, *Stolen Time*, revisits the same themes as an impoverished student gets a tidy fee from a mysterious tribunal for agreeing to spend two weeks in the "Hotel from Hell".

★**Panos Karnezis.** Karnezis has become the most accessible, and feted, Greek writer since the millennium. He grew up in Greece but now lives in London, writing in English; however, his concerns remain utterly Greek. *Little Infamies* is a collection of short stories set in his native Peloponnese during the late 1950s and early 1960s; *The Maze* is a darker-shaded, more successful novel concerning the Asia Minor Catastrophe. More recent works include *The Birthday Party*, based on events in the life of Aristotle Onassis and daughter Christina, and *The Convent*, a gentle whodunnit with nuns.

GREEK POETRY

Modern Greece has an intense and dynamic **poetic tradition**. Two Greek poets – George Seferis and Odysseus Elytis – have won the Nobel prize in literature; along with C.P. Cavafy, from an earlier generation, and Yiannis Ritsos they are the great names of modern Greek poetry. Good English translations of pretty much all of their work are widely available, or try these anthologies:

Peter Bien, Peter Constantine, Edmund Keeley, Karen Van Dyck, eds *A Century of Greek Poetry, 1900–2000* (o/p). Superb bilingual anthology, with some lesser-known surprises alongside the big names.

Nanos Valaoritis and Thanasis Maskaleris, eds *An Anthology of Modern Greek Poetry* (o/p). English-only text, but excellent biographical info on the poets and good translations by two native Greek-speakers.

THE CLASSICS

Many of the classics make excellent companions for a trip around Greece; reading Homer's Odyssey when battling the vagaries of island ferries puts your own plight into perspective. Most of these good beginners' choices are published in a range of paperback editions. Particularly outstanding translations are noted.

★**William Allan** *Classical Literature: A Very Short Introduction*. Exactly as it promises: an excellent overview.

Herodotus *The Histories*. Revered as the father of narrative history – and anthropology – this fifth-century BC Anatolian writer chronicled both the causes and campaigns of the Persian Wars, as well as the assorted tribes and nations inhabiting Asia Minor.

★**Homer** *The Iliad* and *The Odyssey*. The first concerns itself, semi-factually, with the late Bronze Age war of the Achaeans against Troy in Asia Minor; the second recounts the hero Odysseus's long journey home, via seemingly every corner of the Mediterranean. The best prose translations are by Martin Hammond, and in verse Richmond Lattimore. For a stirring if very loose verse *Iliad*, try also Christopher Logue's recent version, *War Music*.

Ovid *The Metamorphoses*. Ovid was a first-century AD Roman poet, but his masterpiece includes accessible renditions of the more piquant Greek myths, involving transformations as divine blessing or curse. Excellent

verse translation by David Raeburn; prose version A.D. Melville.

Pausanias *The Guide to Greece*. Effectively the first-ever guidebook, intended for Roman pilgrims to central mainland and Peloponnesian sanctuaries. Invaluable for later archeologists in assessing damage or change to temples over time, or (in some cases) locating them at all. The two-volume Penguin edition is usefully annotated with the later history and nomenclature of the sites.

Plato *Apology*. The most accessible of Plato's works relates the fascinating defence put up by his mentor, Socrates, against the state charges of corrupting the youth, as well as his dignified acceptance of the death penalty.

★**Thucydides** *History of the Peloponnesian War*. Bleak month-by-month account of the conflict, by a cashiered Athenian officer whose affiliation and dim view of human nature didn't usually obscure his objectivity.

Xenophon *The History of My Times*. Thucydides' account of the Peloponnesian War stops in 411 BC; this eyewitness account continues events until 362 BC.

Nikos Kazantzakis *Zorba the Greek; The Last Temptation of Christ; Christ Recrucified/The Greek Passion; Freedom and Death; The Fratricides; Report to Greco*. Kazantzakis can be hard going, yet the power of his writing shines through. *Zorba the Greek* is a dark, nihilistic work, worlds away from the two-dimensional film. By contrast, the movie version of *The Last Temptation of Christ* – specifically Jesus's vision, once crucified, of a normal life with Mary Magdalene – provoked riots among Orthodox fanatics in Athens in 1989. *Christ Recrucified* (*The Greek Passion*) resets the Easter drama against the backdrop of Christian/Muslim relations, while *Freedom and Death*, perhaps his most approachable, chronicles the rebellions of nineteenth-century Crete. *The Fratricides* portrays a family riven by the civil war. *Report to Greco* is an autobiographical exploration of his Cretan-ness.

Artemis Leontis (ed) *Greece: A Traveler's Literary Companion*. A nice idea, brilliantly executed: various

regions of the country as portrayed in (very) short fiction or essays by modern Greek writers.

★**Petros Markaris** *The Late Night News* (*Deadline in Athens* in US)*; Zone Defence;* and *Che Committed Suicide*. Inspector Haritos is an unmistakeably Greek cop, and these detective tales, while thoroughly engrossing on their own, also offer a real insight into the realities of life in modern Greece.

Alexandros Papadiamantis *Tales from a Greek Island; The Murderess*. The island is Skiáthos, Papadiamantis' birthplace. These quasi-mythic tales of grim fate come from a nineteenth-century writer ("the inventor of modern Greek fiction") comparable to Hardy and Maupassant.

Dido Sotiriou *Farewell Anatolia*. A perennial favourite since publication in 1962, this chronicles the traumatic end of Greek life in Asia Minor, from World War I to the 1922 catastrophe, as narrated by a fictionalized version of Sotiriou's father.

ANCIENT GREECE

★**Mary Beard and John Henderson** *The Classics: A Very Short Introduction*. A brilliant short introduction to all elements of Classics: art, architecture, history and mythology.

Walter Burkert *Greek Religion: Archaic and Classical*. Superb overview of deities and their attributes and

antecedents, the protocol of sacrifice and the symbolism of festivals. Especially good on relating Greek worship to its predecessors in the Middle East.

A.R. Burn *Penguin History of Greece*. A classic account; packed and informative on everything from philosophy to military history.

Paul Cartledge *Alexander the Great: The Truth Behind The Myth*. An evocative, meticulous and accessible biography, stinting neither on the man's brutality nor his achievements.

Paul Cartledge *Cambridge Illustrated History of Ancient Greece* or *Ancient Greece: A Very Short Introduction*. Two excellent general introductions to ancient Greece; choose between brief paperback or large illustrated tome.

★**Paul Cartledge** *The Spartans: An Epic History*. Reassessment of this much-maligned city-state which was secretive and a source of outsider speculation even in its own time.

★**M.I. Finley** *The World of Odysseus*. Reprint of a 1954 warhorse, pioneering in its investigation of the historicity (or not) of the events and society related by Homer. Breezily readable and stimulating.

Simon Hornblower *The Greek World 479–323 BC*. A well-presented, up-to-date survey of ancient Greece at its zenith,

from the end of the Persian Wars to the death of Alexander.

Oswyn Murray *Early Greece*. The story of Greece from the Minoans and Mycenaeans through to the beginning of the Classical period.

Robin Osborne *Greece in the Making 1200–479 BC* and *Greek History: The Basics*. The former is a well-illustrated paperback on the rise of the city-state; the latter a short new introduction to ancient Greek history. Both are scholarly, if at times a little hard-going.

Robin Lane Fox *Alexander the Great* and *The Classical World: An Epic History of Greece and Rome*. The first is an absorbing study on Alexander that mixes historical scholarship with imaginative psychological detail. *The Classical World* is a racy and entertaining romp through several centuries, written by someone who knows his stuff.

F.W. Walbank *The Hellenistic World*. An historical overview of Greece under the sway of the Macedonian and Roman empires.

MEDIEVAL AND MODERN HISTORY

Timothy Boatswain and Colin Nicolson *A Traveller's History of Greece*. Well-written overview of crucial Greek periods and personalities, from earliest times to the end of the twentieth century.

★**Richard Clogg** *A Concise History of Greece*. If you read only one title on "modern" Greek history, this should be it: a remarkably clear account, from the decline of Byzantium to the economic crisis, with numerous maps and feature captions to the well-chosen artwork.

C.M. Woodhouse *Modern Greece: A Short History*. Woodhouse was a key liaison officer with the Greek Resistance during World War II, and later a Conservative MP. Writing from a more right-wing perspective than Clogg, his account – from the foundation of Constantinople to 1990 – is briefer and drier, but scrupulous with facts.

BYZANTINE, MEDIEVAL AND OTTOMAN GREECE

David Brewer *Greece, the Hidden Centuries: Turkish Rule from the Fall of Constantinople to Greek Independence*. Readable yet authoritative history of this little-explored era of Greek history.

Nicholas Cheetham *Medieval Greece* (o/p). A general survey of the period's infinite convolutions in Greece, with Frankish, Catalan, Venetian, Byzantine and Ottoman struggles for power.

★**Roger Crowley** *Constantinople: The Last Great Siege, 1453*. Thrillingly readable narrative of perhaps the key event of the Middle Ages, and its repercussions throughout Europe and the Islamic world.

Paul Hetherington *The Greek Islands: Guide to Byzantine and Medieval Buildings and Their Art*. A readable, well-illustrated and authoritative gazetteer to most island monuments of the period, though there are some peculiar

omissions.

★**John Julius Norwich** *Byzantium: The Early Centuries*; *Byzantium: the Apogee* and *Byzantium: The Decline*. Perhaps the main surprise for first-time travellers to Greece is the fascination of its Byzantine monuments. This is an astonishingly detailed yet readable – often witty – trilogy of the empire that produced them. There's also an excellent, one-volume abridged version, *A Short History of Byzantium*.

INDEPENDENT GREECE

David Brewer *The Greek War of Independence*. The finest narrative of revolutionary events (with some black-and-white illustrations), strong on the background of Ottoman Greece as well as the progress of the war.

★**John S. Koliopoulos and Thanos M. Veremis** *Greece: The Modern Sequel, from 1831 to the Present*. Thematic rather than chronological study that pokes into corners rarely illuminated by conventional histories; especially good on Macedonian issues, brigandage and the Communists.

★**Michael Llewellyn Smith** *Ionian Vision: Greece in Asia Minor, 1919–22*. Still the best work on the disastrous Anatolian campaign, which led to the population exchanges between Greece and Turkey.

WORLD WAR II AND THE CIVIL WAR

★**Antony Beevor** *Crete: The Battle and the Resistance*. The historian best known for his Stalingrad and Berlin epics actually made his debut with this short 1992 study, which first aired the theory that Crete was allowed to fall by the British to conceal the fact that they'd cracked the Germans' Enigma code, in order to win the more strategic campaign in North Africa.

Winston Churchill *The Second World War, Vol. 5: Closing the Ring*. Includes the Allied Aegean campaigns, with

BOOKS FOR KIDS

The Greek myths and legends are perfect holiday reading for kids; they're available in a huge number of versions aimed at all ages, often lavishly illustrated.

Terry Deary *Groovy Greeks; Greek Tales;* and the *Fire Thief* trilogy. The first of these is from Deary's familiar *Horrible Histories* series, the three books of *Greek Tales* take a sideways look at famous myths, and the *Fire Thief* is a comedy-fantasy series based on Prometheus, who stole fire from the gods.

Caroline Lawrence *The Roman Mysteries.* The final two volumes of this authentically detailed series of Roman-era mystery books for 8- to 11-year-olds, *The Colossus of Rhodes* and *Fugitive from Corinth*, are set in Greece.

Mary Renault *The King Must Die; The Last of the Wine;*

The Masks of Apollo; The Praise Singer; and *The Alexander Trilogy.* The style may be a tad dense and dated, but these retellings of great Greek stories remain classics of historical fiction.

Rick Riordan *Percy Jackson* series. A modern setting infused with Greek mythology as Percy Jackson, 12 years old and dyslexic, discovers he is the modern-day son of a Greek god. Gripping bestselling tales.

Francesca Simon *Helping Hercules.* Fans of *Horrid Henry* will enjoy this clever retelling of Greek myths by the same author, where young heroine Susan sorts out the not-so-heroic heroes.

---

detailed coverage of battles on and around Rhodes, Léros, Sámos and Kos.

Alan Clark *The Fall of Crete.* Racy and sensational military history by the late maverick English politician, if less thorough than Beevor's tome (and lacking maps). Detailed on the battles, and more critical of the command than you might expect from a former cabinet minister.

★**David H. Close** *The Origins of the Greek Civil War.* Excellent, even-handed study that focuses on the social conditions in 1920s and 1930s Greece that made the country so ripe for conflict; draws on primary sources to overturn various received wisdoms.

★**Mark Mazower** *Inside Hitler's Greece: The Experience of Occupation 1941–44.* Eccentrically organized, but the

scholarship is top-drawer and the photos magnificent. Demonstrates how the utter demoralization of the country and incompetence of conventional politicians led to the rise of ELAS and the onset of civil war.

Adrian Seligman *War in the Islands* (o/p). Collected oral histories of a little-known Allied unit: a flotilla of *kaïkia* organized to raid the Axis-held Aegean islands. Boy's Own stuff, with service-jargon-laced prose, but lots of fine period photos and detail.

★ **C.M. Woodhouse** *The Struggle for Greece, 1941–49.* Masterly, well-illustrated account of the so-called "three rounds" of resistance and rebellion, and how Greece emerged without a communist government.

ART AND ARCHEOLOGY

John Boardman *Greek Art.* An evergreen study in the *World of Art* series, first published in 1964. For more detailed treatment, there are three period volumes entitled *Greek Sculpture: Archaic Period, Classical Period* and *The Late Classical Period.*

A.R. and Mary Burn *The Living Past of Greece: A Time Traveller's Tour of Historic and Prehistoric Places* (o/p). This wide-ranging guide covers sites from Minoan through to Byzantine and Frankish, with clear plans and lively text.

Costis Davaras *Guide to Cretan Antiquities.* A fascinating guide to the antiquities of Crete, by a distinguished archeologist. Cross-referenced in gazetteer form, it has authoritative articles on all major sites up to the Ottoman era, as well as topics as diverse as Minoan toilet articles and the disappearance of Cretan forests. Widely available at Cretan museums.

Reynold Higgins *Minoan and Mycenaean Art.* Concise, well-illustrated roundup of the culture of Mycenae, Crete and the Cyclades, again part of the *World of Art* series.

J. Alexander MacGillivray *Minotaur: Sir Arthur Evans*

and the Archaeology of the Minoan Myth. Taking as its starting point Evans' manipulation of the evidence at Knossós to fit his own prejudices and beliefs, this is also a fascinating look at the development of modern archeology and the history of Crete.

Constantine E. Michaelides *The Aegean Crucible: Tracing Vernacular Architecture in Post-Byzantine Centuries.* It's difficult to pigeonhole this sprawling, interdisciplinary study by a Greek-American architecture professor on how island settlements – especially the Cycladic kástra, Ýdhra, Santoríni, fortified monasteries – came to be as they are, drawing on history, geology, climatic influences, agriculture and popular religion. The text, erudite without being technical, is directly keyed to copious illustrations and maps.

R.R.R. Smith *Hellenistic Sculpture.* Appraisal of the art of Greece under Alexander and his successors; another *World of Art* title.

James Witley *The Archaeology of Ancient Greece.* An excellent overview of current scholarship, not overly academic.

PEOPLE AND CULTURE

Juliet du Boulay *Portrait of a Greek Mountain Village.* Ambéli village on Évvia, during the 1960s: an absorbing narrative of a bygone way of life in. A sequel, *Cosmos, Life, and Liturgy in a Greek Orthodox Village*, explores how the Church underpins the interior lives of the villagers.

Bruce Clark *Twice a Stranger: How Mass Expulsion Forged Modern Greece and Turkey.* The build-up to and execution of the 1923 population exchanges, and how both countries are still digesting the experience eight-plus decades on. Compassionate and readable, especially the encounters with elderly refugees and oral histories.

Adam Hopkins *Crete: Its Past, Present and People* (o/p). Excellent general introduction to Cretan history and society with interesting detail on diverse topics like the Battle of Crete, daily life, mass tourism and herbology, though it's beginning to show its age (1977).

John Cuthbert Lawson *Modern Greek Folklore and Ancient Greek Religion: A Study in Survivals.* Exactly as it says: a fascinating, thorough study still applicable a century after first publication.

Michael Llewellyn Smith *The Great Island: A Study of Crete* (o/p). Long before he became a known scholar (and twice ambassador to Greece), Llewellyn Smith debuted with this fine volume emphasizing folk traditions, including a lengthy analysis of Cretan song.

Anthony J. Papalas *Rebels and Radicals: Icaria 1600–2000.* The lowdown on that most peculiar of mid-Aegean islands, delving into its Ottoman past, American diaspora links, unexpected Communist affiliations and recent touristic development.

David Sutton *Memories Cast in Stone: The Relevance of the Past in Everyday Life.* A 1990s ethnology of Kálymnos, where tenacious "traditional" practices such as dynamite-throwing *paniyíria* and dowry-collecting confront the new, pan-EU realities.

★**John L. Tomkinson** *Festive Greece: A Calendar of Tradition.* Copiously photographed gazetteer, by date, of festivals and events; whether Christian, pagan, political or just plain bizarre.

FOOD AND WINE

★**Rosemary Barron** *Flavours of Greece.* The leading Greek cookbook – among many contenders – by an internationally recognized authority. Constantly reprinted, with over 250 recipes and background info.

Andrew Dalby *Food in the Ancient World from A to Z; Siren Feasts: A History of Food and Gastronomy in Greece* (o/p); and *Tastes of Byzantium: The Cuisine of a Legendary Empire* (o/p). All scholarly works, the first of these is literally an A–Z, laid out encyclopedia-style, of ancient foods and food

terms. *Siren Feasts* demonstrates just how little Greek cuisine has changed in three millennia, and is also excellent on the introduction and etymology of common vegetables and herbs. *Tastes of Byzantium* adds the influences of Rome, Turkey and the Middle East.

Konstantinos Lazarakis *The Wines of Greece.* An excellent, up to 2005, overview of what's happening in Greece's eleven recognized wine-producing regions.

ACTIVITIES

See also the Wildlife guides (see box, p.553).

★**Rod Heikell** *Greek Waters Pilot.* An indispensible reference for yachting in the Aegean or Ionian seas, regularly updated; various regional sub-guides are also available.

Loraine Wilson *The High Mountains of Crete: White Mountains, Psiloritis & Lassithi Ranges.* The best of several guides to the island, with nearly a hundred hikes of all levels, described by one of the most experienced foreign trek leaders on the island.

Greek

So many Greeks have lived or worked abroad that you will find English-speakers in the tiniest island village. Add the thousands attending language schools or working in the tourist industry – English is the lingua franca of most resorts – and it's easy to see how so many visitors return home having learned only minimal restaurant vocabulary. You can certainly get by this way but it isn't very satisfying, and the willingness and ability to say even a few words will transform your status from that of dumb "tourístas" to the more honourable one of "xénos/xéni", which can mean foreigner, traveller and guest all combined.

Learning basic Greek

Greek is not an easy language for English-speakers but it is a very beautiful one, and even a brief acquaintance will give you an idea of the debt owed to it by Western European languages. Greek **grammar** is predictably complicated; **nouns** are divided into three genders, all with different case endings in the singular and in the plural, and all adjectives and articles have to agree with these in gender, number and case. To simplify things, all adjectives are cited in the neuter form in the lists on the following pages. **Verbs** are even more complex; they're in two conjugations, in both active and passive voices, with passively constructed verbs often having transitive sense. As a novice, it's best to simply say what you want the way you know it, and dispense with the niceties.

TEACH-YOURSELF GREEK COURSES

Anne Farmakides *A Manual of Modern Greek, 1, for University Students.* If you have the discipline and motivation, this is among the best for learning proper, grammatical Greek.

Hara Garoufalia et al *Read & Speak Greek for Beginners* (book & CD). Unlike many quickie courses, this provides a good grammatical foundation; new in 2008.

David Holton et al *Greek: A Comprehensive Grammar of the Modern Language.* A bit technical, so not for rank

beginners, but it covers almost every conceivable construction.

Alison Kakoura and Karen Rich *Talk Greek* (book and 2 CDs). Probably the best in-print product for beginners' essentials, and for developing the confidence to try them.

Aristarhos Matsukas *Complete Greek: Teach Yourself* (book and optional cassettes or CDs). Another complete course; touches on idiomatic expressions as well.

PHRASEBOOKS AND DICTIONARIES

Collins Pocket Greek Dictionary Harry T. Hionides. Very nearly as complete as the *Pocket Oxford* and probably better value for money. The inexpensive *Collins Gem Greek Dictionary* (UK only) is palm-sized but identical in contents – the best day-pack choice.

The Pocket Oxford Greek Dictionary J. T. Pring. A bit

bulky for travel, but generally considered the best Greek–English, English–Greek paperback dictionary.

Rough Guide Phrasebook: Greek Current, accurate and pocket-sized, with phrases that you'll actually need. The English–Greek section is transliterated, though the Greek–English part requires mastery of the Greek alphabet.

The Greek alphabet: transliteration and accents

Besides the usual difficulties of learning a new language, Greek has an entirely separate **alphabet**. Despite initial appearances, this is in practice fairly easily mastered – a skill that will help enormously in getting around independently. In addition, certain combinations of letters have unexpected results. This book's **transliteration system** (see below) should help you make intelligible noises, but remember that the correct **stress** (marked throughout the book with an acute accent or sometimes dieresis) is crucial. With the right sounds but the wrong stress people will either fail to understand you, or else understand something quite different.

The **dieresis** (¨) is used in Greek over the second of two adjacent vowels to change the pronunciation; often in this book it can function as the primary stress. In the word *kaïki* (caique), the use of a dieresis changes the pronunciation from "keh-key" to "ka-ee-key". In the word *païdhákia* (lamb chops), the dieresis changes the sound of the first syllable from "peh" to "pah-ee", but in this case the primary stress is on the third syllable. It is also, uniquely among Greek accents, used on capital letters in signs and personal-name spellings in Greece, and we have followed this practice on our maps.

GREEK	TRANSLITERATION	PRONOUNCED
Α, α	a	*a* as in father
Β, β	v	*v* as in vet
Γ, γ	y/g	*y* as in yes except before consonants or a, o or ou when it's a breathy *g*, approximately as in gap
Δ, δ	dh	*th* as in then
Ε, ε	e	*e* as in get
Ζ, ζ	z	*z* sound
Η, η	i	*i* as in ski
Θ, θ	th	th as in theme
Ι, ι	i	*i* as in ski
Κ, κ	k	*k* sound
Λ, λ	l	*l* sound
Μ, μ	m	*m* sound
Ν, ν	n	*n* sound
Ξ, ξ	x	*ks* sound, never *z*
Ο, ο	o	*o* as in box
Π, π	p	*p* sound
Ρ, ρ	r	*r* sound, lightly rolled as in Scottish
Σ, σ, ς	s	*ss* sound, except *z* before m or g
Τ, τ	t	*t* sound
Υ, υ	y	*i* as in ski
Φ, φ	f	*f* sound
Χ, χ	h before vowels, denoted kh before consonants but pronounced the same	harsh *h* sound, like *ch* in loch
Ψ, ψ	ps	ps as in lips
Ω, ω	o	*o* as in box, indistinguishable from *o*

COMBINATIONS AND DIPHTHONGS

ΑΙ, αι	e	*e* as in get
ΑΥ, αυ	av/af	*av* before voiced consonants and vowels *af* before voiceless consonents
ΕΙ, ει	i	*i* as in ski
ΕΥ, ευ	ev/ef	*ev* before voiced consonants and vowels *ef* before voiceless consonents
ΟΙ, οι	i	*i* as in ski
ΟΥ, ου	ou	*ou* as in tourist
ΓΓ, γγ	ng	*ng* as in angle; always medial
ΜΠ, μπ	b/mb	*b* at start of a word, *mb* if medial
ΝΤ, ντ	d/nd	*d* at start of a word, *nd* if medial

THE QUEST FOR "PURE" GREEK

When Greece achieved independence in 1832, its people were mostly illiterate, and the spoken language – **dhimotikí**, "demotic" or "popular" Greek – had undergone enormous change since the Byzantine and Classical eras. The vocabulary had numerous loan words from the languages of the various invaders and conquerors – especially Turks, Venetians and Slavs – and the grammar had been considerably streamlined since ancient times.

The leaders of the new Greek state, filled with romantic notions of Greece's past glories, set about purging the language of foreign words and reviving its Classical purity. They accordingly created what was in effect an artificial language, **katharévoussa** (literally "cleansed" Greek). Long-forgotten words and phrases were reintroduced and complex Classical grammar reinstated. *Katharévoussa* became the language of the schools, government, business, the law, newspapers and academia. Everyone aspiring to membership in the elite strove to master it.

The split between *katharévoussa* and *dhimotikí* quickly took on a **political** dimension with intellectuals and left-wing politicians championing the demotic form, while the right, notably the colonel's junta of 1967–74, insisted on the "purer" *katharévoussa*. *Dhimotikí* returned permanently after the fall of the colonels, though the Church and the legal profession still persist with *katharévoussa*.

All this has reduced, but not eliminated, confusion. The Metaxás dictatorship of the 1930s changed scores of village names from Slavic, Turkish or Albanian words to Greek ones – often reviving the name of the nearest ancient site. These official **place names** still hold sway on most road signs and maps – even though the local people may use the *dhimotikí* or non-Greek form. Thus for example you will see "Plomárion" or "Spétsai" written, while everyone actually says "Plomári" or "Spétses".

Polite forms and questions

Greek makes the distinction between the **informal** (*essý*) and **formal** (*essís*) second person, like the French "tu" and "vous". Young people and country people often use *essý* even with total strangers, though it's best to address everyone formally until/unless they start using the familiar with you, to avoid offence. By far the most common greeting, on meeting and parting, is *yiásou/yiásas* (literally "health to you").

To ask a **question**, it's simplest, though hardly elegant, to start with *parakaló* (please), then name the thing you want in an interrogative tone.

GREEK WORDS AND PHRASES

ESSENTIALS

Hérete/Yiásas	Hello	Pos se léne?	What's your name?
Kaliméra	Good morning	Me léne …	My name is …
Kalispéra	Good evening	Kýrios/Kyría	Mr/Mrs
Kaliníkhta	Goodnight	Dhespinís	Miss
Adío	Goodbye	Parakaló, o …?	Where is the …?
Tí kánis/Tí kánete?	How are you?	Dhen xéro	I don't know
Kalá íme	I'm fine	Tha se dho ávrio	See you tomorrow
Ke essís?	And you?	Kalí andhámosi	See you again
Ne	Yes	Páme	Let's go
Óhi	No	Parakaló, na me	Please help me
Parakaló	Please	voithíste	
Efharistó (polý)	Thank you (very much)	(Dhen) Trógo/píno	I (don't) eat/drink
Sygnómi	Sorry/excuse me	(Dhen) Mou aréssi	I (don't) like
Miláte angliká?	Do you speak English?	Stinyásas!	Cheers!
(Dhén) Katalavéno	I (don't) understand	Málista	Certainly
Parakaló, na milísate	Speak slower, please	Endáxi	OK, agreed
pió sigá		Anikhtó	Open
Pos léyete aftó sta	How do you say it	Klistó	Closed
Ellinká?	in Greek?	Méra	Day
		Níkhta	Night

Edhó	Here	Tahydhromío	Post office
Ekí	There	Gramatósima	Stamps
Grígora	Quickly	Venzinádhiko	Petrol station
Sigá	Slowly	Trápeza	Bank
Pou?	Where?	Leftá/Khrímata	Money
Pos?	How?	Toualéta	Toilet
Póte?	When?	Astynomía	Police
Yiatí?	Why?	Yiatrós	Doctor
Ti óra ... ?	At what time ... ?	Nosokomío	Hospital
Ti íne/Pió íne ... ?	What is/Which is ... ?		

ACCOMMODATION

ON THE MOVE

Parakaló, éna dhomátio	We'd like a room	Parakaló, o dhrómos yiá ... ?	Can you show me the road to ... ?
yiá éna/dhýo/tría átoma	for one/two/three people	Aeropláno	Aeroplane
yiá mía/dhýo/tris vradhiés	for one/two/three nights	Leofório, poúlman	Bus, coach
me dhipló kreváti	with a double bed	Aftokínito, amáxi	Car
me dous	with a shower	Mihanáki, papáki	Motorbike, scooter
Xenodhohío	Hotel	Taxí	Taxi
Xenónas	Guesthouse	Plío/vapóri/karávi	Ship, ferry
Xenónas neótitas	Youth hostel	Tahyplöö, katamarán	High-speed boat, catamaran
Zestó neró	Hot water	Dhelfíni	Hydrofoil
Krýo neró	Cold water	Tréno	Train
Klimatismós	Air conditioning	Sidhirodhromikós stathmós	Train station
Anemistíras	Fan	Podhílato	Bicycle
Boró na to dho?	Can I see it?	Otostóp	Hitching
Boroúme na váloume ti skiní edhó?	Can we camp here?	Mé ta pódhia	On foot
Kámping/Kataskínosi	Campsite	Monopáti	Trail, path
		Praktorío leoforíon KTEL	Bus station
		Stási	Bus stop

SHOPPING AND SERVICES

Póso (káni)?	How much (does it cost)?	Limáni	Harbour
Tí óra aníyi/ klíni?	What time does it open/ close?	Ti óra févyi?	What time does it leave?
		Ti óra ftáni?	What time does it arrive?
Parakaló, éna kiló portokália?	May I have a kilo of oranges?	Póssa hiliómetra?	How many kilometres?
Póssi, pósses or póssa?	How many?	Pósses óres?	How many hours?
Aftó	This one	Pou páte/pas?	Where are you going?
Ekíno	That one	Páo sto ...	I'm going to ...
Kaló	Good	Thélo na katévo sto ...	I want to get off at ...
Kakó	Bad	O dhrómos yiá ...	The road to ...
Megálo	Big	Kondá	Near
Mikró	Small	Makriá	Far
Perisótero	More	Aristerá	Left
Ligótero	Less	Dhexiá	Right
Lígo	A little	Katefthía/ísia	Straight ahead
Polý	A lot	Éna isitírio yiá ...	A ticket to ...
Ftinó	Cheap	Éna isitírio apló/mé epistrofí	A ticket one-way/ return
Akrivó	Expensive	Paralía	Beach
Mazí (me)	With (together)	Spiliá	Cave
Horís	Without	Kéndro	Centre (of town)
Magazí	Shop	Eklissía	Church
Farmakío	Pharmacy	Thálassa	Sea
		Horió	Village

NUMBERS

énas/mía/éna	1
dhýo	2
tris/tría	3
tésseri/tésseres /téssera	4
pénde	5
éxi	6
eftá	7
okhtó	8
ennéa (or, in slang, enyiá)	9
dhéka	10
éndheka	11
dhódheka	12
dhekatrís/ía	13
dhekatésseri/es/a	14
dhekapénde	15
íkossi	20
íkossi éna	21
triánda	30
saránda	40
penínda	50
exínda	60
evdhomínda	70
ogdhónda	80
enenínda	90
ekató	100
ekatón penínda	150
dhiakóssies/ia	200
pendakóssies/ia	500
hílies/hília	1000
dhýo hiliádhes	2000
prótos/próti/próto	first
dhéfteros/i/o	second
trítos/i/o	third

TIME AND DAYS OF THE WEEK

Tóra	Now
Argótera	Later
Símera	Today
Ávrio	Tomorrow
Khthés	Yesterday
Tó proï	In the morning
Tó apóyevma	In the afternoon
Tó vrádhi	In the evening
Kyriakí	Sunday
Dheftéra	Monday
Tríti	Tuesday
Tetárti	Wednesday
Pémpti	Thursday
Paraskeví	Friday
Sávato	Saturday
Tí óra íne?	What time is it?
Mía iy óra/dhýo iy óra/trís iy óra	One/two/three o'clock
Tésseres pará íkossi	Twenty minutes to four
Eftá ke pénde	Five minutes past seven
Éndheka ke misí	Half past eleven
Se misí óra	In half an hour
S'éna tétarto	In a quarter-hour
Se dhýo óres	In two hours

MONTHS AND SEASONS

Yennáris/Ianouários	January
Fleváris/Fevouários	February
Mártis/Mártios	March
Aprílis	April
Maïos	May
Ioúnios	June
Ioúlios	July
Ávgoustos	August
Septémvris/ios	September

GREEK'S GREEK

There are numerous words and phrases which you will hear constantly, even if you don't have the chance to use them. These are a few of the most common.

Éla!	Come (literally) but also Speak to me! You don't say! etc.	**Étsi k'étsi**	So-so
		Ópa!	Whoops! Watch it!
Oríste!	Literally, Define!; in effect, What can I do for you? Say that again, when used interrogatively. Also used as phone response.	**Po-po-po!**	Expression of dismay or concern, like French "O là là!"
		Pedhí moú	My boy/girl, sonny, friend, etc.
		Maláka(s)	Literally "wanker", but often used (don't try it!) as an informal term of address
Embrós!/Léyete!	Standard phone responses		
Tí néa?	What's new?	**Sigá sigá**	Take your time, slow down
Tí yínete?	What's going on?	**Kaló taxídhi**	Bon voyage

Októvris/ios	October
Noémvris/ios	November
Dhekémvris/ios	December

Therinó dhromolóyio	Summer schedule
Himerinó dhromolóyio	Winter schedule

A food and drink glossary

BASICS

Katálogos	Menu
O logariasmós	The bill
Merídha	Portion
Zestó	Hot
Krýo	Cold
(Horís) ládhi	(Without) oil
Hýma	Bulk (wine, olives etc)
Varelísio/a	Barrelled wine/beer
Hortofágos	Vegetarian
Kréas	Meat
Lahaniká	Vegetables
Neró	Water
Psári(a)	Fish
Thalassiná	Seafood
Mezédhes	Small plates of various food, dips etc
Orektiká	Starters
Pikilía	Mixed selection on plate
Aláti	Salt
Pipéri	Pepper (condiment)
Avgá	Eggs
Méli	Honey
Psomí ...	Bread ...
Olikís	Wholemeal
Sikalísio	Rye
Kalambokísio	Corn
Tyrí	Cheese
Yiaoúrti	Yoghurt
Záhari	Sugar
Zaharíni	Sweetener

FOOD SHOPS, RESTAURANTS AND BARS

Baráki	Bar
Estiatório/Inomayiría	Old-style restaurant mainly featuring baked dishes
Exohikó kéndro	Out-of-town restaurant
Foúrnos	Bakery
Galaktopolío	Café specializing in dairy products
Mezedhopolío	Restaurant specializing in mezédhes
Ouzerí	Restaurant specializing in ouzo and mezédhes
Patsatzídhiko	Restaurant specializing in tripe soup

Psarotavérna	Specialist fish taverna
Psistariá	Grill house
Souvlatzídhiko	Souvláki shop
Tsipourádhiko	Restaurant specializing in tsípouro and mezédhes
Zaharoplastío	Patisserie, confectionary shop

COOKING TERMS

Akhnistó	Steamed
Frikasé	Stew, either lamb, goat or pork, with celery
Iliókafto	Sun-dried
Kokkinistó	Cooked in tomato sauce
Kourkoúti	Egg-and-flour batter
Krasáto	Cooked in wine sauce
Ladherá	Vegetables cooked in an oily sauce
Ladholémono	Oil and lemon sauce
Makaronádha	Any spaghetti/ pasta-based dish
Mayireftá	Traditional oven-baked dish
Pastó	Fish marinated in salt
Petáli	Butterflied fish, eel, shrimp
Psitó	Roasted
Saganáki	Cheese-based red sauce; also fried cheese
(Tis) Skáras	Grilled
Sti soúvla	Spit-roasted
Sto foúrno	Baked
Tiganitó	Pan-fried
Tís óras	Grilled/fried to order
Yakhní	Stewed in oil and tomato sauce
Yemistá	Stuffed (squid, vegetables, etc)

SOUPS, STARTERS AND SNACKS

Avgolémono	Egg and lemon soup
Bouréki, bourekákia	Courgette/zucchini, potato and cheese pie
Dolmádhes, yaprákia; yalantzí	Vine leaves stuffed with rice and mince; with vegetables
Fasoládha	Bean soup

Fáva	Purée of yellow peas
Féta psití	Baked feta cheese slabs with chilli
Galotýri	Curdled creamy dip
Hortópita	Pastry stuffed with greens
Kápari	Pickled caper leaves
Kopanistí, khtypití	Pungent, fermented cheese purée
Kreatópita	Meat pie, usually with mince
Lahanodolmádhes	Stuffed cabbage leaves
Loukanoukópita	Sausage roll
Mavromátika	Black-eyed peas
Melitzanosaláta	Aubergine/eggplant dip
Piperiés florínes	Marinated sweet peppers
Rengosaláta	Herring salad
Revythokeftédhes	Chickpea/garbanzo patties
Skordhaliá	Garlic dip
Soúpa	Soup
Spanakópita	Spinach pie, usually with cheese
Strapatsádha	Eggs scrambled with tomato and onions
Taramosaláta	Cod roe pâté
Tiganópsomo	Toasted oiled bread
Trahanádhes	Crushed wheat and milk soup, sweet or savoury
Tyrokafterí	Cheese dip with chilli
Tyrópita	Cheese pie
Tyropitákia	Small fried cheese pies
Tzatzíki	Yoghurt and cucumber dip
Tzirosaláta	Cured mackerel dip

VEGETABLES

Ambelofásola	Runner beans
Angináres	Artichokes
Angoúri	Cucumber
Ánitho	Dill
Bámies	Okra/ladies' fingers
Briám, tourloú	Ratatouille
Domátes	Tomatoes
Fakés	Lentils
Fasolákia	French (green) beans
Fasóles	Small white beans
Horiátiki (saláta)	Greek salad (with olives, feta, etc)
Hórta	Steamed greens
Kolokythákia	Courgette/zucchini
Koukiá	Broad fava beans
Láhano	Cabbage
Maroúli	Lettuce

Melitzánes imám/ Imám baïldí	Aubergine/eggplant slices baked with onion, garlic and copious olive oil
Patátes	Potatoes
Patzária	Beetroot
Piperiés	Peppers
Pligoúri, pinigoúri	Bulgur wheat
Radhíkia	Wild chicory
Róka	Rocket, arugula
Rýzi/Piláfi sáltsa	Rice (usually with sauce)
Saláta	Salad
Spanáki	Spinach
Yígandes	White haricot beans

FISH AND SEAFOOD

Ahiní, foúskes	Sea urchins
Astakós	Lobster
Atherína	Sand smelt
Bakaliáros	Cod or hake, usually latter
Barbóuni	Red mullet
Fangrí	Common bream
Galéos	Dogfish
Garídhes	Shrimp, prawns
Gávros	Mild anchovy
Glóssa	Sole
Gónos, gonákia	Any hatchling fish
Gópa	Bogue
Hokhlí	Sea snails
Kakaviá	Bouillabaisse
Kalamarákia	Baby squid
Kalamária	Squid
Karavídhes	Crayfish
Koliós	Chub mackerel
Koutsomoúra	Goatfish (small red mullet)
Lakérdha	Light-fleshed bonito, marinated
Lithríni	Red bream, pandora
Melanoúri	Saddled bream
Ménoula	Sprat
Mýdhia	Mussels
Okhtapódhi	Octopus
Petalídhes	Limpets
Platý	Skate, ray
Psarósoupa	Fish soup
Sardhélles	Sardines
Sargós	White bream
Seláhi	Skate, ray
Sfyrídha	White grouper
Skáros	Parrotfish
Skathári	Black bream
Skoumbrí	Atlantic mackerel
Soupiá	Cuttlefish

Strídhia	Oysters
Thrápsalo	Large, deep-water squid
Tónos	Tuna
Tsipoúra	Gilt-head bream
Xifías	Swordfish
Yermanós	Leatherback
Yialisterés	Smooth Venus shellfish

MEAT AND POULTRY

Arní/arnáki	Lamb
Bekrí mezé	Pork chunks in spicy pepper sauce
Biftéki	Hamburger
Brizóla hiriní	Pork chop
Brizóla moskharísia	Beef chop
Exohikó/Kléftiko	Lamb baked in tin foil or in pastry
Frigadhéli	Minced meat dumplings
Gourounópoulo	Suckling pig roast on a spit
Hirinó	Pork
Kalamáki	Small kebab on a wooden skewer
Katsíki/Yídha	Goat
Keftédhes	Meatballs
Kókoras krasáto	Coq au vin
Kokorétsi	Liver/offal roulade, spit-roasted
Kondosoúvli	Spit-roasted pork
Kopsídha	(Lamb) shoulder chops
Kotópoulo	Chicken
Kounéli	Rabbit
Loukánika	Spicy course-ground sausages
Moskhári	Veal
Moussakás	Aubergine/eggplant, potato and lamb-mince casserole with béchamel topping
Païdhákia	Rib chops, lamb or goat
Pantséta	Pork belly
Papoutsákia	Stuffed aubergine/ eggplant "shoes"
Pastítsio	Macaroni "pie" baked with minced meat
Pastourmás	Cured, highly spiced beef
Patsás	Tripe soup
Patsitsádha	beef with pasta in wine sauce
Provatína	Female mutton
Psaronéfri	Pork tenderloin medallions
Salingária	Garden snails
Sofríto	beef fried in garlic sauce

Soutzoukákia	Minced meat rissoles
Souvláki	Any type of kebab
Spetzofáï	Sausage and pepper stew
Stifádho	Meat stew with tomato and boiling onions
Sykóti	Liver
Tiganiá	Pork chunks fried with onions
Yiouvétsi	Baked clay casserole of meat and pasta
Yíros	Rotisserie meat, usually pork

SWEETS AND DESSERT

Baklavás	Honey and nut pastry
Bergamóndo	Bergamot
Bougátsa	Sweet cream pie served warm with sugar and cinnamon. Can be savoury in the north.
Galaktoboúreko	Custard pie
Glyká koutalioú	Spoon sweet (syrupy fruit preserve)
Halvás	Semolina- or sesame-based sweet
Kataïfi	Honey-soaked "shredded wheat"
Karydhópita	Walnut cake
Kréma	Custard
Loukoumádhes	Dough fritters in honey syrup and sesame seeds
Pagotó	Ice cream
Pastélli	Sesame and honey bar
Ravaní	Sponge cake, lightly syruped
Rizógalo	Rice pudding
Sandiyí	Whipped cream

FRUITS

Akhládhi	Big pear
Aktinídhi	Kiwi fruit
Fystíkia	Pistachio nuts
Fráoules	Strawberries
Karpoúzi	Watermelon
Kerásia	Cherries
Krystália	Miniature pears
Kydhóni	Quince
Lemóni	Lemon
Mílo	Apple
Pepóni	Melon
Portokáli	Orange
Rodhákino	Peach
Sýka	Figs
Stafýlia	Grapes

DIALECTS AND MINORITY LANGUAGES

Ancient **dialects** survive in many remote areas of Greece, some quite incomprehensible to outsiders. The dialect of Sfákia in Crete is one such; Tsakónika of the east-central Peloponnese is another, while the dialect of the Sarakatsáni shepherds is apparently the oldest, related to the language of the Dorian settlers.

The language of the Sarakatsáni's traditional rivals, the **Vlachs**, is not Greek at all, but derived from early Latin, with strong affinities to Romanian. In the regions bordering the Republic of Macedonia and southwestern Bulgaria, you can still hear **Slavic Macedonian** spoken, while small numbers of Sephardic Jews in the north speak **Ladino**, a medieval form of Spanish. Until a few decades ago, **Arvanítika** – a dialect of medieval Albanian – was the first language of many villages of inland Attica, southern Évvia, northern Ándhros, and much of the Argo-Saronic; lately the clock has been turned back, so to speak, as throngs of Albanian immigrants circulate in Athens and other parts of the country. In Thrace, there is a substantial **Turkish-speaking** population, as well as some speakers of **Pomak** (a derivative of Bulgarian with a large Greco-Turkish vocabulary), while Gypsies countrywide speak Romany.

CHEESE			
Ayeladhinó	Cow's-milk cheese	**Kafés**	Coffee
Féta	Salty, creamy white cheese	**Krasí**	Wine
		áspro/lefkó	white
		kokkinélli/rozé	rosé
(Kefalo) graviéra	(Extra-hard) Gruyère-type cheese	kókkino	red
		Limonádha	Lemonade
Katsikísio	Goat cheese	**Metalikó neró**	Mineral water
Kasséri	Medium-sharp cheese	**Portokaládha**	Orangeade
Myzíthra	Sweet cream cheese	**Potíri**	Glass
Próvio	Sheep cheese	**Rakí/Tsikoudhiá**	Clear Cretan spirit
		Retsína	Wine made with added pine resin
DRINKS			
Boukáli	Bottle	**Tsáï**	Tea
Býra	Beer	**Tsáï vounoú**	"Mountain" (mainland sage) tea
Gála	Milk		
Galakakáo	Chocolate milk	**Tsípouro**	Clear strong spirit

Glossary

Acropolis Ancient, fortified hilltop.

Agora Market and meeting place of an ancient Greek city; also the "high street" of a modern village (**agorá** in modern Greek).

Amphora Tall, narrow-necked jar for oil or wine.

Áno Upper; common prefix of village names.

Apse Curved recess at the east end of a church nave.

Archaic period Late Iron Age period, from around 750 BC to the start of the Classical period in the fifth century BC.

Arhondikó A lordly stone mansion, often restored as boutique accommodation.

Astikó (Intra) city, municipal, local; adjective applied to phone calls and bus services.

Ayíasma A sacred spring, usually flowing out of church foundations.

Áyios/Ayía/Áyii (m/f/plural). Saint or holy. Common place-name prefix (abbreviated Ag or Ay), often spelled **Agios** or **Aghios**.

Basilica Colonnaded, "hall-" or "barn-" type church adapted from Roman models, most common in northern Greece.

Bema Rostrum for a church oratory.

Bouleuterion Auditorium for meetings of an ancient town's deliberative council.

Bouzoúki Most common Greek stringed musical instrument.

Capital The flared top, often ornamented, of a column.

Cavea Seating curve of an ancient theatre.

Cella Sacred room of a temple, housing the cult image.

Classical period From the end of the Persian Wars in 480 BC until the unification of Greece under Philip II of Macedon (338 BC).

Conch Concave semi-dome surmounting a church apse, often frescoed.

Corinthian Decorative columns, festooned with

acanthus florettes; any temple built in this order.

Dhimarhío Town hall.

Dhomátia Rooms for rent in purpose-built block, without staffed reception.

Dorian Northern civilization that displaced and succeeded the Mycenaeans and Minoans through most of Greece around 1100 BC.

Doric Minimalist, unadorned columns, dating from the Dorian period; any temple built in this order.

Drum Cylindrical or faceted vertical section, usually pierced by an even number of narrow windows, upholding a church cupola.

Entablature The horizontal linking structure atop the columns of an ancient temple; same as **architrave**.

Eparhía Subdivision of a modern province, analogous to a county.

Exedra Display niche for statuary.

Exonarthex The outer vestibule or entrance hall of a church, when a true **narthex** is present.

Forum Market and meeting place of a Roman-era city.

Frieze Band of sculptures around a temple. Doric friezes consist of various tableaux of figures (**metopes**) interspersed with grooved panels (**triglyphs**); Ionic ones have continuous bands of figures.

Froúrio Medieval citadel; nowadays, can mean a modern military headquarters.

Garsoniéra/es Studio villa/s, self-catering apartment/s.

Geometric period Post-Mycenaean Iron Age era named for its pottery style; starts in the early eleventh century BC with the arrival of Dorian peoples. By the eighth century BC, with development of representational styles, the **Archaic period** begins.

Hammam Domed "Turkish" bath, found on Rhodes and certain northeast Aegean islands.

Hellenistic period The last and most unified "Greek empire", created in the wake of Alexander the Great's Macedonian empire and finally collapsing with the fall of Corinth to the Romans in 146 BC.

Heroön Shrine or sanctuary-tomb, usually of a demi-god or mortal; war memorials in modern Greece.

Hóra Main town of an island or region; literally it means "the place". A hóra is often known by the same name as the island.

Ierón The sanctuary between the altar screen and the apse of a church, reserved for priestly activities.

Ikonostási Wood or masonry screen between the nave of a church and the altar, supporting at least three icons.

Ionic Elaborate, decorative development of the older **Doric** order; Ionic temple columns are slimmer, with deeper "fluted" edges, spiral-shaped capitals and ornamental bases.

Kafenío Coffee house or café.

Kaïki (plural **kaïkia**) Caique, or medium-sized boat, traditionally wooden and used for transporting cargo and passengers; now refers mainly to island excursion boats.

Kalderími A cobbled mule-track or footpath.

Kámbos Fertile agricultural plain, usually near a river mouth.

Kantína Shack, caravan or even a disused bus on the beach, serving drinks and perhaps sandwiches or quick snacks.

Kástro Any fortified hill, but most often the oldest, highest, walled-in part of an island hóra, intended to protect civilians.

Katholikón Central church of a monastery.

Káto Lower; common prefix of village names.

Kendrikí platía Central square.

Kouros Nude Archaic statue of an idealized young man, usually portrayed with one foot slightly in front of the other.

Megaron Principal hall or throne room of a Mycenaean palace.

Meltémi North wind that blows across the Aegean in summer, starting softly from near the mainland and hitting the Cyclades, the Dodecanese and Crete full on.

Metope see **Frieze**.

Minoan Crete's great Bronze Age civilization which dominated the Aegean from about 2500 to 1400 BC.

Moní Formal term for a monastery or convent.

Moreas Medieval term for the Peloponnese; the peninsula's outline was likened to the leaf of a mulberry tree, *mouriá* in Greek.

Mycenaean Mainland civilization centred on Mycenae and the Argolid from about 1700 to 1100 BC.

Naos The inner sanctum of an ancient temple; also, the central area of an Orthodox Christian church.

Narthex Western vestibule of a church, reserved for catechumens and the unbaptized; typically frescoed with scenes of the Last Judgement.

Neolithic Earliest era of settlement in Greece; characterized by use of stone tools and weapons together with basic agriculture. Divided arbitrarily into Early (c.6000 BC), Middle (c.5000 BC) and Late (c.3000 BC).

Néos, Néa, Néo "New" – a common prefix to a town or village name.

Nomós Modern Greek province – there are more than fifty of them. Village bus services are organized according to their borders.

Odeion Small theatre, used for musical performances, minor dramatic productions or councils.

Orchestra Circular area in a theatre where the chorus would sing and dance.

Palaestra Gymnasium for athletics and wrestling practice.

Paleós, Paleá, Paleó "Old" – again a common prefix in town and village names.

Panayía Virgin Mary.

Pandokrátor Literally "The Almighty"; generally refers to the stern portrayal of Christ in Majesty frescoed or in mosaic in the dome of many Byzantine churches.

Paniyíri Festival or feast – the local celebration of a holy day.

Paralía Beach, or seafront promenade.

Pediment Triangular, sculpted gable below the roof of a temple.

Pendentive Triangular sections of vaulting with concave sides, positioned at a corner of a rectangular space to support a circular or polygonal dome; in churches, often adorned with frescoes of the four Evangelists.

Períptero Street kiosk.

Peristereónes Pigeon towers, in the Cyclades.

Peristyle Gallery of columns around a temple or other building.

Pinakothíki Picture gallery, ancient or modern.

Pithos (plural **pithoi**) Large ceramic jar for storing oil, grain, etc. Very common in Minoan palaces and used in almost identical form in modern Greek homes.

Platía Square, plaza.

Polygonal masonry Wall-building technique of Classical and Hellenistic periods, using unmortared, closely joined stones; often called "Lesvian polygonal" after the island where the method supposedly originated. The much-(ab)used term **Cyclopean** refers only to Bronze Age mainland sites such as Tiryns and Mycenae.

Propylaion Monumental columned gateway of an ancient building; often used in the plural, **propylaia**.

Pýrgos Tower or bastion; also tower-mansions found in the Máni or on Lésvos.

Skála The port of an inland island settlement, nowadays often larger and more important than its namesake, but always younger since built after the disappearance of piracy.

Skyládhiko Rough-and-ready live bouzouki club

Squinch Small concavity across a corner of a column-less interior space, which supports a superstructure such as a dome.

Stele Upright stone slab or column, usually inscribed with an edict; also an ancient tombstone, with a relief scene.

Stoa Colonnaded walkway in Classical-to-Roman-era marketplaces.

Távli Backgammon; a favourite café pastime, especially among the young. There are two more difficult local variations (*févga* and *plakotó*) in addition to the standard international game (*pórtes*).

Telestirion Shrine associated with ancient mystery rituals.

Témblon Wooden altar screen of an Orthodox church, usually ornately carved and painted and studded with icons; more or less interchangeable with **ikonostási**.

Temenos Sacred precinct of ancient temple, often used to refer to the sanctuary itself.

Theatral area Open area found in most of the Minoan palaces with seat-like steps around. Probably a type of theatre or ritual area.

Tholos Conical or beehive-shaped building, eg a Mycenaean tomb.

Triglyph see **Frieze**.

Tympanum The recessed space, flat or carved in relief, inside a pediment.

Votsalotó Mosaic of coloured pebbles, found in church or house courtyards of the Dodecanese and Spétses.

Yperastikó Long-distance – as in bus services.

ACRONYMS

ANEK Anónymi Navtiliakí Etería Krítis (Shipping Company of Crete Ltd), which runs most ferries between Pireás and Crete, plus many to Italy.

EAM National Liberation Front, the political force behind ELAS.

ELAS Popular Liberation Army, the main Resistance group during World War II and predecessor of the communist army during the civil war.

ELTA Postal service.

EOS Greek Mountaineering Federation, based in Athens.

EOT Ellinikós Organismós Tourismoú, National Tourist Organization.

KKE Communist Party, unreconstructed.

KTEL National syndicate of bus companies; also refers to individual bus stations.

LANE Lasithiakí Anónymi Navtiliakí Etería (Lasithian Shipping Company Ltd), based in eastern Crete.

ND Conservative (Néa Dhimokratía) party.

NEL Navtiliakí Etería Lésvou (Lesvian Shipping Company).

OSE Railway corporation.

OTE Telecommunications company.

PASOK Socialist party (Pan-Hellenic Socialist Movement).

SEO Greek Mountaineering Club, based in Thessaloníki.

SYRIZA Synaspismós tis Rizospastikís Aristerás (Coalition of the Radical Left) – alternative, "Euro"-Socialist party.

Small print and index

Rough Guide credits

Editors: Helen Abramson, Melissa Graham, Matt Milton
Layout: Pradeep Thapliyal
Cartography: Deshpal Dabas
Picture editor: Michelle Bhatia
Proofreader: Susanne Hillen
Managing editors: Natasha Foges, Alice Park
Assistant editor: Sharon Sonam
Production: Janis Griffith

Cover design: Nicole Newman, Michelle Bhatia, Pradeep Thapliyal
Photographer: Chris Christoforou, Michelle Grant
Editorial assistant: Rebecca Hallett
Senior pre-press designer: Dan May
Programme manager: Gareth Lowe
Publisher: Joanna Kirby
Publishing director: Georgina Dee

Publishing information

This ninth edition published April 2015 by
Rough Guides Ltd,
80 Strand, London WC2R 0RL
11, Community Centre, Panchsheel Park,
New Delhi 110017, India
Distributed by Penguin Random House
Penguin Books Ltd,
80 Strand, London WC2R 0RL
Penguin Group (USA)
345 Hudson Street, NY 10014, USA
Penguin Group (Australia)
250 Camberwell Road, Camberwell,
Victoria 3124, Australia
Penguin Group (NZ)
67 Apollo Drive, Mairangi Bay, Auckland 1310,
New Zealand
Penguin Group (South Africa)
Block D, Rosebank Office Park, 181 Jan Smuts Avenue,
Parktown North, Gauteng, South Africa 2193
Rough Guides is represented in Canada by Tourmaline
Editions Inc. 662 King Street West, Suite 304, Toronto,
Ontario M5V 1M7
Printed in Singapore

© Rough Guides 2015
Maps © Rough Guides
No part of this book may be reproduced in any form
without permission from the publisher except for the
quotation of brief passages in reviews.
592pp includes index
A catalogue record for this book is available from the
British Library
ISBN: 978-1-40937-155-7
The publishers and authors have done their best to
ensure the accuracy and currency of all the information
in **The Rough Guide to The Greek Islands**, however,
they can accept no responsibility for any loss, injury, or
inconvenience sustained by any traveller as a result of
information or advice contained in the guide.
1 3 5 7 9 8 6 4 2

Help us update

We've gone to a lot of effort to ensure that the ninth edition of **The Rough Guide to The Greek Islands** is accurate and up-to-date. However, things change – places get "discovered", opening hours are notoriously fickle, restaurants and rooms raise prices or lower standards. If you feel we've got it wrong or left something out, we'd like to know, and if you can remember the address, the price, the hours, the phone number, so much the better.

Please send your comments with the subject line **"Rough Guide The Greek Islands Update"** to ✉ mail@uk.roughguides.com. We'll credit all contributions and send a copy of the next edition (or any other Rough Guide if you prefer) for the very best emails.

Find more travel information, connect with fellow travellers and plan your trip on ⓦ roughguides.com.

ABOUT THE AUTHORS

Nick Edwards Since graduating in Classics & Modern Greek from Oxford, Nick spent many years living in Athens and travelling widely, especially in India. He later settled in Pittsburgh with spouse Maria, until they returned to his native south London in 2008. He's a lifelong Spurs fan, psych music aficionado and believer in universal Oneness.

John Fisher co-wrote the first edition of this book – the first ever Rough Guide – and has been inextricably linked with Rough Guides ever since, much of the time stuck in the office. Now living in London with his wife, Adrienne, and two sons, he is a freelance writer, editor and dispute mediator.

Rebecca Hall After extensive global travels, Rebecca left the UK to return to the country she fell in love with, Greece, where she teaches English, writes and wryly observes that the chaotic nature of her adopted country actually suits her personality very well. Follow her adventures at ⓦlifebeyondborders.co.

John Malathronas was born in Athens but has spent most of his life in London where he has written three travelogues and contributed to nine guidebooks. He is a member of the Guild of Travel Writers and the Society of Authors, as well as a social media addict and a compulsive blogger.

Acknowledgements

Nick Edwards extends thanks to all the good people who helped along the way, especially the following individuals and establishments: Kostas and family at Boukari Beach, Corfu; Maria of Ionian Paradise, Lefkádha; everyone at Pension Limni, Zákynthos; Regina and family in Kefaloniá; the Acropolis on Thassos; the Villa Afroditi on Límnos; the Aphroditi Beach folk and Iy Galini on Lésvos; Theo of To Kyma, Híos; all those at Patras Rooms, Foúrni; finally, the Agriolykos and Ikaria pensions on Ikaría. Cheers to old friends who were handily placed for company and adventures: Georgia, Katherine and Alex on Corfu; Sally and Dom on Kefaloniá; Makarios on Híos; Rob and Roudi on Ikaría; a special mention for continued hospitality and guidance to Marc on Sámos. Thanks to Helen, Alice and Natasha at RG HQ. As always, gratitude to Maria for love and support from afar.

John Fisher would like to thank all those who helped along the way, including Yiorgos Papadavid in Skópelos, Ioannis Retitagos on Ýdhra, Michalis Papadopoulos on Égina, Joanne Poore on Spetses, Kate Donnelly, Lida Karanikolou and Lia Spartali in Athens, Dina Fotou in Édhipsos, Stelios Chronakis in Iráklio, Eleni Vardaki and

Manolis Drimakis in Plakiás, Nikos Perakis in Káto Zákros, Heracles Papadakis in Spíli, Frosso Bora in Réthymno, Yiorgos Tzanopoulos in Áyios Nikólaos, and Alex Stivanakis and Eva Tsialta in Haniá. As always, special thanks to A and the two Js for ruining their holidays.

Rebecca Hall would like to thank many people who helped her on her journey, both physically and metaphorically – a special thanks extends to Nick Edwards, John Fisher and Marc Dubin for their invaluable input; Kim, Adriana and the team of Triton Tours, Rhodes who tirelessly helped with ferry scheduling; and thanks to the many hoteliers, car hire outlets, restaurant and taverna owners throughout the Dodecanese who gave their time and enthusiasm. Of course, not forgetting her editor and team at Rough Guides for supporting her through the process, and her dad for always believing.

John Malathronas would like to thank Dimitra Voziki, Christina Kalogera, Panayotis Papadopoulos, Yannis Hondrokoukis, Tina Damigou, Irene Giannakopoulou, Makis Bitzios, Katerina Pantazopoulou, Nikoletta and Dimitris Lianos.

Readers' updates

Thanks to all the readers who have taken the time to write in with comments and suggestions (and apologies if we've inadvertently omitted or misspelt anyone's name):

Jim Bailey; Simon and Joy Berwick; Charalambos Bizas; Geoffrey Boardman; Richard Bosley; Ifigenia Chatzigeorgiou; Terence Cuff; Andy Forrest; Akis Gliatis; Gwyneth Jones; Mark Jones; Zannis Kostas;

Charalampos Kyteas; Evelyn Moles; Gail Naughton; Barry Parsons; Charlotte Robinson; Peter Rock; Roy Stevens; Lucy Westmore; Matt White.

Photo credits

All photos © Rough Guides except the following:
(Key: t-top; c-centre; b-bottom; l-left; r-right)

Index

Maps are marked in grey

Map symbols

The symbols below are used on maps throughout the book

Main road	★ Transport stop	✡ Synagogue	Lighthouse
Minor road	Ⓜ Metro/subway	Place of interest	Windmill
Motorway	Ⓣ Tram stop	Garden	Vineyards
Pedestrianised road	Ⓗ Helipad	Ruin	Gorge
Steps	Boat	Castle	Steep slope
Unpaved road	Post office	Arch	Shipwreck
Railway	@ Internet access	Gate	Bridge
Path	Hospital	Viewpoint	Building
Wall	ⓘ Information centre	Mountain range	Market
Ferry	Fuel station	Mountain peak	Church
Cable car	Ⓟ Parking	Cave	Stadium
Tram line	Campsite	Swamp	Park
International airport	Mosque	Hot spring	Cemetery
Domestic airport	Monastery	Waterfall	Beach

Listings key

- Accommodation
- Café/restaurant/bar
- Club/venue
- Shop

ROUGH GUIDES

WE GET AROUND

ONLINE start your journey at roughguides.com

EBOOKS & MOBILE APPS

GUIDEBOOKS from Amsterdam to Zanzibar

PHRASEBOOKS learn the lingo

MAPS so you don't get lost

GIFTBOOKS inspiration is our middle name

LIFESTYLE from iPads to climate change

...SO YOU CAN TOO

BOOKS | EBOOKS | APPS